Imray

MEDITERRANEAN ALMANAC

2015-16

Editor

LUCINDA HEIKELL

Consultant editor

ROD HEIKELL

Imray Laurie Norie & Wilson Ltd

Published by
Imray, Laurie, Norie & Wilson Ltd
Wych House, St Ives, Cambridgeshire, PE27 5BT England
☽ +44 (0)1480 462114 *Fax* +44 (0)1480 496109
Email alm@imray.com
www.imray.com
2015

ISBN 978 184623 598 6

British Library Cataloguing in Publication Data
A catalogue record for this book is available from the British Library.

CAUTION
Every effort has been made to ensure the accuracy of this book. It contains selected information and thus is not definitive and does not include all known information on the subject in hand; this is particularly relevant to the plans, which should not be used for navigation. The publisher believes that its selection is a useful aid to prudent navigation, but the safety of a vessel depends ultimately on the judgement of the navigator, who should assess all information, published or unpublished, available to him.

PLANS
The plans in this guide are not to be used for navigation. They are designed to support the text and should at all times be used with navigational charts.

The last input of technical information was September 2014.

Printed in Croatia by Zrinski

Supplements

This almanac is biennial and a supplement for the second year can be downloaded free from our website www.imray.com. This supplement will contain Gibraltar tide tables for 2016, corrections to lights, radio and new harbour information for the year accumulated during 2015.

Advertising

Advertising in the Imray Mediterranean Almanac is handled by
Imray, Laurie, Norie & Wilson Ltd
Wych House, St Ives, Cambridgeshire, PE27 5BT England
☽ +44 (0)1480 462114
Fax +44 (0)1480 496109
Email alm@imray.com

CONTENTS

1. About the Almanac

1.1 INTRODUCTION

An almanac is by its very nature a hybrid beast, incorporating diverse and often incongruous bits of information. In its early forms it was a calendar of the days and months with astronomical and other vaguely related information scattered through the calendar. The yachtsman's almanac is a comparatively modern invention and has accumulated a wonderfully assorted variety of additional information through the years: everything from first aid to recommendations for anchor sizes, radio procedure to astro-ephemeris.

In the planning and preparation of the first editions we were guided by the sort of information we would want to find as yachtsmen in the Mediterranean. They contained the standard core information on lights, radio services, weather services, tides, astro-ephemeris, and harbour information expected in a nautical almanac. In addition they contained much other information, on first aid, marine life, trouble-shooting a diesel, facts and figures on the Mediterranean countries, anchoring and berthing, a glossary of nautical terms in seven languages; all sorts of peripheral but essential information.

This information seemed essential at the time, but readers suggested the almanac was becoming too bulky. As a result we took out much of the information of a non-changing nature and put it in the *Mediterranean Cruising Handbook* (Imray). In the sixth edition you will find information on geography, climate, history and marine life, as well as a nine-language glossary, information on yachts and equipment and sailing techniques specific to Mediterranean sailing. Further technical information covers many aspects of navigation, first aid, radio and weather services. There is also a section giving an over-view of each country through the Mediterranean, offering useful information when afloat and ashore. This edition includes a list of routeing waypoints supported by a foldout chart showing the positions.

The evolving nature of technology affects leisure sailing as much as anything else and this is reflected in the type of information included in this *Mediterranean Almanac* (Imray). As electronic position-finding equipment continues to dominate navigation techniques, and international regulations like SOLAS shape our safety systems, so the almanac changes to incorporate these developments.

SOLAS and its communications arm GMDSS now form the backbone of maritime data dissemination and emergency communications. Likewise, the rise and rise of mobile communications technology has meant extensive details of telephone, email and internet addresses are a necessary addition to radio contacts. The mobile phone is not a substitute for VHF/MF radio in emergency situations. GMDSS has been developed specifically with the intention of providing an integrated (and where possible automated) system for reporting and co-ordinating search and rescue operations. Using a mobile phone in an emergency should remain a last resort.

Section 2 – Safety and Distress is based on DSC Distress communications. In addition to details of all Maritime Rescue Coordination Centres (MRCCs) throughout the Mediterranean, we have also included maps which clearly show the range of coast stations covered by DSC VHF. Non-DSC VHF channels and telephone numbers are also listed here, although more detail of non-DSC coast radio communications will be found in **Section 3 – Radio and Satellite Services.** Also in this section are details of Traffic Separation Schemes, an overview of other radio services such as Navtex and Automatic Identification System (AIS), telecommunications and satellite services. **Section 4 – Weather Services** concentrates on weather data disseminated using recognised Maritime Safety Information (MSI) broadcasts, namely through coast radio, Navtex and INMARSAT satellite. This edition also includes details on how to obtain weather information using bandwidth-restricted means such as HF radio or a GSM phone in addition to conventional internet sources. Weather forecasting in the Mediterranean, where coastal effects are so pronounced, is without doubt a difficult business, and obtaining data from a broad range of sources gives a navigator the best chance of preparing for any unfavourable weather.

As usual there is also a section detailing regulations for each country, including details on VAT, immigration and Marine Reserve or National Park restrictions.

Further sections also include a comprehensive list of major lights, information on chart coverage, tides for Gibraltar, and a passage planning section showing routes and distances between major hubs through the Mediterranean.

The harbour information section, with plans of the major harbours and marinas, is now a core part of every yachtsman's almanac, and the Imray *Mediterranean Almanac* has a significant part of the volume devoted to this information. Harbour plans are restricted to a selection of major harbours or smaller harbours commonly used by yachts, including many of the marinas in the Mediterranean. There are a number of good pilots available for most of the countries around the Mediterranean and where there are gaps we have endeavoured to provide as many harbour plans as possible. On passage you can safely get around the Mediterranean using the harbour plans in the almanac, but if you are exploring a region then you will need the relevant pilot for that country or area.

In line with many of the Imray pilot books, the Almanac is in full colour, bringing, we hope, greater clarity. We have also continued to update waypoints, referenced to WGS84, where possible. Even with a WGS84 datum and the accuracy of GPS, waypoints and electronic position-finding (EPF) equipment should always be used with caution and with regard for their inherent limitations. The receiver giving a position to two or more decimal places of a minute is displaying accuracy outside the capability of the machine, but it nonetheless instils a feeling of confidence in it. Even with the incredible accuracy of EGNOS-enabled GPS

(WAAS in USA), and all the functions of the new EPF equipment: ETA, cross-track error, course and distance to waypoint, integrated steering and radar functions and much more, the navigator is easily lulled into a false sense of security about the certainty of position and course. The accuracy of the position, around 10–20 metres under optimum conditions (5–10m with EGNOS), is far greater than the accuracy of charts surveyed using traditional astronomical sights and standard triangulation techniques. You may know where you are on the earth's surface, but you have nothing accurate on which to plot that position. Charts which provide corrections for latitude and longitude when using EPF equipment compound the problem by using a mean error correction to remedy random errors on the chart. There are other problems associated with the satellites and the receiver – for example, comparing which datum is used on the chart and datum selection on the EPF equipment. The outcome of it all is that old-fashioned coastal pilotage skills and eyeball navigation must not be forgotten when in the vicinity of land or dangers to navigation.

There are enough documented cases of accidents in the Mediterranean, many of them resulting in the loss of a yacht, due to blind reliance on EPF equipment, to prove the practice is not only foolhardy but potentially dangerous to life. It is not only a question of hitting rocks or reefs either; there have been reports of near misses involving vessels which may have been converging on an identical waypoint!

As usual, a supplement for the second year of the almanac will appear on the Imray website www.imray.com towards the end of 2015. Any important changes or amendments will be posted as necessary. Please check the site regularly to keep your copy updated.

We would like to thank everyone who sent in information for this new edition. The editors and the publisher welcome any suggestions for the improvement of the Imray *Mediterranean Almanac*, whether it be about the content and presentation of the general information or amendments to technical information on lights, radio services or harbour information. We will listen to you and where possible will act on your suggestions if they fall within the brief of the almanac. We hope it will help those who use it to get safely and enjoyably around the Mediterranean.

Rod and Lu Heikell
Cowes, 2014

1.2 NOMENCLATURE

The almanac uses the convention common to all hydrographic departments of calling a place and other geographical and maritime features by the term common in that country rendered into English. In Great Britain the Hydrographic Department translates names from the Roman and other alphabets using the system determined by the Permanent Committee on Geographical Names for British Official Use (PCGN). By and large we stick to this system except where a name is so common in English and the transliteration so far away from that name that confusion could result (e.g. Corfu not Kerkyra, the Dardanelles not Çanakkale Boğazi). There are also a few examples where we believe the PCGN principles stick so closely to laid down rules that the name thus rendered is too far from what it should sound like, and so we have slightly adapted the name in a few examples only. Alternative or older names are included in brackets to clarify what could be a confusing situation.

All capes, headlands, points, bays, reefs, rocks, islands, etc. are rendered using the name common in that country. So, for example, Island = 'Isla' in Spanish, 'Ile' in French, 'Isola' in Italian, 'Nisos' in Greek, 'Ada' in Turkish. Terms commonly used on charts and for navigation will be found in the glossary for German, Spanish, French, Italian, Greek, and Turkish terms in *Mediterranean Cruising Handbook*. Imray-Tetra charts for Greece and Turkey have a glossary of common terms used for features on the chart printed on the reverse side.

1.3 ABBREVIATIONS

Compass directions are abbreviated to the first letter in capitals, as is common practice. So N is north, SE is southeast, ESE is east-southeast, etc.

Abbreviations for the light characteristics, radio signals, weather services and buoyage descriptions use the standard notations which are listed in the relevant chapters.

1.4 COMPASS

All compass directions are True. The magnetic variation for different areas is printed on all charts.

1.5 CORRECTIONS

The editors and publisher welcome information which will lead to the improvement of the almanac. While every effort is made to keep this volume as accurate as possible, it is recognised that in the compilation of this volume from numerous diverse sources, some errors will slip through the net. The editors will be grateful if any errors in the almanac are pointed out to them.

Information should be sent to:
The Almanac Editor,
Imray Laurie Norie & Wilson Ltd,
Wych House, The Broadway, St Ives,
PE27 5BT England
✆ +44 (0)1480 462114 *Fax* +44 (0)1480 496109
Email alm@imray.com www.imray.com

Errors should be noted, giving the page number and a reference. If possible a photocopy or tracing of a harbour plan (if relevant) with amendments marked on it would help greatly. Please remember that details must be as objective as possible so that, for example, if a marina is full, it is not marked as having no visitors' berths when in fact none was available. In general the almanac cannot include criticisms of marina management or staff, even when they are justified.

2. SAFETY AND DISTRESS

2.1 DISTRESS SIGNALS

1. The following signals, used or exhibited either together or separately, indicate distress and need of assistance:
   a. a gun or other explosive signal fired at intervals of about a minute
   b. a continuous sounding with any fog-signalling apparatus
   c. rockets or shells, throwing red stars, fired one at a time at short intervals
   d. a signal made by radiotelegraphy or by any other signalling method consisting of the group ··· – – – ··· (SOS in the Morse code)
   e. a signal sent by radiotelephony consisting of the spoken word 'Mayday'
   f. the International Code Signal of distress indicated by NC
   g. a signal consisting of a square flag having above or below it a ball or anything resembling a ball
   h. flames on the vessel (as from a burning tar barrel, oil barrel, etc.)
   i. a rocket parachute flare or a hand flare showing a red light
   j. a smoke signal giving off orange-coloured smoke
   k. slowly and repeatedly raising and lowering arms outstretched to each side
   l. the radiotelegraph alarm signal
   m. the radiotelephone alarm signal
   n. signals transmitted by emergency position-indicating radio beacons
   o. approved signals transmitted by radio-communications systems.
2. The use or exhibition of any of the foregoing signals except for the purpose of indicating distress and need of assistance and the use of other signals which may be confused with any of the above signals is prohibited.
3. Attention is drawn to the relevant sections of the *International Code of Signals*, the *Merchant Ship Search and Rescue Manual* and the following signals:
   a. a piece of orange-coloured canvas with either a black square and circle or other appropriate symbol (for identification from the air)
   b. a dye marker.

DISTRESS SIGNALS

LIFE-SAVING SIGNALS

SOLAS CHAPTER V REGULATION 29

To be used by Ships, Aircraft or Persons in Distress when communicating with life-saving stations, maritime rescue units and aircraft engaged in search and rescue operations.

Note: All Morse Code signals by light (below).

1. SEARCH AND RESCUE UNIT REPLIES

YOU HAVE BEEN SEEN, ASSISTANCE WILL BE GIVEN AS SOON AS POSSIBLE

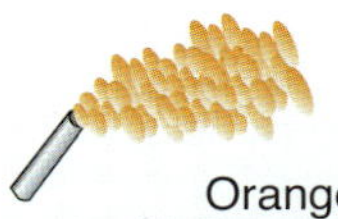

Orange smoke flare

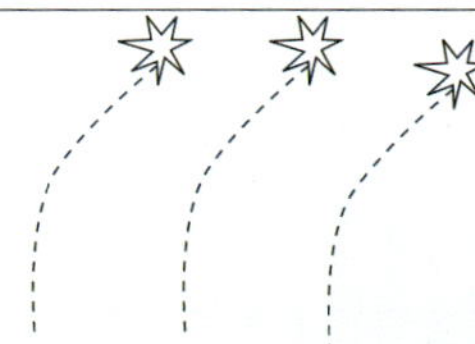

Three white star signals or three light and sound rockets fired at approximately 1 minute intervals

2. SURFACE TO AIR SIGNALS

MESSAGE	ICAO/IMO VISUAL SIGNALS	
REQUIRE ASSISTANCE	V • • • —	
REQUIRE MEDICAL ASSISTANCE	X — • • —	
NO or NEGATIVE	N — •	
YES or AFFIRMATIVE	Y — • — —	
PROCEEDING IN THIS DIRECTION	↑	

Note: Use International Code of Signals by means of light or flags or by laying out the symbol on the deck or ground with items that have a high contrast background.

3. AIR TO SURFACE REPLIES

Note: Use signals most appropriate to prevailing conditions.

MESSAGE UNDERSTOOD

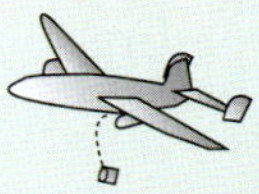

Drop a message.

OR

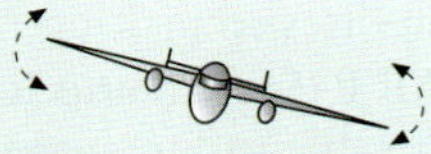

Rocking wings.

OR

Flashing landing or navigation lights on and off twice.

OR T — OR R • — •

MESSAGE NOT UNDERSTOOD

Straight and level flight.

OR

Circling.

OR R • — • P • — — • T —

4. AIR TO SURFACE DIRECTION SIGNALS

SEQUENCE OF 3 MANOEUVRES MEANING PROCEED IN THIS DIRECTION

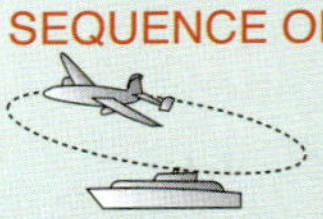

Circle vessel at least once.

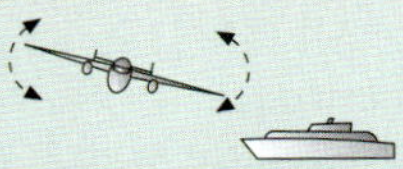

Cross low, ahead of vessel rocking wings.

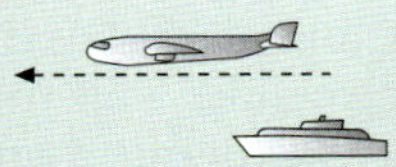

Overfly vessel and head in required direction.

YOUR ASSISTANCE IS NO LONGER REQUIRED

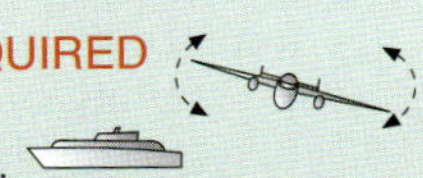

Cross low, astern of vessel rocking wings.

Note: As a non prefererred alternative to rocking wings, varying engine tone or volume may be used.

5. SURFACE TO AIR REPLIES

MESSAGE UNDERSTOOD - I WILL COMPLY

Change course to required direction.

OR T — OR

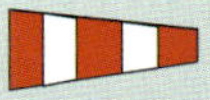

Code & answering pendant "Close Up".

I AM UNABLE TO COMPLY

International flag "N".

OR N — •

6. SHORE TO SHIP SIGNALS

SAFE TO LAND HERE

Vertical waving of both arms,white flag, light or flare

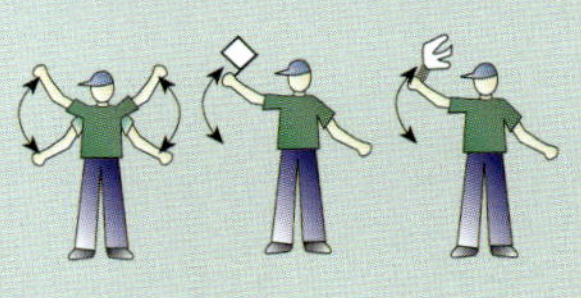

OR K — • —

LANDING HERE IS DANGEROUS ADDITIONAL SIGNALS MEAN SAFER LANDING IN DIRECTION INDICATED

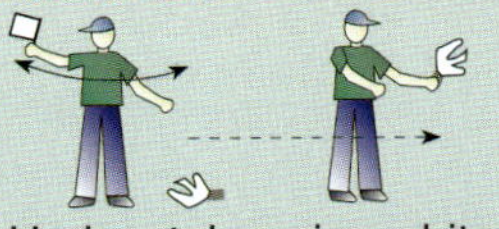

Horizontal waving white flag, light or flare. Putting one flare/ flag on ground and moving off with a second indicates direction of safer landing.

OR

S	• • •	Landing here is dangerous.
R	• — •	Land to right of your current heading.
L	• — • •	Land to left of your current heading.

2.2 SOLAS REGULATIONS

The International Convention for the Safety of Life at Sea (SOLAS) Chapter V is concerned with safety of navigation, some of which applies to smaller vessels. From 1 July 2002 skippers of craft under 150 tons are required to conform to the following SOLAS V regulations. The regulations will almost certainly be applied in piecemeal fashion in the Mediterranean countries (if at all in some). Nonetheless, you should be aware of them. What follows is very much our précis of the regulations and at the time of writing clarification continues.

2.3 GLOBAL MARITIME DISTRESS AND SAFETY SYSTEM (GMDSS)

GMDSS forms part of SOLAS regulations, providing a comprehensive plan for largely automated radio communications between ships and shore stations with worldwide coverage. GMDSS provides a complete system of navigation alerts and distress co-ordination, and consists of several integrated systems which are now required on all ships with the exception of the following:

- Ships other than passenger vessels of less than 300 gross-tonnage
- Passenger ships carrying less than six passengers
- Ships of war
- Ships not propelled by engines
- Fishing vessels under 12m.

GMDSS equipment is not mandatory for such vessels but by gradual phasing-in of equipment and increased availability, pleasure yachts are gradually being equipped with GMDSS equipment.

The integrated system is composed of the following components:

- **DSC (Digital Selective Calling)** VHF, MF and HF will utilise DSC for ship-to-ship, ship-to-shore, shore-to-ship and will also generate a preformatted distress signal giving a location position if connected to GPS or any other position-finding receiver.

SOLAS V

- R19 A radar reflector (3 & 9GHz) must be exhibited. For vessels over 15m it should be 10m² minimum.
- R29 A table of life-saving signals must be available to the skipper/helmsman at all times.
- R31 Skippers must report to the coastguard on dangers to navigation including (R32) wrecks, winds of Force 10 or more and floating objects dangerous to navigation.
- R33 Vessels must respond to distress signals from another vessel.
- R34 Safe Navigation and Avoidance of Dangerous Situations. Vessels must be able to demonstrate that adequate passage planning has been undertaken. Things like weather, tides, vessel limitations, crew, navigational dangers, and contingency plans should be addressed.
- R35 Distress signals must not be misused.

- **MSI (Maritime Safety Information)** NAVTEX and coast radio are the main methods of transmitting navigation and met warnings, met forecasts and other urgent safety related messages. Ship Earth Stations (Satellite phones) and HF Radio are also used to receive long range warnings using the SafetyNET Service.
- **EPIRB (Emergency Position-Indicating Radio Beacon)** Uses COSPAS-SARSAT international satellites to pick up the 406MHz signal.
- **SART (Search and Rescue Radar Transponders)** Portable radar transponders designed to provide a locator signal from survival craft.
- **SESs (Ship Earth Stations)** INMARSAT is currently the only provider of GMDSS satellite communication systems. SESs may be used to transmit voice messages or to receive Electronic Caller Group (ECG) MSI information.

Of all these it is really DSC which most affects pleasure yachts. All GMDSS equipment had to be fitted to ships by 1 February 1999. Ships are no longer required to keep a listening watch on VHF Ch 16 or 2182MHz. It is uncertain yet whether shore stations will likewise stop listening on VHF Ch 16.

GMDSS Radio Communication Requirements

Area	*Description*	*Distance*	*Radio*	*Frequencies*	*EPIRB*[1]	*Survival craft*
A1	Within range of shore-based VHF stations	Depends on antenna height at shore-based VHF station (20–50M)	VHF	156·525MHz (Ch 70) for DSC 156·8MHz (Ch 16) radiotelephone	Either 406MHz COSPAS-SARSAT or L-Band (1·6GHz) INMARSAT	9GHz radar transponder; VHF portable radio (Channel 16 and another frequency)
A2	Within range of shore-based MF stations	about 100M	VHF MF	as above, plus 2187·5kHz DSC 2182kHz radio-telephone 2174·5 NBDP 518kHz NAVTEX	406MHz COSPAS-SARSAT or L-Band (1·6GHz) INMARSAT	as above
A3	Within geo-stationary satellite range (i.e. INMARSAT)	70°N–70°S	VHF MF HF or Satellite	as above, plus 1·5–1·6GHz alerting or as A1 and A2 plus all HF frequencies	406MHz COSPAS-SARSAT or L-Band (1·6GHz) INMARSAT	as above
A4	Other areas (i.e. beyond INMARSAT)	North of 70°N or South of 70°S	VHF MF HF		406MHz COSPAS-SARSAT	as above

1. Emergency Position Indicating Radiobeacon

DSC Distress/Safety Calling Frequencies

VHF Ch 70
MF 2187·5kHz
HF 4207·5, 6312, 8414·5, 12577, 16804·5kHz

SAR co-ordination/on-scene communications

VHF Ch 16, 06 (ship-to-shore/ship-to-ship)
VHF 121·5 & 123·1MHz (ship-to-aircraft – compulsory for passenger carriers)
MF 2182kHz
HF 3023 or 5680kHz (ship-to-aircraft), 4125kHz (ship-to-shore/ship-to-ship)

GMDSS radio communication equipment requirements are based on four sea areas, depending on range limitations of the radio equipment. See table opposite.

2.4 EMERGENCY RADIO & TELEPHONE SERVICES

GIBRALTAR

Emergency telephone numbers

199 Emergency services.

SPAIN

SAR organisation – Sociedad de Salvamento y Seguridad Maritima – is based in Madrid and co-ordinates all SAR operations through MRCC and VTS centres. It is also responsible for pollution control. All MRCC and MRSC stations are 24hr. Coast radio stations (CRS) maintain a continuous listening watch on the distress frequencies, and relay to MRCCs.

MSI announced on VHF Ch 16 and MF 2182kHz before switching to allocated channels.

The main stations to send VHF/MF DSC distress alerts are:

Malaga (S coast) MMSI 002 241 023.

Valencia (W coast) MMSI 002 241 024.

Madrid MRCC
MMSI 002241008
DSC HF 8414·5, 12577kHz
☏ 091 755 9132/9133
INMARSAT C 422 404 710
www.sasemar.es
MMSI 002 241 1011
☏ 0956 211 621
DSC VHF Ch 70, 74

Tarifa MRCC
MMSI 002240994
DSC VHF Ch 70, 10, 16, 67
DSC MF 2187·5kHz, 2182kHz
☏ 0956 684 740

Algeciras MRSC
MMSI 002241001
DSC VHF Ch 70, 15, 16, 74
☏ 0956 580 930

Almeria MRCC
MMSI 002241002
DSC VHF Ch 70, 16, 74
DSC MF 2187·5kHz, 2182kHz
☏ 0950 275 477

Cartagena MRSC
MMSI 002241003
DSC VHF Ch 70, 10, 16
☏ 0968 529 594

Valencia MRCC
MMSI 002241004
DSC VHF Ch 70, 10, 16
DSC MF 2187·5kHz, 2182kHz
☏ 096 367 9302

Palma MRCC
MMSI 002241005
DSC VHF Ch 70, 10, 16
DSC MF 2187·5, 2182 kHz
☏ 0971 728 322

Castellon MRSC
MMSI 002241016
DSC VHF Ch 70, 16, 74
☏ 0964 737 202

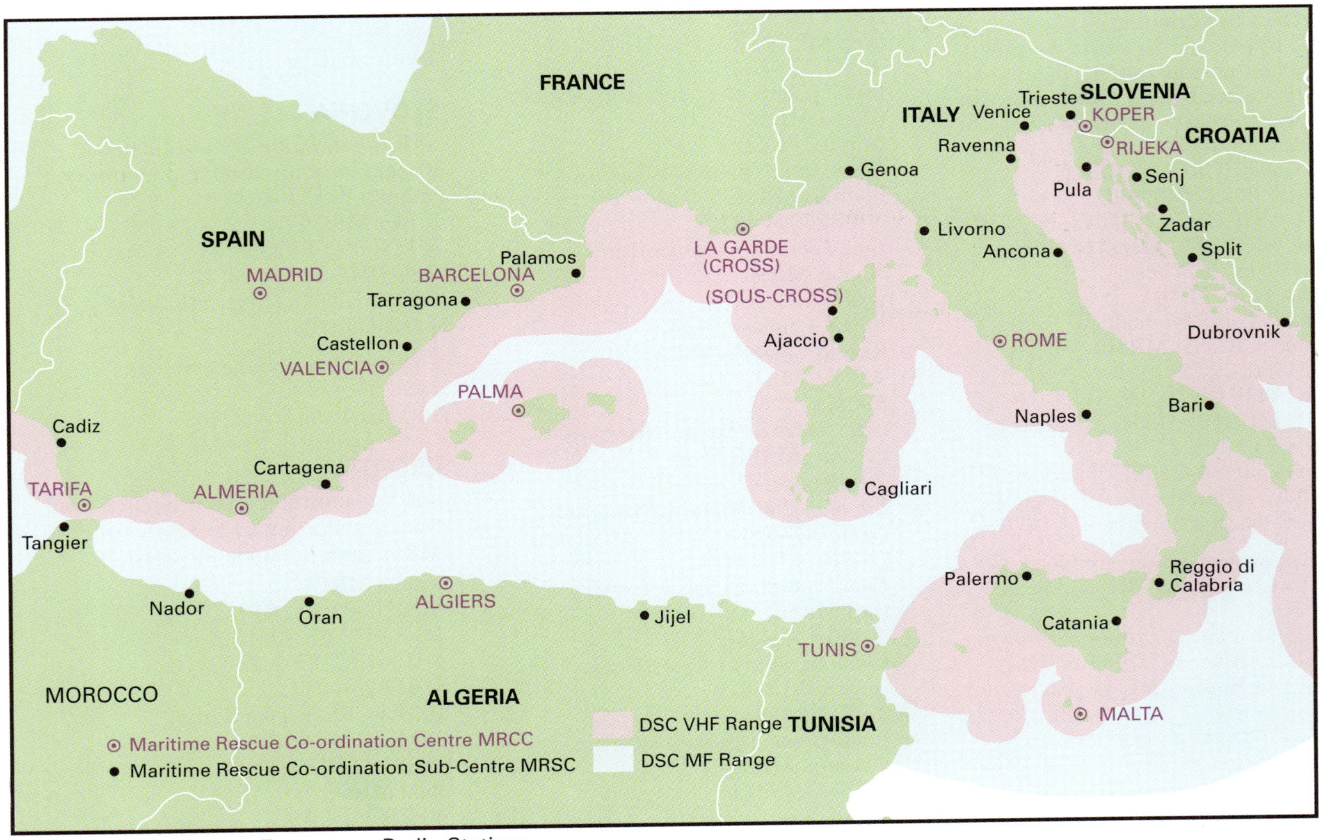

Western Mediterranean Emergency Radio Stations

Tarragona MRSC
MMSI 002241006
DSC VHF Ch 70, 74, 16
✆ 0977 216 203
Barcelona MRCC
MMSI 002240991
DSC VHF Ch 10, 16, 70
DSC MF 2187·5kHz, 2182kHz
✆ 093 223 4733
Palamos MRSC
June to September only.
VHF Ch 13

Emergency telephone numbers
Pan-European Emergency Telephone Number 112
900 202 202 24-hour Marine Emergency Services
003 Emergency services
091 Police
061 Medical Emergency
085 Fire (Bomberos)

FRANCE

SAR organisation – Centres Regionaux Operationnels de Surveillance et de Sauvetage (CROSS) – is based at La Garde (Iles des Lerins) and co-ordinates all SAR operations. It is linked to the COSPAS-SARSAT Control Centre in Toulon to co-ordinate satellite-aided SAR operations.
CROSS also covers
- Marine traffic inside the 12NM coast range including TSS and ITZ tracking.
- Pollution risk (dangerous cargo vessels monitored)
- Fisheries Surveillance
- Data collection.

MSI broadcasts for storm warnings and weather bulletins, and navigation and traffic safety bulletins on vessels which appear to contravene Rule 10 of Col Regs within TSS and ITZ.
La Garde (CROSS) MRCC
MMSI 002275400/002275410
DSC VHF Ch 70, 16, 67, 68, 73, 80
DSC MF 2187·5kHz, 1696kHz, 2182kHz, 2677kHz
✆ 04 94 61 71 10
Email lagarde@mrccfr.eu
Corse (CROSS) MRSC
MMSI 002275420
DSC VHF Ch 70, 16, 67
DSC MF 2187·5kHz, 2182kHz
✆ 04 95 20 13 63
(Service 0730–2300LT Summer 0730–2100LT Winter)
Email ajaccio@mrccfr.eu

Emergency telephone numbers
1616 Coastguard 24hr mobile or landline
✆ 05 61 49 33 33 24-hour Maritime Medical Advice Centre (CCMM)
112 Pan-European Emergency number (Police)
Dial direct from call-boxes
15 Medical (SAMU – Service d'aide medicale urgent)
17 Police (Gendarmerie)
18 Fire (Pompiers)

MONACO (3AC) (3AF)

SAR organisation – Monaco Maritime Police – is linked to La Garde and has an agreement with CROSS for co-operation in SAR operations.
✆ 93 307 300

Emergency telephone numbers also as France.

ITALY

SAR organisation – Commando Generale delle Capitainerie di Porto – is based in Rome and co-ordinates SAR operations nationally and internationally through the Guardia Costieri (coastguard).
CRS maintain a continuous listening watch on international distress frequencies.
MSI broadcasts on CRS VHF and MF including storm warnings and weather bulletins.
Roma MRCC
MMSI 002470001
DSC VHF Ch 70, 16
DSC MF 2187·5kHz, 2182kHz
DSC HF 4207·5, 6312, 8414·5, 12577, 16804·5kHz
✆ 06 656171
Email roma@guardiacostiera.it
www.guardiacostiera.it
CIRM (International Medical Centre)
✆ 065 923 331/2
Email telesoccorso@cirm.it
www.cirm.it
Palermo MRSC
MMSI 002470002
DSC VHF Ch 70, 16
DSC MF 2187·5kHz, 2182kHz
✆ 091 331 538
Email palermo@guardiacostiera.it
Genoa MRSC
✆ 010 241 2222
Email mrsc@mrsc.porto.genova.it
Livorno MRSC
✆ 0586 894 493
Email compliop@portnet.it
Naples MRSC
✆ 081 244 5111
Email 4_mrsc@libero.it
Reggio Calabria MRSC
✆ 0965 6561
Email reggiocalabria@guardiacostiera.it
Cagliari MRSC
✆ 070 605 171
Email cagliari@guardiacostiera.it
Catania MRSC
✆ 095 747 4111
Email catania@guardiacostiera.it
Bari MRSC
✆ 080 521 6860
Email bari@guardiacostiera.it
Ancona MRSC
✆ 071 227581
Email ancona@guardiacostiera.it
Ravenna MRSC
✆ 0544 443011
Email ravenna@guardiacostiera.it
Venice MRSC
✆ 041 240 5711
Email capve6@portovenice.net
Trieste MRSC
✆ 040 676 611
Email mrsctrieste@tiscali.it

Emergency telephone numbers
1530 Coastguard (Guardia Costiera – local Capitaneria)
112 Pan-European Emergency number – Police
112 Police (Carabinieri)
113 Police, Red Cross, emergency first-aid (Pronto soccorso)
115 Fire (Pompiere)
118 Ambulance

MALTA

SAR organisation _ Malta MRCC – is part of Armed Forces Malta (AFM) and co-ordinates SAR operations in Maltese waters assisted by Malta Maritime Authority, Malta Radio and Malta International Airport. Malta Radio maintains a listening watch on international distress frequencies.
MRCC (AFM) Malta
DSC VHF Ch 70, 16
DSC MF 2187·5kHz, 2182kHz
✆ 21 809 279
Email rccmalta@gov.mt
Malta Radio
VHF Ch 16, 01, 02, 03, 04, 28
MF 2182, 2625kHz (0700–1800)
✆ 21 456 767/447 929

Emergency telephone numbers
191 Police
199 Fire
196 Ambulance

SLOVENIA

SAR organisation is co-ordinated by Koper Harbourmaster and monitors international distress frequencies.
Koper MRCC
MMSI 002780200
DSC VHF Ch 70, 16, 12
DSC MF 2187·5kHz, 2182kHz
✆ 0566 32108

Emergency telephone numbers
113 Police
112 Fire/Paramedics

CROATIA

SAR organisation is co-ordinated from Rijeka, and is linked to a series of MRSC stations along the coast.
Rijeka MRCC
MMSI 002 387 010/002 387 020
DSC VHF Ch 70, 10, 16
DSC MF 2187·5, 2182kHz
✆ 051 214 031
Rijeka CRS (Rijeka Radio)
MMSI 002 380 200
✆ 051 217 332
Pula MRSC
VHF Ch 10, 16
✆ 052 222 037

Adriatic Emergency Radio Stations

Senj MRSC
VHF Ch 10, 16
☎ 053 881 301
Zadar MRSC
MMSI 002 387 400/002 387 401
VHF Ch 10, 16
☎ 023 254 880
Sibenik MRSC
MMSI 002 387 500/002 387 501
VHF Ch 10, 16
☎ 022 217 214
Split MRSC
MMSI 002 387 040/002 387 030
☎ 021 389 190
Split Harbourmaster
MMSI 002 3870 100
DSC VHF Ch 70, 07, 16, 21, 23, 81
☎ 021 362 436
Ploce MRSC
VHF Ch 10, 16
☎ 020 679 541
Dubrovnik MRSC
MMSI 002 387 800/002 387 801
☎ 020 418 989
Dubrovnik CRS (Dubrovnik Radio)
MMSI 002 380 300
DSC VHF Ch 70, 16
☎ 020 423 290/665

Emergency telephone numbers
112 Pan-European Emergency Telephone number
9155 Coastguard 24hr (mobiles or landline) to MRCC Rijeka
☎ +385 51 9155 from outside Croatia
92 Police
93 Fire
94 Paramedics

MONTENEGRO

A listening watch on VHF/MF distress frequencies is maintained.

Bar MRCC
MMSI 002 790 001
DSC VHF
DSC MF
☎ 3031 3088

Emergency telephone numbers
92 Police
93 Fire
94 Paramedics

ALBANIA

Coast radio stations keep a listening watch on international distress frequencies.

	VHF	MF
Shengjin	16, 71	2182kHz
Durres	16, 22	2182kHz
Vlore	16, 11	2182kHz
Sarande	16, 06	2182kHz

Emergency telephone numbers
129 Police
127 Ambulance

GREECE

SAR organisation – Hellenic Coastguard – is co-ordinated from Piraeus. All Greek Port Authorities operate SAR units in conjunction with the HCG. CRS (callsign *Olympia Radio*) monitor international distress frequencies.
Five local SAR stations which co-ordinate regional sea areas.

JRCC Piraeus
MMSI 002 392 000 (DSC VHF & MF)
MMSI 237 673 000 (DSC MF & HF)
VHF Ch 16
MF 2182kHz
DSC MF 2187·5kHz
DSC HF 4207·5, 6312, 8414·5, 12577, 16804·5kHz
☎ 210 411 2500

Regional Centres
Ionian
Patras Coast Guard
MMSI 237 673 140
VHF Ch 16
MF 2182kHz
DSC MF 2187·5kHz
☎ 2610 341002
Central Aegean
Mitilini Coastguard
MMSI 237 673 220
VHF Ch 16, 01, 02
MF 2182kHz
DSC MF 2187·5kHz
☎ 22510 40827
North Aegean
Thessaloniki Coast Guard
MMSI 237 673 210
VHF Ch 16
MF 2182kHz
DSC MF 2187·5kHz
☎ 2310 531504
SE Aegean
Rhodos Coastguard
MMSI 237 673 150
VHF Ch 16
MF 2182kHz
DSC MF 2187·5kHz
☎ 22410 22220
SW Aegean
Khania Coastguard
☎ 28210 98888

Sub centres
Aspropirgos Attikis Coastguard
MMSI 002 391000
VHF Ch 16
MF 2182kHz
DSC VHF Ch 70
DSC MF 2187·5kHz
DSC HF 4207·5, 6312, 8414·5, 12577, 16804·5kHz
Kerkira Coastguard
MMSI 237 673 190
VHF Ch 16
MF 2182kHz
DSC MF 2187·5kHz

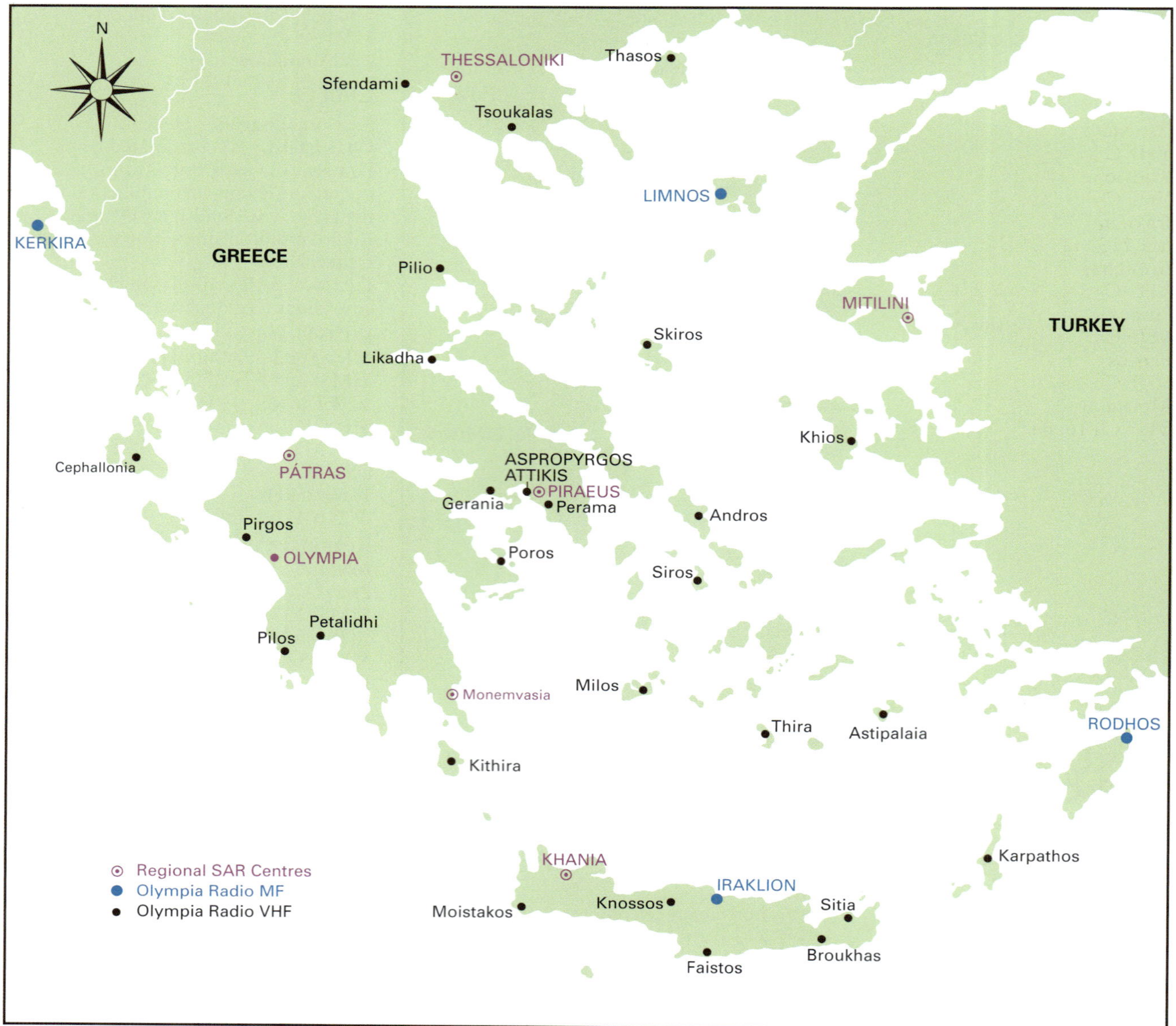

Greek Emergency Radio Stations

Pilos Coast Guard
MMSI 237 673 230
VHF Ch 16
MF 2182kHz
DSC MF 2187·5kHz
Monemvasia Coastguard
VHF Ch 16
MF 2182kHz
Iraklion/Knossus Coast Guard
MMSI 237 673 180
VHF Ch 16, 83, 84
MF 2182kHz
DSC MF 2187·5kHz

OLYMPIA RADIO STATIONS
Olympia
Callsign *Olympia Radio*
MMSI 002 371 000
DSC VHF Ch 70
DSC MF 2187·5, 1695, 1767, 2182kHz
DSC HF 4207·5, 6312, 8414·5, 12577, 16804·5kHz
✆ 210 600 1799
Email shipsva@otenet.gr

Kerkira
VHF Ch 16, 02, 03, 64
MF 2182, 2830kHz
Cephalonia
VHF Ch 16, 26, 27, 28
Patras
VHF Ch 16, 85
Pirgos
VHF Ch 16, 86
Petalidhi
VHF Ch 16, 23, 83, 84
Kithera
VHF Ch 16, 85, 86
Gerania
VHF Ch 16, 02, 64
Poros
VHF Ch 16, 26, 27, 28
Andros
VHF Ch 16, 24
Siros
VHF Ch 16, 03, 04
Milos
VHF Ch 16, 85

Thira
VHF Ch 16, 61, 62
Parnitha
VHF Ch 16, 25, 26, 84
Likhada
VHF Ch 16, 01
Pilio
VHF Ch 16, 03, 60
Sfendami
VHF Ch 16, 23, 24
Tsoukalas
VHF Ch 16, 26, 27
Thasos
VHF Ch 16, 25, 85
Limnos
VHF Ch 16, 82, 83
MF 2182, 2730kHz
Mitilini
VHF Ch 16, 01, 02
Khios
VHF Ch 16, 85
Patmos
VHF Ch 16, 24

Rhodes
VHF Ch 16, 01, 63
MF 2182, 2624kHz
Karpathos
VHF Ch 16, 03
Astipalaia
VHF Ch 16, 23
Knossos
VHF Ch 16, 83, 84
Iraklion
MF 2182, 2799kHz
Broukhas
VHF Ch 16, 28
Sitia
VHF Ch 16, 85, 86
Faistos
VHF Ch 16, 26, 27
Moistakos
VHF Ch 16, 04

Emergency telephone numbers
108 Coastguard 24hr
112 Pan-European – Police
100 Police
171 Tourist police (Athens)
210 171 Tourist police (outside Athens)
166 Ambulance
199 Fire Brigade
191 Forest fire

TURKEY

SAR organisation – General Directorate of Maritime Transport, Maritime Affairs – is based in Ankara and co-ordinates SAR operations in Turkish waters with Sahil Guvenlik (coastguard). CRS maintain a listening watch on international distress frequencies.
GDMT Ankara
☎ 312 232 4783
Email cpt.durmaz@mynet.com

Istanbul
MMSI 002711000
DSC VHF Ch 70
DSC MF 2187·5, 2182, 2670kHz
DSC HF 4207·5, 6312, 8414·5, 12577, 16804·5kHz
☎ 0212 242 9710
Izmir CRS
MMSI 002 715 000
DSC MF 2187·5, 2182, 2629, 2693kHz
☎ 0232 483 3035
Antalya
MMSI 002713000
DSC VHF Ch 70
DSC MF 2187·5, 2182, 2670, 2693kHz
☎ 0312 417 5050
Mersin MRSC
☎ 0324 237 2222/1919
Mersin CRS
MMSI 002 717 000
DSC MF 2187·5, 2182, 2820kHz
☎ 0324 237 1224
Iskenderun CRS
MMSI 002 715 000
DSC MF 2187·5, 2182, 2629, 3648kHz
☎ 0326 613 2121/2122

Emergency telephone numbers
158 Coastguard 24hr
☎ +90 312 158 0000 from outside Turkey. English speaking.
www.sgk.tsk.tr
155 Police
112 Ambulance
110 Fire
177 Forest fire

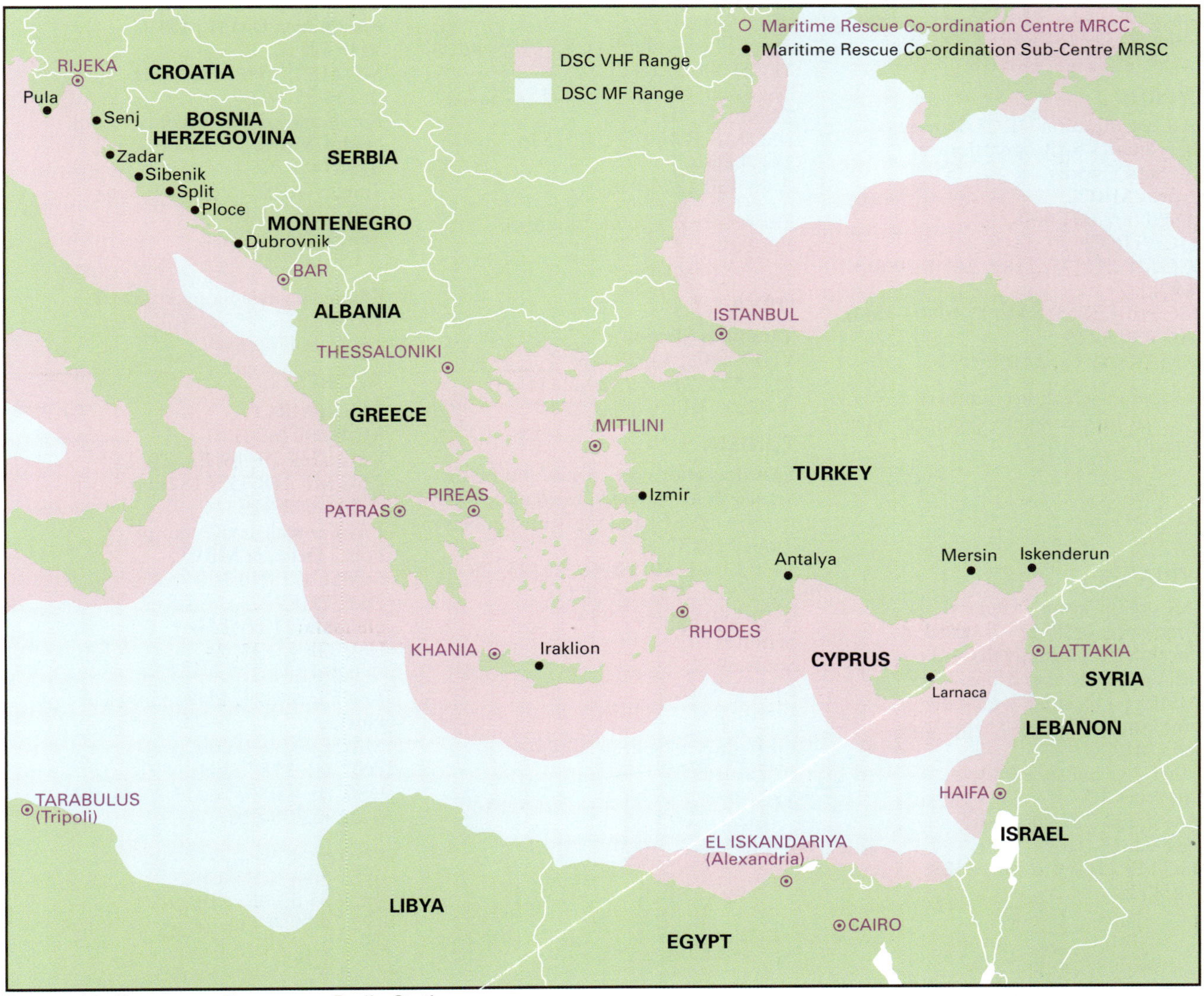

Eastern Mediterranean Emergency Radio Stations

Telephone numbers for regional coastguards are as follows:

Marmara and Straits Area Command at Istanbul ✆ (212) 242 9710, 11, 12
Çanakkale Group Command at Çanakkale ✆ (286) 854 8262
Aegean Sea Command at Izmir ✆ (232) 365 5820, 366 6666, 366 6667
Marmaris Group Command at Marmaris/Muğla ✆ (252) 412 7722, 412 6386
Antalya Group Command at Antalya ✆ (242) 248 1450, 248 1451
Mediterranean Sea Command at Mersin ✆ (324) 237 1919, 237 2222
Samsun Group Command ✆ (362) 445 0333, 445 0334
Trabzon Group Command ✆ (462) 230 0882
Enez ✆ (284) 821 4442
Gneada ✆ (288) 692 2129
Ayvalik ✆ (266) 312 1730
Fethiye ✆ (252) 614 8460
Iskenderun ✆ (326) 614 2311
Karatas ✆ (322) 681 2579
Kaş ✆ (242) 836 2455
Golçuk ✆ (262) 414 6601
Çeşme ✆ (232) 724 8355
Botas ✆ (322) 613 5859
Cevlik ✆ (326) 594 9018

CYPRUS

SAR organisation – RCC Larnaca – co-ordinates SAR operations in southern Cyprus.

Cyprus MRCC
MMSI 002 091 000
DSC VHF Ch 70, 16
DSC MF 2187·5, 2182, 2670, 2700, 3690kHz
DSC HF 4207·5, 8414·5, 16804·5kHz
✆ 02 430 4723
INMARSAT C 421 099 999

Emergency telephone numbers
112 Pan-European Emergency number (Police)
North Cyprus
155 Police
112 First Aid
177 Fire

SYRIA

SAR organisation – General Directorate of Ports – is based in Lattakia (Al Ladhiqiyah) and co-ordinates SAR operations. CRS maintain a listening watch on international distress frequencies.

Syria MRCC
✆ 041 233 333/226 080
Lattakia CRS
MMSI 002 715 000
VHF Ch 13, 16
DSC MF 2187·5, 2182, 2629, 3648kHz

LEBANON

Lebanese Navy maintains a listening watch on VHF Ch 16 and MF 2182kHz.

RCC Beyrouth
✆ 1 629 026

ISRAEL

Israel MRCC
✆ 0464 3311
Haifa CRS (4XO)
MMSI 004 280 001
DSC VHF Ch 70, 16, 24, 25, 26
DSC MF 2187·5, 2182kHz
✆ 0486 99016

Emergency telephone numbers
100 Police
101 Ambulance

EGYPT

Middle East SAR Centre
JRCC Cairo
✆ 02 418 4537
INMARSAT C 462 299 910
MINI-M 762 007 997/999
Egypt El Iskandariya CRS (RCC Cairo)
DSC HF 4207·5, 6312, 8414·5, 12577, 16804·5kHz
Egypt El Iskandariya MRCC (Alexandria)
✆ 03 484 2058
Egypt El Iskandariya CRS (Alexandria)
MMSI 006 221 111
DSC VHF Ch 70, 02, 16, 19, 23, 25, 27, 60, 64, 66, 79, 87
DSC MF 2187·5, 2182, 2576, 2817kHz
✆ 03 480 2226/9500

Emergency telephone numbers
122 Police
123 Ambulance

LIBYA

Tarabulus (Tripoli)
VHF Ch 06, 14, 22, 26
MF 2182, 2197, 2320, 2418kHz
✆ 021 47011

TUNISIA

SAR operations are carried out by the *Service National de Surveillance Cotière* (SNSC) and the Tunisian Navy.

Tunis MRCC
VHF Ch 01, 10, 12, 18, 21, 25, 26
MF 1768, 2182, 2670kHz
✆ 01 240 000/263 999
Sfax RSC
Sousse RSC
Kelibia RSC
Bizerte RSC

Emergency telephone numbers
197 Police
190 Medical (SAMU – *Service d'Aide Medicale Urgent*)

ALGERIA

SAR organisation – Naval Forces Command – MRCC Alger. Algerian Coastguard co-ordinates SAR operations.

Algiers (CNOSS) MRCC
VHF Ch 24, 25, 26, 27, 28, 84, 87
MF 1792, 2182, 2691, 2775kHz
Jijel (CROSS)
✆ 034 474 591
Oran (CROSS)
VHF Ch 24, 25, 26, 27, 28
MF 1735, 2182, 2586, 2719kHz

Emergency telephone numbers
17 Emergency
17 Police
216 066 66 Ambulance
115 Medical Assistance by phone
14 Fire

MOROCCO

SAR organisation – Directorate of the Merchant Marine – is based on the Atlantic coast at Casablanca.
CRS maintain a listening watch on international distress frequencies.
Ocean fisheries dept also maintain a listening watch on distress frequencies from Rabat.

Casablanca DMM MRCC
VHF Ch 16, 20
MF 2182, 2586, 2663kHz
✆ 22 491 162
Email marine@maroconline.com
Nador MRSC
✆ 36 608 706
Tanger MRSC
✆ 03 993 2090
Tanger Radio
✆ 09 935 059

Emergency telephone numbers
19 Police
15 Ambulance/Fire

AZORES

Lisbon MRCC
MMSI 002630100
DSC VHF 70, 16, 23, 25, 26
DSC MF 2187·5, 2182kHz
✆ 214 401 919
Email mrcclisboa@neto.pt
Ponta Delgada MRCC
MMSI 002 040 100
DSC VHF
DSC MF 2187·5kHz
DSC HF
✆ 0296 281 777
Email mrcc.delgada@mail.telepac.pt
Horta
MMSI 002 040 200
DSC MF 2187·5kHz
DSC HF 4207·5, 6312, 8414·5kHz
✆ 0292 208 620

Emergency telephone numbers
292 392 490 Police
292 585 333 Fire Brigade
292 392 931 Emergency Treatment

MADEIRA

Funchal MRSC (Planned)
MMSI 002 550 100
DSC VHF Ch 70
DSC MF 2187·5kHz
✆ 0291 221 105/213 110
Porto Santo (planned)
MMSI 002 550 200
DSC MF 2187·5, 2182, 2657kHz

Emergency telephone numbers
291 757 303 Police
291 222 122 Fire Brigade
291 416 656 Transit Police
291 742 241 District Hospital
291 419 269 Emergency Treatment
291 422 122 Ambulance

CANARIES

SAR organisation – Sociedad de Salvamento y Seguridad Maritima – MRCC Madrid co-ordinates SAR operations. CRS maintain a listening watch on international distress frequencies.
Madrid MRCC
✆ 91 7559132/3
Las Palmas MRCC
MMSI 002 241 005/002 240 995 (VHF)
MMSI 002 241 026 (MF)
DSC VHF Ch 70, 10, 16
DSC MF 2187·5kHz
✆ 928 467 757/955
Tenerife MRCC
MMSI 002 241 007 (VHF)
MMSI 002 241 025 (MF)
DSC VHF Ch 70, 16, 74
DSC MF 2187·5kHz
✆ 922 597 551/2
Email tenerife@sasemar.es

Emergency telephone numbers
091 Polícia Nacional
092 Polícia Local
061 Urgencias Salud (Medical Emergencies)
062 Guardia Civil (only in Gran Canaria, Lanzarote and Fuerteventura)
080 Bomberos (Firefighters) (only in Gran Canaria)

2.5 MAKING A DISTRESS CALL

Making a DSC MAYDAY distress alert

1. Press DSC distress button
2. Select DISTRESS category
3. Press DSC distress button for 5 seconds
4. Wait 15 seconds, or after DSC acknowledgement if sooner
5. Transmit Distress call on VHF Ch 16 or MF 2182MHz:

MAYDAY-MAYDAY-MAYDAY

This is (yacht name or callsign and MMSI) Repeated three times

MAYDAY (yacht name or callsign and MMSI)

Position

Number of people on board

Nature of urgency (collision, sinking, etc) and request assistance OVER

Making a DSC PAN-PAN call

1. Press DSC distress button
2. Select URGENCY category
3. Press DSC distress button for 5 seconds
4. Wait 15 seconds
5. Transmit Pan-Pan call on VHF Ch 16 or MF 2182MHz:

PAN-PAN, PAN-PAN, PAN-PAN
ALL STATIONS, ALL STATIONS,
ALL STATIONS,
This is (yacht name or callsign and MMSI)
Position
Nature of urgency (medical, tow needed, etc) and request assistance OVER.

Note DSC Procedure may vary on different sets.

DSC DISTRESS CATEGORIES

UNDESIGNATED
Sends only your MMSI, position, time of position (as long as the radio is receiving position information).

DESIGNATED
Fire/explosion – Flooding – Collision – Grounding – Listing – Sinking – Disabled & adrift – Abandoning ship – Piracy or attack – Man overboard.

2.6 SALVAGE

Note Full copies of the Lloyd's Open Form Salvage Agreement can be obtained from the Salvage Arbitration Branch, Lloyd's of London, 1 Lime Street, London EC3M 7HA (✆ 020 7623 7100, ext 5849) who should be notified of the services only when no agreement can be reached as to remuneration.

SIMPLE FORM OF SALVAGE AGREEMENT
'NO CURE – NO PAY'
(Incorporating Lloyd's Open Form)

Date

On board the yacht

IT IS HEREBY AGREED BETWEEN

for and on behalf of the Owners of the
(hereinafter called 'the Owners')

AND

for and on behalf of
(hereinafter called 'the Contractor')

1. That the Contractor will use his best endeavours to salve the
and take her into
or such other place as may hereinafter be agreed or if no place is named or agreed to a place of safety.
2. That the services shall be rendered by the Contractor and accepted by the owner as salvage services upon the principle of 'No cure – No pay' subject to the terms conditions and provisions (including those relating to Arbitration and the providing of security) of the current Standard Form of Salvage Agreement approved and published by the Council of Lloyd's of London and known as Lloyd's Open Form.
3. In the event of success the Contractor's remunerations shall be £............ or if no sum be mutually agreed between the parties or entered herein same shall be fixed by arbitration in London in the manner prescribed in Lloyd's Open Form.
4. The Owners their servants and agents shall cooperate fully with the Contractor in and about the salvage including obtaining entry to the place named in Clause 1 hereof or the place of safety. The Contractor may make reasonable use of the vessel's machinery gear equipment anchors chains stores and other appurtenances during and for the purpose of the services free of expense but shall not unnecessarily damage abandon or sacrifice the same or any property the subject of this Agreement.

For and on behalf of the Owners of property to be salved

For and on behalf of the Contractor

3. Radio and satellite services

3.1 COAST RADIO

Coast radio forms part of GMDSS MSI network, broadcasting gale and storm warnings, weather forecasts, navigation and safety information, as well as monitoring the international distress frequencies and relaying information to SAR centres. A range of frequencies is employed to ensure broadcasts can be made over short, medium and long-range using VHF, MF and HF radio. Coast radio is also used by port authorities, pilots, tugs, military and commercial shipping on working frequencies used for communications. Some stations are monitoring 24hr, others are manned only for limited periods. Some stations are linked automatically to central control stations and some are used for data transfer and telephony services. Schedules, frequencies and services are listed later in the section, with further details in ***Section 2 Emergency Services*** *and* ***Section 4 Weather Services***

REGULATIONS FOR THE USE OF RT IN MEDITERRANEAN COUNTRIES

Spain

The following regulations are current.

Regulation for the use of radio by foreign vessels in Spanish ports.

Transmission by radio on frequencies below 30MHz by foreign vessels under way, anchored (or secured alongside) inside Spanish ports, roadsteads and bays is prohibited except in cases of accident or disaster or force majeure.

The prohibition applies to all foreign vessels within three miles of the outer extremities of moles or breakwaters in the case of artificial harbours, or within three miles of the outer points which form the entrance to bays or roadstead.

Frequencies greater than 30MHz can be employed inside ports, roadsteads or bays, provided always they have been assigned by Spanish or International Regulations for port operations services or public correspondence, and are employed for communication with those services, and comply with the special regulations laid down for the particular port, bay or roadstead.

The authorisation to use frequencies greater than 30MHz under the above conditions is automatically rescinded when the harbour signal station or shore pilot station hoists a black ball 50cm in diameter, or when it is ordered by any other means by the above authority.

Special authorisation from the Ministry of the Navy is required if visiting foreign warships wish to use their radio in harbour. Permission will always be granted provided that there is no resultant interference with any Spanish radio station and that a reciprocal agreement exists with the visiting warship's country.

France

The following regulations are current.

Article 1 below refers to superseded abbreviations for the following emission modes:

F3 Frequency modulation telephony
A3 Amplitude modulation telephony
A1 Morse telegraphy

Article 1 French or foreign vessels are forbidden to transmit radio signals in French ports, roadsteads, or anchorages, except for the following:

a. Type F3 emissions in the band 156–162MHz to communicate with:
   i A French coast station open to public correspondence.
   ii A local port operations services.
   iii Another vessel under way in the port or roadstead, if necessary for the safety of navigation.
b. Vessels with no other means of radio communication with land may use type A3 emissions in the band 1605–3800kHz, or type A1 emissions in the band 405–525kHz, only for the purpose of calling stations defined in (a) i and (a) ii above. These messages should be as short as possible.
c. Transmissions for communication with a private radio station authorised under the relevant articles of the Post and Telecommunications Code.
d. Radar transmissions in authorised frequency bands.
e. Transmissions for the tuning or calibration of any shipborne apparatus. These transmissions should be kept to the minimum. If they happen to be on the calling or ship-shore working frequency of a coast station, prior permission should be obtained from the nearest coast station using these frequencies.

Article 2 French or foreign vessels in French territorial waters, within 3 nautical miles of the coast, are forbidden to transmit:

a. Broadcasting programmes, on any frequency band.
b. Signals on frequencies between 4000 and 27500kHz
c. Signals on other frequency bands directed to:
   i Foreign coast stations or ships outside French territorial waters, unless on matters relating to the needs of navigation or the fishing industry.
   ii Stations on land not authorised to receive them.

Transmissions for tuning or calibration should conform to the regulation in Article 1 (e) above.

Article 3 The regulations in Articles 1 and 2 above apply to foreign warships, but not to French warships. These regulations, however, may be temporarily waived by permission of the French naval authorities, in agreement with the Post and Telecommunications Administration.

Article 6 The regulations in this decree do not apply to mobile stations in distress, or to those assisting in search and rescue operations.

Article 7 The terms defined in the radio regulations of the International Telecommunication Union are also so defined in this decree.

Article 8 Penalties for contravening the regulations in this decree are as laid down in Article 72 of the Post and Telecommunications Code.

Article 9 The dispositions of the present decree are also applicable to French overseas territories.

Italy

The following regulations are current.

Radio communication by merchant and pleasure vessels whilst stopping in Italian waters is prohibited, except in the following cases:

1. When advising of, or requesting assistance in case of danger.
2. For reasons of urgency.
3. In the first half hour after arrival.
4. When communication with the land is impeded by reason of force majeure, or sanitary measures.

Persons infringing the regulations are punishable by a fine and/or imprisonment.

Croatia

The following regulation was current in 1992 (from June 1992). It is prohibited to use the shipboard radiotelephony or radiotelegraphy station when ships are in ports and harbours except for piloting, manoeuvring, cargo operations and other ship manipulations.

Greece

The following regulations are current.

1. Ships using radio in Greek territorial waters must conform to the following rules:
   i Transmissions from Greek fixed or mobile stations must not be interfered with.
   ii Transmission must cease immediately, on demand from the appropriate national authorities.
   iii Transmissions on distress frequencies are prohibited, except for distress calls and answers to such calls.
2. The use of radio is forbidden to ships underway or anchored within harbour limits. Exceptionally,when correspondence is already in progress when a vessel crosses the harbour limits, the completion of the signal then being sent is permitted.
3. If a foreign warship wishes to use its radio in circumstances where this is normally prohibited, application must be made in writing to the General Staff of the Navy.

Turkey

The following regulations are current.

Article 27 Communication by radio whilst in port is prohibited. Nevertheless, if it should be impossible to establish communication with the land, the senior naval officer of the port may authorise a vessel to communicate by radio, such communication to be of short duration and solely in respect of matters relating to its management and voyage. Test transmissions for the adjustment of radio apparatus may be carried out with the permission of the coast station. Private messages are not to be received in port.

Article 28 Vessels are expected to comply with instructions from the coast station concerning the time and order for communications in order to avoid interference.

Article 28 Vessels are expected to comply with iusuuctions from the coast station concerning the time and onler for communications in order to avoid interference.

Article 29 In territorial waters, and subject to the observance of the conditions prescribed in Article 28, a vessel may, during its stay in port communicate only with the nearest Turkish coast station. Service messages between vessels of the same company may be exchanged in territorial waters, without being passed through the coast station.

Article 30 The terms of articles 27, 28 and 29 do not apply in cases of distress and danger to life. Messages of foreign vessels and aircraft.
Article 31 The terms of Articles 27, 28, 29 and 30 apply also to foreign vessels entering Turkish territorial waters and ports, and to foreign aircraft which enter Turkish air or which land at Turkish aerodromes and airports. Nevertheless, the Council of Ministers may, should the necessity arise, authorise such vessels and such aircraft to communicate in port, in the air and at airports, without being subject to these restrictions.
Article 32 Every foreign vessel which enters Turkish territorial waters is expected to report to the nearest coast station details of its nationality, name of owners, and also the position of the vessel.
Article 33 Foreign warships and military aircraft which have obtained permission as provided in Article 31 may communicate in the air, and at aerodromes, and in the territorial waters of ports of Turkey, subject to observance of the internal and international rules and regulations intended to safeguard the security of radio communicarions.
Article 50 The present law enters into force as from 1 August 1937.

Israel

The following regulations are current. Ships within the territorial waters of the State of Israel are prohibited from conducting radio communications with any station except under all of the following conditions: That communication will be effected with, or by means of, an Israeli coast station or on authorised frequencies above 26·96MHz. That the minimum required power be utilised. That no interference will result to any other authorised station. These communications shall cease upon notification by an Israeli coast station.

Libya

The following regulations are current. Masters are informed that it is forbidden to operate radio sets in the medium and high frequency wave bands within Libyan Territorial Waters unless such radio sets have been licenced by the General Post and Telecommunications Corporation of the Socialist Jamahiriya.

Algeria

The following regulations are current.
Article 1 Radio transmission from vessels are permitted in Algerian ports, roadsteads, anchorages and territorial waters in the following cases:
- i On VHF frequencies 156–162MHz in order to establish communications with: Algerian coast stations Port operations stations Other moving vessels, only as necessary for navigation.
- ii On telegraphic and telephonic frequencies within bands 405–535kHz, 1605–1625kHz, 1635–1800kHz, 2045–2160kHz to contact the shore if VHF cannot be used. These transmissions may only be used after authorisation from Algerian coast stations.

Article 2 Authorisation must be sought from the nearest Algerian coast station before making test transmissions, these transmissions should be as short as possible and include the vessel's call sign. An artificial sign must be used if the automatic alarm gear is tested.
Article 3 With the exception of the transmissions described in Article 1, all other transmissions are prohibited.
Article 5 Vessels in Algerian ports, roadsteads, anchorages and territorial waters must inform the nearest Algerian coast station or harbour station of the opening and closing times of their radio facility.
Article 6 The rules in Article 3 do not apply to the following situations: i vessels in danger or participating in search and rescue operations; ii vessels flying the flag of a State with which Algeria has established reciprocal arrangements; iii Algerian Naval vessels.
Article 7 Infringements of this Decree will be punished in accordance with Post and Telecommunications Law of 1975.

3.2 CALL SIGN ALLOCATIONS

AMA-AOZ	Spain	TOA-TQZ	France
CNA-CNZ	Morocco	TSA-TSZ	Tunisia
C4A-C4Z	Cyprus	TVA-TXZ	France
EAA-EHZ	Spain	YKA-YKZ	Syrian Arab Republic
FAA-FZZ	France	YMA-YMZ	Turkey
HWA-HYZ	France	ZAA-ZAZ	Albania
IAA-IZZ	Italy	3AA-3AZ	Monaco
J4A-J4Z	Greece	4XA-4XZ	Israel
P3A-P3Z	Cyprus	4XA-4XZ	Israel
SSA-SSM	Egypt	5CA-5GZ	Morocco
SUA-SUZ	Egypt	6AA-6BZ	Egypt
SVA-SZZ	Greece	6CA-6CZ	Syrian Arab Republic
S5A-S5Z	Slovenia	7RA-7RZ	Algeria
TAA-TCZ	Turkey	7TA-7YZ	Algeria
THA-THZ	France	9AA-9AZ	Croatia
TKA-TKZ	France	9HA-9HZ	Malta
TMA-TMZ	France		

3.3 THE STANDARD PHONETIC ALPHABET & NUMERALS

Letter		*Pronunciation*	*Letter*		*Pronunciation*
A	alfa	ALfah	N	november	noVEMber
B	bravo	BRAHvoh	O	oscar	OSScar
C	charlie	CHARlee	P	papa	pahPAH
D	delta	DELLtah	Q	quebec	keyBECK
E	echo	ECKoh	R	romeo	ROWmeoh
F	foxtrot	FOKStrot	S	sierra	seeAIRrah
G	golf	golf	T	tango	TANgo
H	hotel	hohTELL	U	uniform	YOUneeform
I	india	INdeeah	V	victor	VIKtah
J	juliett	JEWleeETT	W	whisky	WISSkey
K	kilo	KEYloh	X	x-ray	ECKSRAY
L	lima	LEEmah	Y	yankee	YANGkey
M	mike	mike	Z	zulu	ZOOloo

Figure	*Pronunciation*	*Figure*	*Pronunciation*
1	wun	6	six
2	too	7	SEV-en
3	tree	8	ait
4	FOW-er	9	NIN-er
5	fife	0	zero

3.4 TRANSMITTING FREQUENCIES

INTERNATIONAL MARITIME VHF FREQUENCIES TABLE

Channel designators		Transmitting frequencies MHz: Ship stations	Coast stations	Notes	Ship to ship	Port operation and ship movements: Simplex	Duplex	Public correspondence
	60	156·025	160·625				X	X
01		156·050	160·650				X	X
	61	156·075	160·675				X	X
02		156·100	160·700				X	X
	62	156·125	160·725				X	X
03		156·150	160·750				X	X
	63	156·175	160·775				X	X
04		156·200	160·800				X	X
	64	156·225	160·825				X	X
05		156·250	160·850				X	X
	65	156·275	160·875				X	X
06		156·300		(1)	X			
	66	156·325	160·925				X	X
07		156·350	160·950				X	X
	67	156·375	156·375		X	X		
08		156·400			X			
	68	156·425	156·425			X		
09		156·450	156·450		X	X		
	69	156·475	156·475		X	X		
10		156·500	156·500		X	X		
	70	156·525	156·525	Digital selective calling for Distress and Safety				
11		156·550	156·550			X		
	71	156·575	156·575			X		
12		156·600	156·600			X		
	72	156·625	156·625		X			
13		156·650	156·650		X	X		
	73	156·675	156·675		X	X		
14		156·700	156·700			X		
	74	156·725	156·725			X		
15		156·750	156·750	(2)	X	X		
	75	Guard-band 156·7625–156·7875MHz(4)				X		
16		156·800	156·800	Distress, Safety and Calling				
	76	Guard-band 156·8125_156·8375Mhz(4)				X		
17		156·850	156·850	(2)	X	X		
	77	156·875			X			X
18		156·900	161·500			X	X	X
	78	156·925	161·525				X	X
19		156·950	161·550				X	X
	79	156·975	161·575				X	X
20		157·000	161·600				X	X
	80	157·025	161·625				X	X
21		157·050	161·650				X	X
	81	157·075	161·675				X	X
22		157·100	161·700				X	X
	82	157·125	161·725			X	X	X
23		157·150	161·750				X	X
	83	157·175	161·775			X	X	X
24		157·200	161·800				X	X
	84	157·225	161·825			X	X	X
25		157·250	161·850				X	X
	85	157·275	161·875			X	X	X
26		157·300	161·900				X	X
	86	157·325	161·925			X	X	X
27		157·350	161·950				X	X
	87	157·375	161·975			X		
28		157·400	162·000				X	X
	88	157·425	162·025			X		
AIS 1 (3)		161·975	161·975					
AIS 2 (3)		162·025	162·025					

Notes

1. The frequency 156·300MHz (channel 06) may also be used for communications between ship stations and aircraft stations engaged in co-ordinated search and rescue operations. Ship stations shall avoid harmful interference to such communications on channel 06 as well as to communications between aircraft stations, ice-breakers and assisted ships during ice seasons.
2. Channels 15 and 17 may also be used for on-board communications provided the effective radiated power does not exceed 1W.
3. These channels (AIS 1 and AIS 2) are used for an automatic ship identification and surveillance system capable of providing worldwide operation on high seas, unless other frequencies are designated on a regional basis for this purpose.
4. The use of these channels (75 and 76) should be restricted to navigation-related communications only and all precautions should be taken to avoid harmful interference to Channel 16, e.g. by limiting the output power to 1W or by means of geographical separation.

RECOMMENDED SINGLE SIDEBAND FREQUENCIES FOR SHIP TO SHIP TRANSMISSIONS (IN KHZ)

4MHz					*8MHz*						
4 000	4 012	4 030	4 045	4 060	8 101	8 113	8 131	8 146	8 161	8 176	8 191
4 003	4 015	4 033	4 048	4146	8 104	8 116	8 134	8 149	8 164	8 179	
4 006	4 018	4 036	4 051	4149	8 107	8 119	8 137	8 152	8 167	8 182	
4 009	4 021	4 039	4 054	4417	8 110	8 122	8 140	8 155	8 170	8 185	
	4 024	4 042	4 057			8 125	8 143	8 158	8 173	8 188	
	4 027					8 128					

3.5 CLASSIFICATION OF EMISSIONS

The following examples of emissions used in ALRS volumes have been compiled from Radio Regulations:

Type of modulation of main carrier	*Nature of signal(s) modulating the main carrier*	*Description of emission*	*Designation*
No modulating signal	–	Continuous wave emission	NON
Amplitude modulation	Signal with quantized or digital information	Continuous wave telegraphy, morse code	A1A
	Telegraphy by on-off keying of a tone modulated carrier: double sideband, morse code		A2A
	Telegraphy by on-off keying of a tone modulated carrier: single sideband, full carrier, morse code		H2A
	Direct-printing telegraphy using a frequency shifted modulating sub-carrier, with error correction, single sideband, suppressed carrier (single channel)		J2B
	Telephony (single channel)	Telephony, double sideband	A3E
	Telephony, single sideband, full carrier (single channel)		H3E
	Telephony, single sideband reduced carrier (single channel)		R3E
	Telephony, single sideband, suppressed carrier (single channel		J3E
	Sound broadcasting	Sound broadcasting, double sideband	A3E
	Composite system	Double sideband eg a combination of telegraphy and telephony	A9W
Frequency modulation	Signal with quantized or digital information	Telegraphy, narrow band direct printing with error-correction (Telex) (single channel)	F1B
	Sound broadcasting	Sound broadcasting	F3E

3.6 COAST RADIO SERVICES

For further details also see Sections *2.4 Emergency Radio Services* and *4.1 Radio Weather Services*

In addition to the frequencies listed below, most coast radio stations maintain a listening watch on the international distress frequencies.

VHF COAST RADIO

All stations monitor Ch 16

Station	*Call sign*	*Manual*	*Auto*	*Autolink*
SPAIN				
Tarifa MRCC[1]		**10, 67**		
Algeciras MRSC[1]		**74**		
Almeria MRCC[2]		**74**		
Valencia MRCC[2]		**10**		
Palma MRCC[1]		**10**		
Castellon MRSC[2]		**74**		
Tarragona MRSC[2]		**74**		
Barcelona MRCC[2]		**Wx10 Nav16**		
Malaga CCR II				
Cadiz CRS		**26**	61	
Tarifa CRS		**81**	23	
Malaga CRS		**26**	25	
Cabo de Gata CRS		**27**	20	
Valencia CCR I				
Cartegena CRS		**04**	65	
Alicante CRS		**85**		
Cabo La Nao CRS		**01**	61	
Palma CRS		**20**	83	
Menorca CRS		**85**	85	
Ibiza CRS		**03**		
Castellon CRS		**25**	63	
Tarragona CRS		**23**	26	
Barcelona CRS		**60**	60	
Bagur CRS		**23**	23	
FRANCE				
CROSS La Garde MRCC[1]		**16**		
CROSS Corse MRSC[1]		**16, 67**		
Neoulos		**16**		
Agde		**16**		
Planier		**16**		
Mt Coudon		**16**		
Pic de l'Ours		**16**		
CORSICA				
Ersa		**16, 67**		
Serra di Pigno		**16, 67**		
Conca		**16, 67**		
Serragia		**16, 67**		
La Punta		**16, 67**		
Piana		**16, 67**		
ITALY				
R – Call sign *Roma Radio*		P – Call sign *Palermo Radio*		
Ligurian Sea				
Monte Bignone	R	**07**	65	03, 23
Castellaccio	R	**25**	83	
Zoagli	R	**27**	85	
Monte Nero	R	**61**	63	
Gorgona	R	**26**	82	
Elba	R		84	
Tyrrhenian Sea				
Monte Argentario	R	**01**	62	04, 27
T. Chiaruccia	R	**64**	81	
Monte Cavo	R	**25**	65	03, 02
Posillipo	P	**01**	23	
Capri	P	**27**	79	
Varco del Salice	P	**62**		
Serra del Tuono	P	**25**	24	82, 86
Sardinia				
Porto Cervo	R	**26**	88	
Monte Moro	R	**28**	66	24, 87
Monte Limbara	R	**85**	86	07, 23
Monte Tului	R	**83**	86	
Monte Serpeddi	R	**04**	78	05, 26
Margine Rosso	R	**62**	63	
Pta Campu Spina	R	**82**	83	
Badde Urbara	R	**87**	03	
Osilo	R	**26**	61	
Sicily				
Sferracavallo	P	**27**		
Ustica	P	**84**	80	
Cefalu	P	**61**	78	
Forte Spuria	P	**85**	02	
Campo Lato	P	**86**	83	03, 26
Siracusa	P	**85**	81	
Gela	P	**26**	61	
Caltabellotta	P	**22**		
Mazara del Vallo	P	**25**	64	
Erice	P	**81**	65	
Pantelleria	P	**22**		
Lampedusa	P	**25**	85	
Grecale	P	**21**	78	84
Ionian				
Capo Armi	P	**62**	82	
Pta Stilo	P	**84**	65	
Capo Colonna	P	**20**	66	04, 07
Monte Parano	P	**26**	61	
Monte Sardo	P	**27**	02	
South Adriatic				
Abate Argento	P	**05**	62	24, 80
Bari	P	**27**		
Casa d'Orso	P	82	02	
Monte Calvario	P	01	03	61, 66
Central Adriatic				
Silvi	R	**65**	63	
Monte Secco	R	**20**	86	
Monte Conero	R	**02**	82	62, 84
Forte Garibaldi	R	**25**	64	
North Adriatic				
Ravenna	R	**27**	03	
Monte Cero	R	**26**	86	23
Piancavallo	R	**01**	26	05, 88
Conconello	R	**83**	25	63
MALTA				
Malta Radio		**01, 02, 03, 04, 28**		
Valetta Port Control		**12, 09**		
SLOVENIA				
Koper HM		**16**		
CROATIA				
Rijeka MRCC		**16, 10**		
Pula HM		**16, 10**		
Senj HM		**16, 10**		
Zadar HM		**16, 10**		
Sibenik HM		**16, 10**		
Split HM		**16, 10**		
Ploce HM		**16, 10**		
Dubrovnik HM		**16, 10**		

Station	*Call sign*	*Manual*	*Auto*	*Autolink*
R _ Call sign *Rijeka Radio*				
S – Call sign *Split Radio*				
D – Call sign *Dubrovnik Radio*				
Rijeka				
Savudrija	R	**16, 81**		
Ucka	R	**16, 20, 24**		21
Kamenjak – Rab	R	**16, 04**		
Susak	R	**16, 20**		
Split				
Sveti Mihovil –				
Uglijan	S	16	07	
Labistica – Split	S	**16, 21**		05
Vidova Gora – Brac	S	16	23	
Hum – Vis	S	16	28	
Dubrovnik				
Uljenje – Peljesac	D	16, 04		
Srdj – Dubrovnik	D	**16,** 07		*81*
Gorica	D	**63**		
MONTENEGRO				
Bar		**16, 24, 87**		
Dobra Voda		10, 12, 16, 20		
Obosnik		16, 24		
ALBANIA				
Shengjin		**16, 71**		
Durres		**16, 22**		
Vlore		**16, 11**		
Sarande		**16, 06**		
GREECE				
Call sign *Olympia Radio*				
Ionian				
Corfu		**02, 03, 64**		
Cephalonia		**26, 27, 28**		
Pirgos		**86**		
Petalidhi (Kalamata)		**23, 83, 84**		
Kithera		**85, 86**		
Patras		**85**		
Saronic				
Gerania		**02, 64**		
Poros		**26, 27, 28**		
Perama		**86**		
Cyclades				
Andros		**24**		
Siros		**03, 04**		
Milos		**16**		
Thira		**16**		
Evia & N Sporades				
Parnis		**25, 26, 84**		
Likhada		**01**		
Pilio		**03, 60**		
Skiros		**16**		
N Greece				
Sfendami (Thessaloniki)		**23, 24**		
Tsoukalas		**26, 27**		
Thasos		**25, 85**		
E Sporades				
Limnos		**82, 83**		
Lesvos		**01, 02**		
Dodecanese				
Patmos		**24**		
Khios		**85**		
Rhodos		**01, 63**		
Karpathos		**03**		
Astipalaia		**23**		

Station	*Call sign*	*Manual*	*Auto*	*Autolink*
Crete				
Knossos		**83, 84**		
Broukhas		**28**		
Sitia		**85, 86**		
Festos		**26, 27**		
Moustakos		**04**		
TURKEY				
Istanbul				
Mahyadag		**16, 25, 67, 82**		
Camlica		**16, 03, 07, 26, 28, 67**		
Akcakoca		**16, 01, 23, 67**		
Sarkoy		**16, 05, 27, 67**		
Keltepe		**16, 02, 24, 67, 81, 84**		
Kayalidag		**16, 01, 23, 67**		
Ayvalik		**16, 28, 67**		
Bandirma		**16, 28, 67**		
Akdag		**16, 02, 24, 28, 67, 84**		
Bodrum		**16, 27, 67**		
Oren		**16, 27, 67**		
Kazakin		**16, 28, 67**		
Dilektepe		**16, 03, 25, 67**		
Palamut		**16, 26, 67, 81**		
Yumrutepe		**16, 01, 24, 67, 82**		
Anamur		**16, 25, 67, 84**		
Cobandede		**16, 04, 67, 82, 85**		
Markiz		**16, 25, 24, 67, 83**		
CYPRUS				
Kionia		**16, 24, 25, 26, 27**		
Olympos				
Pissouri				
SYRIA				
Lattakia (Al Ladhiqiyah)		**16,13**		
Banias		16		
Tartous YKO		20		
Tartous YKI		16, 08		
LEBANON				
Beyrouth		**16**		
ISRAEL				
Haifa (Hefa)		**16, 24, 25, 26, 86, 87**		
EGYPT				
Bur Said (Port Said)		**16, 02, 04, 23, 25, 28, 60, 66**		
El Iskandariya (Alexandria)		**16, 02, 05, 19, 23, 25, 27, 60, 64, 66, 79, 87**		
LIBYA				
Banghazi		**12, 14, 22, 26**		
Tarabulus (Tripoli)		**06, 14, 22, 26**		
TUNISIA				
Sfax[3]		**02, 22, 24**		
Mahida		**27, 28**		
Kelibia[3]		**26,28**		
Tunis		**01, 10, 12, 18, 21, 25, 26**		
Bizerte[4]		**23, 24**		
ALGERIA				
Alger MRCC (CNOSS)		**24, 25, 26, 27, 28, 84, 87**		
Annaba		**24, 25, 26, 27, 28**		
Skikda		**24, 25, 26, 27, 28**		
Tenes				
Arzew		**24, 25, 26, 27, 28**		
Ghazouet		**24, 25, 26, 27, 28**		

Station	Call sign	Manual	Auto	Autolink
MOROCCO				
Al Hoceima		**22, 25, 27, 28**		
Tanger		**24, 25, 26, 27**		
Casablanca		05, **20**, 24, 25, 26, 27		
ATLANTIC ISLANDS				
AZORES				
Horta CRS		11		
Flores	23			
Faial		**24, 25 26**		
Pico		**23, 24, 26**		
São Miguel		**24, 25, 26**		
MADEIRA				
Porto Santo CRS		11		
Porto Santo		**26, 28**		
Pico da Cruz		**25, 28**		
Ponta do Pargo		**23, 26, 27**		
CANARIES				
Lanzarote		**25**		*03*
Fuerteventura		**22**		
Las Palmas		**26**		*84*
Tenerife		**27**		*60*
Gomera		**24**		
La Palma		**20**		
El Hierro		**23**		

1. Stations do not accept public correspondence, excepting distress, safety and urgent traffic only.
2. Stations do not accept public correspondence, excepting distress, safety and urgent traffic, port operations and pollution reports only.
3. 0600–1800
4. 0700–1900

COAST RADIO – MF

All stations monitor 2182kHz

Main operating frequency in bold

Station	Transmit (kHz)	Receive (kHz)
SPAIN		
Almeria MRCC[2]	2182	2182
Valencia MRCC[2]	2182	
Palma MRCC[1]	2182	2812
Barcelona MRCC[2]	2182	
FRANCE		
CROSS La Garde MRCC[1]		
La Garde	2182, 1696, 2677	2182, 2677
SPAIN		
Malaga CCR II		
Chipiona CRS	1656	2081
Tarifa CRS	1704	2129
Autolink	2610	3290
Cabo de Gata CRS	1767	2111
Palma CRS	1755	2099
Autolink	2799	2099
ITALY		
Genova	1667, 2642, **2722**	2182
Livorno	1925, **2591**	2182
Civitavecchia	**1888**, 2710, 3747	2182
Napoli	2632, 3735	2182
Porto Torres	**2719**	2182
Sardinia		
Cagliari	**2680**, 2683	2182
Sicily		
Palermo	**1852**	2182
Messina	**2789**	2182
Augusta	1643, **2628**	2182
Mazara del Vallo	1883, 2211, **2600**	2182
Lampedusa	**1876**	2182
Ionian		
Crotone	1715, **2663**	2182
Bari	1771, **2579**	2182
Central Adriatic		
San Benedetto	1855	2182
Ancona	2656	2182
Trieste	2624	2182
MALTA		
Malta Radio	2625	2182
Rijeka MRCC	2182, 1641, 1656	2182
MONTENEGRO		
Bar	2182, 1720.4, 2191, 2752	2182
ALBANIA		
Shengjin	2282, 2400	2182
Durres	2182, 2282, 2730	2182
Vlore	2282, 2400	2182
Sarande	2282, 2400	2182
GREECE		
Corfu	2182, 1696, 2607, **2830**, 3613	2182
Olympia Radio	1695, 1767	2182
Limnos	2182, **2730**, 3793	2182
Rhodos	2182, 1824, **2624**, 3630	2182
Iraklion	2182, 1615·5, 1726·4, 1741·4, **2799**	2182
TURKEY		
Istanbul	2182, 2670	2182
Canakkale	2182, 1850	2182
Izmir	2182, 1850, 2760	2182
Antalya	2182, 2693	2182
Mersin	2182, 2820	2182
Iskenderun	2182, 2629, 3648	2182
CYPRUS		
Larnaca	2182, 2670, 2700, 3690	2182
SYRIA		
Lattakia (Al Ladhiqiyah)	2182, 3624, 3490	2182
Tartous YKO	2182, 2662	
ISRAEL		
Haifa (Hefa)	2182, 2649	2182
EGYPT		
Bur Said (Port Said)	2182	2182
El Iskandariya (Alexandria)	2182	2182
LIBYA		
Banghazi	2182, 2513, 2816	2182
Tarabulus (Tripoli)	2182, 2197, 2320, 2418	2182
TUNISIA		
Mahida	2182, 1696·4, 1771	2182
Tunis	2182,1768·4, 2670	2182
Bizerte[4]	2182, 1687·4, 2210	2182
ALGERIA		
Annaba	2182, 1911, 2775	2182
Bejaia	(ITU Channels)	
Boufarik Radio	601, 802 (24h), 1207, 1629	2182
Alger MRCC (CNOSS)	2182, 1792, 2691, 2775	2182
Tenes		
Oran (CROSS)	2182, 1735, 2586, 2719	2182

MOROCCO

Tanger	2182, 1911, 2635	2182
Casablanca	2182, 2586, 2663	
ATLANTIC ISLANDS		
AZORES		
Horta CRS	2182	2182
São Miguel	2182, 2741	2182
MADEIRA		
Porto Santo CRS	2182, 2657	2182
Madeira	2182, 2843, 2180	2182
CANARIES		
Lanzarote	2182, 1644	2182, 2069
Las Palmas	2182, 1689	2182, 2114
Autolink	2606	2182, 3283

1. Stations do not accept public correspondence, excepting distress, safety and urgent traffic only.
2. Stations do not accept public correspondence, excepting distress, safety and urgent traffic, port operations and pollution reports only.
3. 0600–1800
4. 0700–1900

COAST RADIO – HF

ITU Channels (H24)

Madrid		804	1201	1637	1801
		810			2229
Monaco	403	804	1224	1607	2225
Roma	412	831	1221	1621	2202
Rijeka	408	810	1229	1611	1812
Olympia	424	806	1232	1640	2217
Istanbul	417	811	1218	1618	
Cyprus	406	807	1208	1603	2212
Haifa		810		1617	

3.7 TRAFFIC SERVICES

Traffic Separation Schemes (TSS) and Vessel Traffic Services (VTS) in the Mediterranean

Leisure craft are not required to comply with VTS, although some ports request all vessels maintain a listening watch on a working channel for navigation warnings.

GIBRALTAR
Gibraltar Straits (Tarifa) VTS and TSS
VTS Monitors all traffic between 05°15′W and 05°58′W.
Call sign *Tarifa Traffic*
MMSI 002240994
VHF Ch 10, 16, 67
DSC VHF
DSC MF
✆ +34 956 684 757/740
Gibraltar Bay VTS
Vessels in Gibraltar Bay should keep a listening watch on VHF Ch 12
VHF Ch 12, 06, 16
Port Captain ✆ +350 77254
Operations Office ✆ +350 77004 78134

SPAIN
Cabo de Gata TSS
Off Cabo De Gato (Spain)
36°35′·0N 02°00′·0W
Cabo de Palos TSS
Off Cabo de Palos (Spain)
38°37′·5N 00°35′·0W
Cabo de la Nao TSS
Off Cabo De La Nao (Spain)
38°40′·0N 00°20′·0E
Approaches to Castellon
Barcelona

FRANCE
Marseille VTS
VHF Ch 12, 14, 16, 73
Marseille Port Control ✆ 0491 39 41 41
Toulon VTS
VHF Ch 06, 12, 16
Harbourmaster ✆ 0494 03 27 60
Porto Vecchio VTS (Corsica)
VHF Ch 12, 14, 16
Bouches de Bonifacio TSS
41°18′·5N 09°03′·5E – 41°23′·0N 09°27′·0E

ITALY
Straits of Messina VTS
All vessels should keep a listening watch on VHF Ch 16 while in the straits.
Taranto Traffic Control
All vessels using Canale Navigable must keep a listening watch on VHF Ch 67 and make contact with Castello Signal Station.
Ravenna Port Control
Port Authority
VHF Ch 16, 11
VHF Ch 12 for bridge opening
✆ 0544 590 222
Email info@port.ravenna.it
www.port.ravenna.it
Approaches to Laguna Veneta (Venice) TSS
45°15′·5N 12°31′·8E

Major Port VTS

Approaches to Genova (including Savona and La Spezia)
Livorno
Piombino
Civitavecchia
Napoli
Torre Anunziata
Castellammare di Stabia
Porto Vecchio (Sardinia)
Golfo d'Olbia (Sardinia)
Cagliari (Sardinia)
Palermo (Sicily)
Catania (Sicily)
Trapani (Sicily)
Otranto
Bari
Brindisi
Ancona
Golfo di Trieste
Monfalcone

MALTA
Valetta Port Control
VHF Ch 16, 12, 09 (leisure craft)
Port Control Office ✆ 21 239 010 / 241 363

SLOVENIA
Koper VTS
Approaches to Koper

CROATIA
Vela Vrata TSS
Between Otok Cres and the Istrian Peninsula
Otok Palagruža TSS (Adriatic)
42°16'·5N 16°09'·5E

GREECE
Rion-Antirrion Bridge VTS
Call sign *Rion Traffic*
VHF Ch 14
Corinth Canal Authority
Call sign *Isthmia Pilot*
VHF Ch 11
✆ 27410 37700
www.corinthcanal.com
Cape Malea (S Peleponnisos) TSS
36°N 23°E
Piraeus VTS
Approaches to Piraeus
Piraeus Port Control
Call sign *Piraeus Traffic*
VHF Ch 13, 16, 19
Port Authority ✆ 210 451 1311/1319
Thessaloniki TSS
40°27N 22°46E
Soudha Bay Port Control (Crete)
Information on naval exercises on VHF Ch 16
VHF Ch 08, 12, 16

TURKEY
Çanakkale Boğazi (Dardanelles) to Bosphorus VTS (including Marmara Deniz)
All traffic including pleasure craft MUST monitor the VTS on VHF Ch 13/14 (Bosphorus VTS sectors are listed in the box below).

The websites www.worldvtsguide.org or www.coastalsafety.gov.tr have the latest directions.

Bosphorus Vessel Traffic Service Sectors

Turkeli	VHF Ch 11
Kavak	VHF Ch 12
Kandili	VHF Ch 13
Kadyköy	VHF Ch 14
Emergency Communications	VHF Ch 06
Met Bulletins	VHF Ch 67

All vessels should maintain a listening watch on VHF Ch 16.
Çanakkale Traffic Control
✆ 0286 212 540
Gelibolu Control
✆ 0286 566 473
Mehmetçik Control
✆ 0286 862 162
Izmit Korfezi (Marmara Sea)
Candarli
Nemrut Koyu
Izmir Korfezi
Iskenderun Korfezi

SYRIA
All vessels entering Syrian waters must contact CRS on VHF Ch 16.

ISRAEL
Approaches to Ashdod

EGYPT
Quanat El Suweis (Suez Canal) VTS
Port Fouad Yacht Centre
VHF Ch 12, 14, 16
✆ 064 330 000/009

LIBYA
All vessels in Libyan waters should maintain contact with a CRS on VHF Ch 16 or Port Radio on VHF Ch 11, 16 as well as keeping a listening watch on VHF Ch 16.

TUNISIA
Cani Islands TSS
37°31'·7N 10°07'·6E
Cap Bon TSS
37°11'·7N 11°06'·3E

ALGERIA
Approaches to Skhida
Approaches to Oran

MOROCCO
Tangier VTS (Gibraltar Straits)
Call sign *Tangier Traffic*
MMSI 002424131
VHF Ch 16, 67
✆ 212 539 937 500

CANARY ISLANDS
TSS between Fuertaventura and Gran Canaria, and Gran Canaria and Tenerife.

3.8 AUTOMATIC IDENTIFICATION SYSTEM (AIS)

AIS is a vessel-tracking tool using VHF frequency radio transmissions to send and receive information on vessels within that range. Each vessel is shown on a screen as a separate icon with a small data box with information such as:

- Name
- MMSI Number
- Rate of turn
- Course over the ground
- Speed over the ground
- Time of last update

AIS can be used as an overlay to chart plotting software and radar or on a stand-alone screen. By 2005 all vessels subject to SOLAS regulations (vessels over 300grt, passenger carrying vessels or fishing vessels over 12m) must be fitted with 'A' System AIS equipment. All vessels over 20m in US waters must also comply. A receive-only system is available for around £200. This unit enables the skipper to identify shipping in the vicinity, but does not transmit information back to the ships. An AIS 'B' system is also available for non-commercial vessels, which works in the same way as the 'A' system, only with fewer data transmissions per minute, but it does mean that 'B' users will be 'seen' by 'A' users.

3.9 NAVTEX

A dedicated service on 518kHz giving information on navigation and weather reports, NAVTEX forms part of the GMDSS Maritime Safety Information (MSI) service. Data is received on a dedicated receiver on screen with storage or by a print-out. The system is in operation in the Mediterranean with information in English and (in some cases) the language of the country of origin. There are a number of message categories, as follows:

A **Navigational warnings**
B **Meteorological warnings**
C Ice reports
D **SAR information and piracy warnings**
E Weather forecasts
F Pilot Service messages
G AIS
H Loran-C messages
I Spare
J Satnav messages
K Other electronic Navaid warnings
L Additional navigational warnings
Z No messages on hand

See *Section 4.2 Navtex Services*, for stations and coverage.

3.10 WEATHERFAX

Weatherfax services are usually accessed using a HF receiver and appropriate computer and software or a dedicated weatherfax receiver. The quality of the charts obtained will depend on the strength of the radio signal, and on the quality of the printer (if used). Some Mediterranean weatherfax stations have been shut down and it is likely that more will go as the information is increasingly sourced from the internet.

See *4.3 Weatherfax Services* for schedules and frequencies.

3.11 GPS (GLOBAL POSITIONING SYSTEM)

The first GPS satellites were launched over 25 years ago. Since then GPS has become the cheapest form of position finding around, with a handheld set now costing less than a decent hand-bearing compass. The speed at which a GPS receiver can do a cold start and produce a position is now around 30 seconds. The ease with which we retrieve data has been simplified by software that enables us to scroll through pages and pick out how we want to view the data. From the stream of position data we get speed over the ground, course heading in true and magnetic, distance off course from a waypoint, and a graphic display of our course.

SDGPS (Satellite Differential GPS) works by a network of ground reference stations receiving GPS signals and then correcting them for known errors. A GPS correction signal is then transmitted to geostationary satellites on the same frequency as GPS signals. An accuracy of 2–3 metres is claimed. Your GPS receiver needs to be WAAS/EGNOS enabled. In **Europe** ***EGNOS (European Geostationary Navigation Overlay Service)*** is the European SDGPS system. ***WAAS (Wide Area Augmentation System)*** is the US equivalent. For more information on EGNOS see the European Space Agency website www.esa.int

Galileo is the EU alternative to GPS. It has already been agreed that Galileo will be fully compatible with both GPS and GLONASS (the Russian system). In practice this means that receivers can get position data from satellites of all three systems. The first Galileo satellites were in orbit in early 2006. The project faltered as doubts over the financial viability of Galileo were raised by the consortium, but in April 2008 the European Commission agreed to make €5 billion available to ensure the project's success. Galileo is now due to be operational in 2015.

Note some GPS manufacturers recommend that in areas where EGNOS is not available, it may actually improve the accuracy of the unit to disable EGNOS until you are back in range of EGNOS or WAAS satellites. Without SDGPS you can expect an accuracy of +/-20m.

The very accuracy of GPS can be misleading and seeing a position to two or three decimal points can induce a false sense of confidence in the user. The problem is simply that we do not have charts accurate enough to make full use of such precise positions.

For more details on GPS see the *Mediterranean Cruising Handbook*, Imray.

3.12 CELLULAR PHONES

GSM Phones

Digital cellular phones with GSM (Global System for Mobile Communications) capacity can be used in all Mediterranean countries, as well as the Azores, Madeira and the Canary Islands.

Your own service provider will need to have an agreement with the main service providers in each country. Check with your service provider for details of their 'roaming rates'. As well as high charges for calls you make, you will also be charged for receiving calls. If using a smartphone you are strongly advised to turn off data roaming. Refer to the section below on Mobile Data.

Local Pay-As-You-Go Services

If you are going to spend some time in any one country

it is worth getting a local SIM card for your phone, with a local number. Initial costs are typically low and usually include a pre-payment for your first calls. Pre-payment top-up cards are readily available and asking the retailer to set it up for you gets round any language problems. If you want to use your existing phone and swap the SIM cards, you may need to request that your phone is unlocked by your service provider before leaving the UK. In most countries where PAYG is available the service also supports data transmissions. If you are leaving the country for some time before returning, some PAYG contracts automatically terminate if they are left unused for more than a couple of months or so; check with the service provider.

Range

Handheld sets are limited to around two watts so you will not be able to transmit when too far away from any particular station. Portables (around five watts) or proper marine installations have a greater range. Portable phones, like VHF sets, are limited by the distance from the receiving and transmitting station and are also shut out by high land. Enclosed bays or high islands and mountains will cast a transmitting shadow over the phone.

Given that much of the Mediterranean is mountainous and hence transmitters must be sited quite high, coverage at sea can be obtained at up to 25–30M off the coast and in some cases we have had coverage at 40M off the coast.

3.13 INTERNET AND DATA ACCESS

There are a number of ways of accessing the internet while cruising:

1. **Wireless Networks (WiFi)** Many marinas, hotels, cafés, bars, libraries and internet cafés have excellent WiFi networks, some of which are provided free of charge, or unsecured, others require a subscription. Subscribers may pay a one-off connection charge and/or 'pay-as-you-go' for minutes/hours/days online access. Costs are reasonable for a fast connection, and you don't need to run up unseen data bills on your SIM card. All you need to do is to identify which network you wish to connect to. Specialised outdoor WiFi aerials connected to WiFi modems are now available. This allows multiple connections through a single aerial with an improved signal in comparison with most built in WiFi aerials.

   Note WiFi is a generic term used here to describe all wireless networks.

2. **Mobile data** Most of us are accustomed to having access to the internet at our fingertips 24/7. For many, going sailing is the perfect antidote. For others though, continued access to a fast connection is imperative. Much depends on which camp you fall into.

   Low use

   Checking emails, weather and light surfing (within the EU)

   A roaming data add-on to your own smartphone contract should be enough. EU data roaming costs have recently been capped at €0.20/MB + VAT, but add-ons to existing contracts at around £2/day for 100MB can be found. For additional surfing and VoIP calls enjoy a coffee while you connect to a high speed WiFi network in a café.

   Medium to high use

   All the above plus constant messaging, Tweeting, downloading, streaming and surfing

   A local SIM card with data will usually be cheaper than roaming costs. The card can be used in several ways:

i. **SIM only** Put the SIM into an unlocked smartphone or tablet, and follow the set up instructions. In most cases it is relatively straightforward. Some phones and data packages will allow 'tethering' of other devices by creating its own WiFi signal (see also 'MiFi' below).

ii. **SIM + data dongle** Many operators will sell a data dongle and SIM as a package with data included, which can mean that set-up is simpler. The dongle connects directly to the tablet or laptop by USB.

iii. **SIM + 'MiFi'** MiFi uses a battery operated mobile WiFi modem, about the size of a small phone, which converts the mobile data signal into a secure WiFi network that permits several data connections to one SIM. No direct connection from the modem to the tablet or laptop is required, which makes it more flexible. Much depends on the quality of the network signal to allow more than one fast connection. Data use obviously goes up if more than one person is using it. As with data dongles and smartphones, the device will need to be unlocked, or from the same network as the SIM. Some smartphones can also operate as a WiFi modem.

Note Very high demand applications like VoIP are better using WiFi, rather than mobile data.

Coverage Mobile data is the most common way to access the internet using smartphones and tablets. In parts of Europe 4G technology is up and running, although in most Mediterranean countries 3G is still the norm. Coverage varies with networks and is by no means 100%. In more isolated bays the much slower GPRS signal will be all that is available.

Costs Hot competition between rival networks keeps costs down, and in countries outside the EU, where the price cap does not apply, it is significantly cheaper than roaming costs. Deals change by the week, and so it is really a case of tracking down the best offers.

For example in Turkey: 10GB data over three months for 79TL (€34).

Roaming costs: €0.20/MB.

3.14 SATELLITE SYSTEMS

Ship Earth Station (SES) Satellite Communications

Inmarsat SESs form part of the GMDSS MSI system. As well as transmitting voice and data calls, some systems can be set up to receive ECG messages – effectively NAVTEX messages when out of the 518kHz range.

Most Inmarsat services are geared to large commercial ships or fishing fleets, and due to the size of the domes and heavy power consumption can only really be considered on superyachts. (For high speed data and voice communications the Fleet Broadband or

Fleet 77/55/33 services should be considered).

Mini-C is a derivative of the Inmarsat C system. Using a suitable antenna, (about the size of a typical GPS antenna,) the Mini-C system is a low power consumption service and can be linked either to a dedicated terminal or with software to a laptop computer. Most also incorporate a 12-channel GPS receiver. Inmarsat C and Mini-C are compatible with the following services:

- Email, Telex, Fax or SMS messaging
- Position reporting and polling
- EGC SafetyNet and FleetNet broadcasts
- Distress Alerting and Distress Priority messages

IsatPhone from Inmarsat is a new compact sat phone with data capability. For more details on Inmarsat products see www.inmarsat.com

Other satellite phone services A number of other satellite phone services are available using either high (GEO), medium (MEO) or low (LEO) earth orbitting satellites:

Iridium Now has a new generation of satellites, Iridium is popular with cruisers. Moderate start-up costs and transmission rates are making it affordable for long-range communications, particularly for ocean passage-making. Coverage is worldwide.

Globalstar Coverage over most land areas and the Mediterranean using LEO satellites, but patchy or non-existent (as yet) for offshore waters.

Thuraya Using one GEO satellite, covers mid-Atlantic to India except for low latitudes. Another GEO satellite planned. The phone incorporates a GPS receiver.

Emsat Uses one GEO satellite, giving coverage of northern Europe and the Mediterranean.

Skymate Uses LEO satellites for text based email services. Limited worldwide coverage.

3.15 VOICE OVER INTERNET PROTOCOL (VoIP)

Using a laptop, tablet or smartphone with a broadband connection, many people are using VoIP to make telephone calls. You need to subscribe to a VoIP provider, and set up an account and username to use the service. Call charges are a fraction of those incurred using a GSM phone, and calls between subscribers of the same provider are free. The only downside for travellers is the need to be connected to a broadband network. Skype is probably the best known service, although there are now many companies offering similar services.

3.16 HF RADIO DATA

You can send text based emails and request GRIB files via HF radio and Pactor modem. Data rates are slow, typically less than 6kb/s, but costs for the service are relatively inexpensive and you can send and receive email directly from your boat, anywhere in the world. Annual contracts are around US$250 and emails are free to send and receive. A Pactor modem costs around £650.

For more information on telecommunications see the *Mediterranean Cruising Handbook*, Imray.

3.17 EPIRBS & SARTS

EPIRB Emergency Position-Indicating Radio Beacon
Uses COSPAS-SARSAT international satellites to pick up the 406MHz signal.

Note EPIRBs using the 121MHz frequency are due to be phased out in February 2009.

SART Search and Rescue Radar Transponders

Portable radar transponders designed to provide a locator signal from survival craft. Operates in the 9GHz frequency band and generates a signal displayed on radar as a line of 12 blips. The blips show bearing and distance (0·6M between each dot) to the target.

3.18 BBC WORLD SERVICE FREQUENCIES

Note To the dismay of thousands of its listeners afloat, in February 2008 the BBC axed its European shortwave service. You may be able to tune into the Middle East or African shortwave stations at certain times, and in a few places there are FM services, but largely the service is now limited to satellite services which require specialised receiving equipment unsuited to the marine environment. The only other way to listen is via internet streaming. For further information see www.bbc.co.uk

Shortwave Frequencies

W Africa

5875	6005	7355	9915	11770	11810
12095	13660	15105	15400	17780	17830

Middle East

1323	1413	6195	7375	11675
12095	13660			

FM Services

The World Service is also carried by a number of local radios stations throughout the Mediterranean, usually as brief news programs during the morning.

For details see:
www.bbc.co.uk/worldservice/europe/radio/italy_1.shtml

4. Weather services

4.1 RADIO WEATHER SERVICES

Note 1. All times are UT except where noted as local.
Note 2. Radio is SSB or VHF for coast radio. Broadcast radio frequencies are given under a separate sub-title.
Note 3. Radio schedules change from time to time. Changes to radio schedules can usually be found on the national meteorological service website for many Mediterranean countries. See ***4·6 Weather on the Internet*** for details.

Gibraltar

GIBRALTAR BROADCASTING CORPORATION
Weather forecast
1458kHz FM 91·3, 92·6, 100·5MHz and AM
0530, 0630, 0730, 1030, 1230 (Monday–Friday)
0530, 0630, 0730, 1030 (Saturday)
0630, 0730, 1030 (Sunday)
General synopsis, situation, forecast, wind direction and strength, sea state, visibility for area up to 5M from Gibraltar in English

BRITISH FORCES BROADCASTING SERVICE (BFBS)
Weather forecasts
FM 93·5, 97·8MHz
0745, 0845, 1005, 1605 LT (Monday–Friday)
0845, 0945, 1202 LT (Saturday–Sunday) 1602 LT (Sunday)
FM 89·4, 99·5MHz
1200 LT (Monday–Friday)
Shipping forecast, wind weather, visibility, sea state, swell, high water and low water times for local waters within 5M of Gibraltar, in English
Storm warnings
FM 89·4, 93·5, 97·8, 99·5MHz
On receipt

TELEPHONE SERVICE
Met Office ✆ 53416 gives standard recorded message
RAF Met Office ✆ 00 44 374 55818 (the call charges can be high to use this service).

PORTS
Weather forecasts in English posted daily at Marina Bay, Sheppard's Chandlery and Queensway Marina.

Spain

See table for details.

TELEPHONE

✆ 906 365 371
Spanish forecast.

PORTS

Weather forecasts in Spanish are posted daily in most marinas.

NEWSPAPERS

In some of the newspapers a synoptic map is published along with a general weather forecast. The national newspapers *La Guardia, Levante* and *La Vanguardia* all contain synoptic maps.

TELEVISION

At approximately 2120 local time the Spanish television weather forecast shows a synoptic map and an annotated weather map for Spain.

SPAIN Weather forecasts and navigational warnings

Station	*VHF/MF*	*Forecast Areas*	*Schedule*
MRCC/MRSC (All Spanish/English)			
Cádiz MRSC	74	Sao Vicente, Cádiz,	0315, 0715, 1115, 1515, 1915, 2315
Tarifa MRCC[1]	10, 67, 73	Gibraltar Straits,	Even H+15 ***Navigational warnings*** On receipt
Algeciras MRSC[1]	74	Alboran	0315, 0515, 0715, 1115, 1515, 1915, 2315
			Navigational warnings On receipt
Almeria MRCC[2]	16, 67, 73	Alboran, Palos	Odd H+15
Cartagena MRSC	10	Palos, Alger,	0115, 0515, 0915, 1315, 1715, 2115
Alicante MRSC	11	Cabrera	Even H+15
Palma MRCC[1]	10	Cabrera, Baleares, Minorque	0735, 1035, 1535, 2035 LT (+1hr in winter)
Valencia MRCC[2]	10, 11		Even H+15
Castellon MRSC[2]	74	Baleares	0900, 1400, 1900
Tarragona MRSC[2]	74		0633, 1033, 1633, 2033 LT
Barcelona MRCC[2]	Wx10 Nav16	Baleares, Leon	Summer 0500, 0900, 1400, 1900
			Winter 0600, 0900, 1500, 2000
Palamos MRSC	13		Summer 0630, 0930, 1330, 1830
Malaga CCR II (Spanish only)			
Chipiona CRS	1656kHz		**0733**, 1233, **1933**
Cádiz CRS	26		**0833**, 1133, **2033**
		São Vicente, Cádiz	***Navigational warnings*** On receipt
Tarifa CRS	81	Gib Straits, Alboran	**0833**, 1133, **2033**
Tarifa CRS	1704kHz		**0733**, 1233, **1933**
			Navigational warnings On receipt
Malaga CRS	26	Alboran, Palos	**0833**, 1133, **2033**
Cabo de Gata CRS	27	Palos, Argel, Cabrera, Baleares	**0833**, 1233, 1733
Valencia CCR I (Spanish only)			
Cabo de Gata CRS	1767kHz	Palos, Argel, Cabrera, Baleares	**0750**, 1303, **1950**
Cartegena CRS	4	Palos, Argel, Cabrera,	
Alicante CRS	85	Baleares	**0910**, 1410, **2110**
Cabo La Nao CRS	2		
Palma CRS	20		**0910**, 1410, **2110**
Palma Radio	16, 03, 20, 85		1120, 1420, 1720
Palma CRS	1755kHz	Cabrera, Baleares	0750, 1303, 1950
Menorca CRS	85	Minorque	**0910**, 1410, **2110**
Ibiza CRS	3		**0910**, 1410, **2110**
Castellon CRS	25		
Tarragona CRS	23	Baleares	**0910**, 1410, **2110**
Barcelona CRS	60		
Begur CRS	23	Baleares Leon	**0910**, 1410, **2110**
Arrecife	1644kHz	Lanzarote	0803, 1233, 1903
Las Palmas	1689kHz	Gran Canaria	0803, 1233, 1903

All times UTC. For LT add 2 hours in summer and 1 hour in winter.

Times in **bold** type: weather and navigation reports, others weather only.

[1] Stations do not accept public correspondence, excepting distress, safety and urgent traffic only.

[2] Stations do not accept public correspondence, excepting distress, safety and urgent traffic, port operations and pollution reports only.

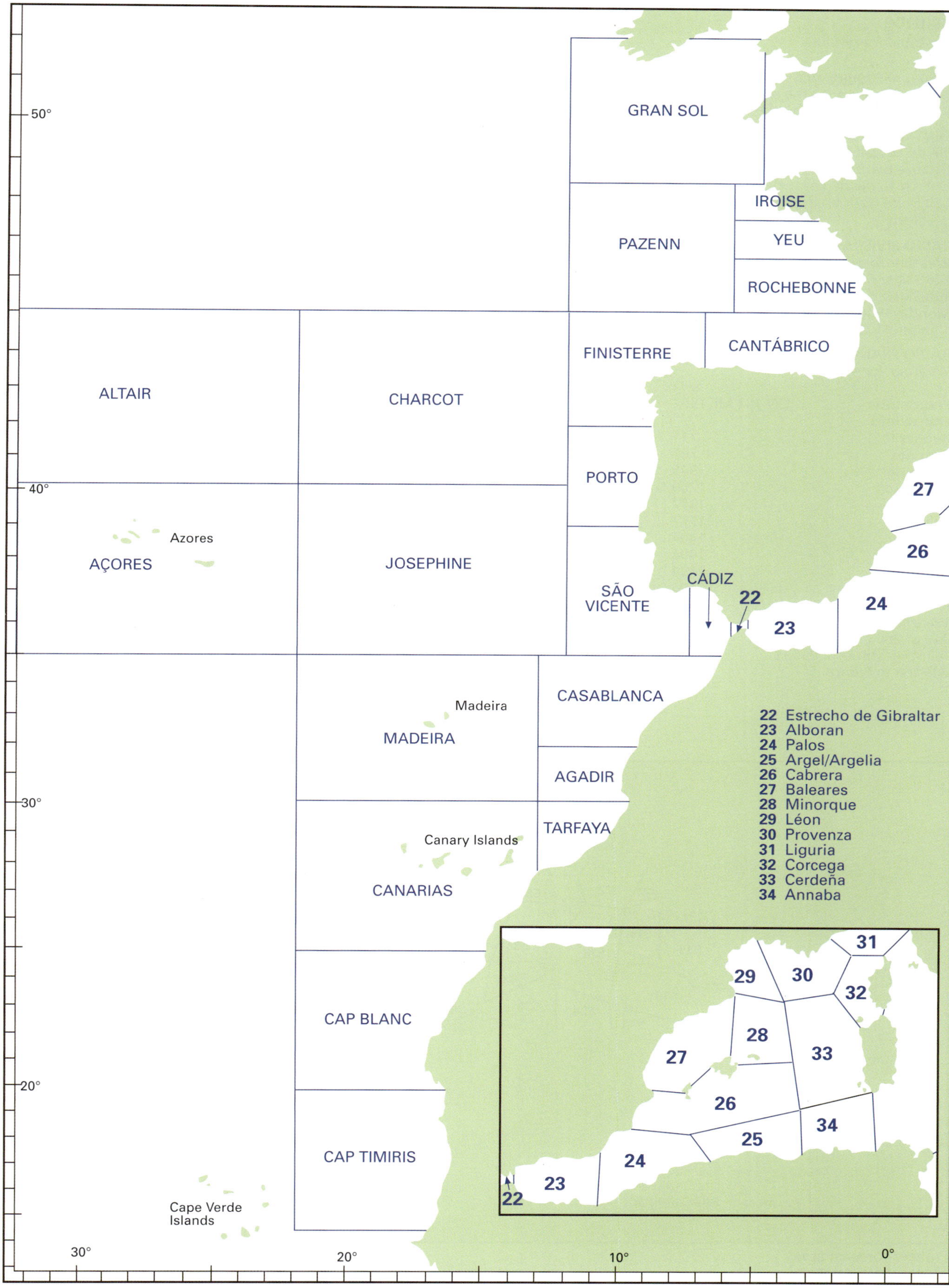
50°
GRAN SOL
IROISE
PAZENN
YEU
ROCHEBONNE
ALTAIR
CHARCOT
FINISTERRE
CANTÁBRICO
PORTO
40°
27
Azores
AÇORES
JOSEPHINE
26
SÃO VICENTE
CÁDIZ
22
24
23
CASABLANCA
Madeira
MADEIRA
AGADIR
22 Estrecho de Gibraltar
23 Alboran
24 Palos
25 Argel/Argelia
26 Cabrera
27 Baleares
28 Minorque
29 Léon
30 Provenza
31 Liguria
32 Corcega
33 Cerdeña
34 Annaba
30°
TARFAYA
Canary Islands
CANARIAS
31
29
30
32
28
33
27
CAP BLANC
20°
26
34
25
CAP TIMIRIS
24
23
22
Cape Verde Islands
30°
20°
10°
0°

Spanish Weather Forecast Areas

France

See table for details.

Note

In summer 2008 a trial for a continuous forecast on VHF Ch 63 was undertaken for the area Port Camargue to St Raphael. This service is being continued for the time being.

CENTRE D'ESSAIS DE LA MEDITERRANEE
(Ile du Levant Firing Range)
Gunfire warnings

VHF Ch 16 (Ile du Levant) Monday–Friday 0800–1800 LT

Call *Delta Neuf* on approach and when within 20 M of Ile du Levant

RADIO RIVIERA
Weather forecasts

106·3MHz Monaco

106·5MHz San Remo and St Tropez

Monday–Friday at 0715, 0815, 1240, 1710, 1915 LT in English for coastal waters between Saint Tropez to Menton and Corsica.

RADIO FRANCE
Weather forecasts

	kHz
France Inter	LW 162 MF 1852
France Info	
Rennes	711
Limoges	792
Toulouse	945
Bordeaux	1206
Marseille	1377
Lille	1377
Brest	1404
Ajaccio	1404
Bastia	1494
Bayonne	1494
Nice	1557

Weather forecasts

162 at 2003 LT

All other stations: 0640 LT

24h fcst in French

RADIO FRANCE-INTERNATIONALE
Weather forecasts

6175kHz at 1130 UT

RFI also broadcasts on MF/HF frequencies with W Atlantic forecasts. See ***Atlantic Islands***.

METEO-FRANCE WEATHER SERVICES

Anywhere in France you can ☎ 0892 68 32 50 or 3250. The short code is only available in France. Costs €0.34/min (additional costs may be incurred if calling from a mobile phone or from outside France).

On connection, press 9 for a 5-day forecast, or code 332 for coastal forecasts (up to 20M offshore), or 333 for offshore forecasts (up to 200M offshore).

Alternatively ☎ 0892 68 08 77 for direct access to the offshore forecast, or dial 0892 68 08 XX where XX is the number of the department required, for a coastal forecast. You will get the latest maritime weather forecast with a general outlook, gale warnings and a detailed forecast for the area you are in, in French at dictation speed.

For further details of French marine weather forecasts including schedules and frequencies see www.meteo.fr/marine/

PORTS

In all marinas in France a weather forecast is posted daily, sometimes with a synoptic chart, in French and sometimes in English as well.

In some ports the Antiope Météo system operates. This shows weather forecasts, synoptic charts and general weather charts on video which constantly scrolls through the complete forecast or allows items to be selected. Usually in the *capitanerie* or marina office if installed.

NEWSPAPERS

Most of the national newspapers have a weather forecast with a general synoptic chart for France. The national newspapers *Le Monde* and *Libération* have synoptic charts.

TELEVISION

On *TF1* and *TF2* there are good general weather forecasts after the news at 1330 and 2030 LT. Wind strengths and directions are mentioned in the commentary.

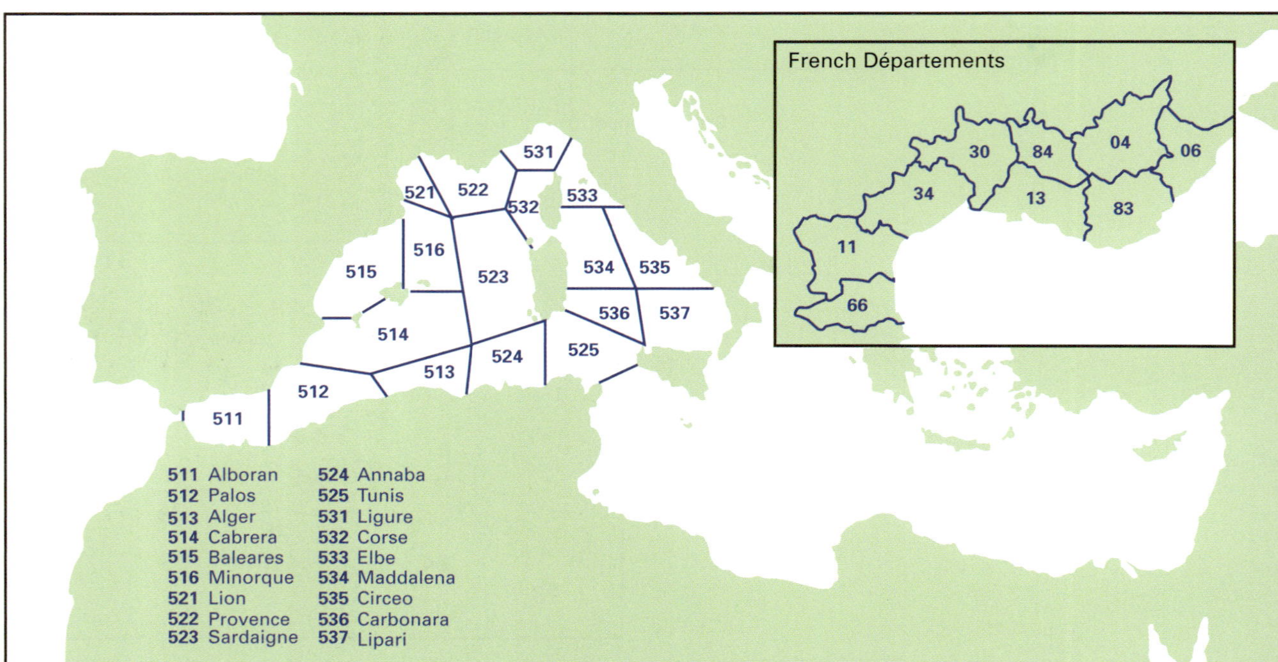

France. Forecast areas

France. Forecast Areas

FRANCE AND MONACO Weather forecasts and navigational warnings

Station	*VHF/MF*	*Forecast Areas*	*Schedule*
CROSS La Garde MRCC (All in French. Also in English where shown)			
			Weather forecasts
La Garde	1696, 2677kHz (announce on 2182)	NW Med[1]	0650, 1433, 1850 (English)
Neoulos	79 (16)	Spanish border to Port Camargue	0703, 1233, 1903
Agde			0715, 1245, 1915
Planier	80 (16)		0733, 1303, 1933
Mt Coudon	63	Port Camargue to St-Raphael	Continuous
Pic de l'Ours	80 (16)		0746, 1316, 1946
Pic de l'Ours	80 (16)	St-Raphael to Menton	0803, 1333, 2033
			Storm warnings
	79, 80 (16)	French coast	On receipt/H+03
	1696, 2677kHz	NW Med[1]	On receipt/4H+03
			(1h, 5h, 9h, 13h, 17h, 21h)
			Navigational warnings
	1696, 2677kHz		0833, 1603
CROSS Corse MRSC (All in French)			
			Weather forecasts
Ersa (Cap Corse)	79 (16)	Corsican coast	0733, 1233, 1933
Serra di Pigno (Bastia)			0745, 1245, 1945
Conca (Porto Vecchio)			0803, 1303, 2003
Serragia (Bonifacio)			0815, 1315, 2015
La Punta (Cargese)			0833, 1333, 2033
Piana (Porto)			0845, 1345, 2045
			Storm warnings
			On receipt/H+10
Monaco Radio (French/English)			
			Weather forecasts
	20 (16)	NW Med[1]	0930, 1403, 1930
	23	St-Raphael to Menton	
	25	Port Camargue to St-Raphael	Continuous
	24	Corsican coast	
	4363, 8728,	W Med[2] 'Large'	0930, 1403, 1930
	13146, 17260kHz	Atlantic 'Grand Large'	0930 UT
		E Med 'Grand Large'	0800, 1030 UT
			Storm warnings
	16, 20/22 4363kHz	NW Med[1]	On receipt/H+03

All times LT except where stated

[1] E Cabrera, Baleares, Minorque, Lion, Provence, Sardaigne, Ligure, Corse, Elbe, Maddalena.

[2] Alboran to Lipari.

Italy

See table for details.

Note

On VHF Ch 68 there is a continuous weather forecast in Italian and English for all sea areas from Alboran (511 on the French forecast areas) to the eastern Mediterranean. The general synopsis is for all of the Mediterranean while the detailed forecast is for all Italian areas. It is updated every six hours with a 12-hour outlook, and an extended outlook for 48 hours in four 12-hour intervals. It can be picked up from the Balearics to western Greece and for a surprising distance out at sea.

RADIOTELEVISIONE ITALIANA-RADIODUE

Weather forecasts

846, 936, 1035, 1116, 1188, 1314, 1431, 1449kHz at 0621, 1432, 2233

Near gale warnings, synopsis, 12h or 18h Fcst and outlook for a further 12h in Italian.

BROADCAST RADIO

RAI 1 (Radiotelevision Italiana/Radio Uno) 567, 658, 1062, 1332, 1575kHz at 0545, 1545 (Saturday–Monday), 2244 (Monday–Friday), 2252 (Saturday–Sunday) LT. In Italian at dictation speed. Gale warnings, area forecasts, further outlook, notices to mariners. The service is not always reliable and times have been known to vary by as much as 30 minutes and occasionally to be omitted altogether.

TELEPHONE SERVICE

Anywhere in Italy you can ring 196 and get a recorded maritime weather forecast. Forecasts are updated regularly. In Italian at dictation speed.

PORTS

In all marinas a weather forecast is posted daily, sometimes with a synoptic map. In Italian and ocassionally in English.

NEWSPAPERS

Most of the national newspapers carry a general weather forecast for Italy with a synoptic map.

ITALY AND MALTA. Weather forecasts and navigation warnings. All in Italian/English.
All times UT except where shown. For LT add 2 hours in summer and 1 hour in winter.

Station	*VHF/MF*	*Forecast Areas*	*Schedule*
Ligurian Sea			
Monte Bignone	07		***Weather forecasts***
Castellaccio	25	Mar di Corsica	0135, 0735, 1335, 1935
Genova	2642kHz	Mar Ligure	***Storm warnings***
Zoagli	27	Tirreno N	On receipt H+03, 33
Monte Nero	61	Mar Ligure	***Navigational warnings***
Livorno	1925kHz	Tirreno N & C (E–W)	0333, 0833, 1233, 1633, 2033
Gorgona	26		
Central Tyrrhenian (N)			
Monte Argentario	01	Tirreno N	***Weather forecasts***
Civitavecchia	1888kHz	Tirreno C (E–W)	0135, 0735, 1335, 1935
T. Chiaruccia	64	Tirreno S (E–W)	***Storm warnings***
Monte Cavo	25	Tirreno N	On receipt H+03, 33
		Tirreno C (E–W)	***Navigational warnings***
			0533, 0933, 1333, 1833, 2333
Central & S Tyrrhenian			***Weather forecasts***
Posillipo	01		0135, 0735, 1335, 1935
Napoli	2632kHz	Tirreno C (E–W)	***Storm warnings***
Capri	27	Tirreno S (E–W)	On receipt H+03, 33
Varco del Salice	62		***Navigational warnings***
Serra del Tuono	25		0533, 0933, 1333, 1833, 2333
Sardinia			
Porto Torres	2719kHz		
Porto Cervo	26	Mar di Corsica	
Monte Moro	28	Mar di Sardegna	
Monte Limbara	85	Tirreno C (E–W)	***Weather forecasts***
Monte Tului	68		0135, 0735, 1335, 1935
Monte Serpeddi	04		***Storm warnings***
Cagliari	2680kHz	Mar di Sardegna	On receipt H+03, 33
Margine Rosso	62	Canale di Sardegna	***Navigational warnings***
Pta Campu Spina	82	Tirreno C & S (E–W)	0303, 0803, 1203, 1603, 2003
Badde Urbara	68	Mar di Corsica	
Osilo	28	Mar di Sardegna	
		Tirreno C (E–W)	
Sicily			
Palermo	1852kHz		
Palermo	81	Tirreno S (E–W)	
Sferracavallo	27	Canale di Sicilia	
Ustica	84		
Cefalu	61		
Forte Spuria	88	Tirreno S (E–W)	
Messina	2789kHz	Ionio N & S	***Weather forecasts***
Capo Lato	86		0135, 0735, 1335, 1935
Augusta	2628kHz	Canale di Sicilia	***Storm warnings***
Siracusa	85	Ionio S	On receipt H+03, 33
Gela	26		***Navigational warnings***
Caltabellotta	82	Canale di Sicilia	0333, 0833, 1233, 1633, 2033
Mazara	2600kHz		
Mazara	25		
Erice	81	Tirreno S (E–W)	
Pantelleria	88	Canale di Sicilia	
Lampedusa	1876kHz		
Lampedusa	25	Canale di Sicilia	
Crecale	87		
Ionian			
Capo Armi	62		***Weather forecasts***
Pta Stilo	84		0135, 0735, 1335, 1935
Crotone	2663kHz	Ionio N & S	***Storm warnings***
Capo Colonna	88		On receipt H+03, 33
Monte Parano	26		***Navigational warnings***
Monte Sardo	68		0333, 0833, 1233, 1633, 2033

South Adriatic			
			Weather forecasts
Abate Argento	05	Ionio N	0135, 0735, 1335, 1935
Bari	2579kHz	Adriatic S	***Storm warnings***
Bari	27		On receipt H+03, 33
Casa d'Orso	81	Adriatic C & S	***Navigational warnings***
Monte Calvario	01		0333, 0833, 1233, 1633, 2033
Central Adriatic			
Silvi	65	Adriatic C & S	
Monte Secco	87		
San Benedetto	1855kHz		***Weather forecasts***
Monte Conero	02		0135, 0735, 1335, 1935
Ancona	2656kHz		***Storm warnings***
Forte Garibaldi	25	Adriatic N & C	On receipt H+03, 33
Ravenna	27		***Navigational warnings***
Monte Cero	26		0433, 0933, 1333, 1733, 2133
Piancavallo	01		
Trieste	2642kHz		
Conconello	83		***Navigational warnings***
			0333, 0833, 1233, 1633, 2033
Venice	26, 27		***Weather forecasts***
			0150, 0750, 1350, 1950
MALTA (All in English)			
Malta Radio	2625kHz	Maltese waters <50M	***Weather forecasts***
			0403, 0803, 1403, 1903
	04 (Call on 16)		***Weather forecasts***
			0703, 1103, 1703, 2203
			Storm warnings On receipt
Valetta Radio	12		***Weather forecasts***
			0903, 1303, 1903, 0003 LT
			(–1hr in winter)

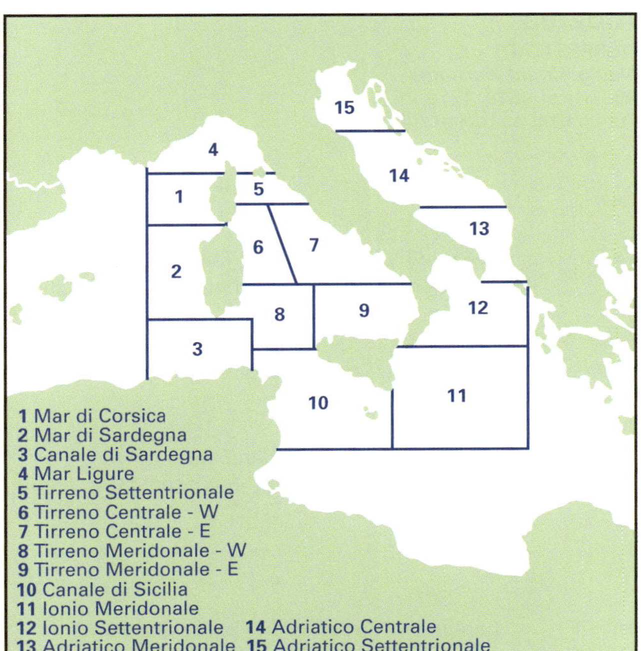

Italy. Forecast areas

Malta

See table for details.

Weather forecasts

12hr forecast for coastal waters of Malta up to 50M offshore.

Storm warnings

On receipt.

Navigational warnings

Local and NAVAREA III warnings for central Mediterranean up to 10 days old are broadcast Monday–Saturday.

All warnings still in force are broadcast on Sundays.

RADIO MALTA

Storm warnings

93·7MHz. On receipt. Warnings of storm, gale or severe weather.

Weather forecasts

93·7MHz at 1545. Daily marine weather report, including wind speed, sea state, air temperature and 12h forecast, for waters around Malta in Maltese.

TELEPHONE SERVICES

Met Office ✆ 284332/284308. Open 24 hours.

PORTS

Weather forecasts posted daily at Grand Harbour Marina, Manoel Island Yacht Yard, and Msida Marina. In English.

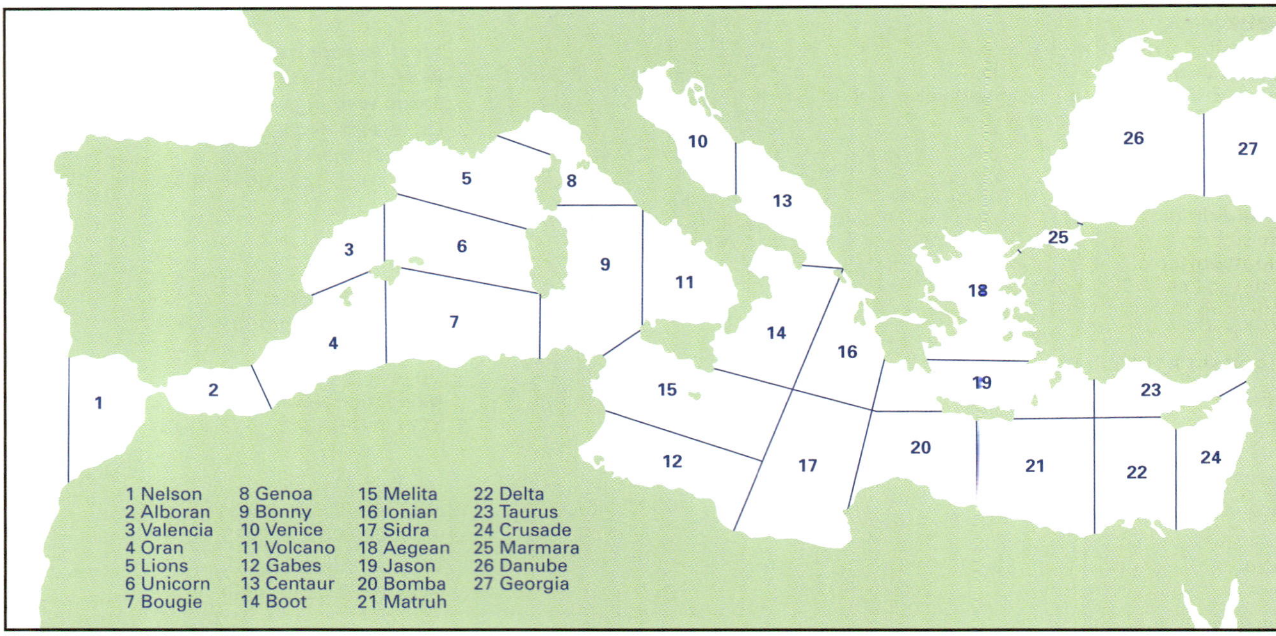

FLEET FORECAST AREAS

Slovenia

RADIO SLOVENIA

Weather forecasts

In Slovenian, English and German.
AM 918kHz, FM 96.5, 100.1, 103.1MHz at 0635, 0955 LT

Marinas post a daily weather forecast for the Adriatic.

Croatia

See table for details.

RADIO ZAGREB

Weather forecasts

In English, German and Italian.
1485kHz and FM 90·5, 100·5MHz at 1130 LT (summer only)

PORTS

Many harbours and all marinas post a daily weather forecast for the Adriatic.

Montenegro

See table for details

PORTS

Most harbours and marinas post a daily weather forecast for the Adriatic.

Albania

DURRES (ZAD)

Navigational warnings

460kHz at 0818, 1218, 1618
For coastal waters of Albania

CROATIA. Weather forecasts and navigational warnings

Station	*VHF/MF*	*Forecast Areas*	*Schedule*
Rijeka Radio Callsign 9AR			
Savudrija	81	Adriatic N & S	0545, 1245, 1945 (Croatian/English)
Ucka	24		Gale warnings on receipt then 0800, 1500, 2200
Kamenjak – Rab	04		
Susak	20		
Pula HM	73	N Adriatic – W Istria	Continuous (Croatian/English/Italian/German)
Rijeka HM	69	N Adriatic – E	
Split Radio Callsign 9AS			
Ucka	21	Adriatic N & S	0545, 1245, 1945 (Croatian/English)
Celevac	28		Gale warnings on receipt then 0800, 1500, 2200
Sveti Mihovil – Uglijan	07		
Labistica – Split	21		
Vidova Gora – Bram	23		
Hum – Vim	81		
Sibenik HM	73	Central Adriatic – E	Continuous (Croatian/English/Italian/German)
Split HM	67	Central Adriatic – E	
Dubrovnik Radio Callsign 9AD			
Hum – Viü	85	Adriatic N & S	0545, 1245, 1945 (Croatian/English)
Uljenje – Peljeüac	04		Gale warnings on receipt then 0800, 1500, 2200
Srdj – Dubrovnik	07	S Adriatic – E	
Dubrovnik HM	73		Continuous (Croatian/English/Italian/German)
MONTENEGRO			
Bar	1720.4kHz 20, 24	Adriatic N & S	0850, 1420, 2050 (Serbo Croatian/English)

All times UT

Greece

Olympia Radio broadcast a forecast for all Greek waters in Greek and English. The forecast covers the Adriatic, Ionian, Aegean, E Mediterranean, Marmara Sea and Black Sea for Z+24 hours with an outlook for a further 12 hours. Gale warnings and a synoptic summary are given at the beginning of the broadcast.

A securite warning on Ch 16 gives all the VHF channels for the different shore stations and you will need to choose whichever shore station is closest to you. In fact, the advice notice on shore stations is often mumbled and at such a speed that it can be difficult to hear, but is worth listening to in case VHF frequencies for the different shore stations are changed. See table for details.

BROADCAST RADIO

Weather forecasts are transmitted on the National Programme in Greek only. The forecasts are at 0430 (1 hour later when DST is in force).

	kHz	*MHz*
Athens	729	91·6
Corfu	1008	99·3
Iraklion	954	97·5
Kavala	1602	96·3
Rhodes	1494	92·7
Khania	1512	104·0
Patras	1485	92·5
Volos	1485	100·7
Zakinthos	927	95·2

Around Athens ERA radio 91·6FM is reported to have a forecast in English at 0630–0700 local time.

For the eastern Mediterranean a marine weather forecast is given by the Austrian short wave service (in German only) on 6150MHz/49m at 0945 and 1400 local time (from 1 May to 1 October only).

GSM WEATHER FORECAST

Dial 108 from any Greek landline or a mobile phone. Give the area required for the forecast, and a 12/24hr forecast is given in English. Available throughout Greek waters.

PORTS

In most of the marinas a weather forecast is posted daily in English.

NEWSPAPERS

Most of the national newspapers carry a general weather forecast usually with a synoptic map.

TELEVISION

On the Greek national channels a good weather forecast with the wind direction and strength (in Beaufort) is given after the news at around 2130 LT.

SMS TEXT MESSAGE FORECAST

Poseidon provide a website weather forecast (see ***4.8 Weather on the Internet)*** and can now send a basic forecast by text message to your mobile phone. It does not seem to work on all mobile phones and you may need to get a Greek SIM card.

Text: **W GPS (coordinates of position for forecast)** and send to 54546.

eg ***W GPS 38 50 20 43*** requests a forecast for the area around Levkas.

The message gives wind strength and direction for 24 hours in three 6-hour intervals.

eg ***24/9 15 4B (NW)*** indicates Force 4 NW wind at 1500 hrs UT on 24 September

The service costs around 25 cents per message.

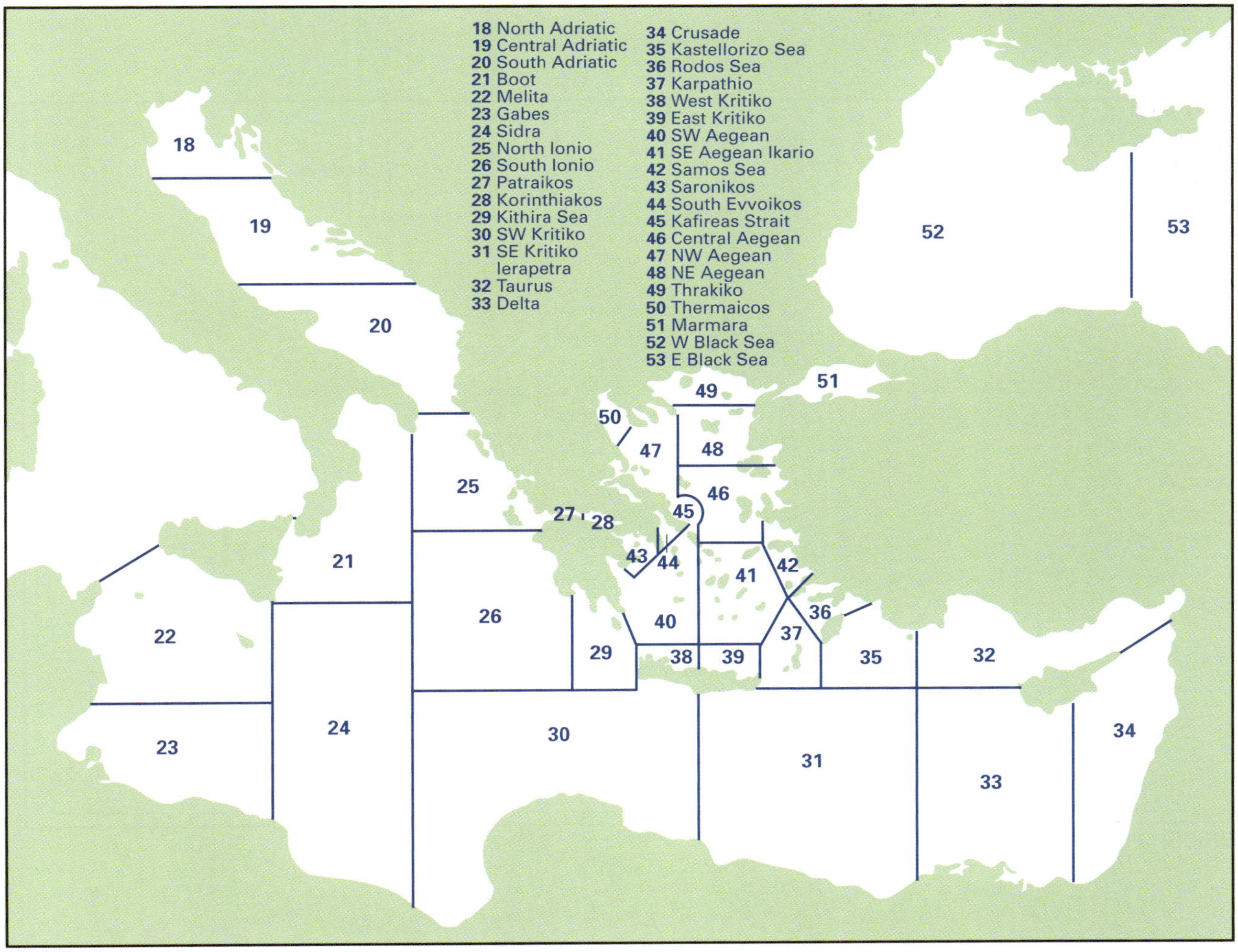

Greece. Forecast areas

GREECE. Weather forecasts and navigational warnings (Greek/English)

Station	*VHF/MF*	*Forecast Areas*	*Schedule*
Olympia Radio			***Weather forecasts***
Corfu	2830kHz		0633, 0903, 1533, 2133
Limnos	2730kHz		***Storm warnings***
Rhodos	2624kHz	All Greek forecast areas	On receipt
Iraklion	2799kHz		
			Navigational warnings
Kerkira/Limnos			0033, 0703, 1033, 1633 UT
Rodhos/Iraklion			0703, 1133, 1733, 2333 UT
Ionian	02, 27, 28, 83, 85		
SW Aegean	04, 25, 27, 85		
NW Aegean	82, 85	All Greek forecast areas	***Weather forecasts***
NE Aegean	23, 60		0600, 1000, 1600, 2200 UT
Central Aegean	01, 25, 85		***Storm warnings*** On receipt
SE Aegean	03, 23, 24, 63		***Navigational warnings***
Kritiko	04, 27, 83, 85		0500, 1100, 1730, 2330 UT

All times UT. For LT add 3 hours in summer and 2 hours in winter

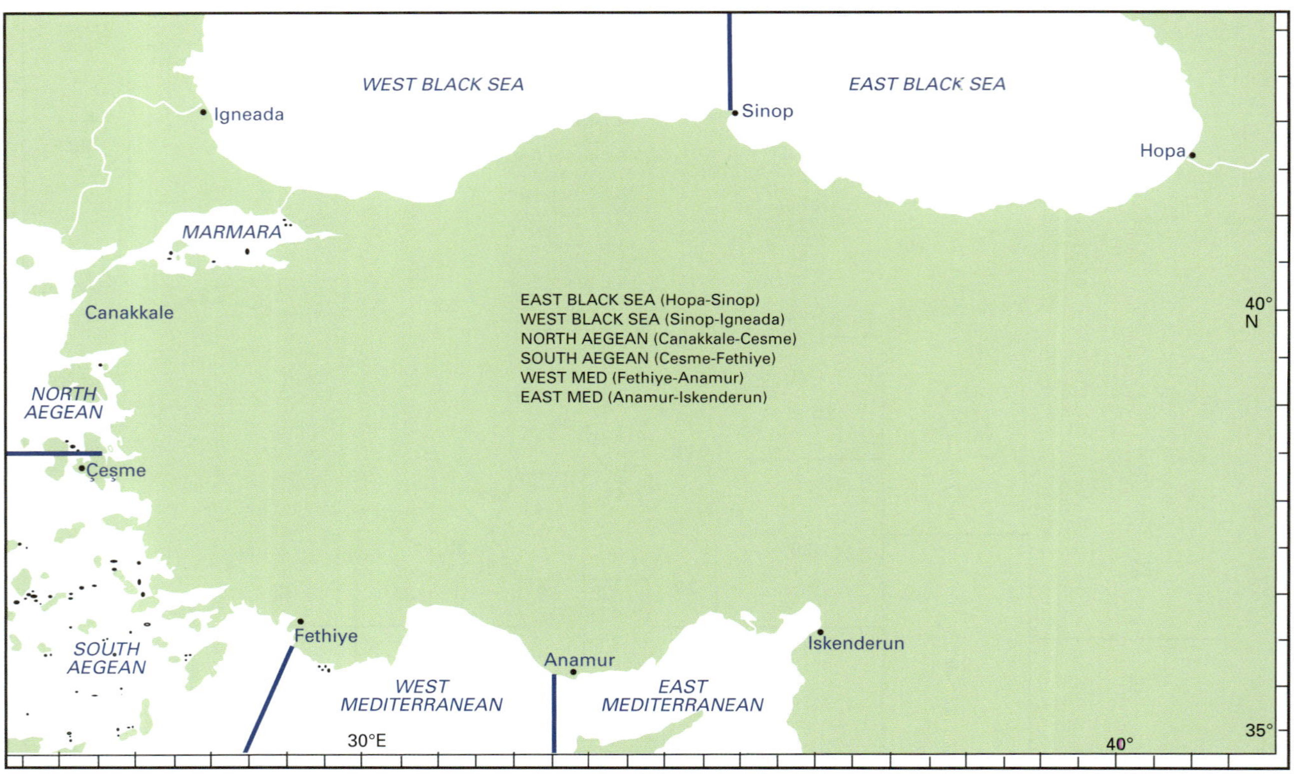

TURKISH FORECAST AREAS

TURKEY. Weather forecasts

Station	*VHF/HF*	*Forecast Areas*	*Schedule*	*Language*
Istanbul Antalya Samsun	67 67 67	Black Sea, Marmara, Aegean Aegean, Mediterranean Black Sea	***Weather observations*** 0730, 0930, 1130, 1330, 1530, 1730, 1930 UTC ***Weather forecasts*** 0700, 1900 UTC ***Storm warnings*** On receipt after forecast	Weather obs in Turkish Weather fcst & Storm warnings in Turkish & English
Istanbul	4405, 8812, 13128kHz	All Turkish forecast areas 15°E–50°E 25°N–50°N	***Weather forecast and storm warnings*** 1000, 1800 UTC	Turkish & English

Weather observations from coastal stations as follows

Istanbul	Inebolu, Zonguldak, Kumkoy, Tekirda, Canakkale, Gokceada, Ayvalik, Dikili, Bodrum, Izmir
Antalya	Ayvalik, Kikili, Bodrum, Izmir, Ku‹adasi, Marmaris, Finike, Antalya, Alanya, Anamur, Mersin
Samsun	Hopa, Rize, Trabzon, Ordu, Samsun, Sinop

MIDDLE EAST. Weather forecasts and navigational warnings in English

Station	*VHF/MF*	*Forecast Areas*	*Schedule*
ISRAEL			***Weather forecasts (Navigational warnings*** in **bold** type)
Haifa (Hefa)	2649kHz 25	Taurus Delta Crusade	0303, **0703, 1103, 1503, 1903**, 2303
LIBYA			***Weather forecasts***
Tarabulus (Tripoli)	2197kHz 2182kHz	10°E to 25°E Libyan coast to 34°N	0833, 1733 ***Navigational warnings*** 0903, 1903

Turkey

See table for details.

BROADCAST RADIO

TRT National Radio FM 96MHz at 0900 LT. Weather forecast in English.

PORTS

In all marinas a weather forecast is posted daily in English and sometimes in German.

NEWSPAPERS

Most of the national newspapers carry a general weather forecast sometimes with a synoptic map.

TELEVISION

On the national television channels a weather forecast with the wind direction and strength is given after the news at 2130–2200.

Cyprus

Weather forecasts and gale warnings for N Cyprus

VHF Ch 16, 67

Navigational warnings

2700kHz. On receipt. At 0733, 1533 for Eastern Mediterranean

BRITISH FORCES BROADCASTING SERVICES ONE (BFBS ONE)

Weather forecasts[1]

Nicosia 89·7MHz, **Akrotiri** 92·1MHz, **Dhekelia** 99·6MHz

Monday–Friday 0635, 0731, 1014, 1310. Saturday 0635, Sunday 0959

Inshore Forecast in English for area between Cape Aspro and Cape Greco. Forecast valid until 1900 LT on day of broadcast

1. All broadcasts are on LT and are approximate

PORTS

In Limassol St Raphael Marina and Larnaca Marina a weather forecast is posted daily. In English.

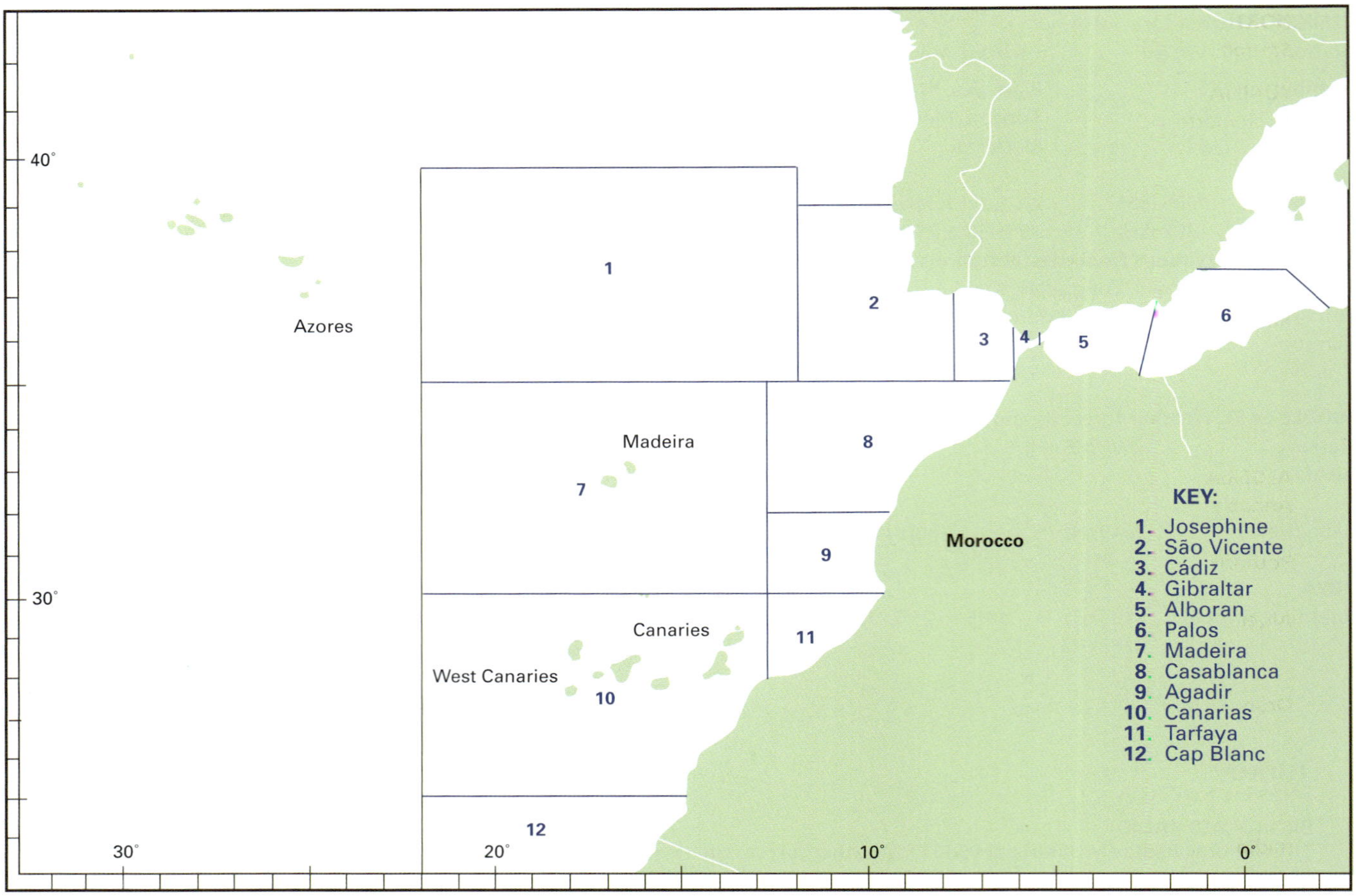

Morocco. Forecast areas

Syria

Weather forecasts available. Syrian Yacht Club.

Israel

See table for details.

PORTS

In all marinas a weather forecast is posted daily. Often in English but if not someone will translate it for you.

Egypt

PORTS

A weather forecast can be obtained at Port Fouad Yacht Centre.

Libya

See table for details.

Tunisia

See table for details.

PORTS

In most marinas a weather forecast is posted daily. In other ports a weather forecast can sometimes be obtained. In French.

Algeria

See table for details.

Morocco

See table for details.

PORTS

In Marinasmir a weather forecast can be obtained. In Ceuta a weather forecast may be available. In Spanish.

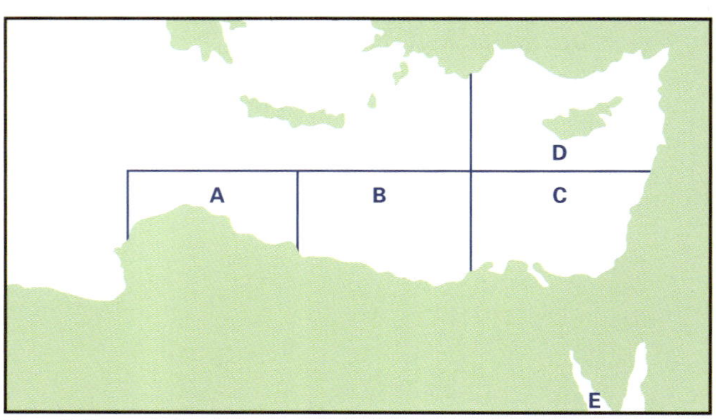

Egypt. Forecast areas

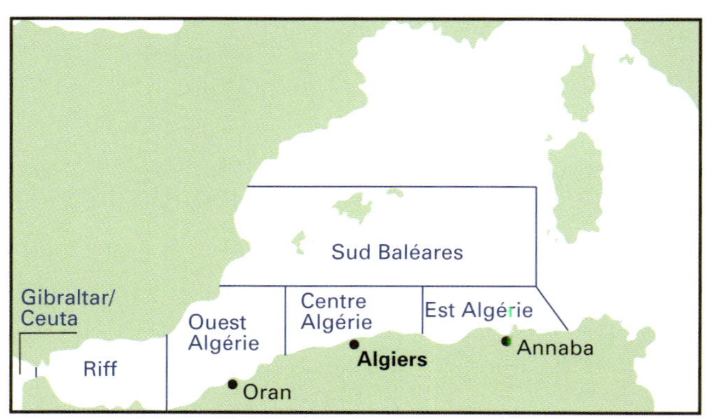

Algeria. Forecast areas

NORTH AFRICA. Weather forecasts and navigational warnings in French

Station	*VHF/MF*	*Forecast Areas*	*Schedule*
TUNISIA			
La Goulette	1743 kHz	Tunisian coast	***Weather forecasts*** 0405, 1905
	2182kHz	Tunisian coast W Med Sea S of 40°N E of 08°E	***Storm warnings*** On receipt H+03
			Navigational warnings 0003, 0403, 0603, 1003, 1303, 1803, 1903, 2103
Tunis	1820/2670kHz	Tunisian coast	***Weather forecasts*** 0805 1705
		Tunisian coast W Med Sea S of 40°N E of 08°E	***Navigational warnings*** 0803, 1203, 2003
Radio Tunis	629kHz		***Weather forecasts*** 0600 (summer) 0630, 1830
	962kHz		***Storm warnings***
	7225kHz	Tunisian coast	1200, 1215, 1230, 1300, 1830, 1900
	11970kHz		
	15225kHz		
ALGERIA			
Annaba	1743kHz		***Weather forecasts*** 0920, 1033, 1720, 1833
	2775kHz		***Navigational warnings*** 0833, 2033 on request
Boufarik	8722kHz		***Weather forecasts*** 0800, 1600
	13095kHz	Algerian waters	
Alger	1792kHz		***Weather forecasts*** 0903, 1703
			Navigational warnings 0918, 2118 on request
	2691kHz		***Storm warnings*** On receipt 0918, 2118
Oran	1735kHz		***Weather forecast***
			Storm warnings On receipt 0833, 2033
			Navigational warnings 0833, 2033 on request
	2586kHz		***Weather forecasts*** 0920, 1033, 1720, 1735
	2719kHz		
Radio Broadcasts – TV Algérienne			
			Weather forecasts
Constantine	1304kHz		1300, 2000
Alger	890kHz		1300, 2000
	6080kHz		2000
	11715kHz	N Africa & W Med	1300, 2000
	11835kHz		1300
Oran	1304kHz		1300, 2000
Tlemcen	746kHz		1300
MOROCCO			
Tanger	1911kHz		***Weather forecasts*** 0915, 1635
			Navigational warnings On receipt H+03
	2182kHz		***Storm warnings*** On receipt H+03
	2635kHz		
Casablanca	2182kHz	Josephine, São Vicente, Cadiz, Gibraltar, Alboran, Madeira, Casablanca, Agadir, Canarias, Tarfaya Cap Blanc	***Storm warnings*** On receipt H+33
	2586kHz		***Weather forecasts*** 0945, 1645
			Navigational warnings On receipt 0918, 2028
Safi	1743kHz		***Weather forecasts*** 0915, 1635
			Navigational warnings On receipt 0928, 1648
	2182kHz		***Storm warnings*** On receipt H+03
Agadir	1911kHz		***Weather forecasts*** 0935, 1615
			Navigational warnings On receipt 1048, 1628
	2182kHz		***Storm warnings*** On receipt H+33
Radio Broadcasts – TV Marocaine			
Tanger	701, 1048, 1187, 1332, 7225kHz FM 90.0, 92.1MHz	Moroccan coasts	***Weather, Storm warnings*** 1228 (English)
			Weather, Storm warnings 0758, 1315, 2015

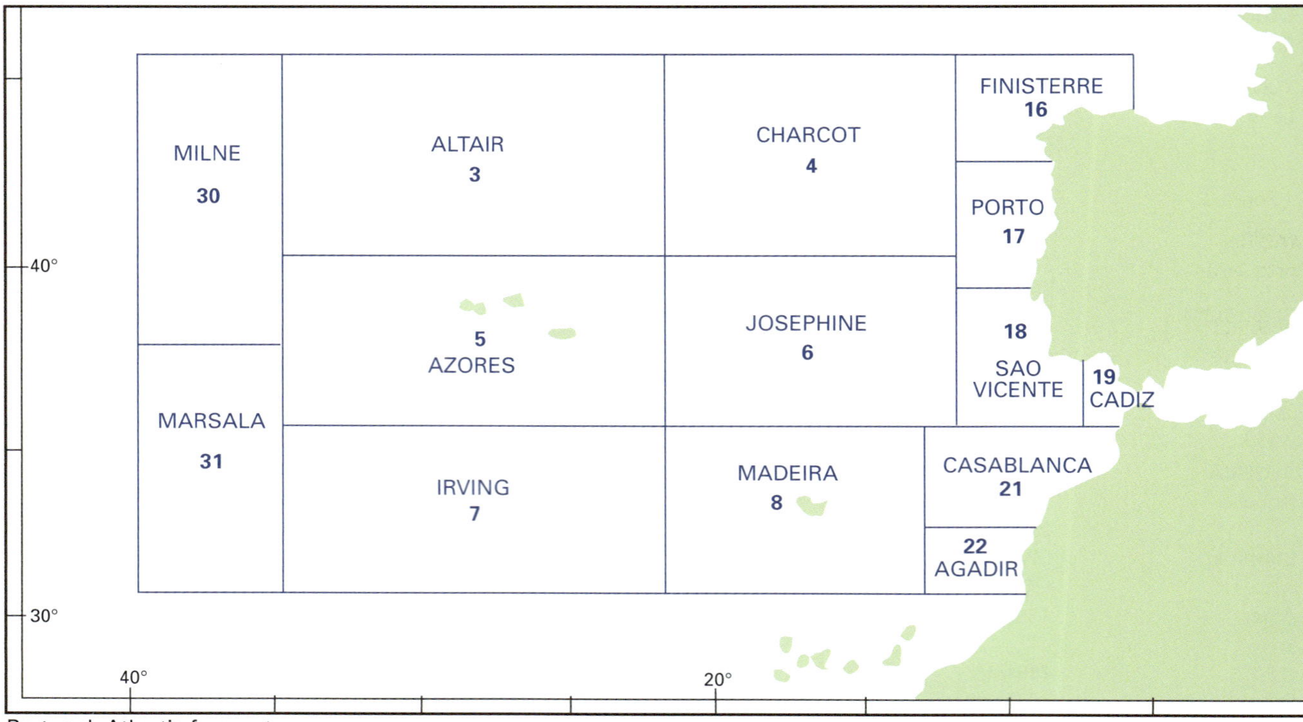

Portugal. Atlantic forecast areas

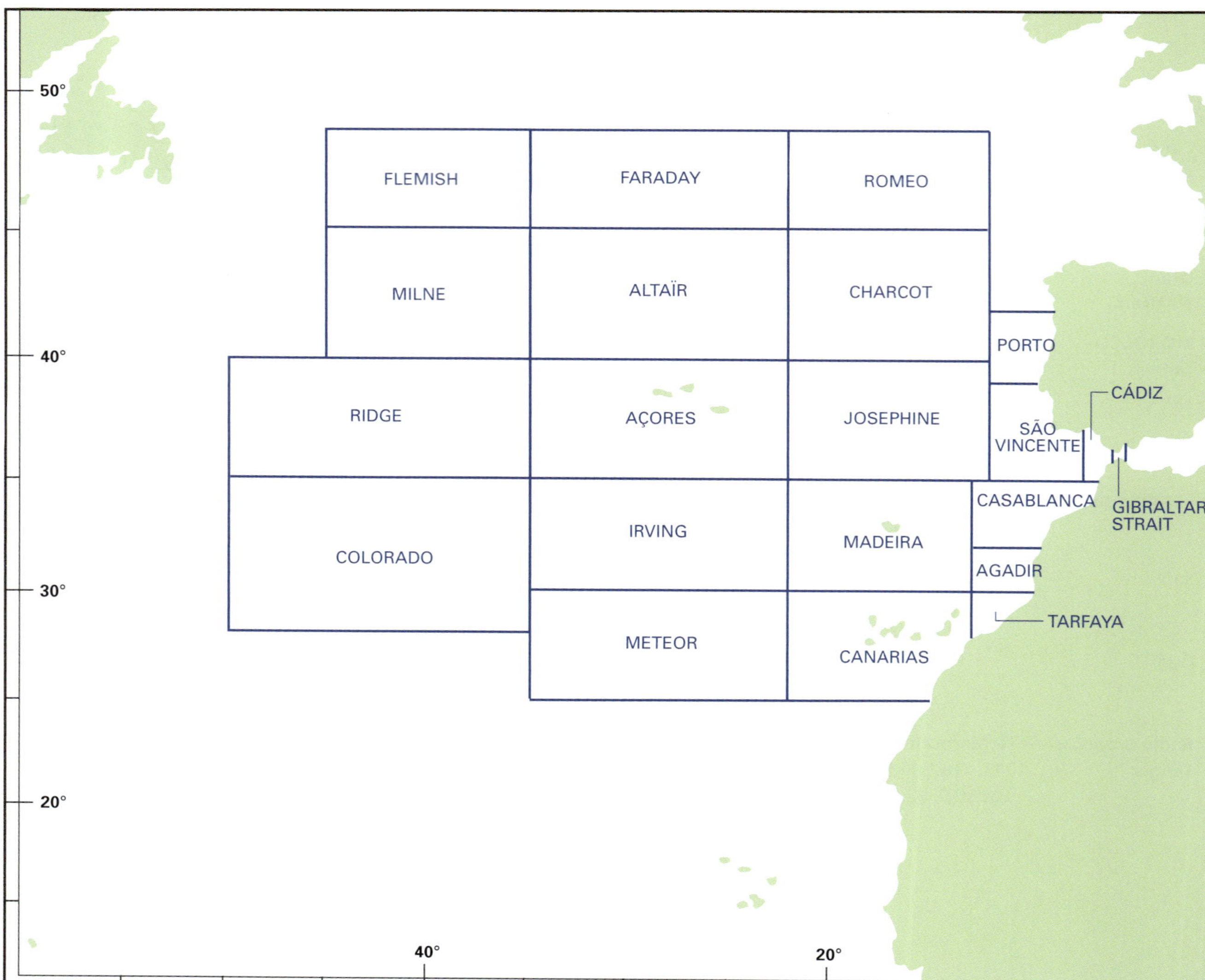

France Atlantic Forecast Areas - Radio France Internationale

ATLANTIC ISLANDS. Weather forecasts and navigational warnings

Station	*VHF/MF*	*Forecast Areas*	*Schedule*
AZORES			
Horta	2657kHz	Altair Açores Irving Milne Marsala,	0935, 2135 (Portuguese/English)
	11	Faial Graciosa, Pico	0900, 2100 (Portuguese)
		São Jorge, Terceira,	
		Corvo Flores	1000, 1900 (Portuguese)
Ponta Delgada	11	São Miguel & Santa Maria	0830, 2000 (Portuguese)
MADEIRA			
Porto Santo	2657kHz	Madeira, Casablanca, Agadir,	0735, 1935 (Portuguese/English)
	11	Madeira & Porto Santo	1030, 1630 (Portuguese)
CANARIES			
Lanzarote	1644kHz	N Atlantic[1]	**0803, 1233, 1903** (Spanish)
	25	Canaries coasts	**0833**, 1333, **2033**
Fuerteventura	22	Canaries coasts	
Las Palmas	1689kHz	N Atlantic[1]	0803, 1233, 1903
	26	Canaries coasts	**0833**, 1333, **2033**
	10	Canaries coasts	***Navigational warnings*** On receipt (Spanish/English)
Tenerife	11, 18, 67	Canaries coasts	Even hr+15
	74	Anaga-Agaeta channel	***Wx*** 0015, 0415, 0815, 1215, 1615, 2015
		Tenerife Gomera	***Navigational warnings*** 0215, 0615, 1015, 1415,
		La Palma El Hierro	1815, 2215 (Spanish/English)
Gomera	24	Canaries coasts	
La Palma	11, 18, 67	Canaries coasts	Even hr+15
El Hierro	23	Canaries coasts	

[1] N Atlantic: Altair, Açores, Charcot, Josephine, Madeira, Casablanca, Agadir, Tarfaya, Canarias, Cap Blanc
Times for Weather & Navigational Warnings are in **Bold** type.

Atlantic Islands

See table for details.

Radio France International broadcasts on MF/HF frequencies with W Atlantic forecasts, which include the Azores, Madeira and the Canary Islands.

6175, 11700, 15300, 15363, 17575kHz at 1130 UT

MARINAS

A weather forecast with synoptic chart is posted in most marinas.

MARINE RADIO NETS

There are several marine radio nets operating in the Med and W Atlantic which broadcast weather forecasts as part of their schedule. In English or Italian/English.

Mediterranean M/M Net	7085kHz	0700 UT
Med Net	8122kHz	0430UT
UK M/M Net	14303kHz	0800 1800 UT
Italian M/M Net	14297kHz	1900 UT (2000 October–March)
Herb's Atlantic Net	12359kHz	2000 UT (check in from 1940 UT)

4.2 NAVTEX (N4) TRANSMITTERS

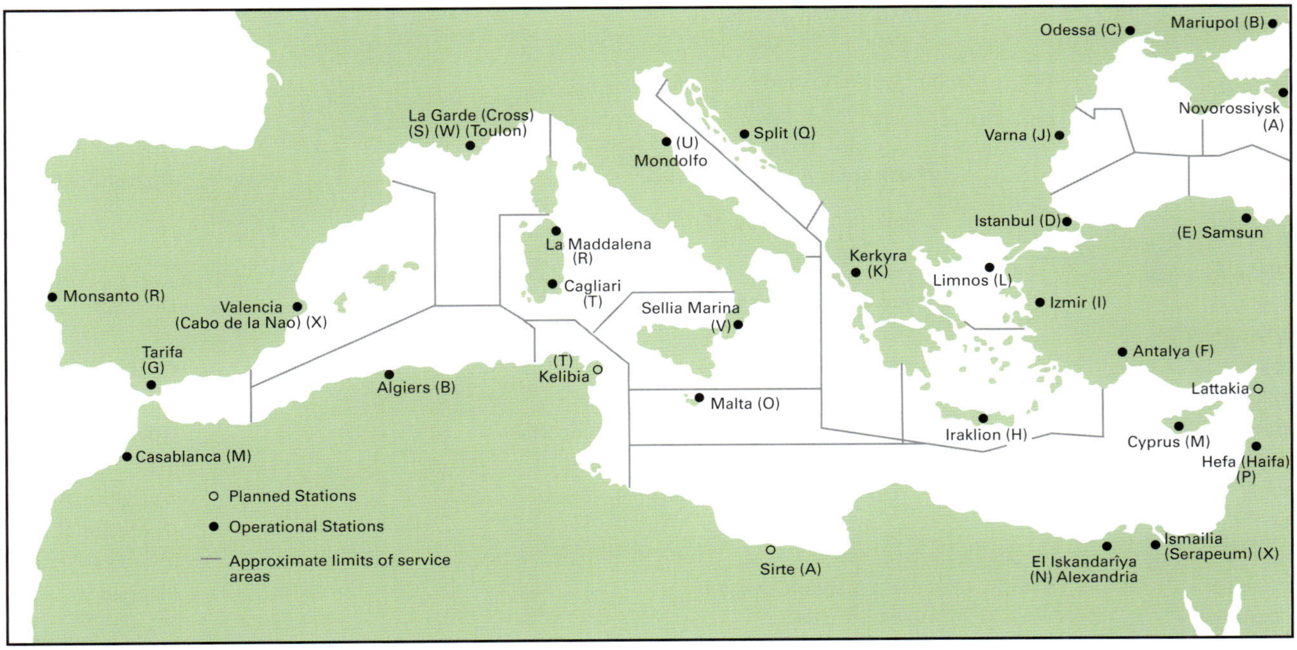

NAVTEX TRANSMITTERS

4.2 NAVTEX (N4) TRANSMITTERS

Country	*Ident. char.*	*Freq kHz*	*Forecast Areas*	*Status of implementation*
Portugal				
Monsanto	R	518	Porto, Sao Vicente, Cadiz	Operational
	G	490		
Spain				
Tarifa	G	518	San Vicente, Cadiz, Gibraltar Strait, Alboran, Palos, Algeria, Agadir, Casablanca	Operational
Valencia (Cabo de la Nao)	X	518	Lion, Provence, Ligure, Corse, Sardaigne, Annaba	Operational
France				
La Garde (CROSS)	W	518	East Cabrera, Baleares, Minorque, Lion, Provence, Ligure, Corse, Sardaigne, Maddalena, Elbe	Operational
	S	490		
Italy				
Sellia Marina	V	518	Ionian Sea (N & S)	Operational
Mondolfo	U	518	Adriatic (N, central, S)	Operational
Sardegna				
La Maddalena	R	518	Ligurian Sea, Tyrrhenian Sea (N, central E & W, S)	Operational
Sicily				
Augusta	V	518	Sicily Channel, Sardinian Channel, Sardinian Sea	Decommissioning
Lampedusa		518		Planned
Croatia				
Hvar (Split)	Q	518	Adriatic (N, central, S)	Operational
Malta				
Malta	O	518	Maltese Waters	Operational
Greece				
Kerkyra	K	518	Boot, N Ionio, S Ionio, Patraikos, Korinthiakos, Kithera Sea	Operational
Limnos	L	518	Samos Sea, Saronikos, S Evoikos, Kafiraeas Strait, Central Aegean, NW Aegean, NE Aegean, Thrakiko, Thermaicos	Operational
Iraklion	H	518	Kithera Sea, SW Kritiko, SE Kritiko Ierepetra, Kastellorizo Sea, Rodos sea, Karpathio, W Kritiko, E Kritiko, SW Aegean, SE Aegean Ikario, Samos Sea	Operational
Turkey				
Izmir	I	518	Aegean, Jason	Operational
Istanbul	D	518	Danube, Marmara	Operational
Antalya	F	518	Taurus	Operational
Samsun	E	518	Georgia, Danube	Operational
Cyprus				
Peras	M	518	SE Kritiko, Delta, Crusade, Taurus	Operational
Israel				
Haifa	P	518	Delta, Taurus, Crusade	Operational
Egypt				
Ismailia	X	518		Operational
Alexandria	N	518	Egypt Wx areas A,B,C,D	Operational
Libya				
Sirte	A	518		
Tunisia				
Kelibia	T	518	Sardinian Channel, Sardinian Sea, Corsican Sea	On trials
Algeria				
Algiers	B	518	Algerian Wx areas	Operational
Morocco				
Casablanca	M	518	Casablanca, Agadir, Canarias, Tarfaya, Cap Blanc	Operational
Açores				
Horta	F	518	Altair, Azores Irving, Milne, Marsala	Operational
Horta	J	490		Operational
Madeira				
Porto Santo	P	518	Madeira, Casablanca, Agadir	Planned
Islas Canarias				
Las Palmas	I	518	Madeira, Casablanca, Agadir, Canarias, Tarfaya, Cap Blanc	Operational

4.3 WEATHERFAX (WX) BROADCASTS

For notes on set-up and use see ***3.10 Weatherfax.***

DWD OFFENBACH Hamburg/Pinneberg

Frequencies & Schedule

3855 (DDH3)/7880 (DDK3)/13882.5 (DDK6)

Time (UT)	Obs time	Forecast	Chart Area
0430/1600	00/12	Surface Weather Chart	NA
0512	18	H+30 Surface pressure	NA
0546/1821	03/15	N Atlantic Tropical Storms	
0717	18	H+30 Surface pressure	NA
0730/1847	00/12	H+48 Surface pressure	NA
0804/1900	00/12	H+84 Surface pressure	NA
0817	00	H+108 Surface pressure	NA
0830/1913	00/12	H+24 Sea, swell, wind	NA
0842/1926	00/12	H+48 Sea, swell, wind	NA
0854/1939	00/12	H+72 Sea, swell, wind	NA
0906	00	H+96 Sea, swell, wind	NA
1050/2200	06/18	Surface weather	NA
1111		Transmission schedule	
1145	06	Surface weather	NA

ATHENS (SVJ4)

Frequencies & Schedule

4481/8105 kHz

Time (UT)	Obs time	Forecast	Chart Area
0845	06	Surface Analysis	A
0857	06	Surface prog H+24	A
0909	06	Surface prog H+48	A
0921–1044	Var	Wave Heights	B, C

4.4 SATELLITE WEATHER SERVICES

SafetyNET

SafetyNET is the SES-based MSI service for GMDSS. A receiver can be fitted to an INMARSAT SES to facilitate reception of satellite-transmitted Enhanced Group Calls (EGC) MSI broadcasts. The Mediterranean comes under the Area of Responsibility NAV/METAREA III covered by the Atlantic Ocean Region – East Satellite footprint. Forecasts for METAREA II are issued from Plomeur, France, and for METAREA III from the LES Thermopylae, Greece. Forecasts and warnings are for areas not covered by NAVTEX broadcasts.

Transmission schedule

METAREA II	
Weather forecasts	0900, 2100
Navigational warnings	0630 & on receipt
METAREA III	
Weather forecasts	1000, 2200
Navigational warnings	1200, 2400 & on receipt

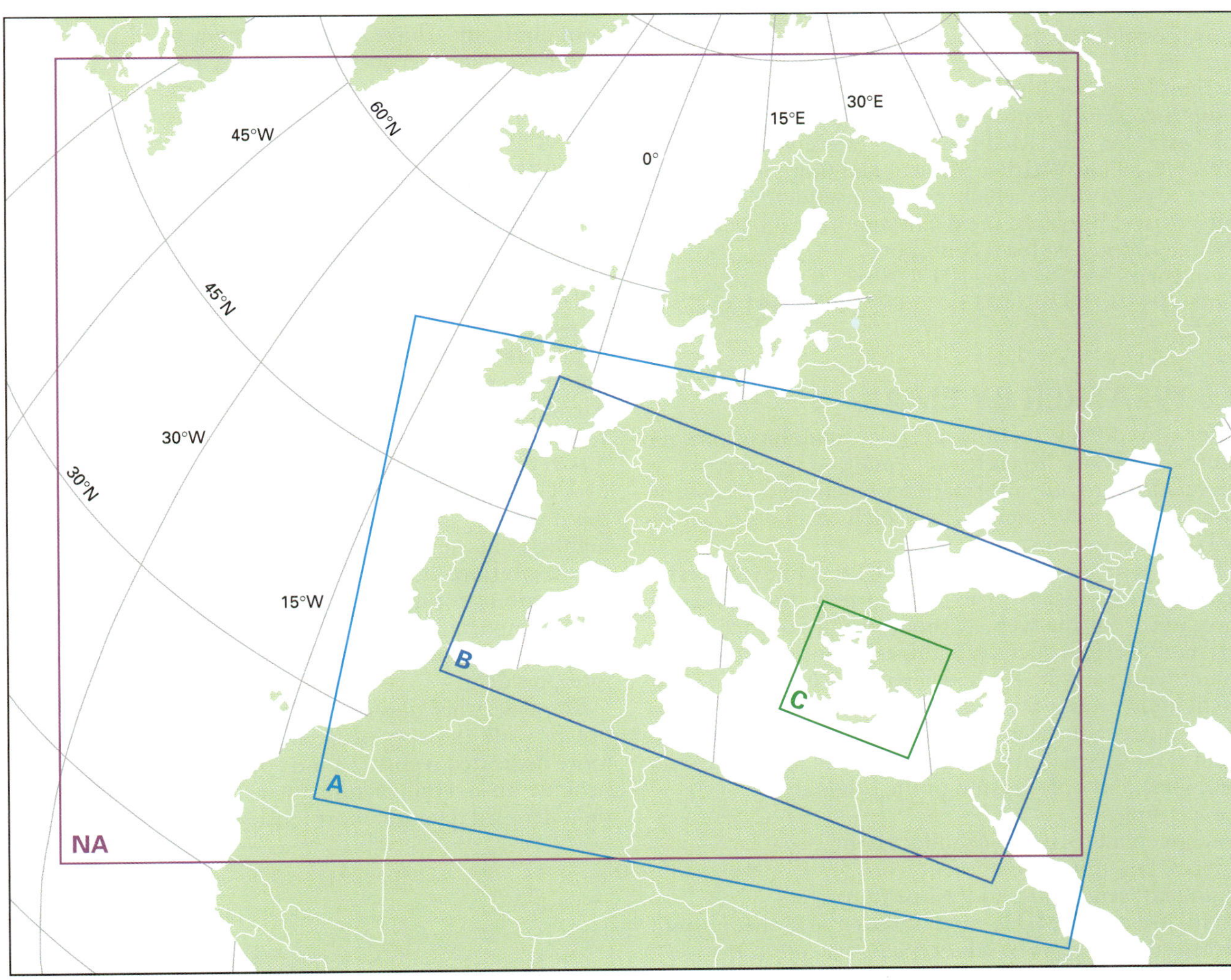

Weatherfax Broadcast Areas

NORTHWOOD (JYA)
Frequencies & Schedule
2618.5, 4610, 8040, 11086.5 kHz
At least two frequencies in use at any time.

Time (UT)	Obs time	Forecast	Chart Area
0000/1200	18/06	Surface Analysis	N
0012/1212	18/06	Surface prog H+24	N
0100/1300		Transmission schedule	
0236/1436	00/12	Surface Analysis	N
0300/1500	00/12	Surface Analysis	N
0348/1548	04/16	Gale warning summary	N
0400/1600	00/12	Surface Analysis	N
0436/1636	00/12	Surface prog H+24	N
0500/1700	00/12	Surface Analysis	N
0512/1712	00/12	Surface prog H+24	N
0524/1724	00/12	Surface prog H+48	N
0612/1800	00/12	Surface Analysis	N
0624/1812	00/12	Surface prog H+24	N
0724/1924	00/12	Surface prog H+48	N
0736/1936	00/12	Surface prog H+72	N
0748/1948	00/12	Surface prog H+96	N
0800/2012	00/12	Surface prog H+120	N
0900/2100	06/18	Surface Analysis	N
1000/2200	06/18	Surface Analysis	N
1012/2212	06/18	Surface prog H+24	N
1100/2300	06/18	Surface Analysis	N
1112/2312	06/18	Surface prog H+24	N
1148/2348	00/12	Gale warning summary	N

Chart area 54°N 82'W – 26°N 45'W – 54°N 51'E – 28°N 12'E
(Western Mediterranean and North Atlantic area)

4.5 RTTY FORECASTS

It is possible to receive text forecasts using Radio Teletype (RTTY) using either a dedicated receiver (such as the NASA Weatherman or NASA HF3), or an SSB radio linked to a laptop with suitable software. RTTY forecasts for the Mediterranean are available from DWD (German Weather Service) Hamburg and include a five day outlook which can be useful for planning longer trips, but lacks the detail required to be accurate enough to forecast local conditions.
Frequencies 4583, 7646, 10100.8kHz
Times 0410, 0930, 1015, 1115, 1550, 1610, 2215, 2315.

4.6 WEATHER BY EMAIL

Refer also to the section on Telecommunications for details on how to retrieve email. This section is intended to provide information on getting forecasts on slow or expensive connections such as dial-up, GPRS or HF radio systems.

Document retrieval using FTP (File Transfer Protocol) is a means of extracting text based weather forecasts from the web, without needing to access the internet. Services such as Saildocs (www.saildocs.com) enable you to 'ask' for a webpage to be sent to your email address as a text only email. Any pictures on the original page are deleted, and the page is reformatted to plain text, so what arrives is a much smaller (read: less kilobytes) text only version of the original.
For example:
Send an email to: query@saildocs.com
Subject: (anything)
Main text: send *http address of webpage*
So to get the GMDSS text forecast for the Eastern Mediterranean from Saildocs type:
Send met.3e
For the Western Mediterranean:
Send met.3w
The link must be exactly as it is on the webpage that you want, with no extra spaces or characters.

More information on Saildocs is available by sending an email to info@saildocs.com, this will return the how-to document (about 5Kb).

Saildocs is provided without charge thanks to the support of Sailmail, a membership-owned SSB radio email service for cruising sailors which operates a network of 14 stations world-wide. For more information on SailMail visit their website at www.sailmail.com

It is also possible to obtain GRIB files using this system (see below).
Note Obtaining forecasts using phones or email should not replace obtaining MSI (Maritime Safety Information) forecasts using VHF or Navtex. Gale Warnings are disseminated first on official MSI services. Saildocs warns users that the retrieval service is completely automated and therefore is susceptible to changes in URLs or other things which will cause the retrieval to fail.

4.7 GRIB WEATHER FILES

GRIB files are highly compressed weather files which cut download speeds compared to earlier compression formats. They contain all sorts of data though commonly they have information on wind speed and direction, barometric pressure and rainfall. The files can be downloaded off the internet or received by email and their small size makes them particularly suitable for receiving using slow modems such as HF radio or expensive GPRS connections. You will need a GRIB viewer, although most GRIB services provide these and the GRIB file free of charge. Subscription services do not seem to offer a great deal more than these, given that the source data for almost all services is the same. GRIB files obtained solely by email must be requested using specially formatted auto-response email requests, which differ according to the provider. Saildocs is a popular email based GRIB service which uses the Airmail GRIB viewer. See www.saildocs.com or www.siriuscyber.net for more details.

A very useful internet based GRIB service is provided by UGRIB. The software can be downloaded free from the internet, and requests can be easily made by highlighting the area requested on a map, and selecting the resolution, duration and spacing of the files. See www.grib.us for details.

It is important to know that GRIB files are entirely computer generated, and have no human at the helm to interpret data.

These weather files are all fairly broad stroke and do not provide the sort of detailed information found in more dedicated websites for a country or sea area. They provide an overall picture for a large sea area rather than detailed data for short local passages.

4.8 WEATHER ON THE INTERNET

WiFi or internet cafés are the cheapest way to access the internet, and are found in many towns across the Mediterranean. Marinas sometimes have an online computer for visitors' use, and some places allow you to plug in your own laptop to connect, or have a WiFi network.

Frank Singleton's Weather Site

An excellent overview of weather for sailors, with comprehensive links to weather sources.

http://weather.mailasail.com

Weather Online

Gives surface wind direction and strength up to a week ahead. Also synoptic charts. Good site.

www.weatheronline.co.uk

JCOMM GMDSS by Meteo France

Official text forecast for GMDSS MSI. Select METAREA III.

http://weather.gmdss.org

DWD German Weather Forecasting

Follow links to Wetter + klima – Wetter Aktuell – Seewetter – Mittelmeer

German language site but easily understood tabled forecasts. Detailed 3-day text forecasts for W Med areas.

www.dwd.de

Predict Wind

Subscription service (£19/year). Good interface and a choice of models.

www.predictwind.com

Passage Weather

Grib viewer with area details for Gibraltar Strait, Bonifacio Strait and Balearics.
Optional low bandwidth interface.
www.passageweather.com

Other general sites

www.windguru.com
www.windfinder.com
www.meteosail.com
www.weatherweb.net (Atlantic)

SPAIN

Spanish State Met Agency

Forecasts in Spanish
www.aemet.es/es/eltiempo/prediccion/maritima

FRANCE

Meteo France

Detailed forecasts for coastal and offshore areas in W Med.
www.meteofrance.com

ITALY

Italian National Meteorological Service

Meteomar text of forecasts as on VHF Ch 68.
www.meteoam.it

Eurometeo

Gives up to a three day forecast with wind strength and sea conditions for all Italian waters.
www.eurometeo.com

Italian aeronautical forecasts
www.meteoam.it

MALTA

Malta Weather

3-day forecasts, text, graphics and synoptic charts
www.maltaweather.com

CROATIA

National Met Service
http://meteo.hr

ALADIN Weather
www.prognoza.hr

GREECE

Poseidon
www.poseidon.ncmr.gr/weather.html

Hellenic National Meteorological Service
www.hnms.gr

SKIRON University of Athens
//forecast.uoa.gr
High Resolution Forecast

Meteo
www.meteo.gr/sailingmapf.asp

TURKEY

Turkish Meteorological Service
www.meteor.gov.tr

ISRAEL

Israeli Meteorological Service
www.ims.gov.il

4.9 WEATHER APPS

Many of the websites listed above now have apps available on iTunes or Google Play (Android), including Predict Wind, Windfinder, Poseidon and Aladin.
As with the websites though, some of the low resolution GRIB programs lack the detail for coastal cruising when the MSI forecasts tend to be more accurate.

5. Regulations and documentation

5.1 NINE-LANGUAGE GLOSSARY OF TERMS USED FOR FORMALITIES

GB Name of yacht and radio callsign
F Nom du yacht et numéro radio
D Name der Yacht und Radiorufnummer
I Nome dell vascello e segnale radio
P Nome do yacht – sinal de chamada
E Nombre de yate – señal de llamada
GR Ὄνομα σκάφου καὶ ραδιοτηλεγράφου
TR Yatin ismi ve Çağirma işaretti
Ime broda (plovila) i broj radio uredaja

GB Country and port of registration
F Pays et port d'enregistrement
D Land und Hafen wo registriert
I Paese e porto di registrazione
P Matricula, porto de registo
E Matrícula, puerto asiento
GR Χώρα καὶ λιμήν ἐγγραφῆς
TR Sicil Memleketi ve limani
Zemlja i luka registracije

GB Registration number
F Numéro d'enregistrement
D Registrationsnummer
I Nummero di registrazione
P Número de Registo
E Número asiento
GR Ἐγγραφή ἀριθμου
TR Sicil numarasi
Registarski broj

GB Net registered tons weight
F Poids net (en tonnes) enregistré
D Netto Registertonnen Gewicht
I Peso netto registrato (in ton.)
P Tonelagem
E Tonelada asiento peso neto
GR Καθαρός κατὰλογος τόννου βαρύτητος
TR Net tonilato
Neto registarska težina

GB Length
F Longueur
D Länge
I Longezza
P Comprimento
E Eslora
GR Μηκος
TR Uzunluk
Dužina

GB Beam
F Largeur
D Breite
I Largezza
P Dargura
E Manga
GR Δοκὸς μέτρου
TR Ğenişlik
Šieina

GB Draught
F Profondeur
D Tiefe
I Profondita
P Calado
E Calado
GR Σχέδιο μέτρου
TR Çektiğisu
Ǧaž

GB Description of vessel
F Description du bâteau
D Beschreibung des Bootes
I Descripzione dell vascello
P Descricao do barco
E Descripción de barca
GR Περιγραφὴ του σκάφους
TR Ğeminin cinsi
Opis broda (plovila)

GB Yacht owner and address
F Propriétaire du yacht et adresse
D Yacht Eigentümer und Adresse
I Indirizzo e nome del propretario
P Nome e endereso do proprietario
E Proprietario – dirección
GR Ἰδιοτὴτης του σκὰφου καὶ διεύθυνσις
TR Yatin sahibî ve adresî
Ime ulasnika i adresa

GB Captain of yacht and passport number
F Nom du capitaine et numéro de passeport
D Kapitän der Yacht und Pass-Nummer
I Capitano dell vascello e nummero di passaporto
P Nome do capitao e no. do passaporte
E Nombre del capitán, número de pasaporte
GR Πλοίαρχος του σκὰφου καὶ ἀριθμός διαβατηρίου
TR Yatin kaptani ve pasaport numarasi
Kapetan broda (jahte) i broj pasoša

GB Names of crew and passport nos
F Noms et no. de passeport des membres de l'équipage
D Namen der Besatzung und Pass-Nummern
I Nomi del equipagio e nummero di passaporto
P Nomes da tripulacao e nos. dos passaportes
E Nombre de los tripulantes, número de pasaporte
GR Ὀνόματα πληρωμάτου καὶ ἀριθμός διαβατηρίου
TR Mürettebatin îsimlerî ve pasaport numalari
Imena posade i brojeui pasosa

GB Time/date of arrival in port
F Heure et date d'arrivée au port
D Ankunftszeit, Datum der Ankunft im Hafen
I Ora e data d'arrivo in porto
P Data e hora da chegada
E Hora y fecha de arribo
GR Ὥρα / ἡμερομηνία ἀφίξεως λιμανιού
TR Limana varis tarîhî ve saati
Vrijeme/datum dolaska u luku

GB Last port of call
F Dernier port d'attache
D Letzter Anlaufhafen
I Precedente porto
P Ultimo porto
E Puerto último – precedente
GR Τελευταιος λιμὴν ἐπισκέψεως
TR Ğeldiği son ziyaret limani
Luka zadnjeg boravišta

GB Next port of call
F Prochain port d'attache
D Nächster Anlaufhafen
I Prossimo porto
P Proximo porto
E Puerto próximo – destino
GR Προσεχής λιμὴν ἐπισκέψεως
TR Ğidecği ilk ziyaret limani
Sljedeča luka

GB Reason for visit
F Raison de la visite
D Grund für Besuch
I Ragiona della visita
P Motivo da visita
E Motivo por visita
GR Λὸγος ἐΠισκέψεως
TR Ziyaret sebebi
Razlog dolaska

5.2 EU LAWS FOR YACHTS

Border Controls around the Mediterranean

The immigration controls outlined below refer solely to the individual. The vessel is considered separately under VAT regulations. Cruising permits and other charges are covered later.

European Union

An area consisting of 28 countries, with agreements on trade, security and immigration:

Austria	Germany	Poland
Belgium	Greece	Portugal
Bulgaria	Hungary	Romania
Croatia	Ireland	Slovakia
Cyprus	Italy	Slovenia
Czech Republic	Latvia	Spain
Denmark	Lithuania	Sweden
Estonia	Luxembourg	United Kingdom
Finland	Malta	
France	Netherlands	

European Economic Area EEA

An area consisting of the EU countries plus several more with special trade and travel agreements. These 'extra' countries are all part of the Schengen area.

Non EU EEA countries:

Iceland Liechtenstein Norway

Switzerland is not in the EEA but has similar agreements.

Schengen Agreement

An agreement between European countries which is intended to guarantee free movement of all people between participating countries. Land border controls have been lifted between participating countries, although controls may be imposed for exceptional circumstances. External borders with non-signatory countries and sea borders retain strict border controls. Anybody entering the Schengen area from outside should expect full immigration controls. Not all EU countries are signatories of Schengen, and the agreement includes the non-EU countries listed above.

EU members not in Schengen:

Ireland	(opted out)
United Kingdom	(opted out)
Cyprus	(due to the partition issue)
Bulgaria	(candidate)
Romania	(candidate)
Croatia	(candidate)

EU citizens, and citizens of Schengen countries may travel and live within any Schengen country on an unlimited basis, but will be considered as a resident of any country where they reside for more than 183 days in one year. A resident must comply with that country's laws on taxes and specific maritime laws, and may become an issue for live-aboards spending a long time in one country.

Non EEA passport holders are permitted to stay in the Schengen area for ***up to 90 days in any six month period***. If visitors spend three months within the area, they must leave the area for at least the next three months. Some people will need to obtain a visa on or before arrival. The Schengen visa is a permit to travel within this area once the application is accepted. It is not a work permit.

The list of visa-exempt countries is listed in Annex II of the Schengen agreement. Those required to obtain a visa are listed in Annex I. Visitors from the following countries do not require a visa, but must travel within the restrictions noted above. The list is not exhaustive and if in doubt check the requirements with your embassy:

Australia	Israel
Brazil	New Zealand
Canada	Switzerland
Croatia	USA

In reality, visitors who do not require visas and who are travelling on their own vessel do not appear to have this time limit enforced and many have stayed longer within the Schengen area without penalty, but there is nothing to say that the regulations will not be enforced, and you may be fined for over-staying. Those who can demonstrate that they are travelling through the area are less likely to hit problems than those who stay for long periods within one country.

If you do require a visa (South African or Turkish nationals for example) it is worth applying for a multi-entry visa to assist with travel arrangements. Visas are not readily extended.

Those wishing to stay longer than three months may need to obtain a residence permit.

Non Schengen Countries Immigration

Non Schengen countries apply their own immigration and visa regulations, but most Mediterranean countries permit stays of up to 90 days. Some countries allow visa extensions, but some follow the Schengen rules of 90 days in any six month period.

Selected European Country Checklist

COUNTRY	EU member	EUROZONE member	EU VAT area	SCHENGEN area
United Kingdom	✓	×	✓	×
Gibraltar	✓	×[a]	×	×
(Channel Islands)	×	×[a]	×	×
Portugal	✓	✓	✓	✓
Azores	✓	✓	✓	✓
Madeira	✓	✓	✓	✓
Spain	✓	✓	✓	✓
Ceuta	✓	✓	×	×
Melilla	✓	✓	×	×
Canary Islands	✓	✓	×	✓
France	✓	✓	✓	✓
Monaco	×	✓	✓[b]	✓[b]
Italy	✓	✓	✓	✓
San Marino	×	✓	×	✓[b]
Vatican	×	✓	×	×
Malta	✓	✓	✓	✓[c]
Slovenia	✓	✓	✓	✓[c]
Croatia	✓	×[a]	✓	×
Montenegro	×	✓	×	×
Albania	×	×[a]	×	×
Greece	✓	✓	✓	✓
Cyprus	✓	✓	✓	×
TRNC	×	×[a]	×	×
Turkey	×	×[a]	×	×

[a] Euros are widely accepted but not official currency.

[b] De-facto VAT and Schengen countries. In Monaco, French authorities are responsible for import VAT and policing the sea border.

[c] Not signatories to Schengen visa 3rd country lists Annex I and II, so those who need visas may differ from countries listed.

VAT

EU-Registered Yachts

Since 1 January 1993 all yachts registered in EU countries are required to have proof that VAT has been paid or that the yacht is exempt from payment. The only exemption is for yachts built before 1 January 1985 which were in an EU country before 1 January 1993. All yachts built after 1 January 1985, and older craft imported into the EU after 1 January 1993, are liable for VAT payment.

If liable, VAT should be paid in the country where the vessel entered the EU, or in the country of registration, and is subject to a customs valuation of the vessel.

Note VAT-paid EU vessels will lose their VAT status if sold outside the EU.

Non-EU Registered Yachts

From 1 July 2002 yachts registered in countries outside the EU and owned by someone who is established outside the EU, are allowed 18 months Temporary Importation (TI) into the EU without incurring VAT liability. At the end of the 18-month period the yacht must leave the EU to discharge its TI liability. Once the TI liability has been discharged by exit from the EU, the vessel may re-enter the EU to begin a new period of TI. There doesn't seem to be an official minimum time that a vessel needs to be out of the EU before it may re-enter to start a new TI period, but it is important that a yacht has established a recognisable time gap, backed up with documentary proof, before attempting to re-enter the EU. Proof of clearing customs out of the EU, into and out of a non-EU country, such as Turkey, Albania or Tunisia, with official documents, and, say, dated berthing receipts from the non-EU country. The lack of an official time limit means that the law is open to a certain amount of interpretation from country to country, and possibly from port to port. For example, it would seem that Spain only allows non-EU yachts six months in the country. It is important to ascertain the local interpretation at the time of entry.

Notes

1. Yachts registered in EU 'non-fiscal' areas, such as the Channel Islands, where the owner is also established, will have similar limitations.
2. Yachts registered in non-EU countries or those such as in 1, but with an owner who is an EU resident, have a much more limited TI period of just one month.
3. Yachts registered in EEA countries, such as Norway, are permitted six months sailing, with six months in storage (or out of the EU), in any one year.
4. The Channel Islands, Gibraltar, Ceuta, Melilla and the Canary Islands are not part of the EU VAT area.
5. If a yacht is hauled out and placed under customs bond in an EU country, it is probable that this time will not count against the 18-month limit. Thus a non-EU yacht can remain within the EU for up to two years, as long as it is hauled out and under customs bond for a period of six months. Yacht owners who are not EU nationals must also leave the EU for this 6-month period. It is essential that these terms be agreed with the relevant customs officials before assuming this interpretation of the ruling.
6. Obviously any non-EU nationals' visa obligations must be observed over and above the VAT regulations.

Small Craft Licences

At the time of publication there was no clear EU directive on small craft licences and it appeared to be up to individual countries to determine agreement on what licence or certificate corresponded with what. The RYA International Certificate of Competence (ICC) is generally accepted as a minimum requirement. Check the RYA website for details www.rya.org.uk

Recreational Craft Directive

On 15 June 1998 the Recreational Craft Directive came into existence. There have been numerous amendments, with the latest 2004 directives becoming mandatory from 1 January 2006. The RCD dictates standards for such things as hull construction, fuel, gas and electrical installations, steering gear, and engine noise and emissions. Below is a brief summary.

- The RCD applies to all recreational craft registered in the EU between 2·5 and 24m LOA.
- Any craft built after 15 June 1998 must have a CE mark and rating.
- Craft built before 15 June 1998 are exempt, as long as they were in the EU before this date.
- If they were imported into the EU after 15 June 1998 they should apply retrospectively. (This is the main point of contention).
- Home-built craft are exempt if not sold for five years. Historical replicas are also exempt.

It appears that the original brief, to have certain common standards of construction for the EU market so that trade within the EU could be facilitated to one kitemark, has been extended to exclude a large number of craft from being sold on the EU market.

In practice most Mediterranean countries are ignoring the requirements of the RCD for the simple reason that it is just not enforceable.

5.3 GENERAL DOCUMENTS

Yacht Registration Documents

Full Part 1 or SSR papers or their equivalent are generally required as minimum proof of ownership by all Mediterranean countries.

Insurance

Most countries expect yachts to carry translations of their Third Party Liability cover.

Radio Licences

A ***Ship Radio Licence (SRL)*** is required in order to install any of the equipment listed below on any UK registered yachts. The relevant operator licences must be held before using the equipment.

- DSC equipment associated with GMDSS
- MF, HF, VHF equipment
- Low powered UHF equipment
- On board repeaters
- 121·5/243MHz and 406/121·5MHz Personal Locator Beacons (PLBs)
- 406MHz and 1·6GHz Emergency Position Indicating Radio Beacons (EPIRBs)
- Satellite communications equipment (Ship Earth Stations)
- RADAR
- Search and Rescue Radar Transponders (SARTs)

A Ship Portable Radio Licence (SPRL) will cover a handheld VHF/DSC VHF or PLB intended for use on more than one vessel.

The SRL will also give a Vessel Callsign, uniquely identifying the vessel within the International Maritime Mobile Service (IMMS). Any DSC or SES equipment will also be allocated a Maritime Mobile Service Identity (MMSI) number.

Radio Operator Licences

From December 2003 UK radio operator licences are administered by OFCOM.

GMDSS Short Range Certificate (SRC) Covers VHF operations in coastal waters. The SRC is the minimum mandatory qualification for yachtsman and other small craft operators on the installation of GMDSS equipment.

GMDSS Long Range Certificate (LRC) MF/HF SSB VHF and satellite communications of both GMDSS and non GMDSS operations.

GMDSS Restricted Radio Operator's Certificate (ROC) Certificate required by Bridge Watch-keeping Officers on SOLAS vessels (>300grt) within GMDSS Sea Area A1.

GMDSS General Operator's Certificate (GOC) Certificate required by Masters, Deck Officers on Merchant Ships and by Professional Yachtmasters (Class 4 unlimited).

EU Health Insurance

The old paper form E111 has been replaced with the European Health Insurance Card (EHIC). Application forms are processed by the post office and the new credit card sized official looking EHIC (valid for five years) will be sent to you. This entitles you to free or reduced costs for medical treatment throughout the EEA and Switzerland. (The EEA or European Economic Area comprises all the EU countries plus Iceland, Liechtenstein and Norway.)

5.4 REGULATIONS COUNTRY BY COUNTRY

GIBRALTAR

Documents Valid passport. Yacht registration papers. Radio licence.

Customs Formalities may now be completed at either of the marinas. Yachts not using a marina currently have no way to clear in.

Entry formalities A yacht should fly a 'Q' flag and head for a marina. A number of forms for customs, immigration and harbour officials must be completed. A list of crew and passengers is required in triplicate. The following regulations should be noted.

i. Any crew member or passenger intending to reside ashore during the time the vessel is in port must report to immigration control at Waterport police station and give the address ashore.
ii. Immigration control should be advised of any guests residing aboard.
iii. If any person has employment in Gibraltar it must be reported to the immigration office.
iv. Crew must not be paid off or enrolled (regardless of nationality) without permission from the immigration office.
v. Before leaving report to the immigration office at Waterport the time and date of departure.

SPAIN

Documents Passport. Yacht registration papers. VAT receipt or other proof of payment. You may be asked for a radio licence, proof of insurance for the yacht and proof of competence to handle a yacht such as the RYA International Certificate of Competence (ICC) or Yachtmaster's certificate. Insurance papers must have a Spanish translation of the Third Party agreement.

Customs (*Aduana*) Spain as part of the EU comes under EU legislation regarding the payment of VAT. Non-EU boats must report to customs on arrival in Spain.

Entry formalities EU flag yachts on which VAT has been paid or which are exempt can enter Spain from other EU countries without formalities. Random checks by customs are carried out. Non-EU flag yachts should report to customs and immigration at the first port of call. Here you will be stamped into the country and issued with a special form. An inventory of yacht equipment and crew lists will be required.

Other Regulations

Black Water New restrictions on black water effectively prohibit discharge of untreated sewage less than 12M offshore. Some ports require yachts to have holding tanks. Fines for discharging black water may be levied.

FRANCE

Documents Passport. Yacht registration papers. VAT receipt or other proof of payment. You may be asked for: proof of insurance for the yacht, proof of competence to handle a yacht such as the RYA ICC.

Customs (*Douane*) France, as part of the EU, comes under EU legislation regarding the payment of VAT. Non-EU boats must report to customs on arrival in France. The non-EU temporary importation of a yacht is carried out under a *Titre de Séjour* obtained at major customs offices.

A yacht registered in a country that does not have a special financial arrangement with France (most do but those that do not include Australia, New Zealand, South Africa and flags of convenience such as Panama, Liberia, Honduras and the Maldives) must pay an additional charge while in French harbours. When it was introduced the tax caused a mass exodus of boats from French marinas which left many of the locals out of work. An unofficial edict from Paris cancelled implementation in practice, but it still remains law.

Entry formalities EU flag yachts on which VAT has been paid or which are exempt can enter France from other EU countries without formalities. Random checks are carried out by customs. Non-EU flag yachts should report to customs and immigration at the first major port of call. Here you will be stamped into the country and a record of your entry made. An inventory of yacht equipment and crew lists will be required.

Yachts chartering in France must have proof VAT (TVA) has been paid on the charter boat and VAT must be paid on the charter fee. Private EU yachts can change crews (including the skipper) as long as no fee is paid for the use of the boat.

Other Regulations

Black Water New restrictions on black water effectively prohibit discharge of untreated sewage less than 12M offshore. Some ports require yachts to have holding tanks. Fines for discharging black water may be levied.

MONACO

Entry formalities

Report to Direction des Ports (Monday–Friday) or Pilot Station (Saturday–Sunday) within 24h. French Customs operate in Monaco. Notify the Pilot Sation on departure (or on the previous day if between 2300–0800).

Other Laws

Monaco Harbour

All vessels leaving the harbour have priority.

Max speed 3 knots.

All vessels must be able to manoeuvre at all times.

Any works affecting manoeuvrability must be reported to the Port Authority.

It is forbidden to leave vessels unmanned.

ITALY

Documents Passport. Yacht registration papers. VAT receipt or other proof of payment. Insurance papers which must have an Italian translation for proof of third party liability. You may be asked for proof of competence to handle a yacht such as the RYA ICC or Yachtmaster's certificate.

Customs *(Guardia di Finanza)* Italy as part of the EU comes under EU legislation regarding the payment of VAT.

Non-EU boats should report to customs on arrival in Italy.

Entry formalities EU yachts on which VAT has been paid or which are exempt can enter Italy from other EU countries without formalities. The old *Constituto in arrivo per il naviglio di diporto* has been shelved for EU-registered yachts with EU nationals on board. Non EU-registered yachts or non-EU nationals should report to the first large port in order to clear into the country with the relevant authorities and apply to the harbourmaster for a *Costituto* (an entry declaration) at the first port.

Yacht Tax 2012 The yacht tax proved universally unpopular and was repealed in 2013 for foreign flag vessels.

Other Laws

1. It is against Italian law to swim in any Italian harbour. Swimmers are subject to hefty fines.
2. It is against Italian law to motorsail within 300m of the shore, except when entering or leaving a harbour.
3. Anchoring is prohibited anywhere around the coast within 200m of a beach or within 100m elsewhere. This rule can often be seen to be flouted, particularly during the high season, but it is a law which is increasingly being enforced, and can attract a fine of €350.

MALTA

Documents Passport. Yacht registration documents. You may be asked for proof of insurance for the yacht and a radio licence.

Customs As part of the EU, Malta comes under EU legislation regarding VAT. All non EU yachts coming from outside Maltese territorial waters must make for Valletta harbour or Mgarr to clear customs. The EU pet passport scheme now applies in Malta, and so pets with the correct official paperwork may enter Malta from another EU country.

Pets on yachts may have special requirements and enquiries should be made well in advance.

Entry formalities A yacht entering Malta should fly a 'Q' flag and a Maltese maritime courtesy ensign (not the same as the national flag). When 10M off Malta call Valetta Port Control VHF Ch 16, 09, 12 to advise them of your arrival. They will usually ask you to call again when you are one mile off to receive instructions. Depending on where you are the following customs clearance procedure applies.

Mgarr, Gozo Berth where directed and clear in. If you arrive at night berth where possible and clear in in the morning.

Grand Harbour If you call in on VHF as you should then you will be directed to go to Grand Harbour. The situation at Grand Harbour is far from convenient with only a very high quay to tie up on if you cannot get on the lower sections of quay used by the customs boats.

You will need several crew lists. Customs procedure is thorough yet polite. EU yachts with EU crew arriving from an EU country may be permitted to berth at a marina and clear in afterwards.

Slovenia

Documents Passport. No visas are required for EU nationals for stays of less than three months Yacht registration papers. A radio licence and proof of insurance may be asked for.

Customs A yacht must report to a Port of entry when entering Slovenian waters.

Entry formalities Sailing permit costs are limited to a small payment for light dues. Around €30 for a 10–12m yacht.

Ports of entry

Permanent	*Seasonal*
Koper, Piran	(1 May–31 October) Izola

CROATIA

Croatia joined the EU on 1 July 2013. It is in line with EU Immigration and VAT rules, although it is not part of the Schengen Area. Reports that customs demanding proof of VAT paid status is causing problems for UK yachts. See RYA for latest www.rya.org.uk.

Documents Passport. Yacht registration papers. Proof of ownership/authorisation. Insurance papers. Proof of VAT status. Proof of competence.

Crew List

Foreign registered yachts must declare a Crew List on entering Croatia. It includes crew and passengers. The list must be re-submitted each time the list changes. If there are no changes made, a yacht has no need to check in with the authorities until departing Croatia.

List of Persons

Foreign registered yachts must declare a List of Persons when replacing crew or passengers in Croatia. The maximum number of people on the list may not exceed 230% of the registered maximum for that vessel. The list must be re-submitted each time the list changes, but should not include children under the age of 12. The number of changes is not limited.

Evidence of Seaworthiness

In accordance with the country of the vessel's flag. Harbourmaster may perform an inspection of the vessel.

Entry formalities All yachts entering Croatia should fly the Q flag and the Croatian courtesy ensign. Yachts approaching Croatia should monitor VHF Ch 16 and expect to be called by patrol vessels.

On entering Croatia, yachts must proceed to a port of entry. Immigration, customs, and the harbourmaster are visited.

All persons on board must also register with the police for the duration of the stay. In practice this can be done in the harbourmaster's or marina office.

Cruising Tax

Following Croatia's accession to the EU the old Vignette has been replaced by the Navigation, safety and pollution prevention fee. The formula for the fee is (Lx20) + (Px2) where L is LOA in metres and P is engine power in kW. Thus, in 2014 the annual fee for a 40HP (30kW) 12m boat would be around 300 Kuna (approx €40). 1 HP (UK) = 0·7457 kilowatt (kW)

For details see the Croatian Ministry of Sea, Tourism, Transport and Development website www.mppi.hr (click on English – Maritime Affairs)

Other charges

Tourist Tax A tourist tax is now paid separately to the Port Authority.

Tourist Tax for a 12m yacht are approximately:

€28 for eight days
€70 for 30 days
€150 for one year

All fishing in Croatian waters requires a permit which can be obtained from the harbourmaster.

Other regulations

When underway, motor boats and sailing boats must not navigate within 50m of the coast. Rowing boats may navigate at a distance less than 50m from the coast. When near beaches, all boats shall navigate at a distance greater than 50m from the enclosure of the marked bathing area i.e. 150m from the coast of a natural beach.

Ports of entry

Permanent		*Seasonal* (1 April to 30 October)
Umag	Zadar	ACI Marina Umag
Poreč	Sibenik	Novigrad
Rovinj	Split	Sali
Pula	Vela Luka	Bozava
Raša-Bršica	Ploče	Primosten
Rijeka	Ubli (Lastovo)	Starigrad
Mali Lošinj	Metkovic	Ravni Zakanj (Kornati)
Senj	Korčula	Komiza (Viš)
	Dubrovnik (Gruž)	Vis (Viš)
		Hvar
		Cavtat

MONTENEGRO

Documents Passport. Visas are no longer required by most nationals for stays of up to 90 days. Yacht registration papers. A radio licence, proof of insurance and some proof of competence may be asked for.

Customs A yacht must report to a Port of entry when entering Montenegrin waters.

Entry formalities Call *Bar Radio* on entering Montenegran waters. A listening watch on VHF Ch 16, 24 is recommended. On arrival at a port of entry call Bar Radio on VHF Ch 16, 24. On first entering a port of entry you must report to the harbour office, customs and frontier police. The Vignette is proof of clearance, light dues and administration fees and should be displayed. Costs for 12m yacht:

€40 one week
€95 one month
€400 one year

(more than double for yachts over 12m LOA)

Other Regulations

Swimming is strictly prohibited outside of marked zones.

Ports of entry

All year round	*Summer only*
Porto Montenegro	Zelenika
Bar	Budva
	Kotor

ALBANIA

Documents Passport. Yacht registration papers.

Customs Yacht registration papers. Crew lists. Numerous photocopies of passports and registration papers.

Entry formalities At the time of publication yachts are treated no differently to commercial shipping when entering Albania. Costs are comparatively high given the small cruising area and must be paid in Euros. For this reason a certain amount of cash must be carried. Before entering an Albanian port call up on VHF Ch 11, 12, or 16. Theoretically there are severe penalties for not informing the authorities by radio prior to your arrival. Upon arrival, berth where directed. Customs and immigration will come aboard (as will other 'officials' and the odd soldier) to inspect passports and the ship's papers. Entry tax is around €60 for craft 12–15m. This covers light dues, clearance dues and some other dues, but not port charges in subsequent harbours.

Note A yacht should not be left unattended while in Albanian waters.

Ports of entry

All year round		*Summer only*
Shenjin	Durres	Himare
Vlore (town)	Sarande	

GREECE

Documents Passport. Yacht registration papers. VAT receipt or other proof of payment. You may be asked for proof of competence to handle a yacht such as the RYA ICC.

Customs (*Telenion*) Greece as part of the EU comes under EU legislation regarding the payment of VAT.

Entry formalities

All yachts entering Greek waters should fly a Greek courtesy ensign. Entry formalities will depend on the flag of the vessel and the nationalities of the crew. This will determine whether it is necessary to visit a port of entry where all the relevent officials will be found.

- Arrivals from outside the Schengen area are no longer obliged to use a port of entry, but must notify the port police in advance (usually on VHF Ch12) and provide two completed signed copies of the new Pleasure Boat's Document (see below) on arrival. Any harbour with a port police presence can be used.
- Non EU registered yachts must obtain a Transit log from Customs officials.
- Non EU passport holders must complete immigration formalities and obtain visas if necessary.

If a full check in is required, a port of entry should be chosen and the authorities should be visited in the following order:

Immigration Passports, visas
Customs VAT, Transit log
Port police PBD, TPP, DEKPA

Pleasure Boat's Document (PBD)

This is a pro forma crew list. One completed copy is retained by the port police on entry to Greece, the other stamped copy must be kept on board at all times. It should be handed in to a port police office when leaving Greek waters.

A copy of the PBD is available to download from the Imray website: www.imray.com (search *Greek Waters Pilot*)

Traffic Document (DEKPA)

All yachts over 7m LOA must purchase a Traffic Document (DEKPA) from the Port Police. The DEKPA may be checked at any time, and must be stamped by the port police annually. This will likely happen on entry to Greece or on launching, when the TPP is paid (see below). It may be re-used even after the yacht has left and re-entered Greece. The cost of the DEKPA is €30.

Greek Cruising Tax (TPP)

The new Greek tax was ratified at the beginning of 2014. It is likely to be implemented in 2015. Payments will be made via a bank or local tax office. The receipt should be kept with the DEKPA and PBD.

- vessels 7-12m LOA to pay €200-400
- vessels over 12m LOA to pay €100 per metre
- for all leisure vessels over 7m, including commercial and charter vessels carrying less than 49 passengers
- vessels over 12m may alternatively pay a monthly fee of €10 per metre
- vessels 'permanently' in Greece may pay the annual tax in advance and obtain a 30% discount
- only vessels in the water will be subject to the tax. Vessels on the hard are exempt.
- no refunds are payable if vessels leave the country.
- Vessels that are caught evading this law will pay a fine equivalent to twice the annual charge.

Transit Log

The Transit Log is a customs record for non-EU yachts visiting the EU. It is valid for six months, and an extension for up to twelve months may be applied for. A yacht may be left in Greece for as long as the Transit Log remains valid. Your passport will be stamped by customs to indicate that the vessel remains in Greece. The Transit Log must be surrendered when the yacht leaves Greece. In addition, all non-EU registered yachts (except those from the EEA) are subject to a Reciprocal Tax of €15 per metre, every three months, levied at the end of the period. This tax will likely be dropped when the TPP is in operation.

Other Documents

Yacht registration papers will usually be requested. Proof of VAT status, insurance cover, radio licenses and certificates of competence may also be requested.

Marinas and boatyards at a Port of Entry will usually assist with the paperwork.

Insurance

You need a certificate stating the amounts for which you are covered and this is required to be carried on board the yacht. Contact your insurance company and they will be able to provide the necessary documentation including a Greek translation.

Ports of entry

Kérkira (Corfu)	(Ionian)
Préveza	(Ionian)
Argostoli (Cephalonia)	(Ionian)
Zákinthos	(Ionian)
Katakólon	(Peloponnisos)
Pílos	(Peloponnisos)
Kalamata	(Peloponnisos)
Patras	(Gulf of Patras)
Itéa	(Gulf of Corinth)
Zéa Marina	(Saronic Gulf)
Glifada	(Saronic Gulf)
Vouliagméni Marina	(Saronic Gulf)
Navplion	(Argolic Gulf)
Ermoúpolis (Síros)	(Cyclades)
Lavrion	(Attic Coast)
Volos	(Northern Greece)
Thessaloniki	(Northern Greece)
Kavála	(Northern Greece)
Alexandroúpolis	(Northern Greece)
Mirina (Limnos)	(Eastern Sporades)
Mitilíni (Lésvos)	(Eastern Sporades)
Khíos	(Eastern Sporades)
Pithagorion (Sámos)	(Eastern Sporades)
Vathi (Samos)	(Eastern Sporades)
Kalimnos	(Dodecanese) (summer only)
Kós	(Dodecanese)
Rhodes	(Dodecanese)
Khania	(Crete)
Iraklion	(Crete)
Ayios Nikólaos	(Crete)

Greek insurance requirements:

1. All yachts must have insurance for liability for death or injury for those on board and any third party for a minimum of €500,000.
2. Insurance for liability for damage of at least €150,000.
3. Liability for pollution resulting from an incident of €150,000.

Yacht damage and salvage

If your boat is damaged, either through your own devices or by a third party, and it is reported to the port police, they are obliged to constrain your yacht until it is proved to be seaworthy. In these cases, the port police will usually require that you have your boat surveyed by a registered yacht surveyor and this can cost anything from €500-1000. Without the survey the port police cannot release your boat. If at all possible try to resolve smaller matters without going to the port police. In major cases of salvage your insurance company will be involved and will employ a surveyor in any case.

TURKEY

Documents Passport. Most foreign nationals, including UK citizens, need to obtain a visa. Yacht registration papers. You may be asked for proof of insurance and proof of competence to handle a yacht such as the RYA ICC or Yachtmaster's certificate.

Entry formalities A yacht entering Turkish waters for the first time must do so at a designated Port of Entry. A 'Q' flag and a Turkish courtesy flag should be flown.

You will have to visit the health office, passport police, customs and harbourmaster, usually, but not always, in that order. You are then free to cruise on the itinerary detailed on the Transit Log which must be produced at any port or on demand from the *Sahil Guvenlik* (Coastguard).

Note

Yachts registered in Cyprus may not enter Turkish waters.

Customs A Transit Log will be issued by customs and in 2014 it cost US$30. It is valid for one year, or one continuous visit, or until the yacht is laid-up, whichever happens first. On issue you must list your intended itinerary and crew list in the Transit Log, and changes to either must also be recorded and authorised by the harbourmaster at the time of the change. When leaving Turkey with the yacht you must surrender the Transit Log, even if you intend to return to Turkey at *any time*.

Foreign flag yachts with the owner aboard can have friends or relatives aboard. If anyone leaves this must be noted on the Transit Log. If new friends arrive a new Transit Log must be purchased. A foreign flag yacht without the owner aboard can enter Turkey and sail to another port to pick the owner up, but cannot change the complement of those on board.

There are plans to digitise the Transit Log such that yachts would carry a printout.

New harbour dues must be paid on entry to Turkey for vessels over 11NRT (this equates to yachts around 10–12m LOA). The dues are around 7TL for vessels up to 45NRT.

The payment process can only be done by an agent who may also complete all clearance procedures at the same time. Agent charges vary from €35–150 so ask around before committing to one agent, and make sure you know what is included. It is possible to complete clearance procedures yourself, up to the payment process.

It may be helpful to carry proof of NRT if your vessel is under 11NRT, as otherwise the harbourmaster will assess your NRT.

Light dues must also be paid by larger vessels over 30NRT. Again tonnage certificates would be helpful.

New Visa Regulations

From April 2014, sticker-type visa stamps are no longer issued on entry. All those who require a visa must apply for an e-visa online before arriving in the country. The visa is multi-entry and costs US$20 for a UK citizen. You must have a passport which remains valid for at least six months beyond the end of the visa period.
www.evisa.gov.tr/en/

All EU, N American and Australasian citizens receive 90 days. South Africa passport holders get just 21 days.

- Maximum stay in Turkey is 90 days in a 180 day period (i.e. you must be out of the country for at least 90 days in every six month period).
- multiple entries into Turkey within the 180 day period are permitted on the same visa (as long as the total days spent in Turkey do not exceed 90 days). i.e. the 90 days do not have to be consecutive
- those who need to stay for longer should apply for a Turkish Residence permit

Residence permit costs

Permit validity	Cost (US$)
1 month	25
3 months	35
6 months	50
1 year	80

Requirements

- a current transit log
- a residence permit book (US$80)
- 6 colour passport photos
- a copy of passport, showing identification page, and most recent entry stamp
- original passport
- a completed application form

Notes

1. Short term residence permits no longer require a marina contract or a bank account.
2. Heavy fines are imposed for over-staying your visa, even by one day.
3. Permits can be obtained by EU and US nationals and no doubt by some other nationals as well.

Other Regulations

Blue Card (Mavi Kart)

The new scheme governing the discharge of black and grey water. It is intended to roll out the scheme to all areas, although at present it only operates in the Muğla area.

1. All boats are required to have a blue card. This can be obtained from all marinas in the area and most will issue the card free of charge. At this time no readers were available for the cards so any inspections (and we know of none) were just to see if you had the card. It is planned to introduce card readers soon.
2. There are no plans to inspect individual foreign flag yachts to see if they have adequate tankage.
3. Monitoring of the blue card will be carried out by the harbourmaster and the coastguard.
4. In the Fethiye-Göçek area yachts were required to present evidence of a pump-out to obtain a new Transit Log.
5. There are pump-out stations in the marinas and these work efficiently. A charge is made for pump-out, usually 15–20TL.
6. Grey water is still included in the SEPA regulations although there is still plenty of boat washing and outdoor showering going on. All the Göçek charter companies use ecological brand detergents, as should everyone. It should be evident that any yachts away from a pump-out station for more than a few days will have filled the holding tank. Here you can draw your own conclusions as to what happens in practice.

Coda

The regulations are intended to be implemented around all Turkish coasts. The Muğla region is the pilot for the scheme and originally it was planned that all of the Turkish coast would be under these regulations by 2013–2014. Given the problems encountered implementing the scheme in Fethiye Körfezi this roll-out is proceeding more slowly.

Note Large fines are levied on yachts discharging waste into the sea, particularly in harbour. The maximum official fine is in the region of €235–310. However fines have been known to be as much as €620 and, in one case, €1,550.

Chartering

Foreign flag yachts can charter in Turkey if registered with an authorised Turkish charter operator and on payment of the requisite fees for registration. Charter yachts entering Turkey (inevitably from Greece) must pay a substantial charter fee (depending on LOA) to cruise around the Turkish coast.

Mobile Phone Registration

Turkish authorities are clamping down on illegal/stolen mobile phones. If you wish to use a Turkish SIM card in your UK handset you must register your mobile phone's IMEI number with customs officials when you enter Turkey. You are advised to carry proof of ownership. Failure to register it will mean your phone may cease to work after a few days. In practice this can be done at most Turkcell shops in major (tourist) towns where the procedure is well understood.

Ports of entry

Istanbul	Izmir	Bodrum	Finike	Taşucu
Bandirma	Kuşadasi	Datça	Kemer	Mersin
Çanakkale	Çesme	Bozborun	Antalya	Iskenderun
Ayvalik	Didim	Marmaris	Alanya	
Dikili	Güllük	Fethiye		
	Turgutreis	Kaş		

CYPRUS

Documents Passport. Yacht registration documents.

Customs Southern Cyprus: Rules on temporary importation and VAT are in line with EU regulations.

Entry formalities Southern Cyprus: A yacht should make for Paphos, Limassol or Larnaca. Southern Cyprus is part of the EU and is in line regarding movement of EU-registered vessels. Customs and immigration are located nearby at ports of entry. In Limassol St Raphael Marina and Larnaca Marina they are located within the marina. A yacht coming from northern Cyprus may be denied permission to enter southern Cyprus and you may be liable for the penalties mentioned below.

Note

1. The government in southern (Greek) Cyprus considers any visit by a yacht to northern (Turkish) Cyprus to be illegal. It should be pointed out that under UN Resolution 34/30 (1979) and 37/253 (1983) the UN views the Government of Cyprus (i.e. presently southern Cyprus) as the legal government of all Cyprus. If a yacht does visit northern Cyprus and then goes to southern Cyprus it can incur heavy penalties. Under the laws of the Republic of Cyprus a fine of up to €17,086 and/or two years imprisonment can be imposed. It is legal to proceed from mainland Turkey directly to southern (Greek) Cyprus.
2. Check in procedures out of hours are subject to a €60 surcharge.
3. Reunification talks are ongoing.

SYRIA

The FCO currently advises against all travel to Syria.

Documents Passport. A visa is required for internal travel. The visa must be obtained on entry and is valid for 15 days. A visa is not required for crew if they do not intend to travel more than a few kilometres outside the port area, ie into and around town. Without a visa, those on board will be issued shore passes which allow you outside the port area for a few kilometres. Yacht registration papers.

Entry formalities The best first port for arrival is Lattakia. Arrival should be planned for daylight. When 12 miles off call port control or the pilot station on VHF Ch 11 or 16. Inform them of your ETA. In theory, pilots are compulsory but free. Syrian Yacht Club in Lattakia will assist with formalities.

Ports of entry

Lattakia Banias Tartus

LEBANON

Note Yachts may not enter Lebanese waters if coming from Israel.

Documents Passport. Passports with an Israeli stamp in them cannot be accepted. Visa required for internal travel. Shore-passes can be issued to crew. Yacht registration papers.

Note Any skipper who is not the owner of the vessel should have a letter of authority from the owner.

Entry formalities Pilotage not required for vessels of less than 50 NRT. Yachts should make for Jounié Marina or Marina Joseph Koury as the first Port of Entry. Technically there are other Ports of Entry but, in practice, they are not for yachts. From July 2003 charges were reported as follows:

$50 entry fee for the yacht
$55 departure formalities
$40 per person exit fee

These are effectively the same charges as made for commercial shipping, but it is not clear if they are still current.

The approach to the Lebanese coast must be made in daylight only. In the approach to Jounié call up Oscar Charlie on VHF Ch 11, 16 when still in international waters (12M+). Only after receiving a clearance number should you close the coast. Once in harbour you will be cleared in by customs, immigration, harbourmaster and the navy. Clearance from Jounié must be obtained from all the above before leaving (clearance from the navy can be obtained on VHF Ch 11).

Ports of entry

Tripoli Jounié Joseph Koury Beirut Sidon Tyre

ISRAEL

Documents Passport. Yacht registration documents. Radio licence.

Customs On arrival customs will check you in along with immigration. You should not go ashore until checked in. You are allowed to keep your boat in Israel for one year before import tax is due.

Entry formalities You are advised to contact a marina in advance for latest entry regulations. When 25–50M off the coast call the Israeli Navy on Ch 16 or 2182kHz to advise of your arrival off the Israeli coast. Call sign *Israeli Navy*. You may or may not get a reply but you are likely to be buzzed or hailed by a navy patrol boat. When asked to stop you should do so at once and give all the details asked for (normally on VHF Ch 16) which usually include: Name of the boat and country of registration, where you have come from and where bound, and the names and nationalities of all those on board. At night the experience can be frightening when the first you know of the encounter is a powerful searchlight trained on the boat. You should continue to advise of your arrival on Ch 16 even if you don't get a reply.

A yacht should fly a Q flag and an Israeli courtesy flag if possible. Yachts coming from Cyprus usually head for Haifa. Yachts coming from Egypt usually head for Ashkelon Marina. On arrival you will be checked in by customs and immigration. If you intend going to any of the Middle East countries or any others where an Israeli stamp in your passport will cause problems, you can ask the immigration police not to stamp your passport. Instead they will issue you with a loose-leaf page with an immigration stamp on it.

Ports of entry

Haifa Tel Aviv Ashdod

EGYPT

Documents Passport. A visa is not required if you are only going to transit the Suez Canal. While in Egypt you must (officially) change a certain amount of money every month or part thereof. Official receipts for the exchange must be shown when you leave. Yacht registration documents. Proof of insurance may be asked for.

Customs A bond may be required on a yacht intending to cruise Egyptian waters. Yachts may be temporarily imported for three months with the bond.

Entry formalities A yacht should fly a Q flag and a courtesy ensign if possible. In the approach to Port Said call up on Ch 16 to inform the harbour authorities of your arrival. Customs and immigration will come to the yacht to arrange entry to Port Said/Fouad (the bonded port area) so you can arrange the transit of the canal. At Alexandria inform the yacht club of your arrival and customs and immigration will come to the yacht.

LIBYA

The FCO currently advises against all travel to Libya.

Documents Passport with Arabic translation and a valid visa. As visas are usually issued only to foreigners working in Libya it is unlikely you will be granted one. Yacht registration documents. Radio licence.

Entry formalities Contact a shipping agent in Libya at least two months in advance and advise on your itinerary.

Contact a tour operator to organise any trips.

Two weeks before arrival fax the shipping agent the yacht passengers manifest, with passport copies for each.

Universal Shipping Agent (with offices in every port)
✆ 21 444 4924 *Fax* 21 444 8083
Email info@unishipco.com or operation@unishipco.com

Permission to enter Libyan waters should be asked for on VHF Ch 16 or 2182 kHz. Thereafter keep Ch 16 open and follow all instructions to the letter.

TUNISIA

Documents Passport with a valid visa if necessary. Yacht registration papers. Proof of insurance may be asked for.

Customs A yacht can be temporarily imported into Tunisia for six months and is renewable. The boat can be left afloat or ashore. On arrival you will be issued a *Triptique (Demande de Permis de Circulation)* which records your date of entry and certain dutiable goods on board which may or may not be sealed by customs. On leaving Tunisia the Triptique must be surrendered to customs.

Note In practice EU-flagged yachts with EU nationals on board can remain in Tunisia for extended periods. However the above is the official line and is applied from time to time.

Entry formalities A yacht entering Tunisia should fly a Q flag and a courtesy ensign if possible. Entry should be made at a Port of Entry (see list). On arrival berth at the appropriate berth for clearing in. Here customs will issue a *Triptique* and usually make only a cursory search of the vessel. EU nationals (with the exception of

Benelux passport holders), USA, and Canadian passport holders do not need a visa. Other nationals including Dutch, Belgian, Luxembourg, New Zealand, Australian and others need a visa. Preferably this should be obtained in advance. If not a temporary visa for seven days can be obtained on entry and this may be extended for a longer stay in one of the cities. It has been reported that New Zealand and Australian passport holders may have problems getting the temporary visa extended. German and USA passport holders get a 4-month visa, others a 3-month visa.

Other Regulations

1. Yachts entering/leaving Tunisia, or when going to/from another Tunisian port are required to visit customs to arrange a visit by a customs officer. Note this also applies if you wish to go for a day sail.
2. Yachts with a marina/yard contract must remit the contract to customs officers before leaving the port.
3. All repairs, hauling, storage, addition/removal of boat parts must only be done after giving a written report to the customs service.
4. Chartering, rental, sale or donation of the yacht or any parts or any other goods under customs must only be done with the agreement of the customs service.

Ports of entry

Tabarka	Bizerte	Sidi Bou Said	Kelibia
El Kantaoui	Sousse	Monastir	Mahdia
Sfax	Gabes	Houmt-Souk	Yasmine Hammamet

ALGERIA

Documents Passport with a valid visa. Yacht registration papers. A Radio Licence may be asked for.

Customs Customs procedure is geared to merchant ships and a yacht technically enters and leaves Algeria each time it enters and leaves port. Customs will always want to visit a yacht and make an inventory of equipment and dutiable goods including alcohol and items like computers, cameras, CD players, binoculars, etc. They are also responsible for currency controls. When you arrive you must make a *Declaration of Gold and Foreign Currencies* and all subsequent currency transactions will be made on this form. It is illegal to bring in drugs or pornographic material and there are strict penalties for doing so. Customs also issue the *Permis d'Escale* which lets you leave the immediate port area.

Entry formalities On entry to Algeria a yacht should be flying a Q flag and an Algerian courtesy ensign. The first port of call should be at an official Port of Entry (listed at the end of this section). At every port you will be visited by immigration (*PAF Police aux Frontières*), customs, the coast guard, and by the harbourmaster (*Capitain du Port*) in commercial ports. These procedures can be time consuming. When leaving a port these officials must be seen again. At the next port the procedure will be repeated.

Nationals from most countries need a visa and this should be obtained in the country of residence if possible. British visas can only be obtained at the Algerian consulate in London. In some cases a visa will be inexplicably refused to some nationals. Nationals of Israel, South Africa, South Korea and Taiwan or anyone who has a stamp from one of these countries in their passport will be refused entry to Algeria. Vessels calling in at an Algerian port will be treated as being in transit which technically means you are not allowed to leave the port area. Crew will be allowed ashore for a limited time. Given the political situation this is all you need as travel inland is not recommended.

MOROCCO

Documents Passport with a valid visa if necessary. Yacht registration papers.

Customs Customs will want an inventory of goods on board and will take a special interest in firearms. These must be declared. Customs monitor yachts proceeding along the coast carefully because of the incidence of marijuana (*kif*) smuggling. There are harsh penalties for possessing drugs of any description.

Note Customs will often stop and search yachts proceeding along the coast or anchored in out-of-the-way bays in case they are smuggling marijuana (*kif*). This can be irritating at times, but there is nothing for it but to grin and bear it.

Entry formalities Ports of Entry are Tanger and Al Hoceima, but yachts also go directly to other ports or Marina Smir. On entry customs, immigration (or the *Gendarmerie*) and the *Capitain du Port* will turn up at a boat. Here passports will be stamped (if necessary) and yacht papers examined. Passports and the yacht papers may be held by the *Capitainerie* or the *Gendarmerie* and released to the boat when it leaves. There used to be no problem when going from Morocco to Ceuta or Melilla (both Spanish *presidos*).

Ports of entry

Annaba	Skikda	Stora	Jijel	Bejaia
Dellys	Sidi Ferruch	Cherchell	Tenes	Mostaganem
Oran	Beni-Saf	Ghazaouet		

AZORES

Documents Passport. Yacht registration papers. Insurance papers, certificate of competence and radio licence may also be asked for.

Customs (*alfandega*) All vessels arriving from outside the EU, and all non-EU boats should report to customs on arrival. The Azores, as part of Portugal, come under EU legislation regarding payment of VAT (*IVA*). On mainland Portugal IVA is 23%, but in the Azores it is currently 16%.

Entry formalities Yachts wishing to clear customs should fly a Q flag. All yachts must clear in and out of each island, visiting the port captain, immigration (*service estrangeros*), finance police (*guardia nacional replicana*), and coastguard (*policia maritima*), where applicable. Yachts arriving at the smaller islands where clearance is not possible should proceed as quickly as possible to a Port of Entry.

Ports of entry

Lajes (Flores) Horta (Faial) Ponta Delgada (São Miguel)

Other ports can complete entry formalities, but the above ports are most used to dealing with yachts.

MADEIRA

Documents Passport. Yacht registration papers. Insurance papers, certificate of competence and radio licence may also be asked for.

Customs As part of Portugal, and as such also the EU, requirements are as for the Azores.

Entry formalities Much the same procedure as for the Azores. Must clear in and out of each island.

Ports of entry

Porto Santo   Funchal

CANARY ISLANDS

Documents Passport. Yacht registration papers. Insurance papers, certificate of competence and radio licence may also be asked for.

Customs The Canary Islands are part of Spain, but remain outside the EU VAT area. EU VAT regulations are therefore not applicable. The Spanish Wealth Tax may still be applied if an individual remains in Spain for more than 183 days in one year, effectively becoming 'resident'. For details see *5.2 EU Laws for Yachts*.

Entry formalities If entering from outside mainland Spain, all yachts should fly a Q flag and clear in. Most marinas will assist with procedures. It is not necessary to clear between islands. It is not compulsory to clear out of the Canaries, but it is advised as the stamped paperwork may be neeeded in your next port of call.

Ports of entry

Arrecife (Lanzarote)
Las Palmas (Gran Canaria)
Santa Cruz (La Palma)
Rosario (Fuerteventura)
Santa Cruz (Tenerife)

5.5 MARINE RESERVES IN THE MEDITERRANEAN

SPAIN

Isola Caprera National Park

Administered by ICONA – *Instituto Nacional para la Conservacion de la Naturaleza*. Permits must be obtained in advance, and are now available online. Details of permitted anchorages are included with the permit.

Cabrera National Park Office
✆ 971 725 010
www.magrama.gob.es/es/red-parques-nacionales/nuestros-parques/cabrera/guia-visitante/default.aspx

Menorca Marine Reserve

Restrictions on anchoring and navigation along the N coast from Cabo Gros to Punta d'Es Murte (Cala Fornells).

Baleares Posidonia Protection

Many bays around the Balearic Islands have mooring buoys laid for the use of yachts. It is forbidden to anchor anywhere on Posidonia beds.

FRANCE

Bouches de Bonifacio Marine Nature Reserve

The reserve covers the area from Golfe de Roccapina to Punta di a Chiappa and includes Les Moines, Iles Lavezzi, Ile Perduto and Iles Cerbicale; some 80,000 hectares (nearly 200,000 acres) in all. Restrictions vary over three zones.

- **Zone 1 National Nature Reserve Standard Regulations**
  Hunting and fishing regulated by the prefecture.
- **Zone 2 Protection renforcée**
  Hunting and commercial fishing prohibited.
  Walking on marked footpaths only. Authorised diving only. No camping.
  Includes Iles Lavezzi, Bruzzi, Cerbicales and Ilots des Moines, Bonifacio Straits.
- **Zone 3 Zone de non prélevement**
  Aiming for total prohibition of fishing and diving.

Parc National de Port-Cros

Navigation and anchoring restrictions on Ile de Porquerolles and Ile de Port-Cross. Holding tanks are mandatory for overnight stays.
www.portcrosparcnational.fr

Parc National des Calanques

Established in May 2012, the park covers much of the coast from the port of Marseille around to La Ciotat, including the islands off the coast.

Restrictions apply to navigation and anchoring. Buoys are used to indicate areas where navigation is restricted – either to motors, to all, or to vessels over 20m.

For the latest information and maps of the restricted areas see www.calanques-parcnational.fr

ITALY

There are three types of restricted zones. The interpretation below is a paraphrase of the convoluted legalese in the Italian original and contains the gist of the regulations with, hopefully, nothing left out.

Zone A Riserva integrale

- It is prohibited to navigate or anchor in the designated area.
- It is prohibited to fish in the area.
- It is prohibited to pollute the area in any way including pumping bilge water or black and grey water.
- It is prohibited to remove any plant and animal life and to interfere with the mineral strata of the area.
- Bathing is restricted to designated areas.

Zone B Riserva generale

- It is prohibited to carry out any form of fishing.
- Navigation and mooring are permitted although there may be specific restrictions at any one reserve.

Zone C Riserva parziale

- Commercial fishing is prohibited.
- Sport fishing may be limited in some areas.

New and existing National Parks and Marine Reserves have changes to their status made on a regular basis and you are strongly advised to consult the respective authority prior to arrival. More detail can be found on the Italian National Parks website www.parks.it or in *Italian Waters Pilot* (Imray).

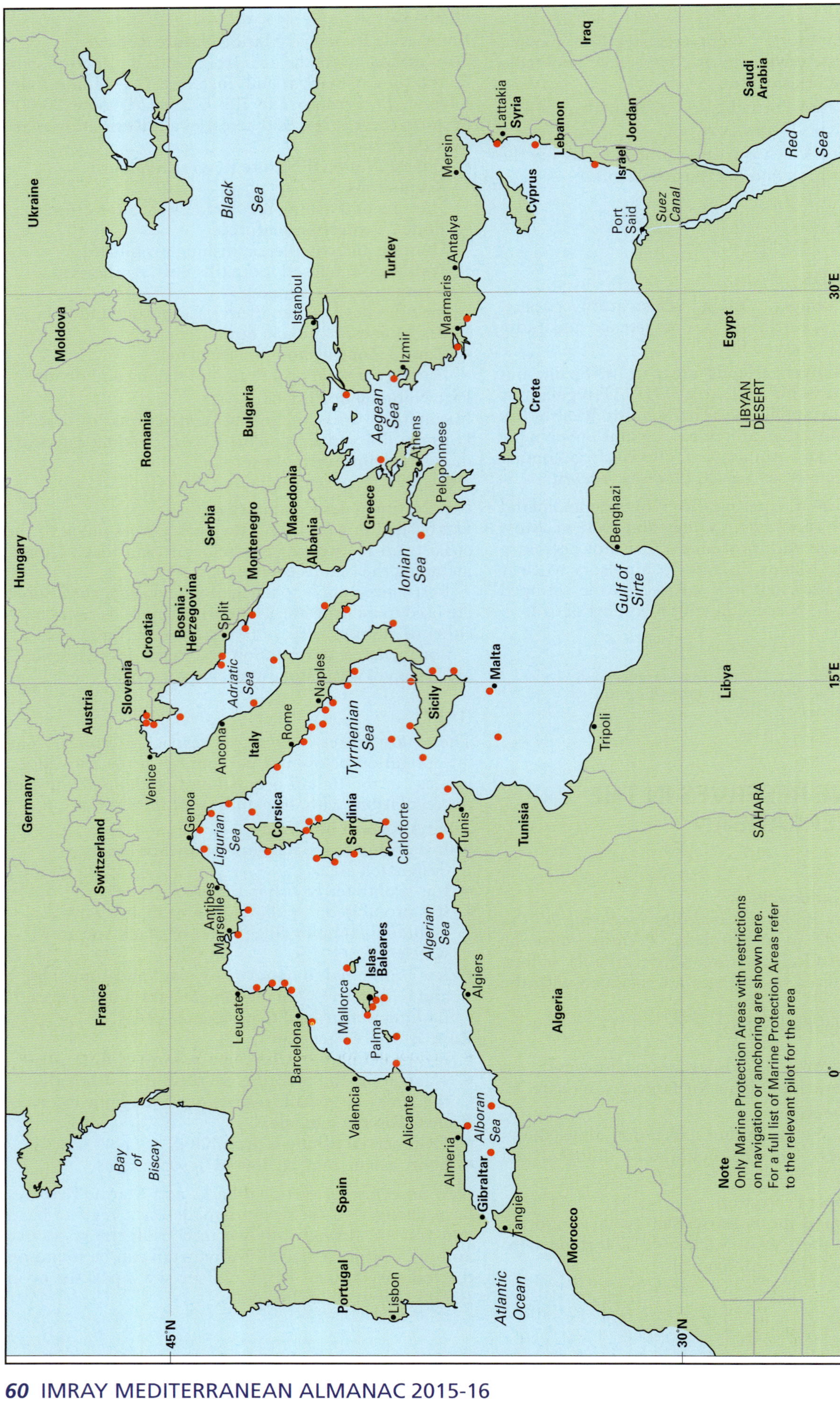

MARINE PROTECTION AREAS IN THE MEDITERRANEAN

Details of the reserves listed below can be found within the section *10.4. Harbour Information – Italy*

Portofino Marine Reserve
Cinque Terre Marine Reserve
Isola di Bergeggi
Tuscan Archipelago National Park
Secche della Meloria
Secche di Tor Paterno Marine Reserve
Isola Ventotene and Isola Santo Stefano Marine Reserve
Baia Giola
Costa degli Infreschi e della Masseta
Punta Campanella Marine Reserve
Santa Maria di Castellabate
Regno del Nettuno
Isola Asinara National Park and Marine Reserve
La Maddalena Archipelago National Park and Marine Reserve
Isola Tavolara and Capo Coda Cavallo Marine Reserve
Capo Carbonara Marine Reserve
Sinis Peninsula and Isola Mal di Ventre Marine Reserve
Capo Caccia Marine Reserve
Capo Gallo and Isola Femmine Marine Reserve
Isola di Ustica Marine Reserve
Tindari Marine Reserve
Isole Cicliopi Marine Reserve
Plemmirio Marina Reserve
Isole Pelagie Marine Reserve
Isole Egadi Marine Reserve
Capo Rizzuto Marine Reserve
Porto Cesaro Marine Reserve
Torre Guaceto Marine Reserve
Torre del Cerrano
Isole Tremiti Marine Reserve
Trieste Marine Reserve
Venice Lagoon

CROATIA

National Parks (with marine restrictions)

There are a number of protected areas with restrictions on navigation:

Limski Kanal
Brijuni Islands National Park
Luka Telascica National Park
Kornati Islands National Park
Mljet National Park

http://croatia.hr/en-GB/Discover-Croatia/Nature

GREECE

Kolpos Lagana Nature Reserve

This important nesting area for the Loggerhead Turtle (*Careta Careta*) has restrictions on navigation and anchoring.

For details see the entry in section *10.11 Harbour information – Greece*

Northern Sporades

The smaller islands in the N and E part of the area are protected under the Mediterranean Monk Seal Protection programme.

TURKEY

There are established marine nature reserves at:

Foça
Gokova Körfezi
Datça-Bozburun
Koycegiz-Dalyan coast
Fethiye-Göçek Körfezi
Patara
Kan-Kekova
Belek (Antalya)
Goksu Delta (Taşucu/Mersin)

Restrictions apply to commercial fishing and to waste water discharge. In Fethiye-Göçek there are additional restrictions on anchoring in some bays.

Olu Deniz near Göçek has been closed to yachts for a number of years to try to curb pollution from diesel engines.

5.6 ASSISTANCE

CONSULS

The following list of what a consulate can and cannot do is from the Stationery Office pamphlet on *Consular Assistance Abroad*.

What a Consul can do

- Can issue emergency passports.
- Can contact relatives and friends and ask them to help with money or tickets.
- Can advise on how to transfer funds.
- Can at most posts (in an emergency) advance money against a sterling cheque for £50 supported by a bankers card.
- Can, as a last resort, and provided that certain strict criteria are met, make a repayable loan for repatriation to the UK. But there is no law that says a Consul must do this and he will need to be satisfied that there is absolutely no-one else you know who can help.
- Can provide a list of lawyers, interpreters and doctors.
- Can arrange for the next of kin to be informed of an accident or a death and advise on procedures.
- Can contact British nationals who are arrested or in prison and, in certain circumstances, arrange for messages to be sent to relatives or friends.
- Can give some guidance on organisations experienced in tracing missing persons.

What a Consul cannot do

- Cannot pay your hotel, medical, or any other bills.
- Cannot pay for travel tickets for you except in very special circumstances.
- Cannot undertake work more properly done by travel representatives, airlines, banks, or motoring organisations.
- Cannot get better treatment for you in hospital (or prison) than is provided for local nationals.
- Cannot give legal advice, instigate court proceedings on your behalf, or interfere in local judicial procedures to get you out of prison.
- Cannot investigate a crime.
- Cannot formally assist dual nationals in the country of second nationality.
- Cannot obtain a work permit for you.

5.7 USEFUL ADDRESSES

EMBASSIES AND CONSULATES
Foreign and Commonwealth Office
☎ 020 7008 1500 (central enquiries)

ALBANIA
TIRANA
British Embassy,
Rruga Skenderberg 12, Tirana, Albania
☎ (355) 4 223 4973/4/5
Fax (355) 4 224 7697

ALGERIA
ALGIERS
Ambassade Britannique, 3 Chemin Capitaine Hocine Slimane (ex Chemin des Glycines), Hydra Algiers
☎ (213) 0 770 085 000
Fax (213) 0 770 085 099

BOSNIA-HERZEGOVINA
SARAJEVO
39a, Hamdije Cemerlica Street
71000 Sarajevo
☎ (387) 33 282 200
Fax (387) 33 282 203
Email britemb@bih.net.ba

CROATIA
ZAGREB
British Embassy, Ivana Lučića 4,
10000 Zagreb
☎ (385) 1 6009 100
Fax (385) 1 6009 111

CYPRUS
NICOSIA
British High Commission, Alexander Pallis Street, (PO Box 21978),
1587 Nicosia, or BFPO 567
☎ (357) 22 861100
Fax (357) 22 861125
Email brithc.2@cytanet.com.cy

ZYGI
British East Mediterranean Relay Station, PO Box 54912, Limassol
☎ (357) 24 332511 / 332341
Fax (357) 24 332595 / 332180

EGYPT
CAIRO
British Embassy, 7 Ahmed Ragheb Street, Garden City, Cairo
☎ (20) 2 27916000
Fax (20) 2 2791 6133
Email cairo.visaapplicants@fco.gov.uk
Email consular.cairo@fco.gov.uk

ALEXANDRIA
British Consulate-General, 3 Mina Street, Kafr Abdou, Roushdi Ramley Alexandria, 21529
☎ (20) 3 5467001
Fax (20) 3 5467177
Email britconsul@dataxprs.com.eg

FRANCE
PARIS
British Embassy, 35, rue du Faubourg St Honoré,75383 Paris Cedex 08 Paris
☎ (33) 1 44 51 31 00
Fax (33) 1 44 51 31 09 (Consular)
Public.Paris@fco.gov.uk

MARSEILLE
British Consulate, 24 Avenue du Prado, 13006 Marseille
☎ (33) 4 91 15 72 10
Fax (33) 4 91 37 47 06

GREECE
ATHENS
British Embassy, 1 Ploutarchou Street, 106 75 Athens
☎ (30) 210 7272 600
Email consular.athens@fco.gov.uk

CORFU
British Consulate, 18 Mantzarou Street, 49 100 Corfu
☎ (30) 26610 30055 / 23457
Fax (30) 26610 37995
Email corfu@fco.gov.uk

CRETE
British Honorary Vice-Consulate, Candia Tower, 17 Thalita Street
Ag. Dimitrios Sq, 71 202 Heraklion Crete
☎ (30) 28102 24012
Fax (30) 28102 43935

RHODES
British Honorary Consulate,
29 Gr. Lambraki Street,
85 100 Rhodes
☎ (30) 22410 22005
Fax (30) 22410 24473

ZAKYNTHOS
British Vice-Consulate, 5 Foskolos Street , 29 100 Zakynthos
☎ (30) 26950 22906
Fax (30) 26950 23769

ISRAEL AND THE PALESTINIAN AUTHORITY
TEL AVIV
British Embassy, 192 Hayarkon Street 6340502
☎ (972) 3 725 1222
Fax (972) 3 524 9176
webmaster.telaviv@fco.gov.uk

ITALY
ROME
British Embassy, Via XX Settembre 80a, I-00187 Roma RM
☎ (39) 06 4220 0001
Fax (39) 06 4220 2333
Email italy.consulate@fco.gov.uk

MILAN
British Consulate General,
Via S. Paolo, 7
I-20121 Milan
☎ (39) 06 4220 2431
Fax (39) 02 8646 5081

LEBANON
BEIRUT
British Embassy,
Embassies Complex Army Street, Zkak Al-Blat, Serail Hill PO Box 11-471, Beirut
☎ (961) 01 9608 00
Fax (961) 01 990 420
Email: visa.beirut@fco.gov.uk
Email: consular.beirut@fco.gov.uk

MALTA
VALLETTA
British High Commission,
Whitehall Mansions, Ta'Xbiex Seafront, Ta'Xbiex XBX 1026,
Malta GC
☎ (356) 2323 0000
Fax (356) 2323 2234
Email bhcvalletta@fco.gov.uk

MOROCCO
RABAT
British Embassy,
28 Avenue S.A.R. Sidi Mohammed, Soussi 10105 (BP 45), Rabat
☎ (212) 537 63 33 33
Fax (212) 537 75 87 09
Email rabat.consular@fco.gov.uk

TANGIER / AGADIR / MARRAKECH
British Honorary Consulates
☎ (212) 537 63 33 33
Email rabat.consular@fco.gov.uk

CASABLANCA
British Consulate-General,
Villa Les Salurges, 36 Rue de la Loire, Polo, Casablanca
☎ (212) 522 85 74 00
Fax (212) 522 85 74 00
Email British.consulate2@menara.ma

MONTENEGRO
PODGORICA - MONTENEGRO
British Embassy, British Embassy
Ulcinjska 8, Gorica C, 81000 Podgorica, Montenegro
☎ (382) 20 618 010
Fax (382) 20 618 020
Email podgorica@fco.gov.uk

SLOVENIA
LJUBLJANA
British Embassy, 4th floor,
Trg Republike 3, 1000, Ljubljana
☎ (386) 200 3910
Fax (386) 1 425 0174
Email info@british-embassy.si

SPAIN

✆ 902 109 356 (in Spain)
(+34) 917 146 300 (if outside Spain)
Email spain.consulate@fco.gov.uk

MADRID

British Embassy,
Torre Espacio,
Paseo de la Castellana 259D
28046 Madrid
Fax (34) 917 146 301

MADRID

British Consulate General,
Torre Espacio,
Paseo de la Castellana 259D
28046 Madrid
Fax (34) 917 146 301

ALICANTE

Edificio Espacio,
Rambla Méndez Núñez 28-32
6ª planta, 03002 Alicante
Fax (34) 965 14 05 28

BARCELONA

British Consulate-General,
Avda Diagonal 477 – 13, 08036
Barcelona
Fax (34) 933 666 221

MÁLAGA

British Consulate, Calle Mauricio
Moro Pareto, 2, Edificio Eurocom,
29006 Malaga
Fax (34) 95 235 9211

MALLORCA

Carrer Convent dels Caputxins, 4
Edificio Orisba B 4ºD
07002 Palma de Mallorca
✆ 902 109 356 / (34) 91 334 2194
Fax (34) 971 71 75 20

IBIZA

British Vice-Consulate, Avenida Isidoro
Macabich 45-1º1ª, Apartado 307,
07800 Ibiza
Fax (34) 971 301 972

TENERIFE

British Consulate, Plaza Weyler, 8, 1º
38003 Santa Cruz de Tenerife
✆ 902 109 356 / (34) 91 334 2194
Fax (34) 922 289 903

GRAN CANARIA

Calle Luis Morote 6-3º
E-35007 Las Palmas de Gran Canaria
Fax (34) 928 267 774

SYRIA

DAMASCUS

At time of publication the British Embassy Damascus has suspended all services and all diplomatic personnel have been withdrawn from Syria.

TUNISIA

TUNIS

British Embassy,
Rue du Lac Windermere,
Les Berges du Lac,
Tunis 1053
✆ (216) 71 108 700
Fax (216) 71 108 789 (Consular)
Email BritishEmbassyTunis@fco.gov.uk

SFAX

Honorary British Consulate, 55 Rue
Habib Maazoun, 3000, Sfax
✆ (216) 74 223 971
Fax (216) 74 299 278

TURKEY

ANKARA

British Embassy, Şehit Ersan Caddesi
46/A, Çankaya, Ankara
✆ (90) 312 455 3344
Fax (90) 312 455 3352
Email info.officer@fco.gov.uk

ANTALYA

British Vice-Consulate,
Gürsu Mahallesi, 324. Sokak No:6
Konyaaltı, Antalya
✆ (90) 242 228 2811
Fax (90) 242 229 2151

BODRUM

British Honorary Consulate,
Cafer Pasa Cad, 2.
Emsan Evleri, No 7, Bodrum
✆ (90) 252 313 0021
Fax (90) 252 313 0017

MARMARIS

British Honorary Consulate,
c/o Yesil Marmaris Tourism and Yacht
Management Inc, Barbaros Caddesi
No. 118, Marina PO Box 8,
48700 Marmaris
✆ (90) 252 412 6488
Fax (90) 252 412 4565

ISTANBUL

British Consulate-General,
Mesrutiyet Caddesi No 34,
Tepebasi Beyoglu, 34435, Istanbul
✆ (90) 212 334 6400
Fax (90) 212 315 6401

IZMIR

British Consulate,
1442 Sokak No. 49,
Alsancak, Izmir PK 300
✆ (90) 232 463 5151
Fax (90) 232 465 0858

TELEPHONE DIALLING CODES

Country	*Code*
Albania	355
Algeria	213
Bosnia Herzegovina	387
Croatia	385
Cyprus	357
Egypt	20
France	33
Gibraltar	350
Greece	30
Israel	972
Italy	39
Libya	218
Malta	356
Monaco	377
Montenegro	381
Morocco	212
Slovenia	386
Spain	34
Syria	963
Tunisia	216
Turkey	90
United Kingdom	44

In all countries dial 00 to access international direct dialling, except the following:
Montenegro dial 99

OTHER ADDRESSES

BRITISH SUB-AQUA CLUB
Telford's Quay, South Pier Road,
Ellesmere Port, Cheshire CH65 4FL
☎ 0800 0093086
Email info@bsac.com

AMATEUR YACHT RESEARCH SOCIETY
BCM AYRS, London WC1N 3XX
☎ 01727 862268
Fax +44 (8700) 526657
Email office@ayrs.org

BRITISH MARINE FEDERATION
Marine House, Thorpe Lea Road,
Egham, Surrey TW20 8BF
☎ 01784 473377
Fax 01784 439678
Email info@britishmarine.co.uk

BRITISH WATER SKI & WAKEBOARD
Unit 3 The Forum, Hanworth Lane,
Chertsey, Surrey, KT16 9JX
☎ 01932 560007
Fax 01932 570028
Email info@bwsf.co.uk

CRUISING ASSOCIATION
CA House, 1 Northey Street,
London E14 8BT
☎ 020 7537 2828
Fax 020 7537 2266
www.cruising.org.uk/contact

HMRC NATIONAL ADVISORY SERVICE
☎ 0300 200 3700
(+44 2920 501 261 outside UK)
www.hmrc.gov.uk

HM REVENUE & CUSTOMS
For postal enquiries relating to importing, exporting, Customs Relief and excise matters
CITEX Written Enquiry Team
HM Revenue & Customs
Crownhill Court, Tailyour Road,
Plymouth, PL6 5BZ
Please include your VAT registration number if applicable and the name and postal address of your business.

IMRAY LAURIE NORIE & WILSON
Wych House, The Broadway, St Ives,
Cambridgeshire PE27 5BT
☎ 01480 462114
Fax 01480 496109
Email ilnw@imray.com

INMARSAT
99 City Road, London EC1Y 1AX
☎ 020 7728 1777
Fax 020 7728 1142
www.inmarsat.com/contact-us/

INTERNATIONAL MARITIME ORGANISATION
International Maritime Organisation
4, Albert Embankment
London
SE1 7SR
United Kingdom
☎ +44 (0)20 7735 7611
Fax +44 (0)20 7587 3210
Email info@imo.orgwww.imo.org

INTERNATIONAL TELECOMMUNICATION UNION (ITU)
www.itu.int

LLOYD'S REGISTER OF SHIPPING
Yacht and Small Craft Depts,
71 Fenchurch Street,
London EC3M 4BS
☎ 020 7709 9166
Fax 020 7488 4796
www.lr.org

MARITIME AND COASTGUARD AGENCY
Coastguard at MCA HQ, Spring Place
105 Commercial Road, Southampton
Hampshire SO15 1EG
☎ 02380 329 486
Email sar.response@mcga.gov.uk
www.gov.uk

METEOROLOGICAL OFFICE
Meteorological Office, Fitzroy Road,
Exeter, Devon EX1 3PB
☎ 0870 900 0100
Fax 0870 900 5050
From outside the UK:
☎ 01392 885680
Fax 01392 885681
Email enquiries@metoffice.gov.uk
www.metoffice.gov.uk

OFCOM OFFICE OF COMMUNICATIONS
Amateur & Maritime Team,
Ofcom Licensing Centre, PO Box
56373, London SE1 9SZ
☎ 020 7981 3131
Fax 020 7981 3061
Email MAAT@ofcom.org.uk
https://licensing.ofcom.org.uk

ROYAL CRUISING CLUB (RCC) PILOTAGE FOUNDATION
www.rccpf.org.uk

ROYAL INSTITUTE OF NAVIGATION (RIN)
1 Kensington Gore, London SW7 2AT
☎ 020 7591 3134
Fax 020 7591 3131
Email admin@rin.org.uk

ROYAL YACHTING ASSOCIATION
RYA House, Ensign Way, Hamble,
Southampton SO31 4YA
☎ 023 8060 4100
Fax 023 8060 4299
www.rya.org.uk

UK SHIP REGISTRY
https://mcanet.mcga.gov.uk/ssr/ssr/

STANFORDS INTERNATIONAL MAP CENTRE
12–14 Long Acre, London, WC2E 9LP
☎ 020 7836 1321
www.stanfords.co.uk

UK SAILING INDEX
www.sail.co.uk

UNITED KINGDOM HYDROGRAPHIC OFFICE
Admiralty Way, Taunton, Somerset
TA1 2DN
☎ 01823 337900
Email customerservices@ukho.gov.uk

YACHT BROKERS, DESIGNERS AND SURVEYORS ASSOCIATION, YBDSA (HOLDINGS) LTD
The Glass Works, Penns Road,
Petersfield, GU32 2EW
☎ 01730 710425
Fax 01730 710423
Email info@ybdsa.co.uk

6. Lights

6.1 INTERNATIONAL PORT SIGNALS

No.	Character	Message
MAIN MESSAGE		
1	Flashing	Serious emergency - all vessels to stop or divert according to instructions
2	Fixed or slow occulting	Vessels shall not proceed
3	Fixed or slow occulting	Vessels may proceed; One-way traffic
4	Fixed or slow occulting	Vessels may proceed; Two-way traffic
5	Fixed or slow occulting	A vessel may proceed only when it has received specific orders to do so
EXEMPTION SIGNALS AND MESSAGES		
2a	Fixed or slow occulting	Vessels shall not proceed, except that vessels which navigate outside the main channel need not comply with the main message
5a	Fixed or slow occulting	A vessel may proceed only when it has received specific orders to do so, except that vessels which navigate outside the main channel need not comply with the main message

AUXILIARY SIGNALS

Auxiliary signals can be added, as required, normally to the right of the column carrying the main message and normally utilising only white or yellow lights.

Such auxiliary signals could, for example, be added to message No. 5 to give information about the situation of traffic in the opposite direction, or to warn of a dredger operating in the channel

6.2 IALA BUOYAGE SYSTEM A

Lateral marks

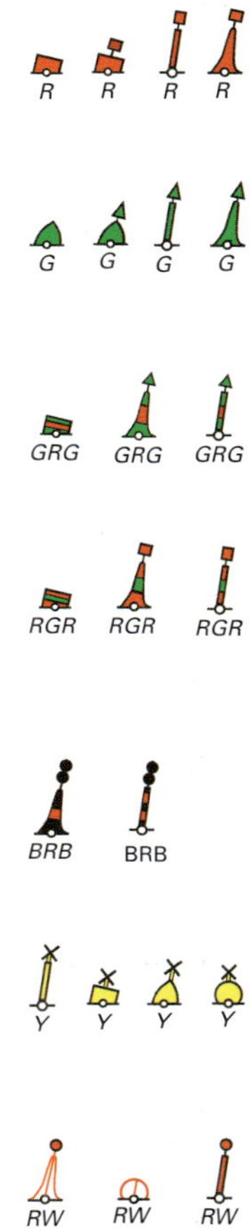

Port hand
All red
Topmark (if any): can
Light (if any): red

Starboard hand
All green
Topmark (if any): cone
Light (if any): green

Preferred channel to port
Green/red/green
Light (if any): Fl(2+1)G

Preferred channel to starboard
Red/green/red
Light (if any): Fl(2+1)R

Isolated danger marks
(stationed over a danger with navigable water around)
Black with red band
Topmark: 2 black balls
Light (if any): Fl(2) (white)

Special mark
Body shape optional, yellow
Topmark (if any): Yellow X
Light (if any): Fl.Y etc

Safe water marks
(mid-channel and landfall)
Red and white vertical stripes
Topmark (if any): red ball

Cardinal marks

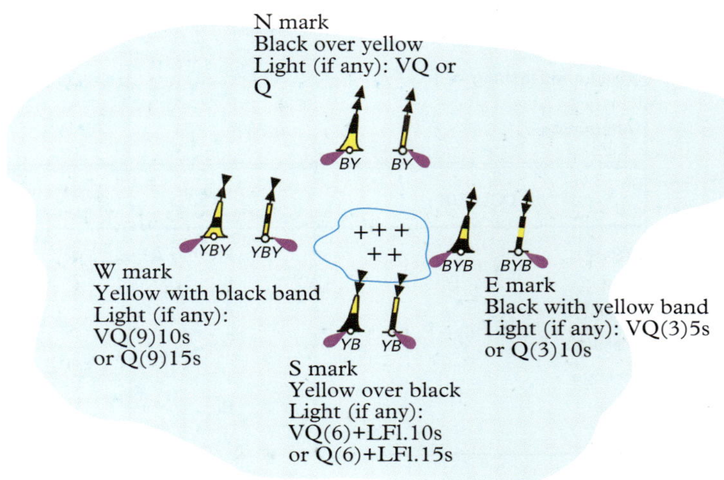

6.3 LIGHT CHARACTERISTICS

CLASS OF LIGHT		International abbreviations	Older form (where different)	Illustration Period shown
Fixed *(steady light)*		F		
Occulting *(total duration of light more than dark)*				
Single-occulting		Oc	Occ	
Group-occulting	*e.g.*	Oc(2)	Gp Occ(2)	
Composite group-occulting	*e.g.*	Oc(2+3)	Gp Occ(2+3)	
Isophase *(light and dark equal)*		Iso		
Flashing *(total duration of light less than dark)*				
Single-flashing		Fl		
Long-flashing (flash 2s or longer)		L Fl		
Group-flashing	*e.g.*	Fl(3)	Gp Fl(3)	
Composite group-flashing	*e.g.*	Fl(2+1)	Gp Fl(2+1)	
Quick *(50 to 79—usually either 50 or 60—flashes per minute)*				
Continuous quick		Q	Qk Fl	
Group quick	*e.g.*	Q(3)	Qk Fl(3)	
Interrupted quick		IQ	Int Qk Fl	
Very Quick *(80 to 159—usually either 100 or 120—flashes per minute)*				
Continuous very quick		V Q	V Qk Fl	
Group very quick	*e.g.*	V Q(3)	V Qk Fl(3)	
Interrupted very quick		IV Q	Int V Qk Fl	
Ultra Quick *(160 or more—usually 240 to 300—flashes per minute)*				
Continuous ultra quick		UQ		
Interrupted ultra quick		IUQ		
Morse Code	*e.g.*	Mo(K)		
Fixed and Flashing		F Fl		
Alternating	*e.g.*	Al.WR	Alt.WR	

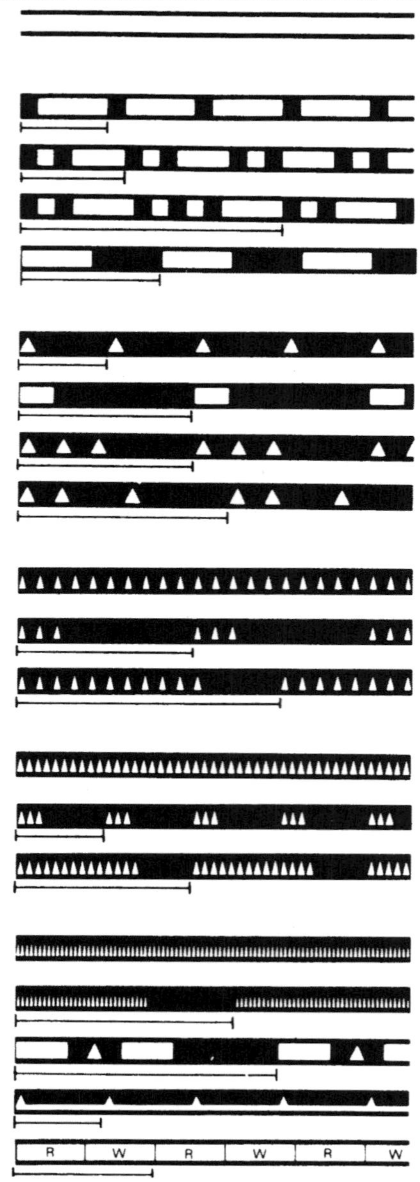

COLOUR	International abbreviations	Older form (where different)
White	W *(may be omitted)*	
Red	R	
Green	G	
Yellow	Y	
Orange	Y	Or
Blue	Bu	Bl
Violet	Vi	

RANGE in sea miles		International abbreviations	Older form
Single range	*e.g.*	15M	
2 ranges	*e.g.*	14/12M	14.12M
3 or more ranges	*e.g.*	22-18M	22,20,18M
PERIOD in seconds	*e.g.*	5s	5sec

ELEVATION is given in metres (m) or feet (ft)

6.4 LIST OF MAJOR LIGHTS

See also *Index of lights*

The following list is of the major lights in the Mediterranean. This normally means a light with a range of seven miles or more. Lights with lesser ranges are included in the harbour information where they can more usefully be consulted along with other harbour information. In a few places (such as the Croatian and Greek islands) a lesser range has been taken where lights are not usefully located with harbour information. For some lights there is a duplication between the two lists where this was thought to be useful.

The identifying number for each light is taken from Admiralty *List of Lights Vol D & E*. This makes it easier to correct lights from *Notices to Mariners*. This means that the order of the lights does not always follow the order of the harbour information, but it can still be easily accessed from the index.

WAYPOINTS

The lights list is arranged with the latitude and longitude of the light after its description so that lights on capes, headlands, islets, major ports and harbours can be used as waypoints. It should hardly need to be mentioned that some lights may be up to half a mile inland although most are within a quarter of a mile or less of the coast. With this in mind the distance off on arrival alarms for GPS sets should be set at one mile minimum. Although every care has been taken by the publisher and editors to ensure the accuracy of the latitude and longitudes given here, no responsibility can be taken for any incidents or mishaps which may arise from their use. The navigator should exercise prudence and caution and must keep a watch at all times when approaching a given waypoint.

The following reference numbers refer to Admiralty *List of Lights and Fog Signals Volume D* (NP 77).

Gibraltar

Amend Lts as follows:

2438 Europa Point
Iso.10s49m19M 197°-vis-042°
067°-vis-125°
Oc.R.10s49m19M+F.R.44m15M
042°-vis-067°
• 36°06'·58N 5°20'·69W

2442 South Mole A Head
Fl.2s10m5M Horn 10s
• 36°08'·03N 5°21'·85W

2456 Aero light
Aero Mo(GB)R.10s405m30M
• 36°08'·57N 5°20'·59W

The following reference numbers refer to Admiralty List of Lights and Fog Signals Volume E (NP 78)

Mediterranean – Spain

0012 Punta Carbonera
Oc.4s39m14M
• 36°14'·7N 5°18'W

0018 La Duquesa Marina S head
Fl.G.5s8m5M
• 36°21'·2N 5°13'·7W

0018·3 N head
Q(3)10s7m5M
• 36°21'·4N 5°13'·6W

PUERTO DE ESTEPONA

0020 Punta de la Doncella
Fl(1+2)15s32m18M
• 36°25'·0N 5°09'·3W

PUERTO JOSE BANUS

0032 E breakwater, Head
Fl(3)G.12s13m5M
• 36°29'·0N 4°57'·3W

PUERTO DE MARBELLA

0056 Marbella
Fl(2)14·5s35m22M
• 36°30'·5N 4°53'·3W

0058 Punta Calaburras
Fl.5s46m18M Aeromarine
• 36°30'·4N 4°38'·4W

0058·5 Fuengirola submerged Jetty Head
Fl(3)G.5m3M
• 36°32'·7N 4°36'·7W

PUERTO DE BENALMADENA

0060·4 S breakwater SW, Head
Fl(2)G.5s9m5M
• 36°35'·6N 4°30'·8W

PUERTO DE MÁLAGA

0062 Málaga E breakwater, Near root
Fl(3+1)20s38m25M
243°-vis-047°
• 36°42'·8N 4°24'·9W

0065 E Breakwater head, S head
Fl.G.5s7m5M
• 36°41'·9N 4°24'·9W

PUERTO EL CANDADO

0072 Torre del Mar o Vélez
Fl(1+2)10s30m13M
• 36°44'·1N 4°05'·8W

PUERTO DE VELÉZ

0074 Punta de Torrox
Fl(4)15s29m20M
• 36°43'·6N 3°57'·4W

0074·8 Punta de la Mona, La Herradwa
Fl.5s140m15M
• 36°43'·40N 3°43'·85W

PUERTO DE MOTRIL

0077 Dique de Poniente head
Fl(2)R.6s11m10M
• 36°42'·9N 3°31'·0W

0080 Cabo Sacratif
Fl(2)10s98m25M
• 36°41'·7N 3°28'·1W

0082 Castell de Ferro. Punta del Melonar (de la Estancia)
Fl(3)13s237m14M
• 36°43'·1N 3°22'·1W

0086 Isla de Alborán S end Summit
Fl(4)20s40m10M
• 35°56'·3N 3°02'·1W

PUERTO DE ADRA

0088 Adra
Oc(3)10·5s49m16M
• 36°44'·9N 3°01'·9W

0089·5 Punta de los Baños
Fl(4)11s22m11M
• 36°41'·8N 2°50'·8W

0090 Punta Sabinal
Fl(1+2)10s34m16M
• 36°41'·2N 2°42'·1W

PUERTO DEPORTIVO ALMERIMAR

0091 Dique Sur head
Fl(4)G.21s13m5M
• 36°41'·9N 2°47'·8W

ROQUETAS DE MAR

0092 Dique sur head
Fl(3)R.9s10m5M
• 36°45'·5N 2°36'·2W

PUERTO DEPORTIVO AGUADULCE

0092·6 Dique head
Fl(2)G.6s5m5M
• 36°48'·8N 2°33'·7W

PUERTO DE ALMERÍA

0093 Almería de San Telmo
Fl(2)12s77m19M
Reserve light range 11M
• 36°49'·7N 2°29'·5W

0096 Dique de Poniente head
Fl.R.5s19m7M
• 36°49'·6N 2°27'·9W

0106 Cabo de Gata
Fl.WR.4s55m24/20M
Siren Mo(G)40s
316°-R-356°-W-316°
Obscured by land within 10M when bearing less than 267°
• 36°43'·3N 2°11'·6W

PUERTO SAN JOSE

0107·7 Punta de la Polacra
Fl(3)14s281m14M
• 36°50'·6N 2°00'·1W

0108 Mesa de Roldán
Fl(4)20s222m23M
• 36°56'·5N 1°54'·4W

PUERTO DE CARBONERAS

0109 Puerto Cementero Dique Este head
Fl(2)G.10s12m5M
• 36°57'·8N 1°53'·8W

0109·4 Muelle de Descarga Dique de Abrigo
Fl.G.10s14m5M
• 36°58′·4N 1°53′·7W

0109·6 Fishing harbour Breakwater
Fl(3)G.12s10m5M
• 36°59′·3N 1°53′·9W

PUERTO DE GARRUCHA
0110 Garrucha
Oc(4)13s19m13M
• 37°10′·4N 1°49′·4W

0111 Dique de Levante head
Fl(3)G.9s13m5M
• 37°10′·7N 1°49′·0W

PUERTO DE AGUILAS
0114 Punta Negra
Fl(2)5s30m13M
• 37°24′·1N 1°34′·7W

0120 Mazarrón
Oc(1+2)13·5s65m15M
Reserve light range 8M
• 37°33′·6N 1°15′·3W

PUERTO DE MAZARRÓN
0124 Cabo Tiñoso
Fl(1+3)20s146m24M
• 37°32′·1N 1°06′·5W

PUERTO DE LA ALGAMECA GRANDE
0125 Breakwater head
Fl(4)R.11s10m7M
• 37°35′·0N 1°00′·3W

0126 Islote Escombreras
Fl.5s65m17M
• 37°33′·5N 0°58′·1W

0126.1 Breakwater head
Fl.G.3s10m10M
• 37°34′·0N 0°58′·7W

PUERTO DE CARTAGENA
0127 Las Losas
Q(6)+LFl.15s5m5M
• 37°34′·5N 0°58′·5W

0128 Dique de Navidad head
Fl(2)R.10s15m10M
• 37°35′·1N 0°59′·1W

0130 Dique de la Curra head
Fl(3)G.14s14m5M
• 37°35′·3N 0°59′·0W

PUERTO DE PORTMAN
0134 Punta de la Chapa
Oc.3·5s49m13M
• 37°34′·82N 0°50′·47W

BAJO DE PORTMAN O DE LA BOLA
0136.5 Los Ponchosos
Q(3)10s8m5M
• 37°37′·4N 0°42′·1W

0136·8 Cabo de Palos
Fl(2)10s81m23M
• 37°38′·2N 0°41′·3W

0136·9 Escollo Las Malvas
VQ(6)+LFl.10s5m5M
• 37°37′·7N 0°41′·9W

PUERTO DE CABO DE PALOS
0137 Cala Avellán marina jetty head
Fl(2)G.7s6m5M
331°-vis-210°
• 37°37′·8N 0°41′·9W

0138 Islote La Hormiga
Fl(3)14s24m8M
• 37°39′·3N 0°39′·0W

0139 Isla Grosa
Fl.3s97m5M
• 37°43′·6N 0°42′·4W

0140 El Estacio
Fl(4)20s32m14M
• 37°44′·8N 0°43′·5W

PUERTO DE TORREVIEJA
0146 E breakwater head
Fl.G.4s15m7M
• 37°57′·9N 0°41′·2W

0147 Guardamar del Segura
Oc.R.1·5s443m15M
7F.R(vert) at intervals of 45m
• 38°04′·4N 0°39′·7W

ISLA TABARCA
0148 Centre
LFl.8s29m15M
• 38°09′·9N 0°28′·3W

0152 Cabo Santa Pola
Fl(2+1)20s152m16M
• 38°12′·6N 0°30′·8W

PUERTO DE ALICANTE
0157·3 South Basin, Harbour Breakwater, Head
Fl(2+1)R.21s18m5M
• 38°19′·15N 0°29′·66W

0157·43 South Basin, Centre
Fl.R.5s12m7M
• 38°19′·48N 0°29′·64W

0158 Dique de Abrigo de Levante head
Fl.G.5s14m10M
• 38°19′·7N 0°29′·4W

0166 Cabo de la Huertas
Fl(5)19s38m14M
• 38°21′·2N 0°24′·3W

PUERTO DE VILLAJOYOSA
0168·5 Breakwater
Fl(2)R.6s8m3M
• 38°30′·4N 0°13′·3W

0172 Islote Benidorm
Fl.5s60m6M
• 38°30′·1N 0°07′·8W

0173·6 Punta del Albir
Fl(3)27s112m15M
• 38°33′·8N 0°03′·0W

PUERTO DE CALPE
0176 Cabo de la Nao
Fl.5s122m23M
190°-vis-049°
• 38°44′·0N 0°13′·8E

PUERTO DE JÁVEA
0179 Breakwater Head
Fl.G.3s11m5M
• 38°47′·7N 0°11′·2E

0180 Cabo de San António
Fl(4)20s175m26M
Vis over an arc of 240°
• 38°47′·2N 0°11′·8E

PUERTO DE DENIA
0184 Dique Norte head
Fl(3)G.11s13m5M
• 38°50′·9N 0°07′·5E

PUERTO DE GANDIA
0193 Contradique head
Fl.R.5s9m5M
• 38°59′·7N 0°08′·8W

0194 Dique Norte head
Fl.G.5s15m7M
• 38°59′·7N 0°08′·7W

PUERTO DE CULLERA
0197 Malecón Norte near head
Fl(4)G.11s10m5M
• 39°09′·1N 0°14′·0W

0198 Cabo Cullera
Fl(3)20s28m25M
• 39°11′·2N 0°13′·0W

PUERTO DE VALENCIA
0200 Dique del Norte elbow
Fl(4+1)20s30m20M
• 39°27′·0N 0°18′·1W

0200·4 Nuevo Dique del Este head
Fl.G.5s21m5M
• 39°26′·0N 0°18′·2W

0209 Manises Airfield
Aero AlFl.WG.4s65m15M Occas
• 39°29′·6N 0°28′·2W

PUERTO DE ALBORAYA
0210 Puebla de Farnals E Breakwater
Fl(2)G.5s9m5M
• 39°33′·5N 0°16′·9W

PUERTO DE SAGUNTO
0212·6 Pantalán de Sierra Menera
Q(3)10s12m5M
• 39°38′·8N 0°11′·7W

0216 Cabo Canet
Fl(2)10s33m20M
• 39°40′·5N 0°12′·5W

PUERTO DE SILES
0217 E breakwater head
Fl(3)G.9s7m5M
• 39°40′·3N 0°12′·05W

0218 Nules
Oc(2)11s38m14M
• 39°49′·6N 0°06′·6W

PUERTO DE BURRIANA
0219 East breakwater head
Fl(2)G.8s12m5M
• 39°51′·5N 0°04′·0W

ISLOTES COLUMBRETES
0222 Monte Colibri
Fl(3+1)22s85m21M Racon
• 39°54′·0N 0°41′·2E

PUERTO DE CASTELLÓN DE LA PLANA
0226 Faro
Fl.8s32m14M
• 39°58′·1N 0°01′·7E

0226·1 E breakwater SW head
Fl(4)G.13m5M
• 39°57′·7N 0°01′·6E

0226·5 E breakwater head. N corner
Q.7m5M
• 39°58′·1N 0°01′·9E

0229·7 Porto Deportivo Orepesa de Mar. Harbour breakwater head
Fl(2)G.7s8m5M
• 40°04′·9N 0°08′·1E

0230 Cabo Oropesa
Fl(3)15s24m21M
• 40°05′·0N 0°08′·8E

PUERTO DEPORTIVO LAS FUENTES
0231·6 Cabo de Irta
Fl(4)18s33m14M
195°-vis-057°
• 40°15′·6N 0°18′·1E

PUERTO DE PEÑISCOLA
0232 Castillo del Papa Luna Peñíscola
Fl(2+1)15s56m23M
184°-vis-040°
• 40°21′·6N 0°24′·6E

PUERTO DE BENICARLÓ
0238 Dique de Levante head
Fl(2)G.5s13m5M
• 40°24′·6N 0°26′·2E

PUERTO DE VINAROZ
0244 Dique de Levante head
Fl.G.5s14m8M
• 40°27′·4N 0°28′·6E

Islas Baleares

ISLA FORMENTERA

0250 Formentera near SE point
Fl.5s142m23M 150°-vis-050°
• 38°39'·8N 1°35'·1E
0251 Cabo Barbaría
Fl(2)15s78m18M
• 38°38'·4N 1°23'·3E
0252 Cala Savina
Fl(4)16s13m7M
• 38°44'·1N 1°24'·9E
0254 Los Puercos o Pou
Fl(3+1)20s28m10M
• 38°47'·9N 1°25'·3E
0256 Isla Espardell N point
Fl(3)7·5s37m7M
• 38°48'·3N 1°28'·6E

ISLA DE IBIZA

0260 Isla Ahorcados S end
Oc(1+2)14s27m10M
• 38°48'·8N 1°24'·7E
0262 Islote Dado Grande
Fl(2)5s13m5M
• 38°53'·5N 1°27'·2E
0263 Puerto de Ibiza. Dique de Botafoch. Head
Fl.G.3s14m7M
• 38°54'·27N 1°26'·92E
0264 Isolote Botafoch Root
Oc.WR.7s31m14M Siren(2)10s
034°-R-045° over Islotes Malvins and Esponja, 045°-W-034°, obscured over Lladós N and S by Isla Grossa
• 38°54'·32N 1°27'·31E
0265 Dique de Abrigo Sur head
Fl(2)R.7s12m3M
Obscd beyond Pta Marloca 025°-070°(45°)
• 38°54'·6N 1°26'·6E
0267·8 Santa Eulalia Marina Breakwater. Head
Fl(3)G.9s11m5M
• 38°58'·9N 1°32'·3E
0268 Isla Tagomago SE end
Fl(1+2)30s86m21M
043·5°-W-037°-R-043·5°over Llosa de Santa Eulalia
• 39°01'·9N 1°39'·1E
0270 Punta Muscarté
Fl.5s93m18M 074°-vis-294°
• 39°06'·9N 1°31'·9E
0273 Puerto de San Antonio Punta Xinxó
Fl(2)G.7s9m5M
075°-vis-275°
• 38°58'·4N 1°17'·0E
0274 Isla Conejera Cabo Blanco
Fl(4)20s85m18M
• 38°59'·6N 1°12'·8E
0276 Islote Bleda Plana
Fl(3)15s28m10M 349°-vis-239°
• 38°58'·7N 1°09'·6E
0278 Islote Vedrá
Fl.5s21m11M 262°-vis-134°
• 38°51'·7N 1°11'·3E

ISLA DE MALLORCA

0282 Isla Dragonera Cabo Llebeitx
Fl.7·5s130m21M 313°-vis-150°
• 39°34'·5N 2°18'·3E
0284 Cabo Tramontana
Fl(2)12s67m14M
095°-vis-230°, 346°-vis-027°
• 39°35'·9N 2°20'·3E
0288 Puerto de Sóller. Punta de Sa Creu
Fl.2·5s35m10M 088°-vis-160°
• 39°47'·8N 2°41'·4E
0289 Cabo Gros
Fl(3)15s120m19M 054°-vis-232°
• 39°47'·8N 2°41'·0E
0296 Cabo Formentor
Fl(4)20s210m22M 085°-vis-006°
• 39°57'·7N 3°12'·7E
0298 Bahía de Pollença. Punta de la Avançada
Oc(2)8s29m15M 234°-vis-272°
• 39°54'·1N 3°06'·7E
0303 El Cocodrilo (Bonaire) Marina. Breakwater Head
Fl(3)R.10s5m5M
• 39°52'·0N 3°08'·6E
0303·7 Punta Sabaté (Cabo del Pinar)
Fl(3)13s47m5M
• 39°53'·6N 3°11'·7E
0304 Bahía de Alcudia Isla Aucanada
Fl.5s25m11M
Vis 140°-109°(329°) Obscured 109°-140°(31°) in Cala Alcudia
• 39°50'·2N 3°10'·3E
0308 Cabo de Pera
Fl(2+3)20s76m20M
• 39°42'·9N 3°28'·7E
0309 Porto Cristo. Morro de sa Carabassa
Fl.5s20m7M
• 39°32'·1N 3°20'·4E
0310 Punta de la Farola
Fl(2)10s42m20M 207°-vis-006°
• 39°24'·8N 3°16'·2E
0311·4 Cala Llonga. Punta d'es Forti
Fl(1+2)20s17m7M
• 39°22'·0N 3°14'·1E
0311·8 Porto Petro. Punta da sa Torre
Fl(3+1)10s22m7M
• 39°21'·3N 3°12'·9E
0311·9 Dique Caló d'es Moix head
Fl(2)R.7s7m5M
• 39°21'·7N 3°12'·7E
0312·6 Cala Figuera de Santañy. Torre d'en Beu
Fl.5s32m10M
• 39°19'·8N 3°10'·6E
0314 Punta Salinas
Fl(2+1)20s17m11M
265°-vis-116°
• 39°16'·0N 3°03'·3E
0314·2 Isla de na Guardia
Fl(4)G.12s7m5M
• 39°18'·7N 3°00'·1E
0315 Punta Puntassa
Fl(3)10·5s18m7M
• 39°18'·8N 2°59'·7E
0315·4 Puerto Deportivo La Rapita dique head
Fl.R.2·5s7m5M
• 39°21'·82N 2°57'·36E
0315·8 Punta Plana
Fl(1+3)12s16m7M
• 39°21'·2N 2°54'·9E
0316 Cabo Blanco
LFl.10s95m15M
296°-vis-321° 336°-vis-115°
• 39°21'·8N 2°47'·3E
0316·3 Puerto Deportivo del S'Arenal Dique de Abrigo. Head
Fl(3)G.9s8m5M
• 39°30'·15N 2°44'·81E
0316·8 Puerto Deportivo del Portixol Espigón exterior Troneras head
Fl(3)R.9s7m5M
• 39°33'·53N 2°40'·10E
0318 Puerto de Palma Puerto Pi Dique del Oeste head
Fl.R.5s19m7M
• 39°33'·16N 2°38'·34E
0318·6 Inner elbow
VQ(6)+LFl.10s16m5M
Obscd inside harbour
• 39°32'·72N 2°37'·94E
0318·8 Harbour S wall
Fl(2)15s41m18M
Vis outside Bahia de Palma 327°-040°
• 39°32'·91N 2°37'·41E
0322 Dique de Levante head SW corner
Fl(2)G.10s6m5M
• 39°33'·55N 2°38'·07E
0329 Palma Nova breakwater head
Fl(4)G.11s7m5M
• 39°31'·44N 2°32'·49E
0330 Punta de Cala Figuera
Fl(4)20s45m22M Siren(2)12s
293°-vis-094°
• 39°27'·46N 2°31'·34E
0332 Islote El Toro
Fl.5s31m7M
• 39°27'·74N 2°28'·31E
0332·5 Puerto Adriano NW head
Fl(2+1)G.14·5s3m1M
• 39°29'·43N 2°28'·64E
0334 Cabo de la Mola
Fl(1+3)12s128m12M
• 39°31'·9N 2°21'·9E

ISLA DE CABRERA

0338 Punta Anciola
Fl(3)15s121m20M
277·5°-vis-169°
• 39°07'·8N 2°55'·4E
0338·3 Cabo Llebeig (Lebeche)
Fl(4)14·5s74m7M
• 39°09'·7N 2°55'·1E
0338·6 Punta da Sa Creueta
Fl.R.4s13m5M
• 39°09'·33N 2°55'·77E
0339 Puerto de Cabrera pier head
Fl(2)R.10·5s5m5M
• 39°09'·10N 2°56'·07E
0340 Isla Horadada (Foradada)
Fl(2)12s42m10M
• 39°12'·5N 2°58'·8E

ISLA DE MENORCA

0342 Cabo D'Artruitx
Fl(3)10s45m18M 267°-vis-158°
• 39°55'·4N 3°49'·5E
0344 Puerto de Ciudadela Punta de sa Farola
Fl.6s21m14M 004°-vis-094°
• 39°59'·8N 3°49'·4E
0345 Entrance N side. Punta El Bancal
Fl(3)R.9s10m5M
• 38°59'·8N 3°49'·5E
0345·9 E point N shore Cala d'en Busquets Dir Lt 045°
DirFl.WRG.5s9m5-3M
White sector marks centre of channel.
Red sector is to the N.
Green sector to the S
• 40°00'·0N 3°49'·7E
0348 Cabo Nati
Fl(3+1)20s42m18M 039°-vis-162°
• 40°03'·1N 3°49'·5E
0350 Cabo Cavallería
Fl(2)10s94m22M 074°-vis-292° Racon
• 40°05'·3N 4°05'·5E
0350·5 Cap de sa Paret
Fl.2s29m7M
• 40°03'·8N 4°08'·0E
0351/0351·1 Cala Fornells Isla Sargantana Ldg Lts 177·2°
Front Q.R.1s14m3M
Rear Iso.R.4s23m3M
• 40°02'·8N 4°08'·2E

0352 Cabo Favaritx
Fl(1+2)15s47m21M
• 39°59'·8N 4°16'·0E
0354 Puerto de Mahón
Punta de Sant Carlos
Oc(2)6s22m13M
183°-vis-143°
• 39°51'·91N 4°18'·41E
0355 Punta del Esperó
Fl(1+2)15s51m7M
• 39°52'·62N 4°19'·66E
0366 Isla del Aire
Fl.5s53m18M
197°-vis-111°
• 39°48'·0N 4°17'·6E
0367 Bajo es Caragol
Q(6)+LFl.15s10m3M
• 39°48'·6N 4°15'·2E

Mediterranean – Spain

PUERTO DE LOS ALFAQUES
0370 Punta de la Baña
Fl(2)12s27m12M
• 40°33'·6N 0°39'·7E
0371·2 Punta Corballera
Fl.WG.4s13m6/4M
000°-G-180°-W-000°
• 40°34'·7N 0°35'·8E
0373 Sant Carles de la Rápita Punta Senieta
Oc(4)R.10s10m11M
• 40°36'·4N 0°35'·1E
0374 Dique de Abrigo head
Fl(2)R.8s8m3M
• 40°36'·6N 0°36'·3E
0377 Cabo Tortosa
Fl.WR.6s18m14/10M
127°-W-047°-R-127° Racon
• 40°42'·9N 0°55'·7E

PUERTO DE FANGAL
0380 El Fangal
Fl(2+1)12s20m12M
• 40°47'·42N 0°46'·11E

PUERTO DE LA AMPOLLA
0380·5 Jetty head
Fl.G.5s10m5M
• 40°48'·5N 0°42'·7E

PUERTO DE AMETLLA DEL MAR
0381·5 East breakwater head
Fl(3)G.9s17m5M
• 40°52'·7N 0°48'·2E
0382·3 Calafat Marina Breakwater
Fl.G.5s9m5M
• 40°55'·6N 0°51'·0E

PUERTO DEPORTIVO HOSPITALET DEL INFANTE
0382·5 Dique SE head
Fl(4)G.11s10m5M
• 40°59'·3N 0°55'·7E

PUERTO DE CAMBRILS
0383 Dique de Levante head
Fl(3)G.9s15m5M
• 41°03'·7N 1°03'·7E
0384 Dique de Poniente head
Fl(3)R.9s13m3M
• 41°03'·8N 1°03'·7E

SALOU
0386 Cabo Salou
Fl(4)20s43m23M
• 41°03'·3N 1°10'·3E

PUERTO DE TARRAGONA
0386·6 Pantalán REPSOL head
Fl.R.5s12m7M
• 41°04'·9N 1°12'·5E
0386.72 Muelle de Galicia head
Fl(2)R.7s8m5M
• 41°05'·32N 1°12'·80E
0388·12 Outer breakwater Head
Fl.G.5s22m10M
Fl.G.5s on post marks marine farm
• 41°04'·7N 1°12'·8E
0392·3 Tarraco International Marina breakwater head
Fl(2)G.10s7m5M
• 41°06'·4N 1°15'·1E

PUERTO DEPORTIVO DE TOREDEMBARRA
0393·7 Punta de la Galera
Fl(5)30s58m17M
• 41°07'·9N 1°23'·7E
0393·8 Dique de Abrigo head
Fl(4)G.11s10m5M
• 41°08'·1N 1°24'·1E
0393·9 Roda de Bara Harbour Breakwater
Fl(3)G.9s8m5M
• 41°10'·0N 1°29'·0E
0393·98 Roc San Cayetaro Pier
VQ(6)+LFl.10s7m5M
• 41°10'·0N 1°28'·8E

PUERTO DEPORTIVO DE COMARRUGA
0394 Dique Oeste head
Fl(2)G.7s7m5M
• 41°10'·6N 1°31'·5E
0394·6 Dique Est head
Fl.R.5s7m5M
• 41°10'·7N 1°31'·6E

PUERTO DEPORTIVO DE SEGUR DE CALAFELL
0394·8 Breakwater head
Fl(4)G.12s8m5M
• 41°11'·1N 1°36'·5E

PUERTO DE VILANUEVA Y GELTRÚ
0396 Punta San Cristóbal
Fl(3)8s27m19M
265°-vis-070°
• 41°13'·0N 1°44'·2E
0396·54 Puerto de Aiguadolç. Dique de Abrigo head
Fl.G.5s12m5M
0396·55 E breakwater T-Jetty Head
Fl(2)G.13s6m1M
• 41°14'·0N 1°49'·5E
0396·62 Puerto de Garraf E Breakwater Head
Fl(3)G.9s7m5M
• 41°14'·9N 1°53'·9E
0396·8 Puerto de Ginesta Outer breakwater head
Fl(2)G.10s8m5M
• 41°15'·4N 1°55'·4E
0398 Río Llobregat entrance N side
Fl.5s32m23M
240°-vis-030°
• 41°19'·50N 2°09'·13E

PUERTO DE BARCELONA
0400 Montjuich
Fl(2)15s108m26M
240·5°-vis-066·6°
• 41°21'·66N 2°09'·96E
0434·71/·72/·73 Puerto Olimpico submerged breakwater
Fl(3)R.8s6m3M
• 41°22'·87N 2°11'·91E
Fl(3)G.8s6m5M
• 41°23'·01N 2°12'·06E
Q(3)10s6m5M
• 41°23'·20N 2°12'·26E

PORTO DEPORTIVO MASNOU
0439·3 Dique de Levante
Fl(2)G.12s10m5M
• 41°28'·4N 2°18'·7E

PUERTO DEPORTIVO PREMIA DE MAR
0439·5 Dique de Abrigo head
Fl.G.3s6m5M
• 41°29'·3N 2°22'·0E
0439·8 Puerto Deportivo Pesquero de Mataro Dique de Abrigo head
Fl(4)G.16s15m5M
• 41°31'·6N 2°26'·7E

PUERTO DEPORTIVO EL BALIS
0440·08 E Breakwater head
Fl(3)G.10s10m5M
• 41°33'·4N 2°30'·4E

PUERTO DE ARENYS DE MAR
0446·5 E breakwater head
Fl(2)G.7s9m5M
• 41°34'·5N 2°33'·4E
0448 Calella. Cerro de la Torreta
Fl(3+2)20s50m18M Aeromarine
• 41°36'·5N 2°38'·7E
0452 Puerto de Blanes Dique de Abrigo corner
Fl.G.3s7m5M
• 41°40'·4N 2°47'·9E
0452·2 Dique de Abrigo Head
Fl(2)G.1M
• 41°40'·4N 2°47'·9E
0452·7 Puerto Deportivo Cala Cañelles Dique de Abrigo head
Fl(4)G.11s5m5M
• 41°42'·2N 2°52'·9E
0453 Cabo Tossa
Fl(3+1)20s60m21M
229·7°-vis-064·2°
• 41°43'·0N 2°56'·0E

PUERTO DE SAN FELIÚ DE GUÍXOLS
0456 Dique Rompeolas head
Fl(3)G.9s10m5M
• 41°46'·6N 3°02'·0E
0459 Playa de Aro. Marina breakwater head
Fl(2)G.9s6m5M
• 41°48'·1N 3°04'·0E
0460 Bajo Pereira (La Llosa de Palamós)
Fl(2)7s10m5M
• 41°50'·2N 3°07'·2E

PUERTO DE PALAMOS
0462 Punta del Molino
Oc(1+4)18s22m18M
• 41°50'·5N 3°07'·8E
0464 Dique de Abrigo head
Fl.G.3s9m5M
• 41°50'·5N 3°07'·2E
0466·7 Marina de Palmós harbour breakwater head
Fl(4)G.10s11m5M
• 41°50'·6N 3°08'·1E
0467 Hormiga Grande Islet N coast
Fl(3)9s14m6M
• 41°51'·8N 3°11'·1E
0468 Puerto Deportivo de Llafranch Dique head
Fl(3)G.11s6m5M
• 41°53'·6N 3°11'·8E
0470 Cabo San Sebastián
Fl.5s167m32M Aeromarine
• 41°53'·68N 3°12'·14E
0471·2 Puerto Deportivo Aiguablava basin entrance east side
Fl(2)G.10s4m5M
• 41°56'·0N 3°13'·0E

0472 Islas Medas summit of largest island
Fl(4)24s87m14M
• 42°02′·9N 3°13′·3E

PUERTO DE ESTARTIT

0473·5 Dique de Levante head
Fl.G.5s9m5M
• 42°03′·0N 3°12′·4E

0474·2 Contradique corner
Fl.R.5s8m5M
• 42°03′·0N 3°12′·2E

0475·3 L'Escala. Breakwater head
Fl(4)R.15s12m5M
• 42°07′·2N 3°08′·8E

PUERTO DEPORTIVO EMPURIABRAVA

0475·5 E Breakwater head
Fl(3)G.7s8m5M
• 42°14′·7N 3°08′·2E

PUERTO DEPORTIVO SANTA MARGARITA

0475·6 Dique de Abrigo
Q(2)G.4s8m5M
• 42°15′·4N 3°09′·0E

PUERTO DE ROSAS

0476 Punta de la Batería o Blancals
Oc(4)15s24m12M
• 42°14′·8N 3°11′·0E

0479 Muelle de Abrigo head
Fl.G.4s8m5M
• 42°15′·1N 3°10′·7E

CADAQUÉS

0484 Punta Cala Nans
Fl(4+1)25s33m8M
• 42°16′·2N 3°17′·2E

0486 Cabo Creus
Fl(2)10s87m20M Aeromarine
• 42°19′·0N 3°18′·9E

PUERTO DE LA SELVA

0488 Punta Sernella
Fl.5s22m13M
• 42°21′·1N 3°11′·2E

0489·2 Puerto Deportivo Llansá breakwater head
Fl(3)R.10s8m5M
• 42°22′·3N 3°09′·7E

EMBARCADERO DE COLERA

0490 E breakwater head
Fl(2)R.6s7m5M
• 42°24′·3N 3°09′·3E

PORT BOU

0491 Breakwater head
Fl.R.5s7m5M
• 42°25′·7N 3°10′·0E

Mediterranean – France

0492 Cap Cerbère
Fl.4s55m15M
• 42°26′·4N 3°10′·6E

0492·2 Cerbère
Fl(2)WR.6s12m9/6M
210°-W-237°-R-210°
• 42°26′·5N 3°10′·2E

PORT DE BANYULS

0493 Île Petite
Fl.WG.4s10m10/7M
193°-W-247°-G-193°
• 42°28′·9N 3°08′·0E

0496 Cap Béar
Fl(3)15s80m30M
146°-vis-056° Partially obscd over Cabo Creus, Ilots Voisin and Cap Cerbère
• 42°30′·9N 3°08′·2E

PORT VENDRES

0497/0497·1 Fort Béar
Ldg Lts 198·5°
Front Q.12m10M
Rear 200m from front DirQ.23m18M
196°-intens-199°
• 42°31′·2N 3°06′·8E

0498 Entrance W side Fort du Fanal
Oc.G.4s29m8M
147°-vis-264°
• 42°31′·3N 3°06′·8E

0498·5
Q.G.9m7M
• 42°31′·3N 3°06′·8E

0504 Môle Abri head
Oc(3)R.12s20m11M 110°-vis-287°
• 42°31′·4N 3°07′·0E

0506 Anse Gerbal Jetée head
Iso.G.4s4m6M
• 42°31′·2N 3°06′·8E

0508 Pointe des Pilotes
Fl.G.4s4m7M
• 42°31′·2N 3°06′·7E

0509 Pointe de la Presqu'ile
Fl.R.4s3m6M
• 42°31′·1N 3°06′·5E

0512 Collioure. Mole head
Iso.G.4s14m8M
135°-vis-278°
• 42°31′·7N 3°05′·3E

0513 Saint Cyprien Jetée sud head
Fl(4)R.15s12m9M
• 42°37′·32N 3°02′·56E

0514 Perpignan-Rivesaltes
Aero Mo(X)8·5s58m33M
• 42°43′·8N 2°52′·6E

0514·5 Canet-Plage
Fl(4)15s27m15M
• 42°42′·5N 3°02′·3E

0515 Jetée sud
Fl(3)R.12s9m9M
• 42°42′·2N 3°02′·6E

0515·2 Jetée nord head
Fl(3)G.12s5m5M
• 42°42′·2N 3°02′·4E

0516·1 Sainte-Marie-la-Mer. S breakwater head
Fl(5)R.20s6m5M
• 42°43′·4N 3°02′·4E

0517 Grau St Ange jetée sud head
Fl(2)R.10s10m10M
• 42°47′·9N 3°02′·4E

PORT LEUCATE

0517·6 Jetée Est head
Fl.R.4s8m6M
• 42°52′·5N 3°03′·3E

0517·7 Jetée Ouest head
Fl.G.4s8m6M
• 42°52′·5N 3°03′·1E

0518 Cap Leucate
Fl(2)10s66m20M
• 42°54′·5N 3°03′·3E

LA NOUVELLE

0522/0522·1 Lts in line 292°24′ jetée sud head
Front Q.1·2s23m14M
Rear 2M from front Q.1·2s53m17M
• 43°01′·5N 3°01′·8E

0524 Jetée Nord head
Iso.G.4s15m6M
Basins within the port marked by strip lights
• 43°00′·9N 3°04′·1E

GRUISSAN

0526 Jetée Sud head
Fl(2)R.6s12m6M
• 43°06′·7N 3°08′·0E

0526·2 Jetée Nord head
Fl.G.4s11m7M
• 43°06′·7N 3°07′·9E

0527·2 Port de Narbonne-Plage, Bassin des Exals
Fl(3)12s24m15M
220°-vis-040°
• 43°10′·3N 3°10′·83E

0527·7 Embouchure de l'Aude Digue E head
Fl(2)G.6s10m8M
• 43°12′·7N 3°14′·6E

0527·8 Digue W head
Fl.R.4s7m5M
• 43°12′·7N 3°14′·5E

PORT DE VALRAS

0528 Dique NE head
Fl.G.4s9m6M
• 43°14′·7N 3°18′·0E

0529 Digue SW head
Fl(4)15s9m9M
• 43°14′·7N 3°18′·1E

AGDE

0534 Rivière de l'Hérault. W jetée head
Oc(2)R.6s14m7M
R and G lights mark the river above this point
• 43°16′·8N 3°26′·6E

0535 E Jetée head
Oc.G.4s14m7M Horn 10s
• 43°16′·8N 3°26′·6E

0535·4 La Lauze
Fl.G.4s10m5M
• 43°16′·0N 3°30′·5E

0536 Yacht harbour digue est head
Fl(3)G.12s8m6M
• 43°16′·1N 3°30′·4E

0536·2 Digue Ouest head
Fl(3)R.12s8m6M
Numerous lights inside the harbour
• 43°16′·1N 3°30′·3E

0538 Îlot Brescou
Fl(2)WR.6s22m13/10M
113°-R-190°-W-113°
• 43°15′·8N 3°30′·1E

PORT AMBONNE

0539 Jetée SW head
Fl(2)R.6s9m6M
• 43°17′·5N 3°31′·8E

PORT DE MARSEILLAN-PLAGE

0542 Digue ouest head
Fl.R.4s7m8M
• 43°19′·0N 3°33′·7E

0542·1 Digue Est
Fl.G.4s8m5M
• 43°19′·1N 3°33′·6E

SÉTE

0544 Mont Saint-Clair
Fl.5s93m27M
W215°-105°
• 43°23′·7N 3°41′·4E

0545 Port des Quilles breakwater W head
Fl(3)G.12s8m5M
• 43°23′·5N 3°39′·9E

0546 Môle Saint Louis head
Fl(4)R.15s34m7M
• 43°23′·9N 3°42′·3E

0547 Épi Dellon middle
Fl(2)R.6s21m3M 080°-vis-268°
• 43°23′·9N 3°43′·2E

0547·5 Head
Iso.R.4s20m11M
• 43°24′·0N 3°43′·9E

0550 Breakwater E head
Fl(3)R.12s15m3M
063°-vis-253°
• 43°23′·8N 3°42′·5E

0551 W head
Fl.G.4s10m6M
• 43°23′·6N 3°42′·1E
0552 Nouvelle dique head
Fl.R.4s10m4M
• 43°23′·7N 3°42′·2E
0556 Nouveau Basin W mole head
Q.R.7m6M
• 43°24′·0N 3°42′·12E
0557 E mole head
Q.G.6m8M
• 43°24′·1N 3°42′·2E
0557·2 Frontignan-La Peyrade. Dique est head
Fl(3)G.12s15m7M
• 43°25′·2N 3°44′·9E
0557·6 Canal Fluvio. W head
Fl(2)WG.6s8m6/4M
• 43°25′·2N 3°44′·71E
0558 Frontignan Marina digue ouest head
Fl.R.4s9m6M
• 43°25′·8N 3°46′·6E
0558·2 Dique est head
Fl.G.4s9m8M
• 43°25′·8N 3°46′·6E

ÉTANG DE THAU

0560 Canal de Sète N entrance E side
Q.G.8m3M
• 43°24′·9N 3°41′·5E
0561 W side
Q.R.8m3M
• 43°24′·9N 3°41′·4E
0562 Rocher de Roquérols
Q(6)+LFl15s7m4M
• 43°25′·8N 3°40′·4E
0566 Méze Jetée est head
Fl.G.4s8m6M
• 43°25′·3N 3°36′·4E
0567 Marseillan detached breakwater N head
Fl(2+1)R.10s5m7M
• 43°21′·2N 3°32′·1E
0567·2 Jetée NE head
Iso.G.4s7m6M
• 43°21′·2N 3°32′·1E
0568 Canal du Midi. Les Onglous E jetée head
Oc(2)WR.6s10m13/10M
217·5°-W-229°-R-217·5°
• 43°20′·4N 3°32′·4E

CARNON

0578 Jetée SW head
Fl(4)R.15s9m7M
• 43°32′·4N 3°58′·7E
0578·2 Jetée est head
Fl.G.4s8m5M
• 43°32′·5N 3°58′·7E

AIGUES MORTES

0580 Port de la Grande Motte Digue ouest head
Fl(2)R.6s12m7M
• 43°33′·1N 4°04′·9E
0580·2 Digue est head
Fl.G.4s9m5M
• 43°33′·1N 4°04′·9E
0582 Grau du Roi Jetée est head
Fl(3)G.15s10m10M
• 43°32′·1N 4°07′·9E
0582·2 Jetée ouest head
Oc(2)R.6s9m7M
• 43°32′·1N 4°07′·9E
0583 Port Camargue Digue d'arrêt head
VQ(9)10s9m9M
• 43°31′·2N 4°07′·3E
0583·2 Jetée ouest head
Fl.G.4s9m9M
• 43°31′·3N 4°07′·3E
0583·4 Jetée est head
Fl.R.4s8m6M
• 43°31′·3N 4°07′·4E
0586 Pointe de l'Espiguette
Fl(3)15s27m24M
• 43°29′·3N 4°08′·5E
0590 Port Gardian Digue ouest head
Fl.R.4s9m7M 117°-vis-075°
• 43°26′·8N 4°25′·4E
0592 La Gacholle
Fl.WRG.4s17m12/9M
300°-G-019°-W-065°-R-085°
• 43°27′·3N 4°34′·2E
0594 Beauduc
Fl(2)R.10s26m18M
• 43°21′·9N 4°35′·1E
0600 Faraman E bank of Vieux Rhône
Fl(2)10s41m23M
• 43°21′·4N 4°41′·3E

GOLFE DE FOS

0602 Canal Saint Louis jetée sud head
Q.WR.14m11/8M
267·5°-R-072°-W-267·5°
• 43°23′·4N 4°52′·2E
0602·1 N side No.1
Fl.G.4s8m7M
264°-vis-144°
• 43°23′·4N 4°51′·0E
0602·2 S side No.2
Fl.R.4s8m7M
024°-vis-264°
• 43°23′·3N 4°51′·0E
0602·32 S side No.4
Fl(2)R.6s8m5M
• 43°23′·3N 4°50′·6E
0602·33 N side No.3a
Q.G.8m5M
• 43°23′·3N 4°50′·1E
0602·6 No.8
Oc.R.4s8m6M 080°-vis-268°
• 43°23′·1N 4°48′·6E
0603 Port Saint Louis du Rhône. Tour Saint Louis Dir Lt 263·5°
DirQ.15m10M
• 43°23′·1N 4°48′·3E
0604/0604·1 Port de Fos Ldg Lts 287°
Front Q.11m11M
284°-intens-290°
Rear 500m from front Q.29m11M
• 43°24′·4N 4°51′·72E
0604·5 Darse 4 elbow
Q(6)+LFl.15s8m8M
• 43°24′·98N 4°53′·81E
0605·2 Darse No.1 Dir Lt 340°
DirOc.WRG.4s25m15-12M
333°-G-339°-W-341°-R-344°
• 43°25′·98N 4°52′·25E
0605·4 LNG pier head
Iso.R.4s10m7M
• 43°26′·9N 4°51′·3E
0606·2 Istres Le Tubé
Aero Mo(F)4s59m23M
• 43°31′·2N 4°57′·1E
0606·8 Pointe de Saint Gervais
IQ(7)WRG.12s45m25-21M
323°-G-340°-W-348°-R-007°
• 43°25′·71N 4°56′·42E
0606·95 Lavéra
VQ(9)10s7m8M
• 43°22′·71N 4°58′·2E
0607 Port-de-Bouc
Oc(2)WRG.6s30m12-9M
321°-G-343°-W-040°-R-087°-W-112°-R-140°-R (unintens)-230°
• 43°23′·6N 4°59′·1E
0607·2 Pointe Saint Antoine
VQ(2)R.1s14m6M
• 43°23′·6N 4°59′·1E
0608 Môle nord head
VQ(2)R.14m6M
• 43°23′·8N 4°59′·1E
0609/0609·1 Ldg Lts 036·7°
Front Q.R.11m11M
027°-intens-047°
Rear 167m from front Q.R.16m15M
026°-intens-048°
• 43°24′·3N 4°59′·6E
0609·4/0609·41 Ldg Lts 029·8°
Front Oc.R.4s11m10M
020°-intens-040°
Rear 184m from front Oc.R.4s17m10M
019°-intens-041°
• 43°24′·3N 4°59′·6E
0609·5 Coaster Basin Digue head
Fl(2)G.6s5m6M
• 43°23′·7N 4°59′·3E
0609·6 Fishing Port Digue head
Fl(2)R.6s3m8M
• 43°23′·9N 4°59′·0E
0609·8 Marina E jetty head
Iso.G.4s6m6M
• 43°24′·1N 4°59′·1E
0610·3 La Gafette N side
Fl.R.4s9m7M
• 43°24′·2N 5°00′·7E
0610·5 SW
Q.5m6M
• 43°24′·1N 5°01′·2E
0610·6 SE
Q(9)15s5m6M Central and southern viaduct piles are illuminated
• 43°24′·1N 5°01′·5E

ÉTANG DE BERRE

0611 Port de la Mède. Les Trois Frères
Fl.G.4s20m7M
F.R and F.G lights along embankment
• 43°24′·3N 5°07′·1E
0615 Point de Berre jetty head
Fl(4)WR.15s12m9/6M
012°-W-057°-R-012°
• 43°27′·6N 5°08′·6E
0616·8 Les Heures Claires breakwater head
Iso.G.4s5M
• 43°29′·9N 5°00′·0E
0617 Anse de Laurons Digue head
Fl.WR.4s7m9/6M
000°-W-110°-R-000°
• 43°21′·3N 5°01′·0E
0620 Carro Digue head
Q.WR.8m9/6M
322°-W-355°-R-322°
• 43°19′·8N 5°02′·6E
0622 Cap Couronne
Fl.R.3s34m20M
Reserve light range 13M
• 43°19′·5N 5°03′·2E
0624 Sausset-les-Pins Ouest head
Fl(3)R.12s10m5M
• 43°19′·7N 5°06′·5E

PORT DE CARRY LE ROUET

0625·3 Îlot de l'Élevine
Q(6)+LFl.15s28m10M
• 43°19′·8N 5°14′·2E
0625·6 Point Esquilladou
Fl(4)WR.15s44m10/7M
233°-R-263°-W-041°
• 43°21′·0N 5°16′·7E

PORTS DE MARSEILLE

0630·02 Port Abri. Passe des Chalutiers E side
Fl.G.4s8m6M
• 43°21′·4N 5°19′·0E

0630·2 Darse de Saumaty. Entrance E side
Iso.G.4s8m7M 030°-vis-210°
• 43°21′·3N 5°19′·4E
0631 Digue de Saumaty W head
VQ(2)20m17M
• 43°21′·3N 5°18′·8E
0634 Passe Nord Digue du large Head
Fl.G.5s15m17M
• 43°20′·8N 5°19′·1E
0635 Digue de Saumaty SE Head
Fl(2)R.6s12m8M
• 43°20′·93N 5°19′·21E
0635·4 Passe de Saumaty Mourepiane ouest
Fl(3)G.12s7m6M
• 43°21′·18N 5°19′·43E
0636 Passe Léon Gourret W side
Iso.G.4s7m3M 125°-vis-308°
• 43°20′·6N 5°19′·6E
0637 E side
IsoR.4s7m4M
• 43°20′·7N 5°19′·7E
0637·2 Passe Nord-est S side
Fl(2)G.6s8m6M
103°-vis-300°
• 43°20′·8N 5°19′·8E
0637·6 N side Digue Transversale E head
Fl(2)R.6s8m2M
• 43°20′·9N 5°19′·9E
0642 Passe de Cap Janet E mole NW corner
Fl.R.4s8m6M
• 43°20′·24N 5°20′·50E
0643 Môle ouest SE corner
Fl.G.4s8m6M
136°-vis-327°
• 43°20′·1N 5°20′·5E
0644 Passe de la Madrague W side NW corner
Fl(2)G.6s8m6M 149°-vis-322°
• 43°19′·7N 5°20′·8E
0646 E side mole NW corner
Fl(2)R.6s8m7M
• 43°19′·8N 5°20′·8E
0654 S entrance Digue des Catalans NW head
Fl(3)G.12s7m6M
• 43°17′·5N 5°20′·8E
PORTS DE MARSEILLE
0656 Digue Saint Marie SW end
VQ(2)R.20m12M
• 43°17′·8N 5°21′·2E
0657 Root
Oc(3)R.12s7m6M
195°-vis-060·5°
• 43°18′·0N 5°21′·5E
0660 Pointe de la Désirade
Fl.G.4s13m9M 003°-vis-271°
• 43°17′·7N 5°21′·2E
0662 Passe de la Joliette Digue du Fort St-Jean head
Oc(3)G.12s7m6M 001·5°-vis-299°, (unintens) 001·5°-009°, 277°-299°
• 43°17′·9N 5°21′·2E
0664 Vieux Port Fort St Jean. St Jean N side of entrance
Q.R.11m5M
• 43°17′·7N 5°21′·7E
0674 Banc du Sourdaras
Q(9)15s12m7M
• 43°17′·0N 5°20′·3E
0676 Ile d'If
Fl(2)6s27m11M
Obscured by Îles de Pomègues and Ratonneau 054°-152°
• 43°16′·8N 5°19′·7E

ÎLE RATONNEAU
0677 W end Ilot Tiboulen
Fl(3)G.12s34m7M
Obscured by Îles Ratonneau 242°-276° and de Pomègues 279°-002°
• 43°16′·8N 5°17′·2E

ÎLE DE POMÈGUES
0679 Cap Caveaux
Iso.4s28m7M
Obscured by Île de Pomègues between 144°-228°
• 43°15′·6N 5°17′·4E
0680 Îlot de Planier
Fl.5s68m23M
Obscured by Île de Riou and adjacent islets when bearing less than 284°
• 43°11′·9N 5°13′·9E

PORT DE POINTE ROUGE
0682 Breakwater head
Fl(2)G.6s10m6M
• 43°14′·8N 5°21′·9E
0684 Îlot Tiboulen-de-Marie
Fl.WG.4s58m11/8M
316°-G-327°-W-142°-G-shore
• 43°12′·8N 5°19′·6E
0685 Îlot les Empereurs
Q(6)+LFl.WR.15s18m7M
222°-R-236°-W-097°-R-112°
• 43°10′·2N 5°23′·7E

PORT CASSIS
0686 Môle neuf head
Oc(2)G.6s17m6M
• 43°12′·8N 5°32′·1E
0687 Batterie des Lecques
Fl.R.4s11m6M
• 43°12′·8N 5°32′·0E
0690 Banc de la Cassidaigne
Fl(2)6s18m7M
• 43°08′·7N 5°32′·8E

LA CIOTAT
0693 Jetée head
Fl.R.4s18m5M
• 43°10′·4N 5°37′·0E
0693·3 Seawall head
Fl(3)R.12s21m6M
• 43°10′·2N 5°37′·0E
0694 Môle Bérouard head
Iso.G.4s15m11M
134·5°-unintens-228·5°
• 43°10′·4N 5°36′·7E
0695 Marina Bassin Bérouard Digue sud head
Fl.G.4s8m7M
• 43°10′·5N 5°36′·8E
0697 Basin des Capucins entrance E side
Fl(2)R.6s7m8M
• 43°10′·7N 5°36′·9E
0698 Port des Lecques Jetée sud NE head
Fl(2)R.6s8m7M
• 43°10′·8N 5°41′·1E
0698·2 SW head
Iso.G.4s10m9M
• 43°10′·7N 5°40′·8E
0698·4 Contre-jetée ouest head
Q.R.3m6M
• 43°10′·8N 5°40′·9E

PORT BANDOL
0700 Jetée sud head
Oc(4)WR.12s9m13/10M
003°-R-351°-W-003°
• 43°08′·0N 5°45′·5E
0701 Jetée est head
Fl.G.4s2m6M
• 43°08′·1N 5°45′·5E

ILE DE BANDOL (BENDOR)
0702 Port de Port Ricard E jetty head
Oc.R.4s5m7M
• 43°07′·8N 5°45′·2E
0702·4 W jetty head
Fl(2)G.6s3m6M
• 43°07′·8N 5°45′·2E
0704 Sanary-sur-Mer. Jetée ouest head
Fl.R.4s9m10M
Obscured when bearing more than 069°
• 43°06′·9N 5°48′·1E
0706 La Coudoulière jetty head
Fl(3)R.12s8m6M
• 43°05′·8N 5°48′·7E

LE BRUSC
0708 Detached breakwater NE end
Iso.G.4s3m6M
• 43°04′·7N 5°48′·2E
0709 Jetty head
Oc(3)WR.12s10m9/6M
156°-W-166°-R-156°
• 43°04′·6N 5°48′·2E
0709·4 Île de la Tour Fondue N point
Fl(4)WR.15s6m8/6M
132°-W-275°-R-132°
• 43°04′·8N 5°47′·4E

PORT DES EMBIEZ
0709·6 Entrance N side
Fl.G.4s5m6M
• 43°04′·9N 5°47′·1E
0709·65 Dir Lt 210°
DirOcWRG.4s3m9-7M
198·5°-G-207°-W-213°-R-221·5°
• 43°04′·8N 5°47′·2E
0710 Île du Grand Rouveau
Oc(2)6s45m15M
Obscured by Île des Embiez 255°-317°, 255°-unintens-297°
• 43°04′·9N 5°46′·1E
0712 Saint-Elme W mole N end
Fl.G.4s9m7M
• 43°04′·5N 5°53′·9E
0713 Cap Sicié
Fl(2)6s47m9M
Obscured by Cap Vieux when bearing more than 094°, and Cap Cépet when bearing more than 252°
• 43°02′·9N 5°51′·6E
0714 Cap Cépet
Fl(3)15s76m20M
• 43°04′·2N 5°56′·8E

TOULON
0716 Saint Mandrier jetée head
Fl(2)R.6s17m9M
Obscured when bearing more than 301°
• 43°05′·2N 5°56′·1E
0717 Grand Jetée S head
Fl.G.2·5s13m11M 186°-vis-165°
• 43°05′·4N 5°55′·5E
0717·8 École de mécaniciens Dique nord head
Fl(2)G.6s4m5M
298°-vis-225°
• 43°05′·0N 5°55′·8E
0719 Pointe de la Vielle head
Q.R.13m5M
• 43°05′·1M 5°55′·3E
0719·5 Anse du Creux-Saint-Georges. Port de Saint-Mandrier Jetée ouest head
Fl.G.4s5m5M
• 43°04′·8N 5°55′·5E
0720 Petite Passe pier head
Iso.RG.4s21m10/10M
266°-G-275°-R-294°-G-145°
• 43°06′·1N 5°55′·6E

0726 Port de Commerce. Dars du Mourillon. Quay Fournell head
Oc(2)R.6s7m6M
• 43°07′·0N 5°55′·8E
0727 S side
Iso.G.4s7m7M
• 43°06′·9N 5°55′·9E
0729 Darse Vielle. W head
Q.R.7m7M
• 43°07′·1N 5°55′·8E
0730 E head N
Q.G.8m7M
• 43°07′·1N 5°55′·8E
0734 Port Militaire. Grands Bassins Vauban. SW corner
Fl(4)G.15s2m6M 261°-vis-091° 3 W floodlights on a quay
• 43°06′·9N 5°55′·4E
0740 Darse de Missiessy entrance W side
Iso.R.4s4m5M
• 43°07′·0N 5°54′·8E
0740·2 E side
Iso.G.4s4m5M
• 43°07′·0N 5°54′·8E
0741 La Seyne-sur-Mer. Jetty NW side
Fl.G.4s6m10M
• 43°06′·2N 5°53′·0E
0741·7 Jetty
Q.3m8M
• 43°04′·9N 5°53′·9E
0741·8 Appontement de Tamaris head
DirOc(4)WRG.12s3m8M
338·5°-G-351·5°-W-353·5°-R-006·5°
• 43°05′·5N 5°54′·1E
0742 Port de Saint-Louis de Mourillon jetée est head
Oc(2)G.6s10m7M
• 43°06′·4N 5°56′·2E
0744 Les Salettes jetée sud head
Oc(4)WR.12s13m10/7M
356°-W-005°-R-356°
• 43°05′·2N 6°04′·8E

ÎLES AND RADE D'HYÈRES

0746 Baie du Niel jetty head
Fl.R.4s5m6M 298°-vis-028°
• 43°02′·1N 6°07′·7E
0748 Le Grand Ribaud
Fl(4)15s35m15M
Obscured by Pointe Escampobariou when bearing more than 108°, by Île du Grand Ribaud 124°-222°, by Cap de l'Estérel when bearing less than 233°, and by Île de Porquerolles 262°-324°
• 43°01′·0N 6°08′·7E
0749 La Tour-Fondue W jetty head
Iso.G.4s7m8M
• 43°01′·7N 6°09′·3E
0750 Ecueils de la Jeaune-Garde
Q.WR.16m6/4M
011°-W-253°-R-282°-W-316°-R-011°
• 43°00′·4N 6°09′·7E
0751 Île de Porquerolles S side Cap d'Armes
Fl(2)10s80m29M
142°-vis-204°, 243°-vis-252°, 266°-vis-119°
• 42°59′·0N 6°12′·4E
0752 Port de Porquerolles pier head
Oc(2)WR.6s8m13/10M
150°-W-230°-R-150°
• 43°00′·3N 6°12′·0E
0754 Port d'Hyères NE jetty head
Fl.G.4s9m10M
• 43°04′·7N 6°09′·6E
0754·2 Dique sud head
Oc.R.4s9m7M
• 43°04′·8N 6°09′·5E
0754·6 Basin 3 E jetty head
Iso.G.4s8m10M
• 43°05′·1N 6°09′·7E
0754·7 Inner jetty S head
Q(6)+LFl.15s8m9M
• 43°05′·0N 6°09′·7E
0754·8 N head
Fl.R.4s2m5M
• 43°05′·1N 6°09′·6E
0755·6 Le Ceinturon (L'Aygade) E breakwater head
Fl(2)G.6s6m6M
• 43°06′·1N 6°10′·5E
0756 Port Pothuau (Les Salins d'Hyères) Jetée est head
Oc(3)WG.12s9m13/10M
260°-G-285°-W-012°-G-060°
• 43°06′·9N 6°12′·1E
0757 Jetée ouest head
Fl(2)R.6s6m6M
• 43°06′·9N 6°12′·1E
0759 Miramar jetée est head
Fl(2)G.6s8m8M
• 43°06′·9N 6°14′·8E
0761 Mararenne River E Breakwater Head
Q(9)15s6m6M
• 43°07′·0N 6°15′·0E
0762 Batterie des Maures
Q(9)10s8m5M
• 43°06′·6N 6°17′·1E
0764 Cap Bénat
Fl.R.5s60m21M 207°-vis-288°, 327°-vis-330°, 001°-vis-042°, 060°-vis-096°
Obscured by Île de Porquerolles 042°-060°, by Île du Levant 288°-327° and by Îles du Port Cros and Bagaud 330°-001° Reserve light 176°-vis-118°
• 43°05′·3N 6°21′·8E

PORT DE BORMES LES MIMOSAS

0765 Jetée est N head
Fl(2)R.6s10m10M
• 43°07′·5N 6°22′·0E
0765·04 S head
Q(6)+LFl.15s9m6M
• 43°07′·3N 6°21′·9E
0765·3 Rocher la Fourmigue
Fl(2)6s8m8M
• 43°06′·4N 6°24′·3E

LE LAVANDOU

0766 Digue sud head
Iso.WG.4s8m13/10M
266°-W-317°-G-332°-W-358°-G-266°
• 43°08′·2N 6°22′·5E
0766·4 Old jetty head
Q(9)15s4m7M
• 43°08′·2N 6°22′·3E

ÎLE DU LEVANT

0769 Port de l'Avis
Fl.G.4s8m6M
• 43°01′·6N 6°27′·2E
0769·5
Q(3)WRG.5s14m8-7M
112°-G-123°-W-131°-R-142°
• 43°01′·8N 6°27′·5E
0770 Le Titan
Fl.5s70m28M 154°-vis-044°
• 43°02′·8N 6°30′·6E

PORT DE CAVALAIRE

0771 Jetée est head
Fl(2)R.6s9m10M
• 43°10′·4N 6°32′·3E
0771·2 Môle central extension. Spur head
Q.7m6M
• 43°10′·4N 6°32′·3E
0772 Cap Camarat
Fl(4)15s130m26M
190°-vis-049°
• 43°12′·1N 6°40′·8E
0774 La Moutte NE rock
Q(3)WR.10s11m9/6M
009°-R-121°-W-009°
• 43°16′·4N 6°42′·7E

SAINT TROPEZ

0778 Jetée nord head
Oc(2)WR.6s15m14/11M
228°-W-245°-R-228°
• 43°16′·4N 6°38′·0E
0779 Jetée sud head
Fl.G.4s6M
• 43°16′·3N 6°38′·0E

PORT DE COGOLIN

0784 Jetée est N head
Fl(2)R.6s7m10M
• 43°16′·1N 6°35′·5E
0784·6 N head
Q.6m9M
• 43°16′·2N 6°35′·3E

PORT GRIMAUD

0786 Jetée nord
Fl.G.4s7m10M
• 43°16′·3N 6°35′·3E
0786·2 S spur head
Fl.R.4s7m6M
• 43°16′·3N 6°35′·2E

SAINTE MAXIME-SUR-MER

0788 Jetée sud head
Q.G.8m8M
• 43°18′·3N 6°38′·3E
0790 Sèche à l'Huile
Q(6)+LFl.WR.15s9m9/6M
075°-R-216°-W-075°
• 43°18′·6N 6°41′·1E
0791 Les Issambres S Breakwater Head
Fl(2)WG.6s8m11/8M
• 43°20′·4N 6°41′·1E
0791·7 Port Ferreol mole head
Fl.WR.4s5m7/5M
250°-W-310°-R-250°
• 43°21′·6N 6°43′·1E

BAIE DE SAINT RAPHAËL

0792.01 Saint Raphaël S head
QG.5m2M
• 43°25′·32N 6°45′·8E
0792·4 Saint Aygulf Jetée est head
Q.R.6M
• 43°23′·6N 6°43′·9E

SANTA LUCIA

0793 Bassin sud breakwater ouest head
Oc(2)WR.6s10m10/7M
040°-W-057°-R-084°-W-122°-R-040°
• 43°24′·5N 6°46′·9E
0793·4 Bassin nord jetée ouest head
Fl.G.4s8m9M
• 43°25′·0N 6°46′·5E
0794 Îlot Lion de Mer
VQ.WR.16m11/8M
275°-W-249°-R-275°
• 43°24′·4N 6°46′·5E

AGAY

0795 Point de la Beaumette
Oc.WR.4s28m15/12M
260°-R-294°-W-032°
• 43°25′·5N 6°52′·3E
0795·5 Le Chrétienne
Q(6)+LFl.15s10m8M
• 43°25′·3N 6°53′·8E

PORT DE LA MIRAMAR

0796 Jetée head
Fl(3)WG.12s12m13/10M
275°-W-348°-G-275°
• 43°29'·0N 6°56'·0E

PORT DE LA GALÈRE

0797 Breakwater head
Q.R.9m7M
• 43°30'·0N 6°57'·4E

0797·8 Pointe Saint-Marc
Fl(2)G.6s7m5M
• 43°30'·0N 6°57'·5E

0798 Théoule-sur-Mer jetée est head
Iso.WR.4s8m9/6M
198°-W-256°-R-198°
• 43°30'·6N 6°56'·4E

LA RAGUE

0798·4 Jetty head
Fl(4)G.15s11m8M
• 43°30'·8N 6°56'·4E

MANDELIEU-LA-NAPOULE

0799 Breakwater head
Fl(3)G.12s9m10M
• 43°31'·3N 6°56'·7E

CANNES

0800 Breakwater head
VQ(3)R.2s23m8M
Obscured by Îles de Lérins when bearing less than 340°
• 43°32'·7N 7°01'·1E

0803 Second Port (Port Canto) Jetée sud head
Fl.G.4s11m11M
• 43°32'·5N 7°01'·8E

0805 Îles de Lérins. Les Moines
Q(6)+LFl.15s12m9M
• 43°30'·0N 7°03'·1E

GOLFE JUAN

0806 La Fourmigue
Fl(2)10s16m7M
• 43°32'·4N 7°05'·0E

0808 Vallauris
Oc(2)WRG.6s167m16/11M
265°-G-305°-W-309°-R-336°-W-342°-G-009°
• 43°34'·1N 7°03'·7E

0809 Port de Mouré Rouge E breakwater head
Fl(4)WG.15s7m9/6M
282°-W-312°-G-282°
• 43°32'·6N 7°02'·6E

0810 Port de Golfe Juan. Jetée sud head
Iso.R.4s6m9M 050°-vis-250°
Synchronised with Iso.R.4s close S
• 43°33'·9N 7°04'·7E

0810·4 Marina outer breakwater
Fl(2)G.6s10m10M
• 43°33'·8N 7°04'·7E

0811 Port Gallice. Jetée ouest head
VQ(3)G.2s10m9M
• 43°33'·8N 7°06'·8E

0812·2 Le Couton S breakwater E head
Fl(2)R.6s6m5M 138°-vis-091°
• 43°33'·6N 7°07'·2E

0814 Pointe de l'Ilette
Oc(3)WRG.12s18m13/9M
185°-W(unintens)-235°-W-045°-R-056°-G-070°-R-090°-W-135°
• 43°32'·6N 7°07'·3E

0818 La Garoupe
Fl(2)10s104m31M
• 43°33'·9N 7°08'·0E

BAIE DES ANGES

0818·6 Marina S breakwater head
Fl(2)R.6s6m7M
• 43°37'·9N 7°08'·3E

0818·7 E breakwater head
Fl(2)G.6s13m9M
• 43°37'·95N 7°08'·37E

ANTIBES

0819 Digue de large head
Fl.R.4s15m11M
• 43°35'·4N 7°08'·0E

0819·6 Epi du Fort Carré head
Fl.G.4s10m5M 186°-vis-148°, 218°-unintens-003°
• 43°35'·3N 7°07'·8E

0821 St Laurent du Var breakwater head
Fl(3)G.12s10m8M
• 43°39'·3N 7°10'·7E

NICE

0822 Jetée du large head
Fl.R.5s21m20M
• 43°41'·4N 7°17'·3E

0823 E pier head
Fl.G.4s5m7M
• 43°41'·5N 7°17'·4E

0824 Bassin du Commerce. W side
Fl(2)R.6s6m7M
• 43°41'·5N 7'17'·3E

0824·2 E side
Fl(2)G.6s6m7M
• 43°41'·5N 7°17'·3W

0825 Basin des Amiraux S side
Fl(3)R.12s6m6M
• 43°41'·6N 7°17'·2E

0826 N side
Fl(3)G.12s6m7M
• 43°41'·6N 7°17'·2E

VILLEFRANCHE

0828 Cap Ferrat
Fl.3s69m25M
226°-vis-167°
• 43°40'·5N 7°19'·6E

0830 E jetty head
Q.WR.8m12/8M
009°-R-148°-R (unintens)-238°-R-286°-W-311°-R-335°-W-009°
• 43°42'·0N 7°18'·7E

0832 Health office mole head
Fl(4)R.15s10m7M
• 43°42'·2N 7°18'·8E

SAINT JEAN

0833 Jetée Abri head
Fl(4)R.15s10m8M
• 43°41'·5N 7°20'·2E

BEAULIEU-SUR-MER

0836 Detached breakwater N head
Q.R.7m10M
• 43°42'·5N 7°20'·4E

0836·2 SW head
Fl(3)G.12s7m3M
• 43°42'·3N 7°20'·3E

0838 Eze-sur-Mer. Port de Silva Maris SE jetty head
Fl(2)R.6s6m9M
• 43°43'·0N 7°21'·2E

0838·4 Cap d'Ail. Digue sud SW corner
Fl.G.4s11m10M
262°-vis-172°
• 43°43'·4N 7°24'·9E

0838·42 NW corner
Fl.G.4s7m6M
• 43°43'·4N 7°24'·9E

PORT DE MONACO

0839 Port de Fontvielle S breakwater head
Fl(2)R.6s10m10M
• 43°43'·7N 7°25'·4E

0839·2 Jetty head
Fl(2)G.6s5m7M
• 43°43'·7N 7°25'·4E

0843 Floating mole (Port Hercule) E head
Fl(3)R.15s8M
• 43°44'·18N 7°23'·91E

0844 W head
Fl(3)G.15s5M
• 43°44'·2N 7°25'·79E

0848 Menton S jetty head
VQ(4)R.3s17m10M
Obscured by Cap Martin when bearing more than 036°
• 43°46'·5N 7°30'·7E

MENTON-GARAVAN

0849 S breakwater head
Fl.R.4s11m10M
• 43°47'·0N 7°31'·4E

Mediterranean – Corse

0852 Cap Corse. Île de la Giraglia
Fl.5s85m28M
057°-vis-314°
• 43°01'·6N 9°24'·4E

0853 Centuri jetty head
Fl.G.4s7m6M
• 42°58'·0N 9°21'·0E

MACINAGGIO

0854 Jetée head
Fl(2)WR.6s8m11/8M
120°-R-218°-W-331°-R-000°-R (unintens)-120°
• 42°57'·7N 9°27'·3E

0855 Cap Sagro
Fl(3)12s10M
Reserve light range 8M
• 42°47'·7N 9°29'·5E

BASTIA

0856 Jetée du Dragon head
Fl.WR.4s16m15/12M
040°-R(unintens)-130°-R-215°-W-325°-R-040°
• 42°41'·6N 9°27'·3E

0860 Jetée Saint Nicolas head
Fl.G.4s9m11M
• 42°41'·8N 9°27'·4E

PORT DE CAMPOLORO

0863 E jetty head
Fl.R.4s7m6M
• 42°20'·5N 9°32'·5E

0864 Alistro
Fl(2)10s93m22M
• 42°15'·6N 9°32'·5E

PORTO VECCHIO

0866 Punta de la Chiappa
Fl(3+1)15s65m23M
198°-vis-027°
• 41°35'·7N 9°22'·0E

0866·4 Rocher Pécorella
Fl(3)G.12s12m6M
• 41°36'·7N 9°22'·3E

0867 Punta San Ciprianu
Fl.WG.4s26m11/8M
220°-W-281°-G-299°-W-072°-G-084°
• 41°37'·0N 9°21'·4E

0869 Punta di Pozzoli
DirOc(2)WRG.6s10m15-13M 258·7°-G-271·7°-W-275·2°-R-288·2°
• 41°36'·6N 9°17'·5E

0870 Dir Lt 224·5°
DirIso.WRG.4s9m11-9M
208·5°-G-223·5°-W-225·5°-R-240·5°
• 41°35'·2N 9°17'·5E

0870·6 Marina E breakwater head
Fl(2)R.6s5m6M
212°-vis-302°
• 41°35'·4N 9°17'·2E

0870·8 NE breakwater head
Fl(2)G.6s4m5M
200°-vis-290°
• 41°35′·5N 9°17′·3E

BONIFACIO STRAIT

0872 Île Lavezzi
Oc(2)WR.6s27m17/14M
243°-W-351°-R-243° but partially obscd 138°-218° Reserve light W 10M R 7M
• 41°20′·1N 9°15′·6E

0874 Lavezzi Rock
Fl(2)6s18m9M Racon
• 41°19′·0N 9°15′·3E

0874·5 Île Cavallo jetty head
Iso.WRG.4s7m6-4M
328°-G-337°-W-344°-R-353°
• 41°21′·7N 9°15′·9E

0875 Perduto Rock
Q(3)10s16m11M
• 41°22′·0N 9°19′·0E

0876 Cap Pertusato
Fl(2)10s100m25M
239°-vis-113°
• 41°22′·0N 9°11′·2E

BONIFACIO

0878 Pointe de la Madonetta
Iso.R.4s28m6M
• 41°23′·1N 9°08′·8E

0882 Pointe Cacavento
Fl.G.4s6m5M
• 41°23′·4N 9°09′·3E

0888 Cap de Feno
DirFl(4)15s21m21M
109·4°-intens-111·4° &
Fl(4)WR.15s23m7/4M
Auxiliary 150°-R-270°-W-150°
Reserve light range W 5M, R 3M
• 41°23′·6N 9°05′·8E

0889 Caldarello jetty head
DirQ.WRG.7-6M
026°-G-035°-W-037·5°-R-046°
• 41°28′·5N 9°04′·39E

0890 Ecueil Les Moines
Q(6)+LFl.15s26m9M
• 41°26′·8N 8°54′·0E

0894 Pointe de Sénétosa
Fl.WR.5s54m20/16M
R over Les Moines 306°-328° but obscured by land as Pointe Latoniccia is approached, 328°-W-306°
• 41°33′·5N 8°47′·9E

PROPRIANO

0896 Scogliu Longu jetty N head
Oc(3)WG.12s16m15/12M
070°-W-097°-G-137°-W-002°
• 41°40′·8N 8°53′·9E

0898 N jetty head
Iso.G.4s11m10M
Obscured by Scogliu Longo LtHo 094°-095°
• 41°40′·8N 8°54′·0E

0899·2 E head
Fl(3)G.12s5m6M
• 41°40′·73N 8°54′·43E

0900 Cap Muro
Oc.4s57m9M
186°-unintens-276°
• 41°44′·4N 8°39′·7E

0902 Îles Sanguinaires Grand Sanguinaire summit
Fl(3)15s98m24M
• 41°52′·7N 8°35′·7E

AJACCIO

0906 Ecueil de la Citadelle
Fl(4)R.15s10m6M
• 41°54′·8N 8°44′·5E

0908 La Citadelle
Fl(2)WR.10s19m20/16M
045°-R-057° over Ecueil de la Guardiola, 057°-W-045°
• 41°55′·0N 8°44′·5E

0910 Jetée de la Citadelle head
Oc.R.4s13m6M
• 41°55′·2N 8°44′·7E

0910·5 Basin de la Ville, N mole dolphin
Q.G.5m6M
• 41°55·20N·8°44·63′E

0912 Port de l'Amiraute S breakwater N head
Fl(2)R.6s5m3M
• 41°55′·9N 8°44′·7E

0914 Aspretto outer jetty head
Q.RG.8m7M
035°-G-300°-R-035° Occas
• 41°55′·4N 8°45′·8E

0915 Interior jetty head
Fl.R.4s6m8M Occas
• 41°55′·3N 8°45′·9E

0915·2 Cargèse S jetty head
Oc(3)WR.12s7m9/6M
025°-R-325°-W-025°
• 42°07′·9N 8°35′·9E

0916 Île de Gargalu
Fl.WR.4s37m8/5M
348°-W-214°-R-348°
• 42°22′·3N 8°32′·2E

0918 La Revellata
Fl(2)10s97m21M
Obscured when bearing less than 060°
• 42°35′·0N 8°43′·5E

0919 Research Station jetty head
Fl.G.4s5m6M
• 42°34′·9N 8°43′·5E

CALVI

0920 NE of citadel
Oc(2)G.6s30m8M
095°-vis-005°
• 42°34′·2N 8°45′·8E

0922 Jetty head
Q.G.10m8M
• 42°34′·1N 8°45′·8E

0923 Breakwater head
Fl.R.4s6m7M
• 42°34′·0N 8°45′·6E

SANT AMBROGIO

0925 Danger d'Algajola
Q.6M
• 42°37′·8N 8°50′·4E

0926 L'Île Rousse, La Pietra
Fl(3)WG.12s64m14/11M
shore-G-079°-W-234°-G-shore
• 42°38′·6N 8°56′·0E

0928 Port de L'Île Rousse jetty head
Iso.G.4s12m8M
Obscured by Grand Île Rousse 111°-143° and by Île Sicota when bearing less than 091°
• 42°38′·5N 8°56′·4E

0930 Pointe de la Mortella
Oc.G.4s43m8M
• 42°43′·0N 9°15′·4E

0932 Pointe de Fornali
Fl.G.4s14m6M 000°-unintens-090°
• 42°41′·3N 9°16′·9E

PORT DE SAINT FLORENT

0933 Jetée nord head
Fl(2)WR.6s6m9/6M
080°-W-116°-R-080°
• 42°40′·8N 9°17′·9E

0935 Pointe Vecchiaia
Fl(3)WR.12s35m10/7M
035°-W-174°-R-035°
• 42°42′·9N 9°19′·5E

Mediterranean – Sardegna

BONIFACIO STRAIT

0936 Santa Teresa di Gallura. Porto Longosardo entrance E side
Fl.WR.3s11m10/8M
030°-R-164°-W-184°-R-210°
• 41°14′·6N 9°12′·0E

0937/0937·1 Isolotto Municca Ldg Lts 196·5°
Front pier head S corner
Oc.R.4s12m3M 181·5°-vis-211·5°
Rear 0·7M from front Fl.R.4s45m7M
151·5°-vis-241·5°
• 41°13′·6N 9°11′·4E

0938 Capo Testa
Fl(3)12s67m22M
017°-vis-256°
Reserve light range 17M
• 41°14′·6N 9°08′·7E

0940 Isola Razzoli NW point
Fl.WR.2·5s77m19/15M
022°-W-092°-R-137°-W-237°-R-320°
Reserve light W17M R13M Racon
• 41°18′·4N 9°20′·4E

0942 Isola Santa Maria Punta Filetto
Fl(4)20s17m10M
173°-vis-016°
• 41°17′·9N 9°23′·1E

0946 Isolotti Barrettinelli di Fuori
Fl(2)10s22m11M
• 41°18′·1N 9°24′·1E

0950 Punta Sardegna
Fl.5s38m11M
• 41°12′·4N 9°21′·8E

0951 Isola Spargi. Secca Corsara
Q(6)+LFl.15s6m5M
• 41°13′·4N 9°20′·2E

0952 Secca di Mezzo Passo
Fl(2)6s7m5M
• 41°12′·22N 9°22′·84E

ISOLA DELLA MADDALENA

0957/0957·1 Rada di la Maddalena Ldg Lts 014°
Front Iso.G.2s50m8M
008·2°-vis-019·8°
Rear 1000m from front
Oc.G.4s150m8M
• 41°13′·3N 9°24′·0E

0958 Secca del Palau SW
VQ(6)+LFl.10s8m5M
• 41°11′·7N 9°23′·2E

0990·2 Secca du Piagge
VQ(9)10s5m5M
• 41°10′·9N 9°23′·33E

0992 Capo d'Orso
Fl.3s12m10M
• 41°10′·6N 9°25′·4E

0994 Secca di Tre Monti
Fl(2)8s5m5M
• 41°09′·3N 9°27′·8E

ISOLA CAPRERA

0996 Punta Rossa
Fl.G.5s9m5M 275°-vis-110°
• 41°10′·1N 9°28′·1E

0998 Isolotti Monaci
Fl.WR.5s26m11/8M
246°-R-268° over Secca dei Monaci-268°-W-317°-R-357° over Secca delle Bisce-357°-W-246°
• 41°12′·9N 9°31′·0E

1000 Isola delle Bisce S side
Fl.G.3s11m8M
255°-vis-110°
• 41°09′·7N 9°31′·5E

1002 Capo Ferro
Fl(3)15s52m24M Aeromarine
Reserve light range 18M
Oc.R.5s42m8M
189°-vis-203° over Secca delle Bisce and dei Monaci
• 41°09'·3N 9°31'·4E

1003 NE point
Fl.R.3s15m8M
• 41°09'·4N 9°31'·6E

PORTO CERVO

1005 N side
Fl.G.4s7m6M
• 41°08'·2N 9°32'·3E

1005·4 S side
Fl.R.4s7m6M
• 41°08'·1N 9°32'·4E

CALA DI VOLPE

1009·56 Porto Rotondo shelter mole
Fl.WR.5s7m7/5M
215°-R-240°-W-215°
During summer season 2 buoys (stbd lateral with ▲ topmark Fl.G.5s2m2M and a port hand lateral with ■ topmark Fl.R.5s2m2M) are laid at the entrance to the tourist landing.
• 41°01'·8N 9°32'·6E

1010 Isolotto Figarolo SE end
Fl.5s71m11M
225°-vis-076°
• 40°58'·7N 9°38'·7E

GOLFO DI OLBIA

1013·8 Capo Ceraso NW
Q.6m5M
• 40°55'·6N 9°38'·1E

PORTO DI OLBIA

1014 Isola della Bocca
LFl.5s24m15M Horn Mo(B)30s
Racon 180°-vis-264°
Reserve light range 11M
• 40°55'·2N 9°34'·0E

ENTRANCE CHANNEL N

1015 Fl.G.5s5m5M
• 40°55'·4N 9°34'·3E

1015·2 S
Fl.R.5s5m5M
• 40°55'·3N 9°34'·3E

ISOLA TAVOLARA

1028 Punta Timone
LFl(2)10s72m15M
Obscured when bearing more than 341° Reserve light range 12M
• 40°55'·6N 9°44'·0E

CAPO CODA CAVALLO

1028·7 Porto Brandinchi
Fl.G.3s6m5M
• 40°48'·8N 9°41'·5E

1028·72 W entrance
Fl.R.3s6m5M
40°48'·8N 9°41'·5E

OTTIOLO

1028·8 Isolotto d'Ottiolo
Fl(2)R.10s5m5M
• 40°44'·2N 9°43'·4E

1028·85 Outer mole head
Fl.G.3s5m5M
• 40°44'·3N 9°42'·9E

1028·9 Inner mole head
Fl.R.3s5m5M
• 40°44'·3N 9°42'·8E

PORTO DI LA CALETTA

1030 Capo Comino
Fl.5s26m15M
148°-vis-010°
Reserve light range 11M
• 40°31'·7N 9°49'·7E

PORTO ARBATAX

1032 Capo Bellavista
Fl(2)10s165m26M
Reserve light range 18M
F.R.145m6M 164°-vis-177·5° over Isolotto Ogliastra
• 39°55'·8N 9°42'·8E

1033 Molo di Levante head
Fl.R.3s9m9M
• 39°56'·6N 9°42'·2E

1034 Spur head
F.R.14m5M
115°-vis-330°
• 39°56'·5N 9°42'·3E

1036 Molo di Ponente head
Fl.RG.3s13m8M
107°-R-147°-G-107°
• 39°56'·4N 9°42'·2E

1042 Capo Ferrato
Fl(3)10s51m11M
• 39°17'·9N 9°38'·0E

1042·1 Baia dei Carbonara
Fl.5s14m6M
009°-vis-058°
• 39°07'·9N 9°29'·9E

1043 Capo Carbonara
Fl.7·5s120m23M
217°-vis-109°
Reserve light range 18M
• 39°06'·2N 9°30'·9E

1048 Isola dei Cavoli NE side
Fl(2)WR.10s74m11/8M
162°-W-073°-R-093°-W-128°
• 39°05'·3N 9°32'·0E

1049 Secca S Caterina
Q(9)15s5m5M
• 39°05'·0N 9°29'·7E

1052·55 Foxi Marina de Capitana outer mole head
Fl.G.3s5m5M
• 39°12'·6N 9°17'·8E

1052·56 Inner mole head
Fl.R.3s5m5M
• 39°12'·6N 9°17'·8E

MARINA PICCOLA DEL POETTO

1054 Cap Sant'Elia S of Forte Sant'Ignazio
Fl(2)10s70m21M
Reserve light range 18M
• 39°11'·0N 9°08'·9E

PORTO DI CAGLIARI

1056·2 Head
Fl.R.3s13m9M
120°-vis-060°
• 39°12'·0N 9°06'·7E

1057 Molo di Levante head
Fl.G.3s13m9M Racon
• 39°11'·7N 9°06'·6E

1065·6 New industrial port
DirWRG.18m5/3M
• 39°13'·3N 9°03'·3E

1065·61 Molo meridionale head
Fl(2)R.6s5M
• 39°11'·5N 9°05'·5E

1065·62 Molo settentrionale head
Fl(2)G.6s5M
• 39°11'·6N 9°05'·8E

SARROCH

1067 Oil Terminal
Fl.3s27m6M
• 39°05'·1N 9°03'·1E

1070 Capo di Pula
Fl(4)15s48m11M
• 38°59'·0N 9°01'·2E

1072 Capo Spartivento
Fl(3)15s81m22M
240°-vis-085°, 093°-vis-094°
Reserve light 18M
• 38°52'·6N 8°50'·7E

PORTO DI TEULADA

1073 Outer mole head
Fl.R.4s8m6M
• 38°55'·6N 8°43'·2E

1073·1 Inner mole head
Fl.G.4s8m6M
• 38°55'·6N 8°43'·1E

1074 Isola del Toro
Fl(2)WR.6s118m11/8M
199°-R over Isolotto la Vacca-205°-W-199°
• 38°51'·6N 8°24'·6E

PORTO DI SANT'ANTIOCO (PONTE ROMANO)

1080 Main light
Fl.5s23m15M
Reserve light 11M
• 39°03'·5N 8°28'·5E

1086 Scoglio Mangiabarche (Mangiabarca)
Fl.6s12m11M
• 39°04'·5N 8°20'·8E

ISOLA DI SAN PIETRO

1090 W end Capo Sandalo
Fl(4)20s134m24M Aeromarine
322°-vis-191° and in Canale di San Pietro 311°-vis-322°
Reserve light range 18M
• 39°08'·8N 8°13'·4E

CANALE DI SAN PIETRO

1092 Isola di San Pietro Carloforte Molo San Vitorio head
Fl.R.3s7m8M
• 39°08'·5N 8°19'·0E

1093·5 Secca dei Marmi NW
Fl.Y.3s6m4M (in line with Front Bn 241·9°)
• 39°09'·0N 8°20'·0E

1093·6 Secca dei Marmi W
LFl.10s6m6M
• 39°08'·6N 8°20'·0E

1094 SSW shore of port
Front
F.R.11m6M (in line with Secca dei Marmi NW 241·9°)
• 39°08'·4N 8°18'·6E

1094·1 Southwestwards
Rear Fl.R.3s75m9M 221°-vis-251°
39°07'·9N 8°17'·6E

1096 Molo della Sanitá head
Fl.G.3s8m6M
• 39°08'·7N 8°19'·0E

1099 Portoscuso Scoglio La Ghinghetta
Fl(2)WR.10s12m11/8M
100°-R-116°-W-153°-R-165°-W-100°
• 39°11'·9N 8°22'·2E

1100·6 Porto Vesme W mole head
Fl.R.3s11m7M
• 39°11'·5N 8°23'·2E

1101 Diga di Levante head
Fl.G.3s11m7M
• 39°11'·5N 8°23'·5E

1103 Isola Piana N end
Fl(2)WR.8s18m7M
209°-R-231° over Secca Grande-W-209°
• 39°11'·6N 8°19'·1E

1103·2 Secca Grande southeastwards
Q.3M
• 39°12'·7N 8°20'·3E

GOLFO DI ORISTANO

1104 Capo Frasca
Fl.6s66m11M
• 39°46′·1N 8°27′·4E

1105·1/1105·11 Porto di Oristano Ldg Lts 130°
Front Iso.2s10m8M
Rear 900m from front
Oc.4s20m10M
• 39°51′·58N 8°33′·80E

1105·2 Porto di Oristano inner mole head
LFl.R.5s10m7M
• 39°51′·9N 8°32′·6E

1105·3 Outer mole head
LFl.G.5s12m8M
• 39°51′·9N 8°32′·2E

1106 Gran Torre. Torre Grande
Fl.R.5s18m8M
• 39°54′·4N 8°31′·0E

1108 Capo San Marco
Fl(2)10s57m22M
215°-vis-155°
Reserve light range 18M
LFl.R.5s55m12M
097·5°-vis-102·5° over Scoglio il Catalano
• 39°51′·6N 8°26′·1E

1111 Isolotto Mal di Ventre summit
Fl.WR.6s26m11/8M
004°-R over Scoglio il Catalano-020°-W-004°
• 39°59′·5N 8°18′·2E

1112 Capo Mannu
Fl(3)12s59m15M
• 40°02′·1N 8°22′·7E

1116·5 Isola Rossa. Bosa Marina Inner mole head
Fl.R.3s11m11M
• 40°17′·1N 8°28′·4E

PORTO DI ALGHERO

1117 Molo S head
Fl.G.3s10m8M
• 40°33′·9N 8°18′·3E

1117·2 New inner mole
Fl.R.3s10m8M
• 40°33′·8N 8°18′·4E

PORTO CONTE

1124 Entrance W point Capo Caccia
Fl.5s186m24M
Reserve light range 18M
• 40°33′·6N 8°09′·8E

1126 E side near Torre Nuova
Fl.3s17m10M
• 40°35′·5N 8°12′·3E

1130 Isola Asinara Punta dello Scorno
Fl(4)20s80m16M
Reserve light range 13M
• 41°07′·1N 8°19′·1E

1132 Rada della Reale NW end
Fl.WR.5s11m7/5M
297°-R-320°-W-297°
• 41°03′·1N 8°17′·6E

1133 Passaggio dei Fornelli, Punta Salippi
Fl.WRG.3s6m6-4M
065·2°-G-068·2°-W-076·2°-R-079·2°
• 40°59′·2N 8°13′·6E

1133·5 Punta Salippi
Fl.WRG.3s6m5-4M
293·3°-G-297°-W-305°-R-308·7°
• 40°59′·2N 8°12′·8E

PORTO DI STINTINO

1134 Shoal
Fl.R.4s6m4M
• 40°56′·19N 8°13′·88E

1134·4 Outer mole head
Fl.G.4s6m8M
• 40°56′·1N 8°13′·8E

PORTO TORRES

1138 Main light
LFl(2)10s45m16M
Reserve light range 12M
• 40°50′·1N 8°23′·8E

1139 Molo di Ponente near head
LFl.G.6s11m11M Racon
Reserve light range 8M
• 40°50′·8N 8°23′·9E

1140 Molo di Levante head
LFl.R.6s11m8M
• 40°50′·7N 8°23′·9E

Mediterranean – Italy

PORTO DI SAN REMO

1149 Molo sud head
LFl.R.5s11m8M
• 43°48′·9N 7°47′·2E

1152 Capo dell'Arma
Fl(2)15s50m24M
Reserve light 18M
• 43°49′·0N 7°49′·9E

MARINA DEGLIA AREGAI TOURIST PORT

1155 Outer mole head
2F.R(vert)9m5M
• 43°50′·2N 7°55′·0E

1155.3 Inner pier
F.R.5m5M
• 43°50′·2N 7°55′·0E

1155.4
2F.G(vert)9m5M
• 43°50′·2N 7°54′·9E

IMPERIA

1156 Porto Maurizo S breakwater 150m from head
Iso.4s11m16M 210°-vis-090°
Reserve light range 11M
• 43°52′·5N 8°01′·7E

1157 Head
Fl.R.3s9m8M
• 43°52′·5N 8°01′·8E

1158 Molo Pastorelli head
Fl.G.7m2M
• 43°52′·6N 8°01′·4E

1162 Oneglia Molo Artiglio head
Fl(2)G.6s14m8M
• 43°53′·0N 8°02′·5E

1164 Oneglia Molo Alcardi head
Fl.R.8m3M
• 43°53′·1N 8°02′·5E

SAN BARTOLOMEO AL MARE

1167 Outer mole head
Fl.R.3s7m5M
• 43°55′·2N 8°06′·4E

1167·1 Inner mole head
Fl.G.3s7m5M
• 43°55′·2N 8°06′·4E

1168 Capo delle Mele
Fl(3)15s94m24M Aeromarine
196°-vis-056° Reserve light range 18M
• 43°57′·3N 8°10′·4E

MARINA DI ANDORA

1168·4 Outer breakwater head
Fl.R.3s7m5M
• 43°56′·9N 8°09′·5E

1168·5 Inner mole head
F.G.3s7m5M
• 43°57′·0N 8°09′·5E

PORTI DI ALASSIO

1171 Outer mole head
Fl.R.3s5M
• 44°01′·1N 8°11′·7E

1171·2 New inner mole head
Fl.G.3s8m5M
• 44°01′·1N 8°11′·6E

RADA DI VADO

1172 Capo di Vado
Fl(4)15s43m14M
Reserve light range 7M
• 44°15′·5N 8°27′·2E

1172·8 Outer mole head
Fl.R.4s10m8M
• 44°15′·7N 8°27′·4E

1175/1175·1 Pontile San Raffaele Lts in line 208° head
Front F.RWR(vert)11m5/3M
Rear 850m from front
Iso.G.2s20m2M
2F.R(vert)18m
• 44°15′·8N 8°26′·7E

PORTO DI SAVONA

1193 New breakwater head
Fl.R.2s12m8M
• 44°18′·8N 8°30′·3E

1196 Molo Sottoflutto head
Fl.G.2s9m7M
• 44°19′·0N 8°29′·8E

VARAZZE

1202 Voltri detached mole W end
Fl.G.4s16m10M
• 44°24′·9N 8°46′·2E

1202·2 N head
Fl.R.3s9m6M
• 44°25′·3N 8°48′·5E

1202·4 Elbow
Fl.2s14m7M
Obscured within harbour
• 44°24′·7N 8°47′·7E

1202·6 Inner mole head
Fl.R.4s11m8M
• 44°25′·0N 8°46′·7E

PORTO DI GENOVA

1206 Lanterna Capo del Faro
Fl(2)20s117m25M &
Oc.R.1·5s119m10M Aeromarine
Reserve light range 18M.
Numerous F.R and Fl.R along the coast between Voltri and Punta Vagno
• 44°24′·2N 8°54′·3E

1208 Diga Aeroporto W end
Oc.3s10m12M
• 44°24′·8N 8°49′·0E

1208·2 Diga di Cornigliano E end
Fl.R.2s13m7M
• 44°24′·0N 8°52′·9E

1208·6 Diga Forano S jetty head
Q.G.10m5M
• 44°24′·1N 8°52′·6E

1211 Multedo entrance No.31
Q.G.8m7M
• 44°25′·0N 8°48′·7E

1211·2 No.32
Q.R.8m6M
• 44°25′·1N 8°48′·6E

1211·3 No.33
Oc.G.2s8m6M
• 44°25′·0N 8°48′·9E

1211·4 No.34
Oc.G.2s8m6M
• 44°25′·1N 8°49′·1E

1211·5 No.35
Oc.R.2s8m5M
• 44°25′·2N 8°49′·0E

1212 Inner mole head
Q.R.10m7M
• 44°25′·1N 8°49′·7E

1212·2 No.36
Fl.G.1·5s6m7M
• 44°25′·1N 8°49′·3E

1212·3 No.37
Fl.R.1·5s8m7M
• 44°25′·1N 8°49′·4E
1212·4 No.38
Q.G.6m7M
• 44°25′·0N 8°49′·7E
1212·5 No. 39
Fl.G.2s6m7M
• 44°25′·0N 8°49′·91E
1215 Calato Olii Minerali E corner
Fl(3)G.7s10m7M
44°23′·9N 8°55′·0E
1216 Molo Duca di Galliera spur NE corner
Fl(3)R.7s10m7M
Obscured from seaward
• 44°23′·8N 8°55′·0E
1217 Spur
Fl.R.3s11m7M
Obscured from seaward
• 44°23′·6N 8°55′·6E
1218
Fl.R.13m4M
115°-vis-303°
• 44°23′·5N 8°55′·9E
1219 Molo duca di Galliera E head
Fl.R.3s18m15M
• 44°23′·3N 8°56′·3E
1220 Inner mole head
Fl.G.4s14m7M
• 44°23′·6N 8°56′·1E
1221 W head
Fl.G.3s10m8M
• 44°23′·8N 8°55′·6E
1225 Calata della Sanita Paleoscapa E corner
Fl.R.3s8m7M
• 44°24′·2N 8°55′·1E
1226 Mole Vecchio head
Fl.G.3s8m7M
• 44°24′·4N 8°55·2E
1230 Punta Vagno
LFl(3)15s26m16M
Reserve light range 11M
• 44°23′·5N 8°57′·2E

CAMOGLI

1236 Outer mole head
Fl.3s11m9M
• 44°21′·1N 9°09′·0E

GOLFO TIGULLIO

1244 Punta de Portofino
Fl.5s40m16M 155°-vis-098°
Reserve light range 11M
• 44°17′·9N 9°13′·1E
1246 Portofino N side
Fl.G.3s7m7M
• 44°18′·2N 9°12′·8E
1248 Punta del Coppo
Fl.R.3s10m7M
• 44°18′·2N 9°12′·9E
1254 Santa Margherita Ligure mole head
Fl.R.4s10m8M
• 44°19′·8N 9°13′·1E
1255 Rapallo. E outer mole elbow
Fl.3s9m9M
• 44°20′·6N 9°14′·1E

PORTO DI CHIAVARI

1257 Molo Foraneo head
LFl.G.3s8m6M
• 44°18′·6N 9°19′·1E
1257·7 Lavagna outer mole head
LFl.R.6s12m6M
• 44°18′·2N 9°20′·6E

SESTRI LEVANTE

1262 Isola del Tino S Venerio
Fl(3)15s117m25M
Reserve light range 18M Racon
• 44°01′·6N 9°51′·0E

BAIA PORTOVENERE

1263 Scoglio Torre della Scuola
Fl(2)6s16m10M
• 44°03′·1N 9°51′·6E

RADA DI LA SPEZIA

1268 Punta Santa Maria
Fl.R.4s11m9M
335°-obscd-347° within a distance of 0·7M Safety distance 30m
• 44°04′·0N 9°51′·1E
1269 Diga Foranea W head
Fl.G.4s11m9M
• 44°04′·1N 9°51′·4E
1270 E head
Fl(2)R.6s10m8M
• 44°04′·8N 9°52′·8E
1274 Punta Santa Teresa
Fl(2)G.6s10m8M
• 44°04′·8N 9°52′·9E
1282 Pontone Societa Arcola
Fl.Y.5s7m5M
• 44°05′·7N 9°51′·3E
1282·2
Fl.G.3s7m5M
• 44°05′·7N 9°51′·45E
1282·4
Fl.R.3s7m5M
• 44°05′·80N 9°51′·48E
1290 Molo Italia head
Fl.R.4s8m8M
• 44°06′·2N 9°50′·1E
1300 Darsena Duca Degli Abruzzi. Diga di Cadimare head
Fl.R.3s6m5M
• 44°05′·2N 9°49′·9E
1302 Diga est S head
Fl.G.3s6m7M
• 44°05′·3N 9°50′·0E
1304 Darsena Duca Degli Abruzzi NE elbow
Fl.3s7m11M
• 44°05′·6N 9°50′·1E
1312 Ldg Lts 306° on sail loft
Front Fl.WRG.3s21m8/6M
297°-G-305·3°-W-306·8°-R-315°
• 44°05′·8N 9°48′·9E
1312·1 Pegazzano
Rear 0·56M from front
Iso.4s48m16M
302°-vis-310°
• 44°06′·1N 9°48′·3E

MARINA DI CARRARA

1328 Molo di Ponente Banchina Chiesa root
Fl.3s22m17M
• 44°02′·1N 10°02′·2E
1328·5 Dir Lt 320°
DirWRG.32m12-10M
PEL 312·8°-F.G-315·3°-AlWG-317·3°-FW-318·3°-AlWR-320·30°-F.R-322·80°
• 44°02·08N 10°02′·17E
1329 Diga Foranea head
Iso.R.2s13m7M
• 44°01′·57N 10°02′·51E
1330 Molo di Levante head
Iso.G.2s10m7M
• 44°01′·7N 10°02′·5E

VIAREGGIO

1340 Outer breakwater
Fl.5s30m24M
F and F.R mark yacht basin
Reserve light 18M
• 43°51′·4N 10°14′·2E
1341 N mole head
Iso.R.3s9m7M
• 43°51′·7N 10°14′·2E
1342 S breakwater head
Iso.G.3s9m9M
• 43°51′·7N 10°14′·0E

SECCHE DELLA MELORIA

1347·8 N end
Fl(2)10s18m10M
• 43°35′·5N 10°12′·7E
1348 S end
Q(6)+LFl.15s18m12M
• 43°32′·8N 10°13′·2E
1348·5 E side
Q(3)10s5m7M
• 43°35′·4N 10°15′·6E

PORTO DI LIVORNO

1356 Livorno
Fl(4)20s52m24M Racon
Reserve light range 18M
• 43°32′·7N 10°17′·8E
1358 Diga Meloria N end
Fl(3)WG.10s12m8/6M
064°-W-138°-G-341°
• 43°33′·5N 10°17′·3E
1360 Diga Marzocco head
Fl(3)R.10s12m7M
• 43°33′·5N 10°17′·5E
1368 Diga Curvilinea S end
Fl.WR.3s22m10/11M
180°-R-078°-W-139° Reserve light Fl.R.3s6M
• 43°32′·6N 10°17′·4E
1370 N end
Fl.RG.3s7m5M
160°-G-288°-R-048°
• 43°33′·2N 10°17′·4E
1374 Diga della Vegliaia W head
Fl.G.3s18m12M
330°-vis-240° Reserve light Fl.G.3s6M
• 43°32′·3N 10°17′·2E
1376·2 Diga Rettilinea head
Fl(2)R.6s8m6M
281°-vis-135°
• 43°33′·1N 10°17′·8E
1380 Mole Mediceo head
Fl(2)G.6s7m5M
Vis inside harbour
• 43°33′·0N 10°17′·8E
1384 Secche di Vada
Fl(2)10s18m12M
• 43°19′·2N 10°21′·9E
1386 Vada, Rosignano Marritimo Cala de Medici marina Outer Mole
Fl.G.3s10m6M
• 43°23′·83N 10°25′·28E
1387 Inner Mole Head
Fl.R.3s8m6M
• 43°22′·77N 10°25′·40E

VADA

1388·2 Elbow
Fl.5s14m5M
• 43°21′·3N 10°25′·7E
1390 Porto Baratti
Fl.3s75m9M
• 42°59′·6N 10°29′·7E

ISOLA GORGONA

1392 Punta Paratella (Maestra)
Fl.5s105m9M
• 43°26′·3N 9°54′·1E

PUNTA CALA SCIROCCO

1396 Punta Cala Scirocco
Fl(2)10s45m9M
43°25′·1N 9°54′·1E

ISOLA CAPRAIA

1400 Punta del Ferraione
LFl.6s30m16M
Reserve light range 11M
• 43°03′·0N 9°50′·7E

ISOLA D'ELBA

1408 Marciana Marina mole head
Fl.G.4s11m7M
• 42°48′·5N 10°11′·9E

1410 Lo Scoglietto
Fl(2)6s24m7M
• 42°49′·7N 10°19′·9E

1412 Portoferraio Forte Stella
Fl(3)14s63m16M
104°-vis-014°&
F.R.60m6M 100°-vis-131°
Reserve light range 11M
• 42°48′·0N 10°20′·0E

1429 Pontile Vigneria
Iso.2s10m5M
• 42°49′·2N 10°26′·0E

1432 Porto Azzurro Capo Focardo
Fl(3)15s32m16M
Reserve light range 11M
• 42°45′·2N 10°24′·6E

1434 Punta San Giovanni
Fl.R.5s15m6M
230°-vis-010°
• 42°45′·8N 10°23′·7E

1436 Mole head
Fl.G.5s6m6M
• 42°45′·8N 10°23′·9E

1438 Monte Poro
Fl.5s160m16M
Reserve light range 12M
• 42°43′·7N 10°14′·2E

1439 Marina di Campo 38m S of tower
Fl.3s34m10M
• 42°44′·5N 10°14′·3E

1444 Punta Polveraia
LFl(3)15s52m16M
Obscured when bearing less than 036°
Reserve light range 11M
• 42°47′·7N 10°06′·6E

1446 Isolotto Palmaiola
Fl.5s105m10M
Reserve light range 11M
• 42°51′·9N 10°28′·5E

ISOLA PIANOSA

1448 Pianosa
Fl(2)10s42m16M
Reserve light range 10M
• 42°35′·1N 10°06′·0E

1454 Scoglio Africa Formiche di Montecristo
Fl.5s19m12M
• 42°21′·4N 10°03′·9E

PORTOVECCHIO DE PIOMBINO

1454·1 Salivoli outer mole head
Fl.R.3s8m6M
• 42°56′·0N 10°30′·0E

1455 Piombino la Rocchetta
Fl(3)15s18m11M
• 42°55′·2N 10°31′·5E

1456 Molo Batteria head
Fl.R.5s10m8M
• 42°55′·8N 10°33′·2E

1460 Torre de Sale outer mole elbow
Oc.3s9m5M
Fl(2)G.6s2M Fl.G.5s2M Fl.G.3s2M
marks dolphins ESE
• 42°57′·1N 10°36′·1E

PORTO DI CARBONIFERS

1460·6 Outer mole head
Fl.R.2s5m5M
• 42°56′·5N 10°41′·0E

1460·8 Inner mole head
Fl.G.2s5m5M
• 42°56′·5N 10°41′·0E

PORTO TURISTICO

1462 Etrusca Marina outer mole head
Fl.G.3s6m5M
• 42°53′·2N 10°46′·9E

1462·2 Inner mole head
Fl.R.3s6m5M
• 42°53′·2N 10°46′·8E

PUNTA ALA

1466 Outer mole elbow
Fl.2s12m7M
• 42°48′·2N 10°44′·0E

1466·2 Inner mole head
Fl.R.2s12m5M
• 42°48′·2N 10°44′·0E

1466·4 Mole head
Fl.G.2s12m5M
• 42°48′·2N 10°44′·0E

CASTIGLIONE DELLA PESCAIA

1468 S mole head
Fl.G.3s8m8M
• 42°45′·6N 10°52′·6E

1470 N mole head
Fl.R.3s8m8M
• 42°45′·6N 10°52′·6W

1471 Puerto Touristico San Rocco mole right entrance
Fl.G.3s7m5M
• 42°42′·9N 10°58′·6E

1471·3 Left entrance
Fl.R.3s7m5M
• 42°42′·9N 10°58′·6E

1474 Formiche di Grosseto Scoglio Formica Maggiore
Fl.6s23m11M
• 42°34′·6N 10°53′·0E

BAIA DI TALAMONE

1476 Talamone
Fl(2)10s30m15M
• 42°33′·1N 11°08′·0E

1477·5 Outer mole head
Fl(2)R.6s10m7M
• 42°33′·3N 11°08′·1E

1480 Punta Lividonia
Fl.5s47m16M
035°-vis-228°
Reserve light range 11M
• 42°26′·7N 11°06′·3E

ISOLA DEL GIGLIO

1486 Punta del Fenaio (del Fienaio)
Fl(3)15s39m16M 026°-vis-249°
Reserve light range 12M
• 42°23′·2N 10°52′·9E

1488 Porto del Giglio Marina E mole head
Fl.R.3s9m7M
• 42°21′·6N 10°55′·3E

1490 W mole head
Fl.G.3s9m7M
• 42°21′·6N 10°55′·3E

1492 Punta del Capel Rosso
Fl(4)30s90m23M 232°-vis-134°
Obscured by Isola di Giannutri over an arc of 8° Reserve light range 18M
• 42°19′·2N 10°55′·3E

ISOLA DI GIANNUTRI

1496 Punta del Capel Rosso
Fl.5s61m13M
195°-vis-106°
• 42°14′·3N 11°06′·5E

PORTO ERCOLE

1500 Forte la Rocca
LFl.WR.7s91m16/13M
177°-R-285°-W-010°
Reserve light range W11, R8M
• 42°23′·4N 11°12′·8E

1502 Punta Santa Barbara mole head
Fl.R.3s9m8M
• 42°23′·6N 11°12′·7E

1504 Cala Galera. Molo frangiflutto head
Iso.WR.2s10m10/7M
197°-W-017°-R-197°
• 42°24′·2N 11°12′·8E

1504·4 Inner mole head
Iso.G.2s10m6M
085°-vis-275°
• 42°24′·2N 11°12′·7E

1505 Valdaliga
Fl.Y.3s6m5M
• 42°07′·4N 11°45′·5E

1505·2 Valdaliga
Fl(3)Y.10s10m5M
• 42°07′·4N 11°45′·1E

1507 Punta Mattonara. Beacon
Fl.Y.3s3M
• 42°06′·5N 11°45′·8E

CIVITAVECCHIA

1508 Monte Cappuccini
Fl(2)10s125m24M
Obscured shore-344°
Reserve light range 18M
• 42°05′·9N 11°49′·0E

1509 Scogliera della Mattonara N head
Fl.R.3s6m8M
• 42°06′·42 11°48′·28E

1510 Antemurale Colombo head
Fl.G.3s6m8M
• 42°06′·18N 11°46′·07E

1514 Banchina Compagnia Roma S corner
Fl.R.3s9m8M
• 42°05′·7N 11°46′·9E

RIVA DI TRAIANO

1518·5 Outer mole head
Fl.G.5s10m6M
• 42°03′·9N 11°48′·6E

1518·7
Fl.R.5s8m5M
• 42°04′·0N 11°48′·7E

FIUMICINO

1524 N mole
Fl.R.3s10m7M
• 41°46′·3N 12°13′·1E

1526 S mole root
Fl.3s20m11M
• 41°46′·2N 12°13′·3E

1526·3 Head
Fl.G.3s10m8M
• 41°46′·20N 12°12′·93E

1528·3 Fiumaru Grande Entrance S Side
Fl.G.5s5m5M
• 41°44′·38N 12°14′·02E

1528·4 River Tevere
DirQ.WRG.1s8m5M
061·5°-G-066·5°-W-071·5°-R-076·5°
• 41°44′·7N 12°15′·0E

1530 Lido di Ostia
Fl.G.4s10m8M
• 41°44′·2N 12°14′·8E

1531
Fl.R.4s10m8M
• 41°44′·2N 12°14′·7E

1538 Capo d'Anzio
Fl(2)10s37m22M
255°-vis-155°
Reserve light range 18M
• 41°26′·7N 12°37′·3E

PORT D'ANZIO

1540·5 Anzio Molo Innocenziano, Head
Fl.R.3s10m5M
• 41°26'·61N 12°38'·28E

NETTUNO

1541·2 Outer mole head
Fl.G.5s11m7M
• 41°27'·1N 12°39'·6E

1541·3 Inner mole head
Fl.R.5s11m7M
• 41°27'·1N 12°39'·6E

1541·7 Rio Martino Entrance mole head
F.R.6m5M
• 41°22'·1N 12°55'·2E

1541·72
F.G.6m5M
• 41°22'·1N 12°55'·2E

1542 Capo Circeo
Fl.5s38m23M
263°-vis-107°
Reserve light range 18M
• 41°13'·3N 13°04'·1E

TERRACINA

1550 Molo Gregoriano head
Fl.R.5s12m9M Safety distance 50m
• 41°16'·9N 13°15'·6E

1551 New harbour outer mole head
Fl.G.5s8m6M Safety distance 25m
• 41°17'·0N 13°15'·5E

GAETA

1558 Monte Orlando
Fl(3)15s185m23M
Reserve light range 18M
• 41°12'·4N 13°34'·7E

1560 Punta dello Stendardo
Fl(2)R.10s20m7M
• 41°12'·6N 13°35'·4E

1562 Molo Sant' Antonio head
Fl.R.3s10m6M
• 41°13'·0N 13°34'·7E

1564 Porto Salvo mole head
Fl.G.3s8m7M
• 41°13'·2N 13°34'·4E

1568 Porto Commerciale. Banchina Salva d'Aquisto head
Fl(2)G.10s10m7M Safety distance 30m
• 41°13'·9N 13°34'·4E

FORMIA

1572 Porto Nuovo inner mole head
Fl.G.3s9m7M
• 41°15'·2N 13°36'·8E

1573 Breakwater head
Fl.WR.3s11m11/8M
252°-W-072°-R-252°
• 41°15'·2N 13°36'·9E

1575·5 Coppola Pinetamare Marina Outer Breakwater Head
Fl.R.5s6M
• 40°58'·44N 15°58'·41E

Marks Harbour Entrance
Fl.Y

1575·8 S Breakwater Head
Fl.G.5s6M
• 40°58'·28N 13°58'·46E

ISOLA PIANOSA

1576 Punta Varo
LFl.8s41m8M
270°-vis-044°
• 40°57'·9N 13°03'·0E

ISOLE PONTINE

1577 Isola di Zannone Capo Negro
Fl(3)10s37m12M
060°-vis-°280°
• 40°58'·3N 13°03'·4E

1580 Isola di Ponza La Rotonda della Madonna
Fl(4)15s61m15M
206°-vis-023°, 070°-vis-080° when more than 1M distant but is obscured by Isola di Zannone through an arc of about 7° Reserve light range 11M
F.R.55m9M 301°-vis-341° over Secche Le Formiche
• 40°53'·7N 12°58'·2E

1582 Scoglio Ravia
Fl.G.3s26m6M
• 40°54'·0N 12°57'·9E

1583 Porto Ponza shelter mole head
Fl.R.3s8m8M
• 40°53'·7N 12°57'·9E

1584 Mole head
Fl.Y.3s12m9M
• 40°53'·7N 12°57'·9E

1588 Punta della Guardia Faraglione della Guardia
Fl(3)30s112m24M
225°-vis-155° obscured by Isola di Palmorola 118°-136°
Reserve light range 10M
Fl.R.5s96m8M 235°-vis-265° over Secche Le Formiche
• 40°52'·6N 12°57'·2E

1592 Isola di Ventotene
Fl.5s21m15M
158°-vis-022° obscd 288°-307° by Isola di S Stafano 025°-vis-030° from an elevation of 9m and at a distance of 1M. Reserve light range 11M
• 40°47'·7N 13°26'·1E

1594 Cala Rossano outer mole
Fl.R.5s8m5M
• 40°48'·1N 13°26'·0E

1595 Inner breakwater
Fl.G.5s6m4M
• 40°48'·1N 13°25'·9E

ISOLA D'ISCHIA

1598 Punta Imperatore
Fl(2)15s164m22M
316°-vis-190° Reserve light range 18M
• 40°42'·6N 13°51'·2E

1608 Porto d'Ischia mole head
Fl.WR.3s13m15/12M
127°-R-197°-W-127° Red sector covering the rubble breakwater to NW
Reserve light ranges W 11M, R 9M
• 40°44'·8N 13°56'·6E

1610 Entrance W side
Fl.G.3s4m8M
• 40°44'·7N 13°56'·5E

1612 E side
Fl.R.3s4m8M
196°-vis-217°
• 40°44'·7N 13°56'·5E

1614 Castello d'Ischia
LFl.6s82m16M
119°-vis-001° Reserve light 12M
• 40°43'·9N 13°58'·0E

1614·3 Secche di Vivara
Q(9)15s5m5M
• 40°44'·7N 13°58'·7E

ISOLA DI PROCIDA

1616 Procida Molo di Ponente head
Fl.G.3s10m8M
• 40°46'·2N 14°01'·7E

1617 Molo di Suttoflutto head
Fl.R.3s10m8M
• 40°46'·1N 14°01'·7E

1618 Punta Pioppeto N head
Fl(3)10s21m11M 076°-vis-287°
• 40°46'·2N 14°01'·1E

1619 Secca del Torrione S head
Q(6)+LFl.15s5m5M
• 40°46'·5N 14°02'·6E

1620 Capo Miseno
Fl(2)10s80m16M 199°-vis-112°
Reserve light range 12M
• 40°46'·7N 14°05'·4E

1622 Baia. Fortino Tenaglia
Iso.R.4s13m8M
• 40°48'·7N 14°05'·0E

BAGNOLI

1628·4 Nisida Molo Dandolo spur head
Fl.G.3s14m7M
• 40°48'·0N 14°09'·9E

1628·7 Secca della Cavallara
Q(6)+LFl.15s5m5M
• 40°47'·1N 14°11'·4E

PORTO SANNAZZARO

1629 Mole head
Fl.R.5s9m8M
• 40°49'·5N 14°35'·5E

1629·4 Inner mole head
Fl.G.5s8m7M
• 40°49'·6N 14°13'·5E

PORTICCIOLO DI SANTA LUCIA

1632 W side mole head
Fl.R.3s9m5M
• 40°49'·7N 14°15'·0E

MOLOSIGLIO

1636 Breakwater head
Fl.R.5s10m8M
• 40°50'·0N 14°15'·3E

PORTO DI NAPOLI

1646 Molo San Vincenzo head
Fl(3)15s25m22M
Inside the port 102°-obscd-233°
• 40°49'·9N 14°16'·3E

1648 Antemurale Thaon de Revel SW end
Fl.G.4s18m9M
• 40°50'·0N 14°16'·6E

1651 E entrance
Fl.G.2s6m7M
• 40°49'·3N 14°18'·4E

1651·2
Fl.G.3s6m7M
• 40°49'·6N 14°18'·2E

1651·4
Fl.R.3s6m5M
• 40°49'·5N 14°18'·0E

1651·5
Fl.R.2s6m5M
• 40°49'·3N 14°18'·0E

1652 Diga Foranea. Emanuele Filiberto Duca d'Aosta E end
Fl.R.4s12m5M Safety distance 20m
• 40°49'·5N 14°18'·0E

1654 W end
Fl.RG.4s
• 40°50'·2N 14°16'·8E

1669 Nuova di Levante SE corner
Fl.G.3s10m8M
• 40°49'·9N 14°17'·9E

PORTO PORTICI

1678 Quay head
Fl.3s16m11M
• 40°48'·6N 14°20'·0E

1680 Porto di Torre del Greco, Outer Mole Head
Fl.R.5s12m9M
• 40°47'·04N 14°21'·69E

TORRE ANNUNZIATA

1684 Molo di Ponente head
Fl(2)R.6s13m4M Safety distance 50m
• 40°44'·6N 14°27'·0E

1685 Molo di Levante
Fl(2)G.6s4m5M
• 40°45′·0N 14°26′·9E
1691 S Harbour Entrance
Fl(3)R.5s12m6M
• 40°42′·94N 14°28′·41E

CASTELLAMMARE DI STABIA
1692 Main light
Fl(2)10s114m16M 095°-vis-223°
Reserve light range 12M
• 40°41′·3N 14°28′·2E
1693 Molo Foraneo head
Fl.G.5s12m8M Safety distance 50m
• 40°41′·9N 14°28′·4E
1695·6 Marina di Mita inner mole head
Fl.G.3s8m5M
• 40°38′·7N 14°24′·5E

SORRENTO
1698 Mole head
Fl.G.3s9m5M
• 40°37′·8N 14°22′·6E
1700 Scoglio Vervece
Fl(2)6s15m7M
• 40°37′·1N 14°19′·4E
1701 Marina della Lobra mole head
2F.G(vert)9m5M
• 40°36′·6N 14°20′·1E
1702 Punta Campanella
Fl.5s65m10M
270°-vis-166°, 066°-obscd-089° by Isola di Capri
• 40°34′·1N 14°19′·5E

ISOLA DI CAPRI
1706 Punta Carena
Fl.3s73m25M
265°-vis-175° Reserve light range 18M
• 40°32′·1N 14°11′·9E
1708 Capo Tiberio (Lo Capo). Scoglio la Longa di Mezzogiorno
Fl(2)10s12m7M
110°-vis-335°
• 40°33′·6N 14°15′·8E
1710 Marina Grande main mole head
Fl.G.3s11m8M
• 40°33′·5N 14°14′·6E
1711 Outer mole head
Fl.R.3s9m8M Safety distance 50m
• 40°33′·5N 14°14′·6E
1716 Isolotti li Galli. Isolotto Gallo Lungo N end
Fl.5s67m6M
• 40°35′·0N 14°26′·1E

PORTO DI AMALFI
1718 Mole head
Fl.R.5s13m8M
• 40°37′·8N 14°36′·0E
1722 Capo d'Orso
Fl(3)15s66m16M
263°-vis-093°
Reserve light range 12M
• 40°38′·0N 14°40′·9E

PORTO DI SALERNO
1729·1 Centara outer mole head
Fl.R.3s8m6M
• 40°38′·65N 14°42′·22E
1730 Molo Faraneo elbow
Fl.3s13m11M
• 40°40′·38N 14°45′·37E
1730·2 Molo di Levante
Fl.G.5s13m9M Safety distance 50m
Racon
• 40°39′·88N 14°44′·69E
1730·4 Molo de Ponente
Fl.R.5s13m8M Safety distance 25m
• 40°40′·0N 14°44′·8E

AGROPOLI
1735 Punta Fortino
Fl(2)6s42m16M
• 40°21′·3N 14°59′·2E
1738 Isolotto Licosa near Punta Licosa
Fl(2)10s13m11M
• 40°15′·0N 14°54′·0E

ACCIAROLI
1739 Outer mole head
Fl.R.3s8m4M
• 40°10′·5N 15°01′·6E

MARINA DI CASALVELINO
1739·7 Outer mole head
Fl.G.3s8m5M
• 40°10′·5N 15°06′·5E
1739·8 Inner mole head outer arm
Fl.R.3s8m5M
• 40°10′·5N 15°06′·5E
1740 Capo Palinuro
Fl(3)15s206m25M
286°-vis-132°
Reserve light 18M
• 40°01′·4N 15°16′·5E
1740·2 Outer mole head
Fl.G.5s10m9M
• 40°01′·8N 15°16′·7E
1742 Scario on beach S of village
Fl(4)12s24m15M
Obscured when bearing more than 025°
Reserve light range 12M
• 40°02′·9N 15°29′·5E
1745 Policastro outer mole
Fl.R.3s7m5M
• 40°04′·1N 15°31′·5E
1745·2 Inner mole
Fl.G.3s7m5M
• 40°04′·1N 15°31′·5E
1746 Sapri. Punta del Fortino
Fl(2)7s13m7M 223°-vis-083°
• 40°04′·2N 15°37′·2E
1747 Maratea N breakwater head
Fl.R.3s8m6M Safety distance 30m
• 39°59′·2N 15°42′·6E
1747·2 S breakwater head
Fl.G.3s8m6M Safety distance 30m
• 39°59′·2N 15°42′·6E
1750 Capo di Bonifati
Fl(2)10s63m15M
Reserve light range 11M
• 39°32′·6N 15°53′·0E
1750·5 Cetraro
Fl.R.4s10m6M
• 39°31′·4N 15°55′·2E
1752 Paola
Fl(3)15s53m15M
315°-vis-160°
Reserve light range 11M
• 39°21′·7N 16°02′·0E
1754·1 Amantea Marina outer breakwater head
Fl.R.3s6m6M
• 39°03′·2N 16°05′·5E
1754·3 Inner breakwater head
Fl.G.3s6m6M
• 39°03′·3N 16°05′·5E
1756 Capo Suvero
Fl(2)10s58m16M 280°-vis-155°
Reserve light range 12M
• 38°57′·1N 16°09′·5E

VIBO VALENTIA MARINA
1757 N mole head. Calata Buccarelli head
Fl.WG.5s17m15/12M Reserve light W10M, G8M
068°-W-230°-G-068°
• 38°43′·4N 16°07′·7E
1758 Molo Cortese head
Fl.R.5s7m7M
• 38°43′·3N 16°07′·7E
1762 Capo Vaticano
Fl(4)20s108m24M
Obscured in Golfo di Sant'Eufemia when bearing more than 205°, partially obscured 208°-215°.
Reserve light range 18M
• 38°37′·1N 15°49′·7E
1763 Gioia Tauro N mole head
Fl.R.4s14m8M
• 38°26′·7N 15°53′·5E
1763·2 S mole head
Fl.G.4s14m8M
• 38°26′·5N 15°53′·4E
1763·35 Dir Lt 103°
DirWRG.22m6M
PEL. 098°-Fl.G-099°-F.G-100·25°-AlWG-102·25°-F-103·5°-AlWR-105·75°-F.R-107°-F.R-108°
• 38°26′·50N 15°54′·38E
1763·7 Bagnara Calabra outer mole head
Fl.G.3s14m5M
• 38°17′·9N 15°49′·0E
1763·8 Inner mole head
Fl.R.3s10m5M
• 38°17′·9N 15°49′·0E
1766 Scilla. On castle
Fl.5s72m22M Reserve light 18M
• 38°15′·4N 15°42′·9E
1770 Punta Pezzo
Fl(3)R.15s26m15M
010°-vis-246°
Reserve light range 13M
• 38°13′·8N 15°38′·2E

VILLA SAN GIOVANNI
1772 Molo di Ponente head
Fl.G.3s14m7M
• 38°13′·1N 15°37′·8E
1773 Molo Sottoflutto head
Fl.R.3s7m6M
• 38°13′·1N 15°38′·0E

REGGIO CALABRIA
1776 Molo di Ponente head
Iso.G.2s14m7M
• 38°07′·7N 15°39′·0E
1777 Molo Sottoflutto head
Iso.R.2s11m6M
• 38°07′·6N 15°39′·1E
1780 Capo dell'Armi
Fl(2)10s95m22M
295°-vis-148°
Reserve light range 18M
• 37°57′·2N 15°40′·8E
1782 Capo Spartivento
Fl.8s63m24M
222°-vis-082°
Reserve light range 18M
• 37°55′·5N 16°03′·7E

Mediterranean – Isole Eolie
1784 Isola Alicudi ferry jetty head
Fl.3s11m10M
• 38°32′·1N 14°21′·7E
1785 Isola Filicudi Scoglio Montenassari
Fl(5)15s20m12M
317°-vis-090°, 095°-vis-255°
• 38°35′·0N 14°31′·7E
1786 Isola Vulcano Punta dei Porci
Fl(4)20s35m16M
251°-vis-093° Reserve light 12M
• 38°22′·1N 14°59′·5E

ISOLA LIPARI
1788 Moletto di Pignataro head
Fl.G.3s11m8M
• 38°28′·7N 14°57′·8E
1792 Marina Corta
Fl(3)15s11m15M
• 38°27′·9N 14°57′·5E
1792·7 Canneto ferry berth
F.G.6m7M
• 38°29′·5N 14°57′·8E

ISOLA SALINA
1796 Punta Lingua
Fl.3s13m11M 186°-vis-076°
• 38°32′·3N 14°52′·3E
1798 Capo Faro
LFl.6s56m18M
137°-vis-357°but only a faint light is perceptible 123°-137°
Reserve light range 11M
• 38°34′·9N 14°52′·3E
1800 Isola Panaria Punta Peppemaria
Fl.WR.5s15m10/8M
319°-R over Scoglio le Formiche-343°-W-319°
• 38°38′·2N 15°04′·7E
1802 Isola Stromboli Scoglio Strombolicchio summit
Fl(3)15s57m11M
• 38°49′·0N 15°15′·2E

Mediterranean – Sicilia

1806 Capo Peloro
Fl(2)G.10s37m19M
112·5°-vis-069°
Reserve light range 13M. Racon
Iso.R.5s22m9M
shore-vis-127° over Secche di Capa Rasocolmo
• 38°16′·1N 15°39′·1E

PORTO DE MESSINA
1814 Punta san Raineri
Fl(3)15s41m22M
Reserve light range 17M
Lts indicate the cable area in the Straits of Messina
• 38°11′·6N 15°34′·5E
1816 Punta Secca
Oc.Y.3s13m10M
097°-vis-335°
• 38°11′·8N 15°34′·4E
1817 Entrance E side Punta san Salvatore
Fl(2)R.5s16m8M
340°-vis-250° The statue of the Madonna della Lettera, 53m high is illuminated
• 38°11′·8N 15°33′·8E
1818 W side port office
Fl(2)G.5s16m8M
• 38°11′·8N 15°33′·51E

GIARDINI-NAXOS
1821 Harbour mole
Fl.R.4s5m8M
• 37°49′·7N 15°16′·59E

PORTO DI RIPOSTO
1822 Molo sopraflutto elbow
LFl.5s15m11M
• 37°43′·68N 15°12′·66E
1823 Head
Fl.R.3s11m5M
• 37°43′·90N 15°12′·64E
1826 Capo Molini
Fl(3)15s42m22M
Reserve light range 18M
• 37°34′·6N 15°10′·6E

PORTO DI CATANIA
1828 Sciara Biscari
Fl.5s31m22M
Reserve light range 18M
• 37°29′·3N 15°05′·2E
1830 Molo di Levante head
LFl.G.5s12m8M
• 37°29′·1N 15°06′·0E
1831 Quay
Fl.G.2s11m5M
355°-vis-175°
• 37°29′·4N 15°06′·0E
1832 Molo di Mezzogiorno head
Fl.R.2s11m5M
• 37°29′·4N 15°05′·8E
1832·5 Breakwater head
LFl.R.5s7m5M
• 37°29′·3N 15°06′·2E
1836 Brucoli
Fl.5s13m11M
Obscured when bearing more than 230°
• 37°17′·1N 15°11′·4E
1838 Capo Sant Croce
LFl(2)12s39m16M
146°-vis-021°
Reserve light range 10M
• 37°14′·4N 15°15′·5E

RADA DI AUGUSTA
1846 Punta Gennalena Ldg Lts 273°51′
Front Iso.4s16m12M
247°-vis-299°
• 37°11′·9N 15°11′·1E
1846·1 Dromo Giggia
Rear 1·55M from front Oc.5s79m17M
245°-vis-301°
Reserve light range 13M
• 37°12′·0N 15°09′·2E
1847 Diga Settentrionale, off head
Fl(2)G.10s12m8M Racon
• 37°11′·8N 15°14′·0E
1848 Diga Centrale, off N head
Fl(2)R.10s14m8M
• 37°11′·6N 15°13′·9E
1860 Penisola Magnisi
Fl(4)12s10m11M
090°-vis-320°
• 37°09′·4N 15°14′·1E

PORTO DI SIRACUSA
1866 Castello Maniace
Fl.G.3s27m9M
188°-vis-330°
• 37°03′·1N 15°17′·7E
1867 Punta Castellucio
Fl.R.3s21m9M
• 37°02′·5N 15°18′·3E
1868 Caderini Ldg Lts 267°12′
Front Iso.R.2s12m17M
224°-vis-274°
Reserve light range 12M
• 37°02′·8N 15°16′·5E
1868·1 Carrozzier
Rear 0·54M from front Oc.5s25m17M
261°-vis-°272°
Reserve light range 10M
• 37°02′·7N 15°15′·8E
1876 Capo Murro di Porco
Fl.5s34m17M
160°-vis-090°
Reserve light range 10M
• 37°00′·0N 15°20′·1E

MARZAMEMI
1882 Cozzo Spadaro
Fl(3)15s82m24M Aeromarine
170°-vis-095° Reserve light range 18M
• 36°41′·1N 15°07′·9E
1884 Capo Passero
Fl(2)10s39m11M
151°-vis-063°
• 36°41′·3N 15°09′·1E

PORTO PALO
1884·5 Punta di Portopalo
LFl.WR.5s8m7/4M
205°-R-230°-W-205°
• 36°40′·0N 15°07′·8E
1886 Isola delle Correnti
Fl.4s16m11M
• 36°38′·7N 15°04′·7E
1888 Scogli Porri
Fl(2)6s7m7M
• 36°41′·1N 14°55′·9E

POZZALLO
1889 Porto Commerciale Farnea Mole E Head
Fl.R.3s11m5M
• 36°42′·55N 14°50′·45E
1889.05 Breakwater Elbow Head
Fl(4)12s18m15M
Reserve light range 11M
• 36°42′·62N 14°49′·83E
1894 Marina di Ragusa
Fl.R.5s12m8M
• 36°46′·9N 14°33′·1E
1896 Capo Scalambri (Scaramia)
Fl(2)8s37m16M
Reserve light range 12M
• 36°47′·2N 14°29′·6E

SCOGLITTI
1898 Scoglitti
Fl(3)10s15m11M
• 36°53′·5N 14°25′·7E
1898·2 Refuge harbour end of anti-silting breakwater
Fl.R.3s5M
• 36°53′·2N 14°25′·6E
1898·3 E Mole Head
Fl.G.3s5M
• 36°53′·2N 14°25′·6E

GELA
1902 Port of refuge. E Mole Head
Fl.G.3s5m8M Safety distance 25m
• 37°03′·7N 14°13′·8E
1902·2 W Mole Head
Fl.R.3s8m8M Safety distance 25m
• 37°03′·8N 14°13′·8E

PORTO DI LICATA
1904 Molo di Levante near root San Giacomo
Fl.5s40m21M
Obscured when bearing more than 095° Reserve light range 18M
• 37°05′·N 13°56′·5E
1905·5 Antemurale, Head
Fl.R.5s8M
• 37°05′·11N 13°56′·41E
1906 Inner Arm
Fl.R.3s9m4M
• 37°05′·3N 13°56′·3E
1908 Diga di Levante head
Fl.G.5s10m8M
• 37°05′·1N 13°56′·6E

PORTO EMPEDOCLE
1916 Molo di Ponente head
Fl.R.3s12m8M
• 37°16′·5N 13°31′·7E
1918 Molo di Levante head
Fl.G.3s9m8M
• 37°16′·8N 13°31′·7E
1922 Capo Rossello
Fl(2)10s95m22M Reserve light 18M
• 37°17′·6N 13°27′·0E

SCIACCA

1927 W mole 30m from head
LFl.R.6s9m8M Safety distance 40m
• 37°30'·1N 13°04'·6E

1928 E mole outer head
LFl.G.6s11m8M
• 37°30'·0N 13°04'·6E

1928·5 Capo San Marco
Fl(3)15s25m18M
• 37°29'·9N 13°01'·3E

PORTO PALO DI MENFI

1929 Outer mole head
Fl.R.4s8m5M
• 37°34'·4N 12°54'·6E

1929·3 Inner mole head
Fl.G.4s8m5M
• 37°34'·4N 12°54'·6E

1930 Capo Granitola
LFl.10s37m18M
Reserve light range 13M
• 37°33'·9N 12°39'·7E

MAZARA DEL VALLO

1932 Nuovo molo di Ponente head
Fl.R.4s13m5M
• 37°38'·5N 12°35'·1E

1933 Diga Antemurale head
Fl.G.4s13m8M
• 37°38'·7N 12°35'·0E

1938 Capo Feto
LFl.10s14m11M
• 37°39'·6N 12°31'·3E

MARSALA

1940 Molo di Ponente head
Fl(2)10s19m15M
Reserve light range 12M
• 37°47'·2N 12°26'·3E

1942 Diga Foranea head
Fl.R.3s11m8M
• 37°46'·9N 12°26'·2E

1944 Molo di Levante head
Fl.G.3s9m8M
• 37°47'·2N 12°26'·4E

1947·5 Punta Scario NW
Q(9)15s5m5M
• 37°54'·2N 12°24'·5E

ISOLA FAVIGNANA

1948 Punta Marsala
Fl(4)15s20m15M
202°-vis-095°
Reserve light range 11M
• 37°54'·3N 12°22'·0E

1949 Porto di Favignana molo foraneo
Fl.R.4s7m7M
• 37°55'·9N 12°19'·6E

1952 Punta Sottile
Fl.8s43m25M Aeromarine
Reserve light range 18M
316°-vis-237°
• 37°56'·0N 12°16'·5E

ISOLA MARETTIMO

1956 Punta Libeccio
Fl(2)15s73m24M
Reserve light range 15M
298°-vis-151°
• 37°57'·3N 12°03'·1E

1962 Isola Levanzo Capo Grosso
Fl(3)15s68m11M
032°-vis-331°
Reserve light range 10M
• 38°01'·2N 12°20'·0E

1966 Isolotto Formica
Fl.4s28m11M
• 37°59'·3N 12°25'·6E

1968 Scoglio Porcelli
Fl(2)10s23m11M
• 38°02'·6N 12°26'·3E

PORTO DI TRAPANI

1970 Scoglio Palumbo
Fl.5s16m15M
Iso.R.2s9m8M
Reserve light range 12M
131°-vis-176° over Secche La Balata and Balatella
• 38°00'·7N 12°29'·4E

1977 Canal entrance outer breakwater head
Fl.R.3s7m8M
• 38°00'·3N 12°29'·8E

1977·5 Inner breakwater head
Fl.G.3s7m8M
• 38°00'·3N 12°30'·0E

1978 Molo del Ronciglio head
Fl.G.10m3M Safety distance 25m
• 38°00'·6N 12°30'·4E

1982 Scoglio Asinelli
Fl(2)6s13m7M
• 38°03'·9N 12°31'·8E

1986 Capo San Vito
Fl.5s45m25M
036°-vis-000° Reserve light range 18M
Iso.R.4s12m8M
165°-vis-225° over rocky shoal N of cape
• 38°11'·2N 12°43'·9E

SAN VITO LO CAPO

1987 Fish harbour Outer Mole head
Fl.G.5s7m5M
• 38°10'·9N 12°44'·1E

1990 Punta Solanto
Fl.WR.3s25m10/8M
122°-R-144°-W-122°
• 38°10'·5N 12°46'·2E

CASTELLAMMARE DEL GOLFO

1992 Castello Normanno
Fl(2)10s19m10M
093°-vis-263°
• 38°01'·7N 12°52'·9E

1993·3 Balestrate outer mole head
Fl.G.3s8m6M
• 38°03'·63N 13°00'·25E

TERRASINI

1994 Punta Raisi
Aero AlFl.WG.35M
• 38°11'·4N 13°06'·5E

ISOLA D'USTICA

1996 Punta Omo Morto
Fl(3)15s100m25M
087°-vis-356° Reserve 18M
Oc.R.5s95m9M
135°-vis-145° over Secca Colombara
• 38°42'·7N 13°11'·9E

2000 Punta Gavazzi
Fl(4)12s40m16M
297°-vis-194°
Reserve light range 12M
• 38°41'·6N 13°09'·3E

2004 Capo Gallo
LFl(2)15s40m16M
077-vis-297°
Reserve light range 13M
• 38°13'·4N 13°19'·0E

PORTO DI PALERMO

2008 N mole Diga Foranea elbow
Fl(4)15s15m15M Racon
• 38°07'·6N 13°22'·5E

2013 Diga foranea head
LFl.G.5s5M
• 38°07'·34N 13°22'·78E

2014 Molo C T Bersagliere head
LFl.R.5s9m8M Safety distance 35m
• 38°07'·5N 13°22'·4E

2023 Capo Zafferano
Fl(3)WR.10s34m16/12M
105°-W-298°-R-over Scoglio Formica-344°-W-355° Reserve light range W12M, R9M
• 38°06'·7N 13°32'·3E

PORTICELLO SAN FLAVIA

2025 Molo foraneo
Fl.G.3s6m5M
• 38°05'·1N 13°32'·6E

TERMINI IMERESE

2030 Molo di Sottoflutto
Fl.R.3s7m5M
• 37°59'·1N 34°42'·7E

2035 Pontile ENEL head
Q.R.20m5M
• 37°59'·2N 13°45'·2E

2036 Cap Cefalù
Fl.5s80m25M Reserve light 18M
• 38°02'·2N 14°01'·7E

2037 Cefalù outer mole head
Fl.G.4s10m5M
• 38°02'·2N 14°02'·5E

2038 Capo d'Orlando
LFl(2)12s27m16M
Reserve light range 12M
• 38°09'·8N 14°44'·9E

2038·1 Porticciolo di Cap D'Orlando
Fl.5s5M
• 38°09'·5N 14°46'·4E

2040 Portorosa Marina outer mole head
Fl.G.4s11m5M
• 38°07'·6N 15°06'·7E

2040·2 Inner mole head
Fl.R.4s11m5M
• 38°07'·6N 15°06'·7E

2042 Capo Milazzo N head
LFl.6s90m16M
Reserve light range 12M
• 38°16'·2N 15°13'·89E

PORTO DI MILAZZO

2044 Molo Poraneo head
LFl.G.5s12m7M
• 38°12'·9N 15°15'·0E

2044·2 Molo Sottoflutto head
LFl.R.5s12m6M Safety distance 30m
• 38°12'·92N 15°14'·84E

2045 85m off Pontile di ponente pier No.1
2F.G(vert)16m5M
• 38°12'·7N 15°15'·8E

2045·2 190m off Pontile di levante pier No.2
F.GR(vert)10m5M
• 38°12'·8N 15°16'·2E

2045·3 Pier No.3 head
2F.R(vert)12m5M
• 38°12'·70N 15°16'·49E

2046 Capo Rasocolmo
Fl(3)10s85m15M
255°-obscd-shore over Secca Rasocolmo. Reserve light range 9M
• 38°17'·7N 15°31'·2E

Malta and Adjacent Islands

GHAWDEX (GOZO)

2050 Gordan Hill summit
Fl.7·5s180m20M
• 36°04'·40N 14°13'·11E

VALLETTA HARBOURS

2061·5 Grand harbour St Elmo
Fl(3)15s34m19M
• 35°54'·13N 14°31'·16E

2062 St Elmo breakwater head
Q.G.16m7M
• 35°54'·15N 14°31'·53E
2064 Ricasoli breakwater head
Q.R.11m6M 120°-obscd157° when firing or searchlight practices are taking place.
• 35°53'·95N 14°31'·38E
2068 Luqa Aero Beacon
Aero Mo(LU)G.9s104m25M
170°-vis-345°
• 35°51'·26N 14°28'·07E
2070 Marsaxlokk Ponta ta'Delimara
Fl(2)12s35m15M
• 35°49'·30N 14°33'·53E
2070·4 Inner breakwater arm
Q.R.9m8M
• 35°49'·23N 14°32'·8E
2070·6 Breakwater head
Fl.R.3s18m6M
260°-vis-042°
• 35°49'·08N 14°32'·97E
2070·7 Container Terminal No2 NE corner
LFl.R.10s9m8M
• 35°49'·38N 14°32'·60E
2070·75
VQ.R.9m6M
• 35°49'·32N 14°32'·41E

ISOLA DI LINOSA
2080 Punta Arena Bianca
Fl.5s9m9M
276·5°-vis-150°
• 35°51'·2N 12°51'·5E
2082 Punta Beppe Tuccio
Fl(4)20s32m16M
107°-vis-345° this arc varies with distance from light, at 6M
103°-vis-346° Reserve light range 12M
• 35°52'·3N 12°52'·7E
2084 Isolotto Lampione
Fl(2)10s40m7M
• 35°32'·9N 12°19'·2E

ISOLA DI LAMPEDUSA
2086 Capo Ponente
Fl(3)15s110m8M
290°-vis-222°
• 35°31'·2N 12°31'·1E
2088 Capo Grecale
Fl.5s82m22M
112°-vis-075° Reserve light range 18M
• 35°31'·0N 12°37'·9E
2089 Porto de Lampedusa Punta Maccaferri
Fl.G.3s17m8M
• 35°29'·7N 12°36'·2E
2090 Punta Guitgia
Fl.R.3s14m8M
• 35°29'·7N 12°36'·0E
2091 Punta Favaloro breakwater head
Fl.R.5s7m7M Safety distance 15M
• 35°29'·8N 12°36'·2E

ISOLA DI PANTELLERIA
2094 Punta Spadillo
Fl(2)10s50m24M Reserve light 18M
• 36°49'·4N 12°00'·8E
2096 Scauri
Fl.5s18m10M
• 36°46'·1N 11°57'·5E
2098 Punta san Leonardo
Fl.3s21m15M Reserve light range 8M
• 36°50'·1N 11°56'·6E
2098·2 W end
Fl.Y.2s8m5M
• 36°50'·7N 11°56'·72E
2100 Molo Cidonio Dir Lt 232°
DirIso.WRG.2s8m7M 213·5°-G-228·5°W-235·5°-R-258·5°
• 36°49'·95N 11°56'·22E
2106 Punta Limarsi
Fl(3)15s35m7M
• 36°44'·2N 12°02'·0E
2107 Punta Trácino (Tracia)
Fl(2)10s49m10M
• 36°47'·8N 12°03'·0E

Ionian Sea – Italy

2108 Punta Stilo
Fl(3)15s54m22M
Reserve light range 18M
• 38°26'·8N 16°34'·7E
2108·5 Roccella Ionica outer mole head
Fl.G.3s11m5M
• 38°19'·40N 16°25'·95E
2108·6 Inner mole head
Fl.R.3s11m5M
• 38°19'·50N 16°24'·94E
2112 Capo Rizzuto
LFl(2)WR.10s37m17/13M
227°-R- over Secche de Capo Rizzuto-270°-W-084°-R over Secca di Le Castella-133°
Reserve light range W11M, R8M
• 38°53'·8N 17°05'·6E
2118 Capo Colonne
Fl.5s40m24M
127°-vis-020° Reserve light range 18M
• 39°01'·5N 17°12'·3E

PORTO DI CROTONE
2120 Porto Nuovo Molo Foraneo head
Fl.R.5s11m8M Safety distance 100m
• 39°05'·7N 17°07'·6E
2121 Nuovo Molo Sottoflutto head
Fl.G.5s13m8M
• 39°05'·5N 17°07'·6E
2122 Bacino Sud Molo Vecchio
Fl(2)G.5s11m8M Safety distance 60M
• 39°04'·6N 17°08'·2E
2123 Moletto Sanitá head
Fl(2)R.5s9m8M
• 39°04'·7N 17°08'·1E
2126 Ciro Marina Molo Foraneo head
Fl.R.3s6m5M
Lights are located on spar jetties within harbour
• 39°22'·4N 17°08'·3E
2128 Punta Alice
Fl(2)10s31m16M
Reserve light range 12M
• 39°23'·9N 17°09'·2E
2130·5 Laghi di Sibari marina
Fl(4)20s23m12M
• 39°43'·8N 16°30'·4E
2131 Approach channel
F.R.6m6M
• 36°44'·1N 16°30'·6E
2132 Capo san Vito
Fl(3)15s46m22M
Reserve light range 18M
• 40°24'·7N 17°12'·2E

TARANTO
2133 Mar Grande approach
Q(9)15s8m5M
• 40°25'·3N 17°10'·5E
2134 Diga di San Vito head
Fl(2)G.7s22m9M Racon
• 40°25'·7N 17°11'·7E
2138 Isolotto San Paolo breakwater head
Fl(2)R.7s12m7M Safety distance 50m
• 40°26'·2N 17°10'·8E
2142·3 Secca della Sirena S side
Q(6)+LFl.15s5m5M
• 40°27'·6N 17°12'·5E
2142·4 W side Inner industrial harbour approach channel
Q.R.6m6M
• 40°27'·7N 17°12'·6E
2142·5 E side
Q.G.6m7M
• 40°27'·6N 17°12'·9E
2144 W mole head
F.R.8m3M
• 40°26'·7N 17°14'·8E
2144.4 Industrial harbour jetty No. 2 head SE corner
F.RG(vert)10m5M
40°28'·4N 17°13'·0E
2144.42 SW corner
F.GR(vert)10m5M
• 40°28'·4N 17°13'·0E
2144·47/2144·48 No. 4 Quay Ldg Lts 341°
Front Q.R.20m6M (occas)
Rear 700m from front Oc.3s42m20M (occas)
• 40°28'·7N 17°12'·3E
2144·5 E detached breakwater E head
Fl.R.5s12m6M
• 40°28'·2N 17°13'·2E
2146 Porto Mercantile mole head
Fl.G.5s12m8M
• 40°28'·5N 17°13'·4E
2150 Canale Navigabile Ldg Lts 193° Secca della Tarantolla head
Front Fl.WG.3s.12m9/7M
057°-G-187·5°-W-198·5°-G-025°
• 40°26'·8N 17°37'·7E
2150·1 Casa Gigante
Rear 1·53M from front Iso.3s21m14M
189·6°-vis-196·4° Reserve light 10M
• 40°25'·4N 17°13'·2E
2152/2152·1 Ldg Lts 013°
Front Q.R.12m6M
009·3°-intens-016·8°
• 40°29'·3N 17°14'·4E
Rear 0·5M from front Fl.3s20m8M
007·5°-vis-018·5°
• 40°29'·8N 17°14'·6E
2153 W side S end Castel San Angelo
2F.R.8m4M Fl.Y occas 4m below the F.R
• 40°28'·3N 17°14'·1E
2153·6 N end
F.R.8m4M Fl.Y occas 4m below the F.R
• 40°28'·5N 17°14'·3E
2154 E side. S end
2F.G.8m6M
• 40°28'·3N 17°14'·1E
2154·6 N end
F.G.8m4M
• 40°28'·5N 17°14'·1E
2159 Buffoluto jetty head
2F.R(vert)7m6M
• 40°29'·1N 17°16'·7E
2160 Outer Industrial Harbour approach
Q(6)+LFl.15s6M
• 40°26'·2N 17°08'·0E
2160·2/2160·4/2160·6
Q(9)15s6M
• 40°27'·2N 17°06'·5E–40°28'·9N 17°06'·6E
2162 Diga Frangiflutti N head
Fl.G.5s14m8M
• 40°29'·5N 17°08'·3E
2162·4 Diga Sottoflutto head
Fl.R.5s14m8M
• 40°29'·7 17°08'·7E

PORTO CESAREO

2164/2164·1 Ldg Lts 034°
Front Iso.2s13m7M
350°-vis-068°
Rear 765m from front
Oc.3s26m10M
• 40°15′·9N 17°54′·2E

GALLIPOLI

2168 Isola Sant'Andrea SW end
Fl(2)10s45m19M
• 40°02′·8N 17°56′·7E

2170 Secca del Rafo
Q.5m5M
• 40°03′·79N 17°58′·60E

2172 Porto Commerciale. Molo di Tramontana head
Fl.G.5s11m9M Safety distance 70m
• 40°03′·6N 17°58′·8E

2172·2 Inner mole head
Fl.R.5s11m9M
• 40°03′·4N 17°58′·9E

2173 Seno del Canneto W breakwater head
F.R.6m3M
• 40°03′·2N 17°58′·8E

2173·2 E mole head
F.G.8m3M
• 40°03′·2N 17°58′·8E

2174 Ugento Torre San Giovanni
Iso.WR.4s.24m15/11M
311°-R over Secche di Ugento-013°-W-120°
Reserve light range W11M, R9M
• 39°53′·1N 18°06′·8E

2174·25 La Terra Rocks
Fl(2)6s7m5M
• 39°53′·0N 18°07′·1E

2174·4 Secce di Ugento
Q(9)15s6m5M
• 39°49′·8N 18°08′·2E

2176 Capo Santa Maria di Leuca
Fl(3)15s102m24M Aeromarine
Shore-obscd-220°
Reserve light range 10M
• 39°47′·7N 18°22′·1E

SANTA MARIA DI LEUCA

2176·5 Harbour mole head
Fl.G.5s9m7M
• 39°47′·7N 18°21′·7E

2176·6 Spur
Fl(2)G.5s8m6M
• 39°47′·87N 18°21′·7E

2176·7 Inner mole head
Fl(2)R.5s8m6M
• 39°47′·8N 18°21′·7E

Adriatic Sea – Italy

2178 Capo d'Otranto
Fl.5s60m18M
Reserve Lt 11M
• 40°06′·4N 18°31′·2E

PORTO DI OTRANTO

2182 La Punta
Fl(3)WR.10s12m13/8M
165°-R over Secca di Misspezza-183°-W-165° Reserve Lt W11M, R7M
• 40°09′·2N 18°29′·5E

2186 S Nicola Mole head
Fl.R.3s11m8M
• 40°08′·9N 18°29′·6E

2188 Torre Sant'Andrea
Fl(2)WR.7s24m15/12M
300°-R over Secca di Misspezza-343°-W-300°
Reserve light range W11M R8M
• 40°15′·3N 18°26′·7E

2192 Punta San Cataldo di Lecce
LFl.5s25m16M
140°-vis-315°
Reserve light range 12M
• 40°23′·4N 18°18′·4E

2193 Power Station
Q.Y.8m5M Marks water outfall
• 40°33′·9N 18°03′·4W

2194 Capo de Torre Cavallo
Q(3)10s5m5M
• 40°39′·8N 18°02′·3E

PORTO DI BRINDISI

2196 Le Pedagne
Fl(2)R.6s21m8M
349°-vis-252°
• 40°39′·4N 17°59′·4E

2198 Diga di Punta Riso head
Fl(2)G.10s12m5M
• 40°39′·7N 17°59′·8E

2202 Castello a Mare
Fl(4)20s28m21M Reserve light
Fl(4)20s18M
• 40°39′·3N 17°58′·1E

2203 Molo Montecatini Edison head
2F.R(vert)11m5M
• 40°38′·9N 17°58′·9E

2204 Diga di Forte a Mare head
Fl.G.3s11m8M
• 40°39′·1N 17°58′·1E

2208 Brindisi-Casale
Aero AlFl.WGW.17s18m24-18M
• 40°39′·1N 17°56′·6E

2210 Canale Pigonati NE end W side
Iso.G.2s9m5M
• 40°38′·7N 17°57′·1E

2212 E side
Iso.R.2s9m5M
• 40°38′·7N 17°57′·2E

2214 SW end W side
F.G.10m4M
227°-vis-070°
• 40°38′·6N 17°57′·0E

2216 E side
F.R.10m4M
018°-vis-227° F.R.2M on two moles at Marina Militare
• 40°38′·9N 17°57′·1E

2222 Punta Torre Canne
Fl(2)10s35m16M
Reserve light range 12M
• 40°50′·4N 17°28′·1E

MONOPOLI

2224 Molo Margherita head
Fl.R.3s15m8M
• 40°57′·3N 17°18′·3E

2226 N breakwater head
Fl.G.3s14m8M
• 40°57′·4N 17°18′·4E

MOLA DI BARI

2228 N mole head
Fl.G.3s14m7M
• 41°03′·6N 17°06′·0E

2228·5 E mole head
Fl.R.3s8M
• 41°03′·7N 17°06′·7E

CALA PORTECCHIA

2230 E mole head
F.R.8m5M
• 41°03′·8N 17°05′·3E

2230·4 N mole head
F.G.8m5M
• 41°03′·8N 17°05′·3E

PORTO DI BARI

2232 Punta San Cataldo
Fl(3)20s66m24M
Reserve light range 18M
• 41°08′·3N 16°50′·7E

2233 Nuovo Molo Foraneo head
Fl.R.3s12m7M Racon
• 41°08′·8N 16°50′·9E

2234 Molo San Cataldo head
Fl.G.3s11m7M
• 41°08′·5N 16°51′·2E

2238 Vecchio Molo Foraneo head
FR.11m4M
• 41°08′·2N 16°51′·7E

2240 Darsena di Levante S side Molo de Ridosso head
Fl.G.5s8m3M
• 41°08′·3N 16°52′·0E

2242 Molo Pizzoli head
FG.11m4M
• 41°08′·0N 16°51′·7E

2243 Molo S Vito head
Fl.Y.2s8m3M
Unreliable
• 41°08′·0N 16°51′·9E

2244 Porto Vecchio Molo San'Antonio head
Fl.G.5s17m9M 190°-vis-130°
• 41°07′·6N 16°52′·8E

MOLFETTA

2248 SW corner
Iso.6s22m16M
Reserve light range 12M
• 41°12′·4N 16°35′·7E

2250 Diga Antemurale NE head
Fl.G.5s13m7M Safety distance 30m
Difficult to distinguish
• 41°12′·9N 16°35′·4E

2252 Molo Foraneo head
Fl.R.5s12m7M Safety distance 30m
• 41°12′·7N 16°35′·5E

PORTO DI BISCEGLIE

2258 E mole head
Fl.R.3s10m8M
• 41°14′·7N 16°30′·4E

2258·2 Molo Liberta W
F.G.10m5M
• 41°14′·8N 16°30′·5E

TRANI

2260 Molo S Antonio 120m from head
Fl.5s9m14M
Reserve Lt range 11M
• 41°16′·8N 16°25′·3E

2261 Head
LFl.R.5s10m8M
• 41°17′·2N 16°25′·3E

2262 Braccio di San Nicola
LFl.G.5s10m8M
• 41°17′·2N 16°25′·9E

PORTO DI BARLETTA

2264 Molo di Tramontana
LFl(2)12s36m17M
Reserve light range 12M
• 41°19′·8N 16°17′·4E

2266 Head
Fl.G.4s12m8M
• 41°19′·8N 16°17′·5E

2268 Diga de Levante head
Fl.R.4s12m8M
• 41°20′·0N 16°17′·7E

PORTO DI MANFREDONIA

2276 Molo di Levante near root
Fl.5s20m23M
Reserve light range 18M
• 41°37′·7N 15°55′·4E

2277 Head
Fl.G.3s14m7M
• 41°37′·2N 15°55′·5E

2278 Molo di Ponente head
Fl.R.3s12m7M
• 41°37′·3N 15°55′·3E

2281 Porto Industriale outer mole head
Oc.G.3s10m7M
• 41°36'·7N 15°57'·0E
2282 Industrial mole head
Oc.R.3s10m7M
• 41°37'·0N 15°56'·9E

MATTINATA
2286 Testa del Gargano Torre Proposti
Fl.5s62m15M
Reserve light range 12M
• 41°46'·9N 16°11'·6E
VIESTE
2288 Isola Santa Eufemia
Fl(3)15s40m25M Aeromarine
124°-vis-348° Reserve light range 18M
• 41°53'·3N 16°11'·1E

RODI GARGANICO
2290·5 Outer Mole Head
Fl.G.3s10m6M
• 41°55'·50N 15°53'·20E

VARANO
2291 W entrance
Fl.R.5s7m5M
• 41°55'·1N 15°47'·7E
2291·2 E entrance
Fl.G.5s7m5M
• 41°55'·1N 15°47'·7E

CAPOIALE
2292 W entrance
Fl.R.5s7m5M
• 41°55'·2N 15°40'·0E
2292·2 E entrance
Fl.G.5s7m5M
• 41°55'·2N 15°40'·0E

ISOLE TREMITI
2294 Isola San Domino Punta del Diavolo
Fl(3)10s48m11M
300°-vis-175°
• 42°06'·3N 15°28'·6E
2296 Isola Caprara
Fl.5s23m8M
110°-vis-020°
• 42°08'·3N 15°31'·2E
2297 Isola San Nicola N end
Fl(4)15s87m12M
Reserve Lt 7M
Obscd over Punta S Maria within 0.3M
• 42°07'·4N 15°30'·6E
2300 Isola Pianosa N coast
Fl(2)10s25m12M
• 42°13'·5N 15°44'·8E

TERMOLI
2303 Citadel
Fl(2)10s41m15M
Reserve light range 11M
• 42°00'·3N 14°59'·8E
2304 N mole head
Fl.G.3s11m8M
• 42°00'·2N 15°00'·5E
2305 S mole 10m from head
Fl(2)Y.6s9m8M
• 42°00'·2N 15°00'·2E

PORTO DI VASTO
2306 Punta Penna
Fl.5s84m25M
Reserve light range 18M
• 42°10'·2N 14°42'·9E
2307·5 W mole head
Fl.G.3s9m7M
• 42°10'·8N 14°42'·7E

ORTONA
2312 Molo Nord root
Fl(2)6s23m15M
Reserve light range 11M
• 42°21'·5N 14°24'·5E
2313 Head
Fl.G.9m5M
• 42°21'·0N 14°25'·4E
2314 Molo sud head
Fl.R.3s9m9M
• 42°20'·9N 14°25'·4E

PESCARA
2315·6 Approaches
Oc(2)Y.10s20m5M
Horn Mo(R)45s
Marks fish farm
• 42°28'·0N 14°19'·3E
2315·7 Detached breakwater (Raffaele Paolucci) W end
Fl.R.6s10m5M
• 42°28'·49N 14°13'·64E
2315·72 E end
Fl(2)G.10s10m5M
• 42°28'·29N 14°14'·08E
2315·73 New mole E end
Fl(2)R.10s10m8M
• 42°28'·29N 14°14'·08E
2319 S Mole
Fl.R.4s13m8M
• 42°28'·1N 14°13'·8E
2320 Molo di Maestro near head
Fl.G.4s13m8M
• 42°28'·1N 14°13'·8E

SAN BENEDETTO DEL TRONTO
2332 San Benedetto del Tronto
Fl(2)10s31m22M
135°-vis-045° Reserve light range 18M
• 42°57'·1N 13°53'·2E
2333 N mole head
Fl.G.3s8m8M
• 42°57'·4N 13°53'·5E
2334 S mole head
Fl.R.3s8m8M
Horn Mo(W)45s
• 42°57'·5N 13°53'·7E
2336 Pedaso
Fl(3)15s51m16M
Reserve light 12M
• 43°05'·4N 13°50'·8E
2337 Porto San Giorgio outer mole head
Fl(2)R.6s8m5M Horn Mo(U)45s
• 43°09'·8N 13°49'·8E
2337·2 Inner mole head
Fl(2)G.6s8m5M
• 43°09'·8N 13°49'·8E

PORTO CIVITANOVA MARCHE
2337·6 Chiesa del Cristo Re
Mo(C)20s42m11M
• 43°18'·6N 13°43'·7E
2338 E mole head
Fl.R.5s10m8M
• 43°18'·9N 13°44'·1E
2339 N mole head
Fl.G.5s9m8M
• 43°18'·8N 13°44'·0E

ANCONA
2344 Colle Cappuccini
Fl(4)30s118m25M
120°-obsc-121·5° by old tower and when bearing more than 306°
Reserve light range 18M
• 43°37'·3N 13°31'·0E
2346 Molo Foraneo nord head
Fl.R.4s11m8M
277°-vis-224° Racon
• 43°37'·5N 13°29'·6E
2346·5 Detached breakwater S end
Fl(2)R.6s10m5M
• 43°37'·25N 13°29'·08E
2348 Della Lanterna mole head
Fl.R.3s8m8M
• 43°37'·4N 13°30'·0E
2349 Molo Foraneo sud head
Fl.G.4s11m7M
• 43°37'·3N 13°29'·7E
2350 Quay 23 near head
Fl.G.3s11m8M
• 43°37'·40N 13°29'·89E
2350·1 Marina Molo di Sottoflutto head
Fl(2)G.10s10m6M
• 43°36'·7N 13°29'·0E
2350·2 Head
Fl(2)R.10s10m6M
• 43°36'·7N 13°28'·9E

SENIGALLIA
2358 E breakwater root
LFl(2)15s17m15M
Reserve light range 11M
• 43°43'·1N 13°13'·3E
2359 Head
Fl.Y.3s9m8M
• 43°43'·3N 13°13'·4E
2360.2 Head
Fl(2)R.6s9m8M Horn Mo(D)45s
• 43°43'·4N 13°13'·3E

FANO
2362 Inner mole root
Fl.5s21m15M
Reserve light range 11M
• 43°51'·0N 13°00'·9E
2364 E Mole head
Fl.R.3s9m8M
• 43°51'·3N 13°01'·0E
2366 W mole head
Fl.G.3s8m8M
• 43°51'·3N 13°00'·9E

PESARO
2372 Monte San Bartolo
Fl(2)15s175m25M
shore-obsc-125°
Reserve light range 18M
• 43°55'·4N 12°53'·0E
2374 E Mole 45m from head
Fl.R.5s10m8M
• 43°55'·5N 12°54'·4E
2376 W Mole 20m from head
Fl.G.5s10m8M
• 43°55'·5N 12°54'·4E

CATTOLICA
2381 E mole root
Mo(O)14s17m15M
Reserve light range 11M
• 43°58'·1N 12°45'·1E
2382 Head
Fl.R.3s10m8M
• 43°58'·2N 12°45'·1E
2384 W mole head
Fl.G.3s10m8M
• 43°58'·2N 12°45'·1E
2390 Riccione E mole head
Fl.R.3s10m5M Horn Mo(M)45s
• 44°00'·5N 12°39'·5E
2390·2 W mole head
Fl.G.3s10m5M
• 44°00'·42N 12°39'·43E

RIMINI
2394 Rimini
Fl(3)12s27m15M
160°-vis-280°
Reserve light range 11M
• 44°04'·4N 12°34'·5E
2395 E mole head
Fl.R.3s10m8M
• 44°04'·9N 12°34'·6E
2397 W mole head
Fl.G.3s7m8M
• 44°04'·7N 12°34'·5E

CESENATICO

2404 Entrance SW side
Fl(2)6s18m15M
Reserve light range 11M
Numerous oil rigs, some marked by lights and fog signals, lie within the area between 1M and 6M NE
• 44°12'·3N 12°24'·1E

2405 Head
Fl.R.5s8m8M Horn Mo(R)45s
• 44°12'·5N 12°24'·3E

2406 W mole head
Fl.G.5s8m8M
• 44°12'·5N 12°24'·3E

CERVIA

2411 Main light
Iso.2s16m11M
Obscured outside of channel by high buildings
• 44°16'·0N 12°21'·3E

PORTO DI RAVENNA

2417·8 Approaches
Fl.10s5m6M
• 44°29'·9N 12°20'·6E

2418 S Mole root
Fl.5s35m20M
Reserve light range 18M
• 44°29'·5N 12°17'·1E

2419 S breakwater head
Fl(2)R.6s10m8M Horn(3)48s
• 44°29'·7N 12°18'·9E

2420 N breakwater head
Fl(2)G.6s10m8M
• 44°29'·8N 12°18'·8E

2421 S Mole head
Fl.R.4s7m8M Horn Mo(H)45s
• 44°29'·6N 12°17'·5E

2422 N mole head
Fl.G.4s7m8M
• 44°29'·70N 12°17'·41E

PORTO GARIBALDI

2426 N mole near root
Fl(4)15s14m15M
Reserve light range 11M
• 44°40'·5N 12°14'·8E

2428 Head
Fl.G.5s9m8M
Horn Mo(G) 48s
• 44°40'·6N 12°15'·0E

2429 Shelter mole head
Q.R.9m5M
• 44°40'·6N 12°15'·3E

2430 S mole head
Fl.R.5s9m8M
• 44°40'·5N 12°15'·0E

BOCCHE DEL PO

2431·5 Porto di Goro entrance channel
Fl(2)10s6m9M
• 44°47'·5N 12°16'·5E

2434 Po di Goro
Fl(2)10s22m17M
Reserve light 13M
• 44°47'·5N 12°23'·8E

2438
Fl(3)Y.9s2m5M
Marks mussel culture zone
• 44°53'·68N 12°32'·04E

2440 Punta della Maestra
Fl(3)20s47m25M
Aeromarine Racon
Reserve light range 18M
• 44°58'·1N 12°31'·8E

2441
Q(3)10s4m6M
• 44°57'·8N 12°35'·4E

ISOLA ALBARELLA

2443 Main light
LFl.6s55m15M
200°-vis-290°
• 45°04'·2N 12°20'·8E

2443·1 Porto Levante W mole head
Fl(2)G.10s9m6M
• 45°04'·5N 12°21'·7E

2443·15 E mole head
Fl(2)R.10s9m8M
• 45°04'·6N 12°22'·2E

2443·3 Eastwards
Iso.Y.2s5m6M
• 45°04'·6N 12°23'·4E

ISOLA BACUCCO

2445·5 Eastwards
Fl(5)Y.20s6m5M
Marks oceanographic research zone
• 45°09'·0N 12°23'·0E

PORTO DI CHIOGGIA

2450 Porto di Chioggia
LFl(2)10s20m15M
Reserve light range 11M
• 45°13'·8N 12°17'·85E

2451 Forte San Felice NW point
Fl(2)R.7s6m8M Horn Mo(N)20s
• 45°13'·8N 12°17'·4E

2452 N breakwater head
Fl.G.3s11m8M
• 45°14'·0N 12°18'·9E

2453 S breakwater near head
Fl(2)R.10s11m8M
F.R.6m6M
• 45°13'·7N 12°18'·9E

2454 S side
Fl.R.3s6m5M
• 45°13'·93N 12°18'·03E

2454·5
Fl.R.3s6m5M
• 45°13'·94N 12°18'·62E

2455·4 N side
Fl.G.3s6m5M
• 45°14'·01N 12°18'·60E

2456 N breakwater root
Fl(2)G.7s9m8M
• 45°14'·1N 12°17'·6E

PORTO DI MALAMOCCO

2462 Oceanographic Platform
Mo(U)15s8M
F.R.3M Horn Mo(U)30s
• 45°18'·8N 12°30'·9E

2463 Fort Rocchetta Pilot tower Dir Lt 287·5°
DirF.WRG.30m6M 285°-G-287°-W-288°-R-290°
• 45°20'·36N 12°18'·70E

2464 Forte Rocchetta SSW if Fort Alberoni
Fl(3)12s25m16M
Reserve light range 11M
• 45°20'·33N 12°18'·68E

2464·4 S side
Fl(3)G.10s6m7M Horn Mo(D)45s
• 45°20'·3N 12°18'·7E

2465
Fl.10s7m6M
• 45°19'·4N 12°23'·1E

2465·4
Fl(2)R.6s6m6M
• 45°19'·5N 12°22'·1E

2465·5
Fl(2)R.10s6m5M
• 45°19'·7N 12°21'·4E

2465·55
Fl(2)G.10s6m5M
• 45°19'·8N 12°21'·4E

2466 N breakwater head
Fl.G.5s18m8M
• 45°20'·0N 12°20'·7E

2467 S breakwater head
Fl.R.3s16m8M
F.R.6m6M
• 45°19'·8N 12°20'·2E

2468 Forte San Pietro. Palata dell Ceppe breakwater head
Fl(3)R.10s11m5M
• 45°20'·1N 12°19'·1E

2469·6 Canale S Leonardo S side
Fl.R.4s6m5M
• 45°20'·3N 12°17'·9E

2470 N side
Fl.G.4s6m8M Horn Mo(N)30s
• 45°20'·4N 12°18'·0E

2470·4 N side
Fl(2)G.10s6m8M
• 45°20'·74N 12°16'·46E

2470·6 N side
Fl(3)G.10s6m8M
• 45°20'·9N 12°15'·5E

2470·8 N side
Fl.G.4s6m8M
• 45°21'·0N 12°15'·1E

VENEZIA PORTO DI LIDO

2480 NE breakwater head
LFl(2)12s26m15M
Reserve light range 11M
Fl(2)G.8s14m7M Horn Mo(N)45s
• 45°25'·3N 12°26'·2E

2481
Fl.10s7m6M
• 45°23'·9N 12°28'·8E

2482
Fl.G.2s6m5M
• 45°24'·6N 12°27'·4E

2482·2
Fl.R.3s6m5M
• 45°24'·5 12°27'·3E

2484 S breakwater head
Fl(2)R.8s14m8M
• 45°25'·0N 12°25'·6E

2486 Ldg Lts 300°40' N side of channel
Front Fl.3s13m11M
Passing light Fl.G.4s3m5M
• 45°26'·3N 12°23'·4E

2486·1 Isola di Murano
Rear 1·72M from front
Oc.6s37m17M Aeromarine
Reserve light range 11M
Dir Lt 300°40'
DirOc.6s21M Vis over 1° only
Reserve light range 11M
• 45°27'·1N 12°21'·3E

2500·4 Canale Vittario Emanuele Entrance NE side
Fl(2)G.10s6m5M
• 45°26'·9N 12°16'·6E

PORTO PIAVE VECCHIA

2504 Piave Vecchia entrance W point
Fl(4)20s45m15M
• 45°28'·6N 12°35'·0E

PORTO SANTA MARGHERITA DI CAORLE

2506 W mole
Fl.R.3s5M
• 45°35'·2N 12°51'·9E

2506·4 E Mole
Fl.G.3s5M
• 45°35'·2N 12°52'·0E

2508 Caorle point E of town
Fl(2)6s12m14M
• 45°36'·0N 12°53'·6E

2518 Punta Tagliamento
Fl(3)10s22m15M
Reserve light range 11M
• 45°38'·2N 13°05'·9E

LIGNANO SABBIADORO
2519·5
Fl.2s6m6M
• 45°39′·7N 13°09′·7E
2521 Pier head
Fl.R.2s7m8M
F (fishing) shown from bridge at Marano 4·9M N
• 45°41′·8N 13°09′·2E

GRADO
2525·7 Approach
Fl.10s5m6M
• 45°39′·6N 13°20′·9E
2526 Canale di Grado. Entrance W side
Fl.WR.3s5m7/5M
193°-R-031°-W-036°
• 45°40′·8N 13°22′·1E
2538 Banco Mula di Muggia
Q(6)+LFl.15s7m6M
• 45°39′·3N 13°26′·3E

PORTO DI MONFALCONE
2543 Approach
Fl.10s5m6M
• 45°44′·6N 13°36′·3E

SISTIANA
2557 Approaches to Triest
Fl.Y.3s5m5M
• 45°38′·6N 13°40′·9E

PORTO DI TRIESTE
2558 Faro della Vittoria Collina Gretta
Fl(2)10s115m22M
Reserve light range 18M
• 45°40′·5N 13°45′·5E
2560 Porto Franco Vecchio breakwater S head
Fl.R.3s7m6M
• 45°39′·3N 13°45′·7E
2562 N head
Fl.G.3s8m8M
• 45°39′·8N 13°45′·4E
2568 Porto Lido mole head
Fl.R.5s7m5M
• 45°38′·9N 13°45′·1E
2576 Porto Franco Nuovo diga nord N head
Fl(2)G.6s9m5M
• 45°38′·5N 13°44′·3E
2578 S head
Fl.R.3s9m8M
• 45°38′·28N 13°44′·37E
2580 Diga Centrale Luigi Rizzo N head
Fl.G.3s9m5M
• 45°38′·19N 13°44′·22E
2582 S head
Iso.R.2s9m5M
198°-vis-148°
• 45°37′·9N 13°44′·3E
2586 Diga Luigi Rizzo N head
Iso.G.2s6m5M 018°-vis-328°
• 45°37′·8N 13°44′·2E
2587 S head
Fl(3)R.10s9m5M
• 45°37′·0N 13°44′·3E

BAIA DI MUGGIA
2594 San Rocco Marina. Outer breakwater head
Fl.G.5s8m5M
• 45°36′·58N 35°45′·16E
2594·1 Inner breakwater head
Fl.R.5s8m5M
• 45°36′·56N 13°45′·12E

VALLONE DI MUGGIA
2603 Porto Industriale
F.R.10m10M
058·2°-vis-069·2°
• 45°36′·80N 13°48′·76E

Adriatic Sea – Slovenia

2607 Rt Debeli off point
Q(9)15s8m8M
• 45°35′·5N 13°42′·2E
2611·7 Ldg Lts 088°
Front Q.Y.1s8m10M
• 45°33′·95N 13°45′·10E
2611·71 Rear Q.Y.1s12m10M
• 45°33′·95N 13°45′·22E

IZOLA
2618 Rt Petelin (Gallo)
Fl.5s7m6M
• 45°32′·5N 13°39′·6E

PIRAN
2624 Rt Madona
Iso.4s13m15M
351°-vis-253°
• 45°31′·8N 13°34′·1E

PORTOROJ
2634 Pier head
Fl.G.2s6m6M
• 45°30′·8N 13°35′·6E

Adriatic Sea – Croatia

2642 Rt Savudrija
Fl(3)15s36m30M Siren(2) 42s
Reserve light range 12M
• 45°29′·4N 13°29′·5E

LUKA UMAG
2644 Pličina Paklena (Pegolota) W side
Fl(2)WR.8s10m8/6M
165°-R-347°-W-165°
• 45°26′·5N 13°30′·3E

LUKA NOVIGRAD
2654 Breakwater head
Fl.WRG.5s7m8-6M
003°-W-025°-R-058°-W-117°-G-003°
• 45°19′·1N13°33′·5E
2658 Luka Mirna Rt Zub
Fl(3)WR.10s11m9/6M
018°-W-325°-R over PliŠina Civran, Veliki and Mali Skolj-018°
• 45°17′·9N 13°34′·4E
2660 Pličina Civran. NW of Pličina Veliki Skolj
Q.7m5M
• 45°16′·96N 13°34′·60E
2660·2 SW
Q(9)15s7m5M
• 45°16′·8N 13°34′·3E

POREC
2662 Hrid Barbaran
Fl.WR.5s9m8/5M
011°-R-062°-W-153°-R-308°-W-011°
• 45°13′·8N 13°35′·4E
2663 Otočić Sv Nikola N breakwater head
Fl.G.5s7m5M
074°-vis-023°
• 45°13′·7N 13°35′·4E
2668 Otočić Altijew
Fl(3)10s9m8M
• 45°11′·9N 13°34′·4E
2672 Pličina Mramori
Fl(2)R.8s13m7M
• 45°08′·9N 13°34′·5E
2674 Otočić Galiner
Fl.2s20m5M
049°-vis-064°, 099°-vis-116°, 185°-vis-025°
• 45°09′·2N 13°35′·9E

VRSAR
2678 Plić Fugaga
Q(6)+LFl.15s6m5M
• 45°07′·7N 13°37′·0E

ROVINJ
2680 Rt Sv Eufemija
Fl.4s19m7M
• 45°05′·0N 13°38′·0E
2687 Marina breakwater head
Fl.G.5s7m5M
• 45°04′·5N 13°38′·0E
2690 Sv Ivan na Pučini
Fl(2)10s23m24M Siren 30s
Distress signals
Reserve light range 12M
• 45°02′·6N 13°37′·1E

FASANSKI KANAL
2692 Greben Kabula
Q.10m9M
• 44°56′·8N 13°42′·8E
2696 Pličina Slavulja (Saluga)
Fl(2)WR.8s8m6M
130°-R-142°-W-130°
• 44°55′·2N 13°47′·1E
2700 Pličina Koteż (Kozada)
Fl.G.3s7m6M
• 44°54′·5N 13°47′·9E
2706 Otočić Sv Jerolim W point
Fl.2s10m5M
349°-vis-221°
• 44°54′·0N 13°47′·3E
2710 Rt Peneda
Iso.4s20m11M
238°-vis-114° Reserve light 7M
• 44°53′·3N 13°45′·5E

LUKA PULA
2718 Rt Prostina
Fl.R.3s9m5M
• 44°53′·5N 13°47′·7E
2720 Rt Kumpar breakwater head
Fl.G.3s9m6M
• 44°53′·2N 13°47′·7E
2734 Rt Verudica
Fl.R.3s11m6M
• 44°50′·0N 13°50′·3E
2738 Hrid Porer
Fl(3)15s35m25M Siren(2) 42s Racon
255°-vis-147°
Reserve light range 12M
• 44°45′·5N 13°53′·8E
2740 Pličina Fenoliga
Fl.R.2s8m5M
• 44°45′·8N 13°54′·2E
2742 Pličina Albaneż
Fl(2)WR.8s15m10/6M
172°-R-227°-W-172°
• 44°44′·1N 13°54′·4E
2744 Hrid Galijola (Galiola)
Fl.5s21m12M Racon
• 44°43′·8N 14°10′·8E
2748 Rt Munat
Fl.WR.2s9m7/4M
312°-W-327°-R-312°
• 44°48′·2N 13°55′·7E
2749 Bodulas SW of islet
Fl(2)G.5s8m5M
• 44°47′·4N 13°56′·9
2750 Rt Marlera
Fl.9s21m9M
186°-vis-038°
• 44°48′·2N 14°00′·4E

OTOK UNIJE
2752 Rt Vnetak
Fl(3)WR.10s17m10/7M
270°-W-158°-R-176°
• 44°37′·2N 14°14′·4E

2756 Rt Lakunji
Fl(4)15s8m8M
• 44°41′·3N 14°17′·0E

OTOK CRES

2760 Otok Zeča SW side
Fl(2)WR.10s13m8/6M
176°-R-194°
• 44°45′·9N 14°18′·3E

2761 Otočić Visoki W side
Fl.3s13m6M
• 44°46′·6N 14°21′·1E

2764 Hrid Zaglav
Fl(3)15s20m10M
• 44°55′·3N 14°17′·6E

RASA ZALJEV

2768 Rt Ubac (Ubas)
Fl.4s16m8M
• 44°56′·7N 14°04′·2E

2782 Rt Crna Punta
Fl(2)10s15m10M
245°-vis-104°
• 44°57′·4N 14°09′·0E

2783 Skvaranska
Fl.5s8m10M
• 44°59′·2N 14°10′·5E

LUKA CRES

2784 Rt Kovačine
Fl(2)6s9m8M
297°-vis-185°
• 44°57′·6N 14°23′·7E

LUKA RABAC

2794 Rt Sv Andrija
Fl(3)8s9m5M
• 45°04′·4N 14°10′·2E

RT MASNJAK

2798·2 Rt Masnjak
Fl(2)8s16m8M 286°-vis-127°
• 45°07′·01N 14°12′·50E

2798·3 W side
Fl(2)R.6s9m5M 136°-vis-317°
• 45°07′·4N 14°12′·00E

2798·4 E side
Fl(2)G.6s9m5M 307°-vis-149°
• 45°07′·37N 14°11′·89E

2799·2 Brestova
Fl(2)R.12s40m13M
• 45°08′·3N 14°13′·7E

2799·4 Rt Sip
Fl.R.5s23m8M
• 45°10′·8N 14°14′·8E

2799·6 Rt Starganac
Fl.G.4s7m8M
• 45°09′·9N 14°18′·4E

2802 Rt Prestenice
LFl.10s17m10M
350°-vis-205°
• 45°07′·2N 14°16′·6E

RIJECKA ZALJEV

2816 Opatija mole head
Fl.R.5s7m6M
• 45°20′·2N 14°19′·0E

2822 Luka Rijeka Mlaka
Fl.10s39m15M
Reserve light range 12M
• 45°20′·0N 14°25′·5E

2824 Riječki Lukobran head
Q(3)G.5s15m8M
• 45°19′·6N 14°25′·4E

BAKARSKI ZALJEV

2855 Rt Srednji
Fl(2)5s12m6M
212·5°-vis-053°
• 45°16′·8N 14°33′·7E

2856 Rt Kavranić
Fl.5s15m6M
• 45°16′·9N 14°34′·1E

OTOK KRK

2863 Omisaljski Zaljev Rt Kijac
Fl(2)R.8s14m8M
331°-vis-224°
• 45°14′·2N 14°32′·4E

2864/2864·1 Ldg Lts 151°
Front Iso.G.2s23m11M
Rear 490m from front
Oc.G.5s32m11M
• 45°12′·7N 14°33′·3E

2866 Rt Tenka Punta
Fl(3)10s9m7M
• 45°13′·7N 14°32′·1E

2870 Rt Manganel
Fl.5s13m8M
• 45°04′·4N 14°26′·2E

2872 Otok Plavnik Rt Veli Pin
Fl.6s20m10M
• 44°58′·8N 14°29′·4E

2873 Otok Cres. Rt Tarej
Fl.R.5s8m6M
• 44°57′·3N 14°29′·5E

2880 Puntarska Draga entrance E side Rt Pod Stražiou
Fl.2s9m5M
• 45°00′·7N 14°37′·6E

2884 Rt Negrit
Fl.G.3s14m5M
• 44°58′·8N 14°37′·3E

2886 Otoeid Galun
Fl(3)10s12m8M
• 44°56′·4N 14°41′·0E

2886·4 Rt Skuljica
Fl.R.3s18m6M
• 44°56′·6N 14°46′·1E

2887 Otok Prvíc Rt Stražica
Fl.6s23m9M
• 44°56′·0N 14°46′·4E

2888 Otok Goli Rt Sajalo
Fl.R.5s8m5M
• 44°51′·0N 14°48′·3E

TIHI KANAL

2890 Otočić Sv Marko
Fl.R.3s15m6M
• 45°15′·2N 14°34′·2E

VINODOLSKI KANAL

2901 Rt Silo
Fl.3s14m7M
• 45°09′·4N 14°40′·4E

2910 Rt Tokal
Fl.6s20m9M
• 45°08′·3N 14°44′·7E

2916 Poluotočić Sv Anton
Fl.3s9m6M
• 45°05′·8N 14°50′·7E

VELEBITSKI KANAL

2922 Senj. Marija Art mole head
Fl(3)10s10m8M
• 44°59′·4N 14°54′·1E

2923 Sv Ambrož mole head
Fl.R.3s10m5M
• 44°59′·5N 14°54′·2E

2928 Luka Lukovo Otočko Rt Malta
Fl.5s9m8M
• 44°51′·5N 14°53′·4E

2938 Jablanac Rt Stokić N of port
Fl.6s50m8M
346°-vis-174°
• 44°42′·6N 14°53′·8E

BARBATSKI KANAL

2943 Hrid Pohlib
Fl.2s7m5M
275°-vis-168°
• 44°41′·9N 14°50′·8E

2943·9 Pličina
Q(2)5s8m8M
• 44°36′·2N 14°58′·2E

2944 Rt Jurisnica
Fl(3)12s10m9M
• 44°34′·4N 14°59′·5E

2945 Hrid Jigljen NW side
Fl.R.2s12m6M
• 44°34′·9N 14°57′·4E

OTOK PAG

2950 Rt Kristofor
Fl.5s62m7M
• 44°28′·5N 15°05′·1E

2953 Pag Ferry pier
Fl(2)R.5s7m7M
• 44°26′·8N 15°03′·4E

2960 Hrid Konj
Fl(3)12s7m6M
• 44°25′·3N 15°13′·1E

2961 Rt Tanka Nožica
Fl.3s8m6M
• 44°19′·9N 15°16′·2E

2962 Kruščica Rt Dugi
Fl.R.3s6m5M
• 44°21′·1N 15°18′·8E

RAJANAC

2964 Otočić Ražanac Veli
Fl.5s16m9M
• 44°19′·0N 15°21′·6E

NOVSKO JDRILO

2973 Rt Baljenica
Fl(2)R.5s10m5M
• 44°14′·8N 15°31′·7E

OTOK RAB

2976 Rt Sorinj
Fl.3s10m6M
• 44°50′·7N 14°41′·0E

2978 Rt Kalifront Donja Punta
Fl(3)10s11m8M
• 44°47′·4N 14°39′·6E

2982 Rt Kanitalj. Kristofor
Fl.5s10m8M
• 44°45′·5N 14°22′·0E

2995 Otok Dolin Rt Donji
Fl(3)10s9m7M
• 44°44′·6N 14°46′·4E

OTOK PAG

2995·6 Stara Novalja
Fl.5s9m5M
• 44°36′·2N 14°52′·6E

2995·8 Rt Zali
Fl.3s9m8M
• 44°36′·8N 14°54′·8E

2996 Tovarnele S point
Fl.WR.6s9m8/5M
141°-R-176°-W-141°
• 44°41′·4N 14°44′·3E

2998 Otočić Dolfin summit
Fl(2)WR.10s30m10/7M
138°-R-153°-W-138°
• 44°41′·5N 14°41′·5E

3002 Otočić Trstenik summit
LFl.WR.10s26m11/8M
042°-W-346°-R-018°-W-032°
• 44°40′·1N 14°35′·0E

OTOK CRES

3006 Rt Suha
Fl.WR.5s6m9/6M
285°-R-319°-W-285°
• 44°36′·2N 14°30′·2E

3008 Hrid Bik
Fl(2)WR.6s11m8/5M
078°-R-150°-W-078°
• 44°32′·4N 14°37′·4E

OTOK LOSINJ

3022 Otočić Murtar
LFl.8s9m8M
• 44°33′·0N 14°25′·6E

3026 Mali Losinj Rt Torunza
Fl.WR.3s10m6/4M
065°-W-072°-R-065°
• 44°33'·7N 14°25'·8E
3028 Rt Poljana
Fl.R.3s9m5M
• 44°33'·2N 14°26'·6E
3032 Rt Kurila
Fl.WR.5s10m8/6M
175°-R-189°
• 44°33'·7N 14°22'·4E
3034 Hrid Silo SE of Srakane mole
Fl.R.5s11m5M
• 44°33'·5N 14°20'·9E
3036 Otok Susak Garba Mountain
LFl(2)10s.100m19M
Reserve light range 8M
• 44°30'·8N 14°18'·5E
3042 Otok Sv Petar SW side
Fl.3s7m5M
• 44°27'·6N 14°33'·6E
3044 Otočić Grujica
Fl(3)15s17m10M Racon
Emergency light F.8M
• 44°24'·6N 14°34'·4E
3045 Pličina Veli Brak
Fl(2)10s12m5M
• 44°26'·5N 14°38'·4E

OTOK PREMUDA
3046 Otočić Kamenjak N end
Fl.5s12m7M
• 44°21'·4N 14°35'·0E
3052 Otočić Grebeni Zapadni NW side
Fl.R.5s21m6M
• 44°19'·9N 14°41'·46E

VIRSKO MORE
3058 Juwni Arat
Q(6)+LFl.15s9m8M
• 44°20'·8N 14°43'·4E
3064 Otočić Morovnik NW Point
Fl.G.5s8m5M
• 44°25'·9N 14°44'·96E
3068 Pohlipski Kanal Otočić Pohlib summit
Fl.5s16m9M
• 44°23'·7N 14°53'·9E
3072 Otok Skrda NW side
Fl(3)15s15m10M
• 44°28'·9N 14°51'·2E
3075 Otok Pag Mandre
Fl.3s7m7M
• 44°29'·0N 14°54'·8E
3077 Rt Zaglav
Fl(3)10s9m7M
• 44°23'·6N 15°02'·6E
3080 Povljana Rt Dubrovnik
Fl.R.3s9m5M
• 44°21'·0N 15°06'·1N
3081 Otok Vir
Fl.10s21m11M
315°-vis-163°
• 44°18'·2N 15°01'·9E
3082 Kanal Nove Povljane. Sidriste Veli Jal
Fl(2)R.5s7m5M
• 44°19'·0N 15°07'·0E

OTOK MOLAT
3092 Rt Vranac
Fl.2s13m5M
• 44°15'·9N 14°48'·15E
3093 Rt Bonaster
Fl(4)15s12m9M
• 44°12'·0N 14°50'·6E

SEDMOVRACE
3094·4 Otočić Golac N side
Fl.3s12m6M
066°-vis-280°
• 44°11'·33N 14°51'·00E
3096 Otočić Vrtlac
Fl.3s7m5M
• 44°12'·1N 14°55'·9E
3097 Otok Tun Veli N end
Fl.WG.5s27m7/4M
092°-W-099·5°-G-213°-W-223°-G-092°
• 44°11'·3N 14°54'·5E
3097·4 Otočić Trata
Fl.R.3s10m6M
• 44°12'·8N 14°55'·6E

DUGI OTOK
3098 Veli Rat
Fl(2)20s41m22M
• 44°09'·1N 14°49'·5E

SREDNJI KANAL
3106 Otočić Tri Sestrice SE island E side
Fl(2)WR.5s16m8/6M
225°-R-234°-W-225°
• 44°10'·3N 15°01'·0E
3106·4 Pličina Sajda
Fl(2)10s3m5M
• 44°11'·3N 15°02'·4E
3108 Otok Sestrunj Rt Trska
Fl(4)15s10m10M
Obscured when bearing more than 323°
• 44°08'·8N 15°01'·8E
3115 Otočić Mrtovnjak
Fl(2)R.10s27m7M
• 44°00'·7N 15°10'·8E
3116 Otočić Karantunić summit
Fl(3)10s30m9M
Passage to Pasmanski Kanal under a bridge 0·7M NE is marked by R & G lights
• 44°00'·5N 15°14'·6E
3116·2 Otočić Balabra Mala
Fl.R.3s10m5M
• 43°56'·8N 15°16'·80E
3116·4 Hrid Galijolica
Fl(2)R.10s11m7M
155°-vis-325°
• 43°52'·7N 15°22'·5E
3117 Otočić Kosara SW side
Fl.5s11m11M
• 43°53'·0N 15°24'·5E

DUGI OTOK
3121 Pličina Beli
Fl(3)8s7m6M
326°-vis-267°
• 44°05'·4N 14°02'·8E
3132 Otok Lavdara NW Point
Fl.3s8m5M
• 43°56'·9N 15°12'·0E
3132·3 Otočić Lavdara Mala
Fl.5s10m8M
• 43°54'·9N 15°14'·2E
3134 Otočić Sestrica Vela
Fl.8s47m20M
Reserve light range 12M
• 43°51'·2N 15°12'·5E

ZADARSKI KANAL
3140 Petrčane Rt Radman
Fl.WR.3s6m7/4M
141°-R-262°-W-141°
• 44°10'·9N 15°09'·6E
3142 Ostri Rat
Fl(3)10s14m15M
• 44°07'·8N 15°12'·5E

OTOK UGLJAN
3160 Otočić Osljak NE point
Fl(4)15s11m8M
• 44°04'·8N 15°13'·0E

ZADARSKI KANAL
3167·5 Otočić Misnjak
Fl(2)5s7m8M
• 44°01'·6N 15°16'·1E
3168 Sukosan Rt Podvara
Fl.WR.5s6m8/5M
207°-R-318°-W-207°
• 44°02'·7N 15°18'·1E

PASMANSKI KANAL
3175 Otočić Ricul S end
Fl.3s8m5M
• 43°58'·6N 15°23'·7E
3180 Otočić Babac W point
Fl(2)5s7m10M
• 43°57'·4N 15°24'·0E
3185 Biograd Na Moru. NW mole head
Fl.G.3s7m5M
• 43°56'·2N 15°26'·6E
3188 Otočić Sv Katarina SW side
Fl(2)8s9m8M
309°-vis-142°
• 43°55'·9N 15°26'·0E
3193 Otočić Ostarije
Fl.3s7m7M
292°-vis-140°
• 43°54'·7N 15°28'·4E
3196 Otočić Artica Vela W islet W side
Fl.5s7m7M
302°-vis-228°
• 43°52'·0N 15°31'·9E
3200 Hrid MiSine
Fl.R.3s9m5M
• 43°48'·7N 15°34'·1E
3202 Otočić Prisnjak near W extremity
Fl(3)10s19m9M
249°-vis-146°
• 43°49'·5N 15°33'·8E

OTOK MURTER
3224 Hrid Kukuljar
Fl.5s11m10M
• 43°45'·6N 15°38'·3E
3225 Otok Smokvica Vela N point
Fl.R.3s13m5M
• 43°44'·1N 15°28'·6E
3225·1 Otočić Babina Guzica Rock 0·3M W of islet
Fl(2)G.5s7m5M
215°-vis-140°
• 43°42'·58N 15°29'·65E
3225·2 Otočić Mrtovnjak N point
Fl(2)10s12m10M
• 43°42'·5N 15°32'·4E
3225·3 Cavlin shoal
Fl(2)5s7m6M
• 43°44'·45N 15°33'·70E
3226 Hrid Blitvenica summit
Fl(2)30s38m24M
Reserve light range 12M
• 43°37'·5N 15°34'·8E
3226·5 Otočić Rapurasnjak
Fl.4s21m7M
• 43'40'·9N 15°35'·5E
3227·7 Hrid Rasohe
Fl(2)R.5s7m5M
188°-vis-061°
• 43°37'·62N 15°44'·12E
3228 Otočić Hrbosnjak
Fl.R.5s25m5M
• 43°38'·8N 15°44'·5E
3229·2 Otočić Ravan W side
Fl.5s12m10M
• 43°39'·6N 15°44'·5E

3229·75 Hr Mala Mare
Fl(2)8s8m5M
• 43°42'·82N 15°38'·32E
3229·8 Brak Prasčiča
Fl(2)10s6m7M
• 43°40'·5N 15°38'·9E
3231 Otok Tijat Rt Tijasćica
Fl(3)10s13m7M
265°-vis-128°
• 43°42'·4N 15°46'·7E

OTOK PRVIC

3242 Plićina Rožnik
Fl.G.5s7m6M
• 43°42'·8N 15°49'·9E

LUKA SIBENIK

3248 Rt Jadrija
Fl(2)R.6s11m9M Horn(2)20s
Reserve light 6M
160°-vis-098°
• 43°43'·3N 15°51'·3E
3271 Prokljansko Jezero Magaretusa
Fl.WR.2s6m6/3M
172°-R-192°-W-172°
• 43°47'·3N 15°52'·0E
3275 Otok Zlarin Rt Rat
Fl(2)5s12m6M
180°-vis-045°
• 43°39'·7N 15°52'·5E
3276 Otočić Dvainka NW point
Fl.5s8m8M
326°-vis-172°
• 43°39'·4N 15°53'·0E

LUKA PRIMOSTEN

3282 Rt Kremik
Fl.3s10m8M
339°-vis-197°
• 43°34'·5N 15°55'·2E
3286 Hrid Mulo
Fl.5s23m21M
Reserve light 12M
• 43°30'·9N 15°55'·4E
3286·5 Grbavac Rock
Fl(2)5s7m7M
• 43°33'·6N 15°53'·3E

LUKA ROGOZNICA

3292·5 Rt Ploča
Fl.G.5s9m5M
• 43°29'·6N 15°58'·4E

DRVENIK KANAL

3293 Otočić Muljica
Fl.3s15m5M
• 43°28'·4N 16°01'·0E
3294 Otočić Murvica
LFl.R.8s15m7M Siren 30s
Reserve light 6M
• 43°28'·0N 16°07'·0E
3295 Otok Drvenik Mali Rt Pasike
Fl(4)15s11m7M
• 43°27'·3N 16°04'·7E
3295·7 Otočić Murvica
Fl(2)8s11m5M
• 43°27'·2N 16°07'·0E

TROGIRSKI ZALJEV

3298 Hrid Galera summit
Fl.5s8m10M
• 43°28'·3N 16°11'·5E
3302 Hrid Celice
Fl(3)10s15m6M
Shows over swing bridge at Trogir
• 43°30'·1N 16°11'·9E

KASTELANSKI ZALJEV

DIVULJE

3317 Aero Iso.R.2s97m12M
• 43°31'·6N 16°16'·5E
3317·2 Aero Iso.2s59m8M
• 43°33'·3N 16°20'·3E
3317·4 Aero Iso.R.2s40m8M
• 43°33'·7N 16°20'·1E
3324 Plićina Silo
Fl(2)10s7m7M
• 43°31'·9N 16°26'·1E
3325 Barbarinac on rock
Fl.R.3s10m5M
• 43°32'·1N 16°27'·0E
3331 Rt Marjan S mole head
Fl.G.3s8m5M
290°-vis-210°
• 43°30'·5N 16°23'·6E
3331·2 Rt Ciovea
Fl(2)8s9m7M
• 43°29'·3N 16°23'·8E
3331·5 Mlin Shoal
Fl(2)10s7m8M
• 43°27'·0N 16°14'·7E

OTOK SOLTA

3331·9 Otočić Stipanska
Fl(2)G.5s8m6M
• 43°24'·4N 16°10'·4E
3332 Maslinica Rt Sveti Nikola
Fl.WR.3s10m7/4M
011°-R-056°-W-011°
• 43°23'·8N 16°12'·4E

SPLITSKA VRATA

3338 Rt Livka
Fl(2)5s11m8M 168°-vis-058°
• 43°19'·8N 16°24'·2E
3342 Otok Brač Rt Rawanj
Fl.5s17m13M Siren(2) 42s
340°-vis-175°
Reserve light range 8M
• 43°19'·2N 16°24'·9E

LUKA SPLIT

3349 Split breakwater head
LFl.G.6s11m10M Siren 30s
285°-vis-252° Reserve light 5M
• 43°30'·1N 16°26'·4E
3350 Marina W mole head
Fl.R.6s9m5M
139°-via-020°
• 43°30'·2N 16°26'·2E
3354 Gat Sv Petra head
Fl(3)8s9m3M
• 43°30'·3N 16°26'·7E

BRACKI KANAL

3380 Otok Brač Puzisča Rt Sv Nikola
Fl.5s20m8M
• 43°21'·7N 16°44'·4E
3384 Povlja entrance E side
Fl.3s7m7M
• 43°20'·4N 16°50'·2E
3387 Baska Voda breakwater head
Fl.R.5s7m5M
• 43°21'·4N 16°57'·1E

HVARSKI KANAL

3388 Makarska Poluotoka Sveti Petar W point
Fl.5s16m11M
321°-vis-141° Reserve light 7M
• 43°17'·7N 17°00'·8E
3392 Rt Lasčatna
Fl(4)15s12m8M
• 43°18'·9N 16°54'·2E
3396 Rt Sumartin entrance E side
Fl.3s8m7M
• 43°16'·8N 16°52'·7E

PAKLENI KANAL

3404 Otok Hvar. Rt Pelegrin
Fl(3)10s21m8M
• 43°11'·7N 16°22'·3E
3406 Otočić Galisnik
Fl.G.3s11m5M
• 43°10'·0N 16°26'·6E
3410 Otočić Pokonji Dol
Fl.4s20m10M
• 43°09'·4N 16°27'·4E

HVARSKI KANAL

3412 Otok Hvar. Uvala Vira. Rt Galijola
Fl.2s8m6M
• 43°11'·9N 16°25'·8E
3418 Rt Kabal
Fl(2)5s16m7M
324°-vis-227°
• 43°13'·5N 16°31'·5E
3420 Luka Vrboska Rt Kriz
Fl.2s5m5M
• 43°10'·6N 16°41'·4E
3426 Otočić Zecevo E point
Fl.5s11m5M
• 43°11'·5N 16°42'·4E
3431 Luka Jelsa E breakwater head
Fl.R.3s6m5M
• 43°10'·0N 16°42'·4E
3431·5 Otok Vodnjak Veli
Fl.6s31m9M
• 43°10'·1N 16°19'·0E

OTOK VIS

3432 Rt Stončica
Fl.15s38m30M
110°-vis-357°
Reserve light 12M
• 44°04'·4N 16°15'·6E
3436 Viska Luka. Otočić Host near NE point
Fl.4s21m8M
• 43°04'·6N 16°12'·6E
3439 Hridi Voliči
Fl.2s8m6M
• 43°05'·2N 16°11'·9E
3440 Otočić Mali Barjak
Fl.3s13m8M
• 43°03'·2N 16°02'·7E
3443 Rt Stupisče
Fl(3)12s18m10M Reserve light 7M
• 43°00'·4N 16°04'·3E
3444 Otok Bisevo Rt Kobila
Fl(2)R.10s18m11M
Reserve light range 7M
• 42°59'·2N 16°01'·5E

KORCULANSKI KANAL

3445 Hridi Lukavci SE rock
Fl.R.3s14m5M
• 43°05'·0N 16°35'·2E
3446 Otok Sćedro. Rt Podsćedro
Fl.WR.6s21m10/6M
087°-R-094·5°-W-087°
• 43°05'·1N 16°40'·2E
3450 Otočić Plićina NW end
Fl(2)10s25m10M
• 43°01'·8N 16°49'·2E
3452 Otočić Proizd W end
Fl.3s11m11M
290°-vis-229°
• 42°59'·0N 16°36'·7E
3461 Rt Velo Dance
Fl(3)10s12m11M
• 42°55'·5N 16°38'·6E
3463 Rt Veli Zaglav
Fl.3s13m7M
• 42°53'·9N 16°51'·2E

PELJESKI KANAL

3470 Otočić Kneža Vela
Fl(2)6s13m8M
• 42°58'·9N 17°03'·5E
3482 Otok Sestrice. NW islet
Fl(4)15s18m11M
• 42°57'·8N 17°12'·7E
3486 Otok Korčula Rt Rawnjie
Fl.6s13m9M
• 42°55'·0N 17°12'·4E

POLUOTOK PELJESAC

3486·5 Rt Osičac
Fl.3s9m8M
322°-vis-270°
• 43°00'·6N 17°00'·6E

3488 Rt Lovisče
Fl(3)10s10m10M
357°-vis-258°
• 43°02'·8N 17°00'·4E

NERETVANSKI KANAL

3490 Otok Hvar Rt Sućuraj
Iso.4s14m11M
• 43°07'·5N 17°12'·1E

3500·5 Ploče (Kardeljevo) Rt Visnjica S side
Fl(2)5s13m7M
• 43°02'·4N 17°25'·3E

3502·2 Rijeka Neretva S mole head
Fl.G.2s5m5M
• 43°01'·1N 17°26'·74E

Adriatic Sea – Bosnia Herzegovina

KLEK-NEUM ZALJEV

3521 Rep Kleka
Fl.3s8m5M
• 42°56'·0N 17°33'·5E

Adriatic Sea – Croatia

MALOG STONA KANAL

3522 Rt Blaca
Fl.5s9m8M
127°-vis-285°
• 42°55'·5N 17°31'·4E

3526 Rt Celjen
Fl.3s10m6M
• 45°52'·2N 17°41'·1E

OTOK MJLET

3535·5 Hrid Crna Seka
Fl(3)WR.10s12m8/5M
060°-W-237°-R-060°
• 42°47'·7N 17°20'·2E

3536 Polače Hrid Kula
Fl.2s11m6M
• 42°47'·2N 17°26'·4E

3537 Sobra. Rt Pusti
Fl.3s14m7M
156°-vis-043°
• 42°44'·7N 17°37'·0E

3537·4 Uvalu Okuklje. Rt Stoba
Fl(2)5s10m6M
• 42°43'·7N 17°41'·1E

3538 Otok Susac Rt Kanula
Fl(2)15s94m24M
253°-vis-213°
Reserve light range 12M
• 42°45'·0N 16°29'·7E

OTOK LASTOVO

3544 Rt Struga
Fl.10s104m27M
259°-vis-095° Reserve light 12M
• 42°43'·4N 16°53'·4E

3548 Otok Prewba
Fl.WR.5s18m8/5M
067°-W-084° 235°-R-023°-W-045°
• 42°45'·2N 16°49'·1E

3551 Otočić Tajan Velji
Fl.5s20m8M
• 42°48'·9N 16°59'·7E

3552 Otočić Pod Mrčaru
Fl(2)6s23m9M
• 42°46'·8N 16°46'·8E

3554 Otočić Glavat
Fl(5)30s45m22M
120°-vis-070°
Reserve light range 12M
• 42°45'·9N 17°09'·0E

MLJETSKI KANAL

3560 Otočić Lirica W point
LFl.10s34m9M
293°-vis-233°
• 42°52'·4N 17°25'·9E

3561 Otočić Olipa
Fl(3)10s31m10M
253°-vis-104°
• 42°45'·5N 17°46'·9E

STRONSKI KANAL

3564 Rt Pologrin (Grbljava)
Fl.3s11m7M
• 42°47'·2N 17°47'·2E

KOLOCEPSKI KANAL

3576 Rt Tiha
Fl(2)8s14m9M
117°-vis-305°
• 42°45'·3N 17°51'·4E

3584 Trsteno Rt Picej
Fl(3)10s10m6M
• 42°42'·7N 17°58'·4E

3586 Otočić Palagruza
Fl.17·5s110m26M
Reserve light range 12M
• 42°23'·5N 16°15'·6E

3588 22m E
Iso.R.2s96m5M
264°-vis over Otoeid Galiola-304°
• 42°23'·5N 16°15'·6E

3590 Otočić Sv Andrija
Fl.15s69m24M
• 42°38'·8N 17°57'·3E

3598 Hridi Grebeni
Fl(3)10s27m10M
• 42°39'·1N 18°03'·2E

3600 Otočić Daksa
Fl.6s7m10M
023°-vis-295°
• 42°40'·2N 18°03'·6E

GRUJ

3601·7 Bridge centre
Iso.2s50m5M
• 42°40'·08N 18°05'·07E

3602 Harbour Rt Kantafig
Fl.2s7m5M
325°-vis-247°
• 42°40'·0N 18°05'·0E

SUPSKI ZALJEV

3614 Cavtat
Fl.WRG.2s10m6-3M
053°-W-083°-R-110°-W-129°-G-158°
• 42°35'·1N 18°13'·0E

3614·5 Pličena Seka Velika
Fl(2)10s8m8M
• 42°35'·1N 18°12'·6E

3615 Otočić Veliki Skolj
Fl(3)15s34m8M
• 42°26'·5N 18°26'·1E

3616 Gornji Molunat entrance N side
Fl.3s8m6M
• 42°26'·9N 18°26'·6E

3620 Rt Ostra (Ostri Rt)
LFl(2)10s73m15M
Reserve light range 10M
• 42°23'·6N 18°32'·2E

Adriatic Sea – Montenegro

BOKA KOTORSKA

3622 Ostrvce Mamula
Fl.3s34m6M
• 42°23'·8N 18°33'·8E

3622·5 Dobree
Fl.G.5s6m6M
• 42°25'·3N 18°33'·1E

HERCEGNOVSKI ZALIV

3624 Herceg-Novi breakwater head
Fl(2)G.5s9m5M
• 42°27'·0N 18°32'·4E

TIVATSKI ZALIV

3630 Kumborski Tjesnac Pristan mole head
Fl.G.3s7m5M
• 42°25'·5N 18°36'·4E

3632 Djenvići bridge head
Fl.R.3s14m6M
• 42°25'·9N 18°36'·6E

3632·5 Baosići mole head
Fl.R.5s5m3M
• 42°26'·5N 18°37'·8E

3638 Rt Seljanovo
Fl.R.3s7m5M
• 42°26'·3N 18°41'·4E

3645 Plićina Tunja
Fl(2)WR.5s8m6/4M
• 42°25'·0N 18°41'·0E

TJESNAC VERIGE

3652 Rt Sv Nedelja
Fl.R.2s7m5M
• 42°27'·6N 18°40'·9E

3658 Turski Rt Cape
Fl(2)5s9m6M
• 42°28'·7N 18°41'·5E

RISANSKI ZALIV

3663·6 Gospa
Fl(2)R.6s5m6M
• 42°29'·2N 18°41'·6E

KOTORSKI ZALIV

3671 Prčanj Markov rt
Fl(2)G.6s7m6M
• 42°28'·0N 18°44'·3E

3676 Cape N Rdakova
Fl.G.5s8m6M
• 42°26'·9N 18°45'·5E

3678 Muo quay head
Fl(2)G.5s5m5M
• 42°26'·1N 18°45'·7E

3682 Kotor NW side
Fl.R.3s8m5M
• 42°25'·6N 18°46'·3E

3683 Rt Plagente Cape
Fl(2)R.5s8m6M
• 42°26'·1N 18°46'·1E

TRASTE ZALIV

3684 Rt Traste Cape
Fl.3s9m5M
010°-vis-278°
• 42°21'·4N 18°41'·6E

3685 Rt Platamuni Cape
Fl.6s32m9M
• 42°16'·1N 18°47'·0E

3686 Otočić Sv Nikola SE point
Fl(3)10s23m8M
248°-vis-113°
• 42°15'·5N 18°51'·8E

BUDVA

3688·5 Katiči
Fl.R.4s25m6M
• 42°11'·71N 18°56'·42E

BARSKO SIDRISTE

3689 Crni Rt Cape
Fl.4s142m25M
• 42°08′·1N 19°00′·9E

3690 Rt Volujica Cape
Fl(2)10s30m20M
Reserve light range 16M
• 42°05′·3N 19°04′·5E

3691 Bar W breakwater head
Fl.G.3s19m6M
• 42°05′·9N 19°05′·0E

ULCINJ

3696 Rt Mendra (Mendre)
Fl(3)10s35m22M
• 41°57′·2N 19°09′·3E

3698 Vrh Trdave
Fl.3s27m8M
• 41°55′·3N 19°12′·4E

Adriatic Sea – Albania

SHËNGJIN

3702 Kepi i Shëngjinit
Fl.R.5s24m10M
• 41°48′·92N 19°35′·10E

3702·2 Breakwater head
Fl.R.3s10m5M
• 41°48′·59N 19°35′·15E

3702·5 Mali Renzit
Fl.5s46m10M
W of Shëngjin Harbour
• 41°48′·90N 19°34′·31E

3703 Ldg Lts 002°
Front Fl.R.6s5M
In centre of jetty
• 41°48′·89N 19°35′·32E

3703·1
Rear Fl.R.5s5M
On base of jetty
• 41°48′·89N 19°35′·30E

3704 Talej
Fl.6s15m7M
On roof of Hydro-Electric Station
• 41°42′·68N 19°35′·22E

3705 Kepi i Rodonit
Fl(2)10s40m8M
• 41°35′·24N 19°26′·68E

3708 Bishti i Pallës
Fl.10s33m10M
• 41°24′·8N 19°23′·5E

3711 Kepi i Durrësit
Fl(2)10s126m11M
• 41°18′·9N 19°26′·4E

DURRËS

3712 S mole head
Fl.R.5s8m6M
• 41°18′·15N 19°27′·33E

3714 E mole head
Fl.G.5s8m6M
• 41°18′·26N 19°27′·39E

3714·1 Dir Lt 019°
DirIso.WRG.2s7m7-5M
015°-G-016·5°-W-017·5°-019° Racon
• 41°18′·92N 19°28′·08E

3714·2
LFl.10s4m6M
• 41°15′·92N 19°26′·73E

3714·55 Talbot shoal
Q(6)+LFl.15s6M
• 41°17′·0N 19°26′·2E

3719 Kala e Turrës (Kepi i Lagit)
LFl.6s20m11M
• 41°08′·8N 19°26′·3E

3720 Karavastase
Fl.8s19m10M
On roof of Hydro-Electric Station
• 40°52′·9N 19°25′·5E

3721 Lumi i Vjosë entrance
Fl.3s12m7M
• 40°38′·9N 19°19′·0E

ISHULLI I SAZANIT

3723 Sazan
Fl(4)15s157m12M
065°-vis-318°
• 40°30′·3N 19°16′·1E

3726·5 Kep i Jugor
Fl.R.3s18m3M
• 40°28′·5N 19°17′·2E

GJIRI I VLORËS (VALONA BAY)

3727 Sqepi i Treporteve
Fl(2)8s70m9M
• 40°30′·7N 19°23′·8E

3729·5 Kepi Kalas
LFl.10s44m11M
• 40°24′·9N 19°28′·9E

3731 Pasha Limanit Sqepi Orikumm
Fl(2)5s21m8M
• 40°19′·68N 19°25′·20E

3732 Sqepi i Sevasinit
Fl(3)8s75m8M
• 40°22′·57N 19°24′·30E

3732·5 Kepi Gjuhezes
Fl.6s58m11M
• 40°25′·35N 19°17′·0E

3733 Grames
Fl.6s52m8M
• 40°13′·0N 19°28′·5E

PORTË E PALERMOS

3734 Kep i Palermos
Fl.8s113m8M
• 40°02′·8N 19°47′·5E

Adriatic Sea – Albania and Greece

3741 Kep i Qefalit
Fl(2)15s147m12M
• 39°54′·5N 19°54′·9E

GJIRI SARANDËS

3742·5 SE side
Fl(4)12s17m9M
• 39°50′·8N 20°01′·4E

Adriatic Sea – Greece

3747 Nísos Othonoi (Fano Island)
Fl.10s103m18M
• 39°51′·9N 19°25′·7E

3748 Nisída Ereikoussa
Fl(3)15s49m6M
• 39°53′·4N 19°35′·7E

KÉRKIRA

3749 Áy Aikateríni
Fl.10s14m6M
• 39°49′·0N 19°50′·9E

3750 Nisídha Peresteraí (Tignoso)
Fl.R.5s23m8M
• 39°47′·6N 19°57′·6E

3754·5 Ífalos Sérpa
Q(3)10s10m7M
• 39°46′·28N 19°57′·67E

3756 Limín Kérkira Ákra Sidhero Citadel
Fl(2)6s78m13M
112·5°-vis-045°
• 39°37′·5N 19°55′·8E

3776 Ákra Levkímmis
Fl.6s8m7M
• 39°27′·6N 20°04′·3E

3779 Vrákhoi Lagoúdhia
Fl(3)14s17m7M
• 39°25′·1N 19°54′·3E

3780 Ákra Kostéri
Fl.3s25m5M
• 39°40′·3N 19°42′·8E

3782 Saigiáda
Fl.3s6m5M
• 39°37′·6N 20°10′·9E

3783 Nisís Prasoúdhi
Fl(2)9s30m8M
• 39°30′·6N 20°09′·4E

ÓRMOS IGOUMENÍTSAS

3784 Ákra Kondramoúrto
Fl.3s11m5M
• 39°29′·9N 20°13′·7E

3784·2 Pier head
2F.R(vert)9m5M
• 39°30′·1N 20°15′·7E

3786 Nísis Sívota
Fl(3)20s87m12M
• 39°24′·4N 20°12′·6E

3788 Ormos Párgas. On point SW of town
Fl(2)6s25m6M
• 39°17′·0N 20°23′·9E

NÍSOS PAXOÍ

3792 Lákka
Fl(3)24s64m20M
• 39°14′·2N 20°07′·7E

3794 Nisís Panagía
Fl.WR.5s26m10/8M
135°-W-250°-R-283°-W-325°
• 39°12′·3N 20°11′·7E

3796 Nisís Andípaxoi Ákra Ovorós
Fl.WR.5s41m20/15M
136°-W-167°-R-185°-W-307°-R-037°-W-060°
Reserve light F.WR
• 39°08′·5N 20°14′·9E

3800 Ákra Mytikas
Fl.WR.3s12m7/5M
347°-W-078°-R-135°-W-147°
• 39°00′·0N 20°41′·9E

AMVRAKIKÓS KÓLPOS

3804 Stenó Prevézis Ldg Lts 066° Aktion
Front Q.Y.5m7M

3804·1 Aiyialós Dhéndrou.
Rear 338m from front
LFl.Y.6s9m7M
• 38°56′·8N 20°45′·9E

3806 Akrí Point
LFl.7·5s4m5M
• 38°57′·5N 20°45′·9E

3811 Ákra Laskára
Fl(2)R.6s12m5M
• 38°57′·4N 20°49′·2E

3820 Ákra Kópraina
Fl(2)WR.16s9m5/3M
169°-W-349°-R-169°
• 39°01′·8N 21°04′·6E

NÍSOS LEVKAS

3832 Fort Agios Mávra Citadel. N battlement
Fl(2)WR.12s17m8/5M
075°-R-120°-W-255°
• 38°50′·8N 20°43′·2E

3835 Nisídha Sésoula
Fl.4·5s37m8M
• 38°41′·8N 20°32′·4E

3836 Ákra Dhoukató
Fl.10s70m20M
• 38°33′·9N 20°32′·6E

NISÍS MEGANÍSI

3840 Ákra Elia
Fl.WR.8s12m10/7M
070°-R-165°-W-019°
• 38°40′·1N 20°48′·5E

ÓRMOS DHREPÁNOU

3842 Nisís Volíos
Fl.WR.1·5s8m5/3M
335°-W-181°, 293°-R-335°
• 38°47′·7N 20°43′·7E

3844 Ákra Kefáli, Drepanon Bay
Fl.4s11m5M
• 38°45′·5N 20°45′·8E

3846 Nisís Formíkoula
Fl.WR.3s17m8/5M
000°-R-180°-W-000°
• 38°34′·0N 20°51′·3E

3848 Atoko Islet S point
Fl.6s25m10M
• 38°28′·5N 20°48′·4E

3852 Ákra Kamilávka
Fl(3)10s24m7M
• 38°40′·4N 20°55′·2E

3854 Nísos Kálamos. Ákra Asprogiáli
Fl.10s13m5M
• 38°39′·2N 20°57′·6E

3856 Nisís Kastos mole head
Fl.R.4s6m5M
• 38°34′·17N 20°54′·78E

NÍSOS ITHÁKI

3858 Ákra Agios Nikoláos
Fl(3)15s15m7M
• 38°29′·4N 20°40′·7E

3860 Port Vathí. Ákra Agios Andreas Setos Gulf
Fl.3s20m5M
• 38°23′·12N 20°42′·15E

3864 Ákra Agios Ioánnis
Fl.10s10m10M
• 38°19′·3N 20°46′·0E

3866 Ákra Pisaitós. Far-Aetos Point. Pisaites Bay
Fl.5s19m6M
• 38°21′·8N 20°40′·0E

KEFALLINÍA

3868 Ákra Kateliós
Fl(2)WR.15s107m11/8M
262°-R-302°-W-100°
• 38°03′·8N 20°44′·7E

3869 Ákra Kapri
Fl(3)WR.9s20m6/4M
190°-W-354°-R-017°
• 38°06′·6N 20°48′·9E

3869·42 NE mole head
Fl.R.4s8m5M
• 38°09′·0N 20°47′·0E

3869·7 Ákra Sarakinato (Poros Bay)
Fl.4s16m5M
• 38°09′·0N 20°47′·3E

3870 Ákra Dekalia (Akra Dikhalia)
Fl(2)R.8s17m5M
• 38°16′·9N 20°40′·6E

3876 Ákra Fiskárdo
Fl.3s28m7M
• 38°27′·7N 20°35′·0E

3880 Ákra Yerogómbos (Gerogompos Cape)
LFl(2)15s58m24M
• 38°10′·9N 20°20′·5E

3882 Nisís Vardhiánoi E end
Fl.WR.7·5s11m6/4M
200°-R-222°-W-080°-R-107°
• 38°08′·0N 20°25′·6E

3890 Ákra Ayíou Theodhóron. Theodori Point. Argostoli Gulf
Fl.3s11m5M
• 38°11′·6N 20°28′·1E

3896 Nisís Kalógiros NE peak
Fl.4s31m8M
• 38°29′·7N 21°01′·9E

3901·5 Provati islet S point
Fl.5s9m6M
• 38°27′·4N 21°02′·7E

3903 Navagio Rock
Fl(2)10s8m6M
• 38°26′·6N 21°02′·9E

NISÍS PETALÁ

3905 Makri Island N Point
Fl.4s10m6M
• 38°22′·4N 21°01′·5E

3906 Nisis Kounéli
Fl.8s28m6M
• 38°21′·1N 21°03′·3E

3908 Ákra Oxeia
Fl(2)15s70m17M
• 38°16′·92N 21°05′·83E

3910 Ákra Páppas
LFl(2)20s7m10M
• 38°12′·9N 21°22′·4E

LÍMIN MESOLÓNGION

3912 Nisís Áyios Sóstis E end
Fl.WR.5s12m17/14M
293°-R-010°-W-059°, 198°-W-203°
• 38°19′·3N 21°22′·4E

3918 Limenisklos Alikon Kato Akhaia. Outer mole head
Fl.WR.3s8m5/3M
120°-W-269°-R-120°
• 38°09′·3N 21°32′·5E

LÍMIN PÁTRON. PÁTRAI

3919 NW breakwater head
Fl.G.5s12m8M
• 38°15′·6N 21°44′·0E

3919·2 Middle
Fl.R.5s7m8M
• 38°15′·59N 21°44′·17E

3927 Fish harbour mole head (Agios Andréas)
Fl.G.6s8m10M
• 38°14′·8N 21°43′·7E

KORINTHIAKOS KÓLPOS

3938 Ákra Andírrion (on the fort of Antirrion Point)
Fl(2)10s16m10M
• 38°19′·7N 21°46′·0E

3938·5 Pioy/Antippioy (Riou/Antirriou Bridge) Main Span centre W side
Iso.4s58m8M Racon
• 38°19′·29N 21°46′·42E

3938·502 N. W side
Iso.R.4s54m6M
• 38°19′·36N 21°46′·39E

3938·504 S. W side
Iso.G.4s54m6M
• 38°19′·22N 21°46′·47N

3938·506 N Span. Centre. W side
Q.42m6M
• 38°19′·57N 21°46′·27E

3938·512 S Span. Centre. W side
Q.42m6M
• 38°19′·03N 21°46′·57E

3938·518 Main Span. Centre. E side
Iso.4s58m8M
• 38°19′·30N 21°46′·44E

3938·52 N. E side
Iso.R.4s54m6M
• 38°19′·36N 21°46′·40E

3938·522 S. E side
Iso.G.4s54m6M
• 38°19′·22N 21°46′·44E

3938·524 N Span. Centre. E side
Q.42m6M
• 38°19′·57N 21°46′-29E

3938·53 S Span. Centre. E side
Q.1s42m6M
• 38°19′·03N 21°46′·59E

3940 Ákra Ríon (Rion Point)
Fl.6s16m6M
• 38°18′·8N 21°46′·9E

3946 Ákra Mórnos (Mornas Point)
Fl(3)15s7m7M
• 38°22′·2N 21°52′·6E

3948 Ákra Dhrépanon (Drepano Point)
Fl.10s10m10M
• 38°20′·4N 21°51′·0E

3948·5 Arakhovitika. Fishing harbour mole head
Fl.G.4s6m5M
• 38°19′·80N 21°50′·47E

3956 Ákra Psaromíta (Psaromyta Point)
Fl(2)15s65m21M
• 38°19′·4N 22°11′·1E

3958 Krissaíos Kólpos. Ákra Andromákhi (Andromachi Point)
Fl(3)15s14m10M
• 38°20′·0N 22°22′·7E

3960 Ormos Galaxidiou. Nisida Apsifia (On the E point of Spsifia Island)
Fl.7s13m5M
• 38°22′·8N 22°24′·2E

3963·2 Marina breakwater head
Q.R.7m5M
• 38°25′·86N 22°45′·40E

3964 Ákra Mákry-Nicólas
Fl.4·5s18m5M
• 38°17′·0N 22°33′·1E

3965·03 Fonía W end. Laimas Point
Fl(2)10s18m7M
• 38°10′·50N 22°56′·78E

3967 Ákra Likoporiá
Fl(2)16s17m10M
• 38°08′·2N 22°29′·5E

3972 Ákra Melangávi (Cape Melagkavi)
Fl.10s60m19M
• 38°01′·8N 22°51′·0E

3973 Angirovólion Kiáto breakwater head
Fl.G.3s9m6M
• 38°00′·9N 22°45′·3E

3976 Dhiórix Korínthou NW entrance Posidonía N mole head
Iso.R.2s10m10M
Dhiórix Korinthíou is marked by lights
• 37°57′·3N 22°57′·6E

3977 S mole head
Iso.G.2s10m10M
Traffic signals 500m SE
• 37°57′·2N 22°57′·5E

NÍSOS ZÁKYNTHOS

3984 Ákra Skinári
Fl.5s66m20M
• 37°55′·9N 20°42′·2E

3985 Nisídha Áy Nikólaos (Point Agios, Nikolaos Is)
Fl.2s15m7M
• 37°54′·4N 20°42′·8E

3986 Kryonéri
Fl(2)16s21m6M
• 37°48′·3N 20°54′·3E

3988 Zakynthou N mole head
Fl.G.1·5s11m5M
• 37°46′·9N 20°54′·4E

3990 Ákri Kerí (Kerry Point)
Fl.10s194m17M
• 37°39′·3N 20°48′·5E

3996 Nisís Kafkalídha
LFl.WR.10s21m12/9M
016°-W-059°-R-092°-W-211°
• 37°56′·5N 21°07′·3E

3997 Ákra Tripití (Trypiti Point)
Fl(3)15s7m7M
• 37°50′·6N 21°06′·7E

3998 Ákra Katakólo
Fl.4s49m15M
• 37°38′·3N 21°18′·9E

4000 Limeras Katakolas, Pier Head
Fl.R.5s10m10M
• 37°38′·8N 21°19′·6E

NISÍDHES STROFÁDHES

4004 Nisís Stamfáni
Fl(2)15s39m17M
• 37°14'·9N 21°00'·2E

4006 Nisís Próti S point
Fl.1·5s13m6M
• 37°02'·1N 21°33'·2E

ÓRMOS NAVARÍNOU

4008 Nísos Pylos SE point
Fl(2)10s32m9M
• 36°54'·4N 21°40'·4E

4009 Neókastro
Fl.G.3s15m6M
• 36°54'·8N 21°41'·3E

NÍSOS SAPIÉNTZA

4015 Ákra Karsí
Fl.3s22m5M
• 36°47'·8N 21°42'·3E

4016 S summit
Fl(3)20s116m18M
• 36°44'·6N 21°41'·8E

4017 Nisís Venético (Venetiko Island)
Fl.9s8m7M
• 36°42'·4N 21°53'·2E

4020 Ákra Livádia (Livadia Point)
Fl.1·5s19m5M
• 36°47'·7N 21°58'·1E

4022 Petalidio Point
Fl.4s7m5M
• 36°57'·6N 21°56'·2E

LIMENAS KALAMATAS

4032 Ákra Kitries
Fl(2)12s32m7M
• 36°55'·0N 22°07'·6E

4036 Port Kardhamíli
Fl.3s10m5M
352°-vis-093°
• 36°53'·2N 22°14'·0E

4038 Ágios Nikolaos
Fl.3s9m5M
• 36°49'·5N 22°16'·8E

4040 Limeni entrance S side
Fl.1·5s17m6M
• 36°40'·9N 22°22'·3E

4042 Mezapos
Fl.3s16m5M
• 36°32'·9N 22°23'·1E

4044 Yerolimena
Fl.3s18m6M
• 36°28'·8N 22°23'·9E

LAKONIKÓS KÓLPOS

4048 Ákra Taínaron (Cape Matapan)
Fl(2)20s41m22M
• 36°23'·2N 22°29'·0E

4050 Pórto Kágio
Fl.5s20m8M
• 36°26'·0N 22°29'·5E

4052 Limín Yíthion Nisís Krani E end
Fl(3)18s25m14M
• 36°45'·3N 22°34'·6E

4060 Órmos Xílis Ákra Xílis 450m NE
Fl.3s11m5M
• 36°39'·4N 22°49'·0E

Aegean Sea – Greece

4065 Vrakhonisís Andidhragonéra
Fl(3)15s14m7M
• 36°14'·2N 23°07'·1E

NÍSOS KÍTHIRA

4066 Ákra Spathí
Fl(3)30s114m20M
062°-vis-319°
• 36°22'·9N 22°57'·0E

4068 Órmos Kapsáli E side
Fl.3s24m10M
• 36°08'·6N 23°00'·0E

4070·6 Vrakhonisís Makrónisos (on Makrónisos Island)
Fl.10s18m7M
• 36°16'·5N 23°04'·8E

NÍSOS ANDÍKITHIRA

4072 Ákra Apolitárais
Fl(2)15s40m17M
• 35°49'·5N 23°19'·6E

4072·4 Órmos Potamós Ákra Kástro
Fl.5s31m6M
013°-vis-227°
• 35°53'·5N 23°17'·7E

4074 Órmos Vátika
Fl.3s16m7M
• 36°29'·5N 23°03'·9E

4076 Ákra Zóvolo (Zovolo Point)
Fl.7s13m12M
• 36°25'·8N 23°07'·9E

4078 Ákra Maléas
Fl.10s40m17M
175°-vis-345°
• 36°27'·1N 23°12'·1E

4080 Nisís Monemvasía E Point
Fl.5s15m11M
• 36°41'·4N 23°03'·6E

PÓRTO YÉRAKAS

4086 Ákra Kástro
Fl.G.3s21m5M
• 36°47'·2N 23°05'·3E

4088 Nisís Falkonéra S end
Fl.5s152m17M
169°-vis-°120°
• 36°50'·4N 23°53'·4E

4090 Nisís Parapóla NW point summit
Fl(2)20s112m22M
342°-vis-319°
• 36°55'·8N 23°27'·2E

ÓRMOS KIPARÍSSI

4094 Ákra Kórtia
Fl.4s42m7M 180°-vis-050°
• 36°59'·1N 23°00'·4E

ARGOLIKÓS KÓLPOS

4098 Ákra Sampatekí (Cape Sabatekí)
LFl.7·5s22m6M
• 37°11'·4N 22°54'·7E

4099 Nísos Spétsai Ákra Mavrókavos
Fl.WR.2s7m5/3M
199°-W-314°-333°-W-019°
• 37°14'·8N 23°10'·0E

4100 Ákra Fanári
Fl.WR.5s27m18/14M
124°-W-254°-R-278°-W-330°
• 37°15'·9N 23°10'·1E

4103 Nisís Petrokáravo
Fl(2)9s22m7M
• 37°17'·1N 23°04'·9E

4104 Ákra Ástrous head
Fl.5s77m7M
• 37°25'·45N 22°46'·18E

4105 Parálion Ástrous. E mole head
F.G.8m5M
• 37°24'·9N 22°46'·0E

4105·5 W mole head
Fl.R.6m5M
• 37°24'·9N 22°46'·0E

4108 Ákra Panayítsa
Fl.1·5s11m5M
• 37°33'·8N 22°47'·6E

4110·4 Ákra Skála
Fl(2)WR.10s23m6/4M
207°-W-315°-R over Ífalos Toló-343°-W-075°
• 37°30'·2N 22°52'·5E

4111 Ákra Agios Nikolaos
Fl(3)WR.15s12m5/3M
301°-W-046°-R over Ífalos Toló-058°-W-220°
• 37°31'·4N 22°56'·1E

4112 Nisís Ipsilí SW point
Fl.5s14m9M
301°-vis-157°
• 37°25'·9N 22°58'·1E

4114 Ákra Kórakas
Fl.7s12m11M
311°-vis-131°
• 37°21'·2N 23°04'·1E

4118 Limín Khelíou entrance NW point
Fl.1·5s22m5M
• 37°18'·9N 23°07'·7E

4119 Áyios Aimilianós S end
Fl.WR.10s7m8/6M
193°-W-314°-R-357°-W-070°
• 37°17'·4N 23°12'·0E

LIMÍN ERMIÓNIS

4124 Nisís Dhokós SE point
Fl(2)WR.12s23m6/4M
219°-W-341°-R-026°-W-063°
• 37°20'·0N 23°21'·4E

NISÍS ÍDHRA

4134 Ákra Zoúrva
Fl(3)20s36m17M
128°-vis-023°
• 37°21'·9N 23°34'·7E

4135 Nisídhes Tselevínia. Nisís Skilli NE Point
Fl.3s31m8M
078°-vis-010°
• 37°26'·7N 23°32'·8E

4136 Nisís Ayio Yeóryios near SE end
Fl(2)15s145m17M
169°-vis-116°
• 37°27'·8N 23°56'·4E

NÍSOS PÓROS

4140 Ákra Dána
Fl.WR.5s31m8/5M
026°-W-200°-R-209°-W-266°
• 37°31'·7N 23°25'·6E

KÓLPOS EPIDHÁVROU

4141·6 Ákra Kalamáki
Fl.2s10m6M
185°-vis-095°
• 37°38'·5N 23°10'·2E

4141·9 Spalathronísi
Fl.8s37m6M
• 37°42'·2N 23°14'·2E

4142 Órmos Sofikoú
Fl.4s11m5M
• 37°45'·6N 23°07'·8E

4143 Nisís Evráios NE point
Fl.10s48m7M
• 37°51'·7N 23°08'·78E

NÍSOS AÍYINA

4144 Ákra Plakákia
Fl(2)15s11m7M
• 37°45'·8N 23°25'·1E

4148 Limín Aíyina NW mole head (S end of E quay. New Aigina harbour)
Fl.5s7m7M
• 37°44'·7N 23°25'·5E

4152 Ákra Toúrlos
Fl.3·6s28m5M
177°-vis-024°
• 37°45'·8N 23°33'·9E

NISÍS MONÍ

4154 Ákra Kostís SW Point
Fl(2)WRG.10s26m11/8M
296°-W-322°-R-336°-W-075°-G-165°-W-173°-R-187°-W-223°
• 37°41'·2N 23°25'·4E

4158 Nisís Lagoúsa E point
LFl.7·5s12m5M
130°-vis-049°
• 37°48'·9N 23°28'·5E

DHIÓRIX KORINTHÓU ISTHMÍA

4160 SE entrance W side
Iso.R.2s10m10M
Traffic signals 350m NW
• 37°55'·0N 23°00'·6E

4160·4 Mole head
Iso.G.2s8m10M
• 37°55'·0N 23°00'·7E

4162 Ákra Sousáki
Fl.G.10s8m12M
May be difficult to distinguish against shore lights
• 37°54'·8N 23°03'·5E

4163·3 Nisís Pákhi E point
Fl.WR.3s13m5/3M
145°-W-030°-R-054°-W-078°
• 37°57'·9N 23°22'·1E

ÓRMOS ÁYIOS YEORYÍOU AND SW APPROACHES

4164 Ákra Káras
Fl.4s8m8M
• 37°57'·5N 23°25'·0E

4164·4 Nisís Revithoúsa E end
Fl.1·5s9m6M
• 37°57'·6N 23°24'·4E

4167 Nisídhes Kanákia
Fl.6s17m5M
288°-vis-254°
• 37°54'·3N 23°23'·6E

4168 Ákra Kónkhi
Fl.4s34m9M
• 37°52'·5N 23°27'·0E

4170 Nisís Psyttáleia NE end
Fl(2)15s47m25M
• 37°56'·7N 23°35'·7E

KINÓSOURA

4171·5 Dhrapetsónas mole head
Fl(2)G.10s14m9M
• 37°57'·0N 23°35'·9E

PÉRAMA

4174 Ákra Fylatoúri
Fl(2)14s13m5M
352°-vis-233°
• 37°58'·9N 23°33'·2E

4174·2 Nisís Arpidhóni W end
Fl.1·5s7m5M
• 37°59'·4N 23°33'·6E

4174·6 Nisís Megáli Kirá W point
Fl.2·5s7m5M
• 38°00'·0N 23°33'·5E

4174·8 Chalyps Cement Factory
2F.G(vert)9m6M
• 38°02'·1N 23°35'·5E

KÓLPOS ELEVÍSNAS

4175·7 Órmos Toúrkolimano. Petrola Pier No.2 head
Iso.R.2s11m9M
• 38°02'·0N 23°30'·6E

4176·1 NW mole head
Fl.R.3s7m5M
• 37°57'·72N 23°29'·60E

4176·2 SE mole head
Fl.G.3s7m5M
• 37°57'·73N 23°29'·73E

PEIRAIAS

4178 Mólos Themistokléous head (S mole)
LFl.G.6s13m9M
Traffic signals
• 37°56'·3N 23°37'·3E

LIMIN PIRAIÉVS

4180 Mólos Vasiléos Yeoryíou head
LFl.R.6s14m9M
• 37°56'·4N 23°37'·4E

4182 Limín Zéas S breakwater head
Fl(2)R.6s10m7M
• 37°56'·0N 23°39'·2E

ÓRMOS FALÍROU

4186 Limín Mounikhías N breakwater head
Fl.G.3s9m6M
205°-vis-145°
• 37°56'·3N 23°39'·7E

4186·2 S breakwater head
Iso.R.2s10m8M
109°-vis-049°
• 37°56'·2N 23°39'·8E

4189·5 Flísvos S mole head
Fl.G.4s11m9M
• 37°56'·11N 23°40'·80E

4189·55 N breakwater head
Fl.R.4s8m7M
• 37°56'·2N 23°40'·8E

4189·6 Limeniskos Alimou Marina W mole head
Fl.G.3s10m9M
• 37°54'·8N 23°42'·1E

4189·8 E mole head
Fl.R.3s10m9M
• 37°54'·7N 23°42'·2E

4190 Áy Kosmás
Q(9)15s9m5M
• 37°53'·6N 23°42'·7E

GLYFADHA

4193 Nisís Fléves
Fl(3)10s41m8M
285°-vis-161°
• 37°46'·0N 23°45'·5E

LIMENÍSKOS VOULIAGMÉNIS

4194 SE mole head
Fl(3)R.12s9m7M
• 37°48'·3N 23°46'·5E

4202 Nisís Patróklou (Gaïdouronissos) N point
LFl.10s7m6M
• 37°39'·5N 23°57'·5E

STENÓN MAKRÓNISOU

4204 Ákra Angálistros
Fl(2)14s32m12M
207°-vis-168°
• 37°38'·8N 24°06'·4E

4208 Ákra Foniás (Fonías Point)
Fl.2·5s13m6M
• 37°41'·2N 24°04'·4E

4208·5 Órmos Gaidhourómandra (Olympic) Marina S mole head
Fl.R.4s7m12M
• 37'41'·8N 24°03'·7E

4209·1 Lavrio N mole head
Fl.G.3s8m5M
• 37°42'·7N 24°04'·0E

4209·3 Liménas Laurión (Lavrio) S breakwater head
Fl.R.3s8m5M
• 37°42'·51N 24°03'·93E

4210 Ákra Vrisáki
Fl.5s21m16M 186°-vis-006°
• 37°44'·7N 24°04'·9E

NÍSOS KÉA

4212 Áyios Nikólaous Ákra Áyios Nikólaous
Fl(2)10s32m15M
• 37°40'·1N 24°18'·9E

4214 Ákra Áyiou Sávvas
Fl.1·5s21m5M
• 37°39'·8N 24°18'·7E

4218 Ákra Tamélos
Fl(2)15s61m17M
• 37°31'·4N 24°16'·6E

NÍSOS KÍTHNOS

4220 Ákra Kéfalos
Fl.4s54m9M
• 37°28'·9N 24°26'·3E

4222 Órmos Loutrón S entrance point
Fl.1·5s14m5M
• 37°26'·6N 24°26'·0E

4223 Ákra Áyios Dhimítrios
Fl.10s23m12M
• 37°18'·1N 24°21'·9E

4224 Ákra Mérikha
Fl.WR.5s23m5/3M
315°-W-340°-R-030°-W-173°
• 37°23'·9N 24°23'·4E

NÍSOS SÉRIFOS

4228 Ákra Spathí
Fl(3)30s67m19M
• 37°06'·82N 24°30'·33E

4230 Ákra Kíklops
Fl(2)14s67m9M
• 37°07'·4N 24°25'·0E

NÍSOS SÍFNOS

4234 Ákra Fílippos
Fl.5s42m9M
• 37°02'·53N 24°38'·37E

4234·5 Ákra Kokkála
Fl(2)10s47m9M
292°-vis-207°
• 37°00'·0N 24°39'·3E

4236·4 Órmos Vathlí. Ákra Maïstros
Fl.2s33m7M
332°-vis-253°
• 36°55'·5N 24°41'·3E

4237 Ákra Stavrós (Stavros Point)
Fl.1·5s26m5M
• 36°56'·4N 24°45'·2E

4238 Nísos Kímolos Órmos Sémina
Fl.G.5s11m5M
Located at SE end of entrance to Agios Minas Bay, Kimolos Island
• 36°48'·4N 24°35'·6E

NÍSOS MÍLOS

4239 Ákra Pelekoúdha (Pelekouda Point)
Fl.2s17m5M
• 36°46'·2N 24°31'·7E

4240 Nisídhes Akrádhia
Fl.10s88m10M
• 36°46'·9N 24°23'·4E

4242 Órmos Mílou. Ákra Bombárdha
Fl.5s36m12M
234°-vis-128°
• 36°43'·3N 24°26'·1E

4244 Nisís Andímilos. Ákra Kokhlídi
Fl.2s60m8M
312°-vis-170°
• 36°47'·1N 24°13'·4E

4246 Nisís Paximádhi
Fl(2)15s26m12M
273°-vis-183°
• 36°37'·97N 24°19'·10E

4248 Vrakhonisís Anánes
Fl(3)12s85m9M
• 36°33'·1N 24°08'·8E

4250 Nisís Áyios Evstáthios N end
Fl(3)15s26m6M
033°-vis-000°
• 36°46'·7N 24°35'·0E

NÍSOS POLÍAGOS

4252 Ákra Máskoula
Fl.5s138m19M
• 36°46'·6N 24°39'·7E

NÍSOS FOLÉGANDROS

4256 Ákra Asprópounda
Fl(3)30s70m17M
306°-vis-138°
• 36°38′·0N 24°51′·6E

4258 Órmos Karavostási entrance
Fl.WR.6s15m10/7M
202°-R-248°-W-322°-R-344°-W-096°
• 36°37′·0N 24°57′·2E

NÍSOS SÍKINOS

4260 Órmos Skála
Fl.5s18m8M
• 36°40′·5N 25°09′·0E

NÍSOS ÍOS

4261 Mole head
Fl.R.3s8m5M
• 36°40′·6N 25°08′·7E

4262 Ákra Fanári
Fl.5s33m9M
• 36°42′·95N 25°15′·58E

NÍSOS THÍRA

4266 Ákra Akrotíri
Fl.10s100m24M
• 36°21′·5N 25°21′·5E

4266·5·Katsouni breakwater head
Fl.G.3s8m5M
• 36°23′·3N 25°25′·7E

4267 Néa Kamméni E side
Fl.3s8m5M
• 36°24′·1N 25°24′·4E

4270 Ammoúdhi Point
Fl.4s71m10M
347°-vis-241°
• 36°28′·0N 25°22′·2E

NÍSOS ANÁFI

4275 Nikolaos Point mole head
Fl.R.3s11m5M
• 36°20′·6N 25°46′·2E

4276 Nisídhes Khristianá Vrakhonisís Eskhati
Fl(3)9s24m10M
• 36°13′·3N 25°13′·8E

NÍSOS AMORGÓS

4277 Ákra Goniá
Fl.8s76m11M
263°-vis-090°
• 36°46′·1N 25°48′·1E

4277·5 Nísis Gramvoúsa
Fl.1·5s14m5M
024°-vis-336°
• 36°49′·2N 25°44′·8E

4278 Órmos Katápola. Ákra Áyios Ilías
Fl(2)10s46m12M
• 36°50′·2N 25°50′·4E

4278·4 Ákra Ákrotíri
Fl.5s95m8M
289·5°-vis-206°
• 36°54′·7N 25°57′·4E

4278·5 Liménas Aiyiáli mole head
Fl.G.3s6m5M
• 36°54′·2N 25′·58′·5E

4279 Nisídhes Liadhi N islet
Fl(2)20s65m9M
• 36°54′·5N 26°10′·0E

4280 Nisís Lévitha. Ákra Spanó
Fl.10s27m11M
161°-vis-075°
• 37°00′·0N 26°29′·9E

4282 Nisís Strongiló
Fl(2)14s50m5M
• 36°56′·8N 24°57′·3E

4283 Nisís Dhespotikó Ákra Koutsouras
Fl.4s39m5M
• 36°57′·9N 25°02′·0E

4284 Vrakhonisídha Pórtes (N rock islet)
Fl(2)10s22m7M
• 37°06′·1N 25°06′·1E

NÍSOS PÁROS

4286 Órmos Paroikiás. Ákra Áyios Fokas
Fl.4s11m6M
226°-vis157°
• 37°05′·5N 25°08′·0E

4289 Stenó Andipárou. Nisís Sálanko
Fl.WR.4s11m5/3M
341°-R-016°-W-135°-R-161°-W-341°
• 37°03′·0N 25°05′·8E

4290 Ákra Kórakas
LFl.12s60m14M
059°-vis-311°
• 37°09′·3N 25°13′·5E

4292 Ákra Kratzi
Fl(3)WG.15s23m12/10M
250°-G-260°-W-250°
• 37°03′·0N 25°16′·7E

4293 Vrákhoi Amarídhes
Fl.WR.4s10m5/3M
015°-W-185°-R-015°
• 37°03′·1N 25°19′·0E

4293·6 Limín Náxou N breakwater head
Fl.R.4s8m7M
• 37°06′·5N 25°22′·2E

4294 Nísos Iráklia Órmos Agios Georgios
Fl.1·5s21m5M
• 36°52′·33N 25°28′·52E

4294·1 Nisís Skhoinoúsa. Órmos Mersiniá
Fl.4s10m6M
• 36°52′·1N 25°30′·5E

4294·15 N Rock
Fl.7s6M
• 36°53′·48N 25°32′·60E

4294·4 Vrakhonisídha Plakí
Fl(2)8s8M
• 36°51′·78N 25°37′·40E

4294·5 Vrakhónisis Kopriá
Fl(2)12s75m10M
• 36°59′·3N 25°38′·3E

4295 Ákra Stavrós
Fl(2)16s50m13M
• 37°12′·1N 25°32′·0E

4295·2 Nisos Donoussa
Fl.R.3s8m5M
• 37°06′·0N 25°47′·7E

4295·5 Nísos Dhenoúsa Ákra Kaloteroúsa
Fl(3)15s147m10M
• 37°08′·2N 25°49′·8E

4295·7 Vrákhoi Boúvais (Melántioi)
Fl.8s52m12M
• 37°14′·4N 25°55′·7E

4296 Nisís Mikrós Avélos
Fl(3)10s40m7M
• 36°49′·7N 25°23′·8E

4298 Vrákhos Mérmingas
Fl.5s17m8M
• 37°11′·7N 25°03′·7E

4299 Vrakhónisis Khtapódhia
Fl(2)10s130m10M
• 37°24′·7N 25°33′·9E

NÍSOS MÍKONOS

4302 Ákra Armenistís
Fl.10s184m22M
022°-vis-241°
• 37°29′·4N 25°18′·9E

4303 Nisísdhes Prasonísia
Fl.3s23m6M
• 37°23′·6N 25°17′·9E

4304 Nisís Náta W summit
Fl.3s16m6M
• 37°22′·0N 25°03′·6E

NÍSOS SÍROS

4306 Nisís Áspro
Fl(2)12s52m7M
• 37°23′·60N 24°59′·66E

4308 Nisís Gáïdharos
Fl.6s67m12M
• 37°25′·7N 24°58′·4E

4310 Ákra Kondoyiánnis (Kontogianni Point)
Fl.3s18m5M
• 37°25′·9N 24°57′·2E

4311 Limín Ermoupolis N breakwater head
Fl.G.3s10m9M
• 37°26′·3N 24°56′·9E

4311·2 S mole head
Fl.R.3s11m9M
• 37°26′·1N 24°56′·9E

4312 Ákra Trímeson
Fl(2)14s62m12M
• 37°30′·9N 24°53′·0E

4313 Psathonísi (on summit of island)
Fl.2s7m5M
• 37°23′·3N 24°51′·7E

4314·5 Foinikas N mole head
Fl.G.4s7m5M
• 37°23′·9N 24°52′·6E

4314·6 S mole head
Fl.R.4s7m5M
• 37°23′·9N 24°52′·7E

4316 Ákra Velostási
Fl(3)12s75m6M
251°-vis-151°
• 37°21′·8N 24°52′·7E

NÍSOS TÍNOS

4318 Vrakhónisis Dhísvato
Fl.10s33m16M
• 37°40′·4N 24°58′·1E

4320 Nisís Planitís
Fl(2)14s80m10M
• 37°39′·6N 25°04′·1E

4322 Ákra Livádha
Fl.15s41m7M
• 37°36′·7N 25°15′·2E

4327 Outer breakwater head
Fl.R.3s10m7M
• 37°32′·3N 25°09′·3E

NÍSOS ANDROS

4330 Ákra Fássa
LFl.10s201m22M
• 37°57′·88N 24°42′·18E

4332 Ákra Kastrí
Fl.6s68m8M
• 37°52′·6N 24°43′·6E

4333 Ákra Kolóna
Fl.3s19m5M
237°-vis-156°
• 37°51′·3N 24°46′·7E

4334 Órmos Kástro. Nisís Tourlítis
Fl(2)15s19m6M
• 37°50′·7N 24°56′·8E

4337·5 Ákra Áyios Kosmás
Fl.3s68m7M
• 37°46′·3N 25°00′·0E

4338 Ákra Griá
Fl.10s86m25M
• 37°54′·0N 24°57′·3E

4342 Vrákhoi Kalóyeroi Rocks
Fl(2)15s38m17M
• 38°09′·9N 25°17′·4E

KÓLPOS PETALIÓN

4346·4 Raftis summit
Fl.2s100m9M
• 37°53′·0N 24°02′·7E

4348 Nisís Foúndi
Fl.3·6s8m5M
• 38°01′·8N 24°14′·9E

4350 Vrakhonisís Dhípsa N point
Fl.4s17m6M
• 38°06′·9N 24°07′·0E

4350·3 Vrakhonisidha Kounéli
Fl.WR.1·5s10m5/3M
100°-W-290°-R-317°
• 38°11′·3N 24°10′·3E

4352 Nisídhes Verdhoúyia. Vrakhonisídha Lígia
Fl(2)16s10m6M
123°-vis-091°
• 38°10′·8N 24°06′·4E

4354 Vrakhonisís Levkasía
Fl.3s17m6M
Obscured by Nisís Parthenópi
• 38°11′·5N 24°05′·6E

4355 Ákra Áyios Marína
Fl(3)15s17m7M
• 38°12′·0N 24°04′·4E

NÓTIOS EVVOÏKÓS KÓLPOS

4357 Órmos Alivéri. Power station mole head
Fl.G.4s10m7M
• 38°23′·5N 24°02′·9E

4360 Órmos Oropoú SE point
Fl.4s5m7M
• 38°19′·7N 23°48′·5E

4362 Liménas Erétria. W side of entrance. Rock
Fl.WR.1·5s7m5/3M
061°-R-342°-W-061°
• 38°23′·0N 23°47′·5E

DHÍAVLOS EVRÍPOU

4366 Stenó Avlídhas-Boúrtzi. Ákra Avlís
Fl(2)12s9m6M
• 38°24′·6N 23°38′·0E

4368 Vrákhos Passándasi
Fl.3s9m5M
• 38°25′·8N 23°37′·0E

4370 Ákra Pérama
Fl.R.3s11m5M
• 38°26′·6N 23°35′·9E

4378 Ákra Kakokefali (NE end of Kakokefali Point)
Fl(2)18s21m12M
• 38°28′·7N 23°36′·3E

VÓRIOS EVVOÏKÓS KÓLPOS

4380 Nea Artaki NW end of Nea Artaki Bat
Fl.1·5s8m5M
• 38°30′·8N 23°37′·7E

4382 Ákra Mníma southeastwards
Fl.3·5s11m6M
• 38°34′·6N 23°31′·9E

4408 Lárimna
Fl.5s8m5M
• 38°34′·1N 23°17′·4E

4408·5 Larko quay W end
Fl.R.5s12m9M
• 38°34′·2N 23°17′·8E

4409 Ákra Stalamáta
Fl(2)8s15m7M
113°-vis-302°
• 38°38′·6N 23°18′·8E

4409·4 Órmos Limnis W entrance point
Fl.1·5s26m5M
• 38°45′·9N 23°18′·8E

NISÍS ATALÁNTI

4412 Nisís Atalánti. Nikolaos Island
Fl.1·5s10m5M
043°-vis-266°
• 38°41′·1N 23°05′·5E

ATALANTIA

4416 Ákra Arkítsa
Fl(2)5s15m19M
• 38°45′·4N 23°02′·1E

KÓLPOS AIDHIPSOÚ

4416·8 Mole head
Fl.G.4s6m5M
• 38°51′·5N 23°02′·4E

4417 Ormos Yialtron S entrance
Fl.3s7m5M
• 38°52′·5N 22°58′·8E

4418 Áyios Konstandinos mole head
F.G.7m7M
• 38°45′·5N 22°51′·6E

STENÓ KNIMÍDHAS

4420 Nisís Strongilí
Fl(2)WR.10s41m12/9M
113°-R-293°-W-113°
• 38°48′·6N 22°49′·3E

DHÍAVLOS KNIMÍDHOS

4422 Ákra Knimís
Fl.WR.2s6m6/3M
098°-W-140°-R-230°-W-278°
• 38°47′·4N 22°49′·5E

4423 Kammena Vourla Marina NE mole head
Fl.R.4s7m6M
• 38°47′·0N 22°47′·1E

4423·1 SW mole head
Fl.G.4s8m6M
• 38°46′·9N 22°47′·1E

MALIAKÓS KÓLPOS

4424 Ákra Khiliomíli
Fl(3)15s10m10M
• 38°51′·1N 22°41′·8E

4427 Liménas Stilídhas mole root
DirLFl.Y.10s11m8M
300°-vis-330°
• 38°54′·6N 22°36′·8E

4430 Ákra Dhrépanon
Fl.6s7m5M
• 38°52′·1N 22°45′·5E

4432 Ákra Vasilína
Oc.WG.5s9m14/11M
025°-G-041°-W-252°
• 38°52′·3N 22°51′·1E

DHÍAVLOS OREÓN

4433·5 Ákra Áy Sostis
Fl.8s16m6M
• 38°56′·7N 22°59′·5E

4434 Ífalos Oréon
Fl(2)12s5m9M
• 38°57′·3N 23°02′·9E

4440 Aryirónisos E end
Fl.5s32m16M
• 39°00′·6N 23°04′·6E

PAGASITIKÓS KÓLPOS (GULF OF VOLOS)

4442 Ákra Kavoúlia
LFl(3)20s22m20M
• 39°05′·9N 23°03′·1E

4444 Metalourgiki Khalyps pier head
Fl.G.3s8m5M
• 39°10′·39N 22°51′·12E

4446 Liménas Vólou. Ákra Sésklo (Séskoulo Point)
Fl.1·5s21m7M
• 39°20′·70N 22°56′·64E

4447·1 Liménas Vólou. Ákra Sésklo NE end
Fl.R.3s8m7M
• 39°21′·0N 22°56′·8E

4449·4 Cement factory W jetty head
Fl(2)10s18m12M
• 39°21′·1N 22°59′·2E

STENÓN KAFIREVS

4451 Nisís Mandhíli
Fl(3)20s83m15M
• 37°56′·1N 24°31′·5E

4451·3 Nisís Arápis
Fl(2)20s34m10M
098°-vis-006°
• 38°09′·63N 24°36′·03E

LIMÍN KÍMIS

4452·08 E mole S end
Fl.G.3s8m6M
• 38°37′·27N 24°07′·68E

4452·3 Ay Grigorios. Koíla
Fl.2s9m5M
• 38°39′·7N 24°07′·7E

4453 Nisís Prasoúdha
Fl.5s42m13M
• 38°39′·9N 24°15′·1E

4453·2 Sarakiniko Point
Fl.8s26m8M
• 38°46′·1N 23°42′·2E

NÍSOS SKÍROS

4454 Ákra Lithári
Fl(3)30s95m16M
189°-vis-067°
• 38°46′·5N 24°40′·9E

4454·1 Treis Boukes
Fl.G.3s8m6M
• 38°45′·9N 24°37′·1E

4454·2 Sarakino Island
Fl.4s63m7M
140°-vis-313°
• 38°45′·53N 24°37′·58E

4454·5 Marmara Point
Fl(2)10s9m7M
• 38°45′·73N 24°34′·30E

4455 Nisídha Valáxa. Ákra Valáxa
Fl.3·3s18m5M
• 38°48′·0N 24°29′·5E

4455·3 Liménas Linariás mole head
Fl.WRG.2·5s7m6-4M
353°-R-021°-W-120°-G-300°
• 38°50′·6N 24°32′·2E

4455·5 Vorio Pódhi N end
Fl.10s42m6M
• 39°01′·2N 24°28′·1E

4455·7 Nótio Pódhi
Fl.3s71m6M
• 39°00′·3N 24°29′·2E

4456 Levkonísia NE islet
Fl(3)15s21m10M
138°-vis-018°
• 38°57′·5N 23°27′·2E

4458 Pondikonísion
Fl(2)WR.15s62m15/12M
077°-W-178°-obscd-187°-W-194°-R-234°-W-317°
• 39°03′·0N 23°20′·4E

4462 Ífalos Levthéris
Fl(2)8s11m9M
• 39°08′·50N 23°20′·67E

4464 Ákra Sépia
LFl.10s105m10M
161°-vis-032°
• 39°11′·3N 23°21′·0E

NÍSOS SKÍATHOS

4466 Vrakhonisís Prassóniso
Fl.6s13m6M
• 39°08′·4N 23°28′·2E

4468 Vrakhonisís Dhaskaloniísi
Fl.3s10m5M
• 39°09′·7N 23°29′·7E

4472 Nísos Répi
Fl(2)WR.10s40m12/8M
183°-W-261°-R-313°-W-020°
• 39°08′·9N 23°31′·8E

NÍSOS SKÓPELOS

4474 Ákra Gouroúni
Fl(3)30s69m20M
029°-vis-244°
• 39°12′·5N 23°35′·6E

4475·4 Limín Skopélou N breakwater head
Fl.G.2s7m6M
• 39°07′·47N 23°44′·12E

4476 Nisís Mikró E end
Fl.4s21m6M
076°-vis-031°
• 39°08′·6N 23°49′·5E

NÍSOS ALONISOS

4478 Ákra Télion
Fl(3)12s21m12M
293°-vis-171°
• 39°08'·4N 23°49'·8E

4479 Nísos Peristéra (SW point of Peristéra Islands)
Fl.3s10m5M
• 39°10'·9N 23°56'·4E

4480 Nisís Pelérissa
Fl.3s25m7M
270°-vis-189°
• 39°18'·9N 24°02'·2E

4482 Nisís Psathoúra N end
Fl.10s41m17M
• 39°30'·3N 24°10'·9E

THERMAÏKOS KÓLPOS

4488 Ákra Kassandra
Fl(2)15s19m24M
• 39°57'·6N 23°21'·8E

4489 Ákra Dhermatás
Fl(2)10s75m11M
131°-vis-345°
• 39°48'·1N 22°51'·1E

4492 Stómion
Fl.3s8m5M
• 39°52'·2N 22°44'·3E

4493 Néa Moudhania W outer mole head
Fl.R.3s7m5M
• 40°14'·3N 23°16'·8E

4494 Ákra Epanomí
Fl(3)18s11m12M
• 40°22'·5N 22°53'·4E

4496 Ákra Atherídha
Fl.5s12m10M
• 40°21'·8N 22°39'·7E

4497 Nisís Kavoúra Axios
Fl(2)15s8m16M
• 40°30'·7N 22°44'·9E

KOLPOS THESSALONÍKIS

4498 Ákra Megálo Émvolon
Fl.10s31m15M
• 40°30'·2N 22°49'·1E

4500 Airport
Aero Al.WG.6s10m13M
• 40°31'·5N 22°58'·6E

4502 Ákra Mikro Émvolon
Fl(3)G.15s16m5M
• 40°35'·03N 22°56'·2E

4502·3 Limeniskos Mikró Émvolon breakwater NW head
Fl.G.2s8m5M
• 40°34'·6N 22°56'·5E

4502·4 SE head
Fl.R.2s9m5M
• 40°34'·3N 22°56'·9E

ÓRMOS THESSALONÍKIS

4503 Yacht club pier Dir Lt 050°
Fl(3)20s9m19M
• 40°36'·6N 22°57'·0E

LIMIN THESSALONÍKIS

4504 No.1 Pier head harbour office
Fl.G.4s17m10M
• 40°38'·0N 22°56'·1E

4505 Detached breakwater W end
Fl.G.4s13m7M
Q.Y marks works in progress 0·5M W and Q.Y 0·8m W (T) 2006
• 40°38'·0N 22°55'·4E

4506 SE end
Fl.R.4s13m7M
• 40°37'·9N 22°56'·0E

4509 Aget Iraklis Cement Terminal
Fl(3)12s9m10M
• 40°38'·3N 22°53'·7E

TORONAÍOS KÓLPOS

4511 Ákra Palioúri
Fl.4s20m7M
183°-vis-071°
• 39°55'·N 23°45'·0E

4512 Porto Koufo Akra Pagona
Fl.G.3s13m5M
336°-vis-249°
• 39°57'·6N 23°55'·0E

4513 Ákra Papadhiá
Fl.WR.3s7m5/3M
269°-W-138°-R-168°
• 40°00'·3N 23°49'·3E

SINGITIKÓS KÓLPOS

4520 Ákra Psevdhókavos
Fl(2)10s52m10M
• 39°57'·0N 23°59'·6E

4524·5 Ífalos Ouranoupolis
Fl(2)10s7m7M
• 40°19'·5N 23°58'·6E

4526 Dháfni
Fl.2·5s17m5M
Obscd by Akri Kastanias when bearing less than 008°
• 40°13'·1N 24°13'·3E

4528 Ákra Pínnes
Fl(3)15s28m9M
284°-vis-140°
• 40°07'·0N 24°18'·5E

4530 Ákra Ákrathos
LFl.10s47m11M
177°-vis-045°
• 40°08'·5N 24°23'·9E

4532 Platí. Ákra Arápis. Nisídhes Stiliária. N islet
Fl.2·5s30m6M
049°-vis-307°
• 40°27'·4N 24°00'·5E

4534 Órmos Statóni
F.R.23m5M
• 40°31'·1N 23°50'·0E

4536 Nisís Kavkanás (Kafkanas Island)
Fl(3)18s23m7M
• 40°37'·1N 23°48'·5E

KÓLPOS KAVÁLAS

4538 Órmos Elevtherón
Fl.3s20m5M
• 40°50'·6N 24°19'·7E

4540 Ákra Kará Ormán
Fl.5s33m15M
• 40°55'·9N 24°24'·9E

4544 Órmos Kaválás W side breakwater head
Fl(2)R.8s11m7M
044°-vis-005°
• 40°55'·9N 24°23'·7E

4545 Órmos Tsari. Neas Kaválás. Fertiliser factory mole head
Fl.G.4s13m7M
• 40°57'·0N 24°28'·9E

4546 Ákra Ammódhis
Fl(2)10s9m7M
265°-vis-134°
• 40°51'·7N 24°37'·8E

4546·3 Ákra Keramotí
Fl.WR.4s6m6/4M
081°-R-095°-W-081°
• 40°51'·4N 24°41'·2E

NÍSOS THÁSOS

4547 Ákra Prínos
Fl.5s5m7M
• 40°45'·7N 24°33'·8E

4547·5 Ákra Atspas (Atspas Point)
Fl(2)10s14m7M
• 40°38'·4N 24°30'·8E

4547·7Ákra Boumbouras
Fl.3s35m7M 200°-vis-126°
• 40°36'·5N 24°46'·5E

4548 Nisís Thasopoúla SE end
Fl.WR.4·5s26m6/4M
237°-R-260°-W-102°
• 40°49'·5N 24°43'·0E

4550 Ákra Fanári
Fl.8s40m6M
• 40°57'·5N 25°07'·8E

ALEXANDROÚPOLI

4554 Main light
Fl(3)15s31m24M
• 40°50'·7N 25°52'·6E

4555 S mole head
Fl.R.3s10m6M
• 40°50'·10N 25°53'·93E

NÍSOS SAMOTHRÁKI

4556 Ákra Akrotíri
Fl.5s12m10M
• 40°28'·6N 25°26'·7E

4556·8 Nisís Zourάfa
Fl(2)10s9m8M
• 40°28'·4N 25°50'·3E

Aegean Sea – Greece and Turkey

ENEZ LIMANI

4557·1 Enez Harbour W breakwater head
Fl.G.5s4m7M
• 40°42'·0N 26°03'·0E

4557·12 N breakwater head
Fl.R.5s4m7M
• 40°41'·9N 26°03'·1E

4557·6 Bakla Burnu
Fl.3s16m12M
• 40°33'·5N 26°44'·9E

4558 Büyük Kemikli Burnu
Fl.5s14m10M
• 40°19'·0N 26°12'·9E

4558·5 Kabatepe Limanı N breakwater head
Fl.R.5s10m6M
• 40°12'·2N 26°16'·0E

4558·6 S breakwater head
Fl.G.5s9m6M
• 40°12'·1N 26°16'·0E

GÖKÇEADA

4559 Aydincik Burnu
Fl(3)20s23m12M
• 40°09'·8N 26°00'·7E

4559·2 Urğurlu Ískelesi breakwater head
Fl.R.3s11m5M
• 40°07'·0N 25°42'·0E

4559·4 Kaleköy
Fl.3s49m7M
• 40°14'·2N 25°54'·0E

4559·6 Kuzu Limanı N breakwater
Fl.G.3s10m10M
• 40°13'·8N 25°57'·3E

4559·7 S breakwater head
Fl.R.3s10m10M
• 40°13'·7N 25°57'·1E

4560 Tavsan Adası
Fl.WR.5s45m14/10M
052°-W-037°-R-052°
Reserve light range W8M, R5M
• 39°56'·2N 26°03'·6E

BOZCAADA

4564 Bati Burnu
Fl(2)15s32m15M
• 39°50'·3N 25°57'·9E

4565 Domlacik
Fl.3s8m8M
• 39°50′·6N 26°05′·5E
4568 Mermer Burnu SE head
Fl.5s35m10M
• 39°48′·1N 26°04′·9E
4568·3 Gülpinar main breakwater head
Fl.G.5s10m7M
• 39°33′·9N 26°05′·8E
4568·31 Auxiliary breakwater head
Fl.R.5s10m7M
• 39°33′·9N 26°05′·8E
4569 Beşiğe Burnu
Fl.3s25m15M
• 39°54′·9N 26°09′·1E
4570 Yenikoy Fishing Harbour breakwater head
Fl.G.5s9m5M
• 39°57′·6N 26°09′·5E

NÍSOS LIMNOS

4572 Ákra Pláka
Fl(3)30s55m22M
• 40°02′·2N 25°26′·8E
4572·2 Lighthouse base
F.R.36m13M
301°-vis-346° over Keros shoals
• 40°02′·2N 25°26′·8E
4574 Ákra Moúrtzeflos
Fl(2)14s59m13M
• 39°59′·2N 25°02′·07E
4575 Ákra Kástron W end of castle
Fl.6s83m11M
• 39°52′·7N 25°03′·2E
4577 Órmos Kondiá Ákra Léna (Lena Point)
Fl.3·3s6m5M
• 39°50′·8N 25°09′·8E
4578 Órmos Moúdhrou Vrakhonisídha Kampi
Fl(2)6s61m10M
• 39°47′·9N 25°14′·2E

NISÍS ÁYIOS EVSTRÁTIOS

4584 Ákra Tripití
Fl(2)10s41m8M
• 39°27′·8N 24°59′·2E
4585 Nisís Ayíou Apóstoloi
Fl.WR.5s34m10/7M
039°-W-294°-R-312°
• 39°34′·0N 25°00′·2E

Aegean Sea – Turkey

4588 Baba Burnu
Fl(4)20s32m18M
• 39°28′·9N 26°03′·9E
4590 Sivrice Burnu
Fl(2)10s16m15M
• 39°27′·95N 26°14′·40E
4591 Kara Burnu
Fl(3)10s14m12M
• 39°33′·6N 26°50′·3E
4592 Boz Burnu
Fl.5s35m10M
• 39°26′·2N 26°48′·8E

Aegean Sea – Greece

NÍSOS LÉSVOS

4594 Ákra Skamnía
Fl.WR.5s14m11/8M
087°-W-104°-R-119°-W-299°
• 39°23′·5N 26°20′·5E
4595 Ákra Mólivos
LFl.WG.10s27m12/8M
068°-W-219°-G-239°-W-263°
• 39°22′·8N 26°11′·1E
4598 Nisídha Megaloníshi
Fl(2)15s53m21M
• 39°12′·8N 25°49′·9E
4598·2 Ákra Saratsina
Fl.WR.3s23m5/3M
000°-W-122°-R-160°-W-219°-R-270°
• 39°11′·4N 25°50′·0E
4598·4 Órmos Sígri berth NW corner
Fl.2s6m5M
• 39°12′·8N 25°51′·0E
4599 Vrak Kalloni
Fl.3s23m6M
355°-vis-330°
• 39°04′·7N 26°04′·7E
4604 Profilaki
Fl.3s27m6M
200°-vis-075°
• 38°58′·3N 26°32′·5E
4605 Ákra Agriliós (Maléa)
Fl(2)12s52m9M
210°-vis-102°
• 39°00′·6N 26°36′·4E
4607 Mitilíni Limín
Fl(3)14s21m6M
122°-vis-027°
• 39°06′·8N 26°34′·1E
4607·6 Outer breakwater head
Fl.G.3s14m7M
• 39°06′·0N 26°33′·8E
4607·8 Breakwater NE end
Fl.R.3s11m5M
• 39°05′·9N 26°33′·8E
4609 Nisidha Panayía
Fl.10s22m7M
• 39°18′·9N 26°26′·9E

Aegean Sea – Turkey

MITILÍNI STRAIT

4610 Günes Adası
Fl.3s66m8M
• 39°19′·7N 26°32′·4E
4612 Çiplak Ada. Fener Burnu
Fl.R.3s18m8M
• 39°17′·2N 26°36′·6E
4613 Korkut Burnu
Fl.3s18m7M
• 39°19′·0N 26°37′·8E
4614 Ayvalík Límani. Alibey Adası. Dalyan Bogazi. Channel N side
VQ(6)+LFl.15s5m7M
• 39°19′·0N 26°38′·1E
4615·3 Dolap Adası
Fl.5s5m8M
• 39°20′·8N 26°40′·9E
4615·4 Madra Çay
Fl(4)15s11m10M
• 39°10′·3N 26°46′·0E
4615·6 Bademli Limanı. Pise Burnu
Fl.WR.5s31m7/4M
240°-W-102°-R-120°-W-140°-R-156°-W-175°
• 39°01′·2N 26°48′·0E

ÇANDARLI KÖRFEZI

4616 Tavsan Adası
Fl(3)10s61m15M
• 38°51′·1N 26°53′·1E
4616·2 Pirasa Adası
Fl.5s44m12M
• 38°51′·8N 26°53′·6E
4616·3 Ilica Burnu
Fl.5s50m9M
• 38°49′·5N 26°53′·7E
4616·4 Aliaga Limanı Tanli Burnu
Q.G.11m10M
• 38°50′·2 26°56′·7E
4616·6 Tuzla Burnu
Q.R.8m8M
• 38°50′·0N 26°57′·8E
4617·9 Aslan Burnu
Fl(2)10s40m10M
• 38°44′·5N 26°44′·5E

IZMIR KÖRFEZI

4618 Eskifoça Fener Adası
Fl.5s25m12M
• 38°40′·6N 26°42′·7E
4620 Degirmen Burnu
Fl.5s17m8M
• 38°40′·2N 26°44′·7E
4621 Büyük Saip Adası NE point (Büyükada)
Fl(2)10s25m10M
• 38°39′·9N 26°31′·2E
4621·2 Mordogan Harbour, Main breakwater. Head
Fl.G.5s8m5M
• 38°31′·12N 26°37′·72E
4621·3 Secondary Breakwater. Head
Fl.R.5s8m5M
• 38°31′·2N 26°37′·75E
4621·5 Azaplar Kayaligi
Fl.R.3s10m12M
• 38°37′·1N 26°44′·6E
4622 Uzan Ada Kösten
Fl(3)15s50m12M
• 38°32′·5N 26°42′·8E
4622·05
Q.R.10M
• 38°31′·2N 26°43′·8E
4622·1 Nergis Adası
Fl(2)10s12m10M
• 38°28′·5N 26°41′·8E
4622·3 Körtan Adalari
Fl.5s7m10M
• 38°25′·30N 26°47′·75E
4622·7 Güzelbahçe
Fl(2)10s14m18M
• 38°22′·79N 26°53′·17E
4623 Çiğli Airfield
Aero AlFl.WG.10s49m10M
• 38°31′·1N 27°00′·5E
4626 Izmir breakwater N head
Fl.G.3s7m10M
• 38°25′·8N 27°07′·9E
4627 Izmir breakwater S head
Fl(2)R.6s7m10M
• 38°25′·4N 27°07′·6E
4630 Karaburun
Fl(4)20s97m12M
045°-vis-225°
• 38°39′·6N 26°21′·7E

Aegean Sea – Greece and Turkey

NISÍS PSARÁ

4632 Ákra Áyios Yeóryios
Fl.10s78m18M
• 38°32′·3N 25°36′·6E

NÍSOS KHÍOS

4638 Ákra Anapómera. Vrakhónisis Gértis
Fl(3)12s33m11M
• 38°36′·3N 26°01′·8E
4640 Órmos Mármaro entrance. Vrakhónisis Margaríti
Fl.3s31m5M
• 38°33′·7N 26°07′·0E
4642 Vrakhónisis Noteable Stróvilo
Fl.5s73m10M
• 38°33′·2N 26°09′·8E

4643·5 Limín Khíou N breakwater head
Fl.G.3s10m12M
• 38°22′·3N 26°08′·7E
4646 S breakwater head
Fl.R.3s10m12M
• 38°22′·2N 26°08′·6E
4648 Nisídha Venétiko
Fl(2)15s78m12M
Obscured by Nísos Khíos 132°-217°
• 38°07′·6N 26°00′·9E
4649 Órmos Mestá
Fl.3s12m7M
• 38°18′·2N 25°55′·5E

NISÍDHES OINOÚSAI

4652 Prassonísia summit
Fl(2)WR.10s17m6/4M
323°-W-301°-R-323°
• 38°31′·5N 26°11′·0E
4654 Nisís Pashá
Fl(2)20s69m11M
• 38°30′·1N 26°17′·6E

ÇESME BOGAZI

4655 Alev Adası
Q(9)15s24m7M
• 38°23′·3N 26°16′·4E
4655·2 Dalyankoy
Fl.5s10m7M
• 38°21′·53N 26°19′·17E
4655·5 Ildir Körfezi. Ufak Ada
Fl(2)10s14m8M
• 38°23′·5N 26°25′·7E
4657 Fener Burnu
Fl.3s10m8M
• 38°19′·3N 26°16′·9E
4658 Süngükaya Adası
Fl.WR.5s43m12/7M
• 38°17′·6N 26°11′·7E
4659 Bozalan Burnu
Fl(2)5s33m7M
• 38°13′·5N 26°23′·4E
4661 Teke Burnu
Fl(3)15s38m8M
• 38°06′·3N 26°35′·6E
4661·5 Sığacík Körfezi. Enek Adası
Fl.10s9m5M
• 38°12′·1N 26°46′·2E
4662 Doğanbey Adası
Fl(2)5s51m8M
• 38°01′·3N 26°52′·9E
4664 Kusadasi
Fl(2)10s20m8M
• 37°51′·89N 27°14′·84E
4665 Bayrak Adası
Fl.5s23m8M
• 37°41′·6N 27°01′·1E
4665·05 Tav‹an Adası
Fl(2)10s30m9M
• 37°39′·1N 27°00′·1E
4665·2 Fener Adası
Fl.5s17m10M
• 37°10′·6N 27°21′·3E
4665·3 Yilan Adası
Fl.G.5s14m7M
• 37°12′·17N 27°33′·07E
4665·4 Çamlik Burnu
Fl(2)5s11m18M
• 37°14′·3N 27°35′·2E
4665·5 Karaburun Feneri
Fl.R.5s18m5M
37°13′·80N 27°31′·63E
4665·6 Incegöl Burnu
Fl.3s13m12M
• 37°13′·83N 27°30′·33E
4665·7 Akbük-Panayir Adası (Altin Ada)
Fl(3)15s35m12M
• 37°19′·7N 26°19′·7E
4665·8 Tekahaç Burnu
Fl.15s15m10M
• 37°21′·33N 27°11′·57E

Aegean Sea – Greece

NÍSOS SÁMOS

4666·2 Prasonisi Island
Fl(2)7s16m7M
• 37°47′·87N 26°57′·77E
4669 Ákra Gátos
Fl(3)14s16m7M
• 37°43′·6N 27°04′·0E
4670 Limín Pithagóriou. Ákra Foniás
Fl.4s15m5M
• 37°41′·3N 26°57′·2E
4678 Ákra Áyois Dhoménikos
Fl.3·6s16m5M
• 37°40′·6N 26°35′·5E
4680 Limín Karlóvasi Ákra Pangózi
Fl.5s28m11M
• 37°47′·8N 26°40′·5E
4682 N breakwater
Fl.G.3s9m3M
• 37°48′·0N 26°41′·0E

NISÍDHES FOÚRNOI

4687 Ákra Trakhíli
Fl(2)15s37m7M
• 37°34′·6N 26°23′·8E
4688 Ákra Saíta (Maláki)
Fl(2)12s40m8M
• 37°39′·39N 26°30′·64E

NÍSOS IKARÍA

4690 Ákra Páppas
Fl.20s75m25M
• 37°30′·7N 25°58′·8E
4692 Ákra Armenistís
Fl(3)12s29m11M
• 37°38′·2N 26°05′·0E
4693 Vrakhónisis Kofinás
Fl.7·5s19m11M
• 37°38′·1N 26°10′·7E
4694 Ákra Dhrápanon
Fl(3)24s36m12M
• 37°41′·5N 26°21′·8E

NÍSOS LÉROS

4698 Órmos Alínta
Fl.3s16m5M
• 37°09′·7N 26°51′·3E
4700 Vrakhónisis Ayía Kiriakí
Fl(3)15s21m5M
• 37°08′·7N 26°53′·4E
4702 Órmos Lakkí Ákra Lakkí
Fl(2)14s68m9M
• 37°06′·8N 26°49′·5E
4703 Ákra Agkistro
Fl.2·5s47m5M
• 37°06′·7N 26°49′·9E

NISÍS KALÓLIMNOS

4708 Nisídha Kalólimnos (Kalolimnos Safonidhi)
Fl.3s29m7M
122°-vis-055°
• 37°03′·6N 27°06′·4E

Aegean Sea – Greece and Turkey

4708·5 Büyük Kiremit Adası
Fl(2)10s89m10M
• 37°05′·4N 27°12′·7E
4708·7 Çatal Ada
Fl(4)20s48m6M
• 37°00′·7N 27°13′·4E
4709 Topan Adası (Atsaki)
Fl.5s54m7M
• 37°00′·4N 27°10′·9E

NISÍS PSÉRIMOS

4711 Ákra Roússa
Fl(2)WR.10s43m12/9M
182°-W-262°-R-281°-W-086°
• 36°55′·3N 27°10′·6E
4711·3 Vrakhónisis Nekrothikes
Fl.WR.5s23m6/4M
049°-W-349°-R-049°
• 36°57′·3N 27°05′·9E
4711·5 Vrakhónisis Safonídhi
LFl.10s64m9M
• 36°53′·2N 26°55′·3E

KÓS CHANNEL

4712 Hüseyin Burnu
Fl(2)15s15m14M
• 36°58′·0N 27°15′·9E
4714 Kargi Adası
Fl.5s33m8M
• 36°57′·6N 27°18′·3E

NÍSOS NÍSIROS

4720 Ákra Katsoúni
Fl(2)9s28m12M
• 36°37′·2N 27°11′·4E
4721 Vrakhónisis Gáïdharos
Fl(2)16s71m10M
• 36°29′·2N 27°17′·2E

NÍSOS KÓS

4722 Ákra Ammóglossa
Fl.R.4s7m9M
080°-vis-320°
• 36°55′·0N 27°16′·8E
4726·6 Ákra Loúros
Fl(3)WR.15s10m6/4M
130°-W-060°-R-130°
• 36°53′·5N 27°20′·2E
4727 Ákra Foúka
Fl.4s23m6M
• 36°51′·6N 27°21′·4E
4727·7 Mastikhari mole head
Fl.G.3s10m6M
• 36°51′·2N 27°04′·6E
4728 Karaada
Fl(2)5s7m5M
• 36°59′·7N 27°25′·5E
4729 Dikilitas Kayasi
Q(6)+LFl.15s6m6M
• 37°00′·9N 27°24′·9E

BODRUM LIMANI

4730 W breakwater head
Fl.R.5s8m8M
• 37°01′·9N 27°25′·5E
4730·4 E breakwater head
Fl.G.5s8m8M
• 37°01′·9N 27°25′·5E
4731 Gokova Korfezi. Ören Burnu
Fl.3s6m8M
• 37°01′·3N 27°58′·4E
4731·2 Orak Adası
Fl.10s17m7M
• 36°58′·1N 27°36′·1E
4731·4 Orta Ada (Snake Island)
Fl.WR.10s15m9/6M
024°-R-056°-W-024°
• 37°00′·0N 28°12′·4E
4731·6 Koyun Burnu
Fl(3)10s13m7M
• 36°55′·6N 28°01′·3E
4731·65 Mersincik Burnu
Fl.WR.3s30m7/5M
154°-R-270°-W-154°
• 36°50′·2N 28°00′·2E
4731·7 Ince Burun (Cape Shuyun)
Fl(2)5s48m10M
• 36°48′·7N 27°38′·5E
4732 Deveboynu Burnu
Fl(2)10s104m12M
315°-vis-183°
• 36°41′·3N 27°21′·8E

4732·5 Ince Burun
Fl(3)15s14m8M
• 36°39′·6N 27°42′·8E

NÍSOS SÍMI

4734 Khondrós
Fl.3s25m5M
• 36°39′·40N 27°49′·22E

4734·2 Nisídha Nímos. Ákra Makria
Fl.4s16m6M
• 36°40′·1N 27°51′·5E

4735·5 Vrakhonisís Kouloundrós
Fl(3)15s30m15M
• 36°30′·9N 27°52′·2E

4736 Nisís Marmarás
Fl.3s38m6M
• 36°33′·7N 27°44′·8E

4737 Ala Burun
Fl(2)10s36m10M
• 36°33′·3N 27°58′·7E

Aegean Sea – Greece

NISÍS KHÁLKI

4738 Órmos Emporeio
Fl.3s12m6M
175°-vis-045°
• 36°13′·6N 27°37′·5E

4739 Vrakhonisídha Nisáki
Fl.WR.6s75m8/6M
232°-R-244°-W-280°-R-297°-W-232°
• 36°13′·3N 27°37′·7E

NÍSOS RÓDHOS

4740 Tragusa
Fl(2)WR.14s60m8/6M
112°-R-125°-W-112°
• 36°13′·4N 27°42′·2E

4741 Kámeros Skála
Fl.3s20m8M
• 36°16′·4N 27°49′·5E

4743 Ákra Milon (Zonári)
Fl.WR.4s10m6/4M
037°-W-286°-R-314° over Ífalos Kolóna.
AlFl.WG.6s and Airport illuminations 7M WSW.
• 36°27′·5N 28°13′·3E

4744 Limín Ródhou Áyios Nikólaos
Fl(2)12s24m11M
• 36°27′·1N 28°13′·7E

4752 Akantia harbour E mole head
Fl.R.5s10m6M
• 36°26′·99N 28°14′·25E

4755 Vrakhos Paximádha
Fl.WR.4s24m9/6M
139°-R-184°-W-139°
• 36°01′·4N 28°05′·6E

4756 Ákra Prasso
Fl(4)30s61m17M
273°-vis-179°
• 35°52′·8N 27°45′·1E

NÍSOS KÁRPATHOS

4757 Ákra Kastéllos
Fl.WR.3s12m7/4M
225°-R-252°-W-134°
• 35°23′·9N 27°08′·3E

4758·2 Nisidha Dhespotiko
Fl.5s12m6M
• 35°30′·9N 27°12′·8E

4760 Ákra Paraspóri
Fl(2)16s49m12M
066°-vis-288°
• 35°54′·3N 27°13′·7E

4760·3 Nisís Stakidha. Vrakhónisos Astakidhopoulo
Fl.3s58m8M
199·5°-vis-148·5°
• 35°52′·6N 26°49′·4E

4760·7 Ounianísia
Fl(2)16s106m7M
• 35°49′·7N 26°27′·8E

4761 Nisís Megálo Sofrána
Fl.10s39m10M
• 36°04′·9N 26°23′·5E

4761·5 Vrakhonisís Strongilí
Fl(2)WR.10s23m7/5M
091°-W-243°-R-258°-W-006°
• 35°26′·4N 27°01′·0E

NISÍS KÁSOS

4763 Ákra Ayios Yeóryios
Fl.WR.3s30m5/3M
083°-R-175°-W-241°-R-251°-W-257°
• 35°25′·3N 26°55′·1E

4763·2 Ákra Avláki
Fl.4s10m6M
• 35°20′·9N 26°50′·9E

4763·5 Vrakhonisís Pláti
Fl(2)16s36m18M
• 35°21′·7N 26°49′·5E

4764 Nisís Kandhelioúsa
Fl.10s55m17M
291°-vis-214°
• 36°29′·9N 26°57′·7E

4764·5 Nisidhes Trianísia Nisís Plakidha
Fl.WR.3s84m9/6M
068°-R-248°-W-068°
• 36°17′·1N 26°44′·5E

NÍSOS ASTIPÁLAIA

4765 Ákra Floúda
Fl(2)14s103m12M
• 36°38′·7N 26°22′·9E

4765·5 Ákra Exópetra
Fl(2)9s31m7M
• 36°34′·9N 26°28′·5E

4768·5 Vrakhonisís Ánidhro
Fl.WR.6s107m9/6M
090°-R-100°-W-090°
• 37°24′·6N 26°29′·4E

NÍSOS PÁTMOS

4770 Ákra Yeranós
Fl.3s36m7M
• 37°20′·4N 26°36′·8E

4770·6 Ákra Áspri
Fl.WR.2s14m7/5M
133°-W-272°-R-320°-W-048°
• 37°19′·7N 26°33′·7E

4771·4 Vrakhonisídhes Kavouronísia
Fl(2)WR.12s10m5/3M
087°-R-232°-W-087°
• 37°17′·5N 26°34′·7E

4772 Ákra Ilías
Fl(3)9s50m9M
182°-vis-086°
• 37°16′·3N 26°34′·3E

NISÍS ÁRKOI

4772·6 Órmos Avgoústa. Ákra Sistérna
Fl.3s14m5M
291°-vis-129°
• 37°22′·8N 26°43′·8E

NISÍDHA LIPSÓI

4773 Ákra Gátos
Fl.3s27m6M
243·5°-vis-088·5°
• 37°17′·6N 26°44′·9E

4775 Vrakhonisídhes Kalapódhia
Fl.4s32m7M
• 37°15′·4N 26°48′·9E

4775·5 Vrakhonisís Saráki
Fl(2)8s23m8M
• 37°13′·8N 26°42′·0E

4776 Nisídha Agathonísion Ákra Stifí
Fl.2s16m6M
186°-vis-033° 308°-obscd by Nisís Kounéli-329°
• 37°26′·7N 26°57′·7E

4777 Nisídha Farmakonísion S summit
Fl(2)14s118m12M
• 37°16′·9N 27°05′·3E

Aegean Sea and Approaches – Kríti – Greece

4778 Nisís Elafónisos
Fl(3)20s43m12M
• 35°16′·2N 23°31′·5E

4780 Nisís Ágria Gramvoúsa NW point
Fl.WR.10s108m17/13M
330°-W-239°-R-255°-W-319°
• 35°38′·9N 23°34′·6E

LIMÍN KHANIÓN

4781 Mole head
Fl.R.2·5s26m7M
• 35°31′·2N 24°01′·0E

4783 Ákra Maléka
Fl(2)12s48m10M
• 35°35′·3N 24°10′·5E

4784 Ákra Dhrépanon
Fl(3)30s56m20M
066°-vis-324°
• 35°28′·5N 24°14′·5E

4786 Nisís Soúdha
Fl.G.4·8s20m6M
245°-vis-120°
• 35°29′·25N 24°09′·2E

LIMÍN RETHÍMNIS

4790 N Mole head
Fl.G.3s10m10M
• 35°22′·5N 24°29′·1E

4791·4 S mole head
Fl.R.4s12m10M
• 35°22′·3N 24°29′·0E

4792 Ákra Khondrós Kávos
Fl.WR.6s57m12/8M
050°-R-097°-W-270°
• 35°25′·67N 24°42′·03E

4794 Ákra Stavrós
Fl(2)15s20m11M
• 35°26′·0N 24°58′·4E

IRAKLÍOU

4798 Outer mole head
LFl.G.6s14m9M
• 35°21′·2N 25°09′·4E

4800 Pier 6 head
LFl.R.6s13m9M
• 35°21′·0N 25°09′·2E

4808 Airport
Aero Al.WG.4s57m15M
• 35°20′·3N 25°10′·8E

NISÍS DHÍA

4810 Ákra Mármara N point
LFl.12s30m9M
• 35°28′·0N 25°13′·0E

4812 Ákra Stavrós
Fl.6s129m12M
• 35°25′·6N 25°14′·4E

4813 Nisís Avgó summit
Fl.5s57m9M
288°-vis-275°
• 35°36′·2N 25°34′·7E

4813·3 Gouves Marina N mole head
Fl.G.4s9m6M
• 35°20′·2N 25°17′·8E

4813·31 S mole head
Fl.R.4s9m6M
• 35°20′·2N 25°17′·8E

4813·5 Órmos Khersónisos mole head
Fl.G.2s10m5M
• 35°19′·3N 25°23′·6E

KÓLPOS MIRAMBÉLLOU

4814 Ákra Áyios Ioánnis
Fl(2)12·8s49m11M
• 35°20′·5N 25°46′·4E

4818 Limin Ayíou Nikolaon mole head
Fl.R.2s10m7M
• 35°11′·7N 25°43′·2E

ÓRMOS SITÍAS

4820 Ákra Vamvakiá
Fl(3)18s24m10M
• 35°13′·5N 26°07′·0E

4824 Nisís Paximádha
Fl.WR.6s36m12/8M
019°-W-284°-R-314°
• 35°23′·1N 26°10′·4E

4824·5 Nisís Yianisádha SE point
Fl.WR.10s14m7/5M
213°-W-275°-R-280°-W-304°-R-310°-W-052°
• 35°19′·6N 26°11′·2E

4826 Ákra Sídheros
Fl.10s45m18M
• 35°19′·0N 26°18′·7E

4828 Ákra Pláka
Fl(2)12s22m10M
• 35°11′·9N 26°19′·1E

Mediterranean – Kríti – Greece

4829 Nisídhes Kaválloi
Fl(3)12s29m6M
• 35°01′·7N 26°13′·7E

4830 Koufonísi
Fl(2)16s73m10M
• 34°56′·0N 26°08′·6E

4832 Gaïdhouronísi
Fl(2)12s12m10M
056°-vis-267°
• 34°52′·8N 25°41′·7E

4833 Ákra Theófilos
Fl(2)12s75m10M
• 34°59′·0N 25°30′·3E

4833·6 Megalonísi
Fl(3)20s67m11M
• 34°55′·4N 24°48′·0E

4834 Ákra Lítinos
Fl.6s33m12M
• 34°55′·4N 24°44′·0E

4838 Nísis Gavdhopoúla NW point
Fl.8s56m12M
• 34°56′·3N 23°59′·4E

4840 Nísos Gávdhos S point
Fl(2)16s37m12M
• 34°48′·3N 24°07′·3E

4842 Nisís Loutró
LFl.10s17m6M
• 35°11′·9N 24°05′·0E

4844 Nisís Skhistó N side
Fl.8s16m8M
• 35°13′·4N 23°40′·3E

Çanakkale Boğazi (Dardanelles) – Turkey

4848 Kumkale Burnu
Fl(2)10s14m18M
• 40°00′·6N 26°11′·9E

4850 Mehmetçik Burnu
Fl.WR.5s50m19/12M
010°-W-350°-R-010°
• 40°02′·7N 26°10′·5E

4852 Anit Limanı
Fl(4)R.15s8m5M
• 40°02′·6N 26°12′·1E

4852·3 Seddülbahir S breakwater
Fl.R.5s5m3M
• 40°02′·5N 26°11′·5E

4852·6 N breakwater
Fl.G.5s5m5M
• 40°02′·6N 26°11′·5E

4853 Karanfil Burnu
Fl(2)R.12s14m10M
• 40°06′·4N 26°19′·7E

4854 Kanlidere Burnu Kepez
Fl.5s10m10M
• 40°05′·7N 26°21′·9E

4855 Sarisiğlar
VQ(9)10s9m9M
• 40°08′·3N 26°23′·9E

4856 Kilitbahir
Fl.R.3s7m15M
• 40°08′·8N 26°22′·9E

4857 Çanakkale Çimenlik Kalesi
Fl.RG.5s16m10M
027°-G-341°-R-027°
• 40°08′·9N 26°23′·9E

ECEABAT

4858/4858·1 Ldg Lts 242°
Front Oc.2·5s40m6M
Rear 132m from front
Q.43m6M
• 40°11′·2N 26°21′·1E

4860 Poyraz Burnu
Fl(2)R.5s7m10M
• 40°12′·2N 26°22′·6E

4862 Nara Burnu
Fl(2)G.10s10m7M
• 40°11′·9N 26°24′·1E

4866 Akban Burnu
Fl(3)R.15s6m12M
• 40°13′·3N 26°25′·4E

4868 Uzum Burun
Fl(2)R.10s11m8M
• 40°16′·2N 29°29′·5E

4870 Gocuk Burnu
Fl.3s12m10M
• 40°16′·8N 26°34′·3E

4872 Karakova Burnu
Fl.R.6s10m10M
• 40°19′·3N 26°35′·3E

4874 Kanarva Burnu Sütlüce
Fl(2)R.10s5m12M
• 40°21′·5N 26°37′·7E

4876 Çardak Burnu
Fl.G.3s12m7M
• 40°23′·2N 26°42′·5E

4876·5 Çardak Banki
VQ(9)10s8m5M
• 40°23′·6N 26°42′·5E

4878 Gelibolu
Fl.5s34m15M Siren(2)30s
• 40°24′·7N 26°41′·0E

4879 Zincirbozan
Fl.10s10m7M
• 40°25′·3N 26°45′·3E

4879·5 Doğanaslan Banki
Q(6)+LFl.15s9m7M
• 40°29′·8N 26°51′·5E

Marmara Denizi – Turkey

4880 Ince Burnu
Fl(3)10s32m16M
• 40°33′·45N 26°59′·80E

KARABIGA

4880·6 Ince Burun Karaburun
Fl(2)10s54m10M
• 40°28′·5N 27°17′·2E

4881 Kale Burnu
Fl.5s23m8M
• 40°24′·7N 27°20′·0E

4881·3 Inner harbour E breakwater head
F.G.5s7m5M
• 40°24′·1N 27°18′·6E

4881·5 Breakwater
F.R.5s7m5M
• 40°24′·0N 27°18′·4E

ERDEK KÖRFEZI

4881·6 Tavşan Adası NE summit
Fl.10s55m12M
• 40°22′·6N 27°47′·3E

4881·7 Cinar Harbour breakwater head
Fl.R.5s8m6M
• 40°23′·3N 27°48′·3E

4882 Türkeli Adası W side. Ekinlik Feneri
Fl.5s18m8M
• 40°30′·9N 27°28′·7E

4884 Kapidağ Yarimadası W end. Balyoz Burnu
Fl(2)10s38m10M
• 40°29′·7N 27°41′·0E

4885 Panalimani Adası
Fl.3s22m12M
• 40°27′·8N 27°40′·1E

BANDIRMA KÖRFEZI

4886 Fener Adası NW point
Fl.5s43m10M
256°-vis-296°, 303°-vis-312°, 028°-vis-256°
• 40°27′·8N 28°04′·0E

4887 Bandirma main mole head
Fl.R.5s10m10M
• 40°21′·57N 27°57′·54E

4888 Auxiliary mole head
Fl.G.5s10m6M
• 40°21′·4N 27°57′·5E

4890 Kapsül Burnu
Fl(2)R.10s20m12M
• 40°28′·7N 28°02′·1E

MARMARA ADASI

4892 Asmaliada
Fl(3)15s40m12M
• 40°38′·0N 27°45′·6E

4892·4 Domuz Burnu
Fl.10s25m9M
• 40°40′·1N 27°38′·1E

4892·8 Marmara fishing shelter main breakwater head
Fl.R.3s10m8M
• 40°35′·1N 27°33′·7E

4892·9 Port Marmara small mole
Fl.G.3s10m8M
• 40°35′·0N 27°33′·8E

4893 Aba Burnu
Fl(2)10s15m5M
• 40°34′·6N 27°34′·6E

4894 Hayirsiz Ada N summit
Fl.3s112m12M
• 40°38′·7N 27°29′·2E

4896 Honköy
Fl(2)10s50m19M
• 40°42′·4N 27°18′·5E

4896·3 Barbaros main breakwater
Fl.G.5s11m7M
• 40°54′·2N 27°28′·2E

4896·4 Minor breakwater
Fl.R.5s10m7M
• 40°54′·2N 27°28′·1E

4896·9 Kargaburun
Aero 2Oc.R.3s196/82m20/16M
Obstruction
• 40°58′·2N 27°52′·4E

4897 Örencik
Fl.6s9m10M
• 40°57′·7N 27°53′·8E

EREHLI
4898 Ereğli
Fl.10s52m16M
• 40°58′·1N 27°57′·7E
4899 Kilkaya Rocks
Q(3)10s9m8M
• 40°58′·4N 27°58′·0E
4899·3 Silivri main breakdwater
Fl.G.5s6m5M
• 41°04′·4N 28°14′·3E
4899·4 Secondary breakwater
Fl.R.5s6m5M
• 41°04′·5N 28°14′·4E

BÜYÜKÇEKMECE
4899·6 Değirmen Burnu
Fl.5s20m10M
• 40°57′·7N 28°37′·3E
4899·8 Marti Burnu
Fl.10s110m10M
• 40°33′·9N 28°31′·3E
4899·9 Değirmen Burnu
Fl.R.3s25m6M
• 40°33′·5N 28°33′·0E

IMRALI ADASI
4899·96 Sivrikaya Burnu
Fl.10s20m12M
• 40°38′·8N 29°00′·5E

GEMLIK KÖRFEZI
4900 Boz Burnu
Fl.5s77m10M Siren(2)30s
• 40°32′·0N 28°47′·0E
4900·2 Arnavutköy Burnu
Fl(2)10s30m12M
• 40°23′·1N 28°52′·1E
4900·6 Tuzla Burnu
Fl.10s14m12M
• 40°25′·2N 29°05′·7E
4900·8 Karacabey
Fl(3)15s13m10M
• 40°23′·5N 28°31′·1E
4901 Yeşilköy
Aero AlFl.WG.8s49m10M
• 40°58′·7N 28°49′·3E
4902 Yeşilköy Burnu E end
Fl(2)10s23m15M
• 40°57′·6N 28°50′·3E

ISTANBUL
4903 Ahirkapi
Fl.6s36m16M
• 41°00′·4N 28°59′·1E
4903·4 Kumkapi shelter breakwater head
Fl.R.3s10m6M
• 41°00′·1N 28°58′·0E
4903·45 Yenikapi IDO jetty head
Fl(2)R.5s9m8M
• 40°59′·9N 28°57′·57E
4903·7 Salipazari Rihtimi
Fl(3)G.10s13m10M
• 41°01′·78N 28°59′·33E
4903·8 Kizkulesi
Fl.WR.3s11m14/11M
000°-W-030°-R-000°
Navigation control station
Lights mark power cable between Kizkulesi and Saraybumu
• 41°01′·3N 29°00′·3E

HAYDARPAŞA
4904 Outer detached breakwater N end
Fl.G.3s15m8M
• 41°00′·61N 29°00′·14E
4904·6 Kadiköy mole head
Iso.4s14m13M
• 40°58′·5N 29°02′·2E
4906·2 SE end
Fl.R.2s15m8M Bell(1)6s
• 40°59′·6N 29°01′·9E

HAYDARPAŞA HAREM
4907 Ferry harbour S breakwater head
Fl(2)G.5s7m6M
• 41°00′·73N 29°00′·44E
4907·2 N breakwater
Fl(2)R.5s7m6M
• 41°00′·88N 29°00′·61E

FENERBAHÇE
4909·4 Yat Limanı W breakwater head
Fl(2)G.10s6M
• 40°58′·5N 29°02′·1E
4909·6 E breakwater head
Fl(2)R.10s6M
• 40°58′·5N 29°02′·2E
4910 Fenerbahçe
Fl(2)12s25m15M
• 40°58′·2N 29°01′·9E
4913 Bostanci pier
Fl.R.2s6m5M
• 40°57′·1N 29°05′·7E
4914 Yildiz Kayaliği
VQ(9)10s5m8M
• 40°56′·2N 29°05′·3E
4915 Dilek Kayaliği
Q(6)+LFl.15s9m8M
• 40°54′·9N 29°05′·4E
4916·2 Pendik
Fl.G.5s11m8M
• 40°51′·6N 29°15′·2E
4916·3 Aydinbey Yarimadası (Pauli) S end
Fl.R.5s7m8Mč
• 40°51′·6N 29°15′·4E
4916·4 Aydinli Limanı breakwater
Fl(2)G.5s8m5M
• 40°51′·1N 29°16′·3E
4916·6 Balikçi Adası
Fl(2)10s31m9M
• 40°49′·2N 29°06′·8E

HEYBELIADA
4917·4 S breakwater head
F.R.3s6m3M
• 40°52′·4N 29°06′·2E
4917·5 Boat harbour mole head
Fl.R.2s6m7M
• 40°52′·9N 29°06′·1E
4918 Sivriada
Fl.3s95m13M
• 40°52′·6N 28°58′·2E
4920 Hayirsizada
Fl.3s17m10M
• 40°47′·5N 29°15′·8E
4920·5 Tuzla Körfezi breakwater head
Fl.R.5s12m5M
• 40°48′·8N 29°17′·6E

IZMIT KÖRFEZI
4922 Yelkenkaya Burnu
Fl.15s20m18M
• 40°45′·4N 29°12′·3E
4924 Dil Burnu
Fl.3s12m10M
• 40°44′·52N 29°30′·92E
4926 Kaba Burnu
Fl(3)10s15m7M
• 40°46′·1N 29°31′·1E
4928 Zeytin Burnu
Fl(2)R.5s10m8M
• 40°44′·5N 29°47′·0E
4929 Gölcük Burnu
Fl.3s9m8M
• 40°43′·9N 29°48′·8E
4931 Yalova W mole head
Fl.G.3s9m8M
• 40°39′·7N 29°14′·7E
4931·2 E mole head
Fl.R.3s9m8M
• 40°39′·7N 29°14′·7E

Istanbul Boğazi (The Bosphorus) – Turkey

4937 Beylerbeyi
Fl(2)R.10s10m9M
• 41°03′·0N 29°02′·0E
4937·4 Defterdar Burnu Ortaköy
Fl(2)G.12s10m7M
• 41°03′·0N 29°02′·0E
4938 Kuruçeşme
Fl(3)G.16s7m10M
• 41°03′·4N 29°02′·2E
4938·3 Çengelköy
Fl(3)R.15s13m9M
• 41°03′·3N 29°03′·1E
4939 Power cable W pylon
Fl.R.193m8M Marks overhead cable
4F.R(vert)
• 41°04′·3N 29°02′·5E
4939·2 E pylon
Fl.R.194m8M
Marks overhead cable
4F.R(vert)
• 41°04′·3N 29°03′·6E
4940 Arnavutköy. Akinti Burnu
Fl.G.3s11m10M
• 41°04′·1N 29°02′·8E
4941 Bebek
Fl(2)G.10s5m5M
Fl.R.3s and Fl.G.3s on buoys mark boat channel into Bebek
• 41°04′·7N 29°02′·8E
4944 Kandilli Burnu
Fl.R.3s27m12M
Navigation control station
• 41°04′·5N 29°03′·4E
4946 Asiyan Burnu
Fl(3)G.15s7m8M
• 41°05′·0N 29°03′·4E
4947 Baltalimani
Fl.G.3s12m5M
• 41°05′·97N 29°03′·25E
4948 Kanlica
Fl(2)R.10s12m8M
• 41°06′·2N 29°04′·0E
4949 Istinye
Fl(2)G.10s14m9M
• 41°06′·9N 29°03′·7E
4949·4 Panbahçe
Fl(3)R.15s14m9M
• 41°07′·0N 29°05′·4E
4949·5 Incirköy
Fl.R.3s16m8M
• 41°07′·7N 29°05′·8E
4949·6 Yeniköy
Q(3)10s6m6M
• 41°07′·5N 29°04′·5E
4949·7 Selvi Burnu SW corner
Fl(2)R.10s13m8M
• 41°08′·6N 29°04′·3E
4950 Kireç Burnu
Fl(3)G.15s11m11M
• 41°08′·92N 29°02′·78E
4952 Büyükdere
Fl.G.3s10m9M
• 41°09′·75N 29°02′·87E
4953 Tellitabya Burnu power cable W side
2Fl.R.2s243m11M
• 41°10′·7N 29°04′·2E
4953·2 E side
2Fl.R.2s249m11M
F.R
• 41°10′·1N 29°05′·2E
4954 Kavak Burnu Anadolukavak
Fl(3)R.15s16m8M
• 41°10′·7N 29°05′·3E

4955 Dikilikaya
Fl(2)G.10s9m12M
• 41°10′·93N 29°04′·75E
4955·2 Poyraz Inner breakwater
Fl.R.4s13m5M
• 41°12′·28N 29°07′·66E
4955·4 Büyük Liman Çali Burnu
Fl(3)G.15s33m5M
• 41°12′·4N 29°06′·3E
4956 Türkeli Feneri
Fl(2)12s58m18M Horn 20s
• 41°14′·1N 29°06′·87E
4956·2 Fishing Harbour breakwater head
Fl.G.3s10m7M
• 41°13′·8N 29°06′·9E
4958 Anadolu Feneri
LFl.20s75m20M
• 41°13′·1N 29°09′·1E

Mediterranean – Turkey

5836 Kadirga Burnu
Fl(3)15s39m12M
• 36°43′·8N 28°18′·0E

MARMARIS LIMANI

5838 Keçi Adası
Fl.R.2s30m7M
• 36°48′·0N 28°15′·5E
5838·2 Yildiz Adası. Ince Burnu
Fl.3s9m5M
• 36°48′·9N 28°16′·0E
5838·4 Yilancik Adası
Fl.WR.5s102m10/7M
086°-R-098°-W-086°
• 36°46′·6N 28°26′·3E

KARAAĞAÇ LIMANI

5838·5 Deliklikaya Burnu
Fl.R.3s100m8M
• 36°49′·9N 28°25′·6E
5838·6 Buğluca
Fl.G.3s67m6M
• 36°50′·3N 28°27′·1E
5838·67 Canakçi Burnu
Fl(2)R.5s10m5M
• 36°51′·27N 28°23′·70E
5838·68
Fl(2)G.5s10m5M
• 36°51′·3N 28°24′·5E
5838·7 Kargili Burnu
Q.60m10M
• 36°51′·6N 28°26′·0E
5839 Delik Adası (Dalyan Adası)
Fl(2)5s35m8M
• 36°47′·8N 28°35′·6E
5839·4 Karaçay
Fl.5s40m5M
• 36°49′·4N 28°33′·0E

FETHIYE KÖRFEZI

5839·45 Baba Adası
Fl(2)5s58m9M
• 36°41′·7N 28°41′·7E
5839·5 Peksimet Adası
Fl.10s35m12M
• 36°34′·1N 28°49′·5E
5839·6 Göçek Island southeastwards
Fl(2)10s7m5M
• 36°42′·8N 28°55′·1E
5840 Göçek Adası E side
Fl(2)10s12m8M
• 36°43′·7N 28°57′·0E
5840·4 Göçek inner harbour
Fl.WR.3s15m7/4M
314°-W-326°-R-314°
• 36°45′·09N 28°55′·82E
5840·5 Yacht harbour W breakwater
Fl.G.5s5M
• 36°44′·91N 28°56′·4E
5840·51 E breakwater
Fl.R.5s5M
• 36°45′·0N 36°56′·5E
5841 Kizil Ada S point
Fl.5s32m15M Racon
• 36°39′·2N 29°02′·5E
5844·2 Dökükbasi Burnu
Fl(2)5s23m10M
• 36°32′·7N 29°00′·6E
5844·4 Kötü Burnu
Fl(2)10s28m12M
• 36°23′·2N 29°06′·2E
5844·6 Çatal Adası
Fl.5s76m9M
• 36°12′·65N 29°21′·0E

Mediterranean – Greece and Turkey

NÍSOS KASTELLORÍZON

5845 Ákra Áyios Stéfanos
Fl.WR.4·5s18m5/3M
060°-W-076°, 086°-W-095°-R-125°-W-254°
• 36°10′·0N 29°35′·4E
5847 Kas Bayindir. Ince Burnu
Fl.3s10m5M
• 36°11′·0N 29°38′·5E
5847·6 Kağdası Mevkil
Fl(2)WRG.10s16m5-4M
297°-G-065°-W-071°-R-093°
• 36°12′·5N 29°36′·9E
5848 Vrakhonisidha Strongylí
Fl.5s107m17M
• 36°06′·6N 29°38′·0E

Mediterranean – Turkey

5848·2 Kekova Adasi SW end
Fl(2)5s55m8M
• 36°10′·3N 29°50′·6E
5848·4 Ölü
Fl.WG.3s26m7/4M
355°-W-358°-G-355°
• 36°10′·8N 29°49′·7E
5848·5 Kekova Burnu (Kekova Adasi NE end)
Fl.5s35m9M
• 36°11′·9N 29°54′·9E

FINIKE KÖRFEZI

5849·4 Barinak E breakwater head
Fl.R.5s13m6M
• 36°17′·6N 30°09′·2E
5849·6 W breakwater head
Fl.G.3s13m6M
• 36°17′·7N 30°09′·1E
5850 Taslik Burnu
Fl(3)10s227m15M
• 36°13′·2N 30°24′·6E
5852 Yardimci Burnu
Fl.R.5s36m8M
• 36°12′·7N 30°24′·3E
5854 Adrasan (Kucuk Cavus Burnu)
Mo(A)15s45m8M
• 36°18′·0N 30°29′·4E
5854·4 Koca Burnu
Fl.10s140m12M
• 36°35′·8N 30°35′·3E
5854·8 On shoal 1020m northwards
Fl(2)10s7m8M
• 36°36′·7N 30°34′·5E

ANTALYA KORFEZI

5855 Antalya Yeni Limanı main mole head
Fl.R.3s12m6M
• 36°50′·1N 30°37′·0E
5855·4 Auxiliary mole head
Fl.G.3s15m6M
• 36°50′·1N 30°36′·8E
5858 Baba Burnu
Fl.5s35m14M
• 36°50′·8N 30°45′·5E
5859 Selimiye Side
Fl.3s14m9M
• 36°46′·0N 31°23′·1E
5860 Alanya Dildarde Burnu
Fl.20s209m20M
249°-vis-108°
• 36°31′·9N 32°59′·6E
5861 Selinti Burnu
Fl.3s33m8M
• 36°14′·2N 32°17′·8E
5862 Anamur Burnu
Fl(2)5s68m15M
• 36°01′·2N 32°48′·1E
5866 Aydincik
Fl.5s23m9M
• 36°08′·7N 33°19′·5E
5866·5 Ovacik main breakwater
Fl.G.5s12m5M
• 36°11′·28N 33°39′·35E
5866·51 Minor breakwater head
Fl.R.5s12m5M
• 36°11′·30N 33°39′·47E
5867 Ovacik Yarimadası
Fl(2)5s43m18M
• 36°08′·17N 33°41′·08E

TAŞUCU KÖRFEZI

5868 Dana Adası
Fl(2)10s70m10M
131°-vis-022°
• 36°11′·87N 33°46′·96E
5871 Ağalar Limanı
Fl.3s23m8M
• 36°16′·6N 33°50′·5E
5871·3 Taşucu S breakwater head
Fl(2)R.10s12m6M
• 36°18′·9N 33°53′·0E
5871·32 N breakwater head
Fl(2)G.10s12m6M
• 36°19′·0N 33°53′·0E
5871·4 Seka main breakwater
Fl.G.3s7m5M
• 36°18′·6N 33°53′·4E
5871·42 N breakwater
Fl.R.3s7m5M
• 36°18′·7N 33°53′·6E
5871·5 Incekum Burnu
Fl.10s13m10M
• 36°15′·88N 33°57′·32E

MERSIN LIMANI

5872 Mersin
Fl(3)10s14m15M
• 36°47′·1N 34°37′·1E
5872·2 S breakwater head
Fl.R.3s9m10M
• 36°47′·2N 34°38′·5E
5872·4 Elbow Dir Lt 220°12′
DirFl.WR.5s10m5/3M
219°-W-221·5°-R-219°
• 36°47′·1N 34°38′·1E
5873 E breakwater head
Fl.G.3s9m10M
• 36°47′·3N 34°38′·6E
5873·2/5873·3 Ldg Lts 040°30′
Front Oc.G.3s19m7M
Rear 189m from front
Oc.G.3s24m7M
• 36°48′·5N 34°39′·6E

5873·6 Karaduvar main breakwater head
F.R.4s13m5M
• 36°48′·3N 34°41′·8E
5873·7 Secondary breakwater head
F.G.4s13m5M
• 36°48′·4N 34°41′·8E
5873·8 Deli Burnu
Fl(2)5s17m5M
• 36°43′·5N 34°54′·5E
5874 Karatas Burnu Fener Burnu
Fl.10s38m20M
• 36°32′·47N 35°20′·38E
5874·4 Karatus shelter main breakwater head
Fl.R.5s10m8M
• 36°33′·5N 35°23′·1E
5874·5 Secondary breakwater head
Fl.G.5s9m7M
• 36°33′·6N 35°23′·0E
5874·6 On island
Fl(2)R.10s10m9M
• 36°33′·5N 35°23′·35E
5875 Yumurtalik
Fl(2)10s30m10M
• 36°47′·7N 35°48′·0E
5875·2 Shelter mole head
Fl.R.5s8m5M
• 36°46′·1N 35°47′·8E
5875·5 Devegeceği
Fl.3s7m7M
• 36°42′·04N 35°43′·9E

Mediterranean – Cyprus

5876 Cape Gata
Fl.5s58m15M
189°-vis-130°
• 34°33′·83N 33°01′·46E
5876·2 Akrotiri sea wall head
Fl.R.10s11m5M
• 34°34′·34N 33°01′·99E

LIMASSOL HARBOUR

5877 Main breakwater head
Q(6)R.10s9m12M
• 34°39′·02N 33°01′·97E
5877·4 Lee breakwater head
Oc.G.7s13m10M
• 34°39′·06N 33°01′·6E
5880 Lighter basin S quay head
Fl.G.3s3M
• 34°40′·11N 33°02′·55E
5880·2 W breakwaer head
Fl.R.3s3M
• 34°40′·15N 33°02′·54E
5880·7 Moni Limassol Sheraton Marina S breakwater head
Fl(2)10s9m10M
• 34°42′·50N 33°10′·05E
5882 Cape Kiti
Fl(3)15s20m13M
• 34°48′·8N 33°36′·2E

LARNACA

5884 Main harbour S breakwater head
Fl.WR.5s8m10/5M
075°-R-270° marks prohibited anchorage area, 270°-W-005° marks anchorage area
• 34°55′·6N 33°38′·9E
5888 Cape Greco
Fl.15s16m12M
• 34°57′·2N 34°05′·0E

FAMAGUSTA HARBOUR

5892 SE Bastion
Fl(2)15s23m16M
150°-vis-290°
• 35°07′·4N 33°56′·8E
5893 NW of town
Fl.WR.7s18m15/11M
178°-W-216°-R-313°
Structure obscured by windmill over a small arc on W bearings when near the anchorage
• 35°08′·5N 33°55′·6E
5898 Cape Elœa
Fl.10s31m5M
• 35°19′·5N 34°02′·8E
5900 Klidhes Islet
Fl(4)20s20m14M
• 35°42′·6N 34°36′·4E
5901 Alici Burnu fishing harbour
Fl(2)15s22m15M
• 35°33′·70N 34°12′·59E
5901·6 Kyrenia main light
Fl(3)R.20s18m20M
• 35°20′·5N 33°19′·78E
5904 Cape Kormakiti
Fl(2)20s30m15M
• 35°24′·0N 32°55′·2E

KARAVOSTÁSI

5906 Xeros pier root
Fl.R.3s19m7M
• 35°08′·56N 32°50′·27E
5907 Ore loading jetty head
Fl.5s18m5M
• 35°09′·02N 32°49′·00E
5907·5 Moulia Rocks
Fl(2)10s6m6M
• 34°43′·42N 32°26′·10E
5907·6 Cape Akamas
Fl(2)15s211m17M
• 35°05′·3N 32°16′·9E

PORT PAPHOS

5908 Paphos Point
Fl.15s36m17M
277°-vis-141°
• 34°45′·63N 32°24′·37E

Mediterranean – Turkey

ISKENDERUN KÖRFEZİ

5910 Sügözu Termik Santrali
Fl(3)R.10s6m5M
• 36°50′·2N 35°53′·0E
5912·5 Toros Gübre W pier head
Fl.R.5s10m5M
• 36°54′·4N 35°59′·0E
5912·6 E pier head
Fl.5s10m5M
• 36°54′·4N 35°59′·5E
5914 Isdemir S mole
Fl.G.3s10m10M
• 36°43′·5N 36°11′·1E
5914·4 N mole
Fl.R.3s10m9M
• 36°43′·6N 36°11′·2E
5915 Iskenderun Limanı W breakwater head
Oc.G.3s13m6M
• 36°36′·3N 36°11′·2E
5916 Iskenderun
Fl.3s45m20M
Obscured 234°-shore
• 36°32′·30N 36°03′·12E
5917 Akinci (Resülhinzir)
Fl(2)5s109m22M
• 36°19′·4N 35°47′·0E

Mediterranean – Syria

5919 Ra's al Basïp
Fl.4s75m14M
• 35°51′·8N 35°48′·0E
5919·4 Ra's Fasurï
Q(3)5s74m5M
• 35°40′·3N 35°46′·3E
5920 Ra's Ibn Hani'
Fl.6s18m12M
• 35°35′·2N 35°42′·9E

AL LADHIQIYAH (PORT DE LATTAQUIÉ)

5921·4 Al Burj
Fl(2)9s22m10M
• 35°30′·9N 35°46′·1E
5921·5 Ldg Lts 115·6°
Front Fl(2)R.5s6M
5921·51 Rear
Fl(2)R.5s6M
• 35°31′·78N 35°46′·10E
5921·6 Breakwater head
Fl.G.4s4m5M
• 35°31′·9N 35°45′·3E

JABLAH (PORT DE JEBLE)

5922·2 E breakwater head
Q.R.6m5M
• 35°21′·6N 35°55′·1E

NAHR HURAYSUN (PORT DE NAHR HAREISSOUN)

5923·5 Ra's al Burj Harf eşŞalīb summit Baniyas
Fl(3)WR.17s98m16/12M
015°-W-175°-R-195°
• 35°08′·8N 35°55′·2E

ŢARTUS (PORT DE TARTOÛS)

5923·8 E breakwater head
Fl.R.4s7m5M
• 34°54′·6N 35°51′·4E

JAZIRAT ARWAD (ÎLE DE ROUÂD)

5924 Jazïrat Arwad (Île de Rouâd)
Fl.5s20m12M
• 34°51′·4N 35°51′·3E

Mediterranean – Lebanon

TRIPOLI

5926 Ramkin Islet
Fl.3·3s22m18M Range 3M(T) 2005
• 34°29′·8N 35°45′·6E
5927 Jetée du Large head
Fl.G.4·5s10m5M
• 34°27′·9N 35°49′·5E
5927·2 Digue Est head
Fl.R.
• 34°28′·03N 35°49′·95E

JEBAÏL

All harbour lights TE 2000
5931
Fl.R.3s15m5M
• 34°07′·5N 35°38′·5E
5931·2
Fl.G.3s7m5M
• 34°06′·0N 35°39′·0E
5932 Tabarja
Fl.3s10m5M
• 34°01′·7N 35°37′·4E

PORT DE JOUNIÈÉ

5933 Yacht basin mole head
Fl(2)G.3s10m8M
• 33°59′·2N 35°37′·4E
5933·1 Quay head
Fl.R.3s8m5M
• 33°59′·5N 35°37′·0E

5933·3 Naval basin jetty head
Fl.G.3s10m8M
• 33°59′·1N 35°37′·1E

BEIRUT

5934 Ras Beyrouth
Fl(2)10s52m22M
• 33°54′·0N 35°28′·2E

5935 Northern mole
Fl.G.5s14m8M
• 33°54′·6N 35°31′·4E

5938 Airfield
Aero Al.Fl.WG.4s42m17M (control tower) & Aero Mo(BL)G.12s42m17M (hangar)
• 33°49′·5N 35°29′·3E

SIDON

5940 Ziri S point
Fl.R.3s10m6M TE 2009
• 33°34′·3N 35°22′·1E

SOUR

5942 Sour
Fl(3)12s15m12M TE 2009
• 33°16′·6N 35°11′·6E

Mediterranean – Israel

5944 Akko
Fl(2)7s16m10M
• 32°55′·1N 35°03′·8E

HEFA (HAIFA) HARBOUR

5945 Har Karmel (Mount Carmel)
Fl.5s179m30M
Partially obscured 235°-236°, obscured 263°-shore
• 32°49′·7N 34°58′·1E

5947 Lee breakwater head
Fl.R.3s14m5M
• 32°49′·4N 35°00′·5E

5952 Qishon harbour N breakwater head
Q(2)R.5s10m6M
• 32°49′·0N 35°01′·3E

5956 Mikhmoret Mevoot Yam
AlFl.WR.15s14m10M
• 32°24′·2N 34°51′·9E

5957 Herzlia Marina main breakwater
Fl.G.5s15m12M
• 32°10′·02N 34°47′·58E

5957·5 Lee breakwater
Fl.R.5s15m12M
• 32°09′·95N 34°47′·62E

TEL-AVIV
JAFFA

5963 Breakwater head
Fl.G.4s7M
• 32°03′·3N 34°45′·0E

ASHDOD PORT

5967 Ashdod
Fl(3)20s76m22M
• 31°48′·8N 34°38′·7E

5968 Main breakwater head
Fl.G.2s7M
• 31°50′·0N 34°38′·2E

5969 N breakwater head
Fl.R.2s7M
• 31°49′·9N 34°38′·3E

5969·2
F(2)5s15m7M
• 31°50′·18N 34°38′·71E

5970 Ashqelon (Ashkelon)
Fl(2)10s15M
• 31°38′·17N 34°32′·48E

5970·5 Marina
Fl(2)G.5s7M
• 31°41′·2N 34°33′·4E

Mediterranean – Egypt

EL ARISH

5973 El Arish
Fl.5s39m18M Racon
• 31°08′·69N 33°48′·88E

5974 W breakwater head
Fl(3)G.5s10m8M
• 31°09′·08N 33°48′·73E

5974·5 E breakwater head
Fl(3)R.5s10m8M
• 31°09′·89N 33°48′·86E

PORT SAID

5978·2 Port Said
Fl.10s47m20M Racon
• 31°16′·50N 32°17′·65E

5978·6 El Bahar Tower
Iso.2s42m15M Horn 2s Racon
• 31°18′·08N 32°21′·47E

5980/5980·1 Ldg Lts 217°40′
Front F.R.36m6M
207°-vis-229°
Ldg Lts difficult to distinguish at night due to ambient lighting
F.R obstruction light on tower top
Rear 0·57M from front
Oc(2)R.10s46m7M 207°-vis-229°
F.R obstruction light on tower top
• 31°14′·6N 32°17′·8E

5988 Ismailia Quay
F.R.11s8M
• 30°35′·1N 32°16′·5E

Suez Bay – Egypt

BÛR IBRÂHÎM (PORT IBRAHIM)

5996/5996·1 Ldg Lts 060°
Front F.12m6M
Rear 200m from front
F.WR(vert)25m10/6M
• 29°56′·3N 32°33′·5E

5997 Detached breakwater W end
Fl.G.2s8m5M
• 29°56′·3N 32°32′·7E

5997·2 E end
Q.8m5M
• 29°56′·3N 32°33′·3E

QAL'A KEBÎRA

6017 Birket Misallât southwards
Fl.3s42m18M Racon
• 29°54′·5N 32°35′·6E

6020 Newport Rock
Fl.5s17m10M
Channels are marked by buoys and buoyant beacons carrying R or G lights
• 29°53′·2N 32°33′·08E

Mediterranean – Egypt

DAMIETTA MOUTH

6156 Damietta entrance E side
Fl(2)30s47m20M Racon
• 31°31′·38N 31°50′·92E

6158 W side
Fl.G.10s14m8M
• 31°31′·7N 31°50′·7E

6158·5 El Girbi
Fl.G.3s4m5M
• 31°30′·5N 31°50′·0E

DAMIETTA PORT

6159 Dir Lt 191°30′ Front
F.R.33m10M
• 31°27′·7N 31°45′·0E

6159·1 170m from front
F.R.41m10M
• 31°27′·60N 31°45′·10E

6159·3 W breakwater
Fl.G.5s10m6M
• 31°29′·5N 31°45′·2E

6159·4 E breakwater
Fl(2)R.10s10m6M
• 31°29′·3N 31°45′·6E

6159·6 No.37
Fl.Bu.2·5s7M
• 31°28′·1N 31°45′·6E

6159·7 Barge Canal E end N side No.35
Fl.G.5s6M
• 31°27′·6N 31°47′·9E

6159·74 S side No.36
Fl(2)R.10s8M
• 31°27′·5N 31°47′·9E

6159·8 W end S side No.33
Fl.G.5s10m7M
• 31°28′·6N 31°45′·4E

6159·84 N side No.34
Fl(2)R.10s3m7M
• 31°28′·7N 31°45′·4E

6162 El-Burullus (Brullos)
Fl(3)20s47m20M Racon
• 31°35′·89N 31°04′·90E

6166 Rosetta
Fl(4)20s47m20M Aeromarine Racon
• 31°26′·62N 30°25′·91E

6168 Gezîret Disûqî (Nelson Island) summit
Fl.5s22m12M Racon
• 31°21′·6N 30°06′·4E

6168·2 Abu Qîr breakwater
Oc.3s17m5M
• 31°19′·9N 30°05′·1E

PORT OF ALEXANDRIA

6170 Eastern harbour. El Silsila breakwater head W end
Fl.R.5s14m5M
• 31°12′·9N 29°53′·7E

6171 W breakwater head
Fl.G.5s21m8M
• 31°12′·9N 29°53′·5E

6173 Râs el-Tîn
Fl(2+1)30s52m21M Racon
• 31°11′·8N 29°51′·7E

6173·5 El Agamy
Fl(2)15s17m15M Racon
• 31°08′·86N 29°47′·22E

6174 Great Pass entrance S side. Great Pass beacon
Fl.4s21m16M Racon
• 31°10′·00N 29°48′·54E

6176 Ldg Lts 113°
Front 2F.R(vert)18m5M
050°-vis-150°
F.13m5M 150°-vis-050°
• 31°09′·3N 29°50′·7E

6176·1 Meks
Rear 740m from front
2F(vert)38m10M
095·5°-vis-169·5°
• 31°09′·2N 29°51′·2E

6176·5 North Shoal
Fl.R.5s5M
• 31°09′·9N 29°49′·0E

6180 Outer breakwater head Awad
Fl.R.3s20m8M
• 31°09′·99N 29°50′·81E

6182 Quarantine breakwater head El Shiro
Fl.G.3s20m8M
• 31°10′·02N 29°51′·08E

6191/6191·1 El Dikheila Ldg Lts 173°
Front Fl.3s14m14M
Rear 650m from front
Iso.2s31m17M
• 31°08′·1N 29°48′·7E
6191·2 Breakwater head
Fl.9m5M
• 31°09′·4N 29°48′·4E
6191·5
3Mo(U)15s10M Horn Mo(U)30s
• 31°08′·9N 29°49′·1E
6192 Sidi Kerir Ldg Lts 142°
Front 2F.R.9m5M
6192·1 Rear 250m from front
2F.R.13m5M
• 31°03′·34N 29°40′·36E
6192·4 N breakwater
Fl.G.2s6m5M
• 31°03′·40N 29°40′·21E
6192·5 E breakwater
Fl.R.4s6m5M
• 31°03′·34N 29°40′·21E
6193 Râs el Shaqîq
Fl(3)15s47m20M Racon
• 30°57′·25N 28°49′·69E
6194 Râs 'Alam el-Rûm
Fl.5s48m12M Racon
• 31°21′·7N 27°20′·6E

MERSA EL FALLAH

6204 Sidi Barrani
Fl(2)15s20m12M Racon
• 31°37′·3N 25°54′·5E
6206 Salûm
Fl(3)20s14m12M
• 31°33′·7N 25°09′·9E

Mediterranean – Libya

PORT BARDIA

6210 Mingar Raai Ruhah
Fl.5s98m12M
• 31°45′·6N 25°06′·5E
6214 Ras Azzaz
Fl.3s16m10M
• 31°58′·2N 24°58′·8E

MERSA TÒBRUCH

Note Navigational lights in Mersa Tobruch reported TE 1996
6220 Main light
Fl(3)15s53m15M
• 32°05′·3N 23°59′·4E
6221 Punta Tòbruch
Fl.G.5s6m6M
• 32°04′·4N 24°00′·6E
6224/6224·1 Marsa Umm Escsciausc Ldg Lts 244°48′
Front Q.21m7M (occas)
Rear 314m from front
Iso.2s26m7M (occas)
• 32°03′·2N 24°00′·8E
6234 Ras's at-Tïn
Fl.5s34m10M
• 32°37′·3N 23°07′·0E

DARNAH

6236 Darnah
Fl(4)20s60m20M
• 32°44′·5N 22°41′·0E
6238 N mole head
Q.G.14m8M
Loading jetty and power station lights 4M WNW
• 32°45′·8N 22°39′·7E
6239 S mole head
Q.R.14m8M
• 32°45′·9N 22°39′·7E

6242 Ra's Al-Hil¸l
Fl(3)17·5s22m10M
Obscured when bearing less than 100°
• 32°55′·4N 22°10′·7E
6244 Susah (Apollonia)
Fl.6s25m11M
• 32°54′·1N 21°58′·0E
6246 Ra's Amir
Fl(2)6s29m11M
• 32°56′·2N 21°42′·5E
6248 Tulmaythah (Tolemaide)
Fl(3)10s21m12M
Emergency light F
• 32°42′·9N 20°56′·7E
6250 Sidi Suwaykir
Fl(4)15s21m13M
• 32°20′·0N 20°17′·3E
6251·5 Ras Sel Mingar jetty head
Fl.3s13m5M
• 32°11′·0N 20°05′·2E

PORT OF BANGHAZI

6251·8 Banghazï Musselman Cemetery
Fl.3s41m17M
• 32°07′·5N 20°03′·8E
6252 Main harbour N breakwater head
Fl.R.3s13m6M
• 32°06′·9N 20°01′·6E
6252·2 W breakwater N head
Fl.G.3s13m6M
• 32°06′·8N 20°02′·0E
6252·4 Dir Lt 066°
DirF.WRG.13m14-9M
062·5°-G-064·7°-W-067·2°-R-069·5°
• 32°07′·1N 20°02′·5E
6254·6 Breakwater head
Iso.5s10m6M
• 32°05′·6N 20°02′·4E

AZ ZUWAYTINAH

6255·4 Radio mast
Q.R.137m15M +F.R.97m+F.R.56m
• 30°50′·0N 20°03′·1E
6255·5/6255·51 Ldg Lts 135°
Front Fl.Y.1·5s7m10M
Rear 750m from front
Oc.Y.10s13m10M
• 30°53′·0N 20°04′·1E
6255·6 Waffeya
Fl(6)10s5M
• 30°54′·0N 20°03′·5E
6255·7
Fl(2)13s31m16M
• 30°53′·8N 20°04′·1E

AL BURAYQAH (MARSA EL-BRÉGA)

6256 W breakwater head
Fl.G.3s12m15M
All lights in Al Burayqah liable to change.
• 30°25′·1N 19°35′·4E
6256·2 E breakwater head
Q.R.12m15M
• 30°25′·0N 19°35′·7E

RA'S LANUF

6266 Water Tower
Q(2)5s50m15M Obstruction
F.R.52m Obstruction
• 30°30′·7N 18°32′·3E
6266·3 Main breakwater head
Fl(2)G.10s18m5M
• 30°30′·63N 18°35′·72E
6266·4 East breakwater head
Fl(2)R.10s18m5M
• 30°30′·48N 18°35′·40E
6266·5/6266·51 Ldg Lts 287°30′
Front F.12m9M
Rear 220m from front
F.17m4M
• 30°30′·90N 18°34′·28E

6267 Ras es Sider
Aero Oc.R.3s120m8M+ Aero F.R.94m
• 30°36′·9N 18°16′·9E
6268 Surt (Sirte)
Fl.5s35m15M
• 31°12′·5N 16°35′·6E

MISURATA (QANR AHMAD)

6274 Ra's al Barq (Ras Zarrùgh)
Fl.5s24m8M
• 32°22′·3N 15°12′·8E
6278/6278·1 Steel Harbour Ldg Lts 262°20′
Front Q.Y.11m7M
Rear 430m from front Iso.Y.6s19m7M
• 32°20′·62N 15°14′·17E
6278·4 N breakwater head
Oc.G.4s12m5M Horn 20s
• 32°20′·89N 15°15′·38E
6280 Zlïpan El-Galab Hill
Fl.3s35m10M
• 32°29′·6N 14°34′·3E
6284 Al Khums. Ra's el-Usif
Fl.3s26m12M
• 32°39′·6N 14°15′·2E
6288 Ra's al-Hallab
Fl(3)15s35m12M
• 32°48′·0N 13°48′·4E
6290 Ra's Tajura
Fl.5s34m14M
097°-obscd-109°
• 32°53′·7N 13°23′·2E
6292 Sidi Otman. Tripoli Ock ba Ben-Nafur
Aero AlFl.WG.10s56m29/24M Occas
• 35°54′·2N 13°16′·4E

PORT OF TARABULUS

6294 Spanish mole root. Tarabulus
Fl(2)10s60m12M
• 32°54′·3N 13°10′·7E
6296·4 No.1
Fl.G.3s13m10M
• 32°56′·1N 13°13′·3E
6296·5 No.2
Fl.R.3s13m10M
• 32°56′·1N 13°13′·7E
6296·6 No.4
Fl(2)R.6s13m10M
• 32°55′·4N 13°13′·7E
6318 Sabratah
Iso.2s20m11M
• 32°48′·8N 12°25′·8E
6320 Mellitah jetty head
Fl.3s13M
• 32°53′·02N 12°14′·73E

ZUWARAH

6322 Main light
Fl.5s15m12M
• 32°55′·5N 12°07′·2E
6323 N mole head
VQ.G.11m8M
• 32°55′·38N 12°07′·57E
6324 S mole head
VQ.R.11m8M
• 32°55′·29N 12°07′·34N
6326 Farwah
LFl.5s17m12M
• 33°06′·4N 11°44′·7E

Mediterranean – Tunisia

6327 Ras El Keft fishing port
Iso.G.6s9m5M
• 33°11′·1N 11°29′·3E
6327·2
Q(3)R.10s9m5M
• 33°11′·1N 11°29′·3E

6328 Zarzis
Oc(2+1)12s15m15M
180°-vis-090°
Emergency light F.R.10M
• 33°29′·7N 11°07′·2E
6328·2 E breakwater head
Fl(2+1)15s11m12M
• 33°28′·7N 11°07′·8E

ÎLE JERBA
6330·2 Aghir
Fl.4·5s7m9M 258°-vis-010°
Reserve light F.G
• 33°45′·2N 11°01′·2E
6332 Rass Taguerness
Fl.5s64m24M
• 33°49′·3N 11°02′·7E
6334 Houmet Souk
Oc(2)7s9m14M
080°-vis-320°
• 33°53′·1N 10°51′·2E
6334·1 Fishing port
Fl.G.4s7m7M
• 33°53′·18N 10°51′·18E
6334.15
Fl.R.5s7m7M
• 33°53′·18N 10°51′·22E
6334·2 No.1
Fl(2)G.7s4m6M
• 33°55′·9N 10°51′·5E
6334·4 No.2
Fl.R.5s4m6M
• 33°55′·9N 10°51′·6E
6334·6 No.3
Fl.G.4s4m6M
• 33°54′·8N 10°51′·5E
6334·8 No.4
Fl.R.5s4m6M
• 35°54′·8N 10°51′·5E
6335 No.5
Fl.G.4s4m4M
• 33°53′·7N 10°51′·6E
6335·2 No.6
Fl.R.5s4m4M
• 33°53′·7N 10′·51·5E
6338 Bordj Djilidj
Fl.R.5s16m9M
• 33°53′·1N 10°44′·6E
6339 Airport
Aero AlFl.WG.10s37m29/26M
• 33°52′·2N 10°47′·3E
6340 El Kantara
F.5m8M
• 33°40′·6N 10°54′·9E
6340·5 Boughrara
Iso.2s7m8M
• 33°32′·3N 10°41′·3E
6342·4 Canal d'Adjim No.1
Fl(3)G.15s5m5M
Canal d'Adjim marked by lit buoys No.2 to No.5
• 33°41′·7N 10°44′·1E
6344 W channel
Fl(2)9s4m7M
340°-vis-250°
• 33°42′·1N 10°36′·3E
6244·5 Jetty head
Fl(5)R.20s5m5M
• 33°41′·0N 10°36′·0E
6345 Zarat entrance N side
Fl(3)G.10s6m5M
• 33°41′·9N 10°21′·8E
6345·2 S side
LFl.R.10s6m5M
• 33°41′·8N 10°21′·8E

GABÈS
6348 Main light
Fl(2)6s13m20M
124°-vis-304°
• 33°53′·6N 10°06′·8E
6349 Fishing harbour Jetée nord head
Fl(2)G.9s10m6M
• 33°53′·6N 10°07′·2E
6350 Jetée sud head
Fl.R.6·5s10m6M
• 33°53′·6N 10°07′·1E

PORT DE GHANNOUCHE
6352 Jetée nord head
Fl.G.4s12m8M
• 33°55′·4N 10°06′·7E
6352·4 Jetée sud head
Fl.R.5s12m10M
• 33°55′·2N 10°06′·5E

SKHIRA
6353 Fishing harbour jetty
Fl(2)G.10s6m6M
• 34°17′·0N 10°05′·7E
6353·1
Fl.R.5s6m6M
• 34°17′·0N 10°05′·6E
6354 Baie des Sur-Kenis
Fl.G.3s32m20M
• 34°19′·7N 10°07′·8E

ZABOUSSA
6359 Rass Tyna
Fl(2)10s55m24M
• 34°39′·0N 10°41′·1E

SFAX
6362 Quai du Commerce
Dir Lt 320°30′
DirOc(2)8s18m13M
319°-intens-325°
• 34°43′·8N 10°46′·1E
6362·5 Fishing harbour S breakwater head
Fl.R.5s4m10M
• 34°42′·7N 10°46′·0E
6362·6 N jetty SW end
Fl.G.4s4m10M
• 34°42′·7N 10°46′·1E
6362·7 Breakwater N head
Iso.R.6s4m10M
• 34°42′·7N 10°46′·3E

PORT DE LOUETA
6364 Port entrance
Fl.R.5s7m6M
• 35°02′·5N 11°02′·1E
6364·2
Fl.G.4s7m6M
• 35°02′·5N 11°02′·1E

ÎLES KERKENNAH
6366·6 Île Chergui Ras Djlija
Fl(2)10s10m6M
• 34°49′·7N 11°14′·8E
6366·65 Ennajet east jetty head
Fl(2)R.10s7m5M
• 34°49′·7N 11°15′·4E
6366·651 W Jetty
Fl.G.7m5M
• 34°49′·8N 11°15′·4E
6366·67 Fishing Harbour
Fl.R.5s10m6M
• 34°49′·7N 11°15′·4E
6366·75 Pier head
Fl.3s10m9M
• 34°51′·8N 10°55′·1E
6366·8 Île Gharbi Sidi Youssef Dir Lt
DirOc(2)WRG.9s9m9/7M
• 34°39′·3N 10°58′·0E
6367 Môle sud head
Fl(2)G.6s8m5M
• 34°39′·3N 10°58′·1E
6367·2 Môle nord head
Fl(3)R.12s8m5M
• 34°39′·4N 10°58′·2E
6368 Rass Kaboudia Tour Khadidja
Fl(2)WR.9s27m19/14M
135°-W-325°-R-135°
• 35°14′·0N 11°09′·4E
6369 Chebba Jetty N
Fl(2)G.9s8m6M
• 35°13′·9N 11°10′·0E
6369·2 S Jetty
Fl(2)R.6·5s8m6M
• 35°13′·9N 11°10′·0E
6369·5 Melloutech Dir Lt
Fl.3·5s10m10M
Fl.G.4s marks beacons 3 & 5. Fl.R.5s marks beacons Nos 4 & 6
Fl.R.5s marks beacon 2, F.G.4s marks beacon 1.
• 35°08′·6N 11°03′·6E

MAHDIA
6370 Cape Afrique
Fl.R.5s26m17M
• 35°30′·4N 11°04′·8E
6371·4 Outer spur head
Fl(2)G.10s6m6M
• 35°30′·0N 11°04′·1E
6372·6 Breakwater SE head
Fl(2)R.10s4m6M
• 35°29′·8N 11°04′·2E
6373 Sayada NW jetty head
LFl(2)G.15s6m6M
• 35°40′·4N 10°53′·6E
6373·2 SE jetty head
LFl(2)R.15s6m6M
• 35°40′·4N 10°53′·6E
6373·6 Téboulba NW
LFl.G.10s7m5M
• 35°39′·5N 10°57′·4E
6373·8 NE pier head
LFl.R.10s7m5M
• 35°39′·5N 10°57′·6E
6373·85 Secondary channel No.1
Fl.G.6s6m6M
• 35°40′·6N 10°59′·1E
6373·9 No.2
Fl.R.6s6m6M
• 35°40′·55N 10°59′·20E

KSIBET EL MEDIOUNI
6373·94 Fishing harbour jetty head
Fl.G.4s10m6M
• 35°41′·3N 10°51′·7E

MONASTIR
6374 Bordj el Kelb
Fl(2)R.6s26m10M
197°-vis-355°
• 35°45′·6N 10°50′·3E
6376·5 New fishing harbour entrance
Fl.G.4s12m5M
• 35°45′·3N 10°50′·3E
6376·6
Fl.R.5s12m5M
• 35°45′·4N 10°50′·3E
6377 Marina E side
Fl.G.4s8m6M
• 35°46′·7N 10°50′·1E
6377·2 S breakwater W side
Fl.R.5s8m6M
• 35°46′·6N 10°50′·1E
6378 N breakwater head
Fl(2)10s11m7M
• 35°46′·6N 10°50′·2E
6380 Île Kuriat
Fl.WR.5s30m18/14M
053°-W-348°-R-053°
• 35°47′·9N 11°02′·0E

SOUSSE
6382 Casbah
Fl.4s70m22M
• 35°49′·4N 10°38′·3E

6384 Jetée Abri
Oc.WR.4s12m10/6M
135°-R-180°-W-045°
Reserve light range 6M
• 35°49'·5N 10°39'·1E
6385 Épi Nord head
Fl.G.4s10m8M
258°-vis-112°
Reserve light range 6M
• 35°49'·5N 10°38'·9E
6385·5 Épi sud head
Fl.R.5s10m8M
Reserve light range 6M
• 35°49'·4N 10°38'·8E
6386 Hammamet Casbah
Fl(2)6s17m15M
255°-vis-165°
Emergency light F 7M
• 36°23'·7N 10°36'·9E
6386·1 Yasmine Yacht Harbour jetty
LFl(2)15s17m12M
• 36°22'·3N 10°32'·8E
6386·3 W breakwater head
Fl.R.5s10m6M
• 36°22'·2N 10°32'·8E
6386·5 E breakwater head
Fl.G.4s8m6M
• 36°22'·2N 10°32'·9E
6387 El Kantaoui pleasure harbour N breakwater head
Fl.G.6s9m6M
• 35°53'·6N 10°36'·0E
6387·3 S breakwater head
Fl.R.6s9m6M
• 35°53'·5N 10°36'·0E
6388 Hergla Jetée du large head
Fl(2)G.10s5m6M
• 36°01'·9N 10°30'·7E
6388·2 Jetée sud head
Fl.R.5s9m6M
• 36°01'·9N 10°30'·6E
6388·3 Nouvelle Jetée sud head
Fl.R.5s9m6M
• 36°01'·8N 10°30'·63E
6389·5 Beni Khiar Jetée du large
Fl(2)G.10s5m6M
• 36°27'·1N 10°47'·8E
6389·6 Jetée sud
Fl.R.5s5m6M
• 36°27'·0N 10°47'·8E

PORT DE KELIBIA

6390 Kelibia
Fl(4)20s82m23M
• 36°50'·2N 11°06'·9E
6390·4 Jetée sud head
Fl(2)8s5m5M
• 36°50'·0N 11°06'·5E
6392 Cap Bon
Fl(3)20s126m30M
068°-vis-310° obscured by Île Zembra 100°-108°
• 37°04'·7N 11°02'·7E
6392·3 Southwards south limit
Fl(3)Y.10s16m9M
Marks S limit of pipeline zone
• 37°00'·4N 11°03'·5E
6392·4 North limit
Fl(3)Y.10s16m9M
Marks N limit of pipeline zone
• 37°01'·6N 11°03'·4E
6392·6 El Haouaria fishing harbour
Fl.G.4s8m9M
• 37°02'·4N 11°03'·9E
6392·62
Fl.R.5s8m8M
• 37°02'·4N 11°03'·9E
6392·64
Fl.5s4m4M
• 37°02'·2N 11°03'·9E
6393 Rās Lahmar
Fl.R.5s7m5M
• 37°02'·9N 10°54'·4E
6394 Djamour es Srir (Îlot Zembretta)
Fl.4s59m6M
124°-vis-099°
• 37°06'·3N 10°52'·4E
6394·2 Djamour el Kébir (Île Zembra) entrance E
Fl.G.4s5m5M
• 37°07'·0N 10°48'·4E
6394·4 W
Fl.R.5s3m5M
• 37°06'·9N 10°48'·4E
6394·5 Sidi Daoud Fishing harbour Jetée Nord head
Fl(2)R.10s3m6M
• 37°01'·1N 10°54'·3E
6394·61 Jetée Sud head
Fl(2)G.10s3m6M
• 37°01'·1N 10°54'·4E
6394·62 Dir Lt
DirIso.2s7m6M
• 37°01'·1N 10°54'·4E

PORT DE LA GOULETTE

6396 Port de Commerce jetée nord S corner No.9
Fl(3)12s13m11M
090°-vis-121°, 215°-vis-035°
Emergency light F.8M
• 36°48'·3N 10°18'·5E
6396·5 Ro Ro berth
Fl.G.4s7m6M
• 36°48'·52N 10°18'·3E
6397 Port de Pêche et Plaisance Dique Nord head
Fl(2)G.10s9m5M
• 36°48'·3N 10°18'·9E
6397·5 Jetty NW side
F.R.13m5M
• 36°48'·3N 10°18'·5E
6399 Dique Sud No.10
Fl.R.5s9m6M
• 36°48'·2N 10°18'·4E
6401 Power Station
Fl.R.1·5s102m8M
• 36°47'·6N 10°17'·0E
6409·23 Tunis Canal No.23
Fl.G.4s3m2M
• 36°48'·59N 10°16'·26E
Inner channel marked by lights Fl.G.3m2M and Fl.R.3m2M
6412 Cap Carthage
Fl.5s146m22M
• 36°52'·3N 10°20'·9E
6414 Île Plane
Fl(2)WR.10s20m15/11M
067°-R-107°-W-067°
• 37°10'·8N 10°19'·7E

LAC DE GHAR EL MALH (PORTO FARINA)

6415·5 Jetty No.1
Fl(3)5s3m8M
• 37°08'·5N 10°12'·6E
6415·7 Jetty No.2
Fl(3)10s3m8M
• 37°08'·5N 10°12'·6E
6416 Îles Cani
Fl(2)WR.10s39m19/16M
237°-W-177°-R-237°
• 37°21'·2N 10°07'·4E

CAP ZEBIB

6418 Fishing harbour jetty head
Fl.G.4s10m6M
• 37°16'·0N 10°04'·0E
6418·1
Fl.R.5s10m7M
• 37°16'·0N 10°04'·1E

BIZERTE

6423 Zarzouna Fishing harbour N wall
Fl(2)G.10s6m6M
• 37°16'·0N 9°53'·7E
6423·4 E jetty
Fl(2)R.10s6m6M
• 37°15'·9N 9°53'·7E
6426 Breakwater N head
F.G.15m8M
• 37°16'·6N 9°53'·4E
6428 E head
Iso.R.4s24m10M
• 37°16'·6N 9°53'·4E
6440 Pointe de Sebra
DirFl.WRG.6s16m8M
• 37°15'·4N 9°51'·5E
6454 Menzel Abderrahmen W jetty
Fl.R.5s9m6M
• 37°13'·8N 9°51'·6E
6456 Ras Engelah
Fl.WR.2·5s38m28/25M
R-shore west of light-R-085°-W-shore
• 37°20'·6N 9°44'·3E
6458 Cap Serrat
Fl(2)WR.10s199m 24/22M
238°-R-261°-W-238°
• 37°13'·9N 9°12'·6E
6459 Sidi Mechregui Fishing Harbour W side
Fl.R.5s10m6M
• 37°10'·2N 9°07'·5E
6459·1 Outer
Fl.G.4s10m6M
• 37°10'·0N 9°07'·5E

ÎLE DE TABARKA

6460 Jazirat Tabarka
Fl.5s72m17M
• 36°57'·8N 8°45'·5E
6462 Fishing harbour Digue Nord head
Fl.G.4s10m6M
• 36°57'·5N 8°45'·9E
6462·4 Digue Est elbow
Fl.R.5s10m6M
• 36°57'·5N 8°45'·7E
6462·6 Digue Interior
Fl.R.5s8m5M
• 36°57'·5N 8°45'·6E

ÎLE DE LA GALITE

6464 Galiton de l'Ouest
Fl(4)20s168m24M
227°-obscd-250° by Île de la Galite. May appear as Fl(2)20s at a distance
Auxiliary F.R.160m23M
064°-vis-069° over Les Sorelles
• 37°29'·9N 8°52'·6E
6465·2 NE corner
Fl(2)G.10s6M
• 37°31'·5N 8°56'·4E

Mediterranean – Algeria

6482 El Kala (La Calle) entrance N side
Iso.R.4s17m9M
Obscured by Pointe Noire when bearing less than 091°
• 36°54'·0N 8°26'·6E
6484 Ras Rosa
Fl(2)6s130m10M
• 36°56'·8N 8°14'·4E

PORT OF ANNABA

6486 Jetée du Lion head
Oc(3)G.12s16m9M
• 36°54′·2N 7°46′·9E

6490 Quai sud head
Oc(2)R.6s16m10M
• 36°54′·1N 7°46′·7E

6504 Fort Gênois
Oc(2)6s61m10M
240°-obscd-263° within 0·5M
• 36°57′·0N 7°46′·6E

6506 Cape de Garde Ras el Hamra
Fl.5s143m30M
• 36°58′·1N 7°47′·1E

6508 Roche Axin
Fl(2)6s16m8M
054°-vis-324°
• 37°03′·2N 7°30′·8E

6510 Ras Toukouch
Oc.WR.4s128m8/5M
140°-W-278°-R-290° over Roche Akcine-W-320°
• 37°04′·7N 7°23′·5E

CHETAÏBI

6516 Cap de Fer (Ras el Hadid)
Fl(3)15s65m19M
312°-vis-254°
• 37°04′·8N 7°10′·4E

6518 El Mersa. Point Sida Bou Merouane
Iso.4s10m7M
• 37°01′·7N 7°15′·2E

SKIKDA

6520 Port Methanier jetée principale head
Fl.G.4s16m10M
• 36°53′·6N 6°56′·9E

6520·2 Jetée secondaire head
Oc.R.4s10m7M
F RG at basin entrance
• 36°53′·5N 6°56′·7E

6522 Jetée nord head
Oc(2)WR.6s21m12/9M
160°-W-288°-R-160°
• 36°53′·6N 6°54′·2E

6523 Traverse Nord head
Fl(2)R.5s10m6M
296°-vis-126°
F.R.4M marks oil berth 750m ESE
• 36°53′·5N 6°54′·3E

6524 Jetée du Château Vert head
Fl(2)G.5s10m5M
109°-vis-011°
• 36°53′·4N 6°54′·3E

6530 Îlot des Singes
Iso.WG.17m10/6M
193·5°-G-216°-W-023°-G-080°
• 36°54′·55N 6°53′·15E

6534 Île Srigina
Fl.R.5s54m20M
Obscured by Pointe Esrah when bearing less than 122°
• 36°56′·3N 6°53′·2E

6538 Port de Collo jetty head
F.G.13m5M
Obscured when bearing less than 221°
• 37°00′·3N 6°34′·5E

6540 Cap Collo
Fl.G.5s26m12M
146°-vis-323°
• 37°00′·9N 6°35′·1E

6542 Cap Bougaroun
Fl(2)10s91m29M
087°-vis-280°
• 37°05′·3N 6°28′·2E

6544 Ras el Moghreb (Atia)
Fl.4s30m10M
• 37°01′·5N 6°15′·9E

JIJEL

6550 Jetée nord main light
Fl(2+1)WR.12s19m12/9M
096°-R-101°-W-096°
Obscured by the heights of Picouleau when bearing less than 094°
• 36°49′·6N 5°46′·9E

6551 Head
Iso.G.4s9m6M
• 36°49′·5N 5°46′·9E

6558 Ras el Afia
Fl.R.5s43m23M
027°-vis-255°
Obscured by Cap Cavallo when bearing less than 064°
• 36°49′·1N 5°41′·5E

6559 Auxiliary light
Fl.R.28m10M
124°-vis-154° over Écuicil de la Salamandre and Banc des Kabyles
• 36°49′·2N 5°41′·5E

6560 Ilot Hadjret Taflkout
Fl(9)15s21m5M
• 36°46′·5N 5°34′·6E

BEJAÏA

6566 Jetée est head
Oc.4s16m12M
Obscured by Cap Bouak when bearing less than 205°
• 36°45′·1N 5°06′·1E

6567 Jetée sud head
Oc(2)R.6s11m10M
• 36°45′·1N 5°05′·9E

6569 Passe Abdelkader S side spur
Fl(2)R.6s8m8M
• 36°45′·0N 5°05′·6E

6569·2 N side jetty head
Fl(2)G.6s8m8M
• 36°45′·1N 5°05′·6E

6570 Passe de la Kasbah S side
Fl(2)R.7s8m8M
• 36°44′·8N 5°05′·3E

6570·2 N side
Fl(2)G.7s8m8M
• 36°44′·9N 5°05′·3E

6572 Cap Carbon
Fl(3)20s220m28M
090°-vis-022°
Obscured by Cap Noir when bearing more than 333°
• 36°46′·5N 5°06′·3E

6573 Auxiliary light
Fl.WR.1·5s32m10/7M
094°-W-114° obscd by coast, 114°-R-126°-W-295°, 295°-W-316° obscd by coast
• 36°46′·6N 5°06′·4E

6578 Cap Sigli
Fl.5s57m17M
Partially obscd between 000° and 010° Aeromarine
• 36°53′·8N 4°45′·6E

6580 Cap Corbelin
Fl(2+1)WR.15s42m13M
001·5°-R-over Roches Mers-el-Farm-104·5°-W-001·5°
Obscured when bearing less than 266°
• 36°54′·7N 4°25′·6E

DELLYS

6584 Point de Dellys
F.R.41m15M
066°-vis-336°
Obscured by Cap Bengut when bearing less than 094°
• 36°55′·4N 3°55′·4E

6588 Jetty head
Oc.4s12m9M
Obscured by Point de Dellys when bearing less than 193°
• 36°54′·8N 3°55′·3E

6590 Quai Sud SE corner
Oc.R.4s12m5M
Obscured by Pointe de Dellys when bearing less than 203°
• 36°54′·8N 3°55′·1E

6592 Cap Bengut Pointe des Jardins
Fl(4)15s63m30M
079°-vis-287°
Obscured by Pointe de Dellys when bearing less than 270°
• 36°55′·4N 3°53′·6E

PORT DE ZEMMOURI BAHAR

6593·4 NE pier head
Q.16m10M
• 36°48′·33N 3°33′·58E

6593·5 NW pier
Fl.G.5s17m7M
• 36°48′·3N 3°33′·6E

6593·7 Harbour entrance secondary pier
F.G.5m6M
• 36°48′·3N 3°33′·7E

6593·8 Main pier
F.R.5m6M
• 36°48′·3N 3°33′·7E

6594 Ras Matifa
Fl(3)15s74m23M Aeromarine
040°-vis-310°
• 36°48′·8N 3°14′·9E

6596 Temenfoust (Le Pérouse) near head of jetty
Iso.R.2s10m7M
Obscured by Cap Matifou when bearing more than 145°
• 36°48′·3N 3°13′·9E

ALGIERS

6602 Port d'Alger Jetée Kheir Eddine head
Fl(2)3s23m20M Horn Mo(N)30s
154°-vis-055°
• 36°46′·7N 3°04′·8E

6604 Spur
Fl.G.4s10m11M
309°-vis-133°
• 36°46′·8N 3°04′·4E

6606 Jetée du Vieux Port N end
Fl.R.4s10m12M
059°-vis-014°
• 36°46′·7N 3°04′·4E

6610 S entrance E breakwater head
Oc.R.4s12m13M
005°-vis-312°
• 36°45′·8N 3°04′·7E

6611 Jetée de Mustapha spur
Iso.G.4s12m12M
295°-vis104°
• 36°45′·9N 3°04′·7E

6612 Bassin de l'Agha S entrance W side
F.R.10m8M
• 36°45′·9N 3°04′·2E

6613 E side
F.G.11m7M
• 36°46′·0N 3°04′·3E

6616 N entrance W side
F.R.10m9M
145°-vis-025°
• 36°46′·3N 3°04′·0E

6617 E side
F.G.10m8M
340°-vis-196°
• 36°46′·3N 3°04′·1E

6620 Roche M'Tahen
Q(3)10s12m8M
• 36°47'·8N 3°04'·0E
6621 Cap Caxine
Fl.5s64m30M
075°-vis-300°
• 36°48'·6N 2°57'·3E
6624 Sidi Fredj Marina
Fl(3)12s42m17M
• 36°46'·0N 2°50'·9E
6624·6 Jetée Principale head
Iso.WG.4s14m11M
190°-W-129°-G-190°
• 36°45'·8N 2°51'·1E
6628 Chréa
Aero Fl(3+1)7s1600m50M
• 36°25'·7N 2°53'·1E
6629 Bouharoun W jetty head
F.R.8m5M
• 36°37'·7N 2°39'·5E
6629·5 Port de Khemisti W jetty
F.G.7m6M
• 36°38'·4N 2°40'·4E

TIPASA
6630 Ras el Kalia
Oc.4s32m12M
341°-unintens-073°
• 36°35'·9N 2°27'·0E
6631 New mole head
F.G.8m6M
Obscured when bearing more than 154°
• 36°35'·7N 2°27'·1E

PORT CHERCHELL
6636 Forte Joinville
Fl(2+1)15s37m21M
• 36°36'·8N 2°11'·4E
6637 Grand Hammam
Q.13m7M
• 36°36'·9N 2°11'·7E
6638 Jetée Joinville head
Iso.G.4s10m7M
• 36°36'·8N 2°11'·5E
6642 S quay
F.R.7m6M
• 36°36'·7N 2°11'·5E
6646 Ras Ténès
Fl(2)10s89m31M
• 36°33'·1N 1°20'·6E

PORT DE TÉNÈS
6648 Outer breakwater W head
Q.1s10m10M
• 36°31'·6N 1°19'·0E
6649 E head
Iso.G.4s10m5M
• 36°31'·7N 1°19'·1E
6650 Jetée NW head
Oc(2)G.6s10m7M
226°-vis-116°
• 36°31'·6N 1°19'·1E
6651 Jetée NE head
Oc(2)R.6s10m9M
193°-vis-096°
• 36°31'·6N 1°19'·1E
6652 Dir Lt 085°
DirF.WG.8M
W sector 1°
• 36°31'·7N 1°19'·6E
6656 Nadji
Fl(3)15s60m26M
• 36°26'·6N 0°56'·4E
6656·5 Îlot Colombi
Oc(2)G.6s29m5M
• 36°26'·3N 0°55'·2E
6658 Ras Ouillis Cap Ivi
Fl.5s118m31M
064°-vis-244°
• 36°06'·9N 0°13'·7E

PORT DE MOSTAGANEM
6660 Jetée du large head
Fl(4)WR.12s17m13/10M
197°-R-234°-W-197°
• 35°56'·1N 0°04'·2E
6661 Spur head
Oc(2)R.6s11m7M
248°-vis-073°
• 35°56'·3N 0°04'·5E
6662 Mole sud head
Oc(2)G.6s13m5M
• 35°56'·1N 0°04'·6E
6664 Môle de Independance head
Fl.G.4s11m6M
• 35°56'·2N 0°04'·6E

PORT D'ARZEW EL DJEDID
6665 Detached breakwater E head
Fl(3)G.5s11m7M
• 35°49'·33N 0°14'·32W
6665·1 W head
Fl(3)R.5s11m7M
• 35°49'·67N 0°15'·48W

PORT D'ARZEW
6669 Jetée abri NE head
Oc.G.4s9m9M
• 35°51'·6N 0°17'·4W
6670 Jetée du large near head
Q(4)6s15m12M
• 35°50'·9N 0°17'·4W
6672 Îlot d'Arzew
Fl.R.5s19m16M
Obscured by Cap Carbon when bearing less than 132°
• 35°52'·5N 0°17'·3W
6674 Ras Aiguille
Fl(3)12s62m26M
Partially obscd 000°-010°
• 35°52'·6N 0°29'·2W

ORAN
6678 Jetée Filaoucène head
Fl(2+1)15s21m22M Horn 60s
• 35°43'·2N 0°37'·6W
6679 Êpi du Large
Iso.G.4s8m7M
• 35°43'·1N 0°37'·6W
6679·4 Traversee du Large
Iso.R.4s9m8M
• 35°43'·0N 0°37'·5W
6680 Epi Ibn Sina
Oc(2+1)G.12s9m6M
• 35°42'·9N 0°38'·0W
6682 Epi Ibn Badis
Oc(3)G.12s9m6M
213°-vis-123°
• 35°42'·8N 0°38'·4W
6684 Ibn Sina eastwards
Oc(2)R.6s9m7M
079°-vis-338°
• 35°42'·8N 0°37'·8W
6684·2 Westwards
F.R.9m7M
342·5°-vis-243·5°
• 35°42'·9N 0°37'·9W
6685·2 Westwards
Iso.R.2s8m6M
• 35°42'·8N 0°38'·1W
6687 Môle Ibn Badis NW corner
F.R.9m7M
359°-vis-332°
• 35°42'·8N 0°38'·4W
6694 Môle Ibn Khaldoun eastwards
Oc(4)R.12s9m7M
• 35°42'·7N 0°38'·6W
6694·2 Westwards
F.R.9m7M
000°-vis-255°
• 35°42'·7N 0°38'·7W

6695 Cale de Halage
Oc.4s9m10M
063°-vis-333°
• 35°42'·6N 0°39'·0W
6695·2 Môle Ibn Tofail
Oc.R.4s9m7M
• 35°42'·6N 0°39'·1W
6696 Môle Ibn Batouta northwards
F.R.9m7M
109°-vis-019°
• 35°42'·7N 0°39'·0W
6696·2 Southwards
Iso.G.4s9m6M
200°-vis-019°
• 35°42'·7N 0°39'·0W
6700 Vieux Port E jetty head
F.R.6m7M
063°-vis-333°
• 35°42'·6N 0°39'·2W

MERS-EL-KEBIR
6704 Hai Zouhour Ldg Lts 259°
Front Oc(2+1)R.12s53m9M
244°-vis-274°
Rear 329m from front
Oc(2+1)R.12s67m16M
• 35°43'·2N 0'42'·4W
6704·4 Jetée nord head
VQ(4)2s13m9M
• 35°43'·6N 0°40'·6W
6704·5 E jetty head
Fl.R.4s14m12M
• 35°43'·5N 0°40'·6W
6705 Quai du Fort W end
F.G.1m5M
• 35°44'·2N 0°42'·0W
6705·4 Môle Nord N end
F.R.2m6M
315°-vis-135°
• 35°43'·8N 0°42'·1W
6705·6 S end
Oc(2)G.6s2m5M
225°-vis-045°
• 35°43'·8N 0°42'·0W
6706 N Grande Môle NE corner
Oc(2)R.6s2m6M
135°-vis-315°
• 35°43'·7N 0°41'·9W
6706·2 SE corner
F.G.2m5M
225°-vis-045°
• 35°43'·6N 0°41'·9W
6706·4 Môle Triangulaire
Q.14m13M
• 35°43'·5N 0°42'·1W
6708 Cap Falcon
Fl(4)25s104m31M
• 35°46'·3N 0°47'·9W
6712 Île Plane
Fl(2)6s24m9M
• 35°46'·3N 0°54'·0W
6714 Îles Habibas
Fl.5s112m26M
• 35°43'·2N 1°07'·9W

BÉNI SAF
6716 Jetée nord head
Iso.G.4s11m7M
072°-vis°-342°
• 35°18'·5N 1°23'·3W
6717 Jetée est head
Oc(2)R.6s9m8M
• 35°18'·N 1°23'·3W
6718 Île Rachgoun
Fl(2)R.10s81m16M
• 35°19'·5N 1°28'·7W

GHAZAOUET

6720 Main light
Fl(3)15s93m26M
058°-vis-248°
Obscured by Plateau de Touent when bearing more than 237°
• 35°05′·9N 1°52′·3W

6722 Jetée nord head
Oc.R.4s17m8M
• 35°06′·3N 1°52′·2W

6722·2 Spur
F.R.8m6M
262°-vis-097°
• 35°06′·3N 1°51′·9W

6724 Môle D
F.G.8m5M
• 35°06′·3N 1°51′·7W

6726 Môle E
F.G.8m5M
• 35°06′·2N 1°51′·9W

6732 Rocher des Deux-Frères
Fl(2)G.6s26m5M
Tower not visible from offshore
• 35°06′·2N 1°52′·2W

Mediterranean – Morocco

ISLAS CHAFARINAS

6752 Isla Congreso S point
Fl.R.4s36m5M
Obscured when bearing less than 110°
• 35°10′·5N 2°26′·3W

6754 Isla Isabel II NW point
Fl.7s52m8M
045°-obscd-080° by Isla Congreso
• 35°11′·0N 2°25′·7W

6756 Muelle de Chafarinas head
Fl(2)R.8s8m4M
• 35°10′·8N 2°25′·6W

6757 Ras El Ma (Cabo del Agua)
Fl(2)6s42m8M
• 35°08′·8N 2°25′·3W

6757·1 Ras Kebdana Dir Lt 294°
DirF.WRG.9m10-7M
276·5°-G-286·5°-W-301·5°-R-311·5°
• 35°08′·9N 2°25′·1W

6757·2 Ras Kebdana N breakwater head
Iso.G.6s12m10M
• 35°08′·9N 2°25′·2W

6757·25 E breakwater head
Iso.R.6s13m10M
• 35°08′·9N 2°25′·3W

PUERTO DE NADOR

6757·6 Muelle de Beni Enzar head
Fl(2)R.6s8m5M
• 35°17′·1N 2°55′·1W

PUERTO DE MELILLA

6758 Melilla
Oc(2)6s40m14M
• 35°17′·7N 2°55′·9W

6762 NE breakwater centre of head
Fl.G.4s32m7M
• 35°17′·33N 2°55′·38W

6763 Head W
Fl.G.4s7m5M
35°17′·32N 2°55′·45W

6765 Minor embarkation dock breakwater head
Fl.R.5s4m5M
• 35°17′·3N 2°55′·9E

6776 Los Farallones
Iso.Y.2s21m6M
• 35°25′·7N 2°56′·4W

6778 Ras Tleta Madari (Cap de Trois Fourches)
Fl(3+1)20s112m19M Siren(3+1)60s
083°-vis-307°
• 35°26′·3N 2°57′·8W

6780 Cala Tramontana Rās Baraket
Oc(2+1)12s49m9M
• 35°24′·1N 3°00′·6W

6784 Ras Tarf (Cabo Quilates)
Fl(3)12s62m8M Aeromarine
• 35°17′·0N 3°40′·8W

AL HOCEÏMA (VILLA SANJURJO)

6785·1 Outer Breakwater Head
Iso.R.4s12m10M
• 35°14′·78N 3°55′·21W

6785·2 Dique de Abrigo Head
Iso.G.4s12m10M
• 35°14′·80N 0°55′·06W

6786 Morro Nuevo Pointe de los Frailes
Fl(2)10s151m20M
082°-vis-275°
• 35°15′·7N 3°55′·7W

6788 Peñón de Vélez de la Gomera
Fl(3)20s47m12M
• 35°10′·5N 4°18′·0W

6789 Puerto de Yebha. Punta Pescadores (Puerto Capaz)
Fl(2)10s38m18M
090°-vis-270°
• 35°13′·2N 4°40′·7W

6789·2 Port de Peche S jetty
Iso.G.4s8M
• 35°13′·0N 4°40′·8W

6789·5 Oued Laou
Oc(2)6s150m18M
• 35°28′·6N 5°06′·6W

PUERTO AL MARTÍL

6820 Sania Ramel
Aero Fl.5s35m54M occas
• 35°35′·5N 5°19′·9W

6824 Ras El Aswad (Cabo Negro)
Fl(2+1)12s135m20M
• 35°41′·2N 5°16′·4W

PUERTO DE AL MEDIQ

6825 Malecón este head
Q.12m13M Horn 60s
090°-vis-270°
• 35°41′·1N 5°18′·5W

The following reference numbers refer to Admiralty *List of Lights and Fog Signals Volume D* (NP 77)

Morocco

2482 Punta Almina, Monte Hacho
Fl(2)10s148m22M
• 35°53′·9N 5°16′·9W

PUERTO DE CEUTA

2484 Dique de Levante head
Fl.R.5s13m5M
• 35°53′·7N 5°18′·5W

2486 Dique de Poniente head
Fl.G.5s13m5M
• 35°53′·8N 5°18′·6W

2493 Punta Círes
Fl(3)10s44m18M
060°-vis-330°
• 35°54′·6N 5°28′·8W

2496 Ksár es Srhir. Alcázar Zeguer mole head
Fl(4)12s16m8M
• 35°51′·0N 5°33′·6W

2498 Punta Malabata
Fl.5s76m22M
• 35°49′·0N 5°44′·9W

TANGIER

2500 Monte Dirección (Le Charf)
Oc(3)WRG.12s88m16-11M
140°-G-174·5°-W-200°-R-225°
• 35°46′·0N 5°47′·3W

2502 Breakwater head
Fl(3)12s14M
• 35°47′·5N 5°47′·6W

2503 S Mole head Quai No.2
Oc(2)R.6s7m6M
• 35°47′·3N 5°47′·8W

2504 Yacht Club jetty head
Iso.G.4s6m6M
• 35°47′·3N 5°48′·1W

2506 Inner harbour entrance N mole head
F.G.4m6M
• 35°47′·3N 5°48′·2W

2507 S mole head
F.R.4m6M
• 35°47′·3N 5°48′·2W

2510 Cap Spartel (Cabo Espartel)
Fl(4)20s95m30M Aeromarine
• 35°47′·47N 5°55′·53W

2512 Tanger Boukhalf
Aero Fl.12s25m25M
067°-vis-115s &
Aero Mo(TG)G (occas)
• 35°43′·5N 5°54′·7W

Archipélago dos Açores

ILHA DE SANTA MARIA

2632 Ponta do Castelo. Gonçalo Velho
Fl(3)13·5s113m25M Aeromarine
181°-vis-089°
• 36°55′·72N 25°00′·99W

2632·2 Espigão
Fl.6s206m12M
• 36°58′·88N 25°02′·85W

2632·3/2632·4 Baía de São Lourenço. Lts in line 273·3° Casa Andrade
Front Iso.R.6s26m7M
Rear 64m from front
Oc.R.7·5s36m6M
• 36°59′·47N 25°03′·39W

2633 Ponta do Norte
Fl(4)15s138m12M
• 37°00′·75N 25°03′·58W

2633·7/2633·71 Ldg Lts 173·4°
Front Fl.3s12m10M
Rear LFl.6s20m10M
• 37°00′·21N 25°09′·54W

2634 Control Tower
Aero AlFl.WG.10s116m25M
021°-vis-121° Shown by day in poor visibility
• 36°58′·35N 25°08′·95W
2635·3 Mole head
LFl.R.5s14m5M
• 36°56′·4N 25°08′·95W
2636 Ponta de Malmerendo
Fl(2)10s49m12M
282°-vis-091°
• 36°56′·37N 25°09′·45W
2638 Ilhéus das Formigas
Fl(2)12s21m12M
• 37°16′·21N 24°46′·85W

ILHA DE SÃO MIGUEL

2640 Ponta do Arnel
Fl.5s65m25M Aeromarine
157°-vis-355°
• 37°49′·39N 25°08′·16W
2640·65 N mole
Oc.G.4s6m6M
• 37°44′·63N 25°14′·76W
2642 Ponta Garça
LFl.WR.5s100m16/13M
240°-W-080°-R-100°
• 37°42′·80N 25°22′·22W
2642·5 Vila Franco do Campo Marina
Fl.G.4s11m9M
• 37°42′·76N 25°25′·79W
2645 Porto da Caloura mole S end
Fl.4s6m9M
• 37°42′·75N 25°29′·75W
2645·4/2645·41 Ldg Lts 333·3°
Front Oc.G.3s10m5M
Rear 9m from front
Oc.G.3s14m5M
• 37°42′·80N 25°29′·75W
2646 Lagoa
Fl.R.3s8m6M
• 37°44′·5N 23°34′·5W
2647 Ponta Delgada breakwater head
LFl.R.6s16m10M
• 37°44′·12N 25°39′·40W
2648 Marina mole
Fl.G.3s12m10M
• 37°44′·32N 25°39′·57W
2652 S Bras Font SE Corner
Fl(4)WRG.8s13m10M
2654 Santa Clara
LFl.5s26m15M
282°-vis-102°
• 37°43′·94N 25°41′·18W
2654·2 Airport
Aero AlFl.WG.10s83m28/23M
282°-vis-124°
• 37°44′·57N 25°42′·49W
2655 Ponta da Ferraria
Fl(3)20s106m27M
339°-vis-174°
• 37°51′·15N 25°51′·05W
2655·4 Mosteiros
Oc.R.3s9m6M 090°-vis-155°
• 37°53′·56N 25°49′·32W
2656 Morro das Capelas
Fl(2)R.12s114m8M
153°-vis-281°
• 37°50′·44N 25°41′·23W
2656·9 Rabo de Peixe. Fishing port mole
Fl.R.5s10m6M
• 37°48′·95N 25°35′·14W
2657 Fishing Harbour, N pier
Fl(2)R.5s7m2M
248°-R-135°
• 37°48′·92N 25°35′·11W
2659 Ponta do Cintrão
Fl(2)10s117m14M
• 37°50′·74N 25°29′·35W
2659·4 Port Formoso
Fl.4s6M
• 37°49′·34N 25°25′·59W

ILHA TERCEIRA

2660 Vila Nova slipway
Iso.6s10m9M
• 38°46′·90N 27°08′·46W
2661 Lajes
Aero AlFl.WG.10s132m28/23M
• 38°45′·60N 27°04′·91W
2662 Praia da Vitória. Ponta do Espírito Santo mole head
Fl.5s19m10M
• 38°43′·59N 27°03′·06W
2662·5 Molhe sul head
Fl.R.3s22m8M
• 38°43′·26N 27°02′·92W
2663·5 São Fernando
Oc.R.3s5m6M
• 38°40′·58N 27°03′·93W
2664 Ponta das Contendas
Fl(4)WR.15s53m23/20M
220°-W-020°-R-044°-W-072°-R-093°
• 38°38′·62N 27°05′·12W
2665 Porto Judeu
Fl.R.3s8m3M
• 38°38′·90N 27°07′·02W
2666 Monte Brasil. Ponta do Farol
Oc.WR.10s27m12M
295°-W-057°, 191°-R-295°
• 38°38′·60N 27°13′·11W
2666·1 Cabos Silveira
Fl(2)R.8s21m9M
• 38°39′·4N 27°14′·0W
2666·2/2666·21 Angra do Heroísmo Ldg Lts 340·9°
Front Fl.R.4s20m7M
Rear 505m from front
Oc.R.6s54m7M
• 38°39′·25N 27°13′·16W
2666·5 Porto Pipas mole head
Fl.G.3s13m6M
• 38°39′·05N 27°12′·98W
2666·7 São Mateus
Iso.WR.6s11m10/7M
270°-R-296°-W-067°
• 38°39′·31N 27°16′·14W
2667 Cinco Ribeiras
LFl.6s22m10M
• 38°40′·55N 27°19′·81W
2668 Ponta da Serreta
Fl.6s99m12M
044°-vis-203°
• 38°45′·95N 27°22′·50W
2669 Biscoitos
Oc.6s12m9M
• 38°48′·0N 27°15′·6W

ILHA GRACIOSA

2670 Ponta do Carapacho
Fl(2)10s188m15M
165°-vis-098°
• 39°00′·8N 27°57′·35W
2672·5 Vila da Praia mole head
Fl.G.3s13m9M
• 39°03′·1N 27°58′·0W
2672·7 Cabo Praia
Fl(2)R.8s5m9M 264°-vis-292° marks submarine cable. By day 2M
• 39°03′·6N 27°58′·33W
2674 Santa Cruz. Fortim do Corpo Santo
Fl.R.4s6m6M
• 39°05′·33N 28°00′·58W
2676 Ponta da Barca
Fl.7s71m20M
029°-vis-031°, 035°-vis-251°, 267°-vis-287°
• 39°05′·63N 28°03′·03W

ILHA DE SÃO JORGE

2680 Ponta da Topo
Fl(3)20s60m20M
133°-vis-033°
• 38°32′·94N 27°45′·34W
2680·2 Ponta do Junçal
Fl.3s64m6M
• 38°35′·68N 27°58′·86W
2681·2 Calheta
Fl.R.3s12m10M
• 38°36′·02N 28°00′·40W
2681·5 Urzelina
Fl.R.6s9m6M
• 38°38′·65N 28°07′·70W
2681·8 Queimada
Fl.5s37m10M
• 38°40′·13N 28°11′·63W
2682·2 Pier head
Fl.R.5s14m7M
• 38°40′·69N 28°12′·25W
2682·3 Cabo Velas
Fl(2)R.8s12m9M
033°-vis-061° marks submarine cable area. By day 2M.
• 38°40′·72N 28°12′·34W
2682·4 Anchorage Lts in line 304·3°
Central front Iso.R.5s12m6M
• 38°40′·70N 28°12′·52W
2682·5 Ermida 803m from front
Rear Oc.R.6s54m7M
• 38°40′·94N 28°12′·98W
2683 Ponta dos Rosais
Fl(2)10s282m8M
• 38°45′·23N 18°18′·79W
2683·5 Ponta do Norte Grande
Fl.6s34m12M
• 38°40′·8N 28°03′·1W

ILHA DO PICO

2684/2684·1 Areia Larga Ldg Lts 082·6°
Front Iso.R.4s8m7M
Shown when weather is suitable for approach
Rear 20m from front
Iso.R.4s12m6M
• 38°31′·64N 28°32′·22W
2687·2 Madalena mole N
Oc.R.3s11m10M
• 38°32′·18N 28°32′·04W
2687·5/2687·51 Ldg Lts 138·9°
Front Fl.G.6s16m5M
Rear 128m from front
Fl.G.6s20m5M
• 38°32′·01N 28°31′·90W
2688 Cais do Pico
Oc.R.6s10m6M
Indicates anchorage when bearing 222°
• 38°31′·63N 28°19′·27W
2689 Prainha
Fl.R.4s11m7M
128°-vis-287°
• 38°28′·51N 28°12′·08W
2689·4/2689·41 Santo Amaro Ldg Lts
Front Oc.R.6s7m7M
Rear Oc.R.6s11m7M
• 38°27′·38N 28°10′·06W
2690 Ponta da Ilha
Fl(3)15s28m24M
166°-vis-070°
• 38°24′·76N 28°01′·90W
2690·02/2690·03 Manhenha Ldg Lts
Front Fl.R.5s9m6M
Rear 19m from front
Fl.R.5s15m3M
• 38°24′·58N 28°02′·20W
2690·1/2690·11 Calheta de Nesquim Ldg Lts
Front Fl.R.5s13m7M
Rear 30m from front
Fl.R.5s18m7M
• 38°24′·18N 28°04′·65W
2690·15 Santa Cruz das Ribeiras mole head
Fl.R.3s7m3M
• 38°24′·35N 28°11′·22W
2690·9 Cabos Galaeo
Fl(2)R.8s8m9M
• 38°25′·5N 28°25′·4W

2691 Ponta de São Mateus
Fl.5s33m13M
284°-vis-118°
• 38°25'·38N 28°26'·97W
2691·4/2691·41 Porto do Calhau Ldg Lts 122°
Front Oc.R.3s10m6M
Rear Oc.R.3s14m6M
• 38°29'·18N 28°32'·39W

ILHO DO FAIAL
2692 Ponta da Ribeirinha
Fl(3)20s135m12M
• 38°35'·75N 28°36'·22W
2693 Marconi Alomoxarife Dir Lt 224·5°
DirFl(2)R.8s9m9M (by day 5M)
224°-vis-225°
• 38°33'·19N 28°36'·58W
2694 Horta breakwater head
Fl.R.3s20m11M
• 38°32'·04N 28°37'·34W
2696 Boa Viagem
DirIsoWRG.6s12m9/6M
• 38°32'·29N 28°37'·57W
2698/2698·1 Feteira Ldg Lts 340·90°
Front Oc.G.6s6m5M
Rear Oc.G.6s9m5M
• 38°31'·43N 28°41'·37W
2699 Vale Formoso
LFl(2)10s111m13M
• 38°34'·87N 28°48'·74W
2700 Ponta dos Cedras
Fl.7s148m12M
• 38°38'·29N 28°43'·36W

ILHA DAS FLORES
2703/2703·1 Porto das Poças Ldg Lts 284·6°
Front Fl.R.3s7m5M
Rear Fl.R.3s17m5M
• 39°27'·00N 31°07'·37W
2704 SE point Ponta das Lajes
Fl(3)28s97m26M 263°-vis-054°
• 39°22'·46N 31°10'·35W
2708 N side Ponta do Albarnaz
Fl.5s100m22M
035°-vis-258°
• 39°31'·12N 31°13'·89W

ILHA DO CORVO
2712 Ponta Negra
Fl.5s22m6M
• 39°40'·11N 31°06'·63W
2714 Canto de Carneira
Fl.6s237m9M
• 39°42'·98N 31°05'·15W

Arquipélago da Madeira

ILHAS DESERTAS
2720 Ilhéu Chão
LFl(2)15s111m13M
• 32°35'·16N 16°32'·5W
2722 Ilha Bugio. Ponta da Agulha
Fl.4s71m13M
163°-vis-100°
• 32°24'·02N 16°27'·57W

ILHA DA MADEIRA
2726 Ilha de Fora E end São Lourenço
Fl.10s102m20M
• 32°43'·60N 16°39'·16W
2727 Pier head
Fl(2)G.5s8m6M
• 32°44'·22N 16°42'·58W
2728 Machico São Roque
LFl.WR.5s11m9/7M
230°-R over dangerous rock-265°-W-230°
• 32°42'·63N 16°45'·60W
2730 Jetty
Fl(3)G.8s6m6M
• 32°43'·01N 16°45'·52W
2738 Porto do Funchal mole head
Fl.R.5s14m8M
275°-vis-075°
• 32°38'·30N 16°54'·17W
2741·3 Cabo Gorgulho, Gorgulho Beach
Fl(2)R.8s22m9M 330°-vis-025° marks submarine cable area. By day 2M
• 32°37'·97N 16°55'·89W
2741·5 Cabos Formosa, Formosa Beach
Fl(2)R.8s6m9M 027°-vis-055° marks submarine cable area. By day 2M
• 32°38'·07N 16°56'·72W
2743 Praia de Vitòria
Q(6)+LFl.15s13m9M
• 32°38'·32N 16°57'·83W
2744 Câmara de Lobos
Oc.R.6s23m9M
304°-vis-099°
• 32°38'·60N 16°58'·29W
2746 Ribeira Brava
Fl.R.5s34m9M
• 32°39'·91N 17°03'·63W
2746·7 Lugar de Baixo
Fl(3)R.8s9m6M
• 32°40'·50N 17°05'·30W
2748 Calhetta E pier head
Fl.G.5s7m6M
• 32°42'·76N 17°10'·01W
2748·2 W pier head
Fl.R.5s8m6M
• 32°42'·78N 17°10'·05E
2750 Paúl do Mar fish market
Oc.R.3s16m6M
• 32°44'·94N 17°13'·19W
2752 W point Ponta do Pargo
Fl(3)20s311m26M
• 32°48'·62N 17°15'·54W
2754 Porto do Moniz. Ilhéu Môle summit
Fl.WR.5s64m10/8M
116°-R over Baixas do Moniz-127°-W-116°
• 32°51'·96N 17°09'·60W
2755 Ponta de São Jorge
LFl.5s270m15M
• 32°49'·86N 16°54'·13W

ILHA DE PORTO SANTO
2756 Ilhéu de Cima
Fl(3)15s123m21M Aeromarine
• 33°03'·06N 16°16'·51W
2757 Porto Santo S breakwater head
Fl.G.4s16m6M
• 33°03'·27N 16°18'·62W
2757·2 N breakwater head
Fl.R.4s12m7M
• 33°03'·36N 16°18'·67W
2757·3 Cabos Cabeco, Cabeco Beach
Fl(2)R.8s9m9M 308°-vis-328° marks submarine cable area. By day 3M
• 33°01'·98N 16°21'·43W
2762 Ilhéu Ferro
LFl.15s129m13M
• 33°02'·11N 16°24'·10W
2763 N coast
Fl(2)10s145m12M
064°-vis-243°
• 33°05'·57N 16°20'·18W

ILHAS SELVAGENS
2768 Selvagem Grande
Fl.4s162m13M
• 30°08'·60N 15°52'·18W
2769 Selvagem Pequena
Fl(2)6s49m12M
• 30°02'·04N 16°01'·56W

Islas Canarias

ISLA ALEGRANZA
2772 Punta Delgada
Fl.3s16m12M
135°-vis-045°
• 29°24'·1N 13°29'·2W

ISLA LANZAROTE
2773·8 Punta de Mujeres
Fl(2+1)R.8·5s9m5M
• 29°08'·5N 13°26'·7W
2774 Arrieta wharf head
Fl.R.2s9m5M
• 29°07'·8N 13°27'·5W
2775 Puerto de los Mármoles Punta Chica pier head
Fl.G.5s12m5M
• 28°57'·9N 13°31'·7W
2780 Puerto de Arrecife mole head
Q(6)+LFl.15s10m3M
• 28°57'·1N 13°33'·0W
2781 Puerto Calero S mole head
Fl(3)G.14s9m6M
• 28°54'·8N 13°42'·4W
2781·5 Marina Rubicón mole head
Fl(4)G.15s3m5M
• 28°51'·3N 13°49'·0W
2781·55 Elbow
Fl(4)R.15s1m5M
• 28°51'·4N 13°49'·0W
2781·7 Playa Blanca mole head
Fl(4)R.11s5M
• 28°51'·5N 13°49'·9W
2782 SW point Punta Pechiguera
Fl(3)30s54m17M
• 28°51'·2N 13°52'·2W

ISLA LOBOS
2786 Punta Martiño
Fl(2)15s28m14M
083°-vis-353°
• 28°45'·8N 13°48'·8W

ISLA DE FUERTEVENTURA
2790 SW point Punta Jandia
Fl.4s32m22M 276°-vis-190°
• 28°03'·8N 14°30'·3W
2791 Punta Pesebre
Oc(2)6s10m10M
• 28°06'·5N 14°29'·4W
2792 Punta Tostón
Fl.8s34m14M
• 28°42'·8N 14°00'·7W
2793·5 Puerto del Rosario. Punta Gavioto
Fl.5s47m20M
• 28°30'·2N 13°50'·5W
2794 Mole head
Fl.G.5s13m5M
• 28°29'·6N 13°51'·3W
2794·5 Caleta de Fustes. Marina mole head
Fl(2)G.12s9m5M
• 28°23'·4N 13°51'·3W
2795 Punta Lantailla
Fl(2+1)18s195m21M Aeromarine
• 28°13'·7N 13°56'·8W
2796 Gran Tarajal mole head
Fl(3)G.7s8m5M
• 28°12'·4N 14°01'·4W
2796·1
Fl(3)R.7s8m5M
• 28°12'·4N 14°01'·5W
2796·5 Puerto de Morro Jable
Fl(2)10s61m20M
• 28°02'·7N 14°19'·9W

ISLA DE GRAN CANARIA
2798 La Isleta
Fl(3+1)20s248m21M Aeromarine
• 28°10'·44N 15°25'·14W
2799 Radio Atlántico
Aero Oc.R.3s1604m40M
Obstruction
• 28°01'·0N 15°35'·1W

2799·2 Roque del Palo
Q(3)10s11m6M
• 28°09'·9N 15°23'·9W
2799·4 Puerto de La Luz Dique Reina Sofia head (Las Palmas)
Fl.G.5s19m10M
• 28°07'·5N 15°24'·3W
2799·5 Outer elbow
Q(3)5s12m8M
150°-vis-000°
• 28°07'·8N 15°24'·3W
2799·66 Ldg Lts 000°
Front Iso.4s14m6M
Rear 609m from front Q.1s30m6M
• 28°09'·3N 15°24'·6W
2800·2 SE Head Muelle León
Fl.R.5s7m5M
• 28°07'·9N 15°24'·7W
2801·2 Muelle León y Castillo head W
Fl(3)G.12s19m7M
• 28°07'·7N 15°25'·1W
2807·5 Punta Melenara
Fl(2)WR.12s32m12M
152°-R-270°-W-152°
• 27°59'·4N 15°21'·9W
2812 Punta Arinaga
Fl(3)WR.10s46m16M
012°-R over Punta Tenefé-052°-W-172°-R over Baja de Gando-212°-W-012°
• 27°51'·8N 15°23'·1W
2812·5 Barranco Tirajana breakwater head
Q(6)+LFl.15s7m5M
• 27°48'·0N 15°26'·0W
2814 Punta Morro Colchas Maspalomas
Fl(1+2)13s59m19M
• 27°44'·1N 15°35'·9W
2815·4 Bahía de Santa Agueda Puerto Cementero Dique Rompeolas head
Q(2)R.6s11m6M
• 27°44'·9N 15°40'·1W
2815·82 Puerto Rico Marina W jetty
F.R.10m5M
• 27°47'·0N 15°42'·9W
2815·94 Punta del Castillete
Fl.5s113m17M
• 27°49'·1N 15°46'·1W
2815·99 Puerto de Las Nieves Agaete dique head
Fl(2)R.9s13m7M
• 28°05'·9N 15°42'·7W
2816 NW side Punta Sardina
Fl(4)20s48m20M
• 28°09'·9N 15°42'·5W

ISLA DE TENERIFE

2818 Punta del Hidalgo
Fl(3)16s51m16M
• 28°34'·58N 16°19'·73W
2820 Punta de Roque Bermejo Anaga
Fl(2+4)30s246m21M
• 28°34'·8N 16°08'·3W
2821 Los Rodeos Airfield
Aero Fl.5s650m37M
• 28°29'·3N 16°18'·4W
2822 Santa Cruz de Tenerife. Dársena sur. Dique del sur head
Fl(2)R.7s18m10M
• 28°28'·7N 16°14'·1W
2822·6 Darsena E. Dique E. Elbow 1 and 2
Q(6)+LFl.15s10m5M
• 28°29'·3N 16°13'·1W
2822·7 Elbow 2 and 3
Q(6)+LFl.15s10m5M
• 28°29'·0N 16°13'·5W
2822·8 Head
Fl(2)G.7s12m9M
• 28°29'·0N 16°13'·7W
2826·7 Dique elbow
Q(3)10s8m5M
• 28°28'·0 16°14'·5W
2826·72 Head E side
Fl(3)G.9s12m9M
• 28°27'·3N 16°14'·8W
2826·82 Contradique head
Fl(3)R.10s7m9M
• 28°27'·3N 16°14'·9W
2827 La Hondura (Puerto Caballo) Muelle de la Hondura head SW Corner
Iso.G.3·4s9m5M
• 28°26'·9N 16°15'·9W
2829 Punta Abona
Fl(3)20s53m17M
213·6°-vis-040·3°
• 28°08'·8N 16°25'·5W
2829·05 San Miguel de Tajao breakwater head
Fl(3)G.9s11m5M
• 28°06'·4N 16°28'·1W
2830 S point. Punta Rasca
Fl(3)12s50m17M
• 28°00'·0N 16°41'·6W
2831 Puerto de los Cristianos mole head
Fl.R.5s12m5M
• 28°02'·8N 16°43'·0W
2831·2 Puerto Colon Dique de defensa head
Fl(2)G.7s10m5M
• 28°04'·68N 16°44'·20W
2831·8 Punta de Buenavista
Fl(4)11s75m20M
• 28°23'·4N 16°50'·1W
2832 W point. Punta Teno
Fl(1+2)20s59m18M
• 28°20'·4N 16°55'·3W
2833 Puerto de la Cruz
Fl(2)7s30m16M
• 28°25'·0N 16°33'·2W

ISLA HIERRO

2836 Punta Orchilla SE of point
Fl.5s131m24M
• 27°42'·3N 18°08'·7W
2838 Puerto de la Estaca pier head
Fl.G.5s13m5M
• 27°46'·8N 17°54'·00W

ISLA GOMERA

2842 Punta San Cristóbal
Fl(2)10s83m21M
• 28°05'·7N 17°06'·0W
2844·7 Puerto de San Sebastian breakwater head E corner
Fl.G.5s15m6M
• 28°05'·0N 17°06'·5W
2845 Puerto de Santiago jetty head
Fl(2)R.7s12m3M
• 28°01'·5N 17°11'·7W
2845·6 Outer Breakwater Head
Fl(3)R.9s1m5M
• 28°04'·70N 17°20'·00W

ISLA PALMA

2846 Punta Cumplida NE side of island
Fl.5s62m23M
104·5°-vis-337°
• 28°50'·3N 17°46'·6W
2848·45 Puerto de Santa Cruz Outer
Fl.G.5s16m5M
• 28°40'·3N 17°45'·8W
2849·51 Punta de Arenas Blancas
Oc(3)8s45m20M
• 28°34'·2N 17°45'·6W
2850 S side Punta Fuencaliente
Fl(3)18s35m14M
• 28°27'·3N 17°50'·6W
2851 Punta Lava
Fl(1+2)20s50m20M
• 28°35'·8N 17°55'·6W
2852 Puerto de Refugio Tazacorte. Dique de abrigo head
Fl(2)R.7s16m5M
• 28°38'·4N 17°56'·6W
2856 Breakwater. Head
Q(9)15s5M
• 28°38'·6N 17°56'·7W

7. Charts

7.1 SYMBOLS USED ON CHARTS

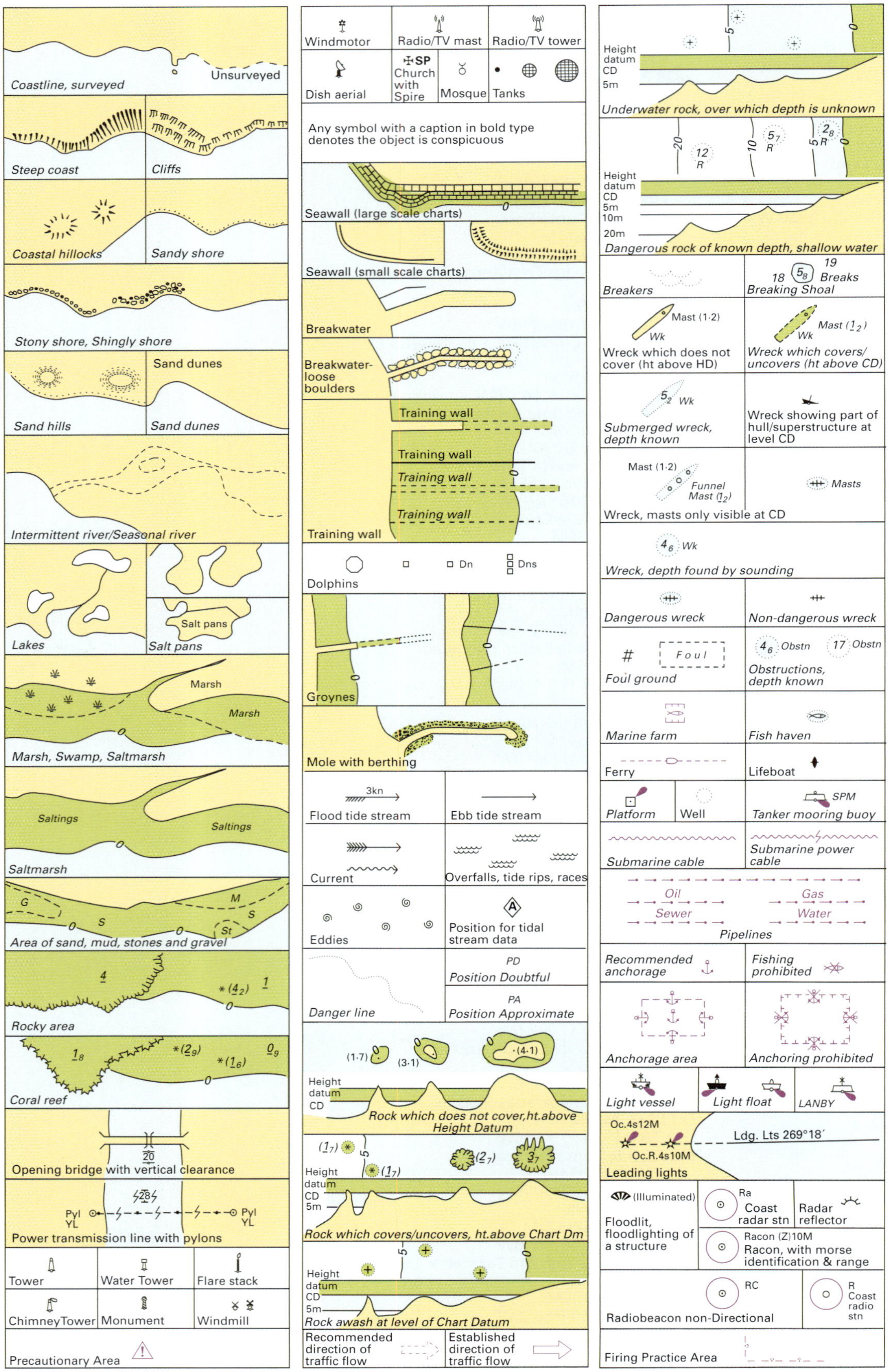

7.2 CHARTS

Imray, British Admiralty, Spanish and French charts are available from:

Imray Laurie Norie & Wilson Ltd
www.imray.com
Wych House The Broadway St Ives
Cambridgeshire PE27 5BT England
+44(0)1480 462114 *Fax* +44(0)1480 496109
Email orders@imray.com

Below are details of Imray charts. Coverage of official hydrographic office charts and publications is available on the appropriate website.

UK: UKHO, www.ukho.gov.uk
France: Service Hydrographique et Oceanographique de la Marine, www.shom.fr
Italy: Istituto Idrografico del la Marina, www.marina.difesa.it
Croatia: Hrvatski hidrografski Institut, www.hhi.hr
Spain: Instituto Hydrografico de la Marina, www.armada.mde.es

Imray charts

M3 **Islas Baleares – Formentera, Ibiza, Mallorca, Menorca**
1:350,000 WGS 84
Plans Puerto de Ibiza, Puerto Colom, Puerto de Palma, Puerto de Máhon, San Antonio, Ciudadela, Alcudia

M6 **Ile de Corse**
1:255,000 WGS 84
Plans Macinaggio, Bastia, Approaches to Calvi, Ajaccio, Approach to Propriano, Bonifacio, Îles Lavezzi

M7 **Bonifacio Strait**
1:65,000 WGS 84
Plans La Maddalena

M8 **North Sardegna**
1:255,000 WGS 84
Plans La Maddalena Archipelago - Southern Group, Golfo di Cugnana, Golfo Spurlatta, Passaggio dei Fornelli, Porto Torres, Approaches to Alghero

M9 **South Sardegna**
1:255,000 WGS 84
Plans Approaches to Arbatax, Approaches to Torre Grande, Canale di San Pietro, Porto di Cagliari, Capo Carbonara, Golfo di Teulada

M10 **Western Mediterranean – Gibraltar to the Ionian Sea**
1:2,750,000 WGS 84

M11 **Gibraltar to Cabo de Gata & Morocco**
1:440,000 WGS 84
Plans Strait of Gibraltar, Gibraltar, Ceuta, Almeria, Estepona, Puerto de Almerimar

M12 **Cabo de Gata to Denia & Ibiza**
1:500,000 WGS 84
Plans Mar Menor, Alicante, Dénia, Torrevieja, Altea, Villajoyosa

M13 **Dénia to Barcelona and Ibiza**
1:440,000 WGS 84
Plans Dénia, Tarragona, Valencia Harbour, Barcelona Harbour, San Antonio (Ibiza)

M14 **Barcelona to Bouches du Rhône**
1:440,000 WGS 84
Plans St-Cyprien-Plage, Puerto de l'Escala, Sète, Cap d'Agde, Roses, Palamos, Port Vendres, Barcelona Harbour, Barcelona Port Vell, Puerto Olímpico

M15 **Marseille to San Remo**
1:325,000 WGS 84
Plans Marseille Vieux-Port & Iles du Frioul, Iles d'Hyères, Golfe de St-Tropez, Antibes, Golfe de La Napoule, Nice, Rade de Villefranche & Cap Ferrat, Monaco

M16 **Ligurian Sea**
1:325,000 WGS 84
Plans San Remo, Approaches to Genova, Golfo Marconi, Approaches to La Spezia, Viareggio, Approaches to Livorno

M17 **North Tuscan Islands to Rome**
1:325,000 WGS 84
Plans Scarlino to Punta Ala, Approaches to Giglio Marina, Approaches to Civitavecchia, Approaches to Fiumocino and Fiuma Grande, Approaches to Anzio

M18 **Capo d'Anzio to Capo Palinuro**
1:325,000 WGS 84
Plans Rada di Gaeta, Golfo di Pozzuoli and Rada di Napoli, Approaches to Acciaroli, Capo Palinuro

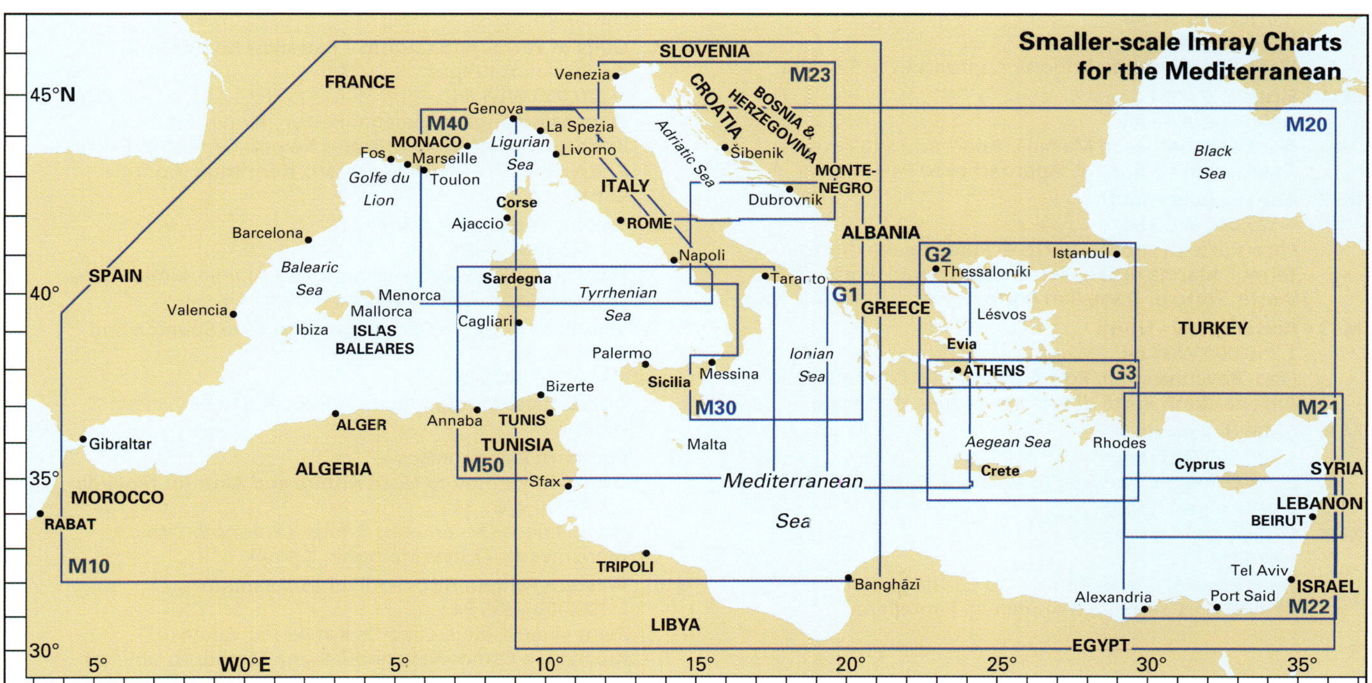

M19 **Capo Palinuro to Punta Stilo**
1:325,000 WGS 84
Plans Golfo di Policastro, Approaches to Vibo Valentia, Isole Alicudi, Stretto di Messina

M20 **Eastern Mediterranean – Sardegna to Port Said and the Black Sea**
1:2,750,000 WGS 84

M21 **Eastern Mediterranean Passage Chart – South Coast of Turkey, Syria, Lebanon & Cyprus**
1:785,000 WGS 84
Plans Larnaca Marina, Mersin, Alanya Limani

M22 **Eastern Mediterranean Passage Chart – Egypt to Israel, Lebanon and Cyprus**
1:785,000 WGS 84
Plans Jounié, Larnaca, Hefa, Bur Sa'id

M23 **Adriatic Sea – Golfo di Trieste to Bar and Promontario del Gargano**
1:750,000 WGS 84

M24 **Golfo di Trieste to Losinji & Rab**
1:220,000 WGS 84
Plans Rovinj, Brijuni Otoci to Pula, Veruda to Medulin Bay, Approaches to Punat, Approaches to Mali Lošinj, Otok Ilovik Channel

M25 **Otok Rab to Sibenik** 1:220,000 WGS 84
Plans Prolaz Zapuntel Passage, Passage Between Otok Molat & Dugi Otok, Zadar, Luka Telašćica, The Kornati Islands, Šibenik and Rijeka Krka, Prolaz Proversa Vela & Mala

M26 **Split to Dubrovnik** 1:220,000 WGS 84
Plans Luka Rogoznica, Trogirski Kanal, Approaches to Split, The Drvenik Islands, Splitska Vrata, Approaches to Hvar & the Pakleni Islands, Approaches to Korčula, Approaches to Ubli, Approaches to Gruž & Dubrovnik Marina

M27 **Dubrovnik to Bar & Ulcinj**
1:220,000 WGS 84
Plans Luka Polače, The Elaphite Islands, Approaches to Dubrovnik, Boka Kotorska, Approaches to Budva, Bar Marina, Ulcinj

M29 **Golfo di Taranto**
1:375,000 WGS 84
Plans Approaches to Brindisi, Approaches to Otranto, Approaches to Gallipoli, Approaches to Crotone

M30 **Southern Adriatic and Ionian Seas – Dubrovnik to Kerkira (Corfu) and Sicilia**
1:850,000 WGS 84
Plans Approaches to Brindisi, Approaches to Siracusa

M31 **Sicilia**
1:400,000 WGS 84
Plans Approaches to Marsala, Approaches to Favignana, Approaches to Trapani, Approaches to Palermo

M32 **Adriatic Italy - South**
1:325,000 WGS 84
Plans Porto di Ortona, Porto di Punta Penna (Vasto), Termoli Marina di San Pietro, Isole Tremiti, Porto di Vieste, Porto di Trani, Bari Porto Nuovo

M33 **Adriatic Italy - North**
1:350,000 WGS 84
Plans Ravenna coast, Porto di Ravenna, Porto di Rimini, Ancona coast, Porto di Ancona, Marina di Pescara

M34 **Golfo di Venezia**
1:220,000 WGS 84
Plans Chioggia, Venezia, Approaches to Grado, Monfalcone, Trieste

M35 **Sicilian Channel**
1:375 000 WGS 84
Plans Bizerte, Cap Gammarth to Carthage, Port de Kélibia, Port Yasmine Hammamet, Pantelleria

M40 **Ligurian and Tyrrhenian Seas**
1:950,000 WGS 84
Plans Monte Argentario, Bonifacio Strait, Golfo di Salerno

M45 **Tuscan Archipelago**
1:180,000 WGS 84
Plans Approaches to Porto Capraia, Approaches to Portoferraio, Bastia, Talamone, Approaches to Porto S. Stefano

M46 **Isole Pontine to the Bay of Naples**
1:180,000 WGS 84
Plans Approaches to Ponza, Approaches to Porto d'Ischia, Approaches to Sorrento, Approaches to Marina Grande (Capri)

M47 **Aeolian Islands**
1:140,000 WGS 84
Plans Approaches to Lipari, Bocche di Vulcano

M49 **West Sicily and Egadi Islands**
Proposed new chart for 2015

M50 **Sardegna to Ionian Sea**
1:1,100 000
Plan Stretto di Messina

G1 **Mainland Greece and the Peloponnisos Passage Chart**
1:729,000 WGS 84
Plans Órmos Falírou

G11 **North Ionian Islands – Nísos Kérkira to Nísos Levkas**
1:185,000 WGS 84
Plans Continuation of North Ionian Islands to Nisís Othoní, Vórion Stenó Kérkiras, Órmos Gouvíon (Nísos Kérkira), Kérkira (Corfu Town) (Nísos Kérkira), Órmos Párga, Continuation of Amvrakikós Kólpos, Limín Alípa (Nísos Kérkira), Órmos Lákka (Nísos Paxoí), Port Gaios (Nísos Paxoí)

G12 **South Ionian Islands – Nísos Levkas to Nísos Zákinthos**
1:190,000 WGS 84
Plans Kólpos Aetoú (N. Itháki), Dhioriga Levkádhos (Levkas Canal), Órmos Argostolíou (N. Kefallínia), Órmos Zákinthou (N. Zákinthos)

G121 **The Inland Sea**
1:95,000 WGS 84
Plans Órmos Ayias Eufima (Cephalonia), Órmos Frikou (N. Itháca), Órmos Fiskárdho (Cephalonia), Vasiliki (N. Levkas), Dhioriga Levkádhos (Levkas Canal), Kálamos Harbour

G13 **Gulfs of Patras and Corinth – Patraïkós Kólpos and Korinthiakós Kólpos**
1:220,000 WGS 84
Plans Mesolóngion, Liménas Pátron, Ríon - Andírrion Bridge, Órmos Aiyíou, Krissaíos Kólpos, Órmos Andíkiron, Kiato, Órmos Loutrákiou, Dhiórix Korínthou (Corinth Canal)

G14 **Saronic and Argolic Gulfs**
1:190,000 WGS 84
Plans Stenó Spétsai, Návplion, Limín Aíginia, Limín Pórou, Órmos Falírou, Marina Alimos (Kalamáki)

G141 **Saronikós Kólpos – Corinth Canal to Ákra Soúnion and Nisos Póros**
1:110,000 WGS 84
Plan Órmos Falírou, Marina Alimos (Kalamáki), Limín Aígina

G15 **Southern Pelopónnisos – Órmos Navarínou to Nísos Kithíra and Ákra Tourkovigla**
1:190,000 WGS 84
Plans Liménas Kalamatas, Órmos Navarínou, Yíthion, Monemvasía, Órmos Methónis, Koróni

G16 **Western Peloponnisos – Killini to Kalamata**
1:190,000 WGS 84
Plans Limín Killinis, Liménas Katakólou, Órmos Kiparissias, Órmos Navarínou, Stenó Methónis, Liménas Kalamátas

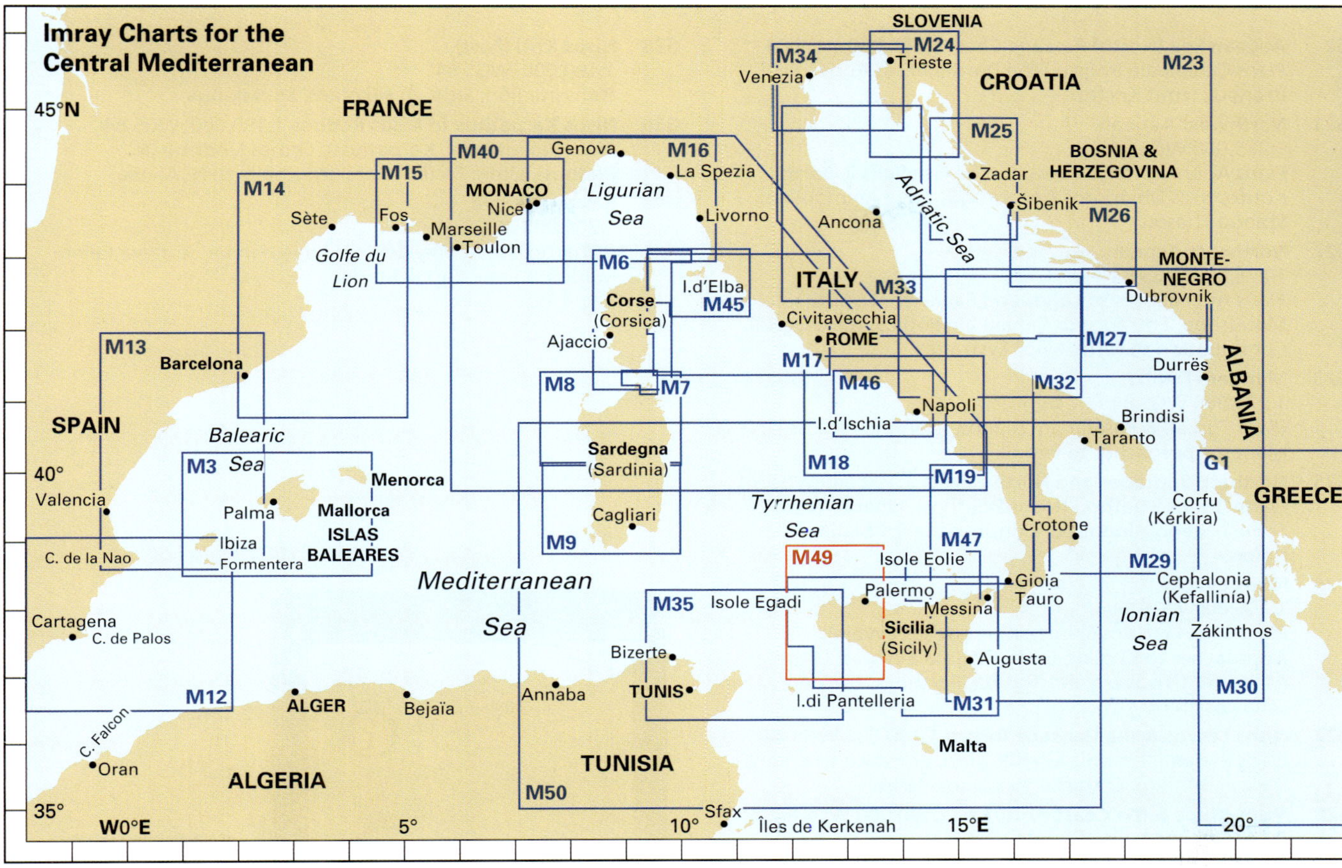

Imray Charts for the Central Mediterranean
45°N
40°
35°
W0°E
5°
10°
15°E
20°
FRANCE
SLOVENIA
CROATIA
BOSNIA & HERZEGOVINA
MONTE-NEGRO
ALBANIA
GREECE
ITALY
MONACO
SPAIN
ALGERIA
TUNISIA
M34
M24
M23
M25
M26
M27
M32
M33
M40
M16
M15
M14
M6
M45
M17
M46
M8
M7
M13
M3
M9
M18
M19
M47
M49
M35
M12
M50
M31
M29
M30
G1
Venezia
Trieste
Genova
La Spezia
Livorno
Zadar
Šibenik
Dubrovnik
Ancona
Adriatic Sea
Ligurian Sea
Sète
Fos
Nice
Marseille
Toulon
Golfe du Lion
I.d'Elba
Corse (Corsica)
Ajaccio
Civitavecchia
ROME
Napoli
I.d'Ischia
Brindisi
Taranto
Durrës
Barcelona
Balearic Sea
Menorca
Mallorca
Palma
Ibiza
Formentera
ISLAS BALEARES
Valencia
C. de la Nao
Cartagena
C. de Palos
Sardegna (Sardinia)
Cagliari
Tyrrhenian Sea
Mediterranean Sea
Crotone
Corfu (Kérkira)
Isole Eolie
Isole Egadi
Palermo
Messina
Gioia Tauro
Cephalonia (Kefallinía)
Ionian Sea
Zákinthos
Sicilia (Sicily)
Augusta
Bizerte
TUNIS
Annaba
I.di Pantelleria
Malta
ALGER
Bejaïa
C. Falcon
Oran
Sfax
Îles de Kerkenah

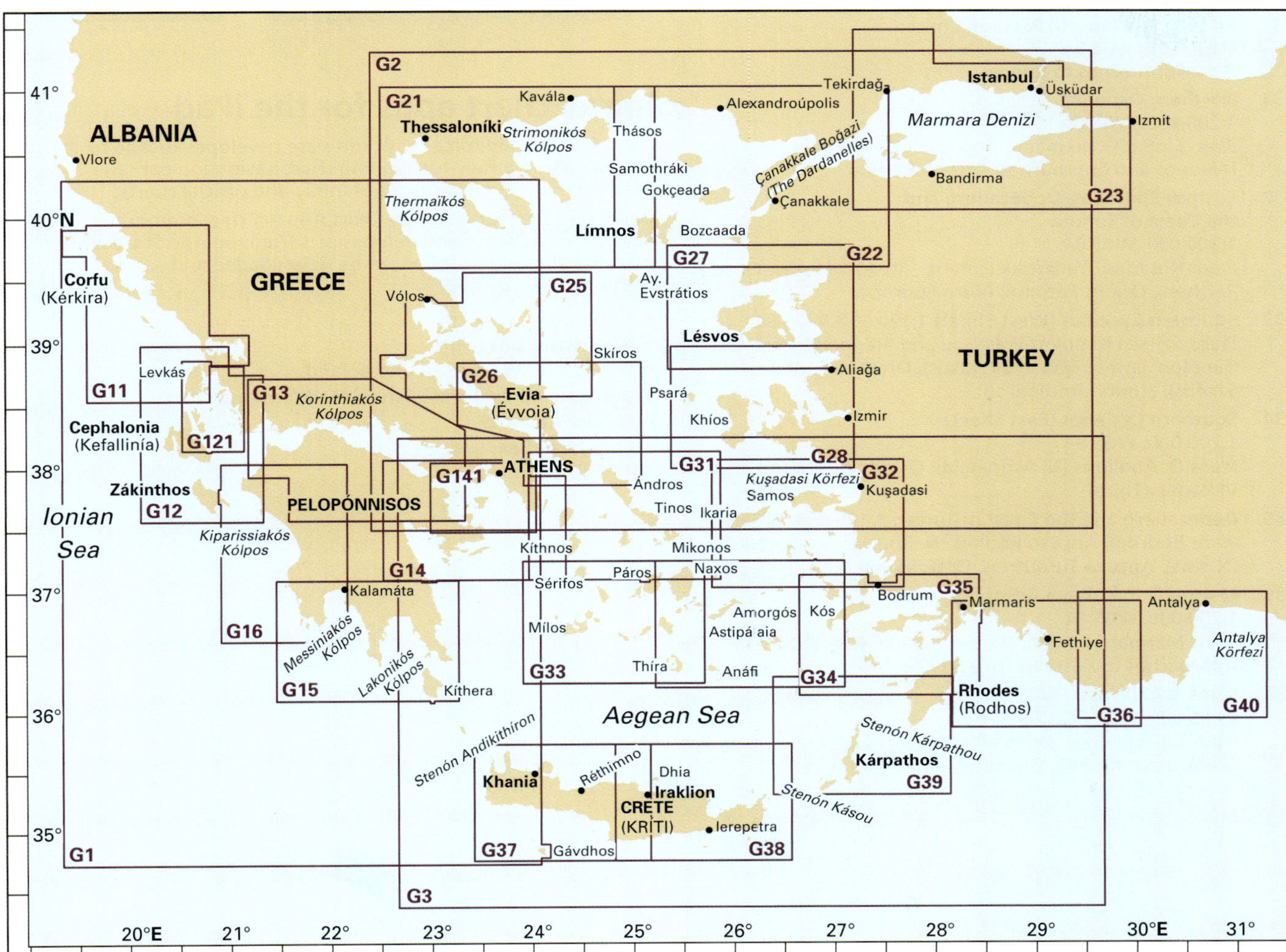

41°
40°N
39°
38°
37°
36°
35°
20°E
21°
22°
23°
24°
25°
26°
27°
28°
29°
30°E
31°
ALBANIA
GREECE
TURKEY
Vlore
G2
G21
G23
G22
G27
G25
G26
G11
G121
G13
G141
G12
G31
G28
G32
G14
G16
G15
G33
G34
G35
G36
G40
G39
G37
G38
G1
G3
Kavála
Alexandroúpolis
Tekirdağ
Istanbul
Üsküdar
Izmit
Marmara Denizi
Bandirma
Çanakkale Boğazi (The Dardanelles)
Çanakkale
Thessaloníki
Strimonikós Kólpos
Thásos
Samothráki
Gokçeada
Thermaïkós Kólpos
Límnos
Bozcaada
Ay. Evstrátios
Vólos
Corfu (Kérkira)
Lésvos
Skíros
Aliağa
Levkás
Evia (Évvoia)
Psará
Khíos
Izmir
Korinthiakós Kólpos
Cephalonia (Kefallinía)
ATHENS
Ándros
Kuşadasi Körfezi
Samos
Kuşadasi
Zákinthos
PELOPÓNNISOS
Tinos
Ikaria
Ionian Sea
Kiparissiakós Kólpos
Kíthnos
Mikonos
Páros
Naxos
Sérifos
Bodrum
Marmaris
Antalya
Kalamáta
Amorgós
Kós
Mílos
Astipá aia
Fethiye
Antalya Körfezi
Messiniakós Kólpos
Lakonikós Kólpos
Thíra
Anáfi
Kíthera
Rhodes (Rodhos)
Aegean Sea
Stenón Andikithíron
Stenón Kárpathou
Kárpathos
Khania
Réthimno
Dhia
Iraklion
CRETE (KRITI)
Ierepetra
Stenón Kásou
Gávdhos

G2 Aegean Sea (North) Passage Chart 1:750,000 WGS 84
Plans Çanakkale Boğazi (The Dardanelles) Apps to İstanbul, Izmit Körfezi

G21 Northwest Aegean
1:275,000 WGS 84
Plans Approaches to Thessaloníki, Néa Skioni, Pórto Koufó, Nisís Dhiáporos Anchorages, Nisís Ammouliani, Stenón Thásou

G22 Northeast Aegean
1:275,000 WGS 84
Plans Approaches to Lágos and Fanárion, Órmos Moudrhou, Entrance to Çanakkale Boğazi, Nara Geçidi, Continuation to Nísos Áyios Evstrátios

G23 Marmara Denizi
1:275,000 WGS 84
Plans Türkeli & Paşalimani Islands, Istanbul, Princes Islands, Approaches to Pendik

G25 Northern Sporades and North Evvoia 1:190,000 WGS 84
Plans Órmos Skíathou (Nísos Skíathos), Linariá (Nísos Skíros), Stenó Alonnísou, Continuation of Maliakós Kólpos

G26 Nísos Evvoia
1:190,000 WGS 84
Plans Linariá (Nísos Skiros), Kímis (Nísos Évvoia), Approaches to Khalkís, Erétria (Nísos Évvoia), Liménas Alivériou (Nísos Évvoia), Rafina, Porthmós Evrípou, Dhíavlos Stenó

G27 Nísos Lésvos & the Coast of Turkey 1:190,000 WGS 84
Plans Bademli Limani, Ayvalik, Sígri, Entrance to Kólpos Kalloní, Mitilíni, Entrance to Kólpos Yéras

G28 Nísos Khíos & the Coast of Turkey 1:190,000 WGS 84
Plans Órmos Mandráki, App. to Khíos, App. to Psará, Çesme Körfezi, Foça Limani, Sigaçik Limani

G3 Aegean Sea (South) Passage Chart
1:750,800 WGS 84
Plan Approaches to Rhodes

G31 Northern Cyclades
1:200,000 WGS 84
Plans Limín Ay Nikoláou, App to Finikas, Órmos Naousis, Mikonos and approaches, Órmos Gávriou

G32 Eastern Sporades, Dodecanese and the Coast of Turkey
1:200,000 WGS 84
Plans Kuşadasi, Yalikavak Limani, , Stenón Sámou, Órmos Parthéni, Órmos Pátmou, Póros Fóurnon

G33 Southern Cyclades (West Sheet) 1:190,000 WGS 84
Plans Stenón Kimólou-Políagou and Stenón Mílou-Kimólou, Órmos Náxou (N Náxos), Órmos Livádhiou (N. Sérifos), Stenón Andipárou

G34 Southern Cyclades (East Sheet)
1:200,000 WGS 84
Plans Ó. Analipsis (N. Astipálaia), Órmos Íou (N. Íos), Vlikadha (Thíra)

G35 Dodecanese and the Coast of Turkey 1:190,000 WGS 84
Plans Bodrum, App. to Ródhos (N. Ródhos), App. to Kós (N. Kós), App. to Turgutreis, Órmos Sími (N. Sími)

G36 Marmaris to Kekova Adasi
1:200,000 WGS 84
Plans Marmaris Limani, Skopea Limani, Göçek, Fethíye, Approaches to Kastellórizo and Kaş

G37 Nísos Kriti (West)
1:190,000 WGS 84
Plans Kali Limenes, Órmos Áy Galínis, Palaiokhora, Órmos Gramvoúsa, Khanía, Órmos Soúdhas, Rethimno

G38 Nísos Kriti (East)
1:190,000 WGS 84
Plans Iraklion, Sitía, Á. Nikólaos, Spinalónga

G39 Nísos Karpathos to Nísos Rodhos 1:190,000 WGS 84
Plans Pigádhia (N. Kárpathos), Órmos Líndhou (N. Ródhos), Limín Fri (N. Kásos), N. Khálki to N. Alimiá

G40 Kaş to Antalya
1:200,000 WGS 84
Plans Kekova Roads, Kekova Adasi, Finike, Antalya Celebi Marina, Kemer Turkiz Marina

Download on the App Store

Imray chart apps for the iPad

Imray have joined forces with software developer Tucabo to produce this is a fully functioning chart navigation package based on high quality images of Imray and official charts.

Download the marine Imray Chart App which contains the navigation software and demo charts from the App Store and then the Imray chart folios can be downloaded and will be ready for use:

- **North Sea**
- **Atlantic Europe**
- **British Isles West coast and Ireland**
- **Western, Central and Eastern Mediterranean**
- **English Channel**
- **Caribbean Sea**

8. Routes within the Mediterranean

8.1 DISTANCE CHARTS

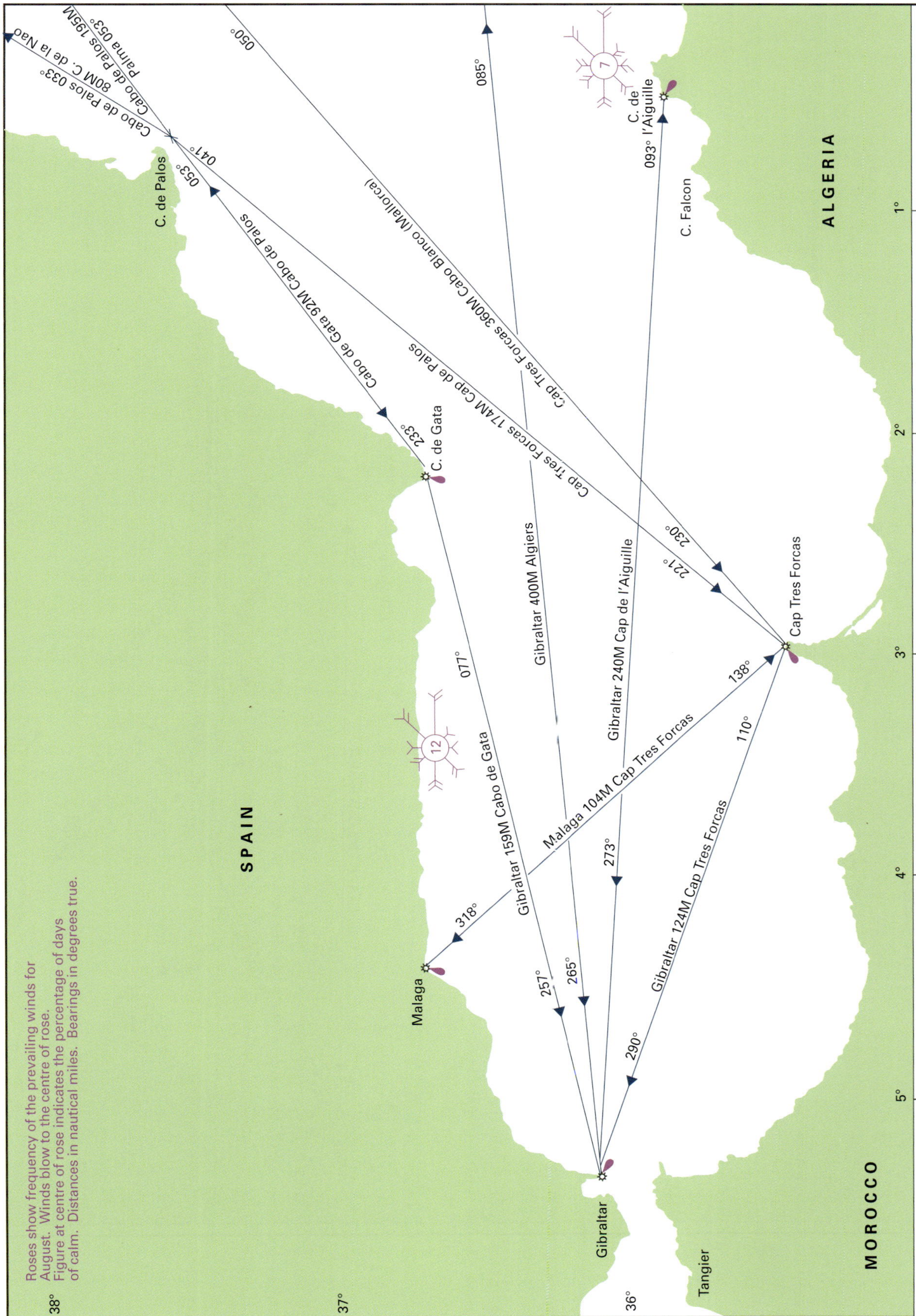

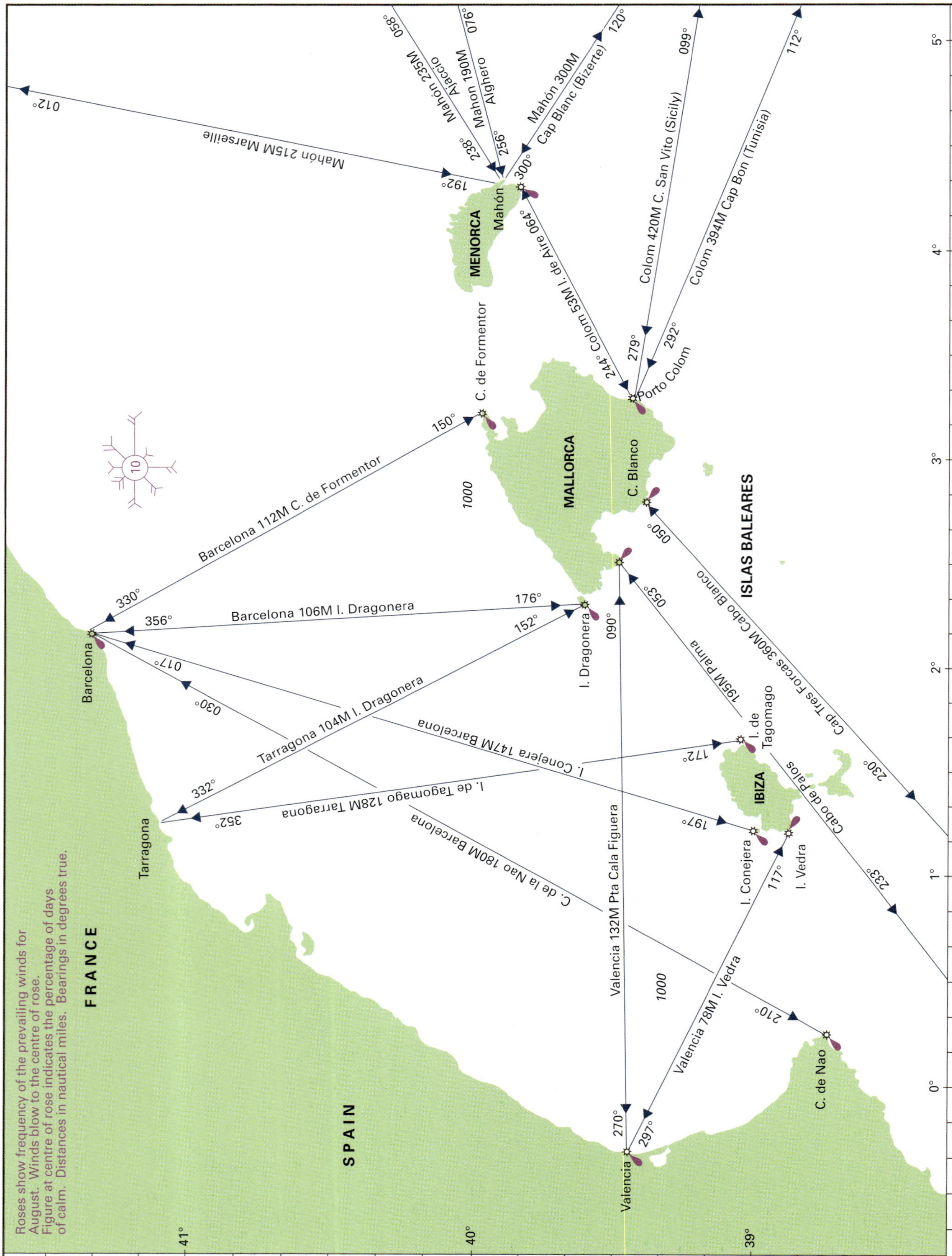
Roses show frequency of the prevailing winds for August. Winds blow to the centre of rose.
Figure at centre of rose indicates the percentage of days of calm. Distances in nautical miles. Bearings in degrees true.
FRANCE
SPAIN
Barcelona
Tarragona
Valencia
C. de Nao
I. Conejera
I. Vedra
IBIZA
I. de Tagomago
I. Dragonera
MALLORCA
C. Blanco
Porto Colom
C. de Formentor
MENORCA
Mahón
ISLAS BALEARES
1000
1000
10
Barcelona 112M C. de Formentor
330°
150°
Barcelona 106M I. Dragonera
356°
176°
Tarragona 104M I. Dragonera
332°
152°
I. Conejera 147M Barcelona
017°
197°
I. de Tagomago 128M Tarragona
352°
172°
C. de la Nao 180M Barcelona
030°
210°
Valencia 132M Pta Cala Figuera
090°
270°
Valencia 78M I. Vedra
117°
297°
195M Palma
053°
Cap Tres Forcas 360M Cabo Blanco
050°
230°
Cabo de Palos
233°
Mahón 215M Marseille
012°
192°
Mahon 235M Ajaccio
058°
238°
Mahon 190M Alghero
076°
256°
Mahón 300M Cap Blanc (Bizerte)
120°
300°
244° Colom 53M I. de Aire 064°
Colom 420M C. San Vito (Sicily)
099°
279°
Colom 394M Cap Bon (Tunisia)
112°
292°
41°
40°
39°
0°
1°
2°
3°
4°
5°

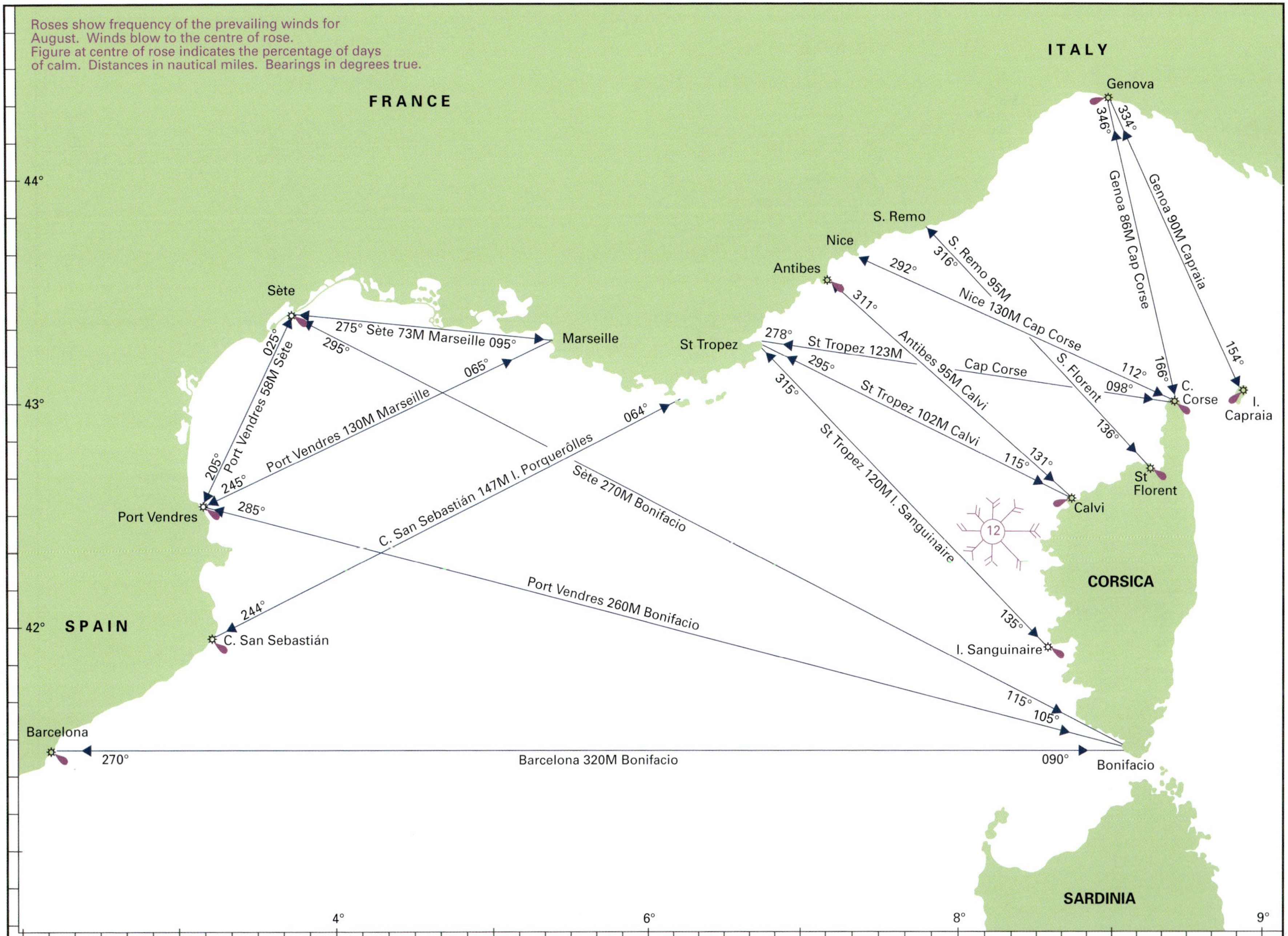
Roses show frequency of the prevailing winds for August. Winds blow to the centre of rose.
Figure at centre of rose indicates the percentage of days of calm. Distances in nautical miles. Bearings in degrees true.
FRANCE
ITALY
SPAIN
CORSICA
SARDINIA
Genova
S. Remo
Nice
Antibes
St Tropez
Marseille
Sète
Port Vendres
C. San Sebastián
Barcelona
C. Corse
I. Capraia
St Florent
Calvi
I. Sanguinaire
Bonifacio
Genoa 90M Capraia
Genoa 86M Cap Corse
S. Remo 95M
Nice 130M Cap Corse
S. Florent
Cap Corse
Antibes 95M Calvi
St Tropez 123M
St Tropez 102M Calvi
St Tropez 120M I. Sanguinaire
275° Sète 73M Marseille 095°
Port Vendres 58M Sète
Port Vendres 130M Marseille
C. San Sebastián 147M I. Porquerôlles
Sète 270M Bonifacio
Port Vendres 260M Bonifacio
Barcelona 320M Bonifacio
346°
334°
154°
166°
112°
098°
136°
316°
292°
311°
131°
115°
278°
295°
315°
135°
025°
205°
245°
065°
285°
064°
244°
115°
105°
270°
090°
12
44°
43°
42°
4°
6°
8°
9°

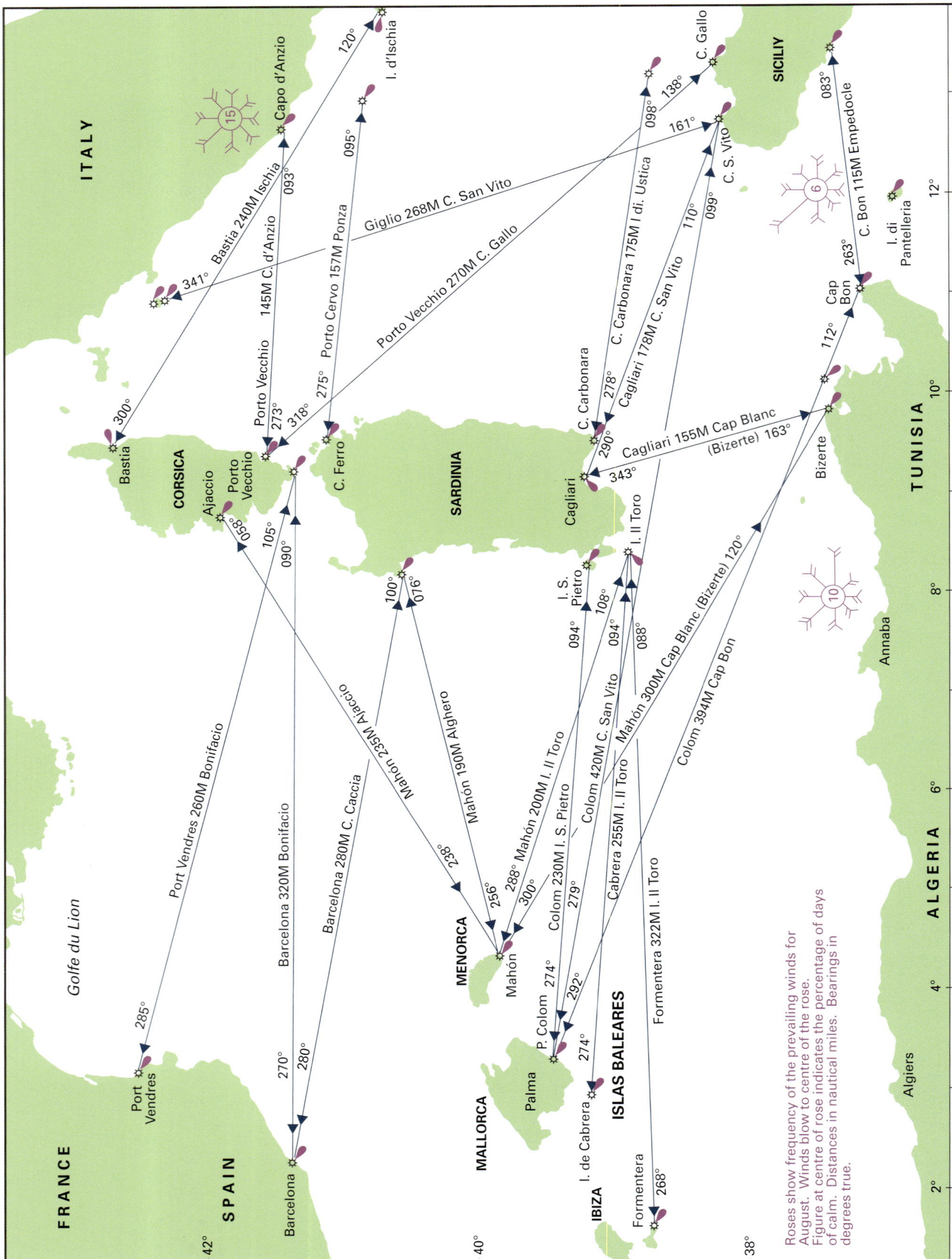

FRANCE
SPAIN
ITALY
CORSICA
SARDINIA
SICILY
TUNISIA
ALGERIA
MENORCA
MALLORCA
IBIZA
ISLAS BALEARES
Golfe du Lion
Port Vendres
Barcelona
Bastia
Ajaccio
Porto Vecchio
C. Ferro
Cagliari
C. Carbonara
I. S. Pietro
I. Il Toro
Capo d'Anzio
I. d'Ischia
C. Gallo
C. S. Vito
I. di Pantelleria
Cap Bon
Bizerte
Annaba
Algiers
Mahón
P. Colom
Palma
I. de Cabrera
Formentera
Bastia 240M Ischia
145M C. d'Anzio
Porto Cervo 157M Ponza
Giglio 268M C. San Vito
Porto Vecchio 270M C. Gallo
C. Carbonara 175M I di. Ustica
Cagliari 178M C. San Vito
C. Bon 115M Empedocle
Cagliari 155M Cap Blanc (Bizerte) 163°
Port Vendres 260M Bonifacio
Barcelona 320M Bonifacio
Barcelona 280M C. Caccia
Mahón 235M Ajaccio
Mahón 190M Alghero
Mahón 200M I. Il Toro
Colom 230M I. S. Pietro
Colom 420M C. San Vito
Mahón 300M Cap Blanc (Bizerte) 120°
Colom 394M Cap Bon
Cabrera 255M I. Il Toro
Formentera 322M I. Il Toro
15
6
10
42°
40°
38°
2°
4°
6°
8°
10°
12°
Roses show frequency of the prevailing winds for August. Winds blow to centre of the rose.
Figure at centre of rose indicates the percentage of days of calm. Distances in nautical miles. Bearings in degrees true.

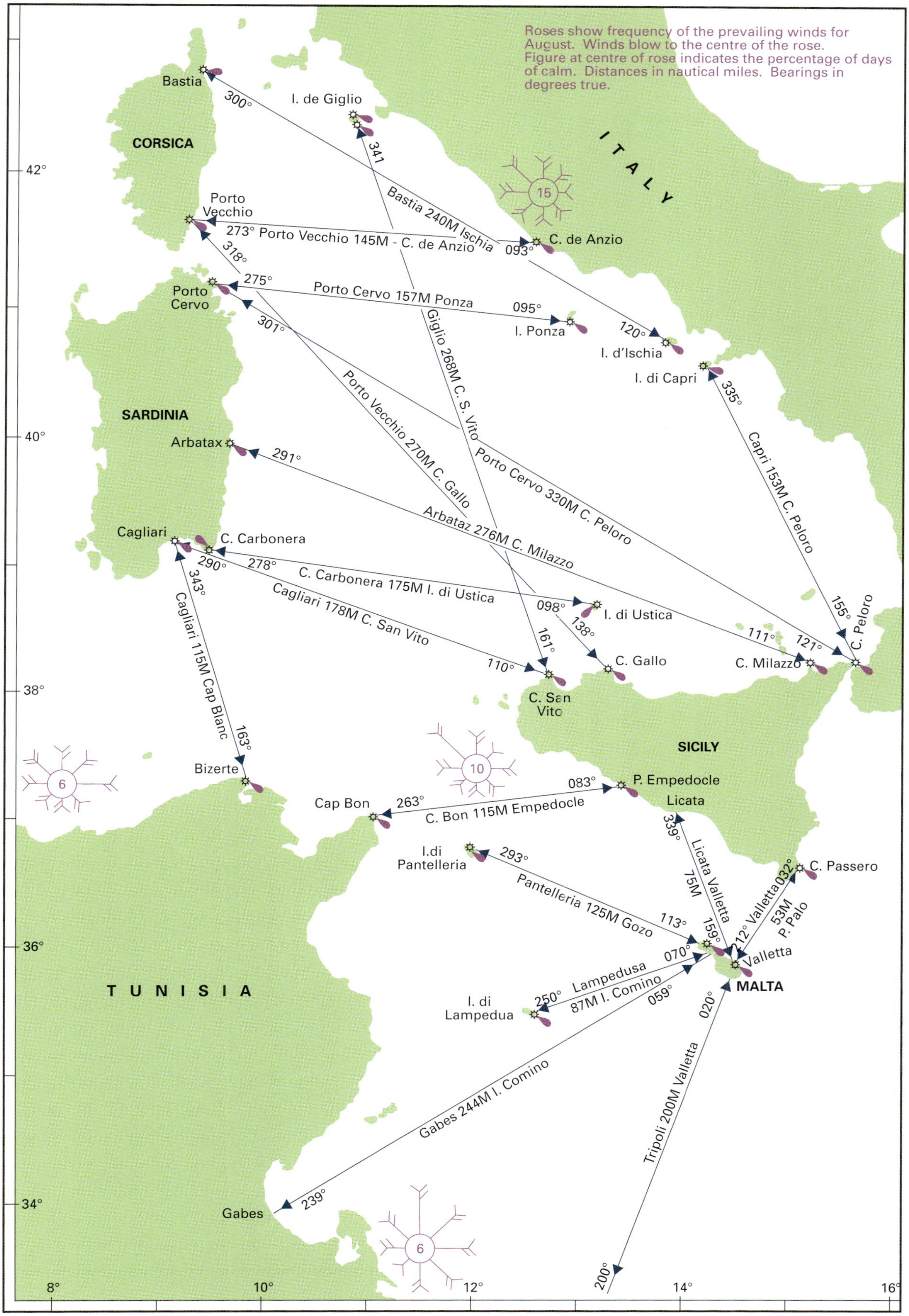

Roses show frequency of the prevailing winds for August. Winds blow to the centre of the rose. Figure at centre of rose indicates the percentage of days of calm. Distances in nautical miles. Bearings in degrees true.
CORSICA
SARDINIA
ITALY
SICILY
TUNISIA
MALTA
Bastia
I. de Giglio
Porto Vecchio
C. de Anzio
Porto Cervo
I. Ponza
I. d'Ischia
I. di Capri
Arbatax
Cagliari
C. Carbonera
I. di Ustica
C. Gallo
C. Milazzo
C. Peloro
C. San Vito
Bizerte
Cap Bon
P. Empedocle
Licata
I.di Pantelleria
C. Passero
Valletta
I. di Lampedua
Gabes
Bastia 240M Ischia
273° Porto Vecchio 145M - C. de Anzio
Porto Cervo 157M Ponza
Giglio 268M C. S. Vito
Porto Vecchio 270M C. Gallo
Porto Cervo 330M C. Peloro
Capri 153M C. Peloro
Arbataz 276M C. Milazzo
C. Carbonera 175M I. di Ustica
Cagliari 178M C. San Vito
Cagliari 115M Cap Blanc
C. Bon 115M Empedocle
Pantelleria 125M Gozo
Licata Valletta 75M
Valletta 53M P. Palo
Lampedusa 87M I. Comino
Gabes 244M I. Comino
Tripoli 200M Valletta
300°
341
093°
318°
275°
095°
301°
120°
335°
291°
290°
278°
343°
098°
138°
161°
110°
111°
121°
155°
163°
263°
083°
339°
293°
113°
159°
112°
032°
070°
250°
059°
020°
239°
200°
15
10
6
6
42°
40°
38°
36°
34°
8°
10°
12°
14°
16°

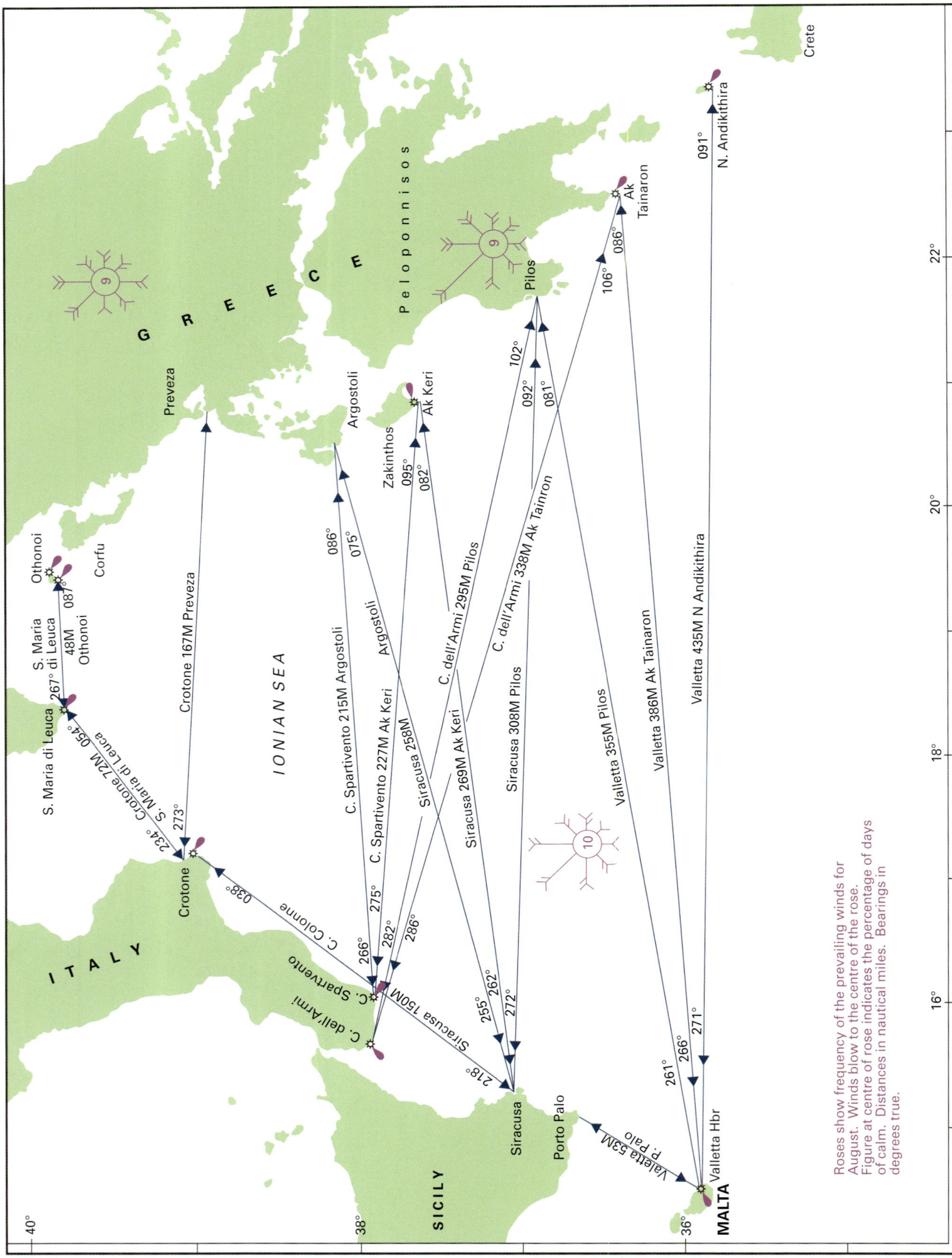
GREECE
Peloponnisos
ITALY
SICILY
MALTA
IONIAN SEA
Crete
Corfu
Othonoi
Preveza
Argostoli
Zakinthos
Ak Keri
Pilos
Ak Tainaron
N. Andikithira
S. Maria di Leuca
Crotone
C. Colonne
C. Spartivento
C. dell'Armi
Siracusa
Porto Palo
Valletta Hbr
S. Maria di Leuca 48M Othonoi
087°
267°
Crotone 72M S. Maria di Leuca
054°
234°
Crotone 167M Preveza
273°
038°
218°
Siracusa 150M C. Spartivento
C. Spartivento 215M Argostoli
086°
266°
075°
Argostoli
C. Spartivento 227M Ak Keri
095°
275°
Siracusa 258M Argostoli
282°
082°
Siracusa 269M Ak Keri
262°
286°
C. dell'Armi 295M Pilos
102°
C. dell'Armi 338M Ak Tainron
106°
Siracusa 308M Pilos
092°
272°
255°
081°
Valletta 355M Pilos
261°
Valletta 386M Ak Tainaron
086°
266°
Valletta 435M N Andikithira
091°
271°
Valletta 53M P. Palo
9
9
10
40°
38°
36°
16°
18°
20°
22°
Roses show frequency of the prevailing winds for August. Winds blow to the centre of the rose. Figure at centre of rose indicates the percentage of days of calm. Distances in nautical miles. Bearings in degrees true.

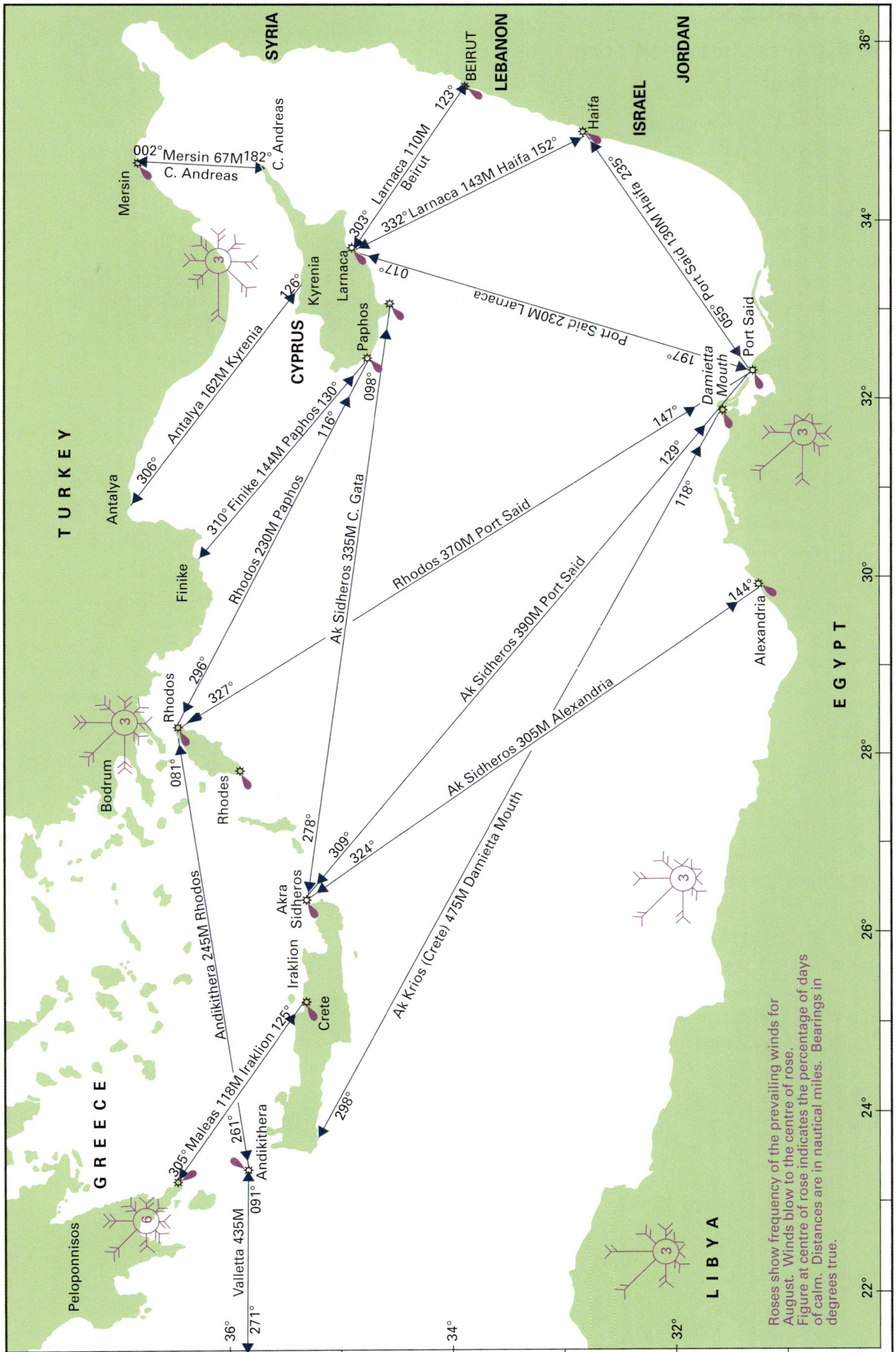
TURKEY
SYRIA
LEBANON
ISRAEL
JORDAN
CYPRUS
GREECE
EGYPT
LIBYA
Peloponnisos
Mersin
C. Andreas
Kyrenia
Larnaca
Paphos
BEIRUT
Haifa
Port Said
Damietta Mouth
Alexandria
Antalya
Finike
Rhodos
Rhodes
Bodrum
Akra Sidheros
Iraklion
Crete
Andikithera
002° Mersin 67M 182° C. Andreas
123° Larnaca 110M Beirut 303°
332° Larnaca 143M Haifa 152°
055° Port Said 130M Haifa 235°
017° Port Said 230M Larnaca 197°
306° Antalya 162M Kyrenia 126°
310° Finike 144M Paphos 130°
296° Rhodos 230M Paphos 116°
Ak Sidheros 335M C. Gata 098° 278°
327° Rhodos 370M Port Said 147°
309° Ak Sidheros 390M Port Said 129°
324° Ak Sidheros 305M Alexandria 144°
298° Ak Krios (Crete) 475M Damietta Mouth 118°
081° Andikithera 245M Rhodos 261°
305° Maleas 118M Iraklion 125°
091° Valletta 435M 271°
36°
34°
32°
30°
28°
26°
24°
22°
3
6
Roses show frequency of the prevailing winds for August. Winds blow to the centre of rose.
Figure at centre of rose indicates the percentage of days of calm. Distances are in nautical miles. Bearings in degrees true.

8.2 DISTANCE TABLES

Approximate distances between ports

* Places common to two or more tables. May be useful when finding distances between ports in separate tables.

Central Mediterranean

	Argostolion	Benghazi	Bizerte*	Cagliari*	Catania	Corfu (Kerkira)*	Crotone	Derna*	Kalamata (Kalamai)*	Khania*	Kithira *	Levkas	Monastir	Otranto*	Pantelleria	Patras (Patrai)	Pilos	Reggio Calabria*	Sfax	Siracusa	Tobruch*	Trapani*	Tripoli (Tarabulus Gharb)	Valetta
Benghazi	373																							
Bizerte*	534	594																						
Cagliari*	576	687	124																					
Catania	265	406	307	369																				
Corfu (Kerkira)*	103	456	558	589	282																			
Crotone	172	443	441	451	145	160																		
Derna*	349	153	692	768	741	439	468																	
Kalamata (Kalamai)*	136	314	611	681	364	224	291	259																
Khania*	247	302	701	771	476	321	396	204	134															
Kithira *	181	283	643	701	391	268	335	207	74	62														
Levkas	71	412	561	579	279	61	171	381	166	267	207													
Monastir	497	511	143	238	276	529	399	617	564	248	593	518												
Otranto*	158	491	506	537	234	84	98	489	286	388	327	132	489											
Pantelleria	429	493	113	198	208	462	331	584	501	592	538	452	89	421										
Patras (Patrai)	69	393	591	627	321	126	229	361	148	248	186	67	553	197	482									
Pilos	101	304	583	628	319	187	254	258	43	147	85	127	532	249	472	106								
Reggio Calabria*	246	424	315	324	49	262	123	475	341	441	396	256	311	213	246	303	303							
Sfax	528	498	222	308	314	567	436	616	592	662	618	554	93	526	151	596	557	351						
Siracusa	261	380	290	391	29	289	157	447	334	436	377	281	248	247	181	316	309	69	287					
Tobruch*	411	231	782	846	549	501	537	85	311	243	250	438	701	553	667	419	314	550	692	526				
Trapani*	418	526	133	176	211	427	288	599	506	595	549	418	161	376	77	466	465	166	226	194	679			
Tripoli (Tarabulus Gharb)	583	354	337	431	304	537	419	482	508	566	524	513	213	509	246	528	486	341	168	276	569	311		
Valetta	323	358	249	329	111	361	234	447	386	466	413	346	184	322	139	377	354	148	222	83	527	171	195	
Zakinthos	36	451	551	597	289	126	198	316	103	207	141	65	506	184	441	52	65	267	552	284	376	431	486	338

Western Mediterranean Sea

	Ajaccio	Alghero	Algiers	Alicante	Barcelona	Bizerte*	Bonifacio*	Cagliari*	Calvi*	Cartagena	Formentera	Gibraltar	Ibiza	Mahon	Malaga	Marinasmir	Marseille*	Mellila	Oran	Palma	Port Camargue	Port Vendres	Propriano	Sete	Tanger	Tarragona	Toulon*
Alghero	96																										
Algiers	408	336																									
Alicante	481	431	198																								
Barcelona	299	284	281	231																							
Bizerte*	302	221	337	503	439																						
Bonifacio*	44	84	399	493	316	261																					
Cagliari*	213	141	324	463	364	124	172																				
Calvi*	54	139	441	496	305	348	89	259																			
Cartagena	525	471	203	61	281	526	527	499	552																		
Formentera	391	343	146	94	171	423	396	377	419	138																	
Gibraltar	756	703	414	295	517	749	762	726	781	239	363																
Ibiza	382	333	153	101	161	417	387	369	409	148	12	379															
Mahon	239	191	198	249	147	308	242	239	265	291	160	514	151														
Malaga	704	651	364	244	464	690	707	669	733	191	319	63	327	471													
Marinasmir	761	707	416	301	518	749	763	726	789	247	376	26	383	526	74												
Marseille*	181	216	411	402	189	428	209	333	167	457	331	689	321	214	636	694											
Mellila	679	621	309	224	444	638	681	628	704	169	297	136	306	444	115	129	619										
Oran	578	514	199	159	365	526	577	521	607	116	208	237	218	426	195	232	537	148									
Palma	332	281	171	166	132	376	536	326	364	214	78	447	70	102	394	451	288	372	281								
Port Camargue	229	256	408	384	166	468	258	382	217	437	313	673	303	222	619	674	57	601	521	274							
Port Vendres	255	264	351	321	91	447	280	368	252	373	252	606	243	174	553	609	111	534	458	209	76						
Propriano	24	91	403	483	305	293	31	205	71	524	391	758	391	239	704	761	197	677	575	333	241	265					
Sete	243	269	404	371	151	466	272	383	231	423	302	655	292	217	606	549	74	586	508	261	21	59	254				
Tanger	783	728	436	321	541	774	784	745	806	266	393	31	403	547	88	38	713	157	254	471	697	631	781	681			
Tarragona	345	325	276	192	49	471	561	398	345	245	149	477	140	168	424	481	236	406	336	129	213	149	349	198	503		
Toulon*	147	189	406	414	201	408	181	318	133	469	339	703	330	214	649	704	41	628	543	296	88	134	161	106	722	247	
Valencia	439	406	229	96	163	501	450	452	456	148	93	382	108	229	329	387	347	311	241	141	326	259	442	309	407	121	359

Ligurian Sea and adjacent ports

	Antibes	Bastia*	Calvi*	Cannes	Cap Corse*	Genova	Livorno	Marseille*	Monaco	Nice	Portoferraio*	Saint Raphael	San Remo	Spezia	St Tropez	Toulon*
Bastia*	126															
Calvi*	95	62														
Cannes	11	134	100													
Cap Corse*	104	22	39	111												
Genova	94	107	111	101	84											
Livorno	138	64	92	146	52	79										
Marseille*	105	220	167	96	197	191	229									
Monaco	15	118	93	23	95	78	126	115								
Nice	9	123	95	17	100	86	132	111	8							
Portoferraio*	15	43	86	157	46	113	47	244	140	145						
Saint Raphael	24	139	102	16	116	113	155	83	38	32	164					
San Remo	32	107	88	39	84	63	112	131	17	25	129	51				
Spezia	126	87	108	134	67	45	39	216	112	119	79	146	97			
St Tropez	32	145	106	25	122	123	161	79	46	40	169	12	61	156		
Toulon*	73	178	133	64	156	159	197	41	83	78	203	52	97	185	48	
Viareggio	137	79	104	142	63	66	20	227	123	129	64	154	107	23	163	196

Aegean Sea

	Ak. Sidheros*	Alexandropoulis	Bodrum	Canakkale	Iraklion	Istanbul	Izmir	Kalamata (Kalamai)*	Kalimnos	Khalkis	Khania*	Khios	Kithira*	Kos	Kusadasi	Mitilini	Navplion	Piraeus	Rodhos*	Skiathos	Thessaloniki
Ak. Sidheros*																					
Alexandropoulis	338																				
Bodrum	119	264																			
Canakkale	303	66	234																		
Iraklion	58	338	158	307																	
Istanbul	434	197	365	131	438																
Izmir	251	182	172	151	256	282															
Kalamata (Kalamai)*	244	374	286	341	189	472	332														
Kalimnos	104	253	24	223	135	354	161	264													
Khalkis	234	228	216	229	212	360	204	227	197												
Khania*	118	337	201	303	61	434	265	135	175	191											
Khios	191	153	116	123	194	254	64	275	101	151	206										
Kithira*	170	319	226	297	117	428	276	74	202	168	62	206									
Kos	113	259	11	228	146	359	166	281	17	212	186	104	218								
Kusadasi	169	217	74	187	193	318	125	294	66	196	213	64	236	67							
Mitilini	239	123	154	84	244	215	57	323	149	186	256	53	265	154	116						
Navplion	219	286	236	274	177	405	249	153	214	136	138	187	94	230	232	237					
Piraeus	207	246	199	222	174	353	198	172	177	94	148	147	108	191	183	192	76				
Rodhos*	119	318	69	288	169	419	226	353	78	256	216	165	259	63	128	215	276	247			
Skiathos	276	151	239	150	253	281	206	254	219	82	247	146	229	233	196	162	206	155	291		
Thessaloniki	369	188	318	182	339	313	257	381	310	171	341	227	324	323	286	216	299	249	381	101	
Volos	311	189	274	178	284	309	221	308	254	81	272	181	249	265	231	196	217	175	346	41	127

Eastern Mediterranean

	Ak. Sidheros*	Alexandria	Antalya	Ashkelon	Beirut	Derna*	Famagusta	Fethiye	Finike	Haifa	Iskenderun	Kyrenia	Ladhiqiyah	Larnaca	Marmaris	Mersin	Paphos	Port Said	Rodhos*	Tartus	Tel Aviv
Ak. Sidheros*																					
Alexandria	304																				
Antalya	253	346																			
Ashkelon	466	247	367																		
Beirut	462	331	318	144																	
Derna*	243	378	486	609	649																
Famagusta	404	324	273	212	108	594															
Fethiye	161	326	136	406	381	396	322														
Finike	202	304	61	353	309	427	251	86													
Haifa	455	281	326	73	73	623	149	384	316												
Iskenderun	493	456	283	311	176	709	143	373	302	242											
Kyrenia	346	321	158	309	185	556	114	237	166	203	159										
Ladhiqiyah	467	394	253	241	99	675	93	349	279	169	79	124									
Larnaca	377	296	227	201	111	568	36	289	217	142	166	142	110								
Marmaris	141	349	167	442	405	378	346	48	108	412	406	267	381	313							
Mersin	426	424	221	308	179	642	115	309	234	241	78	109	93	139	342						
Paphos	301	248	154	215	164	501	105	217	145	173	233	79	182	72	241	177					
Port Said	391	138	348	117	227	508	251	364	321	165	378	291	308	230	393	357	210				
Rodhos*	129	328	156	429	394	359	336	45	98	406	391	258	371	298	26	334	230	375			
Tartus	474	378	301	208	63	671	95	371	298	135	114	144	38	106	402	129	177	283	391		
Tel Aviv	464	263	353	28	115	616	191	395	341	64	287	279	213	179	432	283	199	134	419	179	
Tobruch*	228	308	448	541	592	85	547	376	398	561	664	509	624	519	367	601	451	433	340	619	550

Tyrrhenian Sea and adjacent ports

	Arbatax	Bastia*	Bizerte*	Bonifacio*	Cagliari*	Cap Corse*	Capri	Fiumicino	Ischia	Marsala	Messina	Napoli	Nettuno	Olbia	Palermo	Porto Vecchio	Porto Cervo	Portoferraio *	Reggio Calabria*	Salerno	Trapani*
Arbatax																					
Bastia*	171																				
Bizerte*	162	327																			
Bonifacio*	99	86	261																		
Cagliari*	74	240	124	172																	
Cap Corse*	189	22	347	107	268																
Capri	213	252	284	238	258	266															
Fiumicino	159	136	291	141	225	150	119														
Ischia	201	232	283	221	249	247	18	99													
Marsala	184	327	125	267	180	348	191	241	195												
Messina	303	395	296	358	322	412	162	271	183	176											
Napoli	218	249	296	237	264	262	17	113	17	204	175										
Nettuno	164	164	282	161	226	177	91	29	72	222	283	87									
Olbia	71	111	227	43	141	133	215	132	200	233	325	217	146								
Palermo	206	330	182	279	216	349	155	227	163	62	118	169	204	251							
Porto Vecchio	108	71	267	23	179	91	235	132	218	276	366	235	154	51	286						
Porto Cervo	76	96	236	24	147	116	218	128	202	244	338	217	144	20	256	33					
Portoferraio *	189	43	346	109	258	46	228	111	208	324	381	224	143	131	324	96	117				
Reggio Calabria*	304	397	315	363	324	415	163	272	181	178	7	177	246	337	118	365	342	382			
Salerno	239	276	307	263	280	289	27	142	42	207	158	37	115	239	168	257	241	252	161		
Trapani*	178	316	133	257	176	337	176	228	181	14	161	190	209	223	49	266	235	316	166	193	
Ustica	182	296	180	249	197	314	124	192	131	68	126	138	168	216	39	254	225	284	129	139	55

Adriatic Sea and adjacent ports

	Ancona	Bar	Brindisi	Corfu (Kerkira)*	Dubrovnik	Durres	Monfalcone	Monopoli	Otranto *	Pescara	Pula	Rab	Ravenna	Rovinj	Santa Margherita	Split	Trieste	Venice	Vodice
Ancona																			
Bar	266																		
Brindisi	271	101																	
Corfu (Kerkira)*	383	171	118																
Dubrovnik	215	62	124	213															
Durres	301	54	78	136	105														
Monfalcone	134	351	376	488	292	415													
Monopoli	237	106	38	153	112	112	342												
Otranto *	312	121	42	84	155	88	411	79											
Pescara	81	218	206	319	174	263	205	171	246										
Pula	79	296	321	426	239	362	62	289	356	151									
Rab	93	261	287	393	201	331	123	258	328	143	69								
Ravenna	74	333	344	453	278	395	96	309	386	151	72	115							
Rovinj	90	307	332	438	250	373	48	301	369	163	18	81	68						
Santa Margherita	123	350	376	480	293	418	41	344	410	199	62	124	71	45					
Split	133	158	189	296	102	229	211	161	228	118	157	118	101	160	212				
Trieste	128	347	373	478	290	414	14	340	407	201	60	121	94	43	39	208			
Venice	121	362	384	493	304	429	63	351	428	199	76	136	64	60	25	219	63		
Vodice	104	182	216	319	127	254	172	185	252	109	118	81	162	129	173	41	169	186	
Zadar	88	213	244	353	159	283	139	216	286	126	85	46	131	96	140	72	137	153	36

9. Tides

9.1 TIDAL DIFFERENCES ON GIBRALTAR

Note Predictions for Gibraltar are based on Zone Time –0100.
Where a secondary port lies in a different time zone the differences shown can be applied without further correction to give times directly applicable to the local time zone. Adjustments are only necessary during BST (DST).

	Difference					*Height differences (m)*		
Place	*High water*		*Low water*		*MHWS*	*MHWN*	*MLWN*	*MLWS*
(Zone –0100)								
GIBRALTAR	0000 1200	0700 1900	0100 1300	0600 1800	1.0	0.7	0.3	0.1
SPAIN								
Tarifa	–0038	–0038	–0042	–0042	+0.4	+0.3	+0.3	+0.2
Punta Carnero	–0010	–0010	0000	0000	0.0	+0.1	+0.1	+0.1
Algeciras	–0010	–0010	–0010	–0010	+0.1	+0.2	+0.1	+0.1
GIBRALTAR								
Sandy Bay	–0011	–0011	–0016	–0016	–0.1	–0.1	0.0	
SPAIN								
Málaga	+0015	+0015	+0015	+0015	–0.3	–0.2	0.0	+0.1
Almeria	+0006	+0006	+0006	+0006	–0.5	–0.3	0.0	+0.2
Alicante	–	–	–			Negligible		
ISLAS BALEARES								
Palma de Mallorca	–	–	–			Negligible		
Port Vendres	–0408	–0408	–0409	–0409	–0.6	–0.4	0.0	+0.1
Marseille	–0636	–0636	–0636	–0636	–0.6	–0.3	0.0	+0.2
Toulon	–0453	–0453	–0454	–0454	–0.6	–0.3	+0.1	+0.2
Nice	–0539	0539	–0539	0539	–0.5	–0.3	+0.1	+0.2
MONACO								
Monte Carlo	–0508	–0508	–0509	–0509	–0.5	–0.3	+0.1	+0.3
CORSICA								
Ajaccio	–0528	–0528	–0528	–0528	–0.5	–0.3	0.0	+0.2
SARDINIA								
La Maddalena	+0550	+0550	–	–	–0.7	–0.5	–0.1	0.0
Cagliari	+0610	+0610	+0620	+0620	–0.7	–0.5	–0.2	0.0
Carloforte	+0610	+0610	+0620	+0620	–0.7	–0.5	–0.1	0.0
(Zone GMT)								
MOROCCO								
Tangier	–0010	–0100	–0050	+0010	+1.4	+1.2	+0.7	+0.5
Punta Alboassa	–0035	–0035	–0003	–0003	+0.8	+0.6	+0.4	+0.2
Punta Cires	–0109	–0109	–0104	–0104	+0.2	+0.2	+0.2	+0.1
Ceuta	–0040	–0120	–0140	–0040	0.0	–0.1	–0.1	+0.1
Ensenada de Tetouan	–0045	–0045	–	–	–0.1	0.0	+0.1	+0.1
Baie d'al Hoceima	–0015	–0015	–0055	–0055	–0.4	–0.2	–0.1	0.0
Melilla	–0040	–0040	–	–	–0.4	–0.2	0.9	+0.1
Islas Chafarinas	+0040	+0040	+0105	+0105	–0.6	–0.4	–0.1	0.0
(Zone–0100)								
ALGERIA								
Arzew	+0105	–0105	+0105	+0105	–0.4	–0.2	+0.2	+0.3
Alger (Algiers)	–	–	–	–		Negligible		
GIBRALTAR	0300 1500	0900 2100	0400 1600	0800 2000	1.0	0.7	0.3	0.1
TUNISIA								
Bizerte	–0320	–0430	–0345	–0305	–0.6	–0.4	–0.1	+0.1
La Goulette	–0540	–0540	–0510	–0510	–0.6	–0.3	0.9	+0.1
Monastir	–0230	–0230	–0215	–0215	–0.5	–0.3	+0.1	+0.2
Ras Kapudia	–0105	–0105	–0030	–0030	–0.6	–0.3	–0.1	0.0

Place	Difference				Height differences (m)			
	High water		Low water		MHWS	MHWN	MLWN	MLWS
Kerkennah Banks,								
E Point	–0105	–0105	–0055	–0055	–0.2	–0.3	+0.1	+0.1
Bordj el Hassar	+0210	+0210	+0315	+0315	+0.2	+0.1	+0.3	+0.1
El Abassia	+0043	+0035	–0152	+0152	+0.1	0.0	+0.2	+0.2
Kerkennah Banks								
S Point	+0035	+0035	–0010	–0010	+0.4	+0.2	+0.4	+0.2
Sfax	+0050	+0050	+0015	+0015	+0.7	+0.4	+0.5	+0.2
La Skhirra	+0055	+0055	+0210	+0210	+1.1	+0.7	+0.7	+0.4
Gabës	+0055	+0055	+0125	+0125	+1.1	+0.6	+0.7	+0.4
Bou Grara	+0420	+0420	+0545	+0545	–0.2	–0.2	+0.2	+0.2
Houmt Adjim	+0130	+0130	+0230	+0230	+0.2	0.0	+0.2	0.0
Adjim Bar	+0120	+0120	+0245	+0245	+1.1	+0.7	+0.7	+0.4
Houmt Souk	+0102	+0102	+0240	+0240	+0.7	+0.5	+0.7	+0.6
Ras Tourg-en-Ness	+0105	+0105	+0115	+0115	+0.4	+0.3	+0.5	+0.4
Zarzis	+0100	+0100	+0120	+0120	0.0	0.0	+0.2	+0.1
Ras el Ketef	–0035	–0035	+0040	+0040	0.0	–0.1	+0.3	+0.2
ITALY								
GULF OF GENOA								
Imperia	+0550	+0550	+0640	+0640	–0.7	–0.5	–0.2	–0.1
Genova (Genoa)	+0525	+0525	+0610	+0640	–0.7	–0.5	–0.2	–0.1
La Spezia	+0525	+0525	+0545	+0545	–0.7	–0.4	–0.2	0.0
Livorno	+0550	+0550	+0620	+0620	–0.7	–0.5	–0.2	0.0
Civitavecchia	+0615	+0615	+0625	+0625	–0.6	–0.4	–0.2	0.0
Gaeta	+0620	+0620	+0630	+0630	–0.7	–0.5	–0.2	–0.1
Napoli (Naples)	+0630	+0630	+0640	+0640	–0.6	–0.4	–0.2	0.0
Ischia	+0615	+0615	+0630	+0630	–0.7	–0.5	–0.2	–0.1
Tropea	+0630	+0630	+0600	+0600	–0.6	–0.4	–0.2	–0.1
STRAIT OF MESSINA								
Villa San Giovanni	+0120	+0120	+0120	+0120	–0.8	–0.5	–0.2	0.0
Reggio Calabria	+0020	+0020	+0040	+0040	–0.8	–0.5	–0.2	–0.1
Taormina	+0010	+0010	+0030	+0030	–0.7	–0.5	–0.2	–0.1
Messina	–0230	–0230	–0050	–0050	–0.8	–0.5	–0.2	–0.1
Capo Peloro	+0620	+0620	+0650	+0650	–0.7	–0.5	–0.1	0.0
LIPARI ISLANDS								
Lipari	+0620	+0620	+0640	+0640	–0.6	–0.4	–0.2	–0.1
Sicily								
Milazzo	+0630	+0630	+0610	+0610	–0.6	–0.4	–0.2	–0.1
Palermo	–0615	–0615	+0630	+0630	–0.6	–0.4	–0.2	–0.1
Marsala	+0615	+0615	+0640	+0640	–0.7	–0.5	–0.2	0.0
Mazara del Vallo	+0240	+0240	+0230	+0230	–0.8	–0.5	–0.2	0.0
Porto Empedocle	+0050	+0050	+0100	+0100	–0.8	–0.5	–0.2	0.0
Catania	+0025	+0025	+0500	+0050	–0.8	–0.5	–0.2	–0.1
MALTA								
Valletta	+0050	+0050	+0025	+0025	–0.6	–0.4	0.0	0.1
ITALY								
GOLFO DI TARANTO								
Taranto	+0045	+0045	+0045	+0045	–0.7	–0.5	–0.1	0.0
Otranto	+0050	+0050	+0050	+0050	–0.7	–0.5	–0.1	0.0
GIBRALTAR	0000	0600	0300	0900	1.0	0.7	0.3	0.1
	1200	1800	1500	2100				

(Zone–0200)

Place	High water		Low water		MHWS	MHWN	MLWN	MLWS
GREECE								
Pandeleimon	+0119	+0119	–	–	–0.6	–0.3	0.0	+0.2
Galaxidhion	+0225	+0225	–	–	–0.4	–0.3	–0.1	0.0
Korinthos (Corinth)	+0230	+0230	–	–	–0.2	–0.1	+0.1	+0.1
Evipos Strait								
Khalkis, S side	+0110	+0110	–	–	–0.4	–0.2	+0.1	+0.1
Khalkis, N side	+0222	+0222	–	–	–0.2	–0.2	0.0	–0.1
Dhiavlos Knimidhos	+0703	+0703	–	–	–0.2	–0.2	0.0	–0.0
Volos	+0705	+0705	–	–	–0.3	–0.2	0.0	–0.0
Thessaloniki	+0141	+0141	–	–	–0.5	–0.3	0.0	+0.1

Place	*Difference* *High water*		*Low water*		*MHWS*	*Height differences (m)* *MHWN*	*MLWN*	*MLWS*
TURKEY								
Aydincik Limani	+0020	+0020	–	–	–0.8	–0.6	–0.3	–0.2
Ayvalik	+0102	+0102	–	–	–0.8	–0.6	–0.3	–0.2
Izmir (Smyrna)	+0646	+0646	–	–	–0.2	–0.2	–0.0	–0.1
GREECE								
Nisos Leros	–0250	–0250	–0225	–0225	–0.9	–0.6	–0.2	0.0
Nisos Astipalaia	–0310	–0310	–0245	–0245	–0.8	–0.6	–0.2	0.0
Nisos Kos	–0400	–0400	–0335	–0335	–0.8	–0.6	–0.2	0.0
Nisos Simi	–0400	–0400	–0340	–0340	–0.8	–0.6	–0.2	0.0
Rodhos (Rhodes)	–0440	–0440	–0415	–0415	–0.7	–0.5	–0.2	0.0
Lindhos	–0445	–0445	–0420	–0420	–0.7	–0.5	–0.2	0.0
Kastellorizou	–0450	–0450	–0430	–0430	–0.6	–0.4	–0.1	+0.1
CYPRUS								
Dhavlos	–0457	–0457	–0410	–0500	–0.4	–0.2	+0.1	+0.2
Kyrenia	–0450	–0525	–0446	–0446	–0.4	–0.2	+0.1	+0.1
Limassol	–0510	–0510	–0440	–0440	–0.5	–0.3	0.0	+0.1
Famagusta	–0510	–0510	–0445	–0445	–0.4	–0.2	+0.1	+0.1
GIBRALTAR	0800	1100	0100	0500	1.0	0.7	0.3	0.1
	2000	2300	1300	1700				
LEBANON								
Tripoli	–0442	–0442	–	–	–0.4	–0.3	0.0	0.0
Beirut	–0456	–0456	–	–	–0.6	–0.4	–0.1	0.0
Sidon	–0450	–0450	–0400	–0400	–0.4	–0.2	0.0	+0.1
ISRAEL								
Haifa	–0505	–0505	–	–	–0.4	–0.3	–0.2	–0.1
Ashdod	–0505	–0505	–	–	–0.4	–0.3	–0.2	–0.1
EGYPT								
Port Said	–0630	–0410	–0520	–0410	–0.3	–0.2	+0.2	+0.2
El Iskandariya (Alexandria)	–0435	–0435	–0440	–	–0.5	–0.4	–0.2	–0.1
Salum	–0449	–0449	–	–	–0.8	–0.5	–0.1	0.0
LIBYA								
Bardia	–0510	–0510	–0450	–0450	–0.8	–0.6	–0.2	0.0
Mersa Tobruk	–	–	–	–			Negligible	
Mersa el Brega	+0110	+0110	+0135	+0135	–0.6	–0.3	0.0	+0.1
Misurata	+0100	+0100	+0130	+0130	–0.5	–0.3	0.0	+0.2
Tarabulus (Tripoli)	+0124	+0124	+0154	+0154	–0.5	–0.4	–0.1	0.0

9.2 TIDAL CURVES (GIBRALTAR)

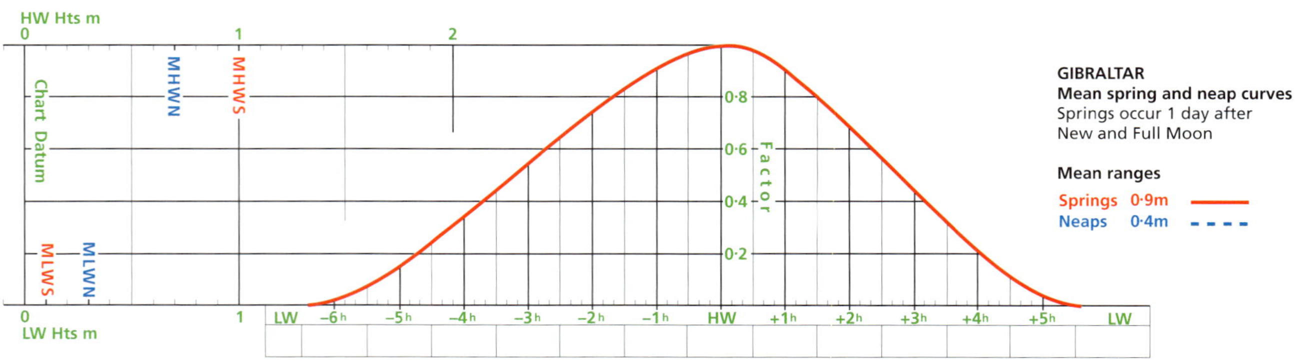

Tidal Prediction Programmes

For those who have a laptop on board there are a number of tidal prediction programmes that can be purchased. Amongst some of the more popular are *Autotide* (Linden), *Totaltide* (UKHO) and *Tidecomp* (Pangolin). Alternatively you can use some of the shareware around such as WXTide. Try searching the web for 'WXTide32' or 'WXTide' for any new support pages. To download, try any of the following sites where WXTide32 can currently be downloaded:
www.simtel.net/simtel.net has FTP servers world-wide, search for 'wxtide' in the Win95/98 – Science collection.

9.3 GIBRALTAR TIDES 2015

Gibraltar tide tables for 2016 will be included in the Mediterranean Almanac Supplement to be published at the end of 2015. This is available from **www.imray.com**

Subtract 1 hour for UT. Summer time (29.3.2015 to 25.10.2015) add 1 hour

GIBRALTAR — GIBRALTAR

LAT 36°08′N LONG 5°21′W

TIME ZONE **-0100**

TIMES AND HEIGHTS OF HIGH AND LOW WATERS

YEAR **2015**

JANUARY

Day	Time	m	Time	m	Time	m	Time	m
1 TH	0004	0.8	0554	0.2	1221	0.8	1829	0.2
2 F	0102	0.8	0645	0.2	1313	0.9	1915	0.1
3 SA	0151	0.8	0728	0.1	1400	0.9	1956	0.1
4 SU	0235	0.9	0808	0.1	1443	0.9	2034	0.1
5 M	0315	0.9	0846	0.1	1524	0.9	○ 2111	0.1
6 TU	0352	0.9	0923	0.1	1603	0.9	2145	0.1
7 W	0428	0.9	0959	0.1	1639	0.9	2218	0.1
8 TH	0501	0.9	1034	0.1	1714	0.8	2250	0.1
9 F	0534	0.8	1109	0.1	1749	0.8	2322	0.1
10 SA	0608	0.8	1145	0.2	1825	0.8	2356	0.2
11 SU	0646	0.8	1225	0.2	1905	0.7		
12 M	0033	0.2	0730	0.7	1315	0.3	1951	0.7
13 TU	0122	0.3	0821	0.7	1417	0.3	☾ 2046	0.7
14 W	0230	0.3	0921	0.7	1534	0.3	2152	0.7
15 TH	0359	0.3	1031	0.7	1653	0.3	2309	0.7
16 F	0516	0.3	1141	0.7	1754	0.2		
17 SA	0016	0.7	0611	0.2	1239	0.8	1843	0.1
18 SU	0111	0.8	0656	0.2	1331	0.9	1927	0.1
19 M	0200	0.9	0740	0.1	1420	0.9	2011	0.0
20 TU	0246	1.0	0825	0.0	1508	1.0	● 2055	0.0
21 W	0332	1.0	0910	0.0	1555	1.0	2139	0.0
22 TH	0417	1.0	0956	0.0	1641	1.0	2222	0.0
23 F	0502	1.0	1041	0.0	1727	1.0	2305	0.0
24 SA	0548	1.0	1128	0.0	1815	1.0	2350	0.0
25 SU	0637	1.0	1218	0.1	1906	0.9		
26 M	0039	0.1	0730	0.9	1314	0.2	2002	0.8
27 TU	0137	0.2	0828	0.8	1421	0.2	☽ 2105	0.7
28 W	0249	0.2	0935	0.8	1545	0.2	2221	0.7
29 TH	0420	0.3	1052	0.7	1719	0.2	2345	0.7
30 F	0541	0.2	1206	0.8	1823	0.2		
31 SA	0052	0.7	0637	0.2	1304	0.8	1909	0.2

FEBRUARY

Day	Time	m	Time	m	Time	m	Time	m
1 SU	0144	0.8	0720	0.2	1352	0.8	1948	0.1
2 M	0226	0.8	0758	0.1	1434	0.8	2024	0.1
3 TU	0304	0.8	0834	0.1	1512	0.9	2058	0.1
4 W	0338	0.9	0909	0.1	1547	0.9	○ 2130	0.0
5 TH	0409	0.9	0943	0.1	1621	0.9	2200	0.0
6 F	0439	0.9	1015	0.1	1652	0.9	2229	0.1
7 SA	0508	0.9	1046	0.1	1723	0.8	2258	0.1
8 SU	0538	0.8	1117	0.1	1756	0.8	2326	0.1
9 M	0611	0.8	1150	0.1	1831	0.8	2357	0.2
10 TU	0649	0.8	1227	0.2	1913	0.7		
11 W	0034	0.2	0736	0.7	1318	0.2	2004	0.7
12 TH	0126	0.3	0833	0.7	1431	0.3	☾ 2107	0.6
13 F	0249	0.3	0945	0.7	1610	0.3	2225	0.6
14 SA	0439	0.3	1107	0.7	1733	0.2	2347	0.7
15 SU	0552	0.2	1218	0.8	1828	0.1		
16 M	0051	0.8	0644	0.1	1315	0.8	1915	0.0
17 TU	0143	0.9	0730	0.1	1406	0.9	1959	0.0
18 W	0231	0.9	0815	0.0	1454	1.0	2043	-0.1
19 TH	0317	1.0	0900	-0.1	1541	1.0	● 2126	-0.1
20 F	0402	1.0	0945	-0.1	1627	1.0	2208	-0.1
21 SA	0446	1.1	1029	-0.1	1712	1.0	2249	-0.1
22 SU	0531	1.0	1112	0.0	1759	1.0	2330	0.0
23 M	0617	1.0	1156	0.0	1848	0.9		
24 TU	0014	0.1	0707	0.9	1245	0.1	1940	0.8
25 W	0105	0.2	0802	0.8	1344	0.2	☽ 2039	0.7
26 TH	0211	0.2	0906	0.7	1507	0.3	2151	0.7
27 F	0346	0.3	1025	0.7	1658	0.3	2320	0.7
28 SA	0526	0.3	1149	0.7	1810	0.2		

MARCH

Day	Time	m	Time	m	Time	m	Time	m
1 SU	0035	0.7	0624	0.2	1252	0.7	1854	0.2
2 M	0127	0.8	0706	0.2	1339	0.8	1931	0.1
3 TU	0208	0.8	0742	0.1	1418	0.8	2004	0.1
4 W	0243	0.8	0816	0.1	1453	0.8	2036	0.1
5 TH	0315	0.9	0849	0.1	1526	0.9	○ 2107	0.1
6 F	0344	0.9	0921	0.0	1558	0.9	2136	0.0
7 SA	0413	0.9	0952	0.0	1628	0.9	2205	0.1
8 SU	0441	0.9	1022	0.1	1658	0.9	2232	0.1
9 M	0510	0.9	1051	0.1	1730	0.8	2300	0.1
10 TU	0542	0.8	1121	0.1	1805	0.8	2330	0.1
11 W	0619	0.8	1156	0.2	1847	0.8		
12 TH	0005	0.2	0703	0.7	1240	0.2	1936	0.7
13 F	0053	0.2	0800	0.7	1347	0.3	☾ 2038	0.7
14 SA	0210	0.3	0911	0.7	1533	0.3	2153	0.7
15 SU	0407	0.3	1039	0.7	1708	0.2	2320	0.7
16 M	0534	0.2	1158	0.7	1809	0.1		
17 TU	0029	0.8	0629	0.1	1259	0.8	1857	0.1
18 W	0123	0.9	0716	0.0	1349	0.9	1941	0.0
19 TH	0211	0.9	0801	0.0	1437	1.0	2025	-0.1
20 F	0258	1.0	0846	-0.1	1524	1.0	● 2107	-0.1
21 SA	0343	1.0	0929	-0.1	1610	1.0	2149	-0.1
22 SU	0427	1.0	1011	-0.1	1654	1.0	2229	0.0
23 M	0511	1.0	1052	0.0	1740	1.0	2309	0.0
24 TU	0556	0.9	1133	0.0	1827	0.9	2350	0.1
25 W	0644	0.9	1217	0.1	1919	0.8		
26 TH	0037	0.2	0737	0.8	1311	0.2	2015	0.7
27 F	0138	0.3	0838	0.7	1425	0.3	☽ 2120	0.7
28 SA	0306	0.3	0951	0.7	1613	0.3	2242	0.7
29 SU	0452	0.3	1118	0.7	1735	0.3		
30 M	0000	0.7	0558	0.3	1226	0.7	1823	0.2
31 TU	0055	0.7	0640	0.2	1313	0.8	1900	0.2

APRIL

Day	Time	m	Time	m	Time	m	Time	m
1 W	0136	0.8	0716	0.2	1351	0.8	1933	0.2
2 TH	0210	0.8	0750	0.1	1426	0.8	2006	0.1
3 F	0242	0.9	0823	0.1	1458	0.9	2037	0.1
4 SA	0313	0.9	0855	0.1	1530	0.9	○ 2107	0.1
5 SU	0343	0.9	0926	0.1	1602	0.9	2137	0.1
6 M	0414	0.9	0957	0.1	1634	0.9	2206	0.1
7 TU	0445	0.9	1027	0.1	1708	0.9	2237	0.1
8 W	0519	0.9	1059	0.1	1745	0.9	2309	0.2
9 TH	0557	0.8	1135	0.2	1827	0.8	2347	0.2
10 F	0642	0.8	1219	0.2	1918	0.8		
11 SA	0037	0.3	0739	0.7	1325	0.3	2018	0.7
12 SU	0153	0.3	0849	0.7	1504	0.3	☾ 2130	0.7
13 M	0339	0.3	1013	0.7	1637	0.2	2252	0.7
14 TU	0508	0.2	1135	0.7	1742	0.2		
15 W	0002	0.8	0609	0.1	1238	0.8	1833	0.1
16 TH	0058	0.9	0658	0.1	1329	0.9	1918	0.0
17 F	0147	1.0	0743	0.0	1417	0.9	2001	0.0
18 SA	0234	1.0	0828	0.0	1504	1.0	● 2044	0.0
19 SU	0320	1.0	0911	-0.1	1549	1.0	2126	0.0
20 M	0405	1.0	0952	0.0	1635	1.0	2207	0.0
21 TU	0449	1.0	1032	0.0	1720	0.9	2247	0.1
22 W	0534	0.9	1111	0.1	1807	0.9	2328	0.1
23 TH	0621	0.9	1153	0.1	1856	0.8		
24 F	0013	0.2	0712	0.8	1241	0.2	1950	0.8
25 SA	0109	0.3	0809	0.7	1345	0.3	2049	0.7
26 SU	0223	0.3	0913	0.7	1510	0.3	☽ 2155	0.7
27 M	0353	0.3	1028	0.7	1635	0.3	2307	0.7
28 TU	0511	0.3	1140	0.7	1735	0.3		
29 W	0007	0.7	0602	0.2	1233	0.7	1819	0.2
30 TH	0052	0.8	0642	0.2	1315	0.8	1856	0.2

Subtract 1 hour for UT. Summer time (29.3.2015 to 25.10.2015) add 1 hour

GIBRALTAR — GIBRALTAR

LAT 36°08′N LONG 5°21′W

TIME ZONE **-0100** — TIMES AND HEIGHTS OF HIGH AND LOW WATERS — YEAR **2015**

MAY

Day	Time	m	Day	Time	m
1	0129	0.8	16	0122	0.9
	0718	0.2		0724	0.0
F	1351	0.8	SA	1356	0.9
	1930	0.2		1938	0.1
2	0204	0.9	17	0210	1.0
	0753	0.1		0809	0.0
SA	1426	0.9	SU	1443	0.9
	2003	0.2		2022	0.0
3	0238	0.9	18	0257	1.0
	0826	0.1		0852	0.0
SU	1500	0.9	M	1530	1.0
	2035	0.1	●	2104	0.0
4	0312	0.9	19	0343	1.0
	0900	0.1		0934	0.0
M	1535	0.9	TU	1615	0.9
○	2108	0.1		2146	0.1
5	0347	0.9	20	0428	0.9
	0933	0.1		1013	0.0
TU	1611	0.9	W	1700	0.9
	2142	0.1		2227	0.1
6	0423	0.9	21	0512	0.9
	1007	0.1		1052	0.1
W	1648	0.9	TH	1745	0.9
	2216	0.2		2307	0.1
7	0501	0.9	22	0558	0.9
	1042	0.1		1131	0.1
TH	1728	0.9	F	1832	0.8
	2254	0.2		2351	0.2
8	0542	0.9	23	0646	0.8
	1121	0.2		1214	0.2
F	1812	0.9	SA	1921	0.8
	2337	0.2			
9	0629	0.8	24	0039	0.2
	1208	0.2		0736	0.7
SA	1904	0.8	SU	1306	0.3
				2013	0.8
10	0030	0.3	25	0139	0.3
	0725	0.8		0831	0.7
SU	1312	0.2	M	1411	0.3
	2002	0.8	☽	2107	0.7
11	0142	0.3	26	0249	0.3
	0831	0.7		0931	0.7
M	1436	0.3	TU	1523	0.3
☾	2109	0.8		2205	0.7
12	0310	0.3	27	0404	0.3
	0948	0.7		1038	0.7
TU	1559	0.2	W	1633	0.3
	2223	0.8		2306	0.7
13	0435	0.2	28	0511	0.3
	1108	0.8		1140	0.7
W	1709	0.2	TH	1730	0.3
	2333	0.8		2359	0.8
14	0543	0.2	29	0602	0.2
	1213	0.8		1230	0.8
TH	1805	0.1	F	1815	0.3
15	0031	0.9	30	0043	0.8
	0637	0.1		0643	0.2
F	1307	0.9	SA	1313	0.8
	1853	0.1		1853	0.2
			31	0124	0.8
				0721	0.2
			SU	1352	0.8
				1929	0.2

JUNE

Day	Time	m	Day	Time	m
1	0203	0.9	16	0238	0.9
	0757	0.1		0837	0.0
M	1430	0.9	TU	1514	0.9
	2005	0.2	●	2047	0.1
2	0242	0.9	17	0324	0.9
	0834	0.1		0917	0.0
TU	1509	0.9	W	1558	0.9
○	2042	0.2		2128	0.1
3	0323	0.9	18	0409	0.9
	0911	0.1		0956	0.1
W	1550	0.9	TH	1641	0.9
	2120	0.2		2208	0.1
4	0404	1.0	19	0452	0.9
	0949	0.1		1032	0.1
TH	1630	1.0	F	1723	0.9
	2200	0.2		2247	0.1
5	0446	0.9	20	0533	0.9
	1029	0.1		1108	0.1
F	1713	1.0	SA	1804	0.9
	2243	0.2		2327	0.2
6	0530	0.9	21	0616	0.8
	1111	0.1		1145	0.2
SA	1758	0.9	SU	1846	0.8
	2329	0.2			
7	0618	0.9	22	0008	0.2
	1158	0.2		0659	0.8
SU	1849	0.9	M	1227	0.2
				1929	0.8
8	0022	0.2	23	0056	0.3
	0712	0.8		0746	0.7
M	1256	0.2	TU	1315	0.3
	1944	0.9		2015	0.8
9	0126	0.2	24	0150	0.3
	0814	0.8		0836	0.7
TU	1406	0.2	W	1413	0.3
☾	2046	0.9	☽	2104	0.7
10	0240	0.2	25	0253	0.3
	0923	0.8		0932	0.7
W	1520	0.2	TH	1519	0.3
	2153	0.8		2159	0.7
11	0400	0.2	26	0404	0.3
	1038	0.8		1036	0.7
TH	1633	0.2	F	1630	0.3
	2303	0.9		2259	0.7
12	0516	0.2	27	0513	0.3
	1148	0.8		1140	0.7
F	1738	0.2	SA	1730	0.3
				2355	0.8
13	0005	0.9	28	0607	0.2
	0618	0.1		1233	0.8
SA	1247	0.8	SU	1818	0.3
	1832	0.1			
14	0100	0.9	29	0045	0.8
	0709	0.1		0650	0.2
SU	1338	0.9	M	1319	0.8
	1919	0.1		1859	0.2
15	0150	0.9	30	0131	0.9
	0754	0.1		0731	0.1
M	1427	0.9	TU	1403	0.9
	2004	0.1		1939	0.2

JULY

Day	Time	m	Day	Time	m
1	0216	0.9	16	0309	0.9
	0810	0.1		0900	0.1
W	1446	0.9	TH	1541	0.9
	2020	0.1	●	2111	0.1
2	0301	1.0	17	0350	0.9
	0851	0.1		0935	0.1
TH	1530	1.0	F	1620	0.9
○	2103	0.1		2148	0.1
3	0347	1.0	18	0429	0.9
	0932	0.1		1009	0.1
F	1613	1.0	SA	1656	0.9
	2147	0.1		2224	0.1
4	0431	1.0	19	0506	0.9
	1014	0.1		1041	0.1
SA	1657	1.0	SU	1730	0.9
	2231	0.1		2300	0.1
5	0517	1.0	20	0542	0.9
	1057	0.1		1114	0.1
SU	1742	1.0	M	1805	0.9
	2318	0.1		2335	0.2
6	0604	1.0	21	0619	0.8
	1143	0.1		1147	0.2
M	1831	1.0	TU	1840	0.8
7	0008	0.2	22	0013	0.2
	0656	0.9		0657	0.8
TU	1235	0.2	W	1224	0.2
	1923	0.9		1919	0.8
8	0105	0.2	23	0056	0.3
	0754	0.9		0742	0.7
W	1334	0.2	TH	1307	0.3
☾	2021	0.9		2003	0.8
9	0210	0.2	24	0148	0.3
	0858	0.8		0833	0.7
TH	1443	0.2	F	1405	0.3
	2124	0.9	☽	2055	0.7
10	0326	0.2	25	0255	0.3
	1010	0.8		0934	0.7
F	1600	0.3	SA	1521	0.4
	2234	0.8		2157	0.7
11	0452	0.2	26	0418	0.3
	1126	0.8		1046	0.7
SA	1716	0.2	SU	1643	0.3
	2343	0.8		2307	0.8
12	0604	0.2	27	0531	0.3
	1231	0.8		1155	0.7
SU	1817	0.2	M	1747	0.3
13	0043	0.9	28	0011	0.8
	0658	0.2		0623	0.2
M	1327	0.9	TU	1251	0.8
	1907	0.2		1835	0.2
14	0136	0.9	29	0105	0.9
	0742	0.1		0707	0.1
TU	1415	0.9	W	1339	0.9
	1950	0.1		1919	0.2
15	0224	0.9	30	0155	0.9
	0822	0.1		0749	0.1
W	1500	0.9	TH	1425	1.0
	2032	0.1		2003	0.1
			31	0243	1.0
				0831	0.1
			F	1510	1.0
			○	2047	0.1

AUGUST

Day	Time	m	Day	Time	m
1	0329	1.0	16	0403	0.9
	0914	0.0		0941	0.1
SA	1555	1.1	SU	1625	1.0
	2132	0.1		2158	0.1
2	0415	1.1	17	0435	0.9
	0957	0.0		1011	0.1
SU	1639	1.1	M	1654	0.9
	2217	0.0		2230	0.1
3	0501	1.1	18	0506	0.9
	1039	0.0		1040	0.1
M	1723	1.1	TU	1724	0.9
	2302	0.1		2302	0.2
4	0548	1.0	19	0538	0.9
	1123	0.1		1110	0.2
TU	1810	1.1	W	1754	0.9
	2349	0.1		2334	0.2
5	0638	1.0	20	0613	0.8
	1210	0.1		1141	0.2
W	1900	1.0	TH	1829	0.9
6	0039	0.2	21	0009	0.2
	0732	0.9		0653	0.8
TH	1303	0.2	F	1218	0.3
	1954	0.9		1910	0.8
7	0139	0.2	22	0053	0.3
	0834	0.8		0744	0.8
F	1408	0.3	SA	1305	0.3
☾	2056	0.9	☽	2002	0.8
8	0254	0.3	23	0154	0.3
	0945	0.8		0845	0.7
SA	1529	0.3	SU	1418	0.4
	2207	0.8		2106	0.8
9	0431	0.3	24	0326	0.3
	1107	0.8		0959	0.7
SU	1659	0.3	M	1600	0.4
	2325	0.8		2223	0.8
10	0554	0.3	25	0500	0.3
	1220	0.8		1119	0.8
M	1806	0.3	TU	1721	0.3
				2342	0.8
11	0033	0.8	26	0601	0.2
	0646	0.2		1224	0.8
TU	1317	0.9	W	1816	0.2
	1855	0.2			
12	0126	0.9	27	0044	0.9
	0727	0.2		0646	0.2
W	1403	0.9	TH	1317	0.9
	1936	0.2		1901	0.2
13	0211	0.9	28	0136	1.0
	0804	0.1		0729	0.1
TH	1443	0.9	F	1404	1.0
	2014	0.2		1946	0.1
14	0251	0.9	29	0224	1.0
	0837	0.1		0811	0.0
F	1520	0.9	SA	1449	1.1
●	2050	0.1	○	2030	0.0
15	0328	0.9	30	0311	1.1
	0910	0.1		0853	0.0
SA	1553	1.0	SU	1534	1.1
	2124	0.1		2114	0.0
			31	0357	1.1
				0936	0.0
			M	1618	1.2
				2158	0.0

136 IMRAY MEDITERRANEAN ALMANAC 2015-16

Subtract 1 hour for UT.
Summer time (29.3.2015 to 25.10.2015) add 1 hour

GIBRALTAR — GIBRALTAR

LAT 36°08′N LONG 5°21′W

TIME ZONE **-0100** | TIMES AND HEIGHTS OF HIGH AND LOW WATERS | YEAR **2015**

SEPTEMBER

Day	Time	m	Day	Time	m
1 TU	0442	1.1	16 W	0433	1.0
	1018	0.0		1009	0.2
	1702	1.1		1648	1.0
	2242	0.0		2230	0.2
2 W	0528	1.1	17 TH	0503	0.9
	1100	0.1		1038	0.2
	1747	1.1		1718	0.9
	2326	0.1		2300	0.2
3 TH	0616	1.0	18 F	0537	0.9
	1144	0.2		1108	0.2
	1835	1.0		1751	0.9
				2333	0.2
4 F	0012	0.2	19 SA	0617	0.9
	0709	0.9		1142	0.3
	1233	0.2		1832	0.9
	1928	0.9			
5 SA	0107	0.3	20 SU	0012	0.3
	0809	0.9		0706	0.8
	1335	0.3		1226	0.4
☾	2028	0.9		1923	0.8
6 SU	0219	0.3	21 M	0108	0.3
	0919	0.8		0808	0.8
	1500	0.4		1336	0.4
	2141	0.8	☽	2029	0.8
7 M	0406	0.4	22 TU	0245	0.4
	1045	0.8		0921	0.8
	1640	0.4		1526	0.4
	2308	0.8		2149	0.8
8 TU	0537	0.3	23 W	0431	0.3
	1204	0.8		1045	0.8
	1751	0.3		1656	0.3
				2317	0.8
9 W	0021	0.8	24 TH	0537	0.3
	0627	0.3		1157	0.9
	1300	0.9		1755	0.3
	1837	0.3			
10 TH	0113	0.9	25 F	0024	0.9
	0705	0.2		0625	0.2
	1343	0.9		1253	1.0
	1915	0.2		1842	0.2
11 F	0153	0.9	26 SA	0117	1.0
	0738	0.2		0707	0.1
	1419	1.0		1340	1.1
	1950	0.2		1926	0.1
12 SA	0229	0.9	27 SU	0204	1.1
	0809	0.2		0749	0.1
	1452	1.0		1426	1.1
	2023	0.2		2010	0.0
13 SU	0302	1.0	28 M	0250	1.1
	0840	0.1		0831	0.0
	1522	1.0		1511	1.2
●	2056	0.1	O	2054	0.0
14 M	0333	1.0	29 TU	0336	1.1
	0910	0.1		0913	0.0
	1551	1.0		1555	1.2
	2129	0.1		2137	0.0
15 TU	0403	1.0	30 W	0420	1.1
	0940	0.1		0954	0.1
	1619	1.0		1639	1.2
	2200	0.1		2219	0.1

OCTOBER

Day	Time	m	Day	Time	m
1 TH	0506	1.1	16 F	0436	1.0
	1036	0.1		1011	0.2
	1724	1.1		1651	1.0
	2301	0.1		2233	0.2
2 F	0553	1.0	17 SA	0511	1.0
	1119	0.2		1042	0.3
	1810	1.0		1727	0.9
	2344	0.2		2306	0.2
3 SA	0644	0.9	18 SU	0552	0.9
	1206	0.3		1118	0.3
	1902	0.9		1808	0.9
				2345	0.3
4 SU	0034	0.3	19 M	0640	0.9
	0742	0.9		1203	0.4
	1305	0.4		1859	0.8
☾	2001	0.8			
5 M	0142	0.4	20 TU	0038	0.3
	0851	0.8		0740	0.8
	1428	0.4		1312	0.4
	2112	0.8	☽	2003	0.8
6 TU	0326	0.4	21 W	0211	0.4
	1012	0.8		0851	0.8
	1608	0.4		1457	0.4
	2240	0.8		2121	0.8
7 W	0502	0.4	22 TH	0358	0.4
	1133	0.8		1012	0.8
	1722	0.4		1627	0.3
	2358	0.8		2250	0.8
8 TH	0557	0.3	23 F	0509	0.3
	1230	0.9		1128	0.9
	1809	0.3		1731	0.3
9 F	0049	0.9	24 SA	0001	0.9
	0634	0.3		0601	0.2
	1312	0.9		1227	1.0
	1847	0.3		1820	0.2
10 SA	0128	0.9	25 SU	0056	1.0
	0707	0.2		0645	0.1
	1347	1.0		1316	1.1
	1921	0.2		1906	0.1
11 SU	0201	1.0	26 M	0143	1.0
	0739	0.2		0727	0.1
	1418	1.0		1402	1.1
	1954	0.2		1950	0.0
12 M	0232	1.0	27 TU	0229	1.1
	0810	0.2		0809	0.1
	1448	1.0		1447	1.1
	2027	0.2	O	2033	0.0
13 TU	0302	1.0	28 W	0315	1.1
	0840	0.2		0851	0.1
	1518	1.0		1532	1.1
●	2100	0.1		2116	0.0
14 W	0333	1.0	29 TH	0400	1.1
	0910	0.2		0933	0.1
	1548	1.0		1617	1.1
	2131	0.2		2158	0.1
15 TH	0404	1.0	30 F	0445	1.1
	0940	0.2		1015	0.1
	1619	1.0		1702	1.1
	2202	0.2		2239	0.1
			31 SA	0531	1.0
				1057	0.2
				1748	1.0
				2321	0.2

NOVEMBER

Day	Time	m	Day	Time	m
1 SU	0620	0.9	16 M	0535	1.0
	1143	0.3		1105	0.3
	1839	0.9		1754	0.9
				2331	0.3
2 M	0007	0.3	17 TU	0623	0.9
	0715	0.9		1152	0.3
	1239	0.3		1844	0.9
	1935	0.8			
3 TU	0107	0.4	18 W	0023	0.3
	0818	0.8		0719	0.9
	1352	0.4		1258	0.3
☾	2039	0.8		1945	0.8
4 W	0232	0.4	19 TH	0142	0.3
	0928	0.8		0826	0.8
	1520	0.4		1427	0.4
	2154	0.8	☽	2057	0.8
5 TH	0405	0.4	20 F	0317	0.3
	1044	0.8		0940	0.8
	1637	0.4		1553	0.3
	2314	0.8		2219	0.8
6 F	0512	0.4	21 SA	0435	0.3
	1147	0.8		1056	0.9
	1732	0.3		1703	0.2
				2335	0.9
7 SA	0012	0.8	22 SU	0535	0.2
	0558	0.3		1159	0.9
	1233	0.9		1800	0.2
	1814	0.3			
8 SU	0055	0.9	23 M	0034	0.9
	0635	0.3		0624	0.2
	1310	0.9		1252	1.0
	1851	0.2		1848	0.1
9 M	0130	0.9	24 TU	0124	1.0
	0709	0.2		0708	0.1
	1344	1.0		1340	1.0
	1926	0.2		1934	0.1
10 TU	0203	1.0	25 W	0211	1.0
	0741	0.2		0751	0.1
	1416	1.0		1427	1.1
	2000	0.2	O	2018	0.0
11 W	0235	1.0	26 TH	0257	1.0
	0813	0.2		0834	0.1
	1449	1.0		1513	1.1
●	2034	0.2		2101	0.0
12 TH	0307	1.0	27 F	0343	1.0
	0845	0.2		0917	0.1
	1523	1.0		1559	1.0
	2107	0.2		2142	0.1
13 F	0341	1.0	28 SA	0428	1.0
	0917	0.2		0959	0.1
	1557	1.0		1644	1.0
	2140	0.2		2223	0.1
14 SA	0416	1.0	29 SU	0512	1.0
	0950	0.2		1041	0.2
	1633	1.0		1730	0.9
	2214	0.2		2303	0.2
15 SU	0454	1.0	30 M	0558	0.9
	1025	0.2		1125	0.2
	1711	1.0		1817	0.9
	2250	0.2		2345	0.2

DECEMBER

Day	Time	m	Day	Time	m
1 TU	0648	0.9	16 W	0610	0.9
	1214	0.3		1146	0.2
	1907	0.8		1834	0.9
2 W	0034	0.3	17 TH	0013	0.2
	0742	0.8		0702	0.9
	1314	0.3		1245	0.3
	2002	0.8		1929	0.8
3 TH	0138	0.3	18 F	0117	0.2
	0840	0.8		0803	0.9
	1426	0.4		1359	0.3
☾	2102	0.7	☽	2034	0.8
4 F	0256	0.4	19 SA	0235	0.3
	0943	0.8		0910	0.8
	1540	0.4		1518	0.3
	2210	0.7		2148	0.8
5 SA	0413	0.4	20 SU	0356	0.3
	1049	0.8		1024	0.8
	1646	0.3		1636	0.2
	2320	0.7		2307	0.8
6 SU	0515	0.3	21 M	0508	0.2
	1146	0.8		1133	0.9
	1740	0.3		1743	0.2
7 M	0015	0.8	22 TU	0015	0.8
	0602	0.3		0606	0.2
	1231	0.8		1233	0.9
	1823	0.2		1837	0.1
8 TU	0058	0.8	23 W	0110	0.9
	0641	0.3		0656	0.1
	1310	0.9		1324	0.9
	1901	0.2		1925	0.1
9 W	0135	0.9	24 TH	0200	0.9
	0716	0.2		0741	0.1
	1347	0.9		1413	1.0
	1938	0.2		2010	0.0
10 TH	0211	0.9	25 F	0247	0.9
	0750	0.2		0824	0.1
	1425	0.9		1500	1.0
	2013	0.1	O	2052	0.0
11 F	0247	1.0	26 SA	0332	1.0
	0824	0.2		0907	0.1
	1503	1.0		1546	1.0
●	2049	0.1		2133	0.0
12 SA	0324	1.0	27 SU	0415	0.9
	0859	0.2		0948	0.1
	1542	1.0		1630	0.9
	2125	0.1		2211	0.1
13 SU	0403	1.0	28 M	0457	0.9
	0936	0.2		1028	0.1
	1621	1.0		1713	0.9
	2202	0.1		2248	0.1
14 M	0442	1.0	29 TU	0538	0.9
	1015	0.2		1108	0.1
	1702	1.0		1755	0.9
	2241	0.1		2326	0.1
15 TU	0524	1.0	30 W	0620	0.8
	1057	0.2		1150	0.2
	1745	0.9		1838	0.8
	2323	0.2			
			31 TH	0005	0.2
				0704	0.8
				1237	0.2
				1923	0.8

10. Harbour information

Harbour information is arranged as follows. Not all harbours will have all the following entries depending on the type of harbour (e.g. some oil terminals unsuitable for yachts have their lights and VHF frequencies listed for completeness) and in a few cases because the data is not available (e.g. a marina under construction).

Data is arranged by country from Gibraltar and going clockwise around the Mediterranean to Morocco.

Data within a country with a long coastline and a large number of harbours is split up into sections of coast and/or islands, normally along the chapter divisions of the relevant Imray pilot for the country.

Data is arranged as follows:

Name of harbour Any alternative names are given in brackets.

Latitude and longitude Often the entrance light to the harbour in which case it will be mentioned in brackets after the latitude and longitude. If no light is mentioned it will be a latitude and longitude derived from some other source. If a waypoint is suffixed WGS84 it has been taken at the harbour entrance by the author. See cautions on using derived latitudes and longitudes with electronic position finding equipment (GPS).

Charts Admiralty chart number for the largest scale chart available is given first followed by the local hydrographic chart number (Spanish, French, etc.) for the largest scale chart available. Imray-Tetra chart numbers are also given for Italy, Greece and Turkey.

Distances Distance to the nearest adjacent harbours in nautical miles. The arrows indicate the previous or next harbour according to the layout in the almanac. Figures are rounded up in most cases as who knows how much or how little clearance is made by the individual navigator when rounding headlands, shoal water, reefs, etc.

Lights Harbour lights and any relevant nearby lights are given in standard abbreviated form. There is some duplication between lights listed with harbour information and *6.3 List of major lights*. This is so light information for the approach to a harbour is grouped with other relevant information for easy reference.

VHF Any relevant channels for a harbour are listed.

Navigation Lists any peculiarities or dangers to navigation in the immediate approach to a harbour.

Berths Details where to berth or where to report for a berth and the type of berth in a marina (laid moorings tailed to the quay or a buoy, finger pontoons, posts or large buoys) if known.

Visitors' berths With few exceptions most marinas have visitors' berths. Some marinas have visitors' berths numbered in three figures while others have just a few. There has been some ire expressed over the fact that yachts arriving in the high season cannot find a berth at a chosen marina and there has been some muttering about whether these berths exist at all. All visitors' berths listed in this book are obtained from the marina concerned and the number of visitors' berths is obtained from figures published or given by the marina.

What it is important to remember is that visitors' berths apply equally to local boats in transit as well as to boats from outside that country. A visitors' berth is for any boat not permanently berthed at the marina in question. The problem is compounded by the fact that some owners will often move their boat to a chosen marina somewhere else for two or three months in the high season. While this leaves a berth free in their normal marina where they have a permanent berth (and continue paying for it), it occupies one of the visitors' berths available at the marina where the boat is to be berthed for part of the high season. You don't need too many of these quasi-visiting boats to clutter up visitors' berths in the high season.

In our experience all marina managers go out of their way to find visiting yachts a berth even in high season. If at all possible try to arrange a berth in known crowded marinas in advance. If you intend to base yourself for a week or more in a marina in the high season then book ahead. Alternatively try to avoid popular parts of the coast in the high season from mid-June to mid-September.

Shelter Brief description of shelter and if untenable or uncomfortable with a particular wind direction.

Data Where relevant the total number of berths, number of berths allocated to visitors, maximum LOA (length overall) the harbour can accommodate, depths in metres from minimum to maximum.

Facilities If available: water, electricity (220 and 380V), WiFi, telephone connection, television connection, showers and toilets, fuel, travel-lift/crane/slipway in tons, yacht repairs, provisions and restaurants.

Remarks Any relevant comments such as work in progress, villages or towns nearby, etc.

Charge bands Under the *Data* section a charge band is given for most marinas and harbours. Prices for the different charge bands are given below, but it must be emphasised that charges change often and arbitrarily. The charge bands are intended to give an indication only. For weekly, monthly, and annual contracts prices come down on a sliding scale, often as much as 50% for an annual contract. Winter rates are usually much less than summer rates.

Charges given here are for a 12-metre yacht in the high season. The high season is a slippery item to define. At one time it used to be just July and August, but some marinas with an eye to bigger profits have been extending the high season either way so it now starts in April or May and may extend until the end of September or October. In general high season charges can be 2x and in some places 3x the low season rate. Winter rates are often much lower and are often negotiable for a 6-month stay.

Key to symbols used on plans

- depths in METRES
- shallow water with a depth of 1m or less
- rocks with less than 2 metres depth over them
- rock just below or on the surface
- a shoal or reef with the least depth shown
- wreck partially above water
- wreck
- dangerous wreck with depth over it
- eddies
- rock ballasting on a mole or breakwater
- above-water rocks
- cliffs
- church
- mosque
- windmill
- wind turbine
- chimney
- pine
- trees other than pine
- houses / buildings

- waypoint
- fish farm
- anchorage
- prohibited anchorage
- harbour with yacht berths
- yacht harbour / marina
- visitors' berths
- port of entry
- customs
- port police

- water
- electricity
- shower
- waste pump-out
- fuel
- travel-hoist

- post office
- tourist information
- airport
- castle
- ruins

- yacht berth
- local boats (usually shallow or reserved)
- beacon
- port hand buoy
- starboard hand buoy
- mooring buoy

Characteristics

- light
- lighthouse
- F. fixed
- Fl. flash
- Fl(2) group flash
- Oc. occulting
- R red
- G green
- W white
- M miles
- s sand
- m mud
- w weed
- r rock
- P.A position approximate

QUICK REFERENCE GUIDES

At the beginning of the chapter on each country there is a quick reference guide which relates to the harbours and anchorages listed in the main section for that country. The quick reference guide gives information with a classification of the shelter offered, mooring, whether fuel, water, provisions and restaurants exist, and an indication of mooring charges. Compressing information about a harbour or anchorage into such a framework is difficult and not a little clumsy but the list can be useful for route planning and as an instant memory aid to a harbour.

Key

Shelter
A Excellent
B Good with prevailing winds
C Reasonable shelter but uncomfortable and sometimes dangerous
O In settled weather only

Mooring
A Stern or bows-to
B Alongside
C Anchored off

Fuel
A On the quay
B Delivered by tanker or available nearby
O None or very limited

Water
A On the quay
B Delivered by tanker or available nearby
O None or very limited

Provisioning
A Excellent
B Most supplies can be obtained
C Meagre supplies
O None

Eating Out
A Excellent
B Average
C Poor
O None

Rating is an indication of the number of restaurants, not of quality.

Charge bands

Charges are for the daily high season rate for a 12m yacht. Prices are in Euros (€). For smaller or larger yachts, make an approximate guess-timate.

1.	No charge	
2.	Low cost	under €25
3.	Low–Medium cost	€26–40
4.	Medium–High cost	€41–55
5.	High cost	€55–70
6.	Very high cost	€70–100
6+.	Highest cost	over €100

GIBRALTAR STRAIT TIDAL STREAMS

EXPLANATION

The figures shown against the arrows are the mean rates at springs.

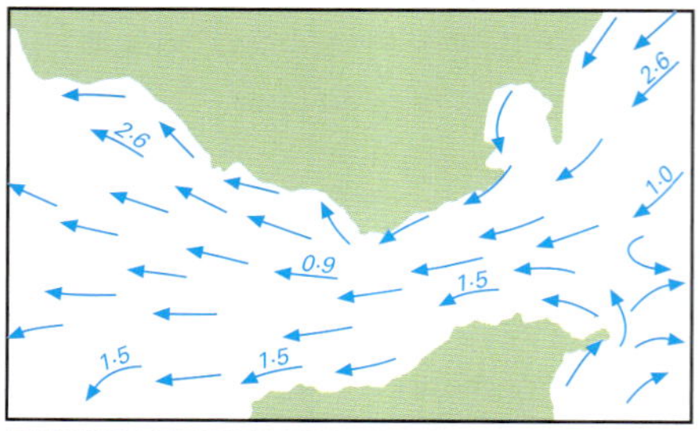

5 HOURS BEFORE HW GIBRALTAR

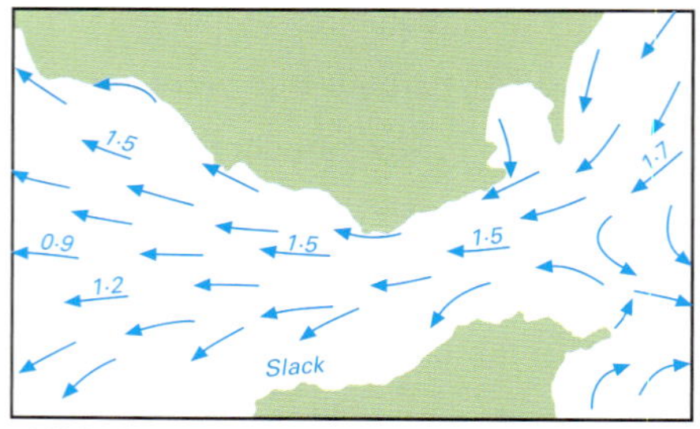

4 HOURS BEFORE HW GIBRALTAR

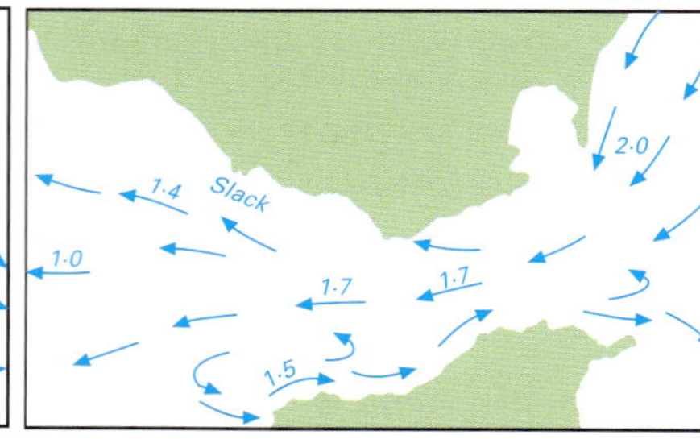

3 HOURS BEFORE HW GIBRALTAR

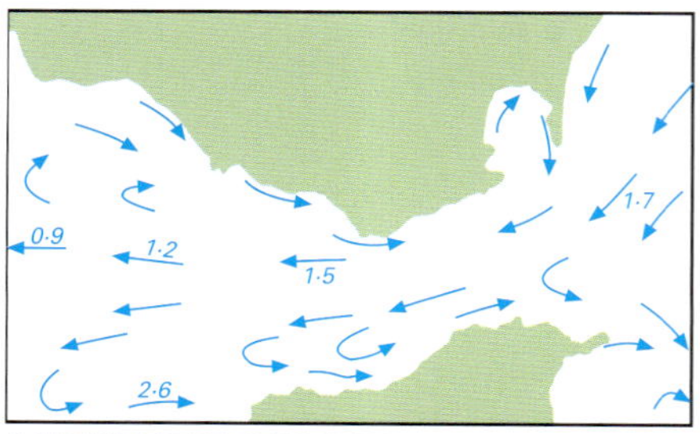

2 HOURS BEFORE HW GIBRALTAR

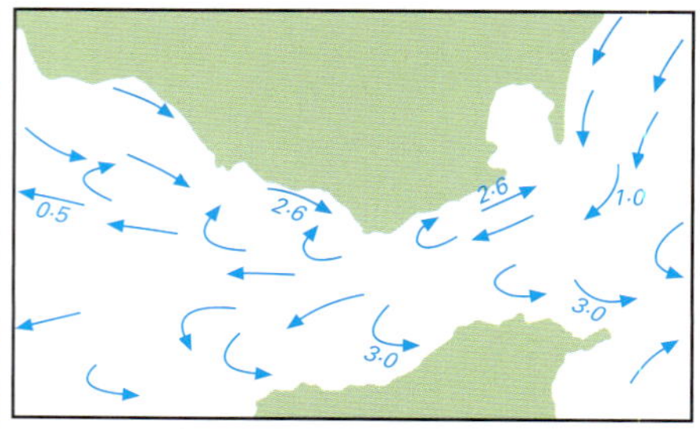

1 HOUR BEFORE HW GIBRALTAR

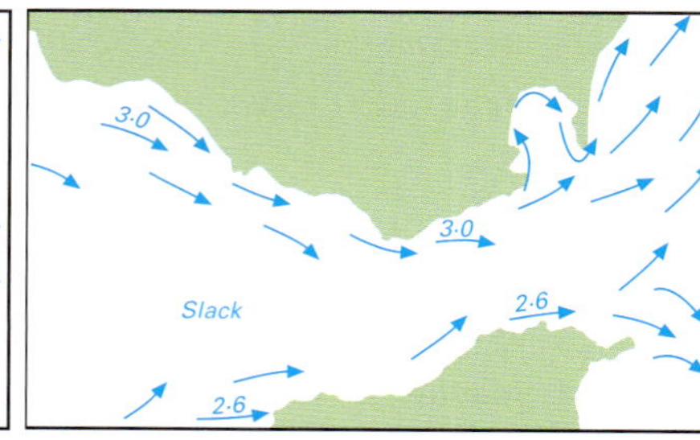

HW GIBRALTAR

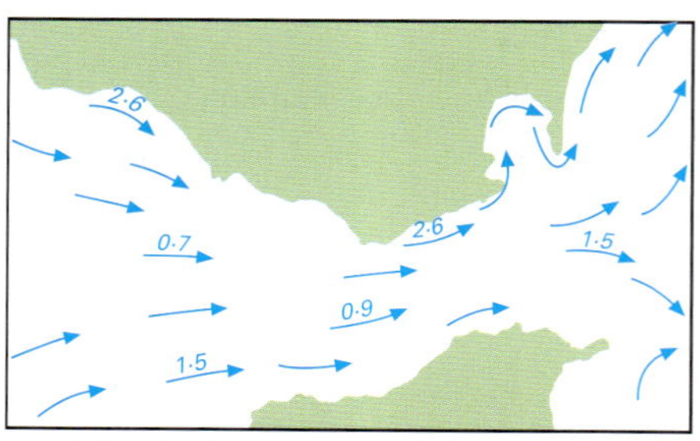

1 HOUR AFTER HW GIBRALTAR

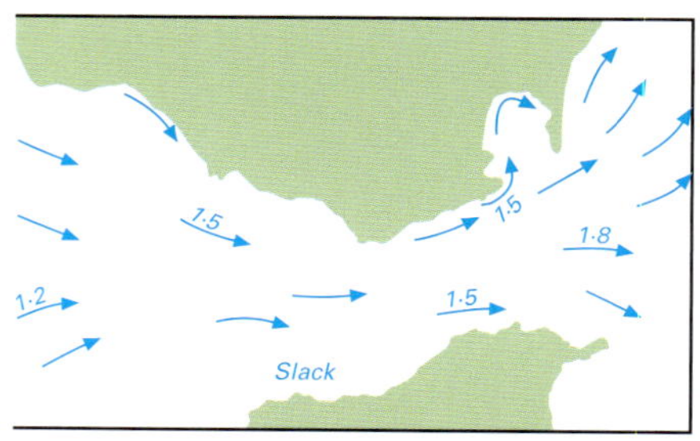

2 HOURS AFTER HW GIBRALTAR

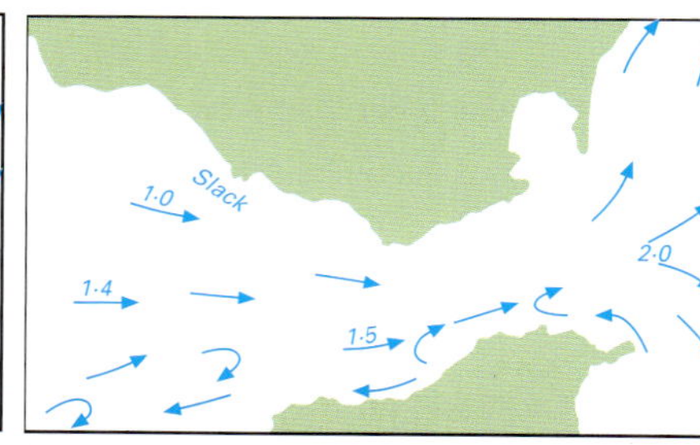

3 HOURS AFTER HW GIBRALTAR

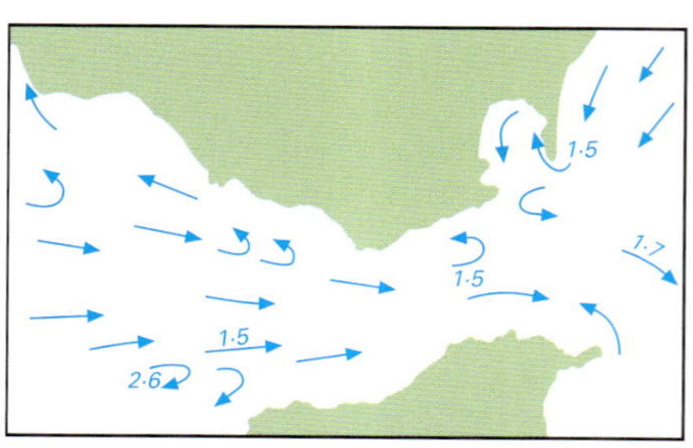

4 HOURS AFTER HW GIBRALTAR

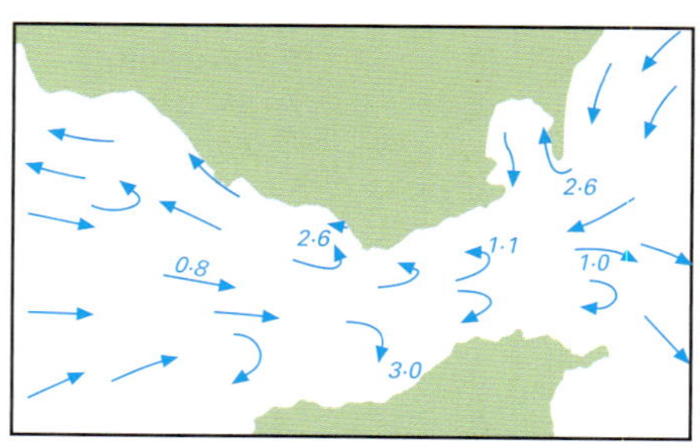

5 HOURS AFTER HW GIBRALTAR

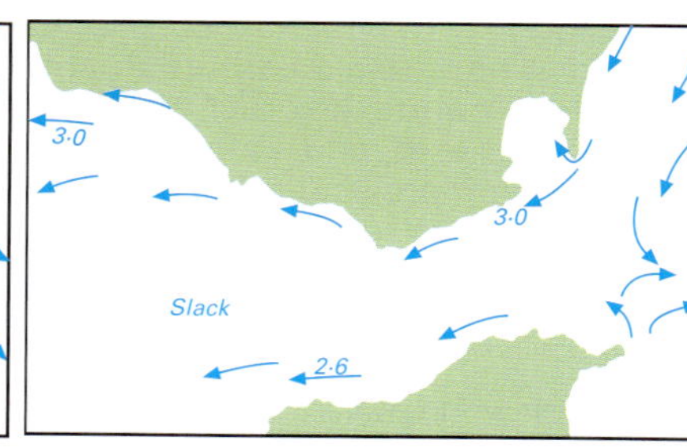

6 HOURS AFTER HW GIBRALTAR

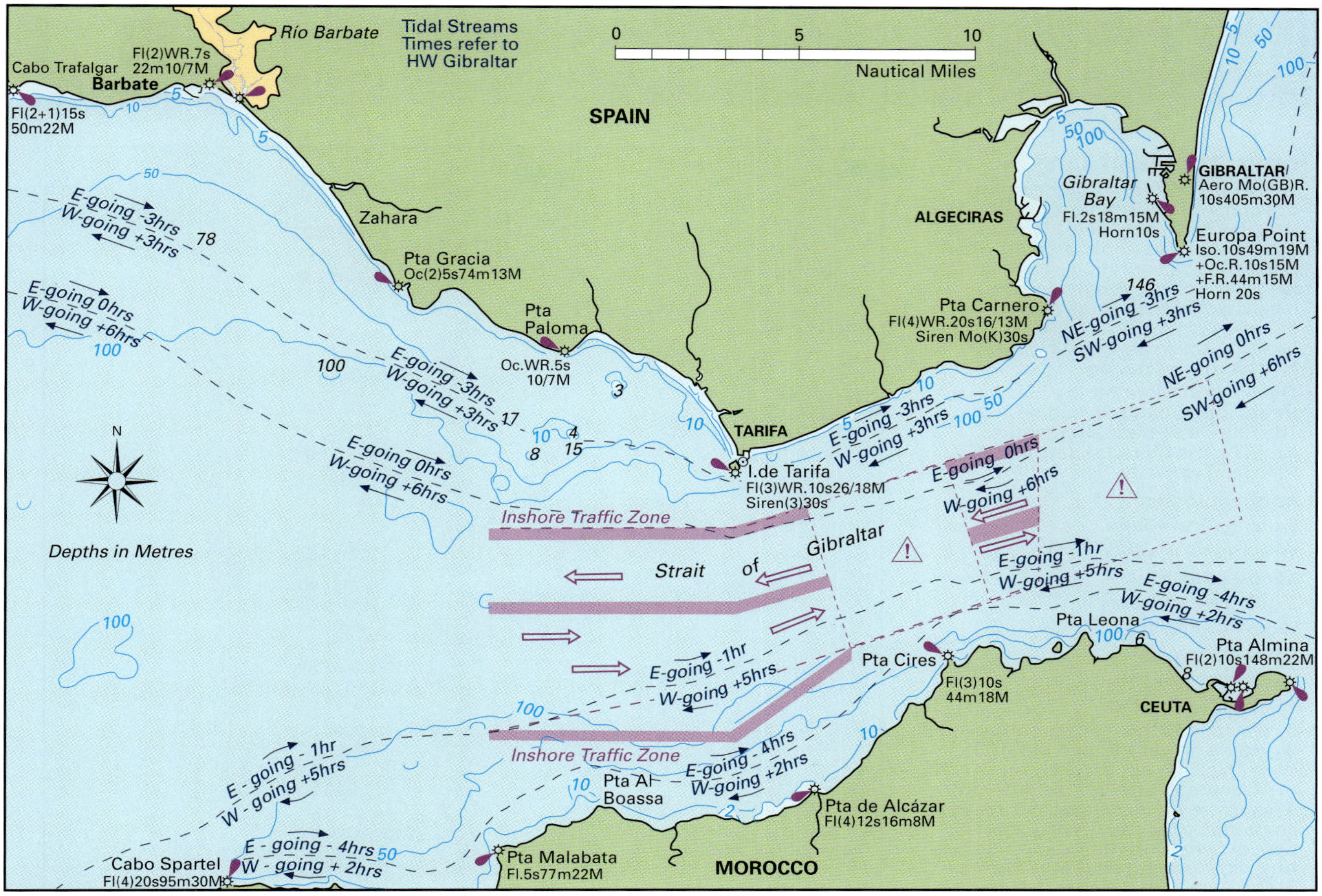

GIBRALTAR STRAIT

MEDITERRANEAN YACHT RALLIES

These are all yacht rallies visiting different ports in one or more countries. Events where races are conducted from a single venue are not listed.

April

Med-Red Rally Runs from Marmaris in Turkey via Tel Aviv in Israel through to the Red sea and then up the Gulf of Aqaba. Last run in 2011.

Gallipoli Rally Runs from Cannakale to Ayvalik in Turkey to commemorate the Gallipoli landings by ANZAC forces in the first world war.

May

EMYR Eastern Mediterranean Yacht Rally. Run annually from Kemer Marina in Turkey (but with feeders from Istanbul onwards) it generally visits eastern Turkey, northern Cyprus, Syria, Lebanon, Israel and Egypt, though it will not necessarily go to all these countries in a single year. Many organised activities en route and usually quite a lot of motoring. www.emyr.org

June

KAYRA Black Sea Rally. Intermittent rally run from Istanbul around the Black Sea. www.atakoymarina.com.tr

MAYRA Marmara Sea Rally. Run biennially from Istanbul around the Sea of Marmara. www.atakoymarina.com.tr

Gibraltar – Morocco Rally Run over the last weekend in June between Ocean Village and Port Smir.

Trophee Bailli de Suffren Cruise in company from St Tropez to Malta. For classic / modern-classic yachts.

July

Aegean Rally Organised by the Hellenic Offshore Racing Club, it is a 400 mile circuit around the Aegean. The regatta starts and finishes near Athens, with two or three stops at selected islands. www.aegeanrally.gr

September

Vasco de Gama Rally Starts in southern Turkey and heads down through Suez into the Red Sea and across to India. Currently the rally only goes as far as Eritrea due to piracy issues in the Gulf of Aden. www.vascodagamarally.nl

Other rallies

Classic Yacht Rallies Organised by CIM (Comité International de la Méditerranée). See www.cim-classicyachts.org

ARC Rally Atlantic Rally for Cruisers. Leaves from Las Palmas, Gran Canaria on the third Sunday of November. Arrives in St Lucia before Christmas. www.worldcruising.org

Christmas Caribbean Rally Runs from Lanzarote to Antigua leaving in early December. www.sailingrallies.com

GIBRALTAR STRAIT TIDES

There is a constant surface current flowing into the Strait of Gibraltar from the Atlantic of between 1–2 knots and this must be taken into account when calculating the duration, set and rate of the tidal streams. What it in effect means is that the overall tide/current equation is most favourable for a west to east passage and least favourable for an east to west passage.

The Strait of Gibraltar in effect has three tidal streams: N, middle and S. The times that these streams flow varies on the Gibraltar data in the following way:

Northern stream

E-going –3 to +3hrs

W-going +3 to –3hrs

Middle stream

E-going HW to +6hrs

W-going –6hrs to HW

Southern stream

E-going –4 to +2hrs

W-going +2 to –4hrs

By playing the three different streams it is possible to get through the strait even if you are not precisely on time for the favourable stream. The different streams can be recognised if there is any wind by the usual 'wind against tide' or 'wind with tide' sea conditions. Any yacht moving across the Strait of Gibraltar must remember that there is a large volume of commercial shipping both in and out of this narrow waterway and that large ships cannot alter course quickly or easily. The overall tidal stream strength and direction can also be altered by surface drift currents set up by strong winds blowing consistently from one direction for several days.

Straits Sailing Handbook by Colin Thomas gives excellent information on transiting the Strait.

Note With increased security around the Gibraltar Straits all ship movements are closely monitored and there is a heavy naval presence. Keep a listening watch on VHF Ch 16 and do not approach any military vessels.

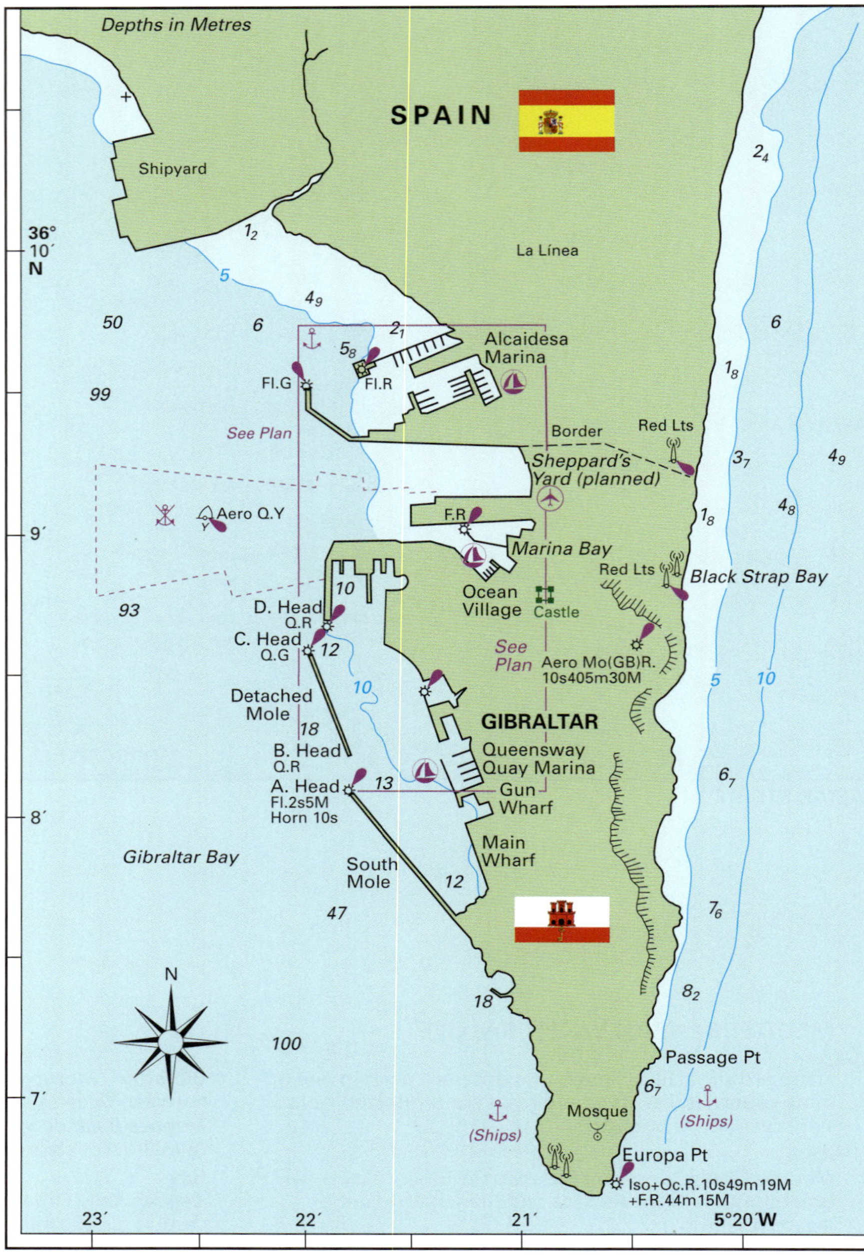

GIBRALTAR

Quick reference guide *For Key to guide see page 139*

	Shelter	Mooring	Fuel	Water	Provisions	Eating out	Charge band
Gibraltar							
Marina Bay	A	AB	A	A	A	A	2
Queensway	A	A	B	A	A	A	3

GIBRALTAR

36°05′·99N 05°20′·56W WGS84

(0·5M S of Europa Point)

BA 144 Imray M11

Entry formalities may be completed at Queensway Quay Marina or Marina Bay.

☆ Europa Point Iso.10s49m19M/Oc.R.10s19M/F.R.44m 15M (197°-vis-042°/042°-vis-067°). South mole A head Fl.2s10m5M Horn 10s. Detached mole B head Q.R.9m5M. Detached mole C head Q.G.10m5M. North mole D head Q.R.18m5M. Cormorant camber 2F.R(vert)5m. Aero light Aero Mo(GB)R.10s405m30M

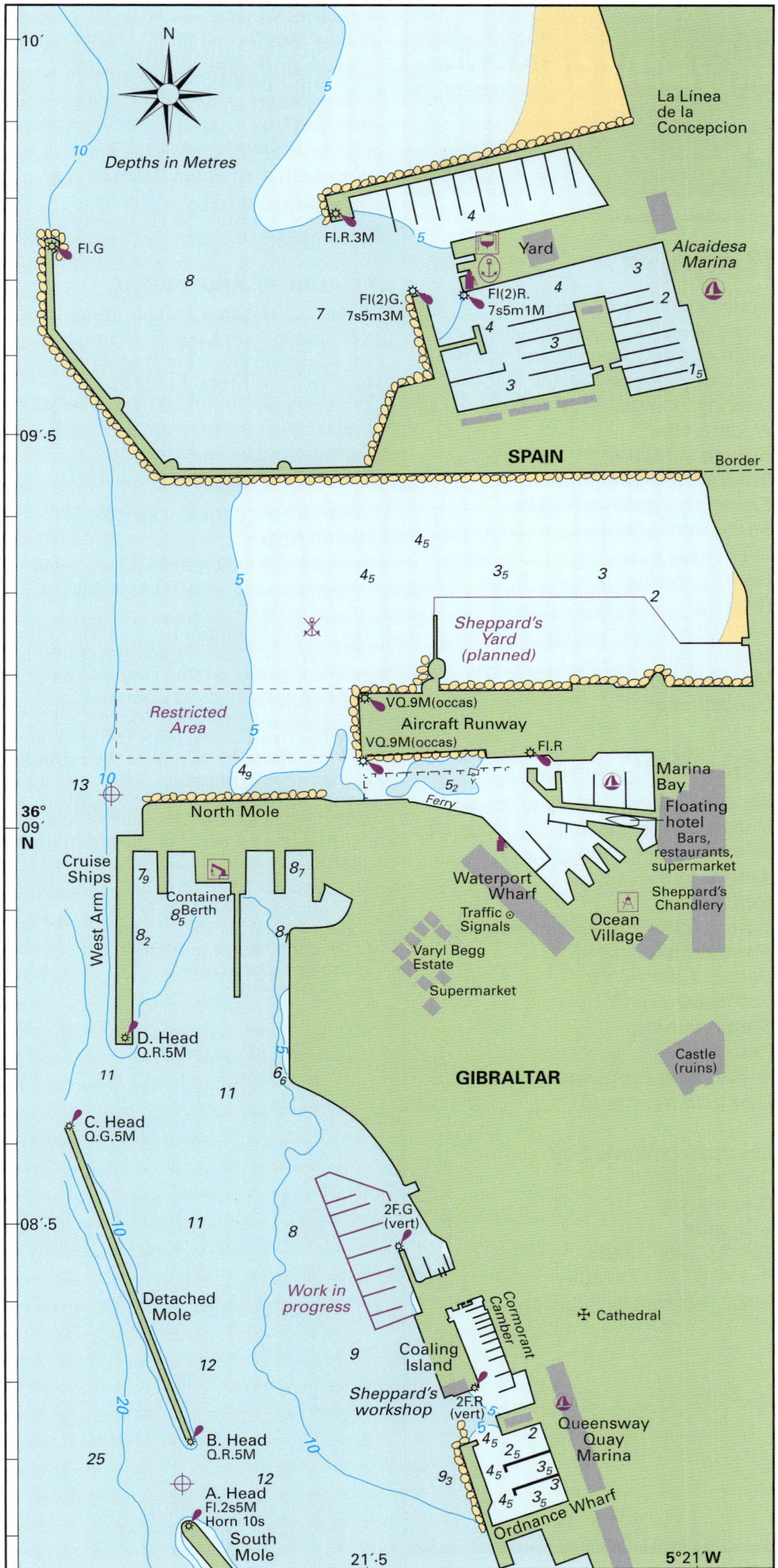

GIBRALTAR YACHT HARBOUR

VHF Ch 06, 12, 13, 14 for port authorities. Ch 12, 14, 16 for pilots.

Navigation The approach to the Rock is unmistakable. Yachts must must give way to naval vessels at all times and observe the traffic separation zones in the Strait.

OCEAN VILLAGE MARINA BAY

36°08′·92N 05°21′·99W WGS84
(N Mole E head)

Marina Bay and the former Sheppard's Marina. Continues to retain a number of transit berths. A number of berths have been lost due to the new 'cruise ship' hotel moored in the harbour, but further new berths are planned.

Note Work is in progress off the north mole at the entrance to Marina Bay. Care needed in the vicinity.

VHF Ch 71.

Berths Where directed. Berthing is stern or bows-to with laid moorings tailed to the quay.

Shelter Some berths suffer from wash from passing craft. Gusts off the rock are bothersome not usually dangerous.

Data 300 berths. Visitors' berths. Max LOA 80m. Minimum 3–4m depths. Charge band 2.

Facilities Water. 220/380V. WiFi. Showers and toilets. Fuel quay nearby. Provisions and restaurants.

Ocean Village Marina Bay
☏ 200 73300
Email pieroffice@oceanvillage.gi
www.oceanvillage.gi
Gibraltar Port Captain ☏ 77254

Remarks

1. Yachts are not permitted to enter Ocean Village Marina Bay (or the fuel station) when the runway lights are flashing.
2. Anchoring off near the runway is discouraged due to height restrictions, and yachts are advised to anchor N of La Línea breakwater (in Spanish waters). If anchoring in Gibraltar waters you are requested to obtain permission from the Port Captain. There is currently no facility for yachts at anchor to clear into Gibraltar.

QUEENSWAY QUAY MARINA

36°08′·10N 05°21′·84W WGS84
(S mole entrance)

☆ 2F.R(vert)/2F.G(vert). Coaling Island new mole head 2F.G(vert)

VHF Ch 71 (0830–2200).

Navigation The marina management strongly advise calling ahead on VHF Ch 71 (callsign *Queensway Quay Marina)* before entering the marina.

Berths Where directed. Laid moorings tailed to the quay.

Shelter Reasonable shelter although strong gusts off the land can be bothersome.

Data 150 berths. Visitors' berths. Max LOA 40m. Depths 2–2·5m. Charge band 3.

Facilities Water. 230/380V. Telephone. WiFi. Showers and toilets. Security gates. Fuel quay planned. Provisions nearby. Restaurants.

Queensway Quay Marina
☎ 200 44700
Email info@queenswayquay.gi

Note Only Camping Gaz and 13kg Kosangas (orange) is available in Gibraltar. All other gas cylinders need to be filled in Spain.

COALING ISLAND MARINA

A new 700 berth marina is under development off Coaling Island as shown in the plan. The marina is principally for local boats up to 8m LOA on pontoons, and for superyacht berths along the outer quay. Construction is underway and completion is planned for 2015/16.

SHEPPARD'S CHANDLERY & BOATYARD

Note The old Sheppard's Marina has been developed as part of the Ocean Village project.

Sheppard's is continuing to offer haul-outs (max 4·5 tons/9m) at the container berth and most repairs from their workshop facilities at Coaling Island (near Queensway Quay Marina). The new boatyard and repairs facility will be located on the N side of the runway. It has run into planning difficulties and completion dates are not available. Sheppard's chandlery remains open in the building adjacent to the old marina, next to Ocean Village.

M. Sheppard & Co Ltd
☎ Chandlery 200 75148/ 77183
☎ Repairs 200 76895
Email admin@sheppard.gi or yachtrep@gibraltar.gi
www.sheppard.gi

10.2 Spain

TIME ZONE UT+1 IDD+34

Quick reference guide

For Key to guide see page 139

	Shelter	Mooring	Fuel	Water	Provisions	Eating out	Charge band
Costas del Sol and Blanca							
Barbate	A	A	A	A	B	B	2/3
Algeciras	A	A	B	A	B	B	2
Alcaidesa Marina	A	A	B	A	A	B	2/3
Sotogrande	A	A	A	A	B	A	3
Duquesa	A	A	A	A	B	A	2/3
Estepona	A	A	A	A	A	A	2/3
José Banus	A	A	A	A	C	B	6
Marbella	B	A	A	A	A	A	4
Marina La Bajadilla	A	A	A	A	B	B	3
Cabopino	B	A	A	A	C	C	3
Fuengirola	B	A	A	A	A	A	2/3
Benalmadena	C	A	A	A	A	A	2/3
Malaga	A	A	A	A	A	A	2/3
Caleta de Velez	B	A	A	A	B	A	2/3
Marina del Este	A	A	A	A	C	B	5
Motril	B	A	A	A	C	B	4/5
Almerimar	B	A	A	A	A	A	2
Roquetas del Mar	A	B	O	A	B	C	2/3
Aguadulce	B	A	A	A	A	A	3
Almeria	B	A	A	A	A	A	3
Puerto de San José	A	A	A	A	A	A	3
Garrucha	B	A	A	A	B	B	3
Juan Montiel Marina	A	B	B	A	C	C	
Aguilas	A	B	B	A	B	B	
Mazarron	A	A	A	A	C	C	
Cartagena	A	A	A	A	A	A	3/4
Tomas Maestre	A	A	A	A	B	A	3
Marina San Pedro del Pinatar	B	A	A	A	C	C	
Puerto de La Horadada	B	A	O	A	C	B	
Puerto de Campoamor	B	A	A	A	C	C	
Torrevieja	B	A	A	A	A	A	3/4
Marina de Las Dunas	A	A	A	A	C	B	3
Santa Pola	A	A	A	A	A	A	4/5
Alicante	A	A	A	A	A	A	4/5
Campello	B	A	B	A	B	A	4
Villajoyosa	B	A	A	A	C	A	4
Altea	B	A	A	A	A	A	4
Marina Greenwich	A	A	A	A	A	A	5
Puerto de Calpe	C	A	A	A	A	A	4
Moraira	C	A	A	A	A	A	4/5
Denia	A	A	A	A	A	A	5/6
Islas Baleares							
Puerto de Ibiza							
Marina Botafoch	A	A	A	A	A	A	5/6
Ibiza Marina	A	A	A	A	A	A	6+
Ibiza Magna	A	A	B	A	A	A	6
Santa Eulalia	A	A	A	A	A	A	5
San Antonio	B	A	A	A	B	A	6
Sabina	C	AB	A	A	A	A	6+
Palma							
Réal Club Náutico	A	A	A	A	A	A	6
Club de Mar	A	A	A	A	A	A	6
Marina Port de Mallorca	AB	A	B	A	A	A	6
Marina Alboran	A	A	B	A	A	A	6
Cala Nova	A	A	A	A	A	A	5
Puerto Portals	A	A	A	A	A	A	6
Porto Adriano	B	A	A	A	C	B	6
Santa Ponsa	A	A	A	A	A	A	5
Puerto de Andratx	A	AC	A	A	A	A	4
Puerto de Soller	C	AC	A	A	B	B	4
Puerto de Pollensa	B	A	A	A	A	A	5
Puerto de Bonaire	A	A	A	A	O	C	6
Puerto de Alcudia	A	A	A	A	A	A	4/5
Ca'n Picafort	A	A	O	A	A	A	5
Cala Ratjada	B	B	A	A	A	A	5
Porto Cristo	A	A	A	A	A	A	5
Porto Colom	C	ABC	A	A	A	A	5
Cala d'Or	A	A	A	A	C	C	5/6
La Rapita	A	A	A	A	A	A	6
S'Estanyol	C	A	A	A	C	C	5
El Arenal	A	A	A	A	A	A	5
San Antonio	A	A	A	A	A	A	6
Mahon	A	AC	A	A	B	B	5/6+
Marina Menorca	A	A	O	A	C	C	4/5
Ciudadela	B	AB	A	A	A	A	5
Cala de Addaya	A	AC	O	A	B	A	2/3
Costas del Azahar, Dorada and Brava							
Gandia	B	A	A	A	A	A	4
Marina Real Juan Carlos I	B	A	A	A	A	A	3
Réal Club Náutico de Valencia	A	A	A	A	C	C	4
Farnals	A	A	A	A	C	C	4
Puerto de Siles	A	A	B	A	B	B	4
Burriana	A	A	A	A	B	B	4
Castellon de la Plana	A	A	A	A	B	B	4
Oropesa de Mar	A	A	A	A	C	C	3
Las Fuentes	A	A	A	A	B	B	4
Benicarlo	B	A	A	A	C	B	5
Vinaroz	B	A	B	A	B	B	
Rapita	A	A	A	A	A	A	
Sant Carles Marina	A	A	A	A	B	B	
Ampolla	B	A	A	A	B	B	
L'Ametlla de Mar	B	A	A	A	B	B	
Sant Jordi Marina	A	B	B	A	C	C	4
Calafat	B	A	A	A	C	C	
Hospitalet de l'Infant	B	A	A	A	B	B	3/4
Cambrils	A	A	A	A	A	A	4/5
Salou	B	A	A	A	A	A	5
Port Tarraco Marina	A	A	A	A	A	A	5
Port Esportiou	A	A	A	A	A	A	5
Torredembarra	B	A	A	A	A	A	5
Roda de Bara	B	A	A	A	C	C	4
Comaruga	B	A	A	A	B	B	
Villanova y la Geltru	A	A	A	A	A	A	5
Aiguadolc	A	A	A	A	C	A	4
Ginesta	A	A	A	A	A	A	4
Barcelona	A	A	A	A	A	A	4
Port Olimpic	A	A	A	A	A	A	4/5
Port Forum Marina	BA	A	A	A	C	C	3/4
Badalona Marina	B	A	A	A			3
El Masnou	B	A	A	A	B	A	
Premia de Mar	B	A	A	A	B	B	4
Port Mataro	B	A	A	A	A	A	4
El Balis	A	A	A	A	C	A	3/4
Arenys de Mar	B	A	A	A	B	A	4
Blanes	B	A	A	A	A	A	4/5
Sant Feliu de Guixols	B	A	A	A	A	A	5
Port d'Aro	B	A	A	A	C	B	5/6
Palamos	C	A	A	A	A	A	4/5
Marina Palamos	A	A	A	A	A	A	5
L'Estartit	A	A	A	A	A	A	6
L'Escala	B	A	A	A	A	A	6
Ampuriabrava	A	A	A	A	A	A	6
Santa Margarita	A	A	B	A	A	A	
Roses	B	A	A	A	A	A	4
La Selva	C	A	A	A	A	A	6
Llança	A	A	A	A	A	A	5/6
Port Bou	B	A	A	A	B	C	5/6

Andalucia

Junta de Puertos de Andalucia has an excellent website with details of marinas covering the south coast of Spain up as far as Villaricos.
Email eppa@eppa.es
www.puertosdeandalucia.com

BARBATE

36°10'·83N 05°55'·34W WGS84

☆ Cabo Trafalgar Fl(2+1)15s49m22M.
Barbate de Franco Fl(2)WR.7s23m10/7M. W breakwater head Fl.R.4s12m5M. Outer breakwater head Fl.G.3s8m2M.
Marina entrance Fl(2)G.2M/Fl.R.4s2M.

VHF Ch 16, 09.
Navigation In summer a tunny net is laid from close off the S breakwater running 2M to the SSW. The normal approach is from the E side of the net. Entry from the W to the N of the net is possible with care. The entrance is buoyed and care is needed of silting around the N breakwater head and close off the W side of the entrance to the marina.

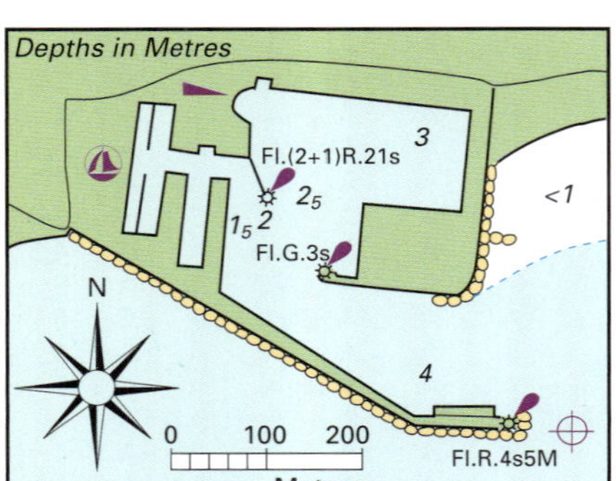

BARBATE

Berths Where directed in the marina. Finger pontoons.
Shelter Good all-round shelter.
Data 300 berths. Max LOA 25m. Depths 2–4m. Charge band 2/3.
Facilities Water. 220V. Showers and WC. Fuel. Travel-hoist. Some repairs. Provisions and restaurants in the town.
Remarks New haul-out and hardstanding facilities being developed.
✆ 956 430 587
Email barbate@eppa.es www.eppa.es

TARIFA

36°00'·6N 05°31'·1W

☆ Tarifa Fl(3)WR.10s41m26/18M. Fl.R.5s/Fl.G.5s.

Ferry and fishing harbour. Very limited space. Anchorage either side of point.
Remarks Care needed of unmarked shoal water to the NE of the harbour.

ALGECIRAS MARINA EL SALADILLO

36°07'·2N 05°25'·6W (port hand outer entrance buoy)
BA 142, 1455 Sp 4451

70M Cadiz ←→ Gibraltar 4M

☆ Entrance outer buoys Q.R/Q.G
S inner jetty head. Fl(4)R.11s4m1M
Breakwater head Fl(4)G.11s5m1M

VHF Ch 09, 16.
Berths 800 marina berths.
Shelter Very good all-round shelter.
Real Club Nautico de Algeciras marina
✆ 956 572 503
www.apba.es

LA LINEA ALCAIDESA MARINA

36°09'·6N 05°22'·0W (Fl(2)G.6s8m4M)

☆ Dique de Capitania head F(2)G.7s5m3M
Puerto Chico jetty head Fl.R.5m3M

VHF Ch 09
Navigation The marina entrance is free of dangers.
Berths Finger pontoons at most berths. Moorings over 30m LOA.
Shelter Good all-round shelter at most berths.
Data 625 berths. Max LOA 80m. 200 berths ashore. Charge band 2/3.
Facilities Water. 220/380V. WiFi. Showers and toilets. Laundry facilities. Pump-out. Fuel quay to be installed. 75-ton travel-hoist. Dry storage. Bicycle hire.
Remarks Close to all amenities and good shopping at La Linea. Five minutes from the Gibraltar frontier.
✆ 956 021 660
www.alcaidesamarina.com
Email marina@alcaidesa.com

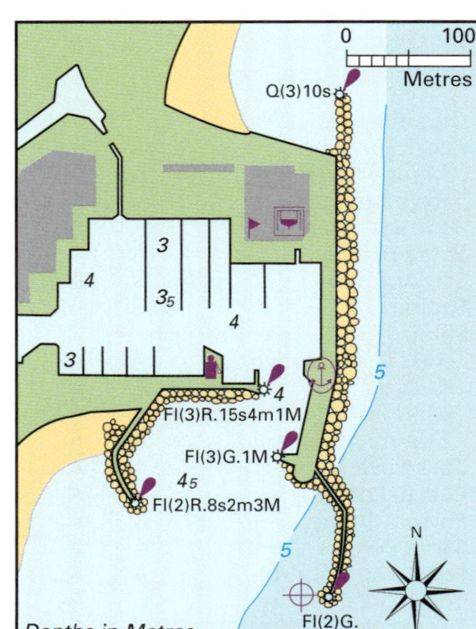

PUERTO DE SOTOGRANDE

Costa del Sol

SOTOGRANDE

36°17'·3N 05°16'·1W
BA 3578 Sp 445A
15M Gibraltar ←→ Duquesa 5M

☆ Breakwater S Head Fl(2)G.10s8m5M. N Head Q(3)10s4M. Contradique head Fl(3)R.15s4m1M. Martello de Escollera Fl(2)R.8s2m3M

VHF Ch 09.

Berths Report to *torre de control* at the entrance.

Shelter Surge with SE–E winds although now less with the new inner breakwater. Inner berths are better.

Data 1,300 berths. Max LOA 70m. Depths 3–4m. Charge band 3.

Facilities Water. 220/380V. Showers and toilets. Fuel quay. 200-ton travel-hoist. All yacht repairs. Provisions and restaurants.

Remarks Associated residential complex shore. Plans to build an additional residential complex and marina nearby.

Puerto deportivo ✆ 956 790 000
www.puertosotogrande.com

DUQUESA

36°21'·2N 05°13'·7W
BA 3578 Sp 453
5M Sotogrande ←→ Estepona 5M

☆ Marina dique de Levante S head Fl.G.5s5M. N spur Q(3)10s5M. Dique Antirena head Fl.R.5s6m3M

VHF Ch 09.

Berths Go on fuel quay and report to *torre de control* for a berth.

Shelter Good shelter.

Data 330 berths. Max LOA 20m. Depths 2–4m. Charge band 2/3.

Facilities Water. 220/280V. Showers toilets, washing machine. Fuel. 70-ton travel-lift. 50-ton crane. Some yacht repairs. Provisions and restaurants.

Capitanía ✆ 952 890 100
Email
duquesa@marinasmediterraneo.com
www.marinasmediterraneo.com

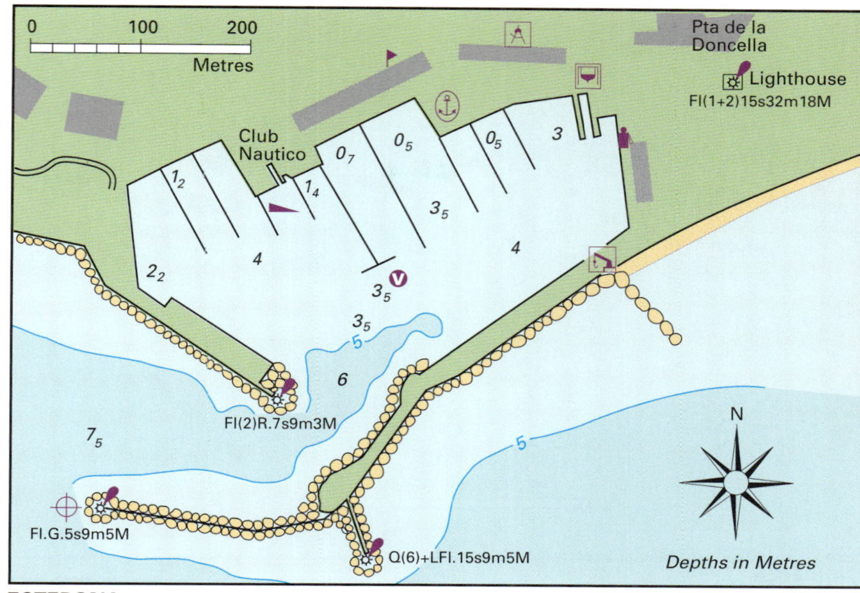

ESTEPONA

ESTEPONA

36°24'·8N 05°09'·4W
BA 3578 Sp 453
5M Duquesa ←→ José Banus 11M

☆ Punta de la Doncella LtHo Fl(1+2)15s18M. Dique de Abrigo Old head Q(6)+LFl.15s5M. Head Fl.G.5s5M. W breakwater head Fl(2)R.7s3M

VHF Ch 09.

Navigation Entrance difficult in S–SW gales. Liable to silting after winter storms.

Berths Where directed.

Shelter Good shelter.

Data 440 berths. Max LOA 35m. Depths 1–4·5m. Charge band 3.

Facilities Water. 220/380V. WiFi. Showers and toilets. 75-ton travel-hoist. Most yacht repairs. Provisions and restaurants.

Puerto deportivo ✆ 952 801 800
Email
estepona@marinasmediterraneo.com

JOSE BANUS

36°29'N 04°57'·3W
BA 3578 Sp 454
11M Estepona ←→ Marbella 3·5M

☆ Elbow Q(6)+LFl.15s3M. Benabolá breakwater W head Fl(3)R.10s7m3M. E breakwater Fl(3)G.12s13m5M. N head Q(6)+LFl.15s4M

VHF Ch 09, 14, 16.

Navigation Entrance difficult in S–SW gales.

Berths Report to *torre de control*. Laid moorings tailed to the quay.

Shelter Good shelter.

Data 915 berths. Max LOA 50m. Depths 1–4·5m. Charge band 6.

Facilities Water. 220/380V. Showers and toilets. Telephone. Fuel quay. 50-ton travel-hoist. Most yacht repairs. Some provisions. Restaurants.

Puerto Banus
✆ 952 909 800
Email torrecontrol@puertobanus.es
www.puertojosebanus.es

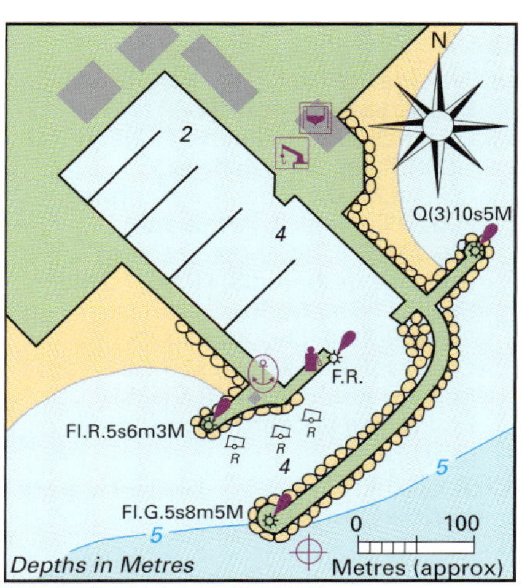

PUERTO DE LA DUQUESA

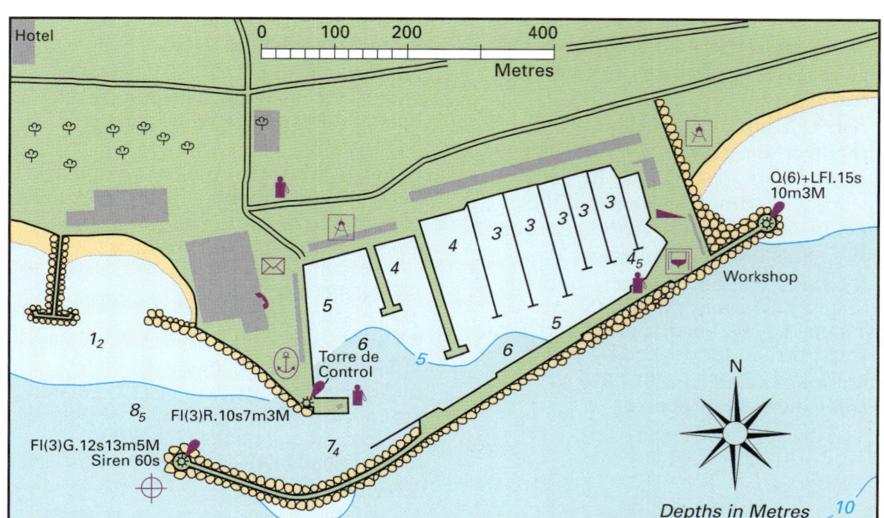

PUERTO DE JOSE BANUS

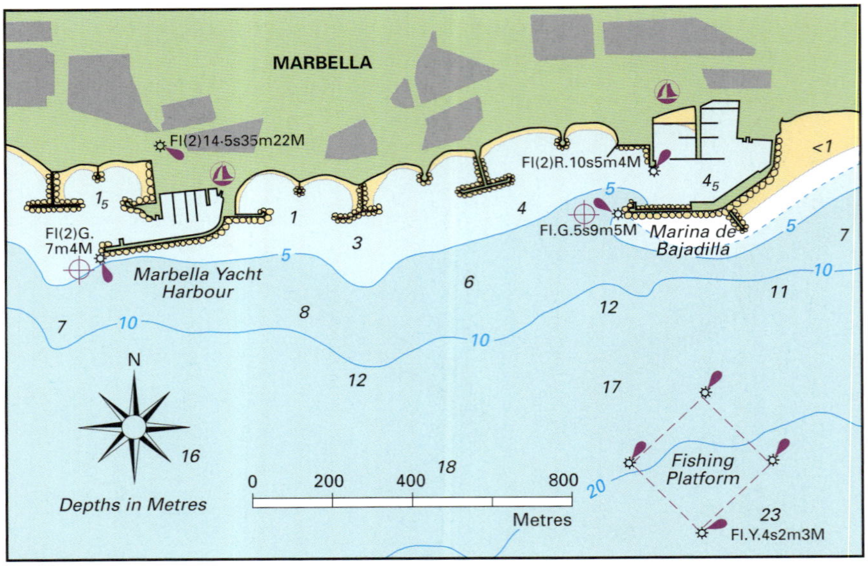

MARBELLA

MARBELLA

36°30'·4N 04°53'·4W
BA 3578 Sp 454
3·5M José Banus ←→ Cabopino 9M

☆ Yacht harbour entrance Fl.R.4s2M/Fl(2)G.7s4M

VHF Ch 09

Navigation Entrance difficult with W–SW gales. Liable to silt.

Berths Where directed.

Shelter Surge with W–SW gales.

Data 378 berths. 100 visitors' berths. Max LOA 20m. Depths 1·5–3m. Charge band 4.

Facilities Water. 220/380V. Showers and toilets. Fuel quay. Provisions and restaurants.

Puerto deportivo ✆ 952 775 700
Email puertodeportivo@marbella.es
Club Maritimo ✆ 952 772 504

MARINA LA BAJADILLA

36°30'·4N 04°52'·5W
BA 3578 Sp45A/454
0.75M Marbella ←→ 8M Cabopino

☆ Entrance Fl.G.5s9m5M/Fl(2)R.10s5m4M.

VHF Ch 09.

Navigation Entry difficult in W–SW gales. Fishing platform ¼M S of the entrance.

Berths Moor at the fuel quay and report to the *capitanía* for a berth.

Data 250 berths. Max LOA 15m. Depths <1–3m. Charge band 2/3.

Facilities Water. 220V. Showers and WC. Fuel quay. Travel-hoist.

Remarks The port is due to undergo a huge transformation into Puerto Al-Thani, a 1200 berth marina and cruise ship port. So far dogged by delays.

Marina la Bajadilla ✆ 952 858 401
Email marbellad@eppa.es

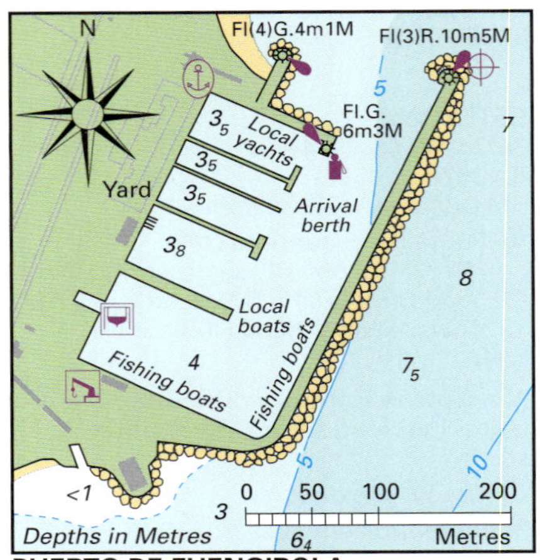

PUERTO DE FUENGIROLA

CABOPINO

36°29'·0N 04°44'·4W
BA 3578 Sp 454
9M Marbella ←→ Fuengirola 6M

☆ Entrance 3F.R(vert)7m4M

VHF Ch 09.

Navigation Entrance silts. Port reported closed due to silting.

Data 250 berths. Limited visitors' berths. Max LOA 16m. Depths 3–4·5m. Charge band 3.

Facilities Water. 220/380V. Showers and toilets. Fuel quay. 30-ton travel-hoist. Some repairs. Mini-market. Restaurant.

Remarks Marina is part of an upmarket development ashore.

✆ 95 2831 975
Email marinacabopino@terra.es

FUENGIROLA

36°32'·6N 04°36'·8W
BA 3578 Sp 455
6M Cabopino ←→ Benalmadena 6M

☆ Submerged jetty head Fl(3)G.5m3M. Entrance Fl(3)R.10m5M. Contradique head Fl.G.6m3M Pier head Fl(4)G.4m1M

VHF Ch 09

Navigation Entry dangerous in E–SE gales.

Berths Where directed.

Shelter Surge with NE winds.

Data 400 berths. Max LOA 20m. Depths 3–4m. Charge band 2/3.

Facilities Water. 220/380V. Showers and toilets. Fuel quay. 40-ton travel-hoist. Limited yacht repairs. Provisions and restaurants.

Remarks New yacht pontoon to be installed.

Puerto deportivo ✆ 952 468 000 / 952 474 197
Email fuengirola@eppa.es

BENALMADENA

36°35'·7N 04°30'·7W
BA 773 Sp 455A
6M Fuengirola ←→ Málaga 9M

☆ Dique de Levante NE head Q(3)10s3M. Laja Bermejo Q(3)10s5M. Entrance Fl(2)G.5s9m5M / Fl(3)G.9s9m4M / Fl(2)R.5s4m3M

VHF Ch 09.

Navigation Care needed of reefs off Laja de Bermejo to the S of the entrance. Laja de Bermejo is marked with an E card buoy lit Q(3)10s5M. There are also some yellow buoys marking Laja de Bermejo.

Berths Report to *torre de control*.

Shelter Some berths uncomfortable with strong W winds.

Data 1,000 berths. Max LOA 40m. Depths 2–5m. Charge band 2/3.

Facilities Water. 220/380V. Showers and toilets. Fuel quay. 50-ton travel-hoist. Most yacht repairs. Provisions and restaurants.

Remarks Close to Málaga Airport. Busy resort with lots of bars and restaurants.

There are plans to expand marina facilities with 800 new berths.

Puerto deportivo ✆ 952 577 022
Email info@puertobenalmadena.org
Capitania ✆ 952 125 000
Harbour Authority ✆ 952 212 706
Email puertodeportivo@benalmadena.com
www.benalmadena.es/puertodeportivo

MALAGA

36°41'·9N 04°24'·9W
BA 1851 Sp 455, 4551
9M Benalmadena ←→ Caleta de Velez 15·5M

☆ Terminal de Amoniaco VQ(3)5s3M. Dique del Este root Fl(3+1)20s25M. Entrance to Ante Puerto Fl(2)G.7s3M/ Fl(2)R.7s4M. NE arm head Q.R.1s12m3M. E breakwater head Fl.G.5s5M. Puerto Pesquero Q.G.2M/Q.R.2M. Inner entrance (Dársena de Heredia) Fl(2)G.7s2M / Fl(4)R.11s7m2M. Small craft basin Fl(3)R.9s2M/Fl(3)G.8s2M. Muelle Canovas Fl(2+1)G.12s2M. Muelle de Romero Robledo Fl(4)R.11s2M. Espigón de la Central Termica Q(3)10s3M

VHF Ch 09, 11, 12, 13, 14, 16 for port authorities and pilots. Ch 09, 16 for RCM.

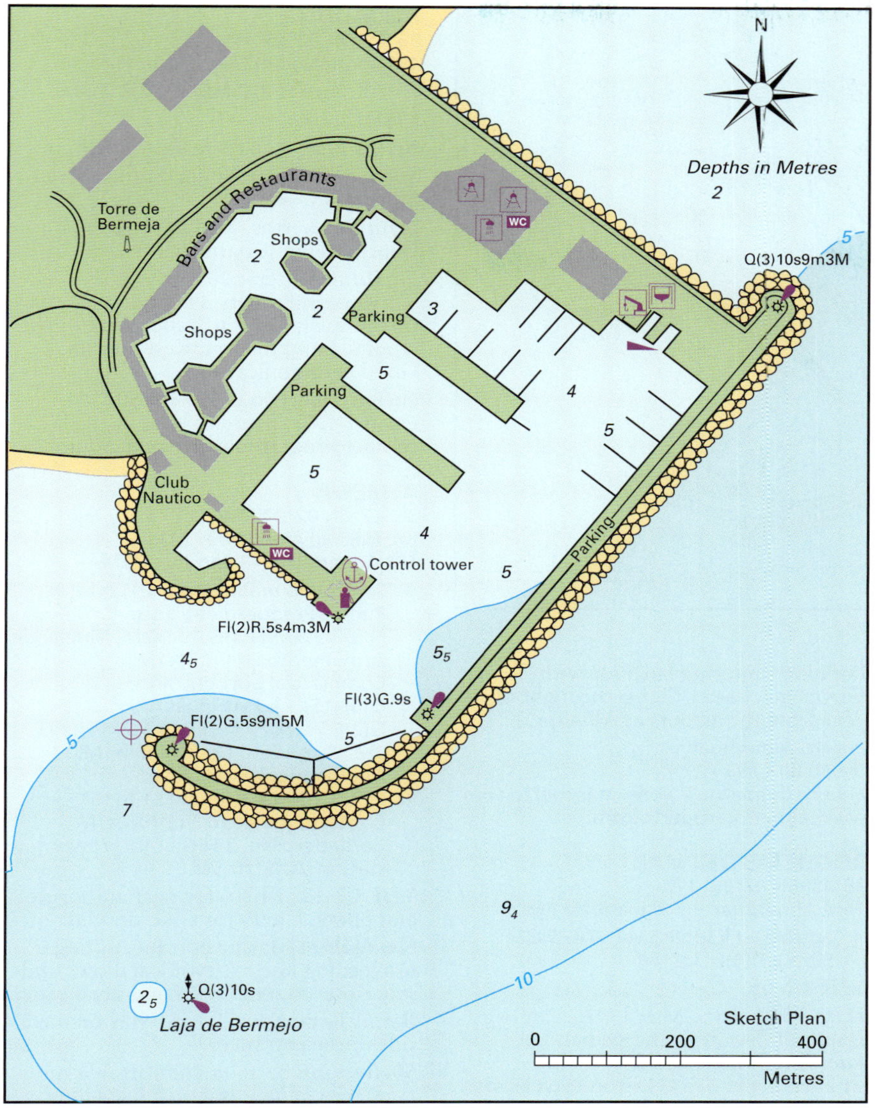

PUERTO DE BENALMADENA

Berths Report to the YC in Dársena de Heredia. Some berths outside Puerto Pesquero.
Shelter Adequate at YC.
Data *YC*: 25 berths. Max LOA 12m. Depths 5–6m.
Facilities *YC*: Water. 220V. Showers and toilets. Fuel. Provisions and restaurants.
Remarks Large commercial harbour. Further extension works and a new 550 berth marina planned.
Réal Club Mediterráneo ✆ 952 226 300
www.realclubmediterraneo.com
Puerto deportivo de Malaga
✆ 952 216 311
www.puertomalaga.com

CANDADO
36°42'·9N 04°20'·7W
☆ Entrance LFl.G.8s7m3M / LFl.R.8s7m3M Torre del Mar o Vélez Fl(1+2)10s13M
VHF Ch 09.
Data 280 berths. Max LOA 15m. Depths 2–4m. Liable to silt.
Puerto deportivo ✆ 952 296 097
www.clubelcandado.com

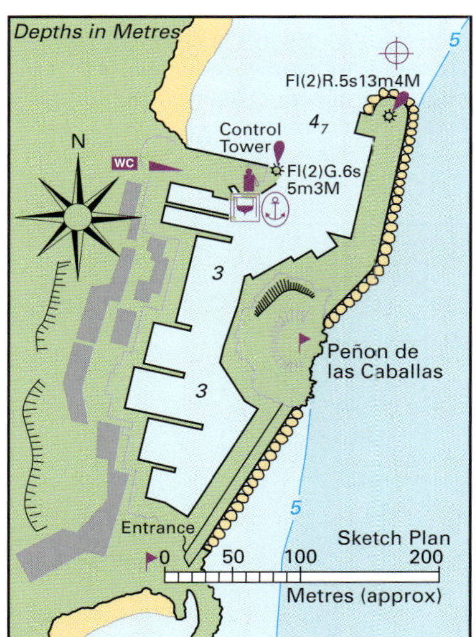

MARINA DEL ESTE

CALETA DE VELEZ (TORRE DEL MAR)
36°44'·9N 04°04'·2W
BA 773 Sp 455, 456
15·5M Malaga ←→ Marina del Este 20M
☆ Espigon Fl.R.4s3M. Entrance Fl.G.5s2M/Fl(2)R.7s3M/F.R
VHF Ch 09.
Navigation Care needed of the *espigón* which is only just above water and extends beyond the light structure.
Berths Where directed.
Data 225 berths. Max LOA 20m. Depths 3–5m. Charge band 3.
Facilities Water. 220/380V. Showers and toilets. Fuel quay. 40-ton travel-hoist. Mechanical and engineering repairs. Provisions and restaurants.
Remarks There are plans to expand the harbour to seaward with an inner harbour of 530 berths, and improve facilities in the marina.
Capitanía ✆ 95 251 1390
Email caleta@eppa.es

MARINA DEL ESTE (PUNTA DE LA MONA)
36°43'·8N 03°43'·4W
BA 773 Sp 456
20M Caleta de Velez ←→ Motril 10M
☆ Punta de la Mona La Herradura Fl.5s15M. Entrance Fl(2)G.6s3M/ Fl(2)R.5s4M
VHF Ch 09.
Berths Report to *torre de control*.
Shelter Good shelter.
Data 230 berths. Max LOA 30m. Depths 3m. Charge band 5.
Facilities Water. 220/380V. WiFi. Showers and toilets. Fuel quay. 30-ton travel-hoist. 3-ton crane. Limited yacht repairs. Some provisions. Restaurants.
Remarks Upmarket marina and development. Some distance to town and shopping.
Capitanía ✆ 958 827 018
Marina ✆ 958 640 801
Email
marinaeste@marinasmediterraneo.com
www.marinasmediterraneo.com

MOTRIL
36°43'·0N 03°30'·9W
BA 1854 Sp 4571
10M Marina del Este ←→ Almerimar 37M
☆ Entrance Fl(2)R.6s10M/Fl(2)G.7s5M. Dique de Levante head Fl(2+1)G.14·5s5M. Espigón head Fl.R.5s1M. Breakwater SE elbow Fl(2+1)G.16s6m3M. Fish harbour breakwater head Fl(2+1)G.16s6m2M
VHF Ch 09.
Berths Report to Club Náutico in NW corner for a berth.
Shelter Uncomfortable with strong E winds.
Data *YC*: 160 berths. Max LOA 20m. Depths 0·5–8m. Charge band 4/5.
Facilities *YC*: Water. 220V. Showers and toilets. Fuel quay. 60-ton travel-hoist. 7·5-ton crane. Limited yacht repairs. Some provisions. Restaurants.
Remarks Further expansion of yacht facilities are planned.
Club Náutico Motril ✆ 958 600 037
Email info@nauticomotril.com

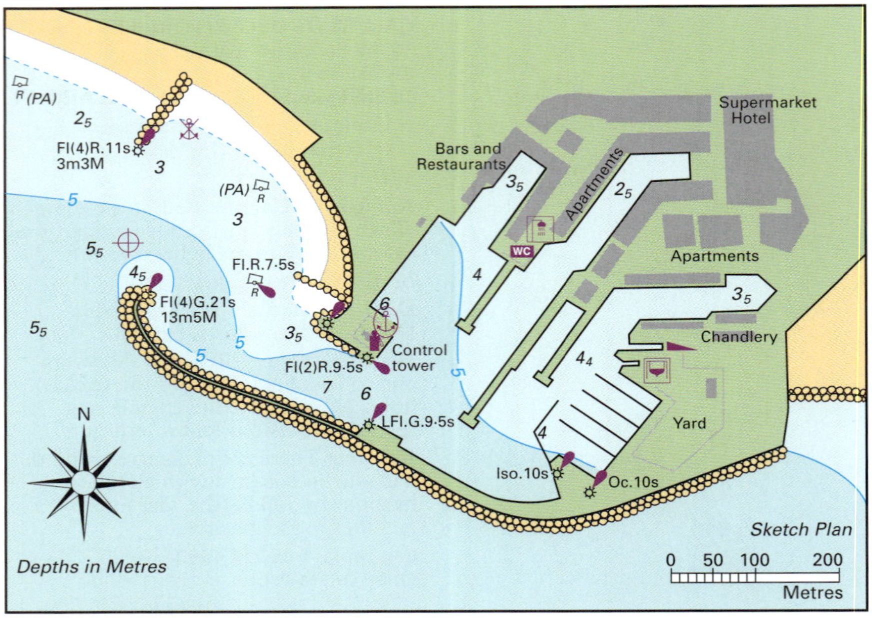

PUERTO DE ALMERIMAR

ADRA

36°44′·6N 03°01′·1W

☆ Main light Oc(3)10·5s16M. Entrance Fl(2)R.6s5M/Fl(2)G.10s8m3M. Inner breakwater head Fl(3)R.10s2M/Fl(3)G.9s2M

VHF Ch 09.

Navigation Care needed of shoal water on inside of outer breakwater.

Berths New pontoons off E breakwater.

Data 250 berths. Max LOA 20m. Depths 3–4·5m. Charge band 3.

Facilities Water. 220V. WC and showers. Fuel reported.

Remarks Marina open in E basin.

Puerto deportivo ✆ 950 805 061
Email adra@eppa.es

Real Club Nautico ✆ 950 403 487

ALMERIMAR

36°41′·68N 02°47′·92W WGS84
BA 774 Sp 4571 Imray M11
37M Motril ←→ Roquetas del Mar 14M

☆ Leading lights Front Iso.10s2M. Rear Oc.10s2M. Entrance Fl(4)G.21s5M/ LFl.G.9·5s2M. Espigón No. 1 Fl(4)R.11s3M. Breakwater E head Fl(2)R.9·5s2M

VHF Ch 09, 16, 74.

Navigation Entry difficult with strong SW winds. Shoal water 500m SE of the entrance marked by buoys. Buoyed channel into the marina.

Berths Report to *torre de control*.

Shelter Some berths uncomfortable with SW winds.

Data 1,000 berths. 200 visitors' berths. Max LOA 60m. Depths 2·5–6m. Charge band 2.

Facilities Water. 220/380V. Showers and toilets. Fuel quay. 60/110-ton travel-hoists. 5-ton crane. Chandlers. All yacht repairs. 400 hardstanding places. Provisions and restaurants.

Remarks Large apartment development ashore. Useful yard with all facilities. Good discounts for winter stays.

Popular wintering harbour with European charter flights throughout the year from the airport at Almeria.

Puerto Almerimar
✆ 950 607 755
Email infomarina@almerimarpuerto.com
www.almerimarpuerto.com

ROQUETAS DEL MAR

36°45′·5N 02°36′·1W
14M Almerimar ←→ Aguadulce 4M

☆ Entrance Fl(3)R.9s5M/Fl(3)G.9s3M Elbow Fl(4)G.11s1M

VHF Ch 09.

Data 400 berths. Max LOA 12m. Depths 1·5–3·5m. Charge band 2/3.

Facilities Water. 220V. WC and showers. Fuel quay. 45-ton travel-hoist.

Remarks Upgrades completed to enlarge marina.

Club Nautico ✆ 950 320 789
www.realclubnauticoroquetas.com

Roquetas del Mar ✆ 950 100 487
Email roquetas@eppa.es

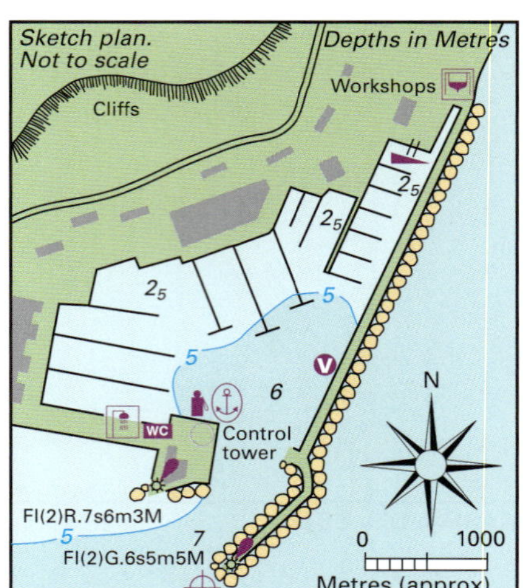

PUERTO DE AGUADULCE

AGUADULCE

36°48′·9N 02°33′·7W
4M Roquetas del Mar ←→ Almeria 5M

☆ Entrance Fl(2)G.6s5M/Fl(2)R.7s3M

VHF Ch 09.

Berths Report to *torre de control*.

Shelter Some berths uncomfortable in SE winds.

Data 765 berths. Max LOA 25m. Depths 2–6m. Charge band 3.

Facilities Water. 220/380V. WiFi. Showers and toilets. Fuel quay. 70-ton travel-hoist. 3·5-ton crane. Some yacht repairs. Supermarket. Restaurants. Good communications.

Puerto deportivo ✆ 950 341 502
Email
contacto@puertodeportivoaguadulce.es

ALMERIA

36°49′·6N 02°27′·8W
BA 1589 Sp 4591 Imray M11
5M Aguadulce ←→ San José 21M

☆ San Telmo main light Fl(2)12s19M. Puerto Pesquero entrance Fl(3)R.9s4M/Fl(4)G.10·5s3M. Muelle de Armamento Fl(4)R.11s1M. Commercial port entrance Q(6)+LFl.15s1M/Fl.R.5s7M/ Fl(2)R.7s1M/Fl(2+1)G.14·5s2M/Fl(2)G.7s 1M. Cargadero No. 1 Fl.R.4s1M. Marina breakwater head Fl(2)G.10s1M. Corner Fl.Y.5s1M. Contradique head Fl(2)R.10s1M. Cargadero No. 2 Fl.G.5s4M. Power station VQ(9)10s5M

VHF Ch 12, 14, 16 for port authorities and pilots. Ch 09 for Club de Mar.

Navigation Marina entrance silting – use leading lines to avoid shallows and stay closer to starboard hand breakwater.

Berths Report to Club de Mar on the E side of the entrance.

Shelter Can be an uncomfortable surge.

Data 280 berths. Visitors' berths. Max LOA 15m. Depths 2·5–7m. Charge band 3.

Facilities Water. 220/380V. Showers and toilets. Fuel quay. 12-ton crane. Some yacht repairs. Provisions and restaurants.

Remarks Club basin close to the town and all its features.

There are plans to expand the harbour to provide 800 new yacht berths.

Club de Mar ✆ 950 230 780
Email cma@clubdemaralmeria.es

ISLA DE ALBORAN

☆ S end summit Fl(4)20s40m10M

Costa Blanca

PUERTO DE SAN JOSE

36°45′·8N 02°06′·1W
21M Almeria ←→ Garrucha 39M

☆ Entrance Fl(3)R.10s7m3M / Fl(3)12s8m5M / Fl.G.7s5M Punta de la Polacra Fl(3)14s281m14M

VHF Ch 09.

Data 240 berths. Limited visitors' berths. Max LOA 15m. Depths 1·5–6m. Charge band 3.

Remarks Small harbour often crowded.

Puerto ☎ 950 380 041
Email correo@clubnauticosanjose.com

PUERTO DE CARBONERAS
36°57'·9N 01°53'·6W (S harbour)

☆ Dique Est head Fl(2)G.10s5M. Elbow Q(3)10s3M. Dique Oeste head Fl(2)R.10s3M. Pucarsa (N harbour) Fl.G.10s5M. Puerto Pesquero Fl(3)G.12s5M / Fl(3)R.12s3M

Commercial and fishing harbours.

Note Work is due to start in the fishing harbour, with plans for a 600 berth marina.

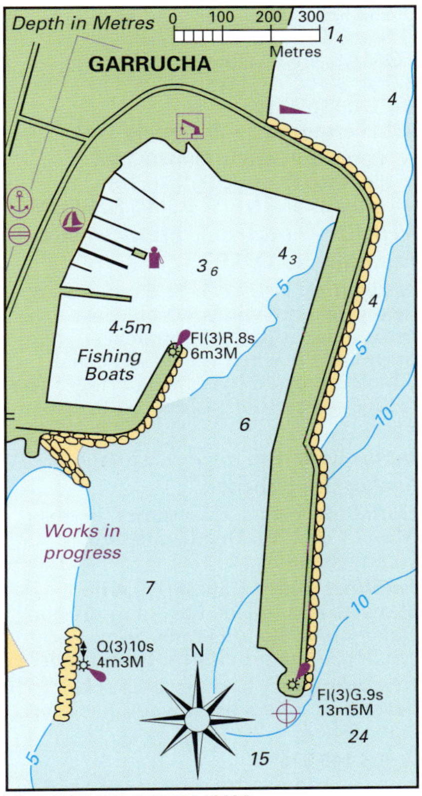

PUERTO DE GARRUCHA

GARRUCHA
37°10'·8N 01°48'·9W
BA 774 Sp 462
39M San José ←→ Aguilas 20M

☆ Garrucha main light Oc(4)13s13M. Bn Q(3)10s3M. Entrance Fl(3)G.9s13m5M/ Fl(3)R.8s6m3M

VHF Ch 16.

Berths Stern or bows-to the pontoons on the W side of the harbour.

Shelter Strong surge in southerlies makes it very uncomfortable.

Data 250 berths. 55 visitors' berths. Max LOA 12m. Depths 1·5–4m. Charge band 3.

Facilities Water. 220/380V. Showers and toilets. Fuel quay. 20-ton crane. Limited yacht repairs. Provisions and restaurants.

Remarks Expansion work is underway with plans for a further 190 berths in the inner harbour.

Puerto Deportivo de Garrucha
☎ 950 460 236
Email garrucha@eppa.es
Club Maritimo ☎ 950 460 048

VILLARICOS LA BALSA
37°14'·8N 01°46'·0W

☆ Breakwater head Fl(4)G.12s5M. Outer breakwater head Fl(4)R.15s4M. Breakwater head Q(2)G.6s8m5M. Outer breakwater centre Fl(2)R.10s3M. Jetty head Fl(3)G.9s3M. T-jetty Fl(3)R.10s3M

Data 90 berths. Max LOA 10m. Depths 2·5m

Remarks Care needed of reef in the entrance. Stay close to breakwater on entry.

☎ 950 467 137

JUAN MONTIEL MARINA
37°23'·7N 01°35'·9W

A new marina close S of Aguilas.

VHF Ch 16.

Berths Stern or bows-to with laid moorings.

Shelter Some berths uncomfortable in strong SE winds.

Data 354 berths. Max LOA 30m.

Facilities Water. 220V. WiFi. WC and showers. Pump-out. Fuel quay. Travel-hoist. Workshops. Hotel and associated facilities.

☎ 968 414 968
Email info@puertodeportivojuanmontiel.com

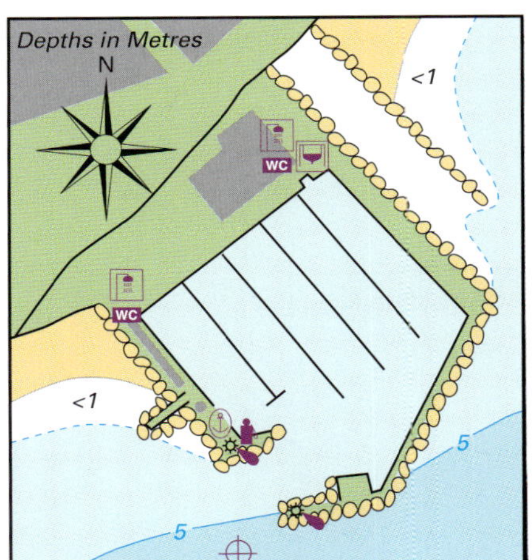

JUAN MONTIEL MARINA

AGUILAS
37°24'·3N 01°34'·4W
BA 1515 Sp 463
20M Garrucha ←→ Mazarrón 19M

☆ Punta Negra Fl(2)5s30m13M. Breakwater head Fl(3)R.9s3M. Contradique head Fl(3)G.9s2M. Dársena Deportiva Fl(2)G.7s3M. Dique Ouest Oc.R.5s2M. Islote Aguilica Fl(2)R.7s5m1M. Southwards Research LtV Mo(U)15s Siren

VHF Ch 09, 16.

Data Yacht harbour 180 berths. 15 visitors' berths. Max LOA 12m. Depths 1·5–2·5m. Charge band 3.

Facilities Water. 220/380V. Showers and toilets. 50-ton travel-lift. Crane. Some repairs. Restaurants.

Remarks Marina often full.

☎ 968 411 951

PUERTO DEPORTIVO DE MAZARRON
37°33'·5N 01°16'·3W
BA 774 Sp 4632
19M Aguilas ←→ Cartagena 14M

☆ YC Jetty head Fl(4)R.10s3M

VHF Ch 09.

Navigation The yacht harbour lies 1M W of the old harbour of Mazarrón.

Berths Where directed.

Shelter Good shelter.

Data 200 berths. 50 visitors' berths. Max LOA 24m. Depths 3–5m.

Facilities Water. 220/380V. Showers and toilets. Fuel quay. 10-ton crane. Limited yacht repairs. Some provisions. Restaurants.

Capitanía ☎ 968 595 253
YC ☎ 968 594 011
www.crmazarron.com

MAZARRON (COMMERCIAL PORT)
37°33'·9N 01°15'·2W

☆ Dique de Abrigo head Fl(4)R.11s5M. Contradique head Fl.G.5s1M. Mole NE Fl(2+1)G.21s1M. Islote La Galerica Fl(4)G.11s3M. Fish market wharf F.1M

Data Max LOA 25m.

ALGAMECA GRANDE
37°35'·2N 01°00'·2W
BA 1194 Sp 4642

☆ Entrance Fl(4)R.11s7M/Fl(3)G.9s3M. Pier F.G.2M

PUERTO DE ESCOMBRERAS
37°34'·2N 00°58'·0W

☆ Entrance Fl.G.3s10M/ Fl(2+1)R.14·5s3M. Muelle Principe Felipe Fl(4)R.12s1M/Fl(2+1)G.16s. Muelle Isaac Peral Fl.R.3s1M / Fl(3)G.9s1M. Methane Gas pier, W head Fl(2)R.7s8m1M. E head Fl(3)R.10s8m1M

Oil terminal. Expansion works in progress.

CARTAGENA
37°34'·92N 00°58'·93W WGS84
BA 1194 Sp 4642
14M Mazarrón ←→ Tomas Maestre 25M

☆ Entrance Fl(2)R.10s10M/ Fl(3)G.14s5M. Muelle de Carbon Fl(2+1)R.14·5s3M. Espalmador floating breakwater head Q.R.4M. Coal wharf head Fl(2+1)R.14·5s3M. Muelle de Alfonso XII W end yacht club Oc.G.3s1M. Marina breakwater Q.G.1M.Yacht marina breakwater Fl(3)R.9s1M. Outer harbour elbow SW Fl(2+1)G.12s1M. Muelle de Santa Lucia NW corner Fl(4)G.12s1M. Santiago breakwater wharf head Fl(4)R.11s1M. Kuelle de Talleres NW corner Fl.G.3s5m1M. Dolphin Fl(2+1)G.16s1M

VHF Ch 11, 12, 14, 16 for port authorities. Ch 09 for RCR and YPC.

Navigation Isolote Escombreras is now joined to Pta del Borracho by a new breakwater. Another new breakwater has been constructed running NW from the islet. There are several prohibited areas around the port. Do not enter Puerto Navale.

Berths Yachts should head for either Real Club Regatas or Yacht Port Cartegena.

Shelter May be a surge in the marina.

Remarks Sympathetic and very Spanish town.

Real Club Regatas Marina

Data 400 berths. 90 visitors' berths. Max LOA 20m. Charge band 4.

Facilities Water. 220/380V. Showers and WC in YC. Fuel quay. Telephone. Limited repair services. Provisions and shopping.

Real Club de Regatas ☏ 968 501 507

Email contacto@clubregatascartagena.es
www.clubregatascartagena.es

Yacht Port Cartagena

New marina lying immediately E of the Real Club de Regatas Marina, along Muelle de Alfonso XII.

Data 310 berths. Max LOA 120m. Depths 7–10m. Assisted mooring. Charge band 3.

Facilities Water. 220/380V. High-speed internet. Satelite TV. Vacuum pump-out. Fuel: direct line/tanker delivery. Heliport. At berth private parking. Yacht club.

Izar Carenas Shipyard

5,500-ton (150x23x9m) syncro-lift.

Specialising in conversion and repair of large luxury yachts.

Yacht Port Cartagena
☏ 968 121 213
Email marina@yachtportcartagena.com
www.cartagenamarina.es

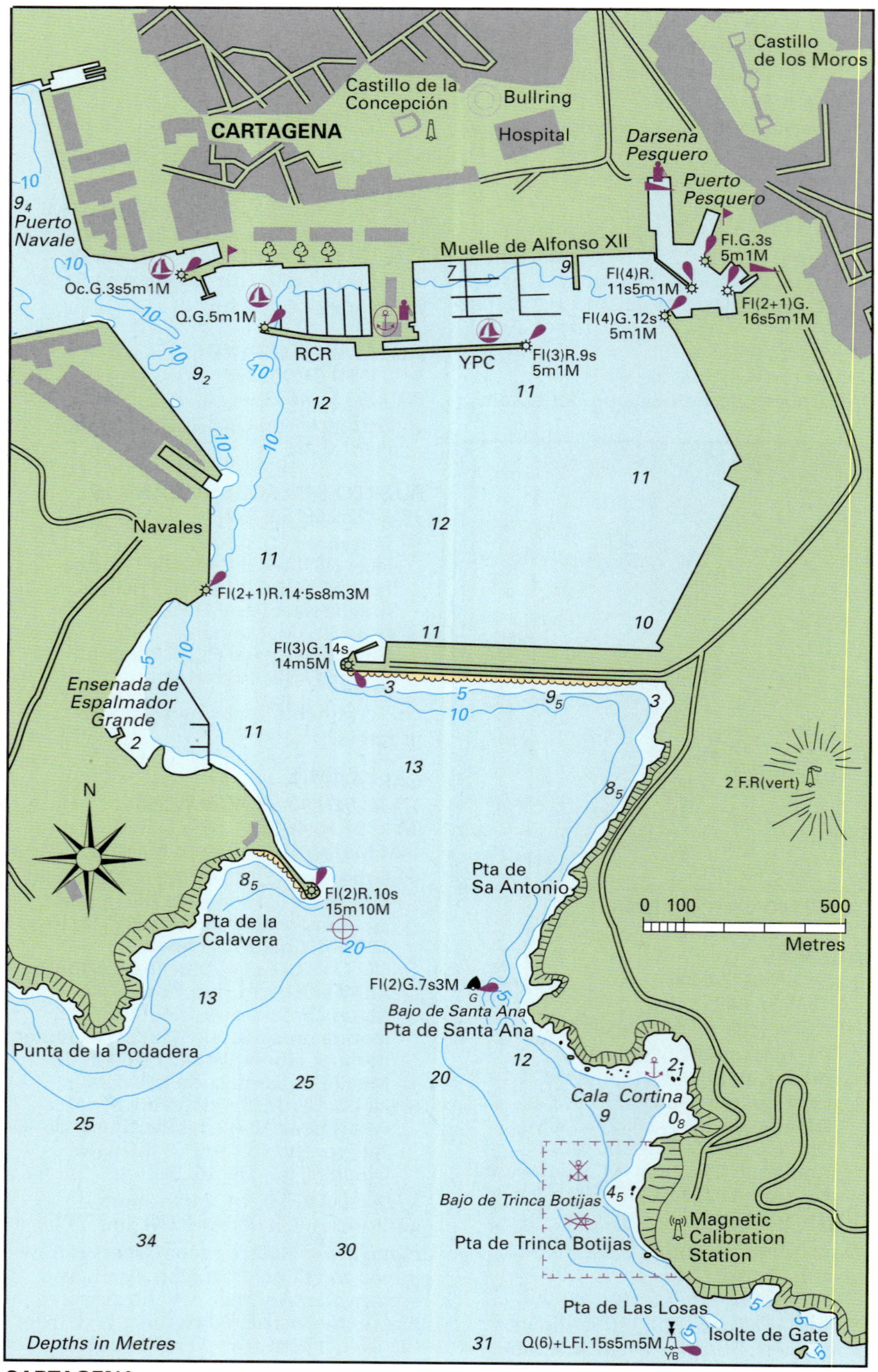

CARTAGENA

CABO DE PALOS

37°37'·9N 00°41'·9W

☆ Entrance Fl(2)G.7s5M/Fl(2)R.7s3M/Fl(2)R.12s 3M. Bn VQ(6)+LFl.10s5m5M

VHF Ch 09.

Data 160 berths. 40 visitors' berths. Max LOA 10m. Depths 2m.

☏ 968 563 515

TOMÁS MAESTRE

37°44'·8N 00°43'·5W
BA 1700 Sp 4710
25M Cartagena ←→ Torrevieja 17M

☆ Punta del Estacio Fl(4)20s14M
Los Escolletes VQ(3)5s7m3M
Interior pier N Fl.R.5s3M/S Fl.G.5s3M

VHF Ch 09 (including bridge comms).

Data Max LOA 25m.

Navigation Entry can be dangerous in heavy onshore winds which cause breaking seas in the approaches. The harbour is reached via a 1½M canal which is crossed by a swing bridge. The bridge opens 1000, 1200, 1400, 1600, 1800.

Berths Report to *torre de control.*

Shelter Good shelter.

Data 860 berths. 325 visitors' berths. Max LOA 25m. Depths 2·5–4m. Charge band 3.

Facilities Water. 220/380V. WiFi. Showers and toilets. Fuel quay. 60-ton travel-hoist. 12-ton crane. Some yacht repairs. Some provisions. Restaurant.

Remarks Outer harbour area is being developed. Old S breakwater has been demolished.

☏ 968 140 816
www.puertomaestre.com

MAR MENOR

Imray M12

An inland sea 12M long and 6M wide separated from the Mediterranean by a long sand bar. Mar Menor has depths of 5–6m over the greater part of its area with gently shallowing sides. There are four islands. The harbour of Tomás Maestre lies at the entrance to Mar Menor.

There are several marinas around the edges of Mar Menor.

Remarks Numerous buoys mark passing channels and floating nets in Mar Menor in the summer.

Puerto Dos Mares

37°40'·0N 00°44'·0W

Data Max LOA 12m. Depths 1–1·9m.

Puerto de la Manga

37°39'·0N 00°43'·0W

Data Max LOA 12m. Depths <1–1·8m.

Puerto de Mar de Cristal

37°39'N 00°46'W

☆ Entrance F.R.2M/F.G.2M

Data Max LOA 10m. Depths 1–2m.

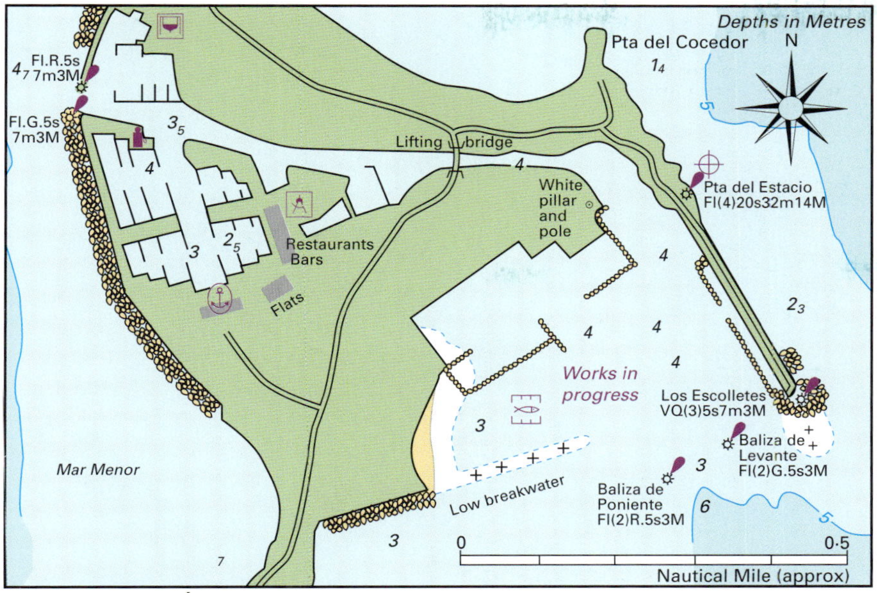

PUERTO DE TOMÁS MAESTRE

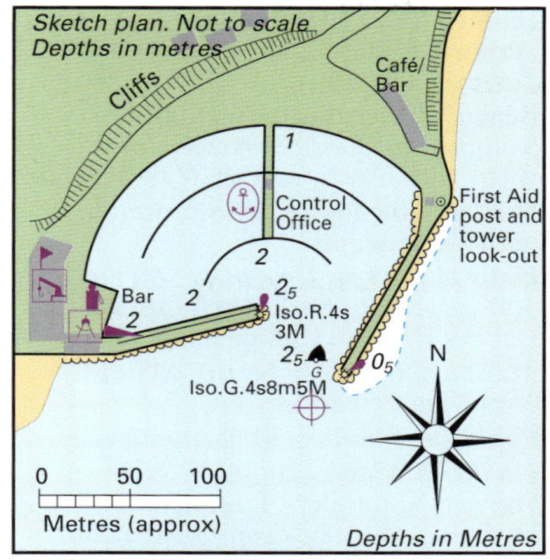

PUERTO DE CAMPOAMOR

Puerto de Los Nietos

37°39'N 00°47'W

☆ Entrance F.R/LFl.R.5s/Iso.G.8s

Data 450 berths. Max LOA 15m. Depths <1–2·5m.

Porto de los Urrutias

37°41'N 00°49'W

☆ Entrance F.G/F.R

Data 250 berths. Max LOA 15m. Depths 1·5–2m.

Puerto de los Alcazares

37°44'N 00°51'W

☆ Fl(3)G.16·5s4M/Fl(2)R14s4M

Data 280 berths. Max LOA 15m. Depths 1–2m.

☎ 968 575 129

MARINA SAN PEDRO DEL PINATAR

37°49'·4N 00°45'·1W

☆ Entrance Fl(4)R.12s3M/Fl(4)G.12s5M

Data 400 berths. Max LOA 15m. Depths <1–2·5m.

Facilities Water. 220V. WC and showers. Fuel. Travel-hoist. Repairs.

CN Puerto San Pedro ☎ 968 182 678

Email info@clubnauticovillasanpedro.com

Marina Salinas ☎ 676 388 790

PUERTO DE LA HORADADA

37°52'·0N 00°45'·3W

☆ Breakwater end Q(3)10s8m3M
Entrance Fl(3)G.10s5M/Fl(2)R.7s4M

VHF Ch 09.

Navigation Depths reported to be mostly <1m inside.

Berths Where directed.

Data 500 berths. Max LOA 12m. Depths mostly 1m in harbour.

Facilities Water. 220V. Showers and toilets. Restaurant.

☎ 966 769 087

Email cnth@clubnauticotorrehoradada.com

PUERTO DE CAMPOAMOR

37°54'·0N 00°44'·8W

☆ Entrance Iso.G.4s5M/Iso.R.4s3M

VHF Ch 09

Navigation There is shoal water in the approaches and care is needed for any craft over 1m draught.

Data 350 berths. Visitors' berths. Max LOA 12m. Depths 1–2m.

Facilities Water. 220V. Showers and toilets. Fuel quay. Some repairs. Mini-market. Restaurants.

☎ 965 320 386

www.cncampoamor.com

PUERTO DE CABO ROIG

37°54'·8N 00°43'·5W

☆ Cabo Roig Marina Fl.G.3s9m5M / Fl.R.3s4m4M

VHF Ch 09.

Navigation Shoal water in the approaches.

Data 250 berths. Visitors' berths. Max LOA 12m. Depths 1–2m.

Facilities Water. 220V. Showers and toilets. Some provisions. Restaurant.

☎ 966 760 176

Email info@marinacaboroig.com

TORREVIEJA

37°57'·9N 00°41'·2W

BA 1700 Sp 4710

17M Tomás Maestre ←→ Santa Pola 13M

☆ Entrance Fl.G.4s7M/Fl(3)R.11·5s3M. Dársena Pesquera Fl(2)G.7s2M. Yacht club jetty Fl(4)R.11s2M. Marina F.R

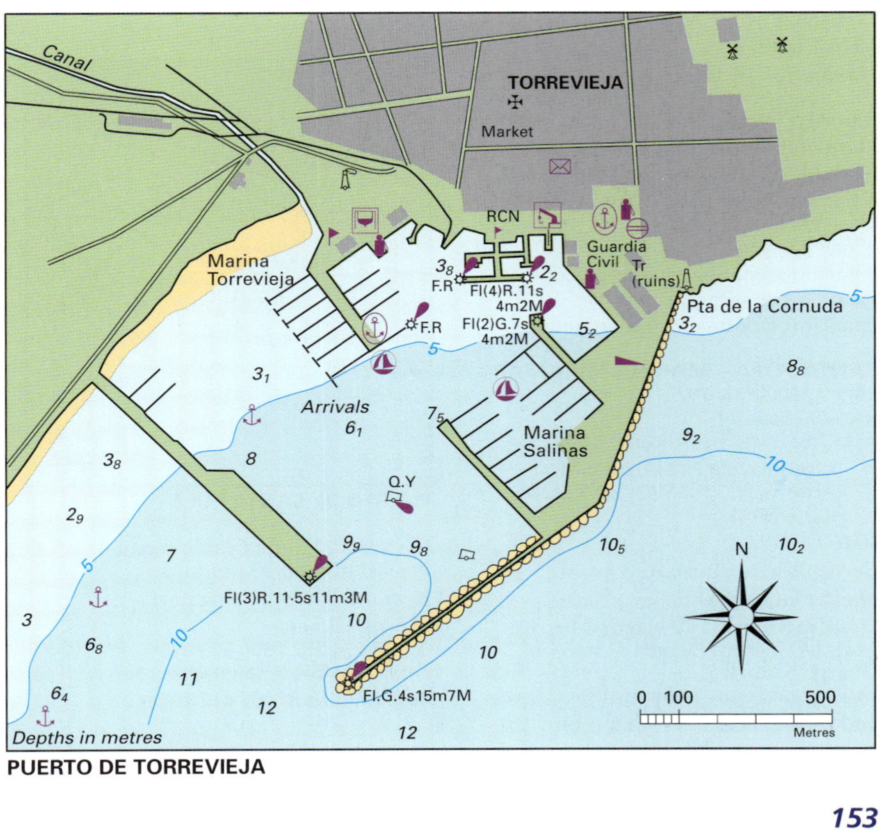

PUERTO DE TORREVIEJA

VHF Ch 06, 11, 14, 16 for port authorities and pilots. Marina de Torrevieja Ch 09.

Berths Where directed at Marina Salinas, Marina de Torrevieja or the yacht club. Anchorage in W of harbour.

Shelter Some berths uncomfortable with S–SW winds.

Data *Marina de Torrevieja* 860 berths. 400 visitors' berths. Max LOA 35m. Depths 1·5–4m. Charge band 3/4.

Marina Salinas 700 berths. Max LOA 35m. Charge band 4.

Real Club Náutico 50 visitors' berths.

Facilities Water. 220/380V. WiFi. Showers and toilets. Launderette. TV. Fuel quay. 80-ton travel-hoist. 12-ton crane. Most yacht repairs. Provisions and restaurants.

Marina de Torrevieja ☎ 96 5 713 650
Email info@puertodeportivomarina internacional.es

Marina Salinas ☎ 965 709 701
Email info@marinasalinas.com

RCN ☎ 965 710 113
Email rcnt@rcnt.com

ISLA TABARCA

☆ Main light LFl.8s29m15M
Breakwater Fl(2)R.6s3M

Natural marine reserve.

MARINA DE LAS DUNAS

38°06'·8N 00°38'·4W (entrance to Río Segura)

☆ Fl(3)R.9s8m5M. Breakwater N head Fl(3)G.9s3M. Inner breakwater pier head Fl(4)G.11s1M. Marina entrance Fl(2+1)G.15s 6m1M / Fl.R.3s6m1M
Mouth of Rio Segura breakwater inner corner Fl(4)R.11s1M
Centre Fl.G.3s1M
W of fishing wharf Q.G.1M
Fishing wharf W head Q.G.1M

VHF Ch 09.

Navigation Inland port reached by the diverted Segura River. 3m least depths reported in channel.

Data 490 berths. 100 visitors' berths. Max LOA 15m. Charge band 3.

Facilities Water. 220V. Fuel quay. Showers and toilets.

☎ 966 726 549
Email info@marinadelasdunas.com

CN Guardamar ☎ 699 302 557
Email info@clubnauticoguardamar.com

SANTA POLA – MARINA MIRAMAR

38°11'·1N 00°33'·7W
BA 1700 Sp 4721
13M Torrevieja ←→ Alicante 16M

☆ Torre Talayola Fl(2+1)20s16M. Entrance Fl.G.5s5M/Q(2)R.5·3s3M. Fl(2)G.7s1M

VHF Ch 09.

Berths Where directed.

Shelter Good shelter.

Data 550 berths. 30 visitors' berths. Max LOA 40m. Depths 1·5–4·5m. Charge band 4/5.

Facilities Water. 220V. WiFi. Showers and toilets. Fuel quay. Pump-out. 10-ton crane. Limited yacht repairs. Provisions and restaurants.

Remarks Large fishing port.

Marina Miramar
☎ 966 694 752 / 650 569 869
Email info@marinamiramar.com
Club Náutico ☎ 965 412 403

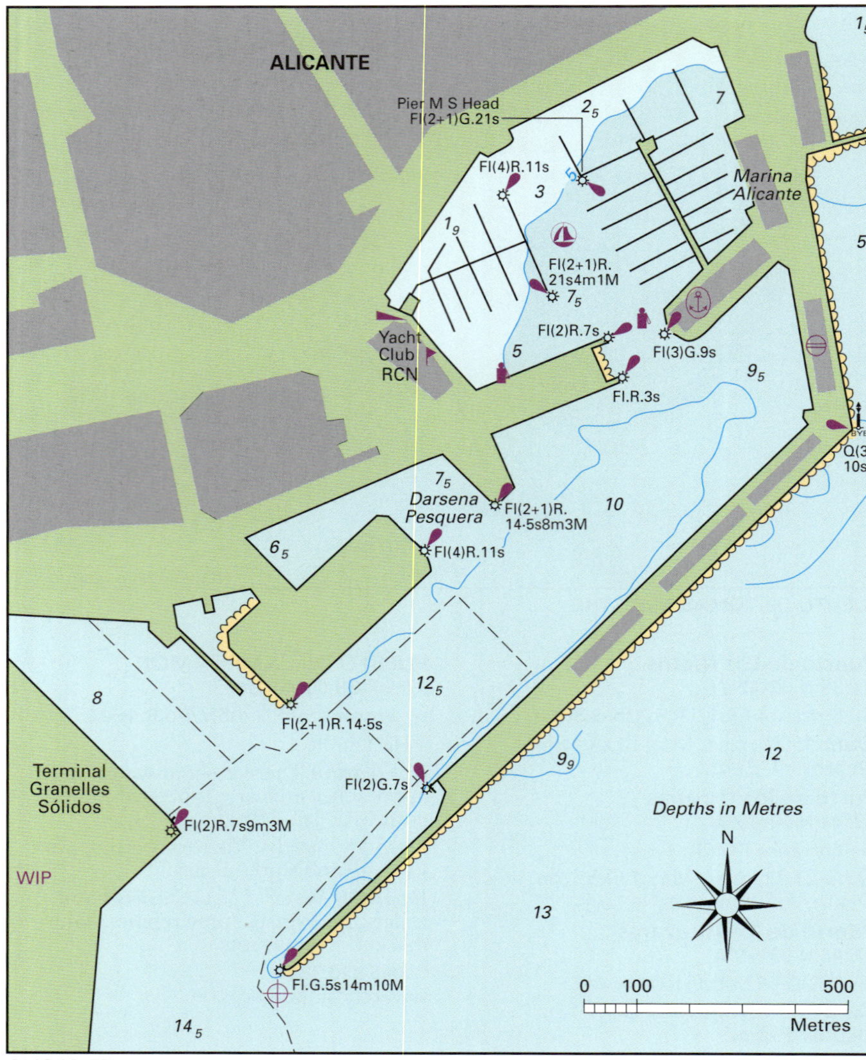

ALICANTE

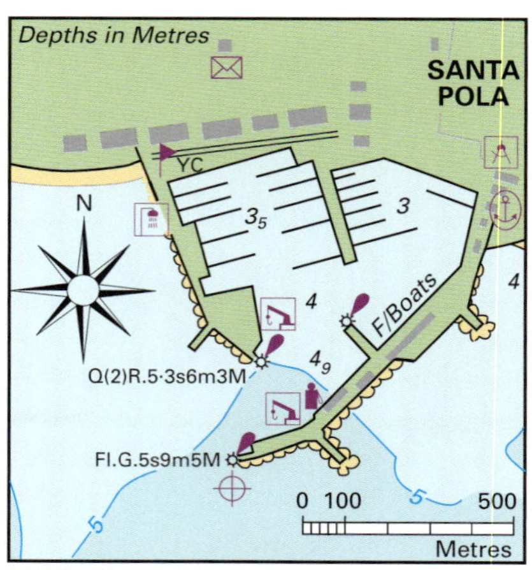

PUERTO DE SANTA POLA

ALICANTE

38°19'·8N 00°29'·3W
BA 469 Sp 4722 Imray M12
16M Santa Pola ←→ Campello 8M

☆ Dique de Abrigo de Levante head Fl.G.5s10M. NE corner Fl(2)R.7s3M. Muelle 11 S corner, container terminal Fl(2+1)R.14·5s5M. Muelle 14 head Fl(2)G.7s. Dársena Pesquera. Muelle 11 head Fl(4)R.11s8m3M
Muelle A head Fl(2+1)14·5s3M. Dársena interior regatta club, outer jetty, S head Fl(2+1)R.21s1M. N head Fl(4)R.11s4m1M. Muelle 5 head Fl(2)R.7s8m3M. Muelles 8 and 10 head Fl(3)G.9s3M. Muelle de Poniente No. 7 head Fl.R.3s8m3M. Muelles 12 and 14 elbow Q(3)10s3M

VHF Ch 12, 14, 16 for port authorities and pilots. Ch 09 for Réal Club de Regatas and Marina Alicante.

Berths Report to fuel berth or nearby until a berth is assigned. *Marineros* assist berthing.

Shelter Good shelter.

Data *RCN* 400 berths. Max LOA 40m. Charge band 4.

Marina Deportiva de Alicante 750 berths. 150 visitors' berths. Max LOA 50m. Depths 4–10m. Charge band 4/5.

Facilities Water. 220/380V. Showers and toilets. Fuel quay. 15/100-ton travel-hoists. Yacht repairs. Provisions and restaurants.

Remarks Large commercial port. Grain silo terminal in the W entrance to the harbour.

Réal Club de Regatas de Alicante
☏ 965 218 600 / 965 921 250
www.rcra.es

Marina Deportiva de Alicante
☏ 965 213 600
Email capitania@marinaalicante.com
www.marinaalicante.com

PUERTO DE SAN JUAN (CLUB NÁUTICO COSTA BLANCA)

38°21'·7N 00°26'·3W

☆ Entrance F.G.3M/F.R.1M

VHF Ch 09.

Data 230 berths. Max LOA 10m. Depths 1·5–3m.

Facilities Water. 220V. Showers and toilets. 8-ton crane. Restaurant.

Remarks Often full.

Club Náutico ☏ 965 265 848
Email info@cnacb.es

Harbour authority ☏ 965 154 491

CAMPELLO

38°25'·5N 00°23'·1W
BA 1700 Sp 473
8M Alicante ←→ Villajoyosa 8M

☆ Entrance Fl.G.3s5M/Fl(2)R.8s3M

VHF Ch 09.

Berths Report to YC for a berth.

Shelter Swell enters with S–SW winds.

Data 475 berths. 250 visitors' berths. Max LOA 15m. Depths *YC*: 1·5–4·5m. Charge band 4.

Facilities Water. 220V. Showers and toilets. Fuel possible. 45-ton travel-hoist. 8-ton crane. Some provisions. Restaurant.

Club Náutico de Campello
☏ 965 633 400
Email info@cncampello.com
www.cncampello.com

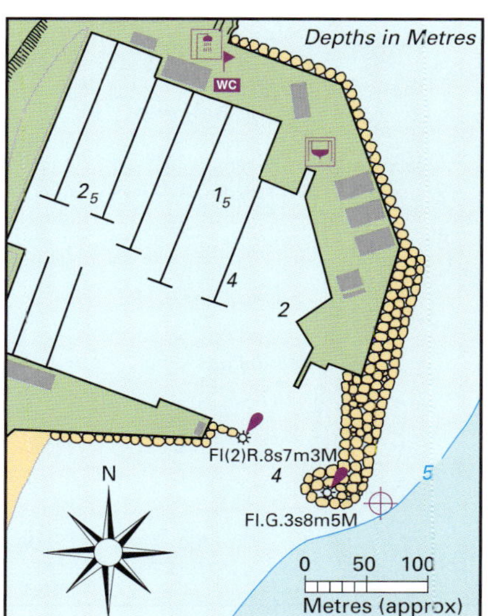

PUERTO DE CAMPELLO

VILLAJOYOSA

38°30'·3N 00°13'·2W
BA 1700 Sp 4731
8M Campello ←→ Altea 13M

☆ Entrance Fl.G.3s5M/Fl(2)R.6s3M/Fl(2)R.6s1M

VHF Ch 09.

Data 325 berths. 160 visitors' berths. Max LOA 20m. Depths 1–7m. Charge band 4.

Facilities Water. 220V. WiFi. Showers and toilets. Fuel quay. 35-ton travel-hoist. 5-ton crane. Slipway. Limited yacht repairs. Some provisions. Restaurants.

Club Náutico ☏ 965 893 606
www.cnlavila.org

BENIDORM

38°31'·9N 00°07'·9W

☆ Islote Benidorm Fl.5s60m6M. Pierhead Fl.G.3s5M. Inner wharf head Fl(3)G.7s1M. Submerged jetty Fl.R.3s3M

Data c.70 berths. Max LOA c.20m. Charge band 4.

Facilities Water. 220V. Showers and toilets. Fuel. Crane. Clubhouse.

Club Náutico Benidorm ☏ 965 853 067
Email info@cnbenidorm.com

ALTEA

38°35'·1N 00°03'·2W
BA 1700 Sp 4732
13M Villajoyosa ←→ Luis Campomanes 7M

☆ Entrance Fl(3)G.9s5m4M/Fl(2)R.6s3M

VHF Ch 09, 16.

Berths Where directed. Laid moorings. Yachts over 15m go outside the outer quay.

Shelter Generally good although strong S–SE winds make 15m+ berths uncomfortable and possibly untenable.

Data 1,700 berths. 150 visitors' berths. Max LOA 25m. Depths 1–3·5m. Charge band 4.

Facilities Water. 220V. Showers and toilets. Fuel quay. 20-ton travel-hoist. Large hardstanding area. Some yacht repairs. Provisions and restaurants.

Remarks Popular with cruising yachts.

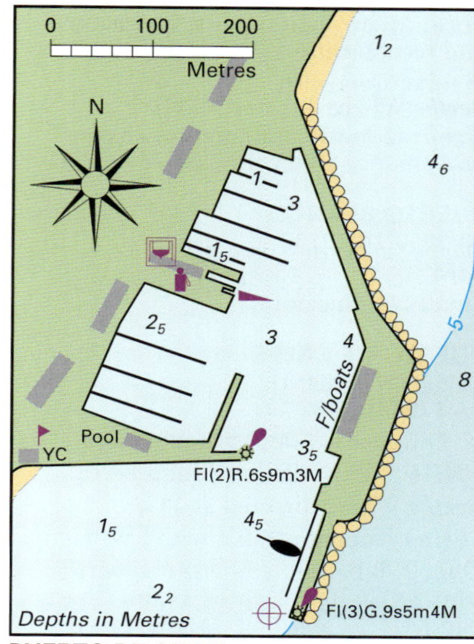

PUERTO DE ALTEA

Club Náutico de Altea ☏ 965 842 185
www.cnaltea.com

LA OLLA DE ALTEA

38°36'·8N 00°01'·9W

☆ Puerto El Portet. Dique Fl(4)G.11s7m1M Contradique Fl(4)R.11s7m3M

LA GALERA

38°37'·3N 00°01'·1W

Small shallow harbour close W of Marina Greenwich.

MARINA GREENWICH

38°37'·6N 00°00'·3W
BA 1700 Sp 4732
7M Altea ←→ Moraira 9M

☆ Entrance Fl(2)G.7s8m5M / Fl(2)R.7s8m1M
Breakwater E head Q(6)+LFl.15s10m3M

VHF Ch 09.

Berths Report to *torre de control*.

Shelter Good shelter.

Data 540 berths. 100 visitors' berths. Max LOA 30m. Depths 2·5–6m. Charge band 5.

Facilities Water. 220/380V. Showers and toilets. Fuel quay. 50-ton travel-

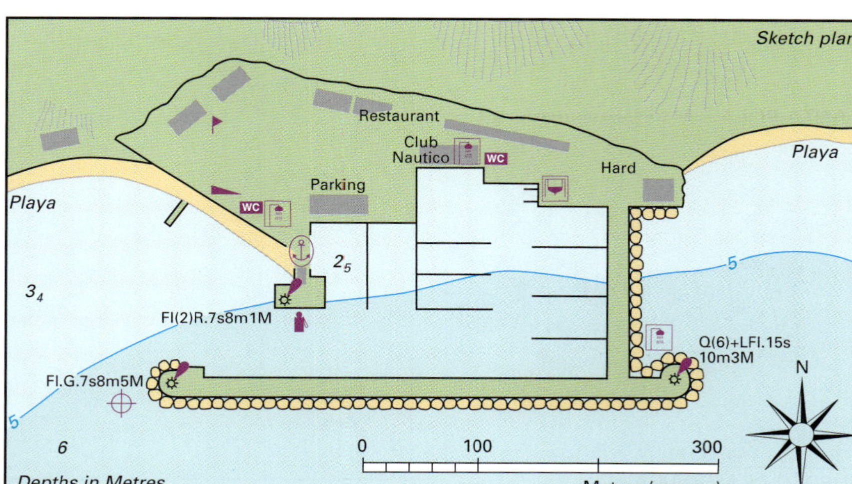

MARINA GREENWICH

hoist. Most yacht repairs. Provisions and restaurants.

Marina Greenwich
☎ 965 842 200
Email marina@marinagreenwich.com
www.marinagreenwich.com

PUERTO BLANCO
38°30′·0N 0°02′·3E
F.3M
Small craft harbour.

PUERTO DE CALPE
38°38′·4N 00°04′·1E
BA 1700 Sp 4732
☆ Entrance Fl.G.4s5M/Fl(4)R.10s3M

VHF Ch 09. Call ahead for a berth.

Berths Where directed at YC.

Shelter Uncomfortable with SW winds.

Data 290 berths. 100 visitors' berths. Max LOA 30m. Depths 1–5m. Charge band 4.

Facilities Water. 220/380V. Showers and toilets. Fuel quay. 10-ton crane. Some yacht repairs. Provisions and restaurants.

Club Náutico de Calpe
☎ 965 831 809
Email info@rcnc.es www.rcnc.es

LAS BASETAS
38°39′·5N 00°05′·2E
☆ Entrance Fl(3)R.9s6m3M / Fl(3)G.9s6m1M

Data 75 berths. Max LOA 10m. Depths 0·5–1·5m.

☎ 965 831 213

MORAIRA (MORAYRA)
38°41′·00N 00°08′·3E
BA 1700 Sp 474
9M Luis Campomanes ←→ Denia 17M
☆ Entrance Fl(2)R.7s2m5M / Fl(2)G.7s10m3M

VHF Ch 09.

Berths Report to YC for a berth.

Shelter Surge with S gales. SW gales can make some berths untenable.

Data 620 berths. Max LOA 30m. Depths 3–7m. Charge band 4/5.

Facilities Water. 220/380V. WiFi. Showers and toilets. Fuel quay. 50-ton travel-hoist. Some yacht repairs. Provisions and restaurants.

Club Náutico de Moraira
☎ 965 744 319
Email info@cnmoraira.com
www.cnmoraira.com

JAVEA
38°47′·6N 00°11′·3E
BA 1700 Sp 4741
☆ Cabo de San Antonio Fl(4)20s175m26M.
Entrance Fl.G.3s5M/Fl(2)R.6s3M.
Inner T-jetty Fl(3)G.9s3M

VHF Ch 09.

Berths Report to YC for a berth.

Shelter Uncomfortable with S–SE winds.

Data Club Náutico: 350 berths. Limited visitors' berths. Max LOA 22m. Depths 2·5–7m.Charge band 4/5.

Facilities Water. 220V. Showers and toilets. Fuel. 65-ton crane. Limited yacht repairs. Provisions and restaurants.

Club Náutico de Javea
☎ 965 791 025
Email info@cnjavea.net

DENIA
38°50′·8N 00°07′·6E
BA 1455 Sp 4741 Imray M12
17M Moraira ←→ Gandia 16M
☆ Entrance Fl(3)G.11s5M/Fl(3)R.10s5M.
Inner entrance Fl(4)G.11s3M / Fl(4)R.11s3M.
Leading lights (229°) Front Fl.WRG.2·5s7M.
Spur head Fl(2+1)G.14·5s5m11M / Fl(2)G.7s.
Club Náutico Fl(2+1)R.21s3m1M

VHF Ch 09, 16.

Navigation With strong N–NE gales there are breaking seas in the immediate approaches.

Berths Head for either Marina de Denia just inside the entrance, the Club Náutico in the SE corner or El Portet to the north. Laid moorings.

Shelter Good shelter.

Data *Marina de Denia* 410 berths. Visitors' berths. Max LOA 60m. Depths 2–4·5m. Charge band 6.
Real Club Náutico de Denia 460 berths. Visitors' berths. Max LOA 20m. Depths 1·5–3·5m. Charge band 5.
El Portet 360 berths. Max LOA 20m. Depths 3m. Charge band 4/5.

Facilities Water. 220/380V. WiFi. Showers and toilets. Fuel quay. 30/60-ton travel-hoist. Yacht repairs. Provisions and restaurants.

Club Náutico de Denia ☎ 965 780 989
Email info@cndenia.es
www.cndenia.es

Marina de Denia ☎ 966 424 307
Email mar@marinadedenia.com
www.marinadedenia.com

El Portet ☎ 966 426 675
Email info@elportetdedenia.es

CABO SAN ANTONIO-JAVEA MARINE RESERVE
Restrictions on diving and mooring.

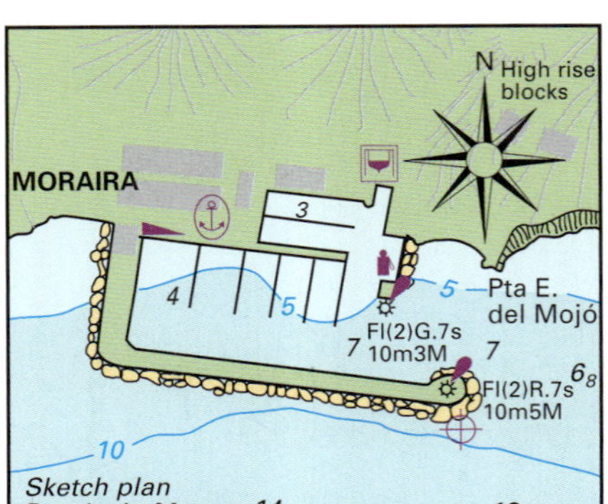

PUERTO DE MORAIRA

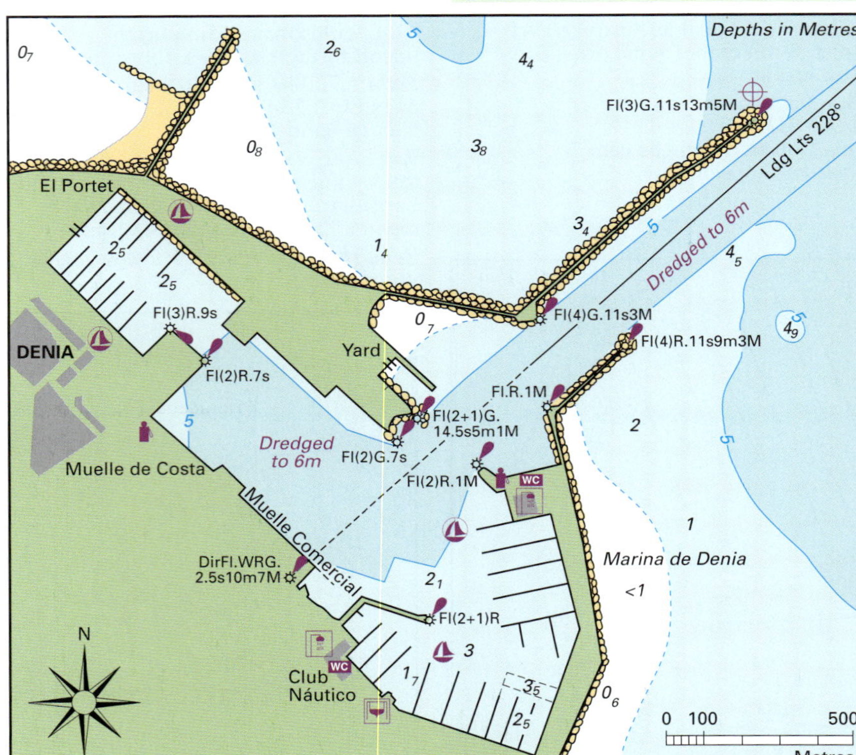

PUERTO DE DENIA

Islas Baleares

Anchoring restrictions

Many anchorages in the Balearics are now restricted for the purposes of protecting Posidonia seagrass beds. Buoys have been laid in many bays and are in place from 1/6–30/9. Reservations must be made for all mooring buoys three days in advance, and for a maximum stay of two consecutive nights in any calendar week. Register on the website, then reserve by phone or on the website. Attendants in RIBs monitor buoy use and are reported to be helpful.

Recommended vessel size for buoys:
Orange/red buoys <8m
White buoys 8–15m
Yellow buoys 15–25m
Green buoys 25–35m

Note This is a different scheme to that in Isla de Cabrera where separate permits must be obtained.

✆ 902 422 435
www.balearslifeposidonia.eu

Please note that the presence of these buoys does not necessarily mean the anchorage is suitable in all winds.

Illes Balears Port Authority

Manages many berths and buoys around the islands and has a useful website where it is possible to pre-book berths.

www.portsib.es

Isla de Ibiza

PUERTO DE IBIZA

38°54'·14N 01°26'·83E WGS84
BA 2834 Sp 4791 Imray M3
11M Sabina ←→ Santa Eulalia 9M

☆ Islote Botafoch, breakwater head Fl.G.3s7M. Root Oc.WR.7s31m14M (045°-W-034°). Marina Botafoch breakwater head Fl(2+1)G.11s3M. T-jetty Fl(2)R.5s1M. Contradique head Fl(2)G.5s1M. Puerto de Ibiza entrance Fl(2)R.7s3M. Puerto Deportivo Nueva Fl(2)G.7s1M. W breakwater SE head Fl(3)R.9s1M.

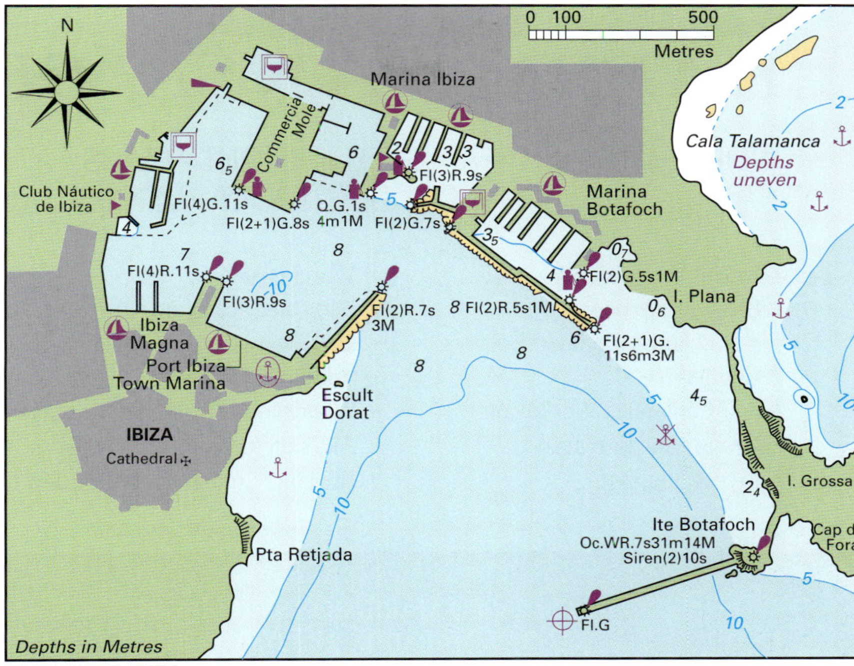

PUERTO DE IBIZA

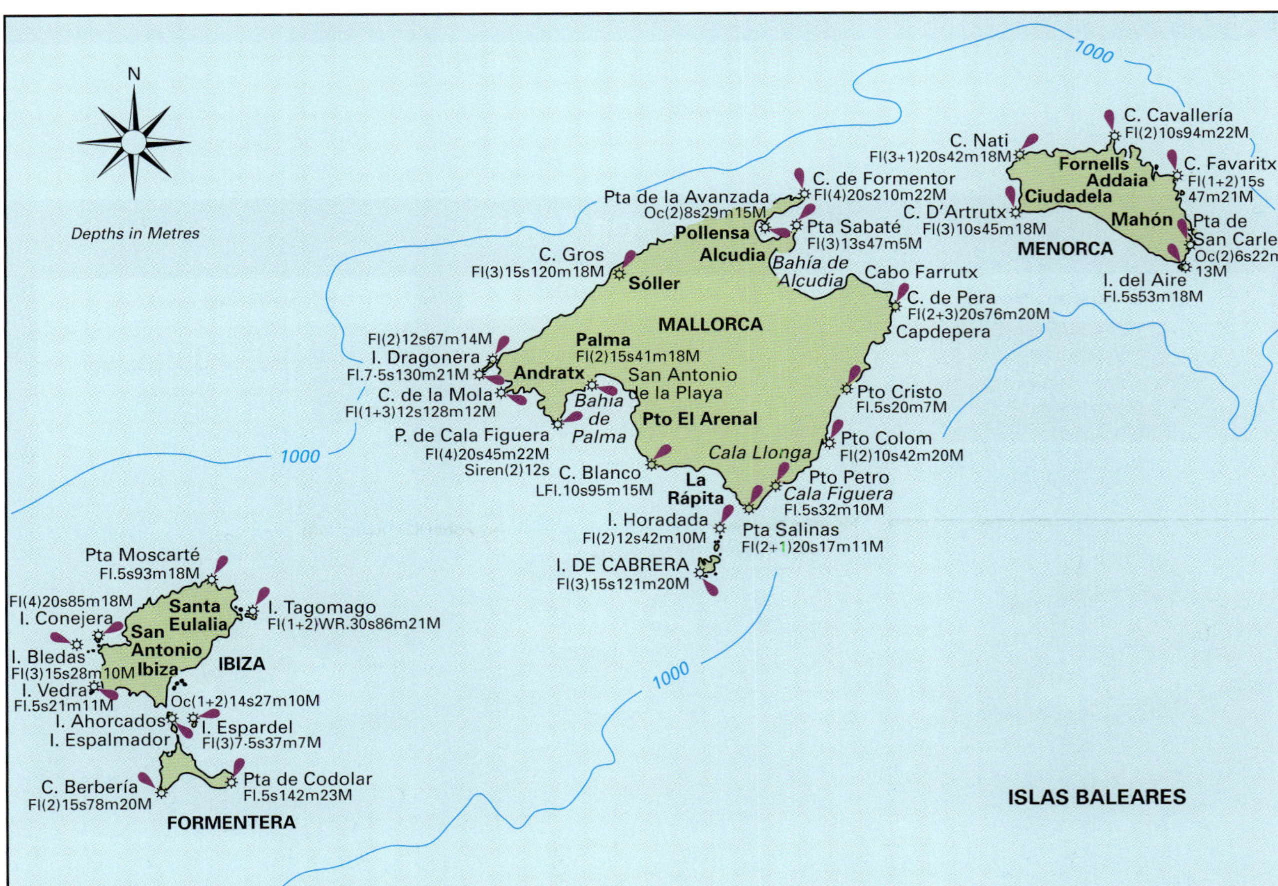

ISLAS BALEARES

W breakwater T-jetty centre Fl(2)R.7s5m1M. Ibiza Marina entrance Q.G.1s4m1M. Oil jetty SE end Fl(2+1)G.8s1M. SW end Fl(4)G.11s1M.

VHF Ch 12, 13, 14, 16, for port authorities and pilots. Ch 09, 06 and 16 for Marina Botafoch and Marina Ibiza. Ch 09 Ibiza Magna.

Navigation Care needed of the islets in the approaches.

Berths Proceed to Marina Botafoch, Marina Ibiza, Ibiza Magna or Port Ibiza Town Marina.

Shelter Good shelter at most berths.

Data Marina Botafoch 425 berths. Max LOA 30m. Depths 3–4m.

Charge band 5/6.

Club Náutico de Ibiza 340 berths. 20 visitors' berths. Max LOA 50m. Charge band 6+.

Marina Ibiza 380 berths. Max LOA 100m. Charge band 6+.

Ibiza Magna 85 berths. Max LOA 60m. Depths 7–10m. Charge band 6+.

Port Ibiza Town 12 berths. Min LOA 60m. Depths 7m. Charge band 6+.

Facilities Water. 220/380V. Showers and toilets. WiFi. Fuel quay. Pump-out. 100/60/27-ton travel-hoists. Most yacht repairs. Provisions and restaurants.

Remarks Marina Botafoch and Marina Ibiza operate launch-ferries to and from the old town. Reports of theft from yachts in Marina Ibiza. Overcrowded in summer months and nearly impossible to find a berth. Anchorage in Cala Talamanca.

Marina Botafoch ☏ 971 312 231
Email info@marinabotafoch.com
www.marinabotafoch.com

Marina Ibiza ☏ 971 318 040

Ibiza Magna ☏ 971 193 870
Email info@ibizamagna.com

Club Náutico de Ibiza
☏ 971 313 363 / 971 310 407
Email cnauibiza@jet.es

Ibiza Yacht Service ☏ 971 310 617
Email ibizayacht@jet.es

Port Ibiza Town Marina tel 971 193 870
www.portibizatown.com

SANTA EULALIA

38°59'N 01°32'·4E
BA 2834 Sp 7A
9M Puerto de Ibiza ←→ Sant Antoni 28M

☆ Entrance Fl(3)G.9s5M/Fl(3)R.9s3M

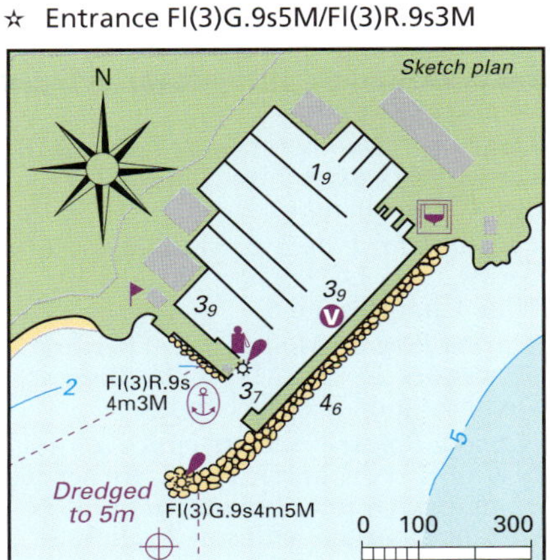

SANTA EULALIA

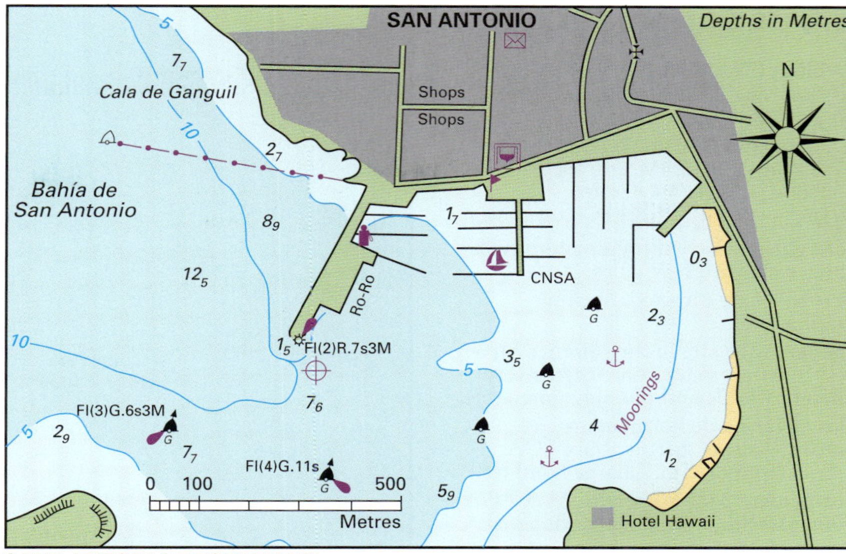

SANT ANTONI DE PORTMANY

VHF Ch 09, 16.

Navigation Entry difficult with strong S–SE winds.

Berths Report to *torre de control* at the entrance.

Shelter Good shelter.

Data 755 berths. Max LOA 25m. Depths 3–5m. Charge band 5.

Facilities Water. 220/380V. Showers and toilets. Fuel quay. 60-ton travel-hoist. Some yacht repairs. Provisions and restaurants.

Puerto Deportivo de Santa Eulalia
☏ 971 339 754

Email ptostaeulalia@interbook.net

SANT ANTONI DE PORTMANY

38°58'·6N 01°17'·9E
BA 2834 Sp 4781 Imray M3, M13
28M Santa Eulalia ←→ Sabina 24M

☆ Pta Chinchó Fl(2)G.7s5M. Breakwater Fl(2)R.7s3M

VHF Ch 09, 16.

Berths New pontoons with laid moorings.

Shelter Good shelter except in strong W–SW winds.

Data Club náutico: 500 berths. Max LOA 30m. Charge band 6.

Port Authority: 245 berths. Max LOA 15m.

Facilities Water. 220V. Showers and toilets. Fuel quay. 20-ton travel-hoist. 4-ton crane. Limited yacht repairs. Provisions and restaurants. Bus to Ibiza.

Remarks Anchoring possible in the bay but keep clear of the ferry turning area. Can be noisy.

Club Náutic Sant Antoni
☏ 971 340 645
Email info@esnautic.com

Port Authority ☏ 971 340 503
Email port.santantoni@portsib.es

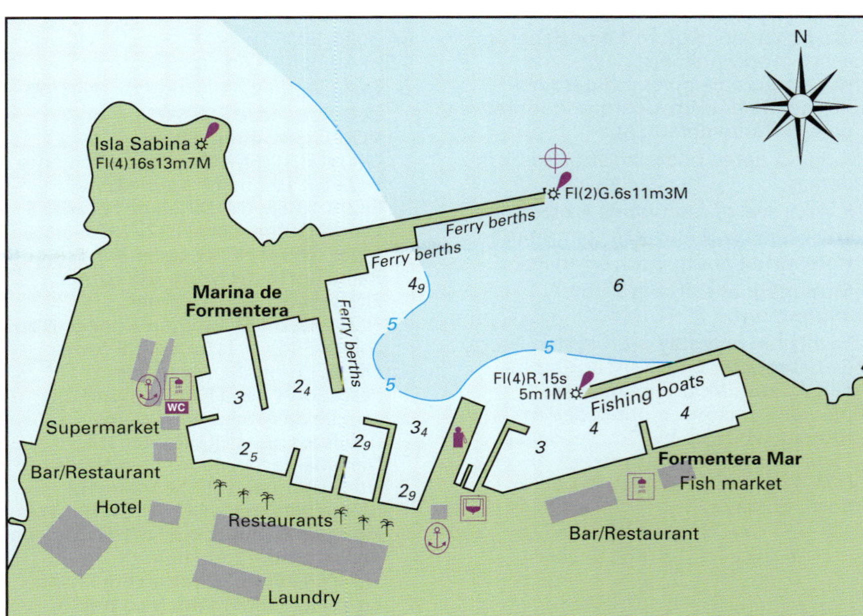

SABINA

Isla de Formentera

SABINA (SAVINA)
38°44′·1N 01°25′·2E
BA 2834 Sp 479

☆ Main light Fl(4)16s13m7M. Isla de Gastabí Q(9)15s4M. Entrance Fl(2)G.6s3M/Fl(4)R.15s1M

VHF Ch 09, 16.

Navigation Entry difficult and possibly dangerous with NW gales.

Berths Where directed, in either marina.

Shelter Adequate in the summer. Strong N–NE winds make some berths very uncomfortable and possibly untenable.

Data **Marina de Formentera** 200 berths. Visitors' berths. Max LOA 24m. Depths 2–5m. Charge band 6+.

Formentera Mar 90 berths. Max LOA 20m. Depths 3–6m. Charge band 6+.

Facilities Water. 220V. Showers and toilets. Fuel quay. 35-ton hoist. Provisions and restaurants.

Marina de Formentera
✆ 971 323 235 / 971 322 346
Email info@marinadeformentera.com

Formentera Mar ✆ 971 322 693
Email info@formenteramar.com

CALA PUJOLS

☆ Leading lights (215°27′). Front Q.R.2M. Rear Iso.R.4s2M

Isla de Cabrera National Park

☆ Cabo Llebeig Fl(4)14·5s74m7M. Punta de Santa Creveta Fl.R.4s13m5M. Puerto de Cabrera pierhead Fl(2)R.10·5s5M

The Cabrera archipelago was declared a marine reserve in 1991. Yachts must obtain a permit to visit Cabrera. Permits can be obtained up to 1 month before a visit. Apply online at www.magrama.go/es/red-parques-nacionales/muestros-parques/cabrera/guia-visitante/default.aspx

- Select dates, boat size etc, and fill in details
- Approval of reservation is given and you will receive an email confirmation.
- Reported not to work on an iPad.

Most marinas will help with applications.

Yachts can only stay overnight in Puerto de Cabrera for one night during July and August. Mooring buoys are provided and are colour-coded as follows: white up to 12m; yellow 12–15m; orange 15–20m; and red 20–30m LOA. Daytime anchorage in Cala Es Borri. €5/day.

ISLA DE CABRERA AND CONEJERA

Isla de Mallorca

PALMA DE MALLORCA
39°32′·92N 02°38′·67E WGS84
BA 3034, 3035 Sp 4211
6·5M Arenal ←→ Portals 5M

☆ Main light Fl(2)15s41m22M. Porto di del Oeste head Fl.R.5s7M. Elbow VQ(3)5s5M. Inner elbow Q(6)+LFl.10s5M. Muelles de Poniente Fl(2+1)R.10s5m3M. Spur elbow Fl(2)R.10s4m1M. Dique de Levante E Wharf Outer corner Fl(2)G.10s6m5M. Inner corner Fl(2)G.10s5m3M. Espigón Rama Corta del Norte NW corner Fl(3)G.9s7m1M. NE corner Fl(3)G.9s7m1M. Espigón Exterior NW corner Fl(4)G.11s7m1M, NE corner Fl(4)G.11s7m1M. Muelle de Pescadores head Fl(4)R.15s6m1M. Muelle de Armamento de los Astilleros head Fl(3)R.9s6m1M. Darsena de San Pedro Club Náutico No. 3 spur head Fl(2)R.14s4m1M. Muelle de Espera Fl(2+1)R.12s6m1M. Pantalan N end Fl.R.3s5m1M. Darsena de San Magin Jetty head Fl(2+1)R.10s1M. Floating breakwater head Fl(2+1)R.15s1M. N corner Fl.R.5s1M.

VHF Ch 06, 14, 16 for port authorities and pilots. Ch 09, 77 for Réal Club Náutico, Ch 09, 16 for Pantalan Mediterraneo, Moll Vell and Club de Mar. Ch 74 for Marina Port de Mallorca. Ch08 for Naviera Balear.

Berths Head for Réal Club Náutico on the NE, Club de Mar on the W or Port de Mallorca in the 'middle'. Other pontoon berths are also available.

Shelter Good shelter at Réal Club Náutico, Marina Port de Mallorca and Club de Mar. Usually good shelter on Pantalan Mediterraneo but can at times be uncomfortable.

Data Réal Club Náutico de Palma 950 berths. Max LOA 25m. Depths 1·5–4m. Charge band 6.

Club de Mar Palma de Mallorca 610 berths. Max LOA 350m. Depths 3–10m. Charge band 6.

Marina Port de Mallorca 150 berths. 30 visitors' berths. Max LOA 30m. Depths 3–6m. Charge band 6.

Naviera Balear Concrete jetties to the NW of RCN. Charter base.Care needed of an underwater obstruction in the N entrance marked with small yellow buoys. c.70 berths. Max LOA c.20m. Depths 2–4m. Charge band 6.

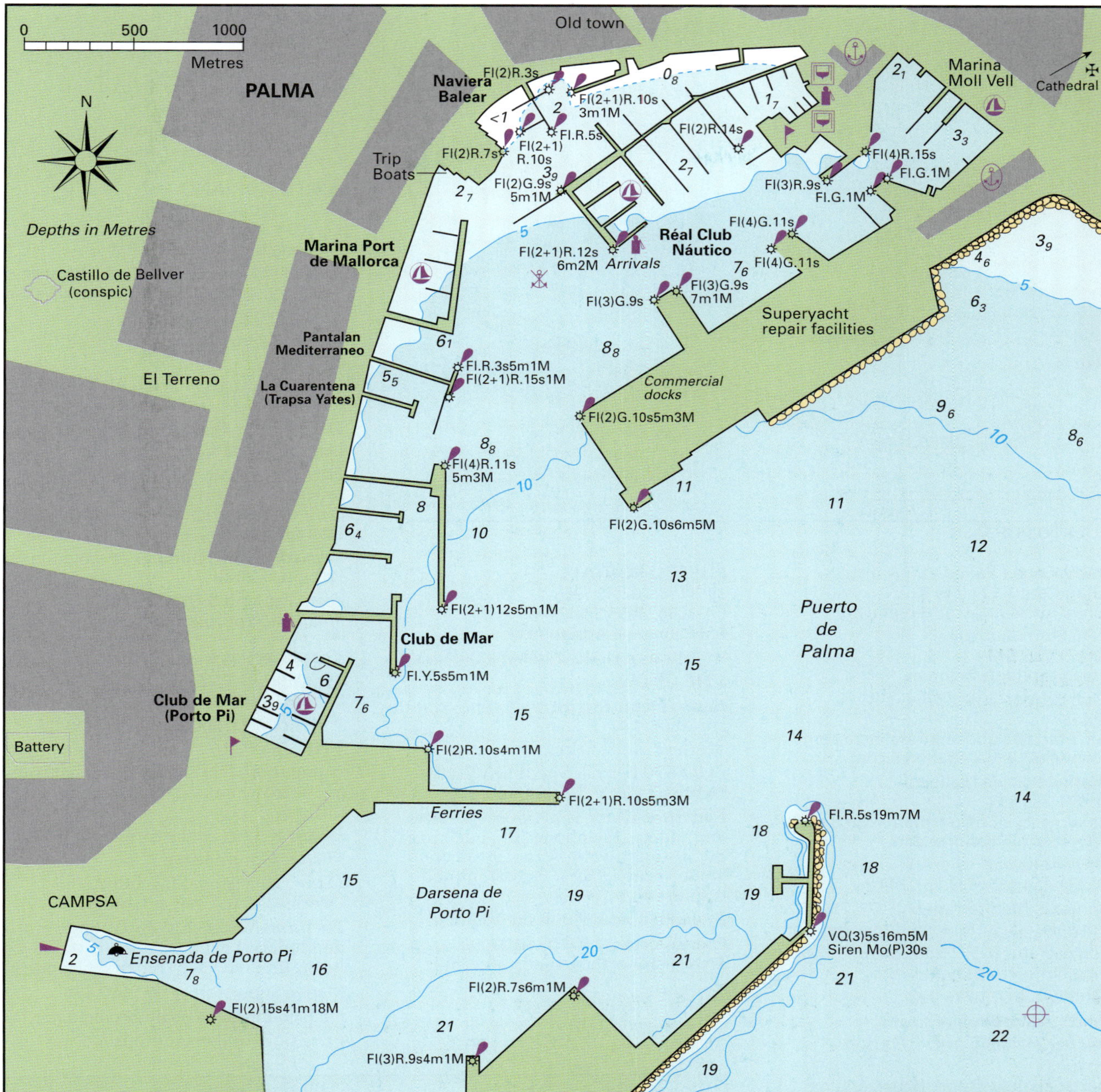

PUERTO DE PALMA DE MALLORCA

CALA NOVA

Pantalan Mediterraneo c.50 berths. 20–100m LOA. Charge band 6.

Trapsa Yates 90 berths. Max LOA 60m. Charge band 5/6.

Marina Moll Vell c.80 berths. 25-40m LOA. Charge band 6+.

Facilities *Réal Club Náutico* Water. 220/380V. Showers and toilets. Fuel nearby. 80-ton travel-hoist. 9-ton crane. All yacht repairs. Chandler.

Club de Mar Water. 220/380V. Showers and toilets. Telephone. Fuel quay. 5-ton crane. All yacht repairs.

Marina Port de Mallorca Water. 220/380V.32/63A. WC and showers. Telephone. 150-ton travel-lift.

Naviera Balear Water. 220V. Showers and toilets. Fuel on SE jetty of RCN.

Pantalan Mediterraneo Water. 220V. Guard.

Trapsa Yates Water. 220/380V. WC. Dry dock and repair services.

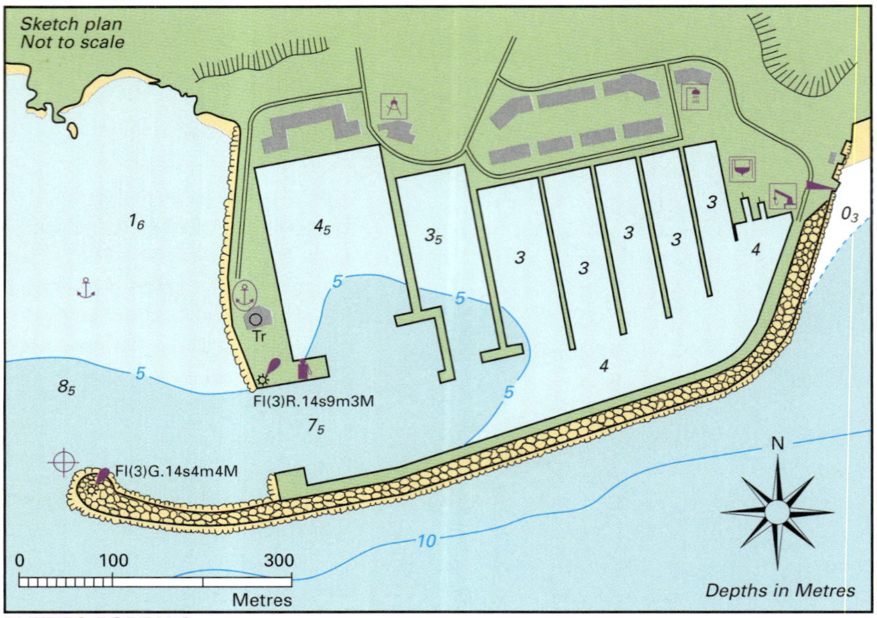

PUERTO PORTALS

Yacht Center Palma
Chandlers ☎ 971 715 612
Email info@yachtcenterpalma.net

Réal Club Náutico
☎ 971 726 848
Email capitania@rcnp.es

Club de Mar ☎ 971 576 605
Email
secretaria@clubdemar-mallorca.com
www.clubdemar-mallorca.com

Marina Port de Mallorca
☎ 971 289 693
Email recepcion@portdemallorca.com
www.portdemallorca.com

Naviera Balear
☎ 971 454 455/ 629 757 944

Pantalan Mediterraneo ☎ 971 718 887
Email info@pantalanmediterraneo.com

Trapsa Yates ☎ 971 730 750
Email info@trapsayates.com

Moll Vell ☎ 971 716 332
Email palma@mollvell.com

Puerto de Palma ☎ 971 715 100
Email
portsdebalears@portsdebalears.com

Yacht Repair Services
☎ 971 710 645 / 46 / 47
Email astillerosmallorca@logiccontrol.es

Audax Marina, Varadero R.C. Náutico de Palma
☎ 971 720 474

CALA NOVA
39°32'·9N 02°36'·0E

☆ Entrance Fl(2)R.7s3M/Fl(2)G.7s3M

Data 215 berths. Max LOA 16m. Depths 2–3m. Charge band 5.

Facilities Water. 220V. Showers and toilets. 25-ton travel-hoist. Limited yacht repairs. Provisions and restaurants.

Cala Nova ☎ 971 402 512
www.portcalanova.com

PUERTO PORTALS
39°31'·8N 02°33'·9E
BA 3034, 3035 Sp 421A
5M Palma ←→ Adriano 8M

☆ Entrance Fl(3)G.14s4M/Fl(3)R.14s3M

VHF Ch 09.

Berths Report to *torre de control* at the entrance.

Shelter Good shelter.

Data 670 berths. Max LOA 70m. Depths 3–7m. Charge band 6.

Facilities Water. 220/380V. Showers and toilets. Telephone. TV. Fuel quay. 80/30-ton travel-hoists. 10-ton crane. Some yacht repairs. Provisions and restaurants.

Remarks Crowded in the summer.

Puerto Portals ☎ 971 171 100
Email marina@puertoportals.com

PALMA NOVA
39°31'·5N 02°32'·6E

☆ Entrance Fl(4)G.11s5M/Fl(4)R.11s3M

Data 80 berths. Max LOA 12m. Depths 1–2m.

Club Nautic ☎ 971 681 055
Email cnpc@eresmas.com

PORTO ADRIANO
39°29'·5N 02°28'·7E
BA 3034, 3035 Sp 421A
8M Portals ←→ Andraix 10M

☆ Islote El Toro Fl.5s31m7M. Entrance Fl(2)G.5s13m5M/Fl(2)R.5s6m4M

VHF Ch 09, 16.

Berths Report to the *capitanía* at the entrance.

Shelter Surge develops with W–NW winds.

Data 490 berths. Max LOA 80/100m. Depths 2–6m. Charge band 6.

Facilities Water. 220V. Showers and toilets. Fuel quay. 50-ton travel-hoist. Limited yacht repairs. Some provisions. Restaurants.

Remarks New buildings designed by Philippe Starck.

Porto Adriano ☎ 971 232 494
Email info@portoadriano.com

SANTA PONSA
39°30'·9N 02°28'E
BA 2832 Sp 4215

☆ Entrance Fl(3)G.9s5M/Fl(3)R.9s3M

VHF Ch 09, 16.

Navigation The entrance and harbour are narrow making manoeuvring difficult.

Berths Report to the *capitanía*.

Shelter Good shelter.

Data 520 berths. Max LOA 20m. Depths 2–8m. Charge band 5.

Facilities Water. 220/380V. Showers and toilets. Fuel quay. 45-ton travel-hoist. Limited yacht repairs. Chandler.

Marine Superstore ☎ 971 690 684
Email marine@yachtcenterpalma.net
Provisions and restaurants.

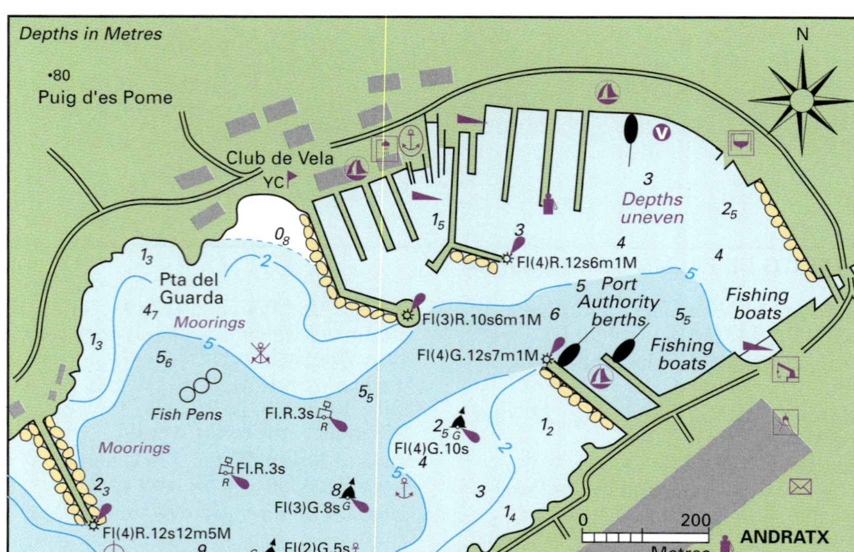

PUERTO DE ANDRATX

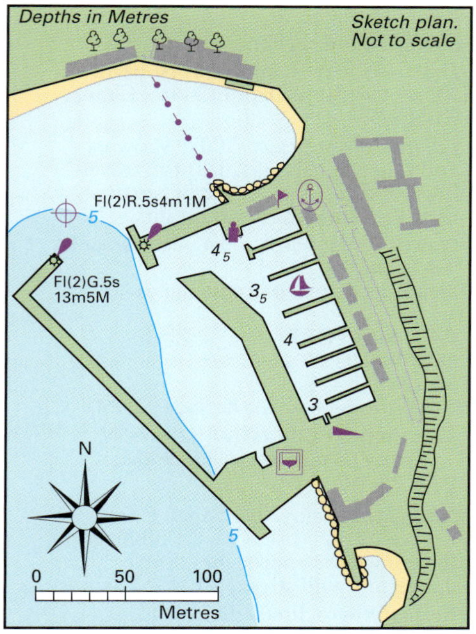

PORTO ADRIANO

Remarks Crowded in the summer.
Club Náutico de Santa Ponsa
☏ 971 694 950
Email cnsp@arrakis.es

PUERTO DE ANDRATX
39°32'·53N 02°22'·75E WGS84
BA 2832 Sp 4214
10M Adriano ←→ Soller 27M

☆ Cabo de la Mola Fl(1+3)12s128m12M. Outer mole head Fl(4)R.12s12m5M. Breakwater head Fl(3)R.10s6m1M. Pier W head Fl.G.4s1M/E head Fl(4)R.12s6m1M. Inner mole head Fl(4)G.12s7m1M

VHF Ch 09, 10 (*Andratx Vela*).

Berths Report to YC on N side for a berth. Laid moorings tailed to the quay or buoys. Alternatively go stern or bows-to under the S mole. New port authority pontoons have been laid near the fish pens.

Shelter Good shelter.

Data *Club de Vela* 475 berths. 120 visitors' berths. Max LOA 35m. Depths 1·5–4m. Charge band 4.

Andratx Port Authority 125 berths. Max LOA 40m.

Facilities Water. 220V. Showers and toilets. Fuel quay. 50-ton travel-hoist. Limited yacht repairs. Provisions and restaurants.

Remarks Anchoring restricted in the bay.

Club de Vela ☏ 971 671 721
www.cvpa.es

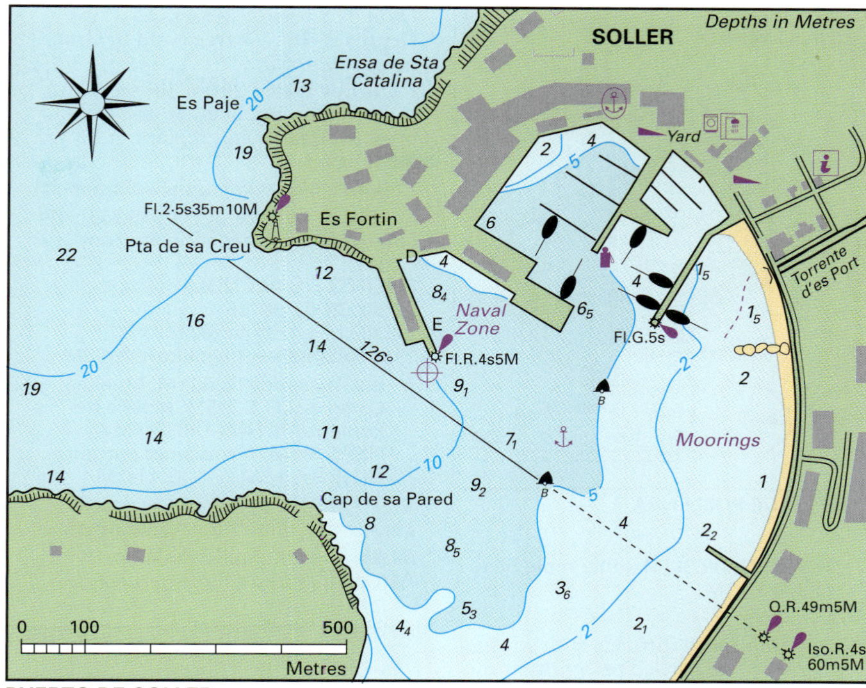

PUERTO DE SOLLER

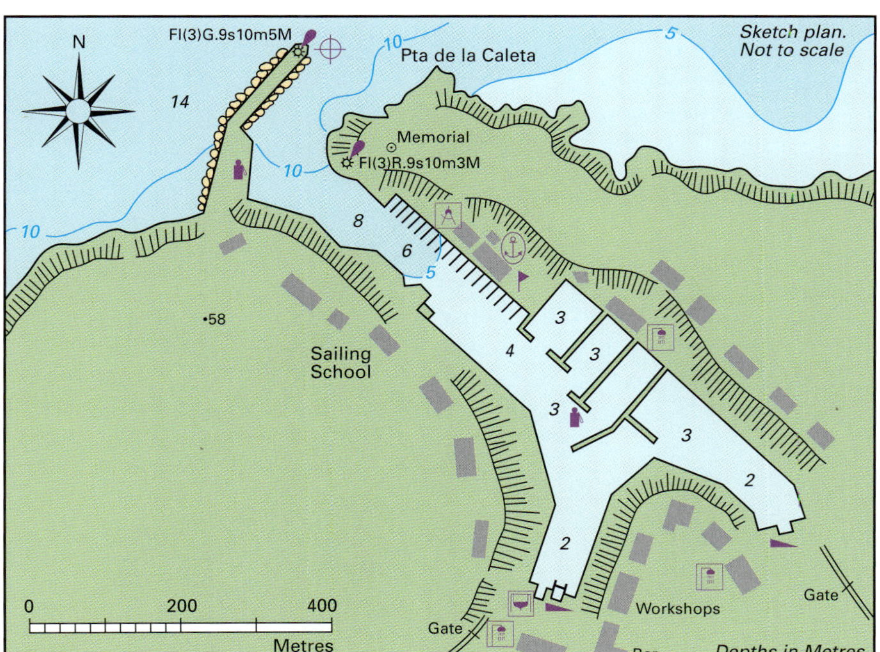

PUERTO DE SANTA PONSA

Andratx Port Authority ☏ 971 674 216
Email port.andratx@portsib.es

ISLA DRAGONERA
39°34'·5N 02°18'·3E

☆ Cabo Llebeitx Fl.7·5s130m21M

PUERTO DE SOLLER
39°47'·8N 02°41'·6E
BA 2832 Sp 4251
27M Andraix ←→ Pollensa 35M

☆ Pta de Sa Creu Fl.2·5s10M. Cabo Gros Fl(3)15s120m19M. Leading lights (124°) Dir.Iso.WRG.4s49m3M. Dique E head Fl.R.4s5M. Inner breakwater SW corner Fl(2+1)R.9s1M. Muelle pontoon head Fl.G.5s4m1M. Pier head Fl(2+1)G.9s4m1M

VHF Ch 16.

Berths New pontoons off the town quay for visitors.

Marina Tramontana berths on the S mole.

Shelter Uncomfortable with strong W winds.

Data c.450 berths. Max LOA c.30m. Charge band 4.

Facilities Water. 220V. Fuel. Provisions and restaurants.

Puerto de Soller ☏ 971 633 316 / 971 186 129
Email port.soller@portsib.es
Marina Tramontana ☏ 971 632 960
www.marinatramontana-portdesoller.es
Club Náutico ☏ 971 631 326

PUERTO DE POLLENSA
39°54'·2N 03°05'·2E
35M Soller ←→ Alcudia 13M

☆ Punta de la Avanzada Oc(2)8s29m15M. Breakwater head Fl(2)G.6s6m5M. E breakwater head Fl(3)G.12s5m1M. Corner Q(3)10s3M. Outer breakwater head Fl(2)R.8s3M. Muelle Servicios S head Fl(3)R.9s1M.

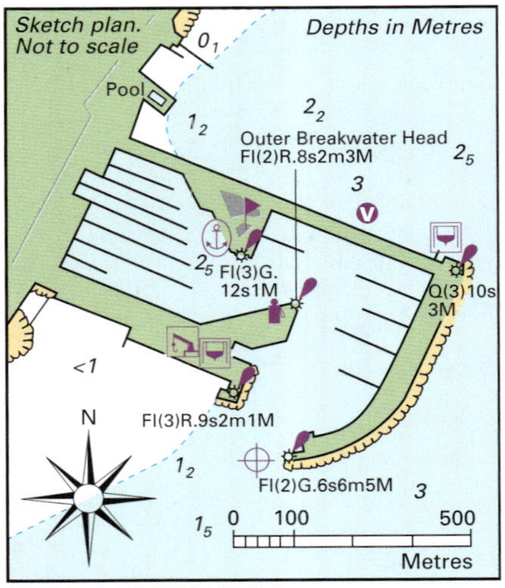

PUERTO DE POLLENSA

N head Fl(3)R.9s1M. Inner mole head Fl(3)G.12s1M

VHF Ch 09.

Navigation Entry difficult with strong SE winds. Care needed of depths at the entrance. Shoal water in the vicinity. Stay close to the end of the outer breakwater.

Berths Where directed.

Shelter Some berths uncomfortable with E–SE winds.

Data 375 berths. 80 visitors' berths. Max LOA 25m. Depths 2–3m. Charge band 5.

Facilities Water. 220/380V. Showers and toilets. Fuel quay. 50-ton travel-hoist. Limited yacht repairs. Provisions and restaurants.

Club Náutico de Puerto Pollensa
☏ 971 864 635
Email oficina@rcnpp.net

Puerto Pollensa ☏ 971 866 867
Email port.pollensa@portsib.es

PUERTO DE BONAIRE (COCODRILO)

39°52'·1N 03°08'·7E
BA 2832 Sp 965

☆ Entrance Fl(3)R.10s5M/Fl(3)G.10s3M

VHF Ch 09.

Berths Stern or bows-to where directed.

Shelter Good shelter.

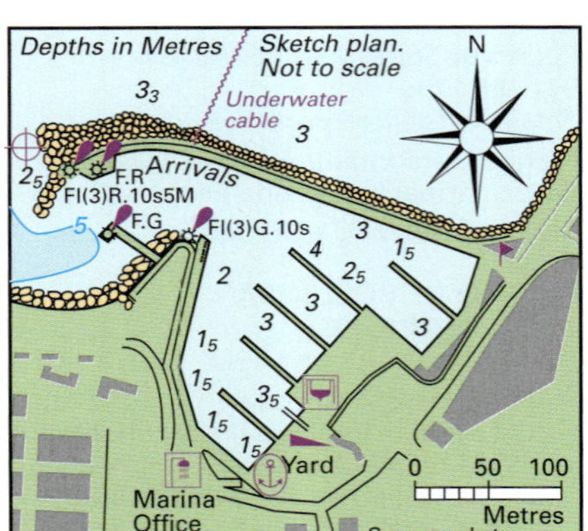

PUERTO DE BONAIRE

Data 325 berths. Max LOA 17m. Depths 2–4m. Charge band 6. Cash only (reported).

Facilities Water. 220V. Showers and toilets. Laundry. Fuel. 30-ton travel-hoist. Limited yacht repairs. Restaurant.

Remarks Crowded in the summer.

Marina de Bonaire ☏ 971 546 955
Email info@marinadebonaire.com

PUERTO DE ALCUDIA

39°50'·3N 03°08'·2E
BA 2831 Sp 425A Imray M3
13M Pollensa ←→ Ca'n Picafort 4·5M

☆ Isla Aucanada Fl.5s11M. Muelle Comercial Fl.G.3s5M. Muelle de Poniente SE Fl(2+1)R.12s3M / Fl(2)G.6s1M. Alcudiamar entrance Fl(3)R.9s5m3M / Fl(4)G.11s1M

VHF Ch 11, 13, 14, 16 for port authorities. Ch 09 for Alcudiamar.

Berths Yachts should make for Alcudiamar and report to *torre de control* for a berth.

Shelter Good shelter.

Data 745 berths. 180 visitors' berths. Max LOA 30m. Depths 2–4m. Charge band 4/5.

Facilities Water. 220/380V. Showers and toilets. Fuel quay. 150-ton travel-hoist. 8-ton crane. All yacht repairs. Gas. Provisions and restaurants.

Club de Amigos de Alcudia, Alcudiamar SA
☏ 971 546 000
Email alcudiamar@alcudiamar.es

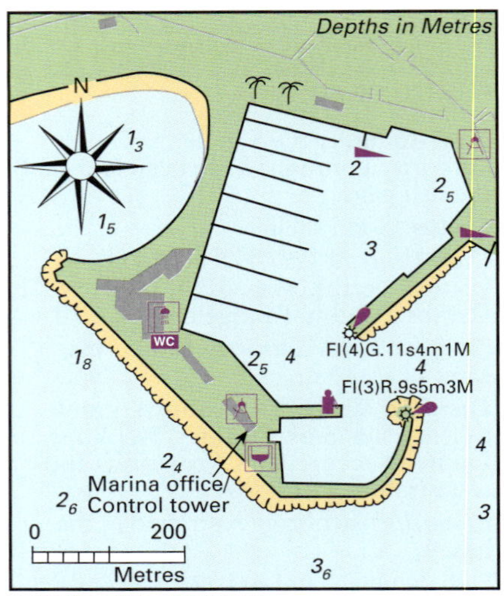

PUERTO DE ALCUDIA

CA'N PICAFORT

39°46'·1N 03°09'·6E
BA 2831 Sp 425
4·5M Alcudia ←→ Cala Ratjada 16·5M

☆ Entrance Fl(2)R.7s5M/Fl(2)G.7s5M. Escury Ca'n Barret VQ(3)10s4M

VHF Ch 09.

Navigation Buoyed channel. Care needed of reef (Escuy de Ca'n Barret) in the immediate approaches. Entry dangerous with strong NE–E–SE winds.

Berths Where directed.

Shelter Good shelter.

Data 465 berths. Max LOA 12m. Depths 2–4m. Charge band 5.

Facilities Water. 220V. Showers and toilets. 6-ton crane. Provisions and restaurants.

Puerto de Ca'n Picafort ☏ 971 850 010
Club Náutico ☏ 971 850 185

SERRA NOVA

39°44'·4N 03°13'·5E

☆ Entrance Fl(3)R.10s5M/Oc.G.8s1M

Data Max LOA 9m. Depths 2–3m.

COLONIA DE SAINT PERE

39°44'·3N 03°16'·3E

☆ Entrance head Fl(4)R.12s5M. Breakwater Fl(4)G.12s3M

New marina now open.

Data c.80 berths. Max LOA c.18m.

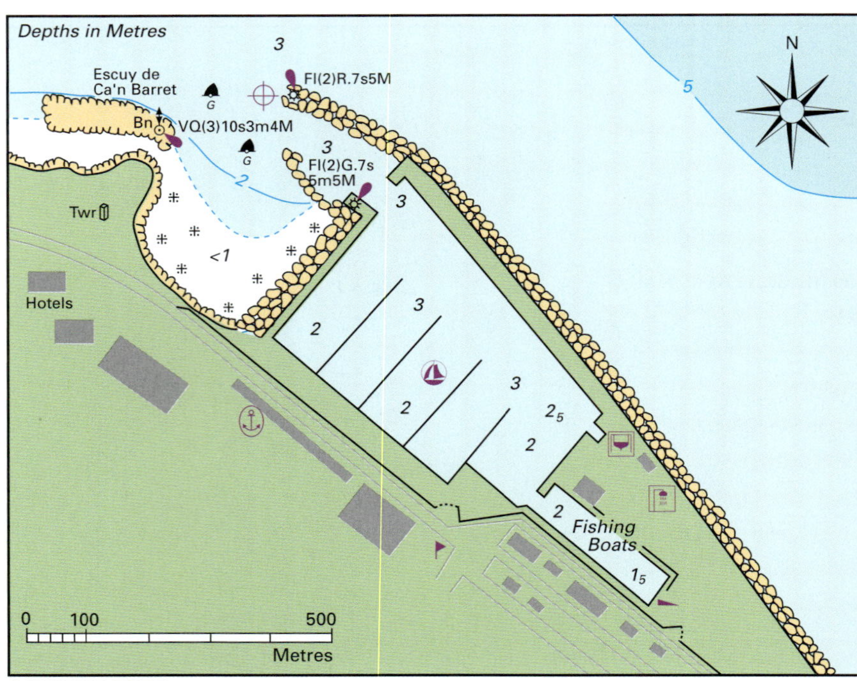

CA'N PICAFORT

Club Náutico ✆ 971 589 147
Capitanía ✆ 971 589 118

CABO FARRUX

☆ Mole head Q(2)R.6s3M

CALA RAJADA

39°42'·6N 03°27'·9E
BA 2831 Sp 4241
16·5M Ca'n Picafort ←→ Porto Cristo 12M

☆ Mole head Fl.G.5s5M. Basin entrance Fl(2)G.6s1M/Fl.R.3s3M. N spur head Fl(2)R.6s1M

Berths Alongside inner side of breakwater. Small yachts may find a berth at the Club Náutico.

Shelter A swell enters with E–SE–S winds.

Data 130 berths. Max LOA 12m. Depths 1–3·5m. Charge band 5.

Facilities Water. 220V. Toilets and showers. Fuel quay. 7-ton crane. Provisions and restaurants.

Remarks Often crowded. Yachts often rafted four or five deep in the summer. Ferry to Ciudadela.

Club Náutico ✆ 971 564 019
Puerto Cala Rajada ✆ 971 565 067
Email port.calarajada@portsib.es

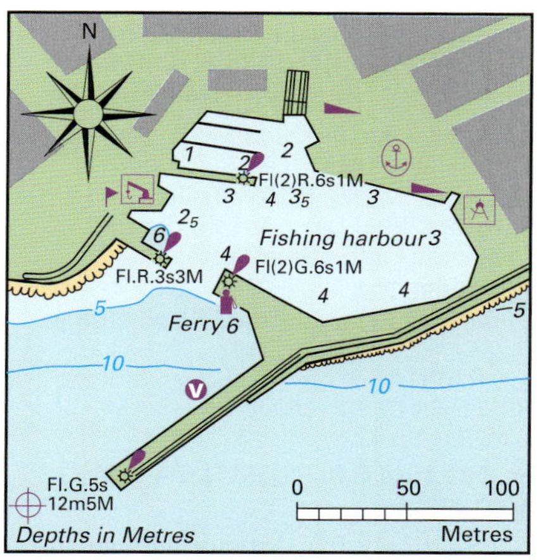

CALA RATJADA

CALA BONA

39°36'·8N 03°23'·6E

☆ Dique Sur Fl(2)R.10s5M. Dique Norte Fl(2)G.10s3M

Data 135 berths. Max LOA 9m. Depths 1–2·5m.

Facilities Water.220V. Fuel to be installed. ATM ashore.

Capitanía ✆ 971 586 256
Email port.calabona@portsib.es

PORTO CRISTO (CALA MANACOR)

39°32'·2N 03°20'·5E
(Cabo del Morro de la Calabaza light Fl.5s7M)
BA 1703 Sp 4241
12M Cala Ratjada ←→ Porto Colom 8M

☆ Cabo de Morro de la Calabaza Fl.5s20m7M. Mole head Fl(3)R.10s3M

VHF Ch 09.

Navigation Entry difficult with NE–E–SE gales.

Berths Stern or bows-to in the marina or on the town quay. Laid moorings tailed to the quay.

Shelter Good shelter.

Data 205 berths. 20 visitors' berths. Max LOA 18m. Depths 2·5–4m. Charge band 5.

Facilities Water. 220/380V. Showers and toilets. Fuel quay. 60-ton travel-hoist. 25/12-ton cranes. Some yacht repairs. Provisions and restaurants.

Club Náutico ✆ 971 821 253
Capitanía ✆ 971 820 419
Email port.portocristo@portsib.caib.es

PORTO COLOM

39°24'·9N 03°16'·3E
BA 2831 Sp 4241 Imray M3
8M Porto Cristo ←→ Puerto de Campos 18M

☆ Punta de la Farola Fl(2)10s42m20M. Punta de la Bateria Fl(4)R.11s5M. Pierhead Fl(3)R.10s1M. Punta de sa Sinia breakwater head Fl(4)R.11s1M

VHF Ch 16 for port authorities. Ch 09 for Club Náutico. Ch 08 for Ports IB.

Berths Report to the YC at the N end for a berth.

Shelter With strong SW winds a surge is set up making some of the YC berths untenable.

Data Club Náutico: 250 berths. 125 visitors' berths. Max LOA 15m. Depths 1·5–2·5m. Charge band 5. Charge band 3 moorings (includes use of showers).

Facilities Water. 220V. Showers and toilets. Fuel quay. 10-ton crane. Provisions and restaurants.

Remarks Anchorage in the NE and SW of the bay.

Note There are plans to dredge the harbour.

Club Náutico
✆ 971 824 658
Capitanía ✆ 971 824 683
Email port.portocolom@portsib.es

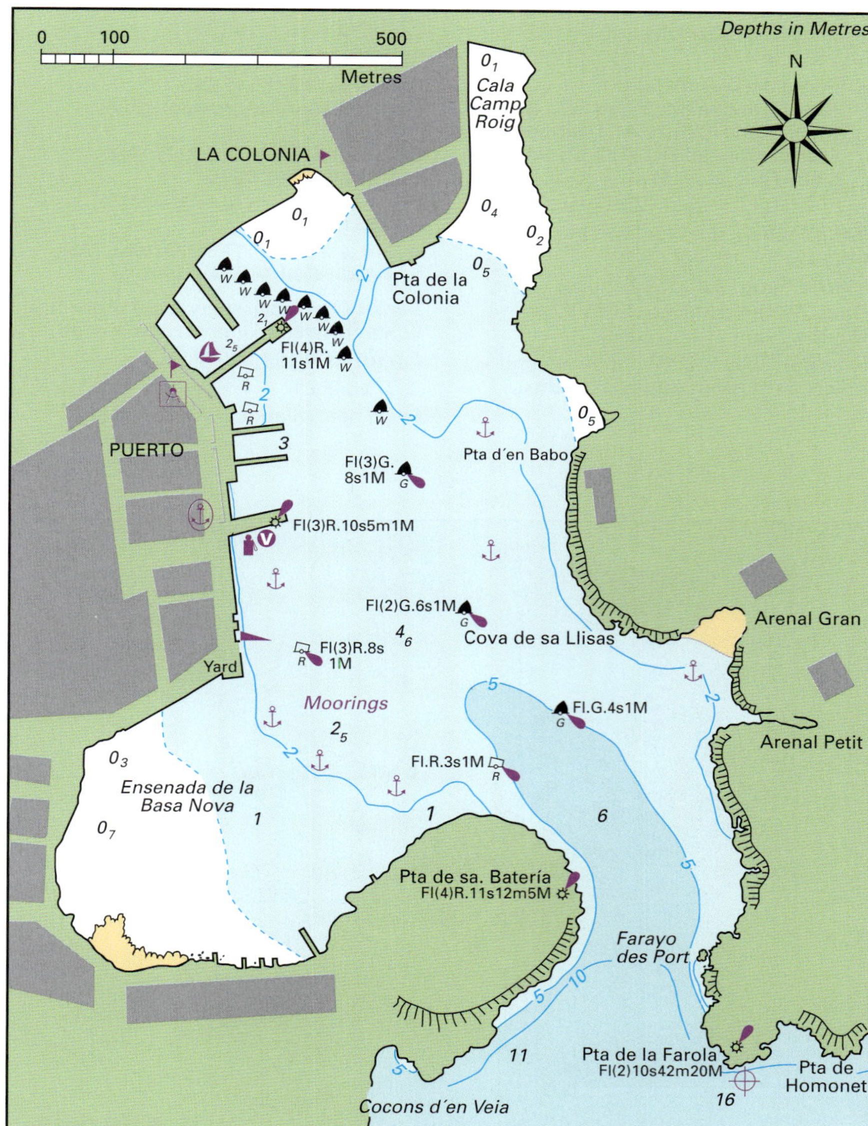

PORTO COLOM

MARINA CALA D'OR (CALA LLONGA)

39°22'·2N 03°13'·9E
BA 2831 Sp 424

☆ Punta des Forti Fl(1+2)20s7M. Cala Llonga N side Fl.G.5s5M. Mole head Fl.R.5s1M

VHF Ch 09.

Navigation Buoyed entrance channel.

Berths Go on the mole and report to the *capitanía* for a berth.

Shelter Good shelter.

Data 570 berths. 20 visitors' berths. Max LOA 25m. Depths 3m. Charge band 5/6.

Facilities Water. 220/380V. Showers and toilets. WiFi. Fuel quay. 60-ton travel-hoist. 5-ton crane. Some yacht repairs. Provisions and restaurants.

Remarks Anchorages around the *cala* are restricted. Anchoring is only permitted on sand.

Marina Cala d'Or ✆ 971 657 070
Email marinacalador@telefonica.net

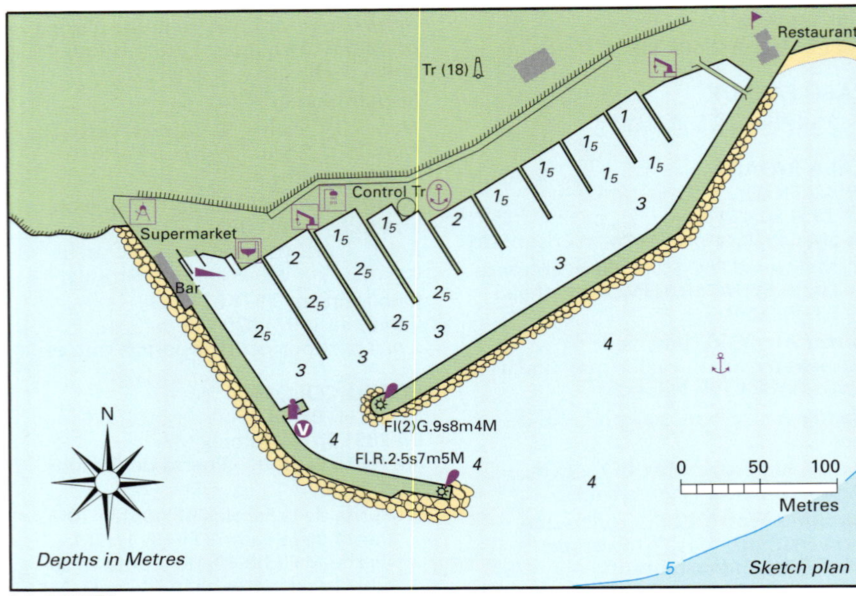

LA RAPITA

PORTO PETRO

39°21'·4N 03°13'·0E (Punta de Sa Torre light Fl(3+1)10s22m7M)
BA 2831 Sp 4231

☆ Punta de Sa Torre light Fl(3+1)10s22m7M. Dique Calo d'es Moix head Fl(2)R.7s5M. Espigón Martillo N head Fl(2+1)G.12s3M. S head Fl(2)G.7s1M

VHF Ch 09 for Real Club Náutico.

Berths Where directed. Anchorage in the bay.

Shelter Surge with E–SE gales.

Data 230 berths. Max LOA 12m. Depths 1–2m.

Facilities Water. 220V. Showers and toilets. Provisions and restaurants.

Remarks Work in progress on new Club Náutico facilities.

RCN ✆ 971 657 657

Capitanía ✆ 971 645 242
Email portportopetro@portsib.es

CALA FIGUERA DE SANTAÑY

39°19'·8N 03°10'·7E
(Torre d'en Beu light Fl.3s12M)
BA 2831 Sp 4231

☆ Torre d'en Beu Fl.5s32m10M. Mole head Fl(3)R.10s5M

Berths On transit quay. Laid moorings. Open to swell from prevailing wind.

Facilities Water. 220V.

✆ 971 645 242
Email port.calafiguera@portsib.es

PUERTO DE CAMPOS (PUERTO COLONIA DE SANT JORDI)

39°19'N 03°00'E
18M Porto Colom ←→ Arenal 19M

☆ Isla de na Guardia Fl(4)G.12s7m5M. Breakwater head Fl(4)R.12s3M. Entrance Fl(2+1)R.10s1M/Fl.G.3s1M

Data 315 berths. Max LOA 9m. Depths <1–2m.

Facilities Water. 220V. Toilets and showers. Fuel quay (2–3m depths). Provisions and restaurants.

✆ 971 656 224
Email port.coloniasantjordi@portisib.es

LA RAPITA

39°21'·6N 02°57'·1E
BA 2831 Sp 422

☆ Entrance Fl.R.2·5s5M/Fl.G.4·5s3M

VHF Ch 09.

Navigation Entry difficult with strong E–SE winds.

Berths Go on quay at the entrance and report for a berth.

Shelter Good shelter.

Data 460 berths. 140 visitors' berths. Max LOA 20m. Depths 1–3m. Charge band 6.

Facilities Water. 220/380V. Showers and toilets. Pump-out. Fuel quay. 50-ton travel-hoist. 7-ton crane. Some yacht repairs. Provisions and restaurants.

Remarks Cabrera permits available here.

Club Náutico La Rapita ✆ 971 640 001
www.cnrapita.com

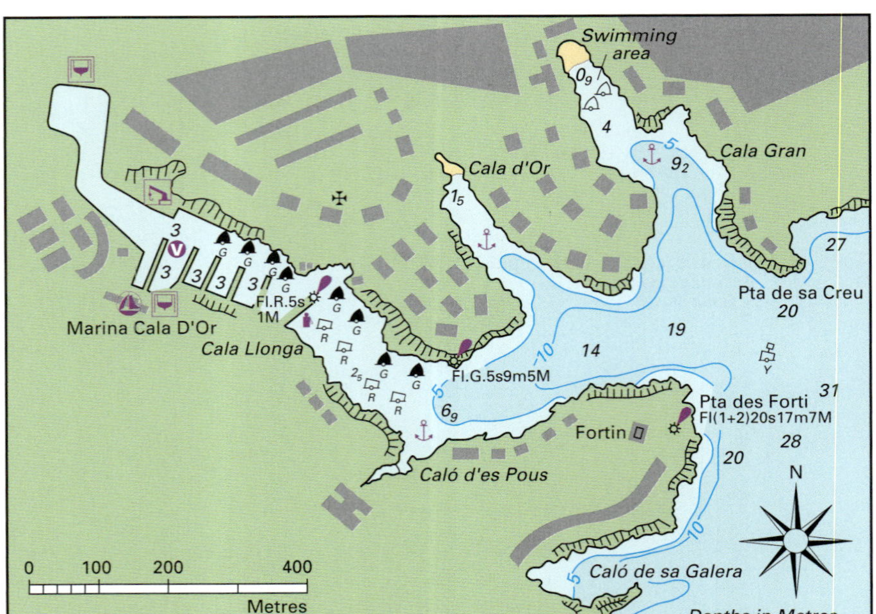

MARINA CALA D'OR (CALA LLONGA), CALA D'OR AND CALA GRAN

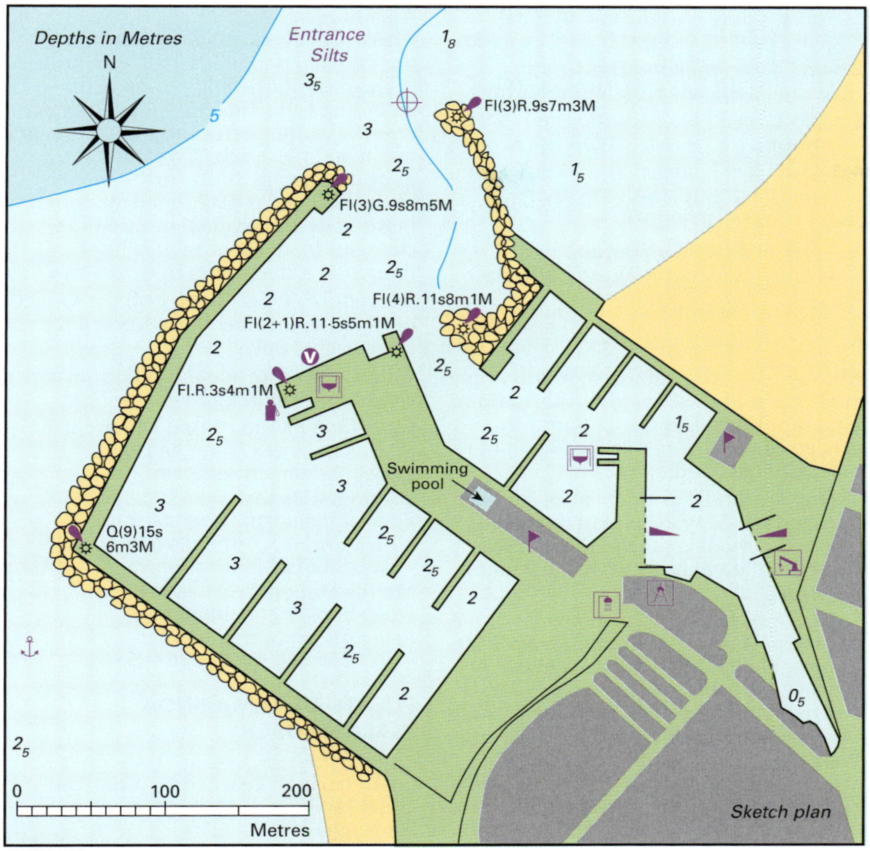

ARENAL

S'ESTANYOL

39°21'·7N 02°55'·3E

☆ Entrance Fl(2)R.6s5M/Fl(2)G.7s1M

Data 285 berths. Max LOA 12m. Depths 1–3m. Charge band 5.

Remarks Plans for the proposed 700 berth marina are at present on hold.

Club Náutico S'Estanyol ✆ 971 640 085
Email cne@cnestanyol.com

EL ARENAL

39°30'·2N 02°44'·9E
BA 3034, 3035 Sp 421A
19M Puerto de Campos ←→ Palma 6·5M

☆ Entrance Fl(3)G.9s5M/Fl(3)R.9s3M. Elbow Q(9)15s3M. Spur Fl(4)R.11s1M. Muelle Interior Fl(2+1)R.11·5s1M/Fl.R.3s1M

VHF Ch 09.

Navigation Entry difficult with strong SW–W winds. Entrance silts. The channel is buoyed on port side.

Berths Go on the central pier and report to the *capitanía*.

Shelter Good shelter.

Data 650 berths. 70 visitors' berths. Max LOA 25m. Depths 1·5–3·5m. Charge band 6.

Facilities Water. 220/380V. Showers and toilets. Laundry. Fuel quay. 50-ton travel-hoist. 10-ton crane. Most yacht repairs. Chandler. Gas. Provisions and restaurants.

Remarks The entrance is dredged periodically.

Club Náutico del Arenal
✆ 971 440 267
www.cnarenal.com

SAN ANTONIO DE LA PLAYA

39°32'N 02°43'·1E
BA 3034, 3035 Sp 421 Imray M3

☆ Entrance Fl(4)R.13s5M/Fl(4)G.13s3M

VHF Ch 09.

Navigation Entry difficult with strong S winds.

Berths Go on quay at the entrance and report to the *capitanía*.

Shelter Good shelter.

Data 400 berths. Max LOA 20m. Depths 1·5–3m. Charge band 6.

Facilities Water. 220/380V. Showers and toilets. Fuel quay. 60-ton travel-hoist. 15-ton crane. Most yacht repairs. Provisions and restaurants.

Club Maritimo de San Antonio de la Playa ✆ 971 745 076
Email cmsa@cmsap.com
www.cmsap.com

CALA GAMBA

39°32'·9N 02°41'·8E

☆ Fl.R.2s5M/Fl.G.2s3M

VHF Ch 09.

Data 225 berths. Depths <1–1·5m.

Facilities Water. 220V. WC and showers. Fuel. 14-ton crane.

Club Náutico ✆ 971 261 849

PUERTO DEL MOLINAR

39°33'·5N 02°40'·6E

☆ Fl(2)R.7s5M/Fl(2)G.7s3M

CALA PORTIXOL

39°33'·6N 02°40'·2E
BA 3034, 3035 Sp 4212

☆ Entrance Fl(3)R.9s5M/Fl(3)G.9s3M. Inner entrance Fl(4)R.11s1M/ Fl(4)G.11s1M

Navigation Entry difficult with strong S winds.

Berths Go on Muelle Interior and report to the YC.

Shelter Some berths uncomfortable and possibly untenable with S gales.

Data 250 berths. Max LOA 12m. Depths 1·5–2·5m.

Facilities Water. 220V. Showers and toilets. 4-ton crane. Slipway. Limited yacht repairs. Provisions and restaurants.

Remarks Limited visitors' berths.

Club Náutico Portixol
✆ 971 415 466 / 971 242 424

NORTH MENORCA MARINE RESERVE

This extends from Cap Gros to Punta des Morter and includes the whole of Cala Fornells. Fishing, scuba diving activities are restricted or prohibited. Between Cap Gros and Illa Bledes and right down the eastern side of Cala Fornells anchoring is forbidden where there are sea grass 'prairies'. These are usually marked by yellow buoys. The western extremity of the zone is marked by a yellow buoy due N of Cap Gros.

Isla de Menorca

MAHON

39°52'·03N 04°18'·53E WGS84
Channel entrance (Fl.R.5s/Fl.G.5s)
BA 2762 Sp 4261 Imray M3
13·5M Cala de Addaya ←→ Ciudadela 36M

☆ Punta de San Carlos Oc(2)6s22m13M. Punta del Esperó Fl(1+2)15s51m7M. Punta del Lazareto Fl(2)G.7s13m3M. Punta de Na Cafayes Fl(3)R.9s3M. Isla Cuarentena o Plana SW point Fl(3)G.9s3M. Punta de Villacarlos Fl(4)R.11s3M. Isla del Rey S side Fl(4)G.11s13m3M. N side Oc.R.4s3M. Punta de la Bassa Oc.G.4s3M. Cala Rata Fl.G.5s7m3M. Punta de Cala Figuera Fl.R.5s1M. Isla Pinta S end Fl(2)G.7s1M. W side Fl(3)G.9s1M. Naval Base pier heads Fl.Y.5s1M/ Fl.Y.5s1M/ Fl.Y.5s1M. Isla del Lazareto E point Fl(2)R.7s1M. Canal de Sant Jordi S side E end Fl(3)R.9s1M, W end Fl(4)R.11s1M

VHF Ch 12, 14, 16, 20, 27 for port authorities and pilots. Ch 09 for S'Altra Banda, Marina Mahon and Club Maritimo. Ch 69 for Pedro's Boat Centre.

Navigation Straightforward with few hazards into the long *cala*. 3kn speed limit in the harbour.

Berths

S'Altra Banda Marina This private company has taken over the Ribera del Puerto concession. Some changes can be expected. The office is on the public quay, and there are 450 yacht berths in four areas:

1. *Public Quay* E of the commercial quay. Laid moorings. Max LOA 30m.
2. *Isla Clementina and Isla Cristina* Artificial islands with laid moorings.
3. *Cala Longa* Five pontoons and mooring buoys. Max LOA 30m.
4. *Isla del Rey* Pontoon. Max LOA 15m.

All moorings and berths charge band 6/6+.

Marina Mahon 160 pontoon berths along the quay on the W side of Cala Figuera. Charge band 6+.

Club Maritimo de Mahon 50 berths on Pta Figuera. Charge band 5.

Marina Menorca 200 berth marina right at the head of the bay. Max LOA 30m. Laid moorings. Depths <1–5m. Care needed of shoal water at the N end of the port. Charge band 5.

Shelter Generally good. (The earthquake in Algeria in May 2003 sent a tsunami across the Mediterranean that caused substantial damage to yachts in Mahon).

Facilities

S'Altra Banda/Club Maritimo Menorca/Marina Menorca/Marina Port Mahon Water. 220V. Pump-out at Marina Menorca. Yachts using 'islands' and moorings have use of a dinghy dock, WC and showers, and rubbish collection. Water tanks can be filled at a third artificial island. Fuel at the YC in Cala Figuera. *Pedro's Boat Centre* have 50/35-ton travel hoists. Hard standing. Some yacht repairs. Provisions and restaurants in the town.

Anchorages

There are several anchorages through the port, but from 2010 all anchoring in the harbour during peak season – including Cala Taulera – is prohibited, unless all other berths and moorings are taken and there is bad weather. It appears that anchoring anywhere else in the harbour is prohibited at all times, but details are retained in case of changes. In all cases anchoring is limited to a maximum of three days.

Isla del Rey Good shelter on the W side of the island, sometimes reserved for large yachts only.

Cala Longa Outside the laid moorings, clear of the main fairway.

Cala Taulera and behind I Cuarentena.

Marina Menorca ✆ 971 365 889
www.marinamenorca.com

S'Altra Banda Marina ✆ 971 594 062
Email info@portsaltrbanda.com

Club Maritimo ✆ 971 365 022
www.clubmaritimomahon.com

Marina Mahon ✆ 971 366 787
Email info@marinamahon.es

Pedro's Boat Centre (yard)
✆ 971 366 968 *Fax* 971 362 455

PUERTO DE TAMARINDA (CALA'N BOSCH)

39°55'·6N 03°50'·2E

Small harbour reached by a narrow canal (10–12m wide) with maximum air height 10m.

✆ 971 387 171
www.cdcalanbosch.com

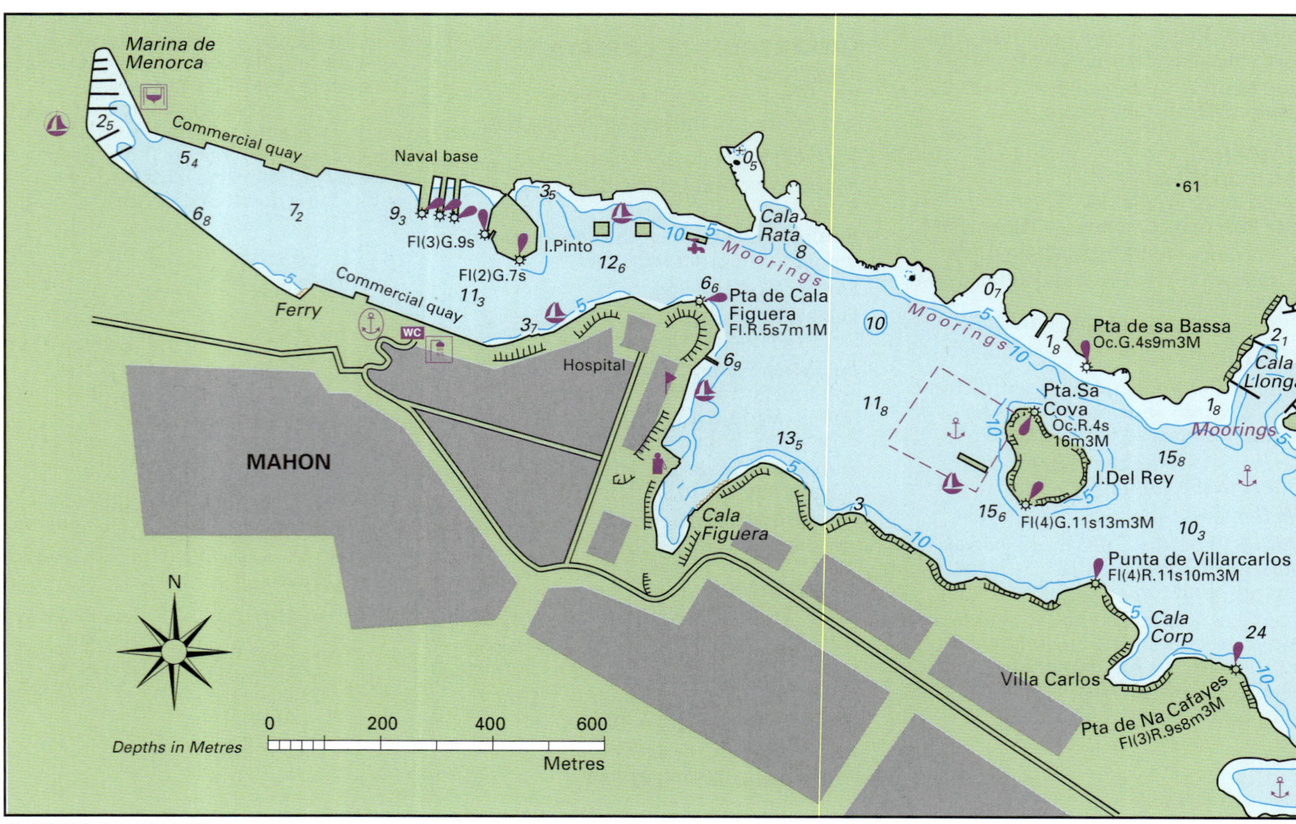

PUERTO DE MAHON

CIUDADELA (CIUTADELLA)

39°59'·8N 03°49'·4E
(Punta de sa Farola light Oc(2+3)14s14M)
BA 2761 Sp 4263 Imray M3
36M Mahon ←→ Fornells 22M

☆ Punta de sa Farola Fl.6s21m14M. Entrance N side Punta El Bancal Fl(3)R.9s5M. S side San Nicolás Fl(3)G.9s3M. Sa Trona Fl(4)G.11s1M. Cala d'en Busquets Fl(4)R.11s1M. E point Dir 045° DirFl.WRG.5s5-3M (W sector marks centre of channel. R sector is to the north. G sector to the south). Muelle Nuevo Fl.G.5s1M. Slipway Fl.R.5s1M.

VHF Ch 16, 09, 14.

Navigation New detached breakwater and commercial port S of Playa Petita. Entry dangerous with SW gales. Entrance difficult to see. Keep an eye on the traffic signals indicating ferries entering or leaving.

3F.R(vert): shipping must clear the channel in <10 minutes.

3Fl.R(vert) and F.GWG(vert): entry prohibited to all shipping except those expressly authorised.

Berths Alongside or rafted out below Club Náutico on the starboard side. Stern or bows-to Public Port pontoons.

Shelter Swell enters with strong W–SW winds.

Data YC 100 berths. Max LOA 20m. Charge band 5.

Facilities Water and electricity. Showers at YC (0900–2300). Fuel quay. 5-ton crane. Provisions and restaurants.

Remarks Fewer berths now a new ferry service has displaced fishing boats from the N quay.

Work in progress developing a new marina in Cala d'en Busquats.

Club Náutico ✆971 383 918
www.cnciutadella.com
Capitanía ✆971 484 455
Email port.cuitadella@portsib.es

FORNELLS

40°02'·9N 04°08'·2E
BA 2761 Sp 4262
22M Ciudadela ←→ Cala de Addaya 6M

☆ Leading lights 178·5° (Isla Sargantana) Front Q.R.3M. Rear Iso.R.4s3M. Dique de Levante head Fl(4)G.11s5M

VHF Ch 09.

Mooring buoys laid in the bay. Anchoring no longer permitted. Pontoon yacht berths in the harbour. Max LOA 12m.

Remarks Navigation and anchoring restricted – Menorca Marine Reserve.

Club Náutico ✆ 971 376 328
www.cnfornells.com
Capitanía ✆971 376 604
Email port.fornells@portsib.es

CALA DE ADDAYA

40°01'·3N 04°12'·5E
6M Fornells ←→ Mahon 13·M

A long indented *cala* with a small yacht harbour.

VHF Ch 09.

Data Puerto de Addaya: 150 berths. Max LOA 25m. Depths 2–3m. Charge band 2/3.

Facilities Water. 220V. Showers and toilets. 10-ton travel-hoist. Limited yacht repairs. Some provisions. Restaurant.

Remarks Moorings now restrict the anchoring area.

Puerto de Addaya ✆ 971 358 649

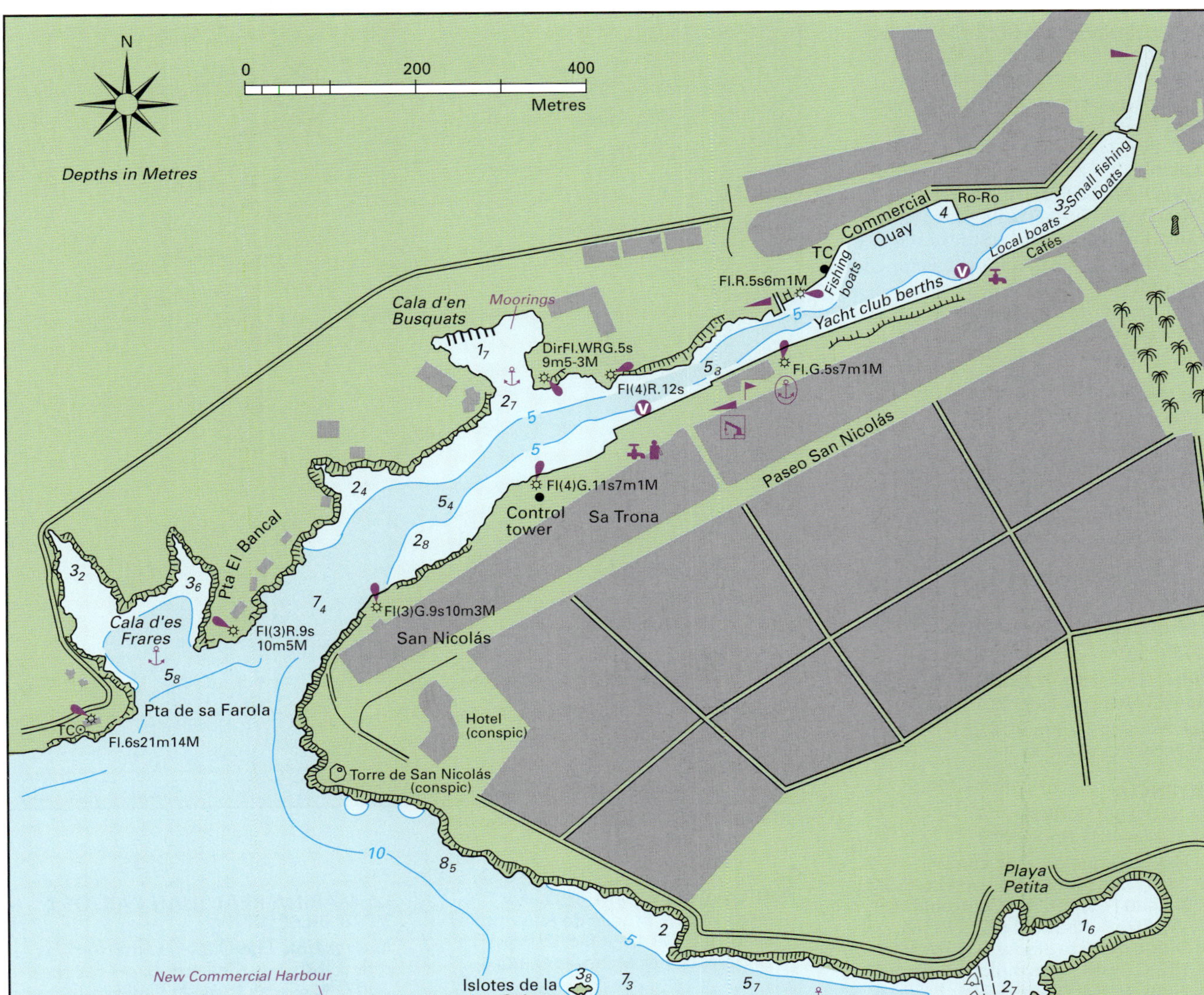

PUERTO DE CIUDADELA

Costa del Azahar

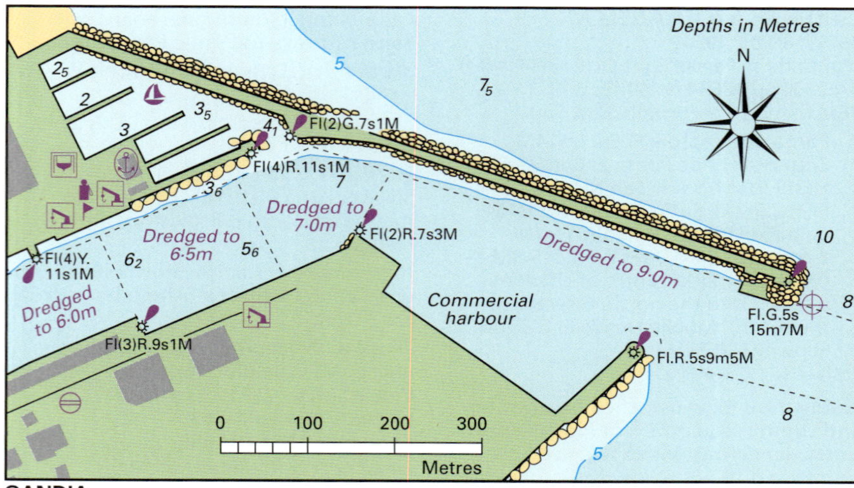

GANDIA

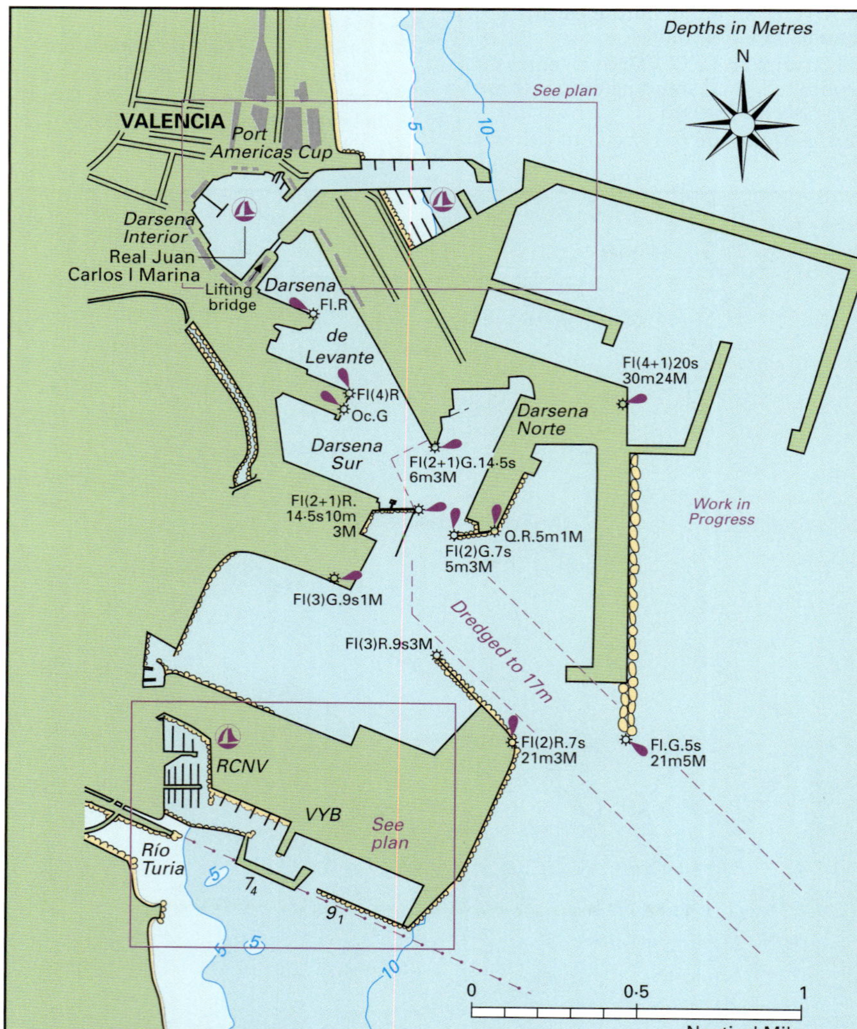

APPROACHES TO VALENCIA

OLIVA

38°56'·1N 00°05'·4W
BA 1701 Sp 475

☆ Entrance Fl(2)G.7s5M. Fl(2)R.7s3M

VHF Ch 09.

Navigation Entrance silts. Depths of 1·7m reported in entrance.

Data 300 berths. 40 visitors' berths. Max LOA 15m. Depths 1·5–2·5m. Charge band 4.

Facilities Water. 220V. Showers and toilets. Fuel. 5-ton crane. Provisions and restaurants.

☎ 962 853 423

CN Oliva ☎ 962 858 612
www.nauticoliva.com

GANDIA

38°59'·8N 00°08'·7W
BA 1453 Sp 4752
16M Denia ←→ Valencia 30M

☆ Entrance Fl.G.5s7M/Fl.R.5s5M. Inner entrance Fl(2)R.7s3M. Yacht basin Fl(2)G.7s1M/Fl(4)R.11s1M. Muelle Frutero Fl(3)R.9s1M

VHF Ch 16 for port authorities. Ch 09 for Club Náutico.

Berths 260 berths. Max LOA 25m. Report to YC for a berth. Visitors' berths on outside of marina wall.

Shelter Uncomfortable with SE gales.

Data Club Náutico 260 berths. Max LOA 20m. Depths 2–3·5m. Charge band 4.

Facilities Water. 220V. Showers and toilets. Fuel. 70-ton travel-lift. 12-ton crane. Provisions and restaurants.

Remarks Outer basin now developed as a commercial port.

Réal Club Náutico de Gandia
☎ 962 841 050
Email rcng@rcngandia.com

CULLERA

39°09'·1N 00°14'·0W
BA 1701 Sp 475

☆ Cabo Cullera Fl(3)20s28m25M. Entrance Fl(2)R.5s3M/Fl.G.3s5M

The Club Náutico de Cullera lies 1M up the river.

MARINA DEL PERELLÓ

39°16'·8N 00°16'·3W

☆ Entrance Fl(3)G.9s4M/Fl(3)R.11s4M

VHF Ch 09.

Data 225 berths. 40 visitors' berths. Max LOA 12m. Depths 1–2m.

Club Náutico El Perello ☎ 961 770 386
www.cnelperello.com

VALENCIA

39°26'·1N 00°18'·1W
BA 562 Sp 4811 Imray M13

☆ Nuevo Dique del Este elbow Fl(4+1)20s30m24M. Head Fl.G.5s5M. N head Fl(3)R.9s3M. Contradique S VQ(6)+LFl.10s3M. E Fl(2)R.7s3M. Dique del Este elbow Q.R.1M. W end Fl(2)G.7s3M. Nuevo dique S corner Fl(3)G.9s1M. Dique del Sur head Fl(4)R.11s3M. Muelle de Levante head Fl(2+1)R.14·5s3M. Espigón del Turia NE corner Fl.R.3s1M. SE corner F(4)G.11s1M. Muelle de Poniente head Fl(2+1)R.14·5s1M. Darsena Embarcaciones Menores Q.R/Q.G

VHF Ch 11, 12, 14, 16 for port authorities and pilots.

LA MARINA REAL JUAN CARLOS I

39°28'·0N 00°18'·5W

Navigation The Darsena Interior was redeveloped as the team bases for the 2007 Americas Cup. A T-pier in the centre of the basin is for superyachts. A canal allows direct access to the

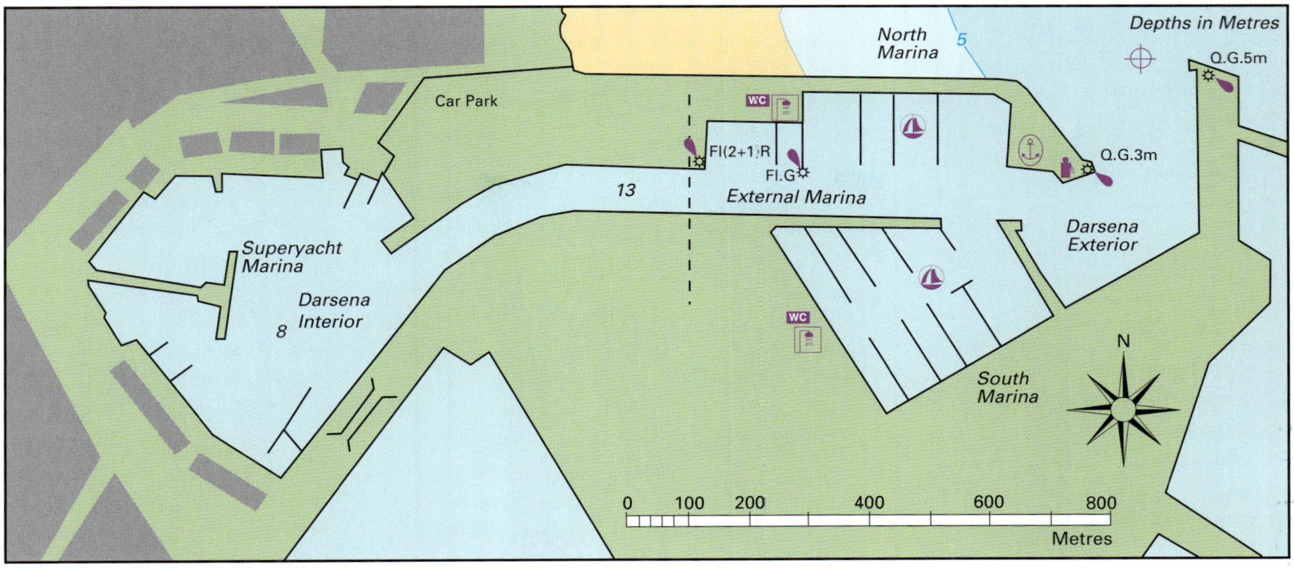

MARINA REAL JUAN CARLOS I

Darsena Interior, and yachts are no longer permitted to enter the commercial harbour. A marina has been developed on the N and S sides of the new access canal.

Note Major expansion work in progress in the commercial harbour, to the S of the entrance to Marina Real Juan Carlos I. Cardinal buoys mark the extent of the work area down to Valencia Yacht Base.

VHF Ch 67.

Berths Call ahead to arrange a berth. Stern or bows-to. Laid moorings.

Shelter Excellent shelter in darsena interior. Some berths in the External Marina will be uncomfortable due to wash from passing craft.

Data 700 berths. Max LOA 25m (external marina) and 150m (superyacht berths). Charge band 3.

Facilities Water. 220/380V. WiFi. Showers and toilets. Laundry. Fuel. Pump-out facilities. Shuttle bus. Provisions and restaurants.

Marina Real Juan Carlos I ✆ 963 812 009
Email info@marinarealjuancarlosl.com

RÉAL CLUB NÁUTICO DE VALENCIA

39°25'·5N 00°19'·4W
BA 562 Imray M13
30M Gandia ←→ Farnals 7M

☆ Entrance Fl(2)R.7s1M/Fl(2)G.7s3M. E side Fl(3)G.9s3M. W side Fl(3)R.9s1M. Darsena Embarcaciones Menores Q.R/Q.G

Navigation Yacht harbour lies at the root of the S breakwater outside the commercial harbour.

VHF Ch 09, 69, 16.

Berths Report to the *capitanía* for a berth.

Shelter Good shelter.

Data 1,200 berths. Max LOA 50m. Some berths to 60m. Depths 4–5m. Charge band 4.

Facilities Water. 220/380V. Showers and toilets. Fuel quay. 50-ton travel-hoist. 10-ton crane. Most yacht repairs. Restaurant.

Remarks Valencia city is approximately 4km away.

Réal Club Náutico de Valencia
✆ 963 679 011
Email rcnv@rcnv.es
www.rcnv.es

VALENCIA YACHT BASE

A superyacht facility which is part of the RCNV Club.

VHF Ch 69.

Data 235 berths. LOA 20–120m. Depths 10m.

✆ 902 272 007
Email info@valenciayachtbase.com
www.valenciayachtbase.com

PUERTO SAPLAYA (ALBORAYA)

39°30'·7N 00°19'·0W

☆ Entrance Fl(3)R.9s4M/Fl(3)G.9s4M

Small boat harbour.

VHF Ch 09.

Navigation Entrance silts and is periodically dredged to 2m. The narrow channel leads into basins lined with apartments.

Club Náutico ✆ 963 550 033
Email cnps@express.es

FARNALS (POBLA MARINA)

39°33'·5N 00°16'·7W
BA 1701 Sp 481A
7M Valencia ←→ Siles 10M

☆ Entrance Fl(2)G.5s5M. Dique Sur Fl(2)R.5s3M

VHF Ch 09.

Navigation Entrance silts. Buoyed entrance channel.

Berths Where directed. Go alongside the outer end of Muelle de Espera if no

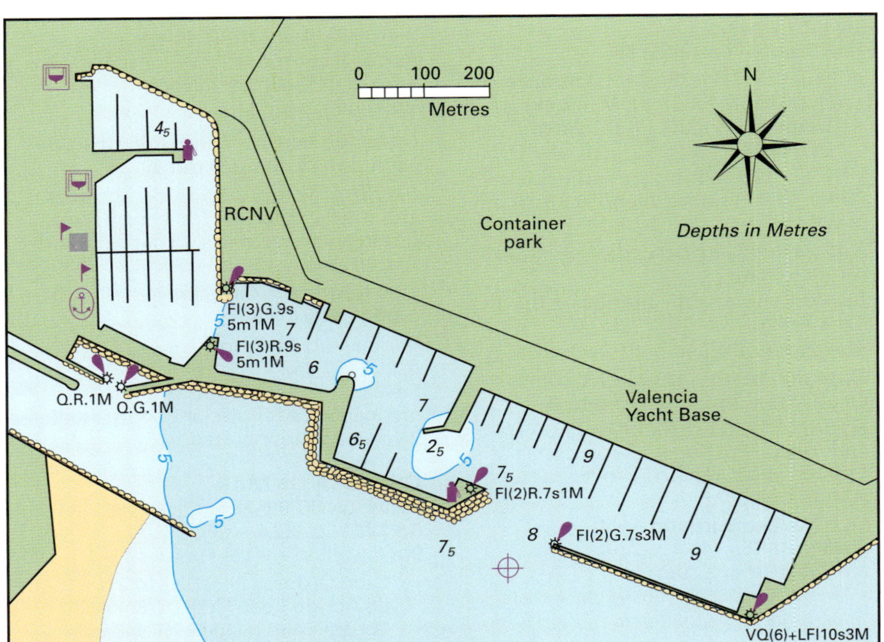

PUERTO DE VALENCIA YACHT HARBOUR

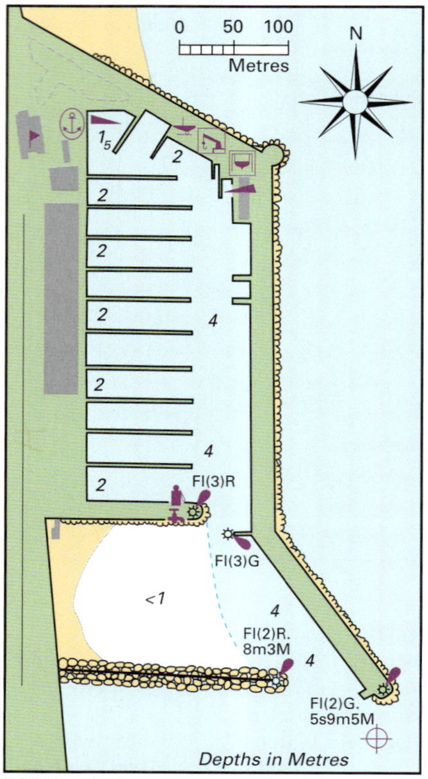

FARNALS (POBLA MARINA)

berth is immediately allotted. Finger pontoons.

Shelter Good shelter.

Data 835 berths. 165 visitors' berths. Max LOA 20m. Depths 2–4m. Charge band 3/4.

Facilities Water. 220V. WiFi. Showers and toilets. Fuel quay. 60-ton travel-hoist. 5-ton crane. Some yacht repairs. Provisions and restaurants.

Remarks There are plans for a massive expansion to double the size of the marina.

Marina ✆ 961 463 223
Email info@poblamarina.es

SAGUNTO

39°37'·7N 00°12'·4W
BA 1460 Sp 835

☆ Outer breakwater S corner Q(3)10s5M. Breakwater T-jetty head Q.G.2M. Outer breakwater elbow jetty head Fl.R.5s3M. Head Fl(2)R.7s3M. Pantalán de Sierra Menera Q(3)10s5M. Muelle Sur SE corner Fl.R.5s3M. Jetty head Fl(2)R.7s3M. Fishing harbour breakwater head Fl(2)G.7s. Outer breakwater head Fl(2)R.7s1M

VHF Ch 09, 12, 16.

Berths Stern or bows-to or alongside near small basin in the NE corner.

Shelter Good shelter.

Facilities Water. Fuel. Provisions and restaurants in the town about 2M N.

Remarks Massive outer commercial harbour.

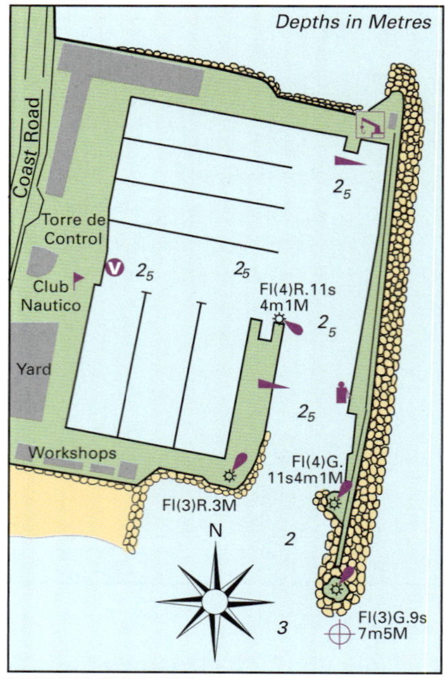

PUERTO DE SILES

PUERTO DE SILES

39°40'·4N 00°11'·9W
10M Farnals ←→ Burriana 13M

☆ Entrance Fl(3)G.9s5M / Fl(3)R.9s5m3M

VHF Ch 09.

Navigation Entry difficult with strong N–NE winds.

Berths Report to *torre de control.*

Shelter Good shelter.

Data 575 berths. Max LOA 12m. Depths 2·5m. Charge band 4.

Facilities Water. 220V. Showers and toilets. 15-ton crane. Limited yacht repairs.

Puerto de Siles ✆ 962 609 223

Club Maritimo ✆ 962 608 132

BURRIANA

39°51'·4N 00°04'·0W
BA 1701 Sp 4822
13M Siles ←→ Castellon 8M

☆ Nules Oc(2)11s38m14M. Entrance Fl(2)G.8s5M/Fl(2)R.8s3M. Muelle Transversal Fl(3)G.10s3M. Jetty Q(3)10s3M

VHF Ch 12, 16 for port authorities. Ch 09 for Marina Burriananova and Club Náutico.

Navigation Care needed of shoal water off the coast.

Berths Report to the marina or the YC for a berth.

Shelter Good shelter.

Data 600 berths. Max LOA 20m. Depths 1–4·5m. Charge band 4.

Facilities Water. 220/380V. Showers and toilets. Fuel quay. 5-ton crane. Limited yacht repairs. Provisions and restaurants.

Club Náutico Burriano
✆ 964 587 055
www.cnburriana.com

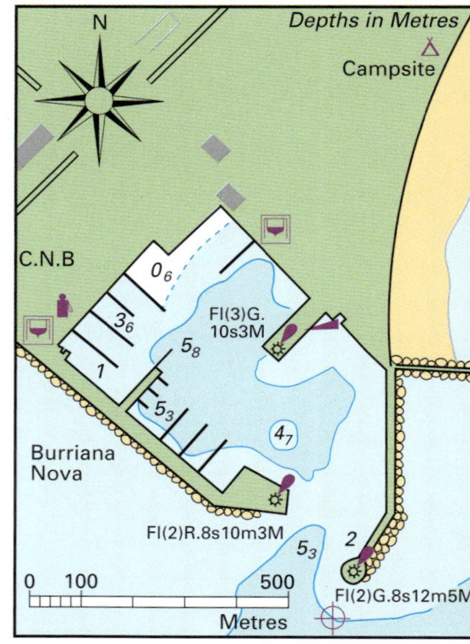

BURRIANA

Burriananova Club de Mar
✆ 964 227 200
Email info@renosmaritima.com
www.burriananova.com

CASTELLON DE LA PLANA

39°57'·5N 00°01'·8E
Sp 4821
8M Burriana ←→ Oropesa 9M

☆ Faro Fl.8s32m14M.
S breakwater E head Fl(4)R.
Dique de Levante SW head Fl(3)G.3M.
SE head Fl(3)G.9s15m5M. Muelle Transversal head SE corner Fl.G.3M.
NW corner Fl(2)G.
E breakwater N corner Q.5M. Muelle Pesquero N head Fl(2+1)R.12s3M.
S head Oc.G.5s2M.
Dry dock slipway Fl(3)R.5s3M.
Oil refinery Oc(2)Y.14s4M/
Oc(2)Y.14s1M/Oc(2)Y.14s1M.

VHF Ch 12, 13, 16 for port authorities. Ch 09 for Club Náutico.

Navigation Care needed of the oil platform in the approaches.

Berths Report to the YC or marina for a berth in the inner harbour.

Shelter Good shelter.

Data 400 berths. Visitors' berths. Max LOA 25m. Charge band 4.

Facilities Water. 220/380V. Showers and toilets. Fuel. 20-ton travel-hoist. Limited yacht repairs. Provisions and restaurants.

Club Náutico de Castellón
✆ 964 282 520 / 697

Marina Port Castello
✆ 964 737 452
Email
marinaportcastello@marinaportcastello.es
www.marinaportcastello.es

OROPESA DE MAR

40°04'·5N 00°08'·2E
BA 1701 Sp 482A
9M Castellon ←→ Las Fuentes 13M

☆ Cabo Oropesa Fl(3)15s24m21M. Dique de Abrigo head Fl(2)G.7s8m5M. Contradique head Fl(2)R.7s6m3M

VHF Ch 09.

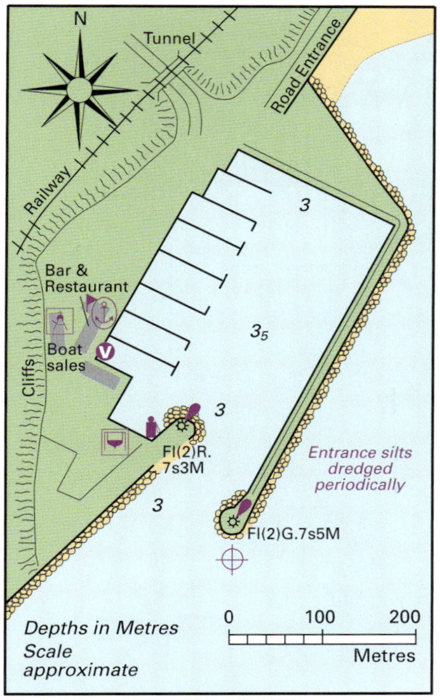

PUERTO OROPESA DE MAR

Berths Report to *torre de control* inside the entrance.

Shelter Good shelter, although swell makes some berths uncomfortable.

Data 665 berths. Max LOA 25m. Depths 2–4m. Charge band 3.

Facilities Water. 220/380V. WiFi. Showers and toilets. Fuel quay. 35-ton travel-hoist. Yacht repairs. Provisions and restaurants.

Puerto Deportivo Oropesa del Mar
✆ 964 313 055
Email info@cnoropesa.com

LAS FUENTES

40°14'·8N 00°17'·2E
BA 1701 Sp 482
13M Oropesa ←→ Vinaroz 16M

☆ Cabo de Irta Fl(4)18s14M. Entrance Oc.G.4s4M/Fl(4)R.14s3M. Pontoon heads F.G/F.R

VHF Ch 09.

Berths Report to *torre de control* on central pier.

Shelter Good shelter.

Data 275 berths. Max LOA 20m. Depths 2–3m. Charge band 4.

Facilities Water. 220/380V. Showers and toilets. Fuel quay. 8-ton crane. Limited yacht repairs. Provisions and restaurants.

Remarks There are plans to expand the marina to the S.

Puerto de las Fuentes ✆ 964 412 084
Email puertolf@telefonica.net

ISOLOTES COLUMBRETES NATURE PARK

Park information centre at the Planetarium Castellon.
✆ 964 282 968

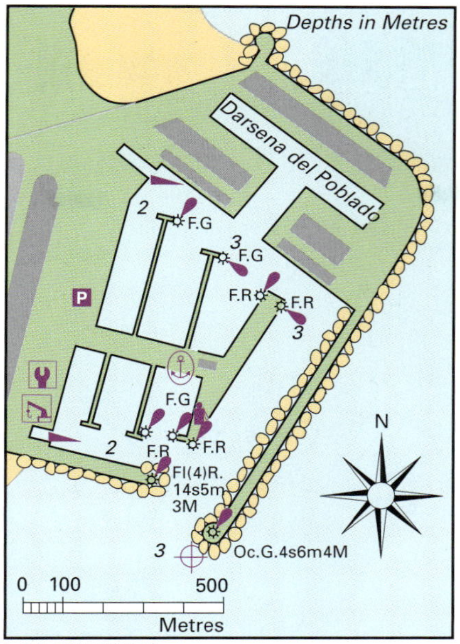

LAS FUENTES

PEÑISCOLA

40°21'·3N 00°24'·2E
BA 1701 Sp 4841

☆ Castillo de Papa Luna Fl(2+1)15s56m23M. Entrance Fl(3)G.9s15m4M / Fl(3)R.9s7m5M. E Cardinal buoy Q(3)10s3M

Navigation Harbour silts.

Berths Harbour normally full with fishing boats. Anchoring now prohibited inside the harbour.

Shelter Uncomfortable and possibly untenable with strong S–SE winds.

Facilities Water. Fuel. Most provisions. Restaurants/cafés.

BENICARLO

40°24'·5N 00°26'·2E
BA 1701 Sp 4841

☆ Entrance Fl(2)G.5s5M/Fl(2)R.6s3M/Fl(3)R.9s3M Espigón head Fl(3)G.9s3M Entrance E side head Fl(2+1)G.15s7m3M

VHF Ch 09.

Berths Marina in N of harbour.

Shelter Uncomfortable with strong S–SE winds.

Data 250 berths. Max LOA 20m. Depths 2–4m. Charge band 5.

Facilities Water. 220V. WiFi. Fuel quay. Travel-hoist. Some repairs. Provisions and restaurants.

Remarks Harbour liable to silting.

Marina Benicarlo ✆ 964 462 330
Email info@marinabenicarlo.com

VINAROZ

40°27'·5N 00°28'·6E
Sp 4842
16M Las Fuentes ←→ Rapita 11M

☆ Entrance Fl.G.5s8M. Spur head Fl(2)G.7s3M. Dique de Poniente head Fl.R.3s3M. Muelle Transversal Fl(3)G.9s3M

VHF Ch 09.

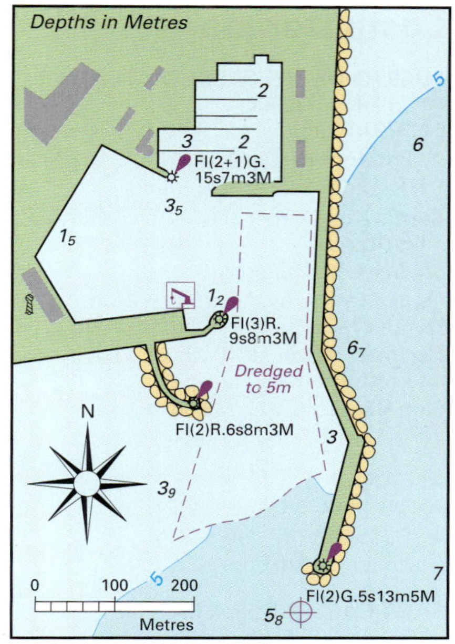

PUERTO DE BENICARLO

Berths Stern or bows-to in NW corner.

Shelter Uncomfortable with S winds.

Data YC 150 berths. Max LOA 16m. Depths 0·5–2·5m.

Facilities Water. 220V. Showers and toilets. Limited yacht repairs. Provisions and restaurants.

Sociedad Náutica de Vinaroz
✆ 977 730 706

Club Nautico ✆ 964 451 705
www.clubnauticovinaroz.com

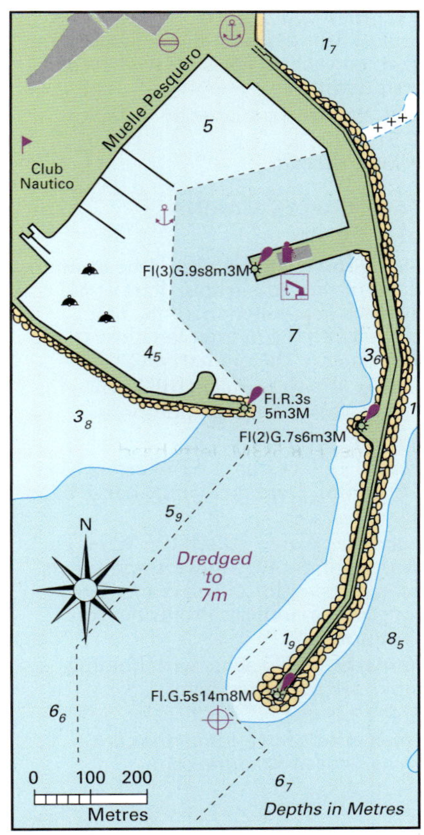

VINAROZ

Costa Dorada

PUERTO DE LES CASES D'ALCANAR

40°33'·0N 00°32'·0E
BA 1701 Sp 485

☆ Entrance Fl(4)R.11s5M/Fl(4)G.11s3M

VHF Ch 09 for Club Náutico.

Berths Report to YC in NW corner for a berth.

Shelter Good shelter.

Data 155 berths. Max LOA 15m. Depths 1–2m in the yacht harbour.

Facilities Water. 220V. Fuel. Provisions and restaurants.

Club Náutico ✆ 977 735 001 / 977 735 014

ALCANAR

40°34'·4N 00°33'·4E

☆ Fl.R.5s3M/Fl(2+1)G.14s2M

Commercial harbour.

SANT CARLES DE LA RAPITA

40°36'·4N 00°36'·3E
BA 1701, 1515 Sp 485
11M Vinaroz ←→ Ampolla 30M

☆ Punta Senieta Oc(4)R.10s10m11M. Entrance Fl(2)R.8s3M/Q.G/ Fl(2+1)G.14·5s2m1M. Muelle de Poniente head Fl.R.3s1M.

VHF Ch 11, 12, 14 for port authorities. Ch 09 for Club Náutico.

Navigation Care is needed of changing depths in the Ebro delta.

Berths Report to YC in NW corner for a berth.

Shelter Good shelter.

Data YC: 480 berths. 120 visitors' berths. Max LOA 15m. Depths 2–3m.

Facilities Water. 220V. Showers and toilets. 30-ton travel-hoist. 6-ton crane. Limited yacht repairs. Provisions and restaurants.

Club Náutico San Carles de la Rapita
✆ 977 741 103
www.cnscr.com

SANT CARLES MARINA

VHF Ch 09.

Navigation The marina in the basin to the E of the old harbour. Part of MDL Marinas, it opened in 2008. The entrance to the marina lies close to the SE corner of the old harbour.

Berths Report to the marina office for a berth. Most berths on pontoons.

Shelter Good shelter.

Data 1,000 berths. c.575 berths. Max LOA 30m. Depths 3–5m. Charge band 4.

Facilities Water. 200/380V. WiFi. Fuel. Waste pump-out. Showers and toilets. 75-ton travel-lift, 5-ton crane. Yard services. Chandlery. Provisions and restaurants.

Remarks Only yachts with holding tanks are permitted here.

✆ 977 745 153
Email info@santcarlesmarina.com
www.santcarlesmarina.com

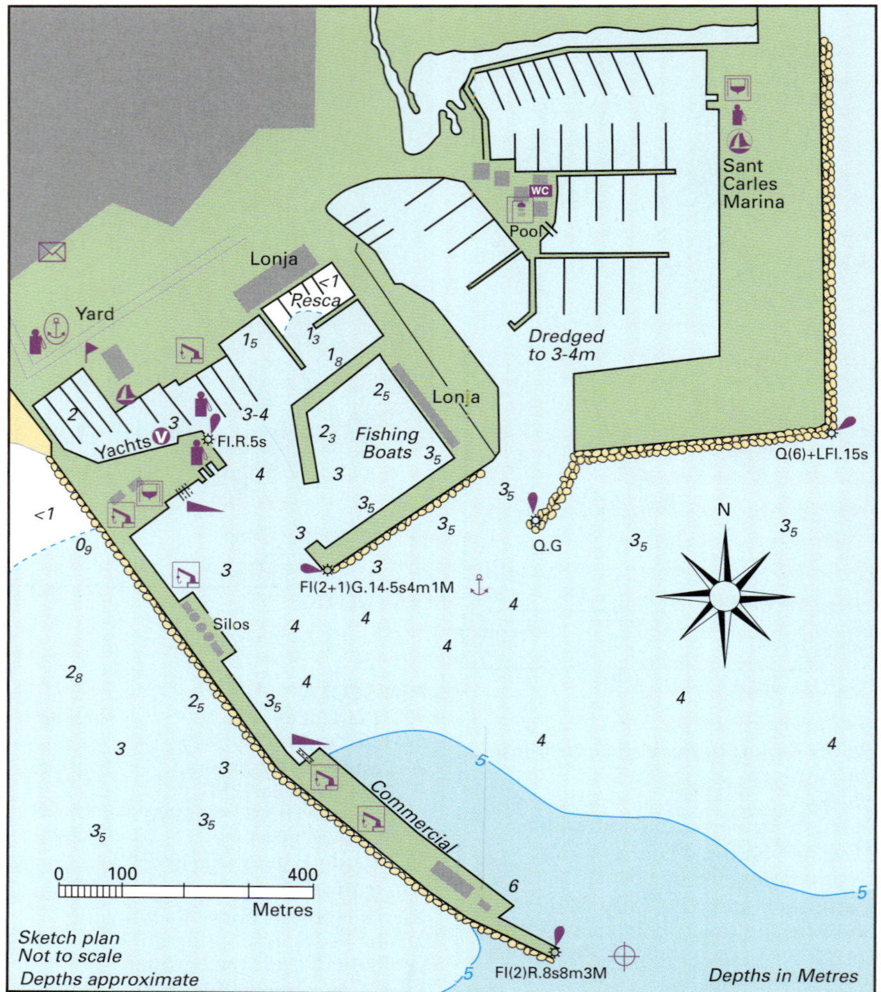

SANT CARLES DE LA RAPITA

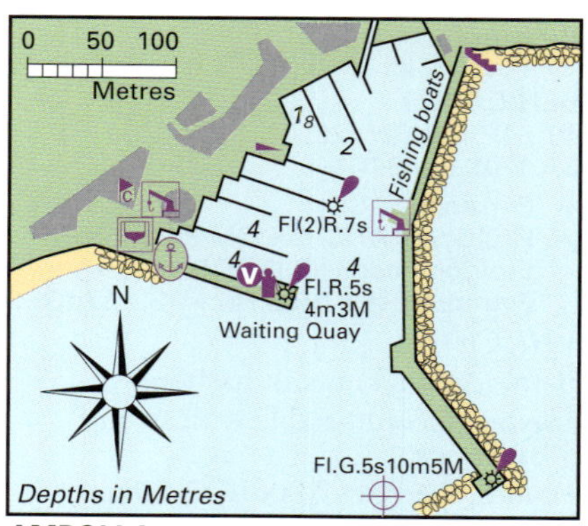

AMPOLLA

AMPOLLA

40°48'·5N 00°42'·8E
BA 1701 Sp 485
30M Rapita ←→ Calafat 11M

☆ T-Jetty head Fl(2)G.7s3M. Outer breakwater Fl.R.5s3M. Breakwater head Fl.G.5s5M. Inner side outer breakwater Fl(2)R.7s1M

VHF Ch 16, 09.

Navigation Entry difficult in strong NE–NW winds.

Berths Go on fuel quay at the entrance and report to the *capitanía* for a berth.

Shelter Good shelter.

Data 430 berths. 125 visitors' berths. Max LOA 15m. Depths 2–4·5m.

Facilities Water. 220/380V. Showers and toilets. Fuel quay. 25-ton travel-hoist. Limited yacht repairs. Provisions and restaurants.

Club Náutico Ampolla
✆ 977 460 211
Email port@nauticampolla.com
www.nauticampolla.com

L'ESTANY GRAS

40°52'·4N 00°47'·7E

☆Entrance Fl(4)G.11s5M / Fl(4)R.11s3M

L'AMETLLA DE MAR

40°52'·7N 00°48'·1E
BA 1701 Sp 486

☆ Entrance Fl(3)G.9s5M/F(3)R.9s3M. Inner breakwater head F(4)R.11s1M

VHF Ch 09.

Berths Report to YC on the SW side for a berth. New yacht pontoons.

Shelter Good shelter.

Data 200 berths. Max LOA 25m. Depths 4–5m.

Facilities Water. 220V. Showers and toilets. Fuel quay. 20-ton crane. Limited yacht repairs. Chandler. Provisions and restaurants.

Club Náutico ☏ 977 457 240
Email cnam@pcserveis.com
www.cnametllamar.com

SANT JORDI D'ALFAMA

40°54'·8N 00°50'·2E

☆ Entrance Fl(2)G.7s8m6M

VHF Ch 09.

Data 130 berths. Max LOA 15m. Depths 1–3m. Charge band 4.

Remarks New marina run by Calafat Marina.

☏ 977 486 327
Email info@portmarinasantjordi.com

CALAFAT

40°55'·7N 00°51'·3E
BA 1701 Sp 486
11M Ampolla ←→ Hospitalet de L'Infant 5M

☆ Entrance Fl.G.5s5M/Fl(2)R.10s4M

VHF Ch 09.

Navigation Entry difficult with strong SE winds.

Berths Report to the *capitanía*.

Shelter Uncomfortable with SW winds.

Data 405 berths. 160 visitors' berths. Max LOA 20m. Depths 2·5–4m.

Facilities Water. 220/380V. Showers and toilets. Fuel. 40-ton travel-hoist. 5-ton crane. Limited yacht repairs. Some provisions. Restaurant.

Puerto Calafat ☏ 977 486 184
Email info@portcalafat.com
www.portcalafat.com

HOSPITALET DE L'INFANT

40°59'·4N 00°55'·7E
BA 1701 Sp 486
5M Calafat ←→ Cambrils 8M

☆ Entrance Fl(4)G.11s5M/Fl.R.2s3M

VHF Ch 09.

Navigation Entry difficult with S gales.

Berths Report to *torre de control*. Poles and finger pontoons.

Shelter Uncomfortable with strong S winds.

Data 585 berths. 100 visitors' berths. Max LOA 18m. Depths 1·5–3m. Charge band 5/6.

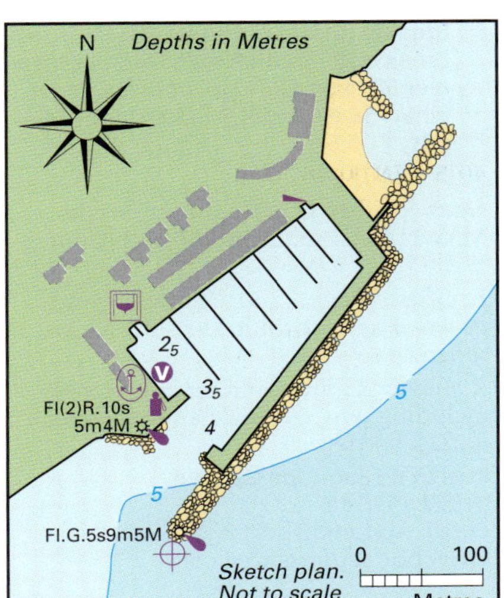

CALAFAT

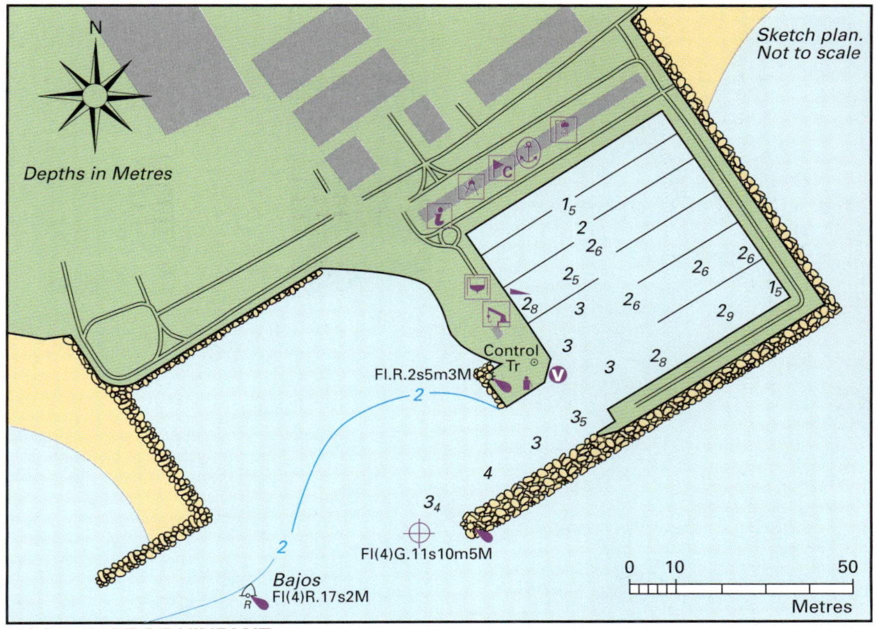

HOSPITALET DE L'INFANT

Facilities Water. 220/380V. Fuel quay. 8-ton crane. Limited yacht repairs. Provisions and restaurants.

Remarks Nuclear power station nearby to the S.

Club Náutico de Hospitalet de L'Infant
☏ 977 823 004
www.cnhv.net

CAMBRILS

41°03'·7N 01°03'·7E
BA 1701 Sp 4861
8M Hospitalet de L'Infant ←→ Tarragona 10M

☆ Entrance Fl(3)G.9s5M / Fl(3)R.9s3M. YC basin Fl(4)G.11s1M

VHF Ch 09.

Berths Report to YC basin on E side of harbour. New pontoons on E quay. Fishing boat pier on W side.

Shelter Good shelter.

Data 525 berths. 50 visitors' berths. Max LOA 20m. Depths 2–3m. Charge band 4/5.

Facilities Water. 220V. Showers and toilets. Fuel quay. 140-ton travel-hoist. 7-ton crane. Limited yacht repairs. Provisions and restaurants.

Club Náutico de Cambrils
☏ 977 360 531
Email info@clubnauticcambrils.com

SALOU

41°04'·3N 01°07'·7E

☆ Entrance Fl(2)G.8s5M/Fl(2)R.8s3M

VHF Ch 09.

Data 230 berths. Max LOA 16m. Depths 1–3m. Charge band 5.

Facilities Water. 220/380V. Showers and toilets. Fuel quay. 10-ton crane. Provisions and restaurants.

Remarks Usually crowded.

Club Náutico de Salou ☏ 977 382 166
Email info@clubnauticsalou.com
www.clubnauticsalou.com

TARRAGONA

41°05'·1N 01°13'·3E
BA 1193 Sp 4871 Imray M13
10M Cambrils ←→ Torredembarra 7M

☆ Mulle de Cantabria elbow Q(6)+LFl.15s1M / Fl(2+1)R.14·5s6m3M. Head Fl(2)R.7s5M. Vehicle terminal SW head Fl(2+1)R.14·5s1M. Platform C Fl(2)R.7s1M. Platform B-20 Fl.R.5s1M. Banya E breakwater Oc.3s1M. Head Fl.G.5s10M. Muelle de Cataluna NE corner Fl(3)G.9s1M. S head Fl(2)G.7s3M. Muelle de Aragón head Fl(4)G.11s3M. Muelle de Reus SE corner Fl(2+1)R.14·5s1M. Lifting bridge W side S head Fl.R.5s1M / centre Fl.R.5s1M / N head Fl.R.5s1M. E side S head Fl.G.2s1M / centre Fl.G.5s1M / N head Fl.G.5s1M

VHF Ch 12, 14, 16 for port authorities.

Navigation Sailing yachts do not have automatic right of way over powered craft.

International Marina Tarraco

New superyacht marina in the darsena interior.

VHF Ch 06.

Navigation Yachts must pass under a lifting bridge into the marina.

Berths 150m reception quay.

Shelter Good shelter.

Data 115 berths. LOA 20–160m. Depths 9m.

Facilities Water. 220/380V. Telephone. Cable/satellite TV. CCTV. Fuel. 275-ton travel-hoist. Helicopter pad. Yacht service companies within the marina. Provisions and restaurants.

IMT ☏ 977 244 173
Email info@porttarraco.com
www.porttarraco.com

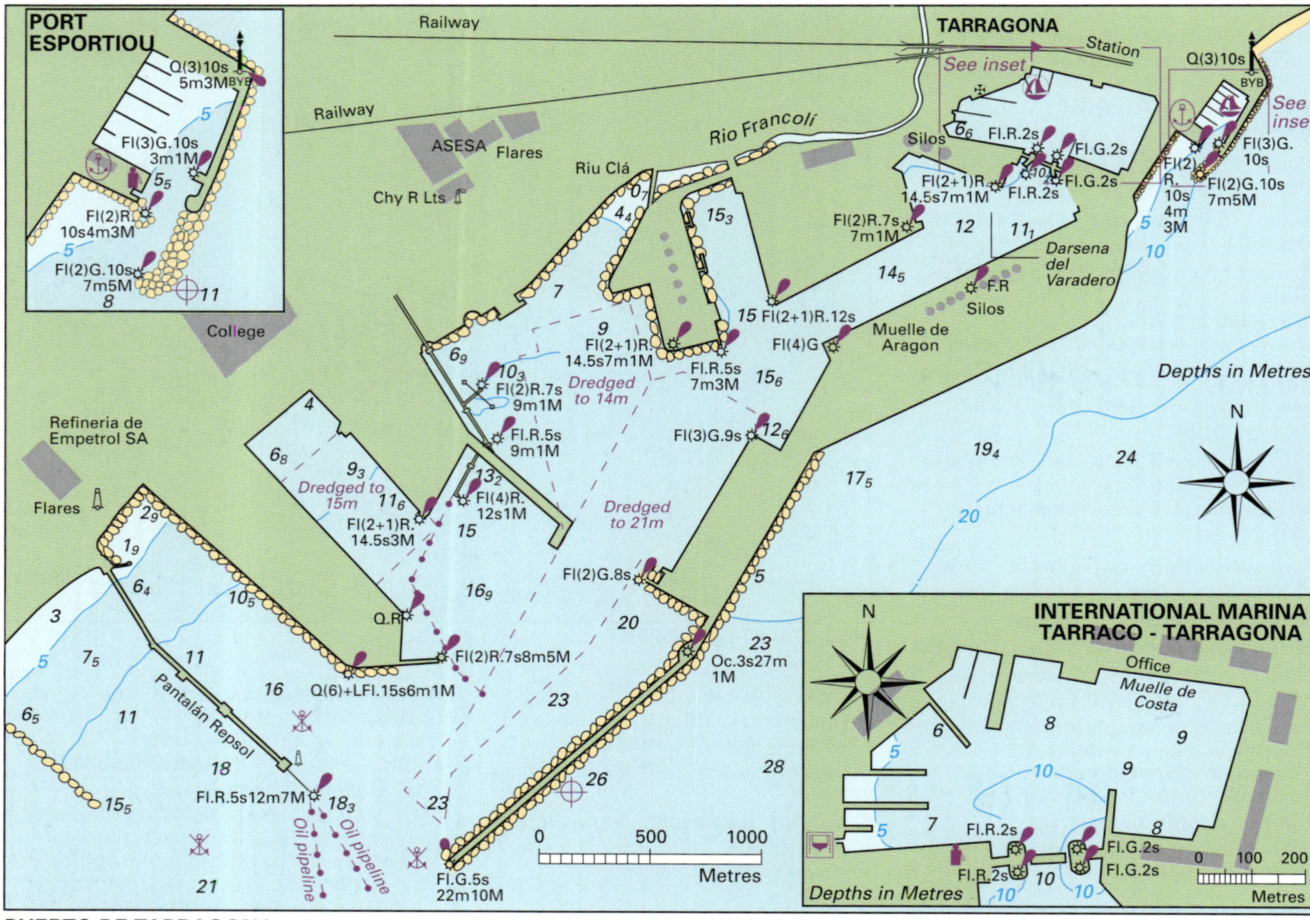

PUERTO DE TARRAGONA

PORT ESPORTIOU DE TARRAGONA

41°06'·3N 01°14'·9E

☆ Outer breakwater Fl.G.5s22m10M Inner breakwater Fl.G.5s9m5M. Pantalan ASESA platform Fl(2)R.7s9m1M

VHF Ch 09.

Navigation This new marina is situated on the outside of the old Mole de Levante.

Berths Where directed.

Data 440 berths. Visitors' berths. Max LOA 20m. Depths 3–10m. Charge band 5.

Facilities Water. 220V. Showers and toilets. Fuel. 50-ton travel-hoist. Some yacht repairs. Provisions and restaurants.

Port Esportiou de Tarragona
✆ 977 213 100
www.portesportiutarragona.com

TORREDEMBARRA

41°07'·9N 01°24'·0E
7M Tarragona ←→ Comaruga 11M

☆ Dique de Abrigo head Fl(4)G.11s10m5M/Fl.G.5s1M/ Fl(4)R.11s3M/Fl.R.5s3M/Q(3)10s3M

VHF Ch 09.

Berths Where directed.

Shelter Some berths uncomfortable with S winds.

Data 820 berths. 200 visitors' berths. Max LOA 20m. Depths 4–6m. Charge band 5.

Facilities Water. 220V. Showers and toilets. Fuel quay. 45-ton travel-hoist. 5-ton crane. Some yacht repairs. Provisions and restaurants.

Port Torredembarra ✆ 977 643 234
Email portorre@arrakis.es
www.porttorredembarra.com

RODA DE BARA (PORT DAURAT)

41°09'·9N 01°28'·9E

☆ Harbour breakwater E corner Fl(3)9s8m5M

New marina.

Data 640 berths. Max LOA 30m. Depths 1·5–3m. Water. 220V. WC and showers. Fuel. 110-ton travel-lift. Repairs. Charge band 4.

✆ 997 138 169
www.novadarsenabara.es
Email info@novadarsenabara.es

COMARUGA

41°10'·7N 01°31'·0E
11M Torredembarra ←→ Vilanova 10M

☆ Dique Oeste head Fl(2)G.7s5M. Muelle Transversal W corner Q(6)+LFl.15s3M. Pasarela de Cierre W head Q(2)R.4s3M/E head Fl.G.5s3M. E corner VQ(6)+LFl.10s3M. Dique Este head Fl.R.5s5M

VHF Ch 09.

Navigation Entrance silts so care needed over depths.

Data 260 berths. 50 visitors' berths. Max LOA 15m. Depths 2–2·5m.

Facilities Water. 220V. Showers and toilets. Fuel quay. 8-ton crane. Provisions and restaurants.

Club Náutico de Comaruga
✆ 977 680 120
Email cnco@clubnautic.com

SEGUR DE CALAFELL

41°11'·0N 01°36'·4E

☆ Breakwater head Fl(4)G.12s5M. Outer breakwater head Fl(4)R.11s3M. Inner pier SE head Fl(2+1)R.14·5s1M. Inner wharf SE corner Fl.R.5s1M. Inner T-jetty Fl.G.5s

VHF Ch 09.

Data 525 berths. 50 visitors' berths. Max LOA 22m. Depths 3–6m. Charge band 5.

Facilities Water. 220V. Showers and toilets. Fuel. 50-ton travel-lift. Most repairs.

Remarks Redevelopment completed including new entrance and expansion to 525 berths.

Puerto de Segur de Calafell
✆ 977 159 119
Email capitania@portsegurcalafell.com
www.portsegurcalafell.com

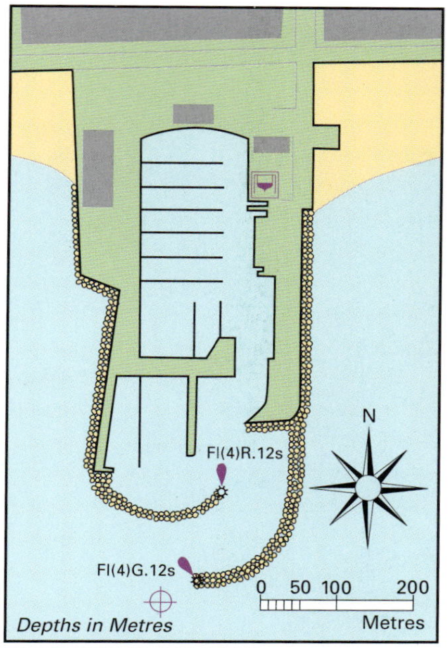

PORT SEGUR-CALAFELL

PORT DE FOIX

☆ Dique de Abrigo E end Q(6)+LFl.15s5M

VILANOVA Y LA GELTRU

41°12'·3N 01°43'·7E
BA 1704 Sp 4881
10M Comaruga ←→ Garraf 7·5M

☆ Puerto San Cristobál Fl(3)8s27m19M.
Nuevo contradique Fl(2)R.7s3M.
Dique de Poniente head Fl(3)R.9s1M.
Dique de Levante S head Fl(2)G.7s5M.
N head Fl(3)G.10s1M.
Espigón Transversal Fl(2+1)R.15s1M.
Fishing jetty centre head Fl(4)R.11s1M. Head Fl(2+1)G.10s1M

VHF Ch 12, 16 for port authorities. Ch 09 for çlub Náutico.

Berths Report to YC in the NW corner for a berth.

Shelter Good shelter.

Data Club Nautico 810 berths. 230 visitors' berths. Max LOA 22m. Depths 1–3m. Charge band 5.

Vilanova Grand Marina 50 berths. LOA 20–80m.

Facilities Water. 220/380V. Showers and toilets. Fuel quay. 30-ton travel-hoist. 200-ton travel-lift, 800-ton lift planned. 15-ton crane. Some yacht repairs. Provisions and restaurants.

Club Náutico de Vilanova y la Geltra ☏ 93 8 150 267
Email cnv@cnvillanova.com

Villanova Grand Marina ☏ 938 105 611
Email info@vilanovagrandmarina.com

AIGUADOLC (SITGES)

41°14'·0N 01°49'·5E
BA 1704 Sp 4882

☆ Entrance Fl.G.5s5M/Fl(2)G.13s1M/Fl.R.5s3M

VHF Ch 09.

Berths Go on fuel quay and report to the *capitanía* for a berth.

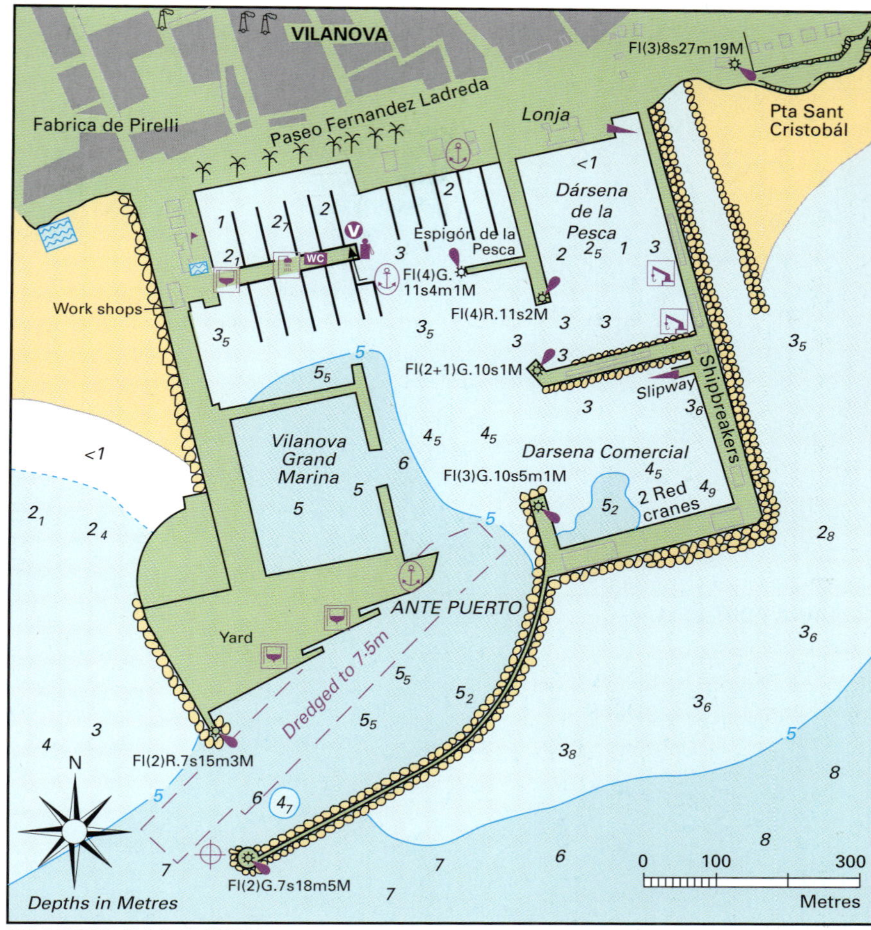

VILANOVA Y LA GELTRU

Shelter Good shelter.

Data 760 berths. 130 visitors' berths. Max LOA 25m. Depths 2–5m. Charge band 4.

Facilities Water. 220/380V. Showers and toilets. Fuel quay. 50-ton travel-hoist. 6-ton crane. Some yacht repairs. Limited provisions. Restaurants.

Port de Sitges ☏ 938 942 600
Email info@portdesitges.com
www.portdesitges.com

YC ☏ 937 432 057

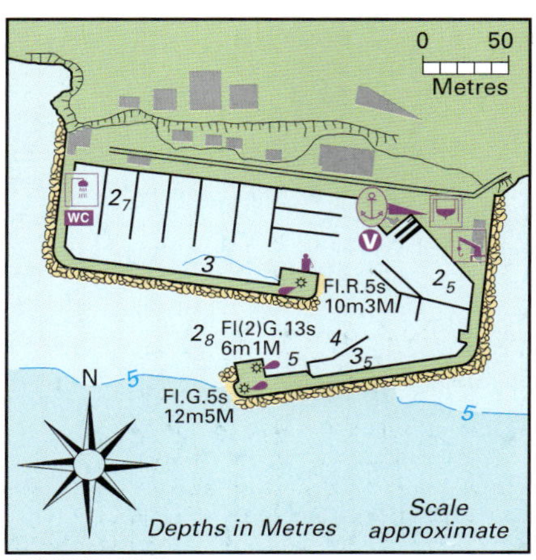

AIGUADOLC

VALLCARCA

☆ Muelle head Fl(4)G.13s4M

Cement works harbour.

PORT GARRAF

41°14'·9N 01°53'·9E
BA 1704 Sp 488A
7·5M Vilanova ←→ Ginesta 2M

☆ Entrance Fl(3)G.9s5M/Fl(3)R.9s3M. Pier head Fl(4)G.20s1M.

VHF Ch 09.

Berths Go on fuel quay just inside the entrance and report to *torre de control*.

Shelter A surge with strong SE winds.

Data 615 berths. 150 visitors' berths. Max LOA 15m. Depths 2·5–5m.

Facilities Water. 220/380V. Showers and toilets. Fuel quay. 20-ton travel-hoist. 6-ton crane. Limited yacht repairs.

Remarks Somewhat isolated situation away from facilities. Liable to silt.

Port Garraf ☏ 936 320 013
Email info@clubnauticgarraf.com

GINESTA (VALBONA)

41°15'·52N 01°55'·46E WGS84
BA 1704 Sp 488
2M Garraf ←→ Barcelona 13M

☆ Entrance Fl(2)G.10s5M/Fl(2)R.10s3M. Espigón de Levante head Q(6)+LFl.15s3M

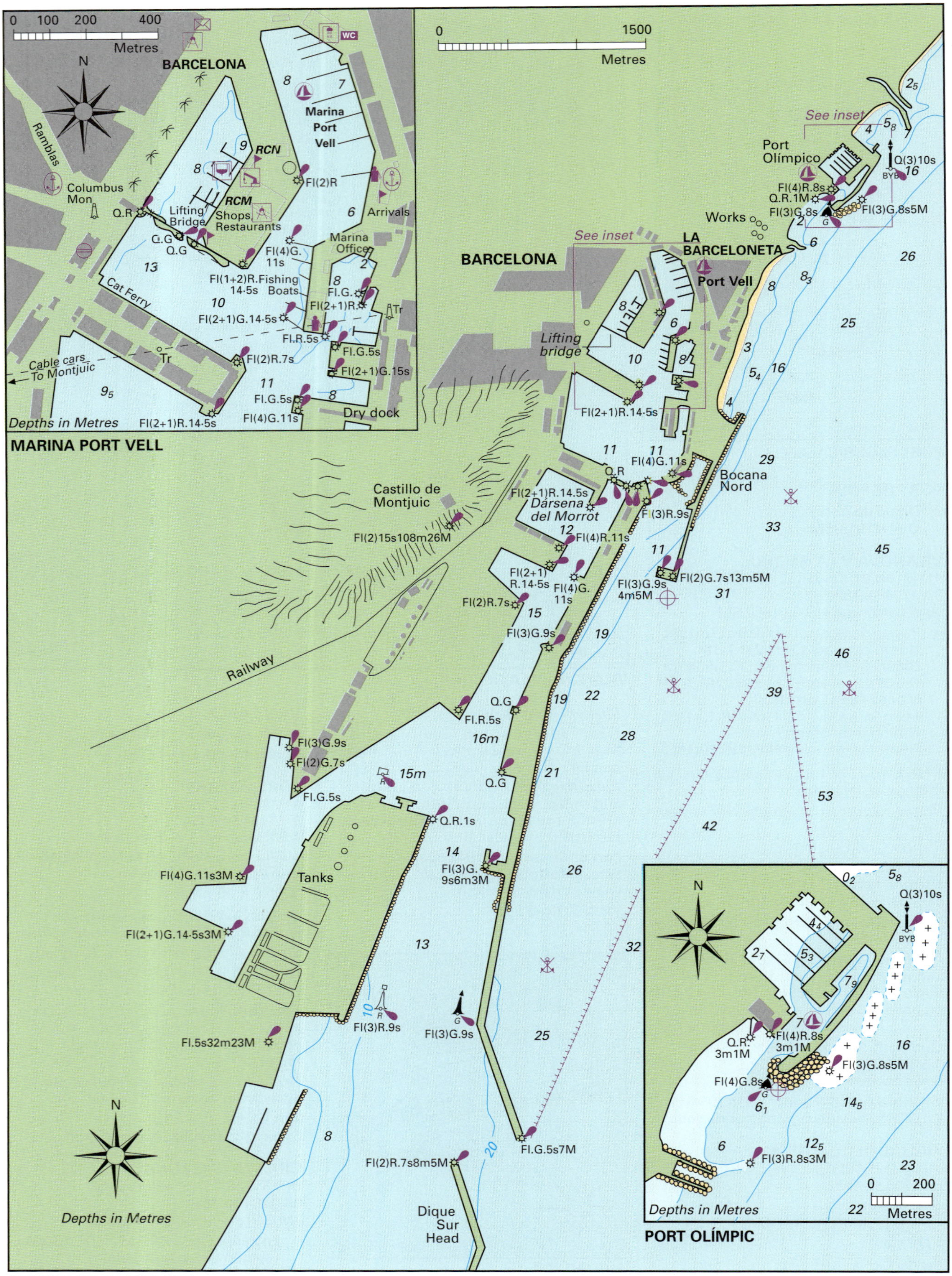

PUERTO DE BARCELONA

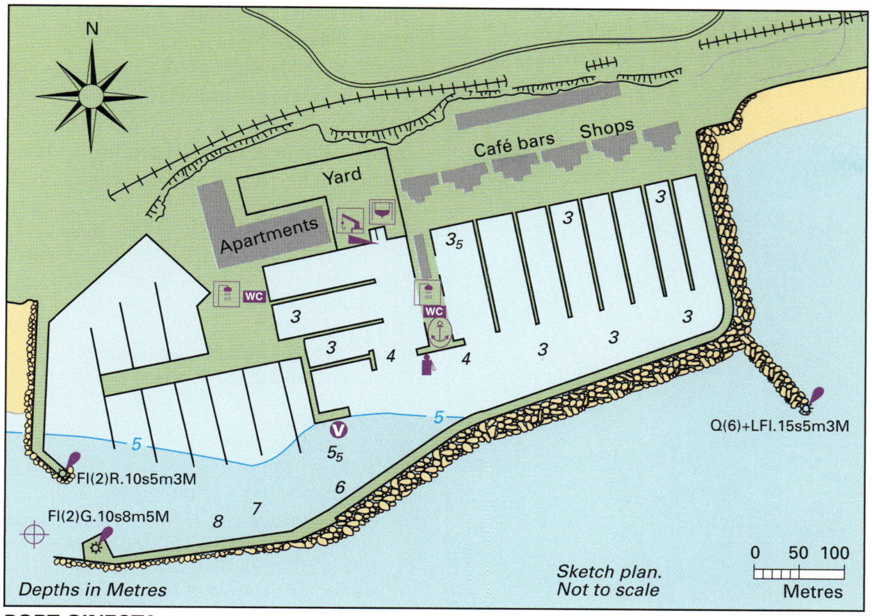

PORT GINESTA

VHF Ch 09.

Navigation Entrance can silt. Deep draught yachts should call to get latest depths.

Berths Go on pier in outer part of the harbour and report to *torre de control*.

Shelter Good shelter.

Data 1,400 berths. 224 visitors' berths. Max LOA 25m. Depths 3–6m. Charge band 4.

Facilities Water. 220/380V. Showers and toilets. Fuel quay. 50-ton travel-hoist. 8-ton crane. Most yacht repairs. Provisions and restaurants.

Remarks Some distance away from Ginesta town centre.

Port Ginesta SA
☎ 936 643 661
Email info@portginesta.com
www.portginesta.com

BARCELONA

41°21'·5N 02°11'·1E (Fl(2)G.7s5M)
BA 1180 Sp 4891 Imray M13, M14
13M Ginesta ←→ El Masnou 11M

☆ Montjuich Fl(2)15s108m26M. Dique del Este Spur Fl(3)G.9s6m3M. E breakwater corner Fl(2)G.7s6m5M. E breakwater head Fl.G5s14m7M. S breakwater Fl.R.5s14m7M. Muelle Príncipe de España S head Fl(4)G.11s6m3M. Muelle de Lepanto Berth No. 1 head Fl(3)G.9s6m3M. Berth No. 2 head Fl(2)G.7s6m3M. S head Fl.G.5s6m3M. Pantalán de Petroleros head Fl(2+1)R.21s6m2M. South Basin SE corner Fl(2+1)G.14·5s6m3M. Muelle Sur S corner Fl.R.5s6m3M. N corner Fl(2)R.7s6m3M. Muelle Adosado S head Fl.G.5s2M. RoRo berth Fl(4)G.11s4m1M. Muelle Contradique S corner Fl(2+1)R14·5s6m3M. Muelle de Poniente S corner Fl(2+1)R.14·5s6m3M. Bridge QG.2m1M. Muelle Occidental S head Fl(2+1)G.14·5s6m3M. Muelle de Cataluña S corner Fl(4)G.11s6m3M. N corner Fl.G.5s6m3M. Muelle de Barcelona SW corner Fl(2+1)R.14·5s6m3M. NE corner Fl(2)R.7s6m2M. Muelle de España S corner Fl(2+1)R.14·5s6m3M. N elbow Fl(2)R.7s3M. Muelle de Baleares SW corner Fl(2+1)G.14·5s6m3M. SE corner Fl.R.5s6m2M. N corner Fl(4)G.11s6m2M. Muelle Nuevo N end Fl.G.5s6m2M. S head Fl(2+1)G.15s4m1M. N entrance harbour breakwater S head SE corner Fl(2)G.7s13m5M. SW corner Fl(3)G.9s4m5M. E breakwater N head S elbow Fl(3)R.9s6m3M. E wharf Inner head E side Fl(2)G.7s5m3M. S head Fl.G.5s6m3M. E mole N elbow Fl(4)R.11s6m3M.

VHF Ch 11, 12, 14, 16 for port authorities. Ch 09 for RCM/RCN. Ch 68 for Marina Port Vell.

Navigation Sailing yachts do not have automatic right of way over powered craft. Racon buoy 06 paints the deep water channel into the main harbour. Yachts should head towards the new entrance to the inner harbour.

Berths Proceed to RCM, RCN or Marina Port Vell at the NE end of the harbour.

Shelter Good shelter.

Data Marina Port Vell 410 berths. Max LOA 180m. Depths 7–10m. Charge band 6+.
RCM 200 berths. 30 visitors' berths. Max LOA 15m. Charge band 4.
RCN 115 berths. 12 visitors' berths. Max LOA 35m.

Facilities Marina Port Vell Water. 220/380V. Showers and toilets. TV. WiFi. Fuel quay. 50/150-ton travel-hoists. All yacht repairs. Provisions and restaurants.
RCM/RCN Water. 220V. Showers and toilets. Fuel quay. 25-ton travel-hoist. 20/5-ton cranes. All yacht repairs. Provisions and restaurants.

Remarks Marina Port Vell Superyacht Marina has berths for superyachts up to 180m LOA. Reopened in 2014.

There is a new project to develop Marina Bocana Nord in the basin near the entrance to the north harbour. No further details are available yet.

Marina Port Vell, Torre de Control
☎ 934 842 300
Email info@marinaportvell.com
www.marinaportvell.com

Marina '92 Yard, Muelle Nuevo 23
☎ 932 214 370

Réal Club Maritimo de Barcelona
☎ 932 217 394
www.maritimbarcelona.org

Réal Club Náutic de Barcelona
☎ 932 216 521
Email info@rcnb.com

PORT OLÍMPIC

41°23'·1N 02°12'E

☆ Outer breakwater Q.R.1M. Breakwater head Fl(4)G.8s. Submerged breakwater Fl(3)R.8s3M / Fl(3)G.8s5M / Q(3)10s5M. Contradique head Fl(4)R.8s1M

VHF Ch 09.

Navigation Marked channel (beacons).

Berths Report to *torre de control*.

Shelter Good shelter.

Data 740 berths. 25 visitors' berths. Max LOA 30m. Depths 3–6m. Charge band 4/5.

Facilities Water. 220/380V. Showers and toilets. Fuel quay. 45-ton travel-hoist. 6-ton crane. Yacht repairs. Provisions and restaurants.

Port Olimpíc ☎ 932 259 220
Email portolimpic@pobasa.es
www.portolimpic.net

POWER STATION

41°25'·5N 02°14'·3E

☆ Muelle Centrals FECSA Jetty 1 Q(3)10s3M

PORT FORUM MARINA

41°24'·9N 02°13'·7E

☆ Breakwater head Fl(4)G.5s5M. Elbow Q(3)10s3M

Motorboat and superyacht marina 3M NE of Port Olímpic, Barcelona.

VHF Ch 09, 73.

Navigation Access to the inner harbour is limited by the bridge crossing the entrance – AH 10m. The outer harbour has no height restrictions.

Berths Where directed. Laid moorings or finger pontoons. All yachts berth in the outer harbour.

Data 200 berths. Max LOA 80m. Charge band 3/4.

Facilities Water. 220/380V. WiFi. TV. Showers and toilets. Fuel. 120-ton travel-hoist. Storage hangar for small motorboats. Provisions and restaurants planned. Ferry, metro, tram and bus to Barcelona.

☎ 93 356 2720 / 25
Email info@portforum.net
www.portforum.net

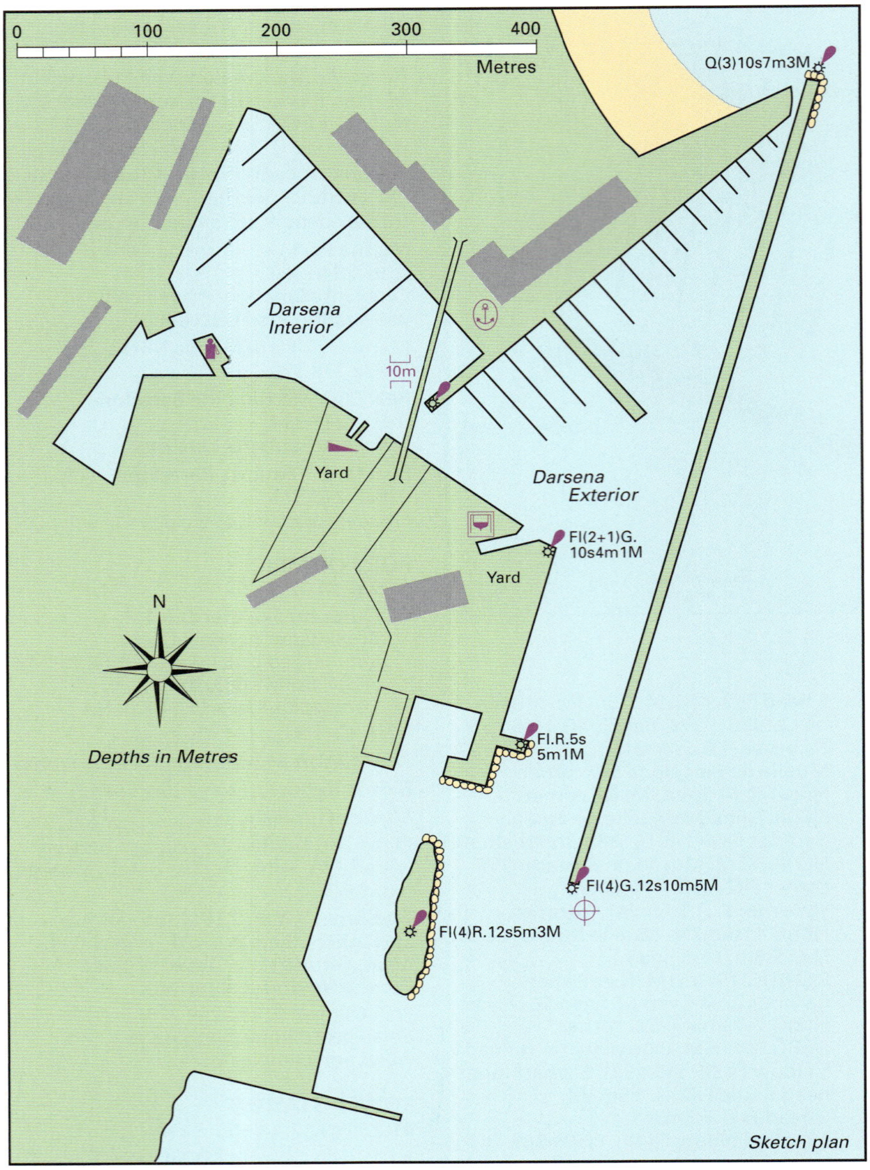

PORT FORUM MARINA

BADALONA MARINA

41°25'·9N 02°14'·6E

☆ Fl(3)G.9s5M/Fl.R.5s1M.

1M N of Port Forum Marina.

VHF Ch 09, 16.

Berths Where directed. Laid moorings.

Data 620 berths. Max LOA 30m. Charge band 3/4.

Facilities Water. 220V. WiFi. Showers and toilets. Laundry. Waste pump-out. Fuel. 75-ton travel-lift, 5-ton crane. 330 places ashore.

✆ 93 320 7500

Email port@marinabadalona-sa.es

www.marinabadalona-sa.es

EL MASNOU

41°28'·6N 02°18'·9E

BA 1704 Sp 4892

11M Barcelona ←→ Mataro 7M

☆ Dique de Levante Fl(3)G.10s2M. Dique de Poniente Fl(3)R.10s2M. Nuevo Dique de Levante Fl(2)G.12s5M. Nuevo Contradique Fl(2)R.12s3M.

VHF Ch 09.

Berths Report to *torre de control* in E basin.

Shelter E basin uncomfortable with strong SW winds.

Data 1,080 berths. 156 visitors' berths. Max LOA 24m. Depths 2·5–4m.

Facilities Water. 220V. Showers and toilets. Fuel quay. 50-ton travel-hoist. 4-ton crane. All yacht repairs. Provisions and restaurants. Train to Barcelona.

Puerto Deportivo de Masnou

✆ 935 403 000

Email portmasnou@infonegocio.com

CN El Masnou ✆ 935 558 817

Email cnm@nauticmasnou.com

PREMIA DE MAR

41°29'·2N 02°21'·5E

BA 1704 Sp 4892

☆ Entrance Fl.G.3s5M/Fl.R.3s3M

VHF Ch 09, 16.

Berths Where directed. Go on W quay at entrance to be allotted a berth.

Shelter Southerlies make some berths uncomfortable.

Data 565 berths. 250 visitors' berths. Max LOA 30m. Depths 1·5–6m. Charge band 4.

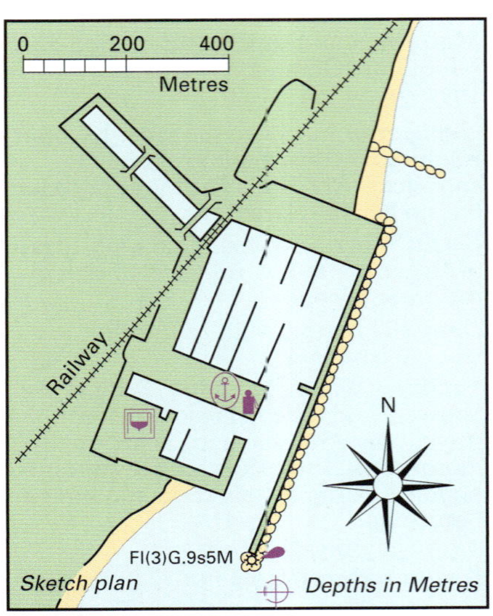

BADALONA MARINA

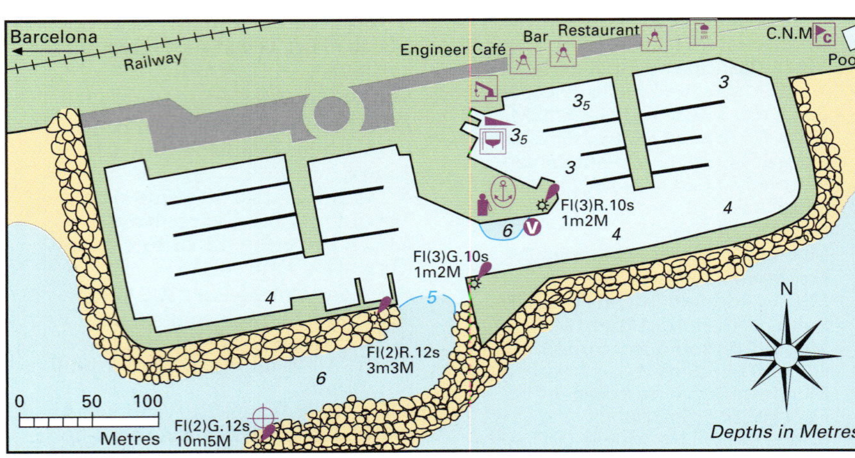

EL MASNOU

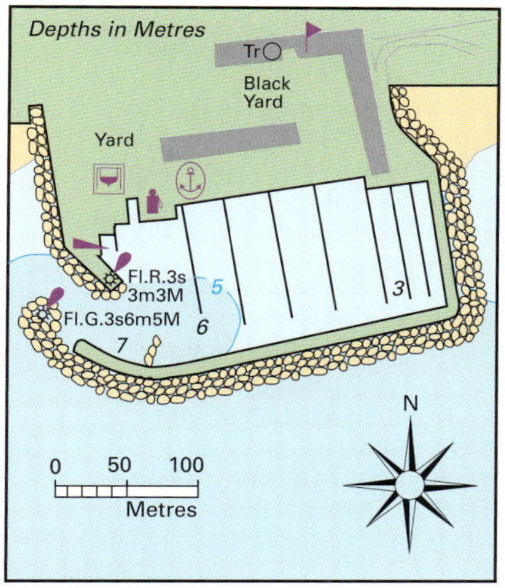

PREMIA DE MAR

Facilities Water. 220/380V. Showers and toilets. Fuel quay. 100-ton travel-hoist. 5-ton crane and slipways. Some yacht repairs. Provisions and restaurants.

Remarks Same group as Port Forum Marina.

Premia de Mar ☏ 937 549 119
Email info@marinapremia.com

PORT MATARÓ

41°31′·6N 02°26′·7E
BA 1704 SP 4893

☆ Entrance Fl(4)G.16s5M/Fl(4)R.8s4M

VHF Ch 09.

Berths Go on fuel jetty just inside the entrance and report to the *capitanía*.

Shelter Uncomfortable with SW winds.

Data 1,080 berths. 230 visitors' berths. Max LOA 30m. Depths 3–7m. Charge band 4.

Facilities Water. 220/380V. Showers and toilets. Fuel quay. 120-ton travel-hoist. 12-ton crane. Most yacht repairs. Provisions and restaurants.

Remarks 20-minute train ride to Barcelona.

Port Mataro ☏ 937 550 961
Email info@portmataro.com
www.portmataro.com

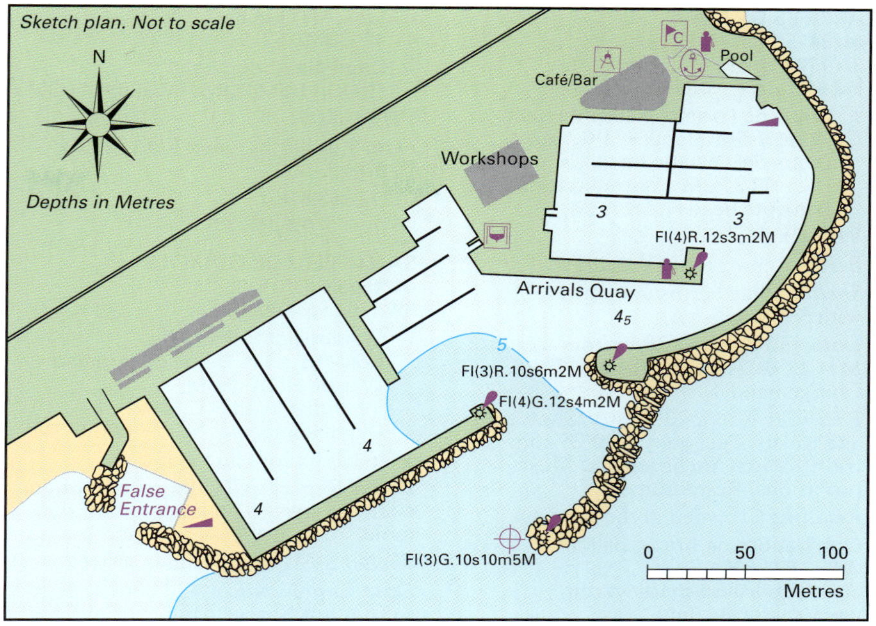

EL BALIS

EL BALIS

41°33′·4N 02°30′·6E
BA 1704 Sp 4911

☆ Entrance Fl(4)G.12s2M/Fl(3)R.10s2M
Dique de Levante spur Fl(3)G.10s5M.
Fuel jetty Fl(4)R.12s2M.

VHF Ch 16, 06.

Berths Go on fuel quay in N basin and report to the *capitanía*.

Shelter Good shelter.

Data 775 berths. 140 visitors' berths. Max LOA 25m. Depths 2·5–4m. Charge band 3/4.

Facilities Water. 220V. Showers and toilets. Fuel quay. 50-ton travel-hoist. 30-ton crane. Most yacht repairs. Some provisions. Restaurants.

Port Balis ☏ 937 929 900
www.cnelbalis.com

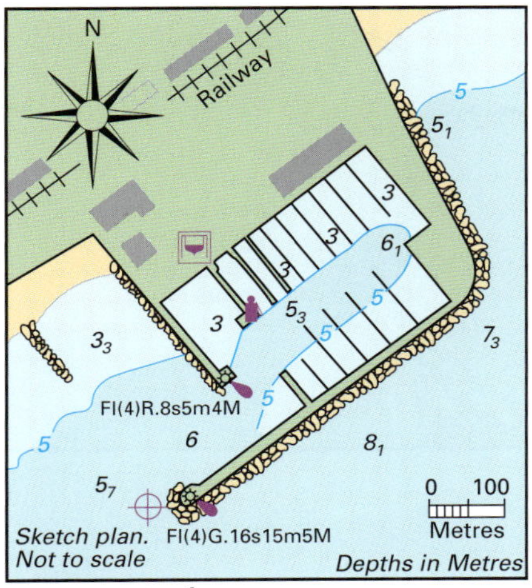

PORT MATARÓ

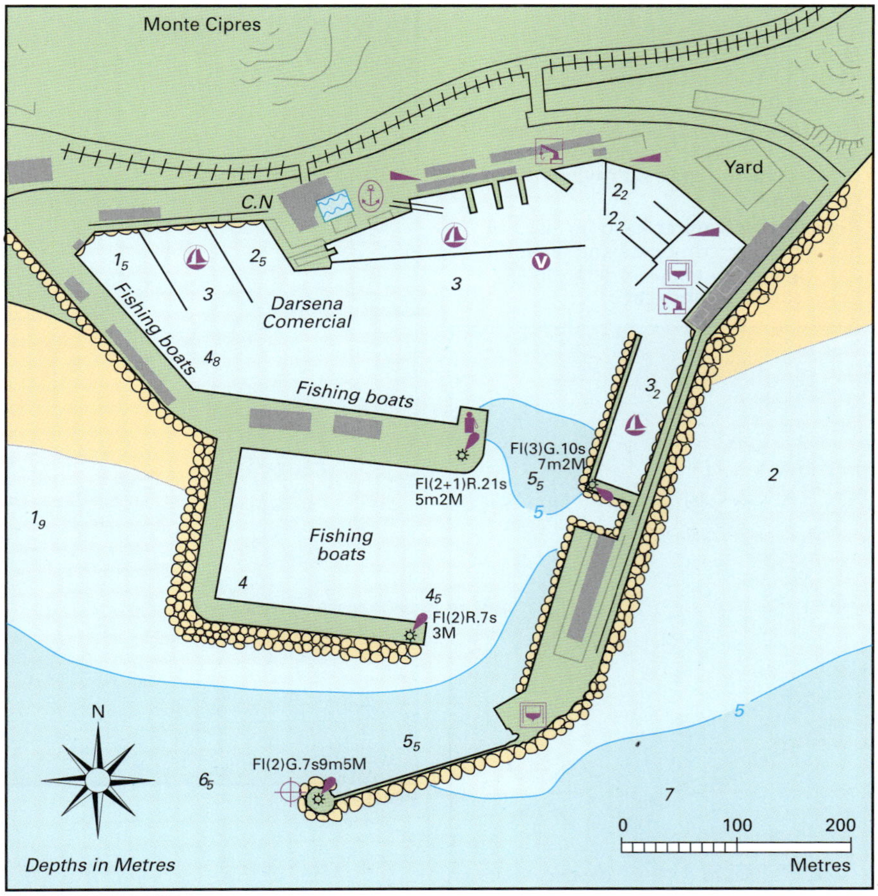

ARENYS DE MAR

ARENYS DE MAR
41°34′·5N 02°33′·5E
BA 1704 Sp 4911
5M Mataró ←→ Blanes 13M

☆ Dique de Portiñol o Levante head Fl(2)G.7s5M. Elbow Fl(3)G.10s2M. Dique del Calvario head Fl(2+1)R.21s2M. Contradique de Poniente head Fl(2)R.7s3M

VHF Ch 04, 09, 23.

Berths Report to the *capitanía*.

Shelter Some berths uncomfortable with SW winds.

Data 450 berths. 120 visitors' berths. Max LOA 22m. Depths 2·5–5m. Charge band 4.

Facilities Water. 220/380V. Showers and toilets. Fuel quay. 150/25-ton travel-hoists. Yacht repairs. Most provisions. Restaurants.

Remarks Crowded in the summer.

Club Náutico de Arenys de Mar
✆ 937 921 600
Email esportiva@cnarenys.com
www.cnarenys.com

Costa Brava

BLANES
41°40′·4N 02°47′·9E
BA 1704 Sp 4913
13M Arenys de Mar ←→ Port d'Aro 16M

☆ Dique de Abrigo head Fl.G.3s5M. Spur head Fl.R.3s3M/Fl(2)R.6s2M.

VHF Ch 09.

Berths Report to YC for a berth.

Shelter Some berths uncomfortable in S–SW winds.

Data 320 berths. 30 visitors' berths. Max LOA 15m. Depths 2·5–6m. Charge band 4/5.

Facilities Water. 220V. Showers and toilets. Fuel quay. 50-ton travel-hoist. Limited yacht repairs. Provisions and restaurants.

Remarks New outer harbour used by fishing boats, trip boats and ferries.

Club de Vela de Blanes ✆ 972 330 552
Email club@cvblanes.cat

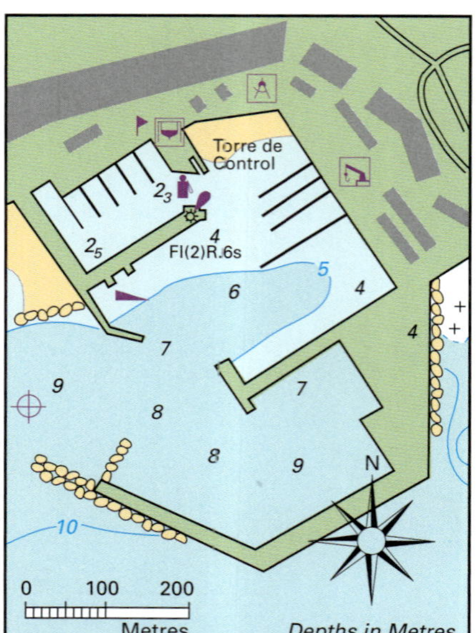

BLANES

CALA CANYELLES
41°42′·3N 02°52′·9E

☆ Dique de Abrigo head Fl(4)G.11s5M/Fl.R.5s1M/Fl(4)R.11s3M

VHF Ch 09.

Data 130 berths. Max LOA 8m. Depths 2–4m.

✆ 972 368 818
www.cncanyelles.com

SANT FELIU DE GUÍXOLS
41°46′·5N 03°01′·9E
BA 1704 Sp 4922

☆ Leading lights (343°) Dir Iso.WRG.3s4M. Dique de refuerzo W head Fl(3)G.9s3M. Inner pier head Fl.G.5s1M. Dique Rompeolas head Fl(3)G.9s5M

VHF Ch 09 for Club Náutico.

Berths Report to YC for a berth or go stern or bows-to on inner half of the mole.

Shelter S–SE winds send in a swell.

Data Club Náutico: 430 berths. Max LOA 60m. Charge band 6.

Facilities Water. 220V. Showers and toilets. Launderette. Waste pump-out. Fuel quay. 3/10-ton cranes. Limited yacht repairs. Provisions and restaurants.

Remarks Anchorage in the bay reported restricted.

Club Náutic Sant Feliu de Guíxols
✆ 972 321 700
Email info@clubnauticsantfeliu.com

PORT D'ARO
41°48′·1N 03°04′·0E
BA 1704 Sp 4922
16M Blanes ←→ Palamos 4M

☆ Breakwater head Fl(2)G.9s5M/Fl(2)R.6·5s3M

VHF Ch 09.

Data 840 berths. Max LOA 25m. Depths 2·5–4m. Charge band 4.

Shelter Uncomfortable even in light NE winds.

Facilities Water. 220/380V. Showers and toilets. Fuel quay. 30-ton travel-hoist. 6-ton crane. Limited provisions. Restaurant.

Port d'Aro ✆ 972 818 929
Email portdaro@clubnauticportdaro.cat

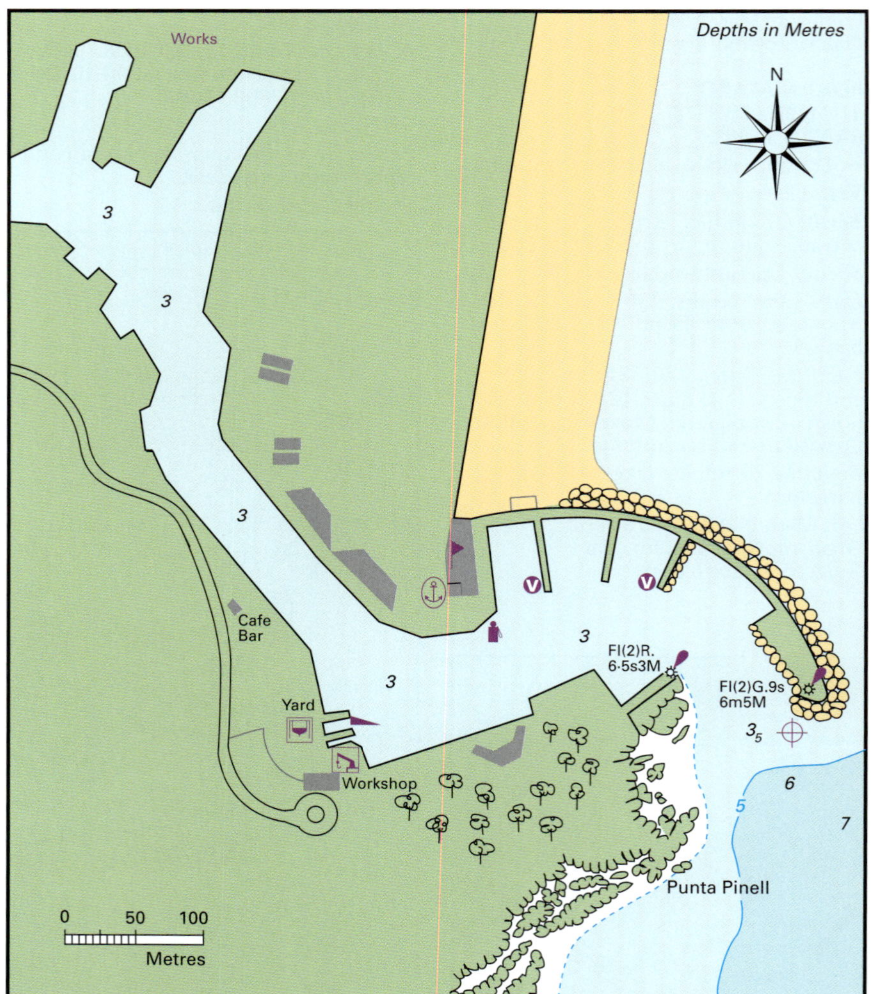

PORT D'ARO

PALAMOS (COMMERCIAL PORT)

41°50′·6N 03°07′·3E

☆ Punta del Molino Oc(1+4)18s22m18M. Dique de Abrigo head Fl.G.3s5M. Old commercial mole head Fl.R.5s3M. Spur Fl(2+1)R.15s3M. Dársena Pesquera Fl(2)G.6s3M/Fl(2)R.6s3M

VHF Ch 09 for Club Náutico.

Berths Report to YC for a berth.

Shelter Uncomfortable and possibly untenable with strong W–SW winds.

Data Club Náutico 250 berths. Max LOA 25m. Depths 3–6m. Charge band 4/5.

Facilities Water. 220V. Showers and toilets. Fuel quay. 2/6/12-ton cranes. Limited yacht repairs. Provisions and restaurants.

Club Náutico Costa Brava ✆ 972 314 324
Email cncb@cncostabrava.com

MARINA PALAMOS

41°50′·7N 03°08′·2E
4M Port d'Aro ←→ L'Estartit 15M

☆ Entrance Fl(4)G.10s5M/Fl(4)R.10s3M. Muelle de Levante head Fl.G.5s3M

VHF Ch 09.

Navigation Entrance difficult in S–SW winds.

Berths Where directed. Finger pontoons.

Data 875 berths. 310 visitors' berths. Max LOA 18m. Depths 2·5–10m. Charge band 5.

Facilities Water. 220/380V. Internet. Showers and toilets. Fuel quay. 30-ton travel-hoist. Limited yacht repairs. Gas. Provisions and restaurants.

Marina Palamos ✆ 972 601 000
Email info@lamarinapalamos.es

ISLA HORMIGA GRANDE

☆ Fl(3)9s14m6M

LLAFRANC

41°53′·6N 03°11′·8E

☆ Mole head Fl(3)G.11s5M

VHF Ch 08.

Data 140 berths. Depths 1–5m. Charge band 5/6.

Facilities Water. 220V. Showers and toilets. Fuel quay. Some provisions. Restaurants.

Club Náutico de Llafranc ✆ 972 300 754

AIGUABLAVA

41°56′N 03°12′·9E

☆ Basin entrance, port side Fl(2)R.6s3M. Starboard side Fl(2)G.10s5M

L'ESTARTIT

42°03′·1N 03°12′·5E
BA 1704 Sp 493
15M Palamos ←→ L'Escala 6M

☆ Dique de Levante head Fl.G.5s9m5M. Dique interior head Fl(2)G.13s3M. Contradique corner Fl.R.5s5M. Head Fl(2)R.13s3M/Fl(3)R.13s1M

VHF Ch 09, 16.

Berths Go on fuel quay and report to the *capitanía*.

Shelter Good shelter.

Data 740 berths. 380 visitors' berths. Max LOA 25m. Depths <1–4·5m. Charge band 6 (July–August).

Facilities Water. 220V. Showers and toilets. Fuel quay. 30-ton travel-hoist. 7·5-ton crane. Some yacht repairs. Provisions and restaurants.

Club Náutico de L'Estartit
✆ 972 751 402
Email info@cnestartit.es
www.cnestartit.es

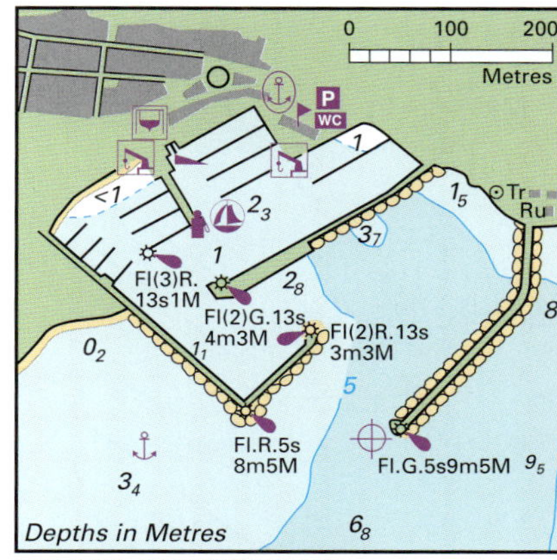

PUERTO DE L'ESTARTIT

LAS ISLAS MEDES

42°02′·8N 03°13′·2E
Isla Mede Grande Fl(4)24s87m14M

Marine Reserve – anchoring and fishing prohibited within 300m.

L'ESCALA

42°07′·1N 03°08′·8E
BA 1704 Sp 493A
6M L'Estartit ←→ Ampuriabrava 7M

☆ Espigón de la Clota Fl(4)G.9s3M. L'Escala breakwater head Fl(4)R.15s5M. Interior breakwater W corner Fl.G.3s1M. Inner breakwater head W Fl(2+1)G.11s3M. Spur Q.6m1M. T-jetty head Fl.R.3s4m3M

VHF Ch 09, 16.

Navigation Care needed of Els Branchs reef in the immediate approach.

Berths Go on fuel quay and report for a berth. Laid moorings tailed to the pontoon.

Shelter Outer berths uncomfortable with N–NW winds.

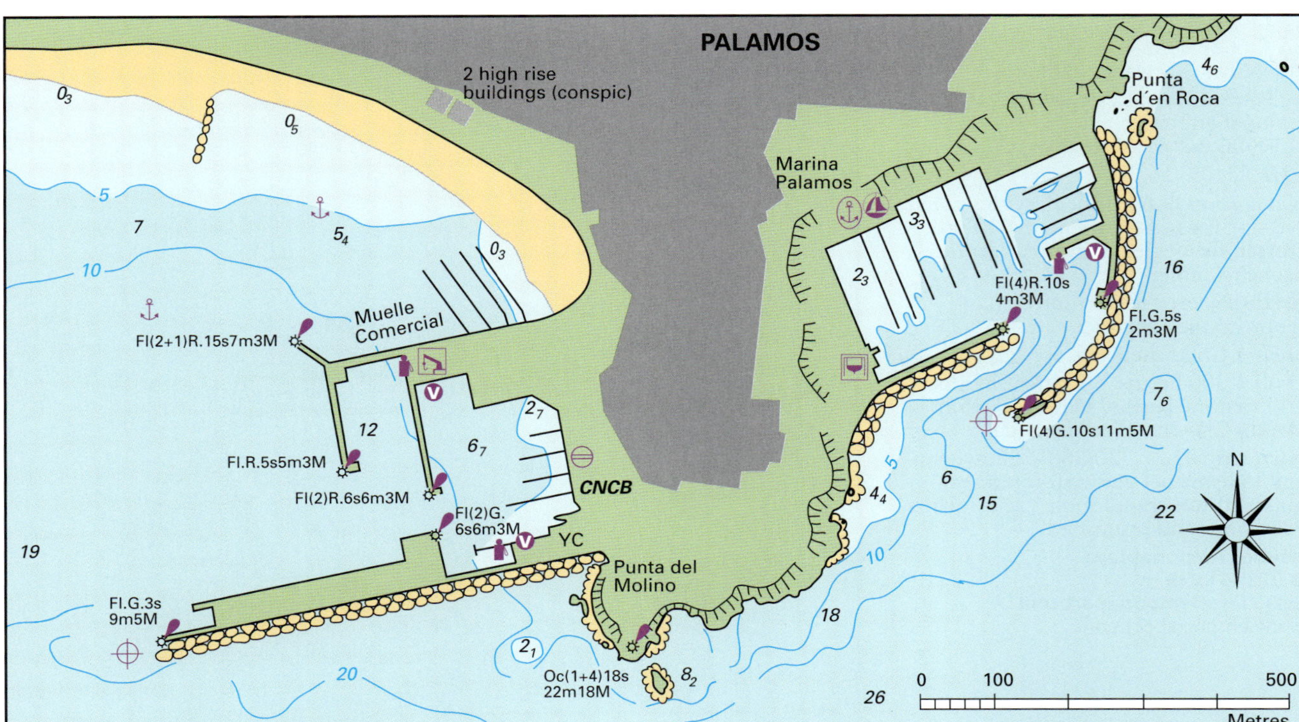

PALAMOS

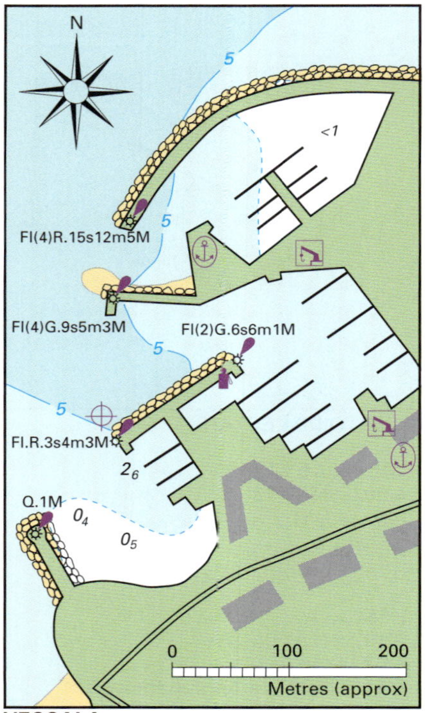

L'ESCALA

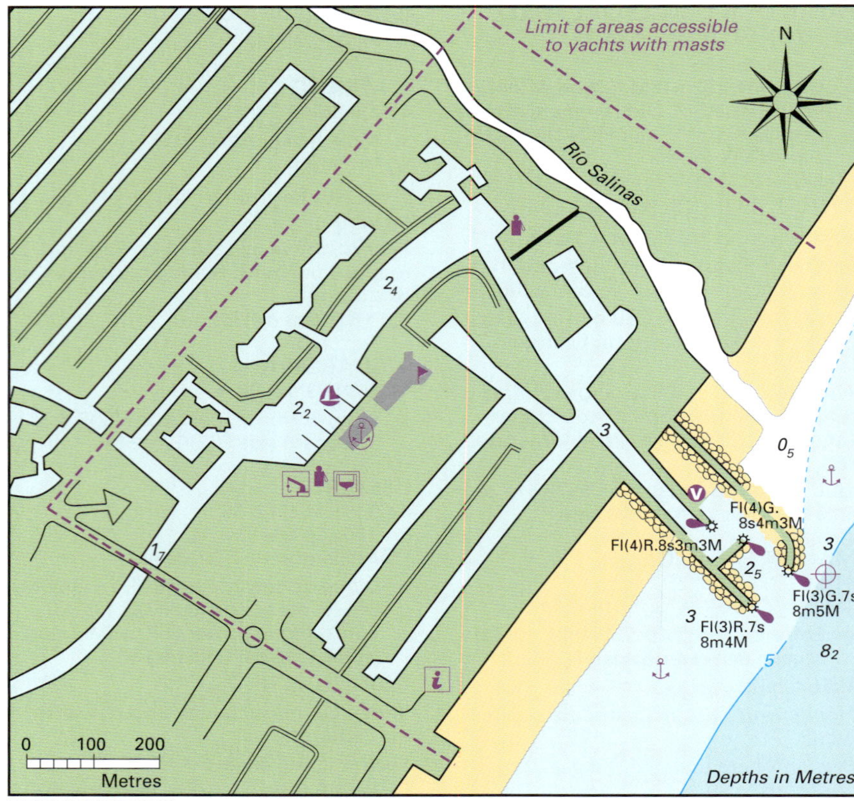

EMPURIABRAVA

Data 600 berths. 200 visitors' berths. Max LOA 15m. Depths 1·5–5m. Charge band 6 (July–August).

Facilities Water. 220V. Showers and toilets. Fuel quay. 8/10-ton cranes. Limited yacht repairs. Provisions and restaurants.

Club Náutico de l'Escala, Puerto La Clota
☏ 972 770 016
Email club@nauticescala.com
www.nauticescala.com

EMPURIABRAVA (AMPURIABRAVA)

42°14'·8N 03°08'·2E
BA 1705 Sp 4932
7M L'Escala ←→ Llança 22M

☆ Entrance Fl(3)G.7s5M/Fl(3)R.7s4M. Inner entrance Fl(4)G.8s3M/Fl(4)R.8s3M

VHF Ch 09, 16.

Navigation Entry difficult with strong NE–E–SE winds. Care needed of other craft in the dogleg entrance. Entrance prone to silting.

Berths Proceed to port interior and report to the *capitanía*.

Shelter Good shelter.

Data 4,000 berths. 500 yacht berths. 100 visitors' berths. Max LOA 25m. Depths 2·5–3m. Charge band 6.

Facilities Water. 220/380V. Showers and toilets. Fuel quay. 50-ton travel-hoist. 10-ton crane. Some yacht repairs. Provisions and restaurants.

Náutica Ampuriabrava
☏ 972 451 239
Email info@empuriaport.com
www.empuriaport.com

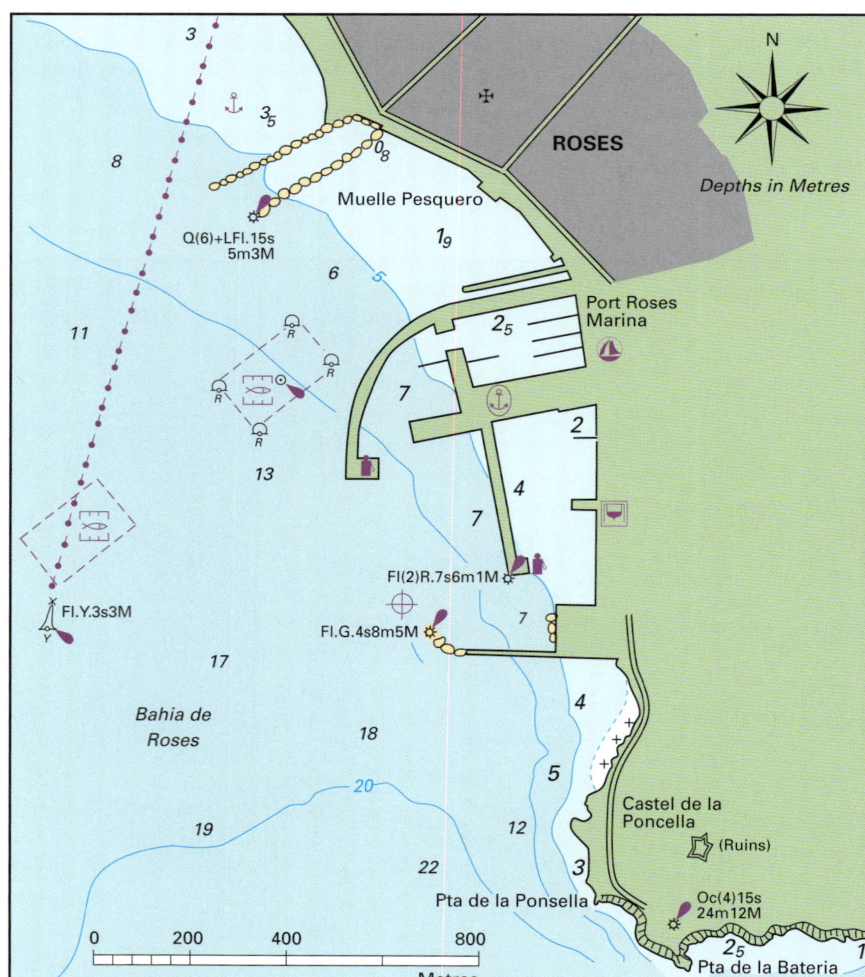

PORT ROSES

SANTA MARGARITA
42°15'·5N 03°09'·1E
BA 1705 Sp 4932

☆ Entrance Q(2)G.4s5M/Q(2)R.4s3M

VHF Ch 09.

Navigation Entry difficult with NE–E–SE winds.

Berths Report to Club Náutico on starboard side of Gran Canal.

Shelter Good shelter.

Data 500 berths. Max LOA 15m. Depths 1·5–2·5m.

Facilities Water. 220V. Showers and toilets. 50-ton travel-hoist. 10-ton crane. Some provisions. Restaurants.

Remarks Entrance liable to silting.

Club Náutico de Santa Margarita
✆ 972 257 700

PORT ROSES (ROSAS)
42°15'·1N 03°10'·7E
BA 1705 Sp 4932

☆ Punta de la Bateria o Blancalls Oc(4)15s24m12M. Muelle de Abrigo head Fl.G.4s5M. Muelle Comercial head Fl(2)R.7s6m1M. Elbow dique transversal head Fl(2)G.7s1M. Playa de Rastell E pier head Q(6)+LFl.15s3M

VHF Ch 09.

Berths Yachts should head for the marina. Berth stern or bows-to where directed. Mooring difficult at visitors' pontoon with E winds.

Shelter Swell with S–SW winds.

Facilities Water. 220V. Fuel quay. Provisions and restaurants.

Data 480 berths. 110 visitors' berths. Max LOA 45m. Depths 2–4m. Charge band 4.

Facilities Water. 220V. Fuel quay. Provisions and restaurants.

Remarks Busy fishing harbour with a yacht marina.

Port Roses ✆ 972 154 412
Email info@portroses.com
www.portroses.com

LA SELVA
42°20'·5N 03°12'·E
BA 1705 Sp 4934

☆ Punta Sernella Fl.5s22m13M. Muelle de Punta del Trench head Fl(4)R.10s5M. Wharf pier head Fl(4)R.11s. Jetty S head Fl(2)G.7s

VHF Ch 09.

Berths Stern or bows-to inside the mole or on the pontoons where directed.

Shelter Adequate shelter in the summer.

Data 325 berths. 55 visitors' berths. Max LOA 20m. Depths 2–7m. Charge band 6 (July–August).

Facilities Water. 220V. WC and showers. Fuel quay. 25/5-ton cranes. Provisions and restaurants.

Club Náutico ✆ 972 387 000
Email nautic@cnps.es
www.cnps.es

COSTA BRAVA MARINE RESERVE
Anchoring restricted or prohibited in some bays.

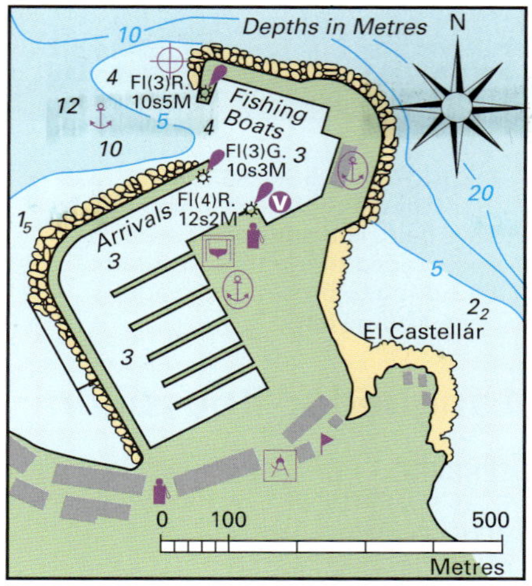

LLANÇA

LLANÇA
42°22'·3N 03°09'·7E
BA 1705 Sp 493
22M Ampuriabrava ←→ Banyuls 7M

☆ Entrance Fl(3)G.10s3M/Fl(3)R.10s5M. Jetty head Fl(4)R.12s2M

VHF Ch 09.

Berths Go on fuel quay and report to the *capitanía*.

Shelter Good shelter.

Data 495 berths. 80 visitors' berths. Max LOA 15m. Depths 2–7m. Charge band 5/6.

Facilities Water. 220/380V. Showers and toilets. Fuel quay. 12-ton crane. Limited yacht repairs. Provisions and restaurants.

Club Náutico de Llança
✆ 972 380 710
Email club@cnllanca.com

COLERA
42°24'·3N 03°09'·3E

☆ Entrance Fl(2)R.7s5M/Fl(2)G.6s3M

Berths Go on inside of W mole and report to the *capitanía*.

Shelter Uncomfortable with *tramontane* (NW).

Data 80 berths. Max LOA 15m. Depths 1·5–4m. Charge band 4/5.

Facilities Water. 220V. Showers and toilets. 2-ton crane. Provisions and restaurants.

Remarks Mooring buoys in Puerto de Cadaques administered by Club Náutico. All other bays up to Cabo Creus are within the marine reserve. Mooring with a permit only.

Club Náutico Sant Miguel de Colera
✆ 972 389 095

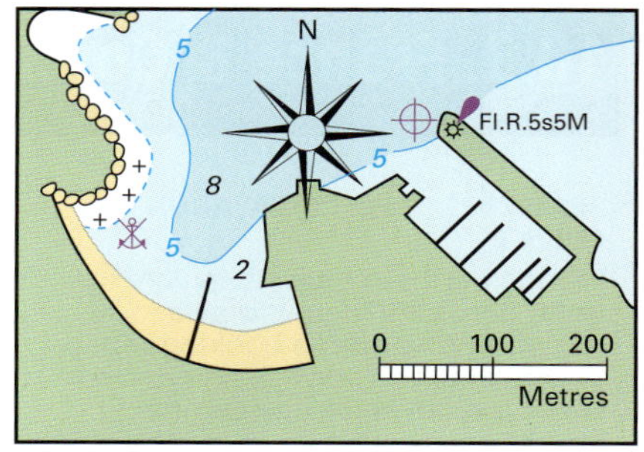

PORTBOU

PORTBOU
42°25'·7N 03°10'E

☆ Breakwater head Fl.R.5s5M. Outer breakwater head Fl.G.5s3M

VHF Ch 09.

Data 300 berths. Max LOA 20m. Depths 10m. Charge band 5/6.

Facilities Water. 220V. Fuel. Hardstanding but no lift-out facilities as yet. Limited yacht repairs.

Marina Portbou
✆ 972 390 712 / 972 390 634
Email portdeportbou@telefonica.net
www.portdeportbou.cat

10.3 France & Corsica

TIME ZONE UT+1 ✆ IDD +33

RESAPORTS BERTH RESERVATION SERVICE

Marina berths in high season are in great demand. There is now a company who offer a booking service to arrange short-term berths and to check availability in any marina around the coast.

You register, and pay an additional fee for each booking made. Covers many ports of the French coast from the Bouches du Rhône to Menton, and along the Italian Riviera. Bookings can be made over the internet or by phone. Open June–September 0800–2000.

✆ 08 20 42 26 00 www.resaports.com

CROSS RESCUE SERVICES

Available by phone on ✆ 1616.

BLACK WATER

New restrictions on black water; some ports require yachts to have holding tanks. Fines for discharging black water may be levied.

***POSIDONIA* SEAGRASS PROTECTION**

In places along the coast white buoys have been laid and yachts are encouraged to use these instead of anchoring to protect the seagrass beds. Charge band 2.

Languedoc-Roussillon

CERBERE

42°26'·5N 03°10'·2E

VHF Ch 09

Berths Three pontoons installed. Visitors berths and moorings for yachts of 14m or less. Anchoring restricted. Charge band 3 /4.

Facilities Water and electricity on the pontoons. Showers and toilets.

Harbourmaster ✆ 0468 88 47 71

Email port-cerbere@orange.fr

BANYULS-SUR-MER

42°28'·9N 03°08'·2E

BA 1705 SHOM 7002

7M Llança ←→ Port Vendres 4M

☆ Entrance Q.WR.4s10/7M/ Iso.G.4s5m2M

CERBERE MARINE RESERVE

Runs from N of Cerbere to Banyuls-sur-Mer, up to 1M off the coast, and is marked with yellow buoys.

- Speed limit 5 kns within 300m of the coast, 8 kns elsewhere
- Amateur fishing only during daylight hours
- Diving permitted
- Anchoring permitted (except where moorings are laid)
- Spear fishing and taking shellfish prohibited

Moorings around Cap l'Abeille and Ilots des Tynes
White buoys for visitors
Anchoring prohibited
Overnight stays are not permitted
✆ 0468 88 56 87
www.cg66.fr/62

VHF Ch 09.

Navigation Approach difficult in strong NE–E winds.

Berths Stern or bows-to where directed. Laid moorings tailed to buoys.

Shelter Good although uncomfortable with strong N winds.

Data 350 berths. 10 visitors' berths.

Quick reference guide *For Key to guide see page 139*

	Shelter	*Mooring*	*Fuel*	*Water*	*Provisions*	*Eating out*	*Charge band*
Cerbère	C	AC	B	B	C	C	3/4
Banyuls-sur-Mer	B	A	B	A	B	A	4/5
Port Vendres	A	A	A	A	B	A	4/5
Collioure	C	C	B	B	B	A	3
Argelès-sur-Mer	A	A	A	A	B	C	4/5
St-Cyprien-Plage	A	A	A	A	B	B	4/5
Canet-en-Roussillon	A	A	A	A	A	A	3/4
Ste-Marie	A	AB	B	A	C	C	3
Port Barcarès	A	A	A	A	C	C	4
Port Leucate	AB	A	A	A	B	B	3/4
Port la Nouvelle	AB	AB	A	A	A	B	2
Port de Barberousse	A	A	B	A	B	B	2
Gruissan	A	A	A	A	B	B	3/4
Narbonne-Plage	A	A	B	A	C	C	3/4
Chichoulet	A	AB	O	A	C	C	3
Valras-Plage	A	AB	A	A	A	B	3/4
Grau d'Agde	AB	B	B	B	B	C	3
Cap d'Agde	A	A	A	A	B	B	4
Marseillan-Plage	A	A	B	A	C	C	4/5
Sète	A	AB	A	A	A	A	3
Frontignan	A	A	A	A	C	C	3/4
Palavas-les-Flots	A	A	A	A	A	A	3/4
Carnon-Plage	A	A	A	A	B	B	4
La Grande Motte	A	A	A	A	B	B	3/4
Grau du Roi	AB	AB	B	A	B	A	3
Port Camargue	A	A	A	A	B	B	4
Port Gardian	A	A	A	A	A	B	4
Port St-Louis-du-Rhône	A	A	B	A	B	C	3
Navy Service Port à Sec	A	B	O	A	C	C	3
Port Napoleon	A	AB	B	A	O	O	3/4
St-Gervais	A	A	A	A	B	C	3
Port de Bouc	A	A	A	A	A	B	3/4
Martigues	A	AB	A	A	A	B	3
Port de Carro	A	A	AB	A	C	C	3/4
Sausset-les-Pins	AB	A	A	A	C	C	4
Carry-le-Rouet	B	A	A	A	C	C	4
Port de la Lave	B	AB	B	A	O	O	3/4
L'Estaque	A	A	A	A	B	C	3/4
Marseille	A	A	A	A	A	A	4
Port du Frioul	AB	AB	A	A	C	C	4
Port de la Pointe-Rouge	A	A	A	A	B	B	4
Les Goudes	C	AB	O	B	O	C	
Cassis	A	A	A	A	B	A	4/5
La Ciotat	A	A	A	A	A	B	3/4
Les Lecques	A	A	A	A	C	C	4
La Madrague	BC	A	O	A	O	C	
Bandol	A	A	A	A	A	A	4/5
Sanary-sur-Mer	B	A	A	A	A	A	4/5
La Coudoulière	B	C	O	B	O	C	4
Port du Brusc	B	A	A	A	C	B	4
St-Pierre des Embiez	A	A	A	A	C	C	5
St-Mandrier	AB	A	A	A	B	B	4
Port Pin-Rolland	B	AB	B	A	O	C	3
Port de la Seyne	A	A	B	A	C	C	4
Toulon	A	A	A	A	A	A	4
Carqueiranne	AB	A	A	A	C	C	3
Port Cros	B	AC	O	B	C	C	4
Port du Niel	B	A	O	A	O	C	5
Port de Porquerolles	AB	A	A	A	C	B	5
Port d'Hyères	A	A	A	A	B	B	5

	Shelter	*Mooring*	*Fuel*	*Water*	*Provisions*	*Eating out*	*Charge band*
Port Miramar	AB	A	A	A	C	C	3
Bormes-Les-Mimosas	A	A	A	A	C	B	5
Le Lavandou	AB	A	A	A	B	A	5/6
Cavalaire-sur-Mer	AB	A	A	A	B	B	4/5
St-Tropez	A	A	A	A	B	A	5/6+
Marines de Cogolin	A	A	A	A	C	C	4/5
Port Grimaud	AB	A	A	A	C	B	5
Ste-Maxime	A	A	A	A	A	A	4/5
Les Issambres	A	A	A	A	C	C	5
Port de Ferreol	B	A	O	A	C	C	4
St-Aygulf	B	A	B	A	C	C	5
Fréjus	A	A	A	A	C	B	5
St-Raphaël (Vieux Port)	A	A	A	A	A	A	4
St-Raphaël (Santa Lucia)	A	A	A	A	B	B	5
Rade d'Agay	C	C	B	B	B	B	5
Figueirette-Miramar	A	A	A	A	O	C	4
La Galère	A	A	A	A	O	C	5
Theoule-sur-Mer	B	A	A	A	C	B	4
La Rague	A	A	A	A	C	C	5
La-Napoule	A	A	A	A	B	B	4
Cannes Marina	A	A	B	A	C	C	
Marco Polo	A	A	B	A	C	C	
Port de Cannes	A	A	A	A	A	A	4
Pierre-Canto	AB	A	A	A	A	B	4
Port de Golfe-Juan	A	A	A	A	C	C	4
Camille Rayon	A	A	A	A	C	C	5/6
Gallice-Juan-Les-Pins	A	A	A	A	C	C	5/6
Vauban-Antibes	A	A	A	A	A	A	5
Baie des Anges	A	A	A	A	B	B	5
St-Laurent du Var	A	A	A	A	C	C	5
Nice	A	AB	A	A	A	A	4
Villefranche	A	A	A	A	B	B	3/4
St-Jean-Cap-Ferrat	A	A	A	A	B	B	4/5
Beaulieu-sur-Mer	A	A	A	A	B	B	4
Port de Cap d'Ail	AB	AB	A	A	B	B	5
Monaco							
Fontvieille	A	A	O	A	B	B	5
Port de Monaco	B	A	A	A	A	A	6
France							
Menton Vieux Port	B	A	B	A	A	A	3/4
Menton-Garavan	A	A	A	A	B	B	5
Corsica							
Calvi	A	AC	A	A	A	A	2/5/6
Cargèse	B	AB	B	A	B	C	5
Ajaccio Vieux Port	A	AB	A	A	A	A	5
Ajaccio Charles							
Ornano	A	A	A	A	A	A	5/6
Propriano	A	A	A	A	B	B	5/6
Baie de Figari Pianottoli	A	AC	O	A	O	C	4
Bonifacio	A	A	A	A	A	A	5
Port de Cavallo	B	A	A	A	C	C	
Porto Vecchio	A	A	A	A	B	B	5/6
Solenzara	A	A	A	A	B	B	4/5
Port de Taverna	A	A	A	A	C	C	4/5
Bastia Vieux Port	B	A	B	A	A	A	5
Port Toga	A	A	A	A	A	A	4/5
Macinaggio	A	A	A	A	B	B	4/5
Centuri	BC	AC	B	B	C	C	
Saint-Florent	A	A	A	A	B	B	5/6
Ile Rousse	B	A	A	A	B	B	4
Sant'Ambrogio	A	A	A	A	C	C	4/5

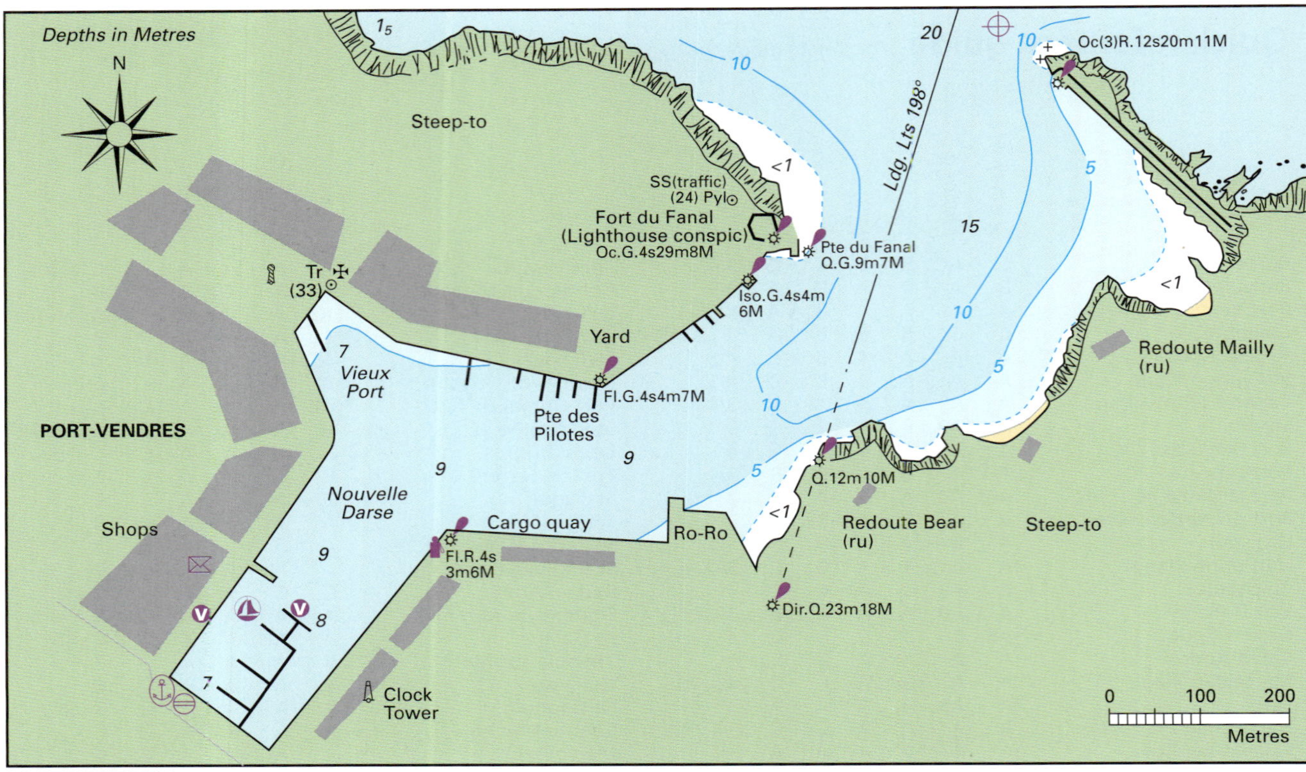

PORT VENDRES

Max LOA 12m. Depths 1–4m. Charge band 4/5.

Facilities Water. 220V. WiFi. Showers and toilets. Fuel 200m. 8-ton crane. Provisions and restaurants.

Bureau du Port de Plaisance
✆ 0468 88 30 32
Email port.banyuls@banyuls-sur-mer.com
www.banyulssurmer.com

PORT VENDRES

42°31′·39N 03°07′·03E WGS84
BA 1506 SHOM 7002 Imray M14
4M Banyuls ←→ Argeles 3M

☆ Entrance Oc(3)R.12s11M / Oc.G.4s8M / Q.G.
Anse Gerbal jetée head Iso.G.4s6M.
Leading lights (198°). Q.12m10M/ DirQ.23m18M. Avant port Fl.G.4s7M/ Fl.R.4s6M

Signal lights: Day and night:

3.F.R.(vert) = Entry prohibited
3.Oc.6s.(vert) = Vessel manoeuvring (VHF Ch12)
Lights off = Entry unrestricted

VHF Ch 12 for port authorities. Ch 09 for Port de Plaisance (summer 0800–2100).

Navigation The *tramontane* gusts into the harbour and raises a sea in the entrance.

Berths Stern or bows-to where directed. Finger pontoons and laid moorings tailed to buoys.

Shelter Good shelter.

Data 230 berths. 20 visitors' berths. Max LOA 40m. Depths 6–8m. Charge band 4/5.

Facilities Water. 220V. Showers and toilets. Fuel. 150-ton hoist. 60-ton crane. Some yacht repairs. Provisions and restaurants.

Remarks Large fishing port. Facilities ashore are largely concerned with the fishing fleet.

Port de Plaisance ✆ 0468 82 08 84
Email port.vendres.plaisance@perpignan.cci.fr

COLLIOURE

42°31′·7N 03°05′·3E
BA 1506 SHOM 6843

☆ Mole head Iso.G.4s8M

VHF Ch 12.

Berths Anchoring prohibited in the bay. 11 moorings in the bay for visitors. Maximum stay 24hrs.

Shelter Untenable in the anchorage with strong N winds.

Data Port 90 berths. Max LOA 6·5m. Depths 1·5–3m.

Moorings Max LOA 12m. Charge band 3.

Facilities Provisions and restaurants.

✆ 04 68 82 05 66
Email portdeplaisance@collioure.net

ARGELES-SUR-MER

42°32′·7N 03°03′·4E
BA 1705 SHOM 6843
3M Port Vendres ←→ St-Cyprien 5M

☆ Entrance Fl.G.4s5m5M/Fl.R.4s4M

VHF Ch 09 (0830–1200 / 1400–2000).

Navigation Entrance difficult to make out. Care needed with strong N winds.

Berths Stern or bows-to where directed. Laid moorings.

Shelter Good shelter.

Data 850 berths and 120 mooring buoys. 30 visitors' berths. Max LOA 24m. Depths 2–4m. Charge band 4/5.

Facilities Water. 220V. Showers and toilets. Fuel quay. 35-ton travel-hoist. Limited yacht repairs. Limited provisions. Restaurants.

Port d'Argeles-sur-Mer ✆ 0468 81 63 27
Email contact@saga-argeles.com

ST-CYPRIEN-PLAGE

42°37′·23N 03°02′·47E WGS84
BA 1705 SHOM 6843
5M Argeles ←→ Port Leucate 17M

☆ Entrance Fl(4)R.15s9M/Fl.G.2·5s4M

VHF Ch 09 (summer 0700–2100, winter 0800–1200 / 1400–1800). CB Ch 30.

Navigation Care needed with strong E–SE winds.

Berths Stern or bows-to, where directed. Finger pontoons or laid moorings tailed to buoys.

Shelter Good shelter.

Data 2,200 berths. 440 visitors' berths. Max LOA 20m. Depths 3–4m. Charge band 4/5.

Facilities Water. 220V. WiFi. Showers and toilets. Fuel quay. 45-ton travel-hoists. 100-ton slipway. Most yacht repairs. Provisions and restaurants.

Remarks Expansion works planned.

Port de St-Cyprien
Harbourmaster ✆ 0468 21 07 98
Email contact@port-st-cyprien.com

CANET-EN-ROUSSILLON

42°42′·2N 03°02′·6E
BA 1705 SHOM 6843

☆ Canet Plage lighthouse Fl(4)15s27m15M.
Entrance Fl(3)R.12s9M/Fl(3)G.12s5M

VHF Ch 09, 16 (summer 0800–2000, winter 0800–1230 / 1330–1830).

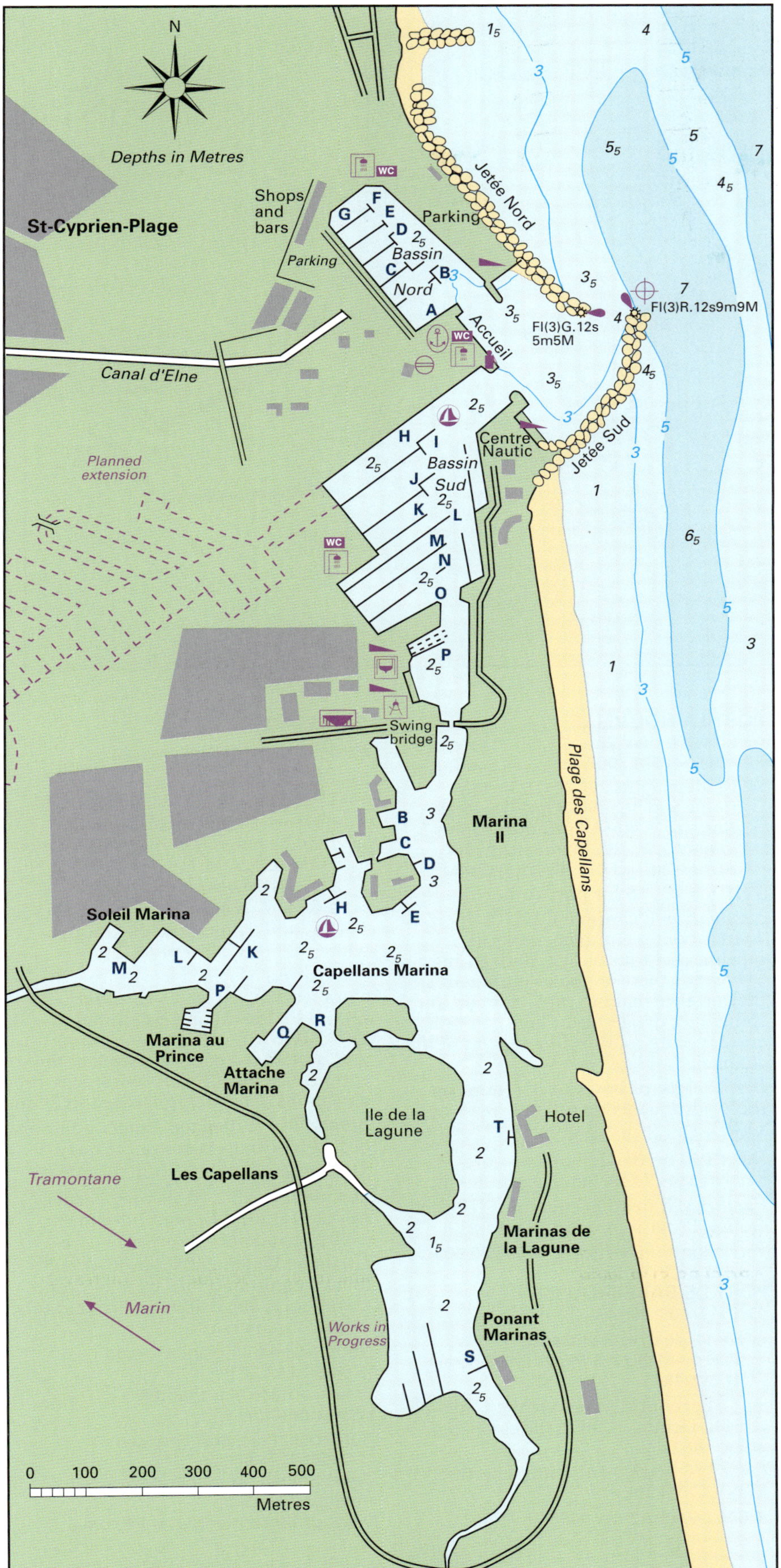

ST-CYPRIEN-PLAGE

Navigation Strong NE–SE winds make entry difficult.

Berths Stern or bows-to where directed. Laid moorings tailed to the quay or a buoy.

Shelter Good although some berths uncomfortable with *tramontane*.

Data 2,200 berths. 50 visitors' berths. Max LOA 40m. Depths 2·5–4·5m. Charge band 3/4.

Facilities Water. 220V. Showers and toilets. Fuel quay. 200/50-ton travel-hoists. 80-ton slipway. Most yacht repairs. Provisions and restaurants.

Remarks Major new development of a new basin on Le Gouffre is now complete.

Canet-en-Roussillon, capitainerie
☎ 0468 86 72 73
Email contact@port-de-canet.com
www.port-de-canet.com

SAINTE-MARIE

42°43'·5N 03°02'·5E

☆ N breakwater head Fl(5)G.20s4M.
S breakwater head Fl(5)R.20s6m5M

Navigation Entrance difficult and possibly dangerous with onshore winds. 1·5m depths in entrance channel.

Berths Where directed.

Data 510 berths. Max LOA 12m. Depths 1·5–2·5m. Charge band 3.

Facilities Water. 220V. 8-ton crane.

Port de St-Marie ☎ 0468 80 51 02
Email info@portsaintemarie66.com
www.portsaintemarie66.com

PORT BARCARÈS (GRAU ST-ANGE)

42°47'·9N 03°02'·4E
BA 1705 SHOM 6844

☆ Entrance Fl(2)R.10s10M/Fl.G.2·5s4M

VHF Ch 09 (summer 0700–2000, winter 0800–1200 / 1400–1800).

Navigation With strong onshore winds entry can be dangerous.

Berths Stern or bows-to where directed. Laid moorings tailed to buoys or posts.

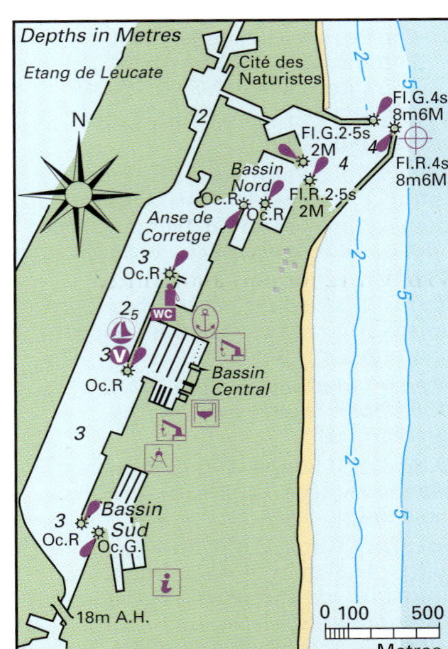

PORT LEUCATE

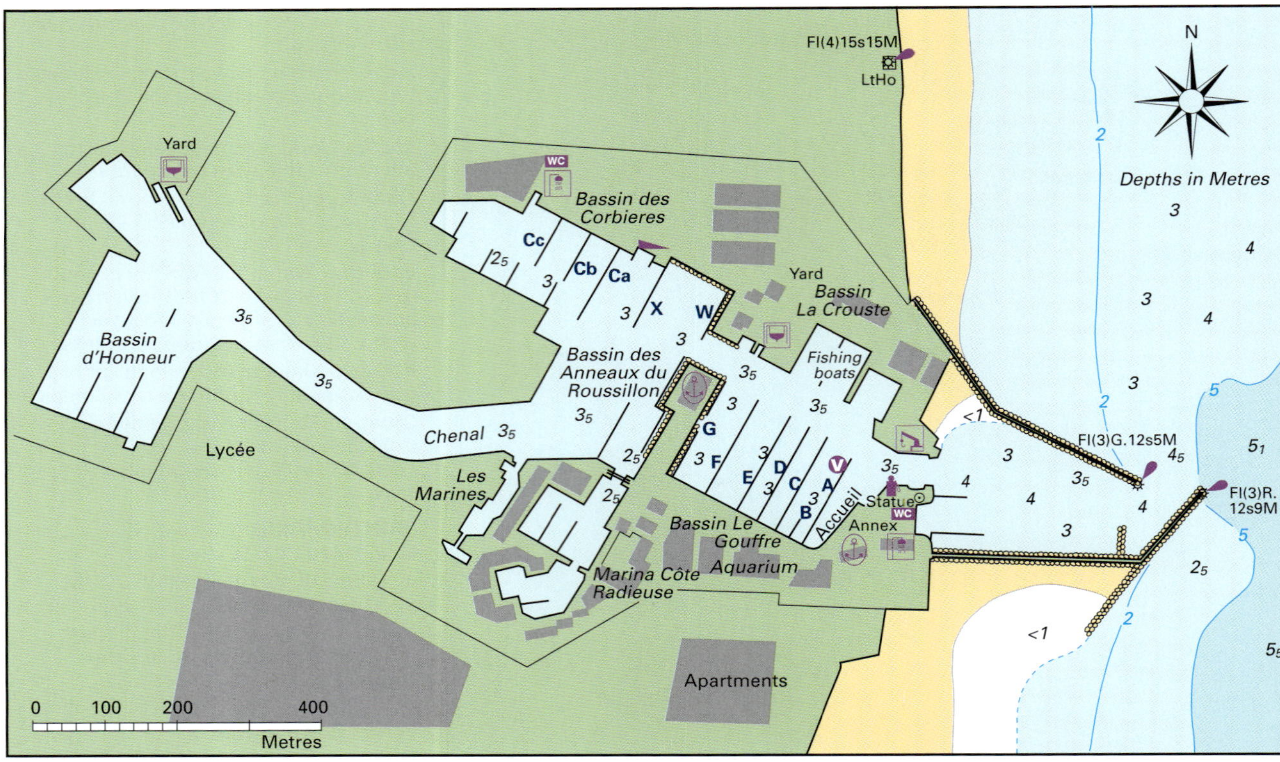

CANET-EN-ROUSSILLON

Shelter Good shelter.

Data 600 berths. 50 visitors' berths. Max LOA 22m. Depths 2–3m. Charge band 4.

Facilities Water. 220V. Showers and toilets. Fuel quay (summer). 5-ton crane. Limited yacht repairs. Some provisions and restaurants.

Capitainerie ✆ 0468 86 07 35
Email capitaine@portbarcares.com
www.portbarcares.com

PORT LEUCATE

42°52′·4N 03°03′·3E
BA 1705 SHOM 7002
17M St Cyprien ←→ Gruissan 15M

☆ Cap Leucate Fl(2)10s66m20M. Entrance Fl.R.4s6M/Fl.G.4s6M. Inner entrance Fl.R.2·5s2M/Fl.G.2·5s2M

VHF Ch 09 (summer 0800–2200, winter 0800–2000).

Navigation Confused swell at the entrance with E–SE winds. Onshore gales can make entry dangerous. Speed limit of 5kns in access channel, 2kns in basins.

Berths Where directed. Visitors normally go in the first basin. Finger pontoons or posts.

Shelter Good shelter although the *tramontane* makes some berths uncomfortable.

Data 1,100 berths. 100 visitors' berths. Max LOA 20m. Depths 2–3m. Charge band 3/4.

Facilities Water. 220V. Showers and toilets. Fuel quay. 45/12/6-ton travel-hoists. All yacht repairs. Provisions and restaurants.

Port Leucate, Capitainerie
✆ 0468 40 91 24
Email capitainerie@port-leucate.fr

PORT LA NOUVELLE

43°00′·8N 03°04′·2E
BA 1506 SHOM 7002

☆ Leading lights 292·4° Q.23m14M (Jetée Sud head)/Q.53m17M. Jetée Nord Iso.G.4s6M. Entrance channel S Bank VQ.5m3M. Marine Farm SW corner Q(6)+LFl.15s4M/Q(3)10s4M

VHF Ch 12, 16 for port authorities.

Navigation E cardinal Q(3)10s approx 1M E of outer entrance marks a pipeline and four buoys. With strong S–E winds there are breaking waves at the entrance making entry difficult and sometimes dangerous. There can be a current of up to 3kns flowing out of the channel.

Berths Stern or bows-to pontoons on the S side (yachts up to 9m).

Shelter Good shelter.

Data 130 berths. Limited visitors' berths. Max LOA 9m. Depths 2–4m.

Facilities Water. Fuel nearby. 6/10-ton cranes. Provisions and restaurants.

Yacht Pontoons Office ✆ 0468 270 609.

PORT DE BARBEROUSSE

43°05′·7N 03°06′·7E

☆ Canal de Grazel entrance Fl.R.4s4M/Oc(2)G.6s3M. Epi central Fl.G.2s1M

Small harbour reached via the Canal du Grazel. Depths 1·2m in the canal and 2m in the basin.

Data 316 berths. 16 visitors' berths. Max LOA 13m.

✆ 0468 49 00 22 *Fax* 0468 75 15 40

GRUISSAN

43°06′·49N 03°06′·18E WGS84
BA 1705 SHOM 6844
15M Port Leucate ←→ Cap d'Agde 17M

☆ Entrance Fl(2)R.6s6M/Fl.G.4s7M. Channel buoys Fl.G/Fl.R(x3). Entrance S side Fl.R.2s3M. N side Fl.G.2s3M. No. 2 Fl.R.2s1M.Basin S entrance Fl.R.2s2M. N entrance Fl.G.2s4M

VHF Ch 09 (summer 0700–2300, winter 0700–1200 / 1400–2100).

Navigation Marine farm off the entrance marked by a S cardinal Q(5)+LFl.15s4M and E cardinal Q(3)10s4M. With strong onshore winds there is a confused swell at the entrance. With S–E gales entry may be dangerous. Channel is dredged to 2·5m.

Berths Where directed. Finger pontoons or laid moorings tailed to the quay.

Shelter Good shelter.

Data 900 berths. 40 visitors' berths. Max LOA 30m. Depths 2·5–3m. Charge band 3/4.

Facilities Water. 220V. Showers and toilets. Pump-out. Fuel quay. 45-ton travel-hoist. Provisions and restaurants. All yacht repairs.

Nautiland hauling and storage
✆ 04 68 43 15 81
Email contact@nautiland.fr
www.nautiland.fr

Bureau du Port, Port Gruissan
✆ 0468 75 21 60
Email accueil.capitainerie@gruissan-mediterranee.com
www.gruissan-mediterranee.com

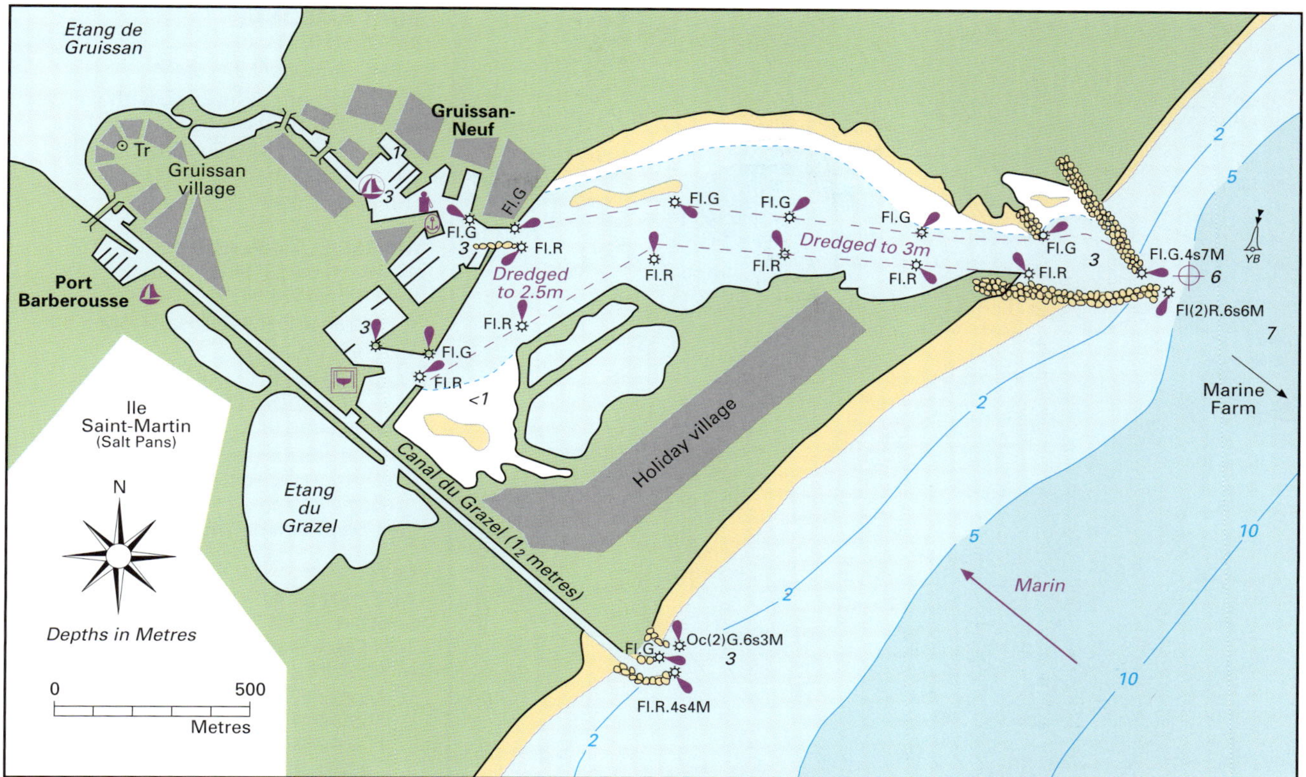

GRUISSAN

NARBONNE-PLAGE

43°10'·4N 03°11'E
BA 1705 SHOM 6844

☆ Main light Fl(3)12s24m15M. Entrance Fl.G.4s1M/Fl.R.4s4M. Inner entrance Oc.R.4s

VHF Ch 09, 16 (summer 24 hrs, winter 0930–1200 / 1530–1800).

Navigation Entry can be dangerous with onshore gales. Least depth 1·8m reported in entrance.

Berths Stern or bows-to where directed. Finger pontoons or laid moorings tailed to the quay.

Shelter Good shelter.

Data 600 berths. Visitors' berths. Max LOA 12m. Depths 2–3m in outer basin. 1·2–1·5m depths in Bassin Brossolette. Charge band 3/4.

Facilities Water. 220V. Showers and toilets. Fuel nearby. 5-ton crane. Limited provisions. Restaurants

Port Narbonne-Plage capitainerie,
✆ 0468 49 91 43

RIVIÈRE AUDE

43°12'·7N 03°14'·6E

☆ Entrance Fl(2)G.6s10m8M/Fl.R.4s7m5M. Marine Farm VQ(6)+LFl.10s9m4M/ VQ(3)5s9m4M

VHF Ch 09 (Cabanes Fleury / Chichoulet) (summer 0700–1700, winter 0800–1200 / 1400–1700)

Navigation Entry dangerous in onshore winds.

Data *Chichoulet* 95 berths. Four visitors' berths. Max LOA 13m. Depths 1·8m. Charge band 3. *Cabanes Fleury* 240 berths. One visitors' berth. Max LOA 12m. Depths 1·8m.

Chichoulet ✆ 0467 32 26 05
Cabanes Fleury ✆ 0468 33 93 32

VALRAS-PLAGE

43°14'·7N 03°18'·1E
BA 1705 SHOM 7054

☆ Entrance to the River Orb Fl(4)15s9M/Fl.G.4s6M. Yacht basin entrance No. 1 Iso.G.4s. No. 2 Iso.R.4s

VHF Ch 09, 16 (24/24).

Navigation Port is situated inside Rivière de l'Orb. With onshore gales entry can be dangerous.

Berths Stern or bows-to or alongside where directed. Finger pontoons or laid moorings tailed to buoys.

Shelter Good shelter in basin. Uncomfortable on outside pontoon.

Data 240 berths. 60 visitors' berths. Max LOA 13m. Depths 1·5–3m. Charge band 3/4.

Facilities Water. 220V. Showers and toilets. Fuel quay. 4-ton crane. Limited yacht repairs. Provisions and restaurants.

Remarks Upstream there are two basins. Bassin Jean Gau 2·5m depths. Port de l'Orb 2m depths.

Port de Valras-Plage
✆ 0467 32 33 64
Email portvalrasplage@wanadoo.fr

GRAU D'AGDE

43°16'·8N 03°26'·6E
17M Gruissan ←→ Sète 13M

☆ Entrance W jetée Oc(2)R.6s7M. E jetée Oc.G.4s7M (Entrance to the Rivière Hérault)

Chantier Allemande boatyard on the east bank.

Data Pontoon. 100-ton travel hoist. Mast stepping. Most repairs.

✆ 0467 94 24 19
Email contact@chantier-allemande.com

CAP D'AGDE

43°16'·08N 03°30'·37E WGS84
BA 1705 SHOM 7003 Imray M14

☆ Ilôt de Brescou: Fl(2)WR.6s13/10M. (113°-R-190°). La Lauze Fl.G.4s5M. E breakwater head Fl(3)G.12s8m6M. W breakwater head Fl(3)R.12s8m6M. Port de la Clape Fl.G/Fl.R. N corner Q.4M. E corner VQ(3)5s4M. Marine Farm W corner VQ(9)10s4M. S corner VQ(6)+LFl.10s4M

VHF Ch 09 (summer 0800–2000, winter 0800–1200 / 1400–1800).

Navigation Care is needed of Le Diamant rock and Roche de l'Ane off the NW and SW sides of the Ilot Brescou. Care is also needed of shoal water fringing Îlot Brescou. The approach should be made between Îlot Brescou and La Lauze beacon.

Berths Go on the pontoon off the *capitainerie* just inside the entrance where a berth will be allocated to you.

Shelter Good shelter although some berths are uncomfortable with the *tramontane*.

Data 2,450 berths. 30 visitors' berths. Max LOA 25m. Depths 2·5–3m. Charge band 4.

Facilities Water. 220V. Showers and toilets. Fuel quay. 13/45-ton travel-hoists. Most yacht repairs. Provisions and restaurants.

Cap d'Agde capitainerie ✆ 0467 26 00 20
Email contact@port-capdagde.com
www.port-capdagde.com

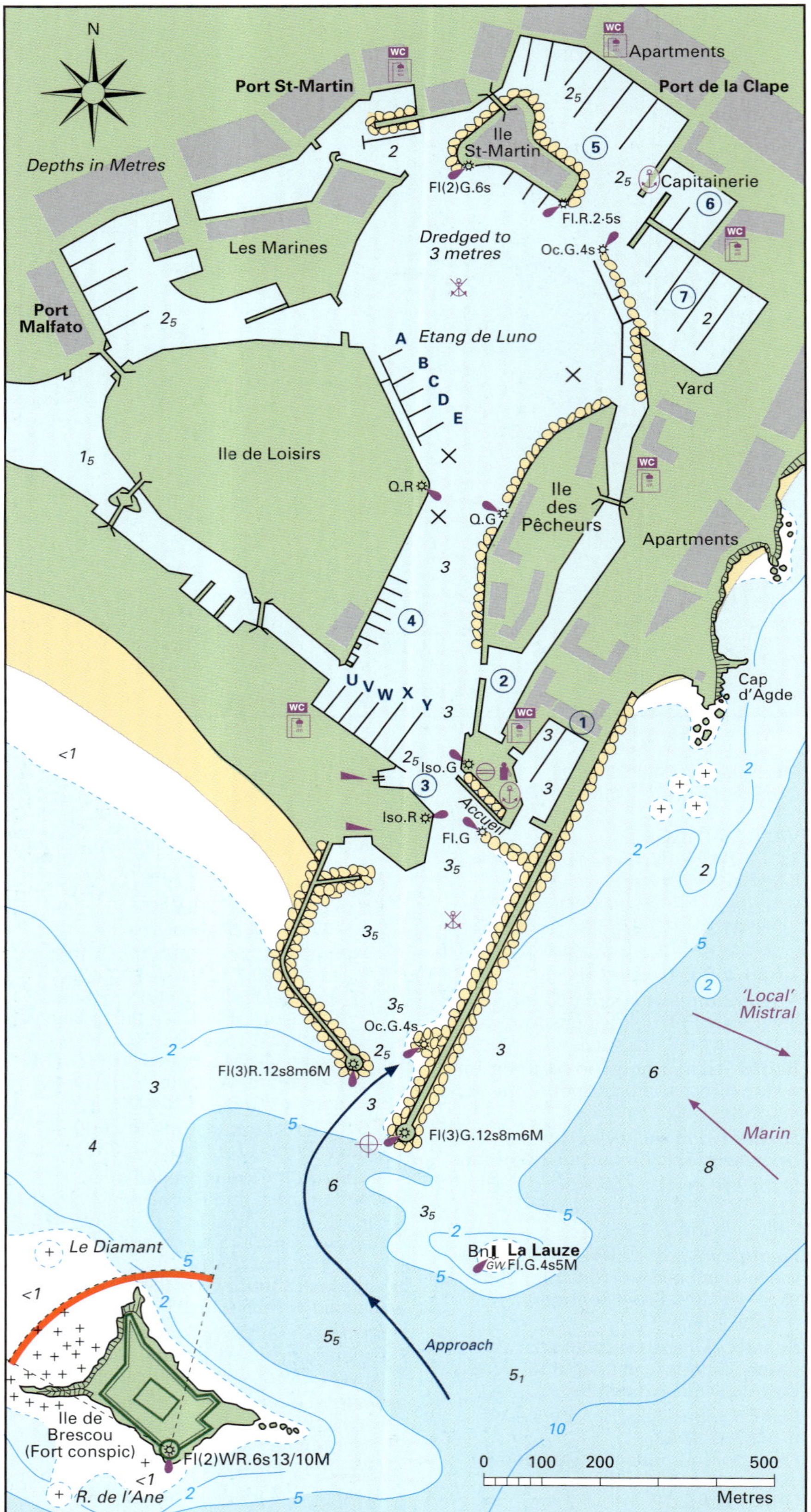

CAP D'AGDE

PORT AMBONNE

43°17'·5N 03°31'·8E

☆ Fl(2)R.6s6M/Fl(2)G.6s4M

Small harbour associated with naturist resort. Depth in access channel 1m.

Data 265 berths. 27 visitors' berths. Max LOA 11m. Depths <1–1m.

✆ 0467 26 00 23

MARSEILLAN-PLAGE

43°19'·1N 03°33'·6E
BA 1705 SHOM 6839

☆ Entrance Fl.R.4s8M/Fl.G.4s5M

VHF Ch 09.

Data 165 berths. 4 visitors' berths. Max LOA 12m. Depths 1·5–2·5m. Charge band 4/5.

The harbour is dredged to 2·5m, but depths may be reduced due to silting.

✆ 0467 21 99 30
Email capitainerie@marseillan.com

SÈTE

43°23'·6N 03°42'·1E
BA 2114 SHOM 7072
13M Cap d'Agde ←→ La Grande Motte 20M

☆ Mont de Sète (Mont St Clair) Fl.5s93m27M. Western entrance Fl.R.4s4M/Fl.G.4s6M. Eastern entrance Iso.R.4s11M / Iso.G.4s / Fl.R.2·5s. Detached breakwater middle Fl(2)R.6s10M. Knuckle Fl(3)R.12s7M. Commercial Port lightbuoy Oc.G.4s. Quai Est Fl(3)G.12s3M. Quai Ouest Iso.G.4s. Entrance to Vieux Port Fl(4)R.15s7M. Mole Masselin Fl(4)G.15s4M. Entrance to Nouveau Bassin Q.R.6M/Q.G.8M

VHF Ch 12, 16 for port authorities. Ch 09 for Port de Plaisance (summer 0700–2100, winter 0800–1800).

Navigation With strong S winds there is a confused swell at the entrance. Commercial traffic has right of way in the approaches and the port at all times. The E entrance is for commercial traffic only.

Berths Stern or bows-to where directed. Visitors normally go on the easternmost pontoon in the Vieux Port. Laid moorings tailed to buoys or the quay.

Shelter Good shelter although uncomfortable with the wash from traffic.

Data 410 berths. 10 visitors' berths. Max LOA 30m. Depths 2–7m. Charge band 3.

Facilities Water. 220V. Showers and toilets. Fuel quay. 7-ton crane. Some yacht repairs. Provisions and restaurants.

Remarks Entrance to the Canal du Rhône à Sète and Canal du Midi across Etang de Thau.

Bureau du Port de Plaisance
✆ 0467 74 98 97
Email portstclair@sete.cci.fr

Note A canal links the Canal Rhône à Sète from Frontignan to the sea approximately 2M to the NE of Sète at a small fishing port between Sète and Frontignan. A long detached

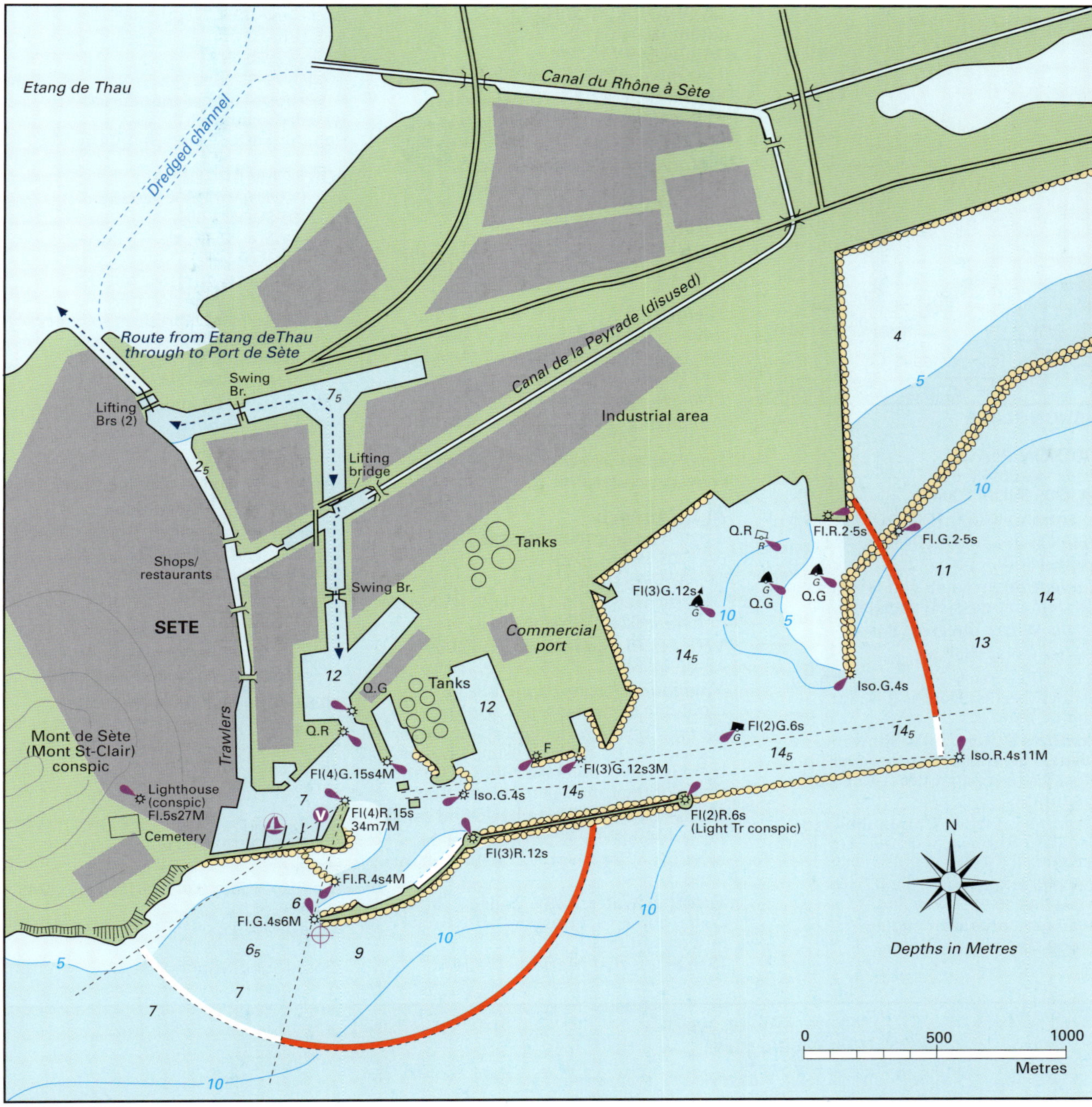

PORT DE SETE

breakwater protects the entrance to the canal and runs SW to Sète commercial harbour E entrance.

PORT DE LA PEYRADE

☆ Entrance Fl(3)G.12s15m7M/Fl(3)R.12s9m6M. Canal Fluvio W head Fl(2)WG.6s6/4M. N Terre plein S head Fl(2)R.6s2M

FRONTIGNAN

43°25′·81N 03°46′·65E WGS84
BA 2606 SHOM 7004

☆ Entrance Fl.R.4s6M / Fl.G.4s8M

VHF Ch 09 (summer 0800–1200 / 1400–1800).

Berths Stern or bows-to where directed. Finger pontoons and poles.

Shelter Good shelter.

Data 600 berths. 60 visitors' berths. Max LOA 18m. Depths dredged to 2·5m. Charge band 3/4.

Facilities Water. 220V. Showers and toilets. Fuel quay. 35/4-ton lifts. Limited yacht repair facilities. Limited provisions. Restaurants.

Port Frontignan
✆ 0467 18 44 90
Email capitainerie@ville-frontignan.fr

PALAVAS-LES-FLOTS

43°31′·45N 03°56′·16E WGS84
BA 1705 SHOM 7004

☆ Entrance Fl(2)R.6s13m6M/Fl(2)G.6s6M. Spur head Fl(3)G.12s2M. Le Lez Fl.R.2·5s4M/Fl.G.2·5s4M

VHF Ch 09, 16 (24/24).

Berths Stern or bows-to where directed. Visitors normally go on outer pontoon. Posts.

Shelter Good shelter.

Data 1,030 berths. 200 canal berths. 50 visitors' berths. Max LOA 20m. Depths 3–4m. Charge band 3/4.

Facilities Water. 220V. Showers and toilets. Fuel quay. 12/45-ton travel-hoists. 5-ton crane. Most yacht repairs. Provisions and restaurants.

Remarks Rivière Lez joins the harbour to the Canal du Rhône à Sète. 1·2m depths in river. Air height under bridges 2m. Base Fluviale Paul Riquet has 230 berths.

Capitainerie ✆ 0467 07 73 50
Email accueil.port@palavaslesflots.com
Paul Riquet ✆ 0467 07 73 48/45

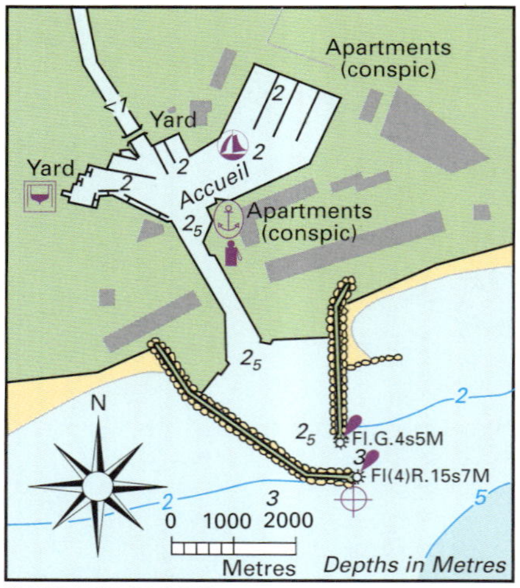

CARNON-PLAGE

CARNON-PLAGE

43°32′·4N 03°58′·6E
BA 1705 SHOM 7004
☆ Entrance Fl(4)R.15s7M/Fl.G.4s5M

VHF Ch 09, 16 (0800–1200 / 1400–1800).

Navigation Strong S winds make entry difficult and possibly dangerous.

Berths Where directed. Posts.

Shelter Good shelter.

Data 700 berths. 240 dry berths. 30 visitors' berths. Depths 2–2·5m. Charge band 4.

Facilities Water. 220V. Showers and toilets. Fuel quay. 13-ton travel-hoist. Most yacht repairs. Provisions and restaurants.

Remarks Canal de Carnon links to Canal du Rhône à Sète. 0·4–1m depths in canal.

Port de Carnon
✆ 0467 68 10 78
Email capitainerie@mauguio-carnon.com

LA GRANDE MOTTE

43°33′·1N 04°04′·9E
BA 1705 SHOM 7004
20M Sète ←→ Port Camargue 3·5M
☆ Entrance Fl(2)R.6s7M/Fl.G.4s5M

VHF Ch 09, 16 (24/24).

Berths Where directed. Report to *capitainerie* at the inner entrance for a berth. Finger pontoons, laid moorings tailed to the quay or posts.

Shelter Good shelter.

Data 1,400 berths. 30 visitors' berths. Max LOA 30m. Depths 2–4m. Charge band 3/4.

Facilities Water. 220V. Showers and toilets. Fuel quay. 50/6-ton travel-hoists. Most yacht repairs. Provisions and restaurants.

Remarks Entrance dredged to 3·7m.

Bureau du Port, La Grande Motte
✆ 0467 56 50 06
Email capitainerie@lagrandemotte.fr
www.lagrandemotte.fr

GRAU DU ROI

43°32′·10N 04°07′·92E WGS84
BA 1705 SHOM 7053
☆ Entrance Fl(3)G.15s10M/Oc(2)R.6s7M. Jetty head Fl(3)R.12s/Fl(3)G.12s (visible only inside the harbour)

VHF Ch 73 (Summer 0830–1200 / 1330–1730)

Navigation Access dangerous in moderate to strong S–SW winds.

Berths Go alongside until swing bridge opens. Port du Peche is usually full, but there is now a pontoon running up the S side of the canal. Berth alongside.

Shelter Good shelter in basin and canal.

Data 120 berths. 31 visitors' berths. Max LOA 9m. Depths 2·5–4m. Charge band 3.

Facilities Water. 220V. Toilets. 18-ton crane. Some yacht repairs. Provisions and restaurants.

Remarks Canal Maritime leads to Aigues-Mortes. Depths 1·8–2m. Max AH 16m.

Bureau du Port
✆ 0466 73 55 06
Email portplaisance.graudurois@terredecamargue.fr
Harbourmaster (bridges) ✆ 04 66 51 91 86

PORT CAMARGUE

43°31′·25N 04°07′·36E WGS84
BA 1705 SHOM 7004
3·5M La Grande Motte ←→ Port Gardian 16M
☆ L'Espiguette Fl(3)15s27m24M. Channel S W breakwater Oc.G.4s7m4M. Port de l'Espiguette Canal Oc.G.4s4M / Oc.R.4s4M. S breakwater VQ(9)10s9M. Entrance Fl.G.4s9M / Fl.R.4s6M

VHF Ch 09, 16 (summer 0800–2000, winter 0800–1800).

Grau du Roi bridge opening times:

Swing Bridge (Pont Tournant)

Summer (01/04–30/09)
Monday–Friday 0800, 1230, 1800
Saturday 0800, 1230, 1730
Sunday and holidays 0800, 1230, 1915

Winter (01/10–31/03)
Monday–Friday 0800, 1230, 1800
Saturday 0800, 1230, 1730
Closed Sundays or holidays.

Sliding Bridge (Pont Levant)

Summer
Monday–Friday 0745, 0815, 1215, 1245, 1600, 1815, 1845
Saturday 0745, 0815, 1215, 1245, 1600, 1930
Sunday and holidays 0745, 0815, 1215, 1245, 1600, 1930

Winter
Monday–Friday 0745, 0815, 1215, 1245, 1600
Saturday 0745, 0815, 1215, 1245, 1600, 1715
Closed Sundays or holidays.

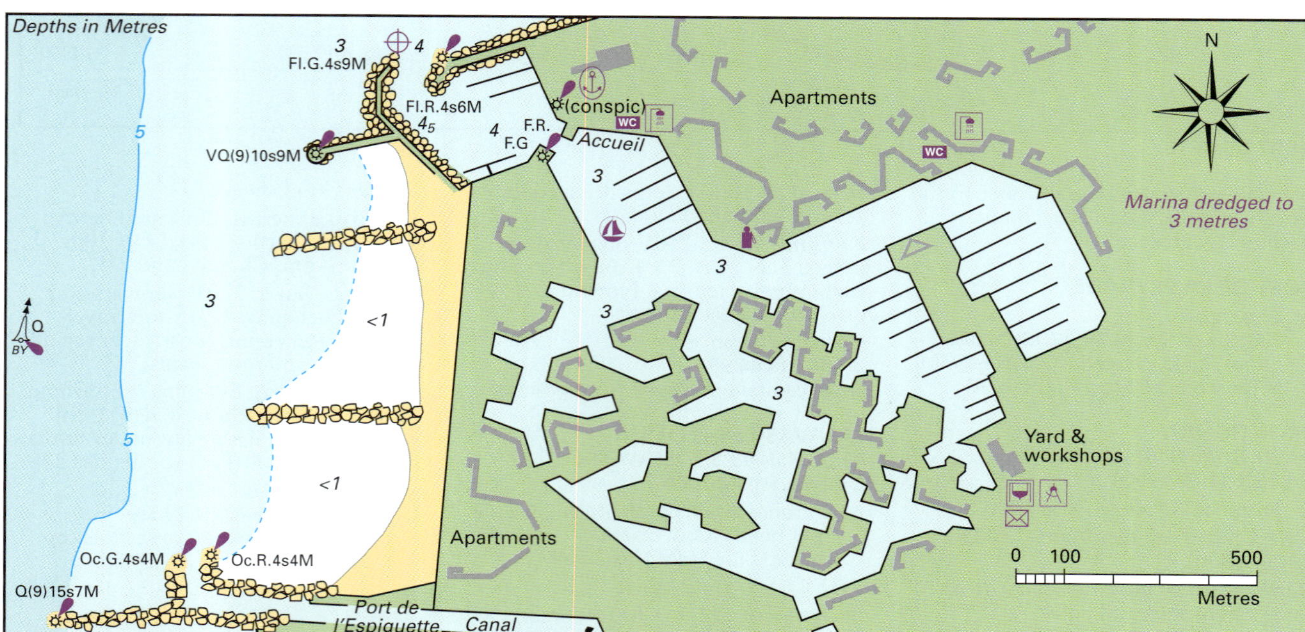

PORT CAMARGUE

Navigation Keep well outside the buoys marking the shoal water off Pointe de l'Espiguette. With S gales, entrance can be difficult. Make the approach from the N.

Berths Where directed. Report to the *capitainerie* in the Avant Port. Laid moorings tailed to buoys or posts.

Shelter Good shelter.

Data 2,600 berths. 400 visitors' berths. 2240 apartment/marina berths. Max. draught 3m. Depths 2–5m. Charge band 4.

Facilities Water. 220/380V. Showers and toilets. Pump-out. Fuel quay. 80/16/5-ton travel-hoist. Slipways. 130-ton crane. All yacht repairs. Provisions and restaurants.

Capitainerie, Port Camargue
✆ 0466 51 10 45
Email capitainerie@portcamargue.com
www.portcamargue.com

Provence

PORT GARDIAN (STES-MARIES-DE-LA-MER)

43°26'·76N 04°25'·41E WGS84
BA 1705 SHOM 7004
16M Port Camargue ←→ Port de Bouc 30M
☆ Lightbuoy Iso.4s.
Entrance Fl.R.4s7M/Fl.G.2·5s2M

VHF Ch 09 (summer 24/24, winter 0800–1200 / 1400–1800).

Navigation Care is needed of shoal water off the mouth of the Petit Rhône. With SE gales entry may be dangerous.

Berths Visitors go on the two outer piers. Laid moorings tailed to the quay or posts.

Shelter Good shelter.

Data 370 berths. 70 visitors' berths. Max LOA 17m. Depths 2–3m. Charge band 4.

Facilities Water. 220V. Showers and toilets. Fuel quay. 14-ton travel-hoist. Limited yacht repairs. Provisions and restaurants.

Capitainerie ✆ 0490 97 85 87
www.portgardian.fr

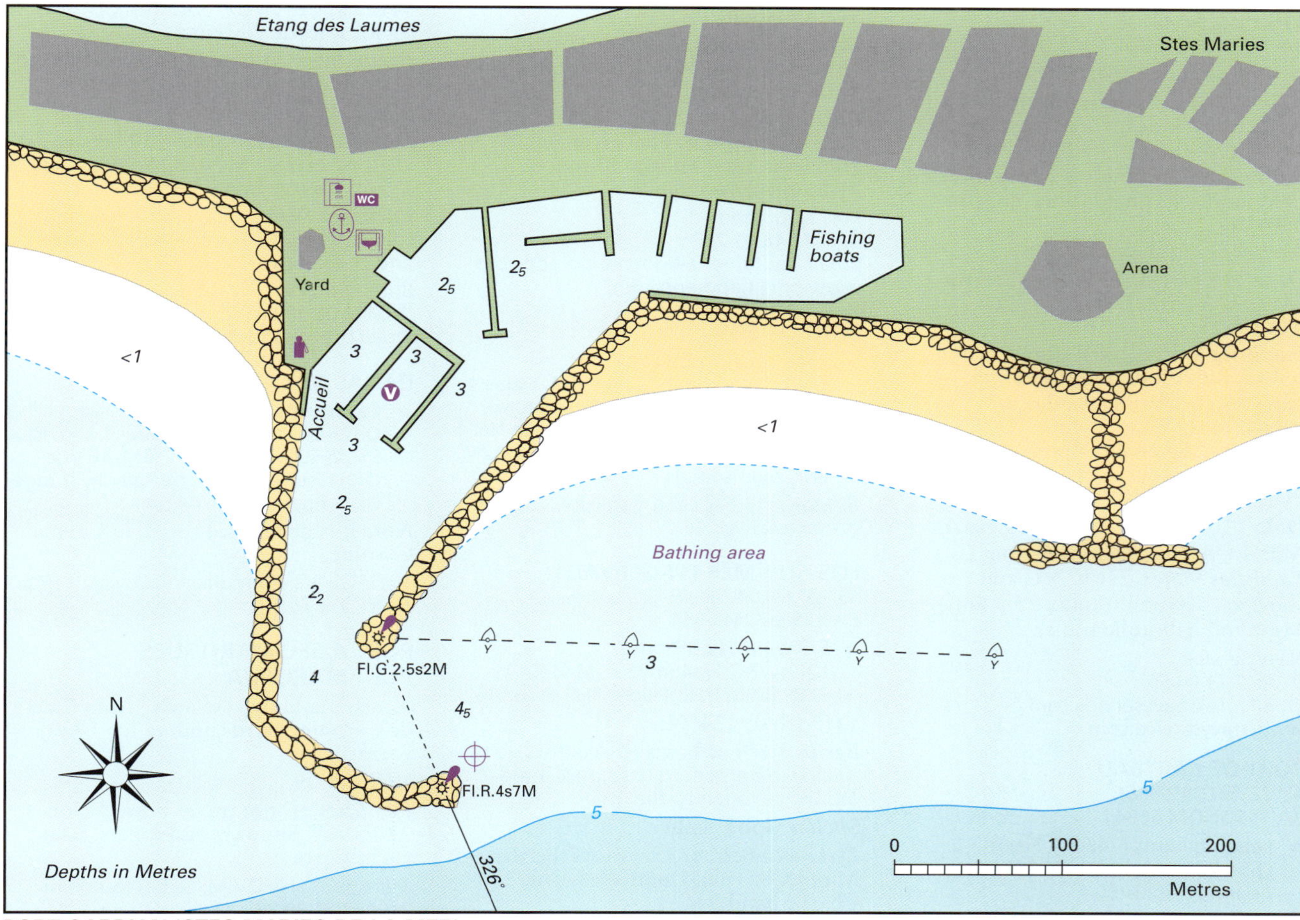

PORT GARDIAN (STES-MARIES-DE-LA-MER)

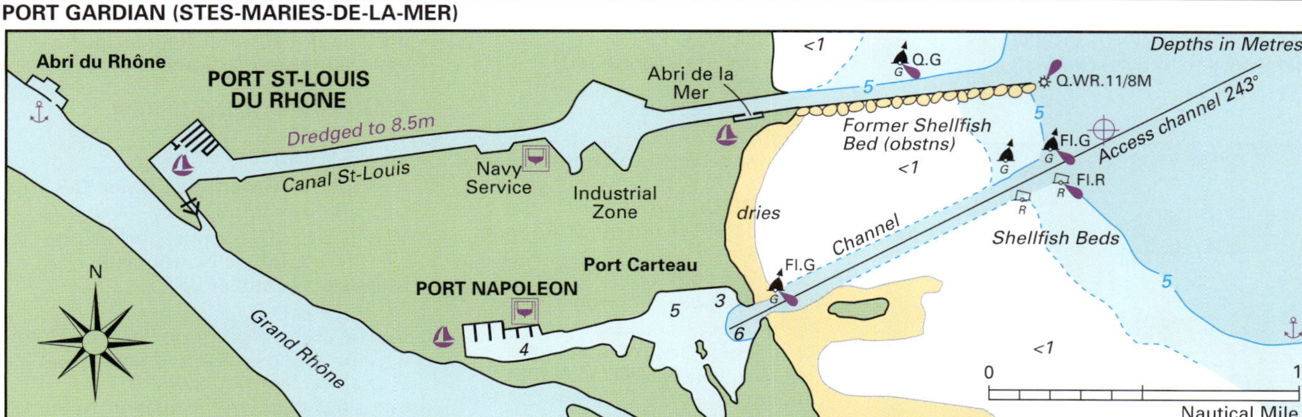

CANAL ST-LOUIS AND PORT NAPOLEON

GOLFE DE FOS
BA 155 SHOM 6684

☆ Omega Landfall buoy Iso.4s8m4M Whis. Balancelle VQ(3)5s4M. Bn No. 2 Fl.R.4s8m6M

CANAL SAINT-LOUIS
43°23′·5N 04°52′·3E

☆ Jetée Sud head Q.WR.14m11/8M (267·5°-R-072°).
N side No.1 Fl.G.4s7M.
S side No.2 Fl.R.4s7M.
N side No.3 E Fl(2)G.6s2M.
S side No.4 Fl(2)R.6s5M.
N side No.3 Q.G.5M.
N side No.5 Iso.G.4s1M.
S side No.6 Oc(2)R.6s3M.
No. 8 Oc.R.4s6M

PORT ST-LOUIS-DU-RHÔNE
43°23′·1N 04°48′·3E
BA 155 SHOM 6684

☆ Tour St-Louis DirQ.15m19M

VHF Ch 16 for port authorities. Ch 19 for Ecluse Maritime. Port de Plaisance Ch 09 (0800–1200 / 1400–1900).

Berths Stern or bows-to where directed. Laid moorings tailed to the quay or buoys.

Shelter Good shelter.

Data 315 berths. 25 visitors' berths. Max LOA 25m. Depths 6–7m. Charge band 3.

Facilities Water. 220V. Showers and toilets. Provisions and restaurants.

Capitainerie (Port de Plaisance)
☎ 0442 86 39 11
Email portdeplaisance@portsaintlouis.fr

PORT A SEC – NAVY SERVICE
Data 1200 places. 23 visitors' berths. Max LOA 26m. Depths 6–7m.

Facilities Water. 220V. WC and showers. 50-ton lift (max 25 × 6m). Multihull hydraulic trailer.

Navy Service
☎ 0442 11 00 55
Email info@navyservice.com
www.navyservice.com

PORT DE CARTEAU
43°22′·5N 04°50′·6E
BA 155 SHOM 6684

☆ Leading lights (242·8°). Front Q.5m7M. Rear Q.10m7M (Reported no longer in use)

PORT NAPOLEON
43°23′·15N 04°52′·40E WGS84 (entrance to buoyed channel)

VHF Ch 74.

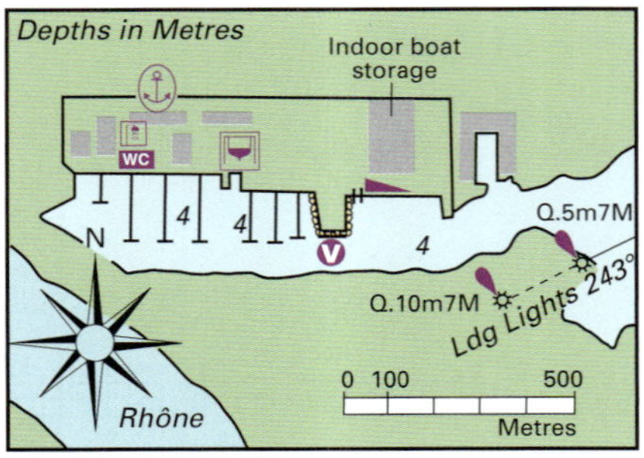

PORT NAPOLEON

Ecluse de Port St-Louis-du-Rhône
Note
1. Rhone side lock opens and closes before the lifting bridge operates.
2. Lifejackets must be worn at all Rhône locks.
From Rhône side call VHF Ch 19.
☎ 0442 86 02 04

Opening times				A			
Rhône écluse	Opens	0600	0815	1150	1150	1605	1845
	Closes	0610	0830	1205	1205	1620	1900
Lifting bridge	Opens	0620	0845	1230	1220	1635	1915
	Closes	0630	0855	1240	1240	1645	1925

Notes A Only on Sunday and holidays

Navigation Along the access channel into Port Carteau on 243°. Port Napoleon lies at the W end of the long indent.

Berths Where directed.

Shelter Good.

Data 250 berths. 2,200 dry berths. 50 visitors' berths. Max LOA 40m. Depths 4m. Charge band 3/4.

Facilities Water. 220V. Showers and toilets. Pump-out. Fuel arranged. 20/65-ton travel-hoist. 30-ton hydraulic trailer.

Port Napoleon
☎ 0442 48 41 21
Email capitainerie@port-napoleon.com
www.port-napoleon.com

PORT DE FOS
☆ Leading lights (287°) Front Q.11m14M. Rear Q.29m14M. Darse 4 elbow Q(6)+LFl.15s8M. Petroleum jetty root No. 1 Fl.G.4s5M. Darse No. 1 Dir light (340°). DirOc.WRG.4s15-12M. LNG pier Iso.R.4s

Remarks Q.R Lt buoy marks work in progress close W.

FOS-SUR-MER (ST-GERVAIS)
43°25′·6N 04°56′·4E
BA 155 SHOM 6684

☆ St-Gervais lighthouse IQ(7)WRG.12s45m25-21M (340°-W-348°-R-007°). Entrance Fl.G.4s7m5M

VHF Ch 09 (24/24).

Berths Stern or bows-to. Visitors go in the basin immediately to port. Laid moorings tailed to the quay.

Shelter Good shelter.

Data 840 berths. 35 visitors' berths. Max LOA 13m. Depths 1·5–3m. Charge band 3.

Facilities Water. 220V. Showers and toilets. Fuel quay. 15-ton crane. Limited yacht repairs. Provisions and restaurants.

Capitainerie
☎ 04 42 47 70 57
Email port.st.gervais@mairie-fos-sur-mer.fr

PORT DE BOUC
43°23′·7N 04°59′·1E (Pointe St Antoine light Fl.Vi.5s)
BA 155 SHOM 6684
30M Port Gardian ←→ Marseille Vieux Port 20M

☆ Fort de Bouc Oc(2)WRG.6s12-9M. Entrance VQ(2)R.6M/Fl.Vi.4s10M. Leading light (036·7°). Front Q.R.11M. Rear Q.R.15M. Leading lights (029·8°). Front Oc.R.4s10M. Rear Oc.R.4s10M. Coaster basin Fl(2)G.6s6M. Fishing port Fl(2)R.6s8M. Marina E jetty Iso.G.4s6M

VHF Ch 12, 16 for port authorities. Ch 09 for Port de Plaisance.

Berths Stern or bows-to where directed. Laid moorings.

Shelter Good shelter.

Data Port de Plaisance: 450 berths. 20 visitors' berths. Max LOA 16m. Depths 2–3m. Charge band 3/4.

Facilities Water. 220V. Showers and toilets. Fuel. 16-ton hoist. Provisions and restaurants.

Bureau du Port
☎ 0442 06 38 50
Email portdebouc@wanadoo.fr

CANAL DE CARONTE
☆ Le Calens N side Q.R.3M, S side Q.G.4M. La Gafette N side Fl.R.4s7M. S side Fl.G.4s4M. SW Q.6M. SE side Q(9)15s6M. Air height Railway bridge 21m. Road bridge 44·5m

Note It is prohibited to sail in Canal de Caronte.

VHF Ch 12 (to request access call *Fos Port Control*).

PORT À SEC-MARTIGUES PORT MARITIMA
Access via buoyed channel from Canal de Caronte. Hardstanding for 1000+ yachts.

VHF Ch 09.

Facilities 16-ton travel-hoist. Water. 220/380V. Showers and toilets. Some yacht repairs.

Martigues SEMOVIM, Le bateau blanc
☎ 0442 41 39 39
Email
port.maritima@semovim-martigues.com
www.semovim-martigues.com

MARTIGUES (JONQUIÈRES)
43°24′·3N 05°03′·1E
BA 155 SHOM 6907

☆ Traverse de Martigues N side Q.R.3M. S side Q.G.3M

VHF Ch 12, 16 for port authorities. Ch 09 for Club de Nautique de Martigues (summer 0830–1200 / 1400–1800).

Berths Visitors' pontoon near the Hotel de Ville. Capitainerie and facilities at Port a Sec. Stern or bows-to. Laid moorings tailed to the quay or to buoys.

Shelter Good shelter.
Data 320 berths. 10 visitors' berths. Max LOA 12m. Depths 1–3m. Charge band 3.
Facilities Water. 220V. Fuel quay. Provisions and restaurants.

CNM, Quai Ste-Anne
✆ 0442 81 17 46
SEMOVIM ✆ 04 42 07 00 00

CAP COURONNE MARINE RESERVE
Extends E to the W edge of Port St-Croix and is marked with yellow buoys. Anchoring and diving is prohibited.

PORT DE CARRO
43°19'·65N 05°02'·61E WGS84
BA 155 SHOM 6767

☆ Cap Couronne Fl.R.3s34m20M. Entrance FlWR.4s9/6M (322°-W-355°)

Data 200 berths. 20 visitors' berths. Max LOA 11m. Depths 1–3·5m. Charge band 3/4.
Facilities Water. 220/380V. 40-ton slipway. 6-ton crane. Provisions and restaurants.

Capitainerie ✆ 0442 80 76 28

SAUSSET-LES-PINS
43°19'·74N 05°06'·53E WGS84
BA 2116 SHOM 6767

☆ Entrance Fl(3)R.12s5M

VHF Ch 09, 16 (summer 0800–1200 / 1400–1900, winter 0800–1200 / 1400–1700).
Berths Where directed. Laid moorings tailed to the quay.
Shelter Uncomfortable with strong S winds.
Data 490 berths. 15 visitors' berths. Max LOA 16m. Depths 1–4m. Charge band 4.
Facilities Water. 220V. Showers and toilets. Fuel quay. 25-ton travel-hoist. Limited yacht repairs.
Remarks Work extending and repairing the W breakwater is complete.

Capitainerie ✆ 0442 44 55 01

CARRY-LE-ROUET
43°19'·68N 05°09'·17E WGS84
BA 2116 SHOM 6767

☆ Pain de Sucre Fl.R.2·5s5M. Entrance VQ.G.5M/Fl.G.2·5s

VHF Ch 09 (summer 0600–1200 / 1400–1930 winter 0800–1200 / 1400–1800).
Navigation Care needed of the shoal marked by L'Estèo beacon (unlit) in the immediate approach.
Berths Where directed. Laid moorings tailed to the quay.
Shelter Strong S winds cause a surge.
Data 560 berths. 20 visitors' berths. Max LOA 16m. Depths 1–2·5m. Charge band 4.
Facilities Water. 220V. Showers and toilets. 10-ton crane. Limited yacht repairs. Provisions and restaurants.

Capitainerie ✆ 0442 45 25 13

CAP DE NANTES MARINE RESERVE
Extends SE from Carry-le-Rouet to the W side of Port du Rouet and is marked by yellow buoys. Anchoring and diving is prohibited.

PORT OUEST MARSEILLE (PORT DE LA LAVE)
43°21'·6N 05°18'·3E

☆ Mole head Fl.R.4s4M

Group Trapani and Carrasco Shipyard.
Data 100 berths. 400 places ashore. Max LOA 30m. Depths 1–3·5m.
Facilities Water. 220V. Showers and toilets. 14-ton lift. 18-ton trailer.

✆ 0491 46 53 40
Email contact@portouestmarseille.com
www.portouestmarseille.com

PORT DE CORBIERES
A new marina close E of Port de La Lave.
Data 300 berths. 20 visitors' berths. Max LOA 50m. Depths 3m. Charge band 3.
Facilities Water. 220/380V. Showers and toilets. Self-service fuel. 20-ton crane. Dry storage.

✆ 0491 03 85 83
www.portcorbieres.com

PORTS DE L'ESTAQUE
43°21'·4N 05°18'·8E Light W end of Digue de Saumaty UQ(2)1s
BA 153 SHOM 7390

☆ Passe de l'Estaque Q.R.3M. Passe des Chalutiers Fl(3)R.12s4M/Fl.G.4s6M. Detached breakwater Q(9)15s3M/ Fl(2)R.6s2M. Mole head Iso.G.4s7M. Digue de Saumaty W head VQ(2)20m17M

Data 1,500 berths. Max LOA 20m. Depths 2–3m. Charge band 2. Visiting yachts should make for Club SNEM (Société Nautique de Mourepiane) via the Passe de l'Estaque: 650 berths, 50 visitors' berths. Max LOA 14m.

SNEM
✆ 0491 46 01 40
Email snemvoile@wanadoo.fr
www.snemvoile.com

A new Port a Sec for motorboats with a limited number of marina berths.

MARSEILLE COMMERCIAL PORT
☆ Passe Nord Fl.G.5s17M/Fl(2)R.6s8M. Passe de Saumaty Fl(3)G.12s6M. Passe Léon Gourret Iso.G.4s3M/ Iso.R.4s4M. Passe Nord-Est Fl(2)G.6s6M / Fl(2)R.6s6M. Passe de Cap Janet Fl.R.4s6M / Fl.G.4s2M. N corner F.2m. Passe de la Madrague Fl(2)G.6s6M/Fl(2)R.6s7M. S entrance, Digue des Catalans Fl(3)G.12s6M. Digue du Large S Fl.R.2·5s. N Fl(2)R.6s. Digue Sainte Marie S end VQ(2)R.12M. Root Oc(3)R.12s6M. Pointe de la Désirade Fl.G.4s9M. Digue du Fort St Jean Oc(3)G.12s6M

VHF Ch 06, 08, 12, 16 for port authorities and pilots.
Note Works in the avant-port Joliette are part of regeneration plan. No yacht berths planned.

MARSEILLE VIEUX PORT
43°17'·7N 05°21'·8E
BA 153 SHOM 7390
20M Port de Bouc ←→ Cassis 16M

☆ (See Marseille Commercial Port). Inner entrance Iso.G.4s1M. Beacons Fl.G.4s3M / Fl(3)G.12s3M

VHF Ch 09. Ch 77 for CNTL.
Berths Visiting yachts should head for the CNTL pontoons (first four pontoons to starboard) or the SNM pontoons (halfway up starboard side). Berth where directed. Laid moorings tailed to the quay or buoys. The *capitainerie* also has a small number of visitors' berths.
Shelter Good shelter.
Data Total 3,200 berths. 40 visitors' berths. Max LOA 100m. Depths 5–7m. Charge band 4.
Facilities Water. 220V. Showers and toilets. Fuel quay.
Remarks Major works underway in the Vieux Port. Projects will run until 2020.

Capitainerie ✆0491 73 93 63 / 0632 87 52 39
Email capitainerie.vieux-port@marseille-provence.fr

Centre Nautique et Touristique du Lacydon (CNTL), Quai Marcel Pagnol
✆ 0491 59 82 00
Email contact@cntl-marseille.com
www.cntl-marseille.com

Sté Nautique de Marseille (SNM), Pavillon Flottant, Quai de Rive Neuve
✆ 0491 54 32 03
Email secretariat@lanautique.com
www.lanautique.com

✉ Libraire Maritime, 26 Quai de Rive neuve, 13007 Marseille
✆ 0491 54 79 26

PARC MARITIME DES ILES DU FRIOULS
There are some restrictions on anchoring and use of engines. Throughout the park anchoring on Posidonia grass is discouraged, and should be avoided if at all possible.

PORT DU FRIOUL
43°16'·7N 05°18'·7E
BA 153 SHOM 7391

☆ Entrance Iso.G.4s4M. Lightbuoy Q(6)+LFl.15s

VHF Ch 09, 16 (summer 0715–1930).
Navigation Entrance difficult with strong S winds.
Berths Visitors' berths on W side near Capitainerie.
Shelter Uncomfortable with S gales.
Data 600 berths. 100 visitors' berths. Depths 2–10m. Charge band 4.
Facilities Water. 220V. Showers and toilets. Fuel quay. 33-ton lift. 12-ton crane. Limited yacht repairs. Most provisions. Restaurants. Ferries to Marseille.

Capitainerie ✆ 0491 59 01 82

PORT DU PRADO
☆ Entrance Fl(2)R.6s4M

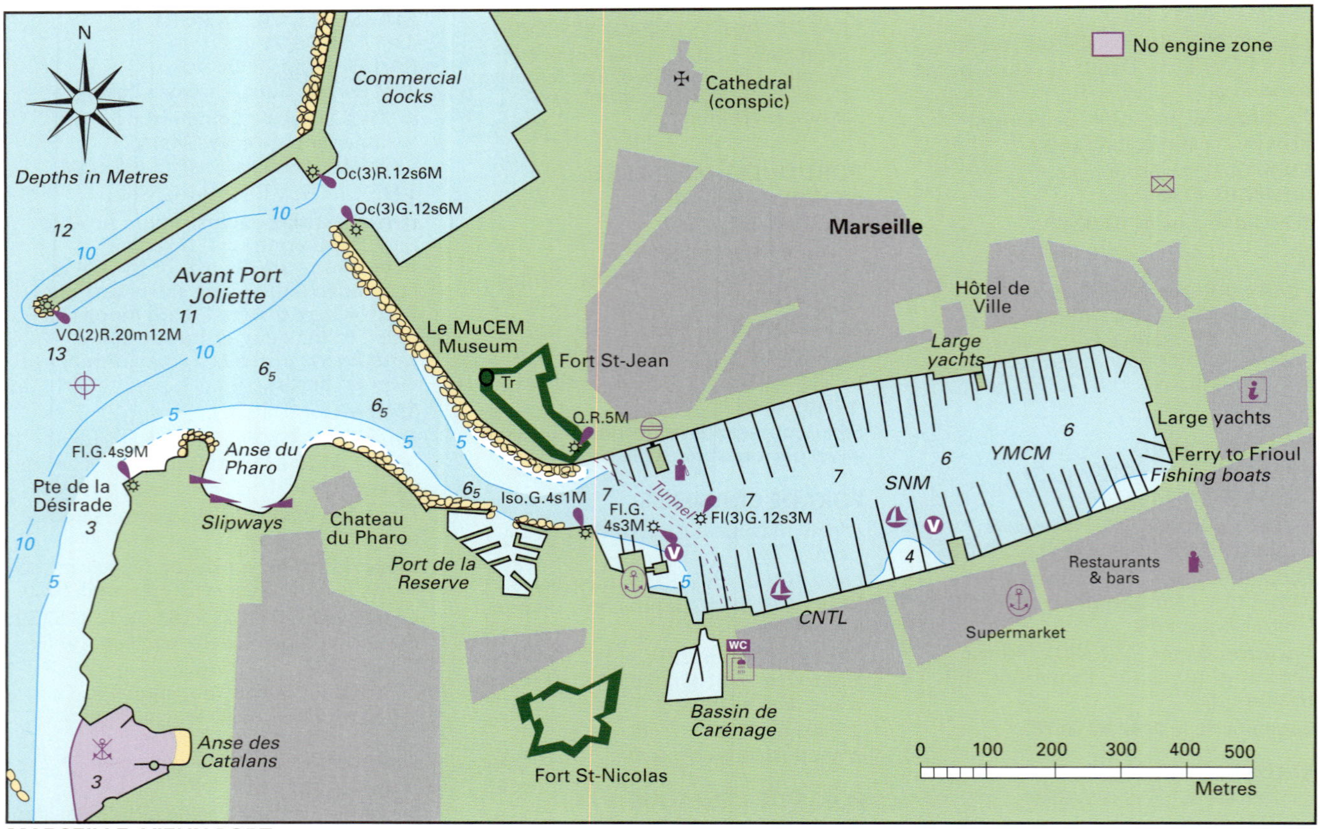

MARSEILLE: VIEUX PORT

PORT DE LA POINTE ROUGE

43°14′·8N 05°21′·9E
BA 153 SHOM 7391
☆ Entrance Fl(2)G.6s6M
VHF Ch 09 (24/24).
Navigation Entrance difficult with the *mistral*.
Berths Stern or bows-to in SE corner. Laid moorings tailed to the quay.
Shelter Good shelter.
Data 1,200 berths. 20 visitors' berths. 600 places ashore. Max LOA 15m. Depths 2·5–6m. Charge band 4.
Facilities Water. 220V. Showers and toilets. Fuel quay. 30-ton travel-hoist. 1·5-ton crane. Most yacht repairs. Provisions and restaurants.
Capitainerie ✆ 0491 73 13 21

CALANQUE DE SORMIOU/ EN VAU/PORT PIN

Yellow buoys restrict anchoring space in Sormiou. En Vau S side no anchoring zone. Port Pin W side no anchoring zone. Vessels over 20m LOA not permitted in Port Pin beyond a line from 43°11'·96N 05°30'·42E to 43°11'·96N 05°30'·54E WGS84.

The head of all the bays are 'no engine' zones.

PORT MIOU

43°12′·1N 05°30′·9E

Calanque with catwalk berths and moorings. Anchoring is prohibited. Max LOA 20m in the mooring area. Max speed 3kn. All fishing is prohibited. No discharge of grey or black water is permitted.

Pick up a mooring in the outer part of the calanque and take a long line ashore to the E side.

VHF Ch 09.

Craft over 50GRT are prohibited.

Charge band 4 (pontoon), 2/3 (moorings).

Capitainerie ✆ 0442 01 96 24 / 0626 84 51 58
Email portmiou@cassis.fr

PORT DES GOUDES

☆ Entrance Iso.G.4s2M

CASSIS

43°12′·8N 05°32′·1E
BA 2116 SHOM 6612
16M Marseille Vieux Port ←→ La Ciotat 6M
☆ Entrance Oc(2)G.6s6M/Fl.R.4s6M
VHF Ch 09 (summer 0800–1200 / 1400–2030, winter 0900–1200 / 1430–1800) ANC/CNC.
Navigation Entrance dangerous with S gales. A dangerous wreck lies 100m S from the harbour entrance.
Berths Where directed on the fuel pontoon or at CNC.
Shelter S gales cause a surge.
Data 400 berths. 20 visitors' berths. Max LOA 15m. Max draught 3·5m. Depths 2–5m. Charge band 4/5.
Facilities Water. 220V. Showers and toilets. Pump-out. Fuel quay. 30-ton slipway. 6-ton crane. Limited yacht repairs. Provisions and restaurants.
Capitainerie ✆ 04 42 32 91 65
Email portdecassis@orange.fr
Cercle Nautique de Cassis, (CNC) ✆ 0442 01 79 04

LA CIOTAT

43°10′·35N 05°36′·68E WGS84 (Vieux Port)
BA 2116 SHOM 6612
6M Cassis ←→ St-Pierre des Embiez 9M
☆ Commercial Port Fl.R.4s5M/Fl(3)R.12s6M. Vieux Port Iso.G.4s11M. Bassin Berouard mole head Fl.G.4s7M. Bassin des Capucins mole head Fl(2)R.6s8M
VHF Port de Plaisance/Vieux Port Ch 09 (summer 0700–2200, winter 0800–1200/1400–1730).
Berths Visiting yachts should head for Bassin Bérouard or Vieux Port. Berth where directed.
Shelter Some berths can be uncomfortable with a strong mistral. Basin Berouard untenable in E–SE gales.

PARC NATIONAL DES CALANQUES

The park covers much of the coast from the port of Marseille around to La Ciotat, including the islands off the coast.

Restrictions apply to navigation and anchoring, particularly in the calanques. Buoys and signs are used to indicate areas where navigation is restricted – either to motors, to all, or to vessels over 20m.

www.gipcalanques.fr

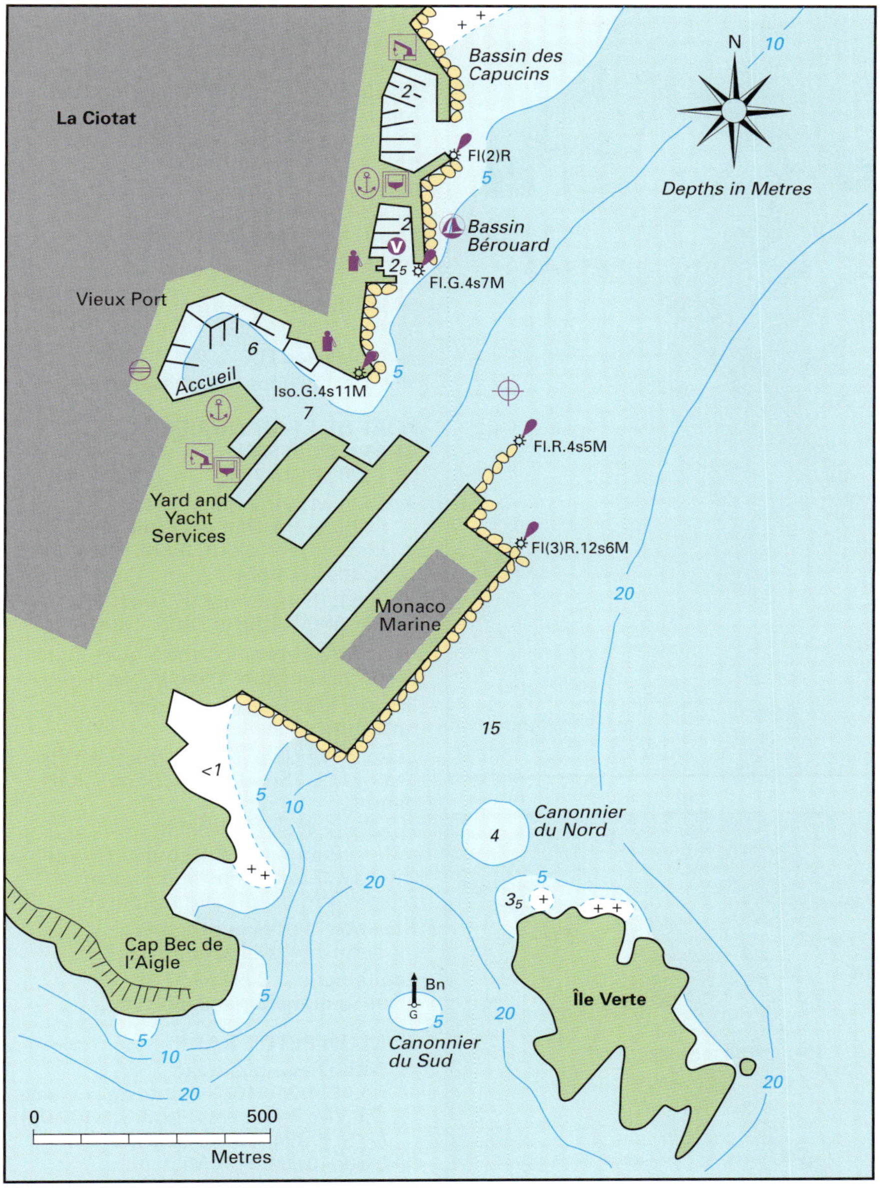

APPROACHES TO LA CIOTAT

Data B. Bérouard 640 berths. 230 dry berths. 25 visitors' berths. Max LOA 18m. Depths 2–4m. Charge band 2/3.

Vieux Port 740 berths. 40 visitors' berths. Max LOA 80m. Depths 5–7m. Charge band 3/4.

Facilities Water. 220V. Showers and toilets. Fuel quay. 36-ton travel-hoist. 10-ton crane. 1·5-ton lift. Monaco Marine 2,000-ton lifting dock, 600-ton gantry crane, 360m dry dock, 16/250-ton cranes, and 80m paint shed. Provisions and restaurants.

B. Bérouard Bureau du Port
☎ 04 42 08 62 90

Vieux Port Capitainerie SEMIDEP-CIOTAT
☎ 04 42 83 80 27
Email capitainerie@semidep.com
www.semidep-ciotat.com

Monaco Marine ☎ 04 42 36 12 12
Email mmlaciotat@monacomarine.com
www.monacomarine.com

Côte d'Azur

LES LECQUES (ST-CYR-LES-LECQUES)

43°10'·7N 05°40'·9E
BA 2164 SHOM 6612

☆ Entrance Iso.G.4s9M/Q.R.6M. Ancien Port Fl(2)R.6s7M

VHF Ch 09, 16.

Navigation Entry difficult with strong S winds.

Berths Visitors go on the first three pontoons. Laid moorings tailed to the quay or buoys.

Shelter S gales cause a surge.

Data 430 berths. Visitors' berths. Max LOA 15m. Depths 2–4m. Charge band 4.

Facilities Water. 220V. Showers and toilets. Fuel quay. 10/15-ton cranes. Limited yacht repairs. Limited provisions. Restaurants.

Remarks The Ancien Port immediately N has only 0·5–1m depths.

Capitainerie ☎ 0494 26 21 98
Email nport-leslecques@wanadoo.fr

LA MADRAGUE

43°10'·1N 05°41'·7E

☆ Fl(4)G.15s4M

Data 200 berths. 30 visitors' berths. Max LOA 8m. Depths 1–1·5m.

Bureau du Port ☎ 0494 26 39 81

BANDOL

43°08'·04N 05°45'·47E WGS84
BA 2116 SHOM 6610

☆ Entrance Oc(4)WR.12s13/10M (351°-W-003°)/Fl.G.4s6M

VHF Ch 09 (summer 0800–2000, winter 0800–1200 / 1330–1700).

Navigation La Cride rock is marked by an E cardinal beacon YBY(♦ topmark). La Fourmigue rock is marked by an isolated danger beacon BRB (: topmark).

Berths Where directed. Laid moorings tailed to the quay or a buoy.

Shelter Good shelter.

Data 1,600 berths. 160 visitors' berths. Max LOA 40m. Depths 1·5–4m. Charge band 4/5.

Facilities Water. 220/380V. Showers and toilets. Pump-out. Fuel quay. 30-ton slipway. 10-ton crane. Most yacht repairs. Provisions and restaurants.

Capitainerie ☎ 0494 29 42 64
Email port-bandol@wanadoo.fr

PORT DE BENDOR

43°07'·8N 05°45'·2E

☆ Entrance Oc.R.4s7M/Fl(2)G.6s6M

Private port. Max 3hr stay. Max LOA 13m.
Sté Ricard ☎ 0611 05 91 52

SANARY-SUR-MER

43°06'·88N 05°48'·04E WGS84
BA 2116 SHOM 6610

☆ Entrance Fl.R.4s10M/Fl(2)G.6s2M

VHF Ch 09 (summer 0800–1200 / 1400–1900, winter 0800–1200 / 1400–1800).

Navigation Entrance channel marked by green buoy on starboard side.

Berths Where directed. Laid moorings tailed to the quay.

Shelter A surge with S gales.

Data 650 berths. 70 visitors' berths. Max LOA 25m. Depths 1–4m. Charge band 4/5.

Facilities Water. 220V. Showers and toilets. Fuel quay. 80-ton slipway. 7-ton crane. Most yacht repairs. Provisions and restaurants.

Capitainerie ☎ 0494 74 20 95
Email capitainerie@sanarysurmer.com

PORT DE LA COUDOULIÈRE

43°05'·8N 05°48'·7E

☆ Entrance Fl(3)R.12s6M

Data 445 berths. Max LOA 11m.

Bureau du Port ☎ 0494 34 80 34

PORT DU BRUSC

43°04'·6N 05°48'·2E

☆ Breakwater NE end Iso.G.4s6M. Jetty Oc(3)WR.12s9/6M

Development and dredging works reported. Charge band 4.

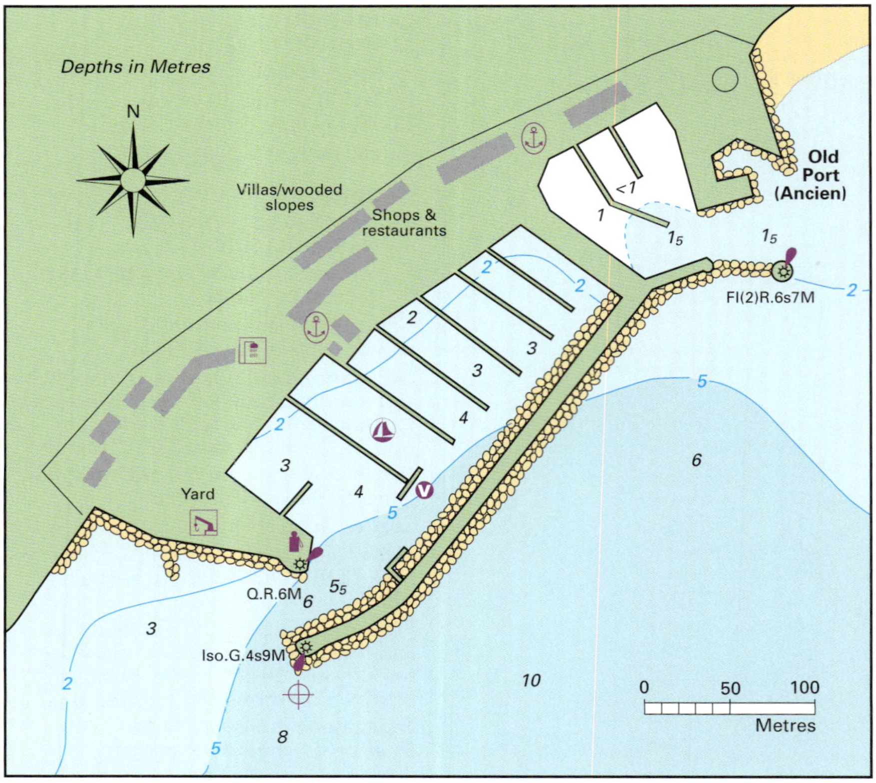

ST-CYR-LES-LECQUES

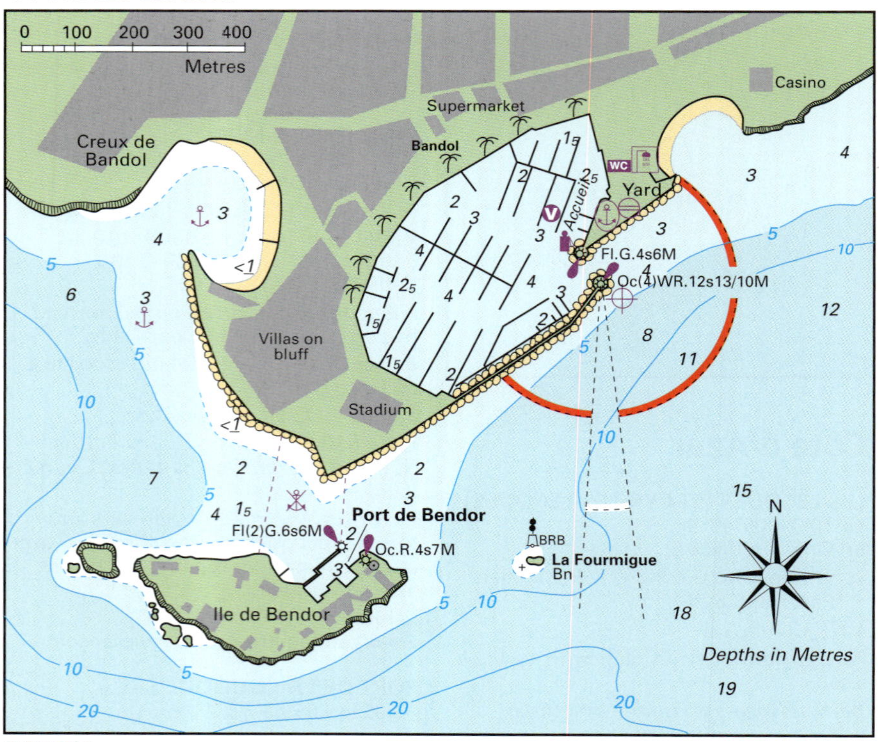

BANDOL

ST-PIERRE DES EMBIEZ

43°04′·9N 05°47′·1E
BA 2116 SHOM 6610
9M La Ciotat ←→ Toulon old port 14M

☆ Ile de la Tour Fondue N point Fl(4)WR.15s8/6M (132°-W-275°). Dir Light (207°-W-213°). DirOc.WRG.4s9-7M. Entrance N side Fl.G.4s6M. Mole des Cargos head Iso.4s1m. Port des Jeunes entrance Fl.R.4s4M

VHF Ch 09 (24/24).

Navigation Care needed of shoal water around Ile des Embiez and Ile du Grand Rouveau. Access to port via a buoyed channel.

Berths Stern or bows-to where directed. Laid moorings tailed to the quay.

Shelter Good shelter.

Data 750 berths. 50 visitors' berths. Max LOA 40m. Depths 1–3·5m. Charge band 5.

Facilities Water. 220V. Showers and toilets. Fuel quay. 15-ton crane. 30-ton slipway. Some yacht repairs. Most provisions. Restaurants.

Bureau du Port, Société Paul Ricard
✆ 0494 10 65 21
Email capitainerie@paul-ricard.com
www.les-embiez.com

SAINT ELME

43°04′·5N 05°53′·9E

☆ Mole head Fl.G.4s7M

Shallow harbour. Depths <1m.

PORT DE ST-MANDRIER

43°05′N 05°55′·8E
BA 2170 SHOM 7093

☆ Saint Mandrier jetée head Fl(2)R.6s9M. Digue N Ecole des Mécaniciens, Fl(2)G.6s5M. Jetée ouest head Fl.G.4s5M

VHF Ch 09 (summer 0730–2000, winter 0800–1200 / 1400–1800).

Berths Visitors go on the S quay. Laid moorings tailed to the quay or buoys.

Shelter The *mistral* makes it uncomfortable.

Data 725 berths. 100 visitors' berths. Max LOA 18m. Depths 2·5m. Charge band 4.

Facilities Water. 220V. Showers and toilets. Pump-out. Fuel quay. 15-ton slipway. 8-ton crane. Some yacht repairs. Provisions and restaurants.

Remarks Works in progress modernising the harbour.

Capitainerie ✆ 0494 63 97 39
Email saint.mandrier@var.cci.fr

TOULON PETITE RADE

☆ Petite Passe pier head Iso.RG.4s21m10M. Pointe de la Vieille Q.R.7M. Petite Passe Iso.RG.4s10/10M (275°-R-294°). Banc de l'Ane VQ(9)10s3M. Port Militaire Fl(4)G.15s6M. Darse de Missiessy. Leading light (351°36′) Front DirF.Vi.3M Rear DirF.Vi.3M. Entrance Iso.R.4s5M/Iso.G.4s5M. Bregaillon Fl(3)G.12s1M. Baie du Lazaret Fl.R.2·5s2M. Terre-Plein Fl(3)R.12s4m2M. Jetty Q.8M

Navigation Sailing yachts do not have automatic right of way over powered vessels.

PORT PIN ROLLAND

43°04′·83N 05°54′·58E WGS84
BA 2170 SHOM 7093

VHF Ch 09 (summer 0800–1200 / 1330–1730).

Data 350 berths. 20 visitors' berths. Max LOA 20m. Depths 1·5–3m. Charge band 3.

Facilities Water. 220V. Showers and toilets. 30/80/320-ton hoists. 8-ton crane. Most yacht repairs.

Port Pin Rolland ✆ 0494 94 61 24
International Marine Services (IMS)
✆ 04 94 30 54 94
Email info@i-m-s.fr

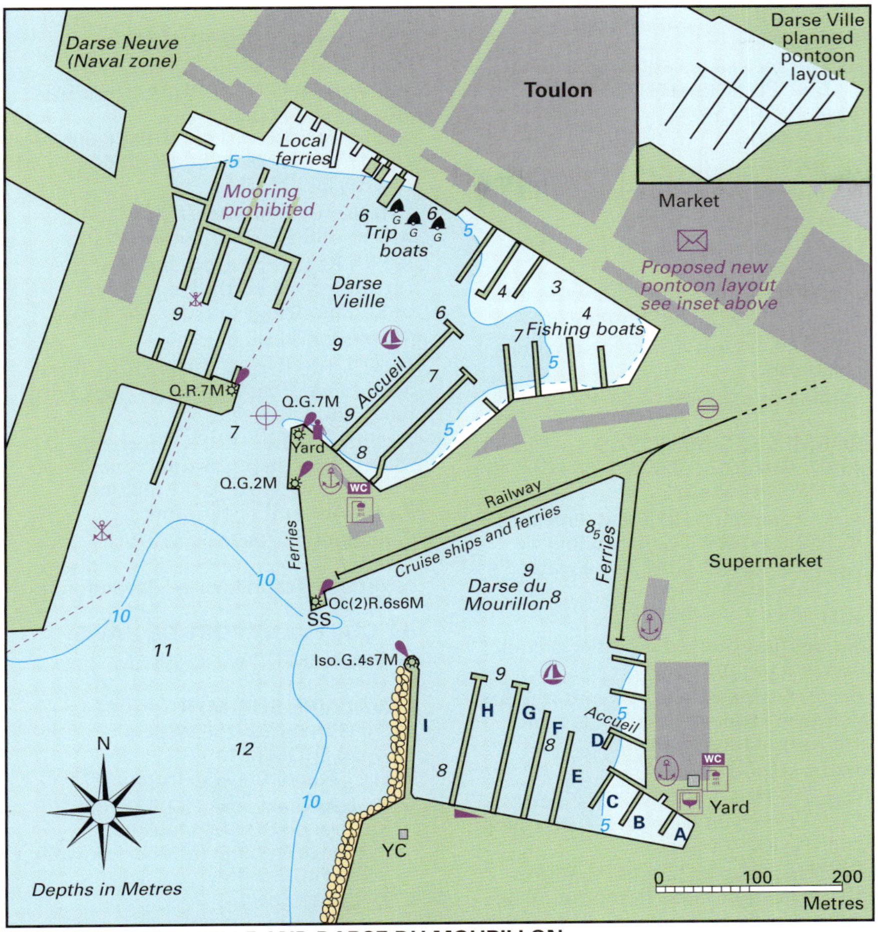

TOULON: DARSE VIELLE AND DARSE DU MOURILLON

MAREPOLIS

43°06'·35N 05°53'·77E WGS84

Yacht storage area and cruise ship harbour in approaches to La Seyne. There are plans to develop a 600 berth marina, superyacht facilities and a cruise ship terminal but the project has stalled for several years.

Several yards on shore for yacht repairs and storage.

PORT DE LA SEYNE

43°06'·18N 05°52'·97E WGS84
BA 2170 SHOM 7093

☆ Entrance N side Fl.G.4s10M

VHF Ch 09 (0800–1200 / 1400–1800).

Data 300 berths. 30 visitors' berths. Max LOA 12m. Depths 1·5–4m. Charge band 4.

Facilities Water. 220V. Pump-out.

Bureau du Port, La Seyne
✆ 0494 87 95 34
Email port.laseyne@var.cci.fr

NAVYSURF

Situated in commercial docks in NW of Baie de la Seyne.

Data 60 berths. 150 dry berths. Five visitors' berths. Max LOA 27m

✆ 04 94 30 84 08

PORT NAUTIC

VHF Ch 09 (summer 0800–1200 / 1400–1900, winter 0900–1200 / 1400–1800)

Data 200 berths. 30 visitors' berths. Max LOA 16m. Depths 2–4m.

Facilities Water. 220V. Showers and toilets. 60-ton crane and 20-ton hydraulic trailer. Some yacht repairs.

TOULON (DARSE VIEILLE/DARSE DU MOURILLON)

43°07'·05N 05°55'·76E WGS84
BA 2170 SHOM 7093
14M St-Pierre des Embiez ←→ Port de Porquerolles 15M

☆ Entrance to Darse du Mourillon Oc(2)R.6s6M/Iso.G.4s7M. Entrance to Darse Vieille Q.R.7M/Q.G.7M/Q.G.2M

VHF Ch 06, 09, 12, 16 for port authorities. Ch 11 for pilots. Ch 09 for Port de Plaisance (summer 0800–1300 / 1400–1900, winter 0800–1200 / 1400–1800).

Berths Report to *capitainerie* in Darse du Mourillon or Darse Vieille for berths. Laid moorings tailed to the quay or buoys. The concrete pontoons are being replaced, and the layout may change.

Shelter Good shelter.

Data 1,000 berths. 60 visitors' berths. Max LOA 45m. Depths 5–9m. Charge band 4.

Facilities Water. 220/380V. Showers and toilets. Pump-out. Fuel quay. 35-ton travel-hoist. 10-ton crane. All yacht repairs. Provisions and restaurants.

Port de Plaisance ✆ 0494 42 27 65
Email tlvd@var.cci.fr
Darse du Mourillon ✆ 04 94 41 23 39
Email tldn@var.cci.fr

ST-LOUIS DU MOURILLON

43°06'·4N 05°56'·2E

☆ Oc(2)G.6s7M

LES SALETTES (CARQUEIRANNE)

43°05'·2N 06°04'·7E
BA 2120 SHOM 7093

☆ Mole head Oc(4)WR.12s10/7M (356°-W-005°). Entrance Fl.R.2·5s1M/ Fl.G.2·5s1M

VHF Ch 09, 16 (0900–1200 / 1400–1700).

Data 400 berths. Visitors' berths. Max LOA 10m. Depths 1–1·5m. Charge band 3.

Facilities Water. 220V. Toilets. Fuel quay. 6-ton crane. Provisions and restaurants.

Capitainerie ✆ 0494 58 56 25

PORT CROS

43°00'·6N 06°22'·7E

Berths Pontoons and mooring buoys in the bay. No electricity. Limited water supplies. Generators prohibited in port. Holding tanks mandatory.

Port Cros HM ✆ 0494 01 40 72

PARC NATIONAL ILE DE PORT CROS

Access, navigation, anchoring and fishing restrictions. Yachts wishing to stop here must have a holding tank. Vessels over 30m are not permitted to moor.

www.portcrosparcnational.fr

PORT DU NIEL

43°02'·1N 06°07'·7E

☆ Jetty Fl.R.4s6M

Data 100 berths. Max LOA 11m. Depths 0·5–3m.

Capitainerie ✆ 0494 58 21 49

LE PRADEAU (LA TOUR FONDUE)

☆ Jetty Iso.G.4s8M

Ferry and trip boat harbour.

ILE DE PORQUEROLLES MARINE RESERVE

Part of the Port Cros National Park.

- navigation within 500m of the coast is prohibited for all vessels over 35m
- jets skis are not permitted within 500m of the coast, except for the access channels
- no anchoring, diving or swimming in zones on the NE, SE and W coasts
- approved anchoring zones on the N coast
- fishing and spear fishing is restricted in certain areas

www.portcrosparcnational.fr

PORT DE PORQUEROLLES
43°00'·3N 06°12'E
BA 2120 SHOM 7282
15M Toulon old port ←→ Le Lavandou 19M

☆ Breakwater head Oc(2)WR.6s13/10M (150°-W-230°)

VHF Ch 12 (summer 0800–2100, winter 0800–1200 / 1400–1600).

Berths Go on central pier to be allocated a berth. The concrete pontoons are being replaced, and the layout may change.

Shelter *Mistral* makes some berths uncomfortable.

Data 500 berths. 200 visitors' berths. Max LOA 40m. Depths 1·5–3m. Charge band 5. Mooring buoys – Max LOA 13m.

Facilities Water (limited hours). 220V. Showers and toilets. Fuel quay. 10-ton crane. Provisions and restaurants.

Capitainerie ☎ 0498 04 63 10

PORT D'HYÈRES
43°04'·8N 06°09'·5E (Fl.G.4s10M)
BA 2120 SHOM 7282

☆ S basin Fl.G.4s10M/Oc.R.4s7M. N basin (bassin 3) Iso.G.4s10M/ Q(6)+LFl.15s9M/Fl.R.4s5M. SE corner Fl.4s

VHF Ch 09 (summer 0600–2300, winter 0800–1200 / 1400–1700).

Berths Visiting yachts normally go to the S basin. Report to *capitainerie* on end of the jetty for a berth.

Shelter Good shelter.

Data 1,350 berths. 120 visitors' berths. Max LOA 16m. Depths 1·5–3m. Charge band 5.

Facilities Water. 220V. Showers and toilets. Fuel quay. 30-ton travel-hoist. 10-ton crane. All yacht repairs. Provisions and restaurants.

Capitainerie ☎ 0494 12 54 40
Email port.hyeres@wanadoo.fr

PORTLAND
43°06'·7N 06°11'·5E

Situated up the Le Gapeau river. 1·6–1·8m depths in river. Max air height 2m.

Data 50 berths. 540 dry berths under cover. Max LOA 8·5m.

☎ 0494 66 46 01
Email portland@free.fr

L'AYGUADE CEINTURON
43°06'·01N 06°10'·41E WG S84

☆ Breakwater head Fl(2)G.6s6M

Rivermouth quay. Entrance silts.

Capitainerie ☎ 0494 66 33 98

LE GAPEAU
43°06'·6N 06°11'·6E

Rivermouth development with dry storage on both banks.

PORT POTHAU (LES SALINS D'HYÈRES)

☆ Entrance Oc(3)WG.12s13/10M/Fl(2)R.6s6M

MIRAMAR
43°06'·9N 06°14'·8E

☆ Entrance Fl(2)G.6s8M/Fl(2)R.6s4M. Digue Est Q(9)+LFl.15s6M

VHF Ch 09 (summer 0800–2000, winter 0800–1230 / 1330–1700).

Berths Where directed. Visitors are normally on outer breakwater pontoon.

Data 1,150 berths. 200 visitors' berths. Max LOA 17m. Depths 1–1·7m. Charge band 3.

Facilities Water. 220V. Showers and toilets. Fuel quay. 15-ton hoist. Some repairs. Chandlery. Provisions and restaurants.

Capitainerie ☎ 0494 01 53 45

BORMES-LES-MIMOSAS
43°07'·53N 06°22'·02E WGS84
BA 2120 SHOM 6616

☆ La Fourmigue Fl(2)6s8M. Entrance Fl(2)R.6s10M/Fl.G (lightbuoy). Pierhead Fl.R.2s1M. Breakwater S end Q(6)+LFl.15s6M

VHF Ch 09, 16 (24/24).

Navigation Buoyed entrance channel dredged to 3m.

Berths Visiting yachts go onto the first pontoon inside the entrance. Laid moorings tailed to the quay.

Shelter Good shelter.

Data 950 berths. 75 visitors' berths. Max LOA 20m. Depths 2–7m. Charge band 5 (July–August).

Facilities Water. 220/380V. WiFi. Showers and toilets. Pump-out. Fuel quay. 45-ton travel-hoist. 20-ton crane. Some yacht repairs. Most provisions. Restaurants.

Capitainerie ☎ 0494 01 55 80
www.portdebormes.com

LE PRADET

☆ Fl.R.2s1M

LE LAVANDOU
43°08'·14N 06°22'·36E WGS84
BA 2120 SHOM 6616
19M Port de Porquerolles ←→ Cavalaire 9M

☆ Entrance Iso.WG.4s13/10M (266°-W-317° & 332°-W-358°)/Fl(2)R.6s3M. Old jetty Q(9)15s7M

VHF Ch 09 (summer 0730–2030, winter 0800–1200 / 1400–1900).

Berths Report to *capitainerie* at the entrance for a berth. Finger pontoons or laid moorings tailed to the quay.

Shelter Good shelter.

Data 1,100 berths. 100 visitors' berths. Max LOA 30m. Depths 2–7m. Charge band 5/6.

Facilities Water. 220V. Showers and toilets. Fuel quay. 25-ton crane. 9-ton travel-hoist. Most yacht repairs. Provisions and restaurants.

Capitainerie ☎ 0494 00 41 10
Email secretariat@capitainerie-lelavandou.fr

ILE DU LEVANT PORT DE L'AVIS

☆ Fl.G.4s6M/Q(3)WRG.5s8-7M

CAVALAIRE-SUR-MER
43°10'·39N 06°32'·25E WGS84
BA 2120 SHOM 6616
9M Le Lavandou ←→ St-Tropez 18M

☆ Outer breakwater Fl(2)R.6s10M. Central pier Q.6M. Vieux Port entrance Q(3)R.5s1M. N breakwater head Fl.G.2·5s4M

VHF Ch 09 (24/24).

Navigation Gusts in the approaches with strong N winds.

Berths Visiting yachts normally make for the Nouveau Port. Report to the *capitainerie* on the pier for a berth. Laid moorings tailed to the quay or buoys. Mooring buoys to N of harbour (summer only).

Shelter Strong N winds make some berths uncomfortable.

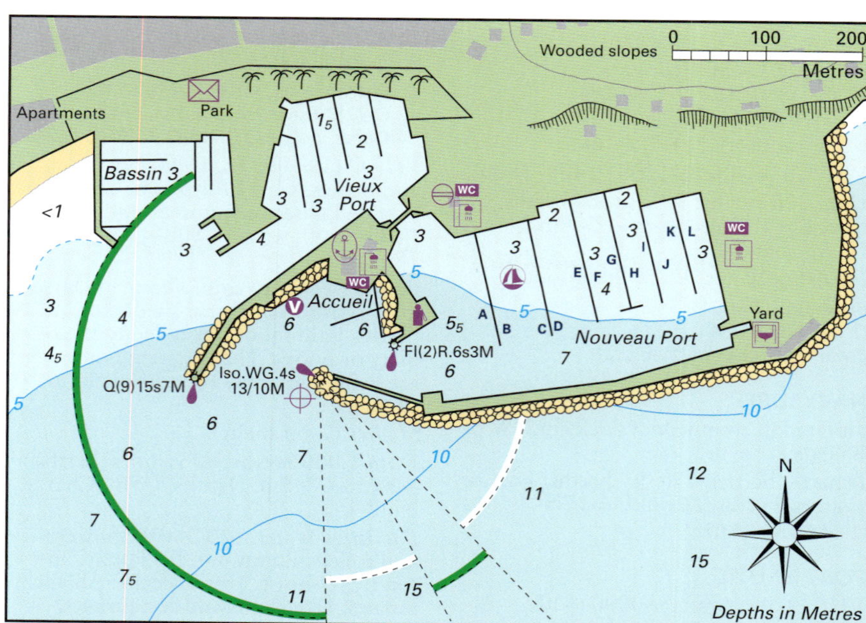

LE LAVANDOU

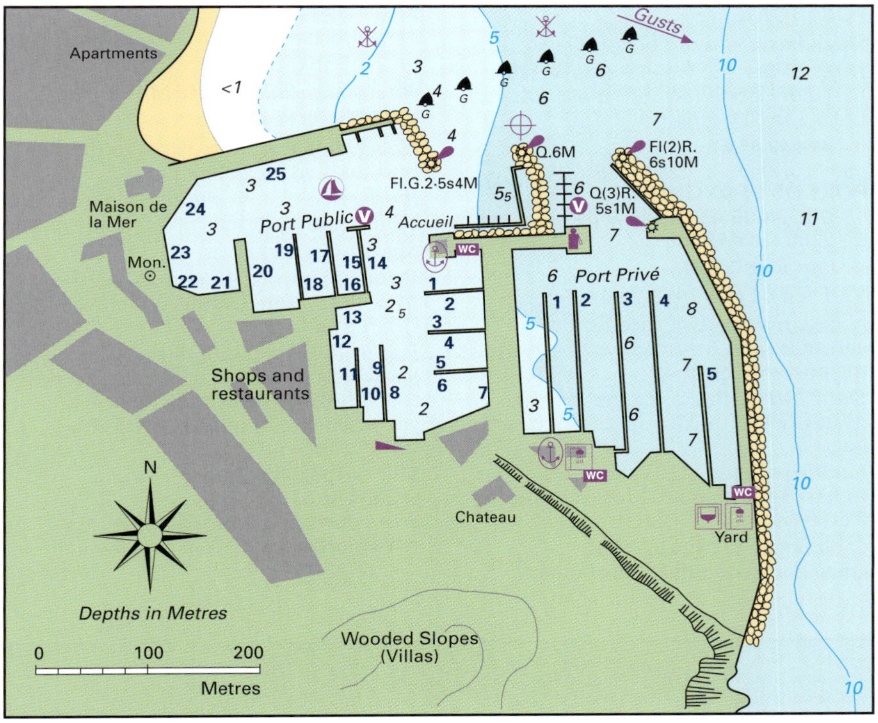

CAVALAIRE-SUR-MER

Data Nouveau Port 580 berths. 40 visitors' berths. Max LOA 21m (+ one 40m berth). Depths 1·5–4m. Vieux Port (Port Privé). 580 berths. Charge band 4/5.

Facilities Water. 220V. Showers and toilets. Fuel quay. 30-ton travel-hoist. Yacht repairs. Provisions and restaurants.

Port Public, Capitainerie
✆ 0494 64 17 81
Email port@cavalaire.fr
www.cavalaire.fr

Port Privé, Capitainerie
✆ 04 94 64 16 01
Email info@port-cavalaire.com
www.port-cavalaire.com

ST-TROPEZ

43°16′·34N 06°38′·00E WGS84
BA 2166 SHOM 7267 Imray M15
18M Cavalaire ←→ St-Raphaël Santa Lucia 11·5M

☆ Entrance Oc(2)WR.6s14/11M (228°-W-245°)/Fl.G.4s6M

VHF Ch 09 (summer 24/24, winter 0800–1200 / 1400–1800).

Berths Where directed. Laid moorings tailed to the quay.

Shelter Some berths uncomfortable with the *mistral*.

Data 800 berths. 100 visitors' berths. Max LOA 50m. Max LOA 50–65m in Vieux Port. Depths 2–6m. Charge band 5 (marina), 6+ (vieux port).

Facilities Water. 220/380V. Telephone. TV. Showers and toilets. Pump-out. Fuel quay. 20-ton crane. 40-ton slipway. Some yacht repairs. Provisions and restaurants.

Remarks Crowded in the summer.

Capitainerie du Port de St-Tropez
✆ 0494 56 68 70
Email
capitainerie@portsainttropez.com
www.port-de-saint-tropez.com

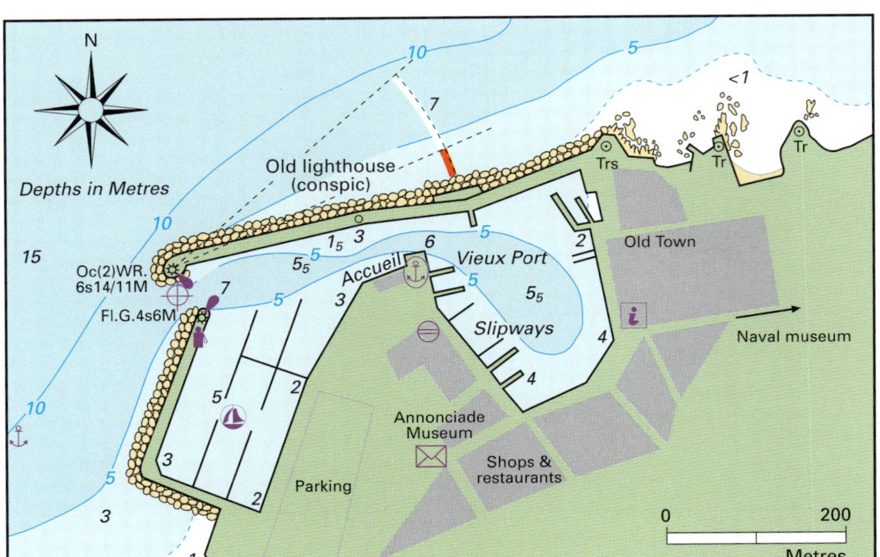

SAINT-TROPEZ ⊕43°16′·34N 06°38′·00E WGS84

MARINES DE COGOLIN

43°16′·1N 06°35′·5E
BA 2166 SHOM 7267

☆ Entrance Fl(2)R.6s10M/Fl.G.2s1M / N head Q.9M

VHF Ch 09 (winter 0800–2000).

Navigation Entrance difficult with strong E winds.

Berths Report to *capitainerie* for a berth. Laid moorings tailed to the quay.

Shelter Good shelter.

Data 1,600 berths. 300 visitors' berths. Max LOA 35m. Depths 2–10m. Charge band 4/5.

Facilities Water. 220V. Showers and toilets. Fuel quay. 150/100-ton travel-hoists. 3/6-ton cranes. Most yacht repairs. Some provisions. Restaurants.

Capitainerie ✆ 0494 56 07 31
Email marines.de.cogolin@wanadoo.fr
www.marines-de-cogolin.com

PORT COGOLIN

43°16′·4N 06°34′·2E

☆ Rivière La Giscle Q.9M S side of entrance.

VHF Ch 09 (summer 0900–1200 / 1400–1830).

Navigation Care needed of the bar at the entrance to the river. Reported depths of 1·5m in the middle of the river and 2–2·25m closer to the S side of the river. Proceed along the river to the basin on the S side.

Berths Where directed. Laid moorings tailed to the quay.

Shelter All round in the basin.

Data 150 berths. Few visitors' berths. Max LOA 15m. Depths 2m in the basin. Charge band 4.

Facilities Water. 220V. Showers and toilets. Fuel at Marines de Cogolin. Chandlers. Bars and restaurants.

Port Cogolin ✆ 04 94 56 30 39

PORT GRIMAUD

43°16′·3N 06°35′·3E
BA 2166 SHOM 7267

☆ Entrance Fl.G.4s10M/Fl.R.4s6M

VHF Ch 09, 12 (summer 0800–2100, winter 0800–1200 / 1400–1900).

Navigation Entrance difficult with strong E winds.

Berths Report to *capitainerie* for a berth. Laid moorings tailed to buoys or finger pontoons.

Shelter Visitors' berths on breakwater can be uncomfortable with strong E winds. Shelter inside is good.

Data Port Grimaud 1,100 berths. 280 visitors' berths. Max LOA 55m. Depths 3m. Charge band 5.

Grimaud Sud 800 berths. 15 visitors' berths. Max LOA 20m. Depths 3m. Charge band 4/5.
Marina Grimaud 500 berths. 60 visitors' berths. Max LOA 20m. Depth 3m. Charge band 5.

Facilities Water. 220/380V. Showers and toilets. Fuel quay. 30-ton travel-hoist. 30-ton travel-hoist (Grimaud 3). 10-ton crane. 60-ton slipway. Some yacht repairs. Provisions and restaurants.

Port Grimaud, Capitainerie
☎ 0494 56 29 88
Email capitainerie@port-grimaud.fr
www.port-grimaud.fr

Grimaud Sud ☎ 0494 56 73 65

Marina Grimaud ☎ 0494 56 02 45
www.marina-port-grimaud.com

STE MAXIME
43°18'·33N 06°38'·25E WGS84
BA 2166 SHOM 7267

☆ Entrance Q.G.8m8M / Fl.R.2s1M. Central pier N corner F.

VHF Ch 09 (summer 0800–2000, winter 0800–1230 / 1400–1800).

Berths Report to the *capitainerie* on the central pier. Laid moorings tailed to the quay.

Shelter Good shelter.

Data *Port Public* 390 berths. 30 visitors' berths. Max LOA 15m. Depths 2–5m. Charge band 4/5.
Port Privé 375 berths. Depths 2–5m.

Facilities Water. 220V. (Telephone and TV in Port Privé.) Showers and toilets. Fuel quay. 10-ton crane. Some yacht repairs. Provisions and restaurants.

Port Public, Capitainerie
☎ 0494 96 74 25
Email semaport@sema83.fr

SAN PEIRE LES ISSAMBRES
43°20'·4N 06°41'·2E
BA 2166 SHOM 7267

☆ Entrance Fl(2)WG.6s11/8M/Fl(2)R.6s4M

VHF Ch 09.

Navigation Care is needed of the reef off Pte des Issambres and off Pte de la Garonne (Bn YB). With strong SE winds entry is difficult.

Berths Visitors normally go on the first pontoon inside the entrance. Laid moorings tailed to the quay.

Shelter Strong S winds make some berths uncomfortable.

Data 445 berths. 10 visitors' berths. Max LOA 13m. Depths 2–3m. Charge band 5.

Facilities Water. 220V. Showers and toilets. Fuel quay. 25-ton hoist. Limited yacht repairs. Some provisions. Restaurants.

Capitainerie ☎ 0494 49 40 29
Email sodeports-issambres@wanadoo.fr

PORT DE FERREOL
43°21'·6N 06°43'·1E

☆ Mole head Fl.WR.4s7/5M (250°-W-310°)

Data 135 berths. 12 visitors' berths. Depths 1–5m. Charge band 4.

Capitainerie ☎ 0494 49 51 56

PORT TONIC
Small basin and dry port.

Data 20 berths. Two visitors' berths. Large dry berth facility ashore. Max LOA 13m. Depths 1·5–2·5m.

☎ 0494 49 47 47

PORT DE ST-AYGULF
43°23'·58N 06°43'·82E WGS84
BA 2166 SHOM 6838

☆ Entrance Q.R.6M

VHF Ch 09 (24/24).

Navigation Care needed as the entrance silts. At present stay close to the port side on entry.

Data 240 berths. 2 visitors' berths. Max LOA 15m. Depths 2–4m. Charge band 5.

Facilities Water. 220V. Showers and toilets. 15-ton crane. Most provisions. Restaurants.

Capitainerie ☎ 0494 52 74 52
Email port.st-aygulf0179@orange.fr

PORT DE FRÉJUS
43°25'·2N 06°45'·1E
BA 2166 SHOM 6838

☆ Entrance Fl(2)R.6s7m6M

VHF Ch 09 (24/24).

Navigation Prohibited area to the S of port marked by yellow buoys.

Berths Report to *capitainerie* for a berth. Laid moorings tailed to the quay.

Shelter Good shelter.

Data 700 berths. 40 visitors' berths. Max LOA 30m. Depths 2–3·5m. Charge band 5.

Facilities Water. 220/380V. TV. Showers and toilets. Fuel quay. 50-ton travel-hoist. 10-ton crane. Limited yacht repairs. Limited provisions. Restaurants.

SEM Gestion Port Fréjus
☎ 0494 82 63 00
Email portfrejus@wanadoo.fr
www.portfrejus.fr

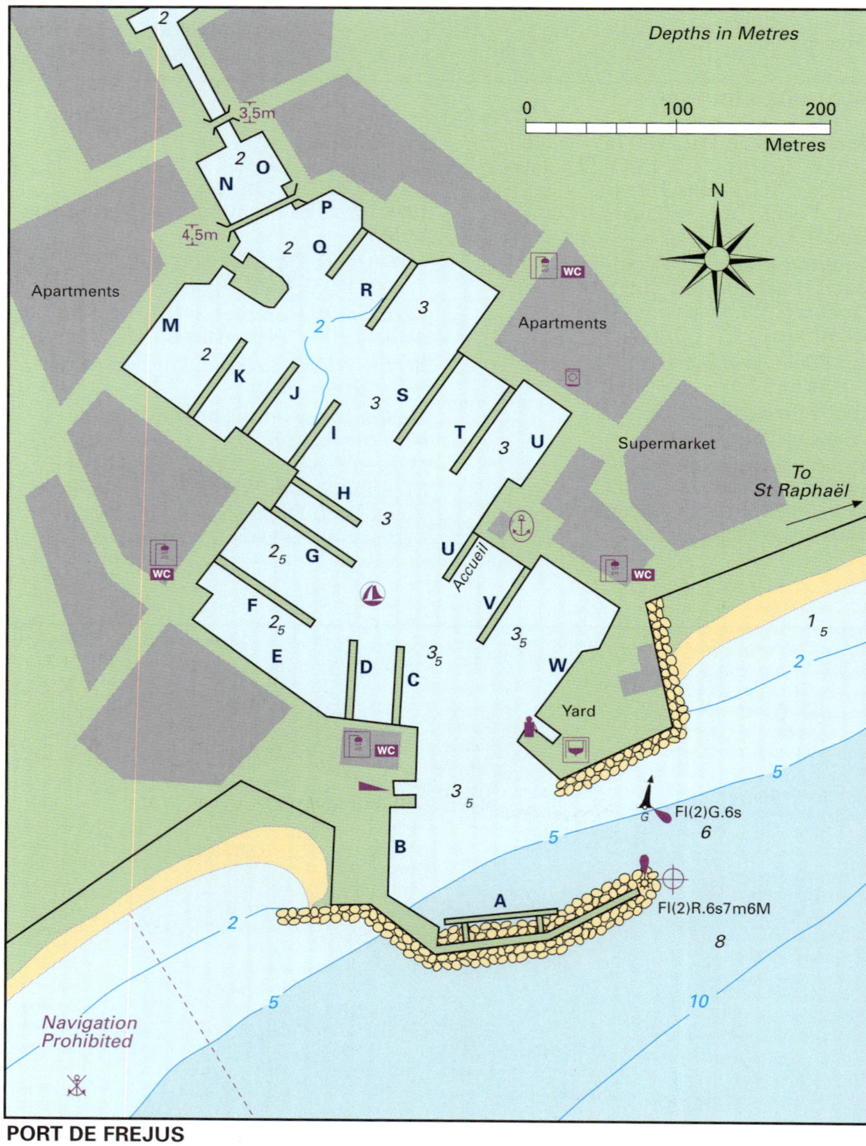

PORT DE FREJUS

ST-RAPHAEL VIEUX PORT
43°25′·4N 06°45′·9E

☆ Entrance Q.G.2M

VHF Ch 12, 16 (summer 0800–1200 / 1400–1900, winter 0800–1200 / 1400 / 1700).

Data 230 berths. Visitors' berths. Max LOA 60m. Depths 1–5m. Charge band 4.

Facilities Water. 220/380V. Fuel quay. 10-ton crane. Provisions and restaurants.

Remarks Work is underway to develop a new superyacht basin on the N side for vessels from 15-45m LOA. S breakwater has been extended.

www.portsdesaintraphael.com

Capitainerie ✆ 0494 95 11 19
Email capitainerie@ville-saintraphael.fr

ST-RAPHAËL – SANTA LUCIA
43°25′N 06°46′·5E
BA 2166 SHOM 6838
11·5M St Tropez ←→ Cannes 15·5M

☆ Lion de Mer VQ.WR.11/8M (275°-W-249°). Lion de Terre lightbuoy Q(6)+LFl. Bassin Nord entrance Fl.G.4s9M. Bassin Sud Oc(2)WR.6s10/7M (040°-W-057°/084°-W-122°)

VHF Ch 09 (24/24).

Navigation There is a deep water passage between Lion de Mer and Lion de Terre.

Berths Where directed in Bassin Nord or Bassin Sud. Laid moorings tailed to the quay or finger pontoons.

Shelter Good shelter.

Data 1,550 berths. 360 visitors' berths. Depths 2–10m. Charge band 5.

Facilities Water. 220V. Showers and toilets. Fuel quay. 50-ton travel-hoist. 2-ton crane. Most yacht repairs. Provisions and restaurants.

Capitainerie ✆ 04 94 95 34 30

Email capitainerie.santa.lucia@ville-saintraphael.com

www.portsdesaintraphael.com

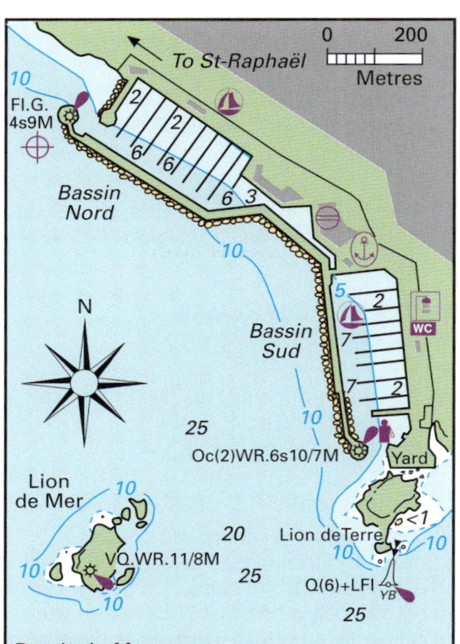

ST-RAPHAËL - SANTA LUCIA

RADE D'AGAY
43°25′·5N 06°52′·3E (Pte de la Beaumette light)

☆ Pte de la Beaumette Oc.WR.4s15/12M. La Chretienne beacon Q(6)+LFl.15s8M.

VHF Ch 09

Anchoring prohibited 1/6-30/9.

Data 123 moorings. Max LOA 16m. Charge band 2.

Capitainerie ✆ 04 94 17 15 57 / 0660 57 79 94
Email ancreavis@ville-saintraphael.fr
www.portsdesaintraphael.fr

LA FIGUEIRETTE-MIRAMAR
43°29′N 06°56′E
BA 2166 SHOM 7409

☆ La Vaquette buoy Q(3)10s2M. Entrance Fl(3)WG.12s13/10M (275°-W-348°)/F.R

VHF Ch 09 (summer 0700–2000, winter 0830–1200 / 1400–1730).

Data 250 berths. 20 visitors' berths. Max LOA 17m. Depths 1·5–2m. Charge band 4.

Facilities Water. 220V. Showers and toilets. Fuel quay. 12-ton crane. Restaurant.

Capitainerie ✆ 0493 75 08 00
Email port.figueirette@wanadoo.fr

LA GALERE
43°30′N 06°57′·4E
BA 2166 SHOM 7205

☆ Pte St Marc Fl(2)G.6s5M. Entrance Q.R.7M/Iso.4s

VHF Ch 09 (July and August 24/24, otherwise 0830–1230 / 1400–1800).

Data 175 berths. 18 visitors' berths. Max LOA 12m. Depths 1·5–3m. Charge band 5.

Facilities Water. 220V. Showers and toilets. Fuel quay. 10-ton crane. Limited provisions. Restaurants.

Capitainerie ✆ 0493 75 41 74
Email port.galere@orange.fr

THEOULE-SUR-MER
43°30′·6N 06°56′·4E
BA 2244, 2245 SHOM 7205

☆ Iso.WR.4s9/6M (198°-W-265°)

VHF Ch 09 (summer 0830–1230 / 1330–1830).

Data 183 berths. Max LOA 13m. Depths 1–2m. Charge band 4.

Facilities Water. 220V. Showers and toilets. Fuel quay. 3-ton crane. Provisions and restaurants.

Capitainerie ✆ 0493 49 97 38
Email port.theole@wanadoo.fr

LA RAGUE
43°30′·85N 06°56′·36E WGS84
BA 2244, 2245 SHOM 7205

☆ Entrance Fl(4)G.15s8M/Fl.R.2·5s2M

VHF Ch 09 (24/24).

Berths Where directed. Report to the *capitainerie* for a berth. Laid moorings tailed to the quay.

Shelter Good shelter.

Data 520 berths. 130 visitors' berths. Max LOA 30m. Depths 2–4·5m.

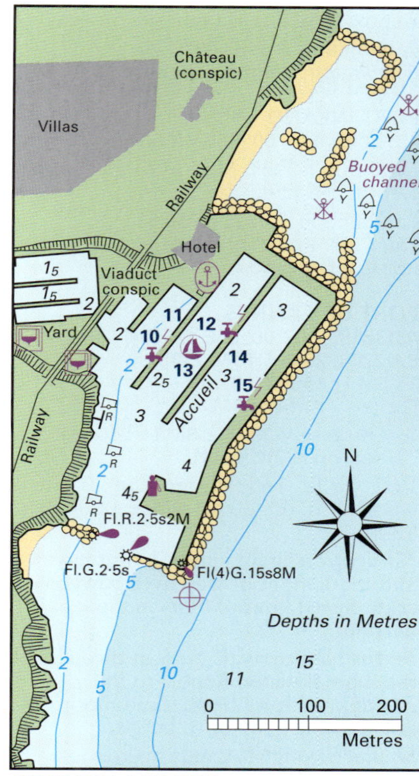

PORT DE LA RAGUE

Charge band 5.

Facilities Water. 220V. Showers and toilets. Fuel quay. 70-ton travel-hoist. 10-ton crane. Some yacht repairs. Some provisions. Restaurants.

Capitainerie du Port de la Rague
✆ 0493 49 81 55
Email portdelarague@cegetel.net

PORT LA NAPOULE
43°31′·30N 06°56′·64E WGS84
BA 2244, 2245 SHOM 7205

☆ Entrance Fl(3)G.12s10M. Spur Q.G.2M/Q.R.2M

VHF Ch 09 (summer 0600–2100, winter 0600–2000).

Navigation Entrance channel buoyed on port side.

Berths Where directed. Report to *capitainerie* on central pier for a berth. Laid moorings tailed to the quay.

Shelter Good shelter.

Data 960 berths. 180 visitors' berths. Max LOA 35m. Depths 1·5–7m. Charge band 4.

Facilities Water. 220/380V. Showers and toilets. WiFi. Fuel quay. 40-ton travel-hoist. 8-ton crane. Slipways. All yacht repairs. Provisions and restaurants.

Yacht Club International de Mandelieu La Napoule ✆ 0492 97 77 77
Email portlanapoule@portlanapoule.com
www.port-la-napoule.com

CANNES MARINA (RIVIÈRE LA SIAGNE)
43°32′·1N 06°56′·3E

VHF Ch 09 (0830–1200 / 1400–1900).

Data 1700 berths. Max LOA 12m.

Depths 1·5–2m. Max air height 4m.
Capitainerie ☎ 0493 49 51 27
Email marina.capitainerie@free.fr

PORT INLAND
42°32′·83N 07°00′·85E WGS84
Data 800 berths. Max LOA 11·5m. Depths 1·5–2m.
Capitainerie ☎ 0493 47 50 68
Email info@port-inland.com
www.port-inland.com

PORT DE CANNES
43°32′·83N 07°00′·85E WGS84
BA 2244, 2245 SHOM 7205
15·5M St Raphaël Santa Lucia ←→ Antibes 9M

☆ Entrance VQ(3)R.2s8M/Le Sécant beacon Fl(2)G.6s4M

VHF Ch 12, 16 (call sign *Cannes Port*) (summer 0700–2000, winter 0800–1800).

Navigation Sailing craft do not have automatic right of way over power craft. Speed limit of 3kns in the harbour.

Berths New arrivals quay at the head of the E breakwater. Report to the *capitainerie* for a berth. Laid moorings tailed to the quay or to buoys.

Shelter Strong SE winds make some berths uncomfortable.

Data 720 berths. 150 visitors' berths. Max LOA 140m. Depths 1–8m (most of the harbour is dredged to minimum 5m). Charge band 4.

Facilities Water. 220/380V. Showers and toilets. Pump-out. WiFi. Fuel quay. 65-ton travel-hoist. 12-ton crane. 70-ton slipway. Most yacht repairs. Provisions and restaurants.

MARITIME REGULATIONS IN BAIE DE CANNES AND ILES DE LERINS

- Jet-skis prohibited all areas within 300m of the coast and the islands. This includes the 10kn zone outlined below, and all access channels in to the coast.
- Max speed 10kn for all vessels in the area formed between a line from Fort Ste-Marguerite to Palm Beach casino, and from Pte Bateguier to the entrance light at Port de Cannes.
- Max speed 5kn for all vessels within 300m of the islands, and in buoyed transit channel between Ile Ste-Marguerite and Ile St-Honorat.
- Max speed 3kn in the authorised mooring area on either side of the transit channel (above).
- No anchoring within 300m of the beach from Port du Beal to Port de Cannes.
- No anchoring between Pte Bateguier and Port de Ste-Marguerite.
- No anchoring between Les Moines and Ile St-Honorat.
- Tenders must only use the authorised buoyed channels to reach the shore. On Iles de Lerins there is just one channel leading into Port de Ste-Marguerite and another into Port des Moines.

www.riviera-ports.com

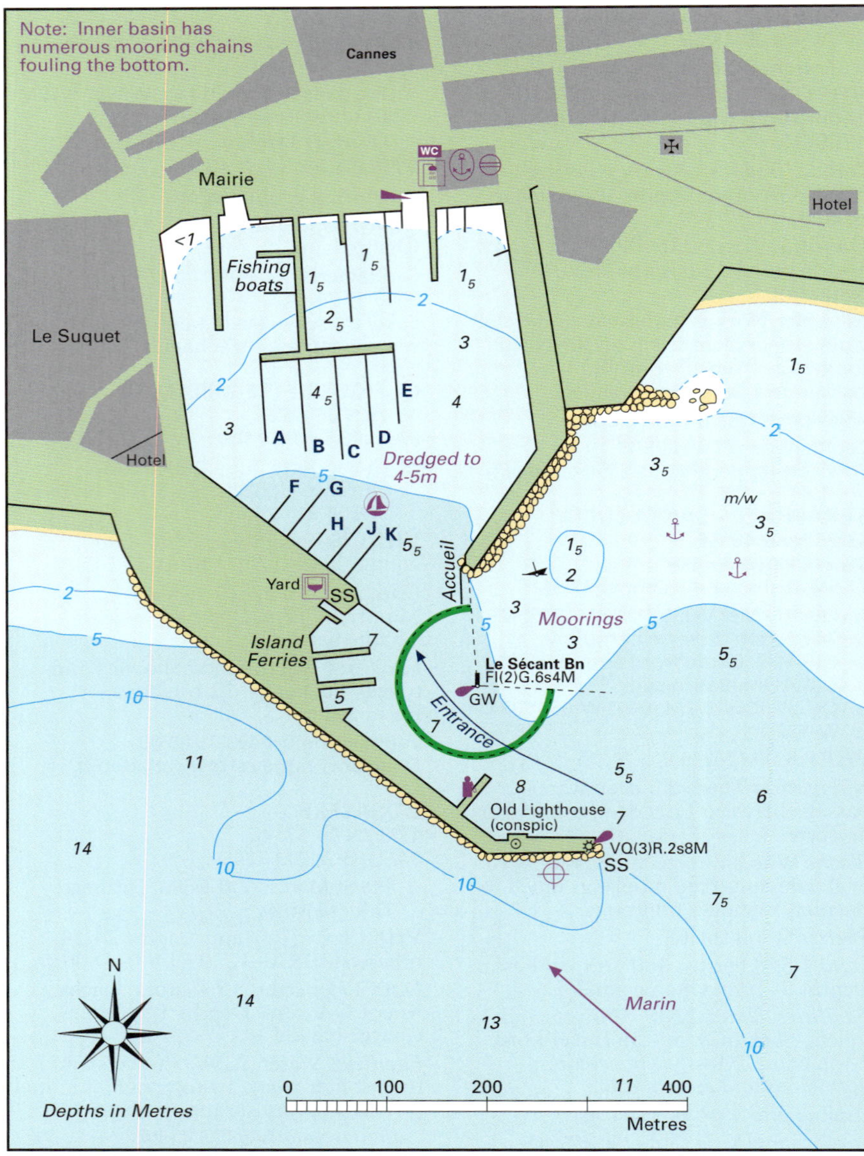

PORT DE CANNES

Remarks No-anchoring zone around the heliport. Anchorage E of the port reserved for cruise ships 01/06–31/08.
Bureau du Port
☎ 0820 42 33 33 / 0492 98 70 20
Email portdecannes-plaisance@cote-azur.cci.fr
www.riviera-ports.com

PORT PIERRE-CANTO
43°32′·47N 07°01′·80E WGS84
BA 2244, 2245 SHOM 7205

☆ Entrance Fl.G.4s11m11M/Fl.R.4s2m3M. Batéguier Q(9)15s4M

VHF Ch 09 (24/24).

Navigation With a strong *mistral* an airbag barrier may be put across the entrance.

Berths Where directed. Report to the *capitainerie* for a berth. Laid moorings tailed to the quay.

Shelter Outer berths uncomfortable with the *mistral*.

Data 650 berths. 100 visitors' berths. Max LOA 70m. Depths 2–7m. Charge band 4.

Facilities Water. 220/380V. Showers and toilets. Fuel quay. 50-ton travel-hoist. 15/6-ton cranes. Most yacht repairs. Provisions and restaurants.

La Croisette, Capitainerie ☎ 0492 18 84 84
Email portpierrecanto@ville-cannes.fr
www.cannes.com

PORT DE MOURÉ-ROUGE
☆ Entrance Fl(4)WG.15s9/6M (282°-W-312°)

PORTS DE GOLFE-JUAN
43°33′·87N 07°04′·77E WGS84
BA 2167 SHOM 7205

☆ La Fourmigue Fl(2)10s7M. Entrance Fl(2)G.6s10M/Iso.R.4s9M

VHF Ch 12 for Port Public (summer 0700–2100, winter 0800–1300). Ch 09 for Port Camille Rayon (24/24).

Navigation La Fourmigue rock is marked by an isolated danger beacon (BRB) with a ⁝ topmark. Le Secanion is marked with a red buoy. Between the two is a shoal patch with least depth 6m.

Berths Report to *capitainerie* on the central pier for a berth. Laid moorings tailed to the quay or a buoy.

Shelter Good shelter.

Data Port Public 860 berths. 260 visitors' berths. Max LOA 22m. Depths 1–3·5m. Charge band 4.
Port Camille Rayon 844 berths. 80 visitors' berths. Max LOA 75m. Depths 2–5m. Charge band 5/6.

Facilities Water. 220V. Showers and toilets. WiFi. Fuel quay. 100-ton travel-hoist. 18/10/6-ton cranes. Most yacht repairs. Provisions and restaurants.

CCI Port Public, Capitainerie
✆ 0493 63 96 25
Email portdegolfe-juan@cote-azur.cci.fr
www.riviera-ports.com

Bureau du Port Camille Rayon
✆ 0493 63 30 30
Email port@portcamillerayon.net
www.portcamillerayon.net

GALLICE-JUAN-LES-PINS

43°33'·75N 07°06'·77E WGS84
BA 2244, 2245 SHOM 7205

☆ Entrance Gallice-Juan les Pins VQ(3)G.2s9M. Port Crouton entrance E head Fl(2)R.6s5M

VHF Ch 09 (call sign *Gallice*).

Navigation Entrance channel buoyed.

Berths Report to *capitainerie* for a berth. Laid moorings tailed to the quay.

Shelter Good shelter.

Data 525 berths. Visitors' berths. Max LOA 45m. Depths 2–3m. Charge band 5/6 (June–September).

Facilities Water. 220/380V. Showers and toilets. Pump-out. Fuel quay. 50-ton travel-hoist. Some yacht repairs. Some provisions. Restaurants.

Capitainerie ✆ 0492 93 74 40
Email contact@port-gallice.fr

VAUBAN-ANTIBES

43°35'·44N 07°07'·91E WGS84
BA 2244, 2245 SHOM 7200
9M Cannes ←→ Nice 10M

☆ Breakwater head Fl.R.4s11M/Fl(2)G.6s (lightbuoy)/Fl.G.4s5M. Mole des Cinq-Cent-Francs head F.Vi.2M. Anse St Roch entrance F.1m/Iso.4s1m/F.R.1m

VHF Ch 09 for Vauban-Antibes and IYCA (24/24).

Berths Report to *capitainerie* for a berth. Laid moorings tailed to the quay or buoys. Craft over 70m report to IYCA.

Shelter Good shelter.

Data 1,700 berths. 250 visitors' berths. Max LOA 50m. Depths 2–7m. Charge band 5.
IYCA 19 berths. Max LOA 165m. Depths 7m.

Facilities Water. 220/380V. Telephone. Showers and toilets. Fuel quay. 150/30-ton travel-hoists. Slipway. All yacht repairs. Provisions and restaurants.

Remarks Project planned to upgrade the harbour and improve pedestrian access around the port. The work will also extend the breakwater to increase berths and for small cruise ships.

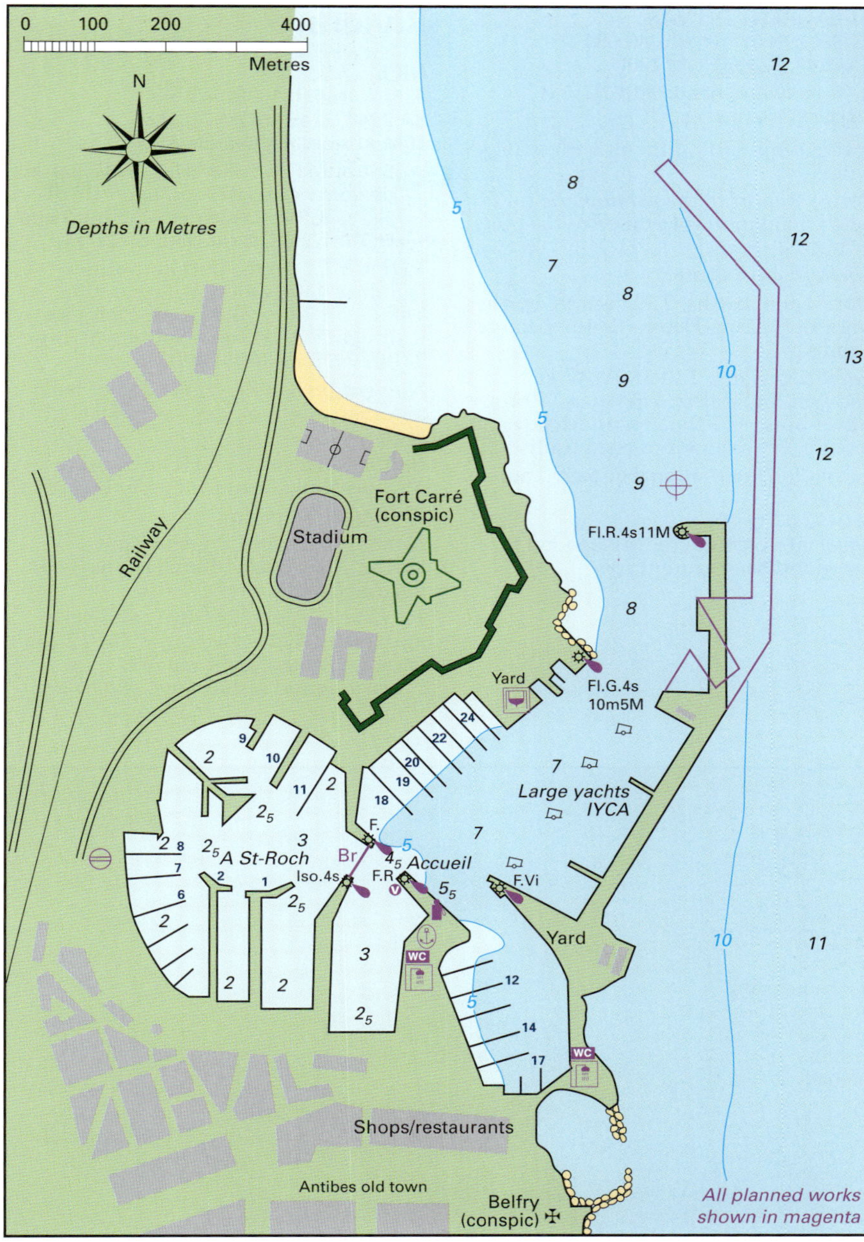

PORT VAUBAN-ANTIBES

Port Vauban, Capitainerie
✆ 0492 91 60 00
Email port@portvauban.net

IYCA ✆ 0493 34 30 30
Email iyca@iycantibes.com

✉ Riviera Charts, Galerie du Port, 11 Rue Fontvieille, 06600 Antibes
✆ 0493 34 45 66
Email sales@rivieracharts.com
www.rivieracharts.com

MARINA BAIE DES ANGES

43°37'·91N 07°08'·31E WGS84
BA 2244, 2245 SHOM 7200

☆ Entrance Fl(2)G.6s9M/Fl(2)R.6s7M

VHF Ch 09.

Navigation Entry difficult with strong E–SE winds.

Berths Report to the *capitainerie* for a berth. Laid moorings tailed to the quay.

Shelter Strong E winds make some berths uncomfortable.

Data 475 berths. 53 visitors' berths. Max LOA 30m. Depths 2–5m. Charge band 5.

Facilities Water. 220/380V. Showers and toilets. Fuel quay. 50-ton travel-hoist. 2·5-ton crane. Some yacht repairs. Provisions and restaurants.

Bureau du Port ✆ 0493 13 32 20
Email
info@portmarinabaiedesanges.com
www.marina-baie-des-anges.com

ST-LAURENT DU VAR
43°39'·29N 07°10'·78E WGS84
BA 2244, 2245 SHOM 7200

☆ Breakwater head Fl(3)G.12s8M

VHF Ch 09 (24/24).

Navigation Entry difficult with strong S winds.

Berths Report to the *capitainerie* for a berth. Laid moorings tailed to the quay or buoys.

Shelter Good shelter.

Data 1,090 berths. 250 visitors' berths. Max LOA 23m. Depths 2–4m. Charge band 5.

Facilities Water. 220/380V. WiFi. Showers and toilets. Fuel quay. 50-ton travel-hoist. 6/4-ton cranes. Most yacht repairs. Provisions and restaurants.

Yacht Club International de Saint Laurent du Var
✆ 0493 07 12 70
Email info.portstlaurent@wanadoo.fr
www.port-saint-laurent.com

Riviera

NICE
43°41'·4N 07°17'·3E
BA 2244, 2245 SHOM 7200
10M Antibes ←→ Beaulieu 5M

☆ Entrance Fl.R.5s20M/Fl.G.4s7M. Bassin de Commerce Fl(2)R.6s7M/ Fl(2)G.6s7M. Bassin des Amiraux S side Fl(3)R.12s6M. N side Fl(3)G.12s7M

VHF Ch 12, 16 for port authorities (summer 0600–0000, winter 0700–1800). Ch 09 for Bureau de Plaisance (call sign *Nice Marina*. Summer 0700–2100, winter 0800–1800).

Navigation Sailing yachts do not have automatic right of way over powered craft.

Berths Must call on VHF in advance. Yachts should head for Bassin Lympia.

Shelter Good shelter.

Data 500 berths. Limited visitors' berths. Max LOA 140m. Depths 3–7m. Charge band 4.

Facilities Water. 220/380V. Showers and toilets. WiFi. Fuel quay. 5/6/12-ton cranes. Limited yacht repairs. Provisions and restaurants.

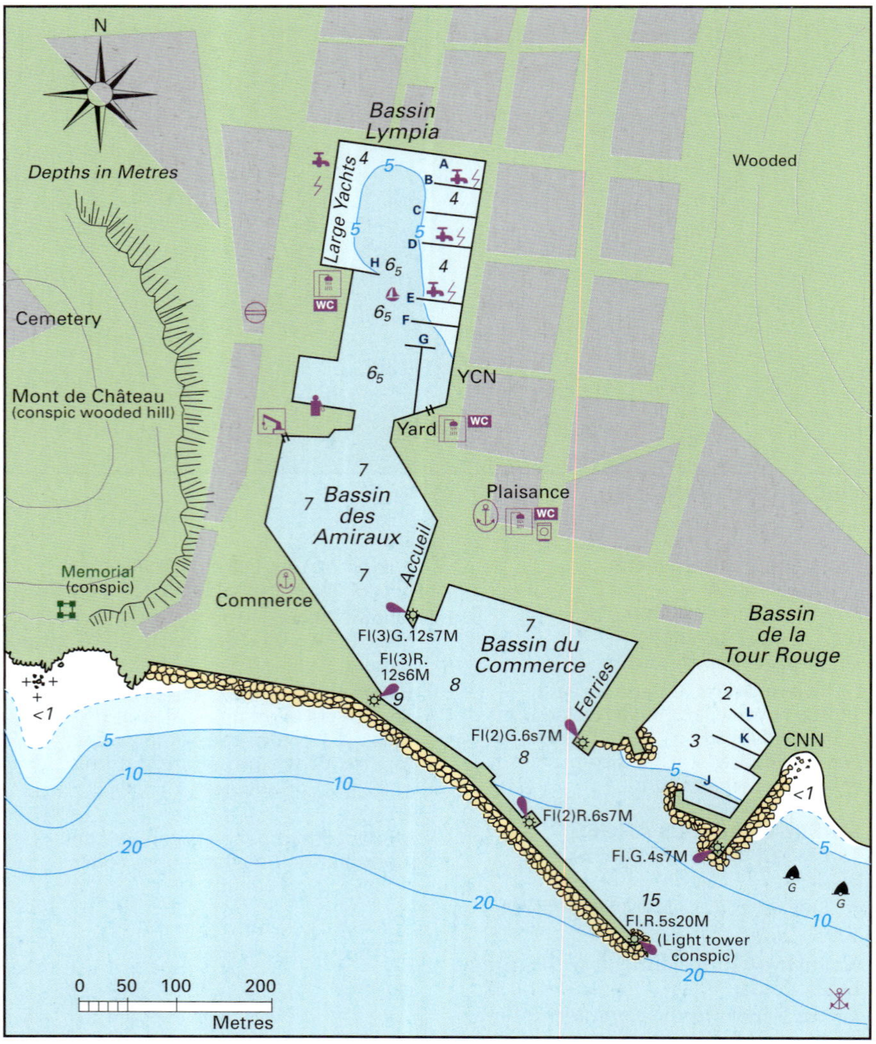

NICE

Yacht harbour office ✆ 0492 00 42 14
Email nice-plaisance@cote-azur.cci.fr
www.riviera-ports.com

RADE DE VILLEFRANCHE
A 5kn speed limit is enforced in the bay, and within 300m of the coast. Pilots are compulsory for craft over 50m LOA. Centre of the bay is a prohibited anchorage at all times. Head of the bay and Anse de l'Espalmador are restricted areas where anchoring is prohibited from 15/6-15/9. Charge band 4/5.

Email pilote-nice@wanadoo.fr

VILLEFRANCHE
43°42'·0N 07°18'·7E
BA 2244, 2245 SHOM 7200

☆ Entrance Q.WR.8m12/8M (286°-W-311°/335°-W-009°). Jetty head Q.G.2M. N mole Fl(4)R.15s7M

VHF Ch 09 (summer 0700–2000, winter 0730–1800).

Navigation 5kn speed limit enforced in Rade de Villefranche.

Berths Where directed. Laid moorings tailed to the quay or buoys.

Shelter Good shelter.

Data 420 berths. Visitors' berths. Max LOA 30m. Depths 1·5–6m. Charge band 3/4.

Facilities Water. 220V. Showers and toilets. WiFi. Fuel quay. 40-ton slipway. 12/30-ton cranes. Limited yacht repairs. Provisions and restaurants.

Capitainerie du Port de Villefranche
✆ 0493 01 70 70 / 01 78 05
Email port.villefranche@cote-azur.cci.fr
www.riviera-ports.com

ST-JEAN-CAP-FERRAT
43°41'·5N 07°20'·2E
BA 2244, 2245 Imray M15

☆ Entrance Fl(4)R.15s8M / Fl.R.4s1m2M / Fl.G.4s1m2M

VHF Ch 09.

Navigation Entry difficult with strong E–SE winds.

Berths Report to the *capitainerie* for a berth. Laid moorings tailed to the quay.

Shelter Good shelter.

Data 560 berths. 10 visitors' berths. Max LOA 30m. Depths 1·5–4m. Charge band 4/5.

Facilities Water. 220/380V. Showers and toilets. Fuel quay. 30-ton travel-hoist. 16-ton crane. Limited yacht repairs. Provisions and restaurants.

Remarks New fuel dock has been completed.

Capitainerie ✆ 0493 76 45 45
Email president@portcapferrat.fr
www.portcapferrat.fr

BEAULIEU-SUR-MER
43°42'·5N 07°20'·4E
BA 2244, 2245 SHOM 6863
5M Nice ←→ Monaco 4·5M

☆ Detached breakwater NE end Q.R.10M. E jetty centre Q.G.7M. SW end Fl(3)G.12s3M. Inner entrance Fl.R.4s4m/Fl.G.4s4m

VHF Ch 09 (24/24).

Navigation Entry should be made by

the Passe Principale at the N end.

Berths Report to the *capitainerie* for a berth. Laid moorings tailed to the quay or buoys.

Shelter Good shelter.

Data 740 berths. 150 visitors' berths. Max LOA 45m. Depths 1·5–5m. Charge band 4.

Facilities Water. 220/380V. Showers and toilets. Pump-out. WiFi. Fuel quay. 100/40-ton travel-hoist. 4-ton crane. Slipway. All yacht repairs. Provisions and restaurants.

Bureau du Port ✆ 0493 01 10 49
Email info@portdebeaulieu.com

PORT DE SILVA-MARIS (PORT D'EZE-SUR-MER)
☆ Fl(2)R.6s9M

CAP D'AIL
43°43'·4N 07°24'·9E
BA 2244, 2245 SHOM 7441
☆ Heliport Mo(MC)30s10m. Entrance Fl.G.4s10M/Fl.G.4s6M/Fl.R.4s5m

VHF Ch 09 (24/24).

Navigation Care needed of the reef running out from Cap d'Aïl.

Berths Report to the *capitainerie* for a berth. Laid moorings tailed to the quay or finger pontoons.

Shelter Strong SW winds make some berths uncomfortable.

Data 253 berths. Visitors' berths. Max LOA 60m. Depths 5–15m. Charge band 4/5.

Facilities Water. 220/380V. Showers and toilets. Fuel quay. 50-ton travel-hoist. 10-ton crane. Slipway. Some yacht repairs. Provisions and restaurants.

Port de Plaisance du Cap d'Aïl
✆ 0493 78 28 46
Email directeur@portcapdail.com
Chantier Naval ✆ 0492 10 60 00
Email info@cncda.com

Monaco

TIME ZONE UT+1 ✆ IDD +377

FONTVIEILLE
43°43'·7N 07°25'·4E
BA 2244, 2245 Imray M15
☆ Entrance Fl(2)R.6s10M/Fl(2)G.6s7M

VHF Ch 09 (summer 0800–2200, winter 0800–2000).

Navigation A reflected swell with strong onshore winds. Entrance difficult to see until close up.

Berths Must call on VHF in advance for a berth. Laid moorings tailed to the quay or finger pontoons.

Shelter Surge in outer part of the harbour with S gales.

Data 275 berths. 15 visitors' berths. Max LOA 30m. Depths 1·5–15m. Charge band 5.

Facilities Water. 220/380V. Showers and toilets. Provisions and restaurants.

Capitainerie ✆ 377 97 77 30 00 / 15
www.ports-monaco.com

PORT DE MONACO (PORT DE LA CONDAMINE, PORT HERCULE)
43°44'·18N 07°25'·92E WGS84
BA 2244, 2245 SHOM 7409 Imray M15
4·5M Beaulieu ←→ Menton 5M
☆ Floating mole (Port Hercule) E head Fl(3)R.15s8M. W head Fl(3)G.15s5M. S and N jetty Q.R/Q.G

VHF Ch 06, 12, 16 for port authorities. Ch 12 for pilot station and marina.

Navigation A reflected swell in the approach with strong onshore winds. Vessels leaving have priority.

Berths Must call on VHF in advance for a berth. Laid moorings tailed to the quay.

Shelter Good shelter with new outer breakwaters.

Data 700 berths. 30 visitors' berths. Max LOA 130m. Depths 2–25m. Charge band 6 (May–September).

Facilities Water. 220/380V. Showers and toilets. WiFi. Fuel quay. Pump-out. 15-ton travel-hoist. 10/20-ton cranes. 40/100-ton slipways. Some yacht repairs. Provisions and restaurants.

Remarks Usually full in the summer.

Capitainerie ✆ 377 97 77 30 00
Email info@ports-monaco.com
www.ports-monaco.com
Pilot station ✆ 377 93 15 85 77

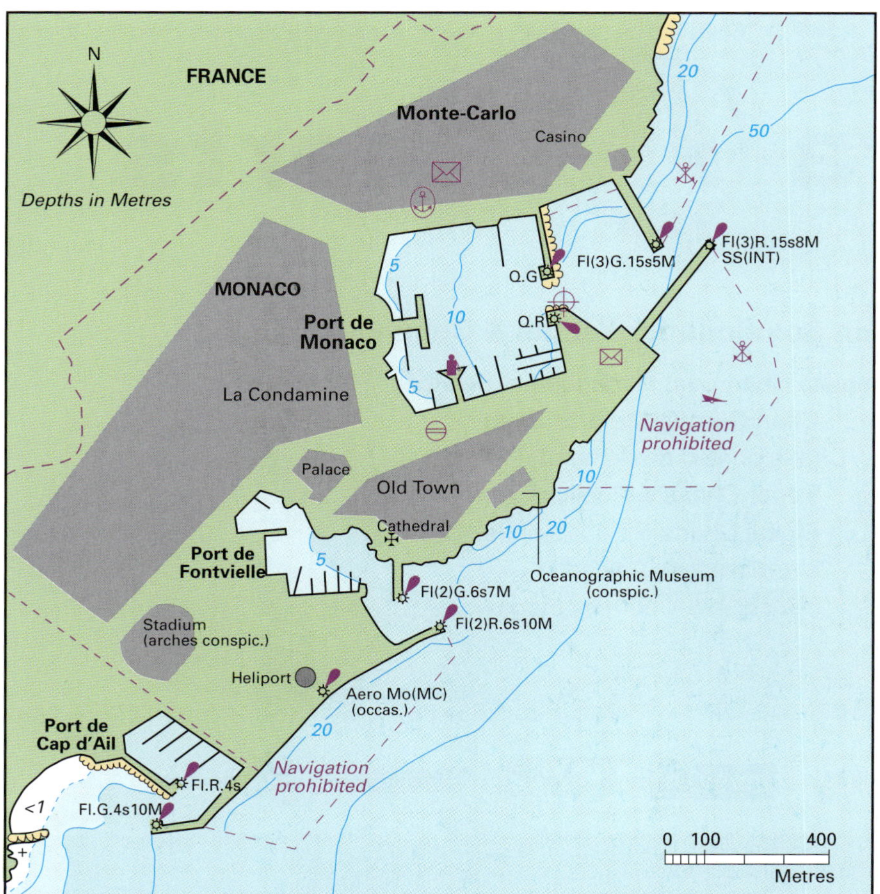

MONACO

MENTON VIEUX PORT

43°46′·58N 07°30′·69E WGS84
BA 2244, 2245 SHOM 7442
5M Monaco ←→ San Remo 13M
☆ Mole head VQ(4)R.3s10M

VHF Ch 09 (summer 0800–1200 / 1500–1900, winter 0800–1200 / 1400–1600).

Data 550 berths. 100 visitors' berths. Max LOA 25m. Depths 1·5–5m. Charge band 3/4.

Facilities Water. 220V. Showers and toilets. Fuel quay. Slipway. Provisions and restaurants.

Capitainerie ☽ 0493 35 80 56

MENTON-GARAVAN

43°47′·0N 07°31′·4E
BA 2244, 2245 SHOM 7017
☆ Entrance Fl.R.4s10M/Fl.G.4s2M

VHF Ch 09 (24/24).

Berths Report to the *capitainerie* for a berth. Laid moorings tailed to the quay.

Shelter Surge on visitors' pontoon in strong E winds.

Data 800 berths. 144 visitors' berths. Max LOA 40m. Depths 2–5m. Charge band 5.

Facilities Water. 220V. Showers and toilets. Fuel quay. 100/50-ton travel-hoist. 2-ton crane. 120-ton slipway. Most yacht repairs. Some provisions. Restaurants.

Port Menton Garavan ☽ 0493 28 78 00
Email
accueil@portdementongaravan.com

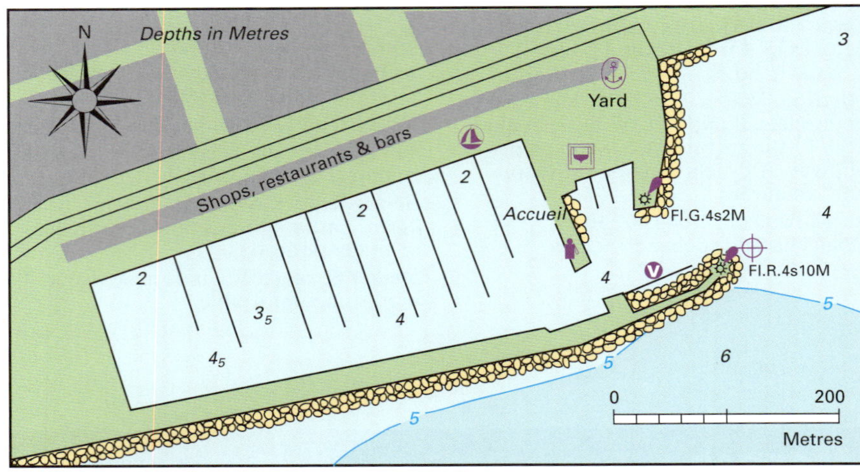

MENTON-GARAVAN

Corsica

Many anchorages in Corsica are now restricted for the purposes of protecting Posidonia seagrass beds. In many bays mooring buoys are now laid and yachts are encouraged to use these (charge band 2) rather than anchoring. Please note that the presence of these buoys does not necessarily mean the anchorage is suitable in all winds.

Resaport Berth Booking Service
You register, and pay an additional fee for each booking made. Covers most ports in Corsica. Bookings can be made over the internet or by phone. Open June–September 0800–2000.
✆ 08 20 42 26 00
www.resaportcorse.com

CALVI
42°33'·97N 08°45'·50E WGS84
BA 1425 SHOM 6980 Imray M6
4M Sant'Ambrogio ←→ Cargèse 35M

☆ Citadel Oc(2)G.6s8M. Commercial mole Q.G.8M. Marina entrance Fl.R.4s7M

VHF Ch 09 (summer 0700–2100, winter 0800–1200/1400–1800).

Navigation Strong gusts into the bay with W winds. Ferry turning area marked with yellow buoys.

Berths Stern or bows-to where directed. Laid moorings tailed to the quay or to buoys. Laid moorings in the bay (June–September).

Shelter Good shelter.

Data 450 berths. 200 visitors' berths. Max LOA 55m. Moorings max LOA 50m (40GRT). Depths 1·5–4m. Charge band 2 (moorings), 5/6 (berth).

Facilities Water. 220V. Showers and toilets. Fuel quay. 50-ton travel-hoist. 15-ton crane. Limited yacht repairs. Provisions and restaurants.

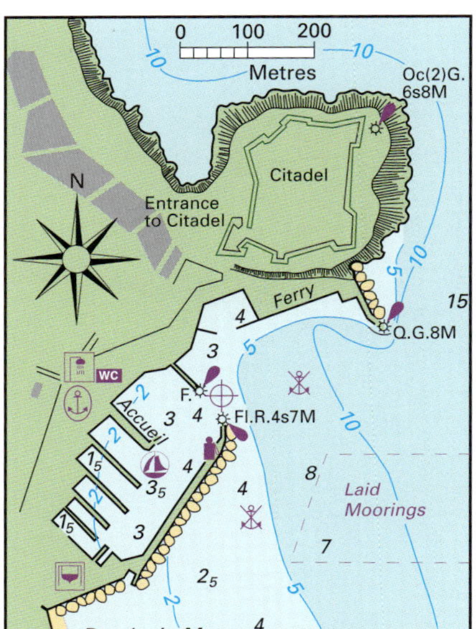

CALVI

CORSICA

Bureau du Port, 'Xavier Colonna'
☏ 0495 65 10 60
Email port-calvi@wanadoo.fr
Moorings VHF Ch 08 ☏ 0495 65 42 22
Email infos@aae-corse.com
www.villedecalvi.fr

GIROLATA

42°20'·7N 08°36'·8E

VHF Ch 09.

Berths Limited berths on pontoon. Mooring buoys in the bay (late May–September). No anchoring permitted.

☏ 0495 50 02 52
Email capitainerie-girolata@hotmail.fr

PORTO

42°15'·99N 08°41'·58E WGS84

Small basin with narrow entrance at Porto in Golfe de Porto. Entrance dangerous in onshore winds. Wooden dock running the length of the N side.

Data 150 berths. 30 visitors' berths. Depths 1–1·8m.

CARGESE

42°07'·86N 08°35'·87E WGS84
BA 1985 SHOM 7050
35M Calvi ←→ Ajaccio 24M

☆ Entrance Oc(3)WR.12s9/6M (325°-W-025°)/Fl(3)G.12s3M

VHF Ch 09 (summer only 0800–2000).

Navigation Care needed of the reef off Pte de Cargèse and the rock in the E approaches to the bay.

Berths Laid moorings tailed to the quay or finger pontoons. Care needed of concrete blocks laid on the bottom, which project above the sea floor, effectively reducing depths over them. Moor bows-to on the end of the outer breakwater. <1m depths S of the southernmost pontoon.

Shelter Good shelter.

Data 235 berths. 35 visitors' berths. Max LOA 15m. Depths 2–5m. Charge band 5.

Facilities Water (limited hours). 220V. Showers and toilets. Provisions and restaurants in the village.

Capitainerie ☏ 0495 26 47 24
Email capitainerie.cargese@wanadoo.fr

AJACCIO

41°55'·21N 08°44'·57E WGS84
BA 1424 SHOM 6851 Imray M6
24M Cargese ←→ Propriano 23M

☆ La Citadelle Fl(2)WR.10s20/16M (057°-W-045°). Ecueil de la Citadelle Fl(4)R.15s10m6M. Jetée de la Citadelle head Q.R.4s8M. Bassin de Charles Ornano head Fl(2)R.6s3M

VHF Ch 06, 12, 16 for port authorities. Ch 09 for Vieux Port (Port Tino Rossi) and Port de Charles Ornano (summer 0800–2100, winter 0800–1200, 1400–1800.)

Navigation Care needs to be taken of reefs and rocks fringing the coast in the approaches.

Berths Vieux Port Where directed on pontoons. Laid moorings at all berths.

Port Charles Ornano Visitors' berth on a pontoon along the outside of the breakwater (June–September). Laid moorings tailed to buoys. Helpful staff.

Shelter The new jetty S of the ferry quay should improve shelter to berths in the Vieux Port. Visitors' berths in Charles Ornano open to wash from all passing boats, but generally quiet at night.

Data Vieux Port (Port Tino Rossi) 260 berths. 100 visitors' berths. Max LOA 60m. Depths 4–10m. Charge band 5. *Port de Charles Ornano* 830 berths. 160 visitors' berths. Max LOA 35m. Depths 0·5–15m. Charge band 5/6.

Facilities Water. 220V. Showers and toilets. Fuel quay. 50-ton travel-hoist. 20-ton crane. Slipway. Some yacht repairs. Provisions and restaurants.

Bureau du Port de Port Tino Rossi
☏ 04 95 51 55 43 / 0495 21 93 28

Port de Charles Ornano, Capitainerie
☏ 0495 22 31 98

LA SCANDOLA MARINE RESERVE

Extends from Pointe Nero around Ile Gargalu S to Punta Rossa. Overnight anchoring is prohibited.

PROPRIANO (PORTU VALINCU)

41°40'·66N 08°54'·39E WGS84
BA 1424 SHOM 6851 Imray M6
23M Ajaccio ←→ Bonifacio 31M

☆ Scogliu Longu Oc(3)WG.12s15/12M (070°-W-097°, 137°-W-002°). Jetée Nord Iso.G.4s10M. Marina breakwater W end Fl(2)6s2m. Marina E entrance Fl(3)G.12s5m6M

VHF Ch 06, 16 for port authorities. Ch 09 for Port Valinco (summer 0800–2000, winter 0800–1200 / 1400–1800).

Navigation Entry difficult with strong W winds. Yachts should head directly for the the E entrance to the YC Valinco basin. The E basin was recently dredged to 3-4m.

Berths Stern or bows-to where directed. Laid moorings tailed to the quay or finger pontoons.

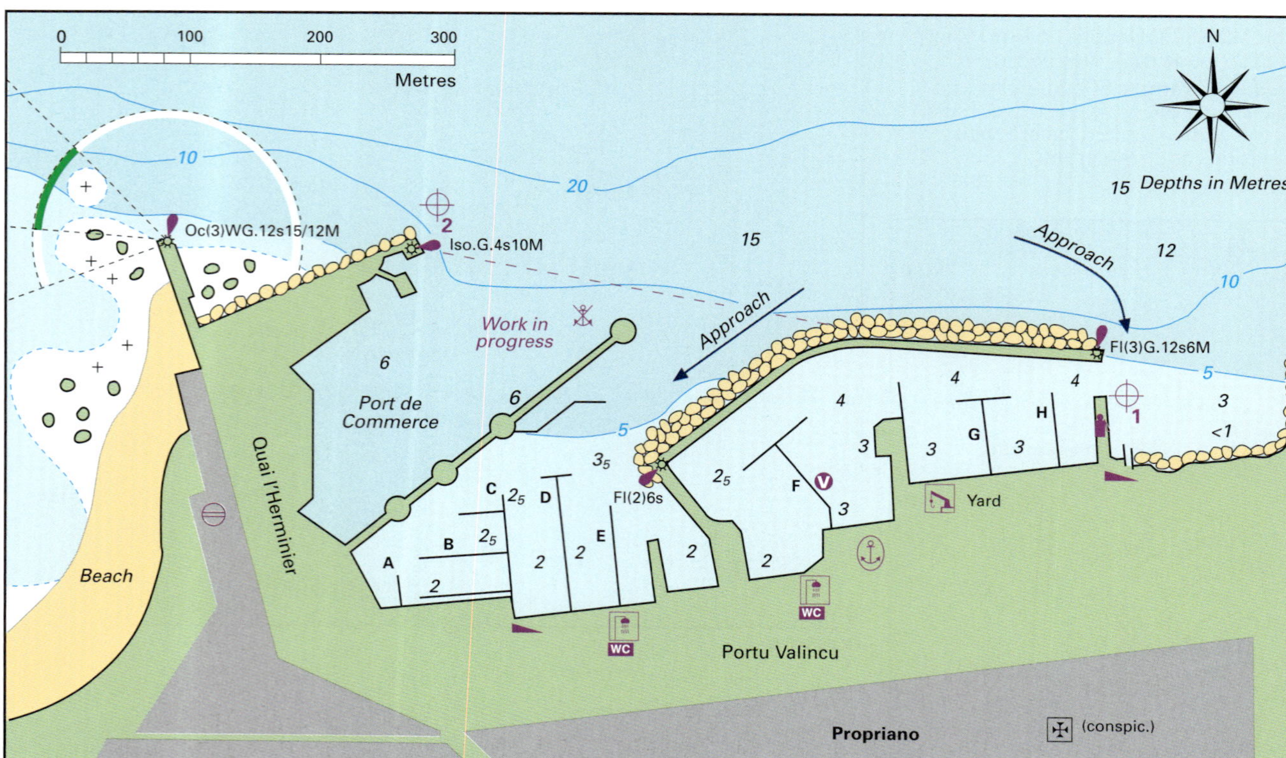

PROPRIANO

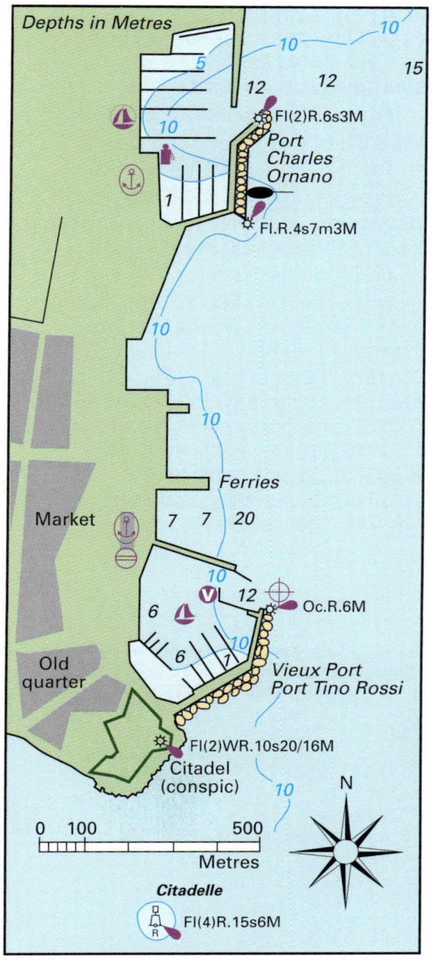

AJACCIO AND APPROACHES

Shelter Good shelter.

Data 420 berths. 40 visitors' berths. Max LOA 35m. Depths 2–5m. Charge band 5/6.

Facilities Water. 220V. Showers and toilets. Fuel quay. 12-ton lift. Limited yacht repairs. Provisions and restaurants.

✆ 0495 76 10 40
Email portuvalincu@orange.fr

PIANOTTOLI-CALDARELLO (BAIE DE FIGARI)

41°28'·5N 09°04'·4E

☆ Jetty head DirQ.WRG.7-6M

VHF Ch 09 (summer 0800–1200, 1400–2000, winter 0900–1200 / 1400–1700).

Navigation Situated at the head of Baie de Figari.

Data 150 berths. 70 visitors' berths. Max LOA 25m. Depths 1–8m. Charge band 4.

Facilities Water. 220V. Showers and toilets.

Bureau du Port ✆ 0495 71 83 57

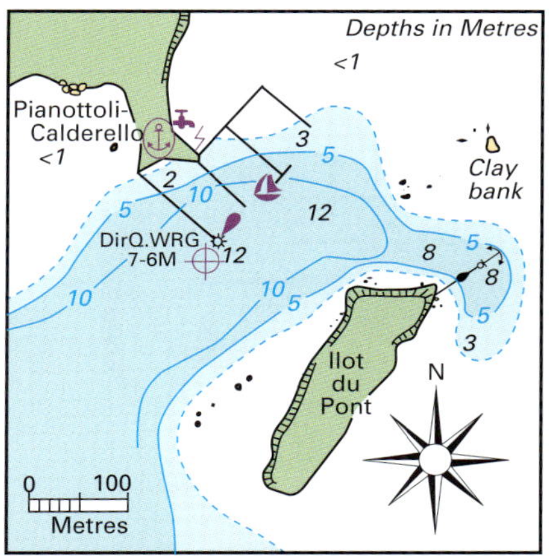

FIGARI: ILOT DU PORT AND PIANOTTOLI - CALDARELLO

BONIFACIO

41°23'·1N 09°08'·8E (Pte de la Madonetta light Iso.R.4s6M)
BA 1424 SHOM 7096
31M Propriano ←→ Porto Vecchio 25M

☆ Pte de la Madonetta Iso.R.4s6M. Pointe Cacavento Fl.G.4s5M. Punta di l'Arinella Oc(2)R.6s3M

VHF Ch 09 (summer 0700–2200, winter 0800–1200 / 1500–1800).

Navigation Entrance to the *calanque* difficult to see until close to.

Berths Stern or bows-to where directed. Laid moorings tailed to the quay or buoys. Supervised mooring with long lines ashore in Calanque de la Catena. Anchoring is prohibited.

Shelter Good shelter.

Data 450 berths. 170 visitors' berths. Max LOA 75m (48-hours notice required). Depths 2–12m. Charge band 5. *Calanque* 80 fore and aft moorings. Max LOA 16m. Charge band 2.

Facilities Water. 220V. Showers and toilets. Fuel quay. 40-ton travel-hoist. 10-ton crane. Limited yacht repairs. Provisions and restaurants.

Remarks Fuel berth suffers from tripboat wash. Care needed.

Bureau du Port de Plaisance
✆ 0495 73 10 07
Email port-bonifacio@wanadoo.fr
www.port-bonifacio.fr

BOUCHES DE BONIFACIO MARINE NATURE RESERVE

The reserve covers the area from Golfe de Roccapina to Punta di a Chiappa and includes Les Moines, Iles Lavezzi, Ile Perduto and Iles Cerbicale. Restriction on navigation and anchoring.

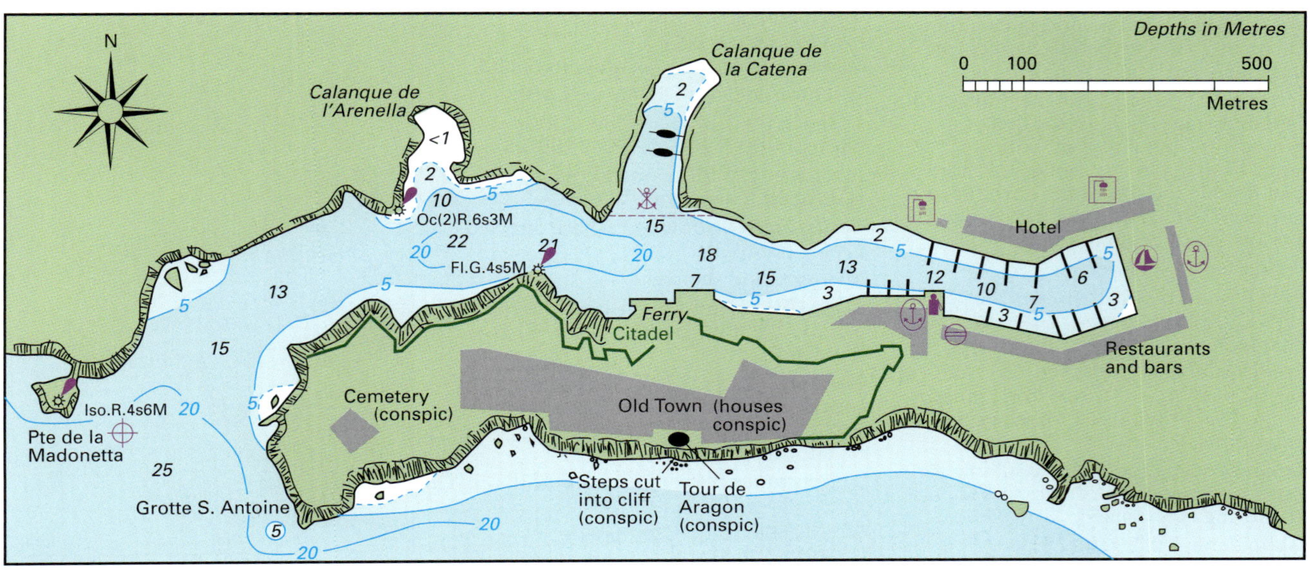

BONIFACIO

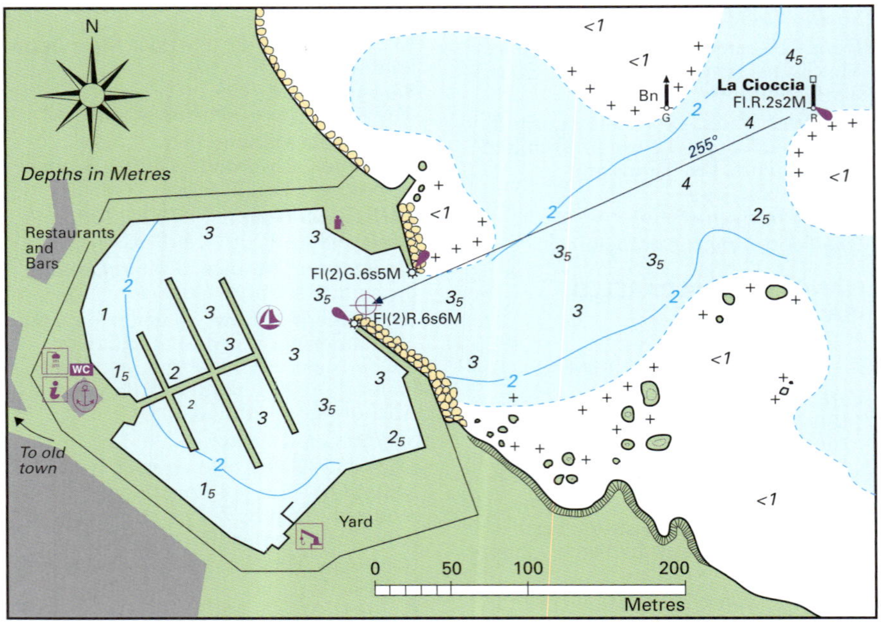

MARINA DE PORTO-VECCHIO

PORT DE TAVERNA

42°20'·44N 09°32'·49E WGS84
BA 1992 SHOM 6823
30M Solenzara ←→ Bastia 22M
☆ Entrance Fl.R.4s6M/Fl.G.4s2M

VHF Ch 09 (summer 0600–2200, winter 0800–1200 / 1400–1800).

Navigation Entrance to the port silts.

Berths Stern or bows-to where directed. Laid moorings tailed to the quay.

Shelter Good shelter.

Data 464 berths. 100 visitors' berths. Max LOA 25m. Depths 1·5–3m. Charge band 4/5.

Facilities Water. 220/380V. WiFi. Showers and toilets. Fuel quay. 50-ton travel-hoist. Some yacht repairs. Limited provisions. Restaurants.

Bureau du Port ✆ 0495 38 07 61
Email porttaverna@wanadoo.fr
www.port-taverna.com

PORT DE CAVALLO

41°21'·8N 09°15'·9E

VHF Ch 67

Navigation Entrance channel buoyed.

Data 240 berths. 35 visitors' berths. Max LOA 20m Depths 2·5–5m.

Facilities Water. 220V. Showers and toilets. Fuel. Mini-market.

MARINA DE PORTO VECCHIO

41°35'·39N 09°17'·16E WGS84
BA 1425 SHOM 6911
25M Bonifacio ←→ Solenzara 18M
☆ Rocher Pecorella Fl(3)G.12s6M. Punta San Ciprianu Fl.WG.4s11/8M (220°-W-281°/299°-W-072°). Commercial harbour DirIso.WRG.4s11-9M (208·5°-G-223·5°/223·5°-W-225·5°). La Cioccia Bn Fl.R.2s2M. Marina entrance Fl(2)R.6s6M/Fl(2)G.6s5M

VHF Ch 09 (summer 0800–2100, winter 0830–1200 / 1400–1730).

Navigation From La Cioccia beacon a course of 255° shows the channel free of dangers into the marina.

Berths Stern or bows-to where directed. Laid moorings tailed to the quay or buoys. Mooring buoys in Golfe de Santa Giulia. There are plans to more than double the size of the harbour in a new basin NE of the existing harbour. Work is yet to begin.

Shelter Good shelter.

Data 450 berths. 150 visitors' berths. Max LOA 40m. Depths 1·5–3m. Charge band 5/6.

Facilities Water. 220V. Showers and toilets. Fuel quay. 30/10/5-ton cranes. Limited yacht repairs. Provisions and restaurants.

Remarks Many moorings available for visitors around Golfe de Porto Vecchio. Anchoring is restricted.

Capitainerie ✆ 0495 70 17 93
Email port@porto-vecchio.fr

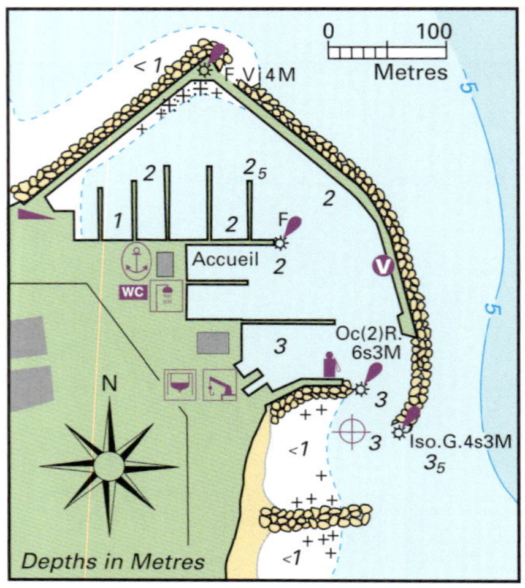

SOLENZARA

SOLENZARA

41°51'·49N 09°24'·24E WGS84
BA 1992 SHOM 6855
18M Porto Vecchio ←→ Campoloro 30M
☆ Entrance Oc(2)R.6s3M/Iso.G.4s3M

VHF Ch 09 (summer 0700–2000, winter 0800–1200 / 1400–1700).

Navigation With strong SE winds entry is difficult. Gusts with W winds.

Berths Stern or bows-to where directed. Finger pontoons.

Shelter Good shelter.

Data 450 berths. 150 visitors' berths. Max LOA 30m. Depths 1–3m. Charge band 4/5.

Facilities Water. 220V. Showers and toilets. Fuel quay. 27-ton hoist. Limited yacht repairs. Provisions and restaurants.

The entrance is dredged periodically to 3m.

Port de Solenzara, Capitainerie
✆ 0495 57 46 42
Email
capitaineriedesolenzara@wanadoo.fr

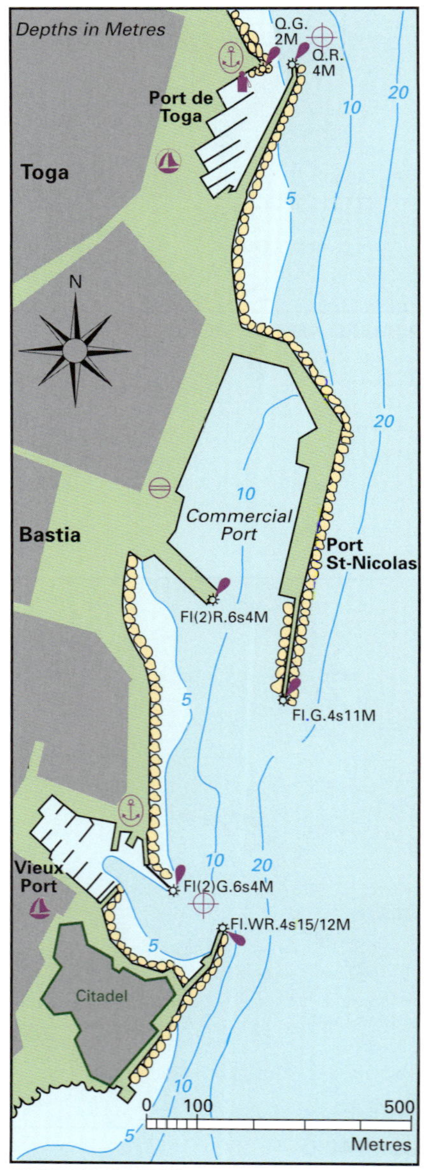

PORT DE BASTIA

BASTIA
42°41'·97N 09°27'·14E WGS84
BA 1425 SHOM 6856 Imray M6
22M Campoloro ←→ Macinaggio 17M

☆ Jetée du Dragon Fl.WR.4s15/12M (215°-W-325°). Mole Génois Fl(2)G.6s4M. Vieux Port entrance Fl(3)R.12s. Jetée St Nicolas Fl.G.4s11M. Ferry pier Fl(2)R.6s4M

VHF Ch 06, 11, 12, 16 for port authorities. Ch 09 for harbourmaster.

Navigation With strong E winds there is a confused sea at the entrance to the Vieux Port.

Berths Stern or bows-to where directed. Laid moorings tailed to buoys on the inside of the N breakwater.

Shelter Uncomfortable with moderate to strong winds from NE–E–SE.

Data 350 berths. 40 visitors' berths. Max LOA 12/30m. Depths 1–6m. Charge band 5/6.

Facilities Water. 220/380V. Showers and toilets. Fuel quay. 10-ton slipway. Limited yacht repairs. Provisions and restaurants.

CNB ☎ 0495 32 67 33

Capitainerie ☎ 0495 31 31 10
Email vieuxport-bastia@wanadoo.fr

PORT DE TOGA
42°42'·58N 09°27'·36E WGS84
BA 1425 SHOM 6856

☆ Entrance Q.R.4M/Q.G.2M

VHF Ch 09 (summer 0800–2200, winter 0800–1200 / 1400–1800).

Berths Report to the *capitainerie* for a berth. Laid moorings tailed to the quay.

Shelter Surge with strong N–NE winds.

Data 355 berths. 60 visitors' berths. Max LOA 25–30m. Depths 2·5–6m. 4m in entrance. Charge band 5.

Facilities Water. 220/380V. Showers and toilets. Fuel quay. Limited yacht repairs. Provisions and restaurants in town.

Port de Toga, Capitainerie
☎ 0495 34 90 70
Email port.toga@orange.fr

SANTA SEVERA
42°53'·26N 09°28'·53E WGS84

Data 80 berths. 20 visitors' berths. Max LOA 12m. Depths 1–3·5m.

MACINAGGIO
42°57'·70N 09°27'·29E WGS84
BA 1425 SHOM 6850 Imray M6
17M Bastia ←→ Saint-Florent 26M

☆ Entrance Fl(2)WR.6s11/8M (218°-W-331°)/Fl(2)G.6s2M

VHF Ch 09 (summer 0700–2100, winter 0800–1200 / 1400–1700).

Navigation With strong N–NE winds entry can be difficult and possibly dangerous.

Berths Stern or bows-to where directed. Laid moorings tailed to the quay.

Shelter Surge with strong NE–E winds.

Data 585 berths. 250 visitors' berths. Max LOA 30m. Depths 1–3·5m. Charge band 5/6.

Facilities Water. 220/380V. Showers and toilets. Fuel quay. 45-ton lift. 2-ton crane. Limited yacht repairs. Provisions and restaurants.

Bureau du Port ☎ 0495 35 42 57

CENTURI
42°58'·02N 09°20'·97E WGS84

☆ Jetty head Fl.G.4s6M. Pass entrance Fl.R.4s2M

Data 60 berths. Planned expansion to 125 berths. Max LOA 10m. Depths 1–2m.

☎ 0495 35 60 06

SAINT-FLORENT
42°40'·89N 09°17'·96E WGS84
BA 1999 SHOM 6850
26M Macinaggio ←→ Ile Rousse 20M

☆ Cap Fornali Fl.G.4s14m6M. Pte Vecchiaia Fl(3)WR.12s10/7M (174°-R-035°). Ecueil de Tignosu Fl.R.4s3M. Entrance Fl(2)WR.6s9/6M (080°-W-116°)/Fl(2)G.6s3M

VHF Ch 09 (summer 0700–2100, winter 0800–1200 / 1500–1800).

Navigation Strong N winds cause a confused sea in the approaches.

Berths Stern or bows-to where directed. Laid moorings tailed to the quay.

Shelter Good shelter.

Data 820 berths. 270 visitors' berths. Max LOA 45m. Depths 1–3m. Charge band 5/6.

Facilities Water. 220/380V. Showers and toilets. Fuel quay. 45-ton travel-hoist. 50-ton crane. Limited yacht repairs. Provisions and restaurants.

Bureau du Port ☎ 04 95 37 00 79
Email capitainerie.saintflo@wanadoo.fr

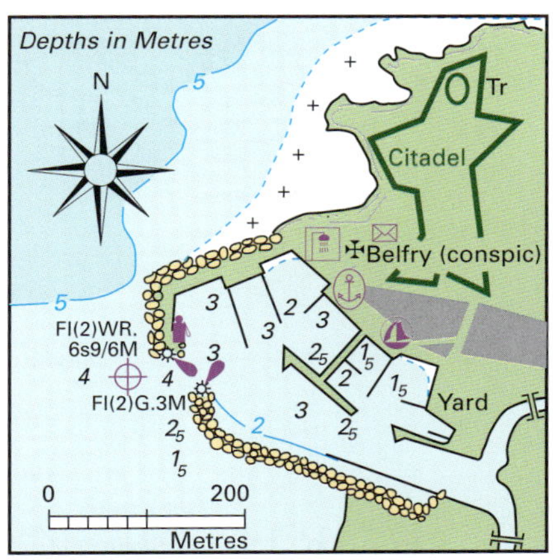

SAINT-FLORENT

ÎLE ROUSSE
42°38'·36N 08°56'·17E WGS84
20M Saint-Florent ←→ Calvi 10M

☆ Ile Rousse, La Pietra Fl(3)WG.12s14/11M (079°-W-234°). Port de Pêche Q(3)10s4M / VQ(3)5s3M. Jetty head Iso.G.4s12m8M.

VHF Ch 09 (summer 0700–2200, winter 0700–1800).

Data 250 berths. 85 visitors' berths. Max LOA 35m. Charge band 4.

Facilities Water. 220V. Showers and toilets. Fuel quay. Provisions and restaurants.

Port Abri de L'Ile Rousse
☎ 04 95 60 26 51

SANT'AMBROGIO
42°36'·1N 08°49'·8E

☆ Entrance Fl(2)G.6s7m3M / Fl(2)R.6s7m3M / Q.6M

Data 220 berths. Limited visitors' berths. Depths 1–2·5m. Charge band 4/5.

Capitainerie ☎ 04 95 60 70 88

10.4 Italy

TIME ZONE UT+1 ☏ IDD +39

Note Anchoring is prohibited anywhere around the coast within 200m of a beach, or within 100m elsewhere. This rule is often flouted, particularly during the high season, but it is a law which is increasingly being enforced, and can attract a fine of €350.

Quick reference guide *For Key to guide see page 139*

	Shelter	Mooring	Fuel	Water	Provisions	Eating out	Charge band
Italy							
Bordighera	B	A	B	A	B	B	3/4
Capo Pino	C	A	O	B	C	C	
San Remo	A	A	A	A	A	A	4
Marina degli Aregai	A	A	A	A	C	C	4
San Lorenzo	A	A		A	C	C	4
Porto Maurizio	B	A	A	A	A	A	4
Oneglia	B	AB	A	A	A	B	
Diano Marina	A	A	B	A	A	A	3
Marina di Andora	B	A	B	A	B	B	4/5
Alassio	A	A	A	A	O	C	5
Loano	B	A	A	A	A	A	5
Finale Ligure	A	A	B	A	O	C	4
Savona	A	AB	A	A	A	A	3
Varazze	A	A	A	A	B	A	6
Arenzano	A	A	O	A	B	B	4/5
Genoa	A	A	A	A	A	A	5/6
Nervi	C	A	O	O	B	B	
Camogli	B	A	A	A	B	A	
Portofino	B	AC	A	A	C	A	6+
Santa Margherita							
Ligure	A	A	A	A	A	A	
Rapallo	A	A	A	A	A	A	6
Chiavari	A	A	A	A	A	A	4
Lavagna	A	A	A	A	A	B	5
Sestri Levante	B	AC	A	A	A	A	
Vernazza	B	A	O	A	C	C	
Portovenere	A	A	B	A	C	B	6+
Le Grazie	B	AC	A	A	B	B	
Fezzano	B	A	B	A	O	C	5/6
La Spezia	A	A	B	A	A	A	4/6+
Porto Lotti	A	A	A	A	C	C	6+
Lerici	B	A	A	A	B	A	6+
Fiume Magra	A	AB	O	O	O	C	3/4
Isola Capraia							
Porto Capraia	A	A	A	A	C	C	5
Isola d' Elba							
Portoferraio	A	A	A	A	A	A	6
Esaom Cesa	A	A	O	A	O	O	6
Edilnautica	A	A	O	A	C	C	6
Cavo	B	A	A	A	C	C	
Rio Marina	C	A	B	A	C	C	5/6
Porto Azzurro	A	A	A	A	A	A	5/6
Marina di Campo	B	AB	B	A	B	A	5
Marciana Marina	B	A	A	A	B	A	6
Isola del Giglio							
Giglio	A	A	A	A	B	B	5
Mainland coast							
Marina di Carrara	B	A	A	A	B	B	3
Viareggio	A	A	A	A	A	A	6
Marina di Pisa	A	AB	A	A	B	B	5
Livorno	A	A	B	A	A	B	5
Marina Cala de Medici	A	A	A	A	A	B	6
Cecina Mare	A	A	A	A	O	C	4
San Vincenzo	A	A	B	A	B	B	6+
Porto Baratti	B	C	O	B	O	C	
Marina di Salivoli	A	A	A	A	B	B	5
Piombino	B	A	B	A	C	C	
Etrusca Marina	A	A	A	A	C	B	6
Punta Ala Marina	A	A	A	A	C	C	6
Castiglione della							
Pescaia	A	AB	A	A	A	A	3
Porto Turistico							
San Rocco	A	A	B	A	B	B	6
Talamone	B	A	A	A	B	B	4/5
Santo Stefano	B	A	A	A	A	A	6

	Shelter	Mooring	Fuel	Water	Provisions	Eating out	Charge band
Porto Ercole	B	A	AB	A	B	B	6
Cala Galera Marina	A	A	A	A	C	C	6
Civitavecchia	A	A	A	A	A	A	
Riva di Traiano	A	A	A	A	B	B	5
Santa Marinella	B	A	B	A	B	A	5/6
Fiumicino	A	AB	A	A	A	A	5
Fiumare Grande							
Darsena Netter	A	A	A	A	C	C	
Marina Porto Romano	A	A	A	A	C	B	5/6
Nautilus Marina	A	B	O	A	C	C	
Tecnomar	A	B	A	A	C	C	
Porto Turistico							
di Roma (Ostia)	A	A	A	A	A	A	5
Anzio	A	A	A	A	A	A	4
Nettuno	A	A	A	A	A	A	5
San Felice Circeo	A	A	A	A	C	C	6
Terracina	A	AB	A	A	A	A	
Gaeta Porto S Maria	B	A	B	B	B	B	
Base Náutica							
Flavio Gioia	A	A	A	A	A	B	6
Caposele	B	A	A	A	C	C	
Formia	B	A	A	A	A	B	4
Pontine Islands							
Ponza Harbour	B	A	A	A	B	A	6+
Ventotene Harbour	A	AB	B	B	C	B	5
Cala Rossano	B	AC	A	A	C	B	4/5
Bay of Naples							
Acquamorta	B	AC	O	O	O	C	
Porto Miseno	A	C	B	B	C	C	
Baia	B	A	A	A	C	C	4
Pozzuoli	A	A	A	A	B	B	5
Nisida	B	A	A	A	B	B	
Sannazzaro	A	A	A	A	B	B	6+
Santa Lucia	A	A	A	A	A	A	6+
Molosiglio	A	A	B	A	A	A	
Marina Vigliena	A	A	A	A	A	A	6+
Portici	B	A	B	A	B	C	
Torre del Greco	B	A	A	A	B	B	5
Torre Annunziata	B	A	A	A	A	B	
Marina di Stabia	A	A	A	A	A	A	6
Marina di Cassano	C	AC	O	O	C	C	
Sorrento	C	AC	A	A	A	A	
Procida							
Procida Marina	B	A	A	A	B	A	6
Chiaiolella	B	A	B	A	C	C	
Ischia							
Porto d'Ischia	A	A	A	A	A	A	6+
Casamicciola	B	A	B	A	A	A	6+
Forio d'Ischia	O	C	B	B	B	B	6
Capri							
Marina Grande	B	A	A	A	B	A	6+
Mainland coast							
Amalfi	C	A	A	A	B	B	6
Cetara	C	A	O	B	C	C	
Salerno	A	A	A	A	A	A	5
Agropoli	B	A	O	A	B	C	4
San Marco di							
Castellabate	C	B	O	A	C	C	
Acciaroli	B	AB	A	A	C	C	5
Palinuro	C	AC	O	O	C	C	4/5
Camerota	A	A	B	B	B	B	5
Scario	A	A	B	B	B	A	6
Policastro	B	A	O	A	O	O	
Sapri	A	AC	A	A	B	B	4
Maratea	A	A	B	A	B	A	5
Cetraro	C	A	O	B	C	C	5/6

	Shelter	Mooring	Fuel	Water	Provisions	Eating out	Charge band
Amantea	B	AB	A	A	C	C	
Vibo Valentia	A	A	A	A	B	B	3
Tropea	B	A	A	A	B	B	5/6
Gioia Tauro	A	ABC	O	B	O	O	
Bagnara Calabria	A	B	O	A	C	C	1/3
Scilla	C	A	B	A	B	B	2
Reggio Calabria	A	A	A	A	A	A	5
Sardinia							
N coast							
Ancora YC	B	A	O	A	C	B	
Stintino	A	A	A	A	B	B	5
Porto Torres	A	A	A	A	A	B	4/5
Castelsardo	B	A	B	A	A	B	3
Marina Isola Rossa	B	B	A	A	B	C	5
Santa Teresa	A	A	A	A	B	B	5
Porto Pollo	B	C	O	O	O	O	
Palau	A	A	B	A	B	A	5
Cannigione	A	AB	A	A	B	B	5/6
Poltu Quatu	A	A	A	A	C	C	6+
I. La Maddalena							
Cala Gavetta	A	A	A	A	A	A	5/6
Porto Massimo	A	A	O	A	C	C	6+
I. San Stefano							
Cala Villamarina	B	BC	O	O	O	O	
I. Porco	C	C	O	O	O	O	
Cala Coticcio	B	C	O	O	O	O	
Porto Garibaldi	B	C	O	O	O	O	
Porto Palma	A	C	O	B	O	O	
East coast							
Porto Cervo	A	AC	A	A	B	A	6+
Cala di Volpe	B	C	O	O	O	C	6
Marina di Portisco	A	A	A	A	C	B	6+
Porto Rotondo	A	A	A	A	C	B	6+
Punta Marana	A	A	A	A	C	C	
Golfo Aranci	C	AC	A	B	C	C	1/3
Baia Caddinas	A	A	O	A	O	C	
Olbia	A	AB	A	A	A	A	5/6+
Puntaldia	A	A	A	A	C	C	6+
Ottiolu	A	A	A	A	C	C	5
La Caletta	A	A	A	A	C	B	4
Cala Gonone	A	A	O	A	C	B	4
S Maria Navarrese	A	A	A	A	C	C	4/5
Arbatax	A	A	A	A	B	B	4
Porto Corallo	A	A	O	B	C	C	4
Villasimius	A	A	A	A	C	C	6
Marina de Capitana	A	A	A	A	C	C	5
South coast							
Marina Piccolo Poetto	A	A	A	A	A	A	4
Cagliari	A	A	A	A	A	A	5
Perd'e Sali	B	A	A	A	B	B	6
Porto Teulada	A	AC	O	A	C	C	5
Porto Ponte Romano	A	B	B	A	C	C	
West coast							
Calasetta	A	B	B	A	C	C	5
Carloforte	B	AC	A	A	B	A	5/6
Porto Vesme	B	B	B	B	C	C	
Portoscuso	A	A	B	A	B	C	4
Buggerru	B	AB	O	A	C	C	
Golfo di Oristano							
Porto d'Oristano	A	BC	O	O	O	O	
Marina Torregrande	A	A	A	A	O	C	4
Bosa Marina	B	AC	B	B	B	B	4
Alghero	A	A	A	A	A	A	5/6
Fertilia	A	A	B	A	C	C	5
Porto Conte	B	A	A	A	C	C	4/5

	Shelter	Mooring	Fuel	Water	Provisions	Eating out	Charge band
Sicily N coast							
San Vito Lo Capo	B	A	A	A	B	B	4
Castellammare del Golfo	B	A	B	A	B	B	4/5
Balestrate	B	AB	O	A	B	B	
Terrasini	B	AC	B	A	C	C	
Sferra Cavallo	C	AC	B	A	B	B	
Fossa del Gallo	B	A	A	A	C	C	
Mondello	B	A	B	A	B	A	
Addaura	C	A	A	A	C	C	
Arenella	A	A	B	B	B	B	6
Marina Villa Igiea	A	A	A	A	B	B	6
Palermo	A	A	A	A	A	A	5
Isola di Ustica							
Cala Sta Maria	B	AB	A	A	B	B	
Sicily N coast							
Porticello	A	A	B	A	B	C	
San Nicolo l'Arena	A	A	A	A	B	B	3
Termini Imerese	A	A	B	A	A	B	
Cefalù	B	AC	A	A	A	A	5
Sant' Agata	C	BC	O	B	C	C	
Capo d'Orlando	B	A	B	B	C	C	4
Portorosa	A	A	A	A	B	B	6
Marina del Nettuno Milazzo	B	A	A	A	A	B	6
Aeolian Islands							
Santa Marina Salina	B	A	A	A	C	C	6+
Rinella	C	AC	O	B	C	C	1
Malfa	C	AC	O	B	C	C	1
Marina Lunga	B	A	A	B	B	A	5/6
Pignataro	B	A	B	B	A	A	5
Marina Corta	B	B	B	A	B	A	
Marina del Nettuno Messina	B	A	A	A	A	A	6
Sicily E coast							
Naxos	C	AC	B	A	B	B	1/3
Riposto Porto dell'Etna	A	A	A	A	B	B	6
Acireale	C	A	B	A	C	C	
Acitrezza	B	A	B	A	B	B	4/5
Ognina	B	A	B	A	C	B	
Catania	A	A	A	A	A	A	3–4
Brucoli	A	BC	B	B	B	C	
Augusta	A	AB	A	A	B	C	
Siracusa Grand Harbour	A	AC	A	A	A	A	5
Porto Marmoreo	B	A	B	A	A	A	
Balata	B	AB	O	B	C	C	2
Marzameni	B	AC	B	A	C	C	4/5
Sicily S coast							
Porto Palo	B	BC	A	A	C	C	
Pozzallo	B	AB	B	B	C	C	
Ragusa	A	A	A	A	B	B	6
Gela	B	AB	B	B	B	B	
Licata	A	ABC	A	A	B	B	6
Marina di Palma	B	AB	O	B	C	C	
San Leone	A	A	A	A	B	C	5
Porto Empedocle	A	AC	A	A	B	B	3/4
Sciacca	B	A	A	A	B	B	5
Palo di Menfi	B	A	B	B	C	C	
Sicily W coast							
Mazara del Vallo	A	A	A	A	B	B	4
Marsala	B	AB	A	A	A	B	4/5
Isola Pantelleria							
Port Pantelleria	A	A	A	B	B	B	1/3
Scauri	A	A	O	B	C	C	1
Pelagie Islands							
Porto Lampedusa	A	AC	A	B	B	B	1
Isole Egadi							
Favignana	A	A	A	A	B	B	5

	Shelter	Mooring	Fuel	Water	Provisions	Eating out	Charge band
Sicily							
Trapani	A	A	A	A	A	A	5
The Ionian							
Saline Joniche	A	A	A	A	O	O	
Rocella Ionica	A	A	B	A	C	C	2
Catanzaro	C	C	B	B	B	C	1
Le Castella	B	A/B	B	B	C	C	3
Crotone	A/B	A	A	A	A	A	3/4
Ciro Marina	A	B	B	O	B	B	
Cariati	B	B	O	O	C	C	
Sibari Marina	A	A	A	A	B	B	3
Taranto	A	B	A	A	A	A	4
Campomarino	A	A	A	A	C	C	
Porto Cesareo	B	C	A	A	B	B	1
Gallipoli	A	A	A	A	A	A	5
Darsena Fontanelle	A	A	A	A	C	C	3
Sta Maria di Leuca	B	A	A	A	B	B	3
Adriatic							
Tricase	A	A	A	A	C	C	
Castro	C	A	O	B	C	C	
Otranto	B	A	A	A	A	B	3
San Foca	A	A/B	O	A	C	C	
Brindisi	A	A/B	A	A	A	A	3
Brindisi Marina	A	A	A	A	C	C	4
Villanova	A	A	B	A	B	B	
Savelletri	A	A	B	A	A	A	
Monopoli	A	A	B	A	A	A	
Mola di Bari	B	A	A	A	A	A	
Bari							
Bacino Grande	B	B	O	A	A	A	
Porto Vecchio	B	A/B	A	A	A	A	
Molfetta	B	A	B	A	A	A	
Bisceglie	B	B	A	A	B	A	3
Trani	B	A	A	A	B	A	4/5
Barletta	B	A/B	A	A	B	A	
Manfredonia	B	A/B	A	A	A	A	
Vieste	A	A/C	A	A	B	A	4/5
Termoli	B	A	A	A	A	A	5
Porto di Punta Penna	C	B	O	A	C	O	
Marina del Sole	B	A	A	A	C	C	5
Ortona	A	A/B	B	A	C	C	
Pescara	A	A	A	A	A	A	5
Giulianova	C	A	B	A	A	A	
San Benedetto del Tronto	B	A	A	A	A	A	4
Porto San Giorgio	A	A	A	A	A	A	4/5
Civitanova	B	A	A	A	A	A	
Numana	B	A	A	A	B	B	
Ancona Marina Dorica	B	A	A	A	A	A	5
Senigallia	A	A	A	A	A	A	4
Marina di Cesari	B	A	B	A	B	B	5
Pesaro	B	A	A	A	A	A	
Marina di Vallugola	A	A	A	A	B	B	3
Marina Porto Verde	A	A	A	A	O	B	5
Rimini Marina	B	A	A	A	A	A	
Cesenatico Marina Onda	A	A	A	A	A	A	5
Cervia Marina	A	A	A	A	B	B	5
Marina di Ravenna	B	A/B	A	A	A	A	5
Porto Garibaldi	A	A	A	A	A	A	5
Albarella	A	A	A	A	O	B	5
Brenta Boat Service	A	A/B	A	A	O	O	
Marina di Brondolo	A	A	A	A	O	C	3
Laguna Veneta							
Chioggia	B	A	B	A	B	B	4
Marina di Lio Grando	A	A	A	A	O	C	5
Sant'Elena	C	A/B	B	B	B	B	5
I. San Giorgio	C	A	A	A	B	B	5
Pta della Salute	C	C	O	C	A	A	6+
Piave Vecchia Marinas	A	A	A	A	C	B	5/6
P. Sta Margherita 4	A	A	A	A	B	B	5
P. Baseleghe	B	A	B	A	C	C	5
Marina Punta Verde	B	A	O	A	C	C	4
Marina Uno	A	A	A	A	C	B	4
Laguna di Marano							
M. Pta Faro	A	A	A	A	B	B	6
M. Pta Gabbiani	A	A	O	A	B	B	
Darsena Centrale	A	A	A	A	B	B	
Marina Stella	B	A	B	A	C	C	
Capan	A	A	B	A	B	B	
M. Sant'Andrea	A	A	B	A	B	B	
M. San Giorgio	A	A	A	A	B	B	5
P. San Vito	B	A	O	B	C	C	4
Monfalcone	B	A	A	A	B	A	5
Sistiana	B	A	O	B	C	C	
Marina San Giusto Trieste	B	A	A	A	A	A	5/6
Porto San Rocco Marina	B	A	A	A	C	C	5
San Bartolomeo	C	A	O	O	O	C	

Ligurian Coast

VENTIMIGLIA

43°47′·.3N 07°35′·85E

Ventimiglia lies on the E side of Capo Mortola, 3M beyond the border with France, at the mouth of the Roya river.

A new marina, Cala del Forte, on the site of the existing fishing harbour remains a work in progress.

Data (when marina completed) 350 berths. 50 visitors' berths. Max LOA 45m. Depths 2–6m.

✆ 340 185 9397
Email info@caladelforteventimiglia.it
www.caladelforte-ventimiglia.it

BORDIGHERA

43°46′·8N 07°40′·7E
BA 1974 It 909 Imray M16

☆ Mole 2F.R(vert)3M

VHF Ch 16, 09 (0700–1900). CB Ch 02.

Navigation A small harbour on the E side of Capo Ampeglio.

Berths There is sometimes room on the pontoon alongside the breakwater at the entrance though this is not always comfortable.

Data 250 berths. Max LOA 20m. Depths 2–5m. Charge band 3/4.

Facilities Water. 220V. Provisions and restaurants.

Remarks The Marina di Sant'Ampeglio project to expand the harbour is yet to begin.

Port Authority ✆ 0184 265 656 / 266 688

MARINA BAIA VERDE

43°47′·9N 07°42′·8E

Navigation A new marina under construction between Bordighera and Capo Pino.

Data When completed, 390 berths. Max LOA 33m.

Facilities Water. 220/380V. WiFi. Showers and toilets. Pump-out. Fuel quay. Boatyard with travel-lift, hardstanding and undercover storage is planned.

✆ 0184 292 308

CAPO PINO

43°47′·8N 07°44′·6E

☆ Entrance F.R.3M/F.G.3M

SAN REMO

43°48′·9N 07°47′·3E
BA 351 It 51 Imray M15
13M Menton ←→ Porto Maurizio 12M

☆ Capo dell'Arma Fl(2)15s24M. Entrance LFl.R.5s8M/LFl.G.5s4M. Porto Communale entrance F.G.4M/ F.R.2M. Porto Sole entrance F.G.2M/F.R.2M

VHF Porto Communale Ch 12, 14, 16 (summer 24/24, winter 0700–1900). Porto Sole Ch 09, 16. CB Ch 02. YC San Remo Ch 12.

Navigation A yacht can choose between the marina (Porto Sole) to the E or the Porto Communale to the W.

Berths Where directed in Porto Sole. Laid moorings tailed to the quay. Porto Communale is always crowded. Visitors' berths on the S breakwater outside the fuel berth.

Shelter Good all-round in Porto Sole. S winds cause a surge in Porto Communale.

Data *Porto Communale* 400 berths. 15 visitors' berths. Max LOA 30m. Depths 1–7m. *Porto Sole* 800 berths. 90 visitors' berths. Max LOA 80m. Depths 2·5–7·5m. Charge band 4.

Facilities Water. 220/380V. WiFi. Showers and toilet. Telephone. Fuel quay. 27-ton travel-hoist. 12-ton crane. 750-ton platform lift and slipways. All yacht repairs. Provisions and restaurants.

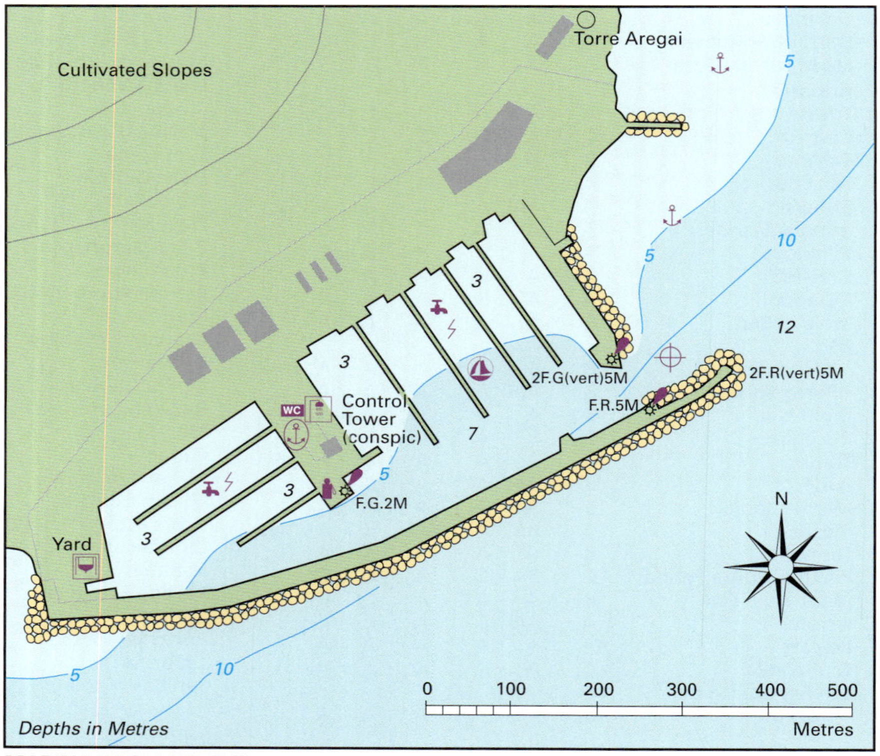

MARINA DEGLI AREGAI

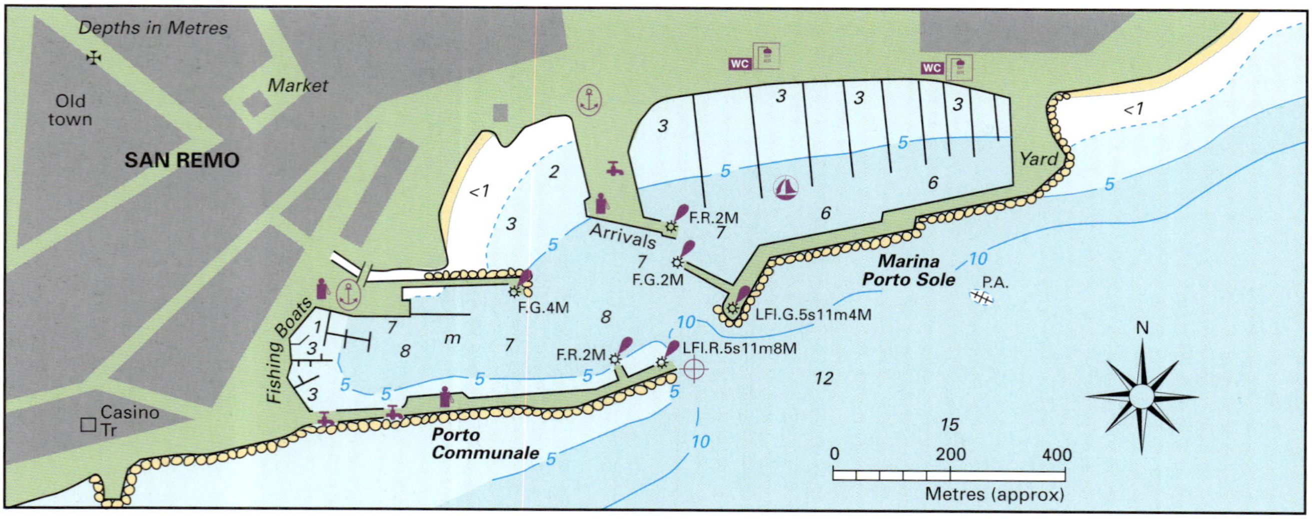

SAN REMO-PORTO COMMUNALE AND MARINA PORTO SOLE

Porto Sole ☎ 0184 5371
Email info@portosolesanremo.it
www.portosolesanremo.it
Porto Communale ☎ 0184 505 531
YC Sanremo ☎ 0184 502 023

ARMA DI TAGGIA
43°49'·9N 07°52'·51E
☆ Outer entrance 2F.G(vert)3M/ 2F.R(vert)3M. Inner F.G.1M/F.R.1M

MARINA DEGLI AREGAI
43°50'·35N 07°55'·00E
BA 1974 It 101 Imray M16
☆ Outer mole 2F.R(vert)5M. Inner pier F.R.5M. Inner mole 2F.G(vert)5M. Inner pier F.G.2M
VHF Ch 09.
Berths Report to the harbourmaster for a berth.
Data 990 berths. 74 visitors' berths. Max LOA 40m + one x 70m. Depths 3–10m. Charge band 4.
Facilities Water. 220/380V. WiFi. Showers and toilets. Launderette. Fuel quay. 100-ton travel-hoist. Some yacht repairs. Covered hard standing. Mini-market. Restaurant.
Marina Degli Aregai, Porto Turistico
☎ 0184 4891
Email info@marinadegliaregai.it
www.marinadegliaregai.it

SAN LORENZO AL MARE
43°51'·3N 07°58'·2E
A marina by the same consortium as the Ventimiglia project opened in 2008.
Navigation The marina lies close N of the small shallow fishing harbour, approximately halfway between Marina Degli Aregai and Imperia. A church is conspicuous on a small promontory between the harbour and the marina.
VHF Ch 09.
Data 360 berths. 36 visitors' berths. Max LOA 20m. Depths 3–4·5m. Charge band 4.
Shelter The marina provides good all-round shelter, although entry may be difficult with strong onshore winds.
Facilities Water. 220V. Pump-out. Fuel dock. Some repairs.
Marina di San Lorenzo al Mare
☎ 0183 9352
Email info@marinadisanlorenzo.it
www.marinadisanlorenzo.it

PORTO MAURIZIO (IMPERIA)
43°52'·49N 08°01'·75E WGS84
BA 1974 It 101 Imray M16
12M San Remo ←→ Marina di Andora 6·5M
☆ Breakwater elbow Iso.4s16M. Breakwater ends Fl.R.3s8M/ Fl.G.3s8M. Spur head Fl.R.3s3M. Inner basin F.R.3M
VHF Ch 16, 09. CB Ch 26.
Navigation Major works now completed.

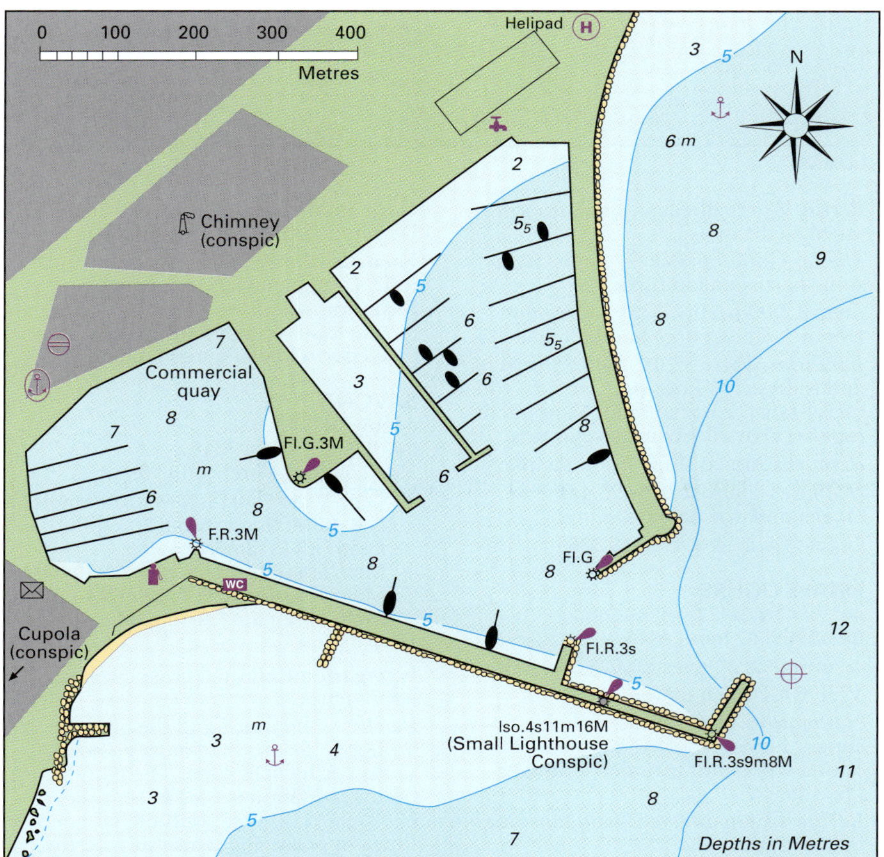

PORTO DI IMPERIA

Berths Stern or bows-to. Laid moorings tailed to the quay.
Shelter Adequate but uncomfortable with SE winds.
Data 1,300 berths. 35 visitors' berths. Max LOA 90m. Depths 2–8m. Charge band 4.
Facilities Water. 220V. Shower and toilet block. Fuel quay. 50-ton travel-hoist. 50-ton slipway. 4/5-ton cranes. Most yachts repairs. Provisions and restaurants.
Port Turistico ☎ 0183 60977 / 0183 667 453
Email ormeggiatori@portodimperia.it
www.portodimperia.it
Port Authority ☎ 0183 666 333

ONEGLIA
43°53'·02N 08°02'·46E WGS84
BA 1974 It 101
☆ Entrance Fl(2)G.6s14m8M / Fl(2)R.6s9m8M
VHF Ch72 for Imperia Yacht
Berths On the quay in the old commercial harbour. 12 superyacht berths. Max LOA 75m. Depth 7-10m. Laid moorings. Water. 220/380V.
☎ 0183 752 900 or 334 287 2273
www.imperiayacht.it

DIANO MARINA
43°54'·53N 08°05'·16E WGS84
☆ F.G.3M/F.R.3M
VHF Ch 16. CB Ch 15.
Navigation Care needed as expansion work is due to start in the W basin.
Data 270 berths (550 when expansion project complete). 10 visitors' berths. Max LOA 15m. Depths 1–2m. Charge band 3.
Port Authority ☎ 0183 753 024
Email porto@gestionimunicipali.com
Circolo Nautico ☎ 0183 494 636

SAN BARTOLOMEO AL MARE
43°55'·23N 08°06'·32E WGS84
☆ Mole head Fl.R.3s5M. Inner mole head Fl.G.3s5M
Porto turistico ☎ 0183 40921
Email info@sanbart.it

MARINA DI ANDORA
43°57'·04N 08°09'·56E WGS84
BA 1998 It 01 Imray M16
6·5M Porto Maurizio ←→ Alassio 5·5M
☆ Capo delle Mele Fl(3)15s24M. Entrance Fl.R.3s5M/F.R/Fl.G.3s5M
VHF Ch 16, 09 (0800–1900). CB Ch 32.
Berths Stern or bows-to. Mostly laid moorings tailed to the quay.
Shelter Adequate except with strong SE winds which send a reflected swell in.
Data 800 berths. Max LOA 18m. Depths <1–4m. Charge band 4/5.
Facilities Water. 220V. 25-ton crane. Provisions and restaurants.
Harbourmaster ☎ 0182 88313/85165
Email info@portodiandora.it
Port Authority ☎ 0182 88899
Circolo Nautico ☎ 0182 86546 / 86106

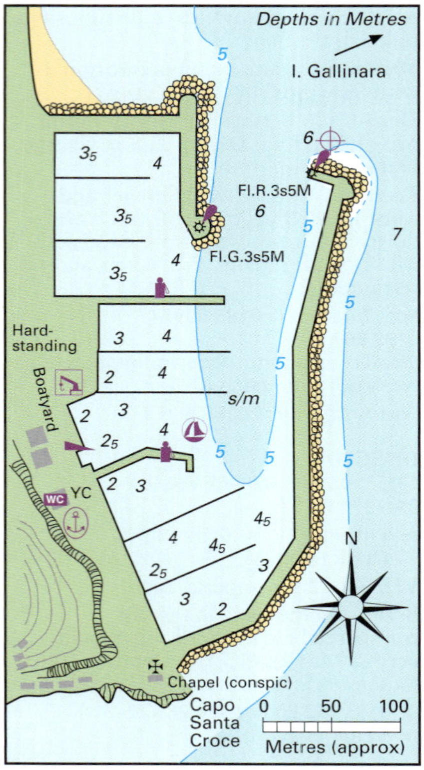

ALASSIO

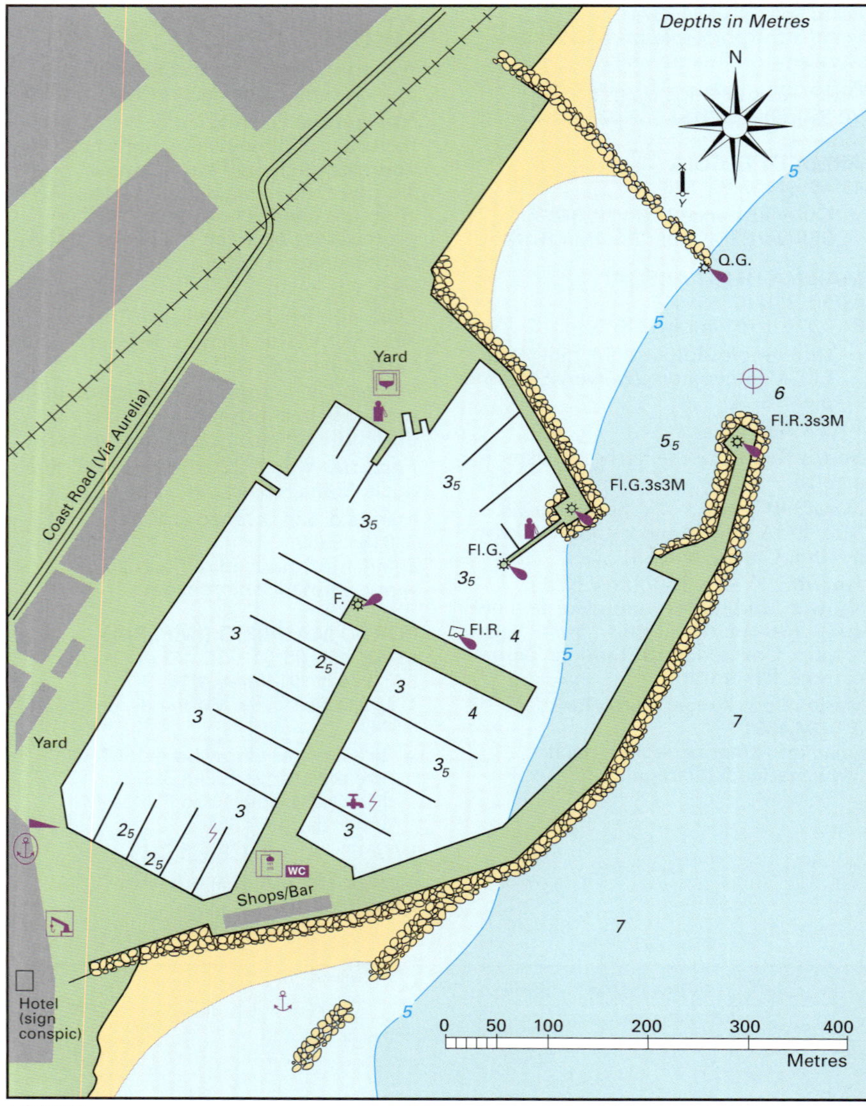

LOANO

ALASSIO

44°01′·15N 08°11′·68E WGS84
BA 1998 It 02 Imray M16
5·5M Marina di Andora ←→ Loano 8M

☆ Entrance Fl.R.3s5M/Fl.G.3s5M. T-pier head F.R.2M

VHF Ch 09, 16, 25 (0900–1200/ 1500–1800).

Navigation Care needed off extremity of the mole where the ballasting extends under water.

Berths Call ahead for a berth. Where directed. Laid moorings tailed to the quay.

Shelter Good shelter.

Data 400 berths. Visitors' berths. Max LOA 30m. Depths 2–5m. Charge band 5.

Facilities Water. 220V. Showers and toilets. Fuel quay. 30-ton crane. Some yacht repairs. Restaurant. ATM.

Marina di Alassio ✆ 0182 645 012
Email info@marinadialassio.net

Port Authority ✆ 0182 640 861

Circolo Nautico ✆ 0182 642 516

GALLINARA ISLAND

44°01′·6N 08°13′·5E (F.R)

☆ F.R.3M/F.G.3M

Data Depths 1–4·5m.

LOANO

44°08′·25N 08°16′·15E WGS84
BA 1998 It 02 Imray M16
8M Alassio ←→ Savona 15M

☆ Entrance Fl.R.3s3M/Fl.G.3s3M. Old inner mole Q.G.3M. Barrier Fl.Y.3s2M x 2.

VHF Ch 16, 09 (Porto Loano).

Navigation Care needed of works in progress outside the harbour.

Berths Where directed. Laid moorings tailed to the quay.

Shelter Good but NE–E winds make some berths uncomfortable.

Data 1,000 berths. Max LOA 65m. Depth 3-5m. Charge band 5.

Facilities Water. 220V. WiFi. Showers and toilets. TV. Fuel quay. 550/70-ton travel-hoist. 25-ton crane. Most yacht repairs. Provisions and restaurants.

Remarks Amico shipyard in the marina.

Marina di Loano ✆ 019 675 445
Email info@marinadiloano.it

Circolo Nautico ✆ 019 668 836

FINALE LIGURE

44°10′·41N 08°22′·13E WGS84
BA 1998 It 02 Imray M16

☆ Entrance 2F.R(vert)3M/2F.G(vert)3M

VHF Ch 16, 09, 69 (0600–1900).

Navigation The entrance is liable to silting. Latest reported depths 2–2·5m. Silting will continue unless dredging takes place.

Berths Where directed. Laid moorings tailed to the quay.

Shelter Good all-round shelter.

Data 550 berths. Max LOA 18m. Depths 2–2·5m. Charge band 4.

Facilities Water. 220V. Showers and toilets. Fuel quay. 25-ton crane. Restaurants.

Circolo Nautico ✆ 019 601 640
Email porto.finaleligure@tin.it

SAVONA

44°18′·8N 08°30′·3E
BA 350 It 53 Imray M16
15M Loano ←→ Arenzano 10M

☆ Capo Vado Fl(4)15s14M. Outer mole Fl.R.4s8M. Nuovo Molo Frangiflutti head Fl.R.2s12m8M.
Molo Frangiflutti head Fl.Y.3s10m4M.
Molo Sottoflutto Fl.G.2s9m7M.
Molo Miramare F.G.10m3M

VHF Ch 09, 16 (24/24).

Navigation Reflected cross swell in S approaches.

Berths Assonautica and the port authority co-ordinate most visitors' yacht berths in Savona. There are berths in Miramare, a YC near the coastguard offices; pontoon Santa Lucia opposite the cruise ship berths; and berths in the Darsena Vecchia.

Note Yachts must wait for the lifting bridge to open at the entrance to the Darsena Vecchia.

The bridge opening times are:
Monday–Friday: Every hour, on the half-hour ie 0630, 0730, 1730, 1830.
Saturday–Sunday: Every half-hour ie 0700, 0730, 0800
Yachts may call ahead to request opening on VHF Ch 09.

Stern or bows-to in Darsena Vecchia. Laid moorings.

Shelter Excellent all-round shelter in the Darsena Vecchia. Some other berths can suffer from wash from passing ships in the harbour.

Data 300 berths. 25 visitors' berths. Max LOA 20m. Depths 4–9m.

Facilities Water. Fuel near YC. 24-ton crane. Provisions and restaurants. Boatbuilders, haul-out and technical services. W-Service (at the entrance to Darsena Nuova).

Note Work in progress on Molo Frangiflutti and the outside commercial basin.

W-Services ☏ 019 848 5379
Email sales@wsrefit.com.com
www.wsrefit.com

Assonautica (Darsena Vecchia)
☏ 019 821 451
Email info@assonauticasavona.it
www.assonauticasavona.it

Savona Port Authority SV Port Services
☏ 019 855 4345
Email svport@portosavona.net
www.porto.sv.it

Lega Navale ☏ 019 854 383

VARAZZE

44°21'·16N 08°34'·27E WGS84
BA 1998 It 909 Imray M16
☆ 2F.R(vert)3M/F.R.3M/F.G.3M

VHF Ch 16, 09.

This marina lies on the N side of Capo dell'Olmo, close W of Varazze town.

Data 800 berths. 70 visitors' berths. Max LOA 35m. Depths 3·5–6m. Charge band 6 (June–September).

Berths Go stern or bows-to where directed. Laid moorings tailed to the quay. Motor boats will use the S side of the marina, and sailing yachts will be directed to berths to the N of C pier.

Shelter There looks to be excellent all-round shelter in the marina.

Facilities Water. 220/380V. Telephone and TV connections. WiFi. Showers and toilets. Fuel quay. 100-ton travel-lift. Hard-standing and covered storage facilities. Most repairs can be arranged. Sailmaker. Chandler. Provisions and restaurants in Varazze town, about 10 minutes walk from the marina. PO. Banks. ATMs. Italgaz and Camping Gaz. Bus and train to Genoa.

Marina di Varazze
☏ 0199 35321
Mooring ☏ 338 364 1506
Fuel ☏ 335 609 7540
Email olga.grassi@marinadivarazze.it
www.marinadivarazze.it

ARENZANO

44°23'·98N 08°41'·22E WGS84
BA 1998 It 909 Imray M16
10M Savona ←→ Genoa E entrance 11M
☆ F.R.3M/F.G.3M

VHF Ch 09.

Navigation An above-water sand bank extends from the extremity of the outer E mole across part of the entrance. Four small conical buoys show the channel.

Berths Where directed. Laid moorings tailed to the quay.

Shelter Good all-round shelter.

Data 186 berths. Max LOA 18m. Depths 1·5–4m. Charge band 4/5.

Facilities Water. 220V. Showers and toilets. 20-ton crane. Restaurants.

Harbourmaster ☏ 010 912 5172
Email posta@portodiarenzano.it

GENOA

44°23'·3N 08°56'·3E (Fl.R.4s15M)
BA 351, 354, 355 It 54, 55, 106 Imray M16
11M Arenzano ←→ 9M Camogli
☆ Lanterna Fl(2)20s25M+Aero
Oc.R.1·5s10M. Diga Aeroporto W end
Oc.3s12M. Diga Cornigliano E end
Fl.R.2s7M. Diga Foranea W end
Q.G.5M. Diga Foranea spur
Fl.G.1·5s2M. E entrance
Fl.R.3s15M/Fl.R.3s7M/Fl.G.4s7M/
Fl.G.3s8M. Genovo-Nervi Marina outer mole head 2F.R(vert)3M

VHF Ch 11, 16 for *capitaneria* (0700–1900).
Ch 67 for Lega Navale Sestri Ponente
Ch 69 for Cantieri Navali di Sestri
Ch 16, 11 (0700–1900) for Abruzzi.
Ch 74 (0830–1830) for MA. RI. NA Service Fiera di Genova.
Ch 74 for Marina Porto Antico.
Ch 71 for Marina Molo Vecchio and Marina Genova Aeroporto.

Navigation With strong onshore winds there is a reflected swell off the two long breakwaters. At either entrance there can be a confused swell. Off Diga Aeroporto there are two oil bunkering stations with floating hoses around

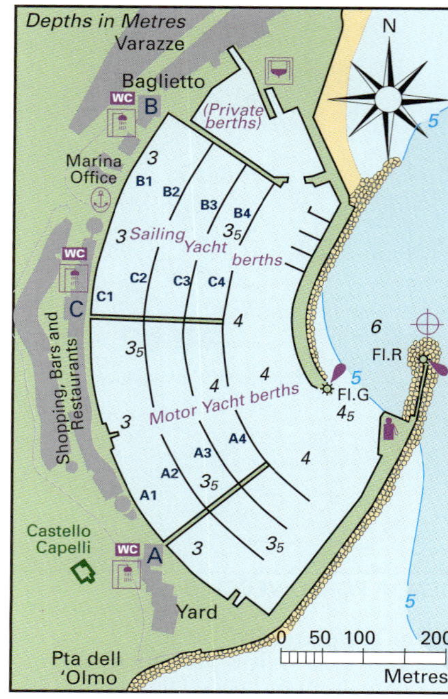

MARINA DI VARAZZE

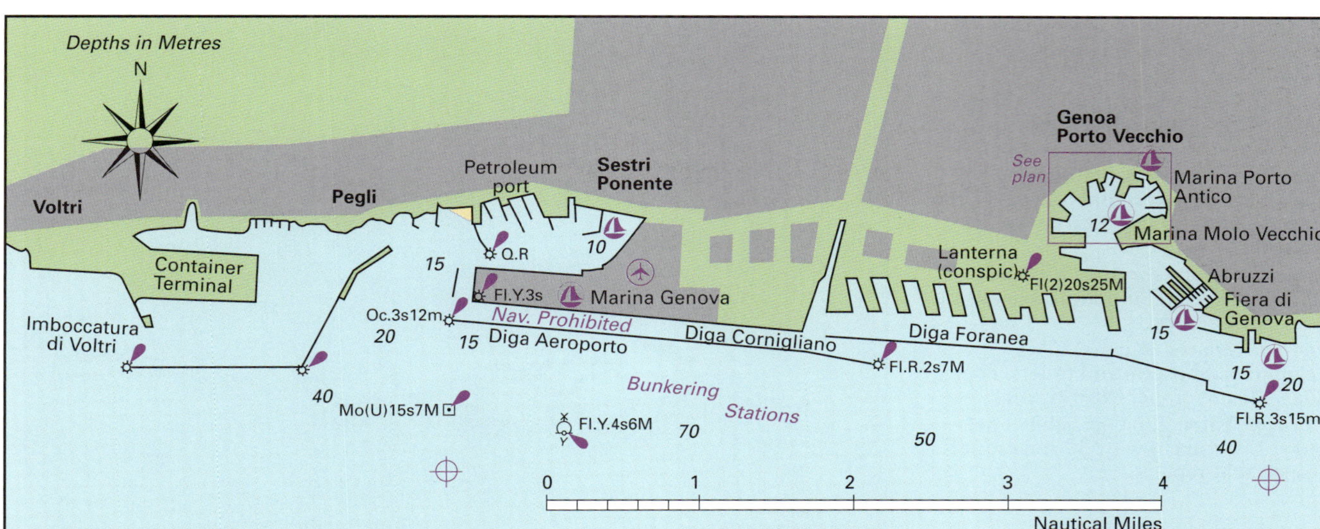

GENOA APPROACHES

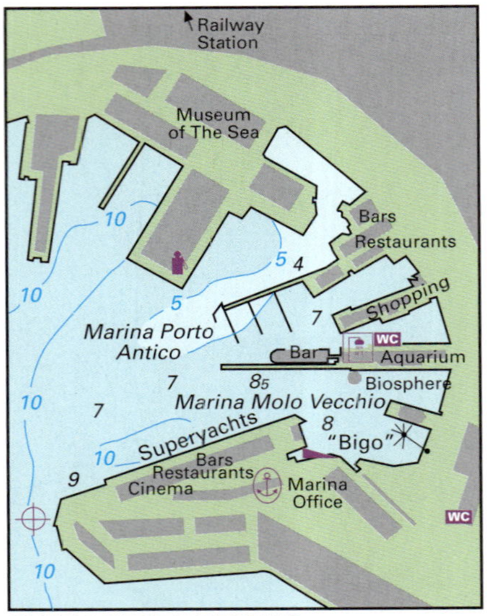

GENOA PORTO VECCHIO

them. The platforms are lit: Mo(U)Y.15s7M. It is prohibited to navigate or moor inside Diga Aeroporto.

Note Vessels with air height over 4m must keep close to the Voltri breakwater when approaching Sestri Ponente. From the end of the breakwater head towards the elbow of the Sestri Ponente N breakwater, then S across to the S breakwater and along to the marina. Keep clear of commercial vessels at all times.

Berths There are five possibilities ranging from Sestri Ponente at the W end to Abruzzi, Fiera di Genova, Marina Porto Antico and Marina Molo Vecchio, the last four in, or near, the centre of Genoa.

Data *Sestri Ponente* 1,200 berths. Max LOA 40m. Depths 2·5–8m. Charge band 4/5.

Marina Genova Aeroporto 500 berths. Max LOA 125m. Depths 8–15m. Charge band 6.

Fiera di Genova 450 berths. Max LOA 25m. Depths 4–7m. Charge band 5.

Abruzzi 300 berths. Max LOA 30m. Depths 6–7m.

Marina Porto Antico 285 berths. Max LOA 40m. Depths 4·5–6m. Charge band 5/6.

Marina Molo Vecchio 160 berths. Max LOA 150m. Depths 9–11m. Charge band 5/6.

Facilities *Sestri Ponente* Water. 220V. Telephone. Showers and toilets. 55-ton crane. Yachts up to 320-tons can be hauled.

Marina Genova Aeroporto Water. 220/380V. WiFi. Pump-out. Fuel dock. Boatyards nearby.

Fiera di Genova Water. 220V. Telephone. Showers and toilets. Fuel quay. 40-ton crane. Most repairs.

Abruzzi Water. 220V possible. Fuel quay. 150-ton slipway. 30-ton crane. Some yacht repairs.

Marina Porto Antico Water. 220/380V. Showers and toilets. Fuel arranged. 30-ton crane.

Marina Molo Vecchio Water. 220/380V. Telephone. Satellite TV. WiFi. Showers and toilets. Fuel arranged. 300-ton travel-hoist. All yacht repairs.

Sestri Ponente Lega Navale
✆ 010 651 2654

Cantieri Navali di Sestri ✆ 010 651 2476
www.cantierisestri.it

Marina Genova Aeroporto
✆ 010 614 3420
Email info@marinagenova.it
www.marinagenova.it

MA.RI.NA Service Marina Fiera
✆ 010 580 760
Email marinaservice@libero.it

Abruzzi Yacht Club Italiano
✆ 010 246 1206
Email info@yci.it

Marina Porto Antico
✆ 010 247 0039
Email porto@marinaportoantico.it
www.marinaportoantico.it

Marina Molo Vecchio
✆ 010 27011 / 340 244 6652
Email mmv@mmv.it
www.mmv.it

Pesto Yacht & Ship Agency
✆ 010 270 1305
Email pesto@pesto.it
www.pestoseagroup.com

Amico & Co.
✆ 010 247 0067
Email amico.yard@amicoshipyard.it
www.amico.it

CAMOGLI

44°21'·1N 09°09'·0E
BA 1998 It 107 Imray M16
9M Genoa E entrance ←→ Portofino 6M

☆ Outer mole head Fl.3s9M. Inner basin Fl.G.5s3M/Fl.R.5s3M. Fuel pier F.GR(vert)3M

Navigation Entrance difficult and possibly dangerous with onshore gales. Care needed of reefs and shoal water off the breakwater.

Berths Stern or bows-to outer end of mole.

Shelter Good in settled weather. A dangerous surge with strong onshore winds.

Data Max LOA 10m. Depths 2–4m.

Facilities Water. Fuel quay. Provisions and restaurants.

Port authorities ✆ 0185 770 032

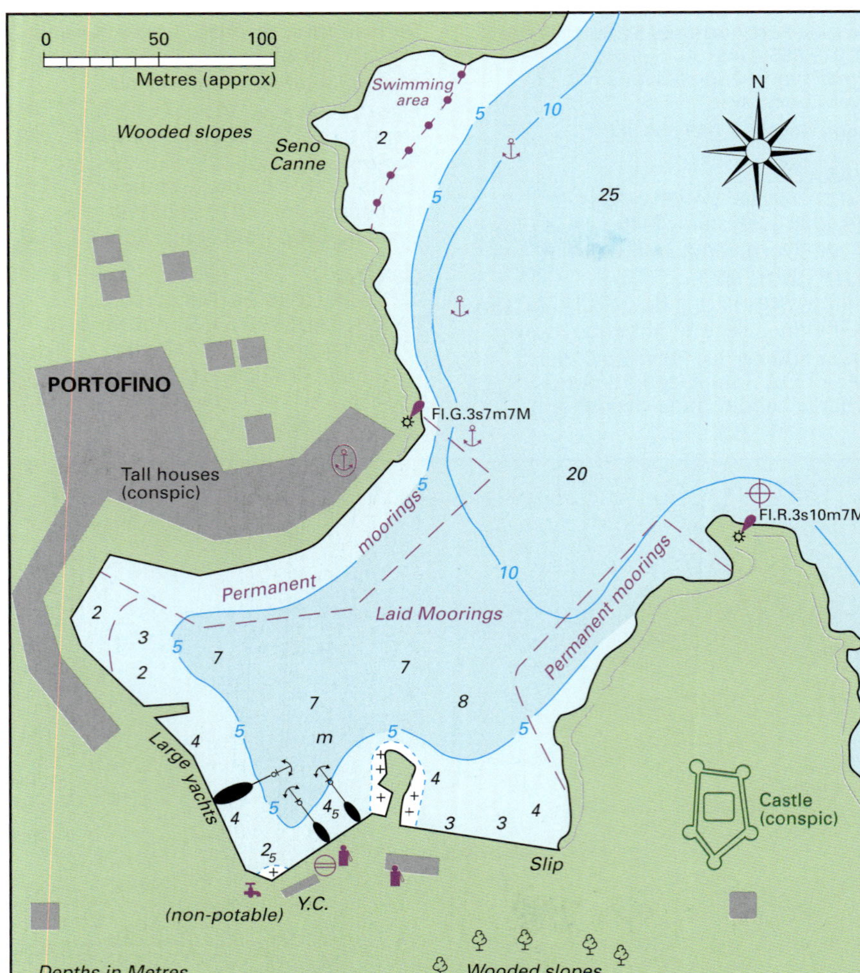

PORTOFINO

SAN FRUTTUOSO
44°18'·85N 09°10'·52E

A cove on the S side of Punta della Chiappa. Moorings (questionable reliability). Limited room for visitors. Charge band 2.

PORTOFINO
44°18'·2N 09°12'·9E
BA 1998 It 909 Imray M16
6M Camogli ←→ Portovenere 32M

☆ Punta Portofino Fl.5s16M. Entrance Fl.G.3s7M/Fl.R.3s7M

VHF Ch 12.

Berths Where directed. Private marina. Larger yachts anchor with long lines ashore.

Shelter Uncomfortable with E winds.

Data 270 berths. Max LOA 80m. Speed limit 3kns. Depths 1–4m. Charge band 6+.

Facilities Water. 220V. Showers and toilets. Fuel quay. Restaurants.

Remarks Usually fully booked in the summer.

✆ 0185 269 580
Ormeggiatori ✆ 0185 269 388
www.marinadiportofino.com
Port authorities ✆ 0185 269 040
Harbourmaster ✆ 0185 269 388

SANTA MARGHERITA LIGURE
44°19'·8N 09°13'·1E
BA 1998 It 909

☆ Mole head Fl.R.4s8M

PORTOFINO MARINE RESERVE
The reserve runs around the square peninsula from Camogli to S of Santa Margherita Ligure. Access channels run to San Fruttuoso and Portofino.
✆ 0185 289 649
www.riservaportofino.it

VHF Ch 11, 16 (summer continuous/winter 0700–1900).

Note Works in progress extending the sea wall.

Berths Stern or bows-to mole where directed. Laid moorings tailed to the quay or a buoy. Anchorage to the N.

Shelter Good shelter.

Data 350 berths. Max LOA 60m. Depths 2–12m. Speed limit 3kns.

Facilities Water. 220V. Telephone. Showers and toilets. Fuel quay. 30-ton crane. 150-ton slipway. Most yacht repairs. Provisions and restaurants.

Consorzio Operatori Portuali
✆ 0185 280 746
Marina di Santa
✆ 0185 205 455 / 335 841 1379
Email ormeggi@comunesml.it
Cantieri Sant'Orsola
✆ 0185 55613 / 282 687
Email cantieri@cantierisantorsola.com
www.cantierisantorsola.it

RAPALLO
44°20'·65N 09°14'·0E
BA 1998 It 909 Imray M16

☆ Elbow of outer mole Fl.3s9M. Entrance 2F.G(vert)3M/2F.R(vert)3M. Molo Langano head F.RG.6m3M

VHF Ch 09, 10, 16, 25 (1000–1900).

Berths Where directed. Laid moorings tailed to the quay. Porto Publico usually full. Anchorage in the N of the bay.

Shelter Good shelter.

Data 400 berths. 30 visitors' berths. Max LOA 40m. Depths 3–7m. Charge band 6.

Facilities Water. 220V. Telephone. Showers and toilets. Fuel quay. 40-ton travel-hoist. 20-ton crane. Most yacht repairs. Provisions and restaurants.

Porto Turistico
✆ 0185 689 369 / 335 617 6495
Email info@portocarloriva.it
www.portocarloriva.it

CHIAVARI
44°18'·7N 09°19'·1E (LFl.G.6s6M)
BA 1998 It 57 Imray M16

☆ Entrance Fl.G.3s5M / F.G.3M / F.R.3M

VHF Ch 16, 10.

Navigation Buoyed entrance channel. Entrance difficult with strong onshore winds.

Berths Where directed. Laid moorings. 24 hrs free on outer mole.

Shelter Good although S winds cause a surge.

Data 460 berths. 35 visitors' berths. Max LOA 25m. Depths 2·5–5m. Charge band 4.

Facilities Water. 220V. Showers and toilets. Fuel quay (not open 2011). 50-ton travel-hoist. 25-ton crane. Most yacht repairs. Provisions and restaurants.

CINQUE TERRE MARINE RESERVE
The reserve runs along the coast from Levanto to Capo di Monte Negro. Vernazza is in Zone C of the reserve. Max LOA in zone C is 24m.
✆ 0187 760 000/061
www.parconazionale5terre.it

Note Mooring buoys have been laid in several bays through the park. Charges €30 (12hrs) €60 (24hrs) up to 50 feet LOA. Not always collected.

Monterosso	15 buoys (8 for <50 ft)
Vernazza	15 buoys (10)
Riomaggiore	20 buoys (8)

Porto Turistico
✆ 0185 364 081
Email info@marina-chiavari.it
www.marina-chiavari.it

LAVAGNA
44°18'·25N 09°20'·55E
BA 1998 It 57 Imray M16

☆ Entrance LFl.R.6s6M / F.G.2M / F.R.2M

VHF Ch 09, 16. CB Ch 31.

Navigation Strong S winds can make it dangerous to enter or leave.

Berths Where directed. Laid moorings tailed to the quay or buoys.

Data 1,050 berths. 40 visitors' berths. Max LOA 50m. Depths 2–5m. Charge band 5.

Facilities Water. 220V. Showers and toilets. Fuel quay. 50-ton travel-hoist. 55-ton crane. 325-ton slipway. All yacht repairs. Provisions and restaurants.

Porto Turistico Lavagna
✆ 0185 321 732
Email dirportlavagna@libero.it
Port Authority ✆ 0185 312 626

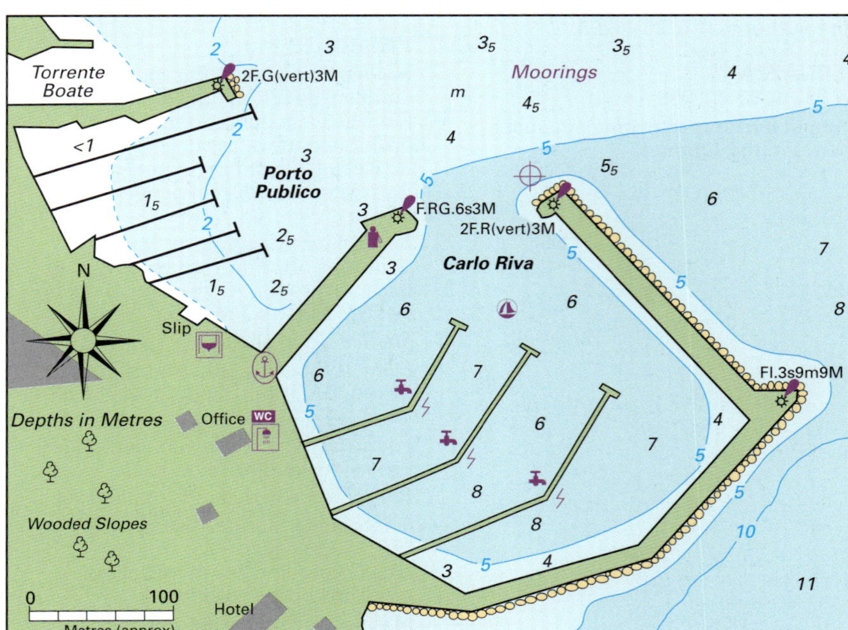

RAPPALO

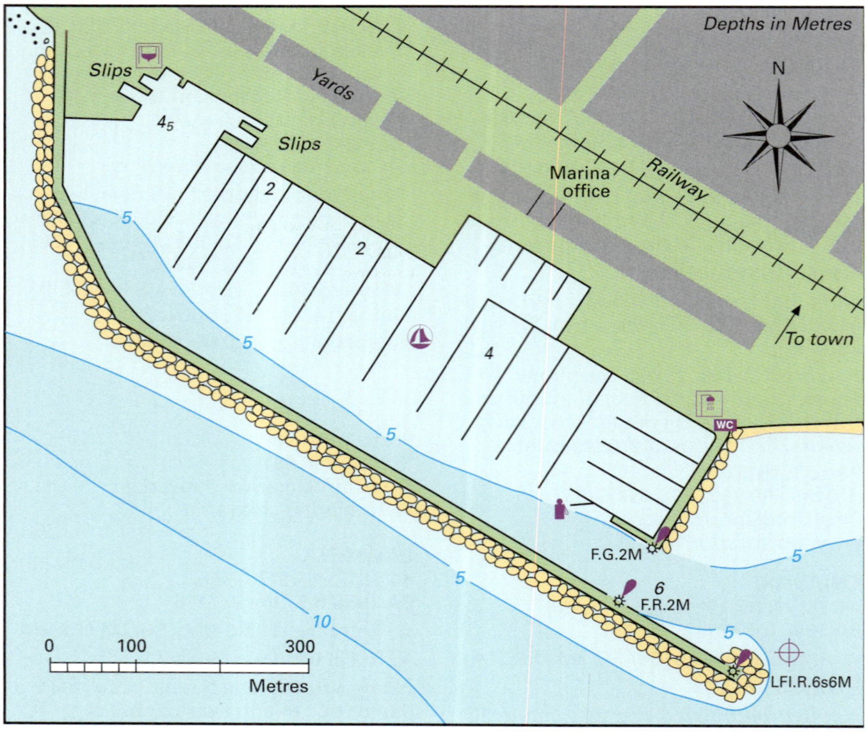

LAVAGNA MARINA

SESTRI LEVANTE
44°16'·4N 09°23'·2E
BA 1998 It 909 Imray M16

☆ Mole head F.G.3M

VHF Ch 09, 16 (0700–1900).

Berths Stern or bows-to mole. Anchorage in the bay.

Shelter Open N.

Data 20 visitors' berths. Max LOA 20m. Depths <1–4m.

Facilities Water. Fuel quay. Restaurants.

Remarks From 1 May–30 September anchoring is prohibited in the bay.

Port Authority ☎ 0185 41295

VERNAZZA
44°08'·1N 09°40'·00E

A small harbour affording adequate shelter in the summer.

Golfo di la Spezia

PARC NATURALE REGIONALE DI PORTOVENERE
☎ 0187 794 823
www.parcnaturaleportovenere.it

PORTOVENERE
44°03'N 09°50·2E (F.R)
BA 118 It 60 Imray M16
32M Portofino ←→ Marina di Carrara 9M

☆ Isola del Tino Fl(3)15s25M. Torre della Scuola Fl(2)6s10M. Entrance F.G.3M/F.R.3M

VHF Ch 09, 11.

Navigation Isola Palmaria has a number of reefs off the N and S. To the E of the Isola del Tino there is a prohibited naval area. The channel between Isola Palmaria and Portovenere has 2·1m depths in the fairway.

Berths Stern or bows-to. Various pontoons offering yacht berths N of harbour proper. Anchorage to the NE or ESE off Isola Palmaria.

Shelter Good shelter.

Data 100 berths. 20 visitors' berths. Max LOA 50m. Depths 1–4m. Charge band 6+.

Facilities Water. Showers and toilets. Provisions and restaurants.

Remarks Crowded in summer.

Portovenere Marina Misenti
☎ 0187 793 042
Email portodiportovenere@alice.it
www.portodiportovenere.it

Marina Misenti ☎ 0187 793 042
www.portodiportovenere.it

Pontile Ignazio ☎ 0187 791 364
Email info@pontileignazio.org
www.pontileignazio.org

Port Authority ☎ 0187 790 768

LE GRAZIE
44°04'·0N 09°51'·1E
BA 118 It 60 Imray M16

☆ Punta S. Maria Fl.R.4s9M. Diga Foranea Fl.G.4s9M. E head Fl(2)R.6s8M. Jetty head Iso.R.2s4M. Punta Santa Teresa Fl(2)G.6s8M

VHF Ch 16.

Navigation Navigation is prohibited in Seno del Varigna. Anchoring is prohibited in Seno della Castagna. Care needed of mussel beds on the NW side of Le Grazie.

Berths Stern or bows-to. Care needed of underwater ballasting. Anchorage in the bay.

Shelter E winds make it uncomfortable.

Data 2–10m in the bay.

Facilities Water. Fuel nearby. 1,000-ton slipway. 10-ton crane. Most yacht repairs. Most provisions and restaurants.

Port Authority ☎ 0187 782 177

Cantieri Valdettaro ☎ 0187 791 687

MARINA DEL FEZZANO
44°04'·9N 09°49'·9E

Navigation A pontoon complex off the yard ashore.

Data 250 berths. 30 visitors' berths. Max LOA 24m. Depths 3–7m. Charge band 5/6.

Facilities Water. 220V. Showers and toilets. 60/200-ton travel-hoists. Most yacht repairs.

Marina del Fezzano
☎ 0187 790 103
Email info@marinadelfezzano.it
www.marinadelfezzano.it

Cantiere Navale ☎ 0187 790 275

PORTO MIRABELLO MARINA
44°06'·19N 09°50'08E WGS84

VHF Ch 73

Navigation A marina on the N side of the breakwater to the N of Darsena Duca Degli Abruzzi.

Berths Go stern or bows-to where directed. Marina staff will assist you. Laid moorings tailed to the quay.

Shelter Good all-round shelter.

Data 380 berths. LOA 14–65m. Depths 3·5–12m. Charge band 6+.

Facilities Water. 220/380V. WiFi. Showers and toilets. Pump-out. Fuel quay. 160-ton travel hoist. Large covered workshop. Most repairs. Bicycle, scooter and car hire. Helipad. Shops, bars and restaurants under development in the marina.

Porto Mirabello ☎ 0187 778 108
Email info@portomirabello.it
www.portomirabello.it

LA SPEZIA COMMERCIAL HARBOUR
44°05′·81N 09°49′·94E WGS84
BA 118 It 59 Imray M16
☆ Entrance Fl.G.4s8M / Fl.R.4s8M
VHF Ch 16 for *capitaneria* (24/24). Ch 71 for *porto turistico*.
Navigation A buoyed channel dredged to 12m leads to the commercial port. Navigation prohibited in Darsena Duca degli Abruzzi, the naval harbour SW of the commercial harbour.
Berths Stern or bows-to in Porto Turistico de Benedetti in the NW basin. There may also be berths at Sardinia Cat, or on Molo Italia in the NE basin.
Data 588 berths. Max LOA 14·5m. Depths 1·5–7m. Charge band 4.
Facilities Water. Fuel quay. Provisions and restaurants nearby.
Assonautica
✆ 0187 770 229 / 331 182 7124
Email asso_sp@libero.it
www.assonautica.it

SARDINIA CAT
The pontoon close N of the Assonautica marina.
✆ 338 145 4374
www.pontilecatamaranilaspezia.com

There are several large ship-builders on the E side of the harbour. Many of these have a number of berths, although they are usually reserved for those using the yard facilities.

NAVALMARE
Navigation The yard lies close N of the E entrance to Rada di La Spezia.
Data 160 berths. Max LOA 40m. Laid moorings.
Facilities 350-ton hoists. Major ship, superyacht and commercial projects.
✆ 0187 562 042
www.navalmare.it

PORTO LOTTI
44°05′·75N 09°51′·54E
BA 118 It 60 Imray M16
☆ F.G/F.R
VHF Ch 09.
Navigation On the E side in the commercial docks.
Berths Where directed. Laid moorings tailed to quay.
Shelter Good.
Data 520 berths. 50 visitors' berths. Max LOA 80m. Depths 2·8–7·5m. Charge band 6+.
Facilities Water. 220/380V. Showers and toilets. Telephone and TV. Fuel quay. 160-ton travel-hoist. 50/12/7-ton cranes. Yacht repairs. Restaurant.
Marina Porto Lotti
✆ 0187 5321
www.portolotti.com

LERICI
44°04′·4N 09°54′·4E (2F.G)
BA 118 It 909 Imray M16
☆ Mole head 2F.G(vert)3M
A small harbour in the E approach to Golfo di La Spezia.
Berths Fore and aft moorings with water-taxi to shore or berth if available on YC pontoon.
Data 220 berths. Max LOA 25m. Depths <1–8m.

BOCCA DI MAGRA
44°02′·7N 09°59′·4E
☆ Entrance Fl.G.5s3M
Number of small harbours and pontoon berths up the Magra River. Care needed when entering with onshore winds. Currently 2m over the bar at the entrance. Channel changes but currently on the W side of the river. Care needed of drying sandbank off Marina del Ponte in the approaches to the bridge.
Remarks Drying sand bar in approaches to Marina del Ponte, close to the bridge.
Porto Bocca di Magra ✆ 0187 608 037
Email info@ameglia servizi.it
www.portoboccadimagra.it
Marina del Ponte ✆ 0187 64670
Email info@marinadelponte.it

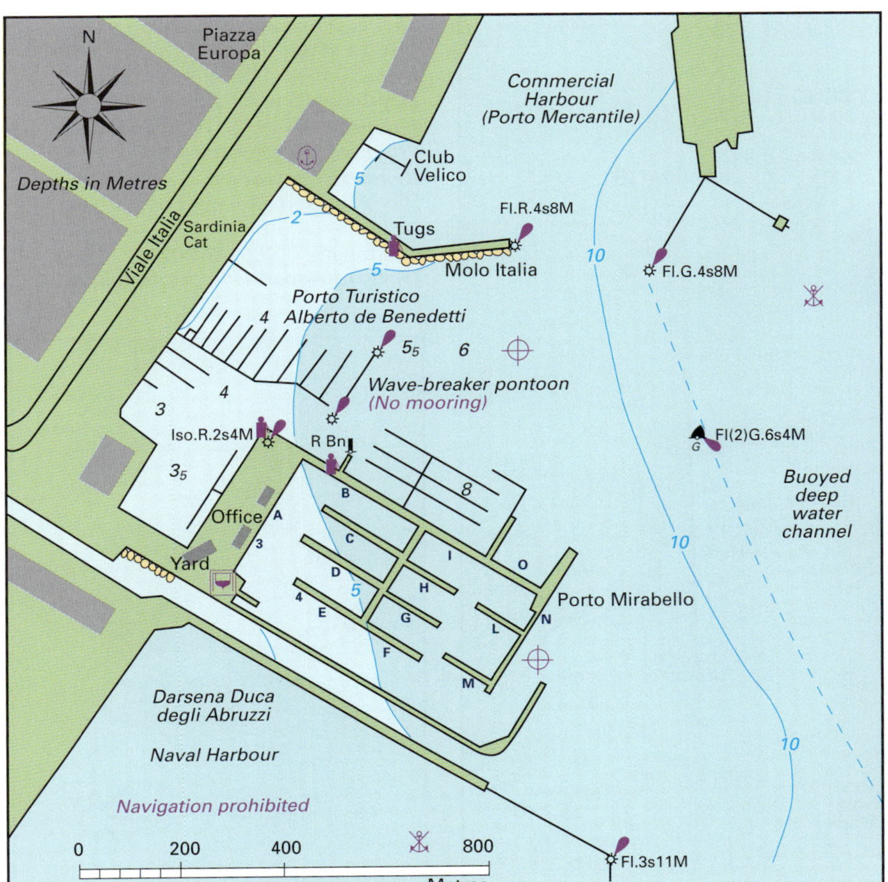

LA SPEZIA

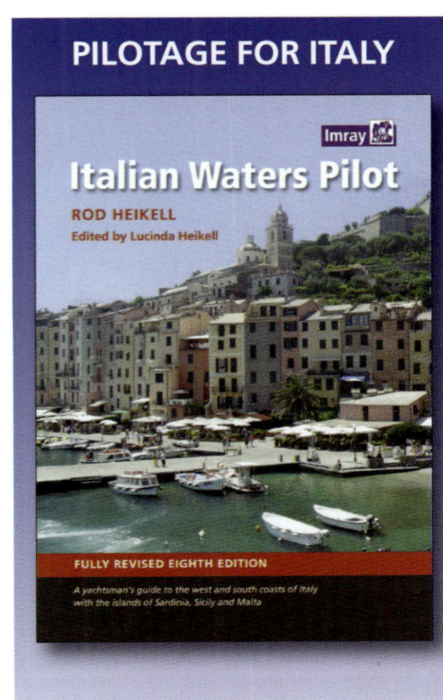

PILOTAGE FOR ITALY
Imray
Italian Waters Pilot
ROD HEIKELL
Edited by Lucinda Heikell
FULLY REVISED EIGHTH EDITION
A yachtsman's guide to the west and south coasts of Italy with the islands of Sardinia, Sicily and Malta

Tuscan Islands and adjacent mainland coast

Capraia

PORTO CAPRAIA

43°03′·1N 09°50′·35E
BA 1999 It 913 Imray M45

☆ Capo Ferraione LFl.6s16M. Entrance Fl.G.3s4M / F.G.3M / Fl.R.3s4M

VHF Ch 69 for moorings.

Navigation Village won't be seen from S and E until the entrance of the bay.

Berths Stern or bows-to on pontoons. Laid moorings for visitors outside the harbour. Charge band 5.

Shelter Adequate shelter in the summer.

Facilities Water. 220V. Fuel nearby. Most provisions and restaurants.

Note The 220V conduit runs along the quay at water level.

Porto Capraia ☎ 0586 905 307 or 338 374 4102
www.portocapraia.it

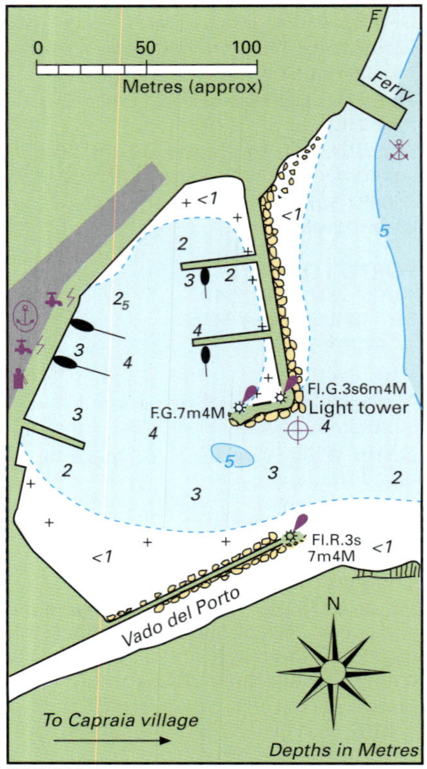

CAPRAIA

TUSCAN ARCHIPELAGO NATIONAL PARK
Isola Gorgona, Isola Montecristo, Isola Pianosa, Isola Capraia, Isola di Giannutri
Access to the main harbours is unaffected.
Via Guerrazzi 1, 57037 Portoferraio
☎ 0565 919 411
Email parco@islepark.it
www.islepark.it

Elba

PORTOFERRAIO

42°48′·7N 10°19′·8E
BA 131 It 72 Imray M45
44M Livorno ←→ Porto Azzurro 14M

☆ Forte Stella Fl(3)14s16M+F.R.60m6M. Scoglietto Fl(2)6s7M. Entrance Fl.R.4s3M / Fl.G.4s3M. Mole No. 1 head Fl.Y.3s6m4M. N mole F.G.3M. S mole F.R.3M. Secca di Capo Bianco Q.5m3M.

VHF Ch 09 for Darsena Medicea. Ch 11, 16 for *capitaneria* (summer 0700–2300, winter 0700–1900). Ch 12 for pilots (24/24).

Navigation Care needed of reef (Secca di Capo Bianco, now lit) off Punta Capo Bianco and the reef around Isoloto Fratelli.

Berths Call ahead for a berth. Port staff assist mooring. Laid moorings tailed to the quay.

Shelter Normally good but S gales cause a surge.

Data 70 berths. Max LOA 70m. Depths 3–10m. Charge band 6.

Facilities Water. 220V. WiFi. Fuel quay. Provisions and restaurants.

Remarks Crowded in the summer. In July/August max length of stay one night.

Capitaneria ☎ 0565 944 024
Email info@marinadiportoferraio.it

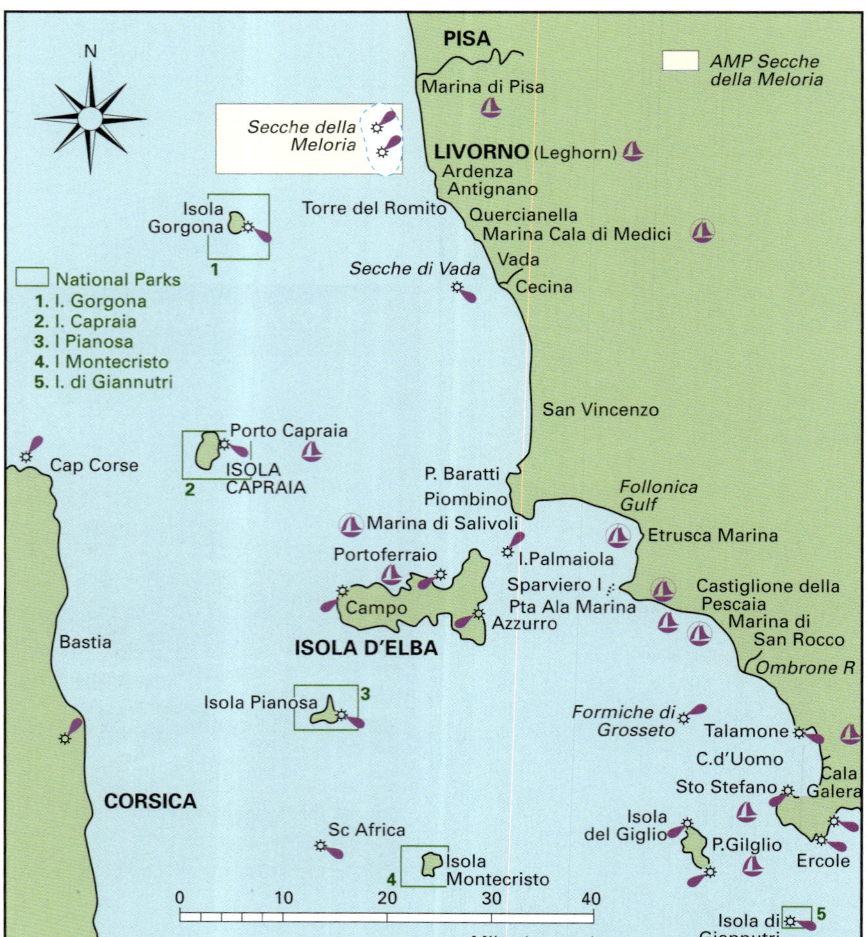

TUSCAN ISLANDS

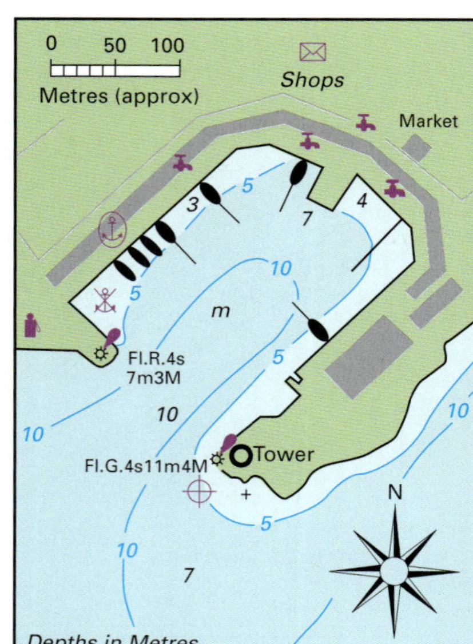

PORTOFERRAIO

CANTIERE NAVALI ESAOM CESA
Data 150 berths. 20 visitors' berths. Max LOA 32m. Depths 2–5m. Charge band 6.
Facilities Water. 220V. Showers and toilets. 260-ton travel-hoist. All yacht repairs.
✆ 0565 919 311
Email commerciale@esaom.it
www.esaom.it

EDILNAUTICA MARINA (ESAOM)
42°48'·4N 10°19'·0E
BA 131 It 72 Imray M45
VHF Ch 09
Navigation Shallows off the coast S of the entrance. Channel into the marina is indistinct.
Berth Where directed. Finger pontoons or laid moorings. Mooring buoys outside the marina. Charge band 6.
Shelter Excellent all-round shelter.
Data 130 berths. Max LOA 35m
Facilities Water. 220V. WiFi. Bicycle hire.
✆ 0565 919 311 / 347 640 1030
Email commerciale@esaom.it

CAVO
42°51'·6N 10°25'·6E (F.R)
BA 131 It 117
☆ Isola Palmaiola Fl.5s10M. Pier 2F.R(vert)3M. Entrance F.G.3M/F.R.3M
VHF Ch 16.
Berths Stern or bows-to. Anchorage to the N.
Shelter Good except with strong N winds.
Data 300 berths. Max LOA 15m. Depths <1–2·5m.
Facilities Water. Fuel. Some provisions and restaurants.
✆ 338 509 7341

RIO MARINA
42°48'·9N 10°25'·8E
☆ Mole head Fl.R.3s3M/Fl/G.3s3M
Data c.100 berths. Max LOA 15m. Depths <1–4m. Charge band 5/6.
Facilities Water and electricity at most berths.
SVAMAR Srl ✆ 0565 962 011
www.portoturisticorioecavo.it

PORTO AZZURRO
42°45'·7N 10°23'·9E
BA 131 It 913 Imray M45
14M Portoferraio ←→ Porto Giglio 32M
☆ Capo Focardo Fl(3)15s16M. Punta San Giovanni Fl.R.5s15m6M. Entrance Fl.G.3s6M
VHF Ch 16.
Berths Several concessions in the harbour. Stern or bows-to where directed. Laid moorings at most berths.
Shelter Good shelter although the *sirocco* causes a surge.
Data 190 berths. Approximately 25 visitors' berths. Max LOA 60m. Depths 2–7m. Charge band 5/6.

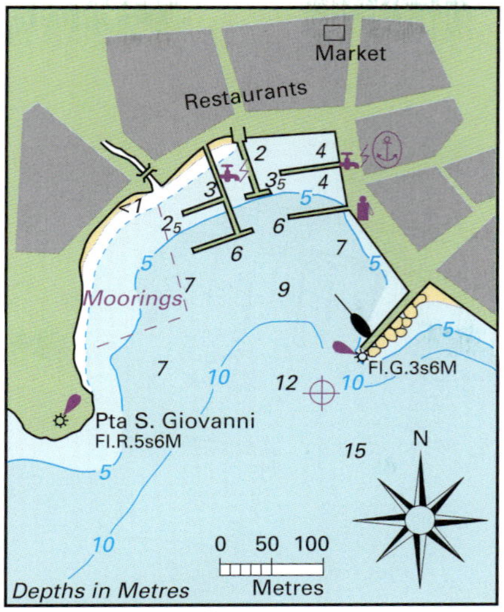

PORTO AZZURRO

Facilities Water. 220V. Fuel quay. Yacht yard on commercial quay in S of bay with hauling facilities. Provisions and restaurants.
Remarks Much of the bay is taken up with moorings (and floating lines) for small craft and work boats.
Porto Azzurro ✆ 0565 921 611
Marina di Porto Azzurro (superyachts)
✆ 0565 914 797 / 347 356 3953
Balfin Marina
✆ 0586 899 827
Email info@balfinsrl.it
Pontile Giovanni Messina
✆ 339 441 9634
Porto Luna Pontoon
✆ 0565 921 158 / 335 787 8832
Email portoluna@tiscali.it
D'Alarcon (S end of quay) ✆ 0565 95263

MARINA DI CAMPO
42°44'·55N 10°14'·35E
BA 1999 It 913 Imray M45
☆ Capo Poro Fl.5s16M. Near tower Fl.3s10M. Mole head Fl.R.5s3M. Pierhead F.R.3M
Berths Stern or bows-to mole. Laid moorings outside the harbour.
Shelter Good shelter although S gales make it uncomfortable.
Data Depths 1·5–8m. Charge band 5.
Facilities Water. Fuel nearby. Provisions and restaurants.

MARCIANA MARINA
42°48'·5N 10°11'·9E
BA 1999 It 913 Imray M45
☆ Mole head Fl.G.4s8M
VHF Ch 09, 16.
Navigation Harbour difficult to identify from seaward.
Berths Laid moorings at most berths on the mole.
Shelter Good shelter although strong E winds cause a surge.
Data 115 berths. Max LOA 30m. Depths 2–7m. Charge band 6.
Facilities Water. 220V. Fuel nearby. 15-ton crane. Provisions and restaurants.
✆ 340 796 0008
Email info@portodimarcianamarina.it
Circolo della Vela ✆ 0565 990 27
www.cvmm.it

Giglio

PORTO GIGLIO
42°21'·6N 10°55'·2E
BA 1999 It 74 Imray M45
32M Porto Azzurro ←→ Riva di Traiano 50M
☆ Entrance Fl.R.3s7M/Fl.G.3s7M
VHF Ch 14, 16 (0700–1300).
Navigation Care needed of ferries entering and leaving.
Berths Stern or bows-to the new pontoon on the E breakwater. Laid moorings.
Shelter Good shelter.
Data 190 berths. Max LOA 15m. Depths 1·5–5m. Charge band 5.
Facilities Water. 220V. Fuel nearby. Provisions and restaurants.
Remarks Crowded in the summer with few berths for visitors.
✆ 0564 806 764

Giannutri

CALA SPALMATOI
42°15'·5N 11°06'·5E
A cove on the E coast offering good shelter from all but strong SE–E winds.

Marina di Carrara to Monte Argentario

MARINA DI CARRARA
44°02'·07N 10°02'·51E WGS84
BA 118 It 61 Imray M16
9M Portovenere ←→ Livorno 31M
☆ Root of W mole Fl.3s17M. Entrance Iso.R.2s3M/Iso.G.2s7M
VHF Ch 16 for *capitaneria* (summer 24/24, winter 0700–1900).
Ch 74 for Club Nautico.
Navigation Head for the YC catwalks on N quay.
Berths Stern or bows-to where directed. Laid moorings tailed to the quay.
Shelter Good shelter although S winds make it uncomfortable.
Data 170 berths. 10 visitors' berths. Max LOA 30m. Depths 2–8m. Charge band 3.
Facilities Water. 220V. Showers and toilets. Fuel quay. Cranes up to 100 tons. Slipway. Most yacht repairs. Provisions and restaurants.
Club Nautico ✆ 0585 785 150

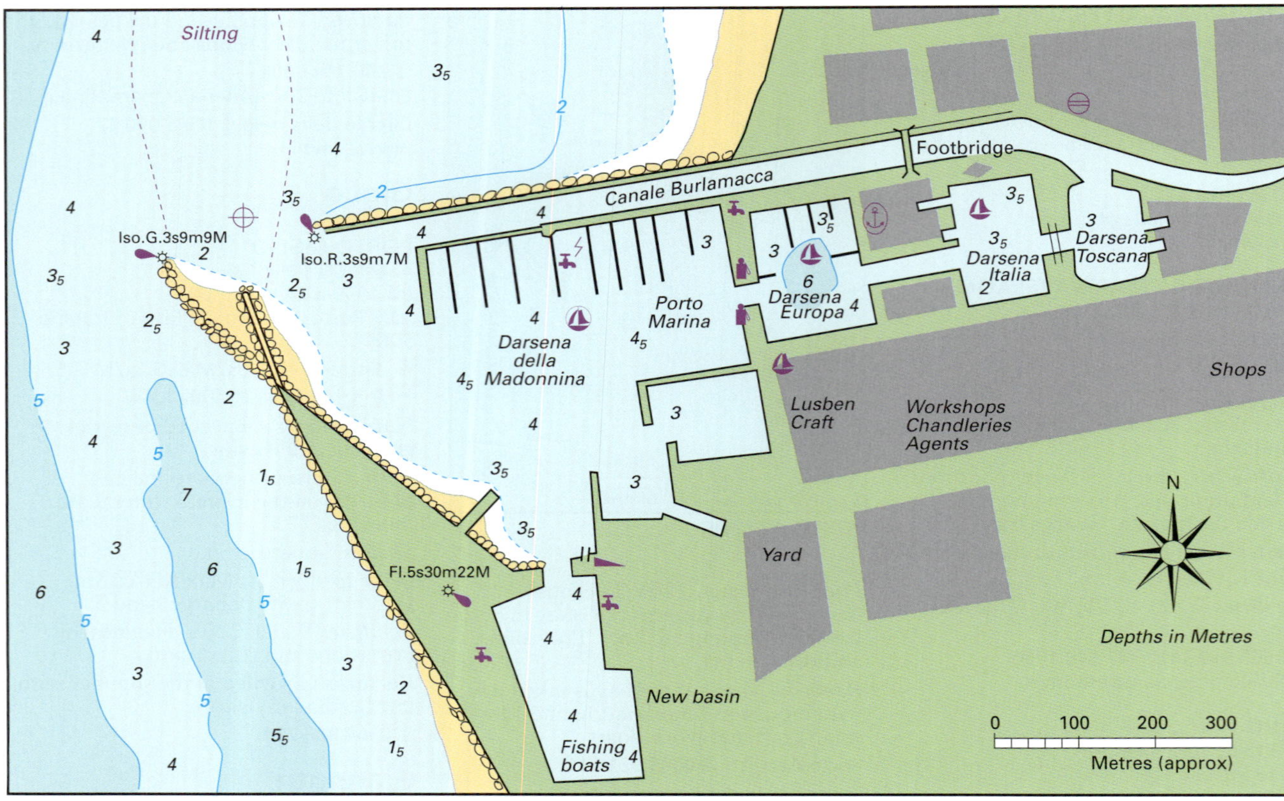

VIAREGGIO

MARINA DI MASSA
44°00'·3N 10°05'·8E

☆ Pier head F.GR(vert)3M

FIUME CINQUALE
43°58'·5N 10°08'·4E

☆ Basin F.R.3M/F.G.3M

FORTE DEI MARMI
43°57'·2N 10°09'·8E

☆ Pier F.R.3M

VIAREGGIO
43°51'·7N 10°14'·1E
BA 1999 It 909 Imray M16

☆ Root of N mole Fl.5s24M. Entrance Iso.R.3s7M/Iso.G.3s9M

VHF Ch 16 for *capitaneria* (summer 0700–2300, winter 0700–1900). Ch 12 for the marina. CB Ch 09.

Navigation As part of the 'Safe Sea Net Harbour System' introduced in December 2009, all vessels over 300GRT are required to contact a local ship agent 24hrs in advance of their arrival, or at the earliest opportunity, for entry and berthing arrangements. Heavy swell at the entrance with strong W–SW winds. A sand bar extends for at least 800m NNE from the end of the breakwater. Approach should be made on a course due E towards a conspicuous hotel on the shore. When the light Iso.R.3s9m7M bears 190° turn towards the entrance, keeping close to the port side when entering.

Yachts drawing over 2·5m are advised to call ahead before entering.

Berths Yachts up to 18m LOA should head for Viareggio Porto Marina in Darsena della Madonnina. Superyacht Services can arrange berths for 24–70m LOA. Lusben Craft may also have berths. Otherwise arrange a berth through the yacht agents.

Shelter Good all-round shelter.

Data Viareggio Porto 1,000 berths. Max LOA 18m. Charge band 6.
Lusben Craft Max LOA 60m. Charge band 6.
Superyacht Services LOA 24–85m. Max draught 4m.

Facilities Water. 220/380V. WiFi. Fuel quay. Pump-out. Slipway up to 200-ton and 60m LOA. 100-ton travel-hoist. 200-ton crane. 1,000-ton electric hoist. All yacht repairs. Provisions and restaurants.

Remarks Base for Benetti, Perini Navi, Lusben Craft, Tecnomarine and others.

Viareggio Porto Marina ☏ 0584 32033
Email approdo@viareggio-portospa.it

Lusben Yard ☏ 0584 384 111

Superyacht Services Yacht Agency
☏ 328 057 9847
Email info@superyachtservices.it

Vannucci Yacht and Ship Agents
☏ 0584 46553
Email info@agenziavannucci.it

Capitaneria ☏ 0584 49500

MARINA DI PISA (BOCCA DI ARNO)
43°40'·8N 10°16'·2E
BA 1999 It 04 Imray M16

☆ Bocca di Arno F.G.3M

Navigation Depths of 4m reported close to N side of the entrance to the river. Much less towards the centre. Overhead cables have been raised – quite large yachts now berth at the yard beyond the cables.

Berths Marina Arnovecchio and Marinova are recommended, but there are many others. Currently no visitors' berths at Lega Navale. Pontoons and catwalks.

Data c.500 berths. Visitors' berths. Max LOA 15(Marinova)–20m (Arnovecchio). Depths 2·5–3·5m.

Facilities Water. 220V. Showers and toilets. Cranes and travel-hoists at many yards.

Marina Arnovecchio ☏ 050 34182 / 348 619 7985
Email arnovecchio@gmail.com
www.arnovecchio.it

Marinova (Mauro Favati) ☏ 050 355 88 / 050 310 037
Email marinova@alice.it

PORTO DI PISA, BOCCADARNO
43°40'·6N 10°16'·0E

A new marina on the S bank of the entrance to the Arno river.

VHF Ch 74

Navigation The entrance to the river is difficult to identify until close to. The town of Marina di Pisa along the coast to the S is easily seen.

Shelter Should provide good all-round shelter.

Data 355 berths. Max LOA 50m. Depths 3–5m.

Facilities Water. 220/380V. WC and showers. Waste pump-out. Fuel quay planned.

Boccadarno Porto di Pisa ☏ 050 36142 or 347 541 3372 (24 hr)
Email info@portodipisa.it
www.portodipisa.it

AMP SECCHE DELLA MELORIA
The most sensitive parts of the reef are now protected and lie within Zone A of the reserve, where all unauthorised navigation is prohibited.
In Zone B navigation by jet skis and motor boats is restricted. Maximum speed 5kns. Anchoring and mooring is restricted.
AMP Secche della Meloria
✆ 050 539 111
www.parcosanrossore.it

MELORIA REEF (SECCHE DELLA MELORIA)

☆ N tower Fl(2)10s18m10M. S tower Q(6)+LFl.15s18m12M. Light buoy E card Q(3)10s5m7M

LIVORNO

43°33'·45N 10°17'·4E (N entrance)
BA 119 It 62 Imray M16
31M Marina di Carrara ←→ Portoferraio 44M

☆ Main light (Avamporto) Fl(4)20s24M. N entrance Fl(3)WG.10s8/6M/Fl(3)R.10s7M. Dir Lt 225·5° Fl.3s5M. Darsena Petroli Fl.R.3s4M/Fl.G.3s3M/Fl.R.3s3M/ Fl.G.3s3M.
S entrance Fl.G.3s9M/Fl.G.3s4M/ Fl.G.3s3M/Fl.G.3s3M/Fl.WR.3s11/9M.
Outer breakwater spur Fl.RG.3s5M.
Porto Mediceo entrance Fl(2)G.6s5M.
Porticciolo di Sant' Iacopo Fl.G.5s3M.
Porticciolo di San Leopoldo Fl.G.8s4M

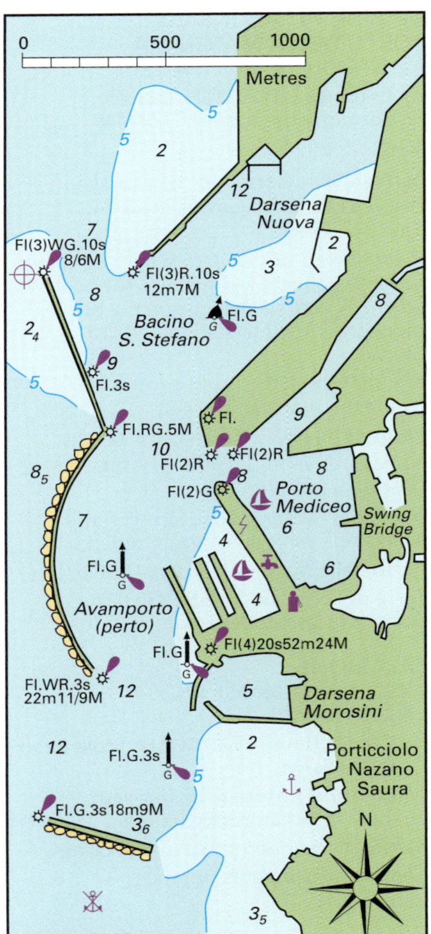

LIVORNO

VHF Ch 16 for *capitaneria* (24/24). Ch 14, 16 for pilots (24/24). Ch 09 for YC.
Navigation Care needed of Meloria Reef lying off Livorno. With strong S winds there is a confused swell in the approaches.
Berths Stern or bows-to outside of Molo Mediceo. Stern or bows-to inside Porto Mediceo. Laid moorings.
Shelter Adequate although uncomfortable with strong S winds.
Data 120 berths. Max LOA 30m. Depths 3–6m. Charge band 5.
Facilities Water (reported not potable). 220V. Fuel quay. 40-ton crane. 500-ton slipway. Some yacht repairs. Provisions and restaurants.
Remarks New superyacht facilities in Darsena Morosini.
Circolo Nautico ✆ 0586 807 354 / 893 015
Ormeggiatori ✆ 0586 894 405
Porto Mediceo ✆ 0586 887 710
Port Authority ✆ 0586 826 011

ANTIGNANO

42°29'·7N 10°19'·3E
☆ Pier Fl.G.3s4M

QUERCIANELLA

43°27'·5N 10°21'·8E
☆ F.R.3M

MARINA CALA DE MEDICI (ROSSIGNANO)

43°23'·54N 10°25'·75E WGS84
VHF Ch 09 (24hr)
Berth Where directed. Marina staff will assist mooring. Laid moorings tailed to the quay.
Shelter Good all-round shelter inside the marina.
Data 650 berths. 60 visitors' berths. Max LOA 40m. Depths 3–8m. Charge band 6.
Facilities Water. 220/380V. TV and telephone. WiFi. Showers and toilets. Self-service laundry. Pump-out facilities. Fuel quay (0900–1200 / 1430–1800). 100-ton travel-lift. Hydraulic trailer. Most repairs. Provisions and restaurants nearby. PO. Banks. ATMs. Buses. Trains to Livorno and Rome. Pisa airport 40km.
Remarks Secche di Vada lies in the S approaches to the marina.
Marina Cala de Medici
✆ 0586 795 223
Mooring ✆ 348 998 5031
Email info@calademedici.net
www.calademedici.net

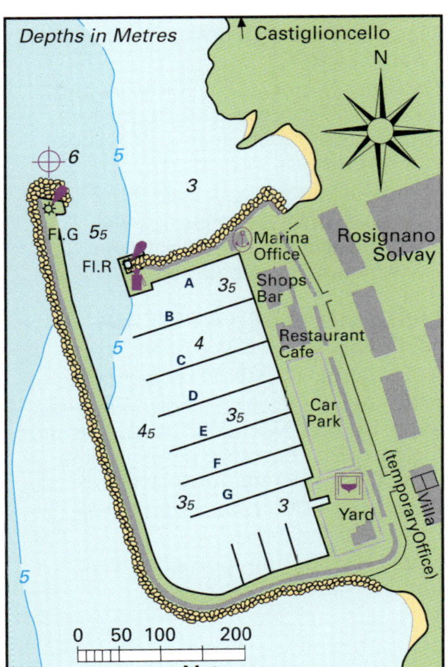

MARINA CALA DE MEDICI

MARINA DI SAN VINCENZO

43°05'·9N 10°32'·2E
☆ F.R.3M/F.G.3M
New large marina on the site of the old shallow small craft harbour.
VHF Ch 09
Navigation With moderate and strong onshore winds there are waves breaking across the entrance and onto the adjacent beach. Yachts must turn beam onto the surf to enter the marina in depths of just 3–3·5m. Extreme caution advised.
Berths Stern or bows-to where directed. Laid moorings tailed to the quay.
Shelter Once inside there is good all round shelter in the marina.
Data 350 berths. Max LOA 27m. Depths 3–4·5m. Charge band 6+.
Facilities Water. 220/380V. WiFi. Showers and toilets. Pump-out (to be completed). Fuel quay (to be completed). 75-ton travel-lift. Repairs can be arranged at the yard. Good shopping in the town. Bars, cafés and restaurant in the marina.
Marina di San Vincenzo ✆ 0565 702 025
Email porto@marinadisanvincenzo.it
www.marinadisanvincenzo.it
Cantiere ✆ 0565 704 717
Email sanvincenzo@golfomola.it

PORTO BARATTI

43°00'·0N 10°30'·3E
☆ Punta delle Pianacce Fl.3s9M
Anchor at the S end of the bay.

MARINA DI SALIVOLI

42°55'·98N 10°30'·47E WGS84
☆ Entrance Fl.R.3s6M
A harbour just S of Piombino. Good all-round shelter.
VHF Ch 16, 09.
Berth Where directed. Laid moorings tailed to the quay.
Data 450 berths. Visitors' berths. Max LOA 20m. Depths 3m. Charge band 5.
Facilities Water and electricity at all berths. Shower and toilet block. Fuel quay. 80-ton travel-hoist. Mini-market. Restaurant and bar.
Marina di Salivoli
✆ 0565 42809 / 48091
Email info@marinadisalivoli.it
www.marinadisalivoli.it

PIOMBINO

42°55'·9N 10°33'·1E
BA 131 It 71 Imray M17

☆ Isola Palmaiola Fl.5s10M. Entrance Fl.R.5s8M/4F.G(horiz)3M. Pier 2F.R(vert)3M. Mole head F.GR(vert)3M

VHF Ch 14, 16.

Note Yachts should not use Piombino except in an emergency.

Port Authority ☏ 0565 229 210
www.porto.piombino.li.it

MARINA DI SCARLINO (ETRUSCA MARINA)

42°53'·18N 10°47'·09E WGS84
VHF Ch 72.

Navigation Porto Turistico on the S side of the entrance to Portiglione Canal. The marina entrance is dredged and buoyed. Deep draught yachts should call ahead for advice on depths. With strong onshore winds care is needed when entering the marina, but it is more difficult than dangerous.

Berth Marina staff will direct you to a berth. Finger pontoons, and laid moorings tailed to the quay for larger yachts (>12m).

Shelter Good all-round protection inside the marina.

Data 550 berths. Visitors' berths. Max LOA 40m. Charge band 6.

Facilities Water. 220/380V. WiFi. Showers and toilets. Fuel quay (0800–1200 / 1500–1900). Cantiere (part of the Nautor Group) in the yard along the S side of the canal. 110-ton travel-lift. 40-ton crane. 60-ton hydraulic trailer. Most repairs. Chandlers. B&G and Simrad dealers.

Cantiere ☏ 0566 867 031
Email info@scarlino-ys.com

Bakery and mini-market in the village 200m away. Restaurants nearby.

Marina di Scarlino ☏ 0566 867 001
Email info@marinadiscarlino.com
www.marinadiscarlino.com

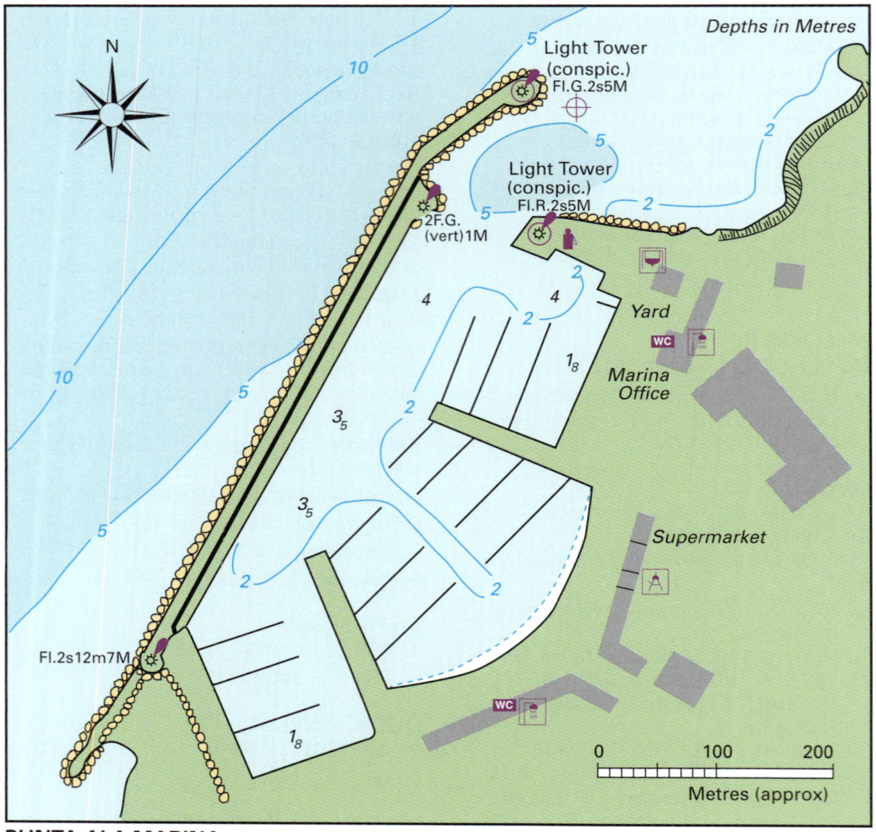

PUNTA ALA MARINA

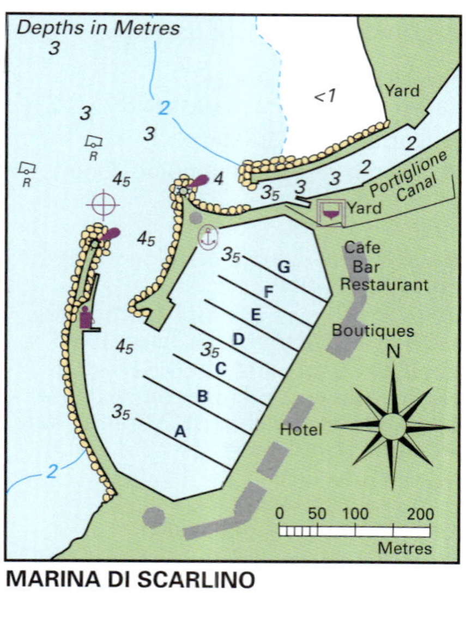

MARINA DI SCARLINO

PUNTA ALA MARINA

42°48'·5N 10°44'·2E
BA 1999 It 05 Imray M17

☆ Elbow Fl.2s7M. Entrance Fl.G.2s5M/Fl.R.2s5M/2F.G(vert)1M

VHF Ch 09, 16.

Navigation Care needed of Scogli Porcellini off Punta Ala.

Berths Where directed. Laid moorings tailed to the quay.

Shelter Good all-round.

Data 895 berths. 90 visitors' berths. Max LOA 32m. Depths 1·8–4m. Charge band 6.

Facilities Water. 220V. Showers and toilets. 100-ton travel-hoist. 50-ton crane. Most yacht repairs. Provisions and restaurants.

Marina di Punta Ala ☏ 0564 922 217
Torre di Controllo ☏ 0564 922 784
Email info@marinadipuntaala.com
www.marinadipuntaala.com

CASTIGLIONE DELLA PESCAIA

42°45'·66N 10°52'·63E WGS84

☆ Entrance Fl.G.3s8M/Fl.R.3s8M

A fishing and yacht harbour inside the River Bruma. Normally 2m depths in the entrance. Entrance dangerous in moderate to strong onshore winds.

Data Max LOA 13m. Depths 0·5–2·5m. Charge band 2/3.

Note Yacht basin reported to have silted to <2m.

MARINA DI SAN ROCCO PORTO DELLA MAREMMA

42°42'·7N 10°58'·8E

☆ Entrance Fl.R.3s5M/Fl.G.3s5M Formiche di Grosseto Fl.6s11M

VHF Ch 09, 16.

Navigation Marina in the Canal San Rocco. Entry dangerous in strong onshore winds.

Berths Stern or bows-to where directed. Larger yachts (11–14m) use the basin on the N side of the entrance. Laid moorings tailed to the quay or to buoys.

Shelter Good all-round protection inside the marina.

Data 560 berths. 56 visitors' berths. Max LOA 14m. Depths <1–3m. Charge band 5/6.

Facilities Water. 220V. Shower and toilets. 20-ton crane. Some repairs.

Porto della Maremma ☏ 0564 330 075
Torre di Controllo ☏ 0564 330 027
Email info@portodellamaremma.it

TALAMONE

42°33'·19N 11°08'·15E WGS84
BA 1999 It 122

☆ Capo d'Uomo Fl(2)10s15M. Mole head Fl(2)R.6s7M

Navigation Entrance by buoyed channel between rocky banks.

Berths Stern or bows-to. Laid moorings.

Shelter Adequate in summer.

Data Max LOA 14m. Depths <1–4m. Charge band 4/5.

Facilities Water. 220V. Fuel quay. Most provisions and restaurants.

☎ 0564 887 003

SANTO STEFANO

42°26'·38N 11°07'·41E WGS84
BA 131 It 74 Imray M17

☆ Punta Lividonia Fl.5s16M. Porto Vecchio 2F.G(vert)3M. Porto Valle Fl.G.3s3M/Fl.R.3s4M

VHF Ch 14, 16 for *capitaneria* (summer 0700–2300, winter 0700–1900). Ch 12 for pilots.

Berths Stern or bows-to.

Shelter Good shelter with breakwater extension.

Data Porto Turistico Domiziano 104 berths. 20 visitors' berths. Max LOA 24m. Depths 4–8m. Charge band 6.

Porto Vecchio 130 berths. Max LOA 40m. Depths 2–5m. Charge band 6.

Facilities Water. Fuel quay. 400-ton slip. Most yacht repairs. Provisions and restaurants.

Between Porto del Valle and Porto Vecchio moorings for visiting yachts are available (June–September).

Porto Turistico Domiziano
☎ 0564 810 845
Email portodomiziano@virgilio.it

Cantierie del'Argentario ☎ 0564 814 063

PORTO ERCOLE

42°23'·63N 11°12'·64E WGS84
BA 1999 It 74 Imray M17

☆ La Rocca LFl.WR.7s16/13M. Entrance Fl.R.3s8M/Fl.G.3s4M

VHF Ch 16.

Navigation Care needed of Burano Reef E of Porto Ercole.

Berths Stern or bows-to. Laid moorings.

Shelter Adequate although prolonged S winds cause a surge.

Data Approximately 600 berths. 10 visitors' berths. Max LOA 14/24m. Depths 1–5m. Charge band 6.

Facilities Water. 220V. Fuel quay (1·5m). 40-ton crane. 500-ton slipway. Some yacht repairs.

Pontili Albatros & Cormorano
☎ 06 375 93152 / 347 356 3953
Email cidonio@cidonio.it
www.pontiliportoercole.it

MARINA DI CALA GALERA

42°24'·10N 11°12'·36E WGS84
BA 1999 It 74 Imray M17

☆ Entrance Iso.WR.2s10/7M (197°-W-017°-R-197°)/Iso.G.2s6M

VHF Ch 09, 16.

Berths Call the marina for a short-stay berth. There are five agencies (listed below) which arrange longer stays. Once you are allocated a berth a marina attendant will come out in a RIB to assist. Laid moorings tailed to the quay.

Shelter Good shelter.

Data 700 berths. 60 visitors' berths. Max LOA 50m. Depths 2·5–5m. Charge band 6.

Facilities Water. 220V. Telephone. Showers and toilets. Fuel quay. 80-ton travel-hoist. 300-ton slipway. Most yacht repairs. Some provisions and restaurants.

☎ 0564 833 010
Email info@marinacalagalera.com
www.marinacalagalera.com

Claudio Mare ☎ 0564 830 135
Covemar ☎ 0564 833 131
Immobiliare Nautica ☎ 0564 832 344
I.M.S. ☎ 0564 832 138
Scott Marine ☎ 0564 832 540
Nauticamato ☎ 339 836 8800

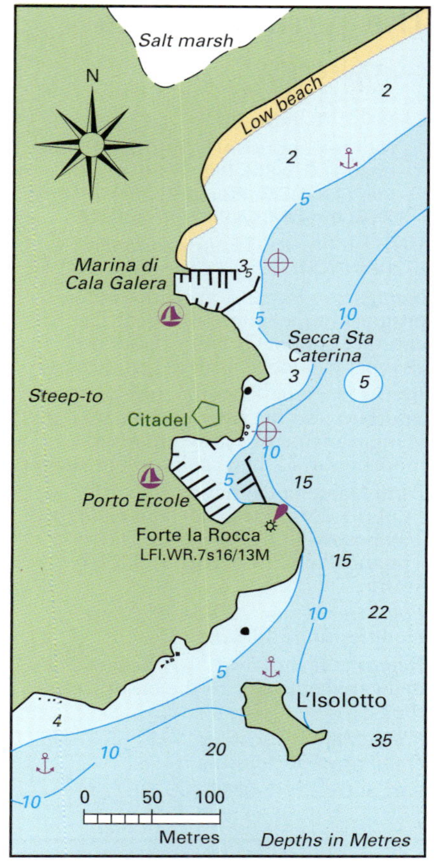

PORTO ERCOLE TO CALA GALERA

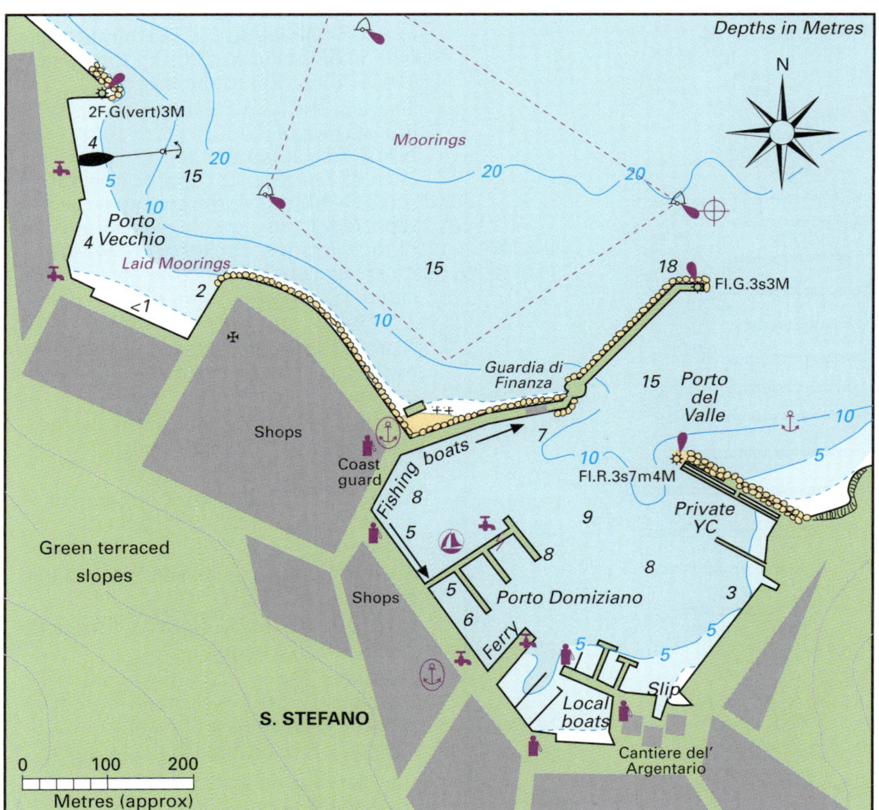

SANTO STEFANO

The Tyrrhenian Sea

CIVITAVECCHIA

42°06'·2N 11°46'·3E
BA 907 It 76 Imray M17

☆ Monte Cappuccini Fl(2)10s24M. Mole head Fl.G.3s8M. Pier 2F.R(vert)3M. Pier Fl.R.4s8M. Pier 2F.R(vert)3M/2F.G(vert)3M. Mole 2F.R(vert)3M

VHF Ch 06, 15, 16 for *capitaneria* (0700–1900). Ch 14 for pilots (24/24).

Navigation Expansion works are in progress in the outer port area. The entrance channel is buoyed, but the channel will move as work progresses.

Berths Darsena Romano and Darsena Traianea and the surrounding area are being transformed into a marina. Laid moorings at all berths. Excellent shelter.

Data Darsena Romano: 70 berths. LOA 15-25m. Darsena Traianea Nord: 100 berths. LOA 10-150m. Darsena Traianea Sud: 14 berths. LOA 40-100m.

Facilities Water. 220/380V. More facilities to be added.

Remarks It is planned to open a dedicated entrance to the basin from the S.

Roma Marina Yachting ✆ 331 657 1096
Email rmy@portdiroma.it

Port authority ✆ 0766 366 226 / 273

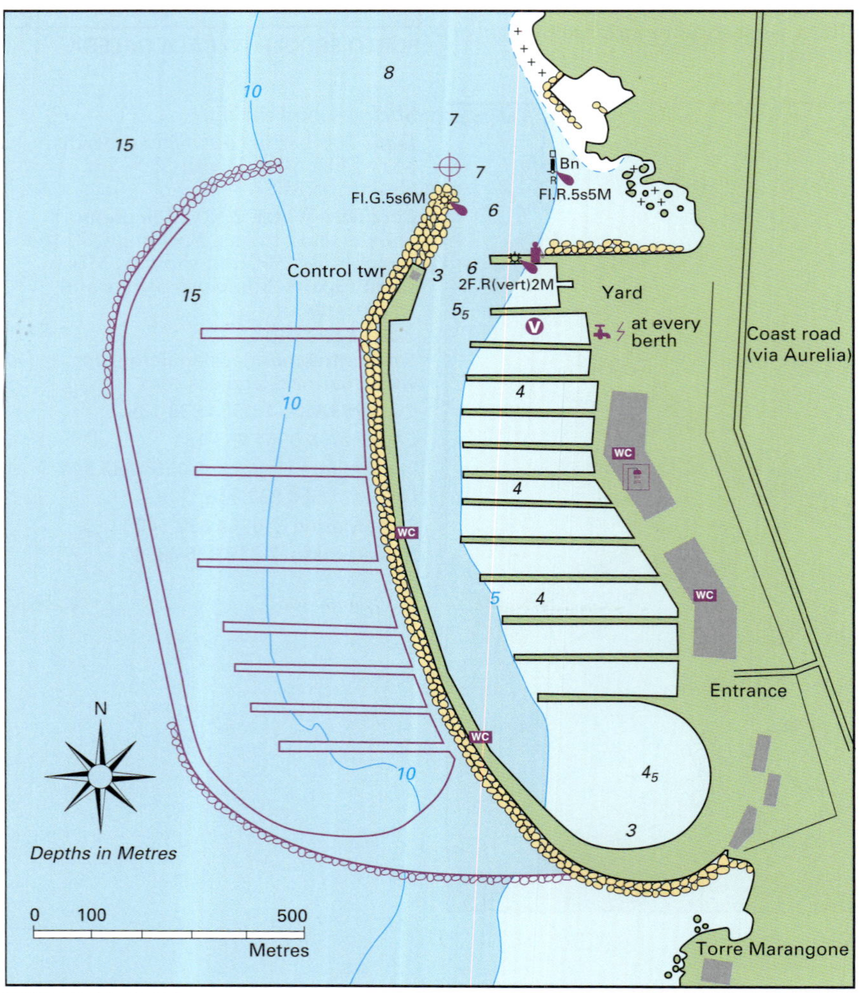

RIVA DI TRAIANO

RIVA DI TRAIANO

42°04'·0N 11°48'·5E
BA 907 It 123 Imray M17
50M Porto Giglio ←→ Fiumicino 28M

☆ Entrance Fl.G.5s6M/2F.R(vert)2M. Beacon Fl.R.5s5M

VHF Ch 09 (24/24).

Navigation The coast is fringed by rocks and the approach should be made on a E–NE course. With strong onshore winds there is a confused swell making entry difficult.

Berths Report to reception quay for a berth. Laid moorings tailed to the quay.

Shelter Good shelter.

Data 1,182 berths. 113 visitors' berths. Max LOA 40m. Charge band 5.

Facilities Water. 220V. WiFi. Showers and toilets. 100-ton travel-hoist. Some yacht repairs. Good supermarket and restaurants.

Remarks Project in planning stage to double capacity of marina as shown in the plan.

Porto Riva di Traiano
✆ 0766 580 193 / 0766 30201
Email direzione@rivaditraiano.com
www.rivaditraiano.com

SANTA MARINELLA

42°02'·07N 11°52'·46E WGS 84
BA 1911 It 75 Imray M17

☆ Entrance 2F.G(vert)3M/2F.R(vert)3M

VHF Ch 16, 09 (Porto Romano).

A small yacht harbour lying 7M from Civitavecchia and 2M E of Capo Linaro. Good shelter.

Berths Two pontoons. Laid moorings tailed to the pontoons.

Data 285 berths. Max LOA 15m. Depths 1·5–5m. Charge band 5/6.

Facilities Water. 220V. WiFi. Fuel quay. 40-ton travel-hoist. 20-ton crane. Provisions and restaurants.

Porto Romano ✆ 0766 513 005
Email info@marinadisantmarinella.com

FIUMICINO (PORTO CANALE)

41°46'·3N 12°12'·9E
BA 906 It 75 Imray M17
28M Riva di Traiano ←→ Anzio 28M

☆ S mole root Fl.3s11M. Entrance Fl.R.3s7M / Fl.G.3s8M / F.G.8m4M

VHF Ch 16 for *capitaneria* (24/24). Ch 12 for pilots (*Piloti Fiumocino*).

Navigation Two oil discharging platforms are situated about 2½M SW and 3M WSW of the entrance to the canal. These platforms are low-lying with masts exhibiting a Mo(A)Y.4s3M / 2Fl.R.5s&4s and a Fl.Y.2s3M respectively. It is prohibited to anchor within a radius of 3M around the entrance to Fiumicino.

Limit of restricted area:
from position 41°46'·02N, 12°09'·2E in a 075° direction for 1410m then in a 040·5° direction for 3350m then in a 106·5° direction to the shore.

There is always a current running W out of the canal which turns to the NNW to run parallel to the coast. The current can reach an appreciable rate: often 3–4 knots with rates up to 6–7 reported. Considerable overfalls occur at the entrance. Yachts over 20 tons must engage a pilot before entering the canal. Call *Roma Radio* on VHF Ch 12, 16.

Note Works in progress at the entrance to the canal on construction of a new commercial harbour.

Berths Stern or bows-to in the basin. Laid moorings tailed to pontoons. Alongside in the canal.

Remarks Dredging work ongoing in canal entrance and in Darsena di Traiano.

Shelter Good in the basin. Adequate in the canal.

Data 200 berths. Max LOA 15m in the basin. Charge band 5.

Facilities Water. 220V. Fuel quay. 50-ton slipway. 10-ton crane. All yacht repairs. Provisions and restaurants.

Capitaneria ✆ 06 658 1911 / 658 1933

Co-operativa del Porto di Traiano (Darsena Traiano) ✆ 0665 82361
Email cooperativa.traiano@tiscalinet.it

Tre Effe Elle (Fulvio's boatyard)
✆ 0665 029 392 / 4 or 335 717 8584

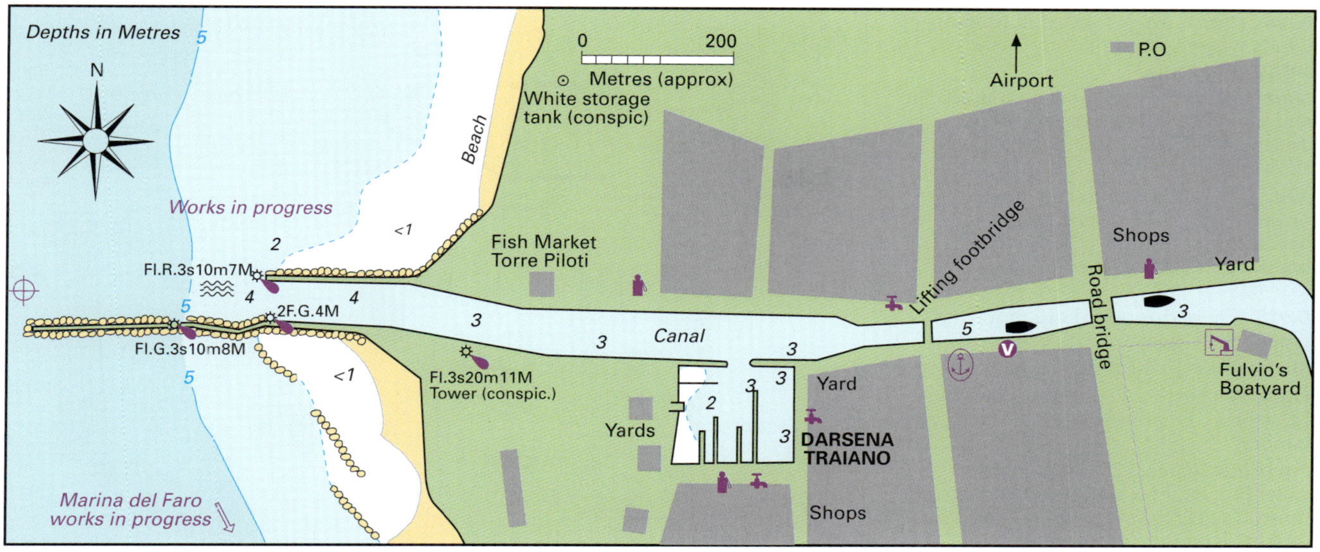

FIUMICINO

Bridge opening times:
Monday, Wednesday, Friday 0630 and 2000
Saturday 0800 and 2000
Sunday 0900, 1400, 2000
None on Tuesday or Thursday
Note Bridge opening times change frequently. Recently the bridges have been unable to open regularly due to mechanical failure.

MARINA DEL FARO PORTO TURISTICO DI FIUMICINO (PORTO DELLA CONCORDIA)

A new marina development between Fiumicino and Fiumare Grande. The usual marina and boatyard facilities can be expected on completion.

Data 1,445 berths (when completed). Max LOA c.60m.
www.portodellaconcordia.it

RIVIERE TEVERE (FIUMARA GRANDE)

41°44'·34N 12°13'·58E WGS84 (River entrance)

☆ Starboard side Fl.G.5s5M. Port side Fl.R.5s5M. Dir Q.WRG.5M (061·5°-G-066·5°-W-017·5°-R-076·5°)

VHF Ch 16 (Porto di Roma, Darsena Netter, Tecnomar) Ch 09, CB 73 (Porto Romano).

Navigation When entering keep close S of the middle of the river. In the summer there are usually yachts coming and going to show the navigable channel. Once into the river proceed up to the island (about 1M upriver) and then take the channel on the N side of the islet.

Berth
Cantieri di Ostia Basin on the S bank.
Marina Porto Romano first basin on the N bank.
Darsena Netter Immediately upriver.
Tecnomar On N bank beyond the islet.
Nautilus Marina Adjacent to Tecnomar.

Cantieri di Ostia

Data Max LOA 20m. Depths 1–3m.
Facilities Water. 220V. 60-ton slip. 12-ton crane. Most repairs.
Canados ✆ 06 564 70155

Marina Porto Romano

Data 200 berths. 100m visitors' quay. Max LOA 25m. Depths 3·5m. Charge band 5/6.
Facilities Water. 220V. Fuel. 70-ton travel-lift. 20-ton crane. Most repairs.
Marina Porto Romano (YC Tevere)
✆ 06 650 2651
Email marina@portoromano.com or cantiere@portoromano.com
www.portoromano.com

Darsena Netter

Data 100 berths. 10 visitors' berths. Max LOA 50m. Depths 3–4·5m.
Facilities Water. 220V. 150-ton slip. 30-ton travel-lift. Most repairs.
Darsena Netter
✆ 06 652 1966 / 67
Email netter@faronet.it
www.netter.it
Nautilus Marina ✆ 06 658 1221

Tecnomar

Data Visitors' berths. Max LOA 30m. Depths 3-4m.
Facilities Water. 220V. Fuel. 300-ton slip. 30-ton travel-lift. Most repairs.
Circolo Nautico Tecnomar
✆ 06 658 0690 / 91
Email info@tecnomar.net
www.tecnomar.net

Nautilus Marina

Data c.100 berths rafted alongside. 30 places ashore. Depths 4-5m. Max LOA c.45m. Charge band 3.
Facilities Water. 220V. Toilets and showers. Restaurant. Security. 50-ton travel-lift. Most engineering, electrical and mechanical repairs.
Nautilus Marina
✆ 06 658 1221
Email info@nautilusmarina.com
www.nautilusmarina.com

PORTO TURISTICO DI ROMA (OSTIA)

41°44'·15N 12°14'·7E

☆ Entrance Fl.R.4s8M/Fl.G.4s8M

VHF Ch 16, 74 (Porto di Roma).

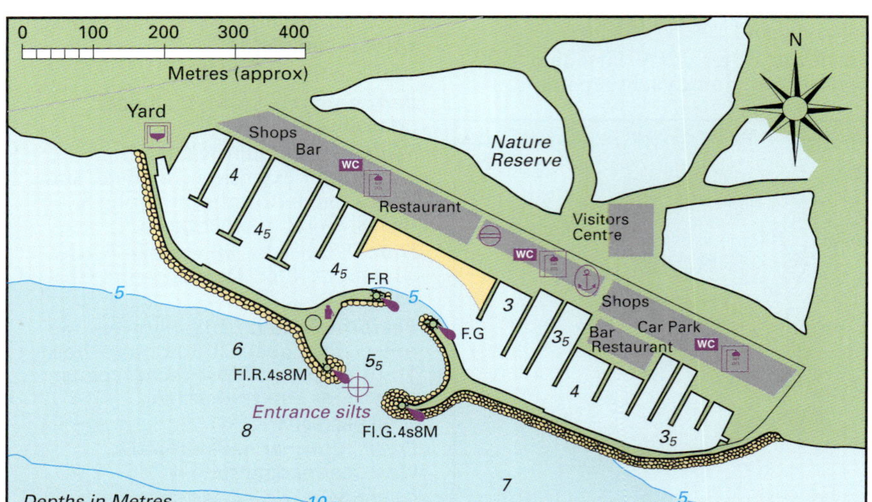

PORTO TURISTICO DI ROMA

Navigation Care is needed in offshore winds when a swell piles up at the entrance.

Note 1. Reports suggest ongoing silting and dredging in the entrance. If in doubt contact the marina before entering.

Note 2. Work is due to start on a project to double the size of the harbour by building a SE opening breakwater around the outside of the marina.

Berth Where directed. Laid moorings tailed to the quay.

Shelter Good all-round shelter

Data 800 berths. Visitors' berths. Max LOA 60m. Depths 3·5–4·5m. Charge band 5.

Facilities Water. 220/380V. Shower and toilet blocks. Fuel quay. 400-ton travel-hoist. Yacht repair facilities. Provisions nearby. Restaurants and bars in the marina and nearby.

Remarks Leonardo da Vinci International Airport 9km. Rome 20km, via bus, metro or taxi.

Porto Turistico di Roma
✆ 06 561 88236 / 88277
Email direzione.porto@portodiroma.it
www.portoturisticodiroma.net

ANZIO

41°26′·62N 12°38′·29E WGS84
BA 906 It 77 Imray M17
28M Fiumicino ←→ San Felice Circeo 26M

☆ Capo d'Anzio Fl(2)10s22M. Entrance Fl.R.3s5M / Fl.G.3s4M / F.G.2M

VHF Ch 12, 16 for port authorities (24/24).

Navigation Care needed of underwater obstructions extending 500m from the coast. With S gales there are breaking waves over the sandbar at the entrance making it dangerous to enter or leave.

A fish farm has been established close off Capo Anzio, marked with yellow buoys. Care needed if approaching at night.

Berths Stern or bows-to. Anchorage in settled weather to the NE.

Shelter Good shelter in the inner basin. A surge in outer harbour with S gales.

Data Depths 2–3m in inner basin. Charge band 1/4.

Facilities Water. 220V. Fuel quay. 300-ton slipway. Some yacht repairs.

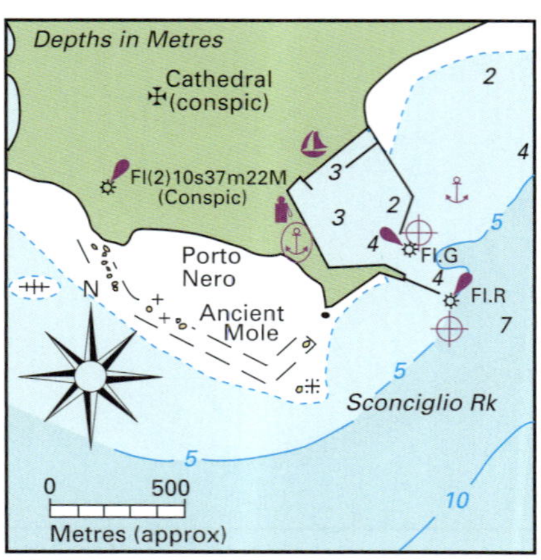

ANZIO APPROACHES

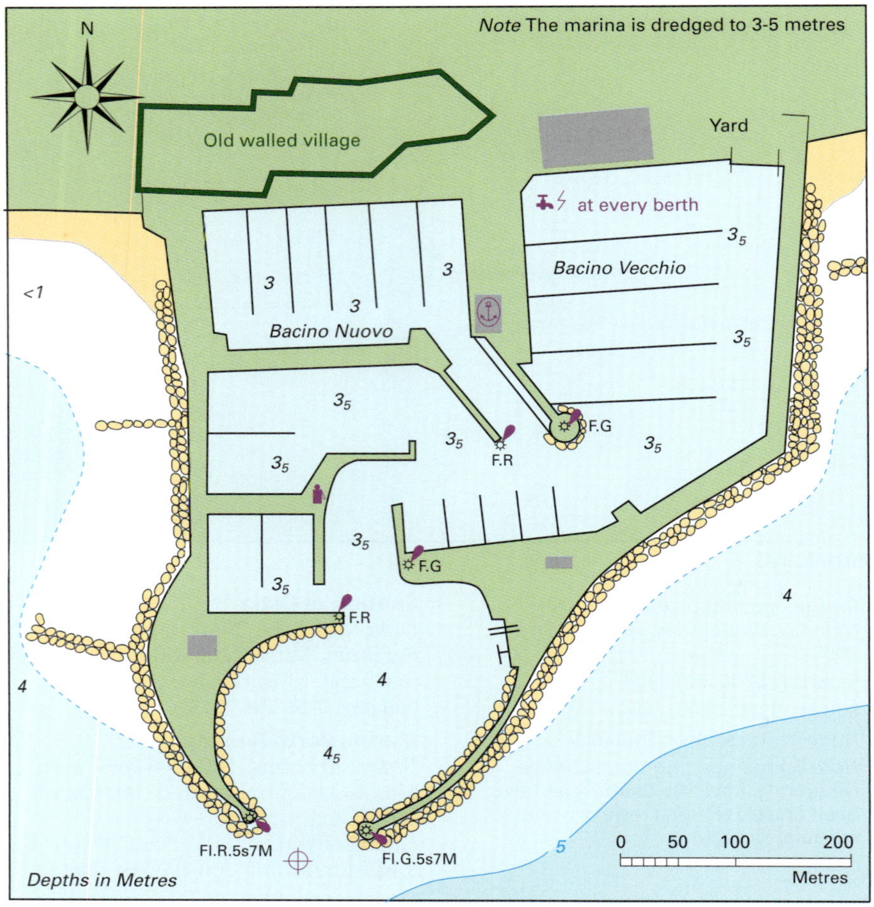

NETTUNO

Provisions and restaurants.

Remarks Entrance continues to silt. Entrance now reported to be close N of the green buoys. Call ahead for latest info or watch ferries on their approach.

Note Harbour extension works planned.

MARINA DI NETTUNO

41°27′·1N 12°39′·6E
BA 906 It 77 Imray M17

☆ Entrance Fl.G.5s7M/Fl.R.5s7M/2F.G(vert)4M. Inner mole F.G.1M/F.R.1M

Navigation The new harbour extension work is complete.

VHF Ch 09, 16 (24/24).

Berths Stern or bows-to. Finger pontoons.

Shelter Much improved with breakwater extension complete. Some berths uncomfortable in strong S winds. Good in inner basin.

Data 970 berths. 80 visitors' berths. Max LOA 40m. Depths 3–5m. Charge band 5.

Facilities Water. 220V. Showers and toilets. Fuel quay. 50-ton travel-hoist. 50-ton slipway. Most yacht repairs. Provisions and restaurants.

✆ 06 980 5404
Email info@marinadinettuno.it
www.marinadinettuno.it

Sailing Yachts ✆ 06 980 5372
Email info@sailingyachts.it

SECCHE DI TOR PATERNO MARINE RESERVE

A rocky shelf approximately 5M off the coast between Ostia and Anzio.
✆ 06 354 03436
www.romanatura.roma.it

Note A firing range E of Nettuno extends out over the adjacent coast. Naval patrol boats control an exclusion zone at least 10M off the coast. Check in Anzio or Nettuno port offices or with Capo Circeo radio.

SAN FELICE CIRCEO

41°13′·5N 13°05′·9E
BA 1911 It 75 Imray M17
26M Anzio ←→ Ventotene 30M

☆ Capo Circeo Fl.5s23M. Entrance 2F.G(vert)2M/2F.R(vert)2M

VHF Ch 09, 16 (Co-operative Ormeggiatori Circeo).

Navigation A sand-bar obstructs much of the entrance. Dredged channel on approximately 287° marked by two port hand buoys. With strong onshore winds waves break at the entrance.

Berths Stern or bows-to. Laid moorings tailed to the quay.

Shelter Good shelter although strong S winds make some berths uncomfortable.

Data 380 berths. Max LOA 20m. Depths 0·5–4m. Charge band 6.

Facilities Water. 220V. Showers and toilets. 40-ton travel-hoist. 30-ton crane. Some yacht repairs. Limited provisions. Restaurant.

Ormeggiatore ☽ 0773 547 336
Fax 0773 546 184
www.circeoprimo.it

TERRACINA
41°16'·96N 13°15'·73E WGS84
BA 1911 It 75 Imray M17

☆ Entrance Fl.R.5s9M/Fl.G.5s6M. Entrance to canal F.R.8m3M / F.G.8m3M

VHF Ch 14, 16 (0700–1900) for port authorities.

Navigation A recent report warns the entrance has silted severely to 1·3–2m with no marked channel. A fishing harbour with yacht berths in outer basin and in inner canal basin.

Data 120 berths in outer basin. 80 berths in canal basin. Max LOA 14m. Depths 1·5–3m.

Remarks Yachts are not permitted to berth alongside in the canal.

SPERLONGA
41°15'·21N 13°26'·17E WGS84

Harbour extended. Depths 1·5-2m. Continuous silting in the entrance. Max LOA 15m. Charge band 6+.

☽ 335 138 9616
www.portodisperlonga.it

GAETA
41°12'·62N 13°36'·54E WGS84
(1M E of Pta Stendardo)
BA 906 It 78 Imray M18

☆ Monte Orlando Fl(3)15s23M. Punta dello Stendardo Fl(2)R.10s7M

PORTO SANTA MARIA
41°12'·6N 13°35'·4E (Punta dello Stendardo light)

A small basin close W of Punta dello Stendardo.

Data 30 berths. Max LOA c.60m. Depths 3·5–10m.

BANCHINA CABOTO

Facilities Water and electricity at most berths.

Capitaneria Gaeta ☽ 0771 460 100
Email gaeta@guardiacostiera.it

PORTO SANT'ANTONIO (BASE NAUTICA FLAVIO GIOIA)
41°13'·09N 13°34'·70E WGS84
BA 906 It 78 Imray M18

☆ Mole head Porto Salvo Fl.G.3s7M. Molo Sant'Antonio head Fl.R.3s6M. Entrance 2F.R(vert)/2F.G(vert)/2F.R(vert)

VHF Ch 09 (24/24).

Berths Where directed. Laid moorings tailed to the quay.

Shelter Good shelter.

Data 250 berths. 15 visitors' berths. Max LOA 60m. Depths 2–4m. Charge band 6.

Facilities Water. 220V. Satellite TV. WiFi. Showers and toilets. 100-ton travel-hoist. 400-ton slipway. All yacht repairs. Provisions and restaurants. Supermarket.

Remarks Yachts are prohibited to berth in Porto Sant'Antonio except in Flavio Gioia. Popular base for wintering over.

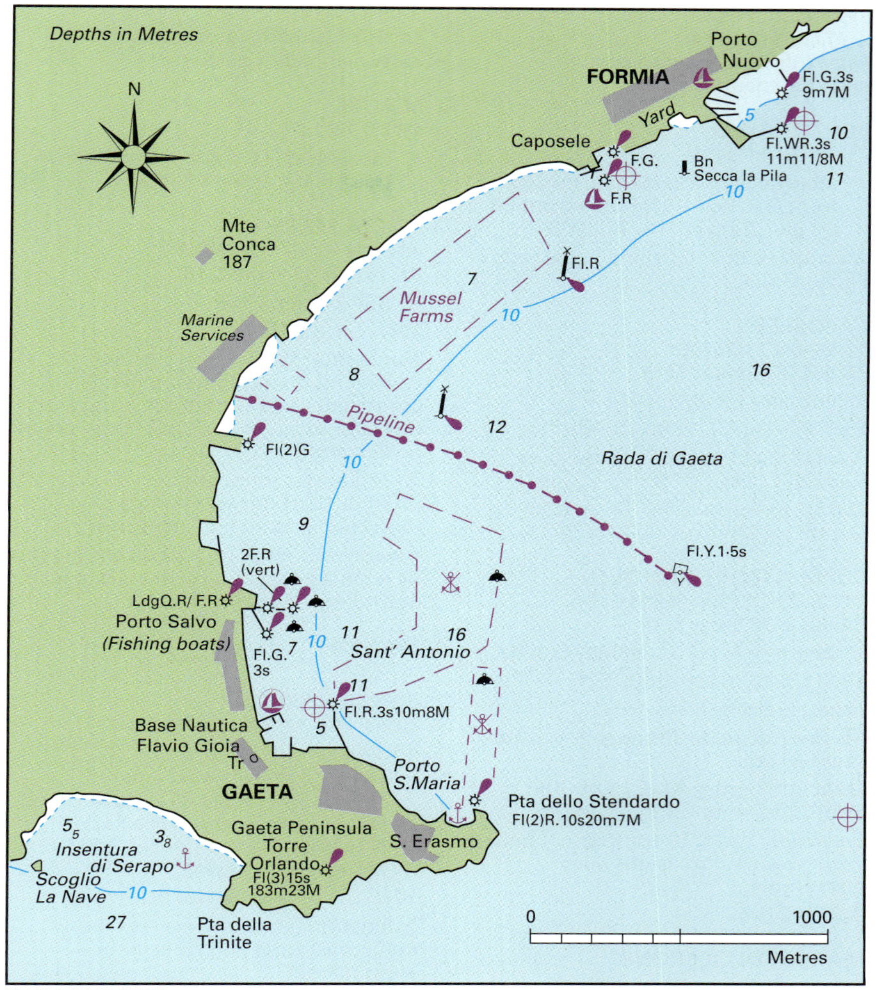

RADA DI GAETA

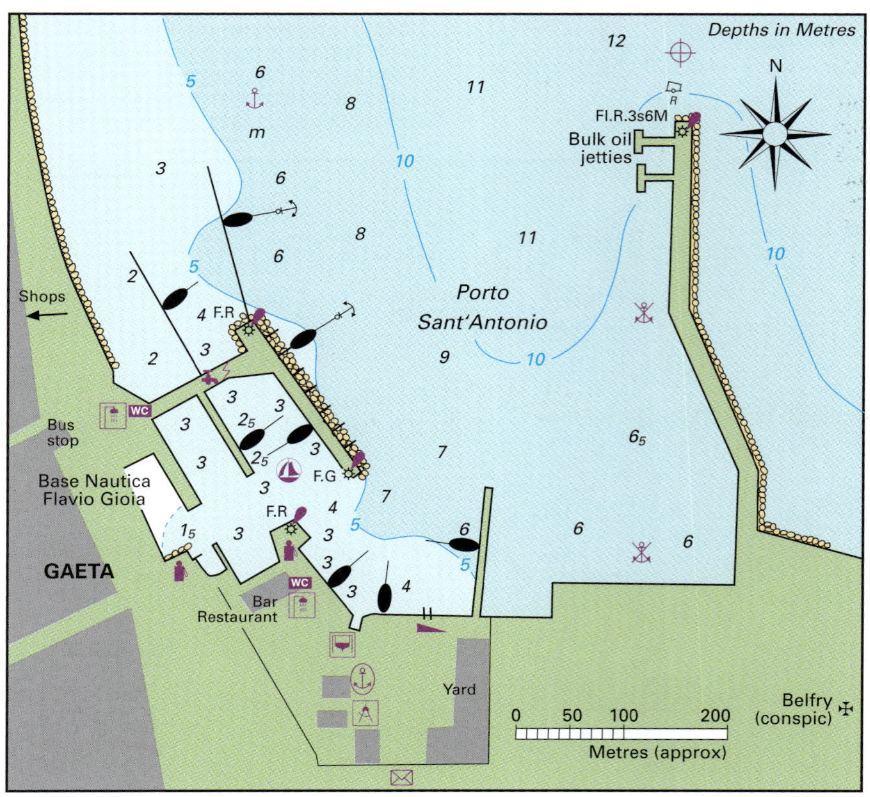

BASE NAUTICA FLAVIO GIOIA

Base Nautica Flavio Gioia
✆ 0771 311 013 / 4
Email info@basenautica.com
www.basenautica.com

PORTO SALVO
41°13'·2N 13°34'·4E

☆ Mole head Fl.G.3s7M. Ldg Lts 269° front Q.R. Rear 190m from front F.R. Oil pier 2F.R(vert)1M. Buoys Q

A commercial and fishing harbour N of Flavio Gioia.

CAPOSELE
41°15'·0N 13°36'·0E
BA 906 It 78 Imray M18

☆ Entrance F.R.2M/F.G.2M

VHF Ch 16, 10 (0800–2000).

A small yacht harbour on the N side of Rada di Gaeta.

Data 130 berths. Max LOA 12m. Depths <1–3m.

FORMIA (PORTO NUOVO)
41°15'·22N 13°36'·96E WGS84
BA 906 It 78 Imray M18

☆ Entrance Fl.WR.3s11/8M/Fl.G.3s7M

VHF Ch 16 (0800–2000).

Berths Stern or bows-to.

Shelter Adequate although SW winds cause a surge.

Data 500 berths. Max LOA 30m. Depths 0·5–6m. Charge band 4.

Facilities Water. 20-ton crane. Limited yacht repairs. Provisions and restaurants.

✆ 0771 215 52

MARINA DI CICERONE

A new project to build a marina to the S of the main harbour. Work is as yet sporadic, and no completion dates are available.

Data (when open) 600 berths. Max LOA 70m.

✆ 06 3759311
email info@marinadicicerone.com
www.marinadicicerone.com

SCAURI
41°15'·1N 13°42'·1E

☆ Mole head Fl.G.5s4M. Inner basin W side F.R.4M. E side F.G.4M

PINETA MARE
40°59'N 13°58'·3E
BA 1911 It 09 Imray M18

☆ Breakwater F.R.6M

VHF Ch 12, 16.

Navigation With onshore winds a considerable swell piles up in the approaches and entrance making entry difficult. In an onshore gale entry could be dangerous.

Note The harbour continues to silt. In 2010 the harbour was completely inaccessible to all but small craft.

Remarks Camper & Nicholsons plan to develop a new 1200 berth marina here. Start dates as yet unavailable.

Ponza

PONZA HARBOUR
40°54'·06N 12°58'·24E WGS84
BA 1908 It 82 Imray M46

☆ La Rotonda della Madonna Fl(4)15s15M/F.R.9M 301°-vis-341° over Secche Le Formiche. Ravia Rock Fl.G.3s6M. Breakwater Fl.R.3s8M. Mole head Fl.Y.3s9M

VHF Ch 14, 16, 09 (see below).

Navigation Care is needed of the numerous rocks and reefs in the approaches.

Berths Limited room on the quay. Anchoring possible inside the marked area. Pontoons around the bay. All have laid moorings at most berths. Depths vary but generally it is only the outermost berths with sufficient depths for most yachts. Max LOA c.25m.

Larger yachts by arrangement. Charge band 6+.

Shelter Normally adequate in the summer. Open NE.

Facilities Water. 220V. Fuel quay. Provisions and restaurants.

Port Authority ✆ 0771 800 27

Ponzamare VHF Ch 09
✆ 0771 80679 / 809 678
Email ponzamare@ponzamare.it
www.ponzamare.it

Ciccio Nero VHF Ch 11
✆ 0771 80697
Email info@ciccionero.it
www.isolaponza.it

Gennarino al Mare ✆ 0771 80071

Enros VHF Ch 12, 16
✆ 0771 80012 / 339 830 9246
Email nauticaenros@tiscali.it
www.nauticaenros.it

Ecomare VHF Ch 68
✆ 338 204 6081

La Fenicia ✆ 338 926 6716

Cantieri Parisi
✆ 0771 80544 / 333 796 2895
Email info@cantieriparisi.it
www.cantieriparisi.it

Cantiere Nautico Porzio
✆ 0771 809 830
Email info@cantierenauticoporzio.com

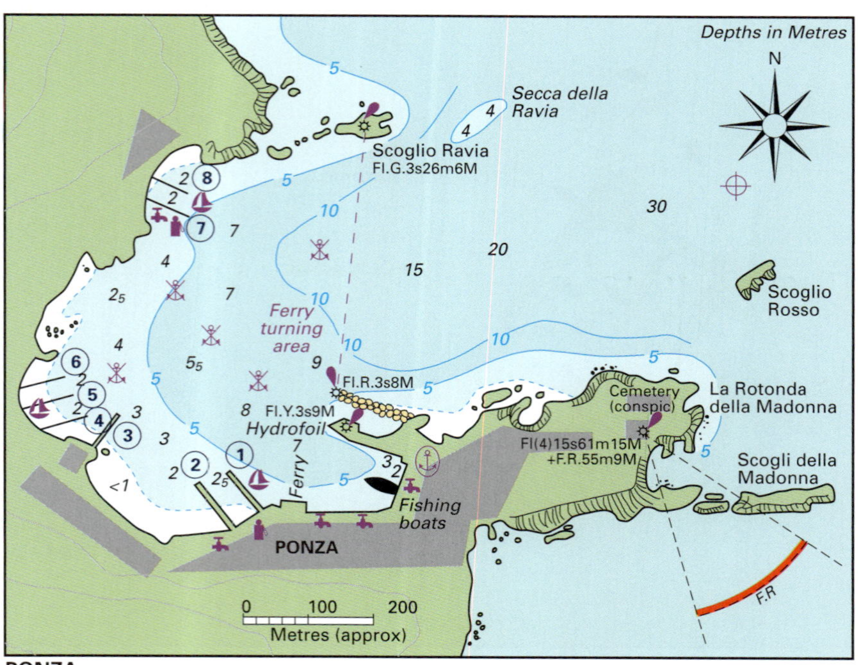

PONZA

Isola Ventotene

ISOLA VENTOTENE AND ISOLA SANTO STEFANO MARINE RESERVE
Ventotene harbours lie within Zone C.
Ventotene Port Authority
✆ 0771 85291 Comune ✆ 0771 85014

VENTOTENE HARBOUR
40°48'·24N 13°26'·03E (Cala Rossano entrance)
40°47'·8N 13°26'·1E (Porto Vecchio entrance)
BA 1908 It 126 Imray M46
30M San Felice Circeo ←→ Ischia 23M

☆ Lighthouse Fl.5s15M. Cala Rossana Fl.R.5s5M / Fl.G.5s4M

VHF Ch 16, Ch 12 for marina

Navigation Larger yachts (over 12m) should go to Cala Rossano. Yachts under 12m can squeeze into the old harbour.

Berths Bows-to in Porto Vecchio on the W quay. Go bows-to to avoid underwater obstructions close to the quay. Stern or bows-to the pontoon with laid moorings or stern-to the N end of the breakwater in Cala Rossano.

Shelter Adequate in Cala Rossana.

Data *Porto Vecchio* 10 berths. Max LOA 12m. Depths <1–3m. Charge band 5.

Marina di Ventotene 30 berths. Laid moorings. Water. 220V. Good shelter.

Facilities Water and 220V on the pontoon and on E quay in Porto Vecchio. Fuel near Cala Rossana. (Anchor with a long line ashore when pontoon absent). Most provisions and restaurants.

Marina di Ventotene ✆ 348 252 5982
www.ormeggimarinadiventotene.com

Porto Vecchio Giro (Enrico) ✆ 0771 85122

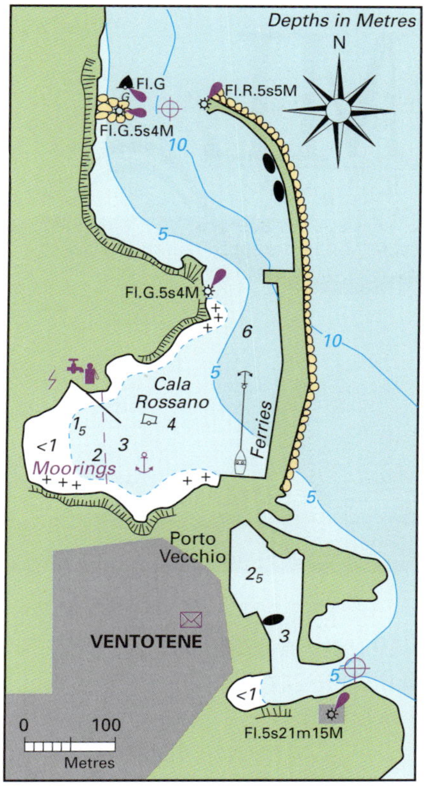

VENTOTENE - CALA ROSSANA AND PORTO VECCHIO

Bay of Naples

AMP CAMPI FLEGREI

This new AMP includes the Baia and Gaiola Reserves, and has been extended to include parts of the coast around Capo Miseno (the anchorage may be affected) and Aquamorta. See park website for details. At present there is a provisional Zone B classification.

www.parcodeicampiflegrei.it

ACQUAMORTA

40°47'·4N 14°02'·45E

A part constructed harbour off Pta di Tre Fumi on the NE side of Canale di Procida. Anchor off inside.

Data Depths 1–6m.

PORTO MISENO

40°47'·33N 14°05'·48E WGS84

BA 916 It 83 Imray M46

☆ Capo Miseno Fl(2)10s16M. Light Bn Fl.3s3M

Anchorage in the outer part of the bay. Laid moorings in inner part of the bay. Trip line recommended.

BAIA

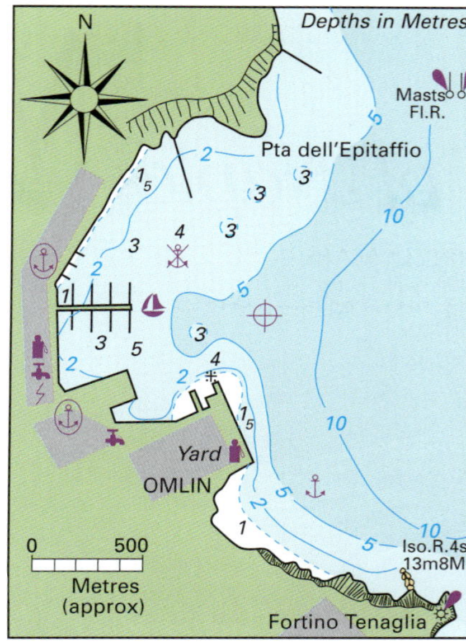

BAIA

BAIA MARINE RESERVE

An underwater (Parco Sommerso) marine reserve has been established off Baia. Navigation, anchoring and mooring is prohibited off Punta dell Epitaffio.

✆ 081 442 21 22

Email info@areamarinaprotettabaia.it

www.areamarinaprotettabaia.it

Baia Parco Sommerso

✆ 081 442 2122

//parcoarcheologicalsommersodobaia.it

40°49'·0N 14°04'·7E

BA 916 It 83 Imray M46

☆ Fortino Tenaglia Iso.R.4s8M

A bay just under 2M N of Porto Miseno.

Data 200 berths. Depths <1–4·5m. Charge band 4.

Facilities Water. 220V. Showers and toilets. Fuel quay. 250-ton slipway. 60-ton crane. Large yard (OMLIN) with all facilities. Provisions and restaurants nearby.

Remarks Anchoring is restricted in the bay.

✆ 081 868 7059

POZZUOLI

40°49'·26N 14°06'·75E WGS84

BA 916 It 83 Imray M46

☆ Breakwater head F.G/F.R/Fl.G.3M. Pontile Pirelli head F.Y.4M

VHF Ch 14, 16 (0700–1900) Ch 72 for Sud Cantieri.

Navigation Head for the N side of the harbour.

Berths Where directed. Laid moorings. Crowded.

Shelter Good shelter.

Data 150 berths. Max LOA 60m. Depths 1–8m.

Facilities Water. 220V. Showers and toilets. Fuel quay. 40/80-ton travel-hoist. Most repairs. Provisions and restaurants in Pozzuoli up the hill.

Sud Cantieri ✆ 081 526 1140

Email info@sudcantieri.it

GAIOLA MARINE RESERVE

An underwater (Parco Sommerso) marine reserve has been established off Punta Gaiola, between Nisida and Capo Posillipo.

✆ 081 240 3235

Email sanc@interbusiness.it

www.areamarinaprotettagaiola.it

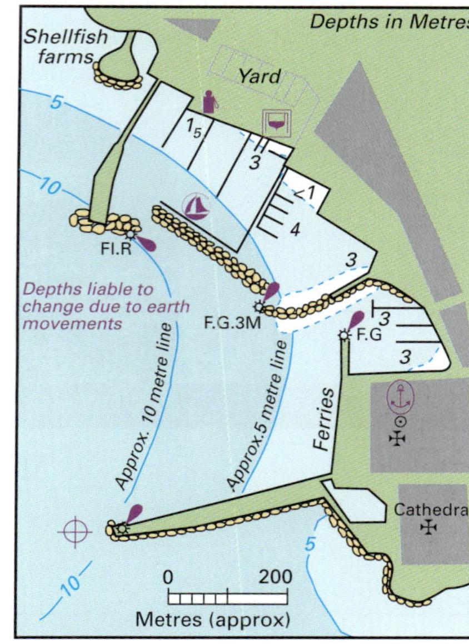

POZZUOLI

NISIDA

40°47'·9N 14°10'·1E

☆ Molo Dandolo spur head Fl.G.3s7M

Navigation Yacht harbour is on the N side of the causeway connecting Nisida to the mainland coast.

Data 400 berths. Max LOA 26m. Depths <1–6m.

Facilities Water. 220V. Fuel quay. Provisions and restaurants nearby.

Onda Azzura ✆ 081 570 8000

SENA ✆ 081 762 2194

SECCA DELLA GAIOLA AND SECCA LA CAVALLARA

☆ Bns Q.Y.10m4M / Fl(2)Y.10s4M / Q(6)+LFl.15s5M

A reef extends SSE from Punta della Gaiola. The southern part of it, Secca La Cavallara, is awash in places.

SANNAZZARO (MERGELLINA)

40°49'·7N 14°13'·6E

BA 916 It 84 Imray M46

☆ Entrance Fl.R.5s8M/Fl.G.5s7M

VHF Ch 09 for Soc. Luise & Sons.

Berths Stern or bows-to.

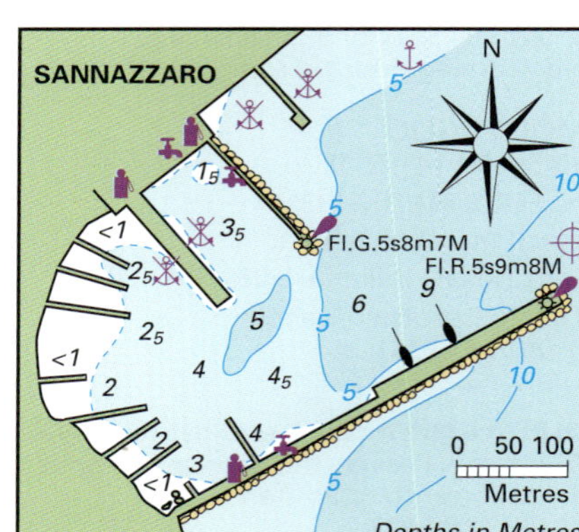

SANNAZZARO

Shelter Good shelter.

Data Max LOA 75m. Depths <1–8m. Charge band 6+.

Facilities Water. 220V. Fuel quay. 20-ton crane. Some yacht repairs. Provisions and restaurants.

Marina Molo Luise ☎ 081 963 3396
Email luise@luise.it
www.luise.com

SANTA LUCIA

40°49'·8N 14°15'·1E

☆ Entrance Fl.R.3s5M/Fl.G.3s4M

Navigation A small yacht harbour under Castell del'Uova. Good shelter.

VHF Ch 77.

Data 150 berths. Max LOA 25m. Depths 2–5m. Charge band 6+.

Facilities Water. 220V. Fuel. 15-ton slip. 10-ton crane. Repairs.

Remarks Can be difficult and expensive to get a berth here.

Coop. Servizi Nautici S.L. (Luciano)
☎ 081 764 5517 or 335 589 4502
www.ormeggioslucia.com

MOLOSIGLIO

40°50'·0N 14°15'·4E

☆ Fl.R.5s8M/Fl.G.5s3M

Small private harbour.

Lega Navale Italiana ☎ 081 551 1806

Circolo Canottieri Napoli
☎ 081 551 2331

PUNTA CAMPANELLA MARINE RESERVE
The reserve covers the coast and islands from Sorrento to Positano.
☎ 081 808 9877
www.puntacampanella.org

PORTO DI NAPOLI

40°49'·8N 14°16'·4E (San Vicenzo head Fl(3)15s22M)
BA 915 It 84 Imray M46

☆ Molo San Vicenzo F(3)15s25m22M. E entrance Fl.G.2s7M/Fl.G.3s7M/Fl.R.3s5M/Fl.R.2s5M. Diga Foranea Fl.R.4s5M/Fl(2)R.10s4M. Darsena di Levante SE corner Fl.G.3s8M

VHF Ch 11, 16 for *capitaneria* (24/24). Ch 12 for pilots (24/24).

MARINA VIGLIENA (PORTO FIORITA)

40°50'N 14°18'·2E

VHF Ch 16, 72

Data 850 berths. LOA 12–80m. Depths 2–4·5m. Charge band 6+.

Facilities Water. 220V. WiFi. Showers and toilets. Fuel quay. 50-ton travel-hoist. Yacht repairs. Provisions and restaurants nearby.

The marina is being re-developed and expanded. At present transit berths are limited. The data above is for the completed marina.

Porto Fiorito ☎ 081 245 7531
Email info@marinavigliena.it

PORTO PORTICI

40°48'·7N 14°20'·0E

☆ Breakwater Fl.3s11M. Mole Fl.G.3s3M

TORRE DEL GRECO

40°47'N 14°21'·8E (Fl.R.5s)
BA 916 It 914 Imray M46

☆ Entrance Fl.R.5s9M / Fl.G.5s3M

VHF Ch 14, 16 (0700–1900).

Berths Stern or bows-to where directed. Laid moorings.

Shelter Good shelter although strong S winds make it uncomfortable.

Data 500 berths. Max LOA 15m. Depths 2–8m. Charge band 5.

Facilities Water. 220V. Fuel quay. Limited yacht repairs. Provisions and restaurants.

Capitaneria ☎ 081 881 2200

Circolo Nautico ☎ 081 881 9150

Luigi (No. 3 pontoon) ☎ 338 101 0402

TORRE ANNUNZIATA

40°44'·5N 14°27'·2E
BA 916 It 94 Imray M46

☆ Entrance Fl.R.2M / F.G.7m2M. Beacon Fl(2)G.6s5M. Molo Darsena Pescatori head F.R.4M

Data Six pontoons with water and electricity.

Circolo Nautico ☎ 081 536 4318

MARINA DI STABIA

☆ Entrance Fl(3)G.5s6M/Fl(3)R.5s6M
Inner entrance 2FG/2FR.2M

Navigation A new marina lying 1·5M S of Torre Anunziata and 1M N of Castellamare di Stabia.

VHF Ch 69.

Berths Stern or bows-to with finger pontoons. Laid moorings for larger yachts.

Shelter Good shelter. Some berths uncomfortable with strong S winds.

Data 900 berths. Max LOA 80m. Depths 3·5–6m. Charge band 6.

Facilities Water. 220/380V. WiFi. Showers and toilets. Laundry. Fuel quay. 220-ton travel-hoist. Large slipway. Repair facilities. Café, bar and restaurant in the marina.

Remarks A good place to leave a yacht for a visit to Pompeii and Herculaneum.

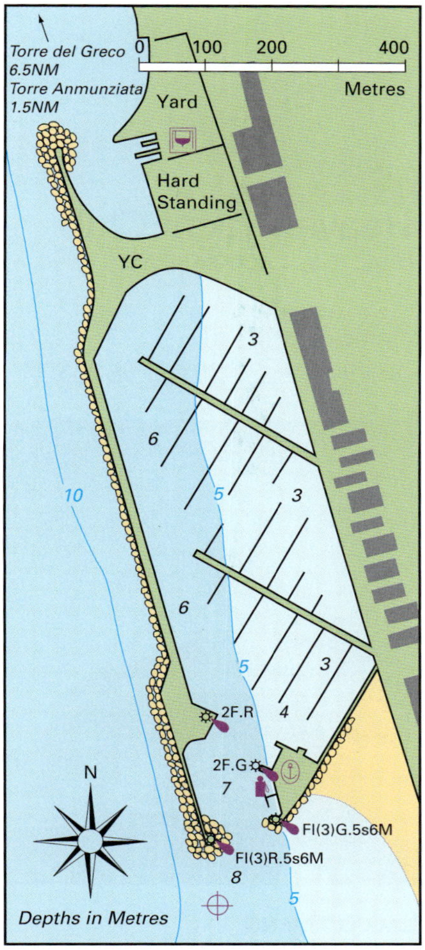

MARINA DI STABIA

Marina manager Piero Sarcinella
☎ 081 871 6871
Email info@marinadistabia.it
www.marinadistabia.it

CASTELLAMMARE DI STABIA

40°42′·2N 14°28′·6E
BA 916 It 95 Imray M46
☆ Main light Fl(2)10s16M. Entrance Fl.G.5s8M/2F.R(vert)3M
Data 200 berths. Max LOA 30m. Depths 1·5–10m. Water and fuel on the quay. Charge band 6.
Cesino Agenzia Marittima
☎ 081 872 4564
Portodavide ☎ 081 871 0107 / 337 942 330
Email info@portodavide.it

MARINA DI EQUA

40°39′·7N 14°25′·0E
☆ Entrance 2F.G(vert)4M/2F.R(vert)

MARINA DI META

40°38′·8N 14°24′·4E
☆ Mole Fl.G.3s5M.

MARINA DI CASSANO

40°38′·56N 14°23′·92E WGS84
☆ Mole F.G.3M
Data 180 berths. Max LOA 14m. Depths 2·5–8m.
Consorzio Nautico Sant'Agnello
☎ 081 878 8436

SORRENTO (MARINA PICCOLA)

40°37′·89N 14°22′·76E WGS84
☆ Breakwater Fl.G.3s5M
VHF Ch 09
Data 250 berths. Max LOA 40m. Depths <1–6·5m. Fuel (May-Oct) and water on the quay.
Porto Turistico Marina Piccola
☎ 081 878 6760 or 347 918 6864 (Francesco)
Email info@portoturisticosorrento.com

Procida

PROCIDA MARINA (MARINA GRANDE)

40°46′·12N 14°02′·02E WGS84
BA 908 It 82 Imray M46
☆ Entrance Fl.G.3s8M/Fl.R.3s8M
VHF Ch 06, 16 (0700–1900).
Navigation Yachts should make for the E basin.
Berths Porto Turistico in the E basin. Yacht quay on E side of W basin. Laid moorings.
Shelter Good shelter in Porto Turistico.
Data 490 berths. Max LOA 30m. Depths 1–3m. Charge band 6.
Facilities Water. 220/380V. Shower and toilets. Fuel. Provisions and restaurants. Ferry to Naples.
Marina di Procida ☎ 081 896 9668
Email info@marinadiprocida.191.it

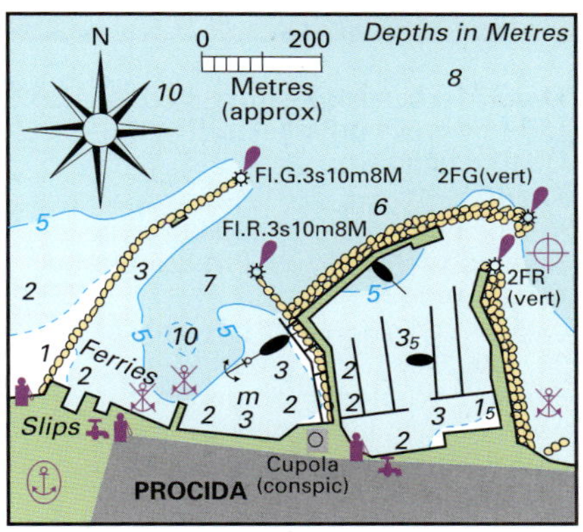

PROCIDA MARINA

CHIAIOLELLA

40°45′·5N 14°01′·9E
BA 908 It 129 Imray M46
☆ Entrance 2F.G(vert)4M/2F.R(vert)4M
A small harbour on the S of the island. Good shelter although southerlies cause a surge.
VHF Ch 16, 11 (0700–1900)
Data c.200 berths. Max LOA 18m. Depths 1–5m.
Facilities Water. 220V. Fuel quay. Some provisions and restaurants.
Marina di Chiaiolella ☎ 081 810 1611
Ippocampo ☎ 081 658 7667
www.ippocampo.biz
Nautica Costamare
☎ 081 896 9029
Meditur ☎ 081 810 1934
Yachting Santa Margherita
☎ 081 896 8074
Email info@yachtingsantamargherita.com

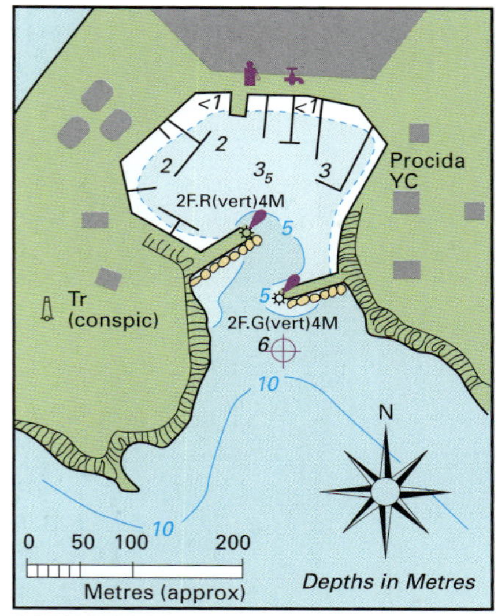

CHIAIOLELLA

Procida Yachting Club Co-op.
☎ 081 810 1481
Email info@procidayachting.it

Ischia

PORTO D'ISCHIA

40°44′·95N 13°56′·77E WGS84
BA 916 It 82 Imray M46
23M Ventotene ←→ Capri 18M
☆ Breakwater Fl.WR.3s15/12M (127°-R-197°). Entrance Fl.G.3s8M/Fl.R.3s8M

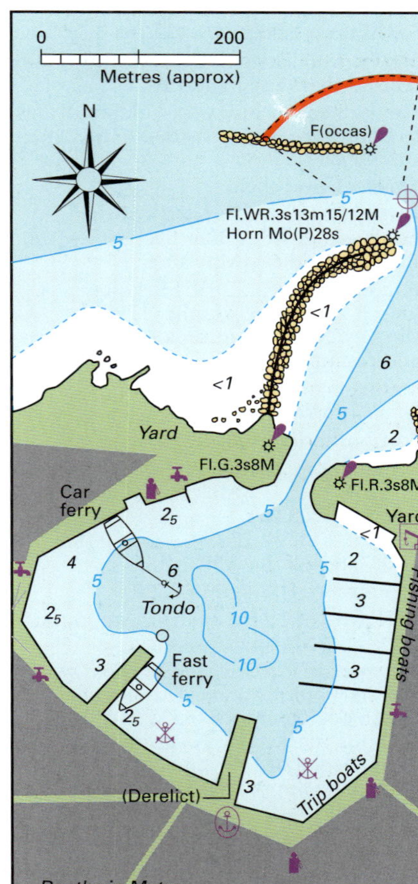

PORTO D'ISCHIA

VHF Ch 16, 15 (0700–1900). Ch 74 for Marina Ischia

Navigation The entrance is narrow and constantly in use by ferries.

Berths Stern or bows-to. Laid moorings to pontoons. Very crowded in the summer.

Shelter Good shelter.

Data 200 berths. Limited visitors' berths. Max LOA 30m. Depths 2–10m. Charge band 6+ (May-Oct).

Facilities Water. 220V. Fuel quay (depth 2m). 30-ton crane. 12-ton slipway. Some yacht repairs. Provisions and restaurants.

Marina Ischia ☏ 081 333 4070
Email info@marinaischia.it

Port Authority ☏ 081 991 417

Ormeggiatori Battellieri ☏ 081 981 419

CASAMICCIOLA

40°45'·1N 13°54'·7E
BA 908 It 82 Imray M46

☆ Entrance Fl.G.4s5M/F.R.2M

VHF Ch 16, 09 for Marina Aragonesi. Ch 08 for Marina Casamicciola.

Navigation Care needed of shoal water E of harbour. Care needed of reef (Secca del Sancturio) 0·5M NW of harbour, marked by N cardinal buoy. Care needed of 1·5–2m depths in immediate approach to Marina Aragonesi.

Berths Stern or bows-to at either marina. Laid moorings tailed to the quay.

Shelter Adequate.

Data 350 berths. Visitors' berths. Max LOA 50m. Depths 1–7m. Charge band 6+.

Facilities Water. 220V. Showers and toilets. Pump-out. 30-ton crane. Limited yacht repairs. Provisions and restaurants.

Cala degli Aragonesi ☏ 081 980 686 / 337 846 220
Email info@caladegliaragonesi.it
www.caladegliaragonesi.it

Casamicciola Marina ☏ 081 507 2545 / 333 888 7975
Email info@marinadicasamicciola
www.marinadicasamicciola.it

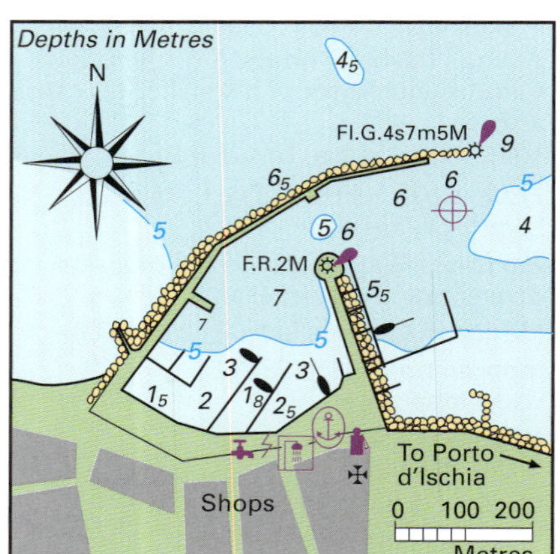

CASAMICCIOLA

LACCO AMENO

40°45'·3N 13°53'·4E

New quay built over the outer breakwater with berths on outside for superyachts.

Seventh Heaven YC (Luise Associates)
☏ 081 963 3396
www.luise.it

MARINA DI PITHECUSAE (COMMUNE DI LACCO AMENO)

New small craft marina in basin at E end of harbour. New pontoon Il Fungo (summer only) off W side of the wharf.

VHF Ch 10.

☏ 081 994 821

Nautica Mare
VHF Ch 10
☏ 348 372 9563

FORIO D'ISCHIA

40°44'·5N 13°51'·5E
BA 908 It 82 Imray M46

☆ Inner mole Fl.RG.3s4M. Breakwater Fl.R.3s2M

Marina under development with pontoons off the NE breakwater.

SANT'ANGELO D'ISCHIA

40°41'·8N 13°53'·8E

Small harbour with yacht berths.

Data Max LOA 60m. Depths 2–5m. Charge band 6.

Ischia Yacht ☏ 081 999 102
Email info@ischiayacht.it

Capri

CAPRI MARINA GRANDE

40°33′·6N 14°14′·7E
BA 908 It 914 Imray M46
18M Ischia ←→ Agropoli 35M

☆ Entrance Fl.G.3s8M/Fl.R.3s8M

VHF Ch 16, 14 (0700–1900) for port authorities. Ch 71 for Porto Turistico.

Navigation Care is needed of ferries and hydrofoils coming and going.

Berths Stern or bows-to. Laid moorings tailed to the quay.

Shelter Normally good but strong N winds make it uncomfortable.

Data 300 berths. Visitors' berths. Max LOA 60m. Depths 3–10m. Charge band 6+.

Facilities Water. 220V. Fuel quay. 40-ton crane. Some provisions and restaurants.

Remarks Large yacht berths handled by Luise International & Co and J. Luise & Sons.

Consorzio Porto Turistico di Capri
✆ 081 837 8950
Email prenotazioni@portoturisticodicapri.com

Luise Associates ✆ 348 386 8538
Email capri@luise.it
www.luise.com

Gruppo Ormeggiatori Capri
✆ 081 837 7158

Tecnomar Boat Capri ✆ 081 837 9659
Email info@tecnomarcapri.com

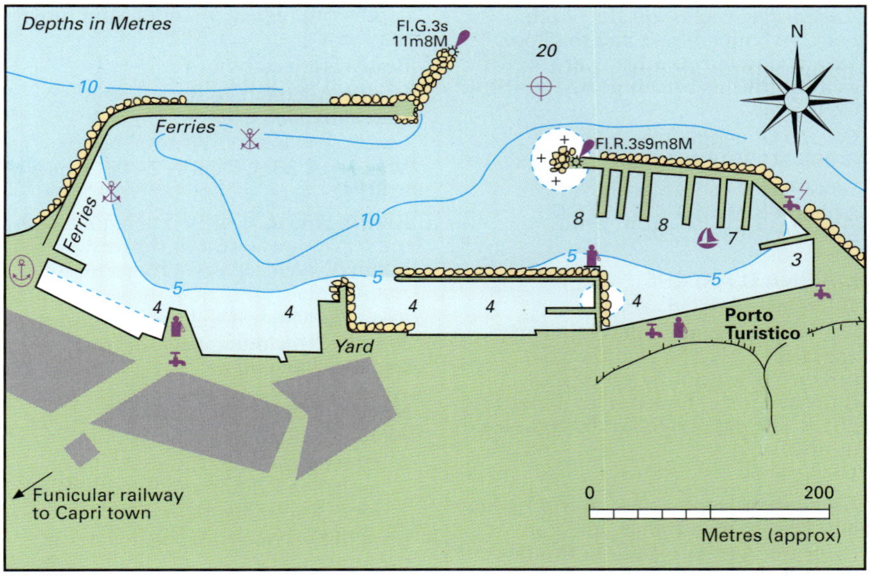

CAPRI

AMP REGNO DI NETTUNO (NEPTUNE'S KINGDOM MARINE RESERVE)

Restrictions on navigation, anchoring and mooring throughout the area.

Notes

1. Most visitors will require authorization in advance before entering Zone B. PDF forms requesting permission are available to download on the website. Contact the AMP for details and authorization.
2. Fees and authorization depend on LOA, engine emissions, holding tanks and type of anti-fouling.
3. Within 300m of the coast the maximum speed is 5kns.
4. Within 600m of the coast the maximum speed is 10 0kns.
5. Access to sea caves restricted to rowed boats or inflatables.
6. Discharge of black or grey water or solid waste is prohibited.
7. Anchoring prohibited in Posidonia beds or areas of coral, overnight, or close to mooring buoys.
8. Yachts may only pick up designated mooring buoys, and not take those reserved for dive or trip boats.

✉ Area Marina Protetta Regno di Nettuno, Piazza municipio 9, 80075 Forio, NA ✆ */Fax* 081 333 2941
Email info@nettunoamp.it

Mainland coast

AMALFI

40°37′·79N 14°36′·05E WGS84
BA 908 It 914 Imray M18

☆ Entrance Fl.R.5s8M/2F.G(vert)3M

A mole off the town provides adequate shelter in settled weather.

Data c.50 berths. Max LOA c.60m. Depths 1·5–8m. Charge band 6.

Facilities Water. 220V. Fuel quay. Provisions and restaurants.

Remarks Crowded in the summer.

Pontoon Aniello Esposito
✆ 338 219 3421 / 893 5226

Pontoon Il Faro ✆ 338 999 8710
Email info@ormeggioilfaro.it

Coppola Marina
✆ 089 873091 or 347 3495 280
Email info@amalfimooring.com

CETARA

40°38′·8N 14°42′·3E

☆ Entrance Fl.R.3s6M/Fl.G.3s3M

SALERNO

40°40′·3N 14°45′·6E
BA 907 It 96 Imray M18

☆ Porto Nuovo entrance Fl.R.5s8M/Fl.G.5s9M. Elbow Fl.3s11M. Inner basin 2F.G(vert)3M. E breakwater Fl.G.6s2M. Porto Masuccio 2F.G(vert)3M/2F.R(vert)3M

VHF Ch 11, 16 for port authorities (0700–1900). Ch 14, 16 for pilots.

Navigation A yacht should make for the pontoons on the E side of Porto Nuovo or at Santa Teresa.

Santa Teresa is being developed as a marina and works continue in the area.

Berths Stern or bows-to.

Shelter Adequate. S–W winds make some berths very uncomfortable.

Data Porto Nuovo Visitors' berths. Depths 0·5–6m. Charge band 5. *Santa Teresa* 600 berths (when completed). Max LOA c.15m. Depths 2–7m. Charge band 5.

Facilities Water. 220V. 30-ton crane. 150-ton slipway. Some yacht repairs. Provisions and restaurants.

Notes

1. There are plans to double the size of the porto turistico Porto Masuccio, but no start dates for the project are available.
2. There are plans to develop another harbour in the area to the SE of the porto turistico, in the Pastena area, and will include berths for fishing boats.

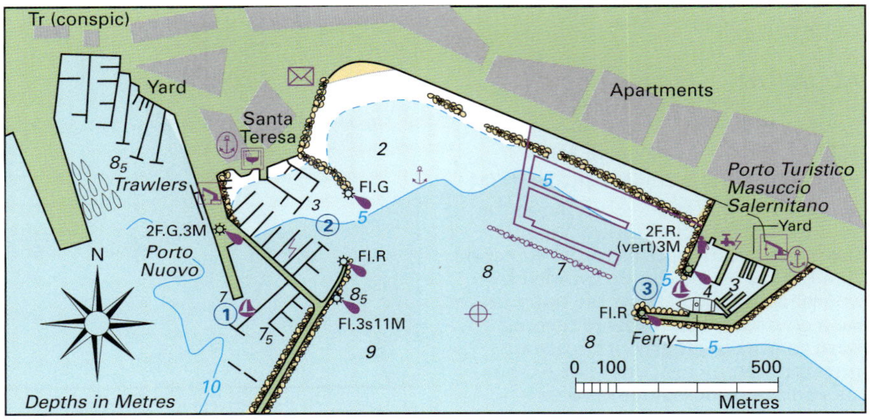

SALERNO

Anchorage Anchor off the beach between Santa Teresa and the Porto Turistico in fair weather. Care needed as a dinghy has been reported stolen overnight.

Gruppo Ormeggiatore
✆ 089 241 201 / 241 543

Santa Teresa concessions:
Azimut Yachting ✆ 089 253 572
Elidiport ✆ 089 232 927

MARINA D'ARECHI
40°38'78N 14°48'53E WGS84

A new marina under development approximately 3M SE of porto turistico Masuccio Salernitano.
It opened, on completion of phase 1, in 2013. The data refers to the completed project.

VHF Ch 74

Navigation Depths of 10m from 200m out. Depths at entrance 7m.

Data 1,000 berths. Max LOA 60m.

Facilities Water. 220V. WiFi. Showers and toilets. Pump-out. Fuel quay. 220-ton travel-lift and repair facilities.

Marina d'Arechi ✆ 089 278 8801
Email info@marinadarechi.com
www.marinadarechi.com

AGROPOLI
40°21'·28N 14°58'·98E WGS84
BA 908 It 10 Imray M18
35M Capri ←→ Acciaroli 15M

☆ Punta Fortino Fl(2)6s16M. Entrance Fl.G.5s5M/2F.R(vert)3M (F.G/Fl.Y temp)

Berths Stern or bows-to where directed. Laid moorings at some berths. Poor holding on quay berths.

Shelter Generally good although N gales cause a surge.

Data 500 berths. Max LOA 50m. Depths <1–6m. Charge band 4.

Facilities Water. 220V. Fuel quay. Provisions and restaurants in town.

Consorzio Euromar ✆ 0974 824 545
Email euromar@oneonline.it

Pietro of Yachting Club Agropoli (outer pontoon) ✆ 338 542 6082

Canottieri Agropoli (next pontoon)
✆ 0974 821 884

La Rosa dei Venti ✆ 368 322 3182

SAN MARCO DI CASTELLABATE
40°16'·27N 14°56'·07E WGS84
BA 908 It 915, 11

☆ Entrance Fl.G.4s2M

Small harbour.

ACCIAROLI
40°10'·50N 15°01'·66E WGS84
BA 1908 It 11 Imray M18
15M Agropoli ←→ Camerota 22M

☆ Entrance Fl.R.3s8m4M / 2F.G(vert)3M

Navigation The two reefs lying in the southern approaches, Secca Vecchia (least depth 2m) and Secca del Generale (sea breaks on it), can be avoided by approaching the head of the outer mole on a course of due E before turning hard to port to enter. Both reefs are now marked by beacons. The harbour silts and despite regular dredging depths can reduce to 1m or less close to the quay.

Berths Stern or bows-to.

Shelter Adequate in settled weather. Untenable in S gales.

Data c.100 berths. Visitors' berths. Max LOA 20m. Depths 2–4m. Charge band 5.

Facilities Water. 220V. Fuel quay. 160-ton travel-hoist. 16-ton slipway. Limited yacht repairs. Provisions and restaurants.

Remarks Major development works complete, including new fuel quay to starboard on entry.

MARINA DI CASAL VELINO
40°10'·5N 15°06'·9E

☆ Outer mole head Fl.G.3s5M. Inner mole head, outer arm Fl.R.3s5M. Inner arm 2F.R(vert)

A small harbour with shoal water in the approaches.

Data c.80 berths. Max LOA 20m. Depths <1–4m.

Facilities Provisions and restaurants.

PISCIOTTA MARINA
40°06'·1N 15°13'·7E

☆ Outer mole Fl.R.4s. Inner mole 2F.G(vert)4m

Silted to less than 1m.

PALINURO
40°02'·0N 15°16'·7E
BA 1908 It 11

☆ Capo Palinuro Fl(3)15s25M. Breakwater Fl.G.5s9M

Data 100 berths. Max LOA 20m. Depths <1–10m. Charge band 4/5.

Facilities Water. 220V. WiFi. Provisions and restaurants in Palinuro.

Co-op. Palinuro Porto Pepoli Gerardo
✆ 0974 931 604 *Mobile* 339 877 6562
Email info@palinurocoop.com
www.palinurocoop.com

PARC NAZIONALE CILENTO E VALLO DI DIANO (CILENTO AND DIANO VALLEY NATIONAL PARK)

There are two new Marine Protected Areas within the National Park.

AMP Santa Maria Castellabate covers the coast from Pta Tresino to Pta dell'Oligastro, with special protected areas where unauthorized navigation is prohibited, around both capes and over the Secche di Licosa.

AMP Costa degli Infreschi e della Masseta runs around Pta Iscoletti from Camerota to Pta del Monaco S of Scario, with Zone A protection around Pta Iscoletti.

MARINA DI CAMEROTA
39°59'·87N 15°22'·78E WGS84
BA 1908 It 11 Imray M18
22M Acciaroli ←→ Cetraro 39M

☆ Entrance Fl.R.4s3M/Fl.G.4s3M

VHF Ch 16. Ch 09 for Marina.

Navigation Reefs and shoal water surround Isolotto del Camerota and a yacht should keep well to seaward. Strong S winds cause a confused swell at the entrance. The entrance to the harbour is prone to silting but a narrow entrance channel is maintained with minimum 2m depths (usually 4m). Keep in the centre of the entrance to stay in the channel.

Yellow buoys approximately 2·5M S of entrance mark a fish farm. Further unlit buoys lie to seaward, with floating ropes attached. Care needed, especially at night.

Berths Stern or bows-to.

Shelter Good shelter although prolonged S winds cause a surge.

Data 250 berths. Max LOA 25m. Depths <1–4m. Charge band 5.

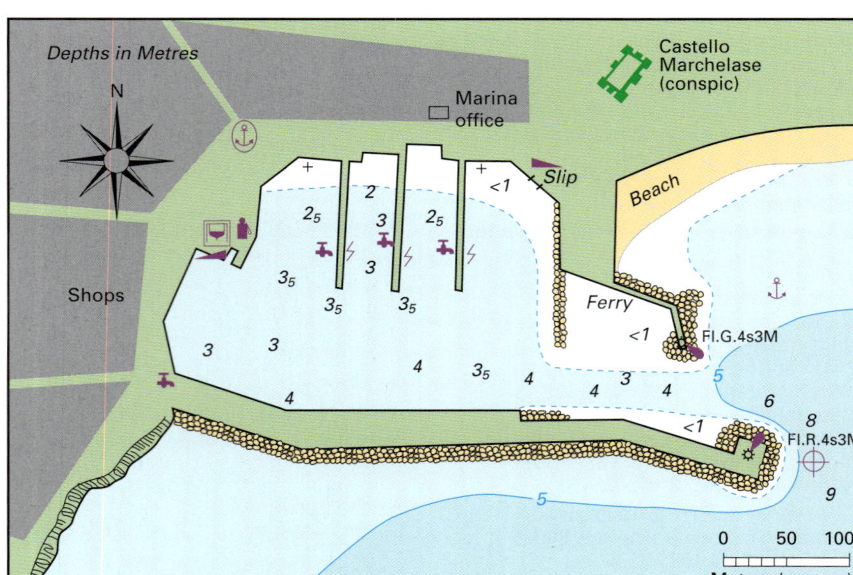

MARINA DI CAMEROTA

Facilities Water. 220V. Toilets and showers. Fuel quay. 200-ton travel-lift. 12-ton crane. Provisions and restaurants.

Marina di Camerota 'La Marina de il Leone di Caprera' ✆ 0974 939 813
Email info@portodicamerota.it
www.portodicamerota.it

Capitaineria ✆ 0974 939 184

MARINA DI SCARIO
40°03′·15N 15°29′·72E WGS84

☆ Scario main light Fl(4)12s15M. Entrance F.G.3M/Fl.R.3s4M

Fishing harbour affording good shelter.

Data 160 berths. Max LOA 30m. Depths 2–5m. Laid moorings. Water. 220V. Charge band 6.

POLICASTRO
40°04′·23N 15°31′·64E WGS84

☆ Entrance Fl.R.3s5M/Fl.G.3s5M

Fishing harbour affording good shelter.

Data 150 berths. Max LOA 15m. Depths <1–3m.

Remarks Being developed as a porto turistico with new pontoons and quays. When finished will have water and electricity, showers and toilets.

SAPRI
40°03′·94N 15°37′·44E WGS84

☆ Punta del Fortino (Carlo Pisacane) Fl(2)7s7M. Mole head F.G. Breakwater Fl.R.3s

Berths Harbour expanded and pontoons with moorings laid in new porto turistico. Other pontoons in NE corner of bay.

Data c.300 berths. Max LOA 40m. Charge band 4.

Facilities Water. 220V. Fuel quay. Travel-hoist. Provisions and restaurants in village.

Sapri Ormeggiatori Peter ✆ 348 333 5327 / 0973 605 536

San Giorgio ✆ 0973 603 305

MARATEA
39°59′·21N 15°42′·40E WGS84
BA 1908 It 11 Imray M18

☆ Entrance Fl.G.3s6M/Fl.R.3s6M. Inner entrance F.G.4M/F.R.4M

VHF Ch 16, 06.

Navigation With onshore winds a swell piles up at the entrance.

Berths Stern or bows-to where directed. Laid moorings tailed to the pontoons.

Shelter Good shelter. Strong southerlies cause a surge.

Data 250 berths. Max LOA 35m. Depths 2–7m. Charge band 5.

Facilities Water. 220V. Fuel quay. 10-ton crane. Limited provisions. Restaurants.

✆ 0973 877 307

DIAMANTE
39°40′·54N 15°49′·03E WGS84
BA 1908 It 11 Imray M18

A small damaged harbour under Punta di Diamante.

Note Development of the porto turistico has been delayed. No completion dates are available. Currently not much here except a damaged breakwater, and little shelter.

CETRARO
39°31′·44N 15°55′·28E WGS84
BA 1908 It 12 Imray M18
39M Camerota ←→ Vibo Valentia 50M

☆ Breakwater Fl.R.4s6M/2F.R(vert)3M. Inner mole 2F.G(vert)3M

VHF Ch 16.

Berths Yachts should go stern-to or alongside where directed. Most berths now on pontoons with laid moorings.

Data Depths 1·5m–5m. Charge band 5/6.

Facilities Water. 220V. Showers and toilets.

✆ 0982 91300
http://portocetraro.it

AMANTEA
39°06′·9N 15°04′·5E

VHF Ch 16.

Navigation A porto turistico to the S of the town of Amantea. It is mostly full with small local boats, and visiting yachts should not depend on finding a berth here.

Berths Alongside on the wedge-shaped quay or inside the S breakwater.

Shelter Adeaquate shelter, although southerlies will make some berths uncomfortable, and may become untenable.

Data c.200 berths. Max LOA 15m. Depths reported 2–4m.

Facilities Water. 220V. Fuel. 25-ton crane.

Capitaineria
✆ 0982 48565 / 338 670 0136

VIBO VALENTIA
38°43′·22N 16°07′·79E WGS84
BA 805 It 134 Imray M18
50M Cetraro ←→ Reggio 49M

☆ Entrance Fl.WG.5s15/12M (068°-W-230°)/Fl.R.5s7M. Gioia Tauro N mole head Fl.R.4s14m8M.

VHF Ch 11, 16 for *capitaneria* (0700–1900). Ch 16, 12 for Marina Carmelo. Ch 10, 16 for Marina Stella del Sud.

Berths Marina Carmelo (2) or Marina Stella del Sud (1). Stern or bow-to. Laid moorings tailed to the quay.

Shelter Good shelter.

Data Max LOA 14–16m. Depths <1–7m. Charge band 3.

Facilities Water. 220/380V. Showers and toilets. Fuel quay. 24-ton crane. Some yacht repairs. Chandlers. Provisions and restaurants.

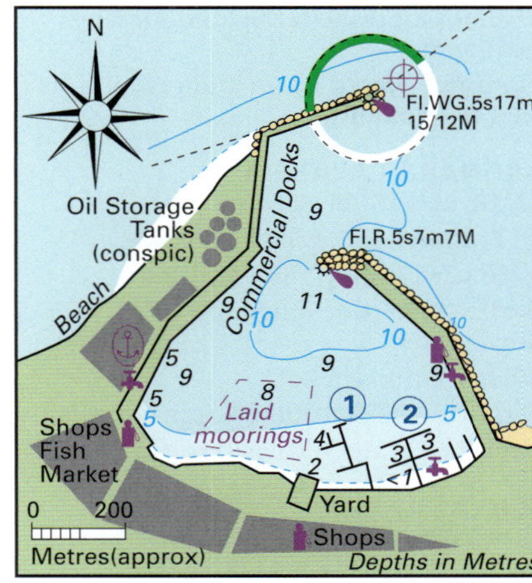

VIBO VALENTIA MARINA

Marina Carmelo ✆ 0963 572 630
Email info@marinacarmelo.it
www.marinacarmelo.it

Marina Stella del Sud ✆ 0963 573 202
Email stellasud@tin.it
www.marinastelladelsud.it

TROPEA MARINA
38°41′·04N 15°54′·39E WGS84
BA 1941 It 13 Imray M18

☆ Breakwater 2F.G(vert)4M

Navigation Care needed of 2–2·5m sandbank extending S from entrance.

VHF Ch 09.

Data 750 berths. 70 visitors' berths. Max LOA 60m. Depths 2–5m. Charge band 5/6.

Facilities Water. 220/380V. Toilets and showers. Laundry facilities. 50-ton travel-hoist. Fuel quay. Repairs.

Porto di Tropea
✆ 0963 61548
Email info@portoditropea.it
www.portoditropea.it

Cantiere Navale ✆ 0963 61885
Email info@cantieretropea.it
www.cantieretropea.it

GIOIA TAURO
38°26′·66N 15°53′·32E WGS84
BA 1018 It 13 Imray M18

☆ Entrance Fl.R.4s8M/Fl.G.4s8M. Inner basin Fl(2)G.6s4M/ Fl(2)R.6s4M /Fl.G.3s4M/Fl.R.3s4M

VHF Ch 16 (0800–2000).

Data c.50 berths. Max LOA 20m. Depths inner basin 3–4m.

Remarks Large commercial harbour.

Port Authority ✆ 0966 52130

PORTO PALMI (TAUREANA)
38°23′·48N 15°51′·64E WGS84

New harbour 3M south of Gioia Tauro.

Data c.100 berths. Depths 2-5m. Max LOA c.16m. Charge band 4/5.

Berths Stern-to where directed or where there is a space. Depths shelve to less than 1m along the E side of the harbour.

Shelter Good shelter behind massive breakwaters.
Facilities Water. Cafés and restaurants nearby in summer.

BAGNARA CALABRIA
38°18'·06N 15°48'·88E WGS84
☆ Entrance Fl.G.3s5M/Fl.R.3s5M
VHF Ch 11, 16 (0700–1300)
Berths Alongside outer end of breakwater.
Shelter Good shelter.
Data Depths 5–10m. Charge band 1/3.
Facilities Water. Provisions. Café/bar.

SCILLA
38°15'·43N 15°43'·01E WGS84
BA 1018 It 138 Imray M18
☆ Castle Fl.5s22M
Berths Mooring buoys for visiting yachts.
Giovanni Arena ✆ 338 9713 413
Email giovarena@libero.it

Strait of Messina (Stretto di Messina)
See also ***Sicily***

VILLA SAN GIOVANNI
38°13'N 15°37'·9E (Fl.G.3s)
BA 917 It 145 Imray M47
☆ Mole head Fl.G.3s7M. Root F.G.3M. Molo Sottoflutto head Fl.R.3s7m6M. E mole head F.R.3M. Pierhead 2F.G(vert)4M. Ferry piers 3F.G(vert)4M/F.RGR(vert)3M/ F.GR(vert)3M/F.R.3M
Ferry port.

REGGIO CALABRIA
38°07'·70N 15°39'·00E WGS84
BA 917 It 145 Imray M47
49M Vibo Valentia ←→ Capo Spartivento 30M
☆ Entrance Iso.G.2s7M / Iso.R.2s6M. Pier F.G.3M/F.R.3M
VHF Ch 11, 16 for *capitaneria* (24/24). Ch 09 for yacht harbour.

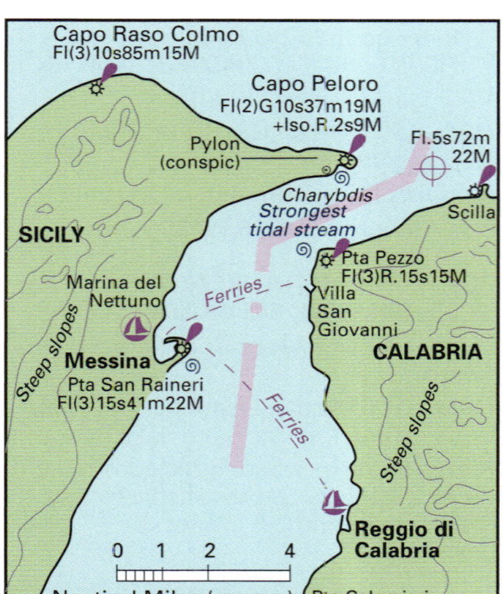

STRAIT OF MESSINA

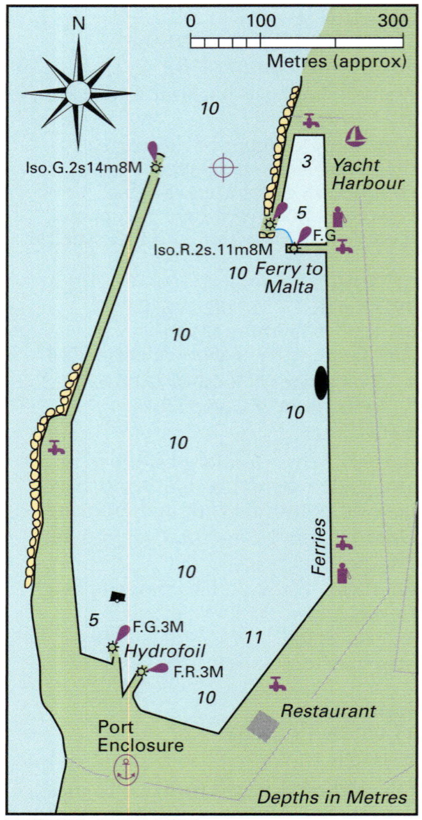

REGGIO CALABRIA

Navigation With wind against tide there is a confused sea in the approaches. Strong gusts off the high land.
Berths Stern or bows-to. Laid moorings tailed to the quay. If yacht basin is full go stern and bows-to or alongside in commercial harbour.
Shelter Normally adequate but strong N winds cause a surge.
Data Limited visitors' berths. Max LOA 12m. Depths 4–7m. Charge band 5.
Facilities Water. 220V. Fuel quay (reported not open in 2011). Limited yacht repairs. Provisions and restaurants in town (15-minute walk).
✆ 0965 47914

Sardinia

STINTINO
40°56'·1N 08°14'·0E
BA 1204 It 289 Imray M8
31M Capo Caccia ←→ Porto Torres 9M
☆ Shoal Fl.R.4s4M/Fl.G.4s8M. Outer mole head Fl.G.4s8M.
Porto Minore mole E & W entrance Fl(2)R.6s3M/Fl(2)G.6s3M. Porto Mannu Breakwater E and W entrance F.G.3M/F.R.3M. Marina E and W mole head F.G/F.R
VHF Ch 09, 12, 14, 16 (Porto Torres). Ch 09 for Stintino Marina.
Navigation Care needed of the shoal (marked by a beacon) between the two inlets.
Berths Stern or bows-to in either inlet or on pontoons at the marina.
Shelter Good shelter.
Data Stintino Marina: 270 berths. 50 visitors' berths. Depths 2–11m. LOA 12–40m. Charge band 5.
Porto Mannu: Max LOA 20m. Depths 2–2·5m. Charge band 5.
Facilities Water. 220V. Fuel quay. 40-ton crane. Provisions and restaurants.
Stintino Marina ✆ 334 740 4583
Email marinadistintino@gmail.com`
Coop. Turistico Stintino ✆ 079 523 516
Nautilus ✆ 079 523 721

PORTO TORRES
40°50'·69N 08°23'·95E WGS84
BA 1202 It 286 Imray M8
9M Stintino ←→ Castelsardo 14M
☆ Main light LFl(2)10s16M. Entrance LFl.G.6s11M/LFl.R.6s8M. Porto Interno 2F.RG(vert)3M/2F.G(vert)3M. Old inner basin F.G.3M/F.R.3M.
VHF Ch 09, 12, 14, 16 for port authorities. Ch 16, 74 for Cormorano Marina.
Navigation With strong onshore winds there is a reflected swell off the new oil terminal breakwater. A yacht should make for the old inner basin on the E side of the harbour.
Berths Stern or bows-to where directed. Laid moorings.

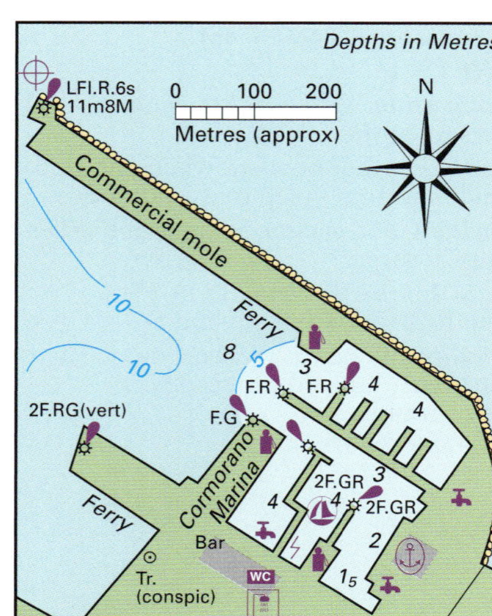

PORTO TORRES

SARDINIA

Shelter Good shelter.

Data *Cormorano Marina* 150 berths. Max LOA 30m. Depths 1–4m. Charge band 4/5.

Facilities Water. 220V. WiFi. Fuel quay. 50-ton crane. 80-ton travel hoist. 200-ton slipway. Limited yacht repairs. Hauling and storage ashore in La Darsena or Marina Service in Zona Industriale. Provisions and restaurants.

ISOLA ASINARA NATIONAL PARK AND MARINE RESERVE

The reserve surrounds the island and there are restrictions on anchoring. Mooring buoys under control of Cormorano Marina, Porto Torres.
☏ 079 512 290
www.asinaramarina.com
Porto Torres Port Authority
☏ 079 502 258
Asinara Park Co ☏ 079 503 388
www.parcoasinara.it

Lorenzo Nuvoli ☏ 079 512066
Email lorenzonuvoli@tiscalinet.it
Cormorano Marina
☏ 079 512 290 / 349 245 3887
Email info@cormorano.com
www.cormoranomarina.it

Marina Service Porto Torres

Hauling and storage facility in Zona Industriale run by Felice Cusimano.

Facilities 80-ton travel-hoist. Repairs can be arranged or done yourself. Steel boat cradles.

☏ 368 554 4262 / 338 898 7834
Email marinaservice@alice.it
www.felicecusimano.it

CASTELSARDO

40°54'·97N 08°42'·28E WGS84
BA 1204 It 289 Imray M8
14M Porto Torres ←→ S. Teresa di Gallura 29M

☆ Entrance Fl.R.3s4M/Fl.G.3s4M. Isola Frigiano breakwater F.G

VHF Ch 09.

Navigation With NW winds a heavy swell piles up in the entrance. Light on end of NE breakwater reported unlit.

Berths Stern or bows-to.

Shelter Good shelter although strong NE winds make it uncomfortable.

Data 500 berths. Max LOA 25m. Depths 1–5m. Charge band 3.

Facilities Water. 220V. Fuel quay. Chandler. Sails agent. 50-ton travel-lift. 15-ton crane. Most repairs. Provisions and restaurants 20 minutes' walk.

Porto di Castelsardo (docking)
☏ 079 471 339

PORTO MARINA ISOLA ROSSA (MARINA TRINITA D'AGULTU)

41°00'·8N 08°52'·3E

☆ Outer mole head Fl.R.5s4M. Inner mole head Fl.G.5s4M

Navigation New marina to the SW of Isola Rossa. The marina is regularly dredged to 5–6m. Care needed of silting in the approaches (2–3m depths are reported).

Berths Visiting yachts go alongside the inside of the breakwater.

Data 280 berths. Max LOA 20m. Depths 2·5–6m. Charge band 5.

Facilities Water. 220V. Showers and toilets. Fuel quay (2·5m). Small crane. Provisions and restaurant.

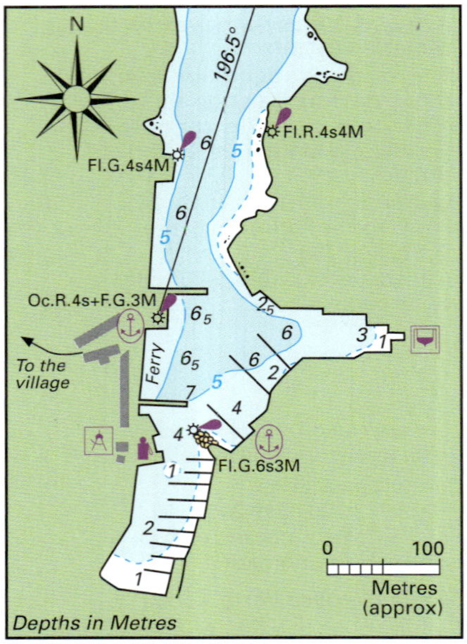

S. TERESA DI GALLURA

Porto Marina Isola Rossa
☎ 079 694 184
Email info@portoisolarossa.com
www.portoisolarossa.com

SANTA TERESA DI GALLURA (LONGOSARDO)

41°14′·7N 09°11′·8E
BA 1213 It 912
29M Castelsardo ←→ Palau 10M

☆ Capo Testa Fl(3)12s22M. E side entrance Fl.WR.3s10/8M (030°-R-164°-W-184°-R-210°) / Fl.R.4s4M. Isolotto Munica Fl.G.4s3M/ Fl.G.4s4M / Fl.R.4s4M. Leading lights 196·5° Oc.R.4s3M/F.G.3M and Fl.R.4s7M

VHF Ch 16, 12.

Navigation Two shoals lie in the approaches to Santa Teresa with least depths of 3–4m.

Berths Where directed.

Shelter Good shelter.

Data 600 berths. Max LOA 35m. Depths 2–5m in inner basin. Charge band 5.

Facilities Water. 220V. Fuel quay. 15-ton crane. Provisions and restaurants. 100-ton travel-lift.

Marina Santa Teresa Porto Turistico
☎ 0786 751 936
Email portostg@tin.it
www.portosantateresa.com

PORTO POLLO (PUDDU)

41°12′·4N 09°19′·7E

A well sheltered bay adjacent to Liscia.

PALAU

41°10′·96N 09°23′·25E WGS84
BA 1213 It 325 M8
10M S Teresa di Gallura ←→ Porto Cervo 7·5M

☆ Punta Palau Fl(2)G.10s4M. Tourist dock head Fl.G.4s5m3M. Marina entrance F.R.3M/F.G.3M

VHF Ch 16, 09.

Navigation Care needed of shoal water in the approaches marked by a W cardinal bn.

Berths. Where directed. Laid moorings tailed to the quay.

Shelter Good shelter.

Data 400 berths. Max LOA 18m. Depths 2–4m. Charge band 5.

Facilities Water. 220V. 50-ton travel-hoist. 20-ton crane. Provisions and restaurants.

Remarks La Maddalena permits available here.

Comune Porto Turistico ☎ 0789 708 435
Email portoturistico@palau.it

CANNIGIONE

41°06′·58N 09°26′·69E WGS84
BA 1213 It 324

☆ Mole head F.G.3M

VHF Ch 11, 16 (0700–1900). Ch 09 for mooring buoys.

Berths Stern or bows-to.

Shelter Good shelter although the afternoon breeze can be uncomfortable.

Data 400 berths. Max LOA 25m. Depths 1–4·5m. Charge band 5/6. 35 moorings at head of bay. Max LOA 35m. Depths 2·5–6m.

Facilities Water. Fuel quay. 20-ton crane. Provisions and restaurants.

Remarks Work to extend the breakwater is complete.

Sardomar ☎ 0789 884 22
Email coop.sardomar@tiscali.it

Consorzio Marina di Cannigione
☎ 346 806 5848
Email consorziomc@tiscali.it
www.marinacannigione.it

POLTU QUATU (MARINA DELL'ORSO)

41°08′·6N 09°29′·7E
BA 1213 It 324

☆ Entrance Fl.R.5s4M/Fl.G.5s4M

VHF Ch 09, 16.

Berths Where directed. Laid moorings tailed to the quay.

Shelter Good shelter.

Data 450 berths. 50 visitors' berths. Max LOA 35m. Depths 2–4m. Charge band 6+ (July–August).

Facilities Water. 220V. Telephone. TV. Fuel quay. 15-ton crane. Mini-market. Restaurant.

☎ 0789 994 77
Email polquatu@tin.it

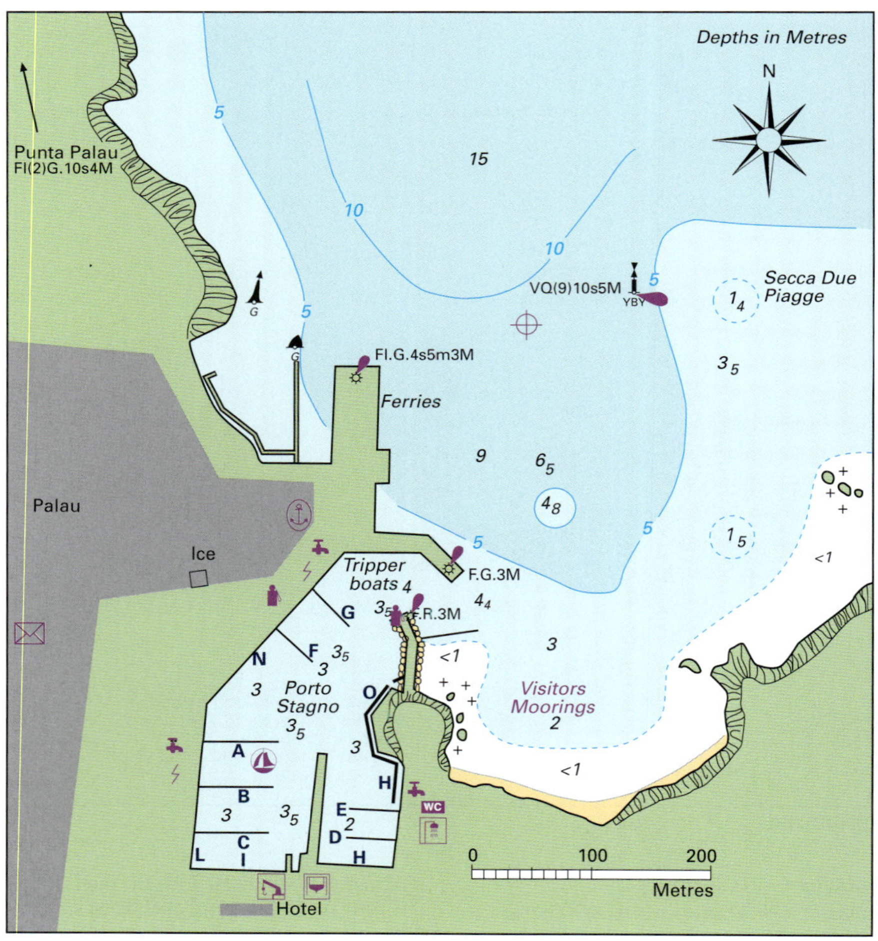

PALAU

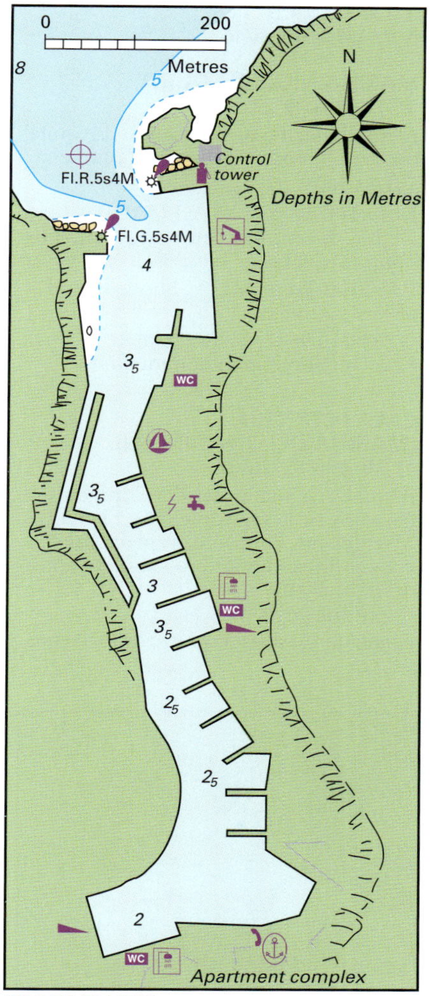

POLTU QUATU

La Maddalena archipelago

LA MADDALENA ARCHIPELAGO NATIONAL PARK AND MARINE RESERVE
Extensive coverage of the islands of the N and NE coast of Sardinia.
Yachts visiting the area between 1 May–31 October must obtain a permit.

Yacht length	*Day permit*	*2 week permit*	*Month permit*
8–10m	2€/m	€130	€250
11–13m	2€/m	€165	€320
14–16m	2€/m	€195	€380
17–19m	3€/m	€460	€900
20–24m	4€/m	€760	€1500
25–29m	4€/m	€920	€1800
30–34m	4€/m	€1060	€2100
35-40m	4€/m	€1230	€2400
40m +	4€/m	€1470	€2900

✉ Parco Nazionale Arcipelago La Maddalena, Via G.Cesare 7, 07024 La Maddalena
✆ 0789 790 211 224
Email info@lamaddalenapark.it
www.lamaddalenapark.it (Italian)
www.lamaddalenapark.net (English)
www.parks.it

✉ Consorzio Parco Blu, Piazza Principe Tommaso 4, 07024 La Maddalena
✆ 0789 723 053

Note Mooring buoys are provided in many bays within the Marine Reserve in order to preserve the Posidonia (seagrass).

From June to September anchoring overnight is not permitted, but those with a permit and a holding tank, using a mooring, are permitted to stay. Yachts should download and keep a copy of the regulations or, better, get the latest edition when you buy your permit.

ISOLA RAZZOLI

☆ NW corner Fl.WR.2·5s19/15M

ISOLA SANTA MARIA

☆ Punta Filetto Fl(4)20s10M. Isolotti Borrettinelli di Fuori Fl(2)10s11M

ISOLA BUDELLI

Mooring buoys at Cala Sud and Deadman's Reef passage.

ISOLA SPARGI

☆ Secca Corsara, S card Q(6)+LFl.15s5M

Anchorages at Cala d'Alga, Cala Corsara and Cala Ferrigno.

Isola della Maddalena

MEZZO PASSAGE
41°12'·04N 09°22'·86E WGS84
Western approaches.

☆ Secca di Mezzo Passo Fl(2)6s5M. Secca del Palau VQ(6)+LFl.10s5M/Fl.Y.5s4M. Leading lights (014°). Front Iso.G.2s8M. Rear Oc.G.4s8M. Leading lights (066·2°). Front F.G.3M. Rear F.G.3M

LA MADDALENA (CALA GAVETTA)
41°12'·60N 09°24'·31E WGS84
BA 1212 It 281

☆ Entrance F.G.3M/F.R.3M. Commercial harbour, pierhead Fl.Y.3s7m3M. Cala Chiesa, Punta Chiara breakwater head Fl.R.3s5m3M

VHF Ch 16, 11 (0700–1900) for port authorities. Ch 74 for porto turistico.
Berths Stern or bows-to.
Shelter Good shelter,
Data 300 berths. Max LOA 12m. Depths 2–8m. Charge band 5/6.
Facilities Water. Fuel quay. 10-ton crane. 10-ton slipway. Provisions and restaurants.
Port Authority ✆ 0789 730 121
Email cgavetta@yahoo.it

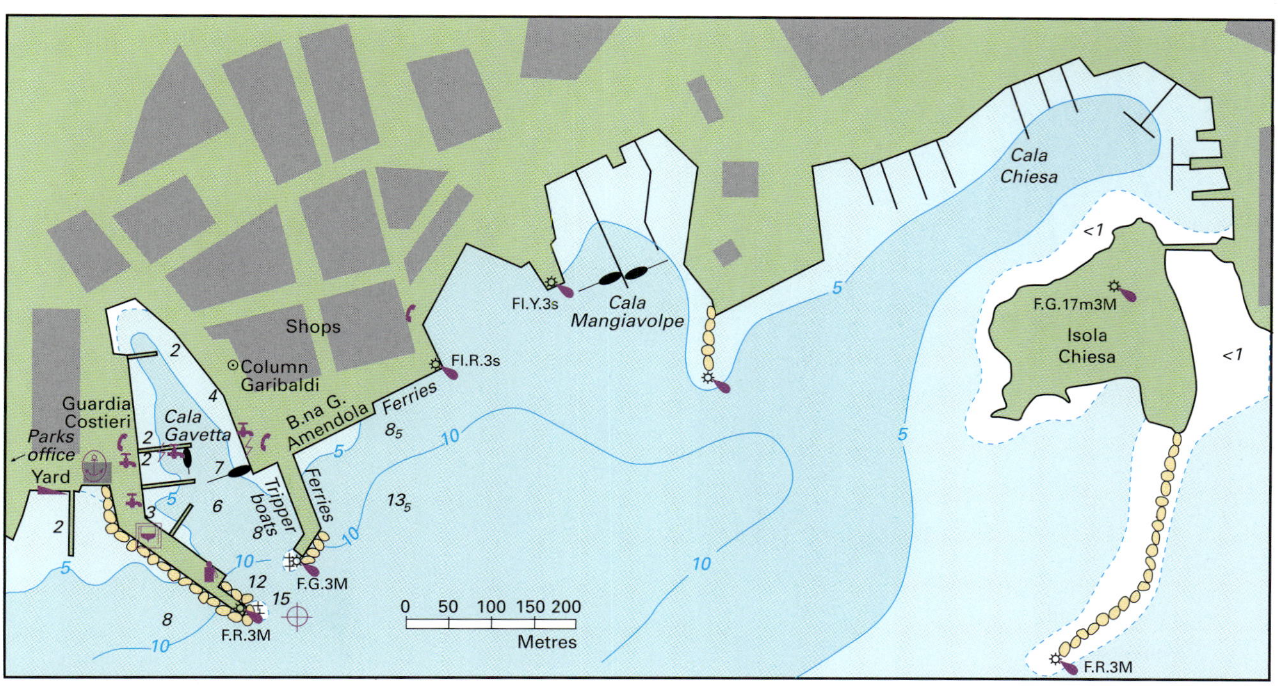

LA MADDALENA

MARINA DI CALA MANGIAVOLPE

VHF Ch 16, 09 (0700–1900).

Navigation New marina in the old military docks.

Data 120 berths. Max LOA 40m. Laid moorings in the bay. Max LOA 80m. Water and electricity.

Marina di Cala Mangiavolpe
☎ 331 865 9946

PORTO ARSENALE LA MADDALENA (CALA CAMICIA)

VHF Ch 69

Navigation From the W pass through '13ft channel' with least depths 4m. An isolated hazard to the W of the harbour is marked by buoys.

Data 450 berths. Max LOA 114m.

Facilities Water and electricity. Toilets and showers. Waste pump-out. Laundry. WiFi. 40-ton crane. 100-ton travel-hoist. Slipway. Repair services.

☎ 0789 794 225
Email info@portoarsenalelamaddalena.com
www.lamaddalenahyc.com

MARINA DEL PONTE

41°12'·9N 09°26'·4E

Navigation Marina under development under the W end of the Maddalena-Caprera causeway.

Data 120 berths. Max LOA 18m. Depths 1–6m reported. Charge band 5/6.

☎ 368 553 858
Email marinadelponte@tiscalinet.it

PORTO MASSIMO (PORTO LUNGO)

41°15'·4N 09°25'·6E
BA 1213 It 324

☆ Entrance F.R.3M/F.G.3M

VHF Ch 16, 09 (0700–1900).

Navigation Difficult to see exactly where the marina is from the N.

Berths Stern or bows-to. Laid moorings tailed to the quay.

Shelter Good shelter.

Data 200 berths. Max LOA 35/50m. Depths 1–5m. Charge band 6+.

Facilities Water. 220V. 10-ton crane. Limited provisions. Restaurant.

ITAS ☎ 0789 728 133
☎ 348 885 7973
www.portomassimo.it

MARINA NIDO D'AQUILA

41°12'·90N 09°22'·92E

A small marina in Cala Nido d'Aquila on the SW corner of Isola Maddalena.

VHF Ch 09, 16.

Data 100 berths. Max LOA 20m. Depths 1–6m. Laid moorings tailed to pontoons. Charge band 6+.

Facilities Water. 220V. Showers and toilets planned.

☎ 334 710 9642 / 0789 720 053
Email info@marinanidodaquila.it

CALA PETICCHIA (MARINA DEI GIARDINELLI)

41°13'·65N 09°26'·3E

A small marina under development between Isola Giardinelli and Isola Maddalena. Pontoons in place. At present looks limited to smaller shoal draught craft.

☎ 346 304 3058
Email marinadipeticciaurso@gmail.com

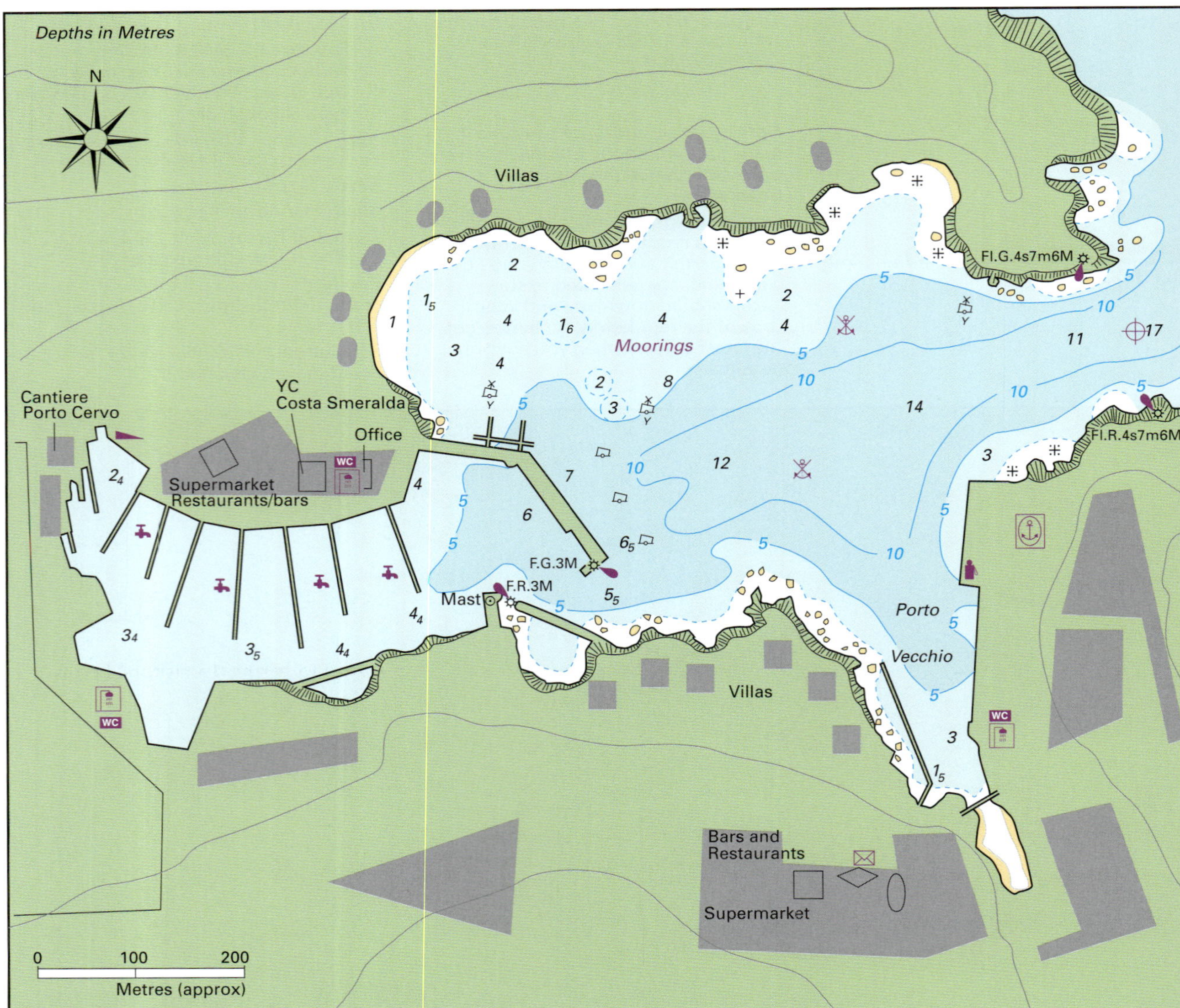

PORTO CERVO

Isola Caprera

PORTO PALMA

41°11′·1N 09°26′·9E

A large bay on the S side of Isola Caprera. Care must be taken of above and below water rocks fringing the coast and of two reefs on the E side of the bay. Moorings in N of bay.

PORTO CERVO

41°08′·24N 09°32′·34E WGS84
BA 1211 It 319 M8
7·5M Palau ←→ Olbia 20M

☆ Secche del Cervo (Cervo Rock) Q(3)10s4M. Entrance Fl.R.4s6M/Fl.G.4s6M. Leading lights (252°22′) Front Iso.R.2s3M. Rear Oc.R.4s3M. Marina entrance F.G.3M/F.R.3M

VHF Ch 16, 09, 11 (0700–1900) (Cervo Radio). Weather forecast on Ch 88.

Navigation Care needed of Cervo Rock (Secche del Cervo) 0·6M NE of Porto Cervo entrance marked by an E cardinal beacon.

Berths Where directed. Laid moorings tailed to the quay. The anchorage is now laid with moorings.

They may be booked in advance through Porto Cervo Marina. Charges €75 (12hrs) €150 (24hrs) up to 15m LOA.

Anchoring is prohibited in the vicinity of the moorings. There may be room for catamarans or shoal draught craft close in.

Data 700 berths. 100 visitors' berths. Max LOA 100m. Charge band 6+.

Facilities Water. 220/380V. Telephone. TV. Showers and toilets. Fuel quay. 40-ton travel-hoist. 350-ton slipway. All yacht repairs. Provisions and restaurants.

Remarks Costa Smeralda YC hosts many international racing events including the Sardinia Cup.

✆ 0789 905 111
Email info@marinadiportocervo.com

CALA DI VOLPE

41°04′·89N 09°32′·38E WGS84

☆ Punta Ligata Fl.3s3M. Entrance Fl.G.4s1M/Fl.R.4s1M

Popular anchorage.

The bay is laid with 19 moorings for vessels up to 300ft LOA. Anchoring is prohibited in the vicinity of the moorings and anchoring in the bay is restricted in high season. You may be asked to move by the coastguard. Contacts as for moorings at Porto Cervo.

MARINA DI PORTISCO

41°09′·92N 09°31′·62E WGS84
BA 1211 It 323

☆ Entrance Fl.G.4s3M/F.R.1M/Fl.R.4s3M

VHF Ch 16, 69

Berths Stern or bows-to where directed. Laid moorings tailed to the quay.

Shelter Good shelter.

Data 600 berths. 65 visitors' berths. Max LOA 90m. Depths 3–12m. Charge band 6+.

Facilities Water. 220/380V. WiFi. Showers and toilets. Fuel quay. 70-ton travel-lift. 65-ton crane. Limited provisions. Restaurant.

✆ 0789 335 20
Email info@marinadiportisco.it
www.marinadiportisco.it

PORTO ROTONDO

41°01′·84N 09°32′·52E WGS84
BA 1211 It 323

☆ Breakwater Fl.WR.5s7/5M. Entrance Fl.G.2s3M/Fl.R.2s3M

VHF Ch 09.

Navigation May be a confused swell in the narrow entrance.

Berths Where directed. Laid moorings tailed to the quay or buoys.

Data 630 berths. 63 visitors' berths. Max LOA 35m. Depths 1–5m. Charge band 6+.

Note 8 super-yacht berths.

Facilities Water. 220/380V. 120/150A. Showers and toilets. Fuel quay. 60-ton crane. Shipway to 45m LOA. Most yacht repairs. Some provisions. Restaurants.

✆ 0789 342 03
Email reservation@marinadiportorotondo.it
www.marinadiportorotondo.it

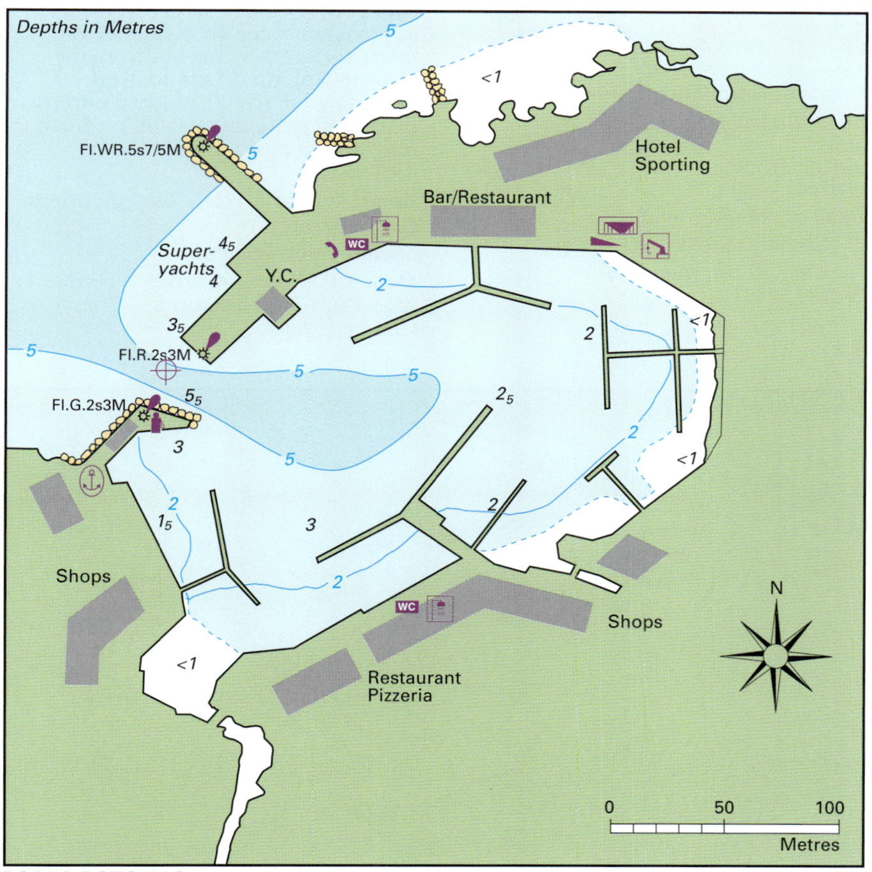

PORTO ROTONDO

PUNTA MARANA

41°00′·3N 09°33′·5E

☆ Entrance Iso.R.6s3M. Mole head Iso.G.6s3M

VHF Ch 09.

Navigation Buoyed narrow entrance channel.

Data 320 berths. Max LOA 14m. Depths 2–2·5m.

Facilities Water. 220V. Showers and toilets. Fuel quay. Restaurant.

Yachting Club Marina ✆ 0789 32088

GOLFO ARANCI

40°59′·6N 09°37′·1E
BA 1202 It 322

☆ Main pier Oc.R.3s3M.
SE mole Oc.G.3s3M.
Basin N side F.G.4M / F.R.4M

PORTICCIOLO BAIA CADDINAS

40°59′·7N 09°36′·2E

☆ Entrance Fl.G.2s2M/Fl.R.2s2M. T mole head F.RG(vert)1M

VHF Ch 09 (0700–2000).

Data 115 berths. 15 visitors' berths. Max LOA 15m. Depths <1–3m.

Facilities Water. 220V. Showers and toilets. Fuel quay. 20-ton crane. Limited yacht repairs. Limited provisions. Restaurant.

✆ 0789 468 13

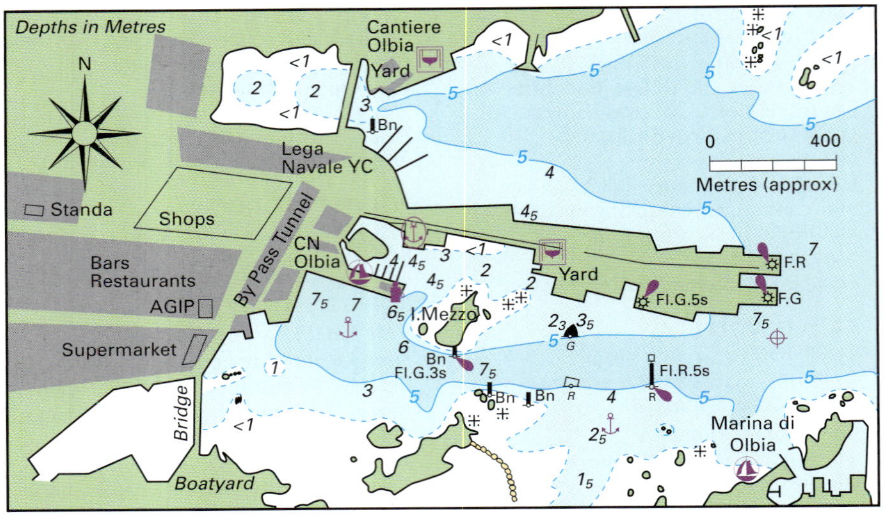

OLBIA

Cantiere Navale Isola Blanca All repair facilities
☏ 0789 210 18
Port Authority ☏ 0789 21243

MARINA DI PUNTALDIA
40°48'·8N 09°41'.5E
☆ Entrance Fl.G.3s5M/Fl.R.3s5M/2F.G(vert)2M
VHF Ch 09.
Navigation Care needed of reef immediately E of entrance. Approach is from the NE.
Data 400 berths. Max LOA 24m. Depths 2–4·5m. Charge band 6+.
Facilities Water. 220V. Showers and toilets. Fuel quay. Some repairs. Mini-market. Restaurant.
☏ 0784 864 589
Email info@marinadipuntaldia.it
www.marinadipuntaldia.it

PORTO DI SAN TEODORO
40°46'·8N 09°40'·7E
A new porto turistico under construction roughly halfway between Marina di Puntaldia and Porto Ottiolu. The breakwaters are complete, but as yet there are no quays or infrastructure. Care is needed as reefs and shoal water extend off the coast in places here.

PORTO OTTIOLU
40°44'·3N 09°42'·9E
BA 1992 It 322
☆ Isolotto d'Ottiolo Fl(2)R.10s5M. Entrance Fl.G.3s5M/Fl.R.3s5M
VHF Ch 09, 16.
Navigation Care is needed in the S approaches of the above and below water rocks extending out from the coast to Isolotto d'Ottiolo. Reef extending NE from Isolotto d'Ottiolo marked at extremity by a N cardinal buoy (lit) at position 40°44'·35N 09°43'·5E.
Berths Where directed. Laid moorings tailed to the quay.
Shelter Good shelter.
Data 405 berths. 40 visitors' berths. Max LOA 30m. Depths 2·7–3m. Charge band 5.

OLBIA
40°55'·77N 09°38'·03E WGS84 (0·2M N Ceraso Bn)
BA 1210 It 318
20M Porto Cervo ←→ Porto Brandhingi 15M
☆ Isola della Bocca LFl.5s15M. Isola di Mezzo Fl.G.3s4M. Pierhead F.G.3M. E end F.R.3M. Entrance channel N and S Fl.G.5s5M/Fl.R.5s5M/ Fl(2)G.6s4M/Fl(2)R.6s4M/Fl.G.5s4M/ Fl.R.5s4M/Fl.G.3s4M/Fl.R.3s4M/ Fl.R.5s4M/Fl.R.3s4M/Fl.R.2s4M/ Fl.G.5s4M/Fl.R.5s4M
VHF Ch 11, 16 for *capitaneria*. Ch 06, 09, 12, 14 for pilots.
Ch 16, 09 for the YC.
Navigation Off Capo Ceraso and Punta Ruia there are numerous rocks extending up to nearly half a mile offshore. The reef with Isoletto Barco Sconcia on it is marked at its extremity by a buoy. 1M W lies Punta Ruia and midway between the point and the cape, a reef off some islets extends northwards. It is marked at its extremity by a N cardinal buoy and exhibits a Q.6m5M. Merchant vessels regularly use Olbia and they have right of way in the channel.
Shelter Good shelter.
Facilities Provisions and restaurants in town. There are now five yards with travel-hoists and a further three yards with cranes that can haul yachts. There are workshops attached to all these yards.
Remarks The whole port area is being developed. The commercial port is to be relocated to the N side of the harbour somewhat W of No. 5 and No. 6 beacons. To the E of the development are six boatyards of which three have travel-hoists and workshops ashore.
Thefts reported from yachts at anchor.
Circolo Nautico Olbia
☏ 0789 26187
Cantieri Costa Smeralda (also in Porto Rotondo) ☏ 0789 57087
Email info@cantiericostasmeralda.com
Olbia Boat Service 160-ton travel-hoist.
VHF Ch 16, 09.
☏ 0789 53060
Email obs.obs@tiscali.it
CS Nautica Crane ☏ 0789 57497
Nausika 50-ton travel-hoist
☏ 0789 57181

MARINA DI OLBIA
40°54'·67N 09°31'·48E
A new marina in the S approaches to Olbia.
VHF Ch 09.
Data 270 berths. Max LOA 80m. Min depths 3–5m. Charge band 6+.
Facilities Water. 220/380V. WiFi. Showers and toilets. Laundry. Fuel quay.
☏ 0789 645 030
Email info@moys.it

Alternative berths in Olbia
1. Alongside old commercial quay (Pontile B. Brin)
2. *Circolo Nautico Olbia*. A small club between Pontile B. Brin and Ile Lucresa.

Data Limited visitors' berths. Max LOA 16m. Depths 2–4m. Charge band 5.

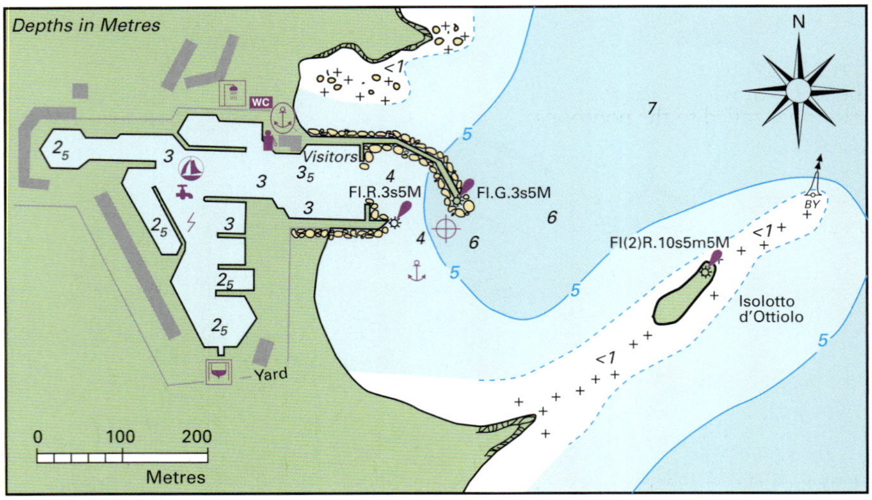

PORTO OTTIOLU

Facilities Water. 220V. Fuel quay. Showers and toilets. 40-ton travel-hoist. 22-ton crane. Some yacht repairs. Most provisions and restaurants.

Port Authority ✆ 0784 846 211
Email portottioulu@isitalia.it

Ottiolu Marina ✆ 0784 846 205
Email info@ottiolu.org

LA CALETTA

40°36′·6N 09°45′·4E
BA 1992 It 43 M8
14M Porto Brandhingi ←→ Arbatax 43M

☆ Entrance Fl.G.3s2M / Fl.R.3s2M

VHF Ch 16

Navigation The Pedrami Rocks extend nearly 1M eastwards from the coast to the N of La Caletta.

Berths Stern or bows-to. Laid moorings. Now four pontoons on NE side of central T-jetty and additional four pontoons on the SW side of T-jetty.

Shelter Good shelter although strong SE winds cause a surge.

Data 300 berths. Max LOA 18m. Depths 2–5m. Charge band 4.

Facilities Water. Fuel. Provisions and restaurants.

Cicolo Nautico La Caletta ✆ 0784 810631
www@circolonauticolacaletta.it

CALA GONONE

40°16′·84N 09°38′·33E WGS84
BA 1992 It 43

☆ Entrance F.G.3M/F.R.3M

VHF Ch 16.

Berths Stern or bows-to. Anchorage just outside W mole.

Shelter Adequate shelter although SE winds cause a surge.

Data Max LOA 12m. Depths 1–5m. Charge band 4.

Facilities Water. Fuel on quay. 9-ton crane. 23-ton slipway. Some provisions and restaurants.

Remarks Often crowded and difficult to find a berth.

✆ 0784 932 61

SANTA MARIA NAVARRESE (MARINA DI BAUNEI)

39°59′·37N 09°41′·68E WGS84

☆ Outer breakwater head F.G.4M. Inner pier head F.G.1M. Entrance breakwater head F.R.4M.

VHF Ch 16, 74.

Berth Berth where directed. Laid moorings tailed to the pontoons.

Shelter Good shelter.

Data 340 berths. Max LOA 30m. Depths 4–7m. Charge band 4/5.

Facilities Water. 220V. Showers and toilets. 40-ton travel-lift. 15-ton crane. Some repairs. Café/bar in the marina.

ISOLA TAVOLARA AND CAPO CODA CAVALLO MARINE RESERVE
The reserve covers the coast from Capo Ceraso to Punta d'Ottiolu and the islands off the coast.
Olbia Port Authority ✆ 0789 21243

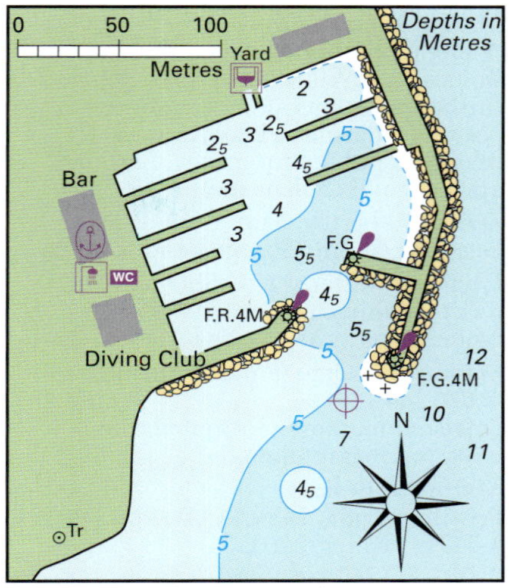

SANTA MARIA NAVARRESE

Provisions and restaurants in village 10 minutes away.

✆ 0782 614 020
Email info@portosantamaria-baunei.it
www.portosantamaria-baunei.it

ARBATAX

39°56′·76N 09°42′·08E WGS84
BA 1210 It 316 Imray M9
43M La Caletta ←→ Villasimius 56M

☆ Capo Bellavista Fl(2)10s26M/F.R.6M (164°-vis-177·5°). Entrance Fl.R.3s9M/F.R.5M/Fl.RG.3s8M. Torre 2F.G(vert)3M

VHF Ch 11, 16 (0700–1900) for port authorities. Ch 09.

Berths Stern or bows-to in the marina basin. Laid moorings tailed to the pontoons.

Shelter Good shelter.

Data 400 berths. 150 visitors' berths. Max LOA 60m. Depths 4–10m. Charge band 4.

Facilities Water. 220V. Fuel quay. 200-ton hoist. Provisions and restaurants.

Remarks Large commercial port.

✆ 0782 667405
Email info@marinadiarbatax.it
www.marinadiarbatax.it

PORTO CORALLO (MARINA DI VILLAPUTZU)

39°26′·4N 09°38′·4E
BA 1983 It 44 Imray M9

☆ Entrance Fl.G.4s4M/Fl.R.4s4M/F.G.3M

VHF Ch 74.

Berths Stern or bows-to or alongside pontoons where directed

Shelter Good shelter.

Data 300 berths. Max LOA 30m. Depths 2–4m. Charge band 4.

Facilities Water. 220V. Fuel quay. 50-ton travel-hoist. Restaurant. Limited provisions.

Remarks A dangerous wreck lies just off the coast close S of the marina entrance at 39°24′·7N 09°38′·5E.

Marina di Villaputzu
✆ 393 923 8334 / 8909
Email info@marinadivillaputzu.it
www.marinadivillaputzu.it

CAPO CARBONARA MARINE RESERVE
Includes Isola Serpentara and Isola dei Cavoli and the adjacent coast to Capo Boi. Villasimius lies within Zone C of the reserve.

Comune di Villasimius ✆ 070 790 234
www.ampcapocarbonara.it

VILLASIMIUS (FORTEZZA VECCHIA)

39°07′·41N 09°30′·23E WGS84
BA 1983 It 45 Imray M9
56M Arbatax ←→ Cagliari 20M

☆ Marina entrance Fl.G.3s4M/Fl.R.3s4M

VHF Ch09 (24 hr)

Navigation Breakwater extension reported to cover the reef extending NNW of the entrance. Care needed in the approaches.

Berths Where directed. Laid moorings.

Shelter Good all-round shelter.

Data 750 berths. Visitors' berths. Max LOA 60m. Depths 1–6m. Charge band 6.

Facilities Water. 220V. WiFi. Showers and toilets. Launderette. Fuel quay opens summer only. Chandler. Mini-market and supermarket. ATM. Gas. Restaurant.

Marina di Villasimius ✆ 070 797 8006
Email info@marinavillasimius.it
www.marinavillasimius.it

MARINA DI CAPITANA (PORTO ARMANDO)

39°12′·28N 09°17′·9E WGS84
BA 1983 It 45 Imray M9

☆ Entrance Fl.G.3s5M / Fl.R.3s5M. Inner dock entrance F.G.2M

VHF Ch 74, 16.

Navigation Entrance straightforward.

Berths Stern or bows-to.

Shelter All-round shelter.

Data 450 berths. 90 visitors' berths. Max LOA 27m. Depths 3m. Charge band 5.

Facilities Water. 220V. Showers and toilets. Fuel quay. 40-ton hoist. Some yacht services. Supermarket nearby. Restaurant and snack bar. Bus to Cagliari.

✆ 070 805460
Email marinadicapitana@tiscali.it
www.marinadicapitana.it

MARINA PICCOLA DEL POETTO

39°11′·6N 09°09′·8E
BA 1983 It 299 Imray M9

☆ Entrance Fl.Y.5s3M / Fl.R.5s1M

VHF Ch 16, 74.

Berths Where directed.

Shelter Good shelter although strong N winds make it uncomfortable.

Data 300 berths. Max LOA 18m. Depths 2–3m. Charge band 4.

Facilities Water. 220V. Fuel. 50-ton crane. Some provisions. Restaurant.

Remarks Usually crowded and difficult to find a berth.

YC Cagliari ✆ 070 370 350

CAGLIARI
39°11′·60N 09°06′·48E WGS84
BA 1208 It 311 Imray M9
20M Villasimius ←→ Teulada 32M

☆ Capo St. Elia Fl(2)10s21M. Entrance Fl.G.3s9M/Fl.R.3s9M/. Bns Fl(2+1)G.5s3M/Fl(2+1)G.7s3M/ Fl(2+1)R.7s3M. Pennello Sant' Elmo head Fl.Y.5s4M. Pennello Bonaria SE F.R.3M, NW F.G.3M. Molo Sabaudo F.R.3M. Inner basin entrance Fl.G.4s6m3M / Fl.R.4s7m3M

VHF Ch 11, 16 for port authorities (0700–1900). Call sign *Cagliari Radio*. Ch 09, 12, 16 for pilots. Ch 74 for Marina di Sant'Elmo. Ch 13 for Marina del Sole.

Navigation A yacht can make for one of the marinas in the SE corner, or the inner basin.

Berths

Marina Del Sole First pontoons in the SE corner of the harbour. Laid moorings. Excellent shelter.

Data 220 berths. 30 visitors' berths. Max LOA 30m. Depths 5–8m. Charge band 5.

Facilities Water. 220V. Fuel can be delivered. 40-ton crane. Repairs.

✆ 070 308 730
Email marinadelsole@tiscalinet.it
www.marinasole-santelmo.com
www.approdomarinasole.com

Marina di Sant' Elmo
A single pontoon between Marina di Bonaria and Marina del Sole. Four further pontoons along the shore between Marina del Sole and the S breakwater. Laid moorings. Berthing assistance. Excellent shelter.

Data 300 berths. Max LOA 18m. Depths 1·5–9m. Charge band 5.

Facilities Water. 220V. Showers and toilets. Pump-out. Security. 35-ton crane. Repairs and storage.

Marina di St'Elmo (Enrico Deplano)
✆ 070 344 169
Email marinasantelmo@gmail.com
www.marinasantelmo.it

Marina di Bonaria
Private marina. Max LOA 30m. Depths 1·5–7m. Water. 220V.
✆ 070 300 240

Motomar Sardo
Small marina in NW corner. Laid moorings.

Data 50 berths. Max LOA 35m. Depths 1·5–2m. Water. 220V. 50-ton crane. Some repairs.

✆ 070 665 948

Cantiere Navale di Ponente
Fuel quay (depths 4m). 30-ton travel-hoist. Most repairs can be arranged.
✆ 070 662 290

Cagliari Inner Harbour and Marina Portus Karalis
Pontoon and quay berths in the inner harbour.

VHF Ch 09.

Berths Where directed. Laid moorings.

Shelter Excellent all-round shelter.

Data 140 berths. Max LOA 18–100m. Depths 8–15m. Charge band 5 (July–August).

Facilities Water. 220/380V. WiFi. Showers and toilets (to be completed). Pump-out. Laundry.

Portus Karalis ✆ 070 653 535
Email portuskaralis@gmail.com
Port Authority ✆ 070 669 467

PERD'E' SALI
39°01′·70N 09°02′·00E WGS84
BA 1990 It 45

VHF Ch 16, 74.

Berths Stern or bows-to.

Shelter Good.

Data 200 berths. 50 visitors' berths. Max LOA 18m. Depths 1·5–2m. Charge band 6.

Facilities Water. 220V. Fuel quay. Restaurant and bar. Taxi for provisions and other restaurants.

Remarks Depths just 1·3m in the entrance. Very crowded with little room to manoeuvre inside.

Saromar ✆ 070 925 3145

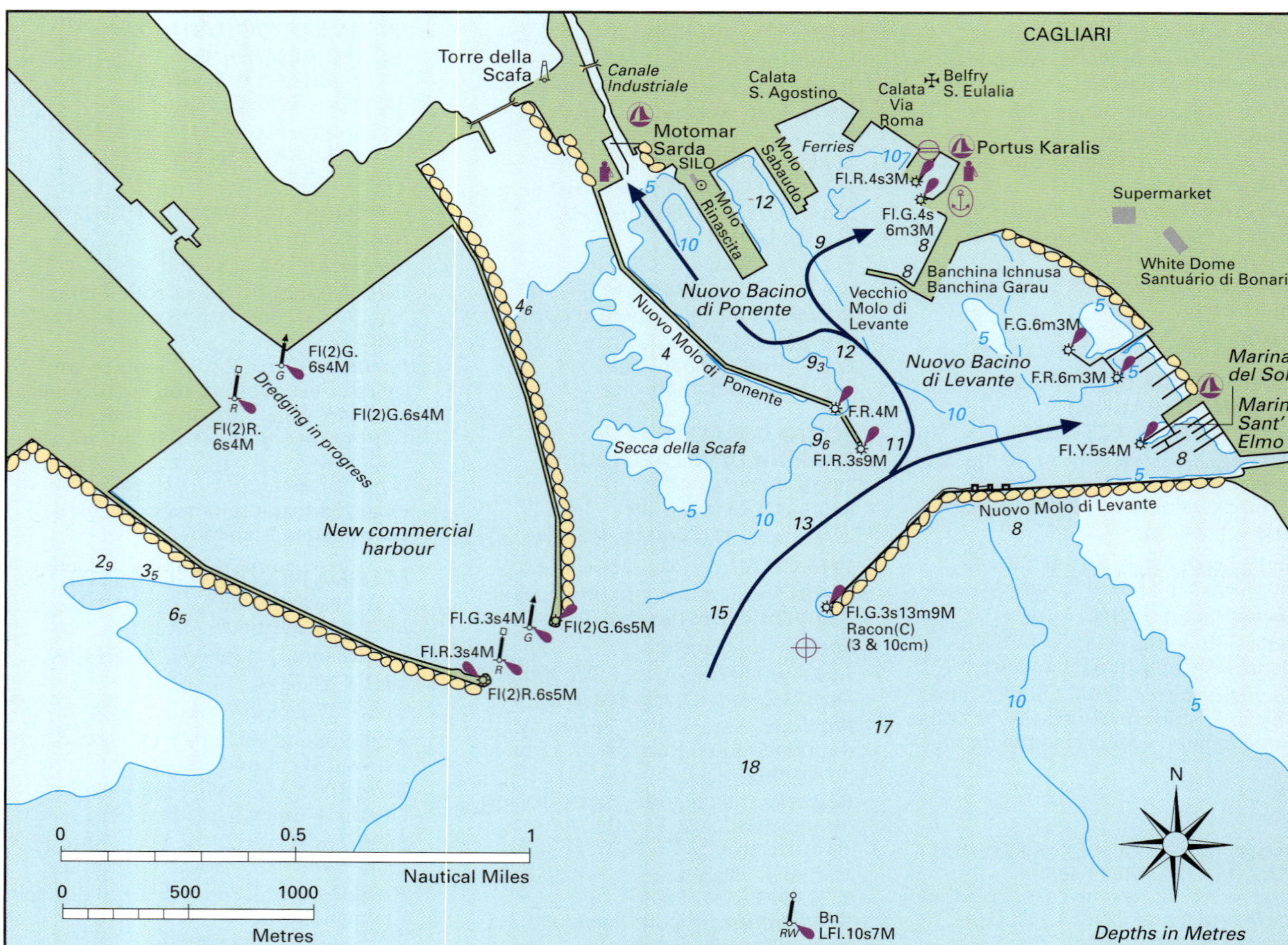

CAGLIARI

CALA VERDE
38°56'·1N 08°56'·5E
BA 1990 It 46
☆ Entrance Fl.G.5s3M/Fl.R.5s3M

VHF Ch 16, 10.

Navigation A dangerous rock in the entrance is reported with 1·6m over. Although there is 2m inside, the fouled entrance effectively reduces draught to 1·5m.

Berths Where directed.

Shelter Good shelter.

Data 100 berths. Eight visitors' berths. Max LOA 12m. Depths 2m, but see *Navigation* note above.

Facilities Water. 220V. Fuel. 6-ton crane.

Curimar ☎ 070 921 214

PORTO TEULADA
38°55'·67N 08°43'·39E WGS84
BA 1990 It 46
32M Cagliari ←→ Carloforte 30M
☆ Outer mole head Fl.R.4s6M. Inner mole head Fl.G.4s6M. Internal Pennello F.R.2M

VHF Ch 09.

Berths Stern or bows-to where directed. Laid moorings.

Shelter Good.

Data 250 berths. Visitors' berths. Max LOA 25m. Depths 2–6m. Charge band 5.

Facilities Water. 220V. WiFi. Pump-out. 25-ton travel-hoist. Café bar and limited provisions nearby.

Remarks Anchorage in the bay.

☎ 070 928 3705
Email info@marinaditeulada.com

PORTO PONTE ROMANO
39°02'·7N 08°29'·0E (Fl.G.3sBn)
BA 1207 It 296
☆ Main light Fl.5s15M. Channel beacons Fl.G.3s4M/Fl.R.3s4M (×2). Wharf F.GR(vert)3M

VHF Ch 14, 16 (0700–1900) for port authorities.

Berths Alongside or stern or bows-to.

Shelter Open S.

Data Depths 2–7m. Charge band 1.

Facilities Water. Provisions and restaurants.

CALASETTA
39°06'·91N 08°22'·53E WGS84 (2F.G(vert)
BA 1207 It 294 Imray M9
☆ Beacon Q.5M. Entrance 2F.G(vert)3M/2F.R(vert)3M

VHF Ch 74, 16 (0700–1900) for Calasetta Marina.

Navigation The N cardinal beacon (Q.5M) marks the edge of the channel into the harbour and must be left to starboard when entering the harbour.

Berths Stern or bows-to in the Porto Turistico. Pontoons in place. Visitors' berths on N breakwater or outer pontoon.

Shelter Good shelter although strong E–SE winds are uncomfortable.

Data 300 berths. Max LOA 20m. Depths 0·5–5m. Charge band 5.

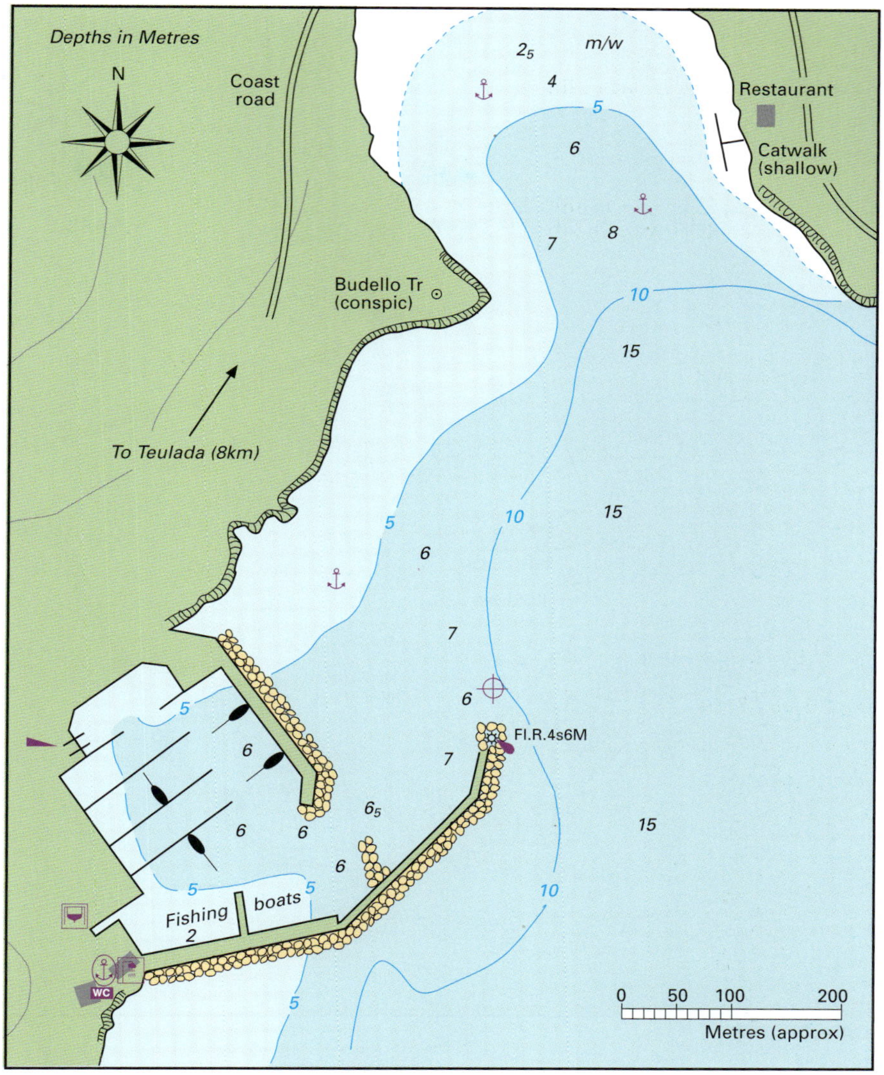

PORTO TEULADA

Facilities Water. 220V. Fuel quay. Most provisions and restaurants.

Calasetta Marina ☎ 0781 88083
Email info@portocalasetta.it

CARLOFORTE
39°08'·5N 08°19'·0E (Fl.R.3s)
BA 1202 It 297 Imray M9
30M Teulada ←→ Marina Torre Grande 46M
☆ Entrance Fl.R.3s8M/Fl.G.3s6M. Leading lights (273°27') Front F.R.3M. Rear F.R.3M. Secca dei Marmi NW Fl.Y.3s4M. W LFl.10s6M. Front (Bn) F.R.6M. Rear (Bn) Fl.R. Piers 2F.R(vert)3M/ F.GR(vert)3M/2F.G(vert)3M. Fishing harbour S pier head 2F.R(vert)2M. N pier head 2F.G(vert)2M

VHF Ch 11, 16 for port authorities (24/24). Ch 15 for Marine Sifredi. Ch 09 for Marinatour.

Navigation Care needed of shoal water in the approaches, especially Secca dei Marmi.

Note

1. Secca dei Marmi is now recorded as having 1·5m over it.
2. The entrance to the fishing harbour is very narrow and care is needed. Depths 2m.

Berths Some of the yacht berths around the harbour are made very uncomfortable by the near constant wash from ferries and other craft, particularly in the busy summer period. From the NW corner of the harbour running southwards:

Marine Sifredi
Operates the basin in the NW corner and two pontoons in the SE corner.

Data 250 berths. Max LOA 60m. Laid moorings. Depths 2–5m. Water. 220/380V. Shower and toilets. Charge band 5.

☎ 0781 857 008
Email info@marinesifredi.it
www.marinesifredi.it

Marinatour Marina di Carloforte
Operates the pontoon immediately S of Marine Sifredi and the pontoons off the public quay.

Data 250 berths. Laid moorings. Max LOA 55m. Depths 2–6m. Water. 220V. Charge band 5/6 (August).

☎ 0781 854 110/ 330 430 091
Email info@marinatour.it
www.marinatour.it

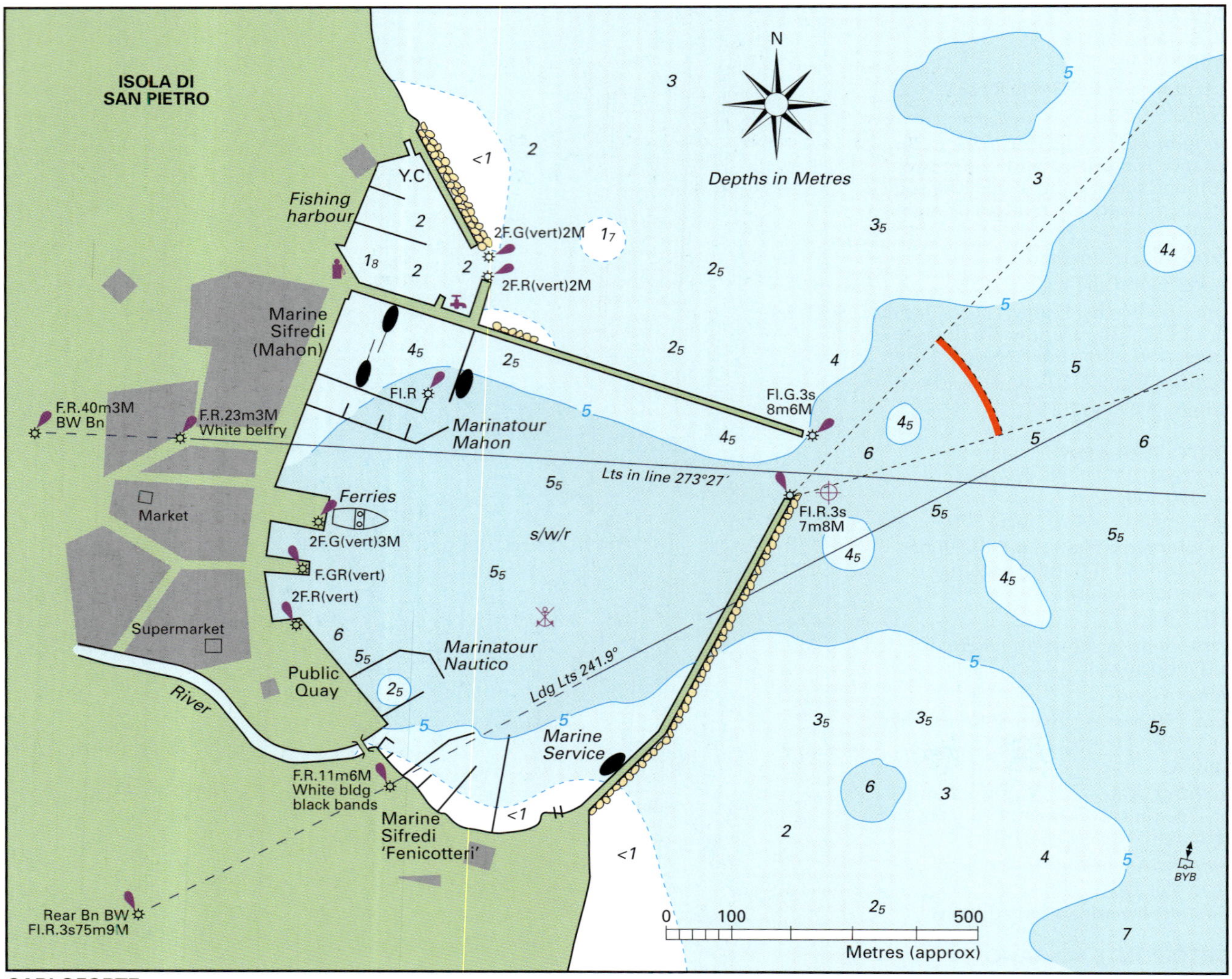

CARLOFORTE

Carloforte town quay Bow or stern-to the new quay.

No laid moorings or services although they may be installed in the future. Stays notionally restricted to 48 hours.

Data c.20 berths. Max LOA c.20m. Depths 2·5–6m. Charge band 3.

Lega Navale
Private YC immediately S of the river.

✆ 0781 855 618

Marine Service Yacht Carloforte
Pontoon in the SW corner.

Data 40 berths. Laid moorings. Depths 1–5m. Water. 220V. Shower and toilets. Charge band 5.

✆ 0781 856 533 / 338 203 8746
Email marineservice@tiscalinet.it
http://web.tiscali.it/carloforteservizi/

Anchorage in the SW corner

Note Anchoring is reported to be prohibited, unless arriving after dark.

Anchor in the SW of the harbour off the entrance to the river. Sand, mud and weed, good holding. Old mooring chains and anchors on the bottom so a trip line may be wise. Some (ferry) wash. Good shelter.

Facilities Water. Fuel quay in the fishing harbour. 90/10-ton cranes. 30-ton slipway. Provisions and restaurants.

PORTO VESME

39°11′·4N 08°23′·1E
BA 1202 It 295

☆ Beacons
Fl.G.3s4M/Fl.R.3s4M/Fl.G.3s3M/
Fl.R.3s3M/Fl.G.3s3M/Fl.R.3s3M.
Entrance
Fl.G.3s7M/Fl.R.3s7M/2F.R(vert)3M

VHF Ch 12, 16 (0700–1900) for port authorities.

Large commercial harbour. Fl.R.3s7M marks works in progress close SW (T).

PORTOSCUSO

39°11′·9N 08°22′·9E
Imray M9

☆ Scoglio la Ghingetta
Fl(2)WR.10s11/8M 116°-W-153°/165°-W-100°. Entrance 2F.R.4M/F.G.4M

VHF Ch 16, 09 (0700–1900).

Berths Stern or bows-to where directed.

Shelter Good shelter.

Data 400 berths. Depths 2–3·5m. Charge band 4.

Facilities Water. 3-ton slipway. Provisions and restaurants.

Saromar ✆ 0781 507 248

BUGGERRU

39°24′·1N 08°23′·8E

☆ Entrance
Fl.R.3s4M/Fl.G.3s4M/2F.R(vert)1M

VHF Ch 16.

Navigation Entrance difficult with moderate to strong NW winds. Entrance silts with 1–1·5m in entrance.

Berths Stern or bows-to alongside in the inner basin.

Shelter Surge with westerlies.

Data Max LOA 10m. Depths 1·5–2·5m.

Facilities Water. 4-ton crane. Some provisions. Restaurant.

Remarks Depths in entrance 3–6m. Depths inside just 1m.

✆ 0781 544 28

PORTO ORISTANO (S GIUSTA)

39°51′·9N 08°32′·2E (LFl.G.5s)
BA 1205 It 291

☆ Entrance LFl.G.5s8M/LFl.R.5s7M. Ldg Lts 130° front Iso.2s8M. Rear Oc.4s10M

VHF Ch 16 for port authorities.

Large commercial harbour.

Remarks Tecnomar (of Fiumicino, Rome) are opening a marina and shipyard in the basin here.

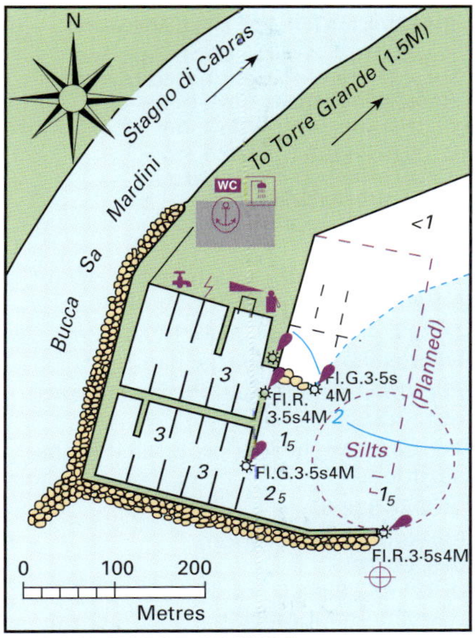

MARINA TORRE GRANDE

Ormeggiatori ☎ 0783 74159
Email info@tecnomar.net
www.tecnomar.net

MARINA TORRE GRANDE

39°54'·3N 08°29'·4E
BA 1205 Italian 293 Imray M9
46M Carloforte ←→ Bosa Marina 32M

☆ Pier S Fl.R.3·5s4M/Fl.R.3·5s4M. Pier N Fl.G.3·5s4M/Fl.G.3·5s4M. T-pier Fl.R/Fl.G

VHF Ch 16, 09.

Navigation Care needed of shoal water in W–SW approaches and fish farms close S. Make approaches from the S to the buoyed channel.

Berths Stern or bows-to.

Shelter Good shelter.

Data 400 berths. Visitors' berths. Max LOA 25m. Depths 1·5–3m. Charge band 4.

Facilities Water. Fuel. 220V. 50-ton travel-hoist.

Marine Oristanesi ☎ 0783 221 89
Email info@marineoristanesi.it
www.marineoristanesi.it

BOSA MARINA

40°17'·1N 08°28'·5E
BA 1985 It 911
32M Marina Torre Grande ←→ Alghero 19M

☆ Breakwater head Fl.R.8m3M. Pierhead Fl.R.3s11m11M

Note A new breakwater runs in a curve across the entrance to Fiume Temo. Keep close to Isola Rossa in the approaches to the river.

VHF Ch 16, 14 (0700–1900) Ch 09, 73 for river berths.

Berths Stern or bows-to on the quay in the bay. Anchorage off the beach in the bay. Nautica Pinna is an established boatyard with pontoon berths in the river. Go stern or bows-to in Nautica Pinna or in the new basin. Laid moorings tailed to the pontoons.

Shelter Adequate although sometimes uncomfortable in the bay. Uncomfortable with onshore winds in River Temo.

Data *Quay* c.20 berths. Depths 1–12m. Charge band 4.

River Temo 200 berths. Max LOA 25m. Depths 1·5–3m. Charge band 4.

Facilities Water and fuel quay in River Temo. 10-ton slipway. Provisions and restaurants.

Remarks Anchoring is prohibited N of a line from the end of the N pier to the end of the rough semi-submerged mole in the NE corner of the bay.

Circolo Nautico Bosa ☎ 0785 376 174
R. Pirisi ☎ 0785 375 550
Nautica Pinna ☎ 0785 373 554 / 331 806 3356
Email info@nauticapinna.it
Il Porticciolo di Bosa ☎ 0785 375 550

ALGHERO

40°33'·87N 08°18'·49E WGS84
BA 1202 It 911 Imray M8
19M Bosa Marina ←→ Capo Caccia 7M

☆ Isoletto della Maddalena Fl.R.5s4M. Entrance Fl.G.3M/Fl.R.3M. Pier head 2F.R(vert)2M. Inner basin entrance 2F.G(vert)3M/2F.R(vert)3M. Nuova Darsena entrance F.G.4M/F.R.5M

VHF Ch 16, 11 (0700–1900). Ch 74, 16 for Aquatica. Ch 09 for town quay, Marina di Sant'Elmo and Ser-Mar.

Isoletto della Maddalena tower is now red. Hull of a wrecked yacht also visible (2010).

Berths Stern or bows-to on the town quay or at your choice of pontoons shown below. One or more companies will meet you inside the entrance to offer you a berth.

Town quay Laid moorings tailed to the quay. Depths 3–5m. Max LOA c.70m.

Aquatica marina 60 berths on pontoons adjacent to the town quay. Max LOA 60m. Repairs and fuel through Atlantis shipyard.

Ser-Mar Two pontoons off the N breakwater. More near town quay. Laid moorings tailed to the quay. Repairs yard.

Marina di Sant'Elmo Pontoons off the S side of the harbour. 100 berths. Max LOA 70m. Depths 4–5m.

Yacht Club Alghero (YCA) Six pontoons in the inner harbour.

Society Centro Alghermar Single pontoon near fuel quay.

Mar de Plata Three pontoons N of the town quay.

Mare Club Italia Four pontoons W of the town quay.

Club Nautico Two concrete piers with pontoons off the central mole.

Ambrosia Single pontoon off the N breakwater. Repairs yard.

Shelter Good shelter although strong onshore winds cause a surge.

Data c.850 berths. Depths 1–4m. Charge band 5/6.

Facilities Water. 220V. Fuel. 15/50-ton cranes. Some yacht repairs. Provisions and restaurants.

Porto di Alghero ☎ 079 989 3117
☎ 339 732 9921
Email info@portodialghero.com
www.portodialghero.com
Aquatica Marina
☎ 079 983 199 ☎ 348 130 3966
Email info@aquaticamarina.com
Atlantis shipyard ☎ /*Fax* 079 976 686

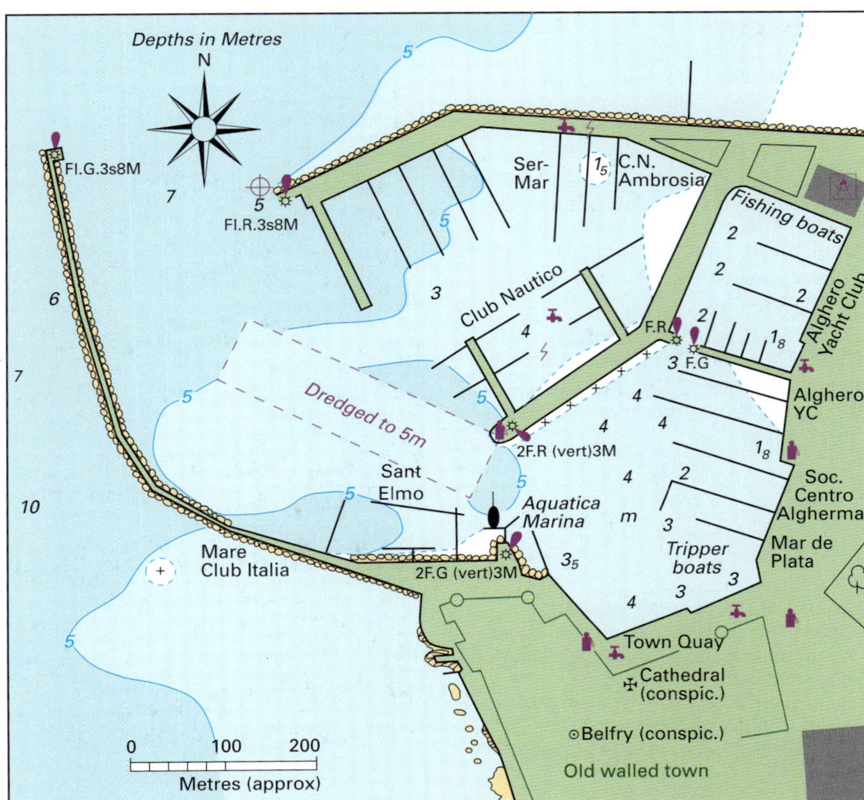

ALGHERO

SINIS PENINSULA AND ISOLA MAL DI VENTRE MARINE RESERVE
Covering the coast from Capo San Marco to Capo Sa Sturaggio, and 7M seawards around Il Catalano and Isola Mal di Ventre.
Comune di Cabras ✆ 0738 290 071
Email info@areamarinasinis.it
www.areamarinasinis.it

Ser-Mar, Federico Crisafulli
✆ 347 772 0544
Email info@ser-mar.it www.ser-mar.it
Marina di Sant'Elmo
✆ 0799 80829 / 333 221 4342
Email info@marinadisantelmo.it
www.marinadisantelmo.it
Yacht Club Alghero (YCA) ✆ 079 952 074
Club Nautico ✆ 079 986 958
Ambrosia ✆ 079 952 179

FERTILIA
40°35'·5N 08°17'·3E
☆ Outer breakwater head F.R.3M. Inner breakwater head F.G.3M
VHF Ch 16.
Two small marinas at the head of Rada di Alghero. Good shelter.
Data 250 berths. Max LOA 25m. Depths 1–4m. Charge band 5.
Facilities Water. 220V. Fuel nearby. 40-ton crane. Yacht repairs. Provisions and restaurants.
Marina di Fertilia (S quay)
✆ 0799 930 002 ✆ 347 183 2122 (English)
Email info@marinadifertilia.it
Base Nautica Cam (W side) ✆ 338 722 2440
Base Nautica Usai Cesare Usai
✆ 0799 30233
Email basenauticausai@tiscalinet.it

PORTO CONTE
40°33'·6N 08°09'·8E Capo Caccia
BA 1202 It 292
☆ Capo Caccia Fl.5s24M. Terre Nuova Fl.3s10M. Marina entrance F.R.1M/F.G.1M
A large almost land-locked bay entered between Capo Caccia and Punta de Giglio. Anchorage on the W and N. Small marina in Cala Torre del Conte.
Porto Conte Marina
VHF Ch 09, 16.
Data 250 berths. 10 visitors' berths. Max LOA 20m. Depths <1–3m.
Facilities Water. 220V. Fuel quay. 12-ton crane. Provisions and restaurants.
✆ 079 942013

CAPO CACCIA MARINE RESERVE
Covers the coast from Capo Galera to Punta delle Gessiere. An access channel leads to Porto Conte.
Comune di Alghero ✆ 079 997 800
www.comune.alghero.ss.it
Comune di Alghero ✆ 079 997 810
Fax 079 997 819
Email info@ampcapocaccia.it
www.ampcapocaccia.it

Sicily

SAN VITO LO CAPO
38°10'·84N 12°44'·23E WGS84
BA 2122 It 252 Imray M31
19M Trapani ←→ Acquasanta (Palermo) 35M
☆ Capo San Vito Fl.5s25M+Iso.R.4s8M. Punta Solanto Fl.WR.3s10/8M. Entrance Fl.G.5s5M/2F.G(vert)3M/2F.R(vert)3M
VHF Ch 16.
Navigation With strong winds there are confused seas off Capo San Vito. Entrance silting on S side and depths less than charted.
Berths Stern or bows-to. Laid moorings tailed to quay.
Shelter Adequate shelter.
Data 200 berths. Max LOA 30m. Depths <1–6m. Charge band 4.
Facilities Water. 220V. Fuel quay. Provisions and restaurants.
Remarks Anchoring reported prohibited E of harbour, but permitted N of the breakwater.
CN La Traina ✆ 0923 972 999
DN Sanvitese ✆ 0923 974 126
CN Costa Gaia ✆ 0923 972037

CASTELLAMMARE DEL GOLFO
38°01'·85N 12°53'·0E
BA 2122 It 252 Imray M31
☆ Castello Normano Fl(2)10s10M. Breakwater head Fl.G.8s3M
VHF Ch 16 (0800–1400).
Berths Stern or bows-to.

RISERVA NATURALE DELL ZINGARO
New nature reserve W of Capo San Vito. There is no designated Marine Reserve but there have been restrictions reported on anchoring.
✆ 0924 35108 *Fax* 0924 35752
Email info@riservazingaro.it
www.riservazingaro.it

Shelter Normally adequate but open NE.
Data c.400 berths. Max LOA 12m. Depths 0·5–8m. Charge band 4/5.
Facilities Water. Fuel. Provisions and restaurants.
Remarks Anchoring prohibited in the harbour.
✆ 0924 312 61
Blu Nautica (N pontoon)
VHF Ch 74
✆ 331 152 8888 (English) / 366 538 9478
www.blu-nautica.it
Sporting Club Veliero (S pontoon)
✆ 0924 32227 / 320 431 5331
Imbarcaderos ✆ 338 753 3733

BALESTRATE
38°03'.1N 13°00'.4E
☆ Outer mole head Fl.G.3s6M
VHF Ch 16.
New harbour in Golfo di Castellamare. The breakwaters are complete, but there are no pontoons or services.
Data 545 berths (when finished). Max LOA 40m. Depths 1–4m.
Facilities Water and 220V to be installed. Slip and travel-lift bay.

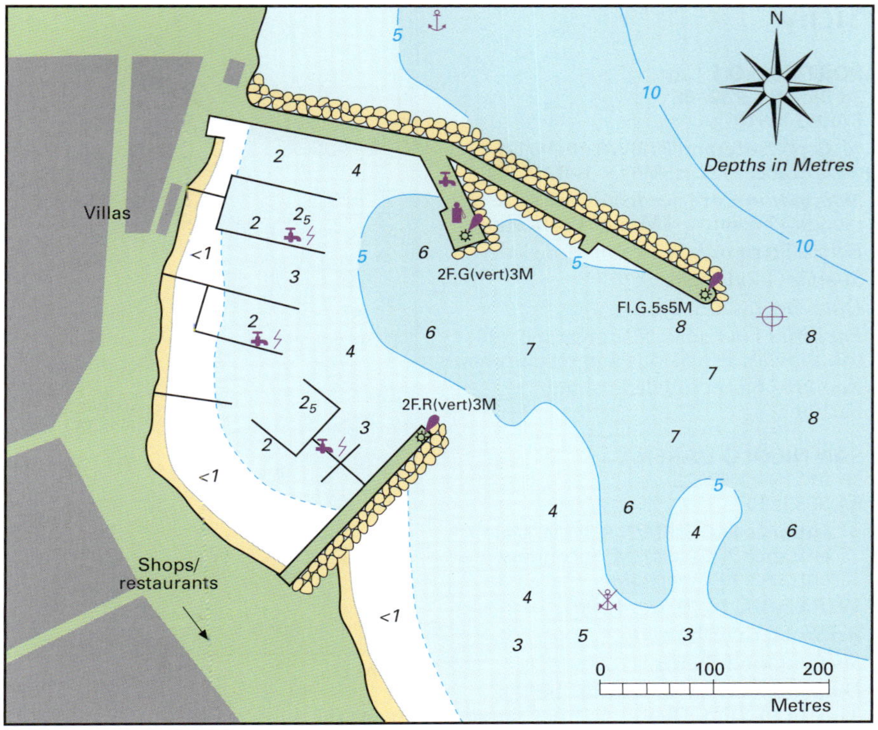

SAN VITO LO CAPO

TERRASINI
38°10'·2N 13°05'·1E

☆ Entrance Fl.G.3s4M / Fl.R.3s4M. Spur Fl.G.4s3M. Mole head 2F.R(vert)1M

Fishing harbour. Prone to silting.

TORRE POZZILLO
38°11'·1N 13°08'·2E

A hauling and storage facility being developed between Terrasini and Femmine, at the NE end of the Palermo airport runway. A travel-hoist bay and slip are sheltered from the NW by a stub mole, with workshops and hardstanding ashore. The facility is reported to haul yachts up to 18m.

SFERRA CAVALLO
38°12'·0N 13°16'·5E

☆ Mole head 2F.R(vert)3M

FOSSA DEL GALLO
38°3'·40N 13°19'·40E

☆ Capo Gallo LFl(2)15s40m16M

A small harbour lying under Capo Gallo. Fuel quay.

Data Max LOA 15m. Depths 2–6·5m. 65-ton travel-hoist. Repairs.

Motomar ☎ 091 453 145
www.motomarcdm.it

CAPO GALLO AND ISOLA FEMMINE MARINE RESERVE

The reserve extends out from the coast to Isola Femmine and around Capo Gallo.

Capitaneria di Porto di Palermo
☎ 091 604 3111

AMP Capo Gallo – Isola delle Femmine
☎ 091 584 802
Email Info@ampcapogallo-isola.com
www.ampcapogallo-isola.org

MONDELLO
38°12'·25N 13°19'·75E

☆ 2F.G(vert)1M

ARENELLA
38°08'·9N 13°22'·5E

☆ F.R

Cala dei Normanni Marina

Data c.50 berths. Max LOA 18m. Laid moorings tailed to pontoons. Water. 220V. Charge band 6.

Altura Club ☎ 091 521595
Mobile 340 0526785
www.alturaclub.eu

Cala dei Normanni ☎ 091 540264
(Pontoon max LOA 10m)
Email info@caladeinormanni.it
www.caladeinormanni.it

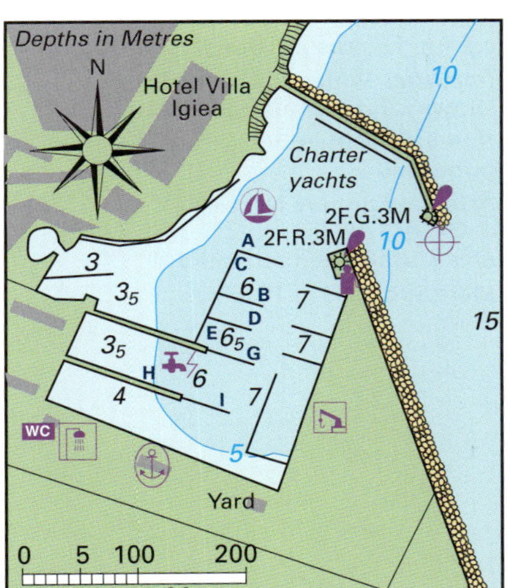

MARINA VILLA IGIEA

Club Nautico Vincenzo Florio
☎ 091 6374425
Email cnvflorio@tin.it
www.chicopaladino.com/cnvf/home.html

Nautica Tramuto ☎ 091 542949

Lega Navale Italiana ☎ 091 363394

MARINA VILLA IGIEA (ACQUASANTA)
38°08'·66N 13°22'·46E WGS84
BA 963 It 256 Imray M31
35M San Vito Lo Capo ←→ Cefalu 33M

☆ Entrance 2F.G(vert)3M/2F.R(vert)3M

VHF Ch 16, 74

Navigation Entrance difficult to see.

Berths Stern or bows-to. Laid moorings.

Shelter Good shelter.

Data 400 berths. Max LOA 65m. Depths 2–12m. Charge band 6.

Facilities Water. 220V. Showers and toilets (poor). Fuel quay. 15/50-ton cranes. Some yacht repairs. Supermarket nearby. Restaurants.

Remarks Close N of Palermo Commercial Harbour.

Marina Villa Igiea ☎ 091 364 123
www.marinavillaigiea.com

PALERMO
38°07'·3N 13°22'·7E
BA 963 It 255 Imray M31

☆ Molo Nord elbow Fl(4)15s15M. Porto Industrial mole head F.G. Entrance LFl.G.5s5M/LFl.R.5s8M. Pierhead 2F.G(vert)3M

VHF Ch 11, 16 for port authorities (0800–2000). Ch 11, 12 for pilots (0700–1900).

Berths Yachts should make for the inside of the S mole. Stern or bows-to or alongside. Charge band 5.

Shelter Good shelter.

Facilities Water. 220V. Fuel quay. 50-ton crane. 100-ton slipway. Some yacht repairs. Provisions and restaurants.

Remarks Crowded in the summer.

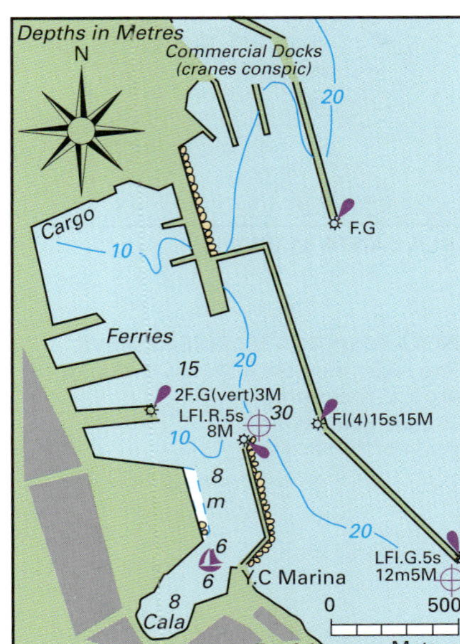

PALERMO

Salpancore ☎ 091 331 055 / 393 992 2120
Email salpancore@infocom.it

Yacht Club del Mediterraneo
☎ 091 581 837
Email ycm@ycm.it

Nixe Yachting
☎ 091 625 7990 / 338 450 4358

Societa Canottieri Palermo
☎ 091 328 467

Nautilus Marine
☎ 091 611 8733 / 335 781 7647
Email nautilus24@nautilusaviation.com

Lega Navale
☎ 389 808 3087
Email palermo@leganavale.it

Isola di Ustica

CALA STA MARIA
38°42'·4N 13°11'·9E
BA 1976 It 251 Imray M31

☆ Punta Gavazzi Fl(4)12s16M. Punta Omo Morto Fl(3)15s25M/Oc.R.5s9M. Mole head 2F.R(vert)3M

VHF Ch 16.

Berths Stern or bows-to or alongside where there is room leaving the hydrofoil berth clear. The harbour is very crowded in the summer.

Shelter Good except with SE–E winds which if strong and prolonged could make the harbour dangerous.

Data Max LOA 15m. Depths 1–7m.

Facilities Fuel quay. Some provisions and restaurants.

☎ 091 844 9045

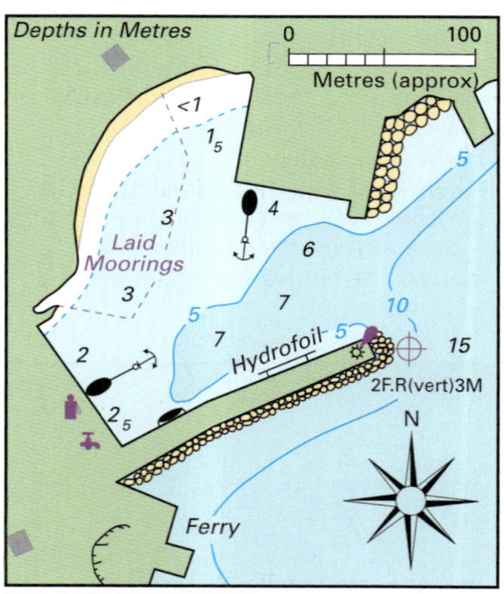

CALA SANTA MARIA

ISOLA DI USTICA MARINE RESERVE
The reserve extends 3M off the coast around the island.
☎ 0981 844 9456
www.ampustica.it

Sicily

PORTICELLO
38°05'·1N 13°32'·6E
BA 963 It 916

☆ Capo Zafferano Fl(3)WR.10s16/12M. Entrance Fl.G.3s5M/Fl.R.3s4M

Navigation Care needed of the rock (Scoglio Formica) 1M E of Porticello.

Berths Stern or bows-to or alongside.

Shelter Good shelter.

Data Depths 1·5–6m.

Facilities Fuel quay. 50-ton crane. 60-ton slipway. Provisions and restaurants.

Remarks Busy crowded fishing harbour.

SAN NICOLO L'ARENA
38°01'·1N 13°37'·2E
BA 963 It 15

☆ Entrance Fl.G.3s3M/Fl.R.3s3M. Main entrance 2F.G(vert)2M. Secondary entrance F.RG(vert)3M

VHF Ch 14, 16 (0700–1900).

Berths Stern or bows-to.

Shelter Good shelter.

Data 450 berths. 45 visitors' berths. Max LOA 20m. Depths 1–5m. Charge band 3.

Facilities Water. 220V. Fuel quay. 15-ton crane. Most provisions and restaurants.

☎ 091 819 0370
Email posta@maresud.it
www.maresud.it
Club Nautico ☎ 0191 812 5002
☎ 339 224 6622
Email info@clubnauticomarinasannicola.it

TERMINI IMERESE
37°59'·20N 14°43'·49E WGS84
BA 963 It 249

☆ N side of harbour Q.R.5M. Diga Foranea outer mole head Fl.G.3s3M. S mole Fl.R.3s5M. Pierhead 2F.G(vert)4M

VHF Ch 16, 14 (0700–1900) for port authorities.

Navigation Yachts should head for the yacht pontoons in the SE corner of the main harbour.

Berths Stern or bows-to.

Shelter Good shelter.

Data Visitors' berths. Max LOA c.25m. Depths 2–10m.

Facilities Water. 220V. 150-ton slipway. Provisions and restaurants.

Remarks Rather desolate at yacht pontoons.

Artemar Cantiere Nautica
☎ 091 811 1890
Email info@artemarnautica.it
Mare Sud ☎ 091 819 0370

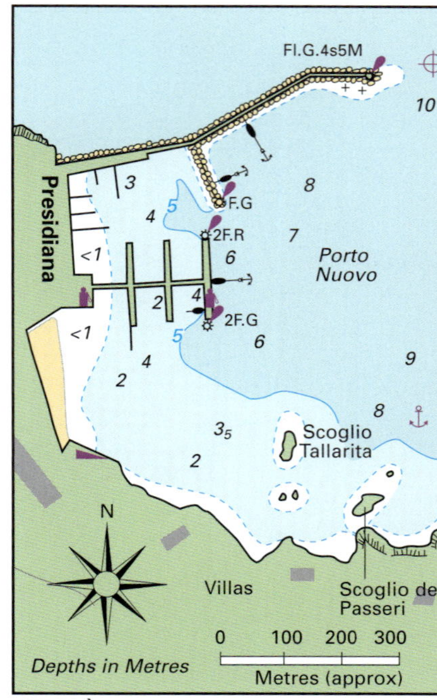

CEFALÙ

CEFALÙ
38°02'·55N 14°02'·28E WGS84
BA 1976 It 15
33M Acquasanta ←→ Vulcano 50M

☆ Capo Cefalu Fl.5s25M. Breakwater head Fl.G.4s5M. Pierhead F.RG(vert)4M

VHF Ch 16, 09.

Berths Stern or bows-to the inside of the fuel quay. Laid moorings tailed to the quay. Larger yachts may be permitted on the quay N of the fuel berth. Limited room to anchor.

Shelter Adequate in the summer, although onshore winds make it uncomfortable.

Data Presidiana Max LOA 25m. Depths 2–6m. Charge band 5.

Facilities Water. 220V. Fuel quay. 100-ton slipway. Provisions and restaurants.

Remarks Town about a 20 minute walk away. Anchorage off the town in calm weather.

Marina Service Cefalù
☎ 338 784 9155

SANT AGATA DI MILITELLO
38°04'·5N 14°38'·4E

☆ S Agata Militello jetty head 2F.RG(vert)8m4M

New ferry port. Two pontoons installed and used by charter companies. Visitors permitted when charter boats out. Care needed of shallows on the N side of each pontoon.

Sicilmarine ☎ 0941 722 933
Yachting Management ☎ 0941 336 392

CAPO D'ORLANDO (PORTICCIOLO DI CAPO D'ORLANDO)

38°09'·49N 14°46'·63E WGS84

☆ Fl.5s5M/Fl.R.3s3M

Harbour on E side of Capo d'Orlando. Prone to silting. YC berths on outer pontoons. Laid moorings. Water. 220V. Fuel quay (shallow).

Data Depths <1–4m.

Remarks There is an ongoing project to extend the breakwater, dredge the basin and install new pontoons for a marina.

PORTOROSA MARINA

38°07'·6N 15°06'·7E
BA 172 It 14 Imray M31

☆ Entrance Fl.G.4s5M/Fl.R.4s5M

VHF Ch 09, 16 (summer 24/24, winter 0800–2000).

Navigation Care needs to be taken in strong NE winds when a swell piles up at the entrance.

Berths Stern or bows-to. Laid moorings tailed to the quay.

Shelter Good all-round shelter.

Data 700 berths. 60 visitors' berths. Max LOA 40m. Depths 2–2·5m. Charge band 6.

Facilities Water. 220/380V. Showers and toilets. Fuel quay. 50-ton travel-hoist. Some provisions. Restaurants.

✆ 0941 874 560
Email info@marinadiportorosa.com
www.marinadiportorosa.com

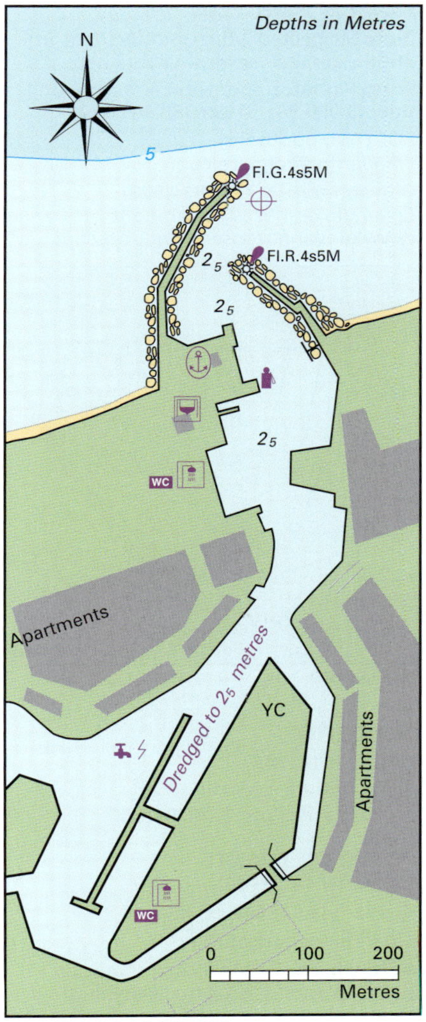

PORTOROSA MARINA

RISERVA NATURALE LAGHETTI DI MARINELLO

New nature reserve on the E side of Capo Tindari.

✆ 090 984 3454

MARINA POSEIDON

A small marina less than a mile N of the entrance to Milazzo harbour.

☆ F.Y.

VHF Ch 09.

Berths Stern or bows-to where directed on the concrete pontoons. Boats over c.12m berth stern-to on the outside pontoon. Laid moorings tailed to the quay.

Shelter Reasonable shelter from northerlies. Open S.

Data 160 berths. Max LOA 35m. Depths 2–5m. Charge band 6 (July–August).

Facilities Water. 220V. Showers and toilets. Fuel quay (0800–2000). Min depths 2m. 60-ton crane. Mechanical and electrical repairs.

Marina Poseidon ✆ 090 922 2564 / 335 847 2415
Email info@poseidonmarina.it

PORTO SANTA MARIA MAGGIORE

Another new pontoon marina close N of Milazzo.

VHF Ch 09.

Berths Stern or bows-to on the pontoons where directed. Larger boats use the outer pontoon.

Shelter Little shelter on the outer berths.

Data 320 berths. Max LOA 100m. Depths 1–6m.

Facilities Water. 220V. Showers and toilets. WiFi.

Cantiere Nautico Disal Nautica hauling and repairs ✆ 090 922 2248
Email info@disalnautica.it
Porto SM Maggiore ✆ 090 922 1002 / 347 634 4620
Email info@portodimilazzo.it
www.portodimilazzo.it

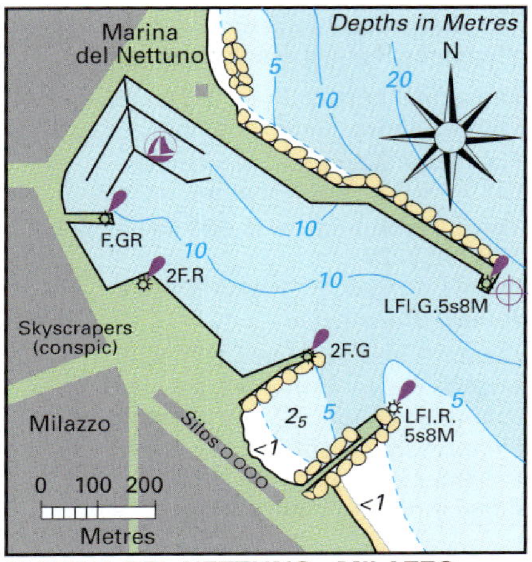

MARINA DEL NETTUNO - MILAZZO

MILAZZO – MARINA DEL NETTUNO

38°12'·9N 15°15'·0E
BA 805 It 245 Imray M31

☆ Capo Milazzo LFl.6s16M.
Entrance LFl.G.5s7M / LFl.R.5s6M.
SW quay 2F.R(vert)3M/2F.G(vert)5M.
Pierhead F.GR(vert)3M. Pier 2 and 32F.GR(vert)5M / 2F.R(vert)5M.
Platform 2Fl.Y.3s3M

VHF Ch 14, 16 (0600–1800) for port authorities. Ch 09 for Marina del Nettuno.

Navigation Yachts should head for the marina in the NE corner of the harbour.

Data 140 berths. Visitors' berths. Max LOA 35m. Depths 6–8m.
Charge band 6.

Facilities Water. 220V. Showers and toilets. Fuel quay. Travel-hoist. Provisions.

Remarks Crowded commercial port.

Marina del Nettuno Milazzo
✆ 090 928 1180
Email info.milazzo@marinadelnettuno.it
www.marinadelnettuno.it/milazzo.html

Aeolian Islands (Isole Eolie)

Stromboli

☆ Strombolicchio (38°49'N 15°15'·2E) Fl(3)15s11M

SCARI

38°47'·91N 15°14'·55E WGS84

The island's main landfall harbour mostly frequented by ferries and hydrofoils.

North of the mole there are mooring buoys (April to October). Boat service to go ashore.

VHF Ch 77.

Data Max LOA 30m. Charge band 5.

✆ 090 986390 / 399
Email info@sabbianerastromboli.com
www.sabbianerastromboli.com

Panarea

☆ Punta Peppemaria Fl.WR.5s10/8M.
Scalo Dittela (38°38'N 15°04'·6E) Fl.G.3s3M

SAN PIETRO

38°38'·37N 15°04'·81E WGS84

Some berths available either side of the jetty at Scalo Ditella. Anchorage off the village.

Note Anchorage prohibited on SE side of the island.

Salina

BA 172 It 14 Imray M47

☆ Punta Lingua Fl.3s11M

SANTA MARINA SALINA

38°33'·22N 14°52'·42E WGS84

☆ Entrance 2F.G(vert)3M/2F.R(vert)4M.
Pierhead 2F.GR(vert)3M

Berths Stern or bows-to in the Porto Turistico S of ferry harbour. Laid moorings.

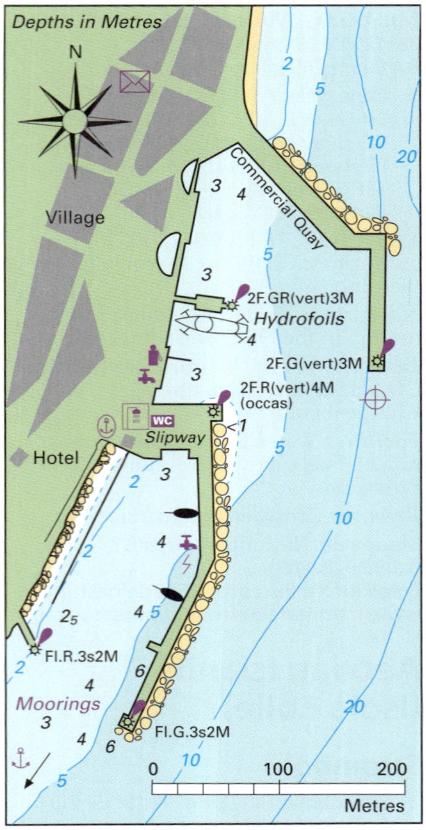

SANTA MARINA SALINA

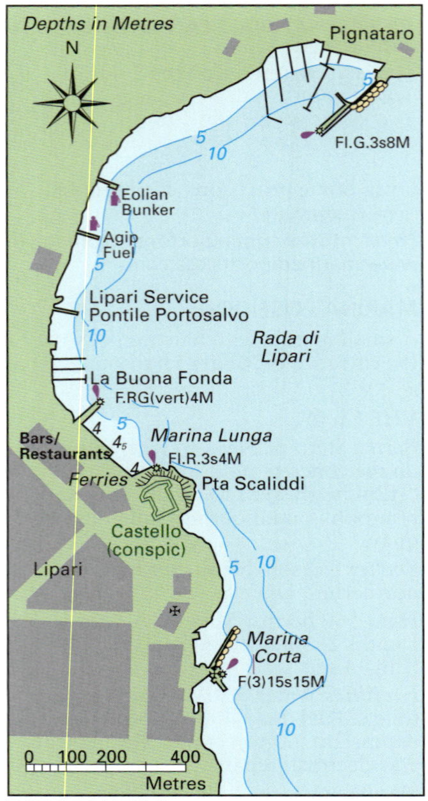

RADA DI LIPARI

Shelter Adequate in the summer.
Data Depths <1–5m Darsena Turistico. Max LOA 50m. Charge band 6+.
Facilities Water. 220V. Fuel. Provisions and restaurants.
Porto delle Eolie ☏ 090 984 3473 / 346 022 0362
Email info@portodelleolie.com

RINELLA
38°32′·7N 14°49′·8E (F.R)
☆ Pierhead F.R

Filicudi

BA 172 It 14 Imray M47
☆ Punta La Zotta Fl(5)15s12M. Porto Filicudi F.GR(vert)4M
20 visitors' moorings. Charge band 4.

Alicudi

BA 172 It 15
☆ Ferry jetty Fl.3s10M

Lipari

BA 172 It 14, 248
☆ Moletto di Pignataro head Fl.G.3s8M

MARINA LUNGA (SOTTOMONASTERO)
38°28′·46N 14°57′·79E WGS84
☆ S quay 2F.R(vert)3M. Pierhead F.RG(vert)4M. Canneto F.G.7M
VHF Ch 16, 11. Ch 72 for Yacht Harbour Lipari.
Berths Stern or bows-to pontoons to the N of the ferry quay. Yachts are no longer permitted to use the town quay. See below for details.
Shelter Normally adequate in the summer. Open E. Suffers from wash of ferries and other craft.
Facilities Water. Fuel pier to N of pontoons (need careful fendering and are unsuitable for dinghies due to protruding metalwork at water level). Provisions and restaurants.
La Buona Fonda A single pontoon immediately N of Marina Lunga.
VHF Ch 16, 13.
Data c. 40 berths. Max LOA c.60m. Depths <1–5m. Laid moorings.
Facilities Water and electricity (220V). Laundry service.
La Buona Fonda ☏ 090 982 2342 / 368 274 944
Email info@labuonafonda.it
www.labuonafonda.it
Yacht Harbour Lipari
T-pontoon N of La Buona Fonda.
Data c.40 berths. Max LOA c.60m. Depths 2–6m. Laid moorings.
Facilities Water and electricity (220/380V). Some repairs.
Yacht Harbour Lipari ☏ 090 981 3152 / 338 330 7227
Email info@yachtharbourlipari.it
Pontile Portosalvo
Data 40 berths. Max LOA 50m. Depths 4–5m. Pontoons and laid moorings in place. Charge band 5/6.
Filippo Saglimbeni, Pontile Portosalvo ☏ 0368 719 0843
Email info@portosalvo.net
Lipari Service
Pontoon close S of fuel piers (May–October) 40 berths. Max LOA 60m.
☏ 090 988 6156 / 330 370 123
Email info@lipariservice.it

MARINA CORTA
38°27′·35N 14°57′·22E
☆ Fl(3)15s11M

PORTO DELLE GENTI
38°27′·35N 14°57′·22E
VHF Ch 16
Berths Moorings for visitors in the bay S of Marina Corta.
Max LOA 15m. Boat service to go ashore.
Ormeggio Portinente
Mobile 334 3473390
Email info@ormeggioportinente.it
www.ormeggioportinente.it

PIGNATARO
38°28′·69N 14°57′·88E WGS84
☆ Mole head Fl.G.3s8M
VHF Ch 74 for Porto Pignataro.
Berths Stern or bows-to, pontoons.
Shelter Good shelter in the summer. Open S.
Data 400 berths. Depths 2–8m. Charge band 5.
Facilities Water. 220V.
Note Suspected Marrobio incident in 2008 damaged several yachts here.
Porto Pignatori (pontoon and quay on E side) ☏ 090 981 5199 / 338 301 1700
EOL (Two pontoons)
Email info@eolmare.com
Giovannazzo ☏ 339 181 4598
Email giovannazzo1@virgilio.it
www.giovannazzoservizinautici.com

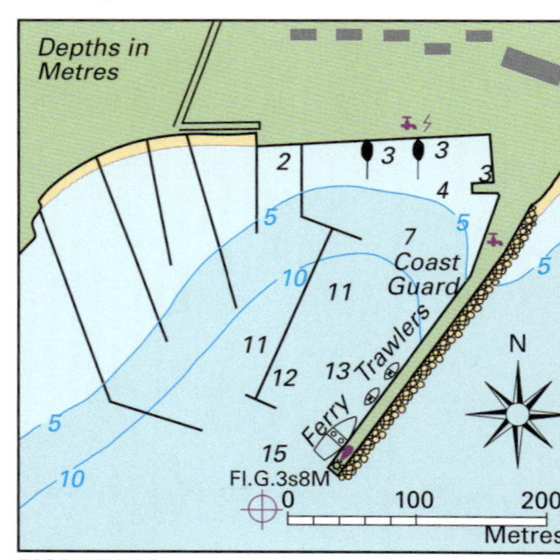

PIGNATARO

Vulcano

BA 172 It 14, 248
50M Cefalu ←→ Messina 40M
☆ Punta dei Porci Fl(4)20s16M

PORTO DI LEVANTE
38°25′·1N 14°57′·4E
☆ Pierhead 2F.G(vert)3M
Small ferry harbour.
VHF Ch 16, 14 for Centro Nautico Baia Levante. Ch 13 for Marina di Vulcanello.

Yacht pontoons with laid moorings. Mooring buoys. Water. 220V. Charge band 6.

Note An unmarked shallow reef extends 80m southwards from the shore to the anchoring area.

Nautico Centro Baia Levante (S pontoons)
✆ 339 337 2795

Marina di Vulcanello (N pontoon)
✆ 090 9385769
www.marinadivulcanello.com

Strait of Messina

STRETTO DI MESSINA

38°15'·86N 15°41'·42E WGS84 1·75M E of Capo Peloro
BA 1018, 917 It 23, 138 Imray M47
40M Vulcano ←→ Taormina 25M

Tidal streams

Under normal conditions the N-going stream begins at about one hour 45 minutes before high water at Gibraltar. The S-going stream starts at four hours 30 minutes after high water at Gibraltar. Both these times are for the streams off Punta Pezzo.

SACCNE FUEL PONTOON

At Paradiso approximately 1½M N of Messina is the Saccne Fuel Pontoon. Diesel, petrol and water available on the quay or nearby. Depths 3–4m. Supermarket nearby.

VHF Ch 16 (0700–2100).

Saccne ✆ 090 310221 / 349 596 7075

MESSINA

38°11'·9N 15°33'·8E
(Punta Salvatore light)
BA 917 It 244

☆ Punta San Raineri Fl(3)15s22M. Punta Secca Oc.Y.3s10M. Punta San Salvatore Fl(2)R.5s8M. W side Fl(2)G.8M. Piers 1-6 F.R.3M / F.GR(vert)3M / F.RGR(vert)3M / F.GR(vert)3M / F.GR(vert)3M / F.G.3M

VHF Ch 11, 16 for port authorities (24/24). Ch 11, 12, 15, 16 for port authorities (0800–2000). Ch 12, 16 for pilots (24/24).

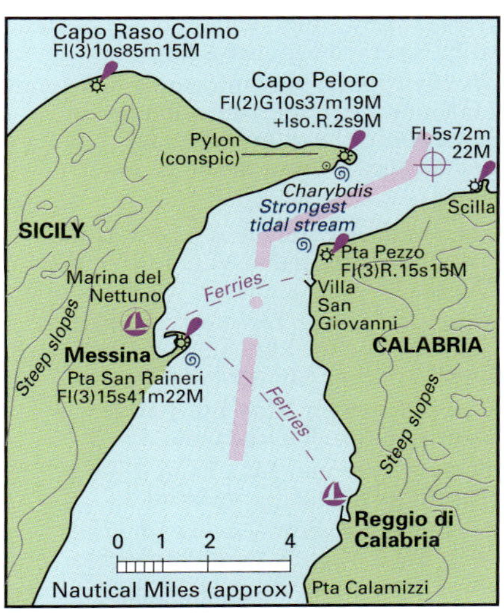

STRAIT OF MESSINA

MESSINA – MARINA DEL NETTUNO

38°11'·8N 15°33'·6E

☆ Fl.R.3s3M

VHF Ch 09. Call before entering.

Navigation The marina is situated on the starboard side just outside the entrance to Messina harbour.

Berths Finger pontoons.

Shelter Many berths suffer from continuous wash from harbour vessels, making berths uncomfortable and causing significant wear to mooring lines. In strong onshore winds it is unlikely the outer protecting pontoon would stop a surge penetrating.

Data 160 berths. Visitors' berths. Max LOA 35m. Charge band 6.

Facilities Water. 220V. Showers. Provisions and restaurants.

Marina del Nettuno
✆ 090 344 139
Email info.messina@marinadelnettuno.it
www.marinadelnettuno.it

GIARDINI NAXOS

37°49'·7N 15°16'·6E
BA 1018 It 918

☆ Harbour mole head Fl.R.4s8M

Navigation Off the quay it is reported (variously) that there is either a shoal patch or a wreck – or both. Great care is needed in the vicinity of the mole.

Berths Stern or bows-to the new yacht pontoons or anchor off.

Note Care needed of rusty protrusions 1m down from top of quay.

Shelter Adequate. Open N.

Data Depths <1–6m. Charge band 1/3.

Facilities Water. 220V. Provisions and restaurants.

Pontoon Walter ✆ 347 621 0852

Marina Yachting ✆ 328 373 8669

RIPOSTO – MARINA PORTO DELL'ETNA

37°44'·1N 15°12'·6E
BA 1018 It 918 Imray M31

☆ Main light LFl.5s11M. Entrance Fl.R.3s5M/Fl.G.3s4M

VHF Ch 74, 16 (0700–1900)

Navigation Yachts should head for Marina di Riposto – Porto dell'Etna. Care needed of works in progress in the N of the harbour.

Berth Stern or bows-to where directed. Laid moorings.

Shelter Good shelter inside the marina. Berths on the N side of the N mole are more exposed.

Data 360 berths. Visitors' berths. Max LOA 50m. Charge band 6.

Facilities Water. 220/380V. Toilet and shower block. Security. Fuel quay. 160-ton travel-hoist. Repairs. Hauling facilities.

Porto dell'Etna ✆ 095 779 5755
Email info@portodelletna.com
www.portodelletna.com

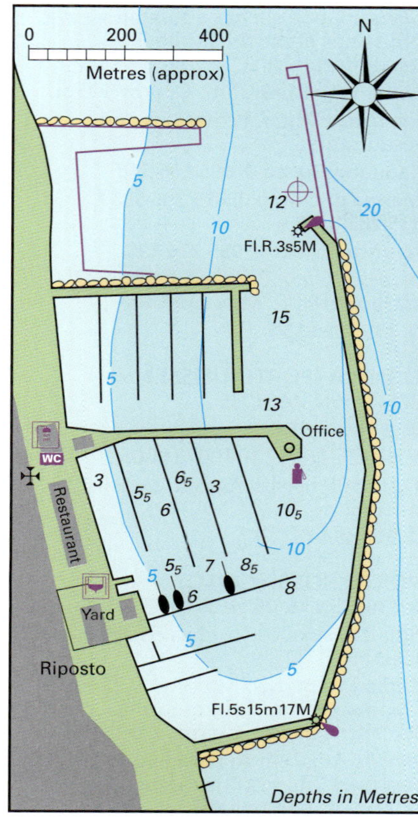

RIPOSTO MARINA DELL'ETNA

ISOLE CICLOPI MARINE RESERVE
Enclosing the islands and the adjacent coast from Capo Molini to close N of Ognina. Access to Aci Trezza is immediately W of the NW corner of Zone A, marked with a yellow buoy.
✉ Visitors' Centre, Via Provinciale 226, Acitrezza
✆ 095 711 7322 *Fax* 095 711 8358
Email amp@isoleciclopi.it
www.isoleciclopi.it

ACIREALE (STAZZO)

37°38'·8N 15°11'·5E

Berths Pontoon on breakwater. Max LOA 12m.

Nautica Glem ✆ 335 782 8354
www.nauticaglem.it

ACITREZZA

37°33'·4N 15°09'·85E
BA 1018 It 22 Imray M31

☆ Capo Molini Fl(3)15s22M. Acitrezza bn Fl.Y.5s5M. Acicastello Molo Porticciolo N corner Fl.R.4s3M

Navigation The depths around the Ciclopi are variable and a yacht should enter and leave Acitrezza to the N of the Ciclopi.

Berths Stern or bows-to. Usually full. In settled weather anchor off to the S of the harbour, keeping close to the breakwater to avoid entering Zone A of the reserve. Otherwise pick up the buoy laid by Ormeggiatori.

There is a buoyed passage to the SW of Zone A, best attempted in daylight only.

Shelter Good shelter although strong NE winds make the harbour uncomfortable.

Data Max LOA 25m. Depths 1–5m.

Facilities Water. Provisions and restaurants.

Capitano Grasso ✆ 095 636 346

Marina di Ciclopi ✆ 095 295 535 / 335 782 8358

Nautica Acimar ✆ 095 276 190

Nautica Glem Pontoon first on starboard side. Max LOA 6m

✆ 335 782 8354

OGNINA (PORTO ULISSE)

37°31′·55N 15°07′·3E

☆ Entrance F.R

VHF Ch 16, 12 (0700–1900)

Data 500 berths approx. Depths 1–10m.

✆ 095 494 152

PORTO ROSSI (CAITO)

37°30′.75N 15°06′.4E

Small basin close to the centre of Catania.

Data 250 berths. Max LOA 25m. Depths <1–5m. Laid moorings. Excellent shelter. Charge band 4/5.

Berths Adjacent to travel hoist depths just over 2m. Entrance dangerous with strong onshore winds.

Note Depths less than charted with 2.5m in the entrance, shelving rapidly inside the harbour.

Facilities Water. 220V. Fuel. Restaurants, bars and provisions.

Porto Turistico ✆ 095 374 966
www.portorossi.com

CATANIA

37°29′·1N 15°05′·9E
BA 994 It 272, 274 Imray M31

☆ Sciara Biscari Fl.5s22M. Entrance LFl.G.5s8M/LFl.R.5s5M. Inner entrance Fl.G.2s5M/Fl.R.2s5M. Airport Aero AlFl.WG (occas)

VHF Ch 12, 16 for port authorities (0700–1900). Ch 12, 14, 16 for pilots. Also see ***Data*** for YC.

Navigation Confused swell at the entrance with S winds.

Berths Stern or bows-to. YC1/YC2/YC3/YC4. Laid moorings.

Shelter Adequate but S winds cause a surge.

Data YC1 Club Náutico 45 berths. Max LOA 25m. Depths 4–8m. Charge band 3/4.

VHF Ch 77

✆ 095 531 443

YC2 Náutico Etneo 100 berths. Max LOA 25m. Depths 4–10m. Charge band 3/4.
VHF Ch 06

✆ 095 531 347

YC3 Circolo Náutico NIC 160 berths. Max LOA 15m. Depths 3–12m. Charge band 3.
VHF Ch 16, 09

✆ 095 531 178

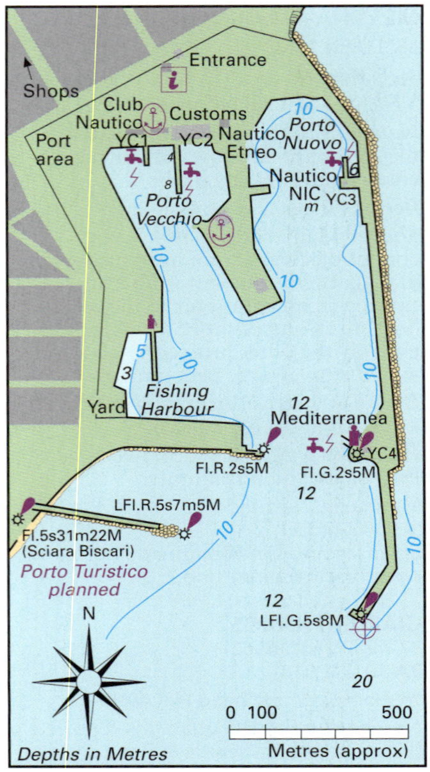

CATANIA

YC4 Mediterranea Yacht Club 90 berths. Max LOA 25m. Depths 3–10m.

VHF Ch 16, 09

✆ 095 534 139

Facilities Water. 220V. Fuel. Cranes to 50 tons. 150-ton slipway. Some yacht repairs. Provisions and restaurants.

Remarks Large commercial harbour with four yacht clubs.

BRUCOLI

37°17′·2N 15°11′·2E
13M Catania ←→ Siracusa 17M

☆ Fl.5s13m11M

MARINA DI BRUCOLI

A new pontoon marina on the E side of the bay to the E of the river.

Berths Go stern or bows-to where directed. Laid moorings tailed to the pontoon. Anchorage in the bay depending on wind and swell.

Data 150 berths. Max LOA c.15m. Depths 2–6m.
Marina di Brucoli ✆ 0931 981 808 / 335 782 8354
Email marinadibrucoli@nauticaglem.it

AUGUSTA

37°11′·9N 15°11′·1E
BA 966 It 271 Imray M31

☆ Leading lights (273°·51′) Front Iso.4s12M. Rear Oc.5s17M. Entrance Fl(2)G.10s8M/Fl(2)R.10s8M. Porticciolo di Terre Vecchie mole FR(vert)3M/Q(9)15s5M. Darsena Servizi mole Fl.G.5s4M/Fl.R.5s4M. Cala del Molo F.G.4M. W side jetties and wharves lit

PLEMMIRIO MARINE RESERVE

AMP Plemmirio was established in 2005 to protect the unusual geological and biological characteristics of the Maddalena Peninsula on the southern part of Siracusa. The reserve covers 2,500 hectares of protected sea and has recently been declared a World Heritage site by Unesco.

✉ Consorzio Plemmirio, Piazza Euripide 21, 96100 Siracusa
✆ 0931 449 310 *Fax* 0931 449 954
Email info@plemmirio.it
www.plemmirio.it

VHF Ch 11, 16 for port authorities (0700–1900). Ch 12 for pilots. Ch 82 for *ormeggiatori*.

Torrevecchia is now a designated military area and yachts are prohibited.

Cala del Molo and Darsena Servizi are for port authority vessels only.

Cantiere Golden Bay may have room for visiting yachts.

Three pontoons. Laid moorings. Max LOA 18m.

Porto Xifono is the only other option.

Golden Bay ✆ 0931 512 352
www.goldenbaysrl.com

SIRACUSA

37°03′·06N 15°17′·77E WGS84
BA 966 It 269 Imray M30, M31
17M Brucoli ←→ Porto Palo 24M

☆ Capo Murro di Porco Fl.5s17M. Punta Castelluccio Fl.R.3s9M. Castello Maniace Fl.G.3s9M. Leading lights (267°12′). Front Iso.R.2s17M. Rear Oc.5s17M. Porto Piccolo entrance 2F.G(vert)3M/ 2F.R(vert)3M. La Darsena F.G.3M/F.R.3M

VHF Ch 09, 11, 16 for port authorities (0700–1900). Ch 14 for pilots.

Navigation Care should be taken of the Pizzo Rocks bordering the coast to the NE of the northern harbour and of the Cani Rocks (Scog. del Cani) 300m E of the old town.

Berths Stern or bows-to in Grand Harbour or in the yacht marina. Laid moorings. New marina planned, see below.

Note Grand Harbour Quay is now bordered by a high wall and is reported to be reserved for cruise ships.

Shelter Can be uncomfortable in Grand Harbour when the afternoon breeze blows onto the quay. Several anchorages around the large bay.

Data

Marina di Archimede A new marina planned. 550 berths. Max LOA c.80m. Depths 4–10m.

Siracusa Marina Yachting c.50 berths. Visitors' berths. Max LOA c.40m. Depths 5–9m. Charge band 5.

Grand Harbour Max LOA 50m. Depths 4–8m. Charge band 5.

Porto Marmoreo Max LOA 15m. Depths <1–3m. Charge band 3.

Facilities *Siracusa Marina Yachting* Water. 220V. Shower and toilet block.

Grand Harbour Water. Fuel quay. 220V. 100-ton crane. 50-ton slipway.

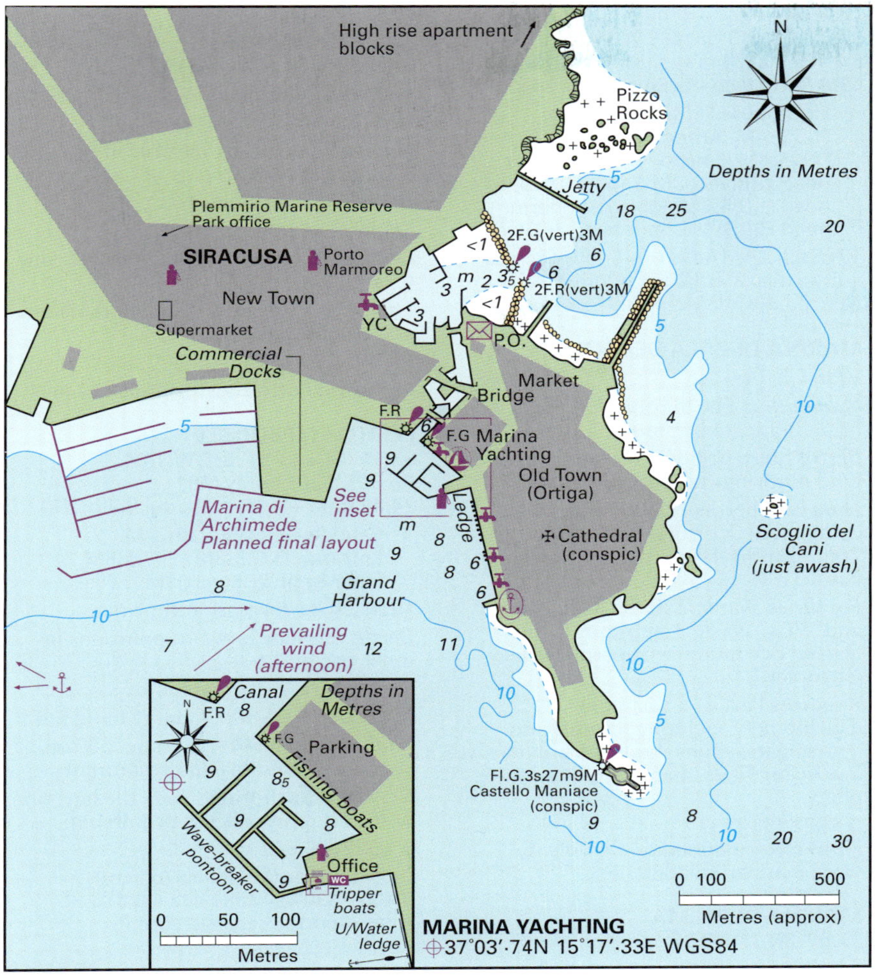

SIRACUSA

Limited yacht repairs. Provisions and restaurants.

Note There have been several dinghy thefts here.

Capitaneria ✆ 0931 666 16

Grand Harbour SOGEAS (Societa Gestione Acque Siracusa) ✆ 0931 481 311 / 335 827 6998 www.sogeas.it

Marina Yachting ✆ 0931 419002 / 333 413 3344 *Email* info@marinayachtingsr.it www.marinayachtingsr.it

Cantiere Marina Yachting ✆ 0931 756 515

LA BALATA

36°44′·4N 15°07′·2E

☆ Pier head F.G(vert)2M

Data 100 berths. Visitors' berths. Max LOA 10m. Depths <1–2·5m.

NAUTICA CALANNA

Berths Pontoon berths. Max LOA 12m.

✆ 338 741 2884
www.nauticacalanna.com

ISOLA PICOLA

36°44′·3N 15°07′·2E

☆ 2F.R(vert)2M

MARZAMEMI

36°43′·99N 15°07′·40E WGS84
BA 1941 It 20 Imray M31

☆ Entrance Fl.G.5s4M/Fl.R.5s3M

VHF Ch 16, 06 for Marina Sporting. Ch 09 for Yacht Marzamemi.

Berths Stern or bows-to. Laid moorings.

Shelter Adequate in the summer.

Data Marina Sporting 150 berths. Visitors' berths. Max LOA 20m. Depths 1–7m. Charge band 5.

Yacht Marzamemi c.130 berths. Max LOA c.50m. Depths 1·5–5m. Charge band 5.

Club Nautico Pontoon in NW corner. 30 visitors' berths. Max LOA 12m. Depths 1–5m.

El Cachalote Pontoon in SW. Max LOA 20m. Charge band 4/5.

Facilities Water. 220V. Showers and toilets. Fuel supplied. Some provisions and restaurants.

Marina Sporting ✆ 0931 841 505

Yacht Marzamemi ✆ 0931 841 776 / 331 269 5554
Email info@yachtmarzamemi.it

Club Nautico ✆ 0931 801 107

El Cachalote ✆ 331 926 5249
www.elcachalote.com

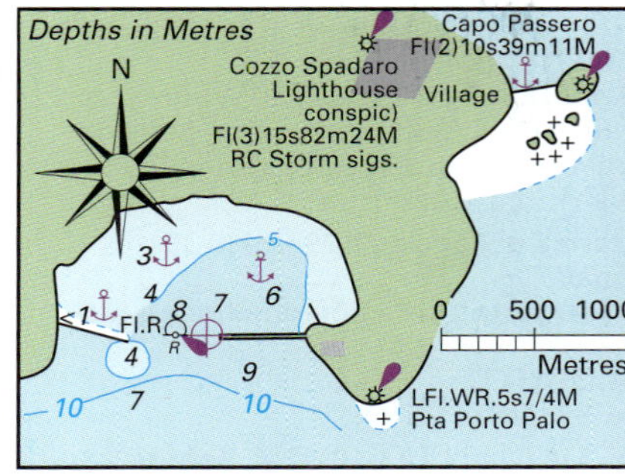

PORTO PALO

PORTO PALO

36°40′·09N 15°07′·18E WGS84
BA 1941 It 20 Imray M31
24M Siracusa ←→ Licata 65M

☆ Cozzo Spadaro Fl(3)15s24M. Capo Passero Fl(2)10s11M. Mole head Fl.G.3s3M. Fuel platform Q.Y.3M

VHF Ch 16

Berths Stern or bows-to. Anchorage behind moles (care needed of permanent moorings).

Shelter Adequate in the summer.

Data Max LOA 25m.

Facilities Water. Fuel. 60-ton slipway. Restaurant.

Remarks 600 berth marina planned.

POZZALLO

36°42′·7N 14°50′·11E WGS84

☆ Main light Fl(4)12s15M. Breakwater head F.R.3M

VHF Ch 16, 13.

Berths Yacht pontoons in main harbour.

Data c.25 berths. Max LOA c.15m. Depths 4–5m.

Facilities Water. 220V. Fuel quay. Cantieri Navale Scala 150-ton travel-lift. Most repairs.

Note 400 berth marina planned for outer harbour.

Lega Navale ✆ 0932 798 028

Ocean Plastic Nautica Pozzallo ✆ 0932 957 344 / 958 606 / 338 548 1683

DONNALUCATA

36°45′·7N 14°38′·1E

☆ Mole head 2F.G(vert)3M

MARINA DI RAGUSA

36°46′·54N 14°32′·94E WGS84

☆ Fl.R.5s8M

New marina approximately 15M W of Pozzallo, and 35M SE of Licata.

VHF Ch 74.

Berth Where directed. Pontoons with laid moorings at all berths. Small red buoys mark concrete mooring blocks which reduce depths to less than 2m in places.

Shelter Good shelter, although some berths may be uncomfortable in strong southerlies.

Data 800 berths. Visitors' berths. Max LOA c.50m. Depths 2–5m. Min depth reported 2·5m (in 2010). Charge band 6 (July–August).

Facilities Water. 220/380V. Showers and toilets. WiFi. Fuel quay. 160-ton travel-lift. Yard and repair facilities. ATM. Bar restaurant.

Marina di Ragusa ☎ 0932 230 301
Email info@portoturisticomarinadiragusa.it

SCOGLITTI
36°53'·4N 14°25'·6E

☆ Main light Fl(3)10s11M. Refuge harbour end of anti-silting breakwater Fl.R.3s5M. Mole head Fl.G.3s5M. F.R.5M (only visible within port)

VHF Ch 15, 16 (0700–1900).

Navigation Great care needed of uneven depths in the approaches. The harbour silts and is dredged periodically.

Berths Stern or bows-to on pontoons. Some laid moorings.

Data c.50 berths. Max LOA c.20m. Depths 2–3·2m. Charge band 3/4.

Facilities Water. 220V. Fuel.

La Ponente ☎ 0932980860
Email info@laponente.com

Scoglitti Beach Club (Office) ☎ 393 438 2045, (Dock) ☎ 339 527 3045.

GELA
37°03'·7N 14°13'·8E
BA 965 It 263 Imray M31

☆ Entrance Oc.G.4s3M/Oc.R.4s3M. Port of Refuge Molo di Levante head Fl.G.3s8M. Molo di Ponente head Fl.R.3s8M

VHF Ch 15, 16 for port authorities (0700–1900). Ch 06, 12, 16 for pilots.

Navigation Entrance silts. Variable depths.

Berths Stern or bows-to.

Data Depths 1–5m.

LICATA
37°05'·06N 13°56'·48E WGS84
BA 965 It 267 Imray M31
65M Porto Palo ←→ Empedocle 24M

☆ Lighthouse Fl.5s21M. E head Fl.G.3s4M. Antemurale head Fl.R.5s5M. E head Fl.R.5s8M. Spur head 2F.R(vert)3M. Diga di Levante head Fl.G.5s8M. Molo di Ponente head Fl.R.3s4M. Spur head 2F.G(vert).

VHF Ch 14, 16 (0700–1900) for port authorities. Ch 12 for pilots. Ch 74 for Marina di Cala del Sole.

MARINA DI CALA DEL SOLE
VHF Ch 74

Navigation The marina is in the NE basin in Licata harbour.

Berths Stern or bows-to where directed. Laid moorings tailed to the quay.

Data 325 berths (1,500 berths when completed). Visitors' berths. Max LOA 70m. Depths 4–6m (dredged). Charge band 5.

Facilities Water. 220/380V. Showers and WCs. Waste pump-out. WiFi. Self-service laundry. Supermarket. Chandler.

Remarks Part of a vast new development including houses and apartments, shops, boutiques, extensive leisure facilities, and a desalination plant.

☎ 0922 183 7137
Email info@marinadicaladelsole.it
www.marinadicaladelsole.it

MARINA DI PALMA
37°09'·8N 13°34'·8E
Small fishing harbour.

SAN LEONE
37°15'·4N 13°34'·8E
BA 965 It 264 Imray M31

☆ Marina entrance Fl.R.3s4M/Fl.G.3s3M

VHF Ch 16 (0700–1900).

Navigation Depths variable in harbour. Max draught outer part of harbour 2m.

Berths Stern or bows-to.

Shelter Open SE.

Data Max LOA 15m. Depths 1–2·5m. Charge band 5.

Facilities Water. Fuel. Some provisions and restaurants.

YC ☎ 0922 411 243

Consorzio Porto Turistico ☎ 0922 24444

PORTO EMPEDOCLE
37°16'·44N 13°31'·63E WGS84
BA 965 It 265 Imray M31
24M Licata ←→ Mazzara del Vello 51M

☆ Capo Rossello Fl(2)10s22M. Entrance Fl.G.3s8M / Fl.R.3s8M. Inner basin 2F.R(vert)3M

VHF Ch 16 for port authorities.

Berths Stern or bows-to pontoons in inner basin.

Shelter Good shelter.

Data Depths 4–8m. Charge band 3/4.

Facilities Fuel. 40-ton crane. 50-ton slipway. Provisions and restaurants.

Remarks Anchoring inside the harbour or in the approaches is prohibited.

☎ 0922 636 640

Diportivo Sea Assistance (berths)
☎ 0922 530 024 / 389 487 6828
www.diportivoseaassistance.it

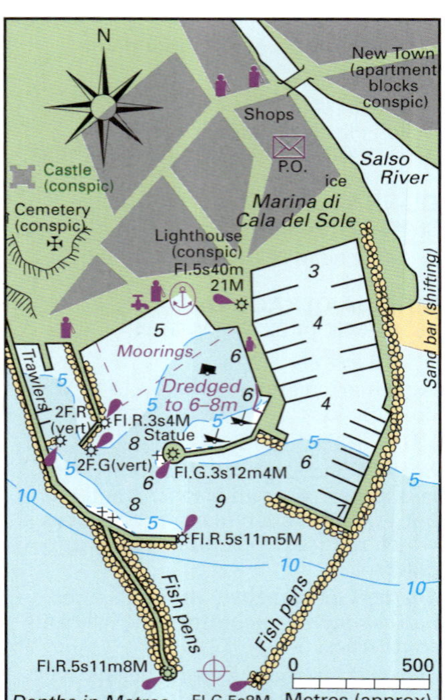

LICATA

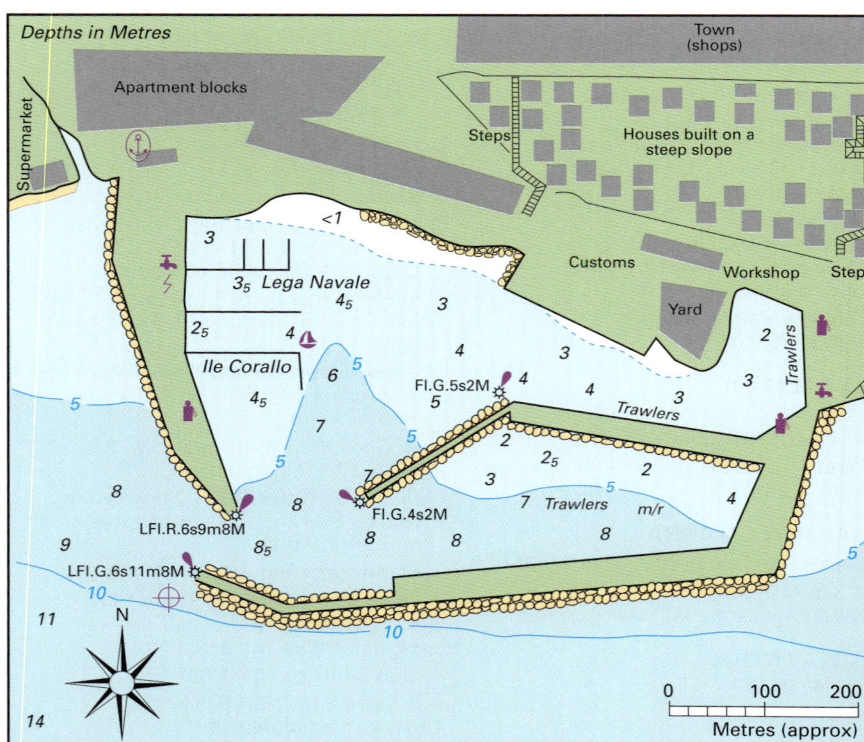

SCIACCA

SICULIANA MARINA
37°19'·9N 13°23'·3E

A small new harbour has been excavated out of the sandbanks off the town of Siculiana Marina. The breakwaters are complete, but there is nothing else here. As with many harbours along this coast, silting looks like it could be a problem here.

SCIACCA
37°30'·03N 13°04'·49E WGS84
BA 2123 It 258 Imray M31

☆ Entrance LFl.G.6s8M/LFl.R.6s8M. Molo Levante old head Fl.G.4s2M. Head Fl.G.5s2M

VHF Ch 16. Ch 12 for Il Corallo.

Navigation Yachts should head for the pontoons on the W side.

Berths Stern or bows-to. Laid moorings.

Shelter Good shelter in the summer.

Data 150 berths. Max LOA c.20m. Depths 2–5m. Charge band 5.

Facilities Water. Fuel quay. 20-ton crane. 200-ton slipway. Limited yacht repairs. Provisions and restaurants.

Lega Navale ✆ 0925 858 79

CN Il Corallo ✆ 0925 21611 / 328 656 3984
Email info@circollonauticoilcorallo.it

PALO DI MENFI
37°34'·4N 12°54'·6E

☆ Entrance Fl.R.4s5M/2F.R(vert)2M/ Fl.G.4s5M/2FG(vert)2M

Navigation The entrance is prone to silting. Presently variable depths 1·5m in the entrance and 1m in the middle of the harbour.

Data 50 berths. Max LOA 15m. Depths <1–3m.

MARINELLA DI SELINUNTE
37°34'·8N 12°50'·5E

A small and shallow fishing harbour off the town of Marinella.

There are depths of around 2m in the entrance and less inside. Depths are uneven and liable to silting; only shoal draught craft should attempt to enter the harbour. In settled weather a yacht could anchor off the beach in 2–5m.

GRANITOLA MARINA
37°34'·2N 12°39'·4E

A new 50 berth porto turistico is under construction on the NW side of Capo Granitola, just 600m N of Capo Granitola light.

The breakwaters are complete, and pontoons are expected in the near future.

Note There is a fish farm reported approximately 2M S of the harbour in position 37°36'·5N 12°36'·1E. It is marked with small yellow buoys and lies in the path of yachts coasting down past Mazara del Vallo.

MAZARA DEL VALLO
37°38'·44N 12°35'·04E WGS84
BA 2123 It 258 Imray M31
51M Empodocle ←→ Marsala 12M

☆ Capo Granitola LFl.10s18M. Entrance Fl.G.4s8M / Fl.R.4s5M / Iso.Y.2s3M

VHF Ch 11, 16 (0700–1900). CB Ch 09, 10.

Berths Stern or bows-to yacht pontoons on E side. Laid moorings.

Shelter Good shelter.

Data Depths 2–6m. Max LOA 40m. Charge band 4.

Facilities Water. Fuel quay. 200-ton slipway. Provisions and restaurants.

Assoc. Diportisti Nautici Mazarase ✆ 0923 940 136

Yacht Service ✆ 0923 942 864
Email info@eneayacht.it

MARSALA
37°46'·95N 12°26'·05E WGS84
BA 964 It 258 Imray M31
12M Mazara del Vello ←→ Trapani 16M

☆ Main light Fl(2)10s15M. Entrance Fl.G.3s8M/Fl.R.3s8M

VHF Ch 14, 16 (0700–1900) for port authorities.

Berths Stern or bows-to on pontoons in SE corner or on the quay on the S breakwater.

Shelter Adequate in the summer.

Data 200 berths. Visitors' berths. Max LOA 20m. Depths 1·8–3m. Charge band 4/5.

Facilities Water. 220V. Fuel. 160-ton travel-hoist. 20-ton crane. 150-ton slipway. Provisions and restaurants.

Note Care is needed in the vicinity of the pontoons where depths are uneven 1·8–3m.

Associazione Sportiva Mothia ✆ 0923 951 201

Cantiere Nautico Polaris ✆ 0923 999 222
Email info@nauticapolaris.com

Alta Marea Charter Nautico (S pontoon). ✆ 0923 711 260
Email info@altamareacharter.com

Port Authority ✆ 0923 951 030

> **RISERVA NATURALE ORIENTATA**
> It is not permitted to navigate, moor or anchor within 100m of the coast (except Punta dell'Arco, Punta Carace, Punta Polacca and Balata dei Turchi where it is 50m).
> Only canoes and kayaks are permitted. Max speed 10kns within 1,000m of the coast.
> Jet-skis and similar water-craft are also restricted.

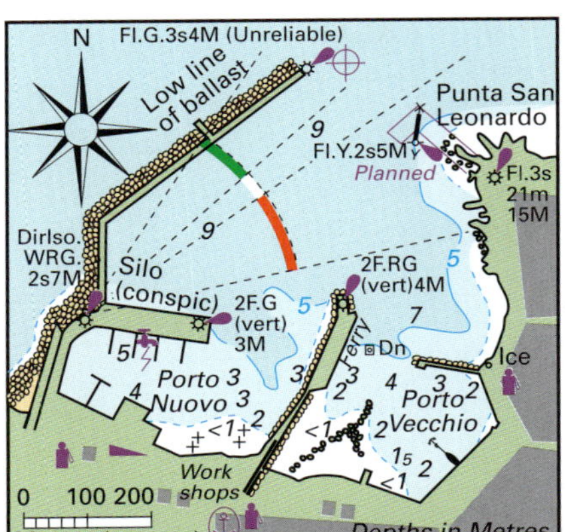

PORTO DI PANTELLERIA

Pantelleria

PORTO DI PANTELLERIA
36°50'·2N 11°56'·4E
BA 193 It 242

☆ Punta San Leonardo Fl.3s15M. Breakwater head Fl.G.3s4M

VHF Ch 16, 14 (0800–2000) for port authorities.

Berths Stern or bows-to or alongside the E basin.

Shelter Good shelter.

Data Max LOA 17m. Depths 1·5–6m. Charge band 1/3.

Facilities Water by tanker. Fuel nearby. 25-ton crane. 20-ton slipway. Most provisions and restaurants.

Remarks Pontoons in W basin full of local craft.

Capitaneria ✆ 0923 911 027

SCAURI
36°46'·0N 11°57'·8E

☆ Scauri Fl.5s10M. Entrance Fl.G.3s3M/Fl.R.3s3M

Data 60 berths. Max LOA 8m. Depths 2–7m.

Cantieri Navali Esposito ✆ 0923 912 813

> **ISOLE PELAGIE MARINE RESERVE**
> Covers the three Pelagie islands:
> Lampedusa
> Linosa
> Lampione
> Porto di Lampedusa is not within the reserve.
> AMP Pelagie ✆ /*Fax* 0922 975 780
> *Email* info@isole-pelagie.it
> www.isole-pelagie.it

Isole Pelagie

Lampedusa

PORTO DI LAMPEDUSA
35°29'·6N 12°36'·0E
BA 193 It 947

☆ Entrance Fl.G.3s8M/Fl.R.3s8M.

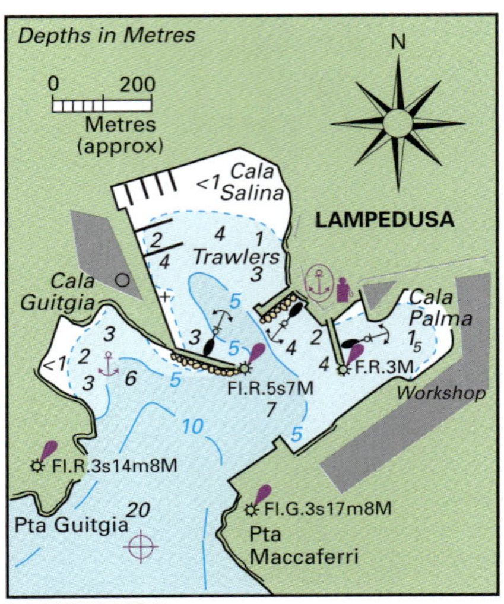

LAMPEDUSA

Breakwater head Fl.R.5s7M. Mole head F.R.3M

VHF Ch 14, 16 (0700–1900) for port authorities.

Berths Stern or bows-to in Cala Palma.

Shelter Good shelter.

Data Cala Palma 10 berths. Max LOA 10m. Depths 1–3m.

Facilities Fuel. 25-ton slipway. Some provisions and restaurants.

Remarks Cala Salina used by fishing boats.

Agenzia Strazzera ☎ 0922 970 809

Isole Egadi

Favignana

FAVIGNANA (CALA PRINCIPALE)

37°56′·09N 12°19′·41E WGS84
BA 964 Italian 259

☆ Mole head Fl.R.4s7M. Pierhead F.GR(vert)4M

VHF Ch 16.

Navigation Care needed of set nets in the tuna season which are now laid around the Egadi Islands and are often poorly marked and poorly lit.

Berths Stern or bows-to. Berths very crowded in summer.

Shelter Adequate in the summer.

Data 100 berths. Max LOA 50m. Depths 1·5–4m. Charge band 5.

Facilities Water. Fuel quay. 6-ton slipway. Provisions and restaurants.

Circolo Nautico ☎ 0923 922 422

Ormeggiatori Isole Egadi ☎ 0923 922 212

ISOLE EGADI MARINE RESERVE
Isole Formica to Isole Marettimo and surrounding waters.
Favignana lies within Zone C.
AMP Egadi ☎ /*Fax* 0923 921 659
Email p.dangelo@ampisoleegadi.it
www.ampisoleegadi.it

ISOLA MARETTIMO

☆ Riserva Marina Fl(2)Y.10s2M (x 2). Marettimo mole 30m from head Fl.R.3s3M

Navigation Entry and exit movements for Porto di Marettimo are prohibited at night because of a lack of lighted marks.

SCALA VECCHIA (MARETTIMO)

VHF Ch 06.

Berths Big Game Marettimo on a pontoon with water and electricity. Charge band 5.

☎ 338 260 2066 / 329 454 4412 / 340 716 4724
Email direzione@marettimoservice.it

CAPO RIZZUTO MARINE RESERVE
Covers the coast from W of Le Castella to the gas platforms off Crotone.
AMP Cap Rizzuto
☎ 0962 795 511 *Fax* 0962 665 247
www.riservamarinacaporizzuto.it

Sicily

TRAPANI

38°00′·12N 12°29′·81E WGS84
BA 964 It 257 Imray M31
16M Marsala ←→ San Vito Lo Capo 19M

☆ Scoglio Palumbo Fl.5s15M+ Iso.R.2s8M. Entrance Fl.R.3s8M/ Fl.G.3s8M. Canal entrance outer breakwater head Fl.R.3s8M. Inner breakwater head Fl.G.3s8M. Detached breakwater E end Fl.R.6s4M. Marina breakwater Fl.G.4s3M/F.R.3M. Pierhead F.R(vert)3M

VHF Ch 16 (0800–2400) for port authorities. Call before entering. Ch 69 for Marina Arturo Stabile and Marina Levante.

Navigation SE breakwater partially completed, not yet joined to E side shore.

Care needed of shallow area c.1·5m between red buoy and mole off the Guardia Costieri building.

Berths Moorings (free) in NW corner off Lega Navale and SE corner. Pontoons between YC and Guardia Costieri with limited visitors' berths from Vento di Maestrale and Columbus Yachting. Marina Levante and Marina Arturo Stabile pontoons off the quay in the NE corner. Limited berths at Trapani Boat Service.

Shelter Good all-round shelter.

Data *Marina Arturo Stabile* 100 berths. Max LOA 40m. Depths 2–6m.

Marina Levante c.50 berths. Max LOA 27m.

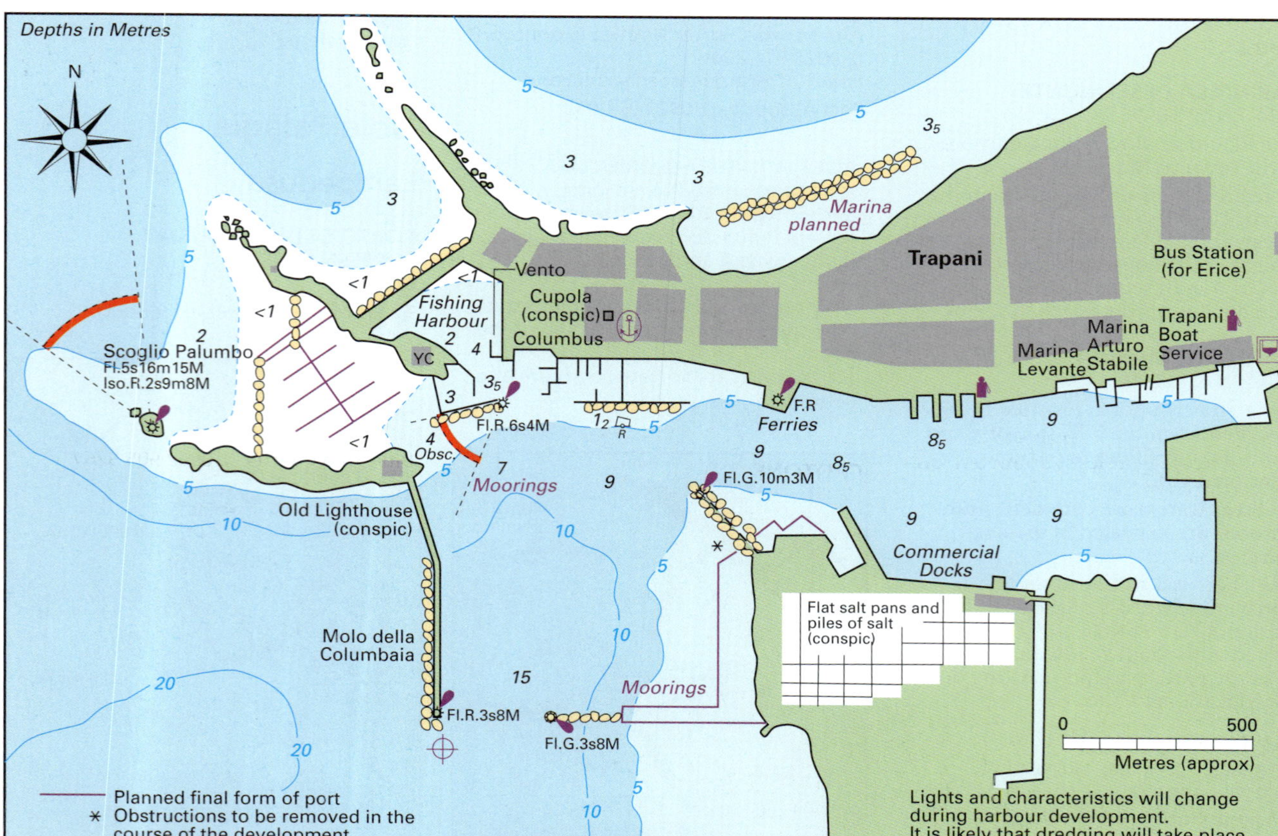

TRAPANI

Vento di Maestrale c.100 berths. Max LOA c.20m. Depths 1–4m.

Columbus Yachting 80 berths. Max LOA c.20m. Depths 1–4m.

All charge band 5.

Facilities Water and 220V at most berths. Fuel on the quay past the short ferry piers. No water. Fuel and water from Trapani Boat Service by arrangement. 40/200-ton travel-hoists. 80-ton crane. 500-ton slipway. Most repairs. Provisions and restaurants.

Port Authority ✆ 0923 289 00
www.portotrapani.it

Marina Arturo Stabile ✆ 0923 28191
✆ 0923 593 967
Email info@marinaarturostabile.it

Marina Levante ✆ 0923 25399 / 333 745 0525 / 329 033 1748
Email info@marinalevante.it

Vento di Maestrale ✆ 0923 26874
✆ 349 627 2840
Email ventodimaestraletp@alice.it
www.pontileventodimaestrale.it

Columbus Yachting ✆ /0923 28341
✆ 393 947 7497
Email columbus.tp@me.com
www.mooringtrapani.com

Boat Service Trapani
✆ 0923 29240 / 349 661 8376
Email info@boatservicetrapani.it

Ionian

SALINE JONICHE
37°55'·56N 15°43'·88E WGS84
BA 1018 It 23

☆ Capo dell'Armi Fl(2)10s22M.

The main entrance has been blocked by a shingle bank for several years.

Note There have been several incidents of aggravated burglary from yachts anchored in this harbour. It is strongly recommended that yachts do not stop here except in an emergency.

ROCELLA IONICA
38°19'·45N 16°25'·55E WGS84
BA 1941 It 24
55M Reggio ←→ Le Castella 48M

☆ Entrance Fl.G.3s5M/Fl.R.3s5M

VHF Ch 16, 14 for PSA.

Navigation The entrance is silting. Care needed of sandbank off the end of the outer breakwater. Approach from the S–SE keeping at least 300m SW off the end of the breakwater. Caution needed as the extent and area of the sandbank is likely to change over time with storms and dredging.

Call PSA ahead for the latest advice. Max draught permitted 2·2m but depths generally more than 2·5m.

With onshore winds there are breaking waves at the entrance and with an onshore gale entry would be dangerous.

Berths Stern or bows-to. Finger pontoons.

Shelter Good shelter.

Data Max LOA 20m. Depths 2–4·5m. 3·5m in the entrance. Charge band 2.

Facilities Water. 220V to be connected. Fuel by tanker. Pizzeria in the marina. WiFi. Provisions and restaurants in the village.

Port Services Agency – Francesco Lombardo administers transit berths. Charge band 2/3.

✆ 338 499 7392
Email psa-ita@libero.it

PORTO BADALATO (LE BOCCE DI GALLIPARI)
38°35'·54N 16°34'·34E WGS84

A small harbour roughly halfway between Rocella Ioniche and Le Castella. The harbour entrance silts and requires ongoing dredging by digger. Care needed as silting likely to reduce depths.

Data c.150 berths. Max LOA c.15m. Depths <1–3m. Few facilities available at the harbour.

✆ 0967 814 306 / 338 870 1702
www.portogallipari.it

CATANZARO LIDO
38°49'·45N 16°37'·85E WGS84

Berths The breakwaters have been re-built and extended. Much of the quay space inside is taken with fishing boats and local craft. Anchor clear of the moorings in the centre of the harbour on shingle, good holding and good shelter. Alternatively go alongside the quay on either side of the entrance, but here you are exposed to wind and swell. Entrance dangerous with onshore winds.

LE CASTELLA
38°54'·51N 17°01'·73E WGS84
48M Rocella Ionica ←→ Crotone 19M

☆ Outer mole head Fl.R.3M. Inner spur head Fl.G.3M

Fishing harbour. Yachts berth on inside end of breakwater or in the marina basin.

Data 100 berths. Visitors' berths. Max LOA 15m. Depths 2–3m. Laid moorings. Water. 220V. Shower and toilets. Charge band 3.

Remarks A sluice on the E side open to the sea causes a surge with onshore winds and is allowing silting along the quay. Laid mooring lines are reported to be inadequate for all but small craft.

Lega Navale ✆ 0962 795 528

Porto Turistico ✆ 333 989 9986

CROTONE
39°04'·67N 17°08'·22E WGS84
BA 140 It 146
19M Le Castella ←→ Santa Maria di Leuca 70M

☆ Capo Colonne Fl.5s24M. Porto Nuovo Fl.R.5s8M/Fl.G.5s8M. Molo Giunti head Fl.G.9m4M. Porto Vecchio Fl(2)G.5s8M/Fl(2)R.5s8M. Platform Luna A Mo(U)15s5M. Platform Luna 27 LFl.10s2M. Platform Luna B Mo(U)15s2M. Platform H Lacina Mo(U)15s5M. Gas pipe Fl(U). Fl(2)Y.10s2M x 4.

VHF Ch 11, 16 (0700–1900) for port authorities. Ch 14, 16 for pilots. Ch 16 for Autonautico Tricoli.

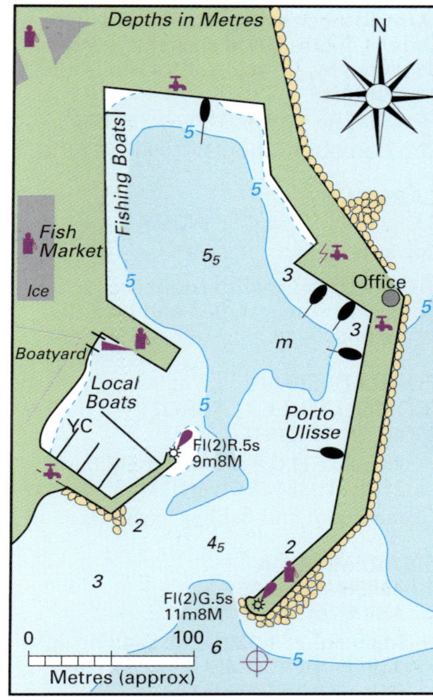

CROTONE – PORTO VECCHIO

Navigation Care is needed of the gas platforms lying in the approaches to Crotone. From Capo Colonne proceed N for 2M and then to Crotone Porto Vecchio on approximately 281°.

Berths Stern or bows-to where directed. Laid moorings tailed to the quay.

Shelter Adequate in the summer but open S. S gales can make it untenable.

Data Depths 2–5m. Charge band 3/4.

Facilities Water. 220V. Fuel quays. Q8 at the S end of the breakwater. Variable depths off the quay; deeper draught yachts should check with the fuel man where to come alongside.

Carmar have duty free fuel from the pier on the W side of Porto Vecchio, and duty paid fuel on the pier in the commercial harbour.

75-ton crane. 150-ton slipway. Provisions and restaurants.

Autonautico Tricoli, Dr Renato G Russo
✆ 0962 22852

Lega Navale ✆ 0962 27240

Carmar ✆ 0962 20156 / 335 740 1734
Email carmarsrl@libero.it

Blue Ship Charter ✆ 0962 905 526 / 338 705 8723
Email pierluigi@seateam.it

Yachting Club ✆ 333 482 5141

De Santis ✆ 338 686 0494

Paolagest ✆ 0962 900736

CIRO MARINA
39°22'·34N 17°08'·19E WGS84

☆ Punta Alice Fl(2)10s16M. Fl.R.3s5M/Fl.G.3s5M

Berths Go alongside where convenient along the breakwater. Can be difficult negotiating a berth here. Both Lega Navale and Guardia Costiera very helpful.

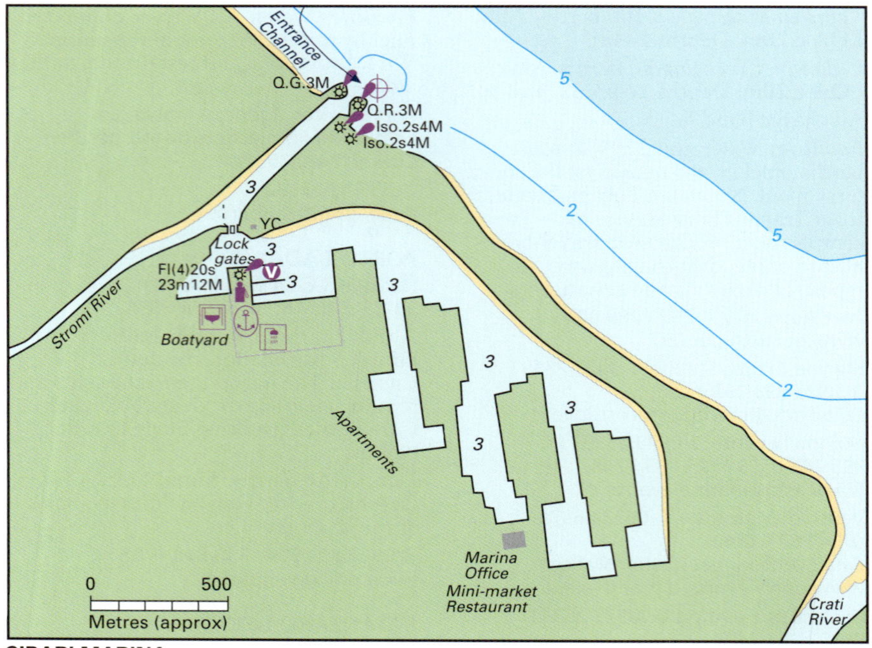

SIBARI MARINA

Data 150 berths. Visitors' berths. Depths 5–6m. Good shelter. Fuel can be delivered by jerrycans. Provisions and restaurants.

Lega Navale ✆ 0962 31766 / 379 007

Ciro Harbour Authority ✆ 0962 611 610

CARIATI

39°30'·34N 16°56'·75E WGS84

Entrance unlit.

Fishing harbour with room for yachts. Pontoons now installed and facilities being improved.

PORTO DI SIBARI (CORIGLIANO CALABRO)

39°40'·3N 16°31'·7E

☆ Entrance Fl.G.3s3M/Fl.R.3s3M.Basin 2F.R(vert)3M/2F.G(vert)3M.

Commercial and fishing harbour.

SIBARI MARINA

39°44'·8N 16°29'·9E

BA 187 It 26

☆ Main light Fl(4)20s12M. Leading light 139° Front Iso.2s4M. Rear Iso.2s4M. Entrance F.R.6M/F.G.6M

VHF Ch 09, 16 (summer 24/24, winter 0730–1700).

Navigation Entrance channel is marked in the summer but care is needed as channel moves. Call the marina on VHF Ch 09/16 and a pilot will come out to guide you in (free service). Entrance difficult and possibly dangerous with onshore winds.

Berths Stern or bows-to where directed.

Shelter Good shelter.

Data 450 berths. 20 visitors' berths. Depths 3m. Charge band 3.

Facilities Water. 220V. Showers and toilets. Fuel quay. 50 travel-hoist. 15-ton crane. Most yacht repairs. Limited provisions and restaurants.

Remarks Past local disputes over responsibility for dredging the access channel led to a halt to the regular dredging work, needed to keep depths in the channel suitable for yachts. Check with the marina office for latest navigation advice before entering.

Cantieri Nautici di Sibari
✆ 0981 79027 / 51
Email cantnaut@tiscalinet.it
www.marina-sibari.it

MARINA DI POLICORO

40°12'·3N 16°44'·5E

A huge leisure complex Marinagri, including Marina di Policoro, around the Fiume Agri, 25M SW of the entrance to Taranto harbour.

VHF Ch 16/74.

Navigation The entrance is dredged to 3·5m, but may silt if not regularly dredged. If in any doubt call ahead before attempting to enter. With strong onshore winds entry could be dangerous.

Berth Stern-to where directed. Bow lines are taken to posts.

Shelter Good all-round shelter inside the basin.

Data 215 berths in the Porto Turistico. Max LOA 30m. Charge band 3.

Facilities Water. 220V. Showers and toilets. Pump-out. Laundry. WiFi. Fuel quay. 100-ton travel-lift. Some repairs. Bar, restaurant, yacht club. ATM.

Marinagri ✆ 0835 960 302
Email info@marinadipolicoro.it

PORTO DEGLI ARGONAUTI (Marina di Pisticci)

40°20'·0N 16°49'·2E

This marina lies 17M WSW of the entrance to Taranto harbour.

Care is needed as it is likely the entrance will silt unless dredged regularly. If in any doubt call ahead for advice on depths before entering.

VHF Ch 16.

Navigation With strong onshore winds the entry could be dangerous.

Berth Stern or bows-to on concrete piers with laid moorings tailed to the pier.

Shelter Good all-round shelter inside the basin.

Data 450 berths. Max LOA 30m. Depths dredged to 4m. Charge band 3.

Facilities Water. 220/380V. Showers and toilets. Pump-out. Fuel quay. Travel-lift.

Porto Degli Argonauti ✆ 0835 470 218
Email info@portodegliargonauti.it

TARANTO

40°24'·7N 17°12'·2E
(Capo San Vito light)
BA 1643 It 148

☆ Capo San Vito Fl(3)15s22M. Mar Grande entrance Q(9)15s8m5M/Fl(2)G.7s9M. Beacon Q(9)15s6M. Secca della Sirena S side Q(6)+LFl.15s5M. W side Q.R.6M. E side Q.G.7M. Detached breakwater Q.R.4M/F.GR(vert)3M. Porto Mercantile E detached breakwater Fl.R.5s7M/Q.G.4M. Basin entrance Fl.G.5s8M/F.GR(vert)4M. Passagio Piccolo Ldg lights (193°) Front Fl.WG.3s9/7M. Rear Iso.3s14M. Ldg lights (013°) Front Q.R.6M. Rear Fl.3s10M

VHF Ch 12, 16 for port authorities.

Berths Yacht berths at Taranto Yacht/Marina Taranto in Porto Mercantile.

Shelter Good all-round shelter, but uncomfortable with strong southerlies.

Data c. 200 berths. Max LOA 50m. Depths 2–7m. Charge band 4.

Facilities Water. 220V. WC and showers. Fuel nearby. Gas. 50-ton crane. Repairs. Provisions and restaurants. Banks. ATMs.

Marina di Taranto
✆ 0994 712 115
Email info@molosanteligio.com
www.molosanteligio.com

Taranto Yacht ✆ 0994 712 115
Email info@tarantoyacht.it
www.tarantoyacht.it

Taranto Port Authority
✆ 0994 711 611
Email authority@port.taranto.it
www.port.taranto.it

CAMPOMARINO

40°18'·0N 17°35·1'E

☆ Entrance F.G/F.R

Data 250 berths. Max LOA 12m. Depths 1–3m.

✆ 099 971 6025

PORTO CESAREO

40°15'·0N 17°53'·5E

BA 187 It 27

☆ Leading lights (034°) Front Iso.2s7M. Rear Oc.3s10M. Q(3)R.13s3M/Q(3)G.13s3M. Ldg Lts 350°-vis-068°. Q.R 0·8M WNW. The alignment is provisionally replaced by two buoys, one red and one green, Fl.R.3s3M and Fl.G.3s3M.

PORTO CESAREO MARINE RESERVE
Covers Penisola la Strega but does not affect Porto Cesareo.
Comune Porto Cesareo ✆ 0833 858 100
Porto Cesareo Port Office
✆ 0833 560 485

Navigation Care needed of reefs and shoals in entrance.
Berths Anchor in the bay.
Shelter Adequate in the summer.
Data 0·5–4m.
Facilities Water. Fuel quay. Provisions and restaurants.

GALLIPOLI
40°03′·6N 17°58′·8E (LFl.G.5s)
BA 140 It 149

☆ Isola Sant'Andrea Fl(2)10s19M. Secca del Rafo (N cardinal Bn) Q.5M. Commercial Port entrance Fl.G.5s9M/Fl.R.5s9M. Seno del Canneto entrance F.G.6M/F.R.6M

VHF Ch 16 (0700–1900) for port authorities. Ch 16 for pilots. Ch 09 for Bleu Salento.
Navigation Care needed of the reef (Secca del Rafo) N of Commercial Port.
Berths Stern or bows-to Bleu Salento pontoons in Porto Mercantile. Laid moorings.
Shelter Surge in Commercial Port with N–NE winds.
Data 160 berths. Max LOA 60m. Depths 3–8m. Charge band 5.
Facilities Water. 220/380V. Fuel. 20-ton slipway. Limited yacht repairs. Provisions and restaurants.
Marina Bleu Salento ✆ 0833 263 072 or 335 601 9017
Email info@bleusalento.com
www.bleusalento.com

DARSENA FONTANELLE
40°03′·5N 17°59′·45E
VHF Ch 10.
A basin just E of Gallipoli commercial harbour.
Data Max LOA 18m. Depths 1–4m. Charge band 3.
Facilities Water. 220V. Showers and toilets. Fuel quay. Travel-hoist. Yacht repairs. Restaurant.
Darsena Fontanelle
✆ 0833 263 535
www.darsenafontanelle.it

PORTO GAIO
Small marina and boatyard in Darsena Acquaviva, ½M NE of Darsena Fontanelle.
VHF Ch 16, 11.
Berth Stern or bows-to where directed. Larger yachts on outer pontoon. Laid moorings.
Shelter Excellent shelter in the basin. Limited shelter on the pontoon.
Data c.100 berths. Max LOA c.15m. Depths 1–5m.
Facilities Water. 220V. Shower and WC. Fuel. 65-ton travel-lift. Mechanical and electrical repairs.
Remarks 1·5km into the centre of Gallipoli.
Porto Gaio, Darsena Acquaviva
✆ 0833 202 204
Email info@portogaio.it
www.portogaio.it

GRUPPO SEA PROJECT
Immediately SW of Darsena Fontanelle. 140-ton travel-hoist. All yacht repairs.
✆ 0833 263 030

TORRE SAN GIOVANNI D'UGENTO
39°53′·0N 18°06′·6E

☆ Torre San Giovanni Iso.WR.4s15/11M (311°-R-013°). Mole head F.R.3M. La Terra rocks Fl(2)6s5M. New pier head F.G.3M

UGENTO REEF (SECCHE DI UGENTO)
Between Gallipoli and Sta Maria di Leuca a reef extends some two miles offshore. A YBY W cardinal beacon Q(9)15s5M marks the westernmost point of the reef.

TORRE VADO
39°48′·8N 18°16′·8E

☆ Entrance Fl(3)G.6s3M/Fl(3)R.6s3M

Data 150 berths. Max LOA 10m. Depths 1–2m.

SANTA MARIA DI LEUCA
39°47′·6N 18°21′·5E
It 28
70M Crotone ←→ Otranto 22M

☆ Capo Santa Maria di Leuca Fl(3)15s24M and Oc.R.4s11M (094°-vis-

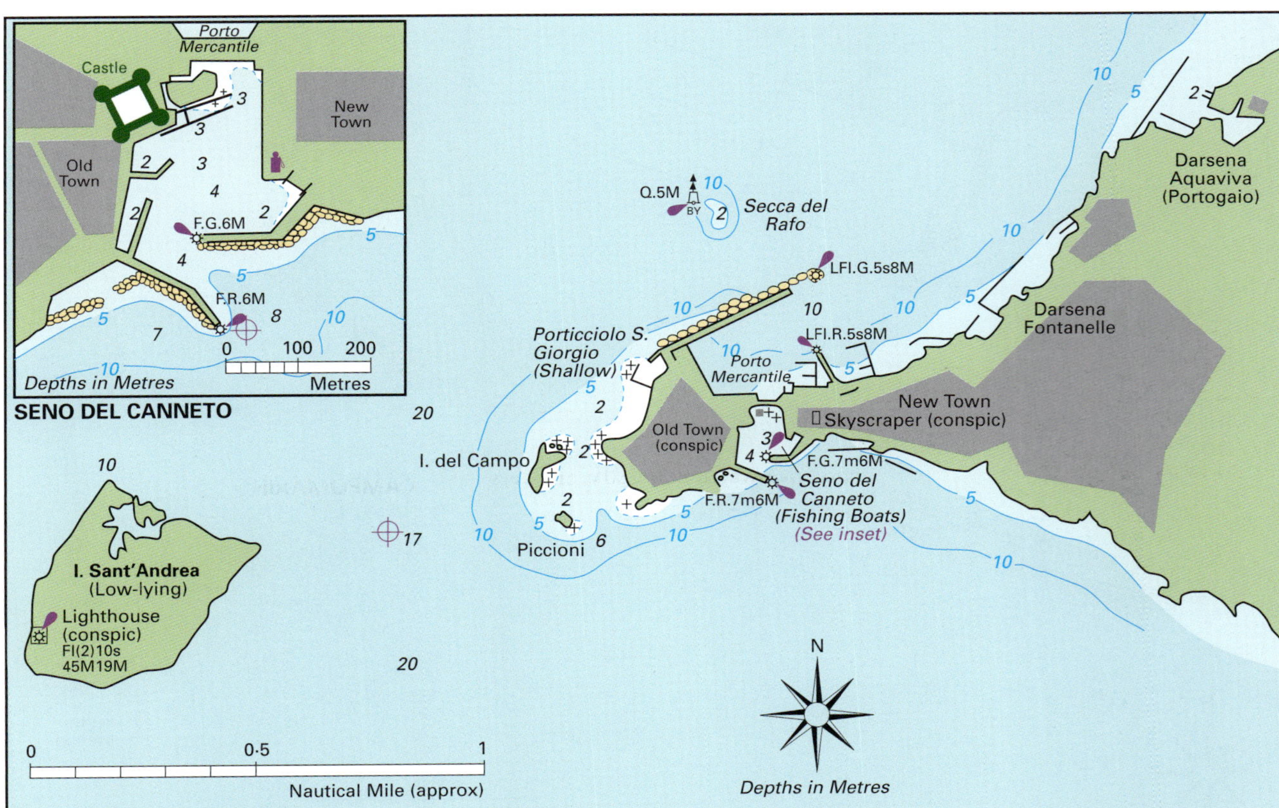

GALLIPOLI APPROACHES

106° over Urgento reef). Mole head Fl.G.5s7M. Spur Fl(2)G.5s6M. Inner mole head Fl(2)R.5s6M

VHF Ch 16, 12 for Porto Turistico (Marina di Leuca).

Navigation N side of entrance silting – depths less than charted.

Berths Where directed. Laid moorings. Yachts in transit should head for pontoons on the W quay and off the NE corner which are administered by the porto turistico Marina di Leuca. Lega Navale has three pontoons in the NW corner.

Shelter Surge with S winds and in fact with most winds. The most comfortable place is on the inner W mole.

Data 250 berths. Visitors' berths. Max LOA 30m. Depths 2–6m. Charge band 3.

Facilities Water. 220V. Showers and toilets. Fuel in inner harbour. Provisions and restaurants.

Marina di Leuca ☎ 0833 758 687
Email info@portodileuca.it

Port Authority ☎ 0833 758 580

Colaci Mare ☎ 0833 758 288

Adriatic

TRICASE (MARINA DI PORTO)

39°55'·9N 18°23'·8E

☆ Iso.G.2s4M

VHF Ch 14, 16.

Data 170 berths. Max LOA 12m. Depths 1–3m.

Facilities Water. 220V. Toilet. 3/15-ton crane.

CASTRO

40°00'·0N 18°25'·75E

VHF Ch 16 (0800–2000).

Navigation Narrow entrance dangerous in strong southerlies.

Data 250 berths approximately Max LOA 14m. Depths <1–5m. Charge band 1/2.

Facilities Water. 220V. Fuel organised.

OTRANTO

40°09'·1N 18°29'·6E
It 189
22M Santa Maria di Leuca ←→ Brindisi 40M

☆ La Punta Fl(3)WR.10s13/9M. St Nichola mole head Fl.R.3s8M

VHF Ch 16 for port authorities.

Berths Stern or bows-to the quay in SE corner.

Shelter Adequate in the summer.

Data Max LOA 12m. Depths <1–7m. Charge band 3.

Facilities Water. Fuel quay. 15-ton crane. Provisions and restaurants.

Gruppo Ormeggiatori (Andrea)
☎ 0836 73028 / 339 799 8073

PORTO DI SAN FOCA (MELANDUGNO)

40°18'·1N 18°24'·3E

☆ Entrance Fl.G.3s5M/F.G.3M

VHF Ch 16. CB Ch 10.

Navigation A new breakwater has been built, creating a new outer harbour. Yachts should not depend on finding a berth here. Variable depths ±1m in the entrance in inner harbour.

Data 400 berths. Max LOA 12m. Depths <1–1·5m.

☎ 0832 881 010 / 183
Email portodisanfoca@libero.it

SAN CATALDO

40°23'·5N 18°18'·2E

☆ Entrance Fl.G.3s5M/Fl.R.3s5M

VHF Ch 16.

Data 200 berths. Max LOA 12m. Depths 1–1·5m.

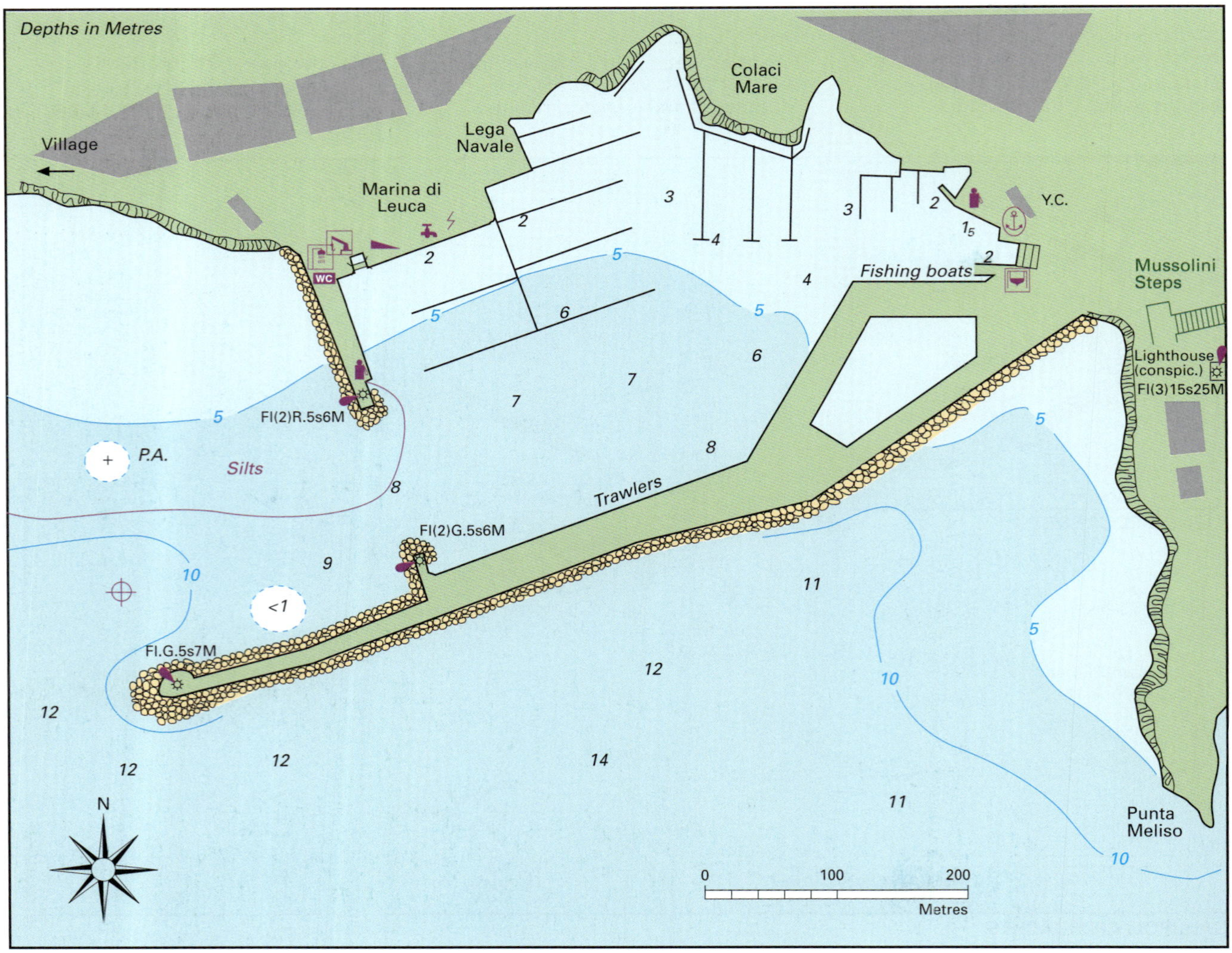

SANTA MARIA DI LEUCA

Note There is a firing range off the coast close N of San Cataldo, extending up to 5M off the coast. Call Otranto or Brindisi *Capitaneria* on VHF Ch 16 for advice on when the ranges are in use.

PORTO FRIGOLE

40°26′·0N 18°15′·1E N entrance

Work in progress reported developing the lagoon near the town of Frigole into a harbour. Bridges built over canals linking the lagoon to the sea limit access to all but small motor boats. New concrete quays line access canals and part of the lagoon.

BRINDISI

40°39′·25N 18°00′·1E
BA 1544, 1545 It 191, 192

☆ Capo de Torre Cavallo Bn Q(3)10s5M. Le Pedagne Fl(2)R.6s8M. Punta Riso breakwater head Fl(2)G.10s5M. Castello a Mare Fl(4)20s21M. Avamporto entrance Fl.G.3s8M/Fl.R.3s5M. Molo Montecatini 2F.R(vert)5M. Banchina di Costa Morena E head F.R.5M. Brindisi-Casale Aero AlFl.WGW.17s24-18M. Canale Pigonati entrance Iso.G.2s5M/ Iso.R.2s5M and F.G.6M/2F.R.6M.

VHF Ch 11, 16 (0700–1900). Ch 12 pilot (24/24). Ch 09 for Lega Navale.

Navigation Care needed in S approaches of reefs and shoals extending up to 1½M off the coast. Approach should be made on a course of due W from Il Trombilla lightbuoy Fl(3)10s.

Berths Yachts should make for the town quay or the Lega Navale quay on the N side of Seno di Ponente. Stern or bows-to or alongside. Anchoring in the harbour is prohibited and subject to a €300 fine.

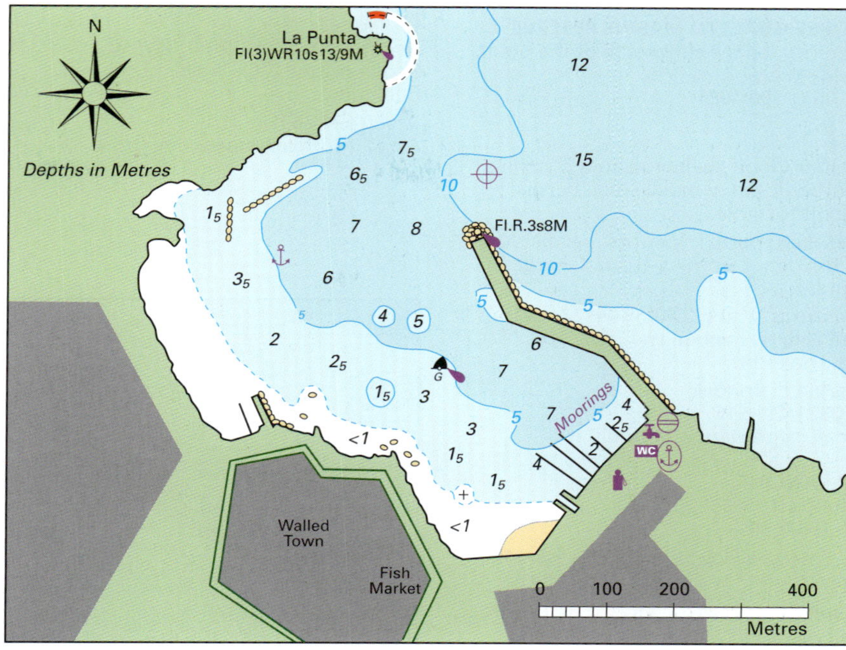

OTRANTO

Shelter Adequate.

Data Lega Navale. 300 berths. Max LOA 18m. Depths 2–7m.

Facilities Water. 220V. Fuel. 10-ton crane. Some yacht repairs. Cantiere Navale Balsamo at the W end of Seno di Ponente, past the Lega Navale. 200-ton slipway. 50-ton travel-hoist. Max LOA 20m. Most repairs. Provisions and restaurants.

☎ 0831 451 565
Email info@navalbalsamo.com
www.navalbalsamo.com

Remarks Yachts may find space to go stern or bows-to in Seno di Levante.

Lega Navale ☎ 0831 418 824

BRINDISI MARINA

40°39′.4N 17°57′.9E

VHF Ch 08, 16.

Navigation Once around the Avamporto entrance head N past Fort Castello del Mare.

Berths Stern or bows-to where directed. Laid moorings.

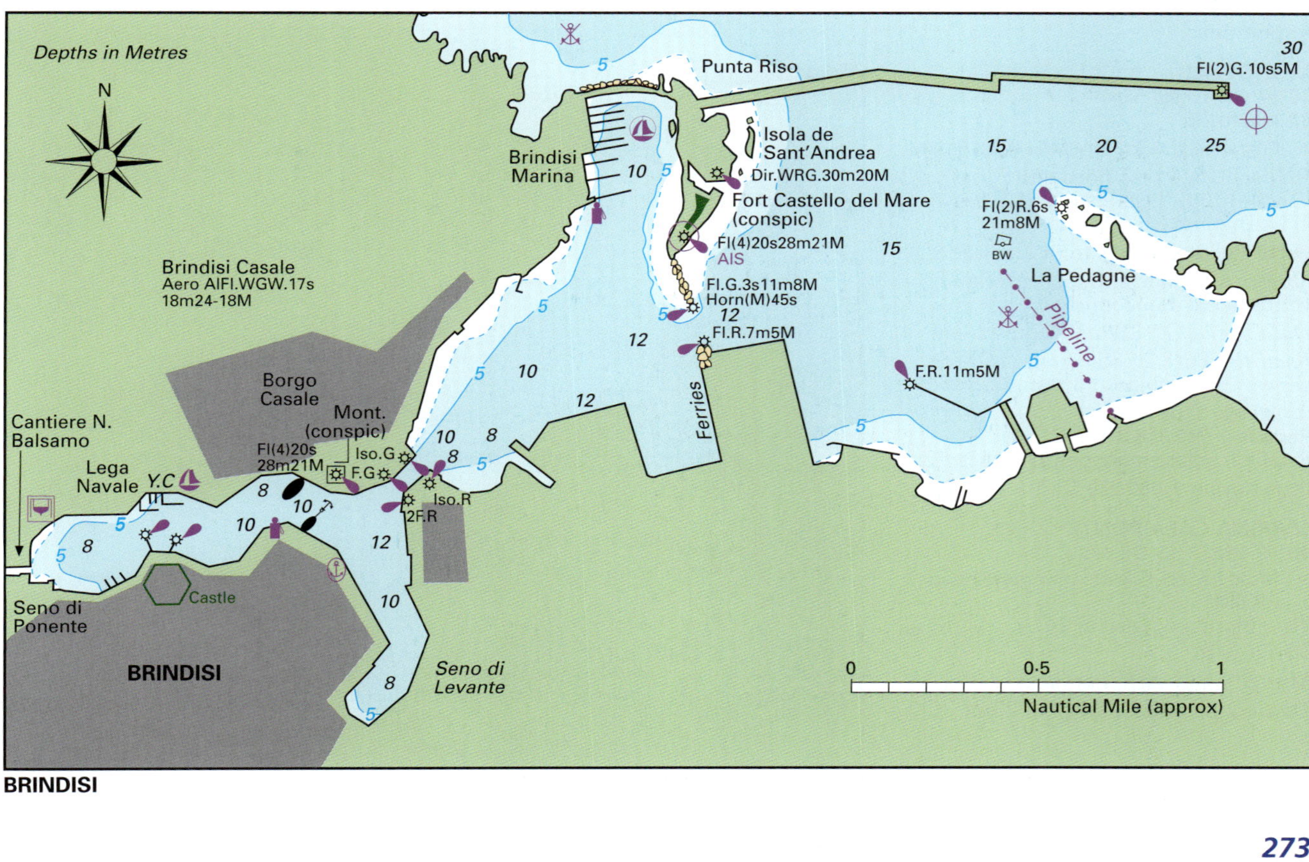

BRINDISI

TORRE GUACETO MARINE RESERVE
Extends for 1M either side of the point.
Brindisi Port Authority
✆ 0831 590 368

Shelter Good shelter although strong southerlies may make some berths uncomfortable.

Data 600 berths. Visitors' berths. Max LOA 35m. Depths 3–10m. Charge band 4.

Facilities Water. 220/380V. Showers and toilets. Fuel quay. Crane and 150-ton travel-lift.

Marina di Brindisi
✆ 0831 411 516
Email info@marinadibrindisi.it

VILLANOVA

40°47′·4N 17°35′·2E
BA 186 It 30

☆ Entrance Fl.G.5s8m4M/Fl.R.5s8m4M

VHF Ch 73.

Navigation Care needed of reef off N end of islet.

Data 250 berths. Max LOA 18m. Depths <1–2·5m.

Facilities Water. 220V. Fuel arranged. 20-ton crane.

Lega Navale ✆ 0831 359 277

SAVELLETRI

40°52′·4N 17°24′·8E (Fl.G.5s3M)
BA 186 It 30

☆ Punta Torre Canne Fl(2)10s35m16M. Entrance Fl.G.5s8m3M/F.R.3M

VHF Ch 16

Berths Stern or bows-to.

Shelter Adequate in the summer.

Data Max LOA 10m. Depths 1·5–3m.

Facilities Water. Provisions and restaurants.

MONOPOLI

40°57′·3N 17°18′·5E
BA 186 It 196

☆ Entrance Fl.G.3s13m8M/Fl.R.3s15m8M

VHF Ch 16, 14 for port authorities (0700–1900). Legal Navale Ch 09. C.N. Daphne Ch 06, 16.

Berths Stern or bows-to or alongside.

Shelter Adequate although strong SE winds make it uncomfortable.

Data Max LOA 100m. Depths 2–6m

Facilities Fuel. 25-ton crane. 150-ton slipway. Provisions and restaurants

✆ 080 930 3105
Repairs ✆ 930 318 8
Email circomare.monopoli@tiscali.it

Lega Navale ✆ 080 930 1341

MARINA CALA PONTE

40°59′·8N 17°13′·3E

☆ Mole head F.G.3M. Inner mole head F.R.3M.

New marina opened in 2014.

VHF Ch 16

Shelter Good shelter at most berths.

Data 320 berths. Max LOA 25m. Depths 2-4·5m.

Facilities Water. 220/380V. WiFi. Showers and WC. Waste pump-out. Fuel quay.

✆ 080 424 7691
Email info@calaponte.com

MOLA DI BARI

41°03′·7N 17°06′·1E
BA 186 It 196

☆ Entrance Fl.G.3s14m7M / Fl.R.3s8M. Braccio di Levante head 2F.R(vert)8m4M

VHF Ch 16 (0700–1900).

Berths Stern or bows-to.

Shelter Good shelter.

Data 110 berths. Max LOA 15m.

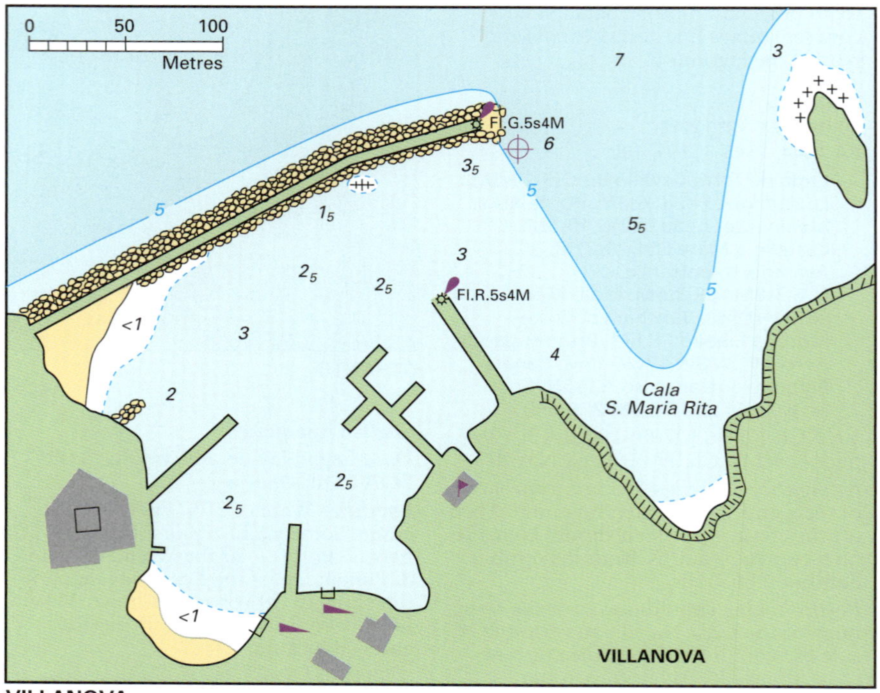

VILLANOVA

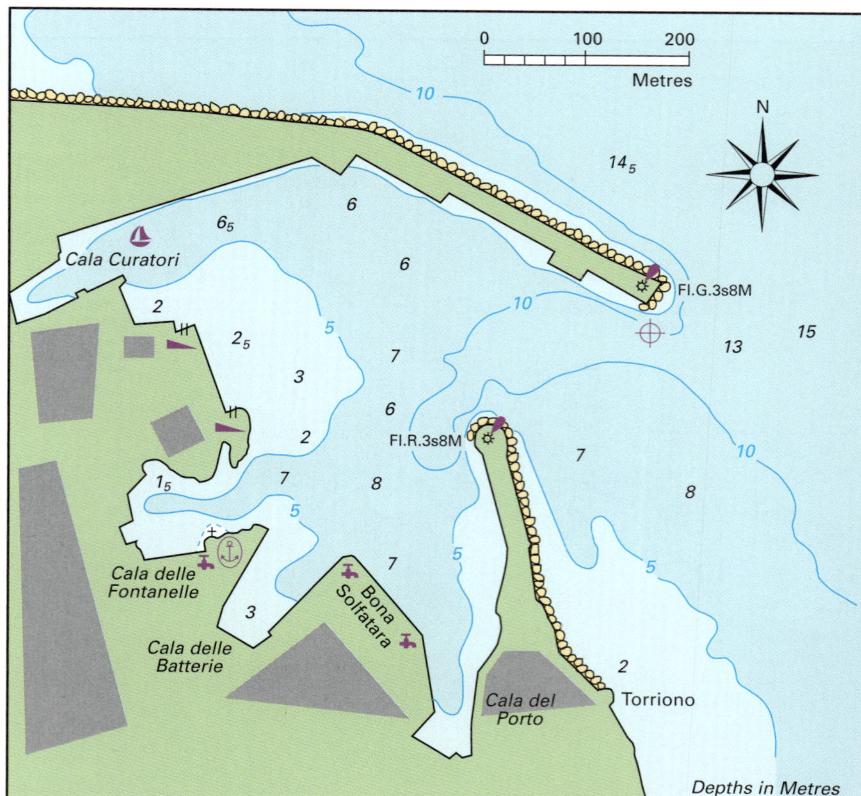

MONOPOLI

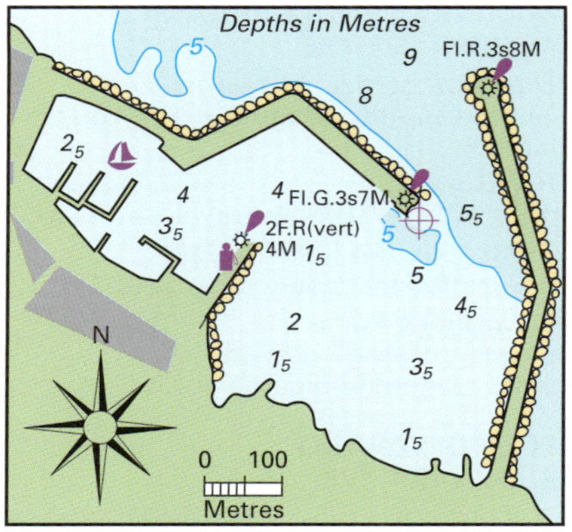

MOLA DI BARI

Depths <1–4m.
Facilities Water. 220V. Fuel arranged. 180/300-ton travel-hoists. Yacht repairs. Provisions and restaurants.
Port Authority ☎ 080 474 1573

TORRE A MARE
41°05′·4N 16°59′·8E
☆ F.G.3M/F.R.3M
Data Depths <1–2m.

BARI (PORTO VECCHIO)
41°07′·6N 16°52′·8E (Fl.G.5s6M)
☆ Entrance Fl.G.5s17m9M (130°-obscd-190°)/F.R
Berths Stern or bows-to in inner basin.
Shelter Adequate although open E.
Data Max LOA 8m. Depths <1–2·5m.
Facilities Water. Fuel quay (shallow). 40-ton crane. Provisions and restaurants.

BARI (BACINO GRANDE)
41°08′·8N 16°50′·9E (Fl.R.3s8M)
BA 140 It 193
☆ Punta San Cataldo Fl(3)20s24M. Entrance Fl.R.3s7M/Fl.R.5s4M/ Fl.G.3s7M. Darsena di Levante Fl.G.5s3M/Fl.R.5s3M. Molo Foraneo 2F.R(vert)6M. Darsena Vecchia Fl.G.5s9M. Darsena Interna F.RG(vert)4M
VHF Ch 11, 16 for *capitaneria* (0700–1900). Ch 12, 16 for pilots (24/24). Ch 09 for Ranieri CN.
Berth Pontoon berths or on the quay in SE corner near the *capitaneria*.
Note Ranieri shipyard with visitors pontoon berths in the W corner. Also refits, fuel, chandler.
Capitaineria ☎ 080 521 2074
Port Authority ☎ 080 521 6860
Ranieri ☎ 340 250 3782
Email info@ranieri-bari.com

SANTO SPIRITO
41°10′N 16°45′·1E (2F.G(vert))
☆ Entrance 2F.G(vert)10m3M/2F.R(vert)10m3M
Data c.200 berths. Max LOA 15m. Depths 1–4m.
Circolo Nautico Costa del Sole ☎ 080 533 7952

GIOVINAZZO
41°11′·4N 16°40′·4E (F.G.4M)
☆ Entrance F.R.8m4M/F.G.8m4M
Small fishing harbour.
Data Max LOA 13m. Depths <1–5m.

MOLFETTA
41°12′·8N 16°35′·5E (Fl.G.5s7M)
BA 186 It 196
☆ Molfetta lighthouse Iso.6s22m16M. Detached breakwater E end Fl.G.5s13m7M. Entrance Fl.R.5s13m7M/F.G.5m4M
VHF Ch 16, 14 for port authorities (0700–1900).
Navigation Care needed of reef on W side of inner basin. Leave buoy to starboard.
Berths Stern or bows-to or alongside.
Shelter Good shelter.
Data 80 berths. Max LOA 30m. Depths 1–6m.
Facilities Water. 15-ton crane. 150-ton slipway. Provisions and restaurants.
Remarks Works in progress in the W corner of the harbour.
Port Authority ☎ 080 397 1076

BISCEGLIE
41°14′·8N 16°30′·5E (F.G.5M)
BA 1443 It 196
☆ Entrance Fl.R.3s10m8M/F.G.10m5M
VHF Ch 16 for port authorities. CB Ch 09.
Data 250 berths. Max LOA 25m. Depths 1–3·5m. Charge band 3.
Facilities Water. 220V. Fuel quay. 8-ton crane. Provisions and restaurants.
Bisceglie Approdi ☎ 080 395 4845
Email bisceglie.approdi@tiscali.it
www.biscegliеapprodi.it
Lega Navale ☎ 080 395 7895

TRANI
41°17′·2N 16°25′94E
BA 1443 It 196
☆ Entrance LFl.G.5s8M/LFl.R.5s8M. Light tower 120m from head Fl.5s9m14M
VHF Ch 16, 14 for port authorities. Ch 16 (Darsena Marina).
Berths Stern or bows-to.
Shelter Strong NE winds make the harbour uncomfortable.
Data 400 berths. Max LOA 30m. Depths 1–4·5m. Charge band 4/5.
Facilities Water. 220V. Fuel quay. 20-ton crane. 25-ton slipway. Some yacht repairs. Provisions and restaurants.
Remarks Port of entry.
Harbourmaster ☎ 0883 583 763
Darsena Comunale ☎ 0883 420 28

BARLETTA
41°20′N 16°17′·7E (Fl.R.4s8M)
BA 1443 It 198
☆ Main light LFl(2)12s36m17M/Fl.G.4s12m8M/ Fl.R.4s12m8M. Entrance F.G.8m1M. Jetty F.R.4M
VHF Ch 16, 11 for port authorities (0700–2000). CB Ch 09.

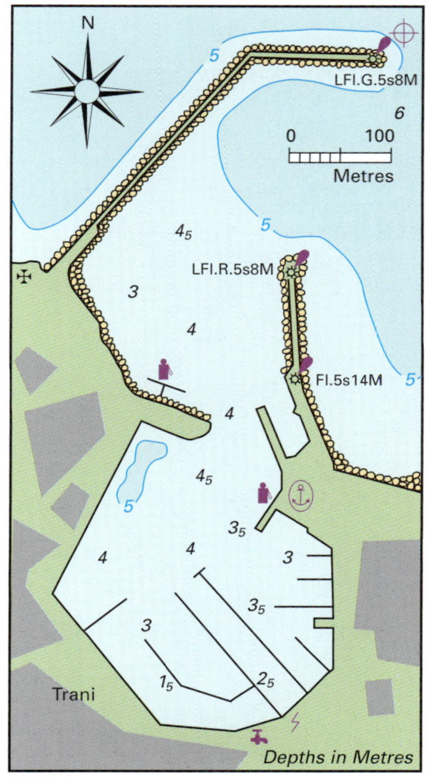

TRANI

Berths Stern or bows-to or alongside W mole or jetty.
Shelter Good shelter although uncomfortable with strong N–NW winds.
Data Depths <1–7m.
Facilities Water. Fuel. 50-ton slipway. Provisions and restaurants.
Remarks Port of entry.

MARGHERITA DI SAVOIA
41°23′·4N 16°08′·2E
☆ Entrance Fl.R.5s4M/Fl.G.5s4M
Data Max LOA 10m. Depths <1–2·5m.
Small basin. Anchorage inside breakwaters.

MANFREDONIA (PORTO VECCHIO)
41°37′·2N 15°55′·5E (Fl.G.3s)
BA 1443 It 199
☆ Manfredonia lighthouse Fl.5s20m23M. Commercial basin Oc.G.3s10m7M / Oc.R.3s10m7M. Entrance Fl.R.3s12m7M / Fl.G.3s14m7M
VHF Ch 14, 16 for port authorities. (summer 24/24, winter 0700–1900).
Navigation A yacht should head for Porto Vecchio. The commercial harbour lies at the seaward end of a 1·5M pier to the E of Porto Vecchio.
Berths Stern or bows-to in inner basin or alongside S mole.
Shelter Good shelter.
Data 365 berths. Max LOA 20m. Depths 1–5m.
Facilities Water. Fuel quay. 50-ton crane. 100-ton slipway. Provisions and restaurants.

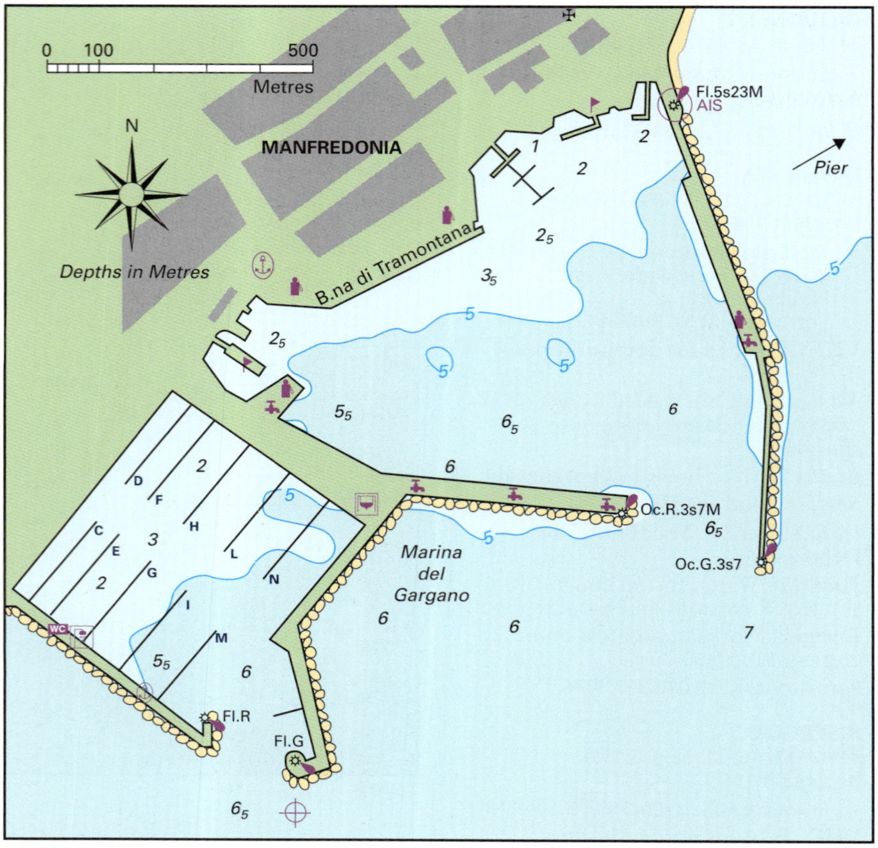

MANFREDONIA

MARINA DEL GARGANO
41°42′·6N 16°04′·8E

☆ F.G.8m3M/Fl.R.3s3M

A new marina off the S side of Manfredonia under the MDL flag. Opened in 2013.

VHF Ch 74

Data 745 berths. Max LOA 60m. Depths 2-6m. Charge band 4.

Shelter Good shelter.

Facilities Water. 220/380V. WiFi. Showers and WC. Waste pump-out. Fuel quay. 130-ton travel-lift.

✆ 0884 542 500 or 334 638 7127
Email info@marinadelgargano.it
www.marinadelgargano.it

MATTINATA
41°42′·6N 16°04′·8E

☆ F.G.8m3M/Fl.R.3s3M

VHF Ch 16.

Data 200 berths. Max LOA 15m. Depths 2–4m.

VIESTE
41°53′·9N 16°10′·8E (F.R.3M)
BA 186 It 32

☆ Isola S. Eufemia lighthouse Fl(3)15s40m25M. Entrance Fl.R.3s8M / Fl.G.3s8M. Jetty head F.G.3M. Inner mole F.R.7m4M

VHF Ch 12, 14, 16 (0700–1900).

Berths Stern or bows-to in inner basin. Anchorage S side of headland.

Shelter Good shelter in the basin.

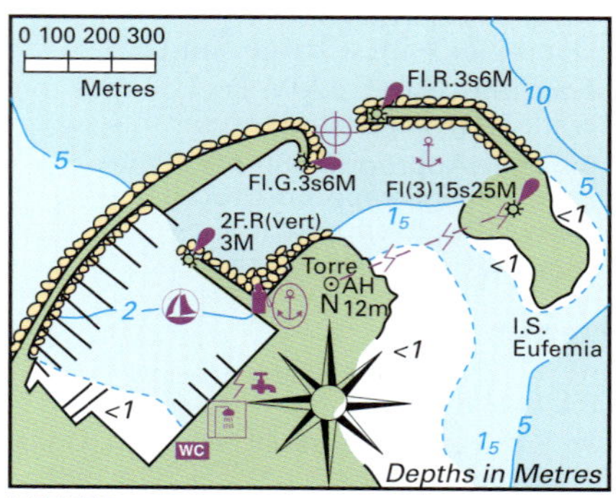

VIESTE

Data c.250 berths. Max LOA 35m. Depths <1–3m. Charge band 4/5.

Facilities Water. 220V. Fuel. Most provisions and restaurants.

Remarks Works in progress developing more berths on the N side of the harbour.

Port Authority ✆ 0884 707 669

Darsena Gargano ✆ 0844 701 675
Email reginaclub@alicposta.it

✆ 0844 707 983 / 330 940 581 (N pontoon)

PESCHICI
41°56′·9E 16°00′·0E

VHF Ch 16, 14 (0800–2000)

Data 50 berths. Max LOA 6m. Depths 1–2·5m.

MARINA DI RODI GARGANICO
41°55′·9N 15°53′·3E

Data 316 berths. 32 visitors' berths. Max LOA 40m. Depths 3–5m. Charge band 6.

Facilities Water. 220V. Showers and toilets. WiFi. 100-ton travel-lift. ATM.

✆ 0884 965 294 / 346 874 7231
Email info@marinadirodigarganico.it

IBS Yachting Point
Email info@ibsgargano.it
www.marinadirodigarganico.it

FOCE DI VARANO
41°55′N 15°47′·7E

☆ Entrance Fl.G.5s5M/Fl.R.5s5M

VHF Ch 16.

Navigation River berths. Entrance silts.

Data 100 berths. Max LOA 10m. Depths 2m.

FOCE DEL CAPOIALE
41°55′·2N 15°40′·0E

☆ Entrance Fl.R.5s5M/Fl.G.5s5M

River berths. Commercial.

Tremiti Islands (Isole Tremiti)

BA 200 It 204

☆ Isola Caprara Fl.5s23m4M (020°-obscd-110°). Isola San Nicola Fl(4)15s87m12M. Punta del Diavolo, I. San Domino Fl(3)10s48m11M (175°-vis-300°)

ISOLE TREMITI MARINE RESERVE
Surrounds the islands in the main group, and also around I. Pianosa. The anchorages are within the reserve.
Isola San Nicola Port Authority
✆ 0882 463 262
Comune di San Nicola
✆ 0882 463 063

SAN NICOLA
42°07′·4N 15°30′·6E

☆ Pier F.G.3M

Short pier used by ferries. Anchorage off to NW. Holding on rock is unreliable.

SAN DOMINO (CALA DEGLI SCHIAVONI)
42°07′·2N 15°30′·0E

Anchorage under Punta Schiavoni. Unreliable holding on rock and weed.

TERMOLI
42°00′·2N 15°00′·5E
BA 200 It 33

☆ Termoli lighthouse Fl(2)10s41m15M. Entrance Fl.G.3s11m8M/F.G.3M. Elbow 2F.G(vert)3M

VHF Ch 16, 14 for port authorities (0700–1900).

Berths Where directed at YC on S mole or in the new marina.

Shelter Good shelter in the summer. Surge with S gales.

Data 120 berths. Max LOA 25m. Depths 1·5–3m. Charge band 5.

Facilities Water. 220V. Fuel quay. 20-ton crane. 80-ton slipway. Limited yacht repairs. Provisions and restaurants.

Marinucci Yachting ☎ 0875 702 238
www.myc.it

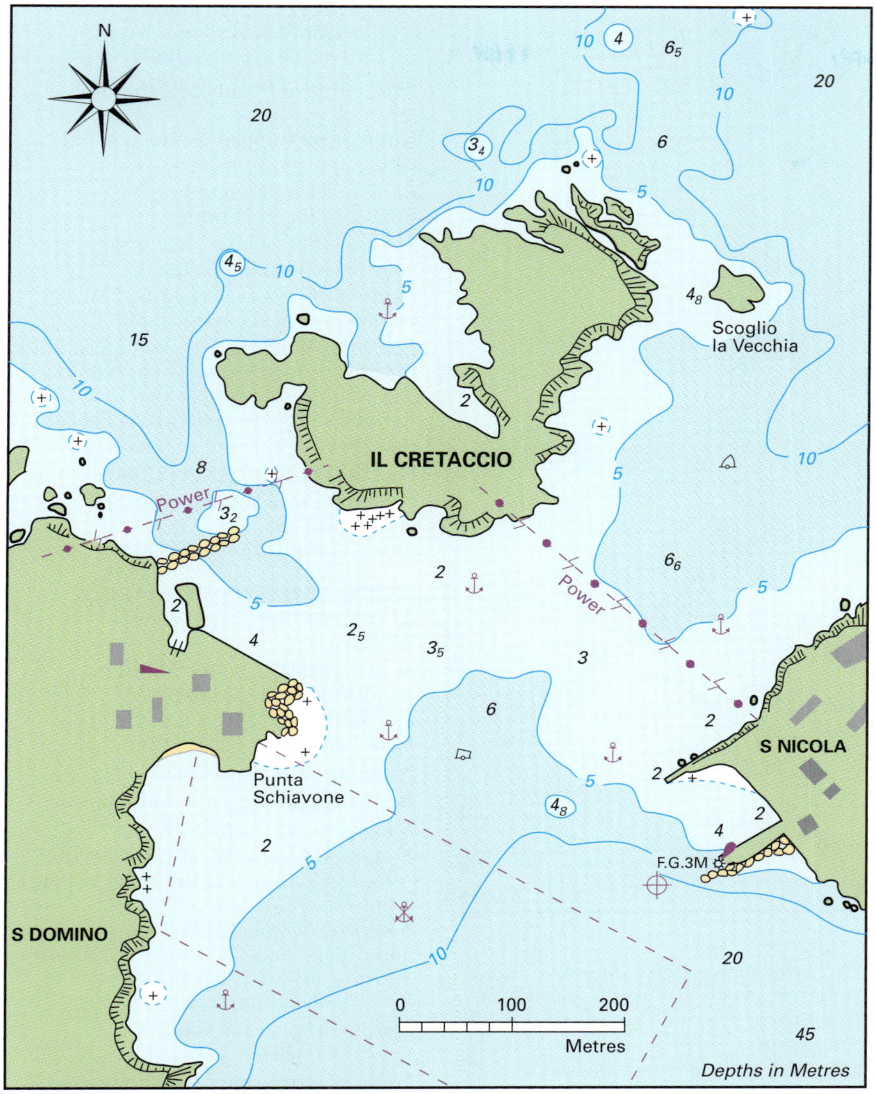

I. SAN NICOLA AND I. SAN DOMINO

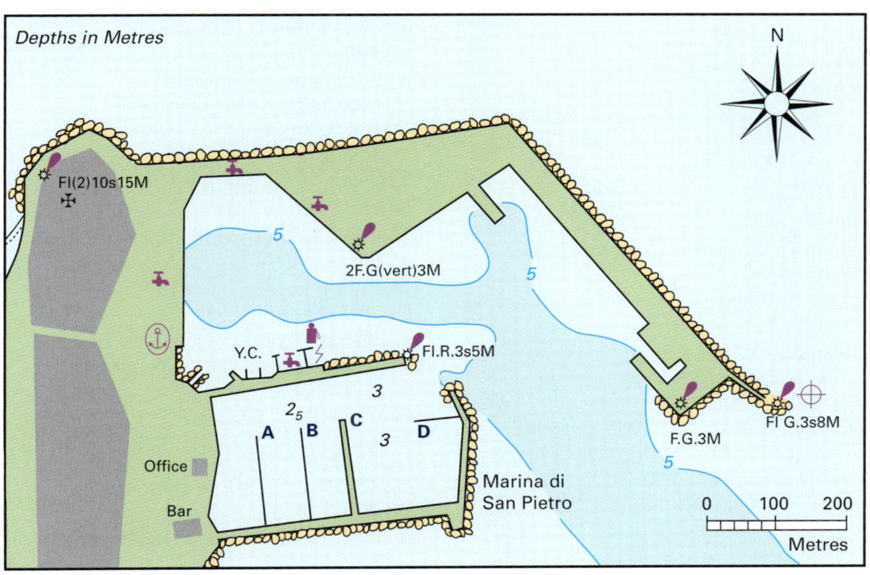

TERMOLI

MARINA DI SAN PIETRO

A marina operated by Marinucci Yachting Club.

Data 250 berths. Max LOA 30m. Depths 3·5–4·5m. Charge band 6+.

Facilities Water. 220V. WiFi. 250-ton travel-hoist.

Marinucci Yachting Club
☎ 0875 705 398
Mooring ☎ 345 475 1783
Email marinadisanpietro@myc.it
www.marinadisanpietro.it

MARINA SVEVA (MONTENERO DI BISACCIA)

42°04'·2N 14°47'·5E

A new porto turistico completed in 2012.

VHF Ch 10

Data 445 berths. Max LOA 35m. Depth 2-4m. Depths 3·5–4·5m. Charge band 6+.

Shelter Good shelter.

Facilities Water. 220/380V. WiFi. WC and showers. Fuel quay. 70-ton travel-hoist.

☎ 0873 803431 or 339 6085696
Email info@smmspa.com
www.marinasveva.com

PORTO DI PUNTA PENNA (PORTO DI VASTO)

42°10'·8N 14°42'·7E (Fl.G.3s7M)
BA 200 It 33

☆ Punta Penna lighthouse Fl.5s84m25M. Entrance Fl.G.3s7M/ Fl.R.3s4M. Inner entrance Fl.G.6s4M/ Fl.R.6s4M

VHF Ch 16, 12.

Berths Alongside in inner basin.

Shelter Adequate in the summer but dangerous surge with N gales.

Data Max LOA 18m. Depths 3–6m.

Facilities Water. 50-ton crane. Limited provisions.

Circolo Náutico Vasto ☎ 0873 584 10

VASTO (PUNTA PENNA)

42°10'·6N 14°42'·7E

☆ Fl.5s.25M / Fl.R.3s.4M / Fl.G.3s.4M / Fl.R.6s4M / Fl.G.6s4M

A new commercial harbour 3M N of the town of Vasto. Limited room for visitors.

MARINA DEL SOLE

42°14'·2N 14°32'·2E

A marina 500m N of Fiume Sangro.

Data 400 berths. Max LOA 12m. Depths 1–2·5m. Charge band 5.

Facilities Water. 220V. Showers and toilets. Fuel.

☎ 0872 608 305
Email marinadelsole@marinadelsole.com

ORTONA

42°21'·0N 14°25'·4E (Fl.G.3s9M)
BA 1443 It 212

☆ Ortona lighthouse Fl(2)6s23m15M. Oc(2)Y.10s20m5M. Entrance Fl.G.5s9m4M / Fl.R.5s9m4M. Mandracchio mole head F.R. Molo Martello head E head F.G.8m3M

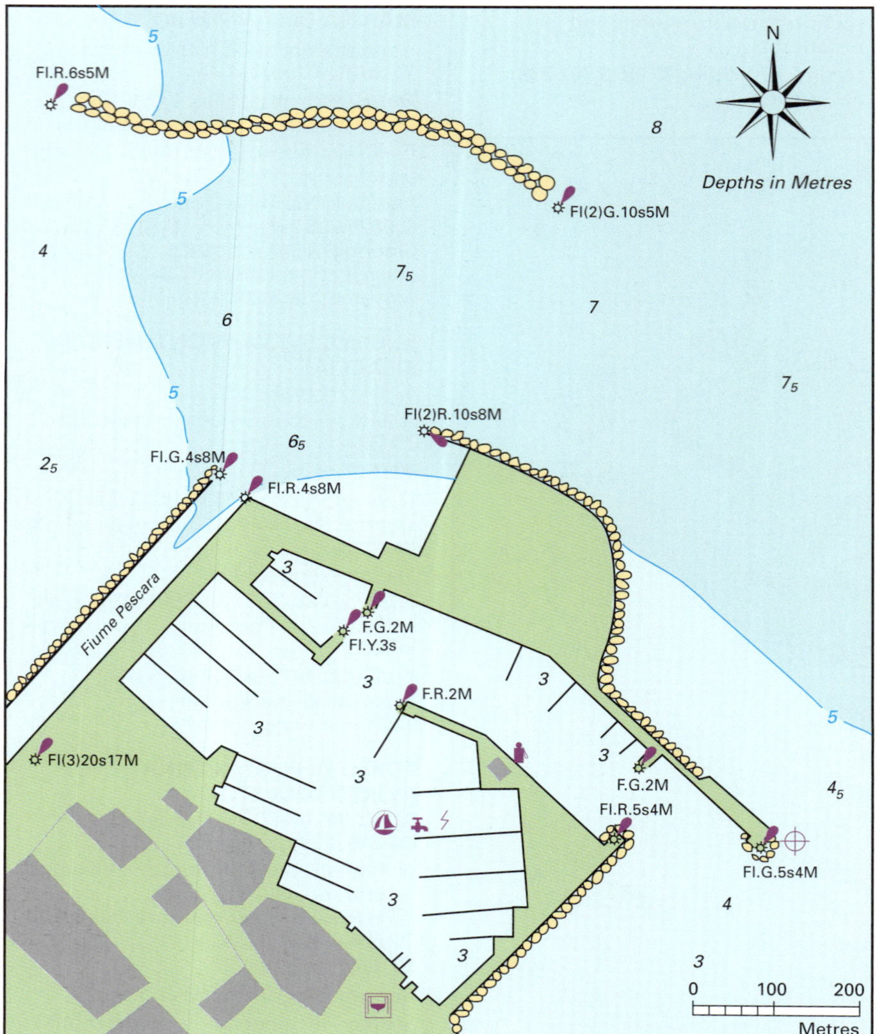

PESCARA

VHF Ch 16, 15 (0700–1900).
Berths Stern or bows-to in SW corner.
Shelter Good shelter except from the E.
Data Max LOA 30m. Depths 1–6m.
Facilities Water. Fuel. 120-ton crane. 80-ton slipway. Limited provisions and restaurants at the harbour.
Remarks Harbour silts. New N breakwater extension.

PESCARA

42°27′·9N 14°14′·2E (Fl.G.5s4M Marina mole head)
It 211

☆ Detached breakwater Raffaele Paolucci W end Fl.R.6s5M. E end Fl(2)G.10s5M. Marina entrance Fl.G.5s4M / F.G.2M / Fl.R.5s4M. Inner entrance Fl.Y.3s/ F.G.2M / F.R.2M.
VHF Ch 06, 16 for Marina.

Berths Yachts should make for the marina. Go stern or bows-to where directed. Laid moorings tailed to the quay.
Shelter Good shelter.
Data 860 berths. 30 visitors' berths. Max LOA 30m. Depths 2–3·5m. Charge band 5.
Facilities Water. 220V. Showers and toilets. Fuel. 40/100-ton travel-hoists. Most yacht repairs. Provisions and restaurants.
Marina di Pescara ✆ 085 454 681
Email contact@marinape.com
www.marinape.com

GIULIANOVA

42°45′·3N 13°58′·7E (Fl.G.5s4M)
BA 200 It 214

☆ Entrance Fl.G.5s8m4M/Fl.R.5s8m4M. Spur F.R.2M. Inner entrance F.G.2M Horn Mo(G)45s

VHF Ch 16, 09 (0700–1900).
Berths Stern or bows-to.
Shelter Uncomfortable with strong northerlies.
Data 240 berths. Max LOA 22m. Depths 2–3·5m.
Facilities Water. Fuel by mini-tanker. 200-ton crane. 150-ton slipway. Provisions and restaurants.
Porto di Giulianova ✆ 085 800 5888
Email info@enteportogiulianova.it
CN Migliori ✆ 085 800 4972
Email info@circolo-migliori.it

SAN BENEDETTO DEL TRONTO

42°57′·5N 13°53′·7E (Fl.R.3s8M)
BA 200 It 213

☆ San Benedetto del Tronto lighthouse Fl(2)10s31m22M. Entrance Fl.G.3s8m8M/Fl.R.3s8m8M Horn Mo(W)45s. Fiume Tronto 2F.R(vert)3M. Eastwards Fl.Y.3s

VHF Ch 11, 16 (0700–1900). CB Ch 07.
Navigation Buoyed channel, prone to silting.
Berths. Where directed on YC pontoons or on N mole.
Shelter Good shelter except with N gales which cause a surge.
Data 380 berths. Max LOA 25m. Depths 2–4·5m. Charge band 4.
Facilities Water. 220V. Fuel quay. 200-ton travel-hoist. Some yacht repairs. Provisions and restaurants.
Remarks A porto turistico has been developed in the S of the harbour.
Port Authority ✆ 0735 592 744
Circolo Nautico Sambenedettese
✆ 0735 584 255
Email info@circolonautico.info

PORTO SAN GIORGIO MARINA

43°09′·8N 13°49′·8E (Fl(2)R.6s)
BA 200 It 35

☆ Entrance Fl(2)R.6s8m5M Horn Mo(U)45s/Fl(2)G.6s8m5M/ F.G(vert)2M

VHF Ch 16, 14. CB Ch 09.
Navigation Buoyed channel.
Berths Where directed. Laid moorings.
Shelter Good shelter.
Data 800 berths. 85 visitors' berths. Max LOA 50m. Depths 3–5m. Charge band 4/5.
Facilities Water. 220/380V. Showers and toilets. Fuel. 100-ton travel-hoist. 200-ton slipway. Most yacht repairs. Provisions and restaurants.
Marina di Porto San Giorgio
✆ 0734 675 263
Email info@marinaportosangiorgio.it

CIVITANOVA

43°18′·9N 13°44′·1E (Fl.R.5s)
BA 200 It 214

☆ Civitanova lighthouse Mo(C)20s42m11M. Entrance Fl.R.5s10m8M / Fl.G.5s9m8M. T-jetty head Fl.R.3s4M

VHF Ch 16 (0800–2400). CB Ch 09.
Berths Stern or bows-to.
Shelter Uncomfortable with strong N winds.
Data 600 berths. Max LOA 18m. Depths 0·5–4m.
Facilities Water. Fuel. 80-ton crane. 150-ton slipway. Provisions and restaurants.
Capitaineria ✆ 0733 810 395

NUMANA

43°30′·5N 13°37′·7E (N entrance)
BA 200 It 35

☆ N entrance 2F.G(vert)3M/2F.R(vert)3M. S entrance F.R.3M/F.G.3M. Centre F.3M

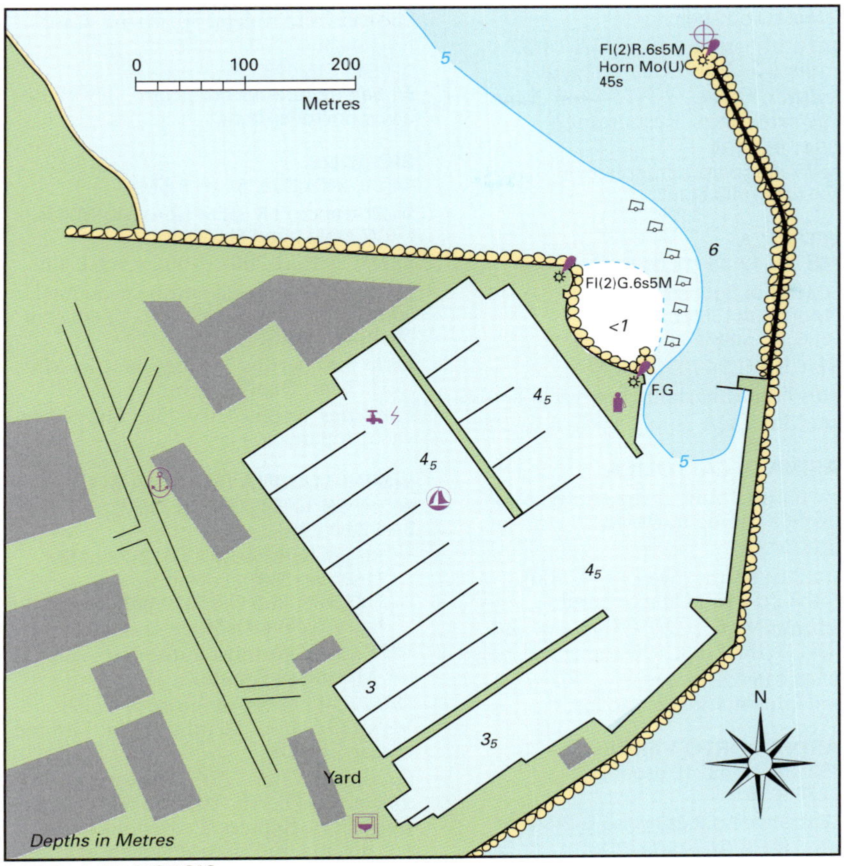

PORTO SAN GIORGIO

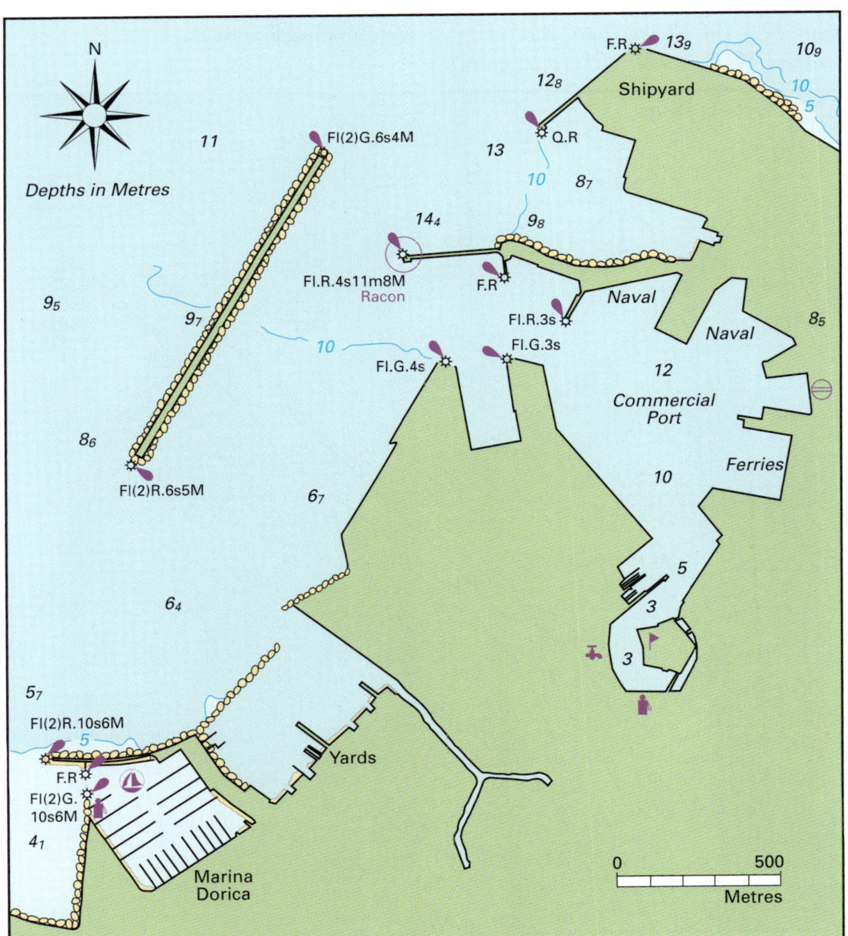

ANCONA

VHF Ch 11. CB Ch 30.

Navigation Entrance by N or S inside detached breakwater.

Berths Stern or bows-to. Laid moorings.

Shelter Adequate in the summer.

Data 780 berths. Max LOA 25m. Depths 1·8–3m.

Facilities Water. 220V. Fuel. 35-ton crane. Some provisions and restaurants.

Port Authority ✆ 071 736 0377

Commune ✆ 0171 933 9835

ANCONA (MARINA DORICA)

43°36′·65N 13°28′·91E

BA 1444 It 209

☆ Colle Cappuccini Fl(4)30s25M. Entrance to commercial port Fl.R.4s8M/Fl.G.4s7M. Detached breakwater S end Fl(2)R.6s10m5M. Molo Foraneo N head Fl(2)G.6s4M. Spur F.R.3M. Inner entrance Fl.R.3s8M/ Fl.G.3s7M. Shipyard Q.R.4M / F.R.3M. Marina Dorica entrance lights Fl(2)G.10s6M/Fl(2)R.10s6M/F.R.3M

VHF Ch 11, 16 (0800–2400). Pilot Ch 12. Marina Ch 16, 08.

Navigation A yacht should make for Marina Dorica SW of the commercial port. Access 0700–2100.

Berths Where directed. Laid moorings.

Shelter Adequate but uncomfortable with strong NW winds.

Data (Marina) 1190 berths. Max LOA 20m. Depths 2·5–4·5m. Charge band 5.

Facilities Water. 220V. Showers and toilet. Fuel. 40-ton travel-hoist. Yacht and superyacht repair centres in the basin N of the marina. Provisions and restaurants.

Remarks May also be berths at the YC in the inner basin of the commercial port.

Marina Dorica ✆ 071 54800

Email info@marinadorica.it

www.marinadorica.it

SENIGALLIA

43°43′·3N 13°13′·4E (Fl.R.3s8M)

BA 1444 It 214

☆ Senigallia lighthouse LFl(2)15s17m15M. Entrance marina Fl.(2)R.6s8M Horn Mo(D)45s3m

VHF Ch 16, 11 (0800–2400). CB Ch 19.

Navigation The marina has a seperate entrance with new breakwater extensions.

Berths Stern or bows-to where indicated. Laid moorings.

Shelter Good shelter.

Data 300 berths. 30 visitors' berths. Max LOA 18m. Depths <1–1·5m. Charge band 4.

Facilities Water. Fuel quay. 40-ton travel-hoist. Some yacht repairs. Provisions and restaurants.

✆ 071 7929 9669

Email info@gestiport.it

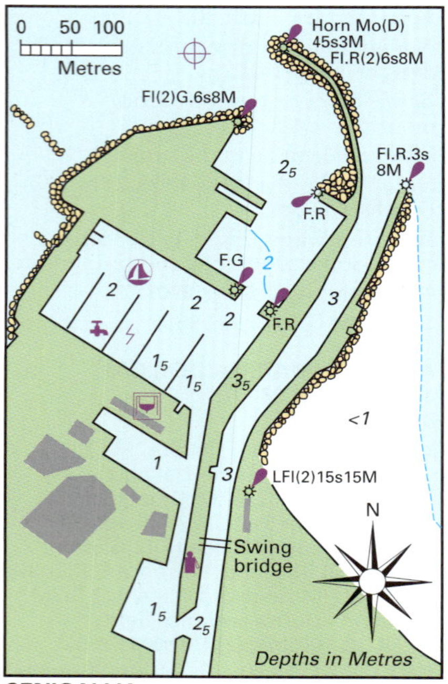

SENIGALLIA

FANO (MARINA DEI CESARI)

43°51′·2N 13°01′E (Fl.R.3s)
BA 220 It 214

☆ Fano lighthouse Fl.Y.3s8m3M. Entrance Fl.G.3s8m8M/Fl.R.3s9m8M. Mole F.GR(vert)8m3M. Marina dei Cesari F.R.3M/F.G.3M

VHF Ch 16, 08 for marina.

Berths Where directed in marina.

Data 420 berths. Max LOA 40m. Depths 1–3m. Charge band 5.

Facilities Water. 220/380V. Showers and toilets. Fuel quay. 75-ton travel-hoist.

Remarks Part of the MDL marina network.

Marina di Cesari ✆ 0721 800 279
Email info@marinadeicesari.it
www.marinadeicesari.it

PESARO

43°55′·5N 12°54′·6E (Fl.R.5s)
BA 220 It 214

☆ Monte San Bartolo Fl(2)15s175m25M. Commercial harbour entrance Fl.G.5s10m8M / Fl.R.5s10m8M

VHF Ch 16, 12 (0700–1900).

Berths Where directed in Porto Turistico, uncomfortable.

Shelter Good shelter but N winds make Porto Turistico uncomfortable.

Data Porto Turistico 400 berths. 15 visitors' berths. Max LOA 25m. Depths 1·5–3·5m.

Facilities Water. Fuel. 10-ton crane. Provisions and restaurants.

✆ 0721 400 016

MARINA DI BAIA VALLUGOLA

43°57′·8N 12°47′·5E (F.R.3M)
BA 220 It 36

☆ Entrance F.G.3M/F.R.3M

VHF Ch 09 (0800–2000). CB Ch 11.

Berths Stern or bows-to. Laid moorings.

Shelter Good shelter.

Data 150 berths. Max LOA 18m. Depths 1·5–2·5m. Charge band 3.

Facilities Water. 220V. 50-ton crane. Some provisions. Restaurant.

✆ 0541 958 134
Email vallugola@vallugola.com
www.vallugola.com

CATTOLICA

43°58′·2N 12°45′·1E (Fl.R.3s)

☆ Cattolica light structure Mo(O)14s15M. Entrance Fl.G.3s7m8M/Fl.R.3s7m8M

VHF Ch 11, 16 (0700–1900).

Berths Fishing harbour. Few yacht berths.

Data Max LOA 20m. Depths 1·5–2·5m.

MARINA DI CATTOLICA

New marina built at the entrance to Cattolica fishing harbour.

VHF Ch 12.

Data 210 berths. Max LOA 30m. Depths 2·5–4m. Charge band 5.

Facilities Water. 220V. Showers and toilets. WiFi. Fuel. 100-ton travel-hoist.

✆ 0541 615 023 or 349 254 2902
Email info@marinadicattolica.it

MARINA PORTO VERDE

43°58′·3N 12°43′·1E (Iso.R.2s)
BA 220 It 36

☆ Entrance Iso.R.2s3M/Iso.G.2s3M

VHF CB Ch 01 (0800–2000).

Data 300 berths. 20 visitors' berths. Max LOA 25m. Depths (1·8m in entrance) 2–3m. Charge band 5.

Facilities Water. 220V. WiFi. Fuel quay. Showers and toilets. 30/15-ton cranes. Restaurant.

✆ 0541 615 023
Email info@portoverde.com
www.portoverde.net

RICCIONE

44°00′·5N 12°39′·5E (Fl.R.5M)

☆ Entrance Fl.R.3s5M Horn Mo(M)45s. W mole head Fl.G.3s5M.

VHF Ch 16 (0700–1900). CB Ch 11.

Navigation Buoyed entrance channel. Min depths 2m. Dangerous to enter in onshore winds.

Data 500 berths. Visitors' berths. Max LOA 12m. Depths 2–5m.

Facilities Water. 220V. Fuel quay. Some yacht repairs.

RIMINI MARINA (MARINA BLU)

44°04′·9N 12°34′·6E (Fl.R.3s5M)
BA 220 It 215

☆ Rimini lighthouse Fl(3)12s27m15M (160°-vis-280°). Entrance Fl.G.3s7m8M/ Fl.R.3s10m8M Horn. Ferry 2F.R(vert)3M

VHF Ch 16 for port authorities. Ch 69 for Marina di Rimini.

Data 650 berths. 60 visitors' berths. Max LOA 45m. Depths 2–4m. Limited visitors' berths.

Facilities Water. 220V. Showers and toilets. Fuel berth. 100-ton travel-hoist. Chandlers. Repairs. Provisions and restaurants. International airport.

Marina di Rimini ✆ 0541 29488
Email info@marinadirimini.com
www.marinadirimini.com

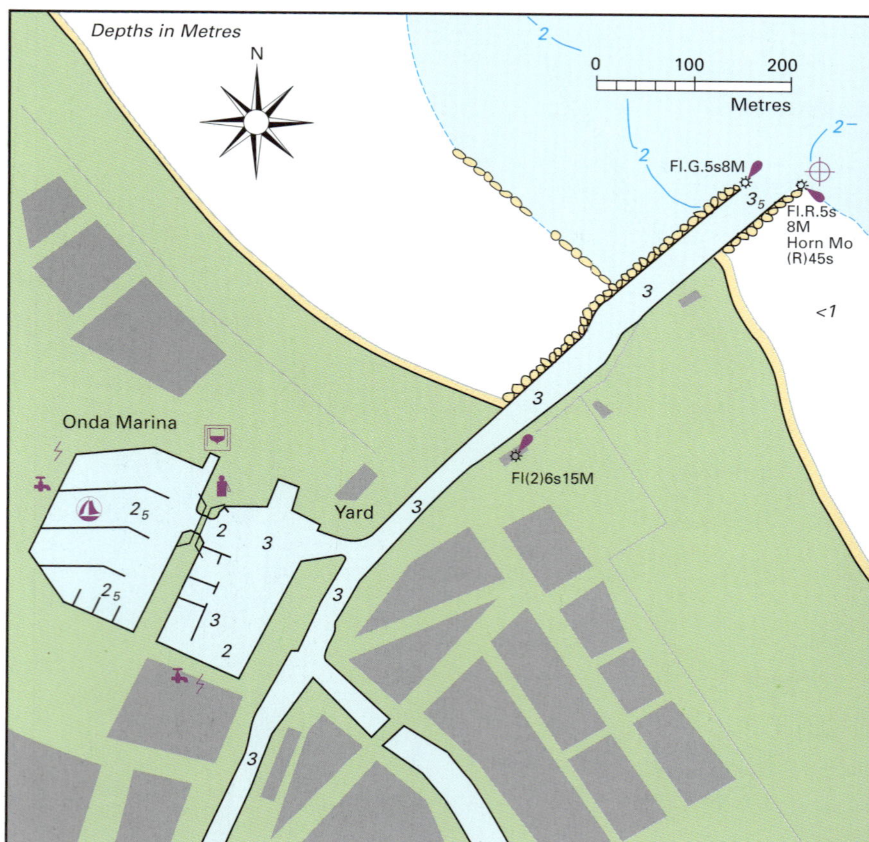

CESENATICO

BELLARIA
44°08′·6N 12°28′·5E (F.R.3M)

☆ Entrance F.R.3M/F.G.3M

Data Max LOA 12m. Depths 1–2m.

CESENATICO (ONDA MARINA)
44°12′·5N 12°24′·3E
BA 1467 It 215

☆ Cesenatico lighthouse Fl(2)6s18m15M. Entrance Fl.G.5s8m8M/Fl.R.5s8m8M Horn Mo(R)45s

VHF Ch 16, 11 (0700–1900). Call sign *Onda Marina*. YC CB Ch 04.

Berths Stern or bows-to in Onda Marina or at the YC.

Shelter Good shelter.

Data 300 berths. 25 visitors' berths. Max LOA 23m. Depths 2–3m. Charge band 3.

YC 80 berths. Four visitors' berths. Max LOA 16m. Depths 2–4m. Charge band 5.

Facilities Water. 220V. Fuel quay. 50-ton travel-hoist. 100-ton crane. 100-ton slipway. Most yacht repairs. Provisions and restaurants.

Onda Marina ☏ 0541 816 77
Email ondamarina@tiscali.it

CERVIA MARINA
44°16′·1N 12°21′·7E (Fl.R.3s4M)
BA 1467 It 215

☆ Cervia lighthouse Iso.2s16m11M. Entrance Fl.G.3s8m4M/Fl.R.3s8m4M Marina elbow 2F.R(vert)3M

VHF Ch 14, 16 (0700–1900).

Navigation Marina entered via the canal.

Berths Where directed in the marina.

Shelter Good shelter.

Data 300 berths. Max LOA 22m. Depths 2–3m. Charge band 5.

Facilities Water. 220V. Fuel quay. 45-ton travel-hoist. 25-ton crane. 50-ton slipway. Some yacht repairs. Provisions and restaurants.

☏ 0544 717 09
Email marinadicervia@tin.it or info@mdcresort.it

MARINA DI RAVENNA
44°29′·8N 12°18′·9E (Fl(2)R.6s)
BA 1445 It 218

☆ Approach beacons Fl.10s6M. Entrance Porto Corsini lighthouse Fl.5s35m20M. Entrance Fl(2)G.6s10m8M/ Fl(2)R.6s10m8M Horn(3)48s. Inner entrance Fl.G.4s7m8M/ Fl.R.4s7m8M Horn(4)45s

VHF Ch 11, 16 for *capitaneria*. Ch 12, 16 for pilots. Ch 16, 10 CB Ch 09 for Marina di Ravenna.

Navigation The outer breakwaters enclosing Porto Corsini and the marina extend nearly 1·5M E of the coast. Yachts should make for Marina di Ravenna or Marinara on the S side of the canal breakwater.

Berths Stern or bows-to. Anchorage on N side of canal entrance.

Shelter Adequate in the summer.

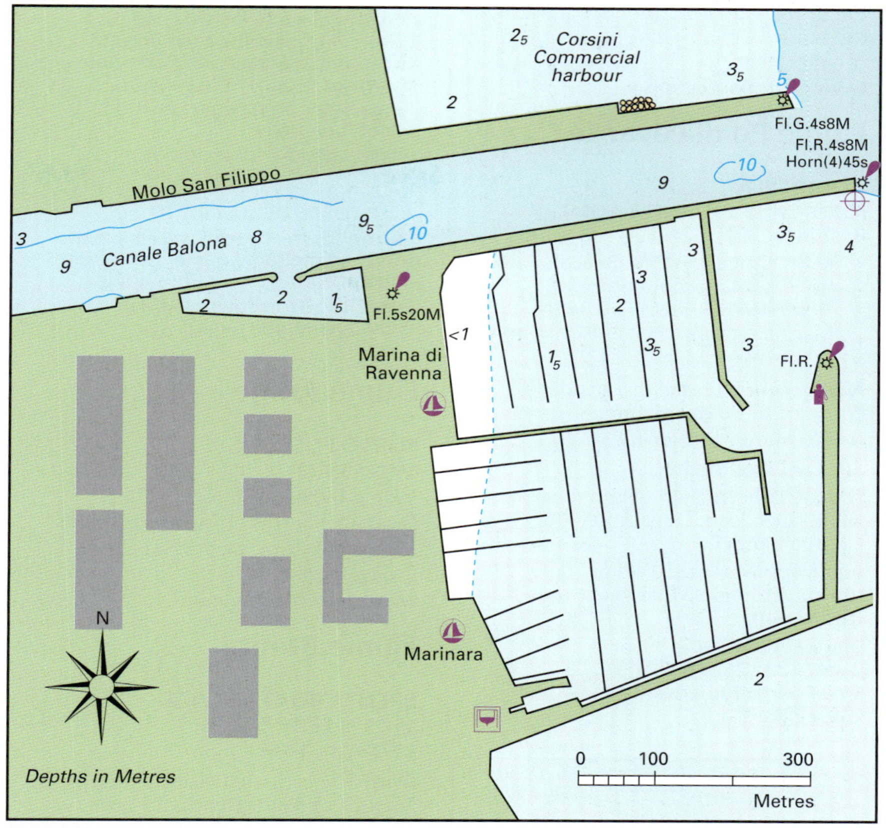

MARINA DI RAVENNA AND MARINARA

Data Marinara c.1200 berths. Visitors' berths. Max LOA 40m. Depths 2–5m. Charge band 5.
Marina di Ravenna 685 berths. Max LOA 15m. Depths 0·5–3·5m.

Facilities Water. 220V. Fuel. 100-ton travel-hoist. 200-ton crane. 300 berths ashore at Porto Corsini up the canal. Yacht repairs. Provisions and restaurants.

Marina di Ravenna CVR ☏ 0544 530 513

Ravenna YC ☏ 0544 531 162

Marinara ☏ 0544 531 644 or 331 387 7999
Email info@marinara.it
www.mdlmarinas.com

Marina Romea
44°30′N 12°17′E

Harbour on Fiume Lamone.

Data 100 berths. Max LOA 12m. Depths <1–2m.

Casalborsetti (Porto Reno Marina)
44°33′N 12°17′E

Basin on Canale di Casalborsetti.

Data 50 berths. Depths <1m.

www.marinadiportoreno.it

PORTO GARIBALDI (LIDO DEGLI ESTENSI)
44°40′·6N 12°15′·0E (Fl.G.5s8M)
BA 1467 It 215

☆ Porto Garibaldi lighthouse Fl(4)15s14m15M. Entrance Fl.G.5s9m8M Horn Mo(G)48s/ Fl.R.5s9m8M/Q.R.5M. Marina Degli Estensi entrance F.G.3M/F.R.3M.

VHF Ch 11, 16 (0700–1900).

Berths Yachts should head for Marina degli Esteni at the end of the port side canal.

Shelter All round shelter.

Data (Marina degli Esteni) 300 berths. 30 visitors' berths. Max LOA 25m. Depths 2·5–4m. Charge band 5.

Facilities Water. 220V. Showers and toilets. Fuel quay. 50-ton travel-hoist. Yacht repairs. Provisions and restaurants.

Marina degli Esteni
☏ 0533 328 428
Email portomarinaestensi@libero.it

GORO
44°47′·5N 12°16′·5E (Fl.G.3s7M)
BA 1467 It 222

☆ Entrance Fl(2)10s9M Fl.R.3s6M/Fl.R.5s6M

VHF Ch 16.

Data 120 berths. Max LOA 13m. Depths 1·5–3m.

Facilities Water. 220V. Fuel arranged. Slipway.

☏ 0533 995 037

PORTO BARRICATA
44°50′·6N 12°28′·0E

☆ Entrance F.G/F.R

VHF Ch 09. CB Ch 16.

Navigation Situated in Fiume Po delle Tolle.

Data 300 berths. 20 visitors' berths. Max LOA 15m. Depths 1–2·5m. Charge band 5.

Facilities Water. 220V. Fuel quay. 5/25-ton cranes.

✆ 0426 89125
www.portobarricata.it

Fiume Po di Levante

ALBARELLA

45°03'·7N 12°21'·5E (Fl.R.4s4M)
BA 1467 It 222

☆ Main light LFl.6s15M. Beacon Iso.Y.2s6M. Harbour entrance Fl(3)9s4M/Fl.R.3s2M/Fl.G.3s.2M. Marina entrance Fl.R.4s4M/Fl.G.4s4M

VHF Ch 09.

Navigation Situated just inside the entrance to Po di Levante.

Berths Stern or bows-to.

Shelter Good shelter.

Data 455 berths. 45 visitors' berths. Max LOA 25m. Depths 2·5–4m. Charge band 5.

Facilities Water. 220V. Fuel quay. 50-ton travel-hoist. Most yacht repairs. Restaurant.

Marina Albarella
✆ 0426 332 262 / 600
Email porto@albarella.it
www.albarella.it

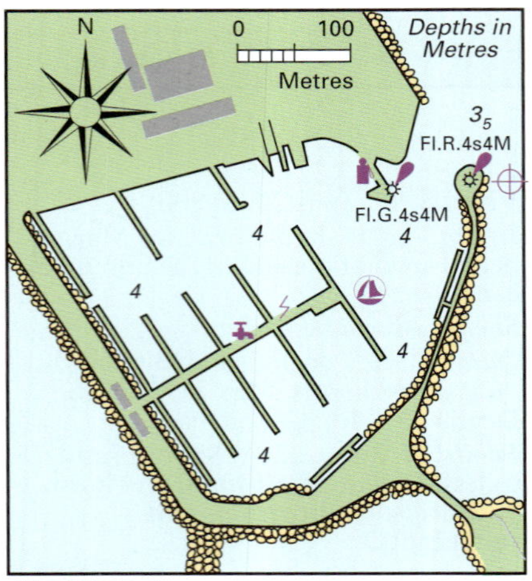

ALBARELLA

MARINA PORTO DI LEVANTE

45°03'·0N 12°22'·0E

☆ Fl(2)G.10s8M / Fl(2)R.10s8M

Data 550 berths. Max LOA 18m. Depths 3–3·5m. Fuel. Charge band 4.

✆ 0426 666 047
www.marinadiportolevante.it

MARINA NUOVA DI PORTO LEVANTE

45°02'·7N 12°19'·2E

VHF Ch 09. CB Ch 31.

Navigation Situated in Po di Levante.

Berth Where directed. Laid moorings to posts or buoys.

Data 200 berths. 10 visitors' berths. Max LOA 10m. Depths 2–4m.

AMP COSTA DEL PICENO

Covers the coastal waters around Grottammare, 10M S of Porto San Giorgio.

Restrictions on navigation and anchoring apply.

www.parcomarinopiceno.it

AMP TORRE DEL CERRANO

Surrounds the coastal waters off the tower of the same name. Navigation and anchoring restrictions apply.

Email info@torredelcerrano.it
www.torredelcerrano.it

Fiume Adige

PORTO FOSSONE

45°08'.5N 12°18'.4E

VHF Ch 09 CB 20

Data 150 berths. 15 visitors' berths. Max LOA 10m. Depths <1–2m.

✆ 0426 68 281
www.portofossone.com

Fiume Brenta

BRENTA BOAT SERVICE

45°11'N 12°16'·5E

VHF CB Ch 09

Data 50 berths. 10 visitors' berths. Max LOA 16m. Depths 1–3·5m.

Facilities Water. 220V. Fuel quay. 20-ton slipway. 15-ton crane. Yacht repairs.

✆ 041 490 033
Email brentaservice@libero.it

MARINA DI BRONDOLO

45°10'·95N 12°16'·4E

☆ Fiume Brenta entrance breakwater head Fl(2)R.6s4m3M

VHF Ch 16, 09.

Navigation Situated in Fiume Brenta.

Data 200 berths. Max LOA 15m. Depths 2–3·5m. Charge band 3.

Facilities Water. 220V. Fuel quay. 10-ton crane.

Marina di Brondolo ✆ 041 490 950
Email info@marinadibrondolo.it
www.marinadibrondolo.it

MARINA DEL SOLE

45°10'·5N 12°16'·1E

Access under bridge limited to motorboats.

Data 260 berths. Max LOA 28m. Depths 2–4m.

✆ 041 490 896
www.marinadelsole.it

Approaches to Venice

There are three entrances to the Laguna Veneta from seaward. These are Porto di Lido to the N, Porto di Malamocco in the centre, and Porto di Chioggia to the S. Porto di Lido is the closest to Venice, and is used by ships proceeding to the industrial port of Porto Marghera. A deep channel also leads to Porto Marghera from Porto di Malamocco. Due to the low-lying nature of the coast, its lack of identifying features, and the shallow depths which stretch almost a mile offshore, it can be difficult to locate these entrances.

Note Work started in 2003 on the Mose project to build flood protection barriers at the three entrances to Venice lagoon. Seventy gates, normally submerged, will be pumped full of air in order to 'float' them into position during exceptionally high tides. Work continues as Phase 2 of the project gets underway, and is due for completion in 2016. At Lido a new island and marina is also under construction as part of the development.

Laguna Veneta

Navigating within Laguna Veneta

Within the Laguna Veneta are many well marked channels which link the three sea entrances, the ports, Venice, and the various settlements together. The larger channels have sufficient depths to allow the passage of ships, whilst many of the smaller canals have less than a metre depth at low water (but almost 2m at high tide). The main channels are lit.

CHIOGGIA

45°14'·0N 12°18'·9E
BA 1473 It 221

☆ Main light LFl(2)10s15M/Fl(2)R.7s8M. N breakwater Fl.G.3s8M. S breakwater Fl(2)R.10s11m8M. Channel beacons Fl.R.3s5M(× 2) and Fl.G.3s5M. N breakwater Fl(2)G.7s8M/Fl.R.5s4M/Fl.G.5s4M. Canal F.R.3M

VHF Ch 16 (0700–1900). Pilot Ch 15, 16 (0700–1900). Darsena Mosella Ch 08. Sporting Club Ch 16.

Navigation Darsena Mosella lies on the E near the beach. Sporting Club is in a basin on the W side of Darsena Interna.

Berths Head for Darsena Mosella or the marina at the Sporting Club.

Darsena Mosella

Data 150 berths. 10 visitors' berths. Max LOA 16m. Depths 2–2·5m. Charge band 4.

Facilities Water. 220V. Showers and toilets. 40-ton crane.

Darsena Le Saline

Data 300 berths. Max LOA 21m. Depths 2–2·5m. Charge band 4.

Facilities Water. 220V. Showers and toilets. 35-ton crane. Fuel 150m away.

Remarks Provisions and restaurants in the town.

Darsena Mosella
✆ 041 404 993
Email info@darsenamosella.it

Sporting Club Marina di Chioggia
✆ 041 400 530
Email info@darsenalesaline.com

MARINA DI CHIOGGIA

45°13'·5N 12°11'·5E

Navigation Lies on Canale Novissimo, SW of Chioggia.

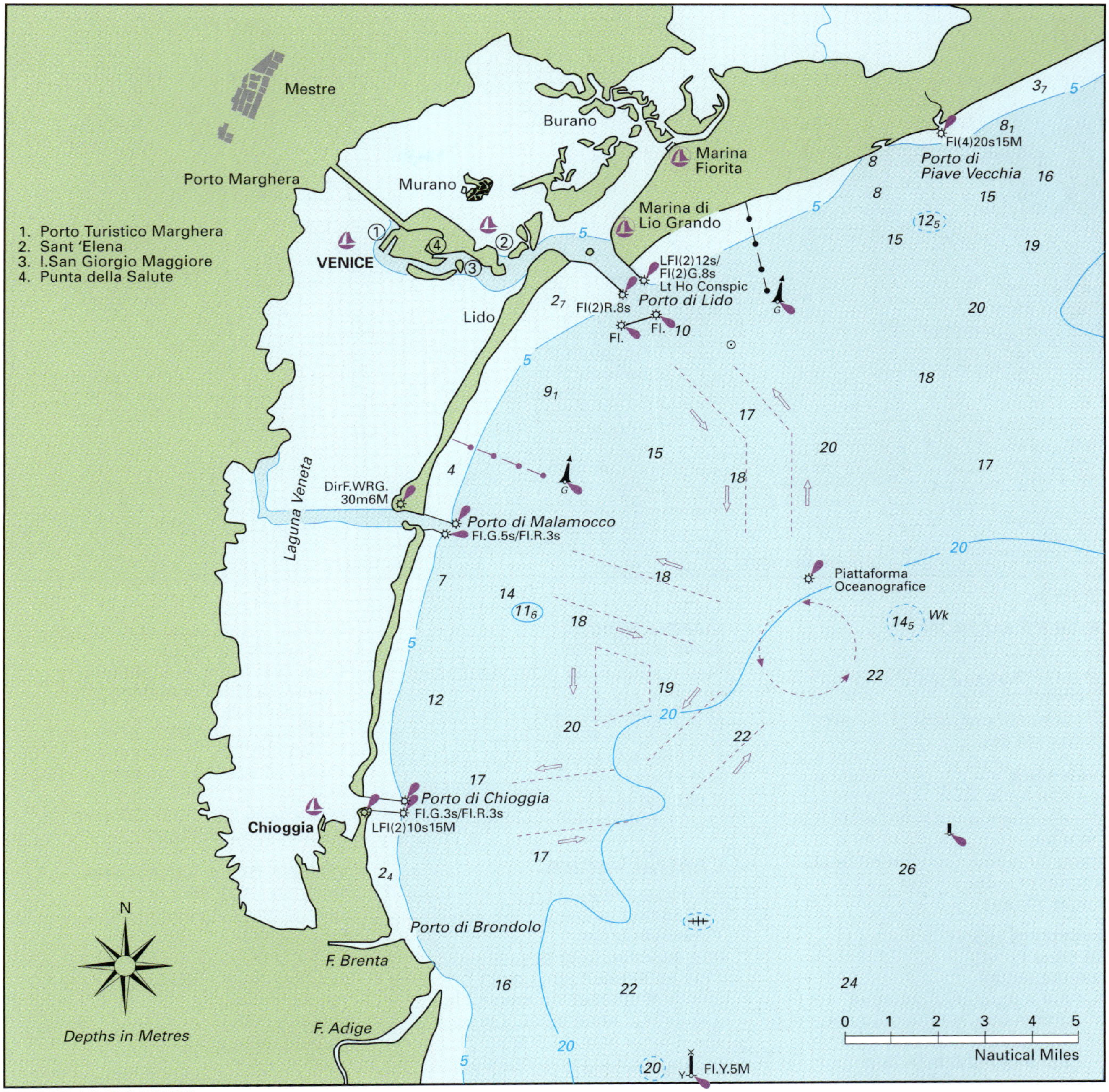

VENICE APPROACHES

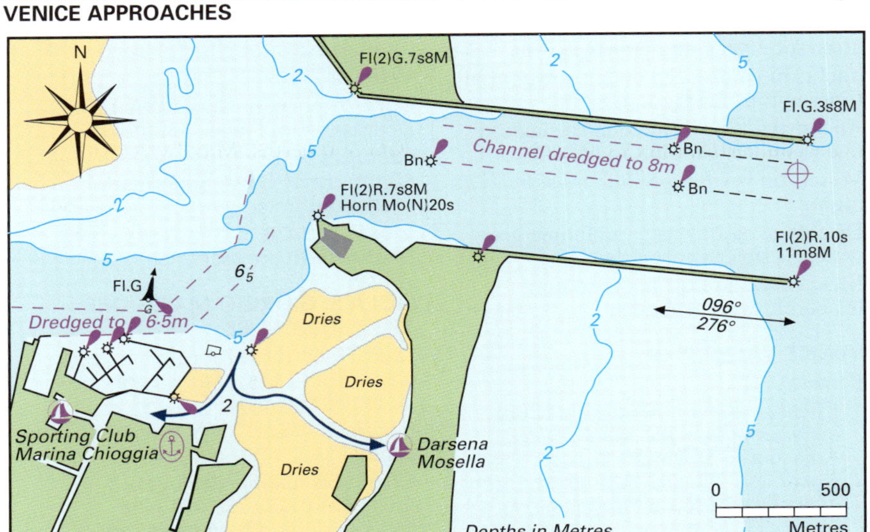

PORTO DI CHIOGGIA

Data 250 berths. Max LOA 15m. Depths 1–2·5m. Charge band 3.

Porto Turistico
☏ 041 499 722
Email portmar@tin.it

PORTO DI MALAMOCCO

45°19'·9N 12°20'·5E
BA 1449 It 223

☆ Fairway beacon Fl.10s7m6M. Outer port hand beacon Fl(2)R.6s6m6M. Inner beacons: port Fl(2)R.6s5M, starboard Fl(2)G.10s5M. Entrance Fl.G.5s18m8M / Fl.R.3s16m8M / Fl.R.6s6M. Training wall Fl(3)R.10s11m5M. Near Rocchetta lighthouse Fl(3)G.10s6m7M Horn Mo(D)45s. Rocchetta lighthouse Fl(3)12s25m16M

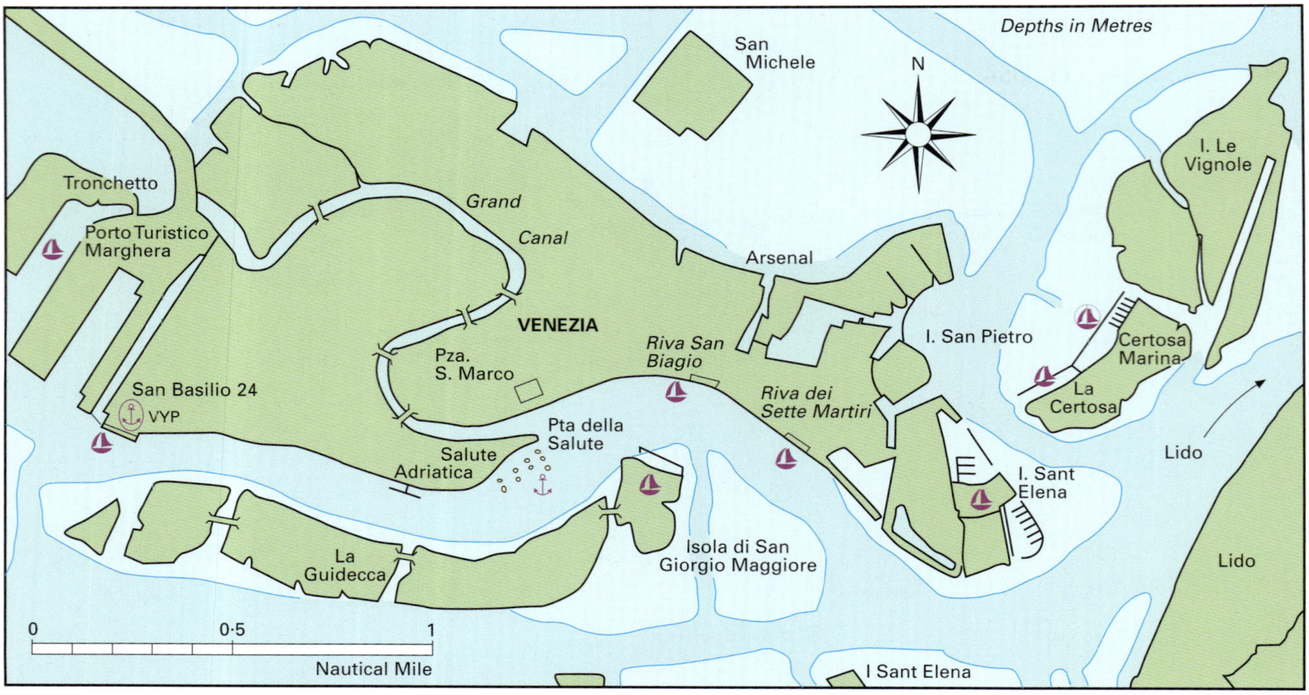

VENICE

MARINA ALBERONI

In Porto di Malamocco.

Data 70 berths. Max LOA 14m. Depths 1·5–2·5m.

Facilities Water. 220V. Fuel quay.

☏ 041 731 046

VEN MAR

45°23′N 12°20′·8E

Navigation Situated on Canale delle Scoasse.

Data 70 berths. Six visitors' berths. Depths 1·5–2m.

☏ 041 770 603

PORTO DI LIDO

45°25′N 12°26′E

BA 1442 It 226

☆ Outer fairway beacon (RW) Fl.10s7m6M. Inner fairway beacon S Fl.R.3s6m5M and (G) Fl.G.2s6m5M. Entrance Fl(2)R.8s14m8M/ LFl(2)12s26m15M Racon/ Fl(2)G.8s14m7M Horn Mo(N)45s. Leading light 300°40′. Front Fl.3s13m11M and Fl.G.4s3m5M. Rear Murano Oc.6s37m17M and DirOc.6s21M

VHF Ch 11, 16 for Venezia *capitaneria* (24/24). Ch 12, 13 for pilots.

MARINA DI LIO GRANDO

45°25′·2N 12°26′·2E

Navigation The marina lies on the NE side of Porto Lido 1M inside the entrance to Laguna Veneta.

Data 200 berths. 10 visitors' berths. Max LOA 40m. Depths 1·5–5m. Charge band 5.

Facilities Water. 220V. Fuel quay (4m depths).

Marina di Lio Grando

☏ 041 966 044

Email marinadiliogrando@libero.it

MARINA FIORITA

45°28′·3N 12°26′·8E

New marina to the N of Marina Lio Grando.

Data 160 berths. Max LOA 60m. Depths 2–6m. Charge band 4/5.

Facilities Water. 220V. WiFi. Showers and toilets.

☏ 041 530 1478

Email info@marinafiorita.com

Central Venice

All traffic and most large yacht berths around the city centre are controlled by Venice Yacht Pier.

Port Procedure and Regulations

Contact Venice Yacht Pier (VYP) or an agency in advance to reserve a berth.

Agents and pilots are mandatory for vessels over 24m.

On approaching Lido breakwaters contact VYP or your agency.

If your berth is at Salute mooring assistance is recommended.

Yachts must proceed under power at all times within the lagoon.

Anchoring is prohibited in the lagoon due to underwater electricity cables.

Vessels on berths at Salute must be lit at night.

Discharge of all waste (including grey water) is strictly forbidden.

Most canals are off-limits to non-residents, even by tender.

VENICE YACHT PIER

Berths

1. *Riva San Biagio* Alongside 120m quay. Depths 9·5m. Water. WiFi. Adjacent to St Mark's Square.
2. *Riva Dei 7 Martiri* Alongside 150m quay. Depths 9·5m. Water. WiFi.
3. *Salute* Mooring posts. c.10 berths. Depths 5·5m. Water.
4. *San Basilio 24* Alongside 120m quay. Depths 9·5m. Water. Fuel. Provisioning.
5. *Adriatica* Alongside 110m quay. Depths 8·5m. Water.

Shelter Most berths are open to wash from passing traffic.

Venice Yacht Pier ☏ 041 533 4177

www.veniceyachtpier.com

VENEZIA ISOLA SANT'ELENA

45°25′·8N 12°21′·9E

Diporto Velico Veneziano. Venice small boat harbour.

VHF Ch 16.

Data 230 berths. Max LOA 15m. Depths 1·5–4m.

☏ 041 523 1927

Email diveven@tin.it

MARINA SANT'ELENA

New marina under development at Cantieri Navali Celli.

VHF Ch 77.

Data 200 berths. Max LOA 120m. Depths 2–4m. Finger pontoons.

Facilities Water. 220V. WC. Showers. 80-ton travel-hoist. Supermarket. Bars and restaurants.

☏ 041 530 1478

Email info@marinasantelena.com

ISOLA S. GIORGIO MAGGIORE

45°25′·8N 12°20′·8E

Data 70 berths. Mooring between posts. Max LOA 15m. Depths 1·5–2·5m. Charge band 5.

Facilities Water. 220V. Fuel quay (4m depths).

Circolo Compagnia della Vela

☏ 041 521 0723 / 339 478 7488

Email segreteria@compvela.com

www.compvela.com

Isola La Certosa

VENTO DI VENEZIA (CERTOSA MARINA)

VHF Ch 72.

Data 300 berths. Max LOA 40m. Min depth 3.5m.

Facilities Water. 220V. WiFi. Showers and toilets. 25-ton crane. Vaporetto to San Marco.

Remarks Les Glénans centre.

✆ 041 520 8588
www.ventodivenezia.it

VENEZIA TRONCHETTO (PORTO TURISTICO MARGHERA)

45°26'·4N 12°18'·5E

VHF Ch 11, 16.

Data 60 berths. 20 visitors' berths. Max LOA 20m. Depths 1–6m.

✆ 041 520 7555

DARSENA FUSINA

Data 150 berths. Max LOA 14m. Depths 1·5–2·5m. Charge band 3.

✆ 041 547 0055
Email info@campingfusina.com

SCAFO CLUB

45°27'·8N 12°17'·0E

VHF Ch 74.

Data 340 berths. Max LOA 13m. Depths 1·5–2·5m.

✆ 041 531 0625

DARSENA DEC

VHF Ch 09.

Data 400 berths. Max LOA 15m. Depths 2–3m.

✆ 041 531 0161

MARINA DI CAMPALTO

45°28'·6N 12°18'·2E

VHF CB Ch 70

Data 200 berths. 10 visitors' berths. Max LOA 16m. Depths 2–2·5m.

✆ 041 903 264 / 900 806
www.cantieremarchi.com

Fiume Sile

PORTO DI PIAVE VECCHIA (LIDO DI JESOLO)

45°28'·6N 12°35'·1E
BA 1483 It 222

☆ Main light Piave Vecchia Fl(4)24s45m18M. Entrance Fl(2)G.6s4M/Fl(2)R.6s4M

Navigation The basins are reached via Fiume Sile. There are five marinas here: Marina del Faro, Marina del Cavallino, Darsena Faro, Porto Turistico di Jesolo and Nautica dal Vi.

Data

Marina del Faro 100 berths. Five visitors' berths. Max LOA 15m. Depths 2–2·5m. Charge band 5.

✆ 041 968 076
Email marinafaro@tin.it

Marina del Cavallino 320 berths. 30 visitors' berths. Max LOA 25m. Depths 3m. Charge band 5/6.

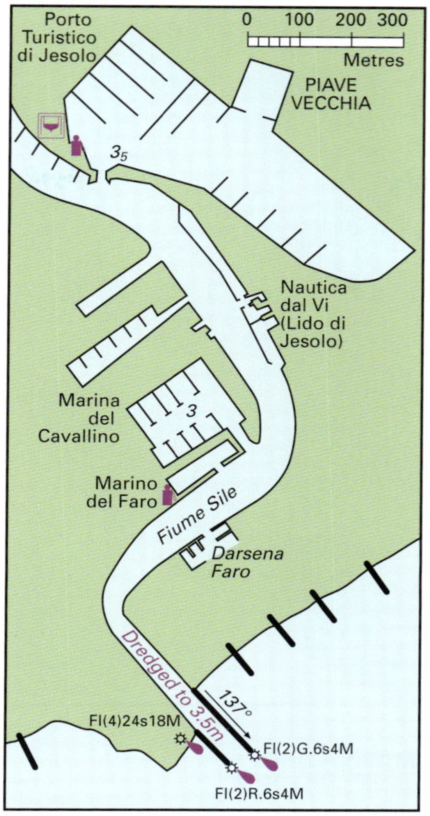

JESOLO – FIUME SILE

✆ 041 968 045
www.marinadelcavallino.com

Porto Turistico di Jesolo 490 berths. 40 visitors' berths. Max LOA 30m. Depths 3·5m. 100-ton travel-hoist. Charge band 5/6.

✆ 0421 971 488
Email info@portoturistico.it

Nautica Dal VI 400 berths. Max LOA 16m. Depths 2–4m.

✆ 0421 971 486
Email dalvi@dalvi.it
www.dalvi.it

MARINA DI PORTEGRANDI

Navigation 8M up canals / Fiume Sile.

Data 300 berths. 30 visitors' berths. Max LOA 25m. Depths 3m. Charge band 4.

✆ 0422 823 263
Email info@marinadeportegrandi.it

Fiume Piave

PORTO DI CORTELLAZZO

45°31'·7N 12°43'·8E (Entrance to Fiume Piave)

☆ W mole Fl.R.3s4M. E mole Fl.G.3s4M

NAUTICA BOAT SERVICE

Access via Fiume Piave.

Data 50 berths. Max LOA 25m. Depths 2–5m. Charge band 5.

✆ 0421 980 016
Email info@nauticaboatservice.com

MARINA DI CORTELLAZZO

☆ Breakwater 2F.R(vert)7m3M

Navigation Upriver from NBS

Data 320 berths. 30 visitors' berths. Max LOA 30m. Depths 2–4m. Charge band 5.

✆ 0421 980 356 / 7
Email marinadicortellazzo@libero.it
www.marinadicortellazzo.it

MARICLEA CLUB (ERACLEA)

45°32'·4N 12°45'·5E

☆ Entrance Fl.R.2s4M/Fl.G.2s4M

VHF Ch 16, 09. CB Ch 30.

Data 180 berths. 30 visitors' berths. Max LOA 13m. Depths 2–3m. Charge band 5.

Facilities Water. 220V. Showers and toilets. Fuel 300m. 12-ton crane.

✆ 0421 662 61
Email info@mariclea.com
www.mariclea.com

PORTO SANTA MARGHERITA (MARINA 4)

45°35'·2N 12°52'·0E
BA 1449 It 38

☆ Caorle Fl(2)6s12m14M. Entrance Fl.G.3s5M/Fl.R.3s5M

VHF Ch 09.

Navigation Marina lies in Fiume Livenza.

Berths Stern or bows-to where directed. Posts.

Shelter Good shelter.

Data 420 berths. 40 visitors' berths. Max LOA 22m. Depths 2–3·5m. Charge band 5.

Facilities Water. 220V. Fuel quay. 30-ton crane. 40-ton slipway. Most yacht repairs. Provisions and restaurants.

✆ 0421 260 469
Email info@marina4.com

DARSENA DELL'OROLOGIO

45°35'·8N 12°52'·3E

☆ F.G/F.R

VHF Ch 09, 16.

Navigation Marina lies in Canale dell'Orologio on the N side of Fiume Livenza.

Data 450 berths. 40 visitors' berths. Max LOA 25m. Depths 3–3·5m. Charge band 5/6.

✆ 0421 842 07
Email info@darsenaorologio.com
www.darsenaorologio.com

PORTO BASELEGHE

45°38'·1N 12°59'·8E

☆ Entrance Fl.G.4s4M/Fl.R.4s4M

VHF Ch 09, 16.

Data 400 berths. 20 visitors' berths. Max LOA 27m. Depths 1–3·5m. Fuel. Charge band 5.

✆ 0431 436 86
Email portobaseleghe@bibionemare.com
www.portobaseleghe.com

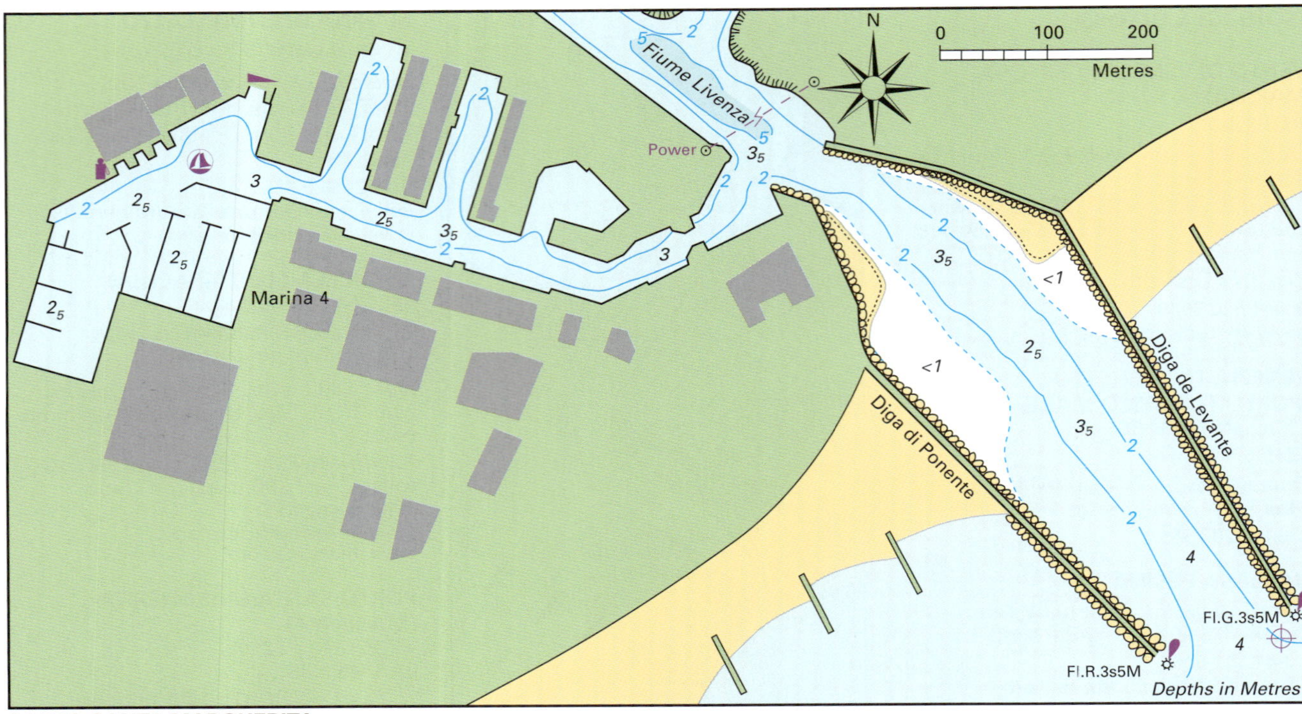

PORTO SANTA MARGHERITA

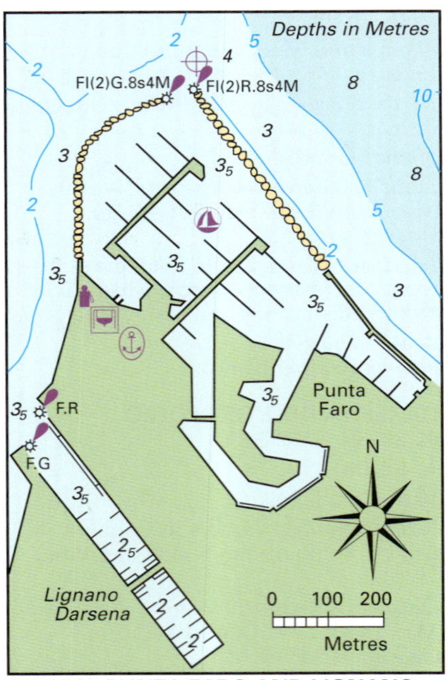

MARINA PUNTA FARO AND LIGNANO DARSENA

Fiume Tagliamento

MARINA PUNTA VERDE

45°39'·3N 13°04'·0E

VHF Ch 09, 16.

Navigation Marina lies 1500m up Fiume Tagliamento.

Data 270 berths. Max LOA 20m. Depths 2·5–3m. Charge band 4.

Facilities Water. 220V. WiFi. Showers and toilets. 10-ton crane.

☎ 0431 427 131

Email marinapuntaverde@libero.it

www.marinapuntaverde.it

MARINA UNO

45°39'·0N 13°05'·7E

☆ Marina Uno entrance Fl.G.3s4M/Fl.R.3s4M. Pier head 2F.R(vert)3M

VHF Ch 10

Navigation Marina lies 500m up Fiume Tagliamento.

Data 420 berths. 50 visitors' berths. Max LOA 20m. Depths 1·5–3m.

Facilities Water. 220V. Showers and toilets. Fuel quay. 200-ton crane. Charge band 4.

☎ 0431 428 677

Email info@marina-uno.com

Laguna di Marano

LIGNANO SABBIADORO

45°41'·8N 13°09'·6E

☆ Punta Tagliamento Fl(3)10s22m15M. Fairway buoy Fl.2s6M. Marina Uno basin entrance E side Fl.G.3s4M. W side Fl.R.3s4M. Pier head 2F.R(vert)3M. Entrance E side Fl.G.5s4M

MARINA PUNTA FARO (TERRAMARE)

45°42'·2N 13°08'·8E

☆ Entrance Fl(2)R.8s4M/Fl(2)G.8s4M. Pier head Fl.R.2s8M

VHF Ch 09.

Berths Where directed. Laid moorings.

Shelter Good shelter.

Data 1,500 berths. 50 visitors' berths. Max LOA 35m. Depths 3–3·5m. Charge band 6.

Facilities Water. 220V. Fuel quay. Showers and toilets. 50-ton travel-hoist. 35-ton crane. Most yacht repairs. Provisions and restaurants.

☎ 0431 703 15

Email info@marinapuntafaro.it

www.marinapuntafaro.it

LIGNANO DARSENA

45°41'·6N 13°08'·6E

VHF Ch 16, 09. CB Ch 01, 02, 03.

Data 400 berths. Max LOA 16m. Depths 2–3m. Fuel quay.

☎ 0431 718 21

MARINA APRILIA MARITTIMA

Vast holiday complex in the SW corner of Laguna di Marana. There are three marinas:

MARINA PUNTA GABBIANI

45°41'·75N 13°04'·4E

☆ F.R

VHF Ch 09, 16.

Navigation Access via buoyed channel, 3m from lagoon. Depths min. 2m.

Data 295 berths. Max LOA 25m. Depths 3m.

Facilities 60-ton travel-hoist. Chandlers. Laundry. ATM.

☎ 0431 528 000

Email info@puntagabbiani.it

www.puntagabbiani.it

DARSENA CENTRALE

45°41'·8N 13°04'·3E

BA 1471 It 39

VHF Ch 09, 16.

Berths Where directed.

Shelter Good shelter.

Data 650 berths. Max LOA 20m. Depths 2–3m.

Facilities Water. 220V. Fuel quay. 60-ton travel-hoist. Most yacht repairs. Provisions and restaurants.

Aprilia Marittima ☎ 0431 531 23

www.cvam.it

MARINA CAPO NORD

45°41'·7N 13°04'·0E

VHF Ch 09.

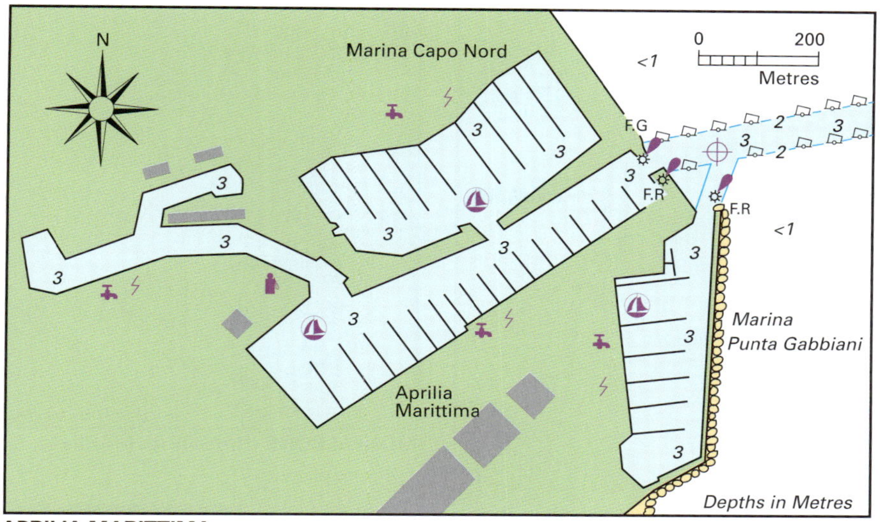

APRILIA MARITTIMA

Data 650 berths. 60 visitors' berths. Max LOA 20m. Depths 3–3·5m.
☏ 0431 53503
www.marinacaponord.it

MARINA STELLA
Navigation Access via Porto Lignano
Data 85 berths. Max LOA 30m. Depths 2·5–5m. 45-ton travel-lift.
☏ 0431 589 288
www.marinastella.it

PORTOMARAN
45°45'·8N 13°10'·1E
Navigation Access via Porto Lignano
Data 400 berths. Max LOA 17m. Depths 1·5–2m.
☏ 0431 67409
Email portomaran@portomaran.com
www.portomaran.com

PORTO BUSO
45°41'·4N 13°15'·3E
☆ Entrance Fl.R.5s5m4M/Fl.G.5s5m4M. Root of E breakwater Fl(2)G.7s8m4M. Beacon Fl.WG.2s5m4/2M

CAPAN
45°45'·3N 13°14'·5E
Navigation Access via Porto Buso
Data 130 berths. Max LOA 20m. Depths 2–3·5m. 45-ton travel-lift.
☏ 0431 620 461

MARINA SANT'ANDREA
45°45'·6N 13°14'·9E
Navigation Access via Fiume Corno (depths 6m).
Data 250 berths. Max LOA 30m. Depths 4–5m.
Facilities Water. 220V. Shower and toilets. Laundry. 80/100-ton travel-hoist. Dry storage.
Remarks Sister marina Izola Marina, Slovenia.
☏ 0431 622 162
Email info@marinasantandrea.it
www.marinasantandrea.it

MARINA SAN GIORGIO
45°10'·2N 13°47'·7E
☆ Entrance F.G/F.R
VHF Ch 14.
Navigation Access via Fiume Corno (depths 6m).
Data 300 berths. 86 visitors' berths. Max LOA 25m. Depths 3·5–4·5m. Charge band 5.
Facilities Water. 220V. Showers and toilets. Fuel quay. 100-ton travel-hoist.
☏ 0431 658 52
Email cantierimarina@cantierimarina.it
www.cantierimarina.it

Grado
45°40'·0N 13°21'·4E
BA 1471 It 235
☆ Banco Mula di Muggia S cardinal Q(6)+LFl.15s6M. Grado fairway beacon Fl.10s5m6M. Grado entrance Fl.WR.3s7/5M Horn Mo(K)45s. Channel junction Fl(2)R.6s4M. Canale di Grado S side Fl.G.3s3M. W mole

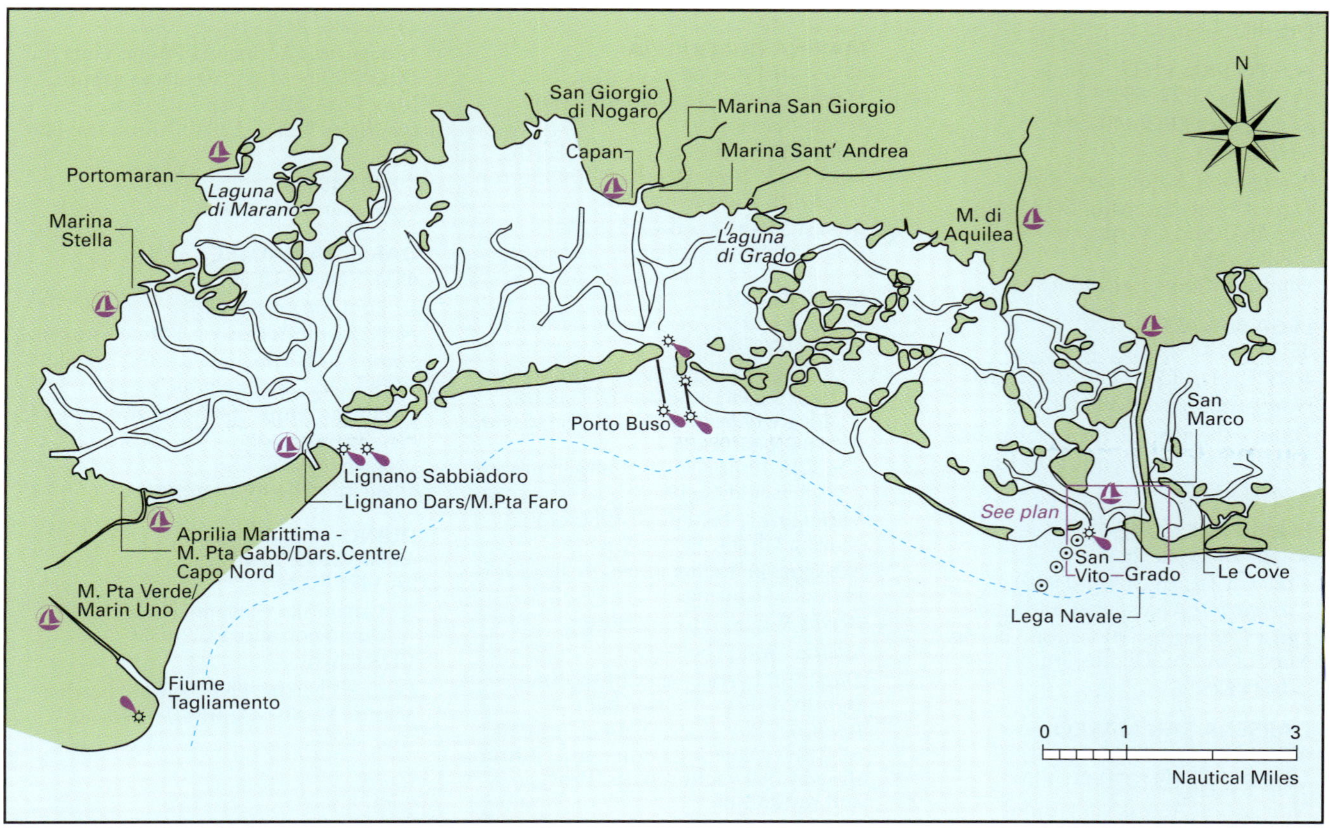

LAGUNA DI MARANO AND LAGUNA DI GRADO

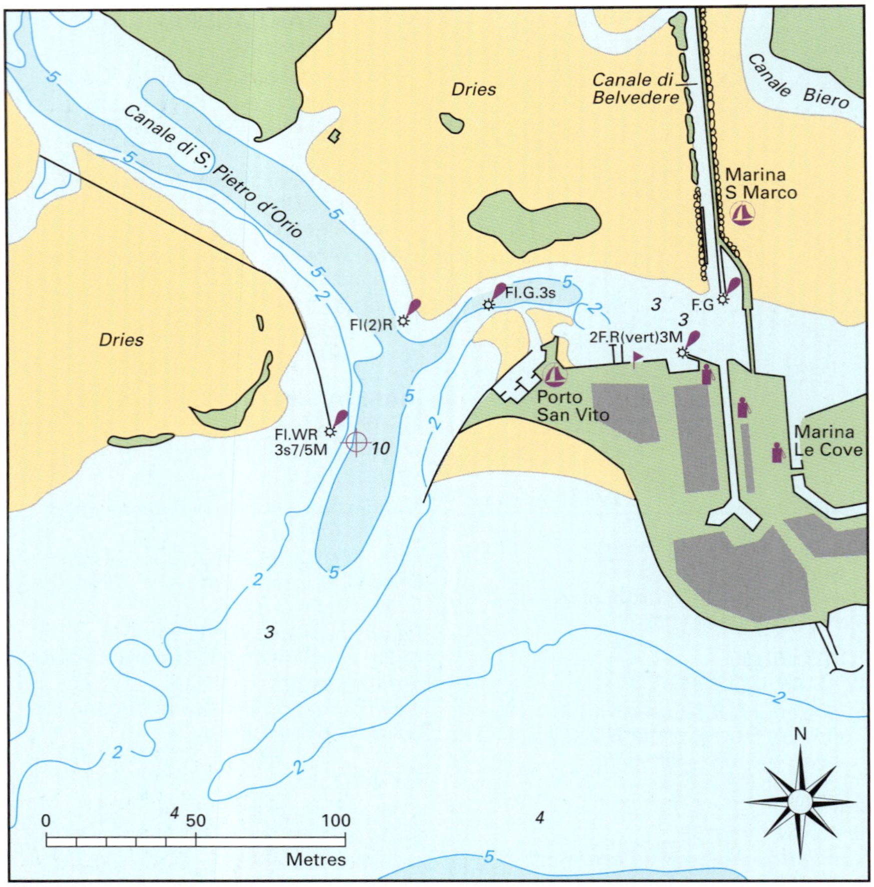

GRADO

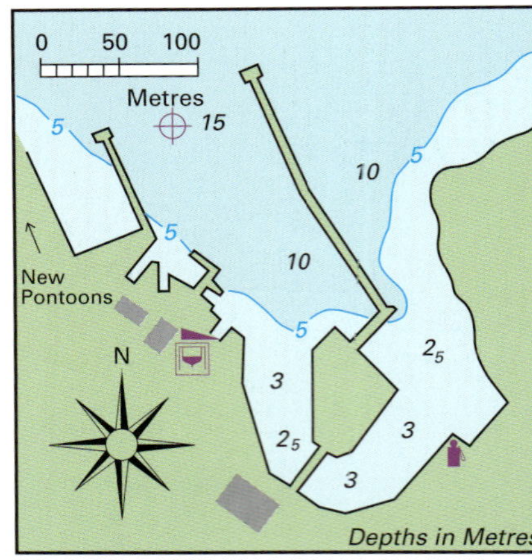

MONFALCONE (HANNIBAL MARINA)

2F.R(vert)3M. Canale di Belvedere F.G.3M. Water intake Fl.Y.3s4M

VHF Ch 16, 15 (0700–2100).

Data 1,700 berths. Max LOA 25m. Depths 1–4m.

PORTO SAN VITO

45°40'·9N 13°22'·65E

☆ Entrance F.R.3M/F.G.3M

VHF Ch 16.

Navigation Access via Grado.

Data 170 berths. Max LOA 20m. Depths 3·5m. Charge band 4.

☎ 0431 83600

Email info@portosanvito.it

LEGA NAVALE

45°41'·0N 13°22'·8E

VHF Ch 16, 15.

Navigation Access via Grado.

Data 50 berths. 12 visitors' berths. Max LOA 15m. Depths <1–4m.

☎ 0431 817 06

MARINA LE COVE

45°40'·9N 13°24'·2E

VHF Ch 16, 15 (0700–1900).

Navigation Access via Grado.

Data 150 berths. 10 visitors' berths. Max LOA 7m. Depths 3m.

☎ 0431 825 96

DARSENA SAN MARCO

45°41'·07N 13°23'·1E

VHF Ch 16, 69 (0700–1900).

Navigation Access via Grado.

Data 80 berths. Five visitors' berths. Max LOA 20m. Depths 1–3m.

☎ 0431 815 48

www.darsenasanmarco.it

MARINA DI AQUILEIA

45°45'·1N 13°21'·3E

Navigation Access via Grado and Fiume Natissa.

Data 300 berths. 20 visitors' berths. Max LOA 20m. Depths 2–4m. 50-ton travel-lift. Charge band 3.

☎ 0431 910 41 *Fax* 0431 919 241

Email info@marinadiaquileia.com

MONFALCONE

45°46'·4N 13°33'·5E (Hannibal Marina)

BA 1471 It 236

☆ Fairway beacon (RW) Fl.10s6M. Outer beacons Fl(2)R.6s4M/Fl(2)G.6s4M. Centre beacons Fl.R.5s4M/Fl.G.5s4M. Inner beacons Fl(2)R.10s4M/Fl(2)G.10s4M. Entrance Fl.R.5s3M/Fl.G.10s3M

VHF Ch 11, 16. Pilot 14. Hannibal Marina Ch 09, 16.

Navigation Yachts normally head for Hannibal Marina.

Berths Where directed. Posts.

Shelter Good shelter.

Data 330 berths. Max LOA 40m. Depths 3–13m. Charge band 5.

Facilities Water. 220V. Fuel. 300/50-ton travel-hoists. 25-ton crane. 200-ton slipway. All yacht repairs. Provisions and restaurants.

Remarks HW Trieste +30 minutes.

Hannibal Marina

☎ 0481 411 541

Email info@marinahannibal.com

COSULICH

45°47'·3N 13°32'·0E

Data Max LOA 12m. Depths 1–5m.

Fiume Timavo

VILLAGIO DEL PESCATORE S. MARCO

45°46'·55N 13°35'·3E

Navigation On E bank of entrance to Fiume Timavo. Access via buoyed channel.

Data 1050 berths. Max LOA 12–15m. Depths 1·5–3m.

☎ 040 209 855

MARINA LEPANTO

45°46'·7N 13°35'·1E

Navigation Access via Fiume Timavo.

Data 200 berths. 250 places ashore. Max LOA 22m. Depths 3–6m.

Facilities Water. 220V. 70-ton travel lift.

☎ 0481 45555

www.marinalepanto.it

DARSENA NAUTEC

45°47'·7N 13°33'·5E

☆ Pontoon ends F.G/F.R

Navigation Access via Fiume Timavo.

Data 200 berths. 10 visitors' berths. Max LOA 25m. Depths 3–6m

Facilities Water. 220V. 60-ton travel-lift. 20-ton crane.

☎ 0481 790 416

Email info@nautecmare.com

DUINO

45°46'·3N 13°36'·0E

BA 1471 It 234

☆ Canale San Giovanni Fl(2)G.10s4M. Duino entrance F.G.7m3M

VHF Ch 16.

Data 50 berths. Five visitors' berths. Max LOA 8m. Depths 0·5–4m.

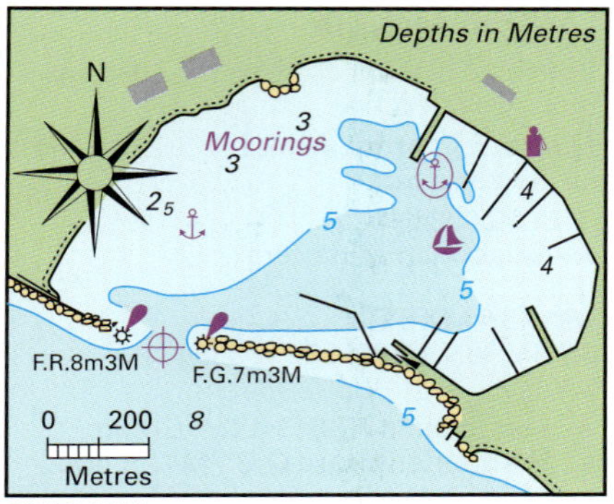

SISTIANA

SISTIANA
45°46'·1N 13°37'·7E
BA 1471 It 239

☆ Entrance F.R.8m3M / F.G.7m3M

VHF Ch 16

Berths Stern or bows-to.

Shelter *Bora* blows strongly here. *Sirocco* causes a surge.

Data 600 berths. 10 visitors' berths. Max LOA 10m. Depths 3–5m.

CANOVELLA DI ZOPPOLI
45°45'N 13°39'E

Data Max LOA 7m.

AURISINIA
45°44'·4N 13°40'·1E

☆ Entrance F.G.3M

Data Max LOA 8m.

SANTA CROCE DI TRIESTE
45°43'·5N 13°41'·4E

☆ F.G.7m3M

VHF Ch 16.

Data 100 berths. Max LOA 10m. Depths <1–3m.

GRIGNANO
45°42'·4N 13°42'·7E (F.G.3M)

☆ Grignano pier F.G.6m3M

VHF Ch 16.

Data 300 berths. Max LOA 20m. Depths 3–6m.

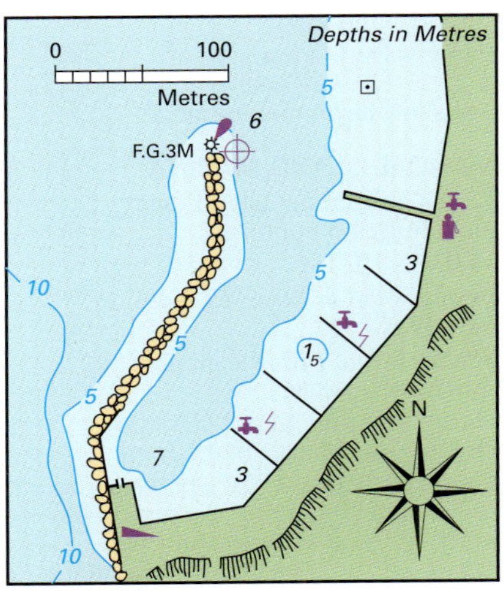

GRIGNANO

BARCOLA
45°40'·9N 13°45'·1E

☆ Faro della Vittoria Fl(2)10s115m22M. Harbour F.G.8m4M

Data 270 berths. Max LOA 12m. Depths 1·5–4m.

TRIESTE
45°38'·5N 13°44'·4E
BA 1473 It 237

☆ Faro della Vittoria Fl(2)10s115m22M N isolated breakwater Fl.G.3s8m8M/ F.G.7m4M/Fl.R.3s7m6M. Baia di Muggia: N isolated breakwater Iso.G.2s6m5M.
S isolated breakwater Fl(3)R.10s9m5M. Porto Lido, mole head, Fl.R.5s7m5M. Mole V N end F.G.7m4M S end F.R.7m4M.

VHF Ch 11, 16 (0700–1900) for port authorities. Pilot Ch 10, 14, 16. Marina Ch 77.

Navigation Yachts should head for Marina San Giusto.

Berths Stern or bows-to at YC. Alongside outer piers.

Shelter Good shelter although NW winds could make some berths uncomfortable at the entrance.

Data Marina San Giusto 225 berths. Max LOA 25m. Charge band 5/6.

Facilities Water. 220V. Showers and toilets. WiFi. Fuel quay. 25-ton travel-hoist. Provisions and restaurants.

Remarks Large commercial port. Free port. Airport nearby.

Marina San Giusto ✆ 040 303 036
Email info@marinasangiusto.it
www.marinasangiusto.it

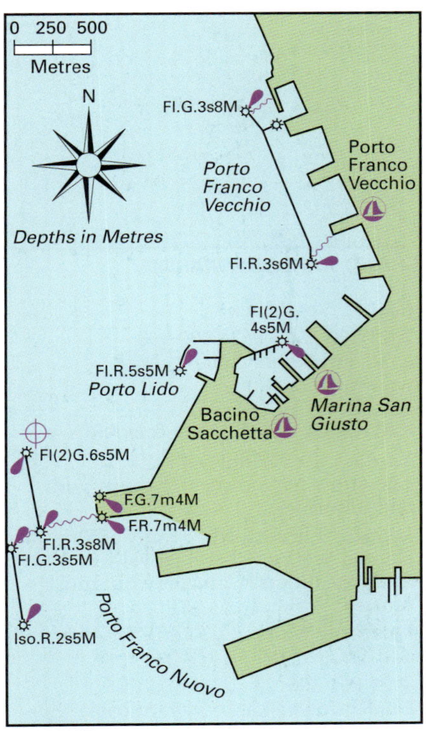

TRIESTE

RISERVA NATURALE MARINA DI MIRAMARE NEL GOLFO DI TRIESTE
Extends around the cape immediately S of Grignano. The harbour lies within Zone B.
Zone A covers a 200m wide channel approximately 1km along the coast from Grignano harbour past Castello Miramare. Navigation, diving and fishing prohibited.
www.parks.it

MUGGIA
45°36'·4N 13°46'·0E
BA 1473 It 238

☆ E mole head F.R.7m3M.
W mole head F.G.7m3M

VHF Ch 11, 16 (0700–1900).

Berths Alongside.

Shelter Good shelter.

Data 300 berths. Max LOA 12m. Depths 2·5–8m.

Facilities Provisions and restaurants.

Remarks Port of entry.

PORTO SAN ROCCO MARINA
45°36'·6N 13°45'·15E

☆ Entrance Fl.G.5s5M/Fl.R.5s5M.

VHF Ch 74.

Berth Where directed. Finger pontoons or laid moorings tailed to the quay.

Data 550 berths. Max LOA 60m. Depths 4–10m. Charge band 5.

Facilities Water. 220V. WiFi. Fuel quay. Shower and toilet blocks. 160-ton travel-hoist. 100/60-ton hydraulic trailers. 22-ton crane. Repairs. Restaurant/bar. Provisions.

Porto San Rocco
✆ 040 273 090
Email infoport1@portosanrocco.it
www.portosanrocco.it

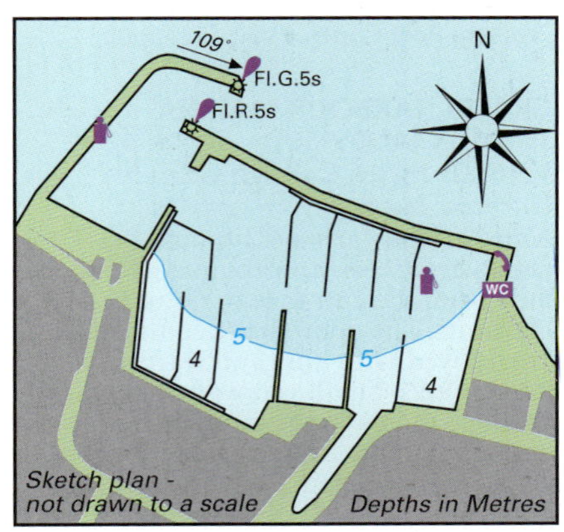

PORTO SAN ROCCO

SAN BARTOLOMEO
45°35'·8N 13°43'·4E
BA 1473 It 39

☆ Rt Grosa (Rt Debeli) Q(9)15s8m8M. Punta Sottile W cardinal buoy Fl(9)15s. Harbour Fl.R.3s6m3M. NW quay F.RG.3M.

Small crowded harbour. Military area to the NE (entry prohibited).

10.5 Malta

TIME ZONE UT+1 ☎ IDD +356

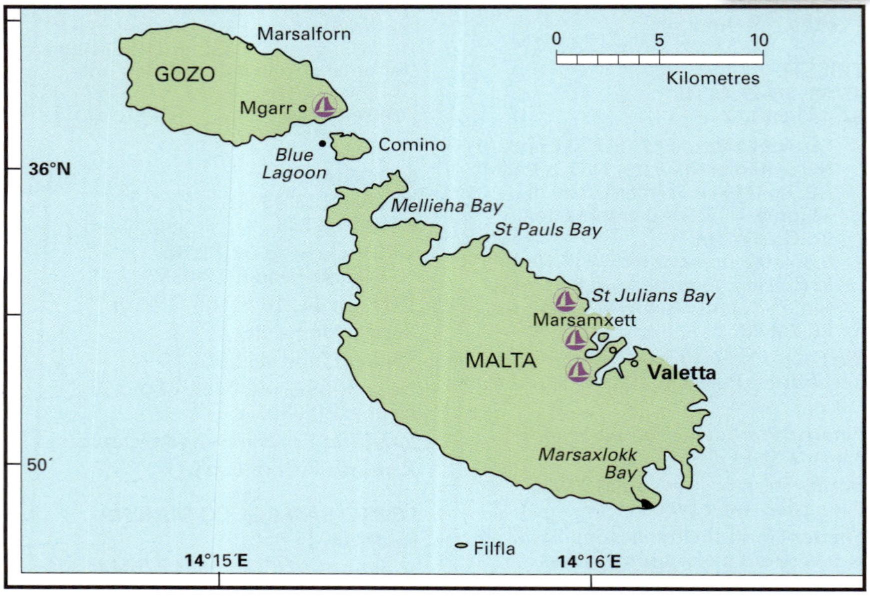

All yachts should call Valetta Port Control when entering Maltese waters, 10M off, and again when entering the port. Customs offices in Grand Harbour and Mgarr (24hr).

Those with EU/EEA passports arriving from an EU/Schengen country, with no pets or declarations, may proceed directly to a marina. Check in advance to agree that you may berth before going to Valetta to complete the paperwork.

All others, and everyone who arrives from outside the EU must complete full customs and immigration clearance in Valetta or Mgarr before proceeding to a marina berth.

Valetta Port Control VHF Ch 16, 09, 12.

GRAND HARBOUR MARINA

35°53′·6N 14°30′·95E

VHF Ch 13, 16 Callsign *Grand Harbour Marina.*

Navigation Marina is situated in Dockyard Creek approximately one mile from the entrance to Grand Harbour. The approaches to the marina are buoyed with port and starboard-hand buoys. Small yellow buoys mark small channels to the inner moorings and slips on the Senglea side of the creek. Care needed at night of small craft moorings close to the channel.

Berth Where directed. Finger pontoons at most berths. Larger yachts use moorings tailed to the pontoons.

Data 285 berths. 50 visitors' berths. Max LOA 100m. Charge band 4.

Facilities Water. 220/380V. WC and showers. Pump-out facilities. Repairs and technical services can be arranged.

Remarks Marina staff can arrange customs and immigration clearance for EU passport holders. Very helpful and attentive staff.

Note Further berths are being developed at the head of the creek at the old No.1 dock.

☎ 21 800 700 *Fax* 21 800 900
Email info@ghm.com.mt
www.ghm.com.mt

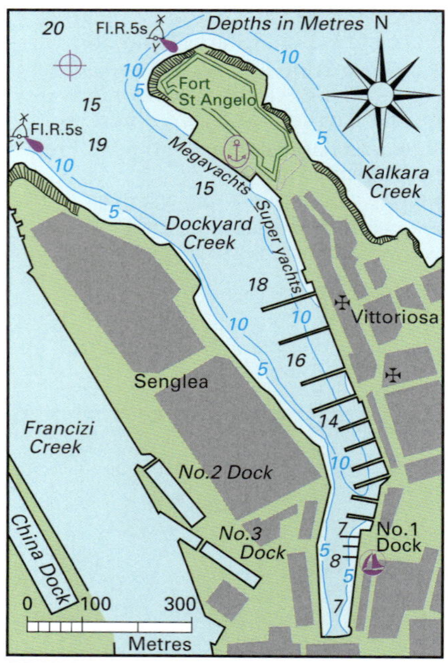

GRAND HARBOUR MARINA

KALKARA BOATYARD & MARINA

Yard on the NE side of Kalkara Creek. They now have three pontoons with laid moorings.

Data 120 berths. Max LOA c.20m. Depths 5-10m. 42-ton travel-lift. 50-ton boat-mover. Can carry out most repairs.

Facilities Water. 220/380V. Showers and WC.

☎ 21 661 306
Email info@kalkaraboatyard.com
kalkaramarina@gmail.com

LAGUNA MARINA

Boutique marina close to the customs quay in Valetta.

Data c.25 berths. Max LAO 15m. Max air height c.5m.

☎ 21 23 0980
www.lagunamarina.com

MARSAMXETT

35°54′·30N 14°30′·98E WGS84
BA 177

☆ Fort St Elmo Fl(3)15s19M. Grand Harbour entrance Q.G.7M/Q.R.6M. Msida Jetty head Q.G.5m2M

VHF Ch 09, 12, 16 (*Valetta Port Control*).

Navigation With strong northerlies and particularly northeasterlies there is a heavy confused swell at the entrance. With a gale from the NE (*gregale*) great care is needed in the entrance.

TA'XBIEX QUAY

VHF Ch 13

Berths Stern-to the quay. Some laid moorings.

Shelter Considerable surge with *gregale* (NE), sometimes dangerous.

Data 200 berths. Max LOA 60m. Depths <1–8m. Charge band 3.

Facilities Water. 220V. Showers and toilets. Provisions and restaurants.

Remarks Part of same group as Msida Creek Marina.

RMYC ☎ 21 33 7049 or 7933 7049 (24/24)
Email info @creekdevelopments.com
www.marinamalta.com

ROYAL MALTA YACHT CLUB

Marina berths on two pontoons off Ta'Xbiex quay near Msida Creek (May-Oct).

Data 65 berths. Max LOA 20m. Charge band 5.

Facilities Water. 220V. Club house facilities available to guests.

☎ 21 33 3109
Email info@rmyc.org

SANDY YACHT MARINA

Currently offers moorings off Ta'Xbiex quay with water-taxi ashore.

Pontoon berths planned in the future. Charge band 2.

Sandy Yacht Marina
☎ 21 331515 / 21 339908
Email info@sym-malta.com

MANOEL ISLAND MARINA

Berths on Manoel Island Quay, including two pontoons.

VHF Ch 10, 16.

Berths Stern or bows-to. Laid moorings.

Shelter Surge with the *gregale*, sometimes dangerous.

Data 70 berths. Max LOA 80m. Depths 5m. Charge band 3.

Facilities Water. 220V. Showers and toilets. Fuel by tanker. 25-ton travel-hoist. 500-ton slipway. All yacht repairs. Provisions and restaurants.

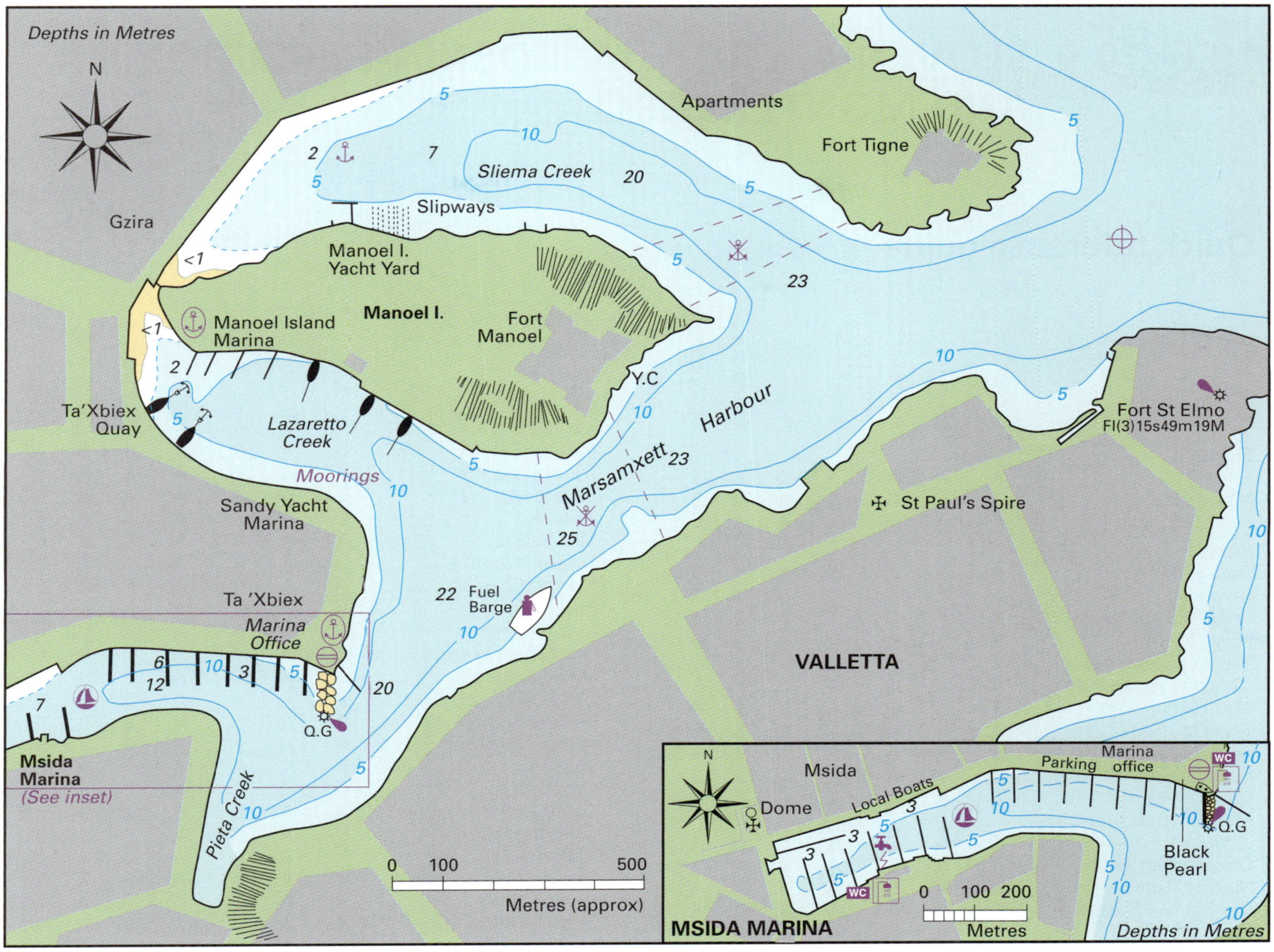

MARSAMXETT

Note Manoel Island marina and Manoel Island Yacht Yard are now under the control of the Manoel Island Harbour Management.

Remarks There are plans to build a protective breakwater across Lazaretto Creek, but no dates are available.

Manoel Island Marina ☏ 21 342 618

Manoel Island Yacht Yard, Gzira
☏ 21 343 900
Email miyy@global.net.mt

MSIDA CREEK MARINA

VHF Ch 13

Berths Stern or bows-to. Laid moorings tailed to the pontoons. Visitors berth alongside the quay near the Black Pearl.

Shelter Good shelter.

Data 700 berths. Depths 3–10m. Max LOA 22m. Charge band 2/3.

Facilities Water. 220V. Fuel by tanker. Provisions and restaurants.

Remarks Crowded in summer. The old Yachting Centre building is now the RMYC clubhouse.

Note The customs and immigration office at Msida closed in October 2008.

Msida Marina
☏ 21 337 049 or 7933 7049
Email info@creekdevelopments.com

Yacht Services

✉ Ripard Larvan and Ripard Ltd, 156 Coast Road, Ta'Xbiex seafront, Gzira, Malta ☏ 21 335 591
Email rlrchandlery@digigate.net

✉ D'Agata Marine, 152 Ta'Xbiex Wharf, Gzira, Malta ☏ 341 533
Email dagata@digigate.net

Marine Services ☏ 440 089 (B'Kara), ☏ 440 089 (Qormi), ☏ 373 822 / 379 019, ☏ 379 040 (St Giljan)

S&D Yachts ☏ 320 577 / 331 515
Email info@sdyachts.com

Cassar Enterprises
☏ 21 225 764 / 21 247 351

Bezzina Ship Repair Yard
☏ 21 624 613 / 21 234 411

Medcomms ☏ 21 335 521
Email medcomms@digigate.net

PORTO MASO

35°55'·25N 14°29'·7E

VHF Ch 13, 16 (call sign *Portomaso)*

Navigation New marina in St Julians Bay. The Hilton Hotel behind the marina is conspicuous.

Berth Where directed. Laid moorings.

Shelter Good all-round shelter. Strong NE winds are reported to cause a surge and entry in such conditions could be dangerous.

Data 150 berths. Visitors' berths. Max LOA 16m. Depths 3–3·5m. Charge band 5.

Facilities Water. 220V. Showers and toilets. Bars and restaurants. Provisions.

☏ 21 387 803 or 7949 5768
Email info@portomasomarina.com
www.portomasomarina.com

MGARR MARINA (GOZO) (MMA)

36°01'·41N 14°17'·93E WGS84

VHF Ch 13, 16.

Navigation Care needed of ferries entering and leaving the harbour.

Berths Where directed in the NE corner of the harbour.

Shelter With E–SE winds a substantial swell enters the harbour and makes most berths uncomfortable, and even dangerous.

Data 200 berths. 30 visitors' berths. Max LOA c.15m. Depths 1·5–5m. Charge band 3.

Facilities Water. 220V. Showers and toilets. Provisions, bars and restaurants.

Remarks All formalities may be completed here all year round, 24/24.

Mgarr Marina ☏ 2099 2501
or 9924 2501 (24/24)
Email info@gozomarina.net

10.6–10.9 SLOVENIA, CROATIA, BOSNIA-HERZEGOVINA AND MONTENEGRO

Quick reference guide *For Key see page 139*

	Shelter	Mooring	Fuel	Water	Provisions	Eating out	Charge band
Slovenia							
Koper	A	A	A	A	O	B	5
Marina Izola	A	A	A	A	A	A	5
Portorož	A	A	A	A	A	A	
Croatia							
Umag Marina	A	A	A	A	A	A	5/6
Novigrad	A	A	A	A	A	A	5
Crvar-Porat Marina	B	A	O	A	O	B	4/5
Poreč Marina	B	AC	A	A	A	A	5
Plava Laguna and Marina Parentium	A	A	O	A	C	B	5
Marina Funtana	B	A	A	A	B	B	4
Vrsar Marina	A	A	A	A	B	B	5
Rovinj Marina	B	A	A	A	A	A	5/6
Pula Marina	B	A	A	A	A	A	5
Marina Veruda	A	A	A	A	C	B	5
Medulin and Marina Pomer	C	A	O	A	C	C	5
Opatija Marina	A	A	B	A	A	A	5/6
Marina Admiral	A	A	B	A	A	A	4/5
Marina Mali Losinj	C	A	A	A	B	B	5
Marina Lošinj	B	A	B	A	B	B	5/6
Cres Marina	A	A	A	A	A	A	5/6
Marina Brodogradiliste Cres	C	B	B	A	A	A	
Krk	B	A	A	A	B	B	
Malinska	B	A	B	A	B	B	
Punat Marina	B	A	O	A	A	A	5
Rab Marina	B	A	A	A	A	A	5
Supetarska Draga	B	A	O	A	C	C	5
Marina Simuni	B	A	O	A	C	C	5
Luka Silba	B	A	O	A	B	B	3
Siroka (Ist)	C	A	O	A	B	B	3/4
Sali (Dugi Otok)	B	A	O	A	B	B	3
Marina Piskera	B	A	O	A	C	C	5/6
Marina Zut	A	A	A	A	C	C	5/6
Iz Marina	B	A	O	A	B	B	5
Marina Preko	B	A	B	A	C	B	5
Olive Island Marina	B	A	O	A	C	C	5
Marina Borik	A	A	A	A	A	A	5/6
Zadar Marina	A	A	O	A	B	B	5
Marina Dalmacija	A	A	A	A	C	C	5
Kornati Marina	A	A	A	A	A	A	5
Jezera Marina	A	A	A	A	C	B	5/6
Hramina Marina	A	A	A	A	B	A	5/6

	Shelter	Mooring	Fuel	Water	Provisions	Eating out	Charge band
Marina Betina	B	A	B	A	B	B	4/5
Tribunj Marina	A	A	O	A	B	C	6
Vodice Marina	C	A	A	A	A	A	5/6
Šibenik	O	AB	A	A	A	A	4
Mandalina	A	A	A	A	B	B	6
Skradin Marina	O	A	B	A	A	A	5/6
Marina Solaris	A	A	O	A	C	C	5
Primosten	B	A	B	A	B	B	
Marina Kremik	A	A	A	A	C	C	4/5
Rogoznica-Marina Frapa	A	A	A	A	B	B	6
Marina Agana	A	A	O	A	B	B	4/5
Trogir Marina	B	A	A	A	C	C	6
Marina Kastela	B	A	O	A	B	B	5
Spinut Marina	A	A	B	A	B	B	5
Split Marina	B	A	A	A	A	A	6
Labud YC	C	A	B	A	B	B	
Zenta Marina	A	A	B	A	B	B	4/5
Lav Marina	B	A	B	A	B	B	5
Makarska	B	A	A	A	B	B	
Marina Baska Voda	B	A	B	A	B	B	5
Tucepi Marina	A	A	O	A	A	A	4/5
Marina Milna	B	A	A	A	B	B	5/6
Marina Vlaska	B	A	B	A	C	C	4/5
Hvar	B	A	A	A	A	A	
Palmižana Marina	B	A	O	A	A	A	6
Starigrad	B	A	O	A	B	B	4/5
Marina Vrboska	A	A	A	A	A	A	5/6
Viska Luka	C	A	O	A	C	C	5
Komiza	C	A	O	A	B	B	4/5
Korčula Marina	B	A	A	A	A	A	6
Marina Lumbarda	B	A	O	A	A	A	4/5
Vela Luka	C	A	A	A	B	B	4/5
Luka Velji Lago Marina	A	A	B	A	C	C	4/5
Podgora	C	A	O	A	B	B	
Ploce	B	A	A	A	A	A	
Orebić	B	A	B	A	A	A	
Ston	A	B	O	O	A	B	
Dubrovnik Marina	A	A	A	A	A	A	6
Gruž Marina	A	A	O	A	A	A	5
Montenegro							
Kotor	B	B	B	A	A	A	
Tivat	A	A	A	A	A	A	5
Budva	A	A	B	A	B	B	5/6
Bar	A	A	A	A	A	A	4

Adriatic Breakdown Services

SEAHELP

Bases in Lignano and San Giorgio (Italy), Portorož (Slovenia), Rovinj, Punat, Mali Lošinj, Zadar, Vodice and Orebič (Croatia).

✆ 060 200 000
www.sea-help.com

EMERGENSEA

Based in Croatia.

✆ +385 98 306 609
www.emergensea.net

10.6 Slovenia

TIME ZONE UT+1 ✆ IDD +386

KOPER (CAPODISTRIA)

45°33'·1N 13°43'·8E (marina entrance)
BA 1471, Imray M24

☆ Entrance Fl(2)R.10s4M/Fl.G.5s4M. Fl.R.5s3M/Fl(2)G.5s3M. N mole head Fl(2)R.10s4M. Ldg Lts 088° Front Q.Y.10M, Rear Q.Y.10M.

VHF Ch 12, 16. Ch 17, 16 for Koper Marina.

Navigation Yachts should head for the marina. Yachts clearing in should go alongside the pier in the old harbour, clear of the ferry berths.

Berths Where directed.

Note Marina extension in S harbour.

Shelter Good shelter although strong W winds cause a surge.

Data 85 berths. Max LOA 18m. Charge band 5.

Facilities Water. 220V. WiFi. Showers and toilets. Laundry. Fuel quay. 70-ton travel-hoist. 50 places ashore. Limited yacht repairs. Restaurant.

Remarks Port of entry.

Marina Koper ✆ 0566 26100
Email info@marina-koper.si
www.marina-koper.si

MARINA IZOLA

45°32'·2N 13°39'·2E
BA 1471, Imray M24

☆ Rt Petelin Fl.5s6M. N mole Fl.R.3s4M. S pier Fl(2)R.10s4M / Fl(2)G.10s4M.

VHF Ch 17.

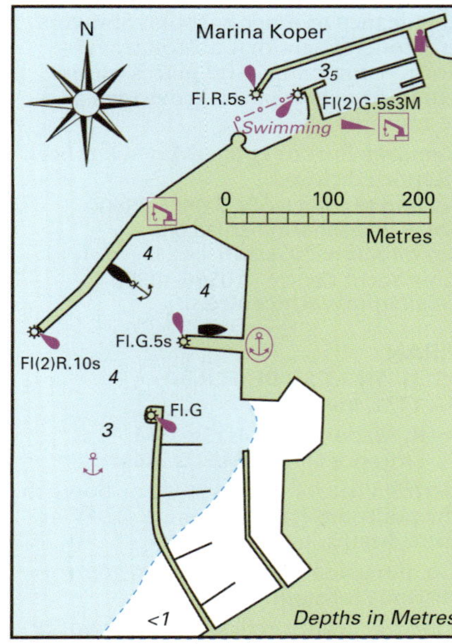

KOPER

Berths Stern or bows-to where directed.

Shelter Good shelter.

Data 700 berths. Visitors' berths. Max LOA 30m. Depths 1·5–3·5m. Charge band 5.

Facilities Water. 220/380V. WiFi. Fuel at entrance to inner harbour. Showers and toilets. Laundry. 50-ton travel-hoist. 4-ton crane. 100 places ashore. Limited yacht repairs. Provisions and restaurants.

Remarks Port of entry (May–October). (Reported closed.)

Porting Marina Izola ✆ 0566 25400
Email info@marinaizola.com
www.marinaizola.com

Izola Yacht Centre ✆ 0566 30990
Email info@yachtcentre.si

PIRAN

45°31'·5N 13°34'·0E (Fl.R.3s)
BA 1471, Imray M24

☆ Rt Madonna Iso.4s13m15M.
Entrance Fl.R.3s4M/Fl.G.3s4M

Berths Visitors' berths stern or bows-to the pontoon. Laid moorings. 220V at some berths. Charge band 4.

Go alongside on the S breakwater for customs formalities.

Remarks Major redevelopment works in progress. Port of Entry.

MARINA BERNADIN

45°30'·8N 13°34'·5E (Entrance)

☆ Fl.R.5s3M/Fl.R.3s3M/Fl.G.3s3M / Fl.G.2s6M

Small marina with associated hotel complex NW of Portorož Marina.

Depths 1·5–2m.

Email marine@h-bernadin.si

PORTOROŽ

45°30'·3N 13°35'·8E (Fl(2)R.5s4M)
BA 1471, Imray M24

☆ Rt Sv Bernard Fl.R.5s3M.
Pierhead Fl.G.2s6M. Marina entrance beacons Fl.R.4s4M / Fl.G.4s4M.
Marina entrance Fl(2)R.5s4M / Fl(2)G.5s4M

VHF Ch 17.

Navigation Entrance to the marina via a buoyed channel. Go on pier near fuel quay.

Berths Posts.

Data 1,000 berths. 50 visitors' berths. Max LOA 24m. Max draught 3·5m. Depths 1–4·5m.

Facilities Water. 220V. Telephone. Showers and toilets. Self-service laundry. ATM. Fuel quay. 60-ton travel-hoists. 5/7·5-ton cranes. Most yacht repairs. Provisions and restaurants.

Marina Portorož
✆ 0567 61100
Email reception@marinap.si
www.marinap.si

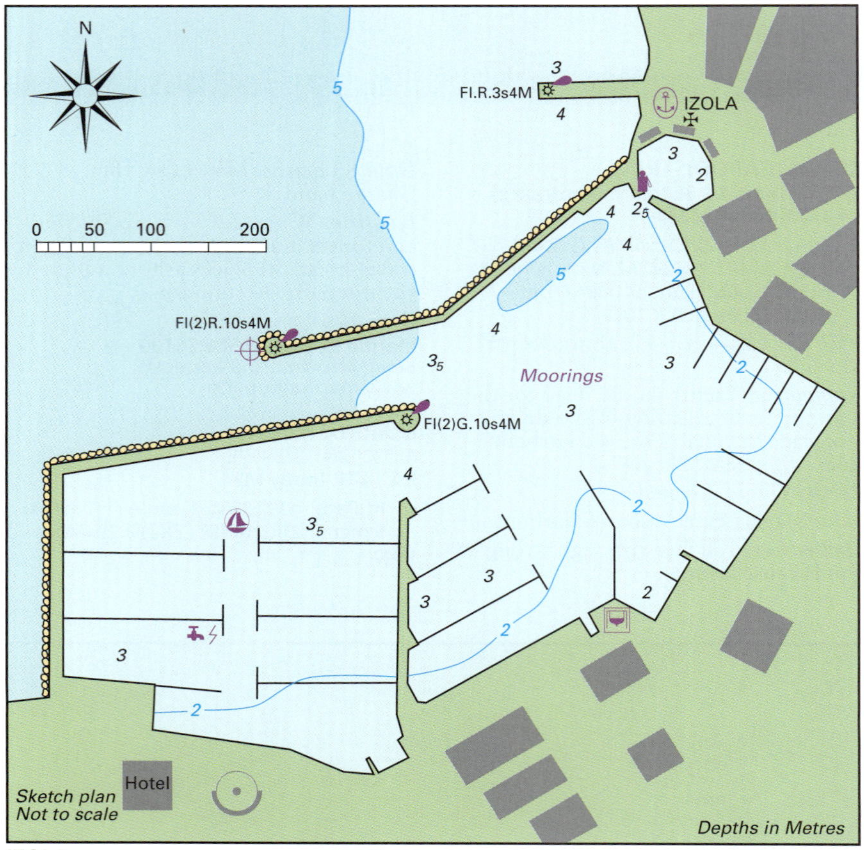

IZOLA

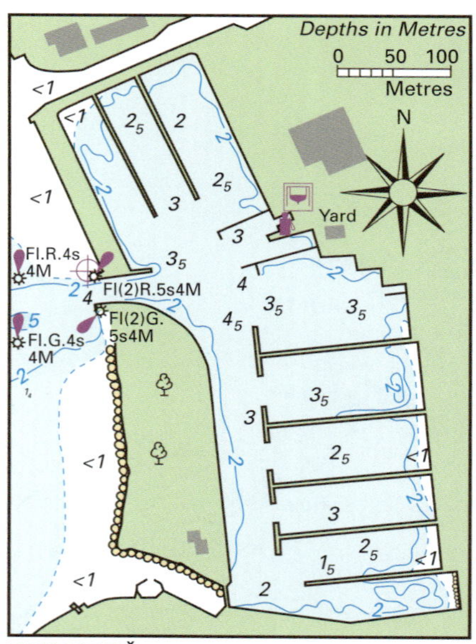

PORTOROŽ

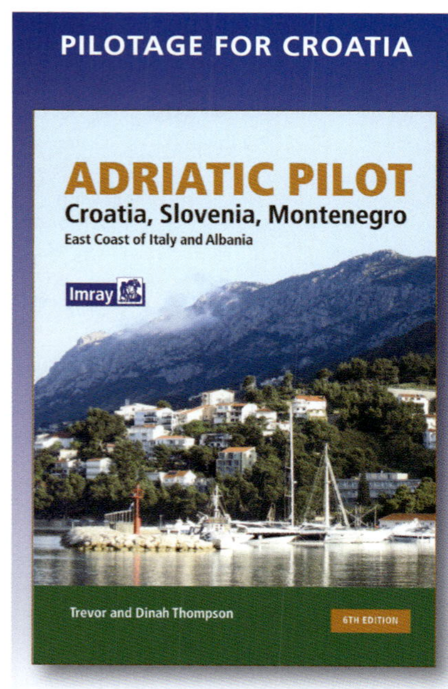

PILOTAGE FOR CROATIA
ADRIATIC PILOT
Croatia, Slovenia, Montenegro
East Coast of Italy and Albania
Imray
Trevor and Dinah Thompson
6TH EDITION

10.7 Croatia

TIME ZONE UT+1 ✆ IDD +385

Tides
Max mean range 0·9m
(decreasing southwards).
Koper 1·00 Dubrovnik 0·35m

Coastguard emergency
✆ 9155
✆ +385 519 155

For a list of authorised mooring buoys (most max LOA 15m)
www.mmpi.hr/default.aspx?id=668
Link to Nautical-anchorages

Mainland coast to Senj

SAVUDRIJA

45°29'·4N 13°30'·2E
Imray M24

☆ Rt Savudrija Fl(3)15s36m30M Siren (2) 42s. Stara Savudrija breakwater head Fl(2)R.5s4M

Small fishing harbour.

UMAG

45°26'·2N 13°30'·9E
BA 201, Imray M24

☆ Pličina Paklena Fl(2)WR.8s8/6M (165°-R-347°). Marina breakwater Q(3)R.5s4M. Mole head Fl.G.5s4M. Inner mole Fl.3s4M

VHF Ch 10, 16 for Port Authority. Ch 17 for ACI Marina Umag (*ACI Umago*).

Navigation Care needed in entrance channel (minimum depths 3m).

Berths Where directed in the marina.

Shelter Good shelter in the marina.

Data 500 berths. Max LOA 40m. Depths 1–4m. Charge band 5/6.

Facilities Water. Showers and toilets. Laundry. Fuel quay. 100-ton travel-hoist. 50 places ashore. Chandler. Some yacht repairs. Provisions and restaurants.

Remarks Port of entry. Mooring buoys available from HM. Charge band 2/3.

ACI Marina Umag ✆ 052 741 066
Email m.umag@aci-club.hr
Umag HM ✆ 052 741 662

LUKA DALJA

☆ F.R.7m1M

NOVIGRAD

45°19'·1N 13°33'·3E (LFl.WRG.5s)
BA 201, Imray M24

☆ Outer breakwater Fl.WRG.5s8-6M (003°-W-025°-R-058°-W-117°-G-003°). Inner breakwater Fl.3s3M. Marina F.G.3M. Sv Anton breakwater head Fl(2)G.5s3M

VHF Ch 17.

Navigation Entrance silts. A small N cardinal buoy marks shoal water at the entrance.

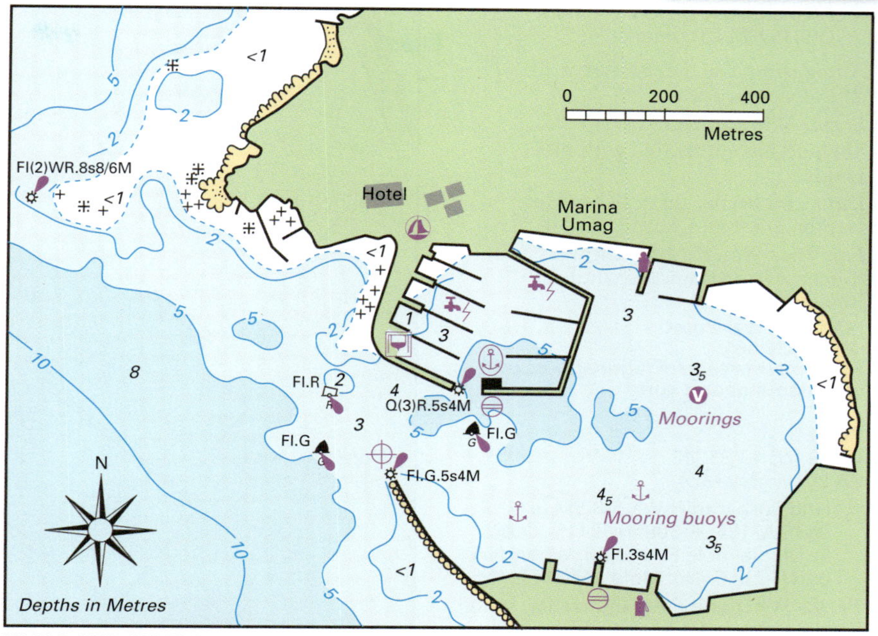

UMAG AND MARINA UMAG

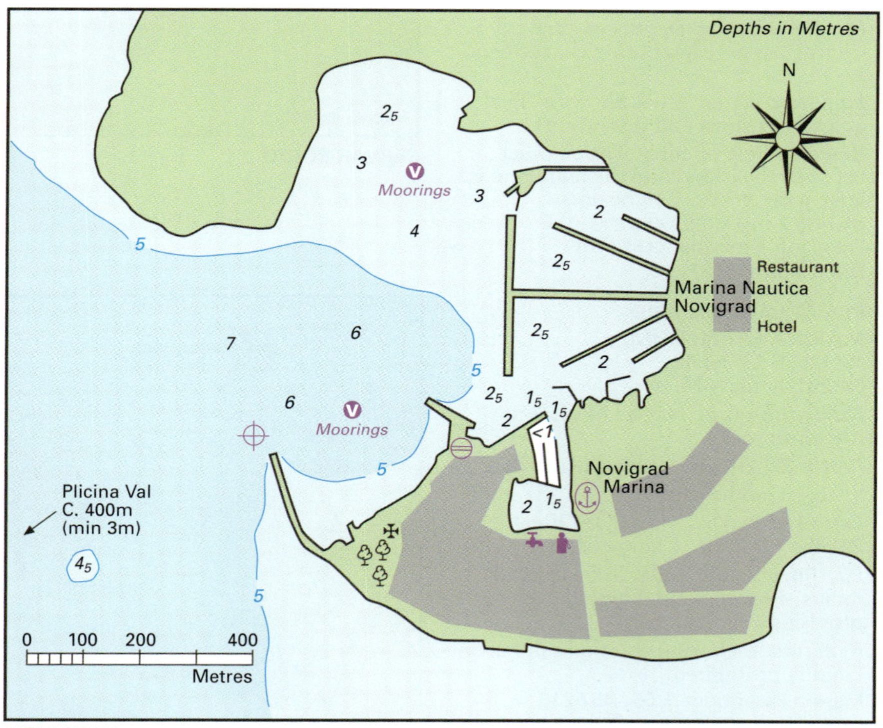

NOVIGRAD

Berths Where directed in the marinas. When checking-in, berth on the customs quay. Mooring buoys in the bay.

Shelter Good shelter in the marina.

Data
Novigrad Marina 365 berths. Max LOA 40m. Depths 1–1·3m. Charge band 4.
Marina Nautica 350 berths. Max LOA 40m. Depths 4m.

Moorings Charge band 2.

Facilities Water. 220/380V. Internet. WiFi. Showers and toilets. Fuel quay. 80-ton travel-hoist. 20-ton crane. Provisions and restaurants.

Remarks Port of entry (April–October)

Marina Laguna Novigrad
✆ 052 757 077 *Fax* 052 757 314
Marina Nautica ✆ 052 600 480
Email marina@nauticahotels.com

LUKA MIRNA

☆ Fl(3)WR.10s9/6M

ČERVAR-PORAT

45°16'·7N 13°36'·2E

☆ Pličina Civran Q.5M ⯁ topmark Q(9)15s5M ⯁ topmark

Navigation The marina lies at the SE end of Červar creek.

Berths Where directed.

Shelter Uncomfortable with NW winds.

Data 260 berths. Max LOA 25m. Depths 1·5–6m. Charge band 4.

Facilities Water. 220V. Showers and toilets. 15-ton crane. Chandler. Restaurant.

Marina Červar-Porat
✆ 052 436 661
Email marina.cervar@lagunaporec.com
www.lagunaporec.com

POREČ

45°13'·7N 13°35'·4E
BA 201, Imray M24

☆ Hrid Barbaran Fl.WR.5s8/5M (011°-R-062°-W-153°-R-308°-W-011°). Otočić Sv Nikola mole Fl.G.5s5M. Wharf NW end Fl(2)R.5s4M. Mole head Fl.2s4M

Berths Where directed in marina. Also berths stern-to on town quay.

Shelter Good shelter in marina, although NW winds send a swell in.

Data 100 berths. Depths <1–3m. Charge band 4. Anchoring charge band 2.

Facilities Water. 220V. Showers. Fuel quay. Provisions and restaurants.

Remarks Port of entry. The channel between the island and the mainland is busy with ferries. Can be noisy.

Marina Poreč ✆ 052 453 213
Email info@marinaporec.com
HM ✆ 052 453117

PLAVA LAGUNA AND MARINA PARENTIUM

45°12'·3N 13°35'·6E
BA 201, Imray M24

Navigation Care needed of off-lying islets and rocks.

Berths Where directed in the marina.

Shelter Good shelter.

Data 185 berths. Max LOA 20m. Depths <1–5·5m. Charge band 5.

Facilities Water. 220V. Showers and toilets. 12-ton crane. Limited provisions. Restaurants.

Remarks Anchoring overnight in Plava Laguna prohibited.

Marina Parentium ✆ 052 452 210
Email marina.parentium@plavalaguna.hr
www.plavalaguna.hr

FUNTANA MARINA

45°11'N 13°36'E

☆ Pierhead F.R.3M

VHF Ch 17. Call before entering.

Navigation Shoal water in N of bay marked with IDM. Shallows in the S approaches are marked with a N cardinal buoy.

Data 180 berths. Max LOA 28m.

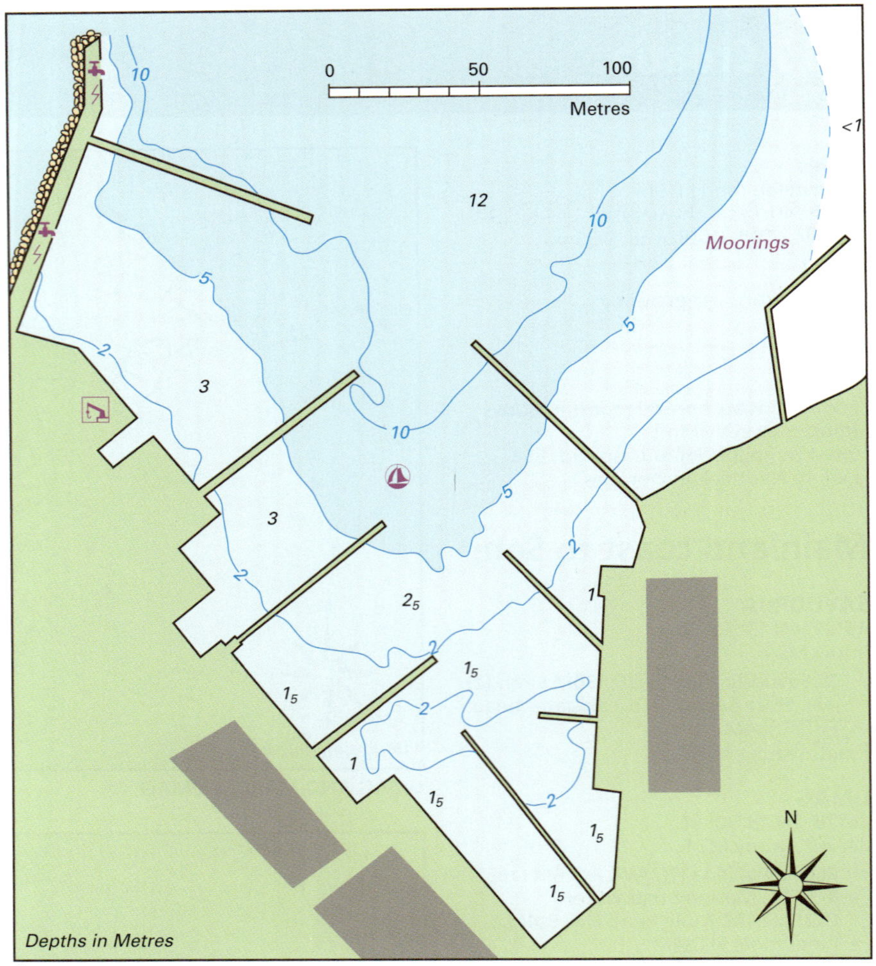

ČERVAR-PORAT

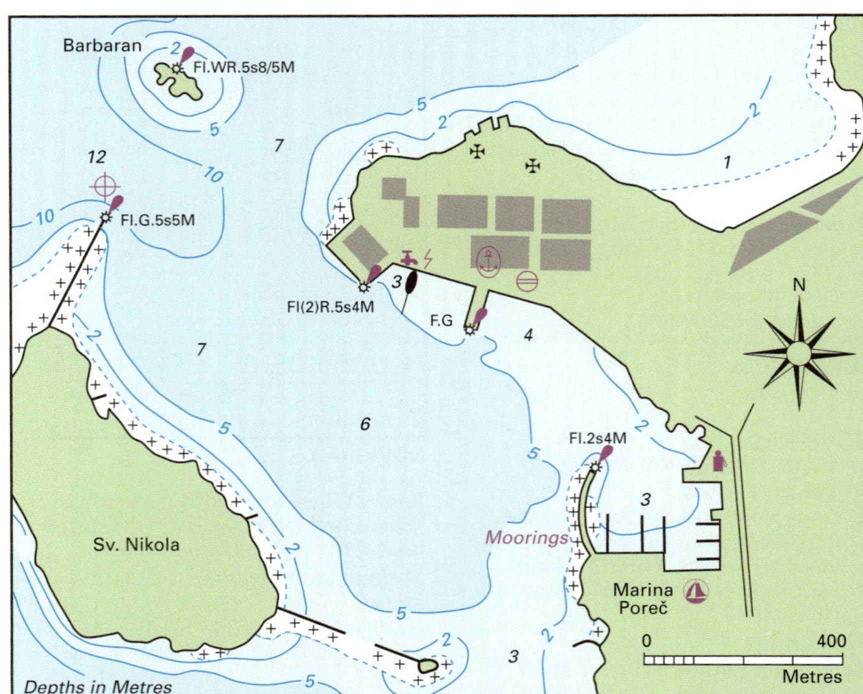

POREČ

Depths 2–4m. Charge band 5.
Facilities Water. 220V. WC. Showers. WiFi. 15-ton crane. Laundry. Café.
Funtana Marina ✆ 052 428 500
Email funtana@montraker.hr
www.montraker.hr

VRSAR
45°09'·2N 13°35'·9E (Otočić Galiner light)
BA 201, Imray M24

☆ Otočić Galiner Fl.2s5M. Mole Fl(2)5s4M. Breakwater head Fl.R.2s3M.

VHF Ch 17. Call ahead to arrange a berth.

Data Marina 220 berths. Max LOA 50m. Depths 4–10m. Charge band 5. Also berths on town quay.

Facilities Water. 220V. WiFi. Showers and toilets. Fuel quay. 30-ton crane. Provisions and restaurants.

Vrsar Marina
✆ 052 441 052 / 053
Email vrsar@montraker.hr
www.montraker.hr

LIMSKI KANAL
An Area of Outstanding Natural Beauty. Navigation by yachts is prohibited.

MARINA VALALTA
45°07'·5N 13°37'·7E
Berths Where directed.
Shelter Uncomfortable with the *bora*.
Data 180 berths. Depths <1–5m. Charge band 4/5.
Facilities Water. 220V. 5-ton crane. Provisions and restaurants in the village.
Remarks A naturist marina.
✆ 052 804 800
Email valalta@valalta.hr
www.valalta.hr

ACI MARINA ROVINJ
45°04'·5N 13°38'·0E
BA 1426, Imray M24

☆ Rt Sv Eufemija Fl.4s19m7M. Uvala quay Fl.G.3s3M. Breakwater Fl.R.3s3M. Mole Fl.G.3s4M. Breakwater SW head F.R. SE head F.G. Marina Fl.G.5s5M

VHF Ch 17 for ACI Rovinj.
Navigation Yachts can pass N or S of O. Sv Katerina.
Berths Where directed in the marina.
Shelter Uncomfortable with strong W–WSW winds, especially on the outer pontoon where it can be untenable.
Data 400 berths. Max LOA 60m. Depths <1–10m. Charge band 5/6.
Facilities Water. 220V. Showers and toilets. Fuel quay on N side of Sv Eufemija. 10-ton crane. Provisions and restaurants.
Remarks Port of entry.
ACI Marina Rovinj
✆ 052 813 133
Email m.rovinj@aci-club.hr

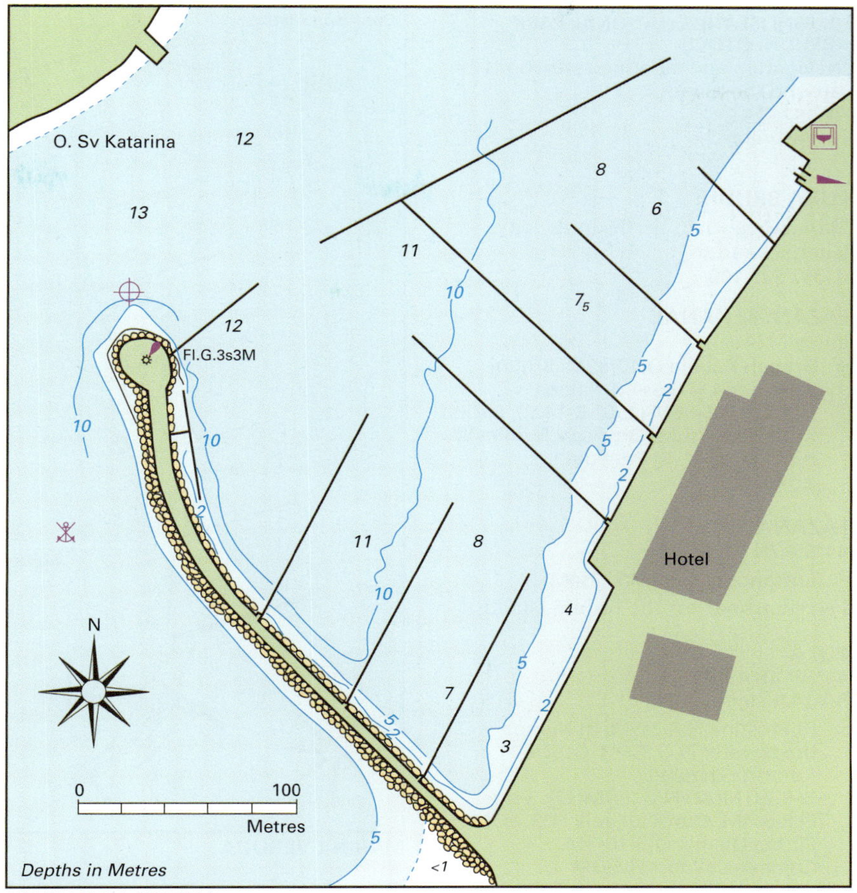

ACI MARINA ROVINJ

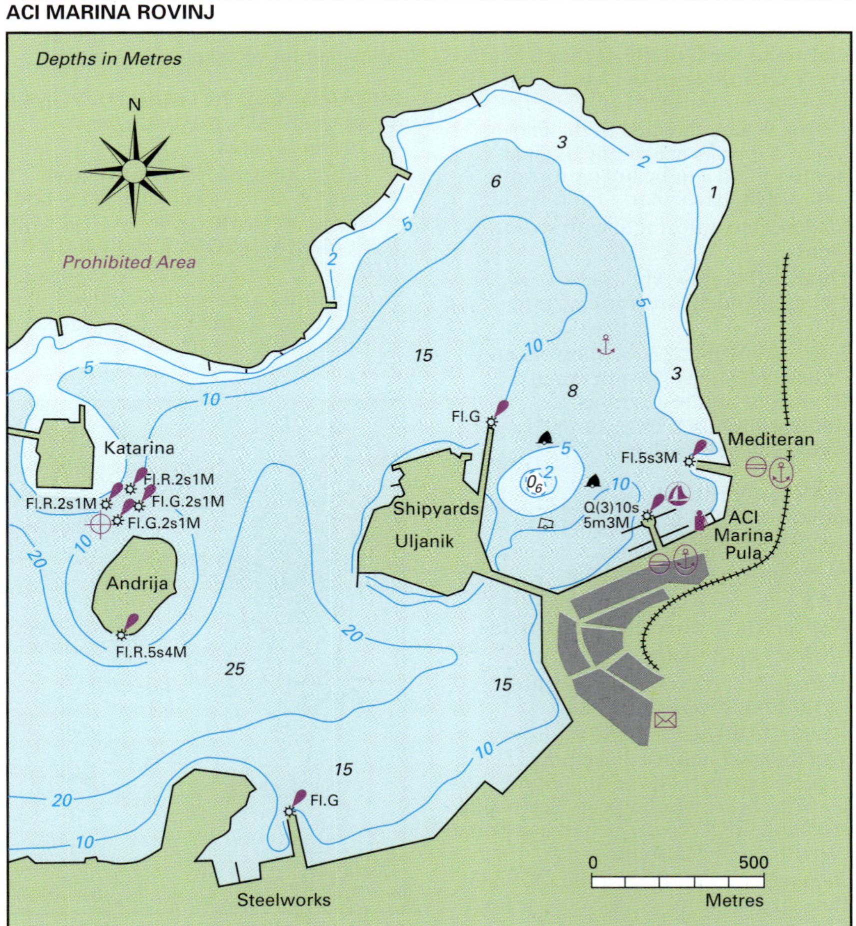

LUKA PULA

BRIONI ISLANDS NATIONAL PARK (BRIJUNI OTOCI)
Navigation and mooring restrictions around the islands.
✆ 052 525 882
www.brijuni.hr

LUKA BRIJUNI

Data Some yacht berths in the bay. Charge band 6+.
✆ 052 525 100

FAŽANSKI KANAL

Imray M24

☆ Greben Kabula Q.10m9M. Brijuni mole head Fl.G.5s4M. Saluga Fl(2)WR.8s8m6M (130°-R-142°). Pličina Kotež Fl.G.3s6M. Otočić Sv Jerolim W point Fl.2s5M. Rt Peneda Iso.4s20m11M

FAZANA

44°55'·7N 13°48'·1E

☆ Entrance Fl.R.2s2M/Fl.2s4M

Ferry harbour for the Brijuni Islands.

PULA

44°52'·4N 13°49'·7E
BA 1426, Imray M24

☆ Rt Proština Fl.R.3s5M. Rt Kumpa breakwater Fl.G.3s6M. Otočić Katarina channel Fl.R.2s1M(x2)/Fl.G.2s1M(x2). S side Fl.R.5s4M. Otočić Uljanik Fl.G.2s3M. Pličina Uljanik Q(3)10s3M. Commercial port Fl.5s3M

VHF Ch 17 for ACI Marina Pula.

Navigation Yachts should head for the marina to the E of the harbour, behind Otok Oljanik or to the Mediteran quay, N of the customs pier.

Berths Where directed in the marina. Visitors' berths are on the outside pontoon and can be uncomfortable with wash, particularly from ferries.

Shelter Uncomfortable with strong W winds.

Data 220 berths. Max LOA 25m. Charge band 5. Anchoring charge band 2/3.

Facilities Water. 220V. Showers and toilets. Fuel quay. 10-ton crane. Provisions and restaurants.

ACI Marina Pula ✆ 052 219 142
Email m.pula@aci-club.hr

MARINA VERUDA

44°50'·0N13°50'·3E
BA 201, Imray M24

☆ Rt Verudica Fl.R.3s6M

VHF Ch 17.

Berths Where directed in the marina.

Shelter Good shelter.

Data 630 berths. Depths 1–5m. Max LOA 40m. Charge band 5.

Facilities Water. 220/380V. Showers and toilets. Laundry. Fuel quay (2·5m, reported closed). 40/15-ton crane. 300 places ashore. Mechanical, electrical, steel and GRP repairs. Chandler. Some provisions. Restaurant.

Remarks Anchorage in Uvala Kanalic. Pula airport 5km.

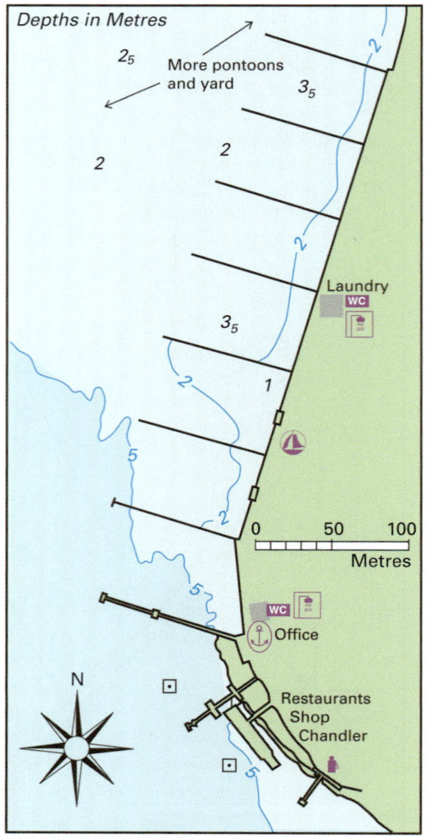

MARINA VERUDA

Marina Veruda ✆ 052 224 034
Email recepcija@tehmarinav.htnet.hr
www.marina-veruda.hr

MEDULIN AND ACI MARINA POMER

44°48'·2N 13°55'·7E (FlWR2s7/4M)
BA 201, Imray M24

☆ Pličina Albanež Fl(2)WR.8s10/6M (172°-R-227°). Hrid Galijola Fl.5s12M. Rt Munat Fl.WR.2s7/4M (327°-R-312°). Rt Marlera Fl.9s9M. Rt Seka Fl.G.2s3M.

VHF Ch 17 for ACI Pomer.

Navigation Large starboard hand beacon close W of Otok Bodulas is conspicuous.

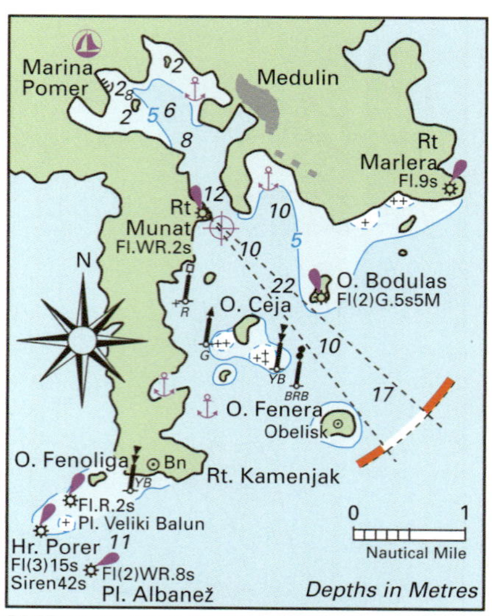

MEDULIN AND MARINA POMER

Berths Where directed at Marina Pomer.

Shelter Uncomfortable with the *sirocco* in the marina.

Data 290 berths. Max LOA 22m. Depths 2–2·5m. Charge band 5.

Facilities Water. 220V. Showers and toilets. 10-ton crane. Some provisions and restaurants in Medulin village.

Remarks Anchorage off the village.

ACI Marina Pomer ✆ 052 573 162
Email m.pomer@aci-club.hr

ZALJEV RAŠA (RAŠA BAY)

44°56'·7N 14°04'·2E

☆ Rt Ubac Fl.4s8M. Rt Mulac Fl.R.2s3M. Rt Kučica Fl.G.2s3M. Rt Sv Mikula Fl.R.2s1M. Uvala Tunarica Fl.R.2s1M. Rt Praščarica Fl.R.2s1M. Uvala Teplica Fl.G.2s1M. Trget Fl.G.2s1M. Rt Crna Punta Fl(2)10s10M. Koromacno Fl.G.3s3M

Moorings at Trget. Enry dangerous with strong southerlies. Tidal range 1·8m.

LUKA RABAC

45°04'·7N 14°09'·7E

☆ Rt Sv Andrija Fl(3)8s9m5M. Quay Fl(2)G.5s6m2M.

Open quay off the town. Laid moorings. Water. 220V.

LUKA PLOMIN (PLOMIN BAY)

45°07'·8N 14°11'·5E

Power station and ferry harbour in long inlet. Poor shelter.

Note In Vela Vrata a TSS is in operation. Expect stronger winds in the channel.

MOŠĆENIČKA DRAGA

45°14'·3N 14°15'·7E

☆ Quay F.G.3M

Small fishing port.

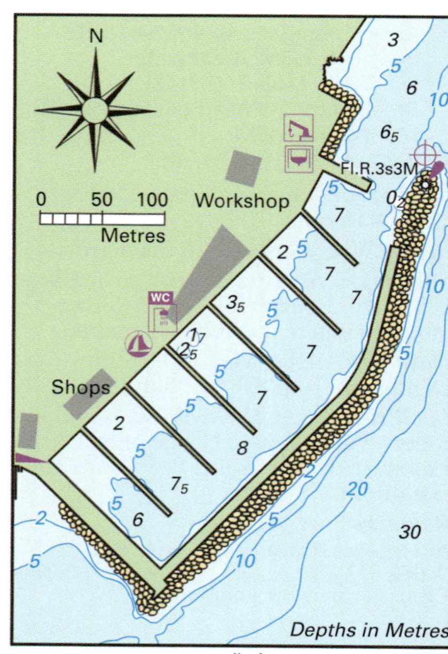

ACI MARINA OPATIJĂ (ICICI)

LOVRAN
45°17′·4N 14°17′·0E
☆ S mole head Fl.G.2s4M
Small boat harbour and tripper boat pier.

IKA
45°18′·3N 14°17′·2E
☆ N side Fl.R.5s2M
Short pier off the village.

ACI MARINA OPATIJA (IČIČI)
45°18′·9N 14°17′·8E
BA 2719, Imray M24
☆ Breakwater head Fl.R.3s3M
VHF Ch 17 for ACI Opatija.
Berths Where directed.
Shelter Good shelter.
Data 300 berths. Max LOA 40m. Depths 2–7m. Charge band 5.
Facilities Water. 220V. WiFi. Showers and toilets. Laundry. 15-ton crane. 35 places ashore. Provisions and restaurants.
ACI Marina Opatija ✆ 051 704 004
Email m.opatija@aci-club.hr

OPATIJA
45°20′·8N 14°19′·8E
☆ Old harbour mole head Fl.R.5s6M
Open quay. No visitors' berths. Fuel quay.

MARINA ADMIRAL
45°19′·6N 14°18′·3E
BA 2719, Imray M24
☆ Breakwater head Fl(2)R.5s4M.
Berths Where directed. Limited visitors' berths.
Shelter Good shelter, although berths near the entrance are uncomfortable with the *bora* and *sirocco*.
Data 160 berths. Max LOA 30m. Depths 2–4m. Charge band 4/5.
Facilities Water. 220V. Fuel at Opatija old harbour. 5-ton crane. Provisions and restaurants.
Marina Admiral ✆ 882 051 271
Email marina-admiral@liburnia.hr

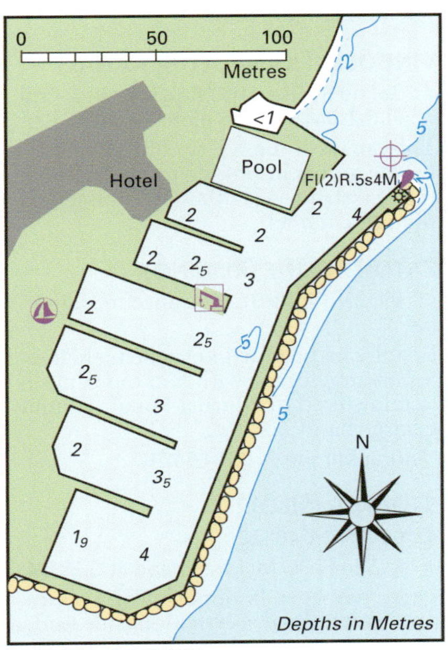

MARINA ADMIRAL

VOLOSKO
☆ Entrance Fl.R.3s3M/Fl.G.3s3M
Little room for visiting yachts.

RIJEKA
45°20′·0N 14°25′·6E
BA 1996, Imray M24
☆ Mlaka Fl.10s39m15M. Lukobran Petar Drapšina Q(3)G.5s8M. Bratislavsko pristaniste, Head F(3)R.6s3M / Fl.G.5s4M. Brgud S breakwater Fl.G.2s4M. Sušak N side Fl.R.2s2M. S side Fl.G.2s3M. RoRo berth Fl.3s4M. Martinšćica Fl.G.3s3M. W pier elbow Fl(2)R.5s4M. Floating dock SW corner Fl(2)G.5s4M. Luka Podurinj Fl.G.3s3M
Large commercial port. Few yacht facilities. Port of entry.

BAKARSKI ZALIV
☆ Kraljevica pier Fl.3s3M. Rt Srednji Fl(2)5s5M. Rt Kavranić Fl.5s6M. Rt Babno Fl.R.2s4M. Bakarac F.R.3M

TIHI KANAL
☆ Otočić Sv Marko Fl.R.3s6M. Otok Krk Rt Glavina Fl.R.5s3M. Rt Vošćica Fl.R.3s3M 106°-vis-346°. Rt Bejavec Fl.R.2s3M. Rt Ertak Fl.2s5M
Bridge linking the mainland to SV Marko and Otok Krk. AH 50m (W channel) or 60m (E channel).

CRIKVENICA
45°10′·3N 14°41′·7E (Fl.G.2s)
☆ Breakwater Fl.G.2s3M. Pier Fl.G.2s4M
Yacht berths on S pier. Depths 2–4m. Laid moorings. Water and fuel on the quay.

SELCE
45°09′·4N 14°43′·3E
☆ Quay head Fl(2)5s7m3M
Hotel jetty. Poor shelter on outside berths.

LUKA NOVI
45°07′·5N 14°47′·6E
☆ Rt Tokal Fl.6s9M. S mole Fl.G.3s2M. Pier Fl.R.3s2M. Hrid Sv Anton Fl.3s6M
Berth alongside the S breakwater. Depths 2·5–5m. Water. 220V. Fuel quay. Laid moorings.

SENJ
44°59′·4N 14°54′·1E
☆ Marija Art. Mole head Fl(3)10s8M. Sv Ambrož mole head Fl.R.3s5M. Sv Juraj mole head Fl.R.2s3M
Berth where convenient, or where there is room in the harbour, depending on the wind direction. Min depths 3m. Poor shelter from the *bora*.

Otok Lošinj

MALI LOŠINJ
44°32′·7N 14°27′·5E
BA 1426, Imray M24
☆ Otočić Zabodaski SE side Fl(2)R.6s4M. Otočić Murtar LFl.8s8M. Otok Koludarc Fl.G.3s3M. Rt Torunza Fl.WR.3s6/4M. Rt Poljana Fl.R.3s5M/Fl.R.4s4M/Fl(2)G.5s3M
Natural harbour at the S end of a deep inlet. Good shelter but uncomfortable in strong NW–W winds. The town quay is not suitable for yachts.
Marina Lošinj Yacht pontoons E of the fuel quay were damaged but expected back in place in 2012. 80 berths. Max LOA 15m. Laid moorings. Water. 220V. Showers and toilets. Charge band 3.
Remarks Port of entry.
Marina Lošinj ✆ 051 234 081
www.marinalosinj.com
Port Authority ✆ 051 231 438

YACHT CLUB MARINA MALI LOŠINJ
44°32′·8N 14°27′·8E
VHF Ch 17.
Navigation The marina lies ½M NE of the town quay.
Berths Where directed. Laid moorings tailed to buoys.
Shelter Uncomfortable with W–SW winds.
Data 150 berths. Max LOA 30m. Depths 2–10m. Charge band 5.
Facilities Water. 220/380V. Showers and toilets. Fuel on W side. 50-ton travel-hoist. 10-ton crane. Some yacht repairs. Laundry. Provisions and restaurants in the town.
Remarks A port of entry.
Note The narrow canal N of the marina leads to the Losinjski Kanal on the E side of the island is dangerous with the Bora. Depths 3m. Width 6m. A swing bridge across the canal opens at 0900 and 1800.
Marina Mali Lošinj ✆ 051 231 005
Email marina@ri.t-com.hr
www.ycmarina.hr

NEREZINE
44°39′·7N 14°24′·2E
☆ Mole head F.R.3M
A small harbour on the Losinjski Kanal. Yacht berths being developed. Shipyard S of the harbour handles yachts.
✆ 051 237 033

LUKA SV. MARTIN
44°32′·0N 14°28′·9E
☆ Mole F.R.3M
Small crowded harbour on E coast opposite Mali Losinj. Poor shelter in *bora*.

LUKA VELI LOŠINJ
44°31′·4N 14°30′·4E
☆ Fl.R.3s3M
Small town and harbour in a narrow inlet, dangerous in N–NE winds.

LUKA KRIVICA
44°29'·7N 14°29'·8E
Almost landlocked basin. Laid moorings. Excellent shelter from the Bora. Charge band 3.

LUKA ČIKAT
44°31'·5N 14°27'·2E
☆ Rt Madona Fl.G.3s3M
Bay open W on W coast opposite Mali Lošinj. Anchoring prohibited at all times except in an emergency.

Otok Susak

SUSAK
44°30'·8N 14°18'·9E (Fl.G.3s)
☆ Otok Susak LFl(2)10s100m19M. Luka Susak breakwater head Fl.G.3s3M
Yacht moorings.

Otok Cres

CRES
44°57'·4N 14°24'·8E (Fl(2)6s8M)
BA 2719, Imray M24
☆ Rt Kovačine Fl(2)6s8M. Rt Križice Fl.G.3s4M. Rt Melin Fl.R.3s3M. New mole Fl.3s2M. Marina entrance Fl(2)R.5s3M/Fl(2)G.5s3M
VHF Ch 17 for ACI Marina Cres.
Berths Where directed in the marina or on the town quay. Also buoys in outer harbour.

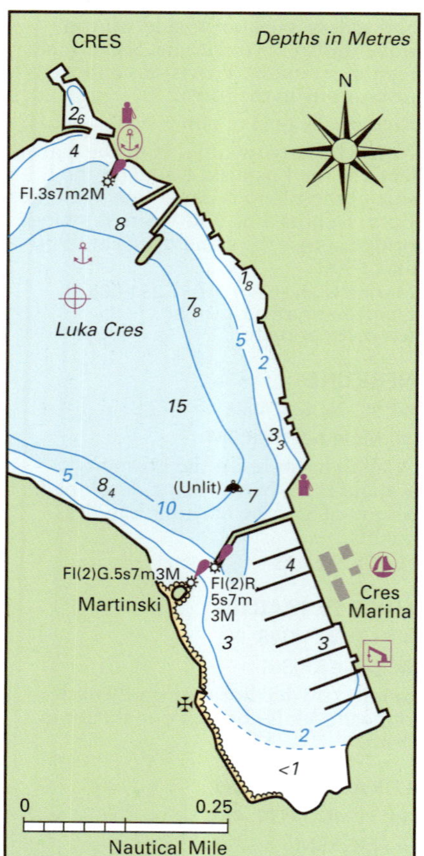

CRES

Shelter Good shelter.
Data 460 berths. Visitors' berths. Max LOA 50m. Depths 2–4m.
Charge band 5 (marina)/3 (town quay).
Facilities Water. 220V. WiFi. Fuel on E quay. 80-ton travel-hoist. 120 places ashore. Yacht repairs. Provisions and restaurants.
ACI Marina Cres ☏ 051 571 622
Email m.cres@aci-club.hr
Cres HM ☏ 051 571 111

MARINA BRODOGRADILISTE CRES
Ship-builder and yacht hauling facility at Cres town, and Marina Punat.
Data 50 berths. Max LOA 100m. 100 places ashore.
Facilities Water. 220/380V. Showers and toilets. 1,000-ton lift cap floating dock (100x11m). 100-ton travel-lift (33x7·5m) with max draught 2·7m. 25-ton crane. Repair workshops. Chandler. Restaurants, hotel and provisions in Cres town. Also Bank, ATM, PO.
Marina Brodogradiliste Cres
☏ 051 571 544
Email brodogradiliste.cres@ri.tel.hr
www.brodogradiliste-cres.hr

POROZINA
45°08'·0N 14°17'·0E
☆ Pierhead Fl.R.3s3M
Ferry terminal.

POGANA
44°36'·9N 14°30'·8E
☆ F.G.3M
Sheltered anchorage with a short pier.
Navigation Rocks and shoal water in the approaches off the S of the island.

OSOR
44°41'·6N 14°23'·7E
☆ Bijar Fl.R.3s4M. Pier Fl.R.1·5s3M
Canal across the isthmus between Cres and Losinj. Depth 2·5m. Width 12m.
Swing bridge opens at 0900 and 1700. N-going vessels have priority.
Pontoon berths in bay on S side. Laid moorings. Water. 220V.

MARTINŠĆICA
44°49'·1N 14°21'·3E
☆ Pierhead Fl.R.4s3M
Sheltered bay N of Osor on the NW coast of Cres.
Yacht berths on the pier clear of the ferry berth. Depths 3–4m. Laid moorings. Water. 220V. Charge band 2/3.
Note Anchoring prohibited.

Otok Krk

KRK
45°01'·4N 14°34'·8E
BA 2719, Imray M24
☆ Entrance Fl.R.4s3M/Fl.G.3s3M
Good shelter in harbour. Yacht berths bows-to on the N quay and W pier. Laid moorings tailed to buoys. Water and fuel quay (depth 2m).
Provisions and restaurants in the town.
Port Authority ☏ 051 221 380

MALINSKA
45°07'·5N 14°31'·9E
☆ Pierhead Fl.R.3s4M
Yacht berths on the pontoon or on the SW pier. Care needed of depths <2m over mooring blocks. Water. 220V. Laid moorings. Provisions and restaurants.
Port Authority ☏ 051 859 346

NJIVICE
45°09'·9N 14°32'·8E
☆ Breakwater head Fl.G.4s3M
Ferry port. Berths inside the S pier. Provisions and restaurants ashore. Expansion of berths planned.

SAPAN
☆ Rt Kijac Fl(2)R.8s8M. Leading lights (151°) Front Iso.G.2s11M. Rear Oc.G.5s11M. Rt Tenka Punta Fl(3)10s7M. Omišalj Fl.4s3M. Sapan quay Fl.G.5s4M
Oil refinery.

OMISALJ - PESJA
45°12'·7N 14°32'·9E
Navigation Keep at least 500m off the oil refinery berths on the W shore. Yacht berths on pontoons off the village.
Data 130 berths. Moorings in the bay. Depths 3m. Max LOA c16m. 5-ton crane.
☏ 051 841 458
Email pesja-nautika@ri.t-com.hr
www.pesja-nautika.hr

VINDOLSKI KANAL (TIHI KANAL)
☆ Soline Rt Glavati Fl.R.5s3M. Hridi Crni Fl.R.2s3M. Klimno pier Fl.R.5s3M
The canal off the NE tip of Krk has a bridge across it, linking to Sv. Marko and the mainland. AH 50m (W channel) or 60m (E channel).

ZATON SOLINE (KLIMNO)
45°09'·8N 14°38'·7E (Entrance to Soline bay)
Landlocked bay with excellent shelter. Secure anchorage with laid moorings is administered by Marina Punat (Klimno). Charge band 2.
Marina Klimno ☏ 051 864 782

STIPANJA (ŠILO)
45°08'·9N 14°40'·2E
☆ Rt Šilo Fl.3s7M. Mole head Fl.G.3s3M
Large bay open N opposite Crikvenica on the mainland. Berth alongside under the breakwater. Depths 3–4m.
Port Authority ☏ 051 852 110

VRBNIK

45°04'·8N 14°40'·8E

☆ Mole head Fl.R.2s3M

Enclosed fishing harbour with a narrow N-facing entrance. Excellent shelter.

BAŠKA

44°58'·1N 14°46'·0E

☆ Rt Skuljica Fl.R.3s6M. Otok Prvíc Rt Stražica Fl.6s9M. Mole head Fl.G.2s4M. W pier Fl.R.3s3M

Open harbour. Stern or bows-to on the SE breakwater. Surge with S winds.

MARINA PUNAT

45°01'·3N 14°38'·1E (Marina Punat)
BA 2719, Imray M24

☆ Punstarka Draga Fl.2s5M. Starboard hand beacons (x3) Fl.G.2s1M. Punat pier Fl.G.4s3M

VHF Ch 17 for Marina Punat.

Navigation Harbour and marina reached via narrow channel. Widening and dredging is planned.

Berths Where directed at Marina Punat on the E side.

Shelter Uncomfortable with strong SW–SW winds in the marina.

Data 800 berths. Max LOA 45m. Depths 2–4m.

Facilities Water. 220V. WiFi. Showers and toilets. Laundry. 100-ton travel-hoist. 600-ton slipway. 400 places ashore. Some yacht repairs. Provisions and restaurants.

Marina Punat ✆ 051 654 111
Email marina-punat@marina-punat.hr
www.marina-punat.hr

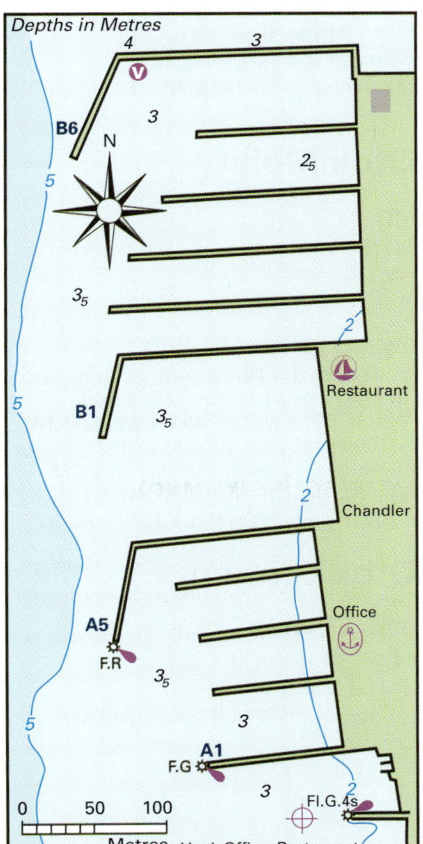

PUNAT

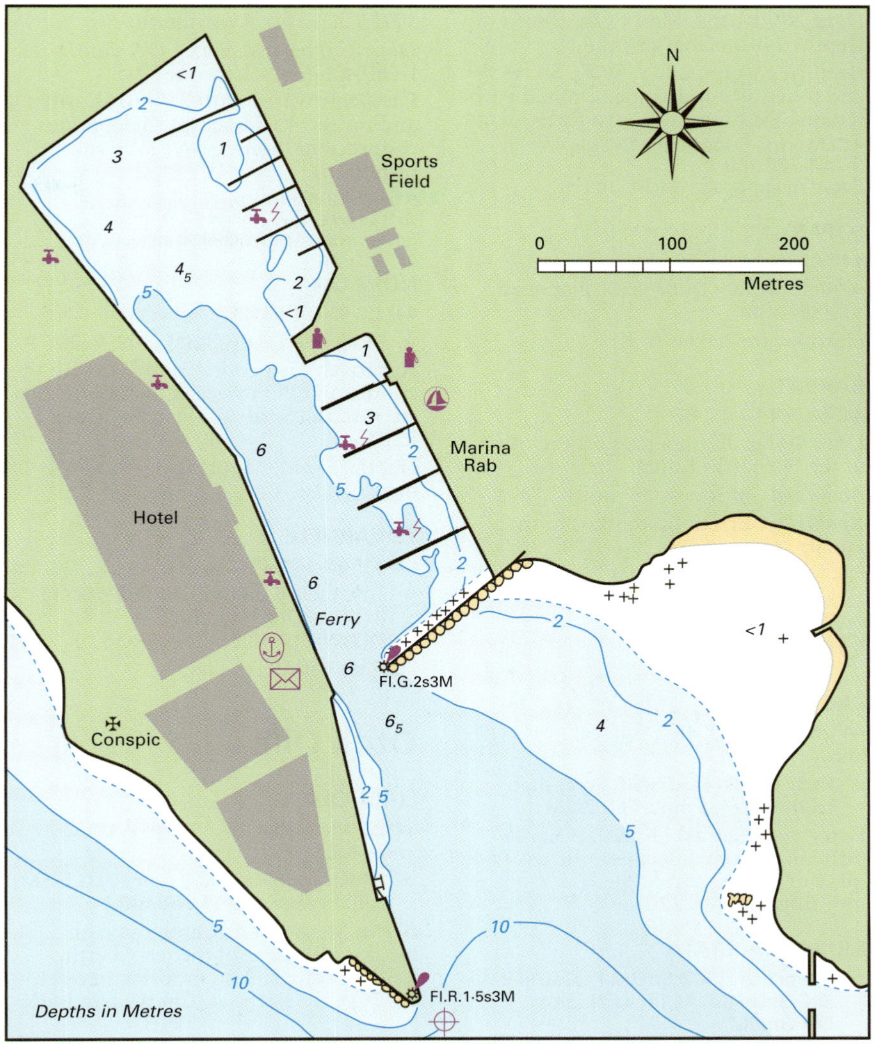

RAB

Otok Rab

RAB

44°45'·2N 14°45'·8E
BA 204, Imray M24, M25

☆ Otok Dolin Rt Donji Fl(3)10s7M. Pličina Fl.G.2s4M. Rt Frkanj Fl.R.2s4M.Rt Sveti Ante Fl.R.1·5s3M. Marina mole head Fl.G.2s3M.

VHF Ch 17 for ACI Marina Rab.

Berths Where directed in the marina. Also a few berths on the town quay. Laid moorings.

Shelter Strong southerlies send a swell into the harbour and make some berths untenable.

Data 150 berths. Max LOA 18m. Depths 1–5m. Charge band 5.

Facilities Water. 220V. WiFi. Showers and toilets. Fuel on centre pier (often busy). 10-ton crane. Limited yacht repairs. Provisions and restaurants.

Remarks Open in summer only (mid-April–end October).

ACI Marina Rab ✆ 051 724 023
Email m.rab@aci-club.hr

KRIŠTOFER

45°45'·5N 14°42'·1E

☆ Rt Kanitalj Fl.5s8M

ACI MARINA SUPETARSKA DRAGA

44°48'·2N 14°43'·6E
BA 202, Imray M24, M25

☆ Rt Sorinj Fl.3s6M. Marina breakwater head Fl.R.5s4M

VHF Ch 17 for ACI Supetarska Draga.

Berths Where directed.

Shelter Uncomfortable with strong NW winds.

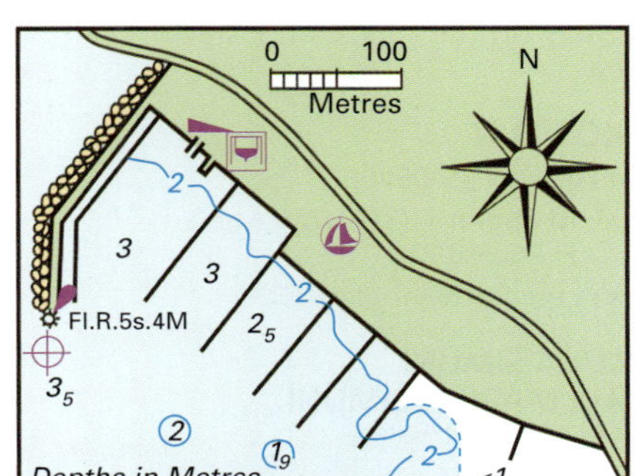

SUPETARSKA DRAGA

Data 280 berths. Max LOA 20m. Depths 1–4m. Charge band 5.
Facilities Water. 220V. WiFi. Showers and toilets. 10-ton crane. Limited yacht repairs. Restaurant. Bus to Rab town.
ACI Marina Supetarska Draga
✆ 051 776 268
Email m.supdraga@aci-club.hr

LOPAR
44°50′·3N 14°43′·5E
☆ Vela Sika Bn Q(9)15s5M. Pier head Fl(2)5s3M
Harbour for ferries to Krk.

BARBAT
44°44′·1N 14°47′·8E
Data 40 berths on jetties off the town in the Barbatski Kanal.
Boatyard. 30-ton travel-hoist.
Remarks Current up to 6kns in the kanal.
Piculjan pier ✆ 051 721 013

Otok Pag

PAG
44°26′·8N 15°03′·4E
Imray M25
☆ Rt Sv Nikola Fl.R.3s4M. Ferry pier Fl(2)R.5s7M. S mole Fl.R.3s2M
Entry via Velebitski Kanal. (Can be difficult in Bora.) Berth on the riverside quay or town quay. Some laid moorings. Water. 220V.

LJUBACKA VRATA
☆ Rt Fortica Fl.R.2s6m3M.Rt Oštrljak Fl.G.3s9m4M. Rt Tanka Nožica Fl.3s8m6M.
A narrow passage joining Pag to the mainland with a road bridge over. AH 30m. Leads from Ljubacki Zaglev into Velebitski Kanal which runs between the E side of Pag and mainland Croatia.

KANAL NOVE POVLJANE
☆ Sidriste Veli Zal Fl(2)R.5s5M. Greben Prutna Fl.R.3s3M. Rt Prutna Fl.R.3s3M. Privlaka Fl(2)G.8m3M
Runs between the W coast of Pag and Otok Vir, leading into Ninski Zaljev and Ljubacki Zaglev. Min. depths in the fairway 4m.

POVLJANA
44°21′·0N 15°06′·0E
☆ Nova Povljana Fl.R.3s5M
Quay off the village on E side of the bay.

KOŠLJUN
44°23′·9N 15°05′·0E
☆ Rt Zaglav Fl(3)10s7M. Mole Fl.RG.5s3/2M
Village with short pier.

LUKA ŠIMUNI
ACI MARINA ŠIMUNI
44°27′·8N 14°57′·5E
☆ Fl.G.3s3M
Marina in the NW corner of the inlet.
VHF Ch 17 for ACI Šimuni.
Data 220 berths. Max LOA 20m. Depths 2–6m. Charge band 5.
Facilities Water. 220V. WiFi. Showers and toilets. 15-ton crane. Telephone connections. Some provisions and restaurant.
ACI Marina Šimuni
✆ 023 697 457
Email m.simuni@aci-club.hr

NOVALJA
44°33′·4N 14°53′·2E
☆ Mole head Fl.RG.3s3M (109°-R-085°)
Approach on a course of 096°, with the church and PO tower in line. Berth stern-to the S side of the pier. Water. 220V.
Depths 3–5m. Mooring buoys in the bay.

TOVARNELE
44°41′·4N 14°44′·4E
☆ Tovarnele S point Fl.WR.6s8/5M (141°-R-176°). Otočić Dolfin Fl(2)WR.10s10/7M (138°-R-153°)
Hamlet with ferry pier.

Otok Olib

LUKA OLIB
44°22′·8N 14°46′·9E
Imray M25
☆ Otočić Morovnik NW point Fl.G.5s5M. Olib breakwater Fl.WR.3s4M
Berths Stern-to on N and S side of breakwater, clear of the ferry berth. Laid moorings. Also mooring buoys to the N of the harbour. Charge band 5/2.

Otok Silba

LUKA SILBA
44°22′·5N 14°42′·5E
Imray M25
☆ Luka Silba mole head Fl.R.3s4M
Yacht berths bows-to on the quay. Laid moorings. Water. 220V. Provisions and restaurants.
Port Office ✆ 023 370 047

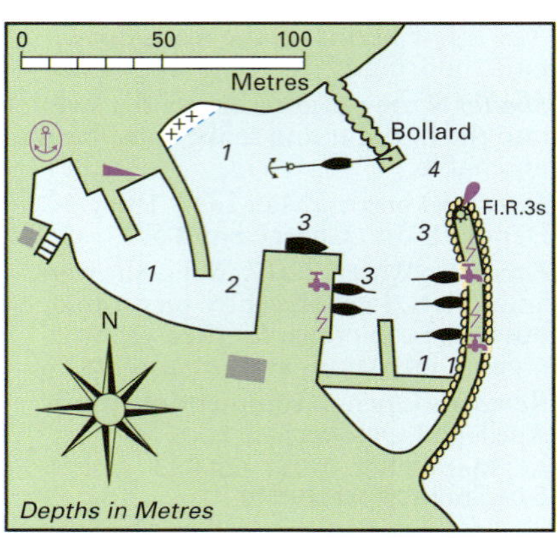

LUKA SILBA

PLIČINA VELI BRAK
44°26′·5N 14°38′·4E
☆ Fl(2)10s5M

SIDRIŠTE ŽALIC (WEST SILBA)
44°22′·4N 14°41′·7E
☆ Mole head Fl.3s3M
Ferry pier off the village. Care needed of submerged pier close N.

Otok Premuda

LUKA KRIJAL
44°20′·2N 14°35′·9E
☆ N mole Fl.R.3s4M
Buoyed approach through reefs.
Yacht berths in harbour. Max LOA 10m. Mooring buoys in the bay.

LOZA
44°20′·8N 14°36′·4E
☆ Fl.R.3s4M
Quay exposed to *bora*.

Otok Ist

ŠIROKA MARINA IST
44°16′·2N 14°46′·3E
☆ Fl.G.3s4M
Yacht berths on the N side of the ferry pier and on the stub pier. Anchoring prohibited W of the piers in the ferry turning area.
Data 66 berths. Laid moorings. Poor shelter. Water. 220V. Charge band 3/4. Open April–November.
Remarks Can get noisy here.
Marina Ist ✆ 023 372 638

Otok Molat

MOLAT
Berths Stern-to clear of the ferry berth. Laid moorings.
Water. 220V. Charge band 5.

BRGULJSKI ZALIV
☆ Rt Bonaster Fl(4)15s9M. O. Golac N side Fl.3s6M. O. Tun Mali S end Fl.R.3s3M. O. Tun Veli Fl.WG.5s7/4M (099·5°-G-213°-W-223°-G-092°). Uvala Vrulje Fl.G.3s4M. Lučina Fl.R.3s4M
60 moorings in the bay. Charge band 2.

Otok Sestrunj

UVALA KABLIN
44°08′·3N 15°00′·8E
☆ Fl.G.3s4M
Harbour on SW side of the island.

Otok Rivanj

RIVANJ

44°09'·2N 15°02'·1E

☆ Rt Zanavin Fl.G.3s8m4M/Fl.R.3s4M. Rivanj pierhead Fl(2)R.4s7m4M

New mole for cruise ships. Crowded harbour. Care needed of strong currents between Rivanj and Sestrunj.

Otok Ugljan

PREKO

44°04'·9N 15°11'·6E
Imray M25

☆ Rt Sv Grgur Fl(2)R.5s4M. O. Ošljak Fl(4)15s8M. Mole head Fl.R.3s3M. Ferry landing head Fl(3)R.8s7m4M

Two small harbours and a ferry pier. Fuel and water quay (depth 2–2·5m). Opposite Zadar on the mainland. Ferry to Zadar.

MARINA PREKO

A new marina off the town of Preko.

VHF Ch 16, 17.

Data 87 berths. Max LOA 20/60m. *Depths* 2-5m. Charge band 5.

Facilities Water. 220V. WiFi. Showers and toilets. Pump-out. Laundry.

Remarks Book ahead with 30% premium (July and August).
✆ 023 286 040 / 230
Email info@marinapreko.com

KALI

44°04'·0N 15°12'·4E

☆ E mole head Fl.R.3s3M

Busy fishing harbour.

KUKLJICA

44°02'·1N 15°15'·5E

☆ N entrance Fl.G.3s4M

Sheltered harbour off the village. Yacht berths on concrete piers. Some laid moorings. Water and 220V at some berths. Anchorage behind NE breakwater.
✆ 023 373 223
www.kukljica.hr

PROLAZ ZDRELAC

Passage between Dugi Otok and Otok Pašman has been widened: 54m wide, 16·5m AH.

UVALA SUTOMISČIĆA

44°06'·1N 15°10'·4E

☆ Rt Sv Grgur Fl(2)R.5s4M

Large bay with numerous piers. Few yacht berths. *See Olive Island Marina.*

OLIVE ISLAND MARINA

44°06'.1N 15°10'.1E (Entrance to bay)

VHF Ch 16, 17.

A new marina on Otok Ugljan opposite Zadar on the mainland.

Data 200 berths. Max LOA 75m. Charge band 5.

Facilities Water. 220V. WiFi. Toilets and showers. 30-ton travel-hoist and repairs to be developed. Chandler. Mini-market. Ferry to Zadar.

Remarks The Mali Zdrelac passage opened for navigation July 2010.
✆ 023 335 808/ 9
Email info@oliveislandmarina.com
www.oliveislandmarina.com

POLJANA

44°05'·5N 15°11'·6E

☆ Fl.G.2s3M

Sheltered harbour N of Preko.

Otok Iž

MARINA IŽ (VELI-IŽ)

44°03'·1N 15°07'·0E
BA 2711, Imray M25

☆ Entrance Fl.R.2s4M

VHF Ch 10, 16

Berths Where directed

Shelter Uncomfortable with strong NE-E winds.

Data 50 berths. Max LOA 25m. Charge band 4/5.

Facilities Water. 220V. Showers and toilets. 25-ton travel-hoist. 150 places

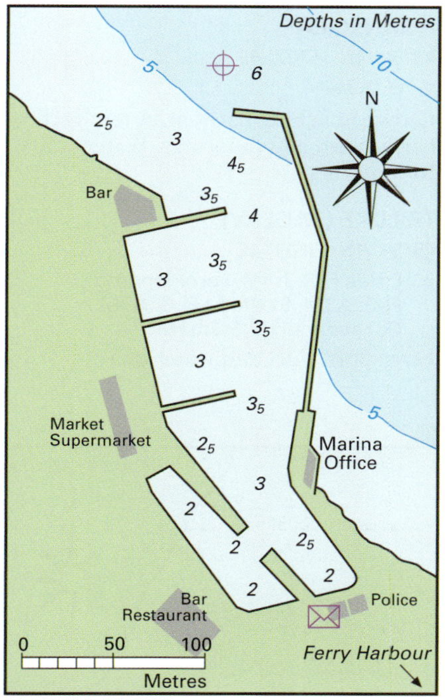

MARINA PREKO

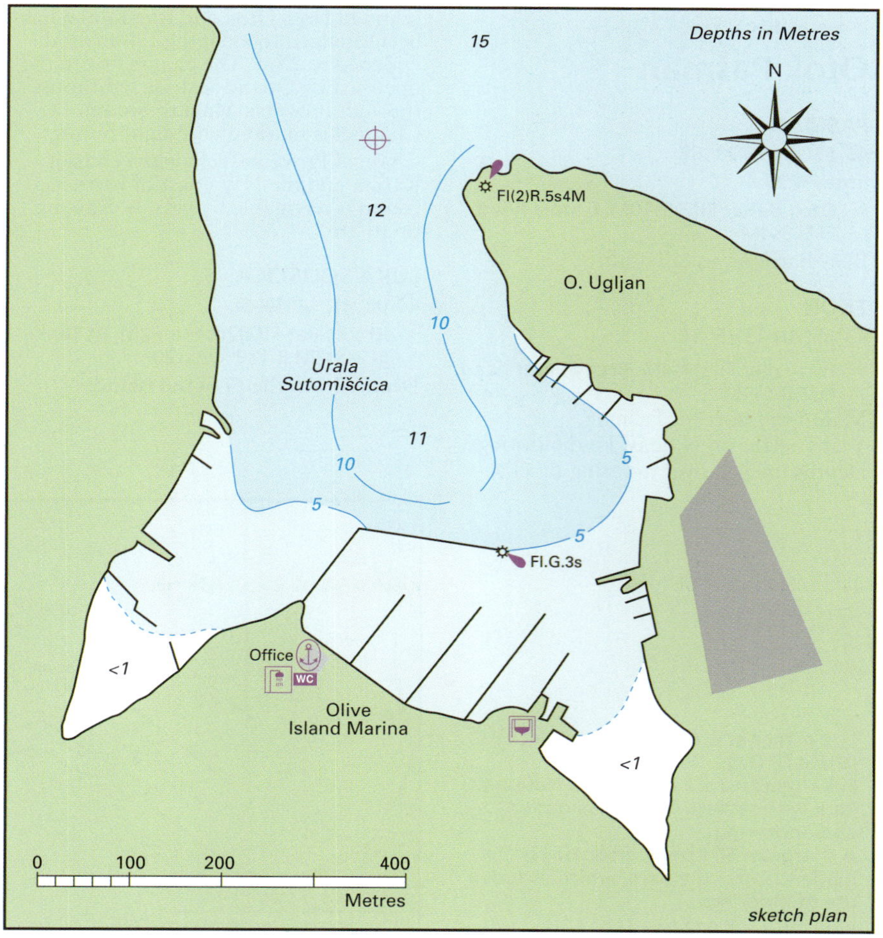

OLIVE ISLAND MARINA

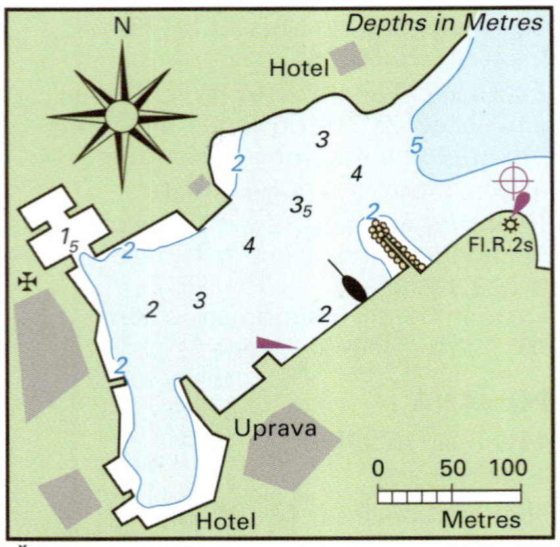

IŽ MARINA

ashore. Some yacht repairs. Provisions and restaurants.

Remarks It is an 'annex' of Marina Zadar.

Marina Veli Iž–Tankerkomerc
☎ 023 277 006 / 186
Email info@marinazadar.com
www.tankerkomerc.hr

MALI IŽ

44°01'·7N 15°08'·7E

☆ Mole head Fl.R.3s4M. Ferry pier Fl(2)G.5s4M.

Short-stay berths on W side of ferry pier.

Otok Pašman

PAŠMAN

43°57'·4N 15°23'·6E

Imray M25

☆ Otok Babać Fl(2)5s10M. E mole head Fl.G.3s4M

Busy harbour, usually full.

TKON

43°55'·4N 15°25'·5E

☆ Ferry pier Fl(2)4s4M. Breakwater head Fl(2)R.5s4M

Main ferry port for Pašman.
Yacht berths on N quay. Laid moorings. Depths uneven over mooring blocks.

LUKA TELAŠĆICA NATIONAL PARK (DUGI OTOK)

Luka Telašćica is a designated National Park with restrictions on navigation and anchoring.
A charge of 60 Kuna/person/day is made to enter the park, which includes use of moorings.
Park Office ☎ 023 313 180

Dugi Otok

SALI

43°56'·1N 15°10'·4E
Imray M25

☆ Otok Lavdara NW point Fl(2)15s5m2M. Rt Bluda Fl.G.3s3M. S breakwater head Fl.R.3s4M.

80 yacht berths bows-to the quay. Depths 1·5–4m. Laid moorings. Water. 220V. Some repairs. Provisions and restaurants. Charge band 3. Ferry to Zadar.

Port Office ☎ 023 377 021 / 042

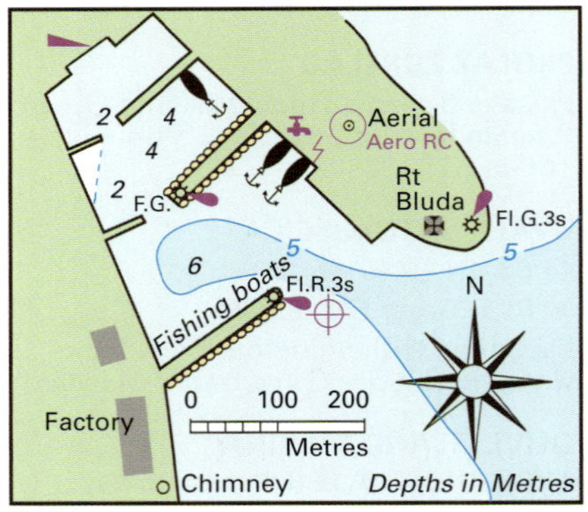

SALI

CHANNEL PROVERSA MALA

Channel Proversa Mala between the island of Dugi Otok and Islet Katina has been dredged to a depth of 4·8m and widened to 25m. The channel from the open sea by Otočić Sestrice lighthouse through Proversa Mala to Srednji Channel is marked with light buoys.

Channel Proversa Vela between Islet Katina and the NW coast of Kornat Island is navigable by vessels drawing up to 2m.

LUKA SOLIŠĆICA

44°09'·1N 14°49'·5E

☆ Rt Veli Rat Fl(2)20s41m22M. Rt Tanki Fl.R.3s3M R 189°-vis-120°

Deep inlet in the N of the island.

MARINA VELI RAT

44°10'·0N 14°50'·6E

Data 110 berths. Laid moorings. Charge band 4/5.

Facilities Water. 220V. Showers and toilets. Restaurant. Ferry to Zadar.

☎ 023 385 823 / 091 2800 034
Email
marinavelirat@baotic-yachting.com
www.cromarina.com

BOŽAVA

44°08'·5N 14°54'·9E

Yacht berths on N quay. Laid moorings. Water. 220V. Provisions and restaurants.

☆ Rt Sv Nedjelja Fl.G.3s4M

UVALA LUČINA (BRBINJ NORTH)

44°05'·0N 15°00·1E

☆ Fl.R.5s3M

Yacht berths inside the ferry berth. Water. 220V. Moorings cover most of the bay.

BRBINJ SOUTH

44°04'·5N 15°00'·9E

☆ Rt Koromašnjak Fl.3s4M

Deep attractive bay. Yacht quay and moorings. Water. 220V.

LUKA

44°00'·1N 15°05'·7E

☆ Otočić Maslinovac Fl.3s4M

Limited berths on town quay. Bows-to best to avoid shallows near quay in places. Water. 220V.

ŽMANŠĆICA

43°58'·4N 15°07'·4E

☆ Fl.G.3s4M

Crowded fishing harbour. A few yacht berths with laid moorings. Water. 220V. Restaurants.

TRILUKE (ZAGLAV)

43°57'·1N 15°09'·4E

☆ E side Fl.R.3s4M. Ferry landing Fl.G.3s3M. Rt Bluda Fl.G.3s3M. O. Lavdara Fl(2)5s5m2M

Ferry port. Fuel and water quay.

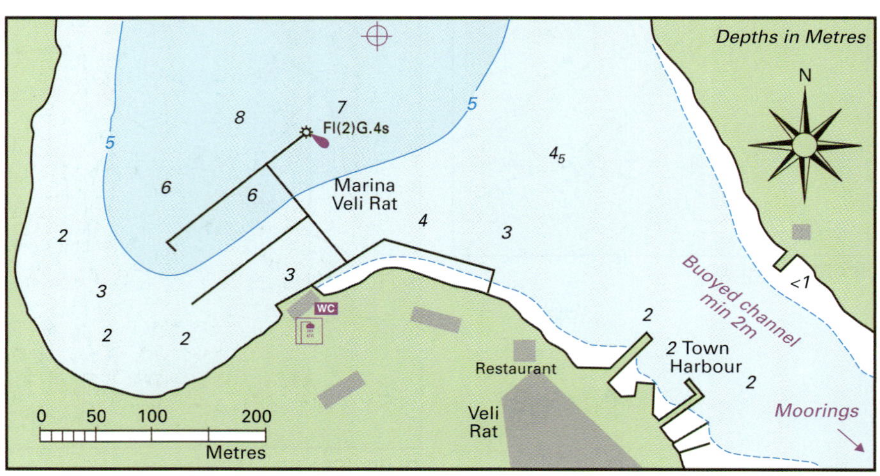

MARINA VELI RAT

KORNATI ISLANDS NATIONAL PARK
Includes the islands Sit, Kornat, Piškera and surrounding islets.
Restrictions on navigation, fishing, diving and anchoring. Permits obtained prior to entry or from a warden.

250 Kuna if purchased in advance – in Marina Dalmacija. 400 Kuna if purchased in the park. (See website for details.)

Note the permit also includes access to Luka Telascica National Park.

Kornati National Park, Murter
☎ 022 435 740
www.kornati.hr

Otok Kornat

VRULJE
43°48′·6N 15°18′·5E

Yacht quay with laid moorings. Moorings in the bay. Popular anchorage. National Park Office ashore.

Otok Piškera

ACI MARINA PIŠKERA
43°45′·6N 15°21′·0E
Imray M25

VHF Ch 17 for ACI Piškera.

Navigation Approach the marina from the SE only.

Data 180 berths. Depths 1·5–3·5m. Max LOA 20m. Charge band 5.

Facilities Water. 220V. Showers and toilets. Restaurant.

Remarks Part of the National Park. Charges levied per person. Open in summer only (April–end October).

ACI Marina Piškera
☎ 091 470 0091 / 92
Email m.piskera@aci-club.hr

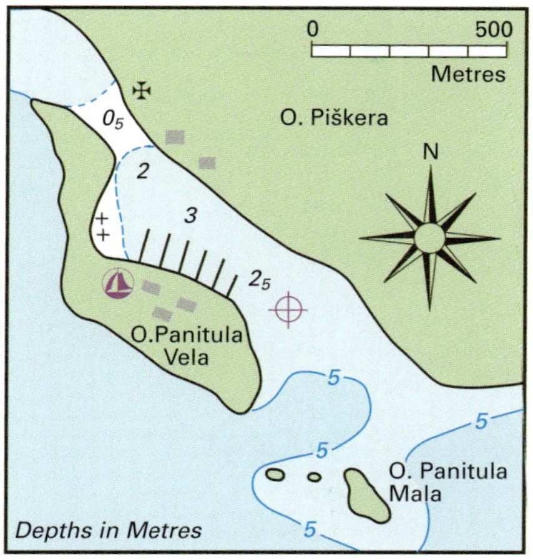

MARINA PISKERA

Otok Žüt

ACI MARINA ŽÜT
45°53′·0N 15°17′·6E

VHF Ch 17 for ACI Žüt.

Navigation Care needed of shoal water in the approaches.

Data 120 berths. Max LOA 38m. Laid moorings. Charge band 5/6. 15 mooring buoys. Charge band 3.

Facilities Water (limited). 220V (limited). Showers and toilets. Restaurant.

Remarks Open in the summer only (mid March–end October).

ACI Marina Žüt
☎ 022 786 0278
Email m.zut@aci-club.hr

Mainland Coast

LUKA SV JURAJ (JURJEVO)
44°55′·8N 14°55′·4E

☆ Fl.R.2s3M

LUKA LUKOVO OTOCKO
44°51′·5N 14°53′·5E

☆ Rt Malta Fl.5s8M. Mole head Fl.R.4s3M

Stern-to under the breakwater. Depths 3–7m. Limited shelter. Few facilities.

JABLANAC
44°42′·3N 14°54′·2E

☆ Pličina Glavina Fl(2)10s4M. Rt Štokić Fl.6s6M. Rt Gradić Fl.R.3s4M. Mole head Fl.G.2s3M

Main ferry port to Rab. Go alongside the pier near the port office.

Note A new ferry harbour is planned at Mali Stinica. When completed more yacht berths will be available here.

KARLOBAG
44°31′·4N 15°04′·5E

☆ Rt Jurišnica Fl(3)12s9M. S mole head Fl.G.3s4M

Go alongside one of the piers, keeping clear of the ferry berth. Depths 2–4m. Ferry to Pag. Poor shelter.

KRUSCICA
44°21′·0N 15°18′·9E

☆ Rt Dugi Fl.R.3s5M

Fishing village.

STARIGRAD-PAKLENICA
44°17′·6N 15°26′·6E

☆ Mole head Fl.R.3s3M

Yacht berths on the pier and the pontoon. Water. 220V.

NOVSKO ZDRILO
☆ Rt Baljenica Fl(2)R.5s5M. Rt Korotanja Fl.G.2s2M. Rt Vranine Fl.G.2s2M. Rt Brzac Fl.R.2s2M. Rt Ždrijac Fl.G.2s3M

Narrow channel S into Novigradsko More. Road bridge crosses the passage. AH min 55m.

Novigradsko More

NOVIGRAD
44°11′·3N 15°33′·2E

☆ Rt Sv Nikola Fl.R.3s4M

Dog-leg inlet. Go alongside on E quay.

VINJERAC
44°15′·5N 15°28′·2E

☆ Mole head Fl.R.3s7m3M

Small village harbour.

RAŽANAC
44°17′·1N 15°21′·1E

☆ Otočić Ražanac Veli Fl.5s9M. Mole head Fl.R.3s4M

Small harbour. Good shelter.

Note From Razanac to Prvlaka *see Otok Pag*.

PRVLAKA
44°15′·9N 15°07′·4E

☆ Fl(2)G.5s8m3M

Shallow, crowded harbour.

PETRČANE
44°10′·8N 15°09′·6E

☆ Rt Radman Fl.WR.3s7/4M (141°-R-262°)

Small harbour. Swell in W–SW winds.

MARINA BORIK
44°07′·7N 15°12′·9E

☆ Breakwater Fl.R.3s4M

Navigation Marina situated one mile NW of Zadar Marina.

Berths Where directed. Finger pontoons. Layout altered.

Shelter Good.

Data 185 berths. Depths 2–6m. Max LOA 40m. Charge band 5.

Facilities Water. 220V. WiFi. Showers and toilets. Pump-out. Fuel. 20-ton travel-hoist. 50 places ashore. Some repairs. Provisions and restaurant. ATM. Bus/ferry to town.

Marina Borik
☎ 023 333 036
Email info@marinaborik.hr
www.marinaborik.hr
www.d-marin.com

MARINA VITRENJAK
44°07′·5N 15°13′·3E
Imray M25

☆ Marina breakwater head Fl(2)R.5s3M

Navigation Situated ½M SE of Zadar harbour. Care needed of shoal water if W of the entrance approaching from the N. The SW extremity is marked with a buoy.

Berths Not licensed for foreign vessels.

Data 250 berths. Depths 1–4m.

Facilities Water. 220V. 2/5-ton cranes. Provisions in Borik.

☎ 023 331 076

MARINA ZADAR

44°07'·2N 15°13'·7E
BA 2711, Imray M25

☆ Oštri Rt Fl(3)10s15M. Istarska Obala Fl.G.2s4M. Marina outer breakwater Fl.R.3s4M

VHF Ch 16, 17.

Berths Where directed. Large yachts (15m+) go under the outer breakwater.

Shelter Good shelter.

Data 300 berths. Max LOA 40m. Depths 1·5–6m. Charge band 5.

Facilities Water. 220V. Showers and toilets. 15-ton crane. 50-ton slipway. 150 places ashore. Some yacht repairs. Provisions and restaurants.

Remarks Yachts wishing to clear customs should go alongside the quay opposite the marina.

Marina Zadar
✆ 023 204 850 / 332 700
Email marina@tankerkomerc.hr
www.marinazadar.com

✉ Charts Plovno podrucje Zadar, Jurja Bijankinja 8, Zadar

MARINA DALMACIJA (SUKOŠAN)

44°02'·7N 15°18'·1E
BA 2711, Imray M25

☆ Rt Podvara Fl.WR.5s8/5M (207°-R-318°). Marina entrance Fl(2)R.5s4M / Fl.R.3s4M / Fl(2)G.5s4M

VHF Ch 17.

Data 1,200 berths. 500 places ashore. Max LOA 80m. Depths 2–6m. Charge band 5.

Facilities Water. 220/380V. WiFi. Showers and toilets. Fuel. 30/80-ton travel-hoists. Limited provisions. Restaurant.

Remarks Large charter base.

Marina Dalmacija
✆ 023 200 300
Email info@marinadalmacija.hr
www.marinadalmacija.hr
www.d-marin.com

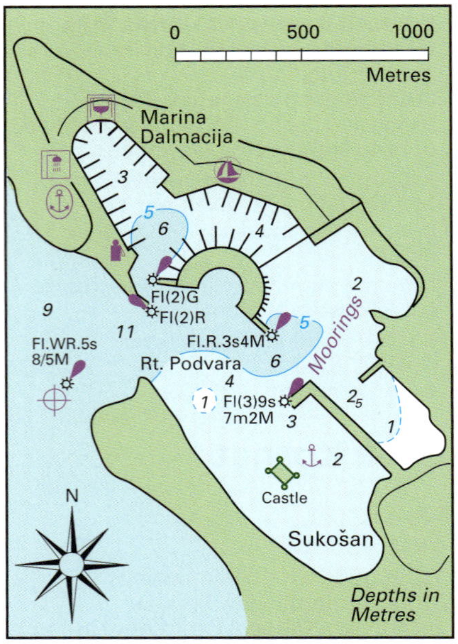

SUKOŠAN (MARINA DALMACIJA)

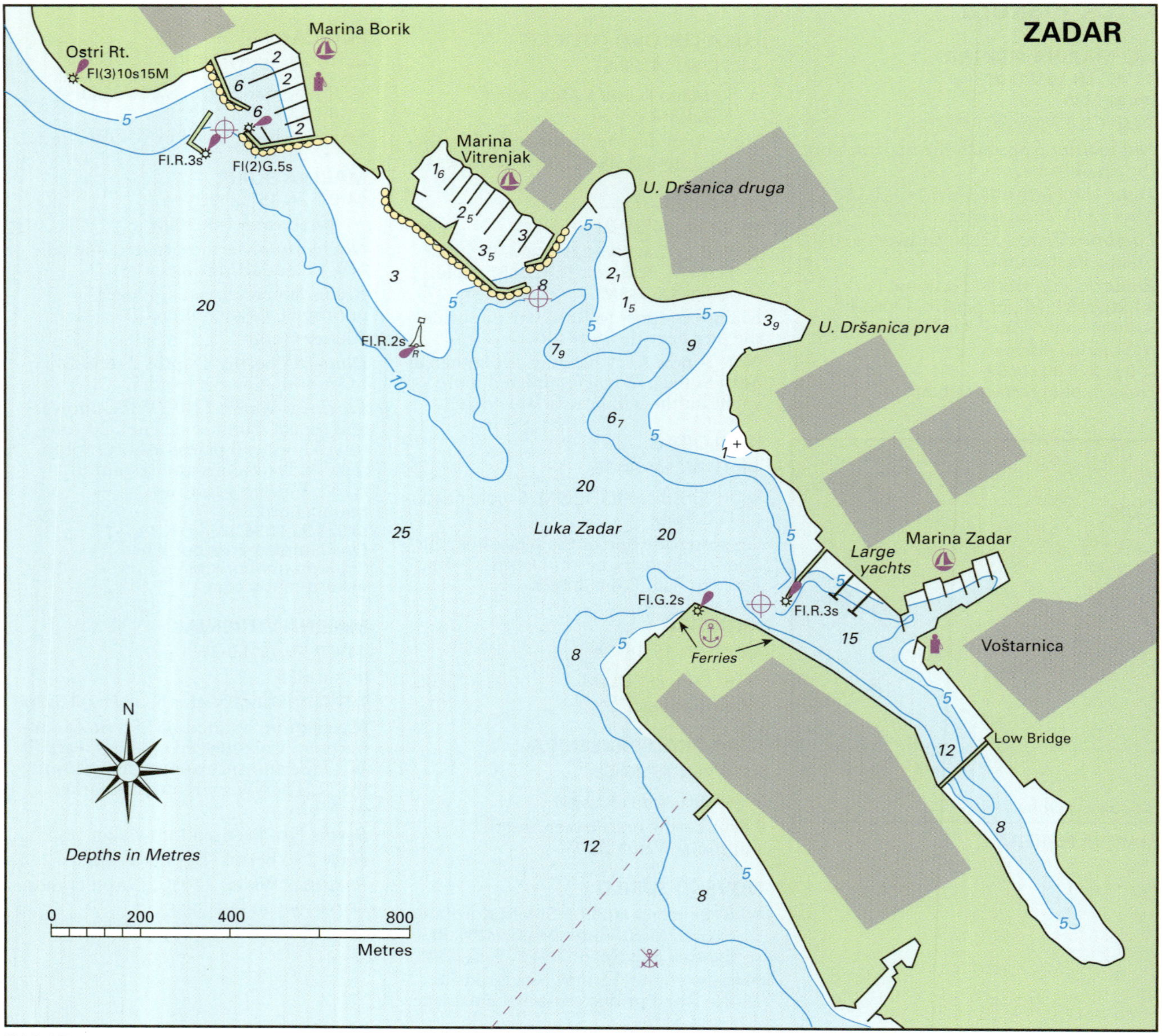

ZADAR

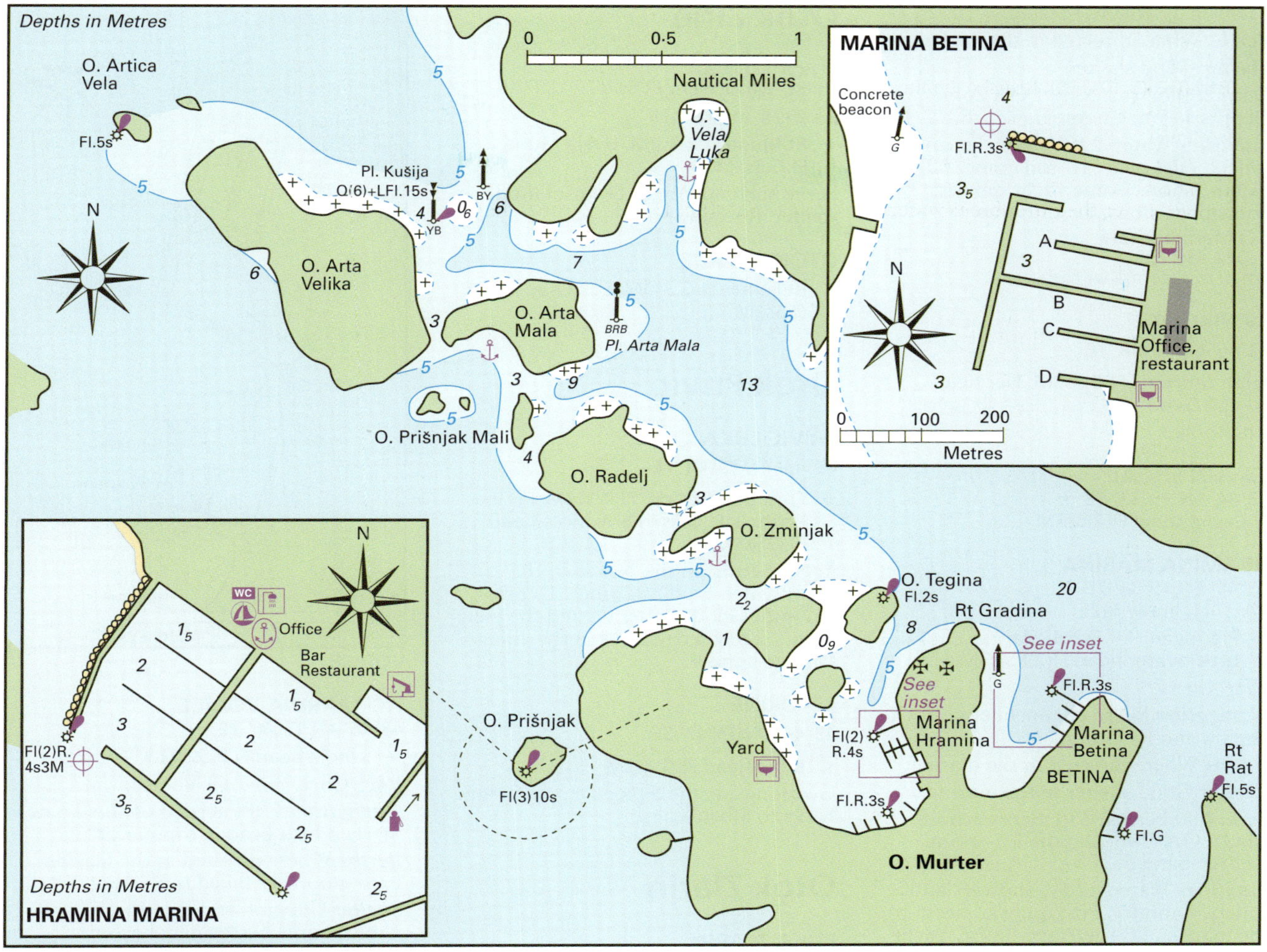

APPROACH TO HRAMINA

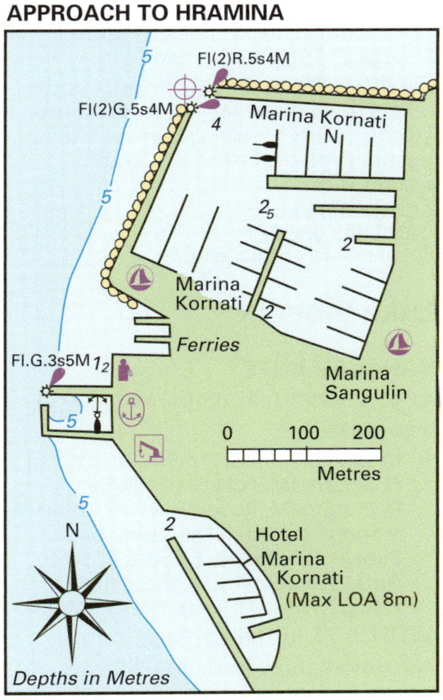

BIOGRAD

TURANJ

43°57'·9N 15°24'·8E

☆ Pličina Minerva Fl.G.3s4M.
Breakwater head Fl(2)G.5s4M

Holiday village and harbour.

FILIP JAKOV

43°57'·6N 15°25'·7E

Small harbour and quay.

BIOGRAD (KORNATI BIOGRAD MARINA AND MARINA SANGULIN)

43°56'·5N 15°26'·7E (Fl(2)G.5s)
BA 2711, Imray M25

☆ Otočić Planac N point Fl.R.3s3M. Otočić Sv Katarina SW side Fl(2)8s8M. Otočić Cavatul NE end Fl.G.3s4M. NW mole head Fl.G.3s5M. Marina entrance Fl(2)R.5s4M/ Fl(2)G.5s4M

VHF Ch 17.

Berths Where directed in either marina.

Shelter Good shelter.

Data 700 (Kornati) 150 (Sangulin) berths. Depths 2–5m. Max LOA 26m. Charge band 5 (Kornati), 4 (Sangulin).

Facilities Water. 220V. Showers and toilets. Fuel quay in the old harbour (1·2m). 50-ton travel-lift. 10-ton crane. 70 places ashore. Limited yacht repairs. Provisions and restaurants.

Kornati Marina ✆ 023 383 800
Email info@marinakornati.com

Marina Sangulin ✆ 023 385 020
Email info@sangulin.hr
www.sangulin.hr/miniweb

PAKOŠTANE

43°54'·3N 15°30'·8E

☆ Breakwater head Fl.G.5s4M

ARTICA VELA

☆ W islet, W side Fl.5s7M

OTOK VRGADA

43°51'·5N 15°30'·5E

☆ Uvala Luka Fl(2)R.5s3M

PIROVAC

43°49'·1N 15°40'·3E

☆ Quay S end Fl.G.3s3M

MURTER CANAL

Bridge opens 0900–0930 / 1700–1730. Depths minimum 1·8m. A 5kn current can run through the canal.

Otok Murter

TIJESNO (TISNO)

☆ Breakwater head Fl.R.5s4M

ACI MARINA JEZERA

43°47'·0N 15°39'·2E
BA 2711, Imray M25

☆ Marina breakwater head Fl.R.5s4M

VHF Ch 17 for ACI Jezera.
Berths Where directed in the marina.
Shelter Good shelter.
Data 200 berths. Max LOA 25m. Depths 1–5m. Charge band 5/6.
Facilities Water. 220V. Showers and toilets. Fuel quay. 10-ton crane. 60 places ashore. Some yacht repairs. Some provisions. Restaurants.
ACI Marina Jezera
☎ 022 439 295
Email m.jezera@aci-club.hr

SV NIKOLA
43°46'·6N 15°38'·1E
☆ Rt Murterić Fl.G.3s3M. Pier head Fl.G.5s4M
Anchorage.

ČAVLIN SHOAL
43°44'·5N 15°33'·8E
☆ Čavlin shoal Fl(2)5s6M

HRAMINA MARINA
43°49'·6N 15°35'·7E
BA 2711, Imray M25
☆ Pier head Fl.R.3s2M. Marina breakwater head Fl(2)R.4s3M
VHF Ch 17.
Navigation 8m in channel between O. Tegina and Rt Gradina.
Berths Where directed in the marina.
Shelter Good shelter in the marina.
Data 400 berths. 250 places ashore. Max LOA 50m. Depths 1·5–3·5m. Charge band 5.
Facilities Water. 220V. Showers and toilets. Laundry. Fuel quay adjacent to the marina. 70-ton travel-hoist. Yacht repairs. Gas. Ship and boat-building industry in Hramina and Betina. Provisions in the village. Restaurants.
Marina Hramina
☎ 022 434 411
Email info@marina-hramina.hr
www.marina-hramina.hr

MARINA BETINA
43°49'·8N 15°36'·4E
BA 2711, Imray M25
☆ Rt Rat Fl.5s5M. Breakwater head Fl.G.5s3M. Boatyard wall Fl.R.3s3M
VHF Ch 17.
Navigation Care needed of rock off Rt Artić.
Data 240 berths. Max LOA 25m. Depths <1–5m. Charge band 4.
Facilities Water. 220V. Showers and toilets. 250-ton travel-hoist. 10-ton crane. 30-ton slipway. 30 places ashore. Yacht repairs. Provisions. Restaurant.
Marina Betina
☎ 022 434 497
Email marina-betina@si.htnet.hr
www.marina-betina.hr

BETINA
43°49'·3N 15°36'·6E
Fishing harbour.

Otok Zirje

LUKA MUNA
43°39'·8N 15°39'·6E
BA 2774, Imray M25
☆ Rt Muna Fl.R.3s2M. Uvala Muna Fl.G.3s2M
Ferry harbour. Yacht berths. Good shelter. Restaurant.

OTOK KAPRIJE
☆ Rt Lemes Fl.G.3s3M. Luka Kaprije Fl.3s3M

Otok Privić

PRIVIĆ LUKA
43°43'·4N 15°48'·1E
☆ O. Lupac. Rt Konj Fl.R.3s2M. Pličina Roženik Fl.G.5s7m6M. Mole head Fl.G.3s3M
Yacht berths on the N side of the breakwater. Laid moorings. Depths 2·5–4m. Good shelter behind the pier. Water. 220V. Provisions in the village. Charge band 4.

SEPURINE
43°44'·0N 15°47'·3E
☆ Mole head Fl.G.3s3M
Go alongside the S pier. Depths 2–4m. Ferry to Sibenik.

Otok Zlarin

LUKA ZLARIN
43°42'·0N 15°50'·2E
☆ N pier head Fl.3s2M
Yacht berths on main pier and inner jetty. Laid moorings. Water. 220V.
YC Zlarin ☎ 022 533 755

Mainland Croatia

OTOK LUKOVNIC
OTOK LOGORIN CHANNEL
Minimum depth 4·2m reported.

TRIBUNJ MARINA
43°45'·1N 15°45'·2E
☆ Fl.G.5s3M. Marina Fl(2)G.5s4M
New marina.
VHF Ch 17 for Marina Tribunj.
Data 240 berths. Max LOA 25m. 150 places ashore. Charge band 6 (July–August).
Shelter Good shelter inside. Outer berths open to wash.
Facilities Water. 220V. Internet. Toilets and showers. Laundry. Fuel. 80-ton travel-lift.
☎ 022 447 140
Email
marina-reception@marina-tribunj.hr
www.marina-tribunj.hr

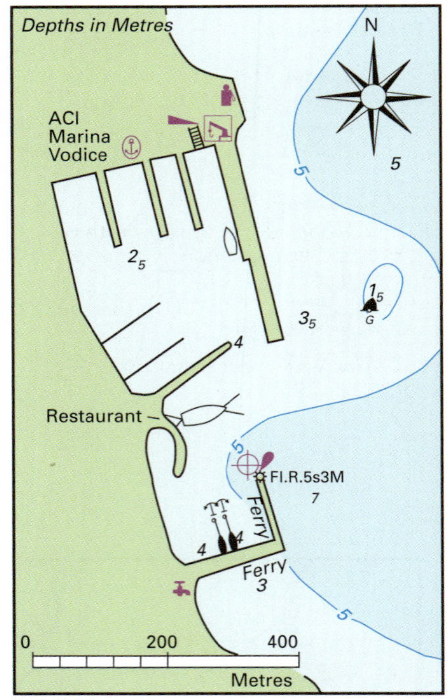

VODICE

ACI MARINA VODICE
43°45'·4N 15°46'·7E
☆ S mole head Fl.R.5s3M
VHF Ch 17 for ACI Vodice.
Navigation Care needed of shoal patch marked by a beacon topmark ⁑.
Berths Where directed in the marina. Laid moorings tailed to the quay.
Shelter Uncomfortable with strong S winds. Some berths may become untenable.
Data 290 berths. Max LOA 40m. Depths 2–5m. Charge band 5/6.
Facilities Water. 220V. Showers and toilets. Fuel quay. 60-ton travel-hoist. 10-ton crane. 55 places ashore. Engine repairs (Volvo). Provisions and restaurants.
ACI Marina Vodice
☎ 022 443 086/221
Email m.vodice@aci-club.hr

Luka Šibenik

KANAL SV ANTE
43°43'·2N 15°51'·4E (Entrance to Kanal)
Imray M25
☆ Rt Jadija Fl(2)R.6s11m9M. Hrid Ročni Fl.G.3s7m3M. Fort Sveti Nikola Fl.G.2s6m4M. Rt Senišna Fl.G.2s8m1M. N Shore Rt Debeli Fl.R.2s6m1M. Rt Baba Fl.R.2s6m1M. S Shore Rt Sveti Ante Fl.G.2s9m4M. N shore Rt Sv Križ Fl.R.2s7m1M. Rt Turan Fl(2)G.5s8m3M.
VHF Ch 71 for Jadria Port Control.
Narrow channel leading to Sibenik. Access to vessels over 50 tons is controlled from Šibenik, and displays signals at the entrance to the Kanal.
Two black balls or 2FG(vert) – the channel is clear.
Inverted red cone or 2FR(vert) – vessel in the channel.

ŠIBENIK
43°43'·9N 15°53'·7E
BA 2773, Imray M25

☆ Rt Turan Fl(2)G.5s8m3M. Pličina Paklena NE edge Fl.G.2s6m3M. Sipad jetty Fl.R.3s3M. Gat Krka Fl.3s4M. Gat Martinska Fl.R.3s2M

VHF Ch 10, 16, 71.
Berths Alongside SE of fuel berth or stern or bows-to on harbourmaster's quay.
Shelter Open NW–W–SW.
Data Max LOA 25m. Charge band 4.
Facilities Water. Fuel quay. 900-ton ship lift. 1,500-ton floating dock. Chandler. Provisions and restaurants.
Port office ✆ 022 217 214 / 218 001
NCP Boat repairs ✆ 022 312 931
Email servis@ncp.hr

MARINA MANDALINA
43°43'·1N 15°53'·8E
VHF Ch 17.
Navigation New marina in the sheltered gulf of Šibenik.
Berths Finger pontoons and laid moorings for larger vessels.
Shelter Good all-round shelter.
Data 430 berths. Max LOA 95m. Charge band 6.
Facilities Water. 220/380V. Showers and toilets. WiFi. 50-ton travel-hoist. 50 places ashore. Most repairs. Bar, restaurant and provisions.
Mandalina Marina ✆ 022 460 800 / 091 391 7516 (24hr)
Email mandalina@d-marin.com
www.marina-mandalina.com
www.d-marin.com

Rijeka Krka (River Krka)

RT VELIKA KAPELA
☆ Fl.G.2s7m3M

RT TRISKA
☆ Fl.G.2s5m1M.
The river runs N from Šibenik to Zaton, then NE into Prukljansko Jezero. A bridge and cable cross the river. AH 27m.

ZATON
☆ Fl.G.5s7m4M
4M N of Šibenik. Go stern-to on the N quay. Some laid moorings. Depths 2m. Water. 220V.

RASLINE
Care needed of shallows on W side of the approaches. Sheltered anchorage and small harbour. Some laid moorings.

ACI MARINA SKRADIN
43°49'·0N 15°55'·6E
BA 2711, Imray M25
☆ Pier SE corner Fl.G.5s3M
VHF Ch 17 for ACI Skradin.
Berths Where directed in the marina
Shelter Difficult with the *bora*.
Data 180 berths. Max LOA 70m. Depths 2–5m. Charge band 5/6.
Facilities Water. 220V. Showers and toilets. Fuel in town. Provisions and restaurants.
Remarks Krk National Park and waterfalls lie upriver from Skradin. Authorised craft only may navigate up river.
Note Restaurants with jetties for yachts on E side of river S of the suspension bridge.
ACI Marina Skradin ✆ 022 771 365
Email m.skradin@aci-club.hr

MARINA SOLARIS (ZABLAĆE)
43°41'·9N15°52'·9E
☆ Fl(2)G.5s6m3M
Marina in a lagoon S of Zablaće.
Data 300 berths. Max LOA 11m. Max depth 2m. 5-ton crane.
Yacht Marina Solaris ✆ 022 364 440
Email info@solaris.hr
www.marina.solaris.hr

PRIMOSTEN
43°35'·1N 15°55'·7E
Imray M25
☆ Rt Kremik Fl.3s10m8M. SE Point Fl(2)R.5s3M. Rt Zečevo Fl(2)G.5s3M. Pličina Peleš Fl.R.2s5M. Vojske W mole head Fl.R.3s3M. Mole head Fl.R.5s3M. Grbvac Rock Fl(2)5s7M
Two small harbours.
Data Yacht berths stern or bows-to on the breakwater or on the W quay. Bows-to better on town quay to avoid underwater rubble off the quay. Laid moorings. Depths 1·5–3m. Mooring buoys in the bay.

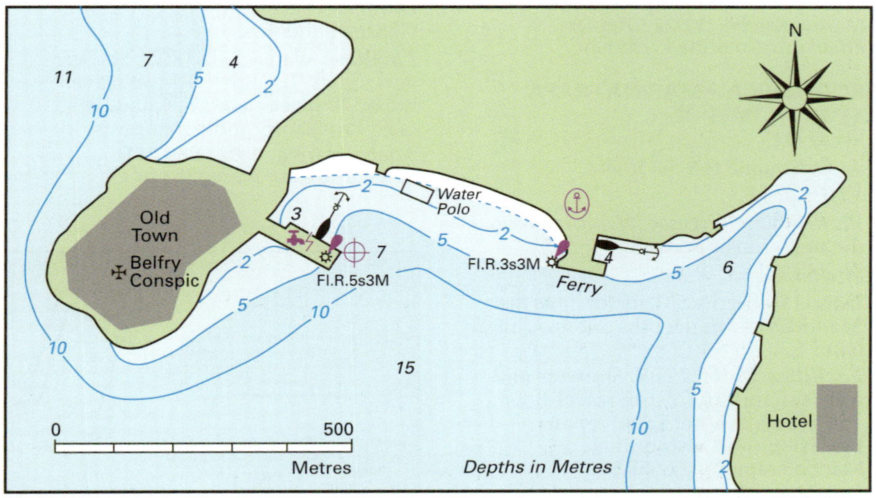

PRIMOSTEN

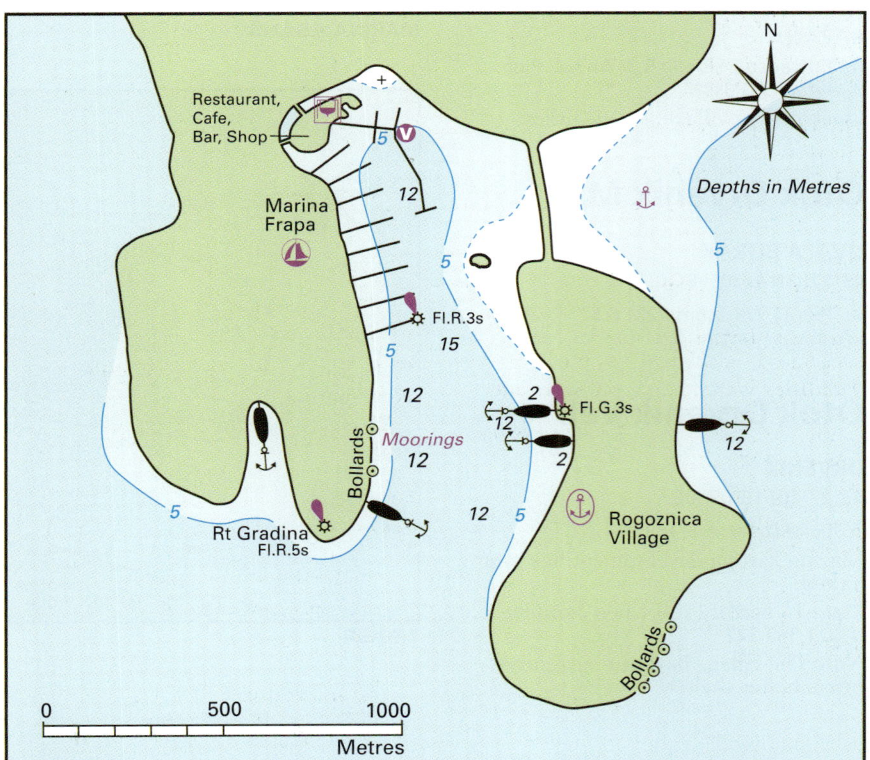

ROGOZNICA

Facilities Water. 220V. Fuel in Kremik Marina. Provisions and restaurants.
Port office ✆ 022 70266 / 098 337 930

MARINA KREMIK
43°33'·8N 15°56'·5E
BA 2712, Imray M25
VHF Ch 17.
Navigation The marina is in the N inlet of Luka Peleš.
Berths Where directed.
Shelter Good shelter.
Data 395 berths. Max LOA 26m. Depths 3–6m. Charge band 4.
Facilities Water. 220/380V. Showers and toilets. 200 places ashore. Chandler. 30-ton travel-hoist. 5-ton crane. Limited yacht repairs. Some provisions. Restaurant. Bus to Primosten.
Remarks Port of entry (summer only).
Marina Kremik ✆ 022 570 068
Email info@marina-kremik.hr

ROGOZNICA – MARINA FRAPA
43°31'·7N 15°58'·3E
Imray M25
☆ Rt Gradina Fl.R.5s15m4M
VHF Ch 17.
Berth Where directed. Visitors go on the new transit pontoon.
Shelter Good.
Data 450 berths. 70 visitors' berths. Max LOA 55m. Depths 3–8m. Charge band 6.
Facilities Water. 220V. Showers and toilets. Laundry. 75-ton travel-hoist. 150 places ashore. Some repairs. Provisions and restaurants.
Marina Frapa ✆ 022 559 900
Email marina-frapa@si.t-com.hr
www.marinafrapa.com

RAŽANJ
☆ Entrance E side Fl.R.3s7m3M. Pier head Fl.G.3s3M
Quay off the village. No facilities.

Otok Drvenik Mali

UVALA BORAK
43°27'·1N 16°05'·8E
☆ Pier Fl.WR.3s6m4/2M (252°-R-258°)
Harbour usually full.

Otok Drvenik Veli

DRVENIK
43°27'·0N 16°09'·0E
☆ Luka Drvenik Fl.R.3s4M
Marina Zirona development has been halted.
Data 15 berths (120 when complete).
✆ 021 362 722
Note The village harbour currently offers better shelter.

Trogirski Zaljev

VINISCE
43°29'·1N 16°07'·1E
Data c.50 berths on two pontoons in Vinisce.
Facilities Limited.
Remarks Marina Mirna is currently closed.
Marina Mirna ✆ 021 892 107

MARINA AGANA
43°30'·8N 16°07'·0E
Imray M26
☆ Fl(2)G.5s7m4M
VHF Ch 17.
Berths Where directed. Anchorage outside marina.
Shelter Good.
Data 135 berths. Max LOA 25m. Charge band 4/5.
Facilities Water. 220/380V. Showers and toilets. Laundry. 40-ton travel-hoist. 70 places ashore. Chandlery. Gas. Provisions and restaurants.
Agana Marina ✆ 021 889 411
Email info@marina-agana.hr

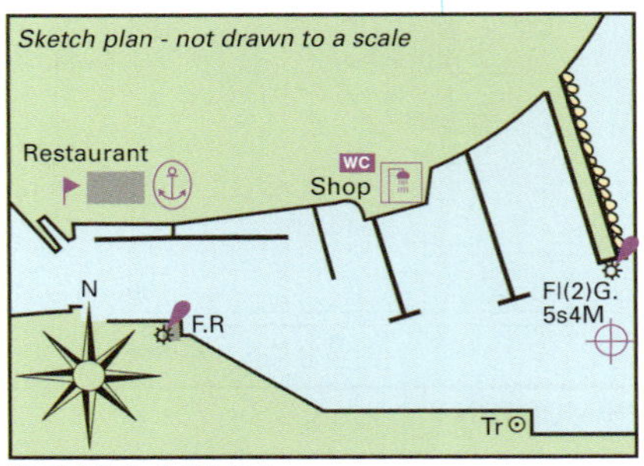

MARINA AGANA

MARINA YC SEGET
43°31'N 16°14'E
New pontoon marina 0.5M W of Trogir.
Data 150 berths. Max LOA 30m. Laid moorings. 100 places ashore. Charge band 5.
Facilities Water. 200V. Showers and toilets. 40-ton travel-hoist. YC restaurant.
YC Seget ✆ 021 798 182
Email reception@yachtclubseget.com
www.cromarina.com

TROGIR
43°30'·7N 16°14'·6E
☆ Hrid Čelice Fl(3)10s15m6M. Rt Pasji Fl.R.5s4M. Marina pier Fl(2)G.5s4M.Rt Čubrijan Fl.G.2s4M
Berths Where directed in the ACI marina Trogir on O. Čiovo. Also berths on Trogir town quay opposite the marina.
Data (Marina) 160 berths. Max LOA 22m. Depths 2–5m. Charge band 5/6.
Facilities Water. 220V. Showers and toilets. Fuel quay. 10-ton crane. Limited provisions. Restaurant.
Remarks 3m air height under bridge at E end. Shuttle ferry to old town.
Note Weekends are busy with charter yachts on change over.
ACI Marina Trogir ✆ 021 881 544
Email m.trogir@aci-club.hr

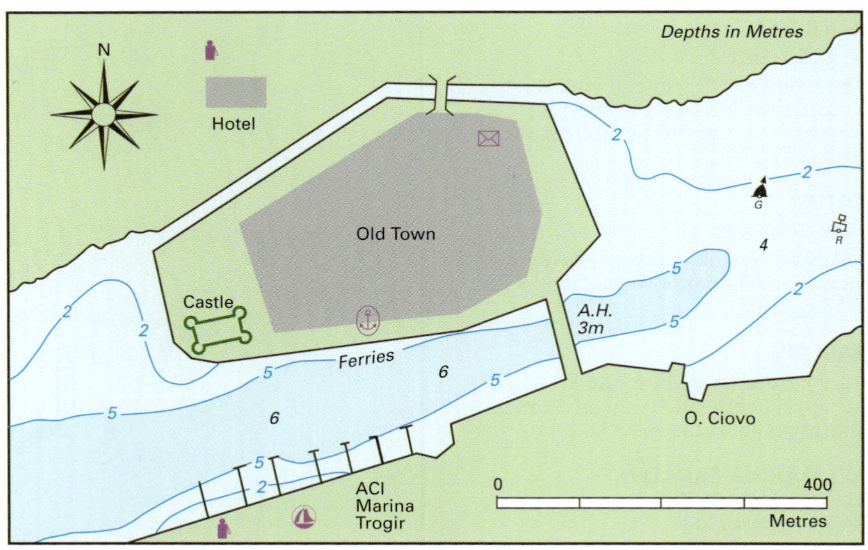

TROGIR

Kaštelanski Zaljev (Bay of Castles)

SLATINE
43°30'·0N 16°20'·7E

☆ Fl.R.3s3M

The harbour and campsite lie to the W of the village. Go alongside the outer breakwater. Depths 1–4m.

Remarks Harbour damaged in a winter storm. Care needed.

DIVULJE
43°31'·4N 16°17'·9E

☆ Mole head Fl.G.3s3M. Resnik breakwater head Fl.G.3s4M. Kaštel Stari mole head Fl(2)G.4s6m4M

KAŠTEL STARI
43°33'·0N16°21'·1E

☆ Pier head Fl(2)G.4s4M

Go alongside on the pier. Depths 2–4m. Close W lies the busier harbour at Kastel Novi.

KAŠTEL LUKSIC
43°33'·0N 16°22'·1E

Small harbour and pier. Alongside. Depths 2–3m.

KAŠTEL KAMBELOVAC
43°32'·9N 16°23'·4N

Fishing harbour, yacht quay and pier. Stern or bows-to. Depths 1·5–4m.

KAŠTEL GOMILICA
43°32'·9N 16°24'·0E

☆ Mole head F.G.3M

Small-boat harbour and quay. Stern or bows-to. Depths 2–3m.

MARINA KASTELA
43°32'·8N 16°24'·4E

☆ Breakwater head Fl(2)G.5s3M

VHF Ch 17.

Navigation Marina close to Split. Care needed of shallows off the industrial port of Split in the approaches.

Berths There are two basins in the marina. Go stern or bows-to where directed.

Data 400 berths. Visitors' berths. 200 places ashore. Depths 2·5–10m. Charge band 5.

Facilities Water. 220V. WiFi. Toilets and showers. 60-ton travel-lift. 40-ton trailer. Provisions and café/bar in the marina.

Remarks Split airport 7km. Large charter yacht base.

Marina Kastela ✆ 021 204 010
Email marina@marina-kastela.hr
www.marina-kastela.hr

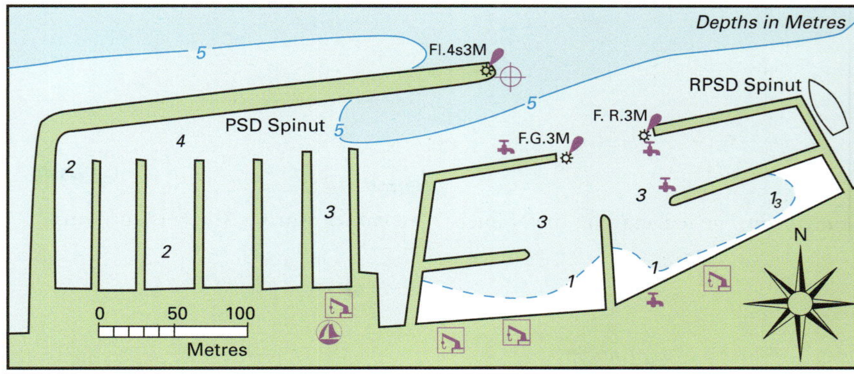

MARINA SPINUT

KAŠTEL SUĆURAC
43°32'·4N 16°26'·6E

Closer to the industrial suburbs of Split. Exposed quay with uneven depths.

VRANJIC
☆ W corner of landing place Fl.R.3s7m4M

Commercial harbour.

SPINUT MARINA
43°31'·3N 16°25'·7E
BA 269

☆ Marina entrance F.R.3M/F.G.3M

VHF Ch 17

Navigation The marina lies on the SE side of Kastelanski Zaljev. Yachts must pass outside the green buoy N of Rt Marjan.

Berths Where directed.

Shelter Good shelter.

Data *Spinut Marina* 780 berths. 100 visitors' berths. Sometimes limited to Croatian Club members only. Max LOA 15m. Max draught 5m. Charge band 5.

Facilities Water. 220V. Showers and toilets. 20-ton crane. Chandlers.

Remarks Bus service into Split.

Port JK Spinut ✆ 021 386 821

RT MARJAN
43°30'·5N 16°23'·6E

☆ S mole head Fl.G.3s8m5M

Oceanographic Institute.

Luka Split

LUKA SPLIT
43°30'·1N 16°26'·4E (LFl.G.6s10M)
BA 269, Imray M26

☆ Entrance LFl.G.6s10M Siren 30s/Fl.R.6s5M. Marina mole head Fl.R.2s3M. Gat Sv Petra head Fl(3)8s3M. Gat Sav Nikole SW corner Fl.3s4M. Grljevac pier head Fl(2)G.5s3M

VHF Ch 09, 12, 16 for port authorities.

Yachts clearing in go on the quay on the E side of the harbour near the port office. For berths there are several choices.

Remarks Split commercial harbour is polluted and smelly. Yachts are recommended to go to Zenta (located outside the commercial harbour) or to Split/Spinut on the N side of the headland.

Note It is reported to be no longer possible for yachts to clear into Croatia here.

ACI MARINA SPLIT
VHF Ch 17 for ACI Split.

Data 365 berths. Max LOA 60m. Depths 2·5–8m. Charge band 6.

Facilities Water. 220V. WiFi. Showers and toilets. Laundry. Fuel quay nearby. 10-ton crane. 30-ton travel-hoist. Limited yacht repairs. Gas. Provisions and restaurants.

Remarks Split airport 20km.

ACI Marina Split ✆ 021 398 599
Email m.split@aci-club.hr

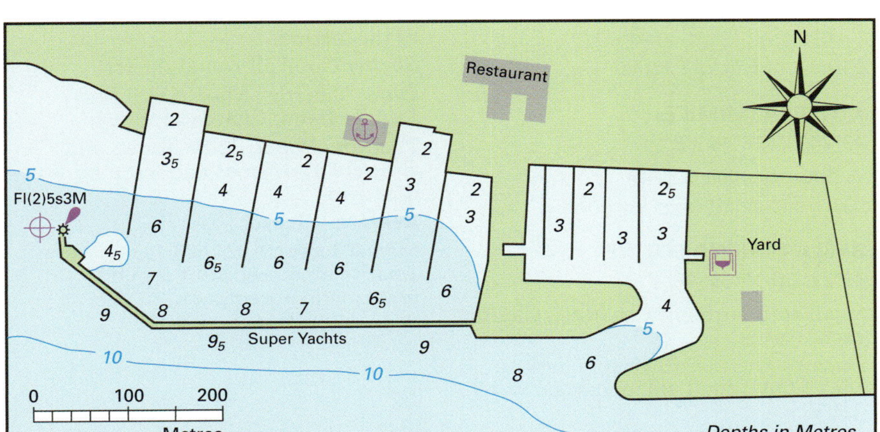

MARINA KASTELA

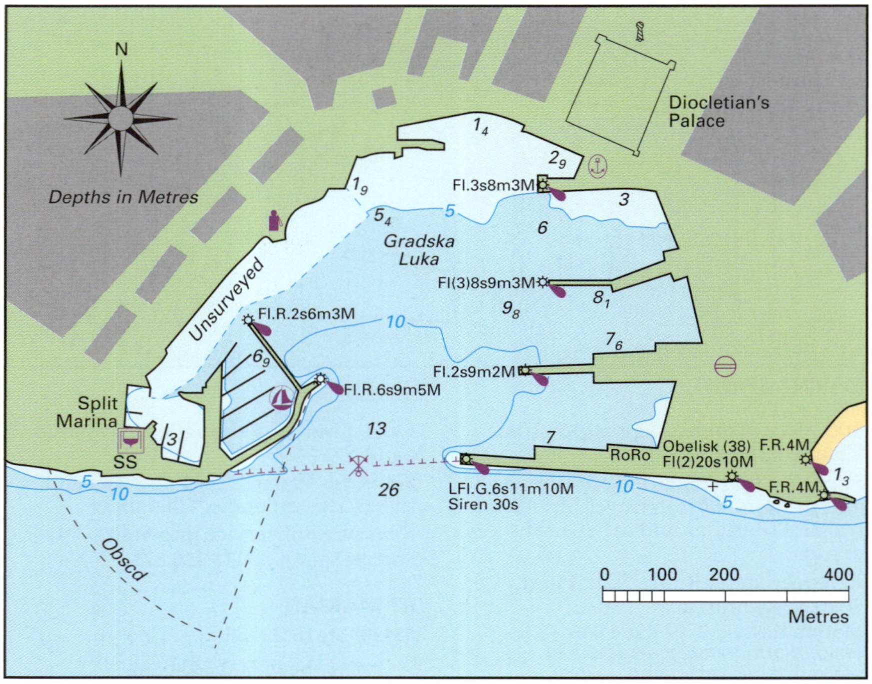

SPLIT AND MARINA SPLIT

LABUD YC

Data 60 berths. Max LOA 8m.

Facilities Water. 220V. Showers and toilets. Fuel quay nearby. Provisions and restaurants.

☎ 021 398 583

ZENTA MARINA

43°30'·0N 16°27'·8E

☆ E breakwater head Fl(2)G.4·5s9m4M. Lts in line 334° (marks pipeline) Front F.R.6m4M Rear F.R.10m4M

VHF Ch 17.

Data 870 berths. Max LOA 14m. Max Draught 5m. Charge band 4.

Facilities Water. 220V. Showers and toilets. 10-ton crane. Limited yacht repairs. Provisions and restaurants nearby.

☎ 021 365 764

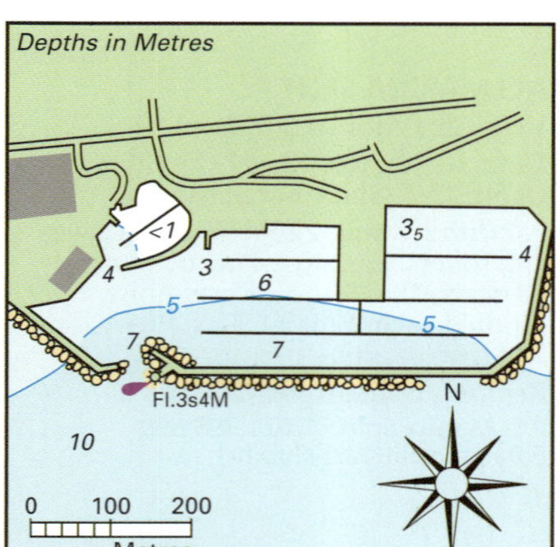

ZENTA MARINA

Luka Stobreč

PODSTANA (MARINA LAV HOTEL)

43°29'·8N 16°32'·1E

VHF Ch 17.

Data 70 berths. Max LOA 35m. Depths 0·5–3m. Water. 220V.

Marina Lav ☎ 021 500 387 / 8
Email info@marinalav.hr
www.grandhotellav.com

KRILO

43°27'·6N 16°36'·1E

☆ Mole head Fl.RG.3s6m2M

Trip boat base.

DUGI RAT

43°26'·4N 16°38'·7E

☆ Fl(2)G.5s7m3M

OMIŠ

43°26'·4N 16°41'·9E

☆ Mole head Fl.WG.3s4/2M (334°-G-038°)

Mouth of Rijeka Cetina.

KUTLEŠA (MIMICE)

43°24'·3N 16°48'·6E

☆ Mole head Fl.G.3s4M

Crowded small-boat harbour.

BRELA MARINA SOLINE

43°22'·0N 16°55'·9E

Small craft harbour with hotel. Charter yacht berths.

Data 100 berths. 50 visitors' berths. Max LOA 12m. Laid moorings. Water. 220V.

Remarks Open May–October.

☎ 021 603 200 / 618 222

MARINA BAŠKA VODA

43°21'·4N 16°57'·1E

☆ Fl.R.5s5M

A marina off the village of the same name.

Data 180 berths. 60 visitors' berths. 30 places ashore. Charge band 5.

Facilities Water. 220V. Provisions and restaurants.

☎ 021 620 909 / 091 515 9976
Email baska-voda@baotic-yachting.com
www.cromarina.com

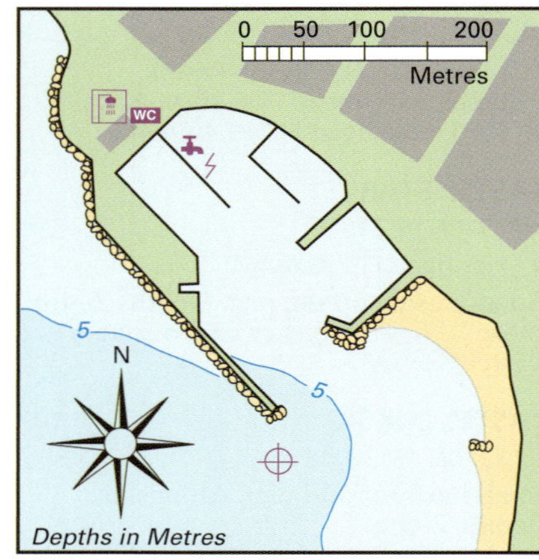

MARINA BASKA VODA

RAMOVA KRVAVICA

43°19'·5N 16°58'·8E

Data 150 berths. Laid moorings. Water. 220V. Charge band 5. Charter base.

☎ 021 621 176
Email ramova.krvavica@gmail.com

MAKARSKA

43°17'·6N 17°01'·3E

☆ Poluotoka Sveti Petar W point Fl.5s16m11M. Mole Fl.3s4M

Yacht berths on the quay. Depths 2–3m. Water. 220V. Fuel quay.

Note A new breakwater has improved shelter.

HM ☎ 021 611 977

TUČEPI MARINA

43°16'·2N 17°03'·4E

VHF Ch 17.

Berths Where directed in the inner part of the marina.

Shelter Good all-round shelter.

Data 70 berths. Max LOA 15m. Depths 1–6m. Charge band 3/4.

Facilities Water. 220V. Toilets and showers. Provisions and restaurants in the town.

Remarks Charter base.

Marina Tučepi ☎ 021 623 155
Email marinatucepi@st.t-com.hr
www.marinatucepi.com

Otok Šolta

ROGAČ

43°24'·0N 16°18'·6E

☆ Ferry pier Fl(2)5s8m3M. Rt Bad Fl.R.3s4M

Yacht berths on N and S quays. Laid moorings. Water. 220V.

STOMORSKA

43°22'·4N 16°21'·5E

☆ Entrance E side Fl(2)R.5s3M

Yacht berths on E quay. Laid moorings. Water. 220V. Restaurants.

MASLINICA

43°23'·8N 16°12'·4E

☆ Rt Sveti Nikola Fl.WR.3s10m7/4M (011°-R-056°)

Small marina and hotel.

Data 50 berths. Depths 1·5–4m. Laid moorings. Water. 220V.

Marina Martinis Marchi Hotel
✆ 021 572 768
Email info@martinis-marchi.com

Otok Brač

ACI MARINA MILNA

43°19'·6N 16°27'·1E

VHF Ch 17 for ACI Milna.

Data 190 berths. Max LOA 40m. Depths <1–3·5m. Charge band 5/6.

Facilities Water. 220V. Showers and toilets. Fuel quay. 10-ton crane. Shipyard nearby. Provisions and restaurants.

ACI Marina Milna
✆ 021 636 306 / 366
Email m.milne@aci-club.hr

MARINA VLASKA

43°19'·7N 16°26'·3E

☆ Fl.R

Marina in the N of Milna Bay, Otok Brac. The marina is 1km from Milna.

VHF Ch 67

Data Three pontoons – 90 berths. Max LOA 15m. Charge band 3/4.

Facilities Water. 220V. Showers and toilets.

✆ 021 636 247
Email info@marinavlaska.com
www.marinavlaska.com

BOBOVISCE

Yacht berths on village quay. Laid moorings. Water. 220V. Charge band 4.

SUTIVAN

43°23'·2N 16°29'·0E

☆ Mole head Fl.R.3s2M

Small harbour.

SUPETAR

43°23'·2N 16°33'·5E

☆ Ferry harbour breakwater head Fl.R.3s5M. Inner breakwater head Fl.G.3s4M

Ferry port to Split. Main town on Brač.

SPLISKA

43°22'·8N 16°36'·5E

☆ Entrance E side Fl.R.2s2M

Forked bay. Quay in E leg. Depths 2–3m. Laid moorings. Water. 220V.

POSTIRA

43°22'·7N 16°37'·8E

☆ Breakwater head Fl.R.2s3M

Fishing port. Works in progress building an extension for yacht berths.

PUČIŠĆA

43°21'·7N 16°44'·3E

☆ Rt Sv Nikola Fl.5s20m8M

Deep inlet open N. Yacht berths on SW quay. Otherwise anchor in harbour clear of the ferry turning area. N quay used by ferry and loading locally quarried stone. Restaurants ashore.

POVLJA

43°20'·4N 16°50'·0E

☆ Fl.3s7m7M

Quiet village. Go stern-to on the quay or on the pier. Some laid moorings.

SUMARTIN

43°16'·8N 16°52'·6E

☆ Mole head Fl.R.3s3M. E side entrance Fl.3s7M

Ferry port with room for yachts on the inner jetty. Laid moorings. Water. 220V.

HM ✆ 021 648 222

BOL

43°15'·6N 16°39'·7E

☆ Fl.G.3s3M

Busy small-boat harbour. Some yacht berths E of the breakwater. Laid moorings. Water. 220V. Fuel quay. Provisions.

HM ✆ 095 454 5610

UVALA LUCICE

Bay on SW side of Otok Brač

25 mooring buoys. Charge band 3. Restaurant.

Otok Hvar

HVAR

43°10'·2N 16°26'·8E (Gališnik light)
BA 2712, Imray M26

☆ O. Sv Jerolim NE point Fl.R.3s12m4M. O. Gališnik Fl.G.3s11m5M. Pier head Fl(2)G.5s4M

VHF Ch 17.

Berths Stern or bows-to on E quay, or moorings stern-to with long line ashore on W side. Depths 3–4m. Charge band 5.

Shelter Uncomfortable with strong SE–S–SW winds.

Facilities Water. 220V. Fuel quay (shallow). Provisions and restaurants.

Remarks Port of entry (summer only). Use quay in N side of harbour.

Port office ✆ 021 741 007 / 091 527 4252

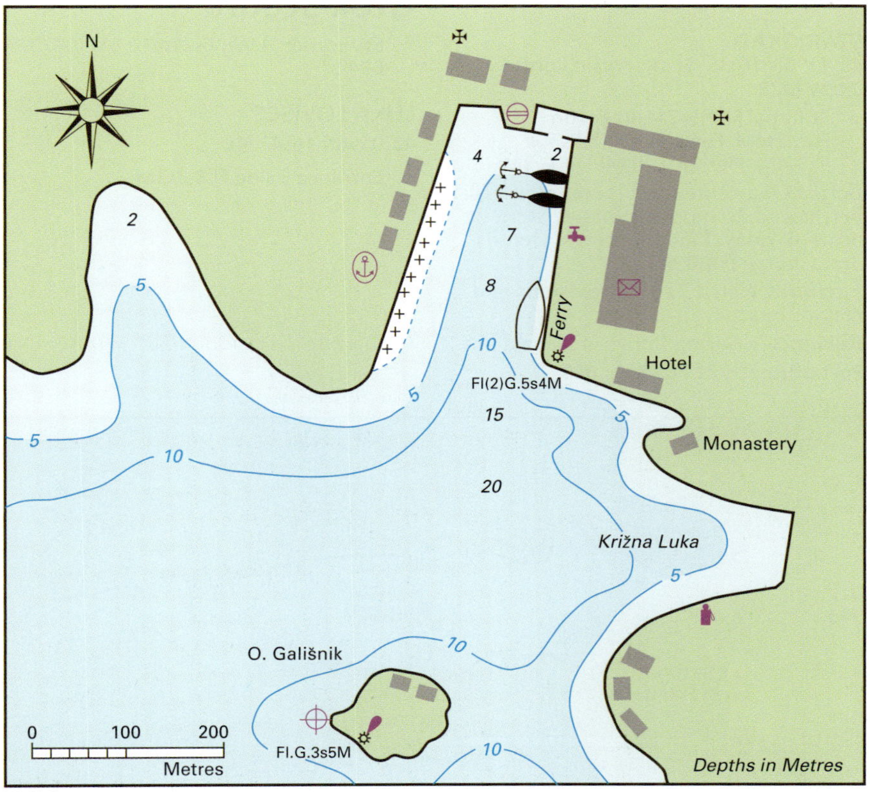

HVAR

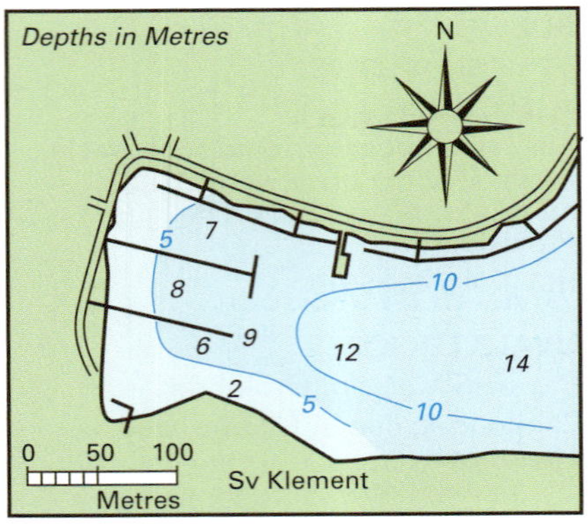

ACI MARINA PALMIZANA

ACI MARINA PALMIŽANA
43°09'·5N 16°24'·0E
Imray M26

Navigation Situated on the NE corner of Sv Klement. Open in summer (mid-April–end October).
Data 200 berths. Max LOA 30m. Depths 2–7m. Charge band 6.
Facilities Water. 220V. WiFi. Showers and toilets. Restaurant. Provisions.
Remarks Care needed as short mooring lines foul easily on propeller.
ACI Marina Palmižana ✆ 021 744 995
Email m.palmizana@aci-club.hr

UVALA PRIBINJA
43°11'·9N 16°25'·7E

Anchorage with mooring buoys. Restaurant.

UVALA VIRA
43°11'·5N 16°26'·0E

☆ Rt Galijola Fl.2s8m6M. Nezadovoljan Fl.R.2s8m3M. Vira Fl.G.2s3M

STARIGRAD
43°11'·0N 16°35'·5E (Rt Fortin light)
Imray M26

☆ Rt Kabal Fl(2)5s7M. Rt Fortin Fl.G.2s4M. Ferry pier Fl(2)5s2M/ Fl.3s4M. Pier F.R.2M. Mole F.G.3M

Berths Quay extension is complete. 70 berths and 20 mooring buoys. Stern or bows-to quay. Laid moorings. Depths 3m. Charge band 6/3.
Facilities Water. 220V. Provisions and restaurants.
Remarks Mooring buoys in Zavala bay.
Port office ✆ 021 765 299 / 060

ACI MARINA VRBOSKA
43°10'·8N 16°40'·8E
BA 2712, Imray M26

☆ Rt Križ Fl.2s5m5M. Quay Fl.R.3s3M

VHF Ch 17 for ACI Vrboska.
Data 125 berths. Max LOA 20m. Depths 2–4m. Charge band 5/6.
Facilities Water. 220V. Showers and toilets. Fuel quay. 5-ton crane. Limited yacht repairs. Provisions and restaurants.
Remarks Also berths on village quay.
ACI Marina Vrboska
✆ 021 774 018
Email m.vrboska@aci-club.hr

JELSA
43°09'·8N 16°42'·0E

☆ Otok Zečevo E point Fl.5s11m5M. North mole head Fl.G.3s4M. Pier head Fl.R.3s5M

Yacht quay with some laid moorings. Depths 2–4m.
HM ✆ 021 761 055

SUCURAJ
43°07'·4N 17°11'·6E

☆ Rt Sućuraj Iso.4s14m11M. Mole head Fl.R.2s3M

Fishing boat and ferry harbour. May be space alongside clear of ferry berth on S quay.

SV NEDJELJA
Small marina for a vineyard and restaurant. Go alongside where directed.
Marina Bilo Idro ✆ 021 745 703
Email zlatanotok@z.hr

Otok Šćedro

☆ SW corner Fl.WR.6s21m10/6M (087°-R-094·5°)

LUKA LOVIŠĆE
43°05'·8N 16°42'·4E

☆ Entrance E side Fl.R.3s3M

Otok Viš

VIŠKA LUKA
43°03'·7N 16°11'·6E
Imray M26

☆ Hrid Krava Fl.R.2s7m4M. Hrid Volići Fl.2s8m6M. Otočić Host NE point Fl.4s21m8M. Prirovo pier Fl.G.3s3M. Ferry pier head Fl.5s3M

Yacht berths at Viš town. Laid moorings between Viš and Kut. There is a charge for anchoring.
Data Charge band 5.
Facilities Water. 220V. Fuel.
Port of Viš ✆ 021 718 746
Email issa.adrianautika@st.t-com.hr

KOMIŽA
43°02'·7N 16°05'·2E

☆ Otočić Mali Barjak Fl.3s13m8M. Rt Stupišće Fl(3)12s18m10M. Mole head Fl.G.3s4M

Yacht berths along breakwater. Laid moorings. Depths 2–3m. Mooring buoys in the bay.
Data Charge band 4/5.
Facilities Water. 220V. Some repairs. Provisions.
Remarks Port of entry (summer only).
✆ 021 713 082 / 849

Otok Korčula

ACI MARINA KORČULA
42°57'·5N 17°08'·5E
BA 196, Imray M26

☆ Ferry pier Fl(2)R.5s3M. E quay Fl.G.3s2M. W harbour breakwater head Fl.R.2s4M. Marina breakwater head Fl.G.5s4M

VHF Ch 17 for ACI Korčula.
Berths Where directed in the marina on the E side of the headland.
Shelter Uncomfortable with the *bora*.

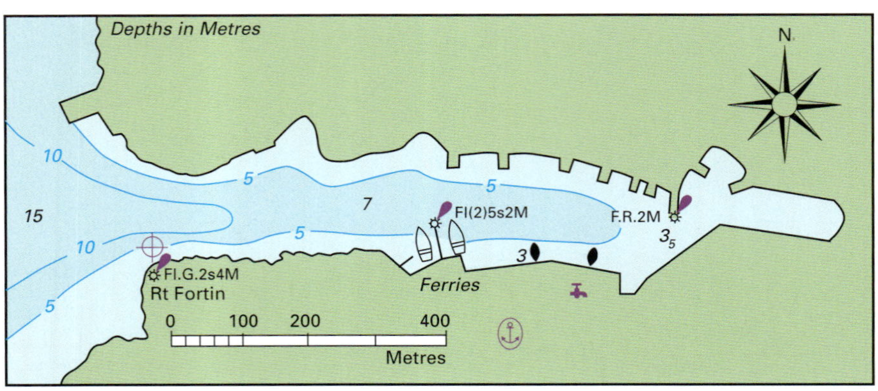

STARIGRAD

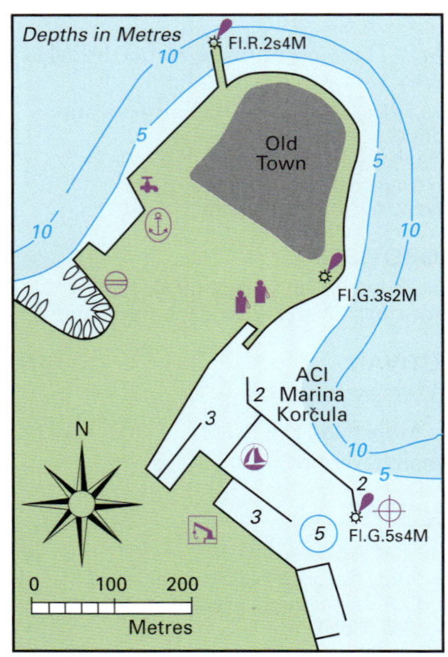

KORČULA

Data 160 berths. Visitors' berths. Max LOA 40m. Charge band 6.

Facilities Water. 220V. WiFi. Showers and toilets. Laundry. Fuel on the SE side of old town. 10-ton crane. 100-ton crane and slipway in boatyard nearby. Limited yacht repairs. Provisions and restaurants.

Remarks Port of entry.

ACI Marina Korčula ☏ 020 711 661
Email m.korcula@aci-club.hr

OTOK BADIJA

42°57'·3N 17°09'·2E

☆ Fl(2)G.5s7m4M

MARINA LUMBARDA

42°55'·5N 17°10'·6E

☆ Fl.R.3s3M

VHF Ch 17.

Data 175 berths. Max LOA 30m. Depths 2–6m. Charge band 4.

Facilities Water. 220V. Showers and toilets. Provisions and restaurants.

Marina Lumbarda ☏ 020 712 489
Email lucica-lumbarda@du.t-com.hr

UVALA ZAVALATICA

42°54'·6N 16°56'·5E

Small harbour.

BRNA

42°54'·3N 16°51'·6E

☆ Rt Veli Zaglav Fl.3s13m7M. Brna Fl.R.3s3M

Usually only room to anchor. Charge band 2/3.

UVALA PRIZBA MALI

42°54'·3N 16°47'·7E

Anchor either side of the peninsula. Holiday village ashore.

VELA LUKA

42°57'·7N 16°43'·1E
BA 196, Imray M26

☆ Otočić Kamenjak S side Fl(2)R.6s10m4M. Rt Vranac Fl.R.2s7m2M. Quay W end Fl.G.3s2M. Pier head Fl(2)5s3M

25 yacht berths stern-to on the quay. Anchorage in N creek.

Data Charge band 3/4.

Facilities Water. 220V. Fuel.

Remarks Port of entry.

HM ☏ 020 812 023 / 091 571 0340

UVALA PRIGRADICA

42°58'·0N 16°48'·5E

☆ Otočić Pločica NW end Fl(2)10s25m10M. Mole head Fl.R.3s3M

Harbour open N.

LUKA RAČIŠĆE

42°52'·5N 17°01'·5E

☆ Breakwater head Fl.G.3s4M

Otok Mljet

MLJET NATIONAL PARK
The W end of the island is protected, and navigation is prohibited in the narrow passage of Zaljev Soline.

POMENA

42°47'·3N 17°20'·9E

Care needed in the approaches. Berth bow or stern-to off restaurants or the hotel. 220V. Depths 2–4m. Charge band 5.

LUKA POLAČE

42°47'·2N 17°26'·2E
BA 196

☆ Hrid Kula Fl.2s11m6M

Sheltered anchorage. Some laid moorings. Restaurants.

KOZARICA

42°46'·7N 17°28'·2E

Harbour usually crowded.

SOBRA

42°43'·6N 17°37'·1E

☆ Rt Pusti Fl.3s14m7M. Ferry jetty head Fl.R.3s3M

Moorings off Villa Mungos.

OKUKLJE

42°43'·6N 17°40'·6E

☆ Rt Stoba Fl(2)5s10m6M. Rt Okuklje Fl.G.2s1M. Pier Fl.G.2s1M

Laid moorings on restaurant jetties.

PODSKOLJ

Bay on E end of Mljet. Three mooring buoys off restaurant Stermasi.

Otok Lastovo

SKRIVENA LUKA

42°43'·8N 16°53'·4E

☆ Rt Stražica Fl.R.3s8m3M

Yacht berths on restaurant jetties. Water. 220V.

UBLI

42°44'·7N 16°49'·8E

☆ Fl.R.2s2M

Ferry berth and quay in SE corner of Luka Velji Lago.

Facilities Customs and fuel quay.

Remarks Port of entry (summer only).

Port office ☏ 020 805 006

LUKA VELJI LAGO (LASTOVO MARINA)

☆ Otočić Pod Mrčaru Fl(2)6s23m9M. Otok Prežba Fl.WR.5s18m8/5M (235°-R-023°).

VHF Ch 17.

Berths Where directed in the marina in the N of the bay. Depths 2m. Laid moorings. Charge band 5.

Facilities Water. 220V. Showers and toilets. Hotel. Diving centre.

Marina Lastovo ☏ 020 802 100
Email info@marina-lastovo.com

LUKA MALI LAGO

Part of Lastovo Marina with berths N of the road bridge. Entry from the N coast of Lastovo. Details as above.

Mainland coast

PODGORA

43°14'·6N 17°04'·5E
Imray M26

☆ Pier head Fl.R.3s4M

Busy resort 2½M SE of Tucepi Marina. Modernised harbour/yacht marina.

Data 100 berths. Laid moorings. Depths 2–4m.

Podgora Marina ☏ 021 625 222

IGRANE

43°11'·7N 17°08'·8E

Fishing harbour. Anchoring space limited by swimming area.

DREVNIK

43°09'·2N 17°15'·2E

☆ Ferry pier head Fl.G.2s3M

Ferry harbour.

GRADAC

43°06'·2N 17°20'·8E

Busy fishing harbour.

PLOČE (KARDELJEVO)

43°02'·4N 17°25'·1E

☆ Rt Višnjica S side Fl(2)5s13m7M. N side Fl.R.2s12m2M. Rt Bad Fl.R.2s9m2M. Gat Oslobodenja W end Fl.G.3s3M

Croatian commercial and ferry port serving Bosnia-Herzegovina.

Berths near the fuel quay. Anchoring permitted in N harbour. Water. Fuel. Some repairs. Provisions.

Remarks Port of entry.

Port office ☏ 020 679 008

RIJEKA NERETVA (NERETVA RIVER)

☆ N mole head (river mouth) Fl.R.2s6m4M/Fl.R.3s6m3M. S mole head Fl.G.2s5m5M. Rogotin S bank Fl.G.3s5m3M. N bank Fl.R.3s5m3M. River lit by 4 pairs of lights Fl.R.3s3M/Fl.G.3s3M

High voltage cable AH 15m. Bridge AH 13m.

Otok Peljesac

MALI STON

42°50'·0N 17°42'·0E
(Fl.R.3s2M Mole head)

☆ Access channel Fl.G.2s1M(x2)/Fl.R.2s1M(x3).

Access via Kanal Mali Ston. Go alongside the quay. Depths 1–3m. Harbour silts to less than 1m in places.

HODILJE
42°51′·5N 17°41′·6E

☆ Mole head Fl.G.2s3M

Yacht berths on jetty.

DRACE
42°55′·1N 17°27′·3E

☆ Mole head Fl.WR.3s4/2M (197°-R-243°)

TRPANJ
43′00′·7N 17°16′·2E

☆ Breakwater head Fl.R.3s4M. E mole head Fl.3s2M

Ferry harbour. Some yacht berths W of ferry quay. Laid moorings. Water. 220V.

UVALA LUKA AND LOVIŠĆE
43°01′·6N 17°02′·0E

☆ Rt Osičac Fl.3s9m8M. Luka Fl.R.3s3M. Rt Lovišće Fl(3)10s10m10M

Yacht quay with laid moorings.
Facilities Water. 220V.

OREBIĆ MARINA
42°58′·4N 17°10′·8E

☆ Ferry mole head Fl.G.3s3M

Berths Head for Peliska Jedra Sailing Club harbour in the SE of the harbour.
Data 240 berths. 30 visitors' berths. Depths 2–3m. Laid moorings.
Facilities Water. 220V. Fuel in the town. Provisions and restaurants. Ferry to Korčula.
✆ 020 713 155 / 098 977 7414

TRSTENIK
42°54′·9N 17°24′·3E

☆ Mole head Fl.R.3s3M

Berths Berth clear of ferry berth on the jetty. Ferry to Ploče.

ŽULJANA
42°53′·4N 17°27′·4E

☆ Otočić Lirica W point LFl.10s34m9M. Mole head Fl.G.3s4M

Small jetty usually full.

Otok Šipan

ŠIPANSKA LUKA
42°43′·8N 17°51′·8E

☆ Pier Fl.R.5s3M

Limited yacht berths. Restaurants.

SUDURAD
42°42′·6N 17°55′·0E

☆ S mole head Fl(2)WR.5s4/2M (235°-R-275°)

Ferry and trip boat harbour. Limited yacht berths.

Otok Lopud

UVALA LOPUD
42°41′·4N 17°56′·6E

☆ Mole head Fl.R.3s3M

Berths available when trip boats leave.

Otok Koločep

GORNJI ĆELO
42°40′·3N 18°01′·3E

☆ Rt Bezdanj (Gornji) Fl(2)8s18m4M.

DONJE ĆELO
42°40′·7N 18°00′·2E

☆ Donje Ćelo mole head Fl.3s6m4M

Ferry harbour. Anchorage in the harbour.

Mainland coast

Stonski Kanal

STON
42°50′·0N 17°42′·2E
Imray M26

☆ Approach channel Fl.G.2s1M(x2)/Fl.R.2s1M(x3). Mole head Fl.R.3s4M

Town at the head of the channel. Opposite Mali Ston on Peljesac. The channel cuts through salt marshes and is dredged to 4m (minimum 2·5m). Go alongside the quay. Depths 2·5–4m. Good all-round shelter.
Facilities Provisions and restaurants in the town.
Port office ✆ 020 754 026

BROCE
42°49′·3N 17°43′·1E

☆ Rt Pologrin (Grbljava) Fl.3s11m7M. Mole head Fl.R.3s4M

Two moles off the village. Depths 1–4m. Dangerous rock 80m off the end of the S mole.

KOBAŠ
42°48′·2N 17°44′·8E

Small cove with a jetty 1½M SE of Broce. Also restaurant jetties. Open S.

DOLI
42°48′·4N 17°48′·0E

☆ Mole head Fl.R.3s2M

Small harbour and factory ashore.

SLANO
42°47′·1N 17°53′·4E

☆ Rt Donji Fl.R.3s16m4M. Quay Fl.G.5s3M

Yacht quay. Laid moorings. Water. 220V. Bar and restaurant. Supermarket. Marina planned in S bay.
✆ 091 9022 672

ZATON
42°41′·1N 18°03′·0E

☆ Rt Bat Fl.R.3s19m4M

Sheltered inlet with a small harbour. Some laid moorings.

Gruž and Dubrovnik

42°40′·0N 18°05′E (Rt Kantafig light)
BA 196, 680, 1578, Imray M27

☆ Hrid Grebeni Fl(3)10s27m10M. O Daksa Fl.6s7m10M. Rt Kantafig Fl.2s7m5M. Petka mole head Fl(2)R.4s8m3M. Rijeka Dubrovačka Mokošica Fl.R.3s4M. Bridge centre Iso.2s5M

VHF Ch 16 for Gruž port authorities. Ch 17 for Dubrovnik Marina.
Navigation Dubrovnik Marina lies 2M upriver from Gruž on Rijeka Dubrovaćka.
Harbourmaster (Lucka Kapetanija Dubrovnik)
✆ 020 418 988.

ACI MARINA DUBROVNIK
40°40′·2N 18°07′·7E

☆ Marina Dubrovnik ACI Marina N breakwater Fl.R.2s2M. S breakwater Fl.G.2s2M

VHF Ch 17.
Berths Where directed.
Shelter Good shelter.
Data 380 berths. Max LOA 60m. Depths 2·5–5m. Charge band 6.
Facilities Water. 220V. WiFi. Showers and toilets. Fuel quay. 100-ton travel-hoist. 140 places ashore. Most yacht repairs. Chandlers. LPG station. Provisions and restaurants.
Remarks Yachts clearing in must go to Gruž. Bus from the marina to Gruž and Dubrovnik. Dubrovnik airport 20 minutes.
ACI Marina Dubrovnik
✆ 020 455 020
Email m.dubrovnik@aci-club.hr

GRUŽ
42°39′·5N 18°05′·5E
Imray M27

☆ Rt Kantafig Fl.2s5M. Petka mole head Fl(2)R.4s8m3M

Commercial port with yacht marina.
Berths Stern or bows-to or alongside S of ferry quay.
Data 40 berths. Depths 3–5m. Max LOA c.40m. Charge band 6.
Shelter Good shelter. Wash from commercial traffic.
Facilities Water. 220V. Provisions and restaurants in nearby Dubrovnik town.
Remarks Port of entry.
Porat Dubrovnik Marina
✆ 020 417 999

DUBROVNIK TOWN

☆ Mole head Fl.R.3s4M. Port office mole head F.WG.2M (254°-G-305°)

Cruise ship port development underway.

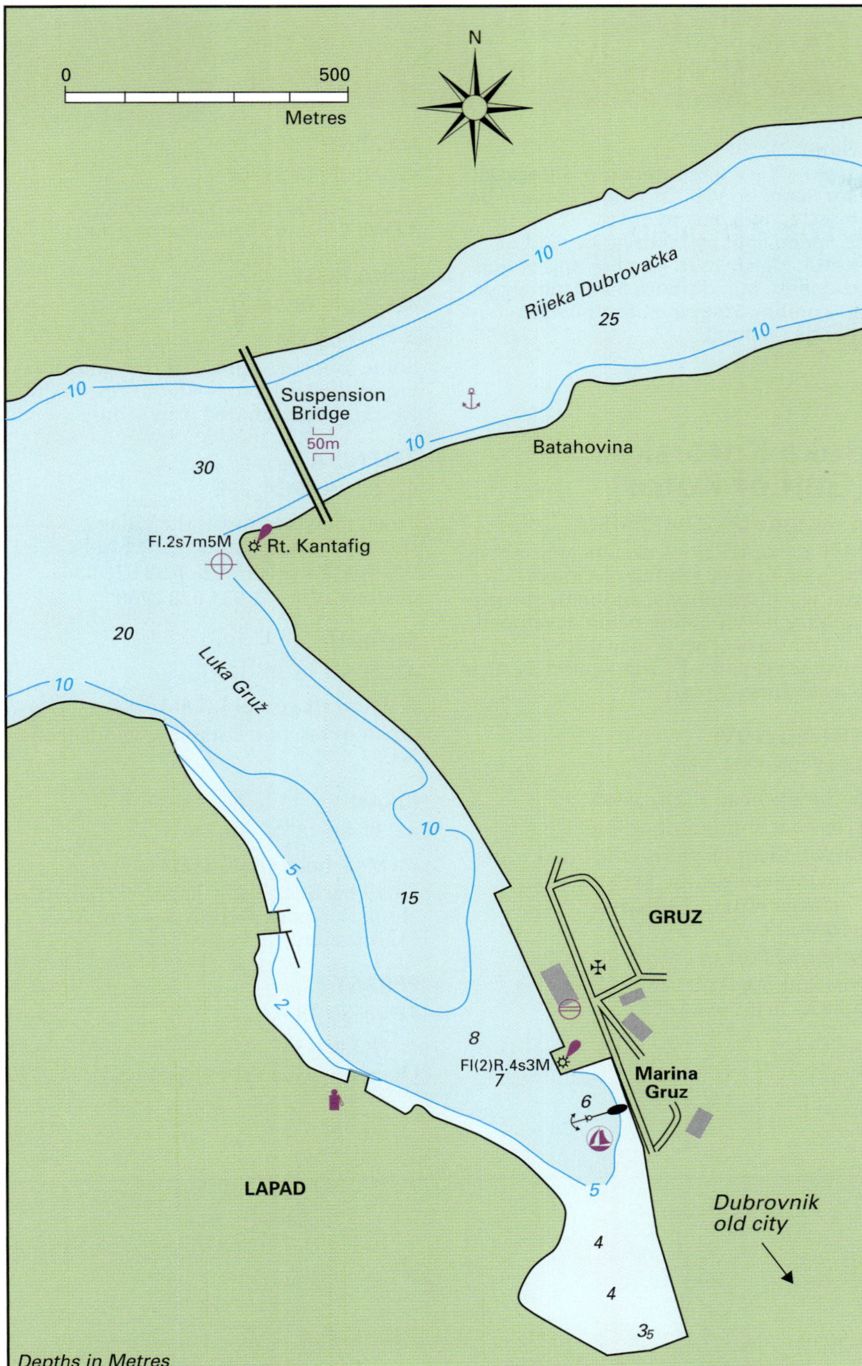

GRUZ (DUBROVNIK)

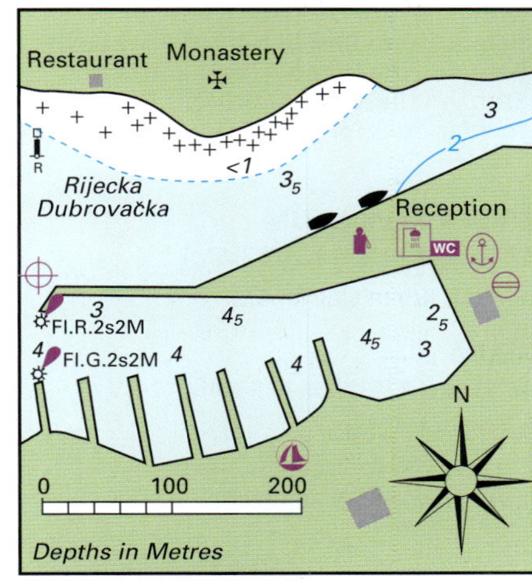

MARINA DUBROVNIK

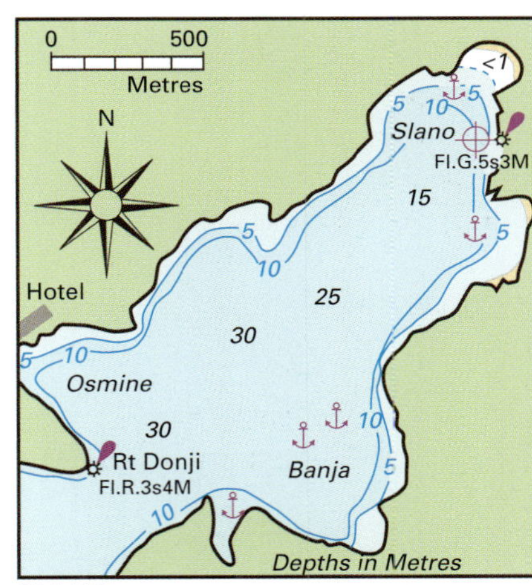

SLANO

SREBRENO

42°37'·2N 18°12'·1E

☆ Breakwater Fl.R.3s2M.

CAVTAT

42°35'·0N 18°13'·0E (Fl.WRG.2s)

☆ Seka Velika Fl(2)10s8m8M. Cavtat Fl.WRG.2s6/3M (083°-R-110°, 129°-G-158°)

Go alongside on the town quay. Usually full of superyachts during high season. Charge band 4.

Remarks Port of entry (summer only). Berth on customs quay.

✆ 020 478 665 / 091 798 5581

MOLUNAT

42°26'·9N 18°26'·6E (Fl.3s)

☆ Otočić Veliki Školj Fl(3)15s34m8M. Gornji Molunat N side Fl.3s8m6M

Anchoring is prohibited unless you have cleared into Croatia.

10.8 Bosnia-Herzegovina

TIME ZONE UT+1 ☏ IDD +387

Note The short Adriatic coastline belonging to Bosnia-Herzegovina lies between the Neretva River and Mali Ston, on the Kanal Mali Ston. There are few facilities for yachts.

ZALJEV KLEK NEUM

42°56'·0N 17°33'·3E (Fl.3s5M)

☆ Rep Kleka Fl.3s8m5M

NEUM

42°55'·2N 17°37'·0E Fl.R3s4M

☆ Fl.R.3s6m4M

Little room for yachts.

Port Authority ☏ 36 880 02

10.9 Montenegro

TIME ZONE UT+1 ☏ IDD+382

Notes

1. On entering Montenegro waters call *Bar Radio* on VHF Ch 16 and you will be directed to a port of entry.
2. Speed limit of 12kns in the Gulf of Kotor. Max 8kns in Kumbor and Verige channels. Min distance 50m from shore in Kumbor. Stopping prohibited in Verige Channel.

Boka Kotorska (Gulf of Kotor)

☆ Rt Ostra LFl(2)10s73m15M

Military restrictions no longer apply in the gulf, except around obvious military installations, and many former military harbours are being developed into marinas. The W side of the entrance is part of Croatia, and as such is a restricted area.

HERZEG NOVI

42°27'·0N 18°32'·3E

☆ S mole head Fl(2)G.5s5M

Trip boat and ferry harbour.

Berths Yacht berths on the breakwater. Laid moorings. Charge band 3.

Facilities Water. 220V. Fuel. YC restaurant.

Remarks Port of entry.

Port authority ☏ 031 678 276
☏ 8832 3015 / 6964 4097

MELJINE

42°27'·2N 18°33'·6E

Yacht berths on two piers. Depths 1-3m.

LUKA ROSE

42°25'·7N 18°34'·7E

☆ Pier F.G.2M

Some mooring buoys off the village. Good shelter from S–SE but open NW. Restaurants. Limited provisions.

ZELENIKA

42°26'·9N 18°34'·25E

Town quay berths off the village. Boatyard and repairs. Travel-hoist.

'Marina' Zelenika yard ☏ 88 678 024

Customs office ☏ 031 678 2760

MORINJ

42°29'·4N 18°39'·3E

☆ Quay NE corner F.G.4M

Open to evening katabatic winds from NE.

RISAN

42°30'·8N 18°41'·9E

☆ Mole head Fl(3)G.6s2M

Small harbour and village. Yacht berths along the quay. Depths 3-4·5m. Max LOA c.17m.

PERAST

42°29'·2N 18°42'·2E

☆ Fl(3)R.7s3M

Open quay off the village.

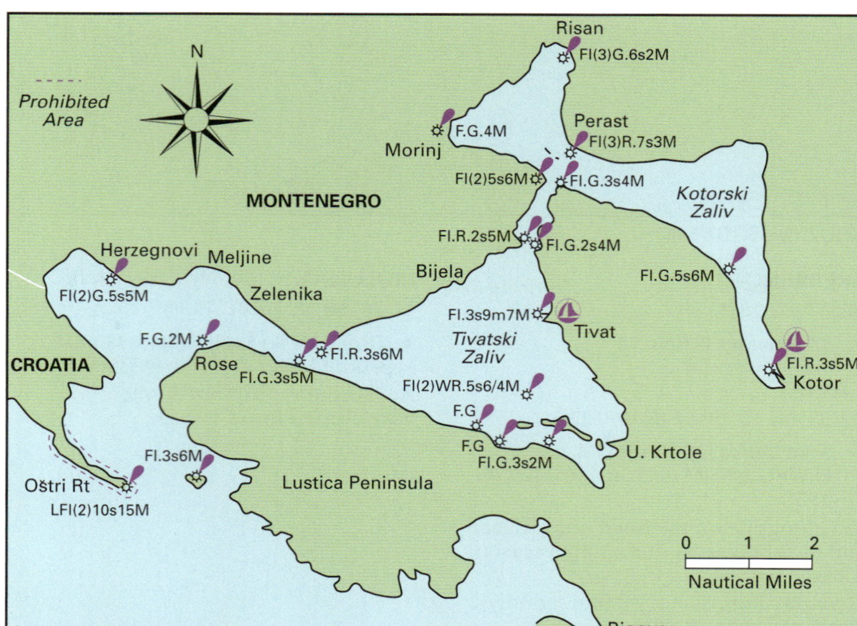

BOKA KOTORSKA
(Gulf of Kotor)

KOTOR
42°25'·6N 18°46'·3E

☆ Quay Fl.R.3s5M

VHF Ch 16.

Berths Go stern-to along the main quay. Depths 2–9m. Charge band 3/4.

Anchorage off S end of main quay.

Facilities Water and electricity on the quay. Fuel. Good provisions and restaurants in the town.

Remarks Port of entry. Popular with cruise ships.

Port authority ✆ 032 304 312
Marina ✆ 082 325 569 / 6722 6555
www.portofkotor.cg.yu

MUO
42°26'·1N 18°45'·7E

☆ Mole head Fl(2)G.5s5M

Open quay off the village. Depths 2–3m.

PRČANJ - MARINA KORDIĆ
42°28'·0N 18°44'·3E

☆ Fl(2)G.6s7M

Data New marina with 25 berths. Laid moorings. Short quay exposed N–NE. Also two berths at Hotel Splendido. Charge band 3/4.

Facilities Water. 220V. 18-ton crane. Open N–NE.

✆ 032 336 162 / 082

TIVAT
42°26'·2N 18°41'·2E

☆ Mole head Fl.3s9m7M (140°-R-167°)

PORTO MONTENEGRO

VHF Ch 16, 71.

Berths Stern or bows-to. Laid moorings at all berths.

Shelter Good shelter in the marina.

Data 250 berths (600 when complete). Max LOA 150m. Depths 2–8m. Charge band 5/6.

Facilities Water. 220/380V. WiFi. Showers and toilets. Laundry. Fuel quay.

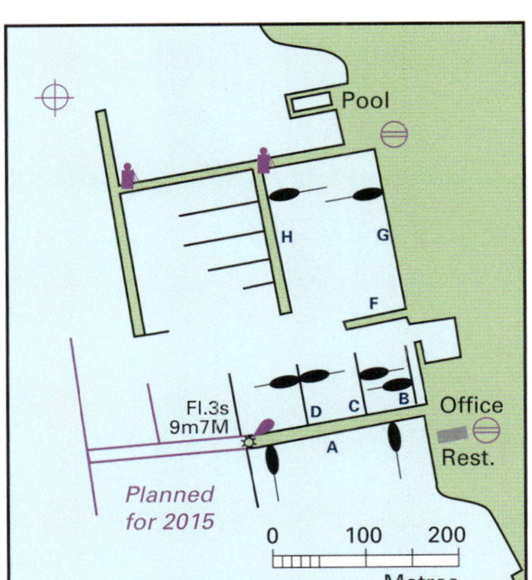

PORTO MONTENEGRO - TIVAT

Remarks Port of entry. Officials in the marina.

✆ 032 660 900 / 661 061
Email berths@portomontenegro.com
www.portomontenegro.com

KALIMANJ MARINA
42°25'·6N 18°42'·0E

0·5M SE of Porto Montenegro.

VHF Ch 16, 71.

Data 330 berths. Max LOA c.10m (or by arrangement). Depths 1·5–3m.

✆ 32 671 039

NAVAR MARINA
42°25'·1N 18°42'·4E

A boatyard adjacent to Tivat airport. 60-ton travel-hoist. Most repairs. Beneteau and Yanmar distributor.

✆ 32 671 674 or 67 620 474
Email service@navaryacht.com

Trašte Zaliv

BIGOVA (TRAŠTE)
42°21'·3N 18°42'·6E

☆ Rt Trašte Fl.3s9m5M

Go alongside the S side of the pier or anchor in 4m. Shelter from N–E–SW.

Restaurant ashore.

LUSTICA MARINA
42°22'·5N 18°39'·9E

A new project to develop two marina basins with hotels and a golf course in the NW side of Zaliv Traste.

www.lusticabay.com
Email info@lusticabay.com

BUDVA - DUKELY MARINA
42°16'·8N 18°50'·6E

☆ Otočić Sv Nikola Fl(3)10s23m8M. Mole head Fl.R.3s3M

VHF Ch 16, 08 for marina.

Navigation Care needed of shoal water in the approaches. Approach from the SSW leaving Sv Nikola to starboard.

Berths Stern or bows-to in the marina off the town.

Shelter Good all-round shelter.

Data 250 berths. Max LOA c35m. Depths 2-4·5m. Charge band 5/6.

Facilities Water. 220/380V. Fuel. Provisions and restaurants in the town.

Remarks Port of entry (May-Oct).

✆ 33 453 294
Email info@dukelymarina.com
www.dukelymarina.com
www.cnmarinas.com

BAR
42°06'·0N 19°05'·4E
BA 683, Imray M27

☆ Rt Volujica Fl(2)10s30m20M. Commercial port entrance Fl.G.3s6M/Fl(2)R.5s3M. Marina N mole Fl(3)G.5s3M. S mole Fl(3)R.5s3M

VHF Ch 14, 16 for port authorities. Ch 73 for OMC.

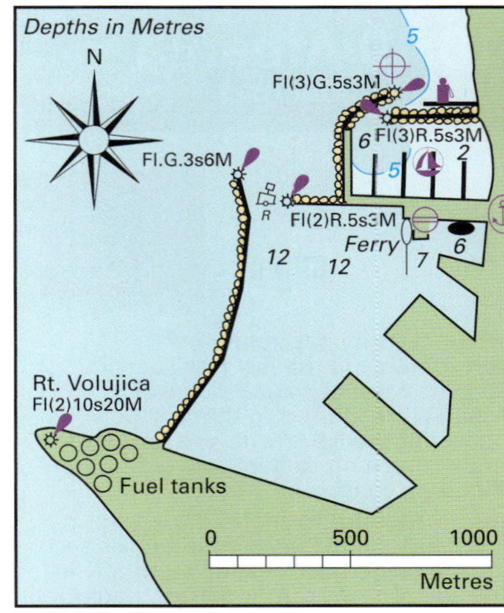

MARINA BAR

Navigation Yachts should make for AD Marina or Nautilus Marina immediately N of the commercial port, or OMC in the NE corner of commercial harbour.

Berths Where directed.

Shelter Good shelter.

Data 50 visitors' berths. 700 places ashore. Charge band 4/5.

Facilities Water. 220V. Fuel. 50/250-ton travel-hoists. 25/35-ton cranes. Provisions and restaurants. Ferries to Bari, Ancona, Trieste.

Remarks Yachts clearing in must go on the customs quay in the commercial port.

AD Marina ✆ 030 317 786
Email info@marinabar.org
OMC Marina St Nikola (Yard)
✆ 085 313 911
Email omc@t-com.me
www.omcmarina.com
Expert Marine (berths) ✆ 069 841 706
Harbourmaster ✆ 030 312 733

ULCINJ
41°55'·3N 19°12'·4E

☆ Vrh Tvrdjave Fl.3s27m8M

Holiday resort around a bay. Limited room on the open quay, clear of the ferry berth.

Remarks No longer a port of entry.

10.10 Albania

TIME ZONE UT+1 ✆ IDD+355

Public security has improved considerably in the last few years. Specific warnings against travel in Albania are limited to the Kosovo border in the NE. Yachts are reported to be returning to harbours along the Albanian coast.

Authorities are formal but friendly. Formalities must be completed for each port. A signed declaration stating that the vessel is not carrying arms, narcotics or stowaways will often be requested. Intended ports of call must be listed.

Photocopies of documents, crew lists and passports are helpful.

Expect to be boarded at sea by military, coastguard, *Kufitare* and the Italian *Guarda di Finanza* officials who are usually checking for stowaways (*clandestinis*).

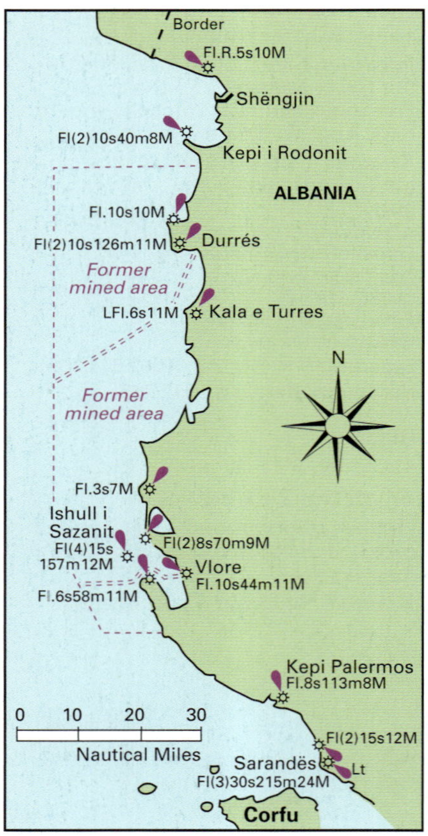

SHËNGJIN

41°48′·5N 19°35′·3E

☆ Kepi i Shëngjinit Fl.R.5s24m10M. Mali Renzit Fl.5s46m10M. Ldg Lights 002° Front Fl.R.6s5M. Rear Fl.R.5s5M

VHF Ch 71, 16 for Port Authority.

Navigation The harbour is reported to have been dredged.

Commercial port. Good shelter. Water and fuel by jerrycans. Some provisions. Bank.

Remarks The port gates are locked from 2200, with no subsequent access.

DURRËS

41°18′·2N 19°27′·3E

☆ S mole head Fl.R.5s6M. E mole head Fl.G.5s6M. Ldg Lts 017° DirIso.WRG.2s7-5M

VHF Ch 10, 16 for port authorities. Ch 15 for harbourmaster.

Navigation Buoyed channel into the port.

Berths Go alongside where directed. Good shelter.

Facilities Water by tanker. Fuel by jerry can from a station nearby. Supermarket.

Remarks Main commercial port for Albania.

Vital Shipping, Mr Llanbi Papa (English-speaking) ✆ */Fax* 0523 7244

Email vital@albmail.com

ISHULLI SAZANIT (SAZAN)

40°28′·5N 19°17′·2E

☆ Kepi I Jugor Fl.R.3s18m3M (S end of island)

Island in the entrance to Vlore. Naval base – entry prohibited.

VLORË (VALONA BAY)

40°26′·8N 19°28′·8E

☆ Kepi i Treporteve Fl(2)8s9M. Outer breakwater lit. Kepi i Gallovecit Fl.G.3s3M. E molehead Fl.G.3s5M. W molehead Fl.R.3s5M

VHF Ch 12, 16 Port Authority.

Vlorë harbour Go alongside on the N breakwater for customs clearance. Care needed of a wreck just underwater close to the quay.

Note Customs clearance must be done here before going to Marina Orikum.

Marina Orikum – see entry below.

Skele i Vlorë 4 piers. Anchor or go alongside as directed. Open NW.

Treporteve Small harbour. Go alongside where directed. Good shelter.

Remarks Oil terminal and fishing port. Ferry to Brindisi.

MARINA ORIKUM

41°18′·2N 19°27′·4E

VHF Ch 15.

Navigation New marina 6M S of Vlore. Approach on a course of 170°. Care needed of a dangerous wreck (2·6m over) 100m NE of the entrance. The entrance channel is buoyed. Keep to the N and W side of entry.

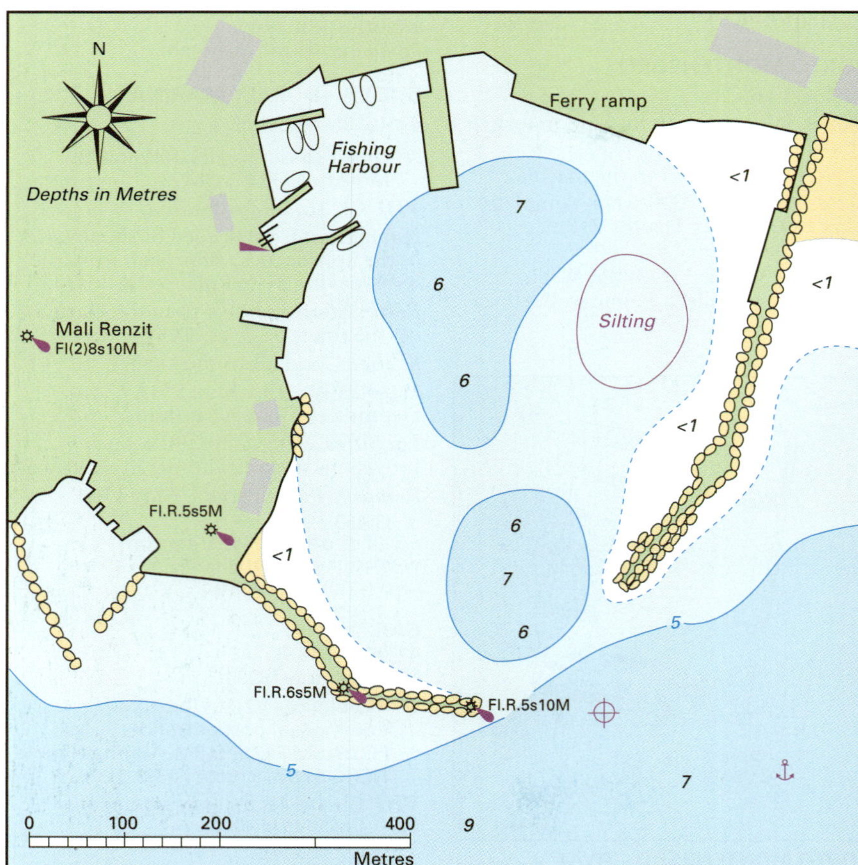

SHENGJIN

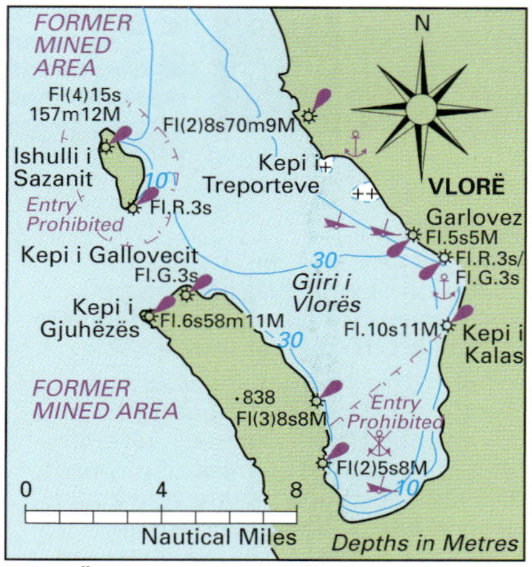

VLORË

Data 40 berths, expanding to 620. Max LOA 21m. Depths min 3m. Charge band 3/4.

Facilities Water. 220V.

☏ 0391 22248 / 06951 370 9415

Email marinaorikum@hotmail.it

www.orikum.it

PASHA LIMINI (KEPI ORIKUM)

☆ Fl(2)5s8M

Naval base in S of Vlorës. Entry prohibited.

GJIRI I SPILES (XIMARE, HIMARE)

40°06'·0N 19°44'·5E

Small quay on NW side (Port Authority) open to SW.

Remarks Port of entry (summer only).

KEPI I PALERMOS

40°03'·7N 19°48'·0E

☆ Fl.8s113m8M (SE entrance)

Military area. Yachts are not permitted to navigate or moor in the N part of the bay. Berth on the pier or anchor on the E side near the church.

Remarks Permission to visit here can be obtained from the agent at Sarandes.

GJIRI I SARANDES

39°51'·5N 20°02'·0E

☆ Fl(3)30s215m24M

Small ferry port serving Corfu.

VHF Ch 11 (Port Authority).

Navigation Shoals in the W approaches are marked with a S cardinal buoy (Fl(5)15s). Red buoy in the bay in the approaches. Leave to port.

Berths Berth on either side of ferry jetty. S side is best. Good security.

Facilities Water. 220V at some berths. ATM in the town. Daily market.

Agent Agim Zholi VHF Ch 10

☏ 355 6925 66576

Email agimzholi@yahoo.com

Spiro Angjeli (Travel Agent)

☏ 0732 4398 *Fax* 0732 3380

Akile ☏ 0692 375 078

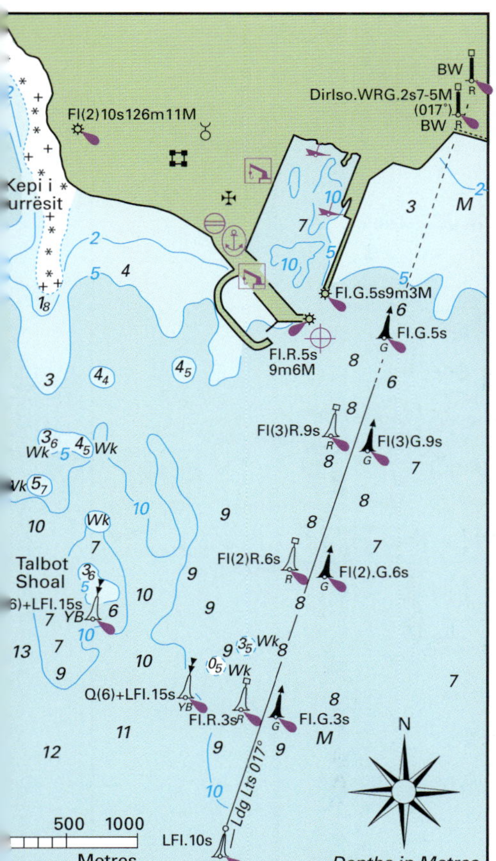

RRËS

10.11 Greece

TIME ZONE UT+2 IDD +30

Security
Security around the Albanian border and North Corfu Channel appears settled, although caution is still advised.

More worrying is the increase in the people-smuggling trade. A number of yachts have been implicated in high profile illegal immigration cases, particularly around the Eastern Sporades and Dodecanese. Increased security around Greece's enormous sea border is now the norm. NATO warships and Greek Coast Guard high-speed RIBs patrol these borders and regularly contact commercial sea traffic. Yachts are rarely contacted but a listening watch on VHF Ch16 is recommended.

Tides
Max spring tides 0·1m to 0·8m (Pagasitikós Kolpós and Evia Channel). Sea levels much influenced by barometric pressure and winds.

Port dues
From August 2014 the charges and collection of port dues have altered. Local agents from the Limeniko Tameio will collect the dues at the quayside.

Where extra facilities are provided (water, electricity, laid moorings) there may be additional charges. A receipt should be offered as proof of payment. The basic cost for a private 12m boat is around €10. Alongside berths are subject to a 25% surcharge. There are discounts for advance payments.

Quick reference guide *For Key see page 139*

	Shelter	Mooring	Fuel	Water	Provisions	Eating out	Charge band
Nísos Othoni							
Ormos Ammou (S Bay)	B	C	O	B	C	C	
Nísos Kérkira							
Kassiopi	C	AC	B	B	B	A	
Gouvía Marina	A	A	A	A	A	A	5
Limín Kérkira (Corfu)	A	AB	A	A	A	A	2
Palaiokastrita	B	AC	B	B	B	A	
Nísos Paxoi and Andipaxoi							
Lákka	B	AC	B	B	C	B	
Gaios	A	A	B	B	B	B	
Mainland coast							
Igoumenítsa	C	AB	B	B	B	B	
Nísos Sívota and Mourtos	B	AC	B	B	B	B	2
Parga	B	AC	B	B	B	A	
Preveza	B	AB	B	A	A	B	2
Vónitsa	B	AC	B	B	B	C	
Nísos Levkas							
Levkas Town	A	A	A	A	A	A	2
Levkas Marina	A	A	A	A	A	A	5
Nidri	B	AC	B	A	B	A	2
Sívota	A	AC	O	A	C	B	
Vasilikí	B	A	B	A	B	B	
Nísos Meganisi							
Spartakhori	B	AC	O	B	C	C	
Port Vathí	A	AC	O	O	C	C	
Odyseas Marina	A	A	A	A	C	C	2/3
Port Atheni	B	AC	O	O	O	C	
Nísos Ithaca							
Frikes	B	A	O	A	C	C	
Kióni	B	AC	O	O	C	C	
Port Vathí	A	AC	B	A/B	B	B	
Nísos Kefallinía							
Argostoli	A	A	A	A	A	B	
Lixouri	B	A	B	B	B	C	
Fiskárdho	A	AC	B	A	B	A	2
Ay Eufimia	B	AC	B	A	C	B	2
Sami	C	AB	B	A	B	C	
Póros	B	AC	B	A	B	B	2
Mainland coast and adjacent islands							
Palairos (Zaverda)	B	A	B	A	B	B	
Vounaki	B	A	A	A	C	C	2
Mitika	C	AC	B	B	C	C	
Astakós	B	A	B	A	B	C	
Nísos Kalamos							
Port Kalamos	B	A	O	B	C	C	
Nisís Kastos							
Port Kastos	B	A	O	O	C	C	
Nísos Zákinthos							
Port Zákinthos	A	A	B	A	A	A	2
Ay Nikólaos	B	AC	B	B	C	C	
The Southern Ionian							
Killini	B	A	B	A	B	B	
Katakólon	A	A	A	A	B	B	2
Pílos Yacht Harbour	A	AB	B	B	B	B	2
Methóni	B	AC	B	B	B	B	
Messianiakós Kólpos							
Koroni	B	C	B	B	B	B	
Kalamata Marina	A	A	A	A	A	A	3/4
Limení	C	C	O	B	C	C	
Lakonikós Kólpos							
Porto Káyio	B	AC	O	O	C	C	
Yíthion	B	AB	B	A	A	A	2
Neapolis	C	AC	B	B	B	B	
Nísos Kithera and Antikithera							
Ay Nikólaos	C	C	O	O	C	O	
Ormos Kapsáli	C	ABC	A	A	B	B	
Patraikós Kólpos							
Mesolóngion	A	ABC	B	A	B	B	3
Patras	B	A	A	A	A	A	
Patra Yacht Harbour	A	A	B	A	A	B	2/3
Korinthiakós Kólpos							
Návpaktos	B	A	A	A	B	B	
Nisís Trizónia	A	AC	O	B	C	C	
Aiyíon	C	AC	B	B	B	A	
Galaxidhi	A	A	B	B	B	A	2
Itéa	A	A	B	A	B	B	2
Andíkiron	B	C	B	B	C	C	
Corinth	A	AB	B	B	A	B	
Nísos Salamis							
Salamís	B	AC	B	A	B	B	
Zea Marina	A	A	A	A	A	A	5
Athens Marina	A	A	B	A	A	A	4/5
Flisvos	B	A	B	A	A	A	5
Kalamáki (Alimos)	A	A	A	A	A	A	4/5
Glifadha 4	A	A	B	A	B	A	
Vouliagméni	A	A	A	A	C	B	5
Várkiza	B	A	B	A	B	B	
Korfos	A	AC	B	A	B	B	
Epidhavros	B	AC	B	A	B	B	
Vathí (Methana)	A	AC	O	A	O	C	
Methana	A	A	B	A	A	B	2
Nísos Aígina							
Limín Aigina	A	A	B	A	A	A	
Perdika	C	AC	O	B	B	B	
Nísos Angistrí							
Angistrí	C	A	O	B	C	C	
Nísos Póros							
Póros	A	AC	B	A	A	A	2
Ermioni	A	AC	B	A	A	B	
Nísos Ídhra							
Limín Idhras	B	A	O	A	A	A	
Nísos Spétsai							
Báltiza (Spétsai)	A	AC	A	A	A	A	
Dápia (Spétsai)	C	A	B	B	A	A	
Porto Kheli	A	AC	B	B	A	B	
Koiládhia	A	AC	O	B	B	C	
Kháidhari	A	C	O	B	B	B	
Toló	C	AC	B	B	A	A	
Navplion	A	AB	B	A	A	A	2
Astrous	A	A	B	A	B	B	
Leonidhion	B	A	B	A	B	C	2
Kiparíssi	B	AC	B	B	C	B	
Ieraka	A	AC	O	O	C	B	
Monemvasía	B	AC	B	B	A	A	2
The Cyclades							
Nísos Kéa							
Ay Nikólaos	B	AC	B	A	B	B	
Nísos Kithnos							
Ormos Fikiadha	B	C	O	O	O	O	
Mérikha	B	AC	B	B	C	C	
Loutra	C	AC	B	B	C	C	
Ay Stefanos	B	C	O	B	O	O	
Nísos Síros							
Ermoúpolis	B	AB	B	B	A	A	
Marina Sirou	A	A	B	A*	A	A	
Finikas	B	AC	B	B	C	B	
Nísos Andros							
Gavrion	B	AC	B	B	B	B	
Batsí	B	AC	B	A	B	B	

	Shelter	Mooring	Fuel	Water	Provisions	Eating out	Charge band
Nísos Tínos							
Tínos	A	A	B	A	A	B	2
Nísos Míkonos							
Míkonos Marina	A	A	B	B	A	A	2
Nísos Sérifos							
Livadhi	B	AC	B	A	B	B	2
Nísos Sífnos							
Kamáres	C	AC	B	A	B	B	2
Ormos Vathí	B	C	B	B	O	C	
Faros	B	C	O	B	C	C	
Nísos Paros							
Paroikia	B	AC	B	B	A	A	
Náoussa	B	AC	B	A	B	B	2
Nísos Naxos							
Naxos Marina	B	A	B	A	A	A	2
Nísos Skhinoússa							
Ormos Mirsini	B	C	O	O	O	C	
Nísos Levitha							
Ormos Lévitha	A	C	O	O	O	O	2
Nísos Mílos							
Adhamas	B	AC	B	A	B	B	2
Nísos Folegandros							
Karavostási	B	ABC	B	O	C	B	
Nísos Íos							
Ios	A	A	B	B	B	B	2
Ormos Manganari	B	C	O	O	O	C	
Nísos Thíra							
Skála Thíra	C	AB	O	B	A	A	
Vlikhada	A	A	B	A	O	C	2
Evia and the Northern Sporades							
Gaidhouromandra (Olympic Marina)	A	A	A	A	C	C	4
Lavrion	B	A	A	A	A	B	
Porto Rafti	B	AC	B	B	B	B	
Rafina	O	A	B	B	B	B	
Karistos	A	A	B	A	A	A	
Voufalo	A	C	O	B	O	C	
Karavos	B	A	B	B	B	B	
Eretria	B	AC	O	O	C	C	
Khalkís	B	AB	A	A	A	A	2
Kólpos Atalántis	B	C	O	O	C	C	
Nea Artaki	B	A	O	O	C	C	
Loutra Adhipsou	B	BC	B	B	B	B	
Limín Stilidhos	B	AB	B	B	A	C	
Orei	B	A	B	A	B	B	2
Pagasitikós Kólpos							
Palaio Trikeri	C	AC	O	B	C	C	
Limín Vathoudhi	A	C	O	B	C	C	
Volos	B	AB	B	A	A	A	2
Northern Sporades							
Nísos Skíathos							
Skíathos	B	AC	B	A	A	A	2/3
Nísos Skópelos							
Loutráki	B	AC	B	A	C	B	
Ormos Agnóndas	B	AC	O	B	O	C	
Limín Skopelou	B	A	B	A	A	A	2
Nísos Alonnisos							
Patitíri	B	A	B	A	B	B	
Steni Vala	B	A	O	B	C	C	
Nísos Pelagos							
Ormos Kira Panayía	C	C	O	O	O	O	
Limín Planitís	A	C	O	O	O	O	
Nísos Skíros							
Limín Linaria	B	A	B	A	B	C	2
East coast of Evia							
Ormos Petriés	B	AC	O	B	C	C	
Kimi	B	A	A	A	C	C	
Northern Greece							
Thessaloniki Marina (Aretsou)	A	A	B	A	A	A	2/3

	Shelter	Mooring	Fuel	Water	Provisions	Eating out	Charge band
Sani Marina	A	A	B	A	C	C	6
Néa Marmaras	B	A	B	A	A	A	2
Porto Carras	A	A	A	A	C	B	6
Porto Koufó	A	AC	B	A	B	B	
Nisís Dhiaporos	A	C	O	O	O	O	
Nisís Ammouliani							
Ammouliani	B	C	B	B	C	B	
Ormos Elevtherón	A	A	B	B	B	B	
Kavala	B	A	B	A	A	A	
Nísos Thasos							
Limín Thasou	A	AB	B	AB	A	A	2
Limín Lágos	A	AB	B	A	B	C	
Alexandroupolis	A	AB	B	A	A	B	2
Nísos Samothraki							
Kamariótissa	A	AB	B	A	B	B	
The Eastern Sporades							
Nísos Limnos							
Mirina	A	A	B	A	A	A	2
Ormos Moúdhrou	A	AC	B	B	B	C	
Nísos Ayios Evstrátios							
Ayios Evstrátios	B	AB	O	A	C	C	
Nísos Lésvos							
Mitilíni	A	A	B	A	A	A	2/3
Mithimna	A	A	O	A	A	A	
Sígri	B	C	O	B	B	C	
Kólpos Kalloni	A	C	O	B	C	C	
Plomárion	B	A	B	A	A	B	2
Kólpos Yeras	A	C	O	O	C	C	
Nísos Psará							
Psará	A	A	O	O	C	C	
Nísos Oinoussa							
Mandráki	A	A	B	A	C	C	2
Nisís Pasha	B	C	O	O	O	O	
Nísos Khios							
Limín Khíos	C	AB	B	A	A	B	2
Khios Marina	A	AB	B	O	C	C	
Marmaro	B	A	B	A	C	C	2
Volissos (Limnia)	B	A	B	B	C	C	
O. Mestá	C	BC	O	A	O	O	
Nísos Ikaría							
Evdhilos	C	A	O	B	B	C	
Ayios Kirikos	O	AC	B	A	A	B	
Nísos Sámos							
Karlóvasi	B	A	B	A	B	B	2
Vathí	O	AB	B	B	A	A	
Pithagorion	A	A	B	A	A	A	2
Pithagorian Marina	A	A	A	A	B	C	5
Nisídhes Foúrnoi							
Foúrnoi	C	C	B	B	C	C	
The Dodecanese							
Nísos Patmos							
Skála Pátmos	B	AC	AB	A	B	A	
Nísos Arki							
Port Augusta	A	AC	O	B	C	C	
Nísos Lipsó							
Ormos Lipso	A	AC	B	A	B	B	
Nísos Léros							
Lakkí	A	A	B	A	A	B	2/3
Partheni	A	C	O	B	C	C	
Ormos Alindas	C	AC	B	A	B	B	
Pandeli	B	AB	O	B	C	B	
Nísos Kalimnos							
Limín Kalímnou	A	A	B	A	A	B	2
Vathí	B	A	O	B	C	C	
Nisís Pserimos							
Psérimos	C	C	O	O	C	B	
Nísos Kós							
Limín Kós	A	A	B	A	A	A	2/3
Kos Marina	A	A	A	A	B	B	3
Ormos Kamáres	B	BC	O	A	O	C	

	Shelter	Mooring	Fuel	Water	Provisions	Eating out	Charge band
Nísos Nísiros							
Mandráki	C	AB	B	A	B	B	
Palon	A	A	O	A	C	B	2
Nísos Tilos							
Livadhi (Tílos)	A	AC	B	A	B	C	2
Nísos Simi							
Sími	B	A	B	A	A	A	2
Panormittis	A	C	O	O	C	C	
Pethi	B	AC	O	B	C	C	
Nísos Rhodos							
Mandráki	A	A	B	A	A	A	2/4
Rhodes Marina*	B	A	B	A	A	A	
Lindos	B	C	O	B	C	A	
Nísos Kastellorízon							
Limin Kastellorizon	B	A	B	A	C	C	2
Nísos Khalki							
Khálki	B	AC	O	A	C	C	2
Nísos Alimia							
Alimia	B	C	O	O	O	O	

*Projected data

	Shelter	Mooring	Fuel	Water	Provisions	Eating out	Charge band
Nísos Karpathos							
Limín Karpathou	C	AB	B	B	A	B	
Trístoma	C	C	O	O	O	O	
Nísos Kasos							
Limín Kasou	C	A	B	B	C	C	
Limin Fri	A	A	B	A	C	C	2
Nísos Astipalaia							
Skála	B	AC	B	A	B	B	2
Maltezana	B	BC	O	O	C	C	
Vathí	A	C	O	O	O	C	
Crete							
Khania	A	A	B	A	A	A	
Soúdha	A	AB	B	B	B	B	
Rethimon	B	A	B	A	A	A	2
Iraklion	A	AB	B	A	A	A	
Ay Nikólaos Marina	A	A	B	A	A	A	2
Sitía	B	A	B	A	A	A	2
Nisís Gramvoúsa	B	C	O	B	O	O	
Palaiokhora	B	AB	B	B	B	B	
Loutró	B	C	O	B	C	C	
Ay Galini	B	A	B	A	B	B	
Kali Limenes	B	C	B	B	C	C	
Ierepetra	B	A	B	B	B	B	

Northern Ionian

Nísos Othoni

ÓRMOS AMMOU

39°50'·2N 19°24'·2E
BA 205 Imray-Tetra G11
50M Santa Maria di Leuca ←→ Gouvia Marina 37M

☆ Othoni Fl.10s103m18M. SW point Fl(2)6s6M. Night approach not recommended

Navigation Care needs to be taken of Ífalos Aspri Petra, a reef lying directly in the southern approach.

Berths Anchor off.

Shelter Adequate from the prevailing NW winds. The stubby breakwater on the W side provides some additional shelter from the ground swell. Open S.

Facilities Some provisions and restaurants ashore.

Remarks An anchorage on the S side of Nisís Othoni commonly used on passage between Italy and Corfu. The small harbour is for the ferry and local boats. Do not anchor in the ferry turning area.

AVLAKI

39°50'·37N 19°24'·79E WGS84

Navigation The fishing harbour to the E of Ammos has been dredged and extended. The appoaches are shallow with uneven depths between 4-10m from some distance out. Approach from the SE with Nisis Mathraki astern.

Berths Yachts can berth alongside on the new quay or catwalk.

Shelter Reasonable from prevailing winds. Untenable in southerlies.

Facilities Water tap nearby.

Nísos Kerkira (Corfu)

KASSIOPI

39°47'·48N 19°55'·40E WGS84
BA 205 Imray-Tetra G11

☆ F.G(occas)

Navigation Small harbour difficult to locate from the distance.

Berths Stern or bows-to.

Shelter Adequate behind the E stub mole.

Facilities Water. Fuel in the town. Provisions and restaurants.

LIMIN GOUVION (GOUVIA MARINA)

39°39'·53N 19°51'·35E WGS84
BA 2407 Imray-Tetra G11
37M Ormos Ammou ←→ Limin Kerkira 3·5M

☆ Lightbuoys Q.G/Q.R. Marina pier head 2F.R(vert)3Mx2

VHF Ch 69.

Navigation Care needed of shallows on S side of the entrance. Follow buoyed channel into the bay.

Berths Stern or bows-to. Laid moorings tailed to the quay in the marina.

Shelter Some berths in the marina uncomfortable with the prevailing NW wind and some dangerous with strong NE winds.

Data 1,235 berths. Visitors' berths. Max LOA 80m. Max draught 5·5m. Charge band 5.

Facilities Water. 220V/380V. Showers and toilets. Fuel quay. 65-ton travel-hoist. Most yacht repairs. Chandlers. Provisions and restaurants.

Remarks Customs officials are not always based in the marina, but by arrangement clearance can be done here. Contact the marina in advance for

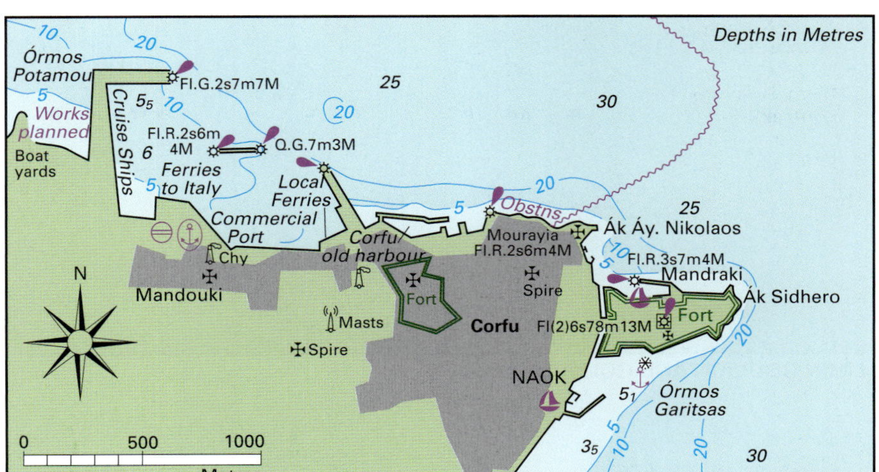

APPROACHES TO CORFU

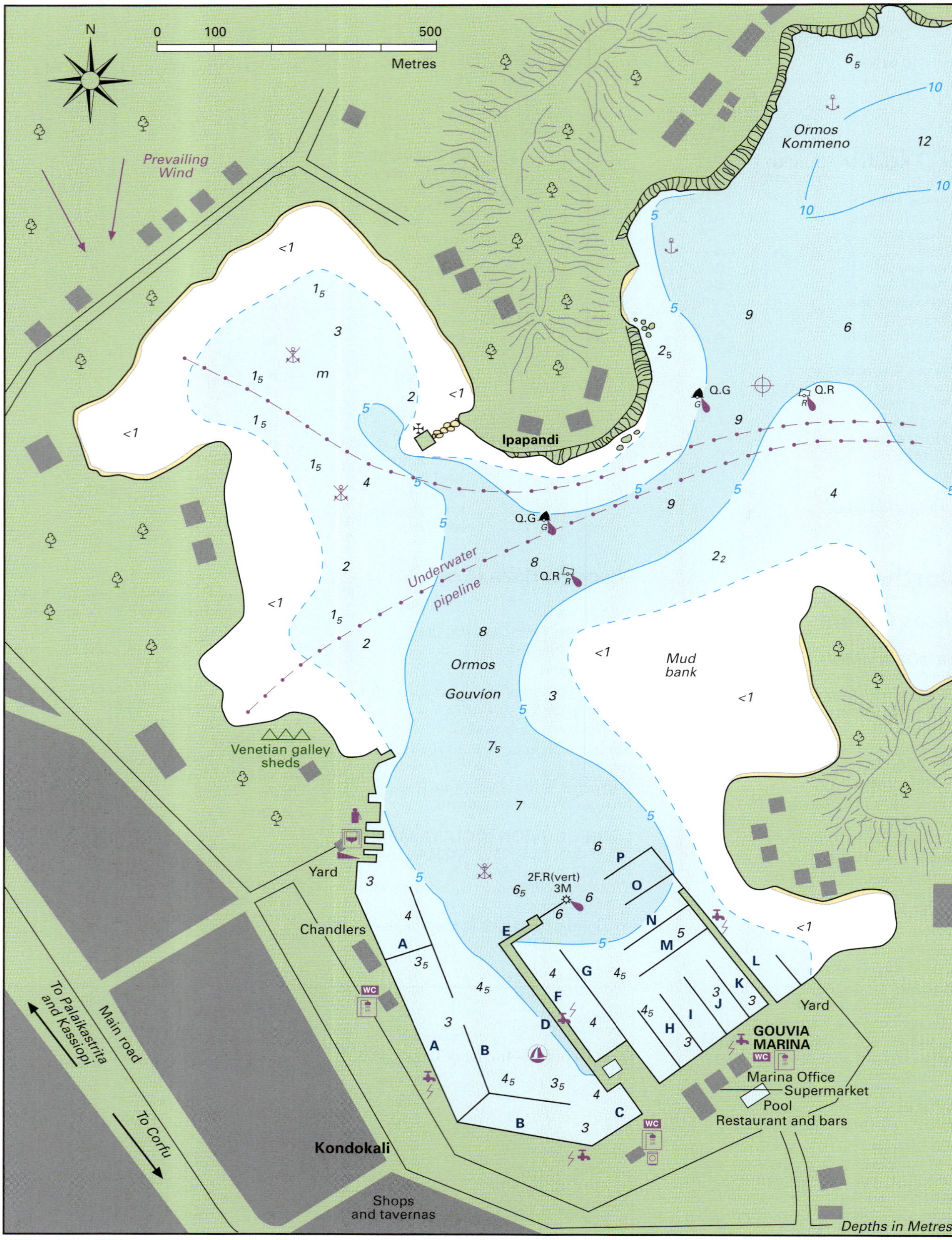

LIMIN GOUVION AND GOUVIA MARINA

advice. Yachts coming from outside the EU must clear in at Corfu town.

Gouvia Marina
☎ 26610 91900
Email k.g@medmarinas.com
www.medmarinas.com

Nautilus Yacht Chandlery
☎ 26610 90343

LIMIN KERKIRA (CORFU)

39°37'·66N 19°55'·15E WGS84
BA 2407 Imray-Tetra G11
3·5M Gouvia Marina ←→ Port Gaios 30M

☆ Ak Sidhero Fl(2)6s13M. Mandraki Fl.R.3s4M. Mourayia pier Fl.R.2s4M. E breakwater Q.R.3M. Detached breakwater Q.G.3M/Fl.R.2s4M

VHF Ch 12, 18 for port authorities.

Navigation Works in progress around the town quay. See notes below.

Berths Depths 2–4m. Care needed of sea level ledge along N quay.

Shelter Good in old harbour E basin.

Facilities Water. Provisions and restaurants.

Remarks A new 80 berth yacht harbour is under construction on the E side of the old harbour. Go stern or bows-to. Laid moorings at some berths.

PETRITI

39°27'·20N 20°00'·19E WGS84

Fishing harbour 11M S of Corfu town. Depths <1–3m. Stern or bows-to under the breakwater.

PALAIOKASTRITA

39°40'·45N 19°42'·58E WGS84
BA 205 Imray-Tetra G11

☆ Ak Kosteri Fl.3s5M. Mole head F.R.3M

Navigation Heavy cross swell with the prevailing NW winds. Care needed of the reef N of the entrance to the harbour.

Berths Stern or bows-to. Anchorage in N bay.

Shelter Good shelter from the prevailing NW wind. Dangerous in southerly gales.

Facilities Fuel in the town. Provisions and restaurants ashore.

Nisoi Paxoi and Andipaxoi (Paxos and Anti-Paxos)

ÓRMOS LAKKA

39°14'·65N 20°07'·75E WGS84
BA 205 Imray-Tetra G11

☆ Ak Lakka Fl(3)24s20M. Entrance lights Fl.R.2s3M/Fl.G.2s3M

Navigation Care needed of the reef (Vos Marmaro) NW of Ak Lakka.

Berths Anchor off. Small yachts go bows-to on some sections of the quay.

Shelter Good except with strong NE winds.

Facilities Water. 220V. Provisions and restaurants ashore.

PORT GAIOS

39°12'·22N 20°11'·47E WGS84
(N entrance)
BA 205 Imray-Tetra G11
30M Limin Kerkira ←→ Preveza 32M

☆ Nisís Panayía Fl.WR.5s10/8M. N entrance Fl.R.3s3M/Fl.G.3s3M. S entrance Fl.G.2s3M/F.R.2M

Navigation Care needed of Ífalos Panayia 2½M E of Gaios. The main harbour is sheltered by two islets with N and S channels. The S channel has just 2–2·5m depths in the entrance. Care needed of traffic in the winding N channel.

Berths Stern or bows-to. If the town quay is full berth at the quay in the N channel. Charge band 2.

Shelter Good with prevailing winds. Uncomfortable and dangerous on town quay with southerly gales. Surge with strong NW winds.

Facilities Water and fuel by mini-tanker. Electricity at some berths. Provisions and restaurants.

Remarks Crowded in the summer. Rats.

Mainland Coast

IGOUMENITSA

39°30'·10N 20°12'·06E WGS84
Entrance to buoyed channel
BA 2408 Imray-Tetra G11

☆ Nisídha Prasoudha Fl(2)9s8M. Ak Kondramoúrto Fl.3s5M. Channel buoys Q.R/Q.G. Pier head 2F.R(vert)5M

VHF Ch 12, 18 for harbour authorities. VTS in operation on Ch 14.

Navigation Entrance through a buoyed channel into Igoumenitsa Bay. Care needed of ferries coming and going.

Berths Stern or bows-to. Anchorage in the bay.

Shelter Reasonable shelter.

Facilities Water. Provisions and restaurants.

Remarks A major ferry port for Italy-Greece. Minimum facilities for yachts.

PLATARIAS

39°27'·12N 20°16'·51E WGS84

Navigation Harbour in the NE corner of Ormos Plataria.

Berths Stern-to on the quay.

Shelter Good shelter from prevailing NW.

Data Depths 2–4m. Max LOA c.20m.

Facilities Water. Fuel by mini-tanker. Tavernas and bars.

MOURTOS AND ADJACENT ISLANDS

39°24'·66N 20°13'·82E WGS84
N entrance
BA 205 Imray-Tetra G11

☆ Nísos Sívota (N end) Fl(3)20s12M. Mourtos pier head Fl.R.1·5s3M. Night approach not recommended

Navigation A 2m bar between the islands and the mainland.

Berths The basin off the town has been completed. Go stern-to on town quay or in basin. Anchorage around the channel and at S end.

Shelter Good in the basin and on the town quay. Surge in basin with strong W winds – possibly dangerous.

Data 50 berths. Depths 1·5–4m. Max LOA c.20m.

Facilities Water and electricity on town quay. Fuel, provisions and restaurants in the village.

PARGA

39°16'·75N 20°23'·55E
BA 205 Imray-Tetra G11

☆ Castle Fl(2)6s6M

Navigation Care needed of reef (Voi Spiridhonia) 100m E of Ak Ay Spiridhonia. Yachts should head for Órmos Valtou and not the pier off the village.

Berths Bows-to in the small harbour or anchor off on the W side of Órmos Valtou.

Shelter Good from the prevailing winds. Dangerous in southerly gales.

Facilities Water-taxi into town. Provisions and restaurants in the village.

Note Some theft reported from yachts.

PREVEZA

38°55'·90N 20°43'·65E WGS84
Entrance to buoyed channel
BA 2405 Imray-Tetra G11
32M Port Gaios ←→ Levkas Canal 7·5M

☆ Channel buoys Q.R/Q.G. Leading lights (066°) Q.Y.7M/LFl.Y.6s7M. Point Akrí LFl.7·5s5M. S mole head Fl.G.2s4M. W mole head Fl.R.2s3M. Limin Preveza pier S end of E mole Fl.G.2s3M

VHF Ch 12, 16 for harbour authorities.

Navigation Buoyed channel into harbour. There can be a 1–3 knot current flowing out of the channel.

Berths Stern or bows-to on the town quay. Alongside in the marina.

Shelter Good from prevailing winds but untenable on the town quay in moderate E–SE winds.

Facilities Water. 220V. Fuel by tanker. Boatyard. Sailmaker. Provisions and restaurants.

Preveza Marina ☎ 26820 23095
Email prevezamarina@gmail.com

J Sails ☎ 26820 61019 or 6932 668 777
Email info@jsails.gr

AKTION

On the opposite side at Aktion, are three boatyards. Yachts up to 300 tons can be hauled. All yacht repairs. Chandlers.

CLEOPATRA MARINA

100 berth marina alongside the boatyard.

VHF Ch 67.

Facilities Water. 220V. WiFi. Showers and toilets. Laundry. Fuel quay. Charge band 3.

Note Strong currents run through the pontoons and can make berthing difficult.

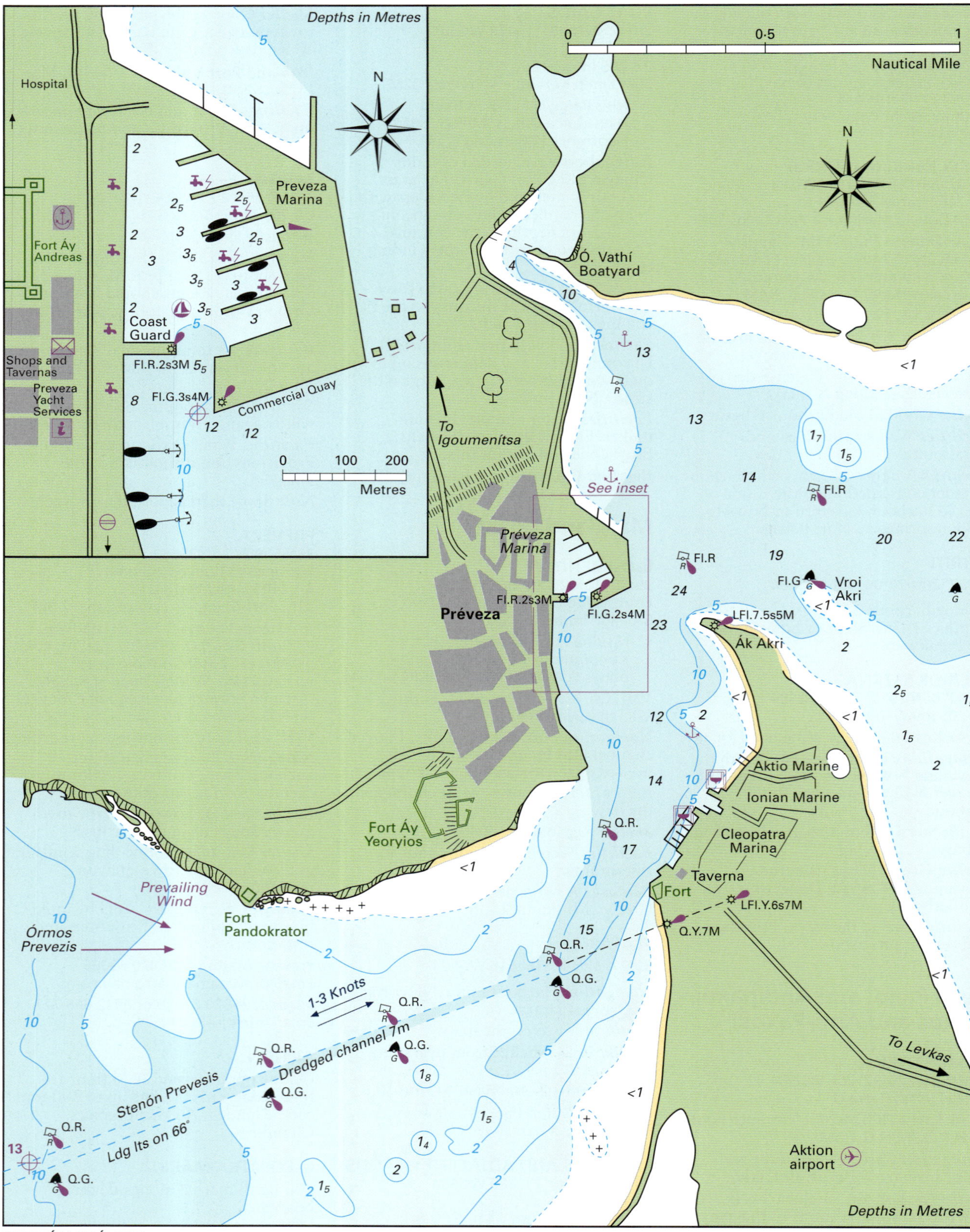

STENÓN PRÉVEZA

Cleopatra Marina 50/300-ton travel-lifts. Hydraulic trailer.
☎ 26820 23015
Email clmarina@otenet.gr
www.cleopatra-marina.gr

Ionian Marine 65-ton travel-lift. Hydraulic trailer.
☎ 26820 24305
Email contact@ionianmarine.com
www.ionianmarine.com

Aktion Marine 70-ton hydraulic trailer.
VHF Ch 09
☎ 26820 61305
Email aktiomar@hol.gr
www.aktio-marine.gr

VONITSA
38°55'·27N 20°53'·31E WGS84
BA 203 Imray-Tetra G11

☆ Mole head Fl.G.1·5s4M

Navigation Situated on the SW side of Amvrakikos Kólpos.

Berths Stern or bows-to town quay. Laid moorings. Depths along the quay 2–3m. Anchorage in Órmos Ay Markou or E side of Nisís Koukouvitsa.

Shelter Reasonable to good from prevailing NW wind.

Facilities Water. Fuel by mini-tanker. Provisions and restaurants.

Nísos Levkas

LEVKAS CANAL
N end 38°50'·79N 20°43'·27E WGS84
S end 38°47'·54N 20°43'·58E WGS84
BA 2405 Imray-Tetra G12

☆ N end Santa Maura Fl(2)WR.12s8/5M. Mole head Fl.G.1·5s3M. S end Ak Kefali Fl.4s5M. Nisís Volios Fl.WR.1·5s5/3M. Channel buoys Q.G/Q.R

VHF Ch 12 for the bridge operator.

Navigation Canal data: 40–100m wide. 3·5–6m depth. Max air height 40m (power cables at S end). Floating bridge on the N end opens every hour on the hour. N end entered around sand spit. Deepest channel is close to the spit. S end entered by a buoyed channel.

Remarks Southbound traffic has right of way through the bridge, though in practice vessels are often waved through together.

LEVKAS
38°49'·98N 20°42'·78E WGS84
BA 2405 Imray-Tetra G12
8·5M Preveza ←→ Nidri 8·5M

Navigation The harbour in the canal lies a short distance down the canal from the N entrance.

Berths Stern or bows-to the town quay.

Shelter Good all-round although some berths difficult in S gales.

Facilities Water. 220V. Fuel quay. Chandler. Some yacht repairs. Boatyard. Provisions and restaurants.

Remarks Busy in the summer although there are always berths available. Some reserved berths.

Contract Yacht Services ✆ 26450 24490
Office *Email* cys@otenet.gr
Store ✆ 26450 24443
Email cysstore@otenet.gr

Levkas Marine Centre ✆ 26450 250 36
Email lmslefkas@otenet.gr

Marine Point Chandlery ✆ 26450 23340
Email lefkasmarinepoint@yahoo.gr

LEVKAS MARINA

VHF Ch 69.

Navigation Situated immediately SE of Levkas town.

Berths Stern or bows-to where directed. Laid mooorings tailed to the pontoons.

Shelter Good shelter although

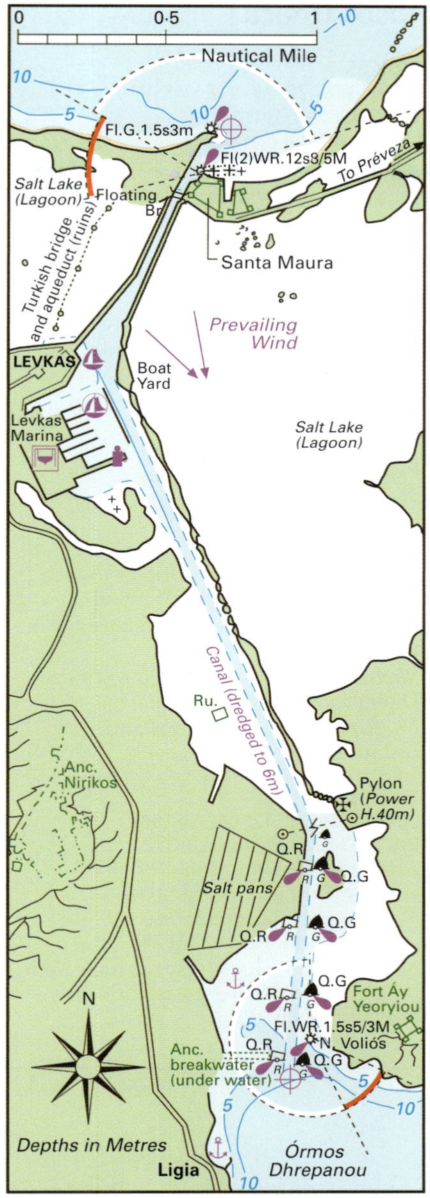

LEVKAS CANAL AND APPROACHES TO LEVKAS

southerlies create a chop.

Data 620 berths. Visitors' berths. Max LOA 40m. Depths 2·5–4m. Charge band 5.

Facilities Water. 220/380V. Showers and toilets. Fuel quay. 60-ton travel-hoist. Bars and restaurants. Mini-market. More in Levkas town.

Levkas Marina ✆ 26450 26645 / 6
Email k.g@medmarinas.com
www.medmarinas.com

Way Point Sails and Rigging
✆ 26450 21461
waypointsails@yahoo.com

NIDRI
38°42'·38N 20°42'·87E WGS84
BA 203 Imray-Tetra G121
8·5M Levkas ←→ Vathi (Ithaca) 21M

Navigation Care needed of 2m patch off Nisís Sparti. No useful lights.

Berths Stern or bows-to town quay. Depths 2–5m. Anchorage in Tranquil Bay and Port Vlikho.

Shelter Adequate on town quay with prevailing winds. All-round in Tranquil Bay and Port Vlikho.

Facilities Water. Fuel by tanker. Chandlers. Boatyards. Provisions and restaurants.

Remarks Busy resort town.

ÓRMOS SIVOTA
38°36'·87N 20°41'·52E WGS84
BA 203 Imray-Tetra G121

Navigation Entrance difficult to spot. No lights.

Berths Stern or bows-to the quay or on the pontoons, although care is needed of shallows in places. Anchorage in the bay.

Shelter Good shelter, except with strong southerlies.

Facilities Water on the quay. Some provisions and restaurants. No ATM.

Remarks Crowded and can get a bit smelly in the summer.

VASILIKI
38°37'·7N 20°36'·4E
BA 2402 Imray-Tetra G121

☆ Ak Dhoukaton Fl.10s20M. Pier head F.G.3M. Mole head Fl.G.3s3M

Berths Stern or bows-to. Depths 1·5–3m.

Shelter Good shelter although gusts into the harbour can be uncomfortable.

Facilities Water on the quay. Provisions and restaurants.

Remarks Works in progress on harbour extension project to expand yacht berths.

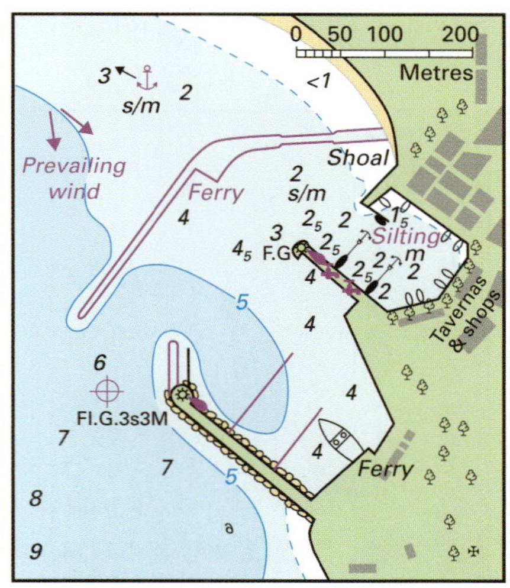

VASILIKI

Nísos Meganísi

VOS HIEROMITI

A reef between Nisís Skorpios and Nísos Meganisi. It is sometimes marked in the summer.

SPARTAKHORI
38°40'·10N 20°45'·82E WGS84
BA 203 Imray-Tetra G121

Navigation Village on the slopes above will be seen. No lights.

Berths Stern or bows-to on the quay or on the pier in the NW or the S of the bay. Some laid moorings.

Facilities Water. Some provisions and restaurants.

PORT VATHI

38°39′·8N 20°47′·0E
BA 203 Imray-Tetra G121

VHF Ch 72 for Odyseas Marina.

Navigation North side of Meganisi. Entrance difficult to see.

Berths Stern or bows-to on the town quay or in the new marina off the town. Laid moorings in the marina. In the middle cove on the SW side of the bay is the Karnayio taverna with a catwalk with about 20 places. Laid moorings. Depths 2–3m.

Shelter Good from prevailing winds although sometimes uncomfortable with NE winds.

Facilities Water. 220V. Fuel by mini-tanker. Some provisions and restaurants.

Odyseas Marina ✆ 26450 51084
Email welcome@odyseasmarina.com
www.odyseasmarina.com

PORT ATHENI

38°40′·20N 20°48′·00E WGS84
BA 203 Imray-Tetra G121

☆ Ak Elia Fl.WR.8s10/7M

Navigation Care needed of the reef dividing the bay.

Berths Anchorage. Stern or bows-to new quay in S.

Shelter Good from prevailing wind. Parts of anchorage open to NE.

Remarks Restaurant. Limited provisions. 20-minute walk to Katomeri village.

Nísos Ithaca

FRIKES

38°27′·60N 20°39′·91E WGS84
BA 203 Imray-Tetra G121

☆ Mole head Fl.R.2s3M

Navigation Care needed of the reef off the islets under Ak Ay Nikolaou. Strong gusts with prevailing NW winds.

Berths Alongside, or stern-to.

Shelter Good from prevailing wind. Open NE.

Facilities Water and fuel can be delivered. Some provisions and restaurants.

Note Wash from fast ferries causes problems.

PORT KIONI

38°26′·84N 20°42′·17E
BA 203 Imray-Tetra G121

☆ F.G.3M

Navigation Entrance difficult to see. Gusts with prevailing NW wind.

Berths Stern or bows-to. Anchorage in bay.

Shelter Good from prevailing winds. Dangerous in S gales.

Facilities Some provisions and restaurants.

VATHI

38°22′·66N 20°42′·06E WGS84
BA 189 Imray-Tetra G12-G121
21M Nidri ←→ Limin Zakinthos 52M

☆ Ak Ay Andreou Fl.3s5M. Nisís Katzurbo Fl.G.4s3M. Nisís Loimokathartíron Q.G.2M

Navigation Straightforward once up to the entrance. Strong gusts with the prevailing NW wind.

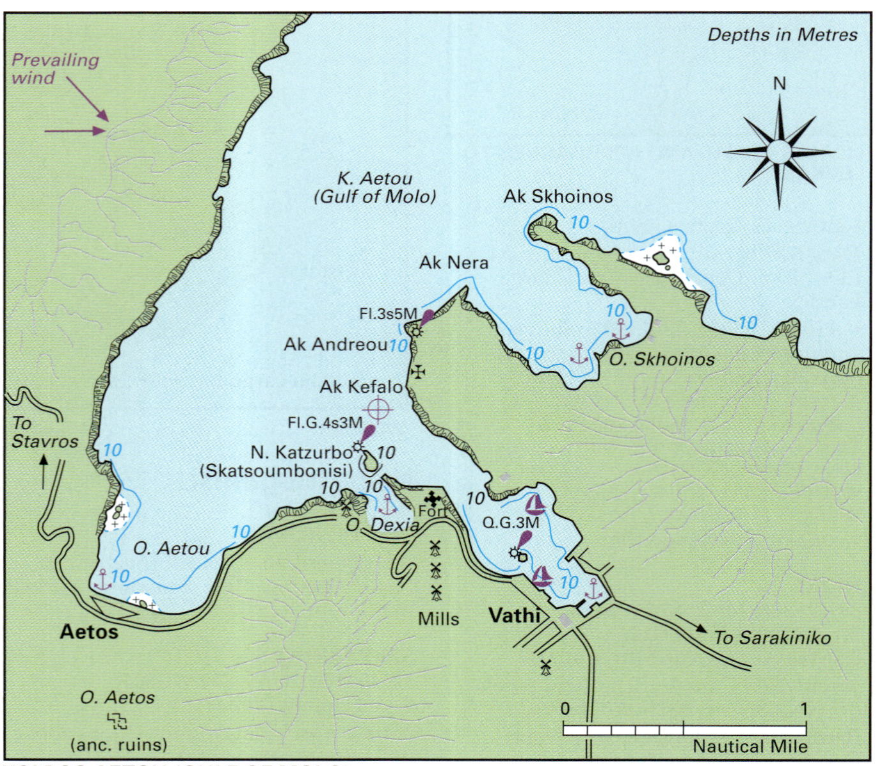

KOLPOS AETOU (GULF OF MOLO)

Berths Stern or bows-to on ferry quay or town pier. Care needed of underwater ledge near the customs office. Stern-to the quay in NE corner. Anchorage off the town or in NE corner.

Shelter Uncomfortable but tenable with prevailing NW wind. Better shelter on N quay.

Facilities Water and fuel by tanker. Provisions and restaurants.

Nísos Cephalonia

ARGOSTOLI (ARGOSTOLION)

38°10′·90N 20°29′·76E WGS84
BA 2402 Imray-Tetra G12

☆ Ak Yero-Gómbos LFl(2)15s24M. Nisís Vardhiánoi Fl.WR.7·5s6/4M. Ak Ay Theodhóroi Fl.3s5M. Beacon Fl.G.3s3M. Marina breakwater Fl.R.3s/Fl.G.3s

Navigation Reefs fringe the coast in the approach to Kólpos Argostoliou. Strong gusts out of the gulf with the prevailing NW wind.

Berths Stern or bows-to.

Shelter Good shelter from the prevailing NW wind under the lee of the customs quay.

Facilities Water on the quay. Fuel by mini-tanker or near the market. Chandlers. Provisions and restaurants.

ARGOSTOLI MARINA

38°10′·90N 20°29′·76E WGS84

☆ N mole head Fl.R.3s3M. S breakwater Fl.G.3s3M

The new marina opposite Argostoli quay was completed some years ago, but as yet there is no infrastructure or management in place.

Data c.250 berths. Max LOA c.30m. Depths 3–3·5m.

LIXOURI

38°12′·1N 20°26′·5E
BA 2402 Imray-Tetra G12

☆ Entrance Fl.R.1·5s3M/Fl.G.1·5s3M

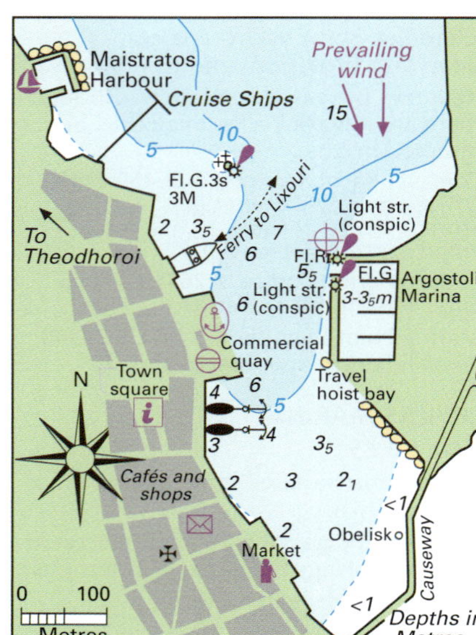

ARGOSTOLI

Navigation On the W side of Kólpos Argostoliou.

Berths Stern or bows-to in the NW corner.

Shelter Uncomfortable with the prevailing wind.

Facilities Water. 220V. Fuel nearby. Provisions and restaurants.

FISKARDHO

38°27′·53N 20°34′·94E WGS84
BA 2402 Imray-Tetra G121

☆ Ak Fiskárdho Fl.3s7M. Short breakwater F.R.2M

Navigation Shallows a short distance off Ak Fiskardho.

Berths Stern or bows-to or anchor off with a long line ashore to N side. Charge band 2.

Shelter Summer thunderstorms with southerly winds can create problems in this busy harbour. A swell is pushed into the bay and makes it uncomfortable and possibly untenable for yachts anchored with a long line ashore on the N side. Wherever you are make sure your anchor is holding well.

Facilities Water. 220V (at some berths). Provisions and restaurants.

Remarks Often crowded in the summer.

ÁYIOS EUFIMIA

38°18′·06N 20°36′·09E WGS84
BA 203 Imray-Tetra G121

☆ Ak Dhekalia Fl(2)R.8s5M. Mole Q.G.3M

Navigation Gusts with the prevailing NW wind.

Berths Stern or bows-to N quay.

Shelter Good with prevailing NW–W wind. Open SE.

Facilities Water. 220V. Fuel nearby. Some provisions and restaurants. Charge band 2.

SAMI

38°15′·30N 20°38′·78E WGS84
BA 203 Imray-Tetra G121

☆ Ak Dhekalia Fl(2)R.8s5M. Mole head Fl.R.2s4M

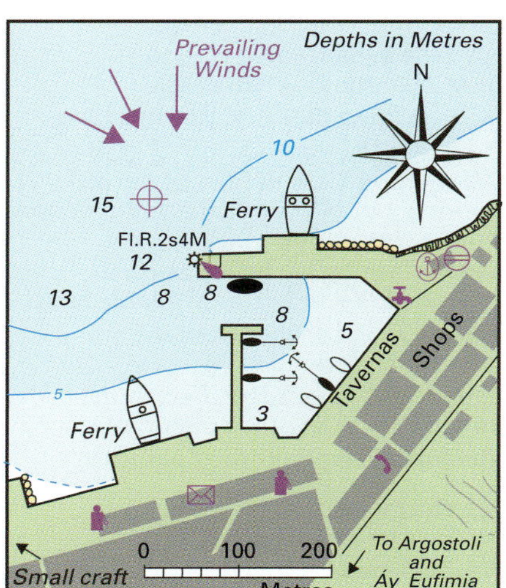

SAMI

Navigation Ferry port at the S end of the Ithaca channel.

Berths Stern or bows-to or alongside.

Shelter Adequate with prevailing NW wind.

Facilities Fuel ashore. Provisions and restaurants.

POROS

38°09′·04N 20°46′·90E WGS84
BA 203 Imray-Tetra G12

☆ Ak Kapri Fl(3)WR.9s6/4M. Breakwater Q.G.3M. Jetty head Fl.R.4s5M

Navigation Difficult to see from the S. Silting reported in the harbour. Care needed for yachts over 2m draught.

Berths Stern or bows-to SW quay.

Shelter Uncomfortable with prevailing NW wind.

Facilities Water. Provisions and restaurants in the village.

IFALOS KAKOVA

2·25M E of Ak Mounda.
38°03′·20N 20°49′·97E WGS84

Navigation Shoal water extends for over one mile SE from the SE corner of Cephalonia.

Mainland coast and adjacent islands

IFALOS IOSSIF

An uncharted rocky shelf in Órmos Palairos in position 38°46′·8N 20°51′·1E WGS84.
The reef lies inside the 20m contour, bearing 274° from Palairos light and 309° from Vounaki light. Depths <1m over an area the size of a tennis court.

PALAIROS (ZAVERDA)

38°46′·94N 20°52′·64E WGS84
BA 203 Imray-Tetra G121

☆ Mole head Fl.G.1·5s3M

Navigation Small harbour in the NE corner of the inland sea.

Berths Stern or bows-to. Care needed of shallows on the E side.

Shelter Good but uncomfortable with strong NE winds.

Facilities Water. 220V on pontoon. Provisions and restaurants.

VOUNAKI MARINA

38°46′·16N 20°52′·62E WGS84

☆ Fl.G.3s3M

VHF Ch 10

Navigation Care needed of shallows immediately N of entrance.

Berth Where directed. Laid moorings tailed to the quay.

Shelter Adequate in the summer. Westerlies might cause a problem.

Data 60 berths. Depths 2–6m. Charge band 2.

Facilities Water. 220V. Showers and toilets. Fuel quay. Yacht repairs. Mini-market. Taverna.

Remarks Charter base.

Vounaki Marina
✆ 26430 419 44

MITIKA

38°40′·05N 20°56′·91E WGS84
BA 203 Imray-Tetra G121

☆ Ak Mitika Fl.1·5s4M

Harbour immediately S of the existing harbour on the E side of Ak Mitika has been badly damaged in winter storms. Much of the outer breakwaters are not visible, but lying just under the surface. Approach with caution. Depths 2–3m. Pontoons in N harbour.

Remarks Reports of theft from yachts in the harbour.

Nísos Kalamos

PORT KALAMOS

38°37′·41N 20°55′·94E WGS84
BA 203 Imray-Tetra G121

☆ Mole head Fl.R.3s3M

Navigation Small fishing harbour on the E side of Nísos Kalamos.

Berths Stern or bows-to.

Shelter Good from prevailing W wind. Dangerous in NW gales.

Facilities Limited provisions. Several restaurants.

Nisís Kastos

PORT KASTOS

38°34′·12N 20°54′·73E WGS84
BA 203 Imray-Tetra G121

☆ Mole head Fl.R.4s5M

Navigation Small fishing harbour on the E side of Nísos Kastos.

Berths Stern or bows-to or anchorage in the bay.

Shelter Good from prevailing W winds.

Facilities Several restaurants.

ASTAKOS

38°31′·91N 21°04′·94N WGS84
BA 203 Imray-Tetra G121

☆ Mole head Fl.R.4s3M

Navigation Gusts with the prevailing NW–W wind.

Berths Stern or bows-to.

Shelter Good from prevailing NW–W winds. Open S.

Facilities Water. Fuel by tanker. Provisions and restaurants.

PLATI YIALI

38°28′·38N 21°04′·81E WGS84

☆ Karlóglossa light Q.R.3M

A large bay with quayed area. Commercial cargo harbour. Entry prohibited.

Nisos Zakinthos

PORT ZAKINTHOS

37°46′·69N 20°54′·36E WGS84
BA 2404 Imray-Tetra G12
52M Vathi (Ithaca) ←→ Katakolon 24M

☆ Ak Krionéri Fl(2)16s6M. Harbour entrance Fl.G.1·5s5M. Ífalos Dhimitri Fl.R.1·5s4M

VHF Ch 12 for harbour authorities.

Navigation Care is needed of Ífalos Dhimitri in the approaches (marked by a red conical buoy). Ferries constantly come and go.

KÓLPOS LAGANA

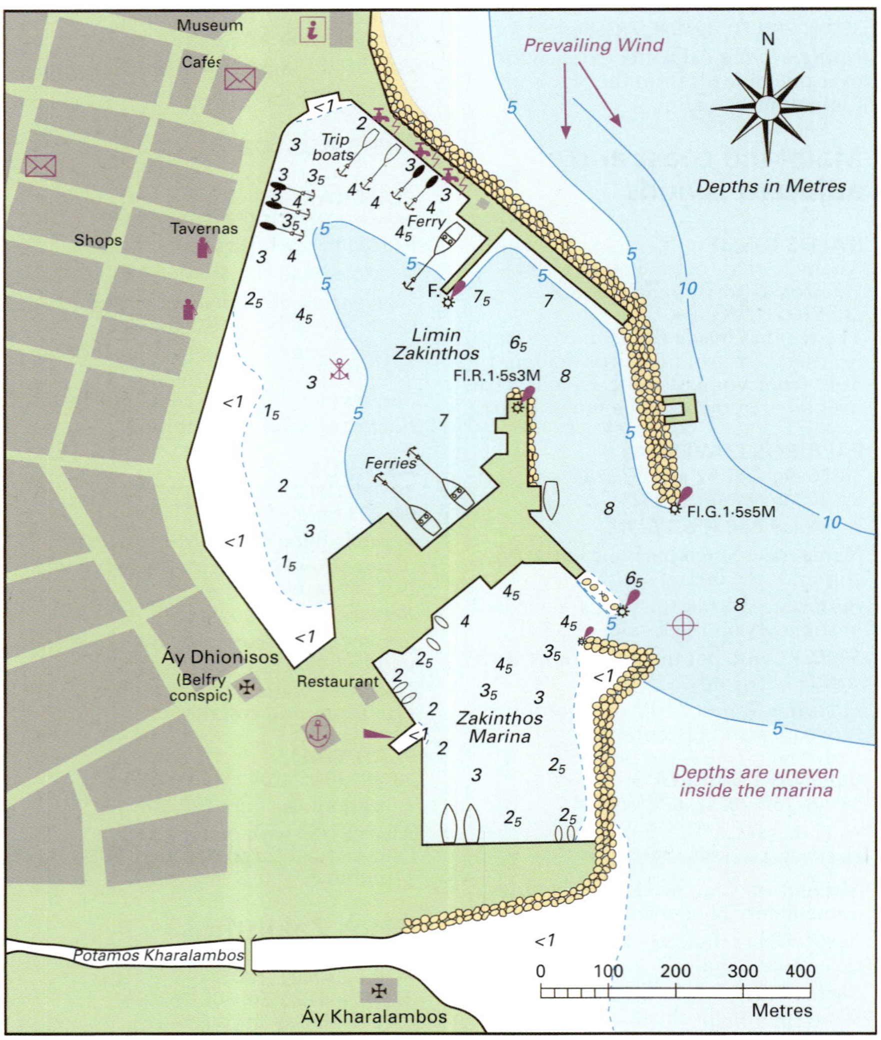

LIMÍN ZÁKINTHOS

Berths Stern or bows-to NE mole or NW quay. Min depths 3m. Charge band 2.

Shelter Good with prevailing NW winds.

Facilities Water. 220V. Fuel by tanker. Provisions and restaurants.

Remarks Trip boats move into the 'marina' during summer season leaving more yacht berths in main harbour.

ZAKINTHOS MARINA

Local boats using the marina but little space or facilities for yachts.

BOATING RESTRICTIONS IN THE BAY OF LAGANAS

The Bay of Laganas on Zákinthos is one of the most important nesting areas for the loggerhead sea turtle (*Caretta caretta*) in the Mediterranean. The coast guard of Zákinthos has issued two Local Port Regulations. According to these, the bay is divided into three zones, in which the following regulations are effective from May to October each year.

Zone A It is forbidden for any boat or vessel to enter or moor within this zone. Fishing with any kind of fishing gear is prohibited.

Zone B It is forbidden for any boat or vessel to travel at a speed greater than 6 kns, and to moor or anchor within this zone.

Zone C It is forbidden for any boat or vessel to travel at speed greater than 6kns within this zone.

What this effectively means is that Yerakas and much of Lagana beach cannot be used from May to October. Yachts should observe the restrictions diligently. Fines (around £200) are made for infringements of the regulations of Órmos Laganas.

ÓRMOS AY NIKÓLAOS

S entrance 37°54′·33N 20°42′·57E WGS84

☆ Nisís Ay Nikólaos Fl.2s7M

Navigation Ferry and fishing harbour under islet of Ay Nikolaos.

Berths Stern or bows-to on the SW end of the new quay around the S side of the bay. Depths 2·5–5m.

Shelter Gusts with the prevailing NW wind. Often a surge in here.

Facilities Water and fuel by tanker. Tavernas and bars. Ferry.

ÓRMOS KERI

Anchoring permitted more than 100m from shore. Good supermarket.

The Southern Ionian

Killini to Kíthera

KILLINI

37°56′·18N 21°08′·86E WGS84
BA 2404 Imray-Tetra G13, G16
16M Zákinthos ←→ Patras 38M

☆ Nisís Kavikalidha LFl.WR.10s12/9M. Entrance Fl.G

Navigation Care needed of the reef running out NW of the harbour. Ferries coming and going.

Berths Fishing harbour has been extended. Yacht berths available here.

Shelter Good shelter from the prevailing W wind.

Facilities Water. 220V. Fuel in the town. Provisions and restaurants.

Remarks Ferry port for Zákinthos.

KATAKOLON

37°38′·81N 21°19′·66E WGS84
BA 2404 Imray-Tetra G12, G16
24M Zakinthos ←→ Pilos 49M

☆ Ak Katakolon Fl.4s15M. Mole head Fl.R.3s4M

VHF Ch 12, 14 for port authorities. (Not always answered).

Navigation Care needed of reef on the E side of Ak Katakolon. Shallows on NW side of harbour. Give way to cruise ships.

Berths Stern or bows-to on W quay. Anchorage on NW side.

Shelter Good with prevailing winds. Appears to be all-round in basin.

Facilities Water. 220V. Fuel by tanker. Boatyard. Provisions and restaurants.

Remarks Commercial harbour close to the site of Olympia by train. Ionian Yacht Services can haul and store yachts ashore. Some yacht repairs.

✆ 06210 213 02 / 213 53

KIPARISSIA

37°15'·51N 21°39'·76E WGS84

Berths Yacht berths stern-to on new E breakwater. Depths 3m.

Facilities Water. Fuel in town. Tavernas.

Remarks New breakwater complete. Shelter much improved.

NISÍDHES STROFADES

Two islands lying approximately 32M due W of Kiparissia and 26M due S of Ak Yerakas on Zakinthos. A light is exhibited on Nisís Stamfáni Fl(2)15s17M.

Part of the Zakinthos Marine Reserve. No specific restrictions for yachts.

PILOS

36°55'·16N 21°42'·02E WGS84 (Marina)
BA 2404 Imray-Tetra G15, G16
49M Katakolon ←→ Methoni 8·5M

☆ Nisís Pilos Fl(2)10s9M. Ak Neókastron Fl.G.3s6M. Pilos pier head F.G.3M. Mole head F.G. Marina N mole head Fl.G.3s3M. S mole head Fl.R.3s3M

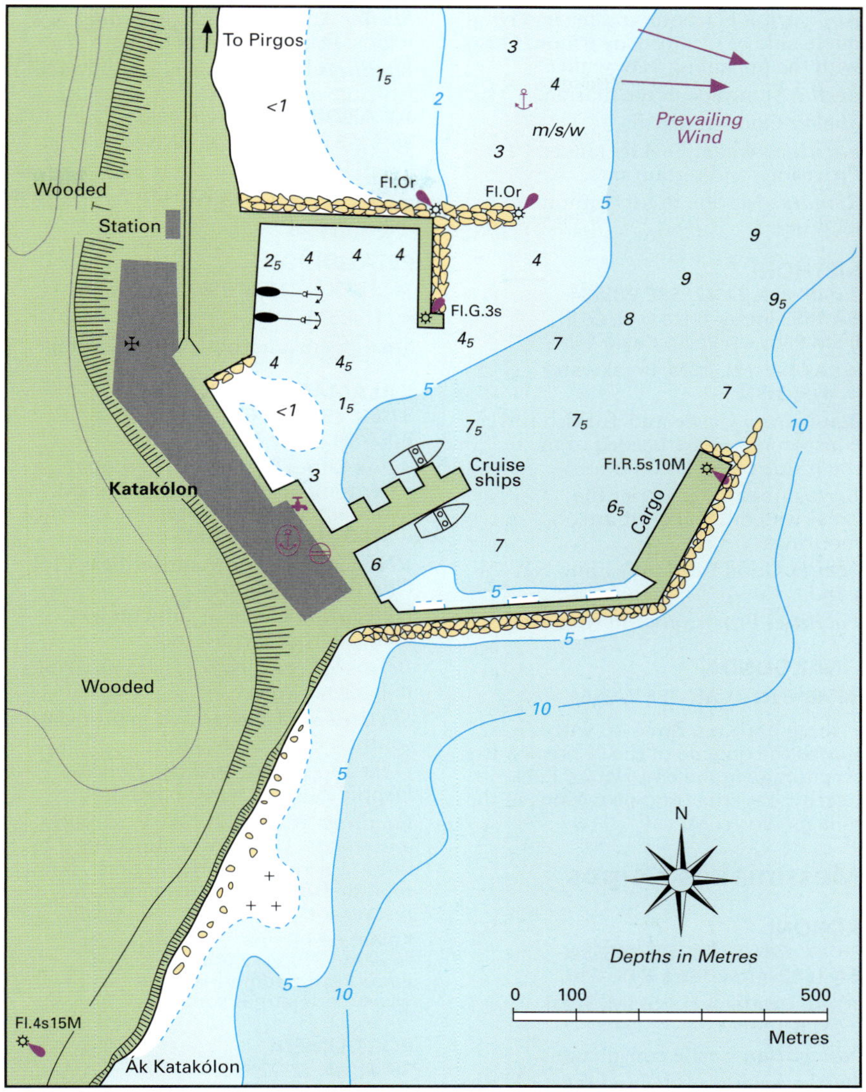

KATAKÓLON

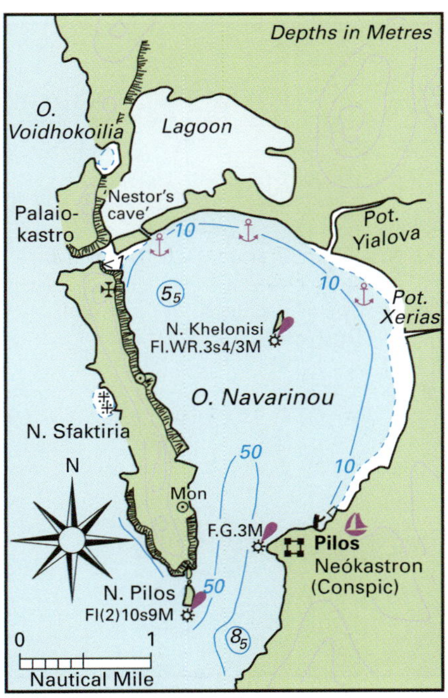

ORMOS NAVARINOU

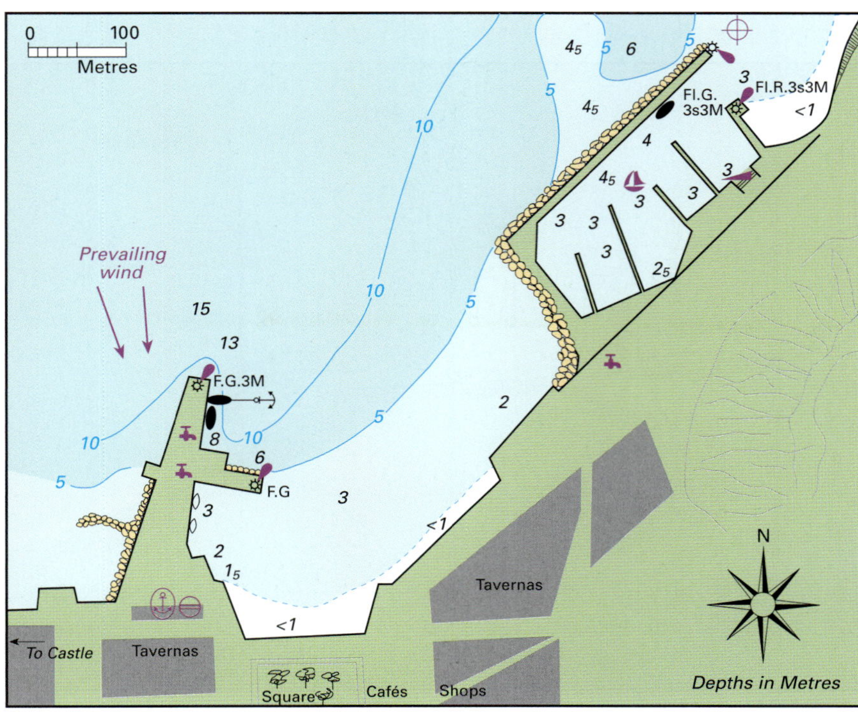

PÍLOS

Navigation Harbour and marina lying on SE side of Órmos Navarinou. Gusts with the prevailing NW winds.

Berths Alongside in the marina.

Shelter Good in marina.

Facilities Water. Fuel by tanker. Provisions and restaurants.

Remarks Marina in use without all facilities.

METHONI

36°48′·83N 21°42′·58E WGS84
BA 1683 Imray-Tetra G15, G16
8·5M Pilos ←→ Porto Kayio 49M

☆ Ak Karsi Fl.3s5M. Breakwater Fl.R.3s3M

Navigation Castle and Turkish tower conspicuous. Care needed of the reef on the E side of Ak Soukouli.

Berths Anchorage under the breakwater. Local craft are on moorings.

Shelter Good from prevailing NW–W wind.

Facilities Provisions and restaurants.

FINAKOUNDA

36°48′·32N 21°48′·38E WGS84

Fishing harbour. Bows-to with a long line to the outside of the N breakwater. Anchorage in the bay. Water. Fuel nearby. Tavernas and provisions in the village. No ATM.

Messiniakos Kólpos

KORONI

36°47′·62N 21°58′·40E WGS84
BA 1683 Imray-Tetra G15, G16

☆ Ak Livádhies Fl.1·5s5M. Breakwater Fl.R.1·5s3M

Navigation Castle conspicuous.

Berths Anchor off behind the mole. Use a trip-line as there are boulders on the bottom.

Shelter Adequate with prevailing NW winds. Dangerous in N gales.

Facilities Provisions and restaurants.

AY ANDREAS

36°51′·81N 21°55′·39E WGS84

Small harbour with 2m in entrance and 2–3m inside. Entrance silting. Crowded with local boats.

PETALIDHION

36°57′·50N 21°55′·95E WGS84

☆ Fl.4s5M

Small fishing harbour and anchorage.

KALAMATA MARINA

37°01′·39N 22°06′·25E WGS84
BA 2404 Imray-Tetra G15, G16

☆ Ak Kitries Fl(2)12s7M. Harbour entrance Fl.R.1·5s3M/Fl.G.1·5s3M. Inner jetty Q.G.3M. Marina entrance Fl.G.3s3M/Fl.R.3s3M

VHF Ch 12 for port authorities. VHF Ch 16, 69 for marina.

Navigation Harbour difficult to identify from the distance.

Berths Where directed. Laid moorings tailed to the quay.

Shelter Good shelter although strong southerlies cause a surge.

Data 255 berths. Visitors' berths. Depths 2–3m. Charge band 3/4.

Facilities Water. 220/380V. Showers and toilets. Laundry facilities. Fuel by mini-tanker. 30-ton travel-hoist. Some repairs. Chandlers. Provisions and restaurants.

Kalamata Marina
✆ 27210 21054 / 21037
Email k.g@medmarinas.com
www.medmarinas.com

PORT LIMENI

36°41′·1N 22°22′·3E
BA 1092 Imray-Tetra G15

☆ Fl.1·5s6M

Lakonikós Kólpos

PORTO KAYIO

36°25′·98N 22°29′·48E WGS84
BA 1092 Imray-Tetra G15
49M Methoni ←→ Akra Maleas 35M

☆ Ak Taínaron Fl(2)20s22M. Entrance Fl.5s8M (unreliable)

Anchorage under Ak Taínaron. Reasonable shelter from westerlies. Untenable in strong NE winds.

YÍTHION

36°45′·64N 22°34′·29E WGS84
BA 1092 Imray-Tetra G15

☆ Nisís Kranai Fl(3)18s14M. Mole head Fl.R.3s3M

Navigation Lighthouse on Nisís Kranai conspicuous.

Berths Ferries now berth on outside of breakwater. Yacht berths stern-to on old ferry quay. Good holding on mud.

Shelter Good shelter from the prevailing S–NE winds.

Facilities Water. Fuel by tanker. Provisions and restaurants.

Remarks Ferry and commercial harbour.

ÓRMOS XÍLIS AND PLÍTRA

36°41′·14N 22°50′·23E WGS84
BA 1092 Imray-Tetra G15

☆ Ak Xílis Fl.3s5M. Mole head Q.G.3M

Large bay and small fishing harbour.

NÍSOS ELAFONISOS AND CHANNEL

(Ormos Sarkiniko) 36°27′·61N 22°57′·03E WGS84
BA 1092 Imray-Tetra G15

☆ Vrakhos Stavros Fl.RG.1·5s2M

NEAPOLIS

36°29′·6N 23°03′·9E
BA 1092 Imray-Tetra G15

Ferry pier off the village. Go alongside or anchor off.

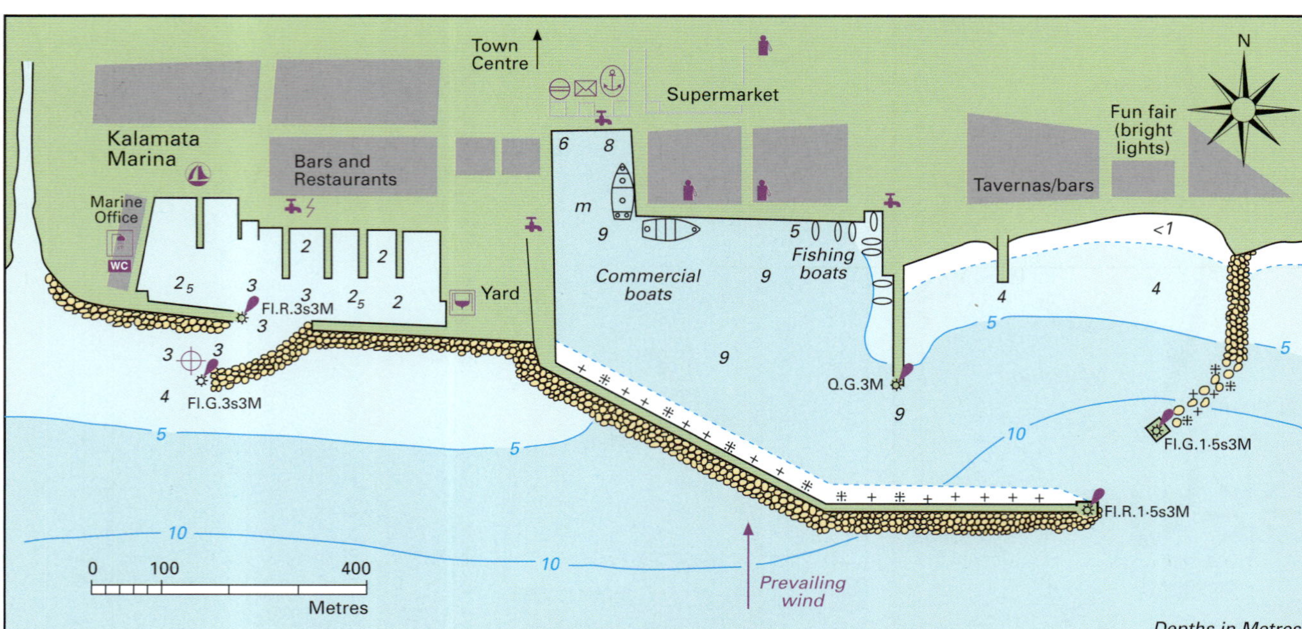

KALAMATA

PALAIOKASTRO
36°29'·52N 23°03'·86E WGS84

☆ Mole hd Fl.G.3s3M

Quiet fishing harbour.

Nísos Kíthera and Andikithera

PELAGIA
36°19'·59N 22°59'·21E WGS84

Small ferry harbour and village.

DHIAKOFTI
36°16'·20N 23°04'·55E WGS84

☆ Fl.R.3s3M

Ferry harbour on W side of Makronisos.

ÁYIOS NIKOLAOS (AVELOMONA)
36°13'·46N 23°04'·89E WGS84
BA 1092 Imray-Tetra G15

☆ Vrak Andidragonéra Fl(3)15s7M. S entrance Fl.G.1·5s3M. Diakofti mole head Fl.R.3s9m3M. Mole head Fl.R.3s3M

A small bay and quayed area on the W side of Kíthera. Indifferent shelter.

ÓRMOS KAPSALI
36°08'·59N 22°59'·91E WGS84
BA 1092 Imray-Tetra G15

☆ E entrance point Fl.3s10M

Navigation Gusts with the prevailing W winds.

Berths Stern or bows-to. Care needed on the quay because of underwater ballasting.

Shelter Adequate with the prevailing W winds. Dangerous in S gales.

Facilities Most provisions and restaurants.

Remarks Anchoring is prohibited in the inner bay.

Patraikós Kólpos (Gulf of Patras)

MESOLONGION (Missalonghi)
38°18'·97N 21°24'·84E WGS84
BA 1676 Imray-Tetra G13

☆ Nisís Ay Sóstis Fl.WR.5s17/14M. Channel buoys and beacons Q.R.3M/Q.G.3M

VHF Ch 69 for marina.

Navigation Outer buoys marking channel are difficult to see. Canal dredged to minimum depth of 6m.

Berths Stern or bows-to in the marina, or anchor off in NW corner.

Shelter Good all-round shelter.

Data 335 berths. Max LOA 80m. Charge band 3.

Facilities Water. 220V. WiFi. Showers and toilets. 120-ton travel-lift to be installed. Hauling by crane at present. Provisions and restaurants in the town about a 15 minute walk away.

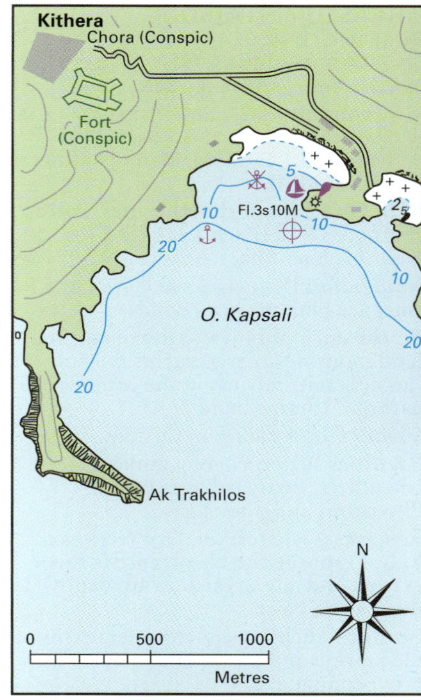

APPROACHES TO ORMOS KAPSALI

Messolonghi Marina
☎ 26310 50190
Email info@messolonghimarina.com

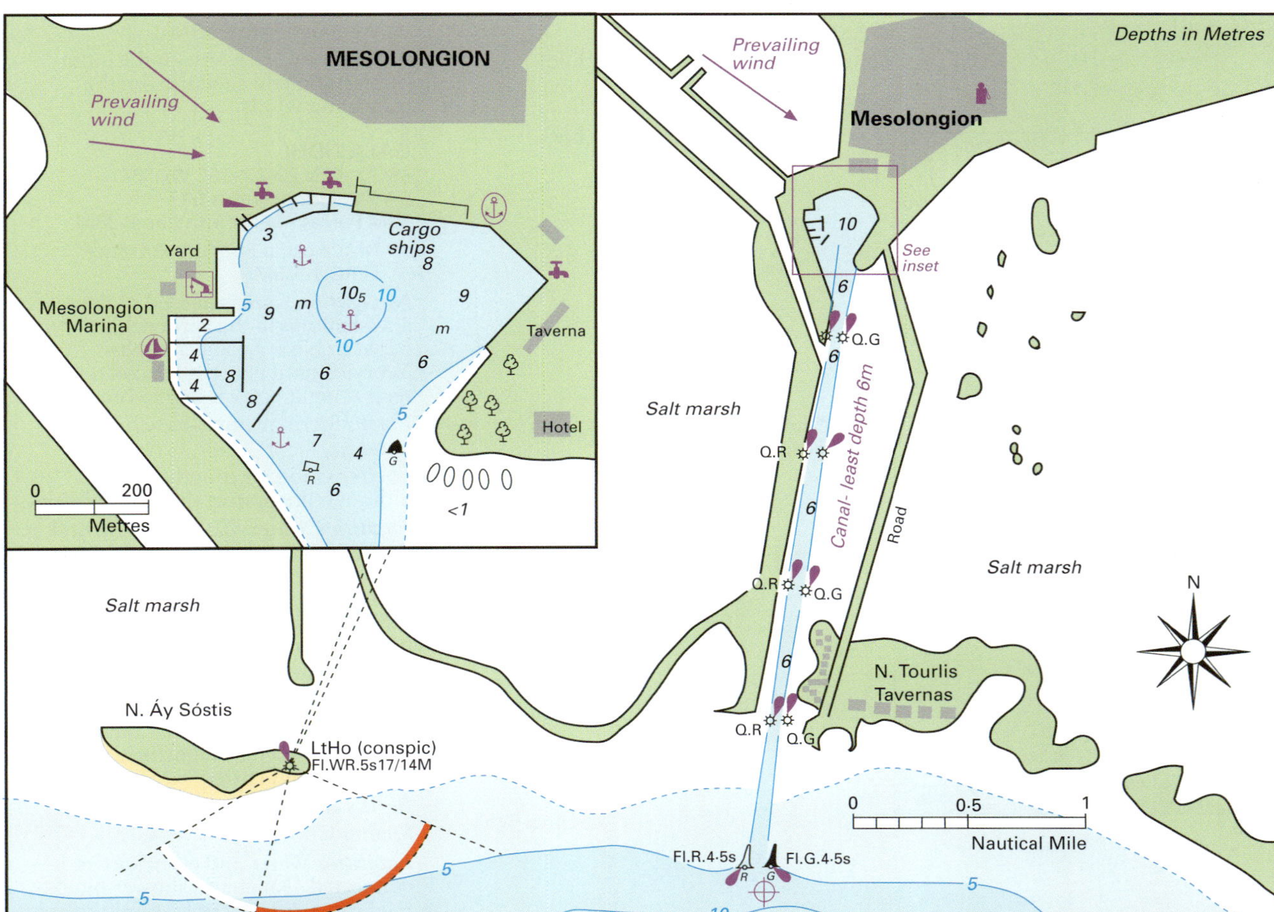

MESOLONGION

PATRAS (LIMIN PATRON)
38°15′·6N 21°44′·0E
BA 2404 Imray-Tetra G13
38M Killini ←→ Galaxidhi 39M

☆ N entrance Fl.G.5s8M. Middle Fl.R.5s8M. Elbow Fl.G.1·5s3M. Pier head Fl.G.1·5s7m3M. Marina entrance F.G.1M/F.R.1M

VHF Ch 12 for port authorities. Patras Traffic VTS VHF Ch 13. Ch 13 for Nautilus Yachting.

Navigation Disturbed swell at N and S entrance with onshore winds.

Berths Stern or bows-to in the marina. Laid moorings. Large yachts (>15m) can negotiate a berth in the commercial harbour. Charge band 2/3.

Shelter Good shelter in the marina.

Facilities Water. Fuel by tanker. Chandlers. Boatyard at marina. Provisions and *tavernas*.

Remarks Main terminal for ferries to Italy. Opposite the N entrance is the marina and a boatyard. 2–4m depths in the marina basin.

Nautilus Yachting can arrange berths in the marina and bunkering, provisioning, etc.

Patras Marina ✆ 2610 453 540 / 429130

Nautilus Yachting ✆ 22610 620061 or 6944 334977 (24/24)
Email ny@nautilusyachting.gr

All clearance paperwork and can arrange pre-payment for Corinth Canal dues.

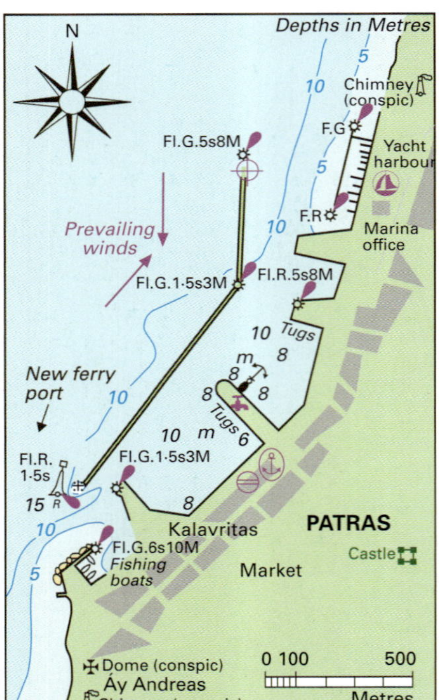

PATRAS

Dhiavolos Ríon and Andírrion (Strait of Rhíon and Andirhíon)

The narrow strait one mile wide at the western entrance to the Gulf of Corinth. The Rion-Andirrion suspension bridge is visible for some distance, and by night is illuminated with blue neon. It has three navigable channels each 560m wide, between four pillars giving an air height of 25–45m.

Yachts must call *Rion Traffic* on VHF Ch 14 when 5M off to obtain permission to transit the bridge. Vessels over 20m LOA should call when 12M off. You will be asked for vessel length and mast height. Yachts will be directed to transit the north or south channels, leaving the central span for commercial traffic. Normally (but not always) E-bound yachts will use the S channel, W-bound the N channel. Try to approach the appropriate channel and avoid crossing the central span close to the bridge. Yachts will be asked to confirm understanding of which span to transit as 'three columns to the left, one to the right' (or vice versa as appropriate).

Each of the three navigable spans is individually lit for navigation and is in line with IALA 'A' scheme; leading from seawards, from W to E.

Centre Span: Iso.R.4s54m6M (N side)/Iso.G.4s54m6M (S side)/Iso.4s58m8M (centre line).

N span: Q.R.35m4M (N side)/Q.G.48m4M (S side)/Q.42m6M (centre line).

S span: Q.R.1s48m4M (N side)/Q.G.1s35m4M (S side)/Q.42m6M (centre line).

Korinthiakós Kólpos (Gulf of Corinth)

NÁVPAKTOS
38°23′·55N 21°49′·72E WGS84
BA 1676 Imray-Tetra G13

☆ Entrance Fl.G.2s3M

Berths Stern or bows-to. Large yachts (>12m) should anchor outside as the harbour is very small.

Shelter Adequate though uncomfortable with strong S and W winds.

Facilities Provisions and restaurants.

NISÍS TRIZÓNIA
38°22′·06N 22°04′·77E WGS84
BA 1676 Imray-Tetra G13

☆ Entrance Fl.4s4M

Navigation The island is difficult to make out against the land behind. Gusts with prevailing winds.

Berths Stern or bows-to in the new 'marina'. Or berth stern or bows-to either side of the breakwater, taking care of underwater ballast off the quay in places. Anchorage in the bay.

Shelter Good all-round shelter although uncomfortable with strong NE winds.

Facilities Water on N side of 'marina'. Limited provisions and restaurants.

AIYIÓN
38°15′·3N 22°05′·0E
BA 2404 Imray-Tetra G13

☆ Pier head Fl.R.1·5s3M

An open bay on S side of the gulf, offering limited shelter from the prevailing winds.

GALAXIDHI
38°22′·69N 22°23′·36E WGS84
BA 2405 Imray-Tetra G13
39M Patras ←→ Corinth Canal 38M

☆ Nisís Apsifía Fl.7s5M. Entrance Fl.RG.1·5s3M

Navigation Care is needed of the reef and shallows in the approach. Proceed between Nisís Apsifia and Nisís Ay Yeoryios until past the beacon on the reef. A night entry is not recommended.

Berths Stern or bows-to. Charge band 2.

Shelter Good all round shelter although uncomfortable with N gales.

Facilities Water. 220V. Fuel by tanker. Provisions and restaurants.

ITEA
38°25′·73N 22°25′·45E WGS84
BA 2405 Imray-Tetra G13

☆ Pier head Fl.RG.3s4M

VHF Ch 12, 24 for port authorities.

Navigation New 'marina' immediately W of town pier. Straightforward approach and entry.

Berths Alongside where convenient.

Shelter Good.

Facilities Water and electricity to be connected. Toilet and shower block. Fuel can be delivered by mini-tanker. Provisions and restaurants.

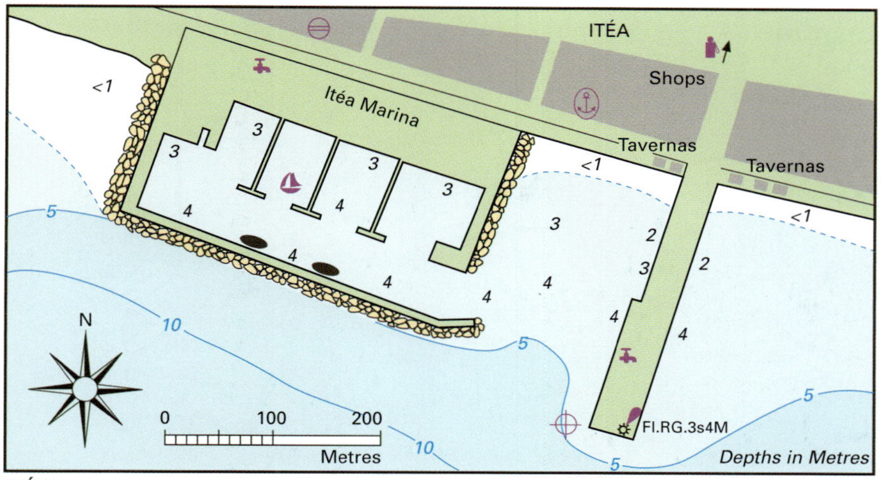

ITÉA

Remarks Nearest safe harbour to Delphi.

ÓRMOS ANDIKÍRON
38°21′·56N 22°38′·00E WGS84
BA 2405 Imray-Tetra G13

☆ Kefáli Fl.3s4M. Buoys Q.R

A large bay with an anchorage on the N side.

ORMOS SARANTI
☆ Fl.R.3s3M

A large bay 6M E of Ak Velanidhia.

PORTO GERMENO
38°09′·5N 23°13′·2E

☆ Germainoú W mole head Fl.R.2s3M. E mole head Fl.G.2s3M

ALEPOKHORÍOU
38°05′·4N 23°11′·2E

☆ S mole head Fl.R.3s3M. Mole head Fl.G.3s3M

KIATO
38°00′·81N 22°45′·28E WGS84

☆ N mole head Fl.G.3s6M. Fishing harbour F.R/F.G

Commercial harbour with room for yachts to go alongside. Extension to fishing harbour now complete. Yacht berths on new breakwater. Good all-round shelter.

CORINTH HARBOUR
37°56′·8N 22°56′·1E (Fl.G.3M)
BA 1600 Imray-Tetra G13

☆ Ak Melangavi Fl.10s19M. Mole head Fl.G.3s3M. Yacht harbour F.R.3M/F.G.3M (unreliable)

Navigation Harbour difficult to identify from distance. There is a confused swell with strong W winds and gusts with strong NE winds.

Berths Stern or bows-to in the yacht harbour. Pontoons are very crowded, with little room for visitors. Max LOA 12m. Some yachts have used the SW corner of the commercial harbour.

Shelter Good shelter in the yacht harbour.

Facilities Water. Fuel by tanker. Provisions and restaurants.

Corinth Canal (Dhiorix Korinthou)
37°57′·19N 22°57′·49E WGS84 (W entrance)
BA 1600 Imray-Tetra G13

☆ Gulf of Corinth Iso.R.2s10M/Iso.G.2s10M

The canal is 3·2M long, 25m (81ft) wide, the maximum permitted draught is 7m (23ft) and the limestone from which it is cut rises to 76m (250ft) above sea level at the highest point. The canal is closed on Tuesdays.

A current of 1–3 kns can flow either way in the canal depending on the wind direction. There are hydraulic bridges at either end which lower to let vessels pass.

Signals

By day	*By night*	*Signal*
Blue flag	One white light	Entry permitted
Red flag	Two vertical white lights	Entry prohibited

A yacht may have to wait up to three hours before entering the canal. Traffic lights control movements. The paperwork and canal fees are done at Isthmia at the Aegean end of the canal. Fuel by mini-tanker.

VHF Ch 11 (*Isthmía Pilot*).

Use the website to calculate the exact transit costs.

Canal Office ✆ 27410 30880 / 30886
www.aedik.gr

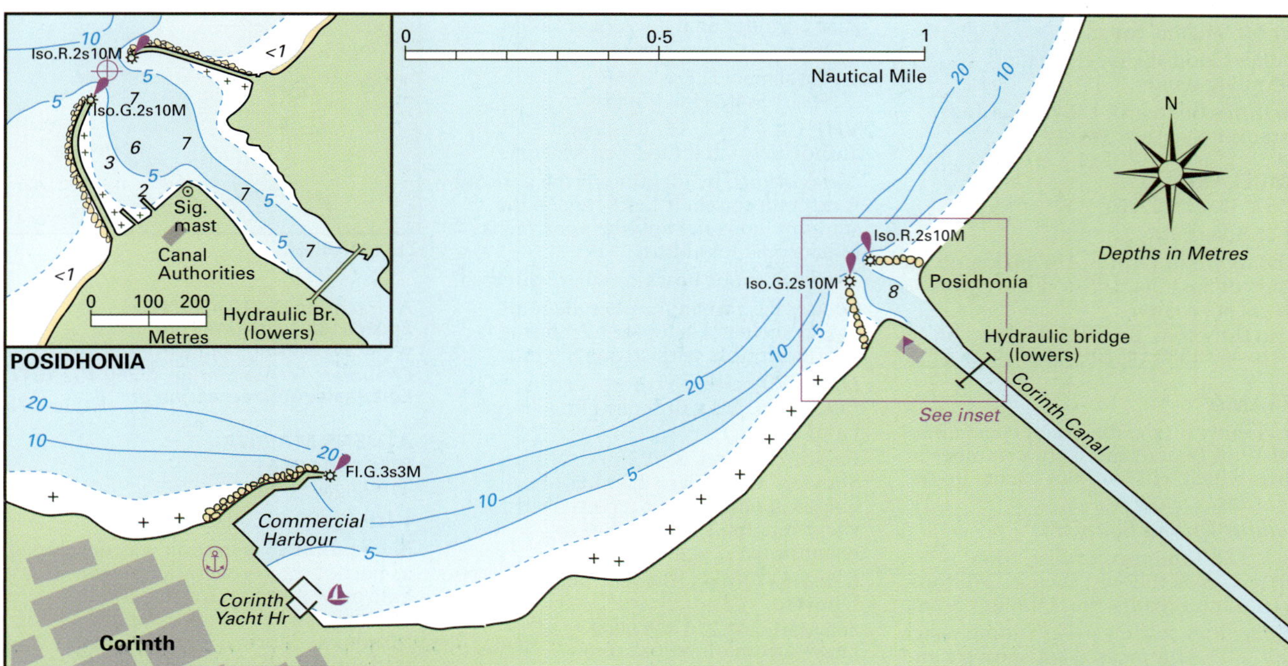

CORINTH CANAL - WEST ENTRANCE

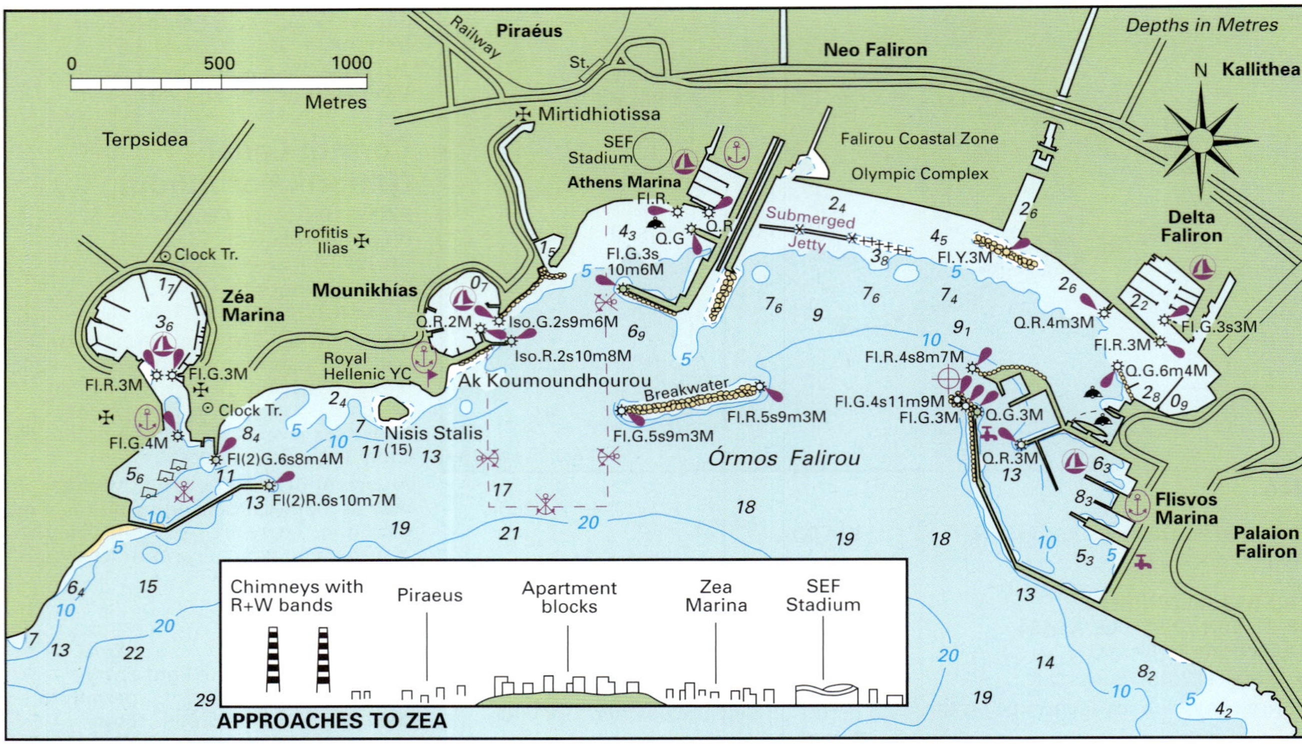

ORMOS FALIROU

The Saronic and Eastern Peloponnese

Nísos Salamis

ÓRMOS SALAMIS

37°57′·7N 23°29′·6E
BA 1657 Imray-Tetra G14

☆ Ak Karas Fl.4s8M. NW mole head Fl.R.3s5M. SE mole head Fl.G.3s5M

Navigation Large bay on the W side of Nísos Salamis

Berths Anchorage at the head of the bay off Salamis town.

Shelter Good shelter from the prevailing wind

Facilities Boatyard. Provisions and restaurants in the town.

AMBELÁKIA

37°57′·1N 23°32′·9E

☆ 2F.G(vert)3M

A boatyard in Órmos Ambelákia on the E side of Salamis. 100-ton travel-hoist. All yacht repairs.

Tasso Lathouras, Bekris Co Ltd
✆ 210 467 1588 / 4120

PERAMA

At Perama on the mainland coast about 3M W of Piraeus there are a number of yards which will haul out yachts up to 200 tons.

Halkitis Urania Boatyard

Uses a 280-ton travel-hoist. Max capacity is as follows: Weight 280 tons. LOA 45m. Breadth 9m. Draught 5·2m.

All facilities at the yard including water, 220/380V, compressed air, showers and toilets, communications, 24-hour security. All yacht repairs carried out or arranged.

Halkitis Urania Boatyard
✆ 210 441 0182 / 402 0256

PIRAEUS COMMERCIAL HARBOUR

☆ Entrance LFl.R.6s9M/LFl.G.6s9M

This large harbour is for ferries and commercial cargo ships only. A yacht should not attempt to enter or berth here.

ZEA MARINA

37°55′·93N 23°39′·22E WGS84
BA 1599 Imray-Tetra G14
32M Corinth Canal ←→ Aigina 16·5M

☆ Entrance Fl(2)R.6s7M/Fl(2)G.6s4M. Paşalimani Fl.R.1·5s3M/ Fl.G.1·5s4M/Fl.G.1·5s4M

VHF Ch 07, 12, 16, for port authorities. Ch 09 for Zea Marina.

Navigation The location of the harbour is difficult to see. It lies between the stadium (conspic) and the apartment blocks on a low bluff.

Berths Stern or bows-to where directed.

Shelter Paşalimani has excellent all-round shelter. The outer harbour is uncomfortable with strong S winds.

Data 670 berths. Visitors' berths. Max LOA 80m. Max draught 6m. Charge band 5.

Facilities Water. 220/380V. WiFi. Showers and toilets. Laundry. Fuel quay. Chandlers. Sail repairs. Most yacht repairs. Provisions and restaurants.

Remarks Often crowded. Theft reported.

Zea Marina ✆ 210 455 9000
Email k.g@medmarinas.com
www.medmarinas.com
www.d-marin.com

ZEA MARINA

A1 Yachting ✆ 210 458 7100
Email a1@a1yachting.com
www.a1yachting.com
Chandlers Tecrep Marine ✆ 210 452 1647
Email sales@tecrepmarine.gr

ATHENS MARINA (SEF MARINA)

37°56′·2N 23°39′·9E

VHF Ch 09 (0700–2200).

Navigation This marina was developed as part of the regeneration of the Faliron waterfront for the 2004 Olympics. The entrance lies close N of Mounikas Marina. The Olympic stadium overlooks the marina and is conspicuous from some distance off.

Berths Go stern or bows-to where directed. Laid moorings tailed to the pontoons.

Shelter Good shelter from the prevailing winds. Strong southerlies can create a surge, making the outer berths uncomfortable.

Data 200 berths. Max LOA 100m (inner basin 28m). Depths 4–6m. Charge band 4/5.

Facilities Water. 220/380V. Telephone. Pump-out facilities at most berths for grey and black water. Toilets and showers. WiFi. Fuel can be delivered by mini-tanker. Provisions, cafés, restaurants and tavernas in Faliron.

Other Buses, trams and metro stops are all adjacent to the marina. Spata Airport 15 minutes (c.€30).

Remarks Prices are based on a calendar day ie the first night you will pay for two days, and thereafter one for each night.

☎ 210 485 3200
Email info@athens-marina.gr

LIMENISKOS DELTA FALIRON

This basin in the NE corner of Ormos Falirou is currently home to the Tzitzifies Kallithea Yacht Club (NOTK).

Data 500 berths. Max LOA c.15m. Depths 2–3m.

Facilities There are few facilities at present.

Note The marina is under the control of Hellenic Olympic Properties and is awaiting further development, which is likely to include new pontoons for yachts in transit, as well as providing a base for local yacht club boats.

☎ 210 413 819
Email info@notk.gr
www.notk.gr

FLISVOS MARINA

37°56'·1N 23°40'·8E
BA 1599 Imray-Tetra G141

☆ S mole head Fl.G.4s9M/Fl.G.3M. N mole head Fl.R.4s8m7M. Marina Q.R.1s3M/Q.G.3M

VHF Ch 09.

Berths Stern or bows-to.

Shelter Good shelter.

Data 300 berths. Limited visitors' berths. Depths 3–13m. LOA 15–120m. Charge band 5.

Facilities Water. Fuel by tanker. 220/380V. WiFi. Provisions and restaurants in Faliron.

Remarks Few visitors' berths. Enquire in advance. Port of entry.

Marina Flisvos
☎ 210 987 1000
Email info@flisvosmarina.com
www.flisvosmarina.com

KALAMAKI (ALIMOS MARINA)

37°54'·8N 23°42'·1E
BA 1599 Imray-Tetra G14, G141

☆ Entrance Fl.G.3s9M/Fl.R.3s9M

VHF Ch 71.

Navigation The location of the harbour is difficult to see. A blue hangar at the old airport SE is conspicuous.

Berths Stern or bows-to. Laid moorings at most berths.

Shelter Good all-round shelter.

Data 900 berths. Depths 2–5m. Charge band 4/5.

Facilities Water. 220V. Showers and toilets. Fuel quay. Yachts craned onto the hard. Chandlers. Provisions and some restaurants nearby.

Remarks Few visitors' berths available.

Alimos Marina Kalamaki
☎ 210 988 0000 ext 203
Email marinaalimou@etasa.gr
www.alimos-marina.gr

ALSITY MARINA AY KOSMAS (OLYMPIC SAILING CENTRE)

37°52'·9N 23°43'·4E

☆ Q(9)15s5M. E mole head Fl.R.4s3M. W mole head Fl.G.4s3M

Data c.200 berths.

The marina is usually full with superyachts.

GLIFADHA MARINA 4

37°52'·3N 23°44'·0E

☆ Entrance F.G.3M/F.R.3M

VHF Ch 09.

Berths Stern or bows-to.

Shelter Good all-round shelter.

Facilities Water. Fuel by tanker. 220V. Showers and toilets. Provisions and restaurants in Glifadha.

Remarks Few visitors' berths available.

☎ 210 894 7920

VOULIAGMENI - ASTIR MARINA

37°48'·3N 23°46'·6E
BA 1657 Imray-Tetra G14, G141

☆ Nisís Fléves Fl(3)10s8M. Entrance Fl(3)R.12s7M, Fl.R.1·5s3M, Fl.G.1·5s3M and Fl.G.1·5s3M

Navigation Care is needed of Vrak Kasidhis Rock and reef 350m S of the W entrance point to the bay.

Berths Stern or bows-to where directed. Laid moorings.

Shelter Good although uncomfortable with strong S winds.

Data Charge band 5.

Facilities Water. Fuel quay. 220V. Showers and toilets. No provisions locally. Restaurant.

Remarks Crowded in the summer.

☎ 210 896 0012 / 0415

Email info@astir-marina.gr
www.astir-marina.gr

VÁRKIZA (VARKILAS)

37°49'·1N 23°48'·3E
BA 1657 Imray-Tetra G14, G141

☆ Entrance F.R.3M

Peloponnese

KORFOS (LIMIN SOFIKOÚ)

37°45'·32N 23°07'·72E WGS84
BA 1657 Imray-Tetra G14, G141

☆ Entrance Fl.4s5M

Navigation Care must be taken of the reef running out from Ak Trelli for 400m. Gusts with W winds.

Berths Anchorage in the bay. Stern or bows-to the quay.

Shelter Good although strong S winds make it uncomfortable and dangerous on the quay.

Facilities Water. Fuel by tanker. Provisions and restaurants.

EPIDHAVROS (PALAIA EPIDHAVROS)

37°38'·27N 23°09'·49E WGS84
BA 1657 Imray-Tetra G14

☆ Ak Kalamaki Fl.2s6M. Beacons Q.G.3M, Q.R.3M. Pier head Fl.R.3s3M

Navigation Entrance difficult to see.

Berths Stern or bows-to. Anchorage in N or SW of bay.

Shelter Good although uncomfortable and possibly untenable with strong E winds.

Facilities Water. Fuel by tanker. Provisions and restaurants.

Remarks Taxis available for excursions to Epidhavros theatre.

VATHÍ (METHANA)

37°35'·60N 23°20'·28E WGS84
BA 1657 Imray-Tetra G14

☆ Entrance F.R.3M

Navigation Harbour on the W side of Methana Peninsula.

Berths Stern or bows-to.

Shelter Good all-round shelter.

Facilities Water. 220V. Some provisions and restaurants.

METHANA

37°34'·47N 23°23'·39E WGS84
BA 1657 Imray-Tetra G14, G141

☆ Headland Fl.G.3s3M. Entrance Q.G.3M/Q.R.3M. Pier head 2F.R(vert)3M

Navigation Harbour lies S of the town. Entrance is very narrow.

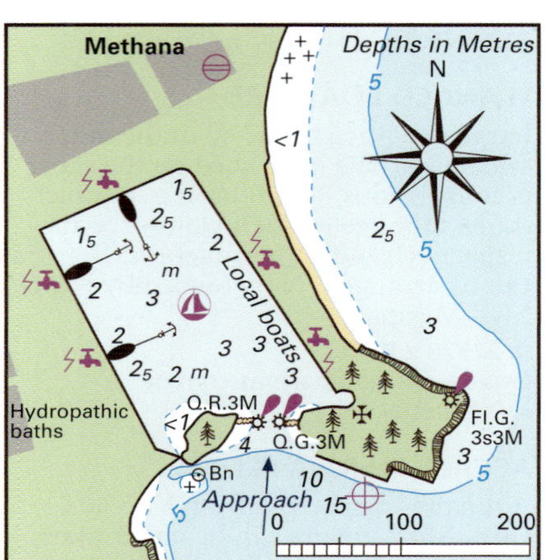

METHANA

Berths Stern or bows-to W quay. Berths also available on ferry pier to the N of the harbour.

Shelter All-round.

Facilities Water. 220V. Fuel by tanker. Provisions and restaurants.

Nísos Aígina

AIGINA

37°44'·66N 23°25'·59E WGS84
BA 1657 Imray-Tetra G14, G141
16·5M Zea Marina ←→ Poros 17M

☆ Entrance Fl.5s7M/F.R/F.G. Marina N mole head Fl.R.3s3M. W breakwater head Fl.G.3s3M.

Navigation Care needed of shoal water extending E from Nisís Metopi across to Aígina. Least depths of 8–9m through the fairway of the channel. Care needed at the entrance of ferries and hydrofoils.

Berths Stern or bows-to on the N quay, or off the café on the S quay.

Shelter Good all-round shelter although strong southerlies send in an uncomfortable swell.

Facilities Water and 220V on the quay. Fuel by tanker. Provisions and restaurants.

Remarks Aigina Marina is only open to local craft.

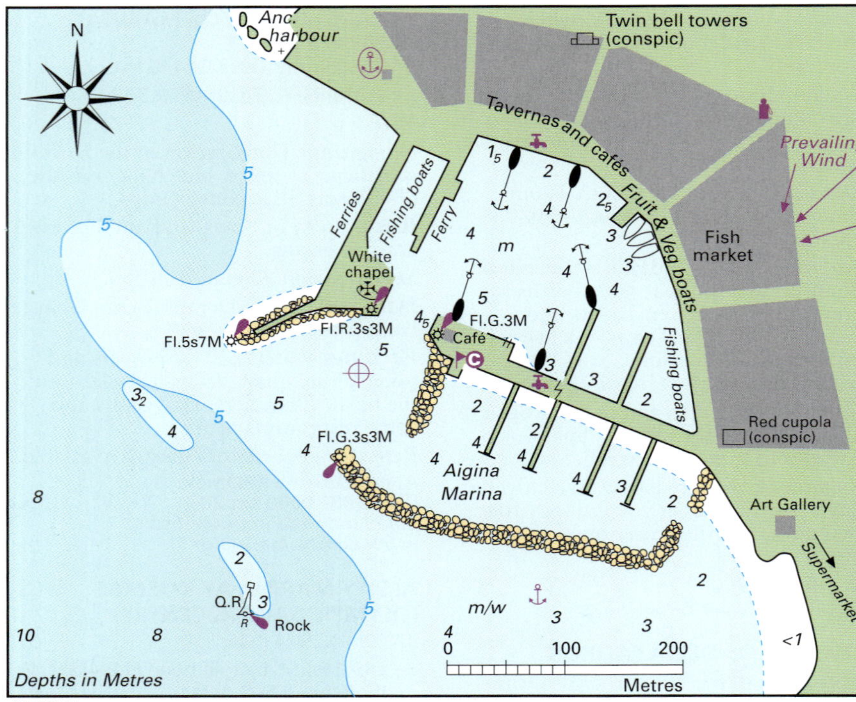

AIGINA

PERDIKA

37°41'·43N 23°27'·06E WGS84
BA 1657 Imray-Tetra G14, G141

☆ Nisís Moni Fl(2)WRG.10s11-8M

Berths Stern or bows-to on inner pier. Limited room.

Facilities Water. Some provisions and restaurants.

KANONIS BOATYARD

37°46'·3N 23°27'·6E

North coast of Aígina. 50/20 ton hydraulic trailers. 2m max. depths.

☎ 22970 241 51 or
Jordanis ☎ 22970 266 45

ASPRAKIS BOATYARD

Adjacent to Kanonis. 60-ton travel-hoist. 2·5m maximum depths. Limited yacht repairs. Few facilities. A bit out of the way but transport can be arranged.

☎ 22970 239 25

PLANACO BOATYARD

Large new yard to the W of the other two yards. The large shed on the shore is conspicuous. 60/260-ton hydraulic trailers for keeled yachts/motorboats respectively. 400-ton travel-lift. Repairs can be arranged. Now owned by K&G Med Marinas.

☎ 22970 29040
Email k.g@medmarinas.com or info@planaco.gr

AEGINA MARINA CENTRE

A repairs yard across from Kanonis yard. Most repairs can be undertaken. Small chandlers.

☎ 22970 53842
Email info@aeginayachtservices
www.aeginayachtservices.com

Nísos Angistri

ANGISTRI

37°43'·00N 23°21'·00E
BA 1657 Imray-Tetra G14, G141

☆ Breakwater Fl.G

Small harbour on the NE corner of Angistri. Stern or bows-to where possible leaving ferry quay clear. Some laid moorings. Depths 2–4m.

Nísos Póros

PÓROS

37°29'·61N 23°27'·74E WGS84 (Ak Stavros)
BA 1599 Imray-Tetra G14, G141
17M Aigina ←→ Hydra 17M

☆ Ak Dána Fl.WR.4s8/5M. Ak Nédha Fl.R.2s3M. Ak Stavrós Fl.RG.3s4/4M 284°-R-309°

Navigation Care is needed of the extensive shallows on the S side of the channel between Póros town and the mainland coast. Care also needed of ferries and hydrofoils in the narrow approach channel.

Berths Stern or bows-to the town quay on the N or S. Care needed of laid mooring chains (no lines) off the S quay in the channel. Pontoon off N quay. Anchorages nearby.

Shelter Good shelter on the S quay except for an uncomfortable wash from ferries and hydrofoils. Adequate shelter on N quay from prevailing winds.

Facilities Water. 220V. Fuel by tanker. Showers and toilets in the bars/cafés. Chandlers. Provisions and restaurants.

Remarks Crowded in the summer, but it is usually possible to find a berth somewhere.

Greek Sails ☎ 22980 23147
Mobile 6944 683678
Email info@greeksails.com
Vikos Marine ☎ 22980 22020
Mobile 6944 986 029
Email info@vikos-marine.com

ERMIÓNI

37°23'·24N 23°15'·68E WGS84
BA 1031 Imray-Tetra G14, G141

☆ Ak Kastrí Fl.1·5s4M. Mole head F.R.2M. Breakwater Fl.G.2s3M

Navigation Care needed of the remains of the ancient mole on the N side of the headland.

Berths Stern or bows-to either side of the mole. Anchorage N of breakwater. Depths 2–4m. Stern-to on S quay.

Shelter Good all-round shelter behind mole.

Facilities Water. Fuel by tanker. Provisions and restaurants.

Remarks New marina planned in NW corner. Work not yet started. Existing berths in old harbour not affected.

Nísos Ídhra (Hydra)

LIMIN ÍDHRAS

37°21'·2N 23°28'·0E (F.G.2M)
BA 1031 Imray-Tetra G14
17M Poros ←→ Spetsai (Baltiza) 15·5M

☆ E side Fl.R.1·5s3M. Entrance F.R.2M and F.G.2M

Navigation Harbour difficult to locate from the distance. Care needed in narrow entrance.

Berths Stern or bows-to where possible. Very crowded in the summer.

Shelter Good from prevailing SE wind. Uncomfortable and dangerous on S quay with strong N winds.

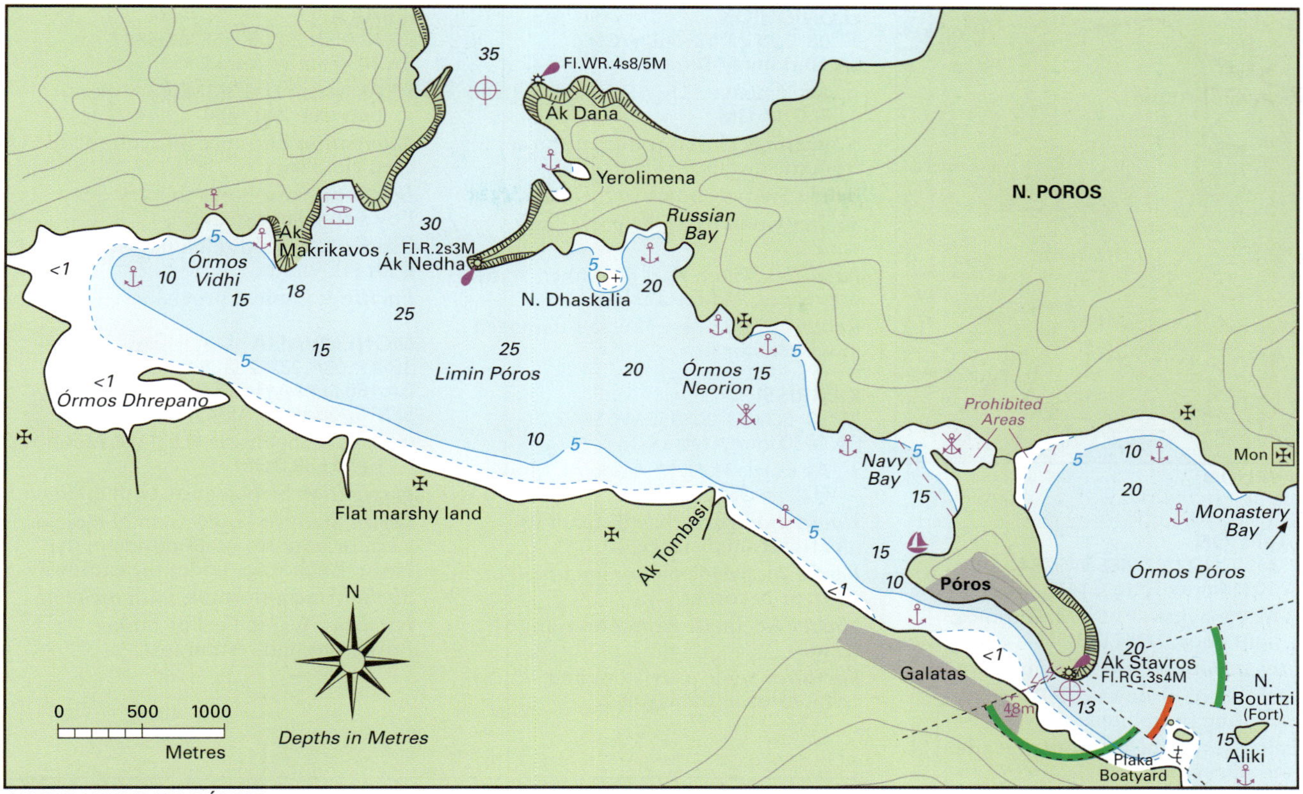

APPROACHES TO PÓROS

Facilities Water. Provisions and restaurants.

Remarks Fouled anchors common. Get here by early afternoon for a berth. Often three deep stern-to on both sides.

Argolikós Kólpos

Nísos Spétsai

SPÉTSAI (BALTIZA CREEK)

37°15'·85N 23°09'·85E WGS84
BA 1031, 1683 Imray-Tetra G14
15·5M Hydra ←→ Monemvasia 38M

☆ Ak Fanári Fl.WR.5s18/14M. Headland Q.R.3M

Navigation Often a confused swell at the entrance with S winds.

Berths Stern or bows-to in inner harbour. Anchor with a long line ashore in outer harbour.

Shelter Good all-round shelter in inner harbour. Sometimes a reflected swell in outer harbour. Water-taxis make significant and uncomfortable wash when coming and going.

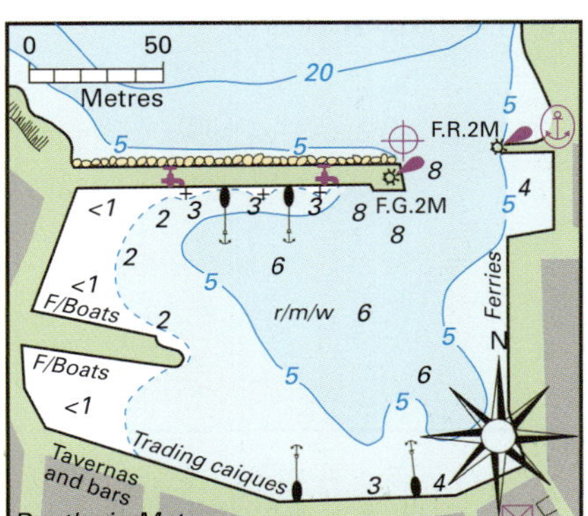

LIMIN IDHRAS

Facilities Water. Fuel. Chandlers. Small boatyards. Provisions and restaurants.

Remarks Large yachts may find a berth at Dapia on the pier W of Spetsai town.

PORTO KHELI

37°18'·67N 23°07'·85E WGS84
BA 1031 Imray-Tetra G14

☆ W side Fl.1·5s5M. E side Fl.G.3s3M (Bn).

Navigation Leave stone beacon to starboard at entrance.

Berths Stern or bows-to on quay. Anchorage in the bay.

Shelter Good all-round shelter.

Facilities Water and fuel by mini-tanker. Boatyard. Provisions and restaurants.

Porto Heli Marine Service (boatyard) ☏ 27540 52380

KOILÁDHIA

37°25'·54N 23°06'·75E WGS84
BA 1031 Imray-Tetra G14

☆ Ak Kókkinos Fl.3s4M. Pier head 2F.G(vert)3M

VHF Ch 77 for shipyard.

Navigation Care needed of reef off S entrance.

Berths Anchorage in the bay.

Shelter Good all-round shelter.

Facilities Water. Some provisions and restaurants.

Two boatyards in the S side of the bay. Access via a buoyed dredged channel. Depths 2–3m. Call ahead for advice on depths.

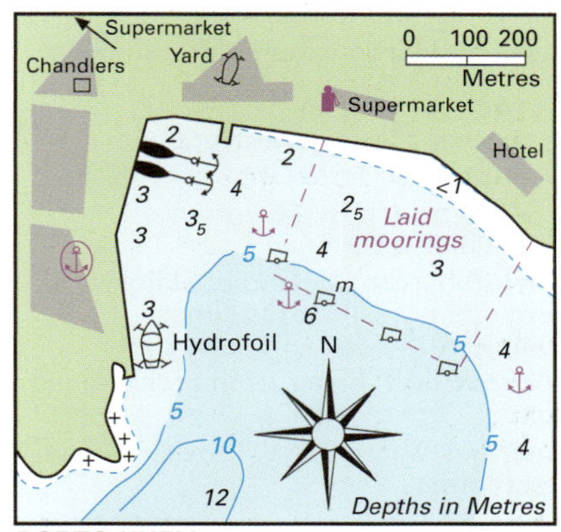

PORTO KHELI

Data 300/70-ton travel-lifts. Hydraulic trailer. Most repairs can be undertaken. Gardiennage.

Basimakopouloi Shipyard ☏ 27540 61409/ 6972 247 814 (or try VHF Ch 77)
Email bashipyard@gmail.com
www.basimakopouloi.gr

Lekkas Shipyard ☏ 27540 61456
Email info@lekkas-shipyard.gr

KHAIDHARI

37°31'·33N 22°55'·94E WGS84

☆ Fl(3)WR15s5/3M

Short pier off the village. Anchorage in the bay. Good all-round shelter.

TOLÓ (TOLON)

37°30'·97N 22°52'·02E WGS84
BA 1031 Imray-Tetra G14

☆ Nisís Toló/Ak Skála Fl(2)WR.10s6/4M. Ak Khäidhari Fl(3)WR.15s5/3M. Ak Megali Fl.2s3M. Mole head 2F.R(vert)3M

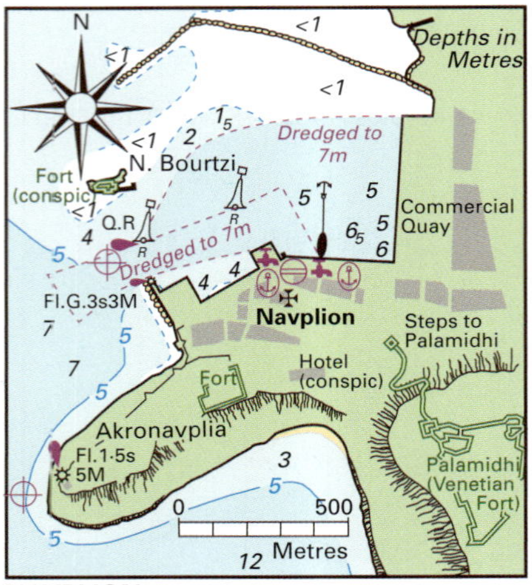

NAVPLION

NAVPLION

37°34′·03N 22°47′·48E WGS84
BA 1031 Imray-Tetra G141

☆ Ak Panayítsa Fl.1·5s5M. Entrance, light buoy Q.R/Fl.G.3s3M

Navigation Entrance channel buoyed.

Berths Stern or bows-to NW quay. Anchoring prohibited.

Shelter Good shelter from prevailing SE wind. Open N–NW.

Facilities Water. Fuel by tanker. Provisions and restaurants.

Remarks Harbour sometimes smelly.

ASTROUS

37°24′·76N 22°46′·01E WGS84
BA 1031 Imray-Tetra G14

☆ Ak Astrous Fl.5s7M. Entrance F.R.5M/F.G.5M

Berths Bows-to on S mole. Major works developing yacht berths almost completed.

Shelter Good shelter from prevailing SE wind.

Facilities Water. 220V. Provisions and restaurants.

Remarks A *katabatic* wind may blow in at night from the W.

TIROS

37°14′·71N 22°52′·06E WGS84

Berths Harbour with yacht berths stern-to on new breakwater extension. Good shelter although the afternoon breeze blows beam on.

Facilities Water available. Restaurants and most provisions.

SABATEKI (Sambateki)

37°11′·4N 22°54′·7E

☆ Ak Sambateki LFl.7.5s22m6M

A harbour just under the cape of the same name.

Berths Go stern or bows-to near the end of the quay where there are depths of 2–4m. Good shelter, and better shelter from southerlies than you'll find at Leonidhion.

Facilities Water nearby.

LEONÍDHION

37°08′·66N 22°53′·66E WGS84
BA 1031 Imray-Tetra G14

☆ Ak Sambatekí LFl.7·5s6M. Mole head Fl.G.1·5s3M

Navigation Harbour difficult to see from the distance.

Berths Stern or bows-to the mole.

Shelter Good from the prevailing winds.

Facilities Water. Fuel by tanker. Some provisions and restaurants.

Remarks End of breakwater damaged in winter storm.

KIPARISSI

36°58′·88N 23°00′·55E WGS84
BA 1030 Imray-Tetra G15

☆ Ak Kortia Fl.4s7M. S side Ak Nisaki Fl.R.1·5s3M

Navigation Large bay difficult to identify from distance.

Berths Alongside pier or anchored off in SE or N corner.

Shelter Adequate from prevailing SE wind.

Facilities Some provisions and restaurants in the village.

IERAKA

36°47′·33N 23°05′·55E WGS84
BA 1030 Imray-Tetra G15

☆ Ak Kastro Fl.G.3s5M obscd except between 240°-200°

Navigation Entrance difficult to see even close to.

Berths Stern or bows-to ferry quay. Bows-to village quay.

Shelter Good although uncomfortable with NE winds.

Facilities Limited provisions. Tavernas.

MONEMVASÍA

36°41′·03N 23°02′·38E WGS84
BA 1683 Imray-Tetra G15
38M Spetsai ←→ Akra Maleas 17M

☆ Nisís Monemvasía Fl.5s11M. Mole head Fl.R.2s3M

Navigation Strong gusts with *meltemi*.

Berths Stern or bows-to on N mole or stern or bows-to or alongside in the basin. Anchorage under the causeway.

Shelter Uncomfortable with *meltemi*.

Facilities Water. Fuel by tanker. Provisions and restaurants.

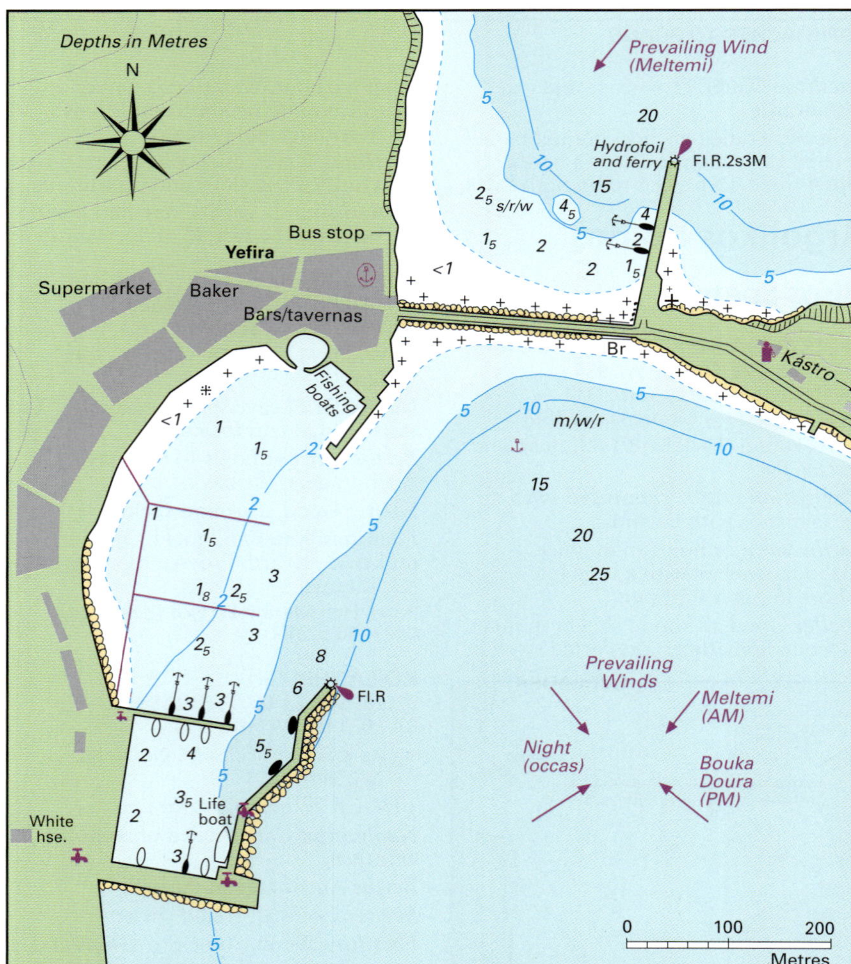

MONEMVASÍA

The Cyclades (Kikládhes Nisoi)

Northern Cyclades

Nísos Kéa

ÁYIOS NIKÓLAOS
37°39'·89N 24°18'·67E WGS84
BA 1038, 1538 Imray-Tetra G31
15M Sounion ←→ Ermoupolis 44M

☆ Ak Ay Nikolaos Fl(2)10s15M. S side Fl.1·5s5M. Korissía Fl.G.3s3M

Navigation Gusts with the *meltemi*.
Berths Stern or bows-to at Korissía or bows-to at Voukari. Anchorage on the N side.
Shelter Good shelter from the *meltemi* although there are gusts into the bay.
Facilities Water. 220V. Fuel by tanker. Some provisions and restaurants.

ÓRMOS KAVIA
37°34'·44N 24°16'·13E WGS84
BA 1038 Imray-Tetra G31

Anchorage under Ak Makropounda. Sheltered from the *meltemi*.

Nísos Kithnos

APOKRIOSIS AND FIKIADHA
37°25'N 24°23'E
BA 1038 Imray-Tetra G31

Two bays N of Mérikha. Órmos Fikiadha affords the best shelter from the *meltemi*. Care is needed of the reef off the E point of Fikiadha. Shelter also in Órmos Kolona. Taverna.

KITHNOS, ORMOS KOLONA TO MERIKHA

MÉRIKHA
37°23'·45N 24°23'·75E WGS84
BA 1038, 1538 Imray-Tetra G31

☆ Ak Mérikha Fl.WR.5s5/3M. Mole head Fl.R.3s3M

Navigation Gusts with the *meltemi*.
Berths Stern or bows-to the NE side or anchorage in the bay.
Shelter Adequate with the *meltemi*.
Facilities Water. 220V. Provisions and restaurants.
Remarks New ferry quay outside harbour breakwater.

LOUTRA
37°26'·66N 24°25'·97E WGS84
BA 1038 Imray-Tetra G31

☆ Ak Kéfalos Fl.4s9M. S side Fl.1·5s5M. Breakwater head Fl.G.3s3M

Navigation Heavy swell at the entrance with the *meltemi*.
Berths Alongside or stern or bows-to in basin.
Shelter Good all round shelter.
Facilities Water. 220V. Fuel by taxi. Some provisions and restaurants.
Remarks Hot springs nearby.

ÁYIOS STEFANOS AND ÁYIOS IOANNIS
BA 1038 Imray-Tetra G31

Two bays on the E coast of Kithnos affording good shelter from the *meltemi*. Care needed of the reef lying 100m SW of the headland separating the two bays.

There is an uncharted wreck reported lying in the NE corner of Órmos Ay Stefanos in 5–6m, with just 1·5–2m over.

Nísos Síros

ERMOUPOLIS
37°26'·2N 24°56'·9E
BA 1038 Imray-Tetra G31
44M Ayios Nikolaos ←→ Mikonos 19M

☆ Nisís Áspronisi Fl(2)12s7M. Nisís Gáïdharos Fl.6s12M. Entrance Ak Kondoyiánnis Fl.3s5M. N Breakwater head Fl.G.3s6M. S Breakwater Fl.R.3s6M/F.Y.3M

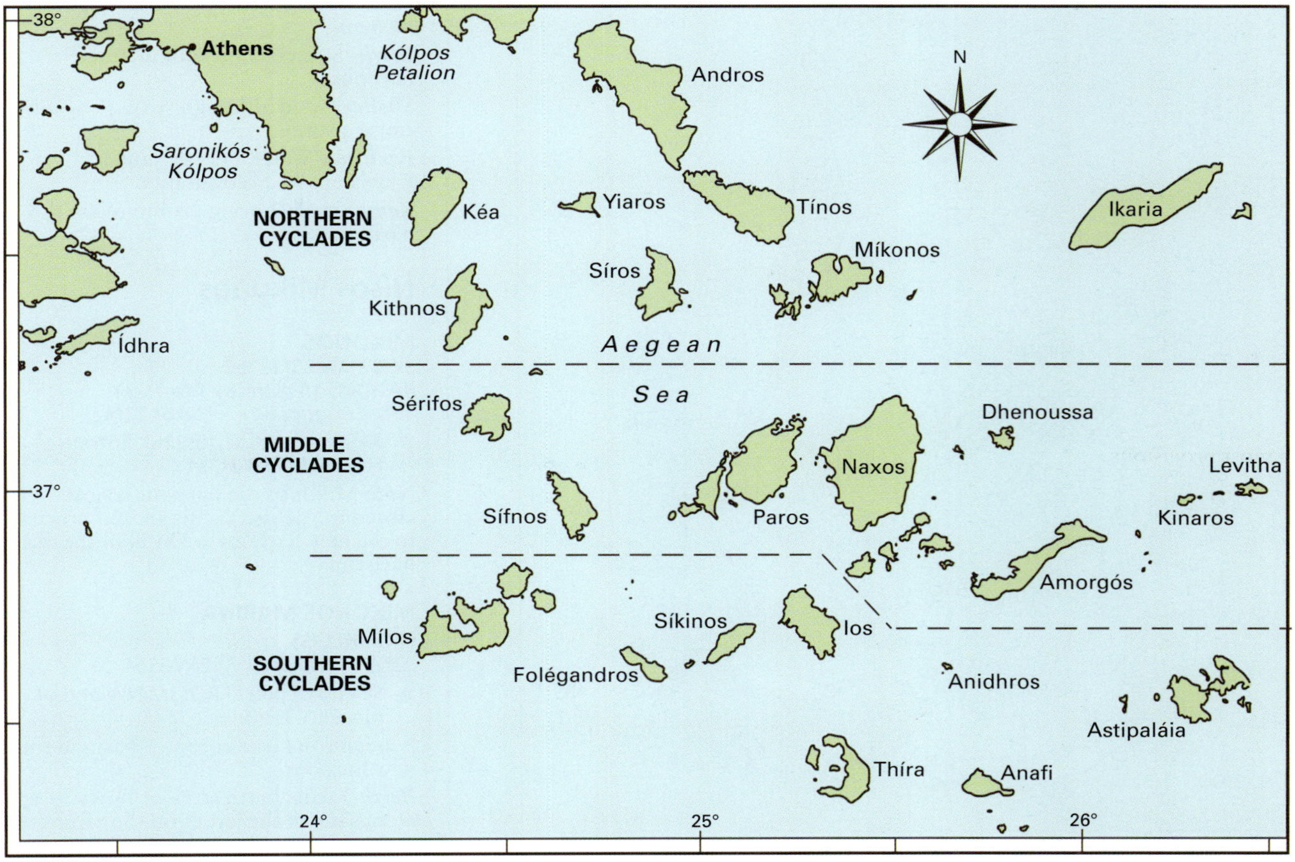

THE CYCLADES

VHF Ch 16, 07, 12 for port authorities.

Navigation Care needed of a reef on the S side (Ífalos Karfomeni). Keep close to outer breakwater.

Berths Stern or bows-to at head of harbour.

Shelter Just adequate. Surge with the *meltemi*. Open S.

Facilities Water. 220V. Fuel by tanker. Limited yacht repairs. Provisions and restaurants.

Port authorities ☏ 22810 826 33 / 826 90

Akilas Mariner – General Ship & Yacht Services ☏ 22810 83682 *or* 6932 622 386

MARINA SIROU

A marina is under development on the S side of Ormos Ermoupolis.

Data c.150 berths. Max LOA c.15m. Depths 2–6m.

Facilities Usual services to be installed.

ERMOUPOLIS BOATYARDS

There are several yards here which can haul yachts.

Lefteris Akilas 65-ton hydraulic lift. 4m depths at slipway.

☏ 22810 236 82

Vangelis Tzortis Sledge and slipway. Used to hauling yachts.

☏ 22810 870 86

The commercial dry-dock can take very large craft. Mechanical and engineering repairs. Chandlers near the yacht yards.

FINIKAS

37°23'·51N 24°52'·48E WGS84
(V. Dhímitra)
BA 1038 Imray-Tetra G31

☆ Psathonisi Fl.2s5M. Vrak. Dhímitra Fl.R.1·5s4M 198°-vis-085° Pier head F.G.3M. N mole head Fl.G.4s5M. S mole head Fl.R.4s5M

Navigation Gusts with the *meltemi*.

Berths Stern or bows-to in basin or on the outside in *meltemi*. Some laid moorings. Anchorage in the bay.

Shelter Good shelter from the *meltemi*.

Facilities Water. 220V. Fuel by tanker. Showers and toilets. Some provisions and restaurants.

Nísos Andros

GÁVRION

37°52'·6N 24°43'·8E
BA 1038, 1538 Imray-Tetra G31

☆ Ak Kastrí Fl.6s8M. Ak Mármara Fl.RG.2s3M (248°-R-005°). Breakwater Q.G.3M

Navigation Care needed of reefs in the approach off Nisís Akamatis and Nisís Plati; Ífalos Vouvi; Ífalos Rosa. Ferries enter and leave at speed.

Berths Stern or bows-to or alongside. Anchorage in the bay.

Shelter Adequate from the *meltemi*.

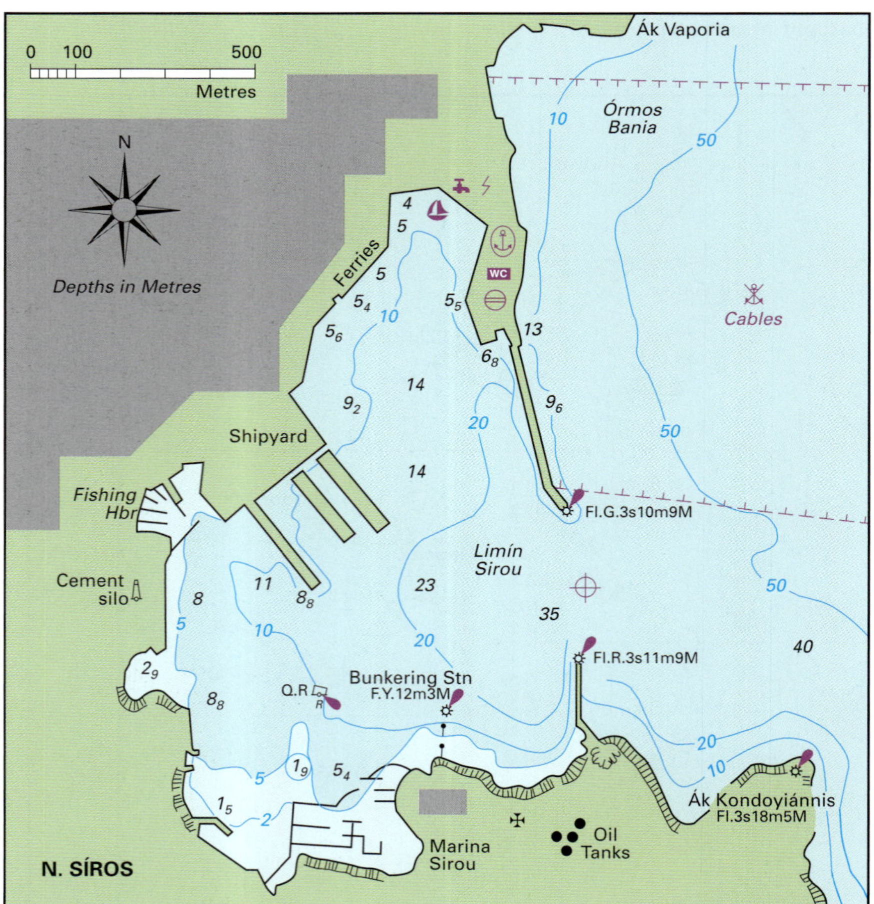

ERMOÚPOLIS

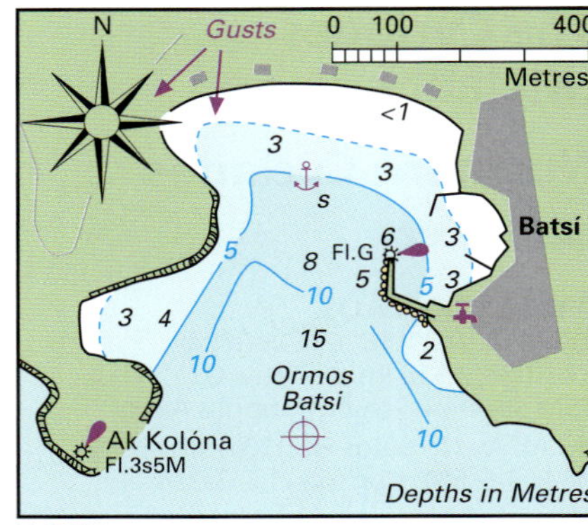

BATSI

BATSÍ

37°51'·21N 24°46'·93E WGS84
BA 1038 Imray-Tetra G31

☆ Ak Kolóna Fl.3s5M. Mole Fl.G.2s3M

Navigation Gusts with the *meltemi*.

Berths Stern or bows-to on the quay, or alongside on the new breakwater extension. Anchorage in the bay.

Shelter Good shelter.

Facilities Water. 220V. Fuel by tanker. Provisions and restaurants.

Nísos Tínos

TÍNOS

37°32'·2N 25°09'·5E
BA 1038, 1041, 1538 Imray-Tetra G31

☆ Entrance Fl.R.3s7M/Fl.G.2s3M. Inner mole Fl.R.2s3M

Navigation Care needed of the reef off Ak Akrotiri. Work completed on breakwater extension. Gusts with the *meltemi*.

Berths Stern or bows-to, in inner harbour.

Shelter Good although strong S winds cause a surge.

Facilities Water. Fuel by tanker. Provisions and restaurants.

Remarks Anchoring prohibited in the harbour.

Nísos Míkonos

MÍKONOS

37°27'·1N 25°19'·6E
BA 1041, 1538 Imray-Tetra G31
19M Ermoupolis ←→ Naxos 22M

☆ Ak Armenistís Fl.10s22M. Entrance Fl.G.3s3M/Fl.R.3s3M

Note Míkonos old harbour is now closed to yachts. Yachts should proceed to the new harbour 1·5M N of the old harbour.

MIKONOS MARINA (TOURLOS)

37°27'·74N 25°19'·54E WGS84

☆ SE end of pier Fl.R.3s3M/NW end of pier Fl.G.3s3M

Navigation Head for the S basin in the new harbour.

Berth Yachts berth stern or bows-to or alongside on the jetties on the SE shore.

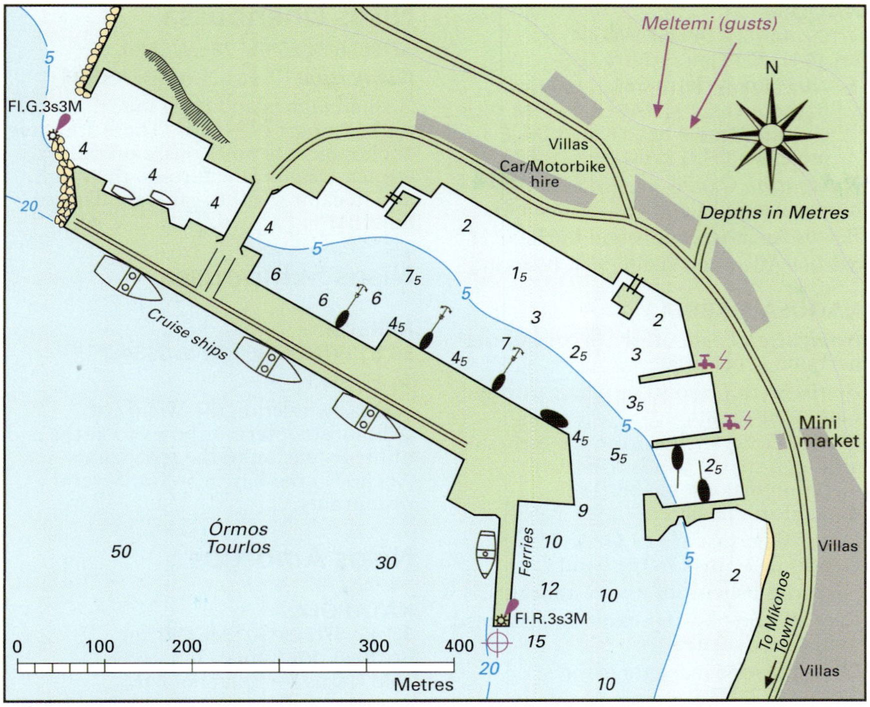

MÍKONOS MARINA

Laid moorings tailed to the quay although some have been damaged.

Shelter in places. Adequate from *meltemi*. Open S.

Facilities Some facilities ashore near the bridge between the basins. Hire car/motorbike agency. It is around 45 minutes walk to Míkonos.

Nísos Delos

DELOS CHANNEL

The channel between Delos and Rinia and the Nisídhes Remmatia is fringed by reefs. When the *meltemi* is blowing the wind funnels through the channel.

All navigation, anchoring or stopping is prohibited within 500m of Nísos Delos. Yachts are permitted to approach Ancient Delos during daylight hours when the archaeological site is open. Otherwise permits to enter the prohibited area must be obtained from Mikonos town.

Middle Cyclades

Nísos Sérifos

LIVADHI

37°07'·97N 24°31'·34E WGS84
BA 1038, 1538 Imray-Tetra G33

☆ Ak Spathí Fl(3)30s19M. Breakwater Fl.R.2s3M. Pier head 2F.R(vert)3M

Navigation Gusts with the *meltemi*. Village on the hill conspicuous.

Berths Stern or bows-to pier. Anchorage in the bay – poor holding in places.

Shelter Good from *meltemi*. Strong gusts.

Facilities Water. Fuel by tanker. Provisions and restaurants.

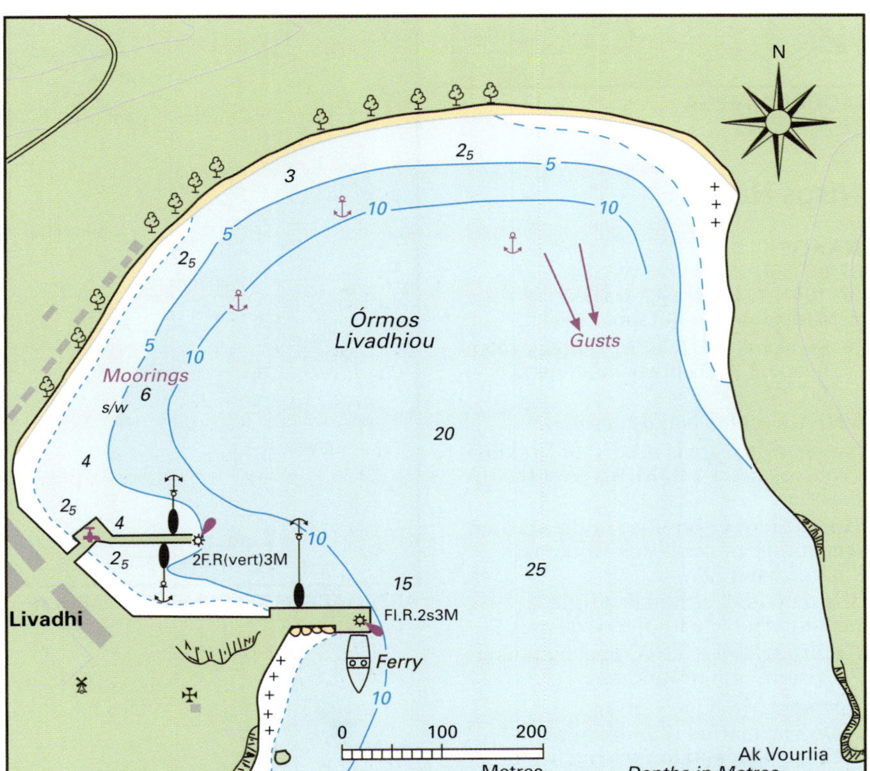

LIVADHI (SERIFOS)

Nísos Sífnos

KAMARES

36°59'·50N 24°39'·21E WGS84
BA 1038, 1538 Imray-Tetra G33

☆ Ak Kokkála Fl(2)10s9M. S side Fl.2s7M. Breakwater Fl.G.1·5s3M

Navigation Strong gusts with the *meltemi*.

Berths Stern or bows-to the quay under the mole. Yacht berths are marked on the quay. Anchorage in the bay.

Shelter Adequate shelter from the *meltemi*.

Facilities Water. 220V. Some provisions and restaurants.

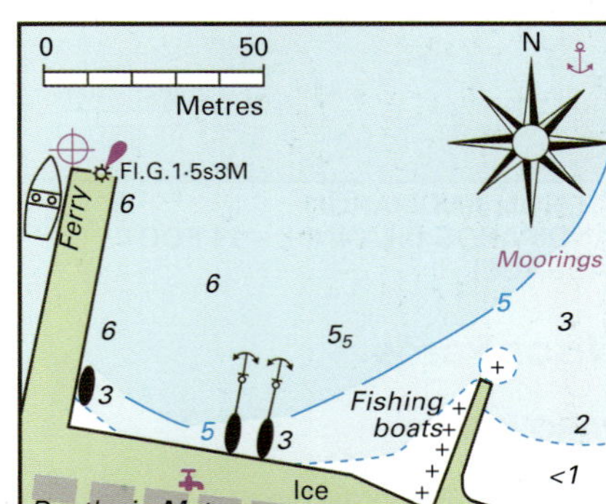

KAMARES

ÓRMOS VATHI

36°55'·62N 24°41'·01E WGS84
BA 1038 Imray-Tetra G33

☆ S entrance Fl.2s7M

A landlocked bay affording good all-round shelter. Anchor in the N of the bay.

PLATI YIALOS
36°55′·6N 24°44′·0E

New harbour in NE corner of the bay.
Berth Stern-to on W quay in 3·5–5m. Laid moorings (2014). Anchorage in the bay.
Shelter Poor shelter in the harbour. Better to anchor off the beach.

FAROS
36°56′·3N 24°45′·2E
BA 1038, 1538 Imray-Tetra G33
☆ Ak Stavrós Fl.1·5s4M
A bay near the SE tip of Sífnos providing good shelter from the *meltemi*. Rock awash off W point of Ak Stavros.
Anchor off the village in 3–12m. Limited provisions and restaurants.

Nísos Andiparos

STENON ANDIPAROU
BA 1038, 1539, 1041 Imray-Tetra G33
The narrow channel between Nísos Andiparos and Nísos Paros running approximately N to S. Yachts normally use the passage on the W side of Nisís Remmatia where there are least depths of 3–4m. The channels should only be attempted by day with due care and attention.

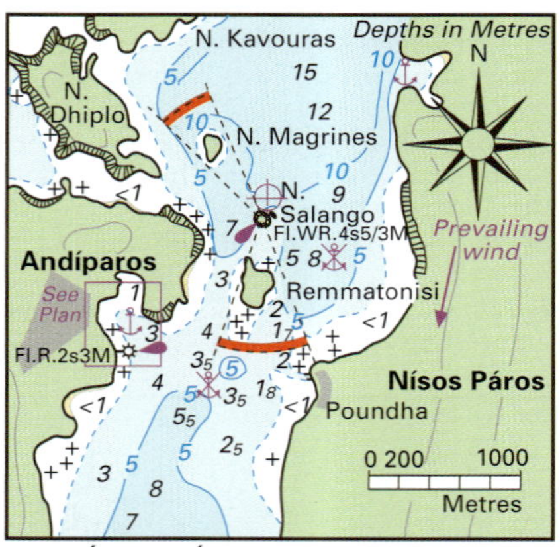

STENÓN ANDÍPAROU (ANDÍPAROS CHANNEL – 14 FOOT PASSAGE)

Nísos Paros

PAROIKIA
37°05′·3N 25°09′·1E
BA 1041, 1539 Imray-Tetra G33
☆ Ak Ay Fokás Fl.4s6M. W mole head Fl.G.2s3M E mole head Fl.R.2s3M
Navigation Care needed of the reef off Ak Ay Fokás.
Berths Stern or bows-to on outside of breakwater. Anchorage in the bay.
Shelter Adequate from the *meltemi*.
Facilities Water. 220V. Fuel by tanker. Provisions and restaurants.
Remarks Main ferry harbour.

NAOUSA
37°09′·44N 25°14′·35E WGS84
BA 1041, 1539 Imray-Tetra G33
☆ Ak Kórakas LFl.12s14M. Naoussa harbour Fl.R.1·5s3M/Fl.G.1·5s3M. Piso Livadhi W mole head Fl.R.3s3M. E mole head Fl.G.3s3M
Navigation Care is needed of the numerous rocks and reefs in the bay.
Berths Anchorages around the bay
Shelter All-round shelter can be found.

NAOUSA MARINA
Navigation Basin off the W side of the harbour at Naousa.
Berths Stern or bows-to where directed. Laid moorings.
Shelter Good shelter from the meltemi, although strong winds from any direction make some berths uncomfortable here.
Data 70 berths. Max LOA c.25m. Depths 3–4·5m. Charge band 2.
Facilities Provisions and restaurants.
Remarks Breakwater extension planned to improve shelter.
Noussa Marina manager Ioannis
✆ 6942 772 023

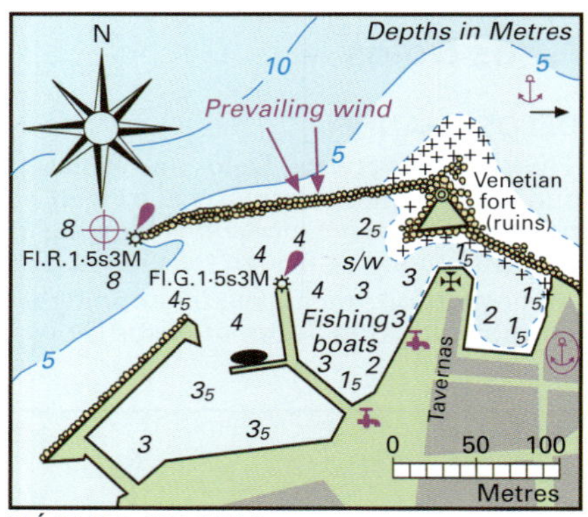

NÁOUSA MARINA

Nísos Naxos

NAXOS
37°06′·36N 25°21′·99E WGS84
BA 1041, 1539 Imray-Tetra G33
22M Mikonos ←→ Katapola 36M
☆ Breakwater Fl.R.4s7M. N breakwater head F.R.3M. S breakwater head F.G.3M
VHF Ch 69 for Naxos marina.
Navigation Care is needed of Vrakhos Frouros, a reef 1·25M WSW of the harbour.
Berths Stern or bows-to in the marina. Anchorage under Nísos Vakkhos. Charge band 2.
Shelter Good, although a little uncomfortable with the *meltemi*.
Facilities Water. 220V. Fuel by tanker. Provisions and restaurants.
Remarks Main ferry port.
Note The marina is under new management and improvements in facilities are planned.

Nísos Dhenoussa

37°08′·63N 25°49′·78E WGS84
Navigation (0·4M N of Ak Kalota)
A small high island lying nine miles off the east coast of Naxos. There are three anchorage: Órmos Roussa on the NE corner, Órmos Dhendro on the south, and in calm weather off the village of Stavros.

Nísos Skhinoússa

MIRSINI
36°51′·97N 25°30′·47E WGS84
☆ Fl.4s6M
A narrow inlet on the W side of Skhinoússa. Stern or bows-to at the end of the extension to the ferry quay. Anchor in the bay in 5–8m. Several restaurants.

Nísos Amorgós

KATÁPOLA
36°49′·87N 25°50′·34E WGS84
BA 1040, 1541 Imray-Tetra G34
36M Naxos ←→ Kalimnos 61M
☆ Ak Ay Iliás Fl(2)10s12M
Navigation Strong gusts and heavy seas with the *meltemi*.
Berths Stern or bows-to the quay.
Shelter Good shelter from the *meltemi*.
Facilities Water. 220V. Some provisions and restaurants.
Remarks Buoys in NE of bay indicate the anchorage area not the swimming area.

APPROACHES TO ORMOS KATAPOLA

Nísos Levitha

ORMISKOS LEVITHA

36°59′·9N 26°29′·8E
BA 1056 Imray-Tetra G34
☆ Ak Spano Fl.10s11M

A land-locked bay on the S coast. Mooring buoys to pick up. Good shelter from the *meltemi*. Restaurant.

Southern Cyclades

Nísos Mílos

ADHAMAS

36°44′·42N 24°24′·14E WGS84
BA 1037, 1539 Imray-Tetra G33
☆ Ak Bombárdha Fl.5s12M

Navigation Gusts and heavy seas at the entrance with the *meltemi*.

Berths Stern or bows-to. Anchorage off the town.

Shelter Good shelter from the *meltemi*.

Data 50 berths. Max LOA c.50m. Depths 1–5m.

Facilities Water. 220V. Fuel by tanker. Provisions and restaurants.

STENON KIMOLOU

36°46′·23N 24°31′·92E WGS84
BA 1539 Imray-Tetra G33

Numerous anchorages around the strait.

Nísos Folegandros

KARAVOSTÁSI

36°36′·84N 24°57′·01E WGS84
BA 1037, 1541 Imray-Tetra G33
☆ N entrance Fl.WR.6s10/7M, 202°-R-248° Mole Q.G.3M

Navigation Care needed of Ífalos Poulioxeresi. Strong gusts and confused seas with the *meltemi*.

Berths Stern or bows-to.

Shelter Adequate but uncomfortable surge with the *meltemi*.

Facilities Limited provisions and restaurants.

ÓRMOS LIVADHI – KARAVOSTASI

An electricity sub-station has been built in Órmos Livadhi, and the bay is crossed with underwater cables. Anchoring is prohibited anywhere in this bay.

Nísos Íos

PORT ÍOS

36°42′·73N 25°15′·72E WGS84
BA 1037, 1541 Imray-Tetra G33
☆ Ak Fanári Fl.5s9M. Breakwater Fl.G.2s3M

Navigation Care needed of the reef off Ak Xeres. Strong gusts with the *meltemi*.

Berths Stern or bows-to as directed. Moorings attached to buoys on E quay. Yellow buoy marks W limit of mooring chain for those using the N quay (no mooring lines). Anchoring prohibited in the bay.

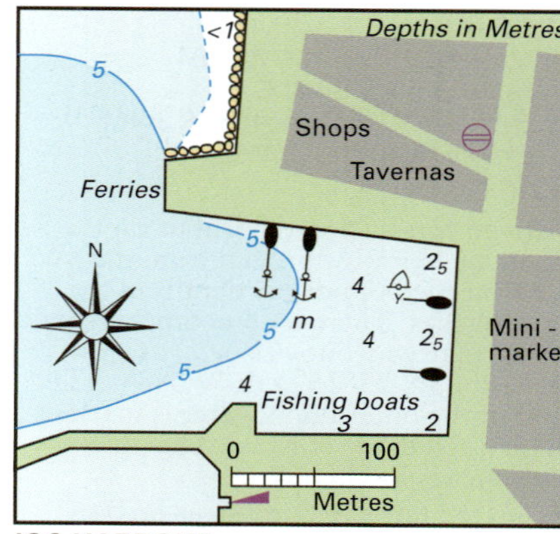

IOS HARBOUR

Shelter Good shelter from the *meltemi*.

Facilities Fuel and water by tanker. Provisions and restaurants.

Remarks Ferries create surge in the harbour.

ÓRMOS MANGANARI

36°39′·05N 25°22′·23E WGS84

A large bay on the S coast of Íos. Anchor near the head of the bay. Good shelter from the *meltemi* although there are gusts. Restaurants.

Nísos Thíra

SKÁLA THÍRA

36°25′·01N 25°25′·54E WGS84
☆ Quay S end Q.R.3M

The S end of the quay is very open and you should not leave a yacht unattended.

Berths Stern or bows-to with a line to the large mooring buoy off the quay. Unsuitable for most yachts.

Shelter A lee from the *meltemi* although there is a slop onto the quay.

ORMOS MILOU

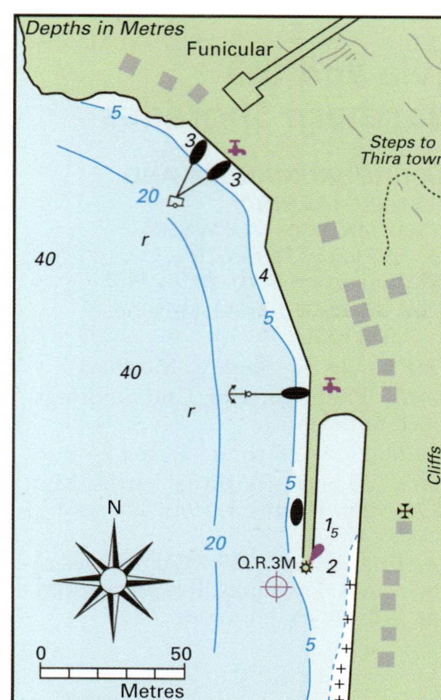

SKÁLA THÍRA

VLIKHADA

36°20′·08N 25°26′·16E WGS84

☆ Fairway buoy Iso.Fl.G
Entrance W mole head Fl.R.3s4M.
E mole head Fl.G.3s4M

VHF Ch 10

Navigation Enclosed harbour on the S coast of Thíra. Approach from the SW. Care needed of uneven depths in the approaches. There is sometimes a small yellow fairway buoy (Iso.2s) at 36°19′·63N 25°25′·55E WGS84. The end of the outer breakwater is marked with a red light (Fl.R.3s). The inner entrance is lit Fl.G.2s.

From the fairway buoy steer on 045° towards the blue hotel on the N side of the harbour. When 250m off turn towards the entrance.

A green buoy (to be left to starboard) now marks the channel into the harbour. Care needed of continuing changes to depths in the approaches, especially following onshore winds. With such winds waves break on the sandbanks and make entering or leaving dangerous.

Note The entrance and harbour continue to silt. Dredging is ongoing and at times depths in the entrance are just 1·5m, although usually there are least depths of 2·1m. Keep to the starboard side of the entrance channel avoiding the rock off the S breakwater. The shallowest part is off the starboard side of the entrance to the inner basin. Care is needed at night of the dredger cables and mooring lines near the entrance to the inner basin.

Berths Alongside on the outer quay.

Data Depths 2–4m. Charge band 2.

Shelter Dangerous in outer harbour in S winds.

Facilities Water. 220V. WiFi. Taverna. Bus to Skála.

Harbourmaster ✆ 22860 82119
Email dimitrios.saliveros@gmail.com

Evia and the Northern Sporades

GAIDHOUROMANDRA AND OLYMPIC MARINA

37°41′·74N 24°03′·80E WGS84
BA 1657 Imray-Tetra G26
5M Sounion ←→ Porto Raftis 14M

☆ Ak Foniás Fl.2·5s6M. Mole head Fl.R.4s12M.

VHF Ch 09 for Olympic Marina.

Berths Where directed. Laid moorings tailed to the quay.

Shelter Good all-round shelter.

Data 700 berths. Visitors' berths. Max LOA 30m. Depths 2–10m. Charge band 4.

Facilities Water. 220V. WiFi. Showers and toilets. Fuel quay. Restaurant and bar. Provisions in Lavrion.

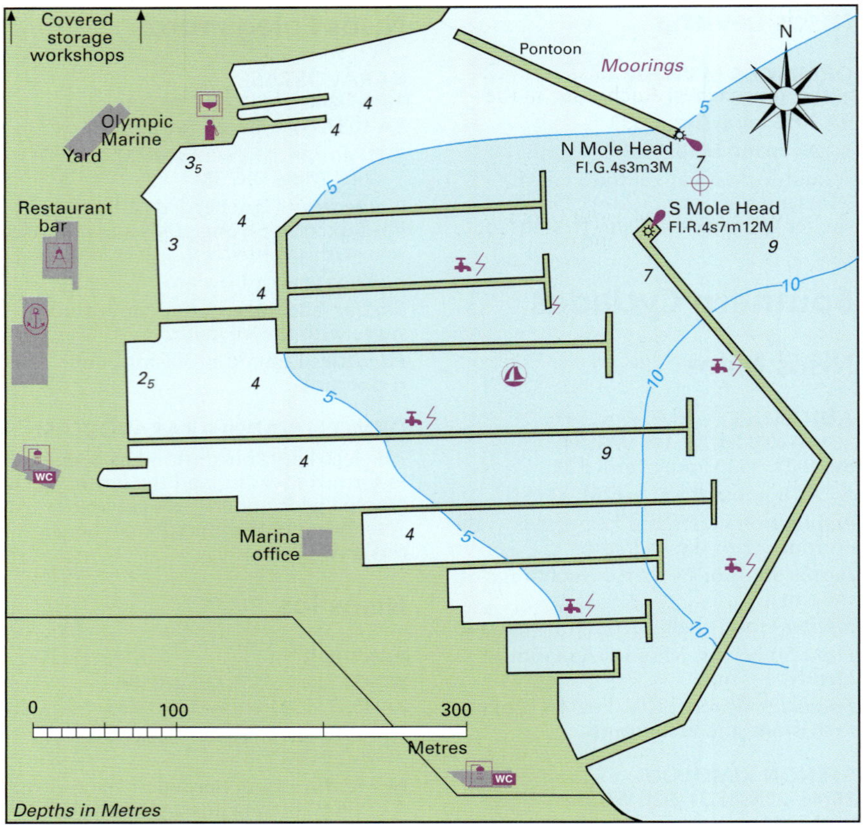

OLYMPIC MARINA

Olympic Marine 1,000 dry berths. Covered workshops. 50/200-ton travel-hoists. 700 places ashore. Yacht repairs.

Olympic Marine ✆ 22920 63700
Email olympicmarine@internet.gr
www.olympicmarine.gr

LAVRION

37°42′·37N 24°04′·01E WGS84
BA 1657 Imray-Tetra G26

☆ Ak Foniás Fl.2·5s6M. Ak Ergastíria Fl.1·5s4M. Entrance Fl.R.3s5M/Fl.G.3s5M.

Berths On waterfront between the piers. Crowded in the summer.

Shelter Good from the *meltemi*.

Facilities Water. 220V. Fuel by tanker. Provisions and restaurants.

Remarks Detached breakwater planned outside the entrance to the harbour.

Port Authority ✆ 22920 25249

PORTO RAFTI

37°53′·2N 24°02′·7E (Raftis light)
BA 1657 Imray-Tetra G26
14M Olympic Marina ←→ Khalkis 49M

☆ Raftis Fl.2s9M. Basin F.R

Navigation Nisís Raftis easily identified. Numerous laid moorings in the bay.

Berths Stern or bows-to at Raftis. Anchorage in NW corner.

Shelter Good shelter although open E.

Facilities Water. Fuel by tanker. Provisions and restaurants.

RAFINA

38°01′·4N 24°00′·7E (F.G.3M)
BA 1657 Imray-Tetra G26

☆ Fl.G.3s3M

Little space for yachts and a considerable surge with the *meltemi*.

KARISTOS

38°00′·7N 24°25′·0E (Fl.G.4M)
BA 1038, 1085 Imray-Tetra G26

☆ Nisís Paximádhi Fl.5s4M. Nisís Mandhíli Fl(3)20s15M. Entrance Fl.G.1·5s4M/2F.R(vert)3M

Navigation Strong gusts with N winds.

Berths Stern or bows-to on town quay. The inner basin is reserved for fishing boats and yachts are not permitted. Go stern-to on the quay to the W of the ferry quay. Depths 5m.

Shelter Good shelter.

Facilities Water. 220V. Fuel by tanker. Provisions and restaurants.

Remarks Useful refuge if bad weather is encountered going through Stenon Kafirevs.

VOUFALO

38°17′·63N 24°06′·47E WGS84

Sheltered anchorage behind a spit off the village. Depths 5–6m. Taverna ashore.

KARAVOS (Aliverion)

38°23′·48N 24°02′·74E WGS84

Large harbour with a power station on the E side. Yacht berths on N or S quay. Water on the quay. Good shelter.

ERETRIA

38°22′·9N 23°47′·5E

Care needed of rocks and shoal water in the approaches. Anchorage in the bay.

DHÍAVLOS EVIRÍPOU – KHALKIS

BA 1554, 1556 Imray-Tetra G25, G26

☆ Ak Avlís Fl(2)12s6M. Light buoys Q.G/Fl.G.2s Vrak Passándasi Fl.3s5M. S side Fl.R.3s5M/2F.R(vert)3M. T-pier head 2F.G(vert)3M. N approach. Ak Kakokefalí Fl(2)18s12M. W bank Fl.G.2s3M. Light buoys Q.G/Q.R

VHF Ch 12 for Bridge Traffic Control.

Berths S harbour: go stern-to on pontoons at Khalkis YC in O. Voukari. Depths 3–5m. Anchorage off YC. N harbour: alongside the E quay. Port Authority office is on the E side, S of the bridge.

Note In places metal bars project out from the face of the quay in the N harbour.

Khalkis Bridge transit charges Around €25 for 12m yacht. 75% surcharge on Fridays and at weekends. Transit will normally be after midnight.

Facilities Water. 220V. Fuel by tanker. Provisions and restaurants.

Remarks Tidal streams through the gap can reach 6–7 kns at springs. In the N harbour the spring range is 0·8m and at neaps 0·2m. The range in the S harbour for springs and neaps is small.

High water occurs in the N harbour approximately one hour and 12 minutes after high water in the S harbour.

Signals

By day	*Meaning*
Three vertical black balls	Bridge closed
Two black cones points together above a cone point down	Bridge open to S-bound vessels
Two black balls separated by a black cone point up	Bridge open to N-bound vessels
By night	*Meaning*
Green, white, red vertical lights	Bridge closed
White fixed light in the middle of the bridge	Bridge closed at night
Green, white green vertical lights	Bridge open to S-bound vessels
Red, white, red vertical lights	Bridge open to N-bound vessels

A siren sounds and a flashing light warns boat traffic that the bridge is opening.

ÓRMOS ATALANTIS

38°40′·58N 23°08′·20E WGS84

BA 1556 Imray-Tetra G25

☆ Nisís Atalantis Fl.1·5s5M. Skala Livanátes breakwater Fl.G.3s3M. Skála Atalantis Fl.G.2s3M

In this large bay on the W side of the gulf there are a number of anchorages affording shelter from the *meltemi*.

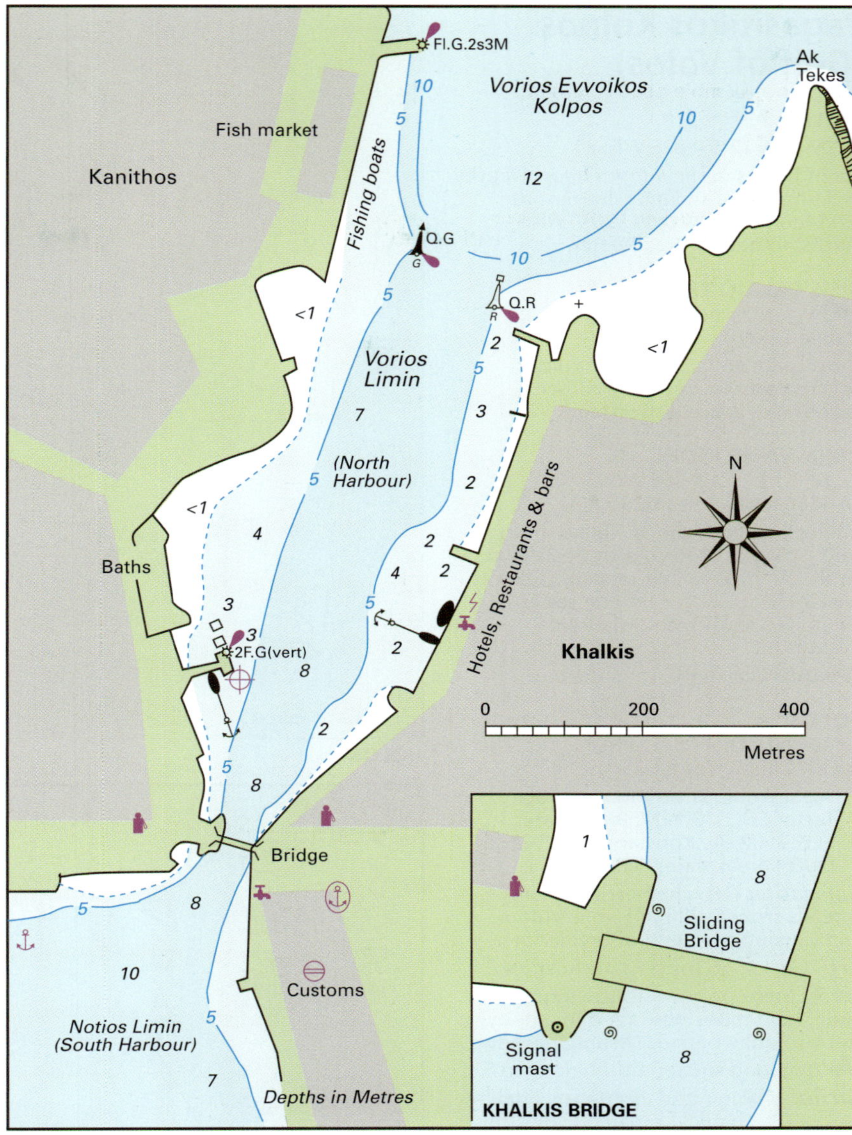

KHALKIS

NEA ARTAKI

38°30′·64N 23°37′·93E WGS84

Trawler port around 2M N of Khalkis. Reasonable shelter from the prevailing wind.

LOUTRA ADHIPSOU

38°51′·44N 23°02′·38E WGS84

Ferry quay and fishing harbour. Go alongside if there is space or anchor off in 5–10m. Good shelter in the harbour.

NISOI LIKHADES

38°49′·43N 22°49′·67E WGS84 (Channel fairway)

Islets off the extreme W arm of Evia. The channel inside the islets just 80–100m off the sandy spit on Evia has good depths.

STILÍDHOS

38°53′·9N 22°37′·9E (Entrance to buoyed channel)

BA 1085 Imray-Tetra G25

☆ Light buoys Fl.G.3s/Fl.R.3s. Beacons Fl.R.2s3M/Fl.G.2s3M. Mole root DirLFl.Y.10s8M

A small harbour reached via a buoyed channel.

OREI

38°56′·88N 23°05′·07E WGS84

BA 1556 Imray-Tetra G25

26M Volos ←→ Skiathos 25M

☆ Panagitsa Fl(2)12s9M. Mole head Fl.R.1·5s3M

Berths Stern or bows-to on N or S quays.

Shelter Good shelter.

Facilities Water. 220V. Boatyard nearby. 25-ton trailer. Provisions and restaurants.

Pagasitikós Kólpos (Gulf of Volos)

AHILIO
39°00'·50N 22°57'·82E WGS84

Yacht berths on new town quay. Depths 3–3·5m. Good shelter. Charter base. Laid moorings. Water. 220V. Also berths on new N breakwater.

NISIS PALAIO TRIKERI
39°09'·16N 23°04'·57E WGS84
(Palaio Trikeri)

Short quay and pier off the village. Taverna ashore. Settled weather anchorages around the island.

LIMIN VATHOUDHI
39°10'·51N 23°12'·56E WGS84
BA 1556 Imray-Tetra G25

An anchorage in the SE corner of the Gulf of Volos protected by Nisís Alatas on the W and the Trikeri peninsula on the E. The anchorage is entered from the N. Good all-round shelter. Restaurant.

Remarks Charter base in the bay.

VOLOS
39°20'·96N 22°56'·81E WGS84
BA 1571 Imray-Tetra G25

☆ Ak Séskoulo Fl.1·5s7M. Cement factory Fl(2)10s12M. Breakwater Fl.G.3s4M. Ay Konstandinou F.G/F.R. Outer breakwater Fl.R.3s

Navigation Detached breakwater extends from S side of Limin Volou. Entry around NE end of breakwater.

VHF Ch 12, 16 for port authorities.

Berths Stern or bows-to town or E mole. Laid moorings tailed to a buoy. Stern-to quay outside 'fishing harbour'.

Shelter Good shelter although open S.

Facilities Water and electricity. Fuel by tanker. Mechanical repairs. Provisions and restaurants.

Remarks Large commercial harbour.

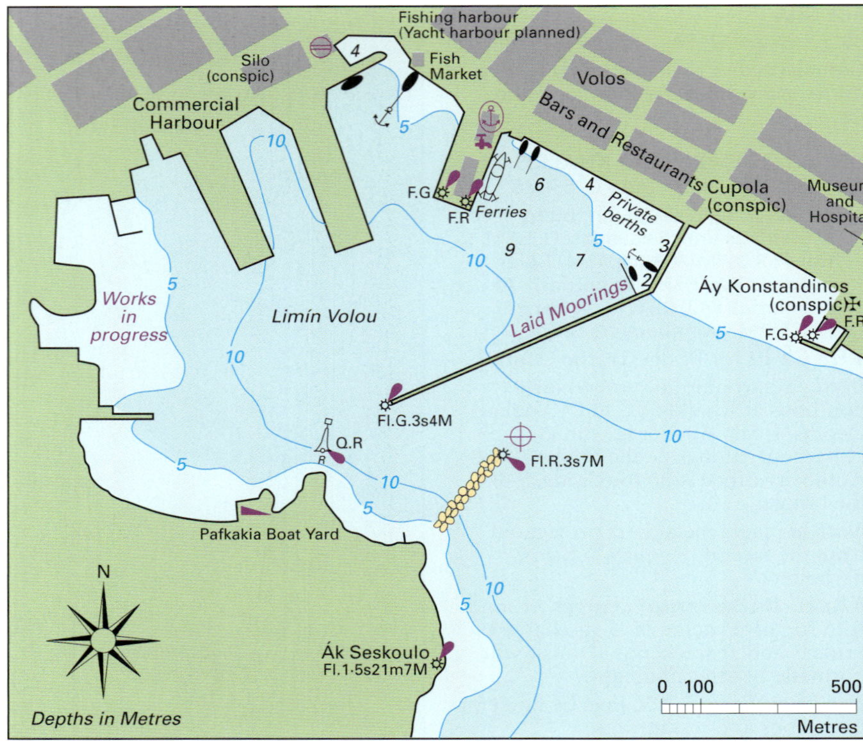

VOLOS

Northern Sporades

Nísos Skíathos

SKÍATHOS
39°08'·29N 23°31'·70E WGS84
BA 1062, 1556, 1571 Imray-Tetra G25
25M Orei ←→ Patitiri 21·5M

☆ Nisís Prassou Fl.6s6M. Nisís Répi Fl(2)WR.10s12/8M. 261°-R-313° Dháskalonisi Fl.3s5M. Mole head Fl.R.1·5s3M

Navigation Nisís Répi lighthouse conspicuous. Yachts must leave N. Dhaskalo to port in the approaches to Skiathos.

Berths Stern or bows-to. Anchorage in the bay. Prohibited anchorage area extended for all craft with AH over 4m.

Shelter Good shelter from the *meltemi* although it blows beam on. Partially open S.

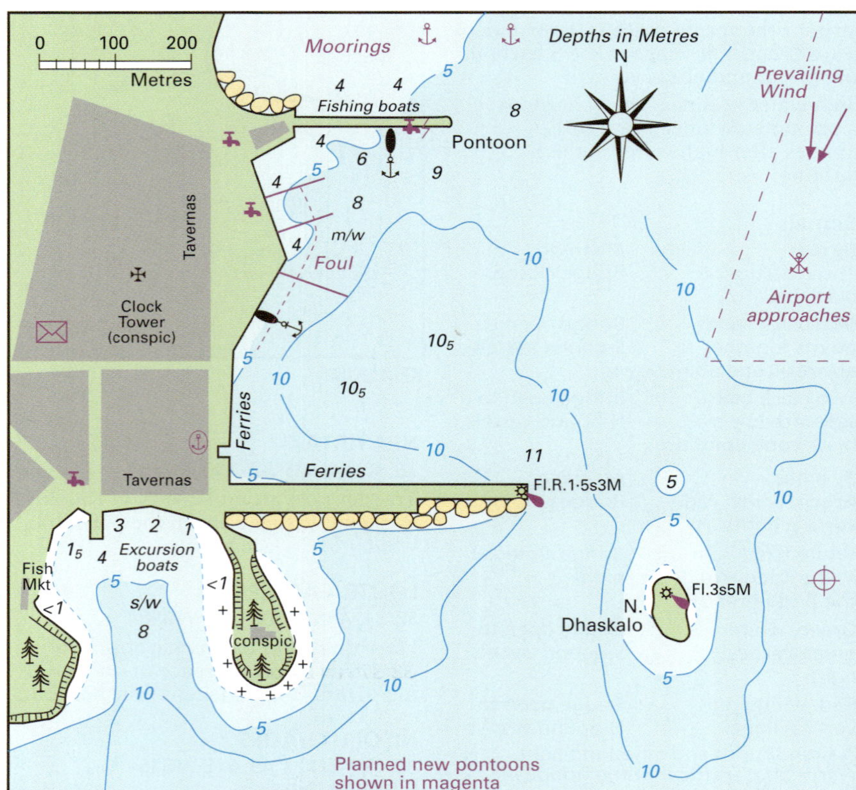

SKÍATHOS

Data Depths 4·6m. Max LOA c.40m. Charge band 2/3.

Facilities Water. 220V. Fuel by tanker. Yard. Provisions and restaurants.

Remarks New pontoons planned.

NATIONAL MARINE PARK OF ALONNISOS, NORTHERN SPORADES NMPANS

The Park comprises Alonnisos and six smaller islands (Peristera, Kyra Panagia, Gioura, Skantzoura, Piperi) and 22 uninhabited islands and rocky outcrops. The area is now divided into three zones, with the main exclusion zone around Piperi islet in the NE corner of the reserve. For more information see www.mom.gr or www.alonnisostravel.gr

Nísos Skópelos

LOUTRAKI

39°09′·79N 23°36′·87E WGS84
BA 1062, 1571 Imray-Tetra G25

☆ Entrance Fl.G.3s3M/Fl.R.3s3M

Berths Stern or bows-to pontoon in NE corner.

Shelter Good shelter from the *meltemi*.

Facilities Some provisions and restaurants.

Remarks Village on the hill above.

NEA KLIMA

39°08′·22N 23°38′·54E WGS84

Harbour recently extended. Berth stern-to in outer harbour. Good shelter from *meltemi*. Open S. Water. 220V.

AGNÓNDAS

39°04′·92N 23°42′·04E WGS84
BA 1571 Imray-Tetra G25

☆ Entrance Fl.R.2s3M/Fl.G.2s3M

An enclosed bay 2·5M E of Ak Miti. Anchor in the bay and take a line ashore or go stern-to or alongside the quay.

Note There is sometimes a dangerous swell from passing ferries.

LIMIN SKOPÉLOU

39°07′·40N 23°44′·11E WGS84
BA 1571 Imray-Tetra G25

☆ Nisís Mikró Fl.4s6M. Entrance Fl.G.2s6M

Navigation With a strong *meltemi* there are steep and dangerous seas in the approaches.

Berths Stern or bows-to N mole. Some laid moorings.

Shelter Uncomfortable with the *meltemi*.

Facilities Water. 220V. Fuel by tanker. Provisions and restaurants.

Nísos Alonnisos

PATITÍRI

39°08′·55N 23°52′·11E WGS84
BA 1062 Imray-Tetra G25
21·5 Skiathos ←→ Linaria 37M

☆ Entrance Fl.R.1·5s3M/Fl.G.1·5s3M

Berths Stern or bows-to.

Shelter Adequate with the *meltemi*. Partially open S and E.

Facilities Water and fuel nearby. Provisions and restaurants.

Remarks Ferry quay is now outside the harbour.

STENI VALA

39°11′·48N 23°55′·75E WGS84

Small cove offering good shelter from the *meltemi*. Shallow in places off the quay. Deepest part midway along quay. Tavernas and a shop ashore.

Nísos Pelagos

KIRA PANAYIA

39°18′·8N 24°02′·3E (Pelerissa light Fl.3s7M)

A large bay on the SW corner of Pelagos. Good shelter from the *meltemi* although there are gusts into the bay.

ÓRMOS PLANITIS

39°22′·02N 24°05′·14E WGS84

A large landlocked bay on the N side of Nísos Pelagos.

There is a least depth of 6m over the bar at the entrance. Anchor in either of the two forks of the bay.

Nísos Skíros

LIMIN LINARÍA

38°50′·6N 24°32′·2E (Fl.WRG.6-4M)
BA 1571, 1062 Imray-Tetra G25
37M Alonnisos ←→ Kimi 23·5M

☆ Sarakino Island Fl.4s7M. Marmara Point Fl(2)10s7M. Nisís Valáxa/Ak Latomion Fl.3·3s5M. Mole head Fl.WRG.2·5s6-4M 353°-R-021°. Órmos Platanias mole head Fl.G.3s3M

Navigation With the *meltemi* there are strong gusts and confused seas in the approaches.

Berths On the SE quay go stern-to, with depths close in of 3–4m, 1·5m near S end.

Shelter Adequate from the *meltemi*.

Facilities Water. 220V. Fuel nearby. Limited provisions and restaurants.

East coast of Evia

ÓRMOS PETRIES

38°24′·5N 24°11′·8E

☆ Fl.5s4M. W breakwater head Fl.R.2s3M. E breakwater head Fl.G.2s3M.

A large bay providing good shelter from the *meltemi*. Care needed of a wreck inside the breakwater end.

KIMI

38°37′·1N 24°08′·2E
BA 1085 Imray-Tetra G26

☆ Nisís Prasoúdha Fl.5s16M. Entrance Fl.R.3s3M/Fl.R.1·5s3M/Fl.G.3s6M. Elbow Fl.G.1·5s2M. Skíros Xenia N breakwater Fl.Y.3s3M. S breakwater Fl.Y.3s3M.

Navigation With the *meltemi* there is a confused sea at the entrance.

Berths Stern or bows-to in the NW corner. Care is needed of shoal water off the W quay.

Shelter Good shelter from the *meltemi* although there may be a surge.

Facilities Fuel and water nearby. Some provisions and restaurants.

Northern Greece

THESSALONIKI

40°35′·2N 22°55′·2E (Ak Mikro Emvolon)
BA 2070 Imray-Tetra G2

☆ Ak Megálo Émvolon Fl.W.10s15M.
Ak Mikró Emvolon Fl(3)G.15s5M

VHF Ch 07, 12, 16 for port authorities.

THESSALONIKI MARINA (ARETSOU)

40°34′·6N 22°56′·5E
BA 2070 Imray-Tetra G2

☆ Breakwater ends Fl.G.2s5M/Fl.R.2s5M

VHF Ch 09, 16 for marina.

Berths Stern or bows-to. Laid moorings.

Shelter Good all-round shelter.

Data 300 berths. Visitors' berths. 3–4m depths. Charge band 2/3.

Facilities Water. 220V. Showers and toilets. Fuel. Yachts craned onto the hard. Mechanical repairs. Provisions and restaurants nearby.

Remarks A yacht should make for the marina and not the commercial port.

Thessaloniki Marina
☏ 2310 444 595 / 8
Email thess-mar@etasa.gr
www.thessaloniki-marina.gr

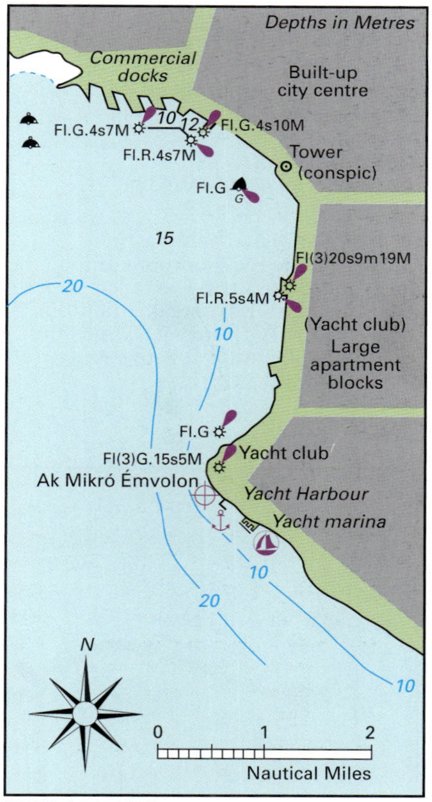

THESSALONIKI

Khalkidhiki

PORTAS CANAL (DHIORIX NEAS POTIDHAIAS)

W entrance 40°11'·77N 23°19'·30E WGS84

This shallow canal cuts the Kassandra peninsula off from the mainland. It is over ½ M long and has a minimum width of 36m. A bridge spans the canal with a vertical clearance of 18m. Minimum depth 2·5m.

SANI MARINA

40°05'·8N 23°18'·4E

☆ Fl.G/Fl.R

VHF Ch 16, 09

Navigation Entrance channel into marina. Call ahead on VHF for navigation advice before entering.

Berths Where directed. If necessary go alongside the reception berth on the starboard side of the channel at the entrance to the basin to be allocated a berth.

Shelter Good all-round shelter inside the marina, but some berths can be uncomfortable with prolonged strong southerlies. Entry could be difficult with strong onshore winds.

Data 215 berths. Max LOA 24m. Depths 2–3m. Charge band 6.

Facilities Water. 220/380V. Fuel. Pump-out. WC and showers. Laundry. Repairs. Bank/ATM. Mini-market. Bars and restaurants.

Sani Marina ✆ 23740 99581
www.saniresort.gr

NEA MARMARA

40°05'·46N 23°47'·03E WGS84
BA 1085 Imray-Tetra G2

☆ Entrance Fl.R.1·5s3M

Berths On the two pontoons among the local craft. Use a trip line tailed back to the bow. The S wavebreaker pontoon is breaking up. With strong S winds this pontoon will undulate with some violence.

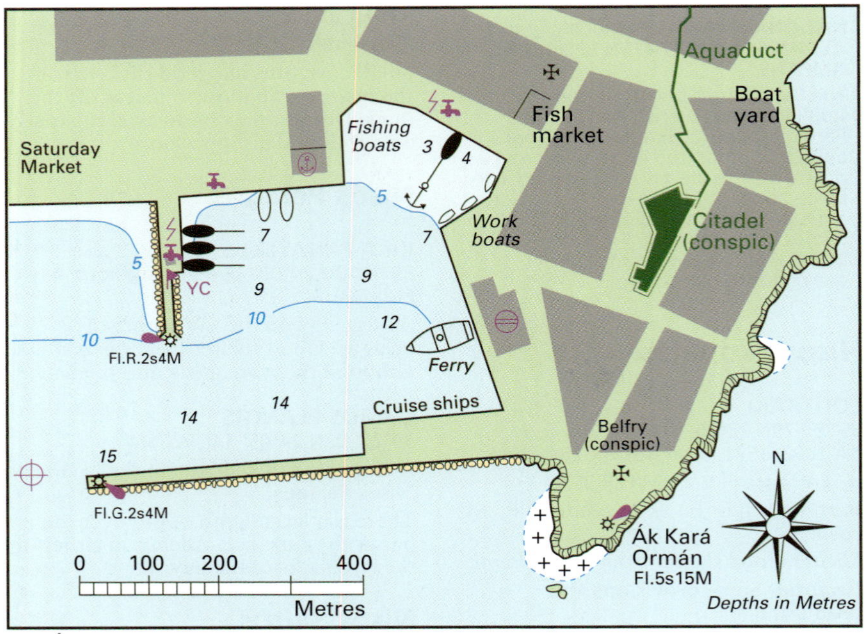

KAVÁLA

Shelter Good shelter although partially open S. Shelter improved with wavebreaker pontoon.

Data Limited visitors' berths. Laid moorings at most berths.
Charge band 2.

Facilities Water. 220V. Provisions and restaurants.

PORTO CARRAS MARINA

40°04'·58N 23°47'·34E WGS84
BA 1086 Imray-Tetra G2

☆ Entrance F.R.3M/F.G.3M. Ldg Lts 095° Front F.Y.3M. Rear F.Y.3M.

Navigation The buoys on the starboard side of the entrance channel have been removed. Min depths 6m in the channel.

Berths Stern or bows-to. Laid moorings.

Shelter Good all-round shelter.

Data 150 berths. Visitors' berths. Depths dredged to 5m. Charge band 6.

Facilities Water. 220V. Fuel quay. Showers and toilets. Crane and covered workshop. Most provisions and restaurants.

Remarks Marina associated with hotel and apartment complex.

Porto Carras ✆ 23750 721 26
Email info@portocarras.com
www.portocarras.com

PORTO KOUFÓ

39°57'·51N 23°54'·81E WGS84
BA 1085 Imray-Tetra G2

☆ Ak Pagona Fl.G.3s5M. Ak Spiliá Fl.R.3s4M

Navigation Entrance difficult to locate.

Berths Bows-to E quay. Anchorage in the bay.

Shelter Good shelter although there are gusts with NE winds and a chop with S winds.

Facilities Water. Fuel by tanker. Provisions and restaurants.

THE AKTI PENINSULA

A 500m exclusion zone around the coast is maintained for all vessels. Anchoring is not permitted in Órmos Vatopedi.

NISÍS DHIAPOROS

40°14'·7N 23°46'·0E Panayia

Behind Nisís Dhiaporos there are a number of sheltered anchorages. Care is needed of the numerous rocks and reefs in the approaches.

PIRGADHIKIA

40°20'·13N 23°43'·21E WGS84

Berths Raft up alongside on the pontoon. Dangerous in S winds.

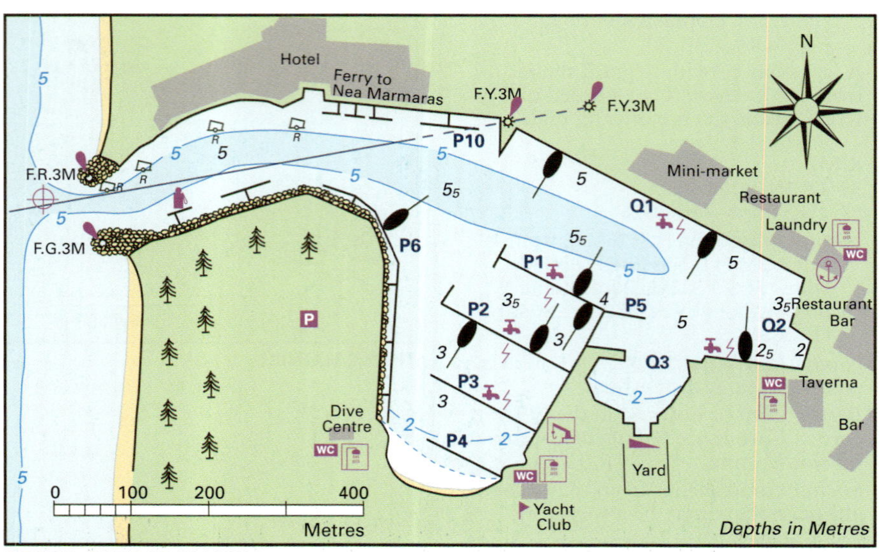

PORTO CARRAS MARINA

Nisís Ammouliani

AMMOULIANI VILLAGE
40°20′·2N 23°55′·3E
BA 1085 Imray-Tetra G26

☆ Ammouliani village Fl.R.3s3M. Nisídhes Dhrénia Fl.WR.2·5s4/3M

This island offers a number of good anchorages according to the wind direction.

The best shelter is off Ammouliani village on the NE of the island.

ELEVTHERÓN
40°50′·6N 24°19′·7E (Fl.3s5M)
BA 1086, 1687

☆ N entrance point Fl.3s5M. Nea Iraklitsa Fl.R.3s3M/Fl.G.3s3M

A large bay 6M S of Kavala. Anchor off according to wind and sea.

Boatyard with 50-ton travel-hoist. Manitsas Marine ✆ 25940 23180

KAVALA
40°55′·82N 24°24′·22E WGS84
BA 1086, 1687

☆ Ormos Kavalas W side Fl(2)R.8s7M. Ak Kára Ormán Fl.5s15M. Entrance Fl.G.2s4M/Fl.R.2s4M. Skála Rakhoníou. Fishing shelter. N Mole head Fl.G.3s3M. S mole head Fl.R.3s3M. Akra Spathi. Grain pier head Fl.R.4s16m3M.

VHF Ch 12, 16 for port authorities.

Navigation Work in progress extending S breakwater.

Berths Stern or bows-to. Limited room. YC very friendly and helpful to visiting yachts.

Shelter Good shelter except from S winds. Will improve with extension to breakwater.

Facilities Water. 220V. Fuel by tanker. Mechanical repairs. Provisions and restaurants.

KAVALA FISHING HARBOUR
40°56′·6N 24°25′·7E

☆ N mole Fl.G.3s3M. S mole Fl.R.3s3M.

LIMIN NEAS KAVALA
40°57′·0N 24°28′·9E

☆ Mole Fl.G.4s7M. Oil terminal 3F.R.3M.

Nísos Thasos

PORT THASOS
40°46′·89N 24°42′·23E WGS84 (Fl.R.3s3M)
BA 1086, 1687

☆ Nisís Thasopoúla Fl.WR.4·5s6/4M. Old harbour Fl.G.2s4M/Fl.R.2s4M Nea Limani N mole Fl.R.3s3M. S mole Fl.G.3s3M

Navigation Head for either harbour.

Berths Alongside either breakwater in Nea Limani. Anchor with a long line ashore in the old harbour.

Shelter Good in both harbours.

Facilities Water. Fuel by mini-tanker. Provisions and restaurants.

Remarks Shelter best in Nea Limani. Old harbour has ambience.

SKÁLA SOTÍROS
40°43′·76N 24°32′·82E WGS84

☆ Fishing shelter S mole head Fl.G.3s3M. N mole head Fl.R.3s3M

SKÁLA KALLIRÁKHIS
40°42′·68N 24°31′·86E WGS84

☆ Fishing shelter S mole head Fl.G.3s3M. N mole head Fl.R.3s3M

SKALA MARION
40°38′.74N 24°30′·72E WGS84

☆ Breakwater Fl.G.3s3M

Fishing village and small open harbour.

LIMENARIA
40°37′·41N 24°34′·58E WGS84

Busy fishing harbour. Care needed of large shoal patch in the entrance. Stay close to the S breakwater.

Remarks Works in progress on major expansion project. Breakwater extension completed.

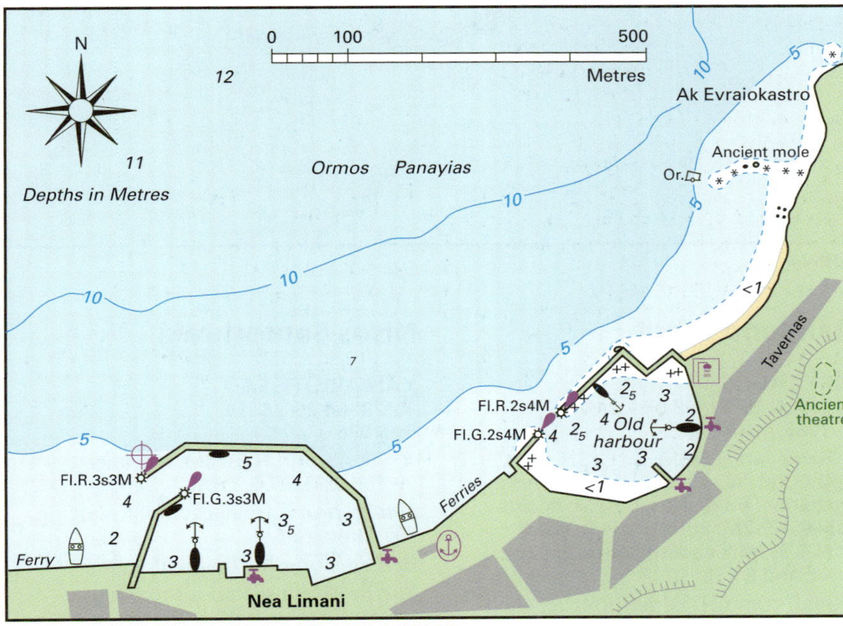

APPROACHES TO THASOS AND NEA LIMANI

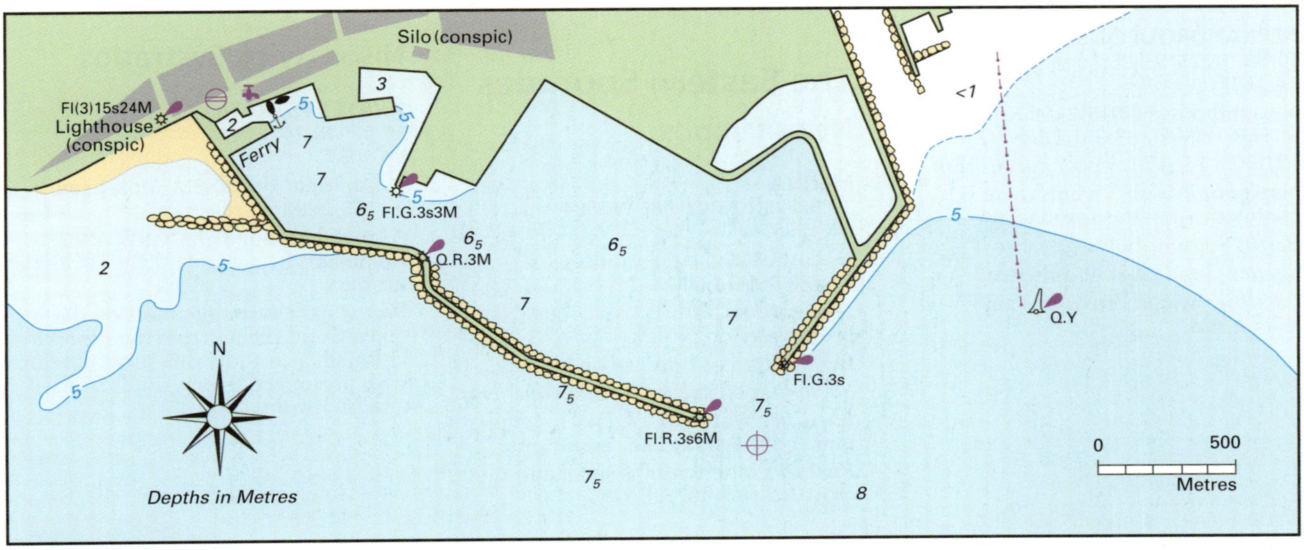

ALEXANDROUPOLIS

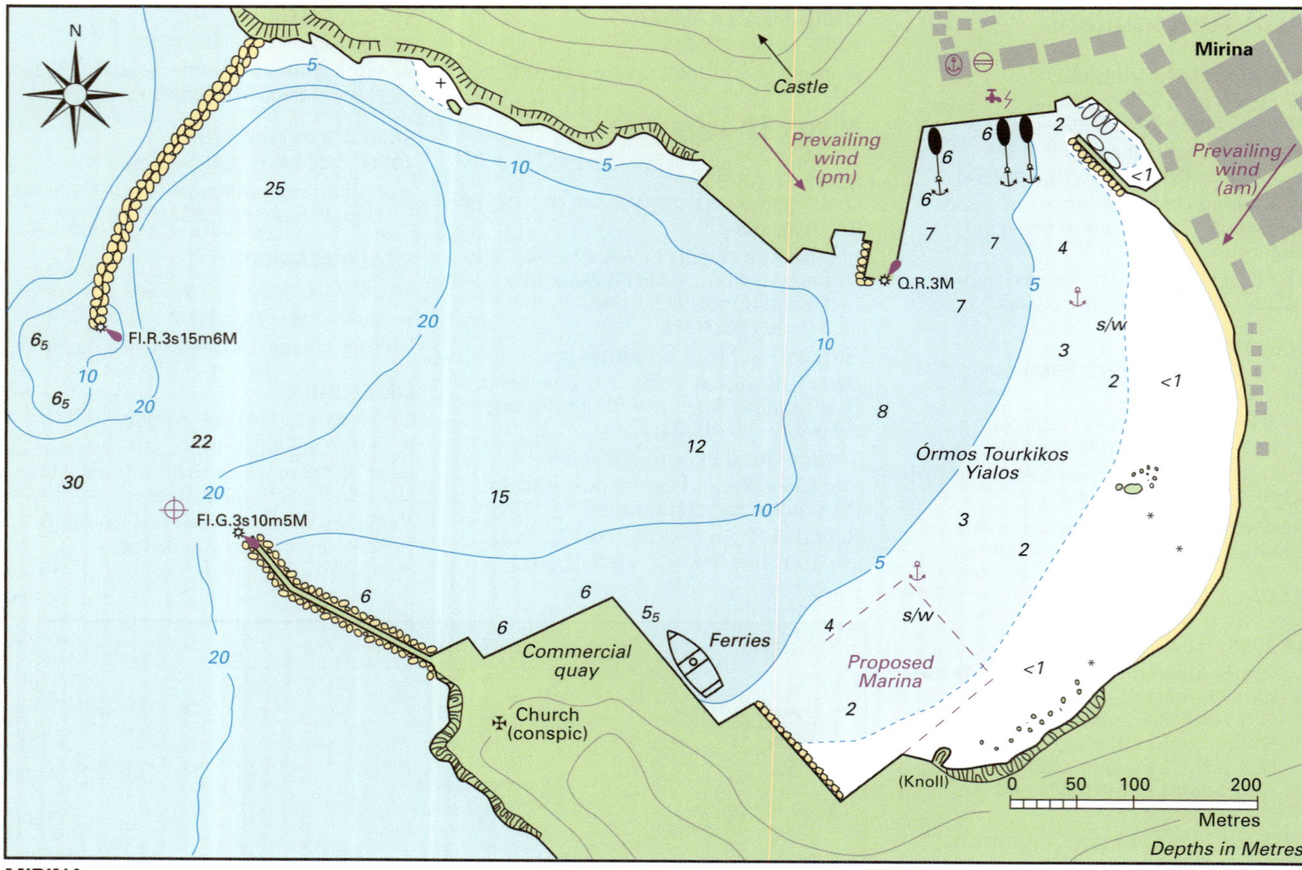

MIRINA

Mainland coast

PORT LÁGOS

41°00'·2N 25°07'·6E (Fl.R.2M)
BA 1086, 1636

☆ Ak Fanári Fl.8s6M. Bn Fl.G. E side Q.G.3M. W side Q.R.3M. Lts marking channel E side Fl.G.1·5s2M. W side Fl.R.1·5s2M. Entrance Fl.R.3s3M/ Fl.G.3s3M. Leading lights on 023·5° F.Y and F.Y.3M

A small commercial harbour reached by a buoyed channel. Good all-round shelter.

ALEXANDROUPOLIS

40°50'·1N 25°53'·9E
BA 1687

☆ Lighthouse Fl(3)15s24M. Entrance Fl.R.3s6M/Fl.G.3s3M. Elbow Q.R.3M

VHF Ch 12, 19 for port authorities.

Navigation With S winds there is a confused sea in the approaches.

Berths Stern or bows-to.

Shelter Good all-round shelter.

Facilities Water. Provisions and restaurants.

Nísos Samothraki

KAMARIÓTISSA

40°28'·4N 25°28'·1E
BA 1086

☆ Ak Akrotíri Fl.5s10M. Entrance Fl.R.3s3M/Fl.G.3s3M.

Navigation Care needed of low-lying Ak Akrotíri.

Berths Alongside on breakwater.

Shelter Good shelter although uncomfortable with S winds.

Facilities Water. Fuel by tanker. Provisions and restaurants.

The Eastern Sporades

Nísos Limnos

MÍRINA

39°52'·29N 25°02'·98E WGS84
BA 1636

☆ Castle Fl.6s11M. Entrance Q.R.3M/Q.G.3M

Navigation Castle conspicuous. New breakwater on N side of bay.

Berths Stern or bows-to on N quay.

Shelter Good shelter from the *meltemi*.

Facilities Water. 220V. Fuel by mini-tanker. Provisions and restaurants.

Remarks Inner basin is small and crowded with local boats.

ÓRMOS MÓUDHROU

39°47'·13N 25°14'·17E WGS84 (N Kastri)
39°51'·01N 25°13'·70E WGS84 (Ak Aspro Kavos)
BA 1636

☆ Nisís Kómbi Fl(2)6s10M. Ak Kávos Fl.3s5M. Móudhros F.R/Q.G/Q.R

Navigation Yachts normally make for Móudhros village.

Berths Alongside pier. Anchorages around the large bay.

Shelter All-round shelter can be found.

Facilities Water. Most provisions and restaurants.

Nísos Áyios Evstrátios

ÁYIOS EVSTRATIOS

39°32'·4N 24°59'·2E
BA 1087

☆ Ak Tripití Fl(2)10s8M. Mole head Fl.R.2s3M

A small harbour 1½M S–SW of Ak Kalamaki. Reasonable shelter from the *meltemi*.

Water and electricity points on the quay. Good shelter from the *meltemi* although a considerable surge develops with prolonged strong winds from almost any direction.

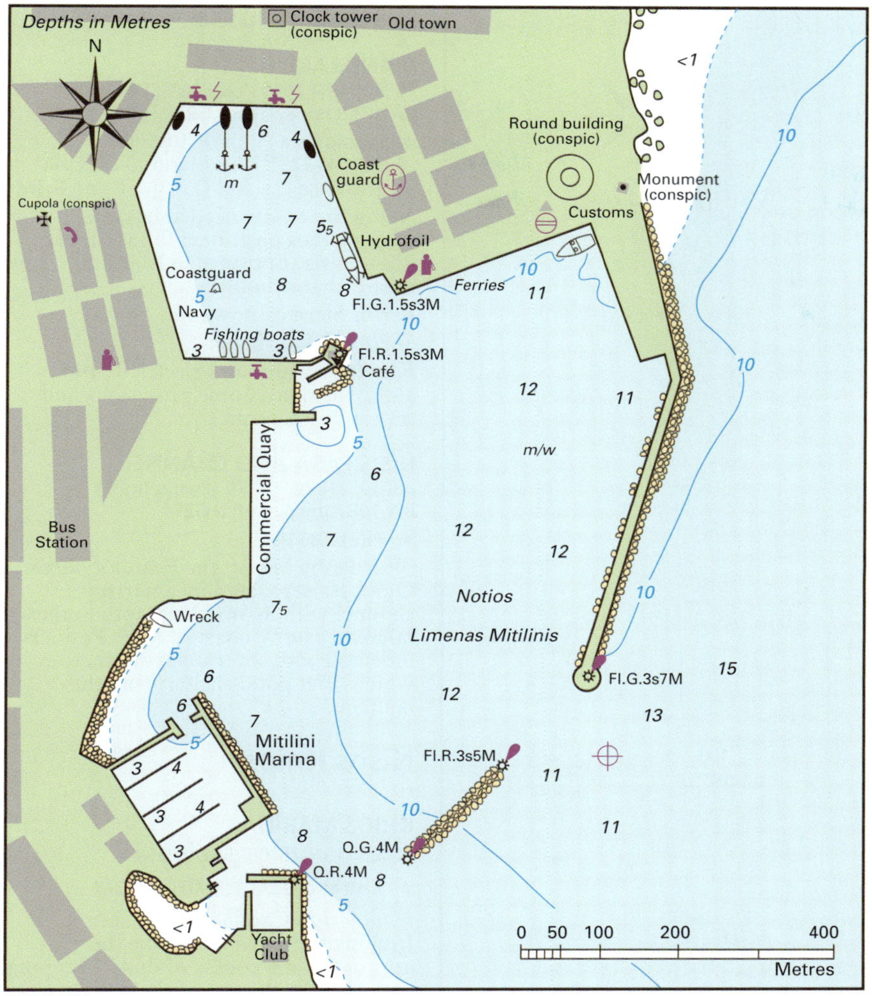

MITILINI

Nísos Lésvos

MITILINI

39°05′·86N 26°33′·83E WGS84
BA 1675 Imray-Tetra G27

☆ Castle Fl(3)14s6M. Breakwater Fl.G.3s7M. Entrance to inner basin Fl.G.1·5s3M/Fl.R.1·5s3M.

VHF Ch 12, 19 for port authorities. Ch 71 for Mytilini Marina.

Navigation Head for the town quay or the marina.

Berths Stern or bows-to on N quay.

Shelter Good shelter although S winds make it uncomfortable.

Facilities Water. 220V. Fuel by tanker. Provisions and restaurants.

Remarks Main ferry port. Smelly in the summer.

MITILINI MARINA

Data c.220 berths. Max LOA 45m. Depths 3–5m. Finger pontoons or laid moorings. Charge band 2/3.

Facilities Water and electricity(220/380V). Toilets and showers. Waste pump-out. WiFi. Laundry. Fuel by mini-tanker. 12-ton crane. 30 dry berths. Some repairs. Diver. Chandler. Mini-market in the marina. Bar-restaurant.

Remarks Under new management.
✆ 22510 54000
Email mytilini@mytilinimarina.com
www.mytilinimarina.com
www.seturmarinas.com

MITILINI LIMIN AKRA KASTRO

39°06′·8N 26°34′·1E
30M Mithimna ←→ Limin Khiou 55M

☆ Outer breakwater head Fl.G.3s14m7M. Mole head Q.R.5m4M. Breakwater NE end Fl.R.3s11m5M. SW end Q.G.11m4M.

Commercial harbour.

PANAYIOUDHA

39°08′·61N 26°31′·84E WGS84

Small crowded fishing harbour.

SKALA THERMIS

39°10′·87N 26°30′·08E WGS84

Reef-bound harbour. Extreme care needed in the approaches.

SKALA SIKAMINEAS

39°22′·48N 26°18′·28E WGS84

Miniature fishing harbour with a conspicuous chapel.

MITHIMNA

39°22′·02N 26°10′·12E WGS84
BA 1061 Imray-Tetra G27

☆ Ak Mólivos LFl.WG.10s12/8M 219°-G-239°. Mithimna F.R.3M. Mole head Fl.R.3s3M

Navigation Care needed of rocks and reef around Ak Mólivos and the harbour.

Berths Stern or bows-to or alongside outer mole. Bad holding.

Shelter Good shelter.

Facilities Water. 220V. Provisions and restaurants.

PORT SIGRI

39°12′·71N 25°50′·94E WGS84
BA 1675 Imray-Tetra G27

☆ Megalonísi Fl(2)15s53m21M. Ak Saratsina Fl.WR.3s5/3M 122°-R-160° and 219°-R-270°. NW corner Fl.2s5M

Navigation N channel should be used only in calm weather and with prudence.

Berths Alongside quay or anchored off.

Shelter Normally adequate but strong W winds can make it untenable.

Facilities Water. Some provisions and restaurants.

KÓLPOS KALLONI

39°04′·7N 26°03′·4E
BA 1675 Imray-Tetra G27

☆ Vrak Kalloni Fl.3s6M. Entrance F.R.3M/F.G.3M.

A large nearly land-locked gulf on the SW of Lesvos. Care is needed when entering by day and a night entry is not recommended.

PLOMÁRION

38°58′·39N 26°22′·26E WGS84
BA 1061 Imray-Tetra G27

☆ Entrance Fl.G.3s3M/Fl.R.3s3M

Berths Stern or bows-to on N and W quay. Laid moorings.

Shelter Poor shelter.

Facilities Water. 220V. Provisions and restaurants.

KÓLPOS YERAS

39°00′·15N 26°33′·17E WGS84
BA 1675 Imray-Tetra G27

The landlocked gulf on the SE of Lesvos. The approach is straightforward by day but should not be attempted at night.

Uncharted reef indicated by Greek authorities on Navtex, in position 38°56′·4N 26°29′·3E SW of the entrance to Kólpos Yeras.

Nísos Psará

PSARÁ

38°32′·4N 25°34′·1E (Fl.R.3M)
BA 1058 Imray-Tetra G27

☆ Ak Ay Yeóryios Fl.10s18M. Entrance Fl.R.1·5s3M. Inner mole F.R.3M

Navigation Care needed of the reefs fringing Nisís Andipsara and Vrak Katonisi.

Berths Stern or bows-to W quay or pontoon in NW corner.

Shelter Good shelter.

Facilities Limited provisions and restaurants.

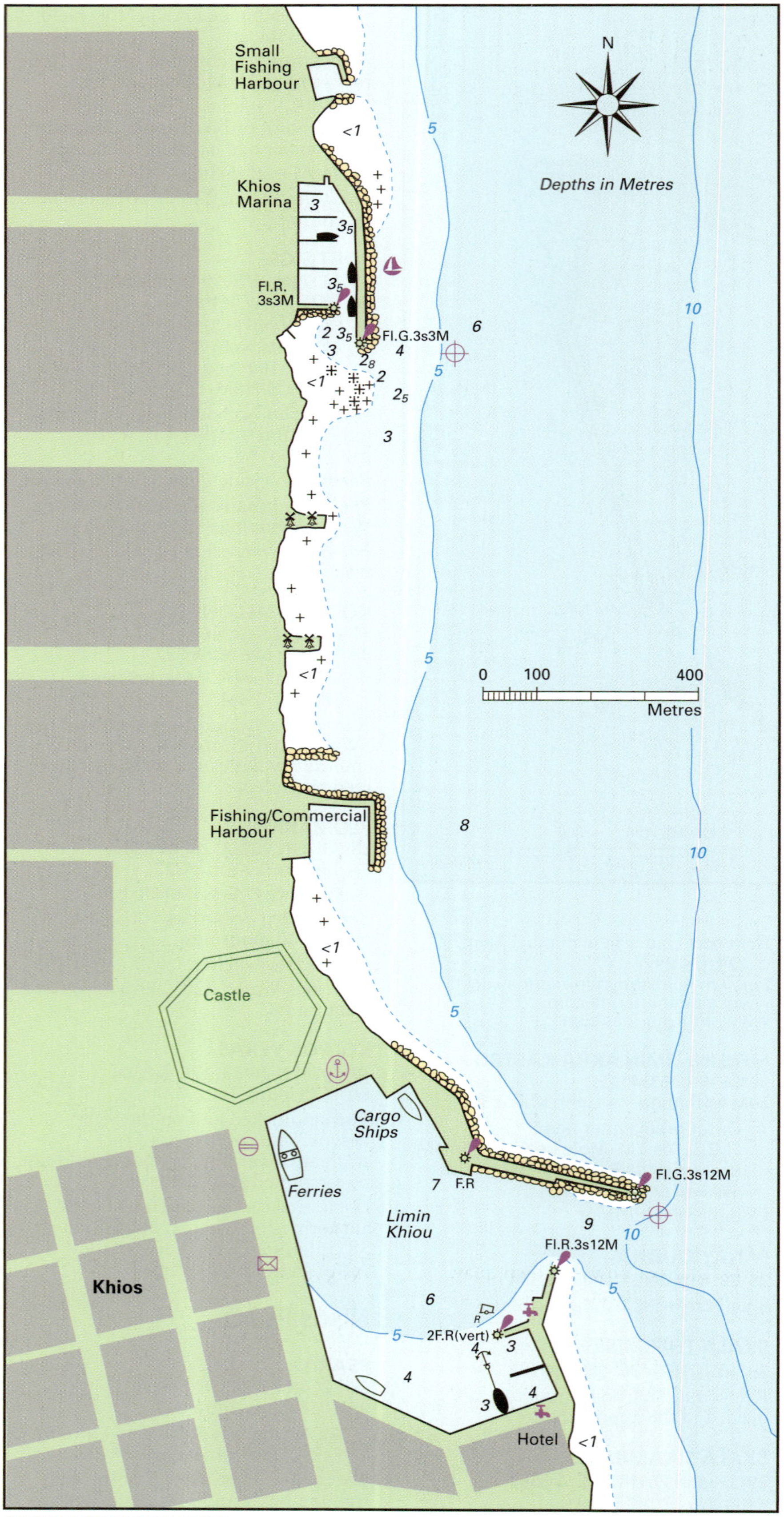

APPROACHES TO KHIOS

Nísos Oinoussa

MANDRAKI

38°30'·41N 26°13'·22E WGS84
BA 1058 Imray-Tetra G27

☆ Prassonísia Fl(2)WR.10s6/4M 301°-R-323°. Nisís Mandraki Fl.2s4M. Entrance Q.G.3M/Q.R.3M. Pier F.G.3M

Navigation Care needed or reefs fringing the coast. Reef 0·5M SE of Prassonisía. Entrance to Mandraki is by the SE channel only.

Berths Stern or bows-to.

Shelter Good shelter.

Facilities Water and electricity boxes along the quay. Some provisions and several restaurants.

NISÍS PASÁ AND CHANNEL

38°30'·1N 26°17'·7E (Pasha light)
BA 1087 Imray-Tetra G27

☆ Fl(2)20s11M

Nisís Pashá lies off the E end of Nísos Oinoussa separated by a narrow channel with 3–5m least depth in the fairway. The W coast of Nisís Pashá is indented with several bays and coves which offer good shelter from the *meltemi*.

Nísos Khios

KHIOS MARINA

38°23'·19N 26°08'·69E WGS84

☆ Entrance Fl.G.3s3M/Fl.R.3s3M

Navigation Care needed of reef fringing the entrance. Make the approach on a course of due W keeping very close to the end of the outer breakwater before turning sharply to starboard.

Berths Alongside where convenient.

Shelter Good all-round shelter.

Facilities Fuel by mini-tanker. Some provisions nearby.

Remarks Basic structure of the marina is complete but there are no facilities.

LIMIN KHÍOU

38°22'·12N 26°08'·72E WGS84
BA 1058 Imray-Tetra G27
55M Mitilini ←→ Ak Mastikho 16M

☆ Entrance Fl.G.3s12M/Fl.R.3s8M/F.R. Pier head 2F.R(vert)3M.

VHF Ch 12, 16 for port authorities.

Navigation There is often a confused sea in the Khios channel with the prevailing N wind blowing against the N-going current.

Berths Stern or bows-to in the SE corner.

Shelter Can be uncomfortable with the *meltemi*. Uncomfortable and possibly dangerous wash from ferries and coastguard.

Facilities Water. Fuel by tanker. Provisions and restaurants.

Remarks Harbour often smelly in the summer.

MÁRMARO (KARDHAMILA)
38°32'·70N 26°06'·61E WGS84
BA 1625 Imray-Tetra G27

☆ Vrak Margaríti Fl.3s5M. Mole head Fl.G.2s3M

Berths Stern or bows-to the inside of the mole.

Shelter Good shelter from the *meltemi.*

Facilities Water. 220V. Most provisions and restaurants.

LIMNIA (VOLISSOS)
38°28'·07N 25°55'·07E WGS84
BA 1625 Imray-Tetra G27

☆ E entrance point Fl.G.3s3M. Inner mole head Fl.R.1·5s3M. Outer mole head Fl.R.3s3M. Night entrance not recommended

Navigation Above and below water rocks fringe the coast.

Berths Stern or bows-to.

Shelter Good shelter.

Facilities Water. Restaurants.

Remarks Village about 2½km away.

MESTÁ
38°17'·60N 25°55'·71E WGS84
BA 1625 Imray-Tetra G27

☆ Fl.3s7M. Entrance Q.G.3M/Q.R.3M

A long inlet on the W coast. Reef lies 300m N of E entrance.

On the SE side of the inlet near the head there are several long quays with good depths off them.

ORMOS KAMARI
38°11'·25N 26°01'·84E WGS84

Small cove offering good shelter from the *meltemi.* Anchor and take a long line ashore.

Nísos Ikaría

ÉVDHILOS
37°38'·1N 26°11'·0E
BA 1056, 1526 Imray-Tetra G32

☆ Vrak Évdhilos Fl.7·5s11M. Mole head Fl.G.2s3M

Berths Stern or bows-to S pier or NW quay (care needed on latter). Anchorage in the bay.

Shelter Just adequate with the *meltemi.* Untenable with strong NE–E winds.

Facilities Some provisions and restaurants.

Note Harbour extension works in progress.

ÁYIOS KIRIKOS
37°36'·8N 26°17'·9E
BA 1056, 1526 Imray-Tetra G32

☆ Mole head Fl.R.3s4M

Navigation Severe gusts with the *meltemi* in the approaches.

Berths Go alongside on N side of centre pier in inner harbour. Care needed of shallows off the stub pier to N. Anchorage in NW.

Shelter Untenable with strong winds from S.

Facilities Provisions and restaurants.

MANGANITIS
37°33'·37N 26°07'·06E WGS84

Small fishing harbour. Go alongside clear of the ferry berth. Surge in strong N winds. Untenable in southerlies. Taverna ashore.

Nísos Sámos

KARLÓVASI
37°47'·68N 26°40'·83E WGS84
BA 1057, 1526 Imray-Tetra G32

☆ Ak Pangózi Fl.5s11M. Entrance Fl.G.3s3M / Fl.R.3s3M

Navigation A confused sea in the approaches with the *meltemi.*

Berths Stern or bows-to or alongside in the SE corner. Care needed as this area silts to less than 2m before dredging.

Shelter Good although uncomfortable with the *meltemi.*

Data c.40 berths. Five visitors' berths. Depths 1·5–3m.

Berth Stern or bows-to. Some laid moorings.

Shelter Good shelter from the prevailing winds.

Facilities Water. 220V. Yard. Provisions in Karlóvasi village. Restaurants.

Note New small craft basin on S side of entrance.

Yacht berths manager Tolis
✆ 22733 00461

VATHÍ
37°45'·34N 26°58'·21E WGS84
BA 1056 Imray-Tetra G32

☆ Ak Kótsikas Fl(2)7s7M. Mole head Fl.R.3s4M

VHF Ch 12 for port authorities.

Berths Go stern or bows-to or alongside the quay S of the ferry quay. There may also be space in the yacht harbour further S.

Shelter Órmos Vathí is completely open to the N–NW.

PITHAGORION
37°41'·19N 26°57'·06E WGS84
BA 1057, 1526 Imray-Tetra G32
27M Karlovasi ←→ Kos 56M

☆ Ak Foniás Fl.4s5M. Entrance Fl.R.2s3M/Fl.G.2s2M

Navigation Strong gusts with the *meltemi.* Leave the beacon at the entrance to the inner basin to port.

Berths Stern or bows-to town quay. Yachts often anchor outside basin to the E.

Shelter Good shelter but the *meltemi* causes an uncomfortable surge.

Facilities Water. 220V. Showers and toilets. Fuel by tanker. Provisions and restaurants.

SAMOS MARINA (PITHAGORION)
37°41'·36N 26°57'·53E WGS84

☆ Entrance Fl.R.3s3M/Fl.G.3s3M

Berth Where directed.

Shelter Good shelter inside the marina.

Data c.150 berths. Depths 3–6m. Charge band 5.

Facilities Water. 220V. Shower and toilet blocks. Laundry. Fuel quay. 80-ton travel-lift. 20-ton mobile crane. Hard-standing. Some repairs. Chandlers. Mini-market and café bar in the marina. Provisions, tavernas and restaurants in Pithagorian.

Samos Marina ✆ 22730 61600
Email moor@samosmarina.gr or info@samosmarina.gr
www.samosmarina.gr

Nisídhes Foúrnoi

FOÚRNOI
37°34'·5N 26°28'·8E
BA 1056, 1526 Imray-Tetra G32

☆ Ak Svistokáminos Fl.WR.3·5s4/3M 034°-R-138°, 172°-R-243°. (Night entrance not recommended)

Navigation Severe gusts with the *meltemi.*

Berths Stern or bows-to in the harbour at the N end of the bay.

Shelter Adequate from the *meltemi.*

Facilities Limited provisions and restaurants.

Remarks Other anchorages around the island.

The Dodecanese

Nísos Patmos

SKALA
37°19'·37N 26°32'·95E WGS84
BA 1531 Imray-Tetra G32

☆ Ak Ilías Fl(3)9s9M. Vrak Kavouronísia, Tragos Rock Fl(2)WR.12s5/3M 087°-R-232°. Ak Áspri Fl.WR.2s5/3M 272°-R-320°. Skalá Fl.R.1·5s3M

Navigation Care needed of reefs in the approaches especially Skopelos Tragos, Ífalos Khelia and Skopeloi Sklavaki.

Berths Stern or bows-to NW quay.

Shelter Adequate shelter from the *meltemi.*

Facilities Water (reported non-potable) and fuel by mini-tanker. Provisions and restaurants.

Remarks Numerous anchorages sheltered from the *meltemi* around the coast.

PATMOS MARINE
A boatyard in the village of Stavros, 3M S of Skala.

Hauling yachts up to 25m on hyrdaulic trailers. Most repairs.

Office on the quay in Skala.

✆ 22470 31903 / 29309
Email tarsanas@12net.gr
www.patmosmarine.gr

Nísos Árki

PORT AUGUSTA
37°22'·59N 26°43'·88E WGS84

☆ N entrance Fl.3s5M

A dogleg inlet on the W side of Árki. Good all-round shelter.

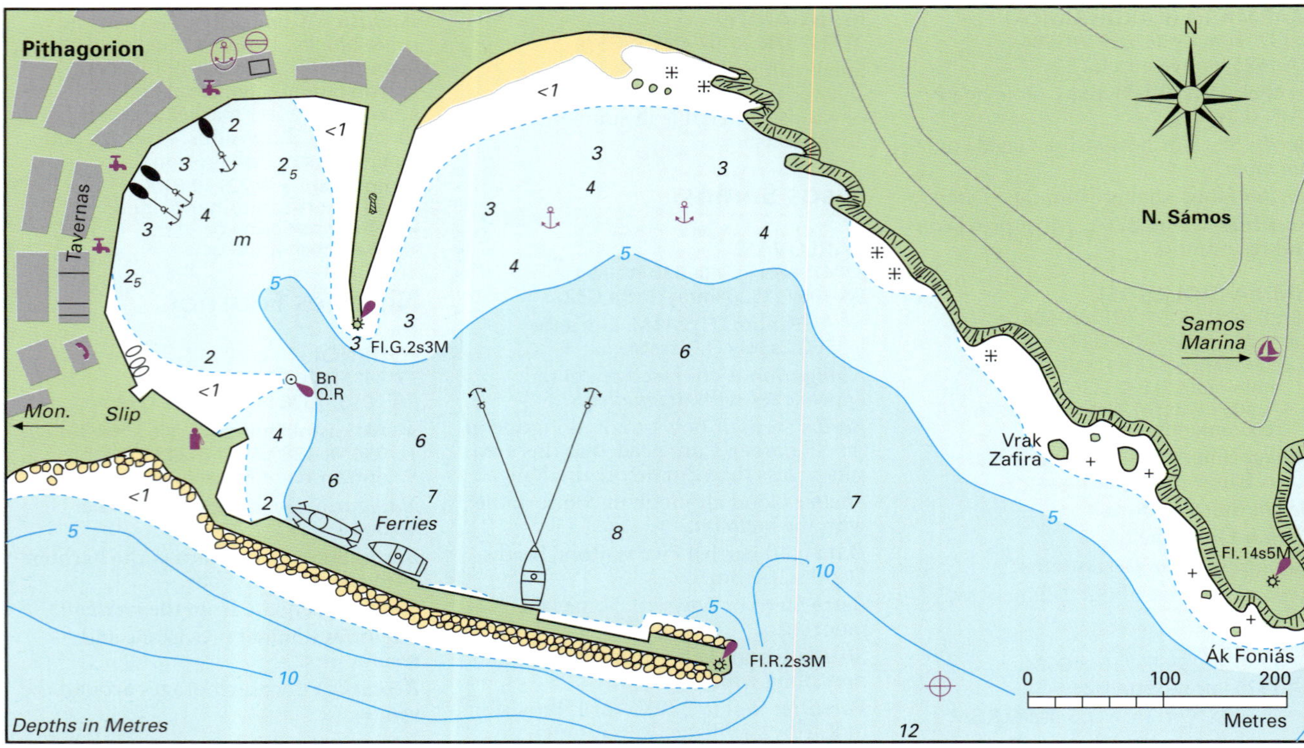

PITHAGORION

Nísos Lipsó

ÓRMOS LIPSÓ

37°17'·67N 26°45'·86E WGS84
BA 1531 Imray-Tetra G32

☆ Ak Gátos Fl.3s6M. Pier head F.R.3M

Berths Stern or bows-to either side of the pier.

Shelter Good shelter from the *meltemi* although there are gusts.

Facilities Water. 220V. Some provisions and restaurants.

Remarks Inner harbour dredged to 3–5m.

Nisís Agathonisi

ÓRMOS AY YEORYIOS

37°26'·65N 26°57'·91E WGS84
BA 1056 Imray-Tetra G32

☆ SW end Fl.2s6M

Berths Coastguard berths on N end of W quay. Ferry berths on S end of W quay. Yachts berth in centre of W quay, and on the N quay, or on the N shore anchored with a long line to a bollard. Otherwise anchor clear of ferry turning area.

Shelter Good shelter from the *meltemi*. Open S.

Facilities Some provisions and restaurants.

NISÍS FARMAKONÍSI

37°16'·9N 27°05'·3E (light on S end)

☆ S end Fl(2)14s12M

The island and anchorage are now a military zone, anchoring and landing on the island is prohibited.

Nísos Léros

ÓRMOS LAKKÍ

37°06'·72N 26°49'·78E WGS84
BA 1531 Imray-Tetra G32

☆ Ak Lakkí Fl(2)14s9M. Ak Ángistro Fl.2·5s5M. Mole head Fl.R.3s4M. Lightbuoy Fl.G.2s2M

VHF Ch 11, 16.

Navigation Strong gusts and confused seas in the approaches with the *meltemi*.

Remarks It is prohibited to approach within 200m of the naval establishment on the S side of Órmos Lakkí.

LAKKI MARINA

37°07'·52N 26°50'·95E WGS84

VHF Ch 11.

Berths Stern or bows-to where directed. Laid moorings tailed to the quay. New pontoons due to be installed as shown in the plan.

Shelter Good shelter from the *meltemi*.

Data c.40 berths. Visitors' berths. Max LOA 40m. Depths 3–5m. Charge band 2.

Facilities Water. 220V. WiFi. Laundry. Provisions and restaurants.

Agmar Marine SA Lakki Marina
✆ 22470 25240 / 24812
Email info@lakki-marina.gr

LEROS MARINA

VHF Ch 10.

Marina and boatyard in the NE corner of Ormos Lakki.

Berths Stern-to where directed. Laid moorings.

Data 220 berths. Max LOA 50m. Depths 3·5–9m. Charge band 2/3.

Facilities Water. 220V. Fuel dock. Shower and toilets. 60/150-ton travel-hoist. Repairs.

Evros Marine SA (Leros Marina)
✆ 22470 26600
Email info@lerosmarina.gr

ÓRMOS PARTHENI

37°12'·0N 26°47'·5E
BA 1056 Imray-Tetra G32

A large dog-leg bay offering good all-round protection on the N side of Leros.

Large boatyard 400/70-ton travel-hoist. Chandler.

Boatyard ✆ 22470 26009 / 26010

ÓRMOS ALÍNDAS

37°09'·62N 26°51'·23E WGS84
BA 1056 Imray-Tetra G32

☆ Ak Kastello Fl.3s5M. Panteli mole head Fl.G.3s3M.

Navigation Strong gusts with the *meltemi*.

Berths Alongside the pier in calm weather or anchored off.

Shelter Just adequate, sometimes untenable with a strong *meltemi*.

Facilities Most provisions and restaurants.

PANDELI

37°09'·00N 26°51'·80E WGS84

Small fishing harbour and popular holiday village. Port regulations (sometimes) restrict yachts from using the harbour August–May. Go alongside the breakwater and/or raft up to other yachts.

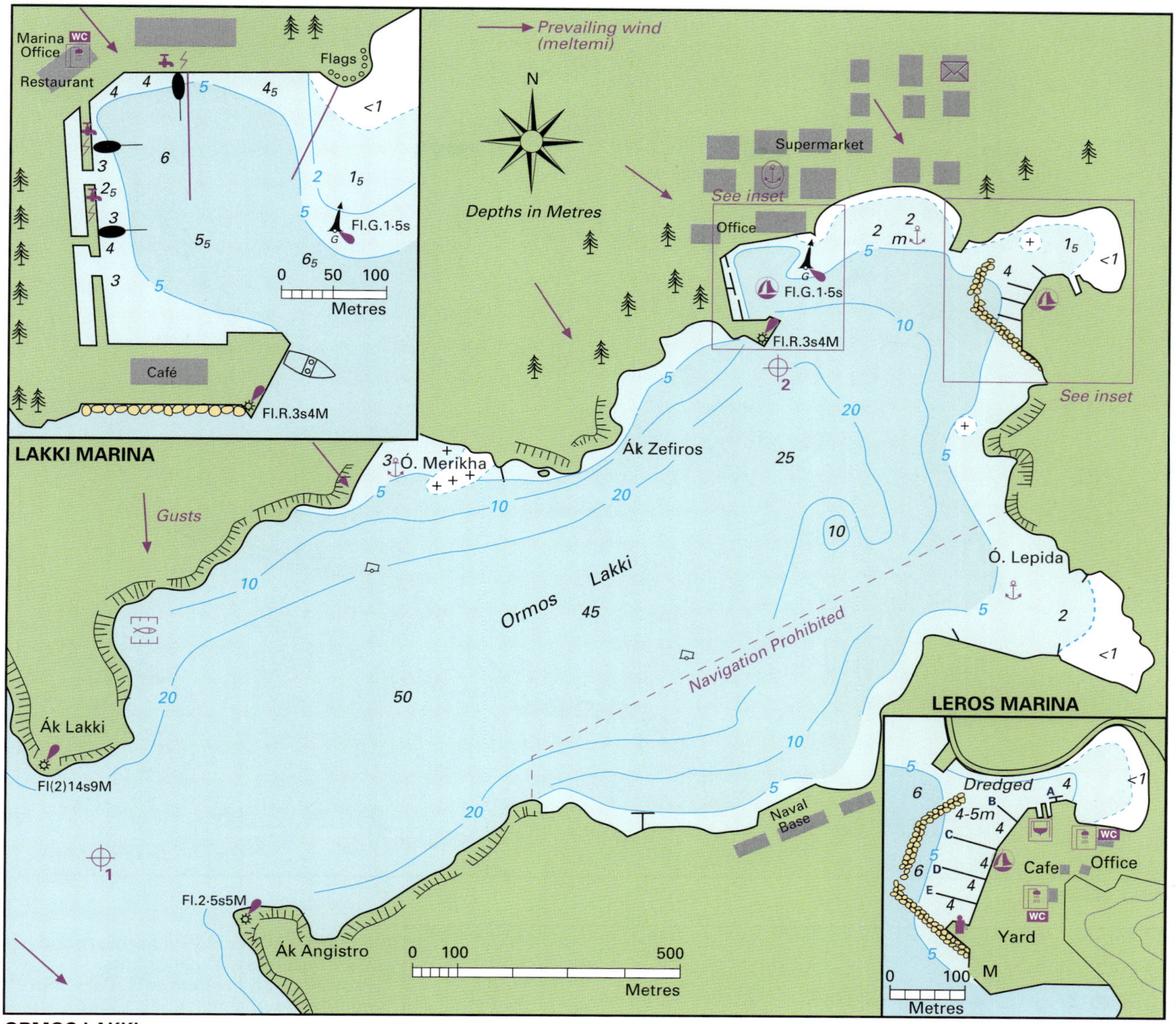

ORMOS LAKKI

Nísos Kalimnos

LIMIN KALÍMNOU

36°56′·84N 26°59′·69E WGS84
BA 1531 Imray-Tetra G34

☆ Entrance Fl.R.3s6M / Fl.G.3s6M

Navigation Strong gusts with the *meltemi*.

Berths Stern or bows-to on NE quay or on S quay.

Shelter Good shelter.

Facilities Water. 220V. Fuel by tanker. Yard. Provisions and restaurants.

Remarks Large commercial and ferry harbour. Port of entry (summer only).

VATHI

36°58′·5N 27°02′·2E

Narrow fjord on SE of Kalimnos. Good shelter.

Nisís Pserimos

PSERIMOS

36°55′·5N 27°07′·8E

Small harbour on the SW side of Pserimos. Good shelter from the *meltemi*. Usually crowded with tripper boats.

Note An old mooring chain crosses the harbour. Use a trip line. The bottom is sand and rock, indifferent holding in places.

Nísos Kós

KÓS

36°53′·88N 27°17′·34E WGS84
BA 1531 Imray-Tetra G35
56M Pithagorion ←→ Rhodes 61M

☆ Ak Ammóglossa Fl.R.4s9M. Ak Foúka Fl.4s6M. Ak Loúros Fl(3)WR.15s4/6M. Entrance Fl.G.3s4M / Fl.R.3s3M

VHF Ch 07, 12 for port authorities.

Navigation Care needed of the shoal water extending from Ak Ammóglossa. Care needed in narrow entrance of craft coming and going.

Berths Stern or bows-to on E side.

Shelter Adequate but uncomfortable with the *meltemi* and wash.

Facilities Water. 220V. Fuel by tanker. Provisions and restaurants. Charge band 3.

Remarks E side berths administered by Kos marina.

KÓS MARINA

36°53′·84N 27°17′·97E WGS84

☆ Entrance Fl.G.4s3M/Fl.R.4s3M

VHF Ch 77.

Navigation A pilot tender will come out to guide you in.

Berths Stern or bows-to where directed. Laid moorings tailed to the quay.

Shelter Good all round shelter.

Data 250 berths. Visitors' berths. Max LOA c.25m. Depths 3–6m. Charge band 4.

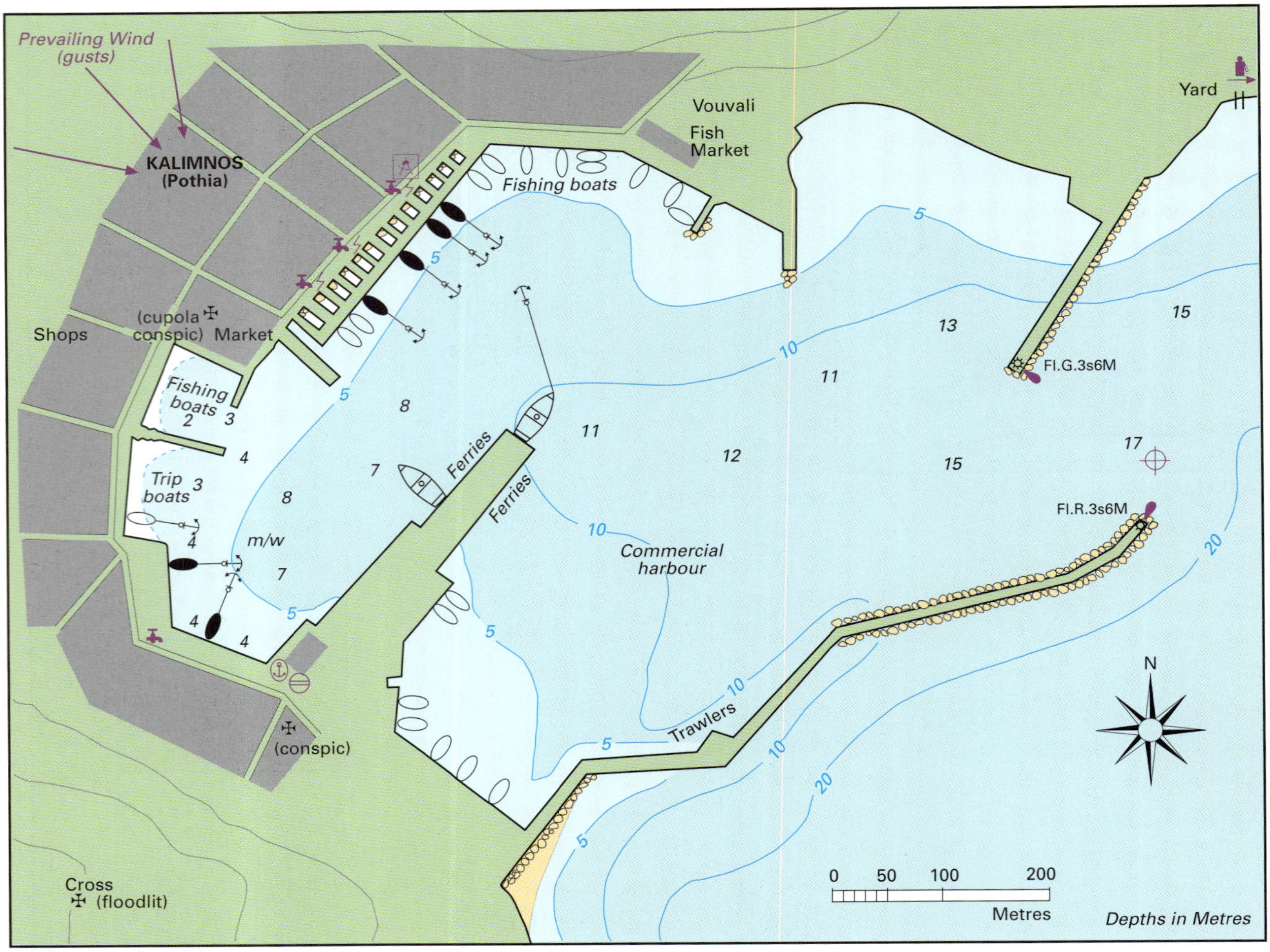

LIMÍN KALIMNOU

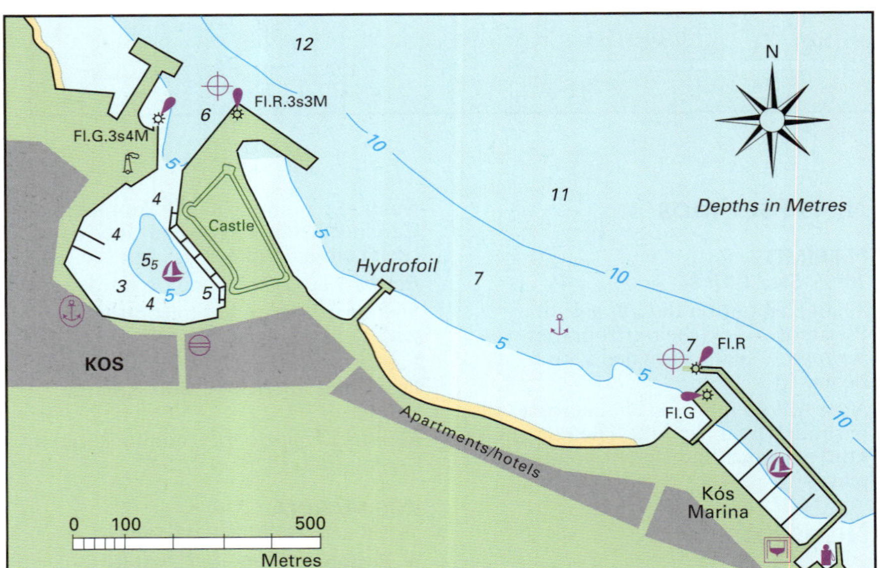

APPROACHES TO KÓS AND KÓS MARINA

Facilities Water. 220V. Showers and WC. Fuel quay. Yacht repairs. Provisions and restaurants. Port police not always on site.

Kos Marina ✆ 22420 57500
Email info@kosmarina.gr
www.kosmarina.gr

ÓRMOS KÁMARES

36°44'·2N 26°58'·3E (Fl.R.3M)
BA 1055 Imray-Tetra G35

☆ Mole head Fl.R.2s4M

Berths Stern or bows-to pier or anchor off.

Shelter Adequate shelter from the *meltemi*.

Facilities Restaurant and bars.

Nísos Nísiros

LIMIN MANDRAKI

36°36'·9N 27°08'·5E (Q.G.3M)
BA 1531 Imray-Tetra G35

☆ Mole head Q.G.3M

Berths Alongside.

Shelter Just adequate and sometimes untenable with the *meltemi*.

Facilities Provisions and restaurants.

PALON
36°37'·24N 27°10'·44E WGS84
BA 1055 Imray-Tetra G35

☆ Ak Katsouni Fl(2)9s12M. Entrance Fl.G.2s3M/Fl.R.2s3M

Navigation Care needed of the reef surrounding Ák Ammodes and fringing the N mole.

Berths Stern or bows-to the N or S quays. Harbour now dredged to 3m.

Shelter Good from the *meltemi* – improved with breakwater extension.

Facilities Water and electricity. Some provisions and tavernas.

Remarks The W breakwater has been extended such that the entrance to the harbour is now from the E.

Nísos Tilos

ÓRMOS LIVADHI
36°25'·02N 27°23'·18E WGS84

☆ Órmos Livádhia Fl.R.3s3M. Pier head Fl.G.3s3M

Berths Stern or bows-to on town quay where directed. Laid moorings.

Shelter Good shelter from the *meltemi*.

Facilities Water. 220V. Provisions and tavernas.

Nísos Simi

LIMIN SIMIS
36°37'·09N 27°50'·40E WGS84
BA 1532 Imray-Tetra G35

☆ Ak Koutsoúmba Fl.3s5M. Quay Fl.G.3s3M

Navigation Location of the harbour difficult to determine from the S and E.

Berths Stern or bows-to where directed.

Shelter Good shelter from the *meltemi*. A surge with S gales.

Facilities Water. 220V. Provisions and restaurants.

Remarks Harbourmaster office now on SE side between ferry berths and fuel dock.

PETHI
36°36'·95N 27°51'·70E WGS84
BA 1055 Imray-Tetra G35

☆ Ak Filonika Fl.6s4M

A large bay SE of Limin Simis. Care needed of an isolated above water rock in the middle of the entrance. Holding unreliable.

PANORMITTIS
36°33'·12N 27°50'·53E WGS84
BA 1532 Imray-Tetra G35

☆ Nisís Marmarás Fl.3s6M. NE side Fl.R.2s3M

Navigation With the *meltemi* there are gusts and confused seas off the entrance.

Berths Anchor in the NE of the bay.

Shelter Good all-round shelter.

Facilities Limited provisions and restaurants.

Nisís Nimos

Nisís Nimos is separated from Nísos Simi by a narrow channel with least depths of 4m in the fairway.

Nísos Rhodos (Rhodes)

LIMIN RHODOU-MANDRAKI
36°27'·12N 28°13'·67E WGS84
BA 1055, 1532 Imray-Tetra G3, G35
61M Kos ←→ Pigadhi 80M

☆ Ak Milon (Zonari) Fl.WR.4s6/4M 286°-R-314°. Ay Nikólaos Fl(2)12s11M. W breakwater head Fl.G.2s4M. Limin Emborikós Fl.R.2s4M. Entrance to Mandraki Fl.RG.3M/F.R/F.G.2M

VHF Ch 07, 12 for port authorities.

Navigation Care needed of the shoal water running out from Ak Milon (Zonari). Care also needed of Ifalos Kolona which runs 250m N from the N side of the entrance to Mandraki. With strong S winds entrance to Mandraki can be difficult.

Berths Stern or bows-to. Some laid moorings. Yachts anchored off the outside of Mandraki E breakwater may be asked to move for cruise ships. Large yachts berth in Limin Emborikos. Call an agent for a berth.

Shelter Good all-round shelter.

Facilities Water. 220V. Fuel by tanker. 40-ton travel-hoist but access limited by depth (normally 2m). Most yacht repairs including sail maker.
A1 Yachting has a large chandlery and will hold mail. Provisions and restaurants.

Remarks Mandraki gets very crowded in the summer with charter boats occupying many of the berths.

Rhodes Marina

Projected Data c.300 berths. Progress patchy – not yet open (2014).

A1 Yachting ☏ 22410 22927
Email rhodes@a1yachting.com

Bluebonnet Maritime & Tourism Ent.
VHF Ch 77 (callsign *Maritime*)
☏ 22410 78780 *Fax* 22410 39750
Mobile (24hr) 6944 434 311
Email maritime@rho.forthnet.gr

Navigo ☏ 6979 286667

LINDOS
36°05'·73N 28°05'·82E WGS84
BA 1532 Imray-Tetra G36

Berths Anchorage.

Shelter Good from the *meltemi* although there are gusts.

Facilities Most provisions and restaurants.

Nísos Kastellorízon

LIMIN KASTELLORÍZOU
36°09'·17N 29°35'·59E WGS84
BA 1054 Imray-Tetra G36, G39

☆ N tip of Kastellorízon Fl.WR.4·5s5/3M. Nisís Strongilí Fl.5s17M. Entrance E side Fl.R.2·4s3M

VHF Ch 16 for port authorities.

Navigation Strong gusts and confused seas in the approaches with the *meltemi*. Care needed of reefs in the E approach.

Berths Stern or bows-to in the SE corner.

Shelter Adequate although uncomfortable with a prolonged *meltemi*.

Facilities Some provisions and restaurants.

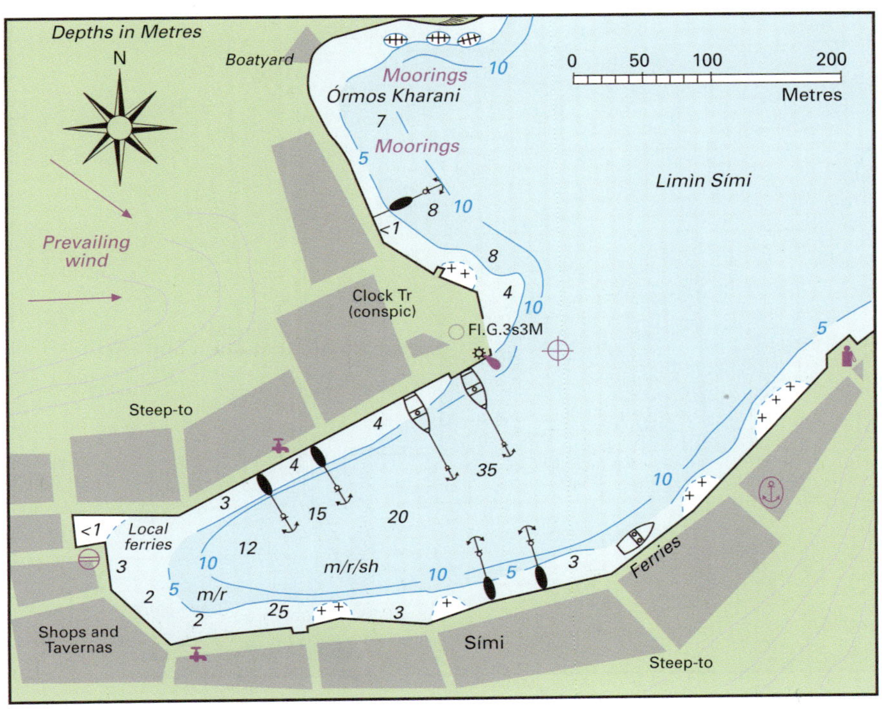

SÍMI

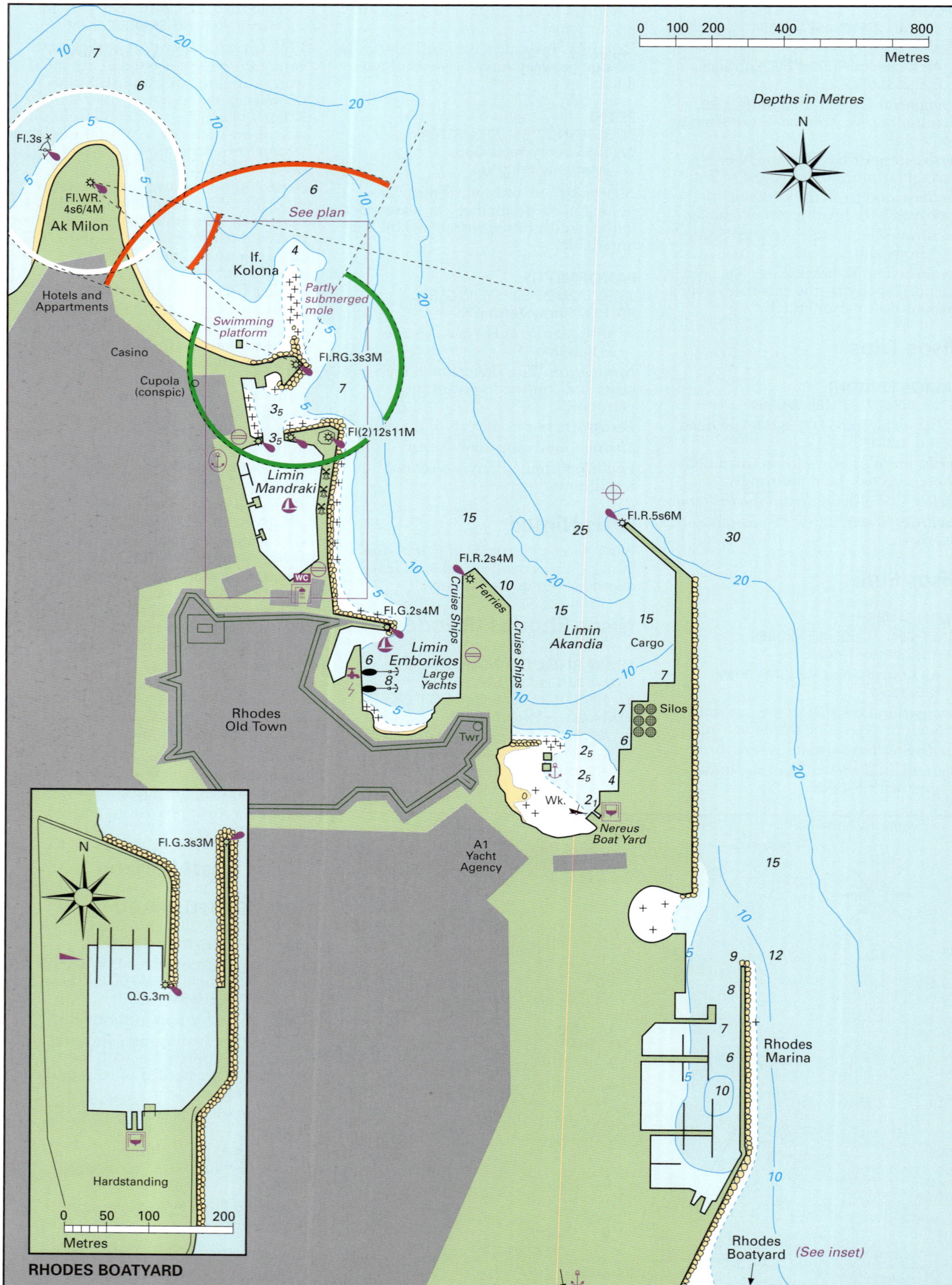

APPROACHES TO RHODES

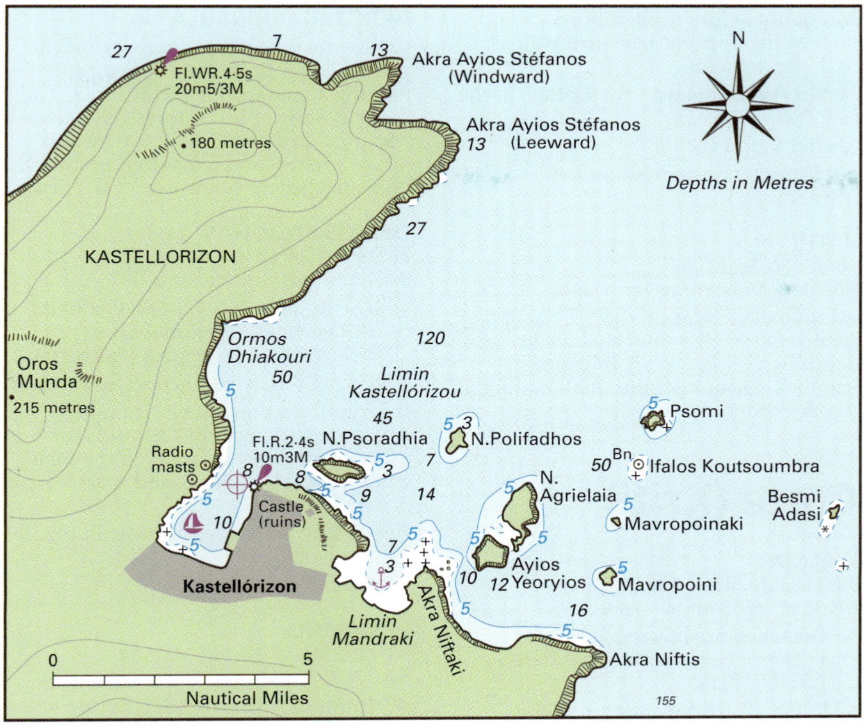

APPROACHES TO LIMIN KASTELLORIZOU

Nísos Khalki

KHALKI (EMBORIOS)

36°13'·3N 27°37'·5E
BA 236 Imray-Tetra G35

☆ Vrak Nisáki Fl.WR.6s8/6M. Tragusa Fl(2)WR.14s8/6M. S entrance Fl.3s6M

Navigation Care needed of numerous rocks and reefs between Nísos Khalki and Nísos Alimia. Special care needed of Xera Rock and the reef immediately due W of Nisáki.

Berths Stern or bows-to pontoon. Anchorage in the bay.

Shelter Adequate shelter from the *meltemi* although there are gusts.

Facilities Water. Most provisions and restaurants.

Nísos Alimia

ÓRMOS ALIMIA

36°15'·8N 27°41'·5E
BA 1055 Imray-Tetra G35

Navigation Care needed of reefs and rocks as for Khalkis. Care needed of reef off S entrance.

Berths Anchorage in the bay.

Shelter Adequate shelter from the *meltemi*.

Nísos Karpathos

PORT KARPATHOS (PIGÁDHIA)

35°30'·72N 27°12'·88E WGS84
BA 1532 Imray-Tetra G39

☆ Órmos Pigádhia Fl.5s6M. Mole head Fl.R.4s3M.

Navigation Severe gusts with the *meltemi*. New breakwater and quay off Garonisos.

Berths Stern or bows-to or alongside.

Shelter Uncomfortable with the *meltemi*. A surge with S gales.

Facilities Water. Provisions and restaurants.

TRISTOMA

35°49'·3N 27°12'·3E (Notia light)
BA 1532 Imray-Tetra G39

☆ Nisís Notía Fl.R.5s4M

A long sheltered inlet on the NW corner of Karpathos. With a strong *meltemi* heavy seas pile up at the entrance and there are fierce gusts off the hills. Entry is by the southernmost passage.

Nísos Kasos

LIMIN KASOU

35°25'·14N 26°56'·03E WGS84
BA 1532

☆ Ak Ay Yeóryios Fl.WR.3s5/3M. 083°-R-175°, 241°-R-251°. Mole head Fl.G.1·5s3M. Village pier Q.R.2M

Navigation With the *meltemi* there are gusts and confused seas in the approaches.

Berths Stern or bows-to.

Shelter Just adequate from the *meltemi*. Violent gusts with S gales.

Facilities Most provisions and restaurants in the village to the W.

LIMIN FRI (Kasos)

35°25'·15N 26°55'·48E WGS84

☆ Limenas Bouka Fl.R.3s3M

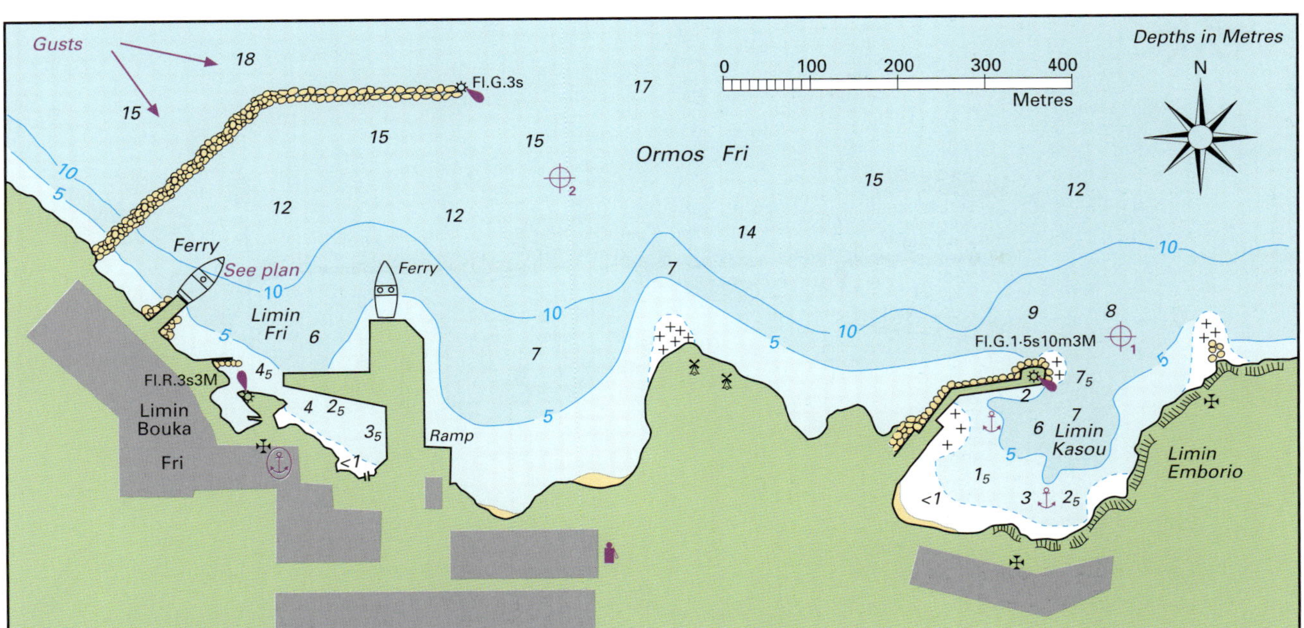

ORMOS FRI (Kasos)

Navigation The new harbour lies ½M W of the fishing harbour of Limin Kasou. Work extending W breakwater has been completed.

The entrance to the new inner harbour is narrow and should not be confused with the entrance to the miniature harbour (Limin Bouka) immediately to the W.

Berths Go alongside where convenient in the inner harbour. The outer quay is used by ferries.

Shelter Good shelter from the *meltemi*. Strong southerlies could make it uncomfortable.

Facilities Water on the quay. Provisions and tavernas.

Nísos Astipalaia

SKÁLA

36°32'·83N 26°21'·53E WGS84
BA 1040, 1541 Imray-Tetra G34

☆ N side Fl.WR.3s5/3M 261°-R-293°. Quay 3F.G.3M/3F.R.3M

Navigation Strong gusts with the *meltemi*. Castle in *chora* conspicuous.

Berths Stern or bows-to on new quay or anchor in the bay. Depths 3m on quay.

Shelter Adequate from *meltemi*. Untenable with strong SE winds.

Facilities Water. 220V boxes. Fuel by tanker. Most provisions and restaurants.

ÓRMOS MALTEZANA

36°34'·48N 26°23'·15E WGS84
BA 1040 Imray-Tetra G34

☆ Nisís Khondró. Fl.4·5s4M. Mole head Fl.G.2s4M.

Navigation Care needed of rocks and reefs in the approaches. Strong gusts with the *meltemi*.

Berths Alongside pier. Anchorage in the bay.

Shelter Good shelter.

Facilities Some provisions and restaurants.

VATHI

36°36'·5N 26°23'·0E
BA 1040, 1541 Imray-Tetra G34

A landlocked inlet on the NE tip of the island. Good all-round shelter. 3m least depth in the fairway of entrance channel. Anchor off the small hamlet in the W corner.

Crete (Kriti)

KHANIA

35°31'·35N 24°01'·09E WGS84
BA 3681, 1707 Imray-Tetra G37

☆ Detached breakwater Fl.G.4s4M. Entrance Fl.R.2·5s7M. Inner harbour F.G.3M/F.R.3M

VHF Ch 12, 16 for port authorities.

Navigation Approach difficult and sometimes dangerous with strong onshore winds. Detached breakwater now mostly submerged.

Berths Stern or bows-to in inner basin. New laid moorings.

Shelter Good shelter although strong onshore winds send solid water over the breakwater and cause a surge.

Facilities Water and 220V. Fuel by mini-tanker. Provisions and restaurants.

Remarks Port of entry. The inner basin is now classified as a marina.

AKROTIRI PENINSULA

Check the firing range activity off the peninsula with the Port Police before making a passage E from Khania. The range is active two or three days a week Monday–Friday, 0700–1500. When active yachts can be diverted up to 20M N. Range safety boats use VHF Ch 12.

ÓRMOS SOUDHAS

36°29'·5N 24°04'·5E
BA 1706, 3681 Imray-Tetra G37

☆ Nisís Soudha Fl.G.4·8s6M. Pier head 2F.R(vert)4M. Ay Nicolaos jetty 3F.G(vert)3M. Vlite jetty 2F.G(vert)3M

VHF Ch 08, 12, 16 for port authorities.

It is reported that yachts are now welcome although they should stay away from the area between the main channel and Soudha Island where there is a military base.

Berths Go alongside the mole in the fishing harbour.

Remarks Port of entry.

RETHIMNO

35°22'·39N 24°29'·22E WGS84
BA 1707, 3681 Imray-Tetra G37

☆ Entrance Fl.G.3s10M/Fl.R.4s10M

Berths Yachts use N pontoon or NE quay.

Shelter Good shelter under E pier.

Facilities Water. Fuel by tanker. Provisions and restaurants.

Remarks Port of entry.

Marina manager ✆ 28310 22408

PALAIOKASTRO

35°21'·27N 25°02'·61E WGS84

New two-basin harbour. Go alongside near the entrance of the N basin. No facilities.

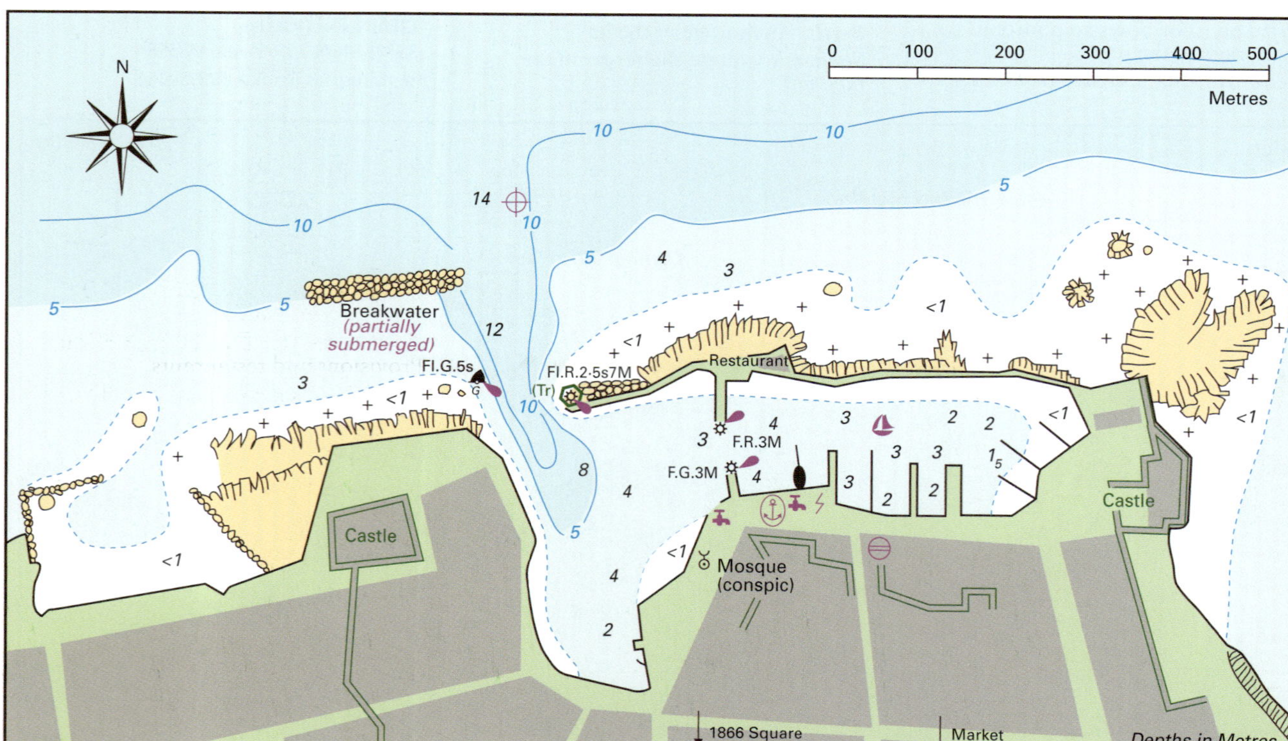

KHANIA

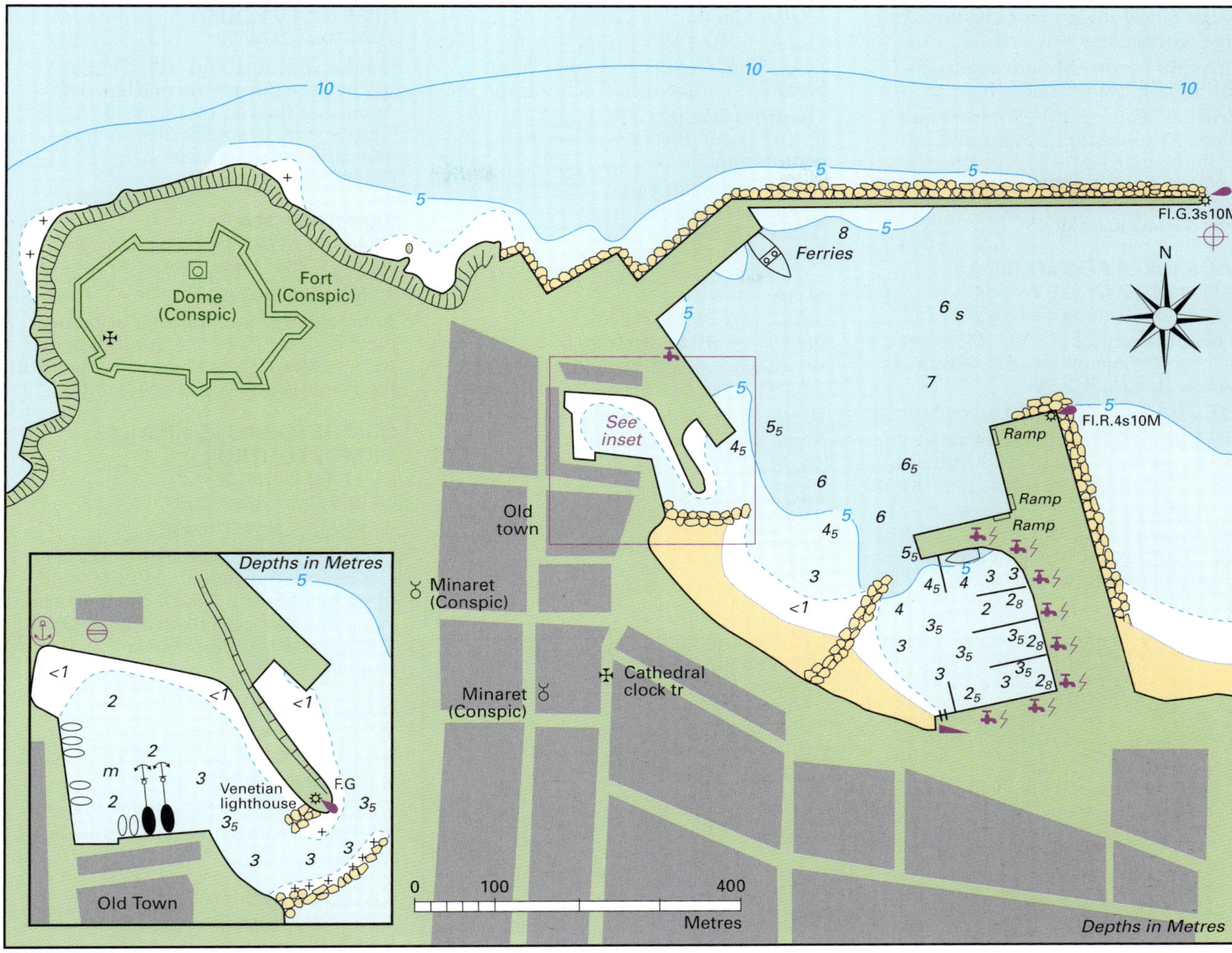

RETHIMNO

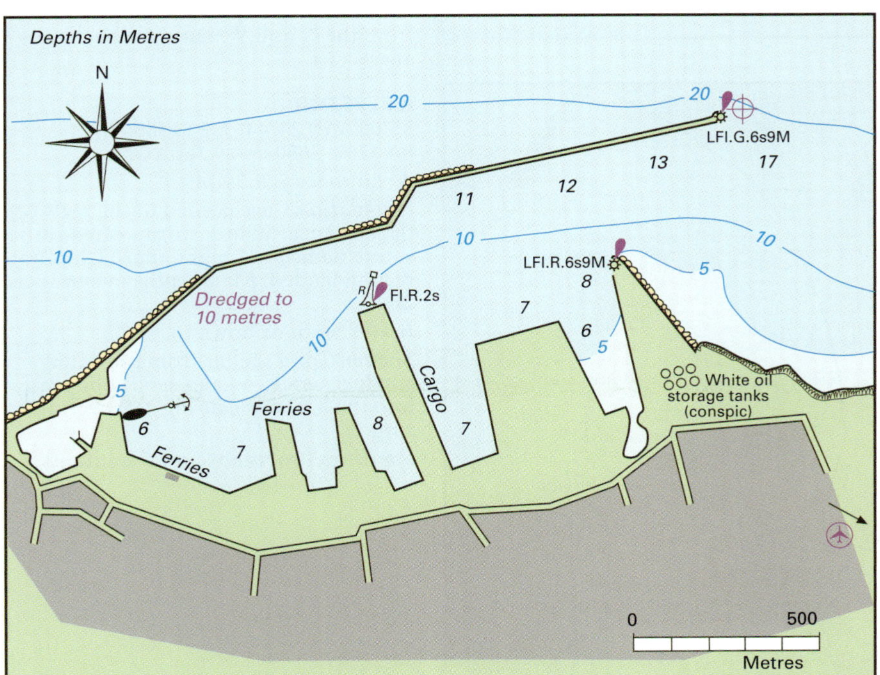

IRAKLION

IRAKLION

35°21′·2N 25°09′·4E (Oc.G light/outer mole head)

BA 1707, 3678 Imray-Tetra G37

☆ Entrance LFl.G.6s9M/LFl.R.6s9M. Airport Aero Al.WG.4s15M

VHF Ch 12 for port authorities.

Navigation Confused swell at the entrance with the *meltemi*.

Berths Stern or bows-to SW quay in outer harbour.

Shelter Good shelter although NE winds cause a surge.

Facilities Water. Fuel by tanker. Yard. Provisions and restaurants.

Remarks Main commercial and ferry port for Crete. Port of entry.

GOUVES MARINA

35°20′·2N 25°17′·8E

Navigation Care needed of extensive shallows off the coast in this region. There are several small harbours to the W of the marina, and another small and shallow harbour close E of the entrance to Gouves marina.

Berth Small private marina. Stern or bows-to. Laid moorings tailed to the quay.

Shelter Good shelter from *meltemi* but surge with strong N winds.

Data c.60 berths. Max draught 3m. Max LOA c.18m. Charge band 2.

Facilities Water. 220V. Showers and toilets. Mini-market, restaurant and bar in the marina.

Gouves Marina ✆ 28970 41112
Email info@portogouves.gr
www.portogouves.gr

ÁYIOS NIKOLAOS MARINA

35°11'·10N 25°42'·99E WGS84
BA 1707, 3678 Imray-Tetra G37

☆ Nisís Mikronísos Fl.3s4M. Mole head Fl.R.2s7M. S mole head Fl.G.3s3M. N mole head Fl.R.3s3M

VHF Ch 12 for Ayios Nikolaos Marina.

Navigation Yachts should head for the marina on the S side of the headland. Yachts drawing more than 2·5m should call ahead.

Berths Stern or bows-to where directed. Laid moorings. Berthing in the old harbour is prohibited to yachts.

Shelter Good.

Data 255 berths. Visitors' berths. Max LOA 50m. Depths 2–4·5m. Charge band 2.

Facilities Water. 220V. Fuel by tanker. 65-ton travel-lift. Provisions and restaurants.

Remarks Port of entry.

Ay Nikolaos Marina
✆ 28410 82384 / 5
Email depaman@otenet.gr

SÍTIA

35°12'·46N 26°06'·70E WGS84
BA 1707, 3679 Imray-Tetra G38

☆ Ak Vamvakiá Fl(3)18s10M. N Mole Fl.G.3s5M. Entrance F.G.3M/F.R.3M

Berths Stern or bows-to in the harbour. Some laid moorings.

Shelter Good shelter from the *meltemi*.

Facilities Water. Fuel on N mole. Provisions and restaurants.

Remarks Port of entry.

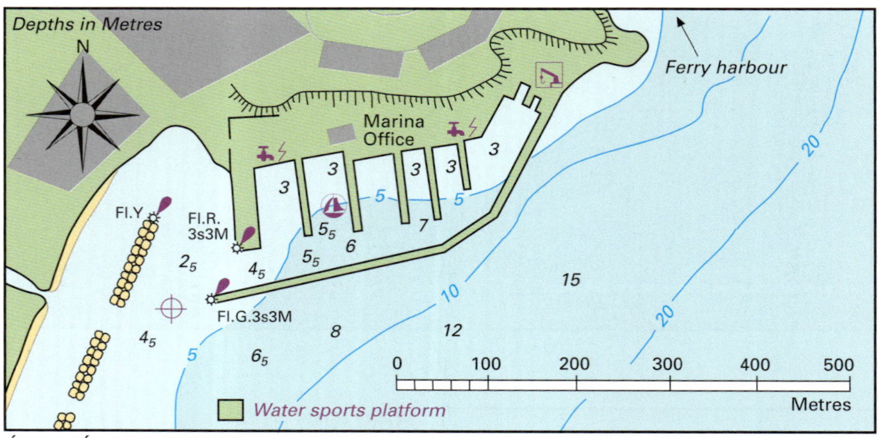

ÁY NIKÓLAOS MARINA

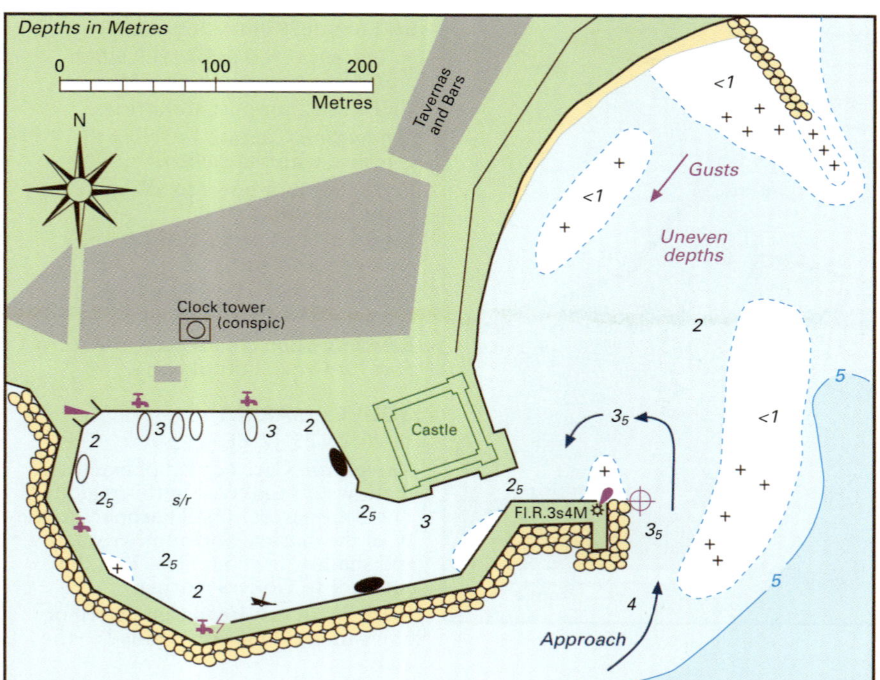

IEREPETRA

NISÍS GRAMVOUSA

35°36'·0N 23°34'·7E

On the SE side of this island there is a bay sheltered from northerly winds. Anchor in the bay on the S side of Nisís Gramvousa. In southerlies anchor under the isthmus formed by Khersonisos Tigani.

PALAIOKHORA

35°13'·4N 23°40'·3E (N. Skhistó light)
BA 1707, 3681 Imray-Tetra G37

☆ Nisís Skhistó Fl.8s8M

An anchorage and harbour lying near the SW tip of Crete. Go alongside or stern or bows-to in the new harbour on the E side of the rocky headland.

ÓRMOS FOINIKIAS AND ÓRMOS LOUTRÓ

35°11'·8N 24°05'·0E
BA 3681 Imray-Tetra G37

☆ Nisís Loutró LFl.10s6M

On either side of Ak Mouros shelter can be found depending on the wind direction. On the W side there is Órmos Foinikias sheltered from NE–E. On the E side there is Órmos Loutró sheltered from N–W–SW.

AY GALINI

35°05'·8N 24°41'·5E (Fl.R.3M)
BA 1707, 3680 Imray-Tetra G37

☆ Mole head Fl.R.3s3M

Small harbour off the village. Open SE–E. Provisions and restaurants in the village.

KALI LIMENES

34°55'·7N 24°48'·3E
BA 1707, 3680 Imray-Tetra G37

☆ Megalonísi Fl(3)20s11M

A small bay on the E side of Ak Litinos. Anchor in the bay where there is shelter from the N and W, but open to the E and S.

IEREPETRA

35°00'·21N 24°44'·33E WGS84
BA 1707, 3680 Imray-Tetra G38

☆ Entrance Fl.R.3s4M

Navigation Care needed of the reefs off the entrance. Winter storms often cause severe damage. A night approach is not recommended. Max depths in entrance 2m.

Berths Stern or bows-to.

Shelter Good shelter from prevailing summer winds. S gales send solid water into the harbour causing a dangerous surge.

Facilities Provisions and restaurants.

Alfamaritime
Yacht charter - Port agent - Travel consultant
• Berthing
• Custom Clearance
• Bunkering
• Provisioning
• Yacht support services
• Travel arrangements
• Tours & Transfers
• Office services
Monitoring VHF Channel 77 call sign 'Alfamaritime'
6, Neorion sq. - P.O.Box 243 - 85100 Rhodes - Greece
Tel: +30 22410 78780 (6 lines) - Fax: +30 22410 39750 - GSM : +30 6944 434 311 (24-hours)
e-mail: maritime@rho.forthnet.gr - www.yachting-greece.net - www.alfamaritime.net
YOUR GREEK CONNECTION

yachtWORKS®
"Your Peace of Mind at Sea"
YACHT MAINTENANCE ~ REPAIR ~ REFIT
Turgutreis
37°00'09"N - 027°15'31"E
Didim
37°20'26"N - 027°15'50"E
Göcek
36°45'36"N - 028°56'31"E
Refit
Engine & generator systems maintenance repairs and overhauling
Marine electric / electronic systems
Full painting and antifouling
Awl Grip Application Center
Teak decking manufacturing and repairs
Stainless steel manufactoring facilities
Rigging service
Ship chandlery
Complete carpentry
Valeting service
Gazi M. Kemal Bulvarı, NO: 48 / A, 48960 Turgutreis - Türkiye • Tel: +90 (252) 382 4445 Fax: +90 (252) 382 7074 • info@yachtworks.info www.yachtworks.info

10.12 Turkey

TIME ZONE UT+2 ✆ IDD +90

The Dardanelles to Istanbul

Gökçeada

KUZU LIMANI
40°13′·8N 25°57′·3E
BA 1608 Imray-Tetra G28
☆ Entrance Fl.G.3s10M/Fl.R.3s10M/F.R.3M/F.G/F.R
Berths Alongside in inner basin.
Shelter Good shelter.
Remarks Ferry port. Village is 7km away.

KABATEPE LIMANI
40°12′·3N 26°15′·9E
BA 2429 Imray-Tetra G28
☆ Entrance Fl.R.5s6M/Fl.G.5s6M

THE DARDANELLES
☆ Kumkale Burnu Fl(2)10s18M

ANIT LIMAN
40°02′·6N 26°12′·1E (Fl(4)R.15s)
☆ Reef Fl(4)R.15s5M. Seddülbahir Fl.3s5M. Harbour F.G.3M/Fl.G.3s3M/F.R.3M

ÇANAKKALE
40°09′·3N 26°24′·4E
BA 2429 Imray-Tetra G28
☆ Kilitbahir Fl.R.3s15M. Çanakkale Fl.RG.3s10M. Ferry pier F.G.3M. Breakwater Fl.G.3s3M. Kösetabya N and S dolphins Q. Jetty head F.R
VHF Ch 16, 17.
Navigation Strong gusts with the *meltemi*. The green conical buoy at the entrance marks a shoal.
Berths Stern or bows-to SW quay. Laid moorings. Charge band 2.
Shelter Adequate in the summer.
Facilities Water. 220V. WC and showers. Fuel. Provisions and restaurants.
Remarks Port of entry. Using an agent to complete clearance is recommended.
Çanakkale Marina ✆ 0286 212 1079

Quick reference guide *For Key see page 139*

	Shelter	*Mooring*	*Fuel*	*Water*	*Provisions*	*Eating out*	*Charge band*
Kuzu Limani	A	B	O	B	O	O	1
Kabatepe Limani	B	AB	O	A	O	C	1
Anit Limani	C	C	O	B	O	O	1
Çanakkale	A	A	B	A	B	B	2
Eceabat	C	A	B	B	C	C	
Gelibolu	B	AC	B	B	C	B	1
Karabíga	B	ABC	B	B	C	C	1
Erdek	A	A	B	A	B	A	2
Port Marmara	A	AB	A	B	C	B	1
Asmaliköy	B	AB	O	B	C	O	1/2
Saraylar	A	AC	B	B	C	C	1
Ilhanköy	B	AB	O	A	C	C	2
Bandirma	A	AB	B	A	A	B	1/2
Zeytinbaği	C	BC	B	A	B	B	1
Mudanya	C	BC	B	A	B	C	
Esenköy	B	C	O	B	C	C	1
Çinarcik	B	A	B	A	B	B	2
Setur Yalova Marina	A	A	A	A	A	A	4/5
Pendik Marina	A	A	A	A	C	B	6
Ataköy Marina	A	A	A	A	C	B	5
Kalamiş Marina	A	A	A	A	B	B	5
West Istanbul Marina	B	A	A	A	B	C	4/5
Istanbul Marina	A	A	A	A	B	B	
Büyükçekmece	C	AC	B	A	C	C	1
Silivri	B	AC	B	B	C	B	1
Marmara Ereğlisi	C	C	B	B	C	C	
Tekirdağ	B	ABC	B	B	B	C	
Hoşköy	A	A	B	B	C	C	
Bozcaada	B	A	B	A	C	B	2
Babakale	B	A	B	B	C	C	2
Sivrice	C	C	O	O	O	O	
Alibey	A	AC	O	B	C	B	1
Setur Ayvalik Marina	B	A	A	A	A	A	4
Dikili	A	AB	B	B	B	B	1
Bademli Limani	A	C	O	O	C	C	
Çandarli	B	C	B	B	B	C	1
Aliağa	B	C	O	O	O	O	
Nemrut Limani	O	C	O	O	O	O	
Yenifoça	B	C	B	B	C	C	
Eskifoça	B	AC	A	A	B	B	1/2
Izmir	B	A	B	A	A	A	1/2
Levent Marina	A	A	A	A	O	C	5
Ildír Körfezi							
Urla Iskelesi	A	A	O	B	B	C	1
Setur Çeşme Marina	A	A	A	A	C	C	5/6
Çeşme Marina	A	A	A	A	B	A	5
Alacati Marina	A	AB	A	A	C	C	4/5
Teos Marina	A	A	A	A	B	B	4
Kuşadasi Marina	A	A	A	A	A	A	4
Didim Marina	A	A	A	A	B	B	4/5
Port Iasos Marina	A	A	B	A	C	C	4
Asin Limani	A	AC	B	A	C	B	1/2
Güllük	C	AB	O	B	B	B	1/2
Torba	A	A	O	B	C	C	1/2
Turk Buku	B	A	B	A	B	A	2
Yalikavak Marina	B	A	A	A	B	A	6
Gümüşlük	B	AC	O	B	C	B	1/2
Turgutreis Marina	A	A	A	A	A	A	5
Ortakent	B	A	B	A	C	B	4/5
Bodrum Marina	A	A	A	A	A	A	5
Cökertme	B	AC	O	A	C	C	
Şehir Adalari	B	C	O	O	O	C	2
Söğüt	B	AC	O	A	C	C	1/2
Değirmen Bükü	A	C	O	B	O	C	
Körmen	A	AC	O	A	C	C	2
Knidos	C	BC	O	O	O	C	2
Datça	B	AC	B	A	A	A	2
Keçi Bükü	A	C	O	A	C	B	
Marti Marina	A	A	A	A	C	C	5
Bozburun	A	AC	B	A	B	B	2
Marmaris	B	AC	A	A	A	A	2
Netsel Marina	A	A	A	A	A	A	5
Yacht Marine	A	A	A	A	C	C	3/4
Ekinçik	B	AC	O	OA	C	C	
Göçek	B	AC	A	A	A	A	5/6
Fethiye Marina	A	A	A	A	A	A	4/5
Kalkan	A	AC	A	A	B	A	4
Kaş Marina	B	A	B	A	A	A	4
Kaş	A	A	B	A	A	A	3/4
Finike Marina	A	A	A	A	B	A	3/4
Cavuş Limani	C	C	O	B	C	C	
Kemer Marina	A	A	A	A	B	A	3/4
Antalya Marina	A	A	A	A	C	C	4/5
Antalya Kaleci Marina	B	A	A	A	A	A	5
Alanya Marina	A	A	B	B	C	C	3/4
Alanya	B	AC	B	A	A	A	
Gazipasa	B	C	O	O	C	C	
Bozyazi Limani	A	AB	O	A	O	O	
Aydincik	A	AC	B	A	C	C	
Yesilovacik	B	AB	B	B	C	C	1
Taşucu	A	A	B	A	B	B	1/2
Kumkuyu	A	A	O	A	C	C	2
Limonlu	B	C	O	O	O	O	
Mersin Marina	A	A	A	A	A	A	3/4
Mersin	A	AC	B	A	A	A	1/2
Iskenderun	A	AC	B	A	A	B	

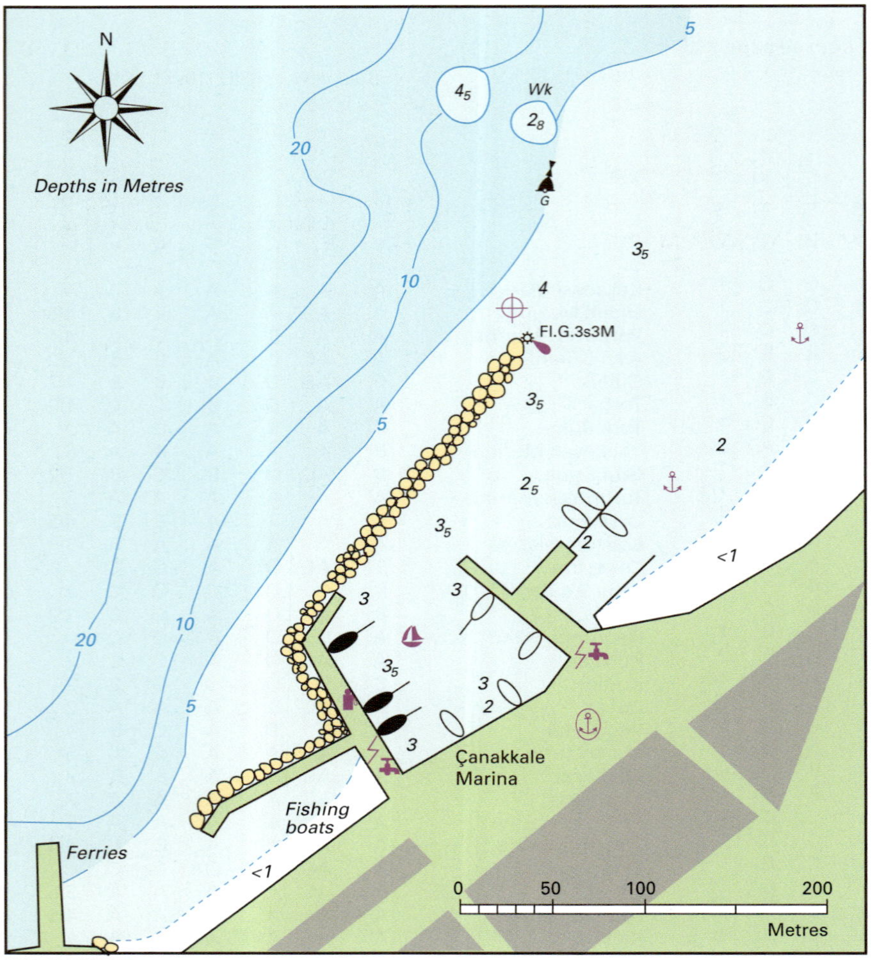

ÇANAKKALE

ECEABAT
40°11′·1N 26°21′·8E

☆ Leading Light 242° Front Oc.2·5s6M Rear Q.6M. Entrance F.R.3M/F.G.3M

LAPSEKI
40°21′·3N 26°41′·5E

A new harbour N of the ferry landing harbour providing alternative mooring to Gelibolu. Care needed of shallows in the approaches from the W–NW with least depths 3m. Once in the harbour a channel to the quay on the E side of the harbour has least depths of 3m. The rest of the harbour is shallow. Go alongside the quay or anchor inside the harbour in convenient depths.

GELIBOLU
40°24′·5N 26°41′·0E
BA 2429 Imray-Tetra G28

☆ Gelibolu Fl.5s15M. Pier F.R

Yachts are no longer permitted to moor anywhere in the harbour. Anchorage in the bay.

Marmara Denizi

ZINCIRBOZAN BANK
☆ Fl.10s7M

DOĞANASLAN BANK
40°29′·8N 26°51′·5E

☆ Q(6)+LFl.15s7M S cardinal beacon YB

A reef and wreck 1M off the coast in the N approaches to the Dardanelles, 6M SW of Ince Burun, 6M NE of Zincirbozan Bank.

KARABÍGA
40°24′·1N 27°18′·6E
BA 224 Tr 2941

☆ Kale Burun Fl.5s8M. Entrance F.G.5M/F.R.5M

Berths Stern or bows-to or alongside.

Shelter Adequate in the summer.

Facilities Some provisions. Restaurant.

ERDEK
40°23′·5N 27°47′·2E
BA 224 Tr 2941

☆ Tavǎn Adasi Fl.10s55m12M. Breakwater head Fl.R.5s6M

Navigation Yachts should not enter the large bay SE of Erdek which is a naval zone.

Berths Stern or bows-to town quay.

Shelter Good shelter.

Facilities Water. Provisions and restaurants.

PAŞALIMANI ADASI
The island lying close to Kapidağ peninsula separated by Narliköy Channel. There are several anchorages around the island.

YIGITLAR
40°29′·.87N 27°31′·62E

Navigation This new harbour lies in Buyuk Liman on the E coast of Avsar Adasi.

Dangers A reef extends for ½M in a NE direction from the end of Buyukliman Burnu in the SE approaches.

Berths Go stern or bows-to or alongside where convenient. The dock in the N corner is used by the Erdek ferry when Turkeli is untenable. Depths of <1–6m have been reported, with shallow areas off the beach and quay on the W side. The bottom is sand and good holding.

Shelter Excellent all-round shelter.

Facilities Water. Fuel in Turkeli. Some repairs. Limited provisions in the village. Market near the mosque on Mondays. Pide restaurant. PO and banks in Turkeli. Ferry to Erdek.

AVSAR RUSBA LIMANI
40°32′·3N 27°30′·4E

A new harbour on Avsar (Turkeli) Adasi, opposite Port Marmara on Marmara Adasi.

Good shelter from the *meltemi*. No facilities. 4km to the village.

Marmara Adasí

PORT MARMARA
40°35′·1N 27°33′·7E
BA 1004 Tr 296 Imray G23

☆ Aba Burun Fl(2)10s5M. Entrance Fl.R.3s10m8M/Fl.G.3s6m8M

Berths Alongside or stern or bows-to.

Shelter Good.

Facilities Water. Fuel. Provisions and restaurants.

Remarks Often crowded with fishing boats.

ASMALIKÖY
40°37′·0N 27°42′·4E
BA 1004 Tr 296 Imray G23

☆ Breakwater head F.G.5m3M

Berths Stern or bows-to or alongside wharf.

Shelter Adequate in the summer.

Facilities Water. Charge band 2.

SARAYLAR
40°39'·5N 27°39'·7E (Fl.G.3s)
BA 224 Tr 2941 Imray G23

☆ Mole head Fl.G.3s7m4M

Berths Stern or bows-to under outer mole or small yachts can go bows-to in fishing harbour.

Shelter Adequate in the summer.

Facilities Limited provisions. Restaurant.

Kapídağ peninsula

ILHANKÖY
40°30'·4N 27°41'·6E

☆ Breakwater end F.R

A small fishing harbour.

Bandírma Körfezi

BANDIRMA
40°21'·6N 27°57'·6E
BA 1006 Tr 2924

☆ Entrance Fl.G.5s10m6M / Fl.R.5s10m10M. S mole 2F.G(vert)2M

Berths Alongside in the E basin or stern or bows-to in the NE corner.

Shelter Good shelter.

Facilities Water. Fuel by tanker. Provisions and restaurants.

Remarks A port of entry.

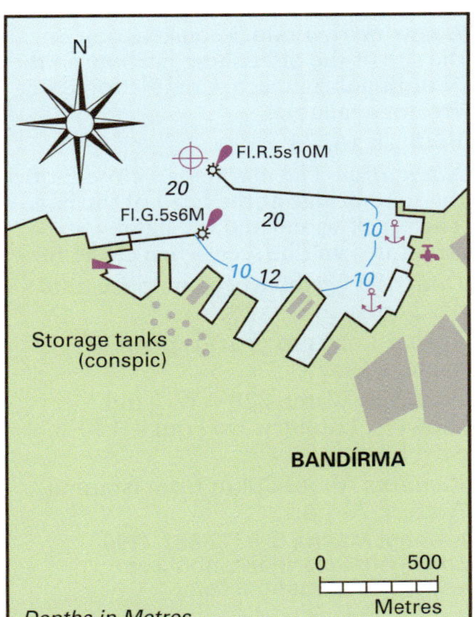

BANDIRMA

ZEYTINBAĞI LIMANI
40°23'·8N 28°48'·2E

A harbour just inside the S entrance point to Gemlik Körfezi. Poor shelter.

MUDANYA
40°22'·6N 28°53'·5E (F.R.2M)
BA 1006 Tr 2924

☆ Arnavutköy Burnu Fl(2)10s30m9M. Mudanya jetty F.R.2M

KATIRLI (ESENKÖY)
40°37'·3N 28°57'·1E

Small harbour affording good shelter.

ÇINARCIK
40°39'·1N 29°07'·8E

☆ Breakwater head F.G.9m3M

Large fishing and ferry port.

SETUR YALOVA MARINA
40°39'·7N 29°16'·4E

VHF Ch 73.

Berths Stern or bows-to where directed. Laid moorings.

Data 265 berths. Max LOA 30m. Depths 2–6m. Charge band 4.

Shelter Good.

Facilities Water. 220V. Showers and toilets. Laundry. WiFi. Waste pump-out. Fuel. 100-ton travel-hoist. Chandler. Bar, restaurant. Close to city centre and ferry port for Istanbul.

✆ 0226 813 1919
Email yalova@seturmarinas.com

ATABAY BOATYARD
40°46'·27N 29°26'·04E

At Gebze. This boatyard has been recommended as giving good service and providing good repair facilities. It is much used by the racing fraternity from Istanbul. 20-ton travel-hoist. Hardstanding. Most yacht repairs can be made.

Atabay Turizm ✆ 0262 655 5854
Email info@atabaymarina.com
www.atabaymarina.com

AYDINLI
40°51'·1N 29°16'·3E

Large harbour offering good shelter from S winds. In N winds anchor off.

RMK Marine (formerly PKM) is a boat-building yard in the harbour. Hauls (and builds) yachts up to 50m. 40/120/320-ton lifts. All yacht repairs.

✆ 216 395 2865
Email info@rmk-yachts.com
www.rmkyachts.com

PENDIK
40°51'·6N 29°15'·2E
BA 497 Tr 291

☆ Harbour entrance Fl.G.5s8M/Fl.R.5s7m8M

Commercial harbour.

PENDIK MARINA
40°52'·0N 29°14'·5E

VHF Ch 73.

A new marina within Pendik harbour.

Data 660 berths. Max LOA 50m. Depths 2–8m. Charge band 6.

Berths Stern or bows-to. Laid moorings.

Shelter Good shelter.

Facilities Water. 220V. WiFi. Showers and toilets. Laundry. Waste pump-out. Fuel quay. 200-ton travel-lift. Repairs. Chandlers. Bars and restaurants.

Remarks Port of entry.

✆ 0216 524 1570
www.seturmarinas.com

PRINCES ISLANDS (PRENSES ADALARI, KIZIL ADALAR)

☆ Balíkçí Adasi Fl(2)10s31m9M. Heybeliada naval harbour F.G.2M/F.R.2M. Su Iskelesi Fl.R.2s7M. Burgaz Adasi Fl.R.3s3M

An archipelago of four major islands and several smaller ones, lying 2–3M off the Asiatic coast in the eastern approaches to the Bosphorus.

MALTEPE BANKI
Opposite Kínalíada an area of shoal water (peppered with a number of reefs) extends out from the mainland coast for 1½M. The extremity of the shoal water is marked by two beacons: Dilek and Yíldíz.

☆ Dilek Kayalíğí Q(6)+LFl.15s8M. Yíldíz Kayaliği VQ(9)10s8M. Bostancí pier Fl.R.2s5m5M

ATAKÖY MARINA
40°58'·22N 28°52'·55E
BA 1198 Tr 292

☆ Airport Aero AlFl.WG.7·5s10M. Yeşilköy Fl(2)10s15M. Entrance F.R/F.R/F.G

VHF Ch 73 (24/24. Callsign *Ataköy Marina*).

Navigation The marina lies 5M SW of the entrance to the Bosphorus and Istanbul.

Berths Stern or bows-to where directed. Finger pontoons. Laid moorings for large yachts.

Shelter Good shelter.

Data 700 berths. Visitors' berths. 100 places in the yard. Max LOA 70m. Depths 4·5–7·5m. Charge band 5.

Facilities Water. 220/380V. WiFi. Satellite TV. Showers and toilets. Fuel quay. 70-ton travel-lift. Larger yachts slipped locally. Most yacht repairs. Provisions. Restaurant.

✆ 0212 560 4270
Email marina@atakoymarina.com.tr
www.atakoymarina.com.tr

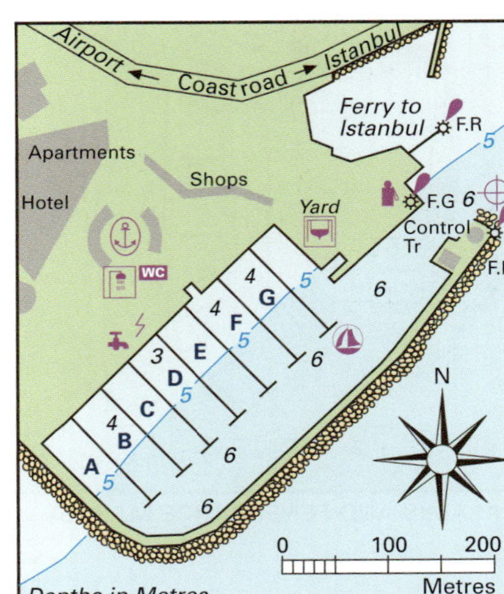

ATAKÖY MARINA

KUMKAPI

41°00'·1N 28°58'·0E
BA 1198 Tr 292

☆ Breakwater head Fl.R.3s10m6M

Small crowded fishing harbour.

SETUR KALAMIŞ MARINA (KALAMIŞ VE FENERBAHÇE)

40°58'·42N 29°02'·15E
BA 1015 Tr 292 Imray G23

☆ Fenerbahçe Br. Fl(2)12s15M. Entrance Fl(2)G.10s6M/Fl(2)R.10s6M. Moda jetty F.R

VHF Ch 72 (Setur Marina).

Navigation The marina lies 4M SE of the entrance to the Bosphorus and Istanbul.

Berths Stern or bows-to. Laid moorings.

Shelter Good shelter.

Data 540 berths in Kalamis. 400 berths in Fenerbahçe. 200 places in the yard. Max LOA 22m. Depths 2–5m. Charge band 5.

Facilities Water. 220/380V. Showers and toilets. Telephone. Fuel by tanker. 70-ton travel-hoist. Some yacht repairs. Provisions and restaurants.

Remarks Limited shower and toilet facilities reported.

Setur Kalamis and Fenerbaçhe Marina
☏ 0216 346 2346
Email kalamis@seturmarinas.com
www.seturmarinas.com

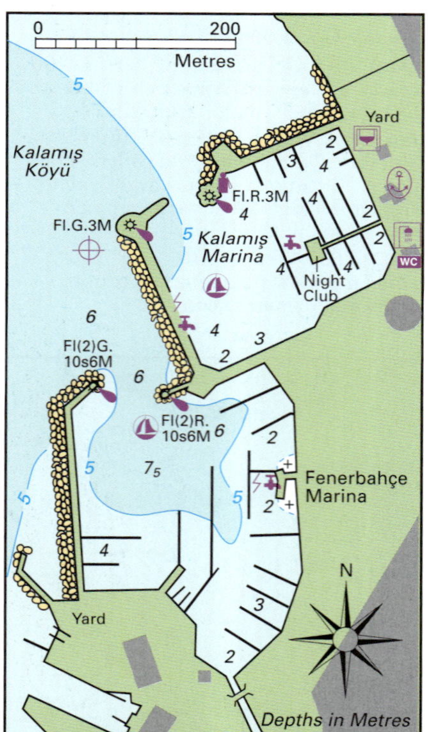

KALAMIŞ AND FENERBAHÇE MARINA

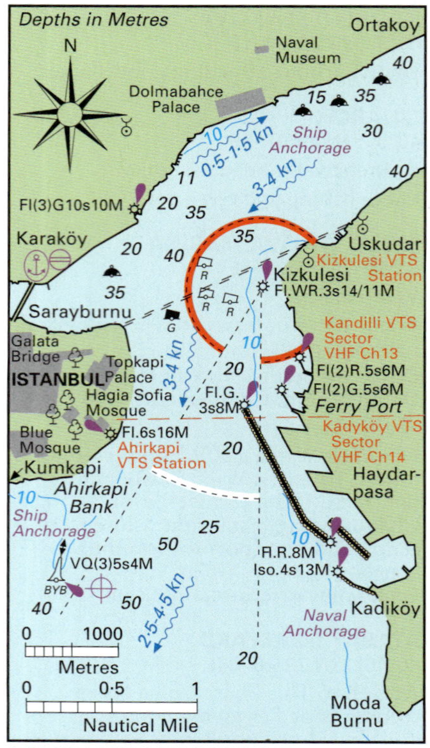

APPROACHES TO ISTANBUL AND THE BOSPHORUS

THE BOSPHORUS (ISTANBUL BOĞAZI, KARADENIZ BOĞAZI)

☆ Fl.6s36m16M. Lightbuoy (wreck) VQ(3)5s8m4M. Salípazari Ríhtímí Fl(3)G.10s13m10M. Kízkulesi Fl.WR.3s11m14–11M

VHF Ch 16, 19 for port authorities. Pilots Ch 16, 71.

Pilotage compulsory for vessels over 300 GRT. Buoyage is arranged from the Black Sea southwards. All buoys conform to IALA system 'A' cardinal markings.

All local traffic including pleasure craft ***must*** monitor the VTS on VHF Ch13/14. Yachts are advised to use the European side when travelling up or down the Bosphorus, the de facto pleasure craft northbound lane, where in places you may find a north-flowing counter-current.

NEW TUNNEL

The new rail tunnel running under the Bosphorus between Uskudar and Saray Burnu opened in October 2013. A new road tunnel is now under construction between Ahirkapi and Haydarpasa.

HAYDARPAŞA

☆ Detached breakwater Fl.G.3s8M/ F.R.8M. Mole head Iso.4s13M. Inner breakwater Fl.R.2s8M / Fl(2)G.6s3M

Ferry port.

North Coast of Marmara Denizi

WEST ISTANBUL MARINA (Ambarli)

40°57'·6N 28°39'·5E

A new marina between Kücükçekmece and Büyükçekmece.

VHF Ch 72.

Navigation Ambarli Liman, the large container terminal immediately E of the marina, and numerous ships at anchor in the vicinity will be seen. Commercial vessels have right of way at all times.

Berths Go stern or bows-to where directed. Laid moorings tailed to the pontoons.

Shelter Good all-round shelter, although some berths may be uncomfortable in strong southerlies.

Data 600 berths. Depths 3–7m. Charge band 4/5.

Facilities Water. 220/380V. Showers and toilets. Laundry. Satellite TV. Waste pump-out. Fuel quay. 75-ton travel-hoist. Stacking system for small craft. Boatyard and technical services. Shops, restaurants and cafés within the development.

Remarks 15km from Istanbul Ataturk Airport.

West Istanbul Marina ☏ 0212 850 2200
Email marina@westistanbulmarina.com

ISTANBUL MARINA

41°00'·9N 28°34'·8E

A new marina under construction on the site of the old fishing harbour in the N of Büyükçekmeçe. Completion dates are not available.

VHF Ch 16, 73.

Navigation The marina lies close E of the road bridge at the head of the bay. The breakwaters and the light structures will be seen when closer in.

Data 595 berths when complete. 200 dry berths.

Shelter Looks to provide good all-round shelter.

Facilities Water. 220V WC and showers. Laundry. Fuel quay. 130-ton travel-hoist.

Remarks About 20km from Istanbul Ataturk Airport.

Istanbul Marina ☏ 0212 882 7190
Email info@marinaistanbul.com
www.marinaistanbul.com

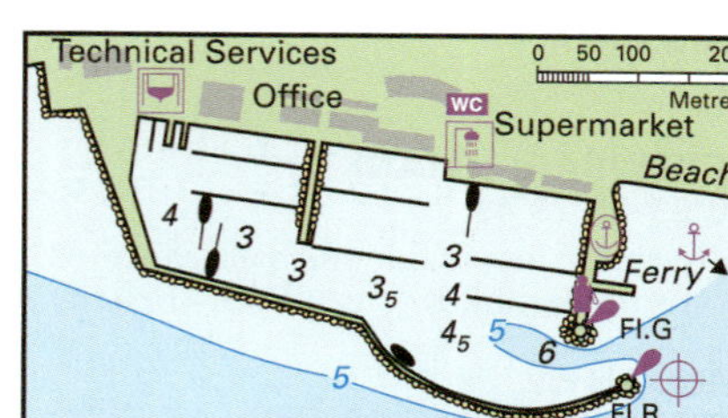

ISTANBUL MARINA - BÜYÜKÇEKMEÇE

BÜYÜKÇEKMECE (MIMARSINAN)
41°00'·9N 28°34'·0E
BA 2286 Tr 2931

☆ Değirmen Burnu Fl.5s10M. Breakwater head F.R.2M

Commercial and fishing harbour.

GUZELCE MARINA (MIMARSINAN WEST HARBOUR)
40°59'·8N 28°30'·6E

VHF Ch 72.

Berths Go stern or bows-to where directed. Laid moorings tailed to the pontoons.

Shelter Good all-round shelter.

Data 250 berths. Max LOA 60m. Depths 1·5–5m. Charge band 4.

Facilities Water. 220/380V. Showers and toilets. WiFi. Fuel by mini-tanker. 500-ton travel-hoist. 120 places ashore. Boatyard and associated technical services.

Remarks 25km from Istanbul Ataturk Airport.

Guzelce Marina ☽ 0212 868 3908
Email info@guzelcemarina.com

SILIVRI
41°04'·4N 28°14'·3E
BA 1005

☆ Entrance Fl.G.5s6m5M/Fl.R.5s6m5M. Jetty F.R.2M

Berths Alongside SW mole. Anchorage in the bay.

Shelter Good shelter from the *meltemi*.

Facilities Fuel nearby. Provisions.

MARMARA EREĞLISI
40°58'·4N 27°57'·9E (Bn)

☆ Main light Fl.10s52m16M. Kilkaya Rocks Bn Q(3)10s8M

Large open bay. Poor shelter.

TEKIRDAĞ
40°58'·4N 27°31'·1E

☆ Pier F.R.3M. Harbour entrance F.G/F.R

Small harbour under commercial pier.

HOŞKÖY
40°42'·6N 27°18'·8E

☆ Fl(2)10s50m19M/F.R

Small fishing harbour prone to silting.

Dardanelles to Çeşme

BOZCAADA LIMANI
39°50'·2N 26°04'·5E
BA 1608 Tr 2131 Imray-Tetra G28

☆ Tavşan Adasi Fl.WR.5s14/10M. Beşiğe Burnu Fl.3s15M. Esek Adalarí Fl.3s8M. Mermer Burnu Fl.5s10M. Harbour entrance Fl.R.3s3M/Fl.G.3s3M

Navigation Care needed of currents which set SW–W to the N of Bozcaada.

Note The breakwater has been extended by 60m and a black conical buoy Fl.G lies 40m off the end of the breakwater extension.

Berths Stern-to on the new wider N breakwater. Some laid moorings. Charge band 2.

Shelter Adequate shelter from the *meltemi*.

Facilities Water. 220V. Fuel by mini-tanker. Provisions and restaurants.

BABAKALE
39°28'·36N 26°04'·08E WGS84

☆ Baba Burun Fl(4)20s18M

Extended fishing harbour under Baba Burun.

Yachts berth stern-to on the NW quay, keeping clear of the trawler berths to the S. Care needed of shoal patches in the N of the harbour. Otherwise good depths at the yacht berths. Good shelter from the *meltemi*, albeit a bit gusty at times. Water on the quay.

Harbourmaster. Charge band 2.

SIVRICE
39°28'·1N 26°14'·6E (Sivrice Burnu light)

☆ Sivrice Burnu Fl(2)10s16m15M

Large bay offering reasonable shelter. Open S.

Ayvalik archipelago
BA 1675 Tr 2145 Imray-Tetra G27

DALYAN BOĞAZI

☆ Fener Burnu Fl.R.3s18m8M. Korkut Br. (Rowley Point) Fl.3s7M. Channel beacon lights: N side VQ(6)+LFl.15s7M. Three pairs Fl.R.3s5M/Fl.G.3s5M

ALIBEY
39°19'·9N 26°39'·4E
BA 1675 Tr 2145 Imray-Tetra G27

☆ Breakwater head F.R.3M

Berths Bows-to N quay. Anchorage under breakwater.

Shelter Good shelter.

Facilities Provisions and restaurants.

SETUR AYVALIK MARINA
39°18'·87N 26°41'·28E WGS84
BA 1675 Tr 2145 Imray-Tetra G27
30M Babakale ←→ Bademli Limani 24M

☆ Entrance Fl.G.3s10m5M/ Fl.R.3s10m5M

VHF Ch 73. Callsign *Setur Marina*.

Berths Stern or bows-to where directed. Laid moorings.

Data 200 berths. Visitors' berths. Depths 3–4m. Charge band 5.

Facilities Water. 220V. Showers and toilets. Fuel quay. 80-ton travel-hoist. Yacht repairs. Provisions and restaurants.

Remarks Port of entry.

Setur Ayvalik Marina ☽ 0266 312 2696
Email ayvalik@seturmarinas.com
www.seturmarinas.com

DIKILI
39°04'·15N 26°53'·12E WGS84
Tr 2141 Imray-Tetra G27

☆ Mole head F.R.9m4M

Berths Stern or bows-to or alongside mole.

Shelter Good shelter from the *meltemi*.

Facilities Water. Provisions and restaurants.

Remarks A port of entry.

BADEMLI LIMANI
39°01'·2N 26°47'·9E (Fl.WR.3s Pisa Br)
BA 1618 Tr 2141 Imray-Tetra G27
24M Ayvalik ←→ Foça 23M

☆ Pise Burun Fl.WR.5s31m7/4M (240°-W-102°-R-120°-W-140°-R-156°-W-175°)

Several anchorages around the islets.

Note An underwater cable runs across from the mainland to Kalem Adasi approximately halfway down the island in position 39°00'·33N 26°47'·89E WGS84.

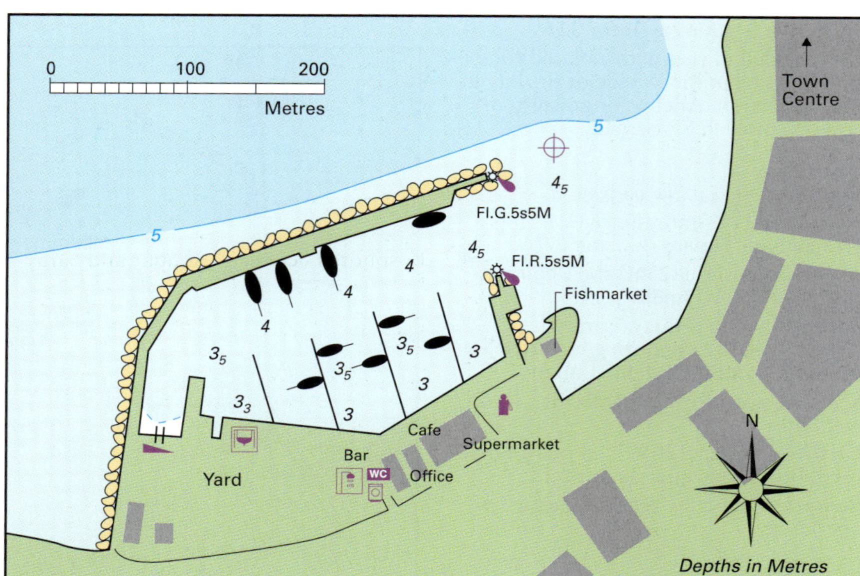

SETUR AYVALIK MARINA

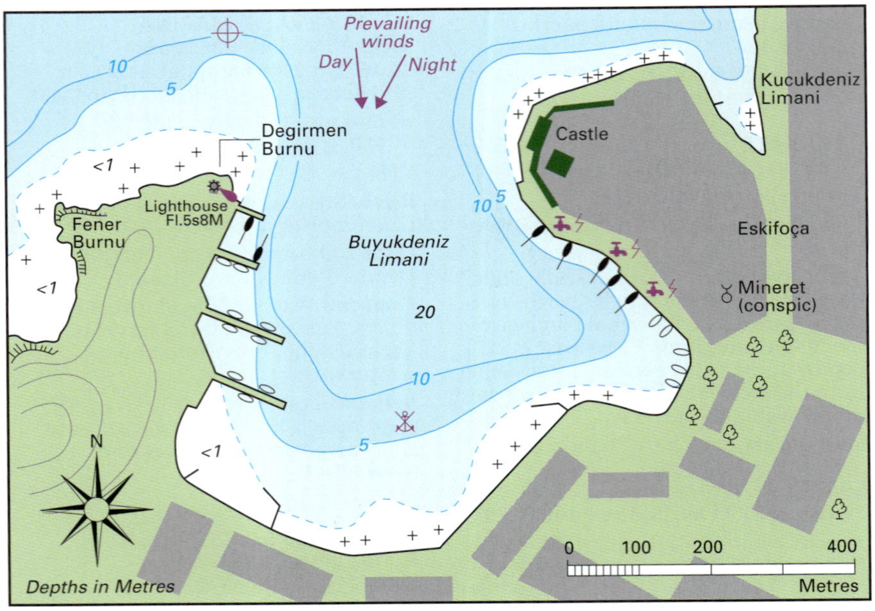

ESKIFOCA

ÇANDARLI
38°55'·44N 26°56'·34E WGS84
BA 1618 Tr 2149 Imray-Tetra G27

Berths Anchorage on the E side of headland affords the best shelter.
Facilities Provisions and restaurants.

ALIAĞA LIMANI
38°50'·2N 26°56'·7E
BA 1618 Tr 2147 Imray-Tetra G27

☆ Entrance Q.G.11m10M/Q.R.8m8M. Jetty F.R

Industrial/oil refinery. Port of refuge.

NEMRUT LIMANI
☆ Habaş jetty F.R Çukurova jetty F.R. Metaş jetty F.R. Landing F.R.3M. Tank F.R.3M. Petkim Refinery F.R.7m2M/F.R

Oil refinery.

YENIFOÇA
38°44'·50N 26°50'·32E WGS84
BA 1618 Tr 2149 Imray-Tetra G27

Care needed of reef with isolated rock extending from the W side of the bay in a NE direction. Anchor or go stern or bows-to mole in SE corner.

ESKIFOÇA
38°40'·19N 26°44'·89E WGS84
BA 1618 Tr 2149 Imray-Tetra G27
23M Bademli Limani ←→ Izmir 27M

☆ Fener Adasí Fl.5s25m12M. Değirmen Burnu Fl.R.3s17m8M

Berths Bows-to E quay. Limited visitors' berths. Anchoring reported prohibited in Büyükdeniz Limani.
Shelter Uncomfortable with the *meltemi*.
Facilities Water. 220V. Fuel quay. Small yard. Provisions and restaurants.
Remarks Fuel quay reported not operating.

Izmir Körfezi

IZMIR
38°25'·4N 27°07'·6E
BA 1522 Tr 2212 Imray-Tetra G28

☆ Channel buoys Fl.R.3s5M/Fl.G.3s4M. N entrance Fl.G.3s7M/Fl.R.3s2M S entrance Fl(2)R.7M

VHF Ch 12, 14 for port authorities.
Berths Stern or bows-to.
Shelter Uncomfortable with the *meltemi*.
Facilities Water. Fuel nearby. Provisions and restaurants.
Remarks A port of entry.

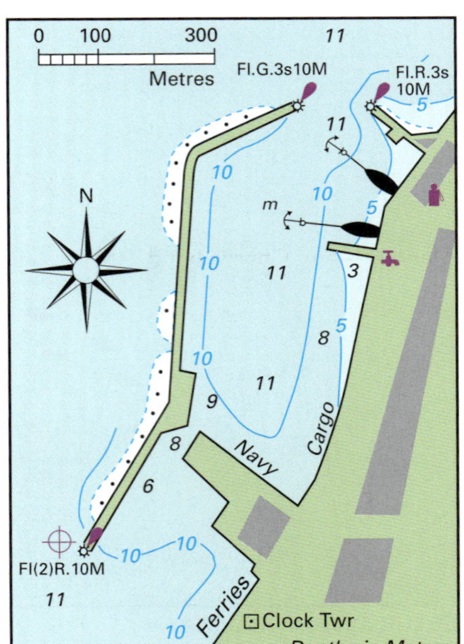

IZMIR OLD HARBOUR

LEVENT MARINA
38°24'·39N 27°04'·14E WGS84

☆ Entrance Fl.R/Fl.G

VHF Ch 16, 73 (Levent Marina).
Berths Where directed.
Shelter Good shelter.
Data 100 berths. Max LOA 25m. Depths 2–6m. Charge band 5.
Facilities Water. 220V. Showers and toilets. Fuel. Some yacht repairs. Restaurant.
✆ 0232 259 7070
Email info@levantmarina.com.tr

URLA ISKELESI
38°22'·0N 26°46'·4E (F.G.3M)
BA 1058 Tr 221 Imray-Tetra G27

☆ Breakwater head F.G.7m3M/Q

Fishing harbour. Good shelter from the *meltemi*.

MORDOĞAN
38°31'·1N 26°37'·6E

☆ Fl.G.5s5M/Fl.R.5s5M

Fishing harbour.

MORDOĞAN YENI LIMANI
38°30'·69N 26°38'·02E WGS84

Large new harbour. Berth alongside where convenient. Good shelter. No facilities.

Ildír Körfezi

SETUR ÇEŞME MARINA
38°19'·5N 26°20'·8E
BA 1058 Tr 222 Imray-Tetra G28

☆ Entrance F.G/F.R

VHF Ch 16, 73 (*Setur Marina*).
Berths Where directed. Some laid moorings.

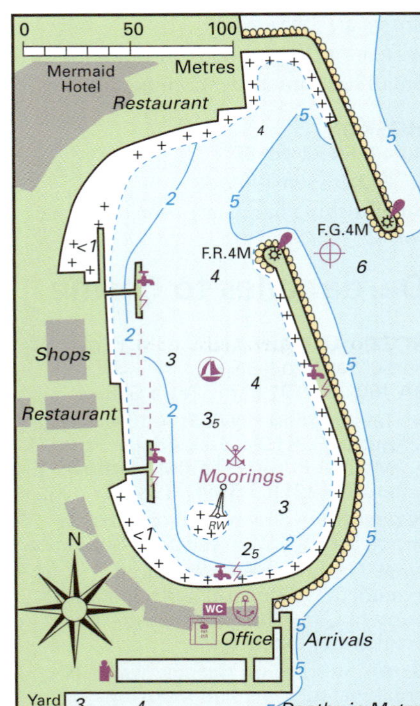

SETUR ÇEŞME MARINA

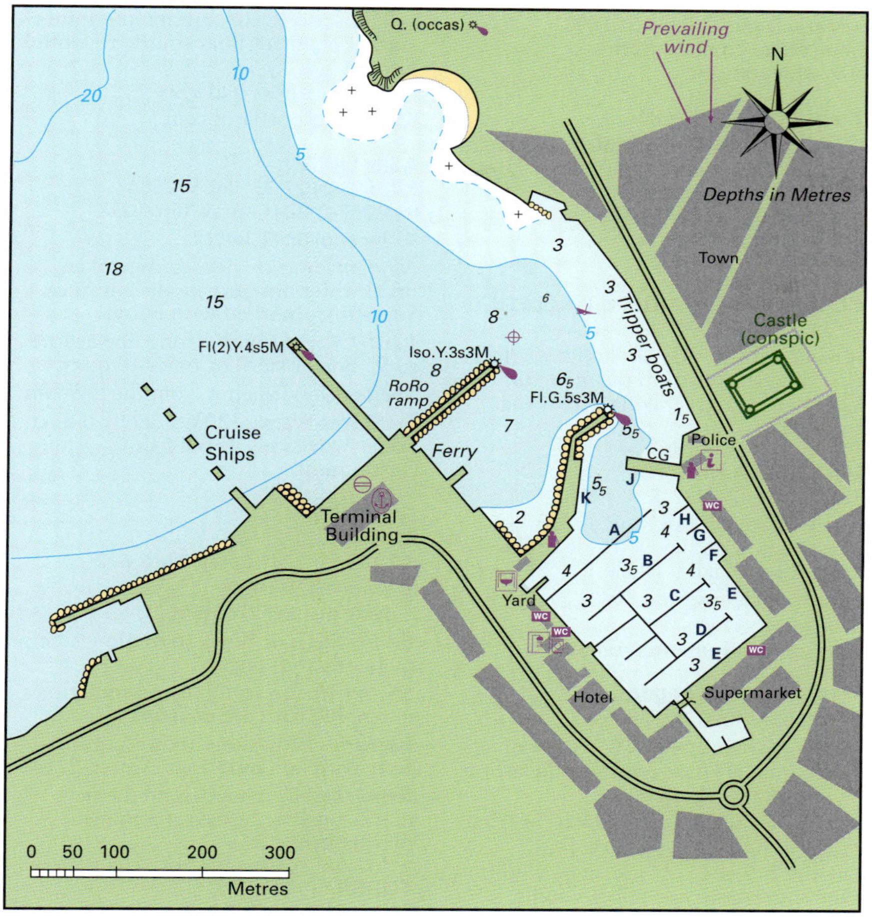

ÇEŞME MARINA

Shelter Good shelter.
Data 180 berths. Limited visitors' berths. Max LOA 35m. Depths 2–5m. Charge band 5/6.
Facilities Water. 220V. Showers and toilets. Fuel quay. 60-ton slipway. Some yacht repairs. Some provisions. Restaurants.
Remarks Port of entry.
Setur Çeşme Marina
✆ 0232 723 1434 / 1631
Email cesme@seturmarinas.com
www.seturmarinas.com

ÇEŞME MARINA

38°19'·40N 26°17'·98E WGS84
BA 1058 Tr 222 Imray-Tetra G28
21·5 Karaburun ←→ Kuşadasi 59M
☆ Kaloyeri Sigleri Fl.5s9m5M. Fener Burnu Fl.3s8M. Entrance Fl.G.5s3M

VHF Ch 72.
Berths Berth where directed. Laid moorings.
Shelter Much improved with new breakwater extension.
Data 400 berths. Max LOA 60m. Charge band 5.
Facilities Water. 220V. Fuel. Waste pump-out. 80-ton travel-lift. Provisions and restaurants in the town.
Remarks Port of entry.
✆ 0232 712 2500
Email info@cesmemarina.com.tr

Çeşme to Güllük Körfezi

AGRILER LIMANI (ALAÇATI KÖRFEZI)

38°13'·5N 26°23'·4E
BA 1058 Tr 22 Imray-Tetra G28
☆ Bozalan Burnu Fl(2)5s33m7M

ALICATI MARINA

38°15'·23N 26°23'·22E WGS84
Navigation Care needed of shoal water on W and N shores of Agriler Limani. Marina entrance may be liable to silting.
Berths Stern or bows-to where directed. Laid moorings.
Data c.260 berths. Max LOA 35m. Depths 2–4m. Charge band 4/5.
Facilities Water. 220V. Fuel. WiFi. 100-ton travel-lift. Restaurant. Mini-market.
Remarks Windsurfing centre nearby.
Port Alacati Marina
✆ 0232 716 9760
Email marina@portalacati.com.tr

SIĞAÇIK TEOS MARINA

38°11'·68N 26°46'·93E WGS84
BA 1057 Tr 2231 Imray-Tetra G28
☆ Eşek Adasí Fl.10s5M. Harbour entrance Fl.R.2M/F.G/Fl.G

Navigation Care needed of reef off N end of Eşek Adasí.

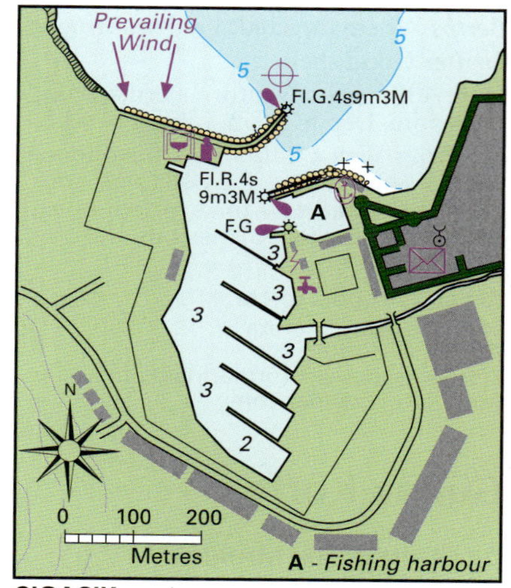

SIGACIK

Berths Yachts berth on the pontoons stern or bows-to where directed. Laid moorings.
Shelter Good shelter.
Data 450 berths.Depths 2–3m. Charge band 4.
Facilities Water. 220V. Showers and toilets. Laundry. Fuel quay. Waste pump-out. 75-ton travel-lift. Repairs. Provisions and restaurants.
Remarks Port of entry.
Teos Marina
✆ 0232 745 8080
Email marina@teosmarina.com

SETUR KUŞADASI MARINA

37°52'·1N 27°15'·6E
BA 1057 Tr 2231 Imray-Tetra G32
59M Çeşme ←→ Bodrum 71M
☆ Güvercin Adasí Fl(2)10s20m8M. Marina entrance E breakwater Fl(2)G.4s8m5M. W breakwater Fl(2)R.4s12m5M.

VHF Ch 16, 73 (0700–1000 / 1200–1500) for port authorities and pilot. Marina, (callsign *Setur Marina*). Ch 16, 73 (summer 0830–2400, winter 0830–1800).

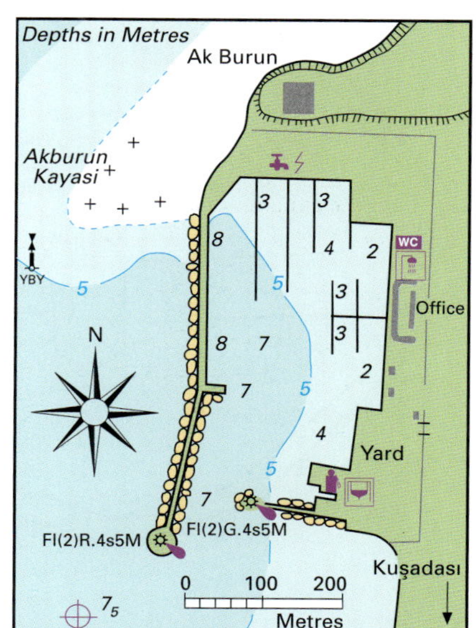

SETUR KUŞADASI MARINA

Berths Where directed. Laid moorings.
Shelter Good shelter.
Data 400 berths. Visitors' berths. Max LOA 55m. Depths 2·7m. Charge band 4.
Facilities Water. 220/380V. Telephone. Showers and toilets. Fuel quay. 80-ton travel-hoist and 150-ton synchro-hoist. Most yacht repairs. Provisions and restaurants.
Remarks A port of entry.
Setur Kuşadasi Marina
✆ 0256 618 1460
Email kusadasi@seturmarinas.com
www.seturmarinas.com

Güllük Körfezi

D-MARIN DIDIM MARINA
37°20'·22N 27°16'·01E WGS84
☆ Fl(2)R.4s3M/Fl(2)G.4s3M
The marina is easy to identify on the headland 4M E of Tekebağ Burnu, and 1M SW of the gulet quay at Altinkum.
VHF Ch 72, 16 (D-Marin Didim).
Berths Stern or bows-to. Laid moorings. A marina RIB will meet you and help you to moor.
Shelter Good all-round shelter.
Data 580 berths. Visitors' berths. Max LOA 70m. Depths 3–10m. Charge band 4/5.
Facilities Water. 220/380V. WiFi. Waste pump-out. Showers and toilets. Fuel quay. 400/75-ton travel-lift. 40-ton hydraulic trailer. 600 places ashore including indoor storage. Chandlers. All repairs can be arranged. Café, Yacht Club restaurant and supermarket in the marina. ATM. Taxis. Car hire.
Remarks Port of entry.
D-Marin Didim ✆ 0256 813 8081
Email didim@d-marin.com
www.d-marin.com

Yachtworks
Professional yacht maintenance, repairs and servicing. Bases in Didim, Turgutreis and Goçek.
Can Sürekli ✆ 0252 813 5244
Email info@yachtworks.info
www.yachtworks.info

ALTINKUM (KARAKUYU ISKELESI)
37°21'·3N 27°17'·2E
A bay on the N side of Güllük Körfezi affording shelter from the *meltemi*. Care needed of reef lying across the entrance.

MANDALYA MARINA
37°19'·97N 27°28'·71E WGS84
A new 'boutique' marina under construction on the west side of the entrance to Kazikli Iskelesi.
Due to open in spring 2015.
✆ 0538 730 3700
www.mandalyamarina.com

PORT IASOS MARINA
37°14'·8N 27°32'·3E
A new marina in the NW corner of Gok Limani. Three pontoons lie off the W side of Gok Limani.
VHF Ch73 (callsign Port Iasos Marina)
Data 50 berths. Max LOA 25m. Depths 2–9m. Laid moorings. Good shelter from the prevailing winds. Charge band 4.
Facilities Water and electricity at all berths. WiFi. Showers and toilets. Fuel by mini-tanker. Restaurant and mini-market planned. Boat shuttle to Gulluk. Taxi.
Port Iasos ✆ 0541 760 4241
Email info@portiasos.com

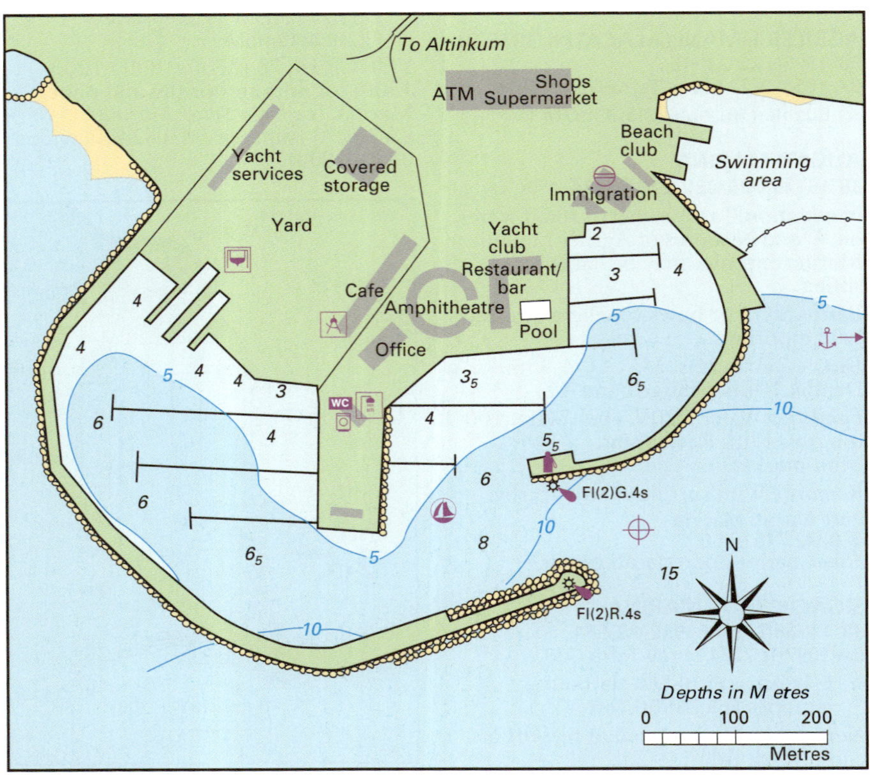

DIDIM MARINA

ASIN LIMANI
37°16'·39N 27°35'·04E WGS84
BA 1057 Tr 2241 Imray-Tetra G32
☆ Incegöl Br. Fl.3s12M
Navigation Care needed of sunken breakwater obstructing the entrance. Sometimes marked with buoys.
Berths Anchor with a long line ashore to W side or stern or bows-to quay.
Shelter Good shelter from the *meltemi*.
Facilities Water. 220V. Fuel by tanker. Some provisions. Fresh fish. Restaurants.

GÜLLÜK
37°14'·4N 27°35'·8E
BA 1057 Tr 2246 Imray-Tetra G32
☆ S side Fl(2)5s18M.
Jetty head Fl(2)Y.8s5M
Berths Stern or bows-to or alongside quay or cargo pier.
Shelter Uncomfortable and sometimes untenable with the *meltemi*.
Facilities Provisions and restaurants. Jetty with laid moorings. Water. 220V.
Remarks The team behind the new marina at Port Iasos is planning a marina here.

TORBA
37°05'·3N 27°27'·15E
A small harbour affording shelter from the *meltemi*.

TURK BÜKÜ (GOLTURKBÜKÜ)
37°07'·74N 27°22'·72E WGS84
Berths Go stern or bows-to the new 'yacht quay' along the outside of the fishing harbour breakwater where directed. Care needed of ballasting off the quay in places. Laid moorings tailed to the quay.
Facilities Water. Provisions and restaurants.
Remarks Laid moorings also in the bay.

PALMARINA YALIKAVAK MARINA
37°06'·40N 27°16'·92E WGS84
☆ Buyuk Kiremit Is. Fl(2)10s89m10M.
Marina Fl.G.5s5M / Fl.R.5s5M
VHF Ch 16, 72
Navigation Care needed of reef in the approaches.
Berths Where directed. Laid moorings.
Data Visitors' berths. Max LOA 45m. Charge band 6.
Facilities Water. 220/380V. WiFi. Showers and toilets. Laundry. Fuel quay. 100-ton travel-hoist. 40-ton trailer. Repairs.
Remarks Port of entry.
Palmarina Yalikavak Marina
✆ 0252 311 0611
www.palmarinayalikavak.com.tr

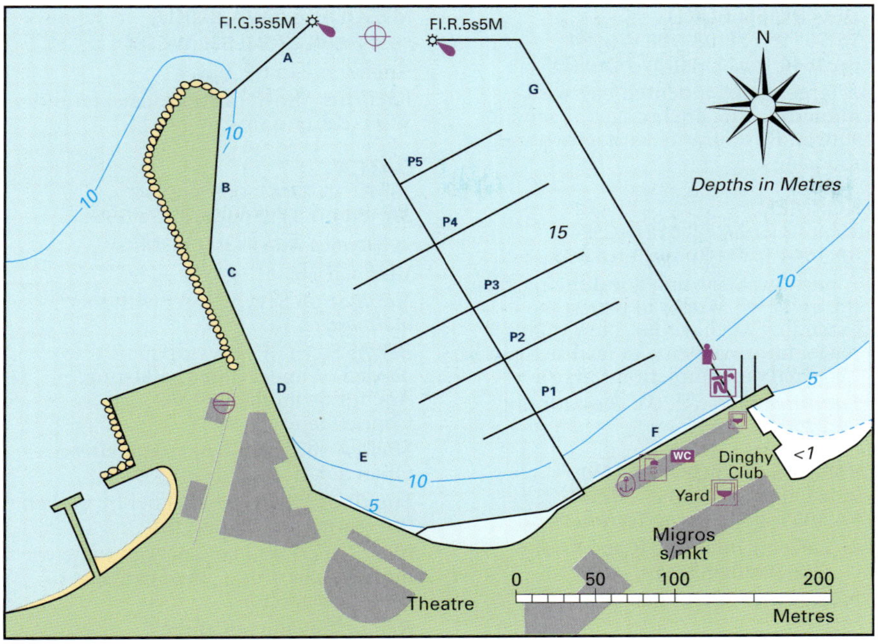

PALMARINA YALIKAVAK MARINA

Gümüşluk to Marmaris

GÜMÜŞLÜK

37°02'·96N 27°13'·72E WGS84
BA 1644 Tr 2248 Imray-Tetra G35

An inlet affording reasonable shelter from the *meltemi*. Care needed of submerged mole in the entrance.

TURGUTREIS MARINA

36°59'·89N 27°15'·30E WGS84
☆ Marina entrance Fl.R.5s/Fl.G.5s

VHF Ch 16, 72 (*D-Marin*)

Navigation The marina lies immediately SE of the fishing harbour at Karatoprak (Turgutreis).

Berths Berth where directed. Finger pontoons. Laid moorings for large yachts (c.+14m).

Data 550 berths. Visitors' berths. Max LOA 50m. Depths 3–8m. Charge band 5.

Facilities Water. 220/380V. WiFi. Showers and toilets. 100-ton travel-lift and repair facilities. Duty-free fuel. Customs and port procedures. ATM. Provisions and restaurants. Ferry to Kos.

Remarks Care is needed of the shallows off the coast and the reefs and islets around Catalada.

D-Marin Turgutreis ✆ 0252 382 9200
Email turgutreis@d-marin.com
www.d-marin.com

ORTAKENT

37°01'·2N 27°20'·8E WGS84

A new small harbour at the N end of Baglar Koyu in the coastal development known as Yali. The basin lies on the west side of a canalised river.

VHF Ch 77.

Berths stern-to where directed by the harbourmaster. Laid moorings tailed to the quay. There are 2·5–3m depths in the outer harbour, shallowing towards the inner berths. Mooring blocks reduce depths in places. Good shelter from the prevailing wind. Showers and toilets. Water and electricity. Charge band 4/5.

MILTA BODRUM MARINA

37°01'·88N 27°25'·44E WGS84
BA 1644 Tr 311 Imray-Tetra G35
71M Kuşadasi ←→ Marmaris 82M

☆ Karada Fl(2)5s5M. Dikilitas reef (Harentem) Q(6)+LFl.15s6M. Entrance Fl.R.5s8M / Fl.G.5s8M.

VHF Ch 73 (24hr). Callsign *Milta Bodrum Marina*. Call ahead for a berth.

Navigation Care needed of Dikilitas Kayasi (S cardinal) in the approaches.

Berths Where directed. Laid moorings tailed to the quay. Usually crowded.

Shelter Good shelter.

Data 450 berths. Max LOA 75m. Depths 2–6m. Charge band 5.

Facilities Water. 220/380V. WiFi. Telephone. Showers and toilets. Waste pump-out. Fuel quay. 70-ton travel-lift. Most yacht repairs. Provisions and restaurants.

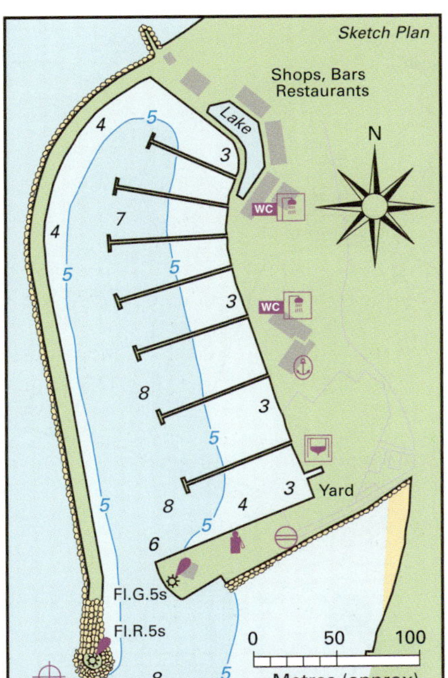

TURGUTREIS MARINA

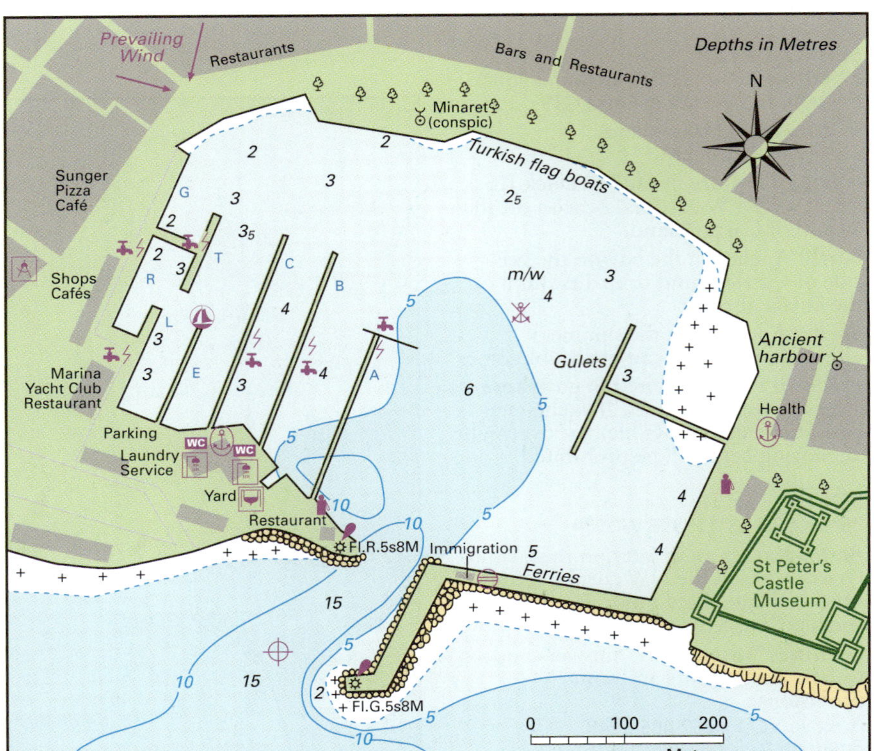

BODRUM - MILTA BODRUM MARINA

Remarks A port of entry.
Milta Bodrum Marina
✆ 0252 316 1860
Email info@miltabodrummarina.com
www.miltabodrummarina.com

Boatyards

At Içemeler SE of Bodrum there are a number of boatyards.

Yat Lift ✆ 0252 316 7842
Email yatlift@yatlift.com
www.yatlift.com
VHF Ch 69 (callsign *Yatlift*)

Betas Agency can arrange hauling and repairs.

✆ 0252 316 1697

COKERTME (FESLEĞEN KÖYÜ)

36°59′·96N 27°47′·52E WGS84

A bay affording shelter from the *meltemi* although there are strong gusts into it.

Various private jetties:
Kaptan Jetty and Restaurant
Laid moorings. Water. 220V. Fuel. Toilet and shower. Mini-market. Restaurant.

✆ 0252 521 0012

Rose Mary Pirate Yachting
Laid moorings. Water. 220V. Fuel. Mini-market. Bar restaurant.

✆ 0252 531 0158 / 9
Email mahirvurmaz@superonline.com
www.rmpirate.8m.com

GOKOVA OREN MARINA

37°01′·55N 27°58′·52E

A new marina under construction close E of the village. Completion due late 2014.

Data 500 berths. Max LOA c.30m.

Facilities All facilities, waste pump-out, fuel, travel-lift, mini-market and restaurant planned.

Email info@gokovaorenmarina.com.tr

ŞEHIR ADALARI

37°00′·0N 28°12′·3E (Snake Island light)
BA 1644 Tr 3111 Imray-Tetra G35

☆ Orta Ada (Snake Island) Fl.WR.10s15m9M

Navigation Care needed of Duck Rock, a reef with a W cardinal beacon off the W end of Castle Island.

Berths Anchor in the bay on the NE side of Castle Island or in Tas Bükü on the adjacent coast.

Shelter Adequate in the summer although NE winds can be troublesome.

Remarks It is prohibited to go ashore after the warden leaves. If yachtsmen persist it is quite possible that overnight anchoring here will be prohibited.

SÖĞÜT

36°56′·92N 28°11′·39E WGS84

Berths Karacasöğüt jetty on the S shore. Gokova YC in the NW corner. Jetties off the village. Laid moorings. Good shelter. Charge band 3/4

Facilities Water. 220V. Showers and toilets. Restaurants and some provisions.

Gokova YC ✆ 0252 465 5148
Email gsc@globalsailing.org
www.globalsailing.org

DEĞIRMEN BÜKÜ

36°56′·18N 28°08′·79E WGS84
BA 1644 Tr 3111 Imray-Tetra G35

A large, much indented bay with numerous safe anchorages around its shores. Restaurants with jetties and moorings.

KÖRMEN

36°46′·31N 27°37′·01E WGS84
BA 1644 Tr 311 Imray-Tetra G35

A harbour affording good shelter from the *meltemi*. Works in progress extending the harbour. New quays in place. Improvements in facilities can be expected on completion (2015).

Facilities Water. 220V. Restaurant. Ferry to Bodrum.

KNIDOS (BÜYÜK LIMANI)

36°41′·01N 27°22′·65E WGS84
BA 1055 Tr 311 Imray-Tetra G35

☆ Deveboynu Burnu (Cape Krio) Fl(2)10s104m12M

Navigation Severe gusts with the *meltemi*.

Berth Alongside on the T-jetty, rafting up if necessary. Anchor with long line ashore if possible.

Shelter Just adequate with the *meltemi*. Open S.

Facilities Water. 220V (after 2000hrs) Restaurant.

PALAMUT

36°40′·17N 27°30′·37E WGS84

Small fishing harbour with yacht berths. Depths 1–3m. Water. 220V. Restaurants and provisions in the village. Charge band 2.

Note Entrance and harbour dredged regularly.

MESUDIYE (OVA BÜKÜ)

36°40′·86N 27°34′·58E WGS84

Anchorage in the bay.

Facilities Showers and toilets. Laundry. WiFi. Restaurants.

DATÇA

36°43′·1N 27°41′·06E WGS84
BA 1644 Tr 3112 Imray-Tetra G35

☆ Uzunca Ada Fl.3s10m3M

VHF Ch 16.

Navigation Severe gusts with the *meltemi*.

Berths Stern or bows-to quay. Care needed of underwater ballasting. Anchorage in the bay W. Charge band 3.

Shelter Adequate from the *meltemi*. Open S.

Facilities Water. 220V. Fuel by tanker. Provisions and restaurants.

Note *Gulets* will lay anchors some way out when berthing. Take care not to foul their anchors.

Remarks A port of entry.
Datça Marina
✆ 0252 712 1098 / 712 1920

DATCA MERMAID MARINA

36°43′·1N 27°41′·5E

A new marina under development close S of Datca town.

No dates for completion are available.
www.datcamermaidmarina.com

KEÇI BÜKÜ

36°46′·70N 28°06′·98E WGS84
BA 1644 Tr 311 Imray-Tetra G35

Berths Stern or bows-to catwalks at S end. Anchorage in the bay.

Shelter Good shelter.

Facilities Water. 220V. Provisions and restaurants.

Remarks Anchoring in the bay.

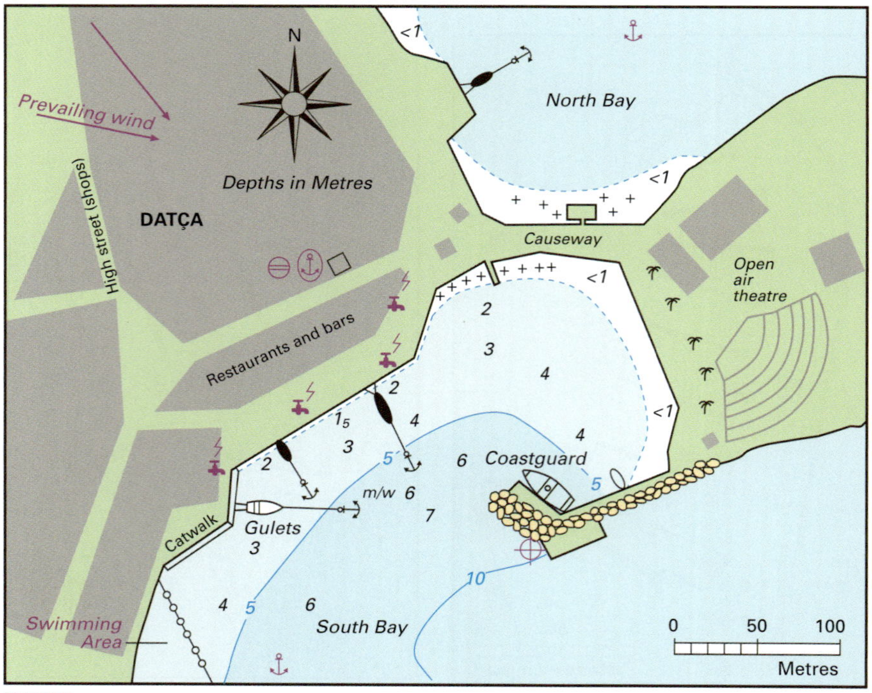

DATÇA

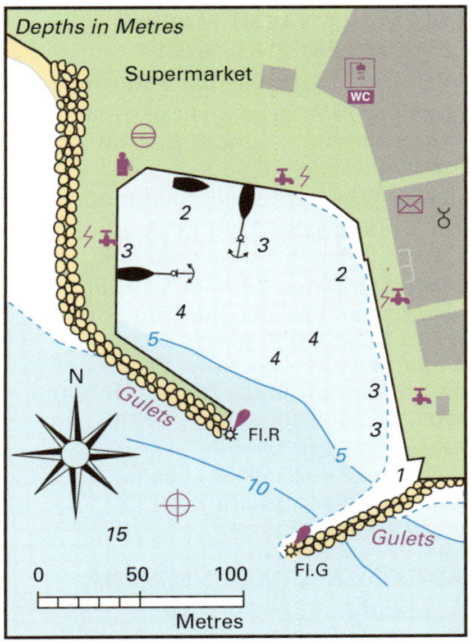

BOZBURUN

MARTI MARINA

36°46'·20N 28°07'·50E WGS84

☆ Fl.R.5m3M/Fl.G.5m3M

VHF Ch 16, 73 (callsign *Marti Marina*).

Navigation The marina lies on the E side of the entrance to Keçi Bükü.

Berth Where directed.

Shelter Excellent shelter except berths on outside of outer pontoons.

Data 300 berths and 80 dockyard capacity. Depths 3–20m. Charge band 5.

Facilities Water. 220/380V. WiFi. Showers and toilets. Fuel quay. 60-ton travel-hoist. Yacht repairs. 24-hour security. Supermarket. Restaurant and bar. Free shuttle service to and from Marmaris.

Marti Marina
✆ 0252 487 1064 / 65 / 67
Email marina@marti.com.tr
www.martimarina.com

BOZBURUN

36°41'·43N 28°02'·52E WGS84
BA 1055 Tr 311 Imray-Tetra G35

☆ Entrance Fl.G/Fl.R

Navigation Care needed of Atabol Kayasi reef in the outer approaches.

Berths Stern or bows-to. Charge band 2.

Shelter Good shelter.

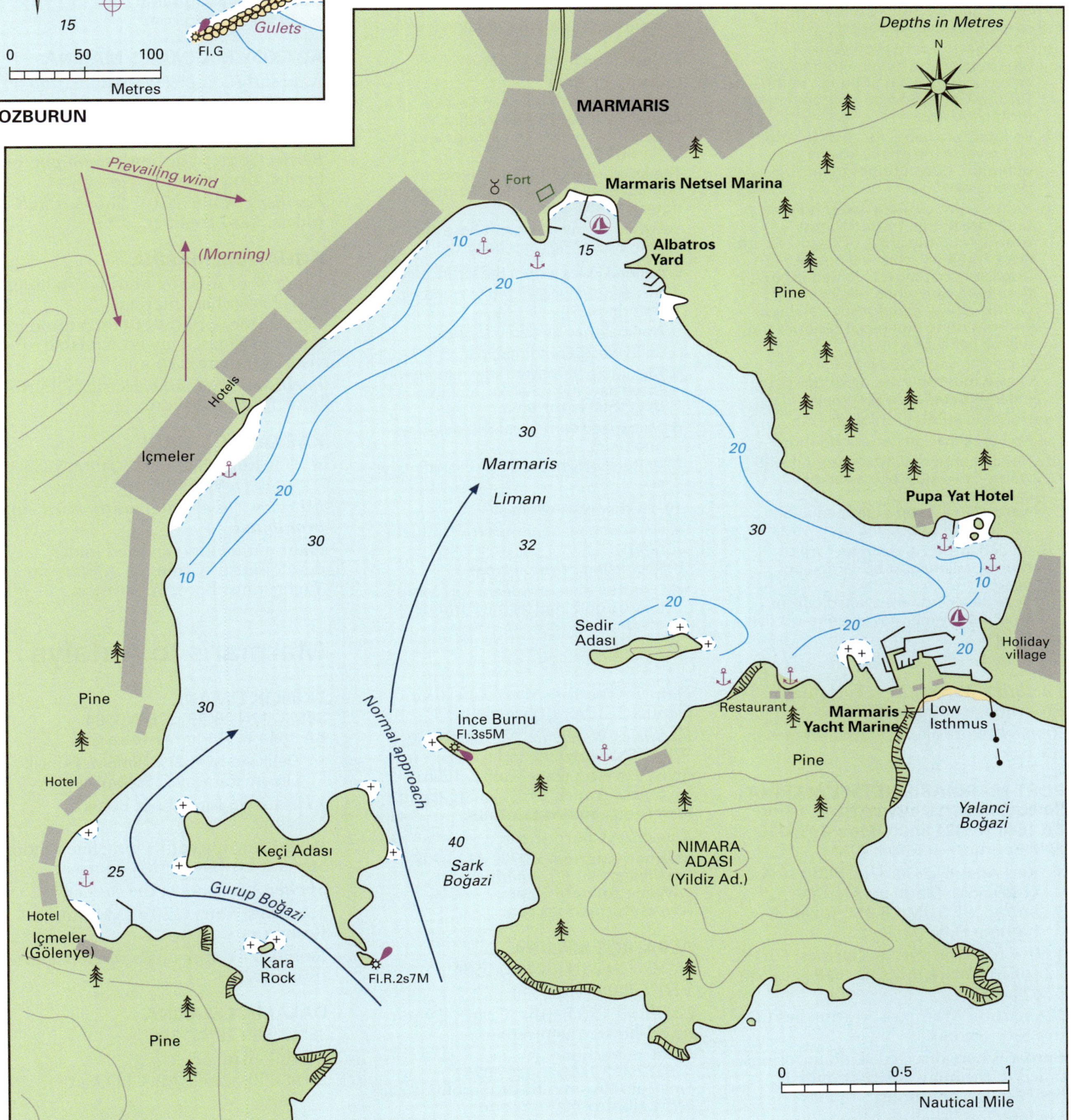

APPROACHES TO MARMARIS

FETHIYE-GÖÇEK SPECIAL ENVIRONMENTAL PROTECTION AREA

Below is an abridged translation of the latest regulations concerning yachts within the SEPA of Fethiye-Göçek. Further restrictions for trip boats, cargo vessels and diving also apply. This is our interpretation of the regulations, and is as accurate as possible, but it does not replace the original Turkish document as the definitive reference.

Ministry of Environment and Forests 04.05.10 number 2540 publication *Principles to Protect the Gulf of Göçek and the Coves in the Göçek/Dalaman region.*

Section 5

These regulations apply to the entire area except where specified.

a. The objective is to protect the biodiversity and the environmental values and to avoid pollution in the Fethiye-Göçek Special Environmental Protection Area

b. Polluters are liable for costs to stop and reverse the effects of any pollution. Costs of fines to be determined

c. Yachts without black water holding tanks are not permitted to stay overnight in the areas of restricted use
Note Foreign yachts will not be inspected, but must be able to show their blue card when asked, and if yachts remain here for several days without using pump-out facilities they will be liable to a fine

c. No anchoring in restricted areas – vessels must only use moorings in the areas as detailed in Section 8

d. Noise pollution prohibited

e. No barbecues on deck or on shore

f. No discharge of waste water or solid waste – this must be passed to collection vessels
Note Waste water is defined as black water, bilge water, and grey water.

g. All documents and digital card to control waste must be carried on board
Note Blue cards are available from most nearby marinas at a one-off cost of 70TL

6. Area prohibited for diving:
area enclosing Kapidag Yarimadasi and most of Skopea Limani

7. Area prohibited to all vessels:
Hammam Köyü (Ruin Bay)

8. Restricted Areas

a. No Anchoring N of a line E-W across the N end of Göçek Adasi

Note There are two ship anchorages within the area

b. Protection of Posidonia sea grass beds

Vessels are prohibited from anchoring, but may secure to mooring buoys and bollards or eye-pads on shore, in the following areas:

- Göçek Adasi NW corner and bay on NE side of Gocek Ad. light
- Tersane Creek
- Corner between 22 Fathom Cove and Seagull Bay
- inner Sarsaya Köyü including Pilloried Cove
- Deep Bay (Siralibuk Köyü)

c. Overnight stays

Anchoring is prohibited in Yassica Adalari including Zeytinli Adasi. All vessels must only use moorings and bollards.

The area around Dil Burnu is out of bounds to all but trip boats during the hours of 1000–2000.

Yachts may stay overnight here, but must only use moorings and bollards.

9. General Rules within the entire area:

a. Vessel numbers limited to numbers of moorings

b. No lines may be taken to trees

c. Solid waste container locations

d. Maximum permitted stay is limited to three days in one place, and max. 11 days total in the area

e. Max speed 6kns in roadsteads, bays and coves

f. Watersports permitted – excluding jet skis

10. Further restrictions

a. Fuel can only be transferred at fuel quays

b. Restriction of vessel types

c. Exceptional permission (short term) may be obtained by the harbour office.

Facilities Water. 220V. Fuel quay. Provisions and restaurants.

Remarks Port of entry. Anchorages in the bay.

PORT MARMARIS NETSEL MARINA

36°50'·91N 28°16'·58E WGS84
BA 1644 Tr 3121 Imray-Tetra G35, G36
82M Bodrum ←→ Göçek 47M

☆ Keçi Adasi Fl.2s30m7M. Yildiz Adasi Fl.3s9m5M. Marmaris Marina entrance F.G.3M/F.R.3M. Town harbour Fl.R

VHF Ch 16 for port authorities. Ch 06, 72 for Marmaris Marina (callsign *Port Marmaris*).

Navigation Marmaris Marina lies in the N of the bay.

Berths Where directed. Laid moorings tailed to the quay. Space is tight between the pontoons.

Shelter Good shelter.

Data 750 berths. Max LOA 40m. Depths 2–12m. Charge band 5.

Facilities Water. 220V. Telephone. WiFi. TV. Showers and toilets. Fuel quay. 100-ton travel-hoist. 12-ton hydraulic trailer. Most yacht repairs. Provisions and restaurants.

Remarks A port of entry.

Marmaris Marina ✆ 0252 412 2708
Email netsel@netselmarina.com
www.netselmarina.com
www.seturmarinas.com

ALBATROS MARINA

36°50'·72N 28°17'·07E WGS84

VHF Ch 06, 16.

Facilities 150 berths. Crane. 20-ton travel-hoist. Yacht repairs.

Albatros Yachting
✆ 0252 412 2456 / 3430 / 0752
Email albatrosmarina@superonline.com
www.albatrosmarina.com

MARMARIS YACHT MARINE

36°49'·26N 28°18'·61E WGS84

VHF Ch 72 (callsign *Yacht Marina*).

Navigation A large yacht marina on the isthmus joining Nimara Adasi to the mainland.

Berths Where directed. Laid moorings.

Data 600 berths. Max LOA 60m. Depths 3–8m. Charge band 3/4.

Facilities Water. 220/380V. WiFi. Showers and toilets. Fuel. 60/330-ton travel-hoist. 1000 places ashore. Chandlers. Most repairs. Provisions and restaurant in the marina. Bus and ferrty to Marmaris town (8km).

Marmaris Yacht Marine
✆ 0252 422 0022 / 0054 / 0063
Email info@yachtmarin.com
www.yachtmarin.com

ADAKOY MARMARIS MARINA

A recently completed small marina on the site of the former Pruva Marina boatyard, close W of Marmaris Yacht Marine.

Berths Go stern or bows-to on pontoon berths. Laid moorings.

Facilities Water. 220V. Showers and toilets. Yard facilities.

AQUARIUM MARINA

Close W of Adakoy Marina is a hotel and charter base marina.

Berths Stern or bows-to on pontoons. Laid moorings. May be available to visitors if there is room.

Facilities Water and electricity. Further hotel facilities ashore.

KARAAGAC LIMANI

☆ Fl.R.3s6M. Fl.G.3s6M. Q10M. Yilancik Adasi Fl.WR.5s10/7M

Military Zone – all unauthorised entry prohibited.

Haul-out facility reported under development within the military area. Yachts must book in advance.

Marmaris to Antalya

EKINÇIK LIMANI

36°49'·12N 28°33'·27E WGS84
BA 1644 Tr 311 Imray-Tetra G36

☆ Delik Adasi Fl(2)5s35m8M. Ekinçik Limanı Karaçay Fl.5s40m5M

VHF Ch 06 for tripper boats to Caunos.

Berths Anchor with a long line ashore. Stern or bows-to at My Marina.

Shelter Adequate in the summer.

Facilities Water. 220V (My Marina). Restaurants.

Remarks Tripper boats run to Caunos from here.

DALAMAN MARINA

36°40'·48N 28°47'·39E

Marina planned.

Data 650 berths. Max LOA 60m.

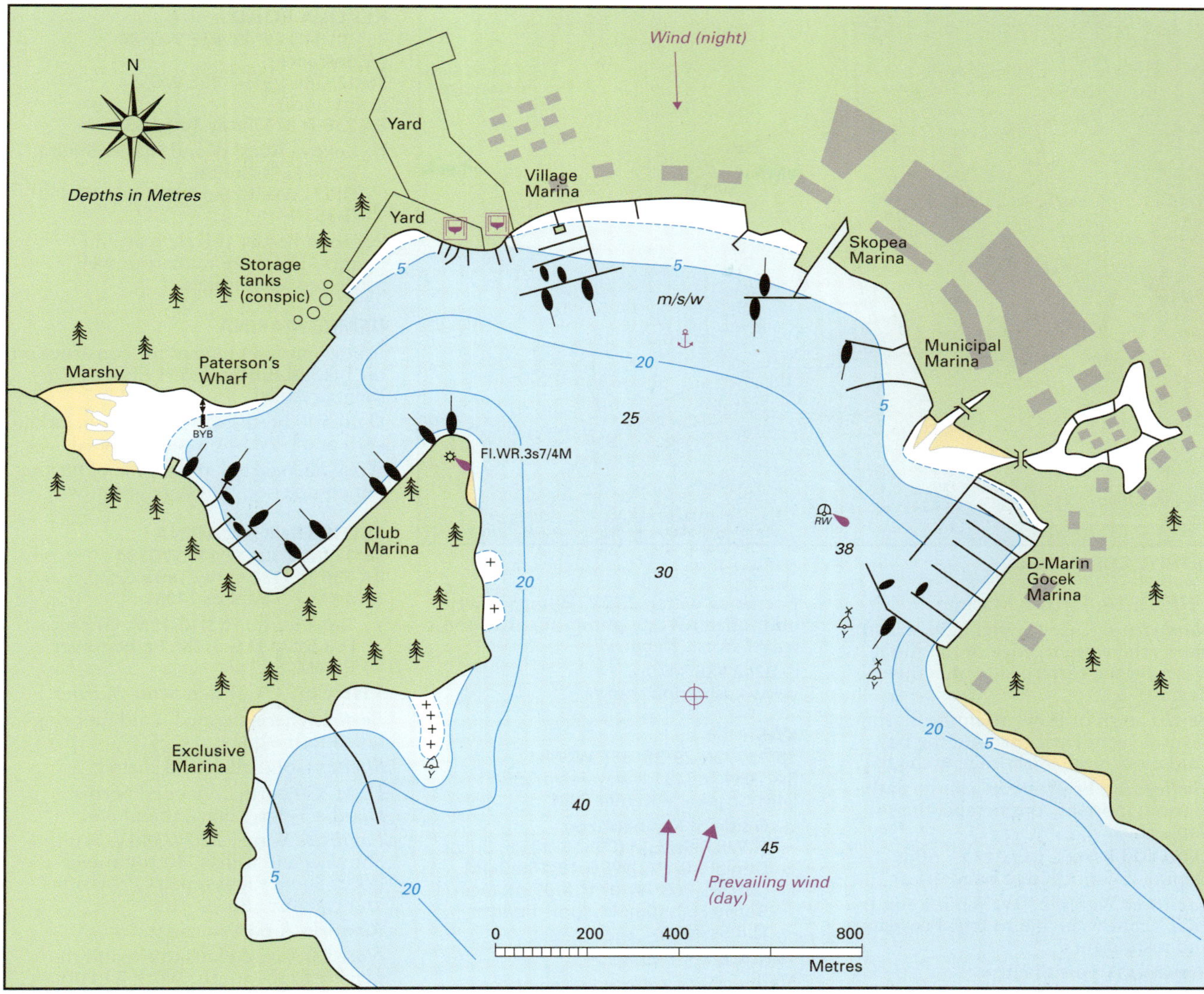

GÖCEK

Facilities All the usual facilities will be available. Travel-hoist planned. 500 places ashore. Five minutes to Dalaman airport.
www.d-marin.com

Fethiye Körfezi

GÖÇEK

36°44′·98N 28°56′·17E WGS84
0·25M E of Göçek Adasi light
BA 1644 Tr 313 Imray-Tetra G36
47M Marmaris ←→ Kaş 54M

☆ Göçek Adasí Fl(2)10s12m8M. Göçek Island southeastwards Fl(2)10s7m5M. Göçek light Fl.WR.3s15m7/4M (326°-R-314°)

VHF Ch 13 for Municipal Marina. Ch 72 for Club Marina (callsign *TAL207 Club Marina*) and Skopea Marina. Ch 73 for Village Marina, D-Marin Göçek Marina and Göçek Exclusive.

Berths Stern or bows-to where directed at any of the marinas.

Shelter Adequate at the Municipal, Village and Skopea Marinas. Good shelter at Club Marina.

Data Municipal Marina 140 berths. Depths 1·5–4m. Charge band 4.
Göçek Belediye Marina ✆ 0252 645 1938
Email marina@gocekmarina.net

Skopea Marina c.50 berths. Max LOA 80m. Depths 2–5m. Charge band 5.
✆ 0252 645 1794
Email info@skopeamarina.com

Village Marina 150 berths. Max LOA 50m. Depths 1–5m. Charge band 5.
✆ 0252 645 2229
www.seturmarinas.com

Club Marina 160 berths. Depths 2–7m. Max LOA c.80m. Charge band 5.

Facilities Water. 220/380V. Waste pump-out. Fuel quay. 200/70-ton travel-lifts. Yacht repairs. Provisions and restaurants.
✆ 0252 645 1800 *Fax* 0252 645 1804
Email info@clubmarina.com.tr
www.turkeyclubmarina.net

GÖÇEK MARINA

36°44′·92N 28°56′·43E WGS84

VHF Ch 73 (*D-Marin Göçek*).

Navigation Situated on the E side of Göçek Bay.

Berth Where directed. Laid moorings tailed to the quay, or finger pontoons.

Shelter Good shelter.

Data 375 berths. Max LOA 45m. Charge band 5/6.

Facilities Water. 220/380V. WiFi. Showers and toilets. 70-ton travel-hoist. Yacht repairs. Bar and restaurants. Provisions.
D-Marin Göçek ✆ 0252 645 1520
Email gocek@d-marin.com

GÖÇEK EXCLUSIVE MARINA

New superyacht facility on the S side of the peninsula on the W side of Göçek harbour.

VHF Ch 73.

Data c.50 berths. LOA 18–100m.
✆ 0252 645 2229
www.seturmarinas.com

FETHIYE ECE MARINA

36°37′·48N 29°05′·97E WGS84
BA 1644 Tr 313 Imray-Tetra G36

☆ Batikkaya VQ.5M. Fethiye Adasi Fl.R.3s3M. Light buoy LFl(9)30s. Wreck buoy Fl.G(occas).

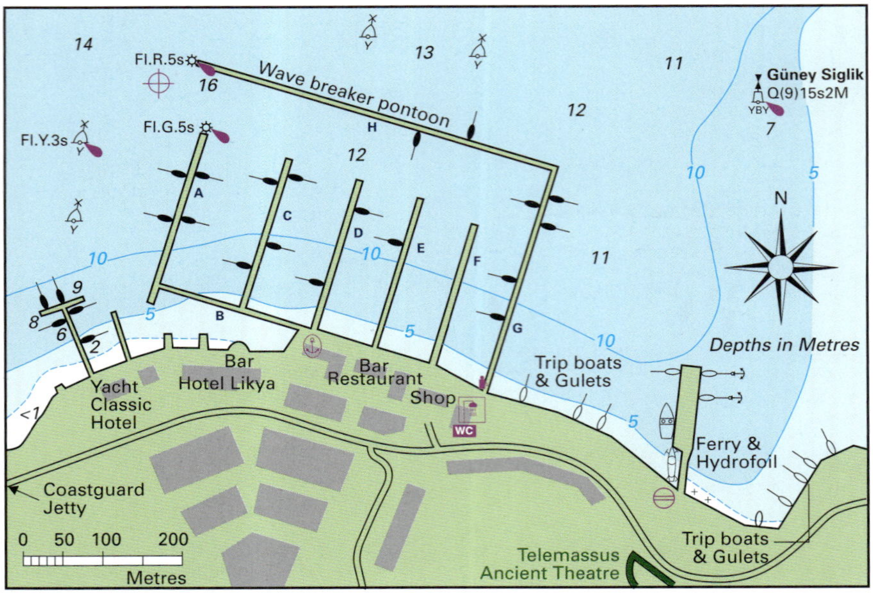

FETHIYE ECE MARINA

VHF Ch 16, 73 (Ece Marina).

Navigation Kuzey Siğliği light structure marks the western edge of the shoal water on the eastern side of Fethiye Bay.

Berths Stern or bows-to in the marina. Several yacht jetties around the bay. Laid moorings. Anchorage in the bay.

Shelter Can be prone to a surge in the marina, more uncomfortable than dangerous.

Data 400 berths. Max LOA 60m. Depths 2–5m. Charge band 4/5.

Facilities Water. 220V. WiFi. Laundry. CCTV. Showers and toilets. Provisions and restaurants.

Remarks A port of entry.

Fethiye Ece Marina ✆ 0252 612 8829
Email marina@ecesaray.net
www.ecesaray.net

KALKAN

36°15'·66N 29°24'·87E WGS84
BA 1054 Tr 313 Imray-Tetra G36

☆ Çatal Ada Fl.5s76m9M. Kalkan harbour entrance Fl.R.5s5M/Fl.G.5s5M

Navigation Strong gusts with the *meltemi*.

Berths Stern or bows-to where directed.

Shelter Good shelter.

Data 50 berths. Depths 2–6m. Charge band 4.

Facilities Water. 220V. Showers and toilets. Provisions and restaurants.

Kalkan Marina
✆ 0242 844 1131 / 844 1020

KAŞ MARINA

36°12'·43N 29°37'·32E WGS84

This new marina opened in 2010.

VHF Ch 73.

Shelter Generally good shelter but with strong westerlies there is some surge on the end of the pontoons. There are plans in place to ameliorate this.

Data 450 berths. Visitors' berths. Max LOA c.60m. Charge band 4.

Facilities Water. 220V. WiFi. Showers and toilets. Waste pump-out. 100-ton travel-hoist. Repairs.

✆ 0242 836 3470
www.kasmarina.com.tr

KAŞ

36°11'·78N 29°38'·55E WGS84
BA 1054 Tr 3131 Imray-Tetra G36
54M Göçek ←→ Kemer 69M

☆ N side of Kastellorízon Fl.WR.4·5s5/3M (095°-R-125°). Bucak Denizinde Fl(2)WRG.10s16m5-4M (297°-G-065°-W-071°-R-093°). Ince Burnu Fl.3s10m5M. Mole head Fl.R.5s5M

VHF Ch 16.

Navigation Confused swell at the entrance with the *meltemi*.

Berths Stern or bows-to where directed. Laid moorings planned.

Shelter Good shelter.

Data 50 berths. Charge band 3/4.

Facilities Water. 220V. Fuel by tanker. Provisions and restaurants.

Remarks A port of entry.

KEKOVA ROADS

36°10'·04N 29°49'·81E WGS84
(W entrance)
36°12'·26N 29°54'·89E WGS84
(E entrance)
BA 236 Tr 321 Imray-Tetra G36

☆ Kekova Adasi W end Fl(2)5s55m8M. E end Fl.5s35m9M. Ölü Fl.WG.3s26m7/4M (355°-W-358°-G-355°)

Pontoon berths at Kale Köy and Uçağiz. There are numerous well protected anchorages.

DEMRE MARINA

A new marina planned for construction on Tasdibi Burnu, 3·5M ENE of Kekova Adasi.

Data 500 berths. All facilities including yard and travel-hoist are planned.

Work had started at the time of writing, but completion dates are unknown.

SETUR FINIKE MARINA

36°17'·69N 30°09'·11E WGS84
BA 236 Tr 3131 Imray-Tetra G37
33M Kaş ←→ Paphos 140M

☆ Taşlik Burnu Fl(3)10s15M. Entrance Fl.R.5s6M/Fl.G.3s6M. Radio tower F.R.4M

VHF Ch 73. Callsign *Setur Marina*.

Berths Where directed. Laid moorings tailed to the quay.

Shelter Good all-round shelter.

Data 350 berths. Visitors' berths. Depths 3–6m. Charge band 3/4.

Facilities Water. 220V/380V. WiFi. Showers and toilets. 80-ton travel-hoist. Some yacht repairs Provisions and restaurants.

Remarks A port of entry.

Note There are plans to expand the marina to the south. Work had not started at the time of writing.

Setur Finike Marina ✆ 0242 855 5030
Email finike@seturmarinas.com
www.seturmarinas.com

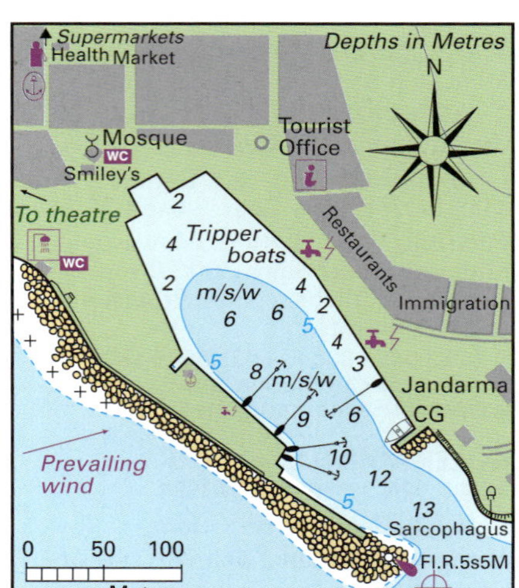

KAS

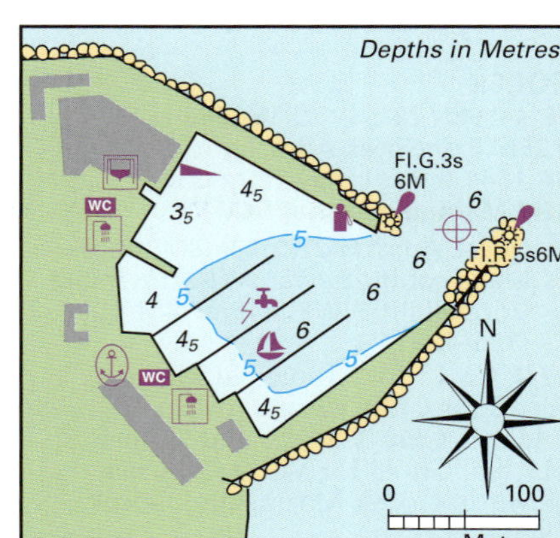

FINIKE

ÇAVUŞ LIMANI
36°17'·8N 20°29'·0E (Çavuş light)

☆ Kucuk Çavuş Burnu Mo(A)15s45m8M

Anchorage off the beach. Thefts reported.

KEMER TURKIZ MARINA
36°36'·14N 30°34'·33E WGS84
BA 236 Tr 3222 Imray-Tetra G37
69M Kas ←→ Antalya 18M

☆ Av Burnu (Koca Br) Fl.10s140m12M. Entrance Fl.G.3s3M/Fl.R.3s3M

VHF Ch 16, 73 (callsign *Kemer Marina* 24/24).

Navigation Care needed of the reef (marked by a beacon and a recent wreck of a coaster) in the N approaches to the marina.

Berths Where directed. Laid moorings tailed to the quay.

Shelter Good shelter.

Data 200 berths. Max LOA 35m. Depths 2–5m. Charge band 3/4.

Facilities Water. 220V. Showers and toilets. Fuel quay. 60–ton travel-hoist. Some yacht repairs. Provisions and restaurants.

Remarks A port of entry.

Kemer Turkiz Marina ✆ 0242 814 1490
Email marina@kemerturkizmarina.com
www.kemerturkizmarina.com

ANTALYA FISHING HARBOUR
36°48'·2N 30°35'·1E

A new fishing harbour on the mainland opposite Sican Adasi. It is reported that yachts are not permitted to use the harbour.

SETUR ANTALYA MARINA
36°49'·96N 30°36'·46E WGS84
BA 242 Tr 3221 Imray-Tetra G37

☆ Commercial harbour entrance Fl.G.3s6M/Fl.R.3s6M. Marina entrance Fl(2)G.4s5m3M / Fl(2)R.4s5m3M

VHF Ch 72 (callsign *Setur Antalya Marina*. Available 0830–2000).

Navigation Numerous ship mooring buoys and underwater pipe-lines S of marina.

Berths Where directed. Laid moorings tailed to the quay.

Shelter Good shelter.

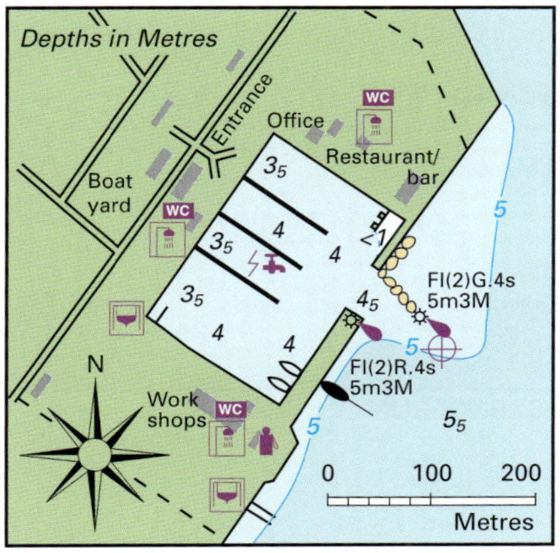

SETUR ANTALYA MARINA

Data 250 berths. Visitors' berths. Max LOA 38m. Depths 3·5–4·5m. Charge band 5.

Facilities Water. 220/380V. WiFi. Showers and toilets. Fuel quay. 60/200-ton travel-hoists. 350-ton slipway. Most yacht repairs. Restaurant. Mini-market.

Setur Antalya Marina ✆ 0242 259 3259
antalya@seturmarinas.com
www.seturmarinas.com

ADOPORT FREE ZONE
Tax-free haul-out area in the NW corner of Antalya commercial harbour. 400 places ashore. 60-ton travel-lift. Winter maintenance and repairs.

✆ 0242 259 2139
Email info@adoport.com.tr
www.adoport.com.tr

ANTALYA KALEÇI MARINA
36°53'·06N 30°42'·06E WGS84
BA 242 Tr 3221 Imray-Tetra G37
15M Kemer ←→ Alanya 68M

☆ Baba Burnu Fl.5s35m14M. Entrance Fl.G.3s4M/Fl.R.3s4M

VHF Ch 12, 16.

Navigation Care needed in the narrow entrance. A small conical buoy marks a wreck W of the harbour.

Berths Limited visitors' berths.

Shelter S winds cause a surge.

Data 50 berths. Max LOA 15m. Depths 1–6m. Charge band 5.

Facilities Water. 220V. Showers and toilets. Fuel quay. Provisions and restaurants.

Kaleçi Turban Marina
✆ 0242 243 4750 / 247 5053

AKSU RIVER MARINA
The Aksu River runs into the sea 8M east of Baba Burnu. There are plans to develop a 1,200-berth marina just inside the river. Work has not started at the time of writing.

MANAVGAT RIVER
36°44'·12N 31°29'·64E WGS84

River navigable for 3M. Care needed of a bar across the entrance. Three visitors' berths at a boatyard on the right bank.

There is a project to develop a marina in the entrance to the Manavgat River. Work had not started at the time of writing. The projected completion date is 2015, although much depends on the planning process. Another project for a marina in Manavgat town is in the very early stages, but no further details were available at this time.

Antalya to the Syrian border

ALANYA MARINA
36°33'·49N 31°57'·01E WGS84

VHF Ch 16, 73.

Berths Stern or bows-to where directed, with laid moorings tailed to the quay.

Shelter Good. Some surge in strong S winds. A new breakwater to further protect the entrance is planned.

Data 250 berths. Depths 3–5m. Charge band 3/4.

Facilities Water. 220V. Showers and toilets. WiFi. Fuel quay. 100-ton travel-hoist. Repairs. Yacht Club. Bar and restaurant. ATM.

✆ 0242 512 1234
Email info@alanyamarina.com.tr
www.alanyamarina.com.tr

ALANYA
36°32'·23N 32°00'·36E WGS84
BA 237 Tr 324

☆ Dildarde Burnu Fl.20s209m20M

Navigation The entrance is not lit, and at night care should be taken in the approaches as large fishing boats sometimes raft up to the E of the breakwater.

Berths Anchor in the outer part of new small boat harbour. Most berths on the quay taken up with tripper boats and local boats.

Shelter Good shelter.

Facilities Water. Fuel by tanker. Provisions and restaurants.

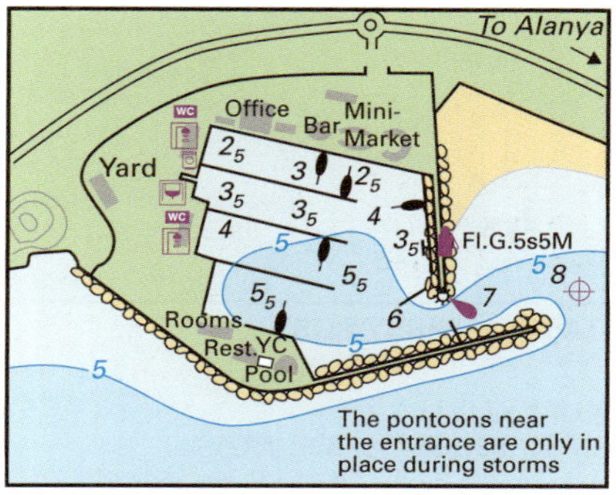

ALANYA MARINA

ALANYA FISHING HARBOUR
36°21'·6N 32°11'·8E

There are plans to build a new fishing harbour approximately 14M S of Alanya. Work had not started at the time of writing, and much depends on the planning process.

GAZIPASA
36°15'·97N 32°16'·63E WGS84

A harbour under the castle at Gazipasa. At present yachts anchor inside the harbour. Marina plans proceeding slowly.

✆ 0242 511 8888 / 0300
Email info@gazipasamarina.com

BOZYAZI LIMANI
36°05'·87N 32°56'·53E WGS84

☆ Fl.R.3s3M/Fl.G.3s3M

Harbour affords good shelter.

AYDINCIK LIMANI
36°08'·73N 33°19'·52E WGS84
BA 237 Tr 331

☆ Aydincik Fl.3s23m9M. Entrance F.G/F.R(occas)

Small harbour and village.

YESILOVACIK

36°11'·24N 33°39'·30E WGS84

☆ Entrance Fl.G.5s5M/Fl.R.5s5M.

A harbour tucked on the N side of Ada Burnu. Go alongside under the outer breakwater. Good shelter.

TAŞUCU

36°18'·87N 33°53'·00E WGS84
BA 242 Tr 331

☆ Incekum Burnu Fl.10s13m10M. Ağalimani Fl.3s8M. Commercial harbour Fl.G.3s5M/Fl.R.3s5M. Ferry harbour Fl(2)R.10s6M / Fl(2)G.10s6M

VHF Ch 16 for port authorities.

Berths Stern or bows-to the quay in the N of the ferry (W) harbour. Laid moorings.

Shelter Good shelter.

Facilities Water. 220V. Provisions and restaurants.

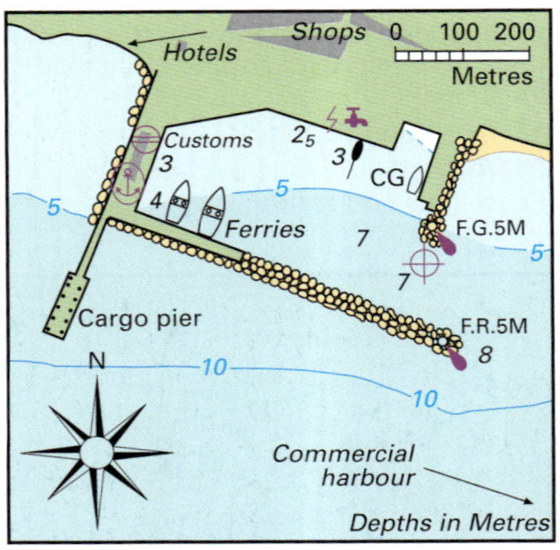

TAŞUCU FERRY PORT

KUM KÜYÜ

36°31'·83N 34°13'·83E WGS84

A new harbour off the resort of Kum Küyü.

Remarks Progress on the marina has stalled for several years, but completion is due in 2015.

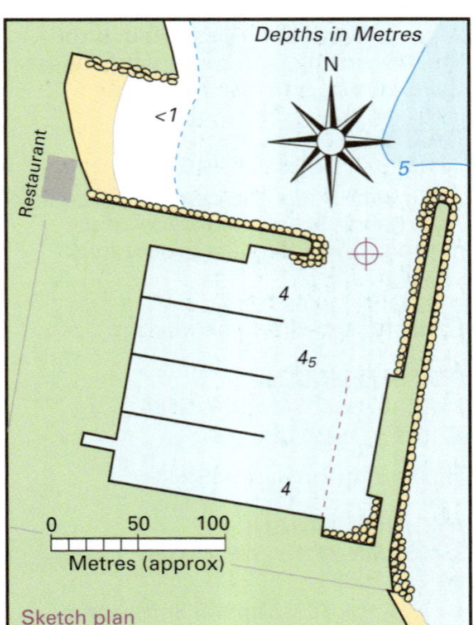

KUM KUYU

LIMONLU

36°33'·9N 34°15'·4E

Small harbour, prone to silting.

ERDEMLI HARBOUR

36°36'·5N 34°19'·6E

A new fishing harbour has been built off the town of the same name. Most berths are taken with fishing boats.

MERSIN MARINA

36°46'·30N 34°34'·09E WGS84

A marina to the W of Mersin commercial harbour.

Berths Go stern or bows-to where directed. Laid moorings tailed to the quay.

Shelter Looks to provide good all-round shelter.

Data 500 berths. Max LOA 50m. Charge band 3 /4.

Facilities Water. 220V. WiFi. Showers and toilets. Waste-pump-out. Laundry. Fuel quay. Duty-free fuel available. 500 places ashore. 100-ton travel-hoist. 30-ton trailer. Most repairs can be arranged. Storage lockers. Chandlers planned. Mini-market in the marina.

Remarks New airport at Tarsus under construction (30km).

Mersin Marina ☏ 0324 329 10 34
www.mersinmarina.com.tr

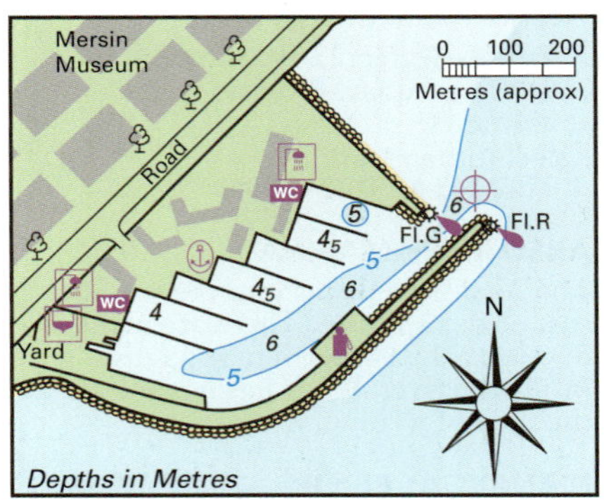

MERSIN MARINA

MERSIN

36°47'·1N 34°38'·5E (Fl.R.3s9M)
BA 2101 Tr 3331

☆ Main light Fl(3)10s15M. Entrance Fl.R.3s10M / Fl.G.3s9M. S breakwater DirFl.WR.5s5-3M. Leading lights (040·5°). Front Oc.G.3s7M. Rear Oc.G.3s7M. Karaduvar entrance F.R/F.G

VHF Ch 06, 12, 16 for port authorities. Pilot Ch 08, 12.

Berths Alongside in W basin. Care needed of 1·5m patch in the middle of the W basin.

Shelter Good shelter.

Facilities Water. Fuel. Provisions and restaurants.

Remarks A port of entry.

Mersin Chamber of Shipping is reported to be very helpful to visiting yachts. Office in modern building near the Hilton Hotel.

☏ 0324 237 3306

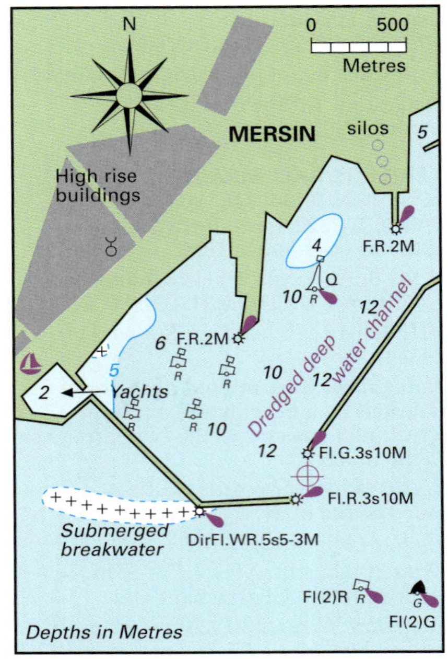

MERSIN

ISKENDERUN

36°35'·51N 36°10'·51E WGS84
(Fishing harbour)
BA 2101 Tr 3342

☆ Main light Fl.3s20M. Entrance Fl.G.3s6M / Fl(2)R.5s3M / F.R.3M. Inner harbour Fl(2)G.5s2M / OcR.3s4M. Fish harbour F.G.3M / F.R.3M

VHF Ch 13, 16 for port authorities. Pilot Ch 16.

Berths Alongside in the fishing harbour. A yacht quay is planned in the fishing harbour.

Shelter Adequate in the summer.

Facilities Water. Fuel. Provisions and restaurants.

Remarks The large commercial harbour is now a restricted area and yachts are not permitted to enter.

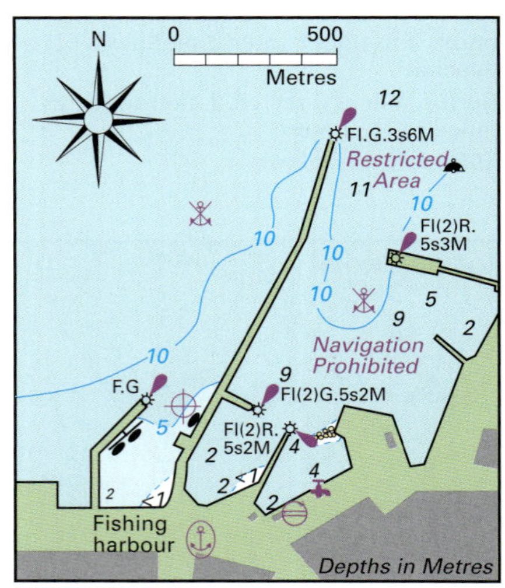

ISKENDERUN

10.13 Cyprus

TIME ZONE UT+2 ✆ IDD (N) +90 ✆ IDD (S) +357

Quick reference guide

For Key see page 139

	Shelter	*Mooring*	*Fuel*	*Water*	*Provisions*	*Eating out*	*Charge band*
Northern Cyprus							
Girne Old harbour	A	A	B	A	B	A	3
Delta Marina	B	A	A	A	B	B	3
Cyprium Bay Marina	A	A	O	A	B	B	
Karpaz Gate Marina	A	A	A	A	C	C	4/5
Famagusta (Gazi Magusa)	A	ABC	B	B	C	C	
Southern Cyprus							
Paphos	B	AC	B	B	A	A	
Limassol Marina	A	A	A	A	B	B	6
St Raphael Marina	A	A	A	A	C	C	3
Larnaca Marina	A	A	A	A	A	A	

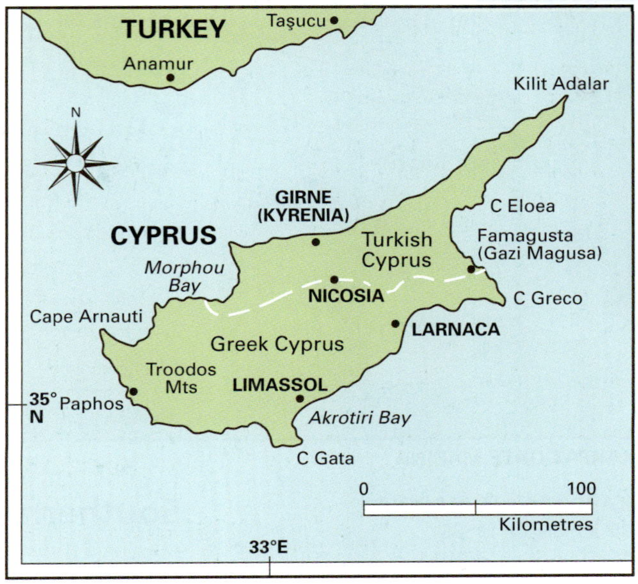

Northern Cyprus

PROHIBITED AREAS

Restrictions along the coast in N Cyprus have been relaxed. Once cleared in, it is possible to visit some of the smaller harbours and anchorages along the coast, although most of these really aren't suitable for overnight stops except in very settled weather.

GIRNE (KYRENIA) MARINA (Old Harbour)

35°20'·56N 33°19'·46E WGS84

BA 849 Tr 344

☆ Kyrenia Fl(3)R.20s20M. Fl.G.5s4M

Navigation Care needed of shoal water in the approaches. The entrance channel is very narrow with little room to pass.

Berths Advisable to call in advance. Berth where directed on the W side of the harbour. Some laid moorings.

Shelter Good all-round shelter.

Facilities Marina office/bar with showers and WC next to Tourist Information centre.

✆ 0392 815 3587 / 4987

DELTA MARINA (Commercial Harbour)

35°20'·49E 33°20'·30E WGS84

☆ Commercial harbour Fl.R.3s4M/Fl.G.3s4M

VHF Ch 16

Navigation Delta Marina (Gemyat) operates along the SW side of the commercial harbour.

Berths Stern or bows-to the catwalk or quay, laid moorings.

Data 75 berths. Max LOA c.25m. Depths 2–5m. Charge band 3.

Shelter Reasonable shelter, but there is sometimes some surge in the harbour. Uncomfortable, not dangerous.

Facilities Water. 220V. Fuel. Showers and WC. Travel-lift, slipway and hardstanding. Most repairs. Chandlers. Café. A short walk into town for provisions, bars and restaurants.

✆ 0392 815 5491 / 92

Email deltamarinacyp@gmail.com

www.delta-marina.com

CYPRIUM BAY MARINA

35°21'·9N 33°39'·8E

A new marina under construction on the N coast, 18M E of Girne. No opening dates available.

Data 445 berths. Max LOA 25m. Depths 3–5m.

Facilities (at completion) Water. 220/380V. WC and showers. Telephone. WiFi. 100-ton travel-lift. 100 places ashore. Technical services. Chandler. Bar-restaurant and café in the marina. 35km to Ercan (local) airport. Larnaca airport (S Cyprus), one hour.

Cyprium Enterprises Ltd ✆ 0533 848 6022

Email info@port-cyprium-marina.com

www.port-cyprium-marina.com

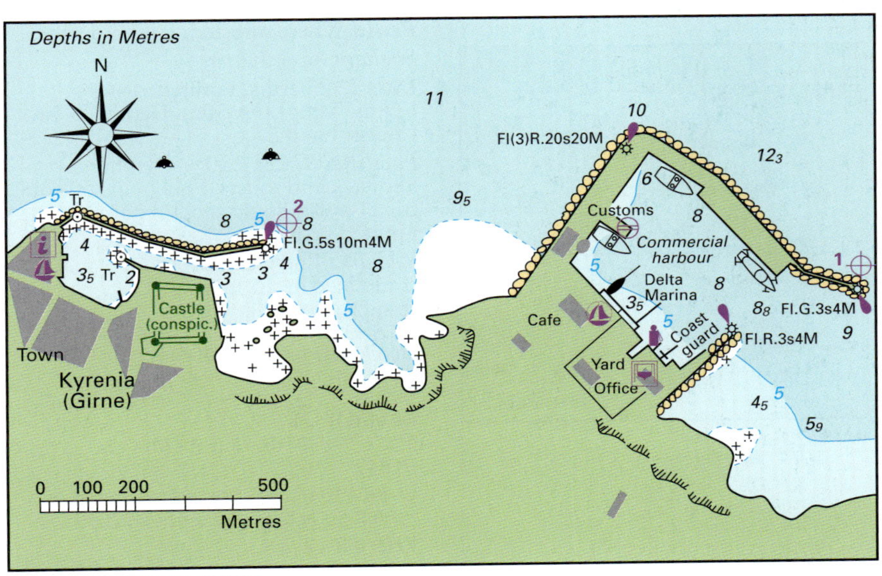

APPROACHES TO GIRNE

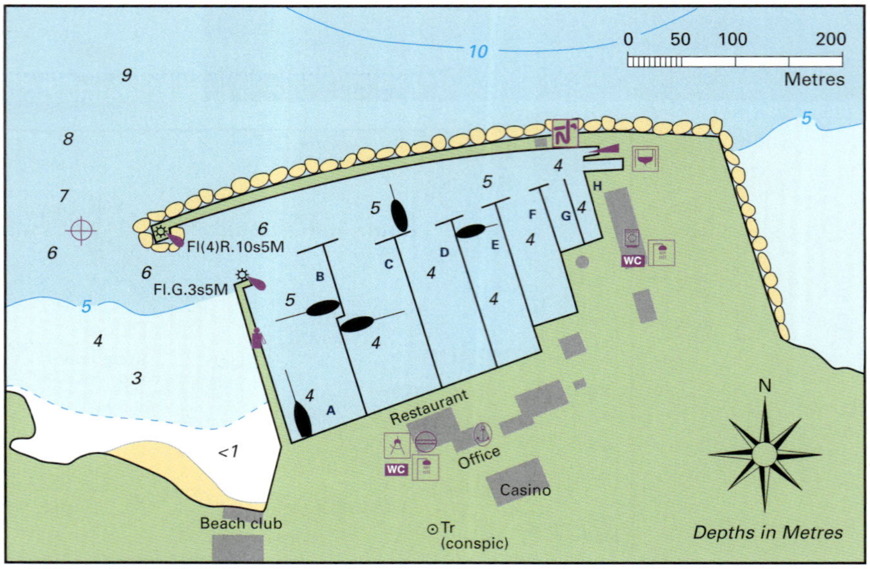

KARPAZ GATE MARINA

KARPAZ GATE MARINA

35°33'·6N 34°13'·6E

Marina opened 2011.

VHF Ch 10, 16. Callsign *Karpaz Gate Marina*.

Berths A RIB will come out to show you to a berth and assist mooring. Go stern or bows-to where directed. Yachts wishing to clear in should go alongside at the far end of the main breakwater. Following completion of the check-in procedures, you will be directed to another berth with stern–to mooring. Laid moorings tailed to the pontoons.

Shelter Good all-round shelter. Yachts are wintered afloat here on dual moorings.

Data 300 berths. Max LOA 55m. Charge band 4/5.

Facilities Water. 220/380V. WiFi. Showers and toilets. Waste pump-out. Laundry facilities. Fuel quay. Duty free available by tanker. 300-ton travel-lift. Most repairs can be arranged. Chandlery. Storage lockers. Mini-market in the marina. ATM. Camping gaz. Bus to Famagusta. International airport at Larnaca. Ercan Airport (near Nicosia) for flights via Turkey.

Karpaz Gate Marina ✆ 0392 229 2800
Email info@karpazbay.com
www.karpazbay.com

FAMAGUSTA

35°08·1'N 33°56·6'E (Q(5)R.10s)
BA 848

☆ SE Bastion Fl(2)15s23m16M.
NW of town Fl.WR.7s15-11M (178°-W-216°-R-313°).
Outer entrance Fl(4)R.5s10m4M
Inshorebreakwater Fl.G.3s10m4M
Inner entrance Q.R.2M

Southern Cyprus

PAPHOS

34°45'·1N 32°24'·4E
BA 849 TR 343
140M Finike ←→ Limassol 43M

☆ Ak Paphos Fl.15s36m17M.
Port entrance Q.R.

Navigation Care must be taken of Vrakhonisos Moulia, a reef and shoal water lying 2M SE of the harbour in the direct approach from the S. The eastern breakwater is partly submerged with the entrance normally marked by a pair of buoys (R/G).

Berths Stern or bows-to T-pier. Anchorage on the W side of the harbour.

Shelter Adequate in the summer. Uncomfortable and may be untenable with strong S winds.

Facilities Water. Provisions and restaurants.

Remarks There are plans to build a marina here.

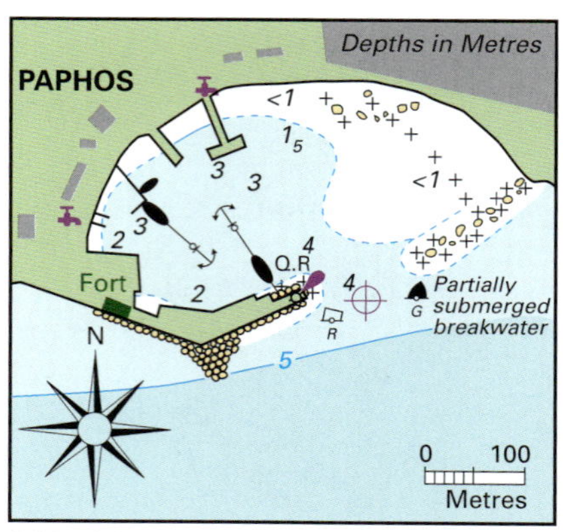

PAPHOS

AKROTIRI

34°34'·0N 33°02'·0E

☆ Entrance Fl.R.10s11m5M/Fl.G.10s11m3M. Akra Yerogómbos Aero Mo(AK)R.37m Ro Ro Berth NE Dolphin Fl(2)R.10s9m3M. SW Dolphin Fl.R.10s7m3M

LIMASSOL

34°39'·0N 33°02'·0E Commercial Port breakwater)
34°39'·8N 33°02'·5E (Fl.G.3s7M. Fishing Harbour)
TR 343
43M Paphos ←→ Larnaca 34M

☆ Commercial port entrance Q(6)R.10s9m12M/Oc.G.7s13m10M. Leading lights (248°) Front F.G.6m2M. Rear Oc.G.5s12m2M. Fishing harbour entrance Fl.G.3s3M / Fl.R.3s3M

VHF Ch 10, 16 (0600–1400).
Pilot Ch 10, 16.

LIMASSOL MARINA

The old fishing harbour has been completely re-developed and the new marina opened in October 2012.

VHF Ch 12, 16.

Berths Go stern or bows-to where directed. Laid moorings tailed to the pontoons.

Shelter The marina should provide good all-round shelter.

Data 640 berths. Max LOA 115m. Depths 2–8m. Charge band 6.

Facilities Water. 220/380V. WiFi, TV and telephone connections. Showers and toilets. Laundry. Waste pump-out. Fuel quay. Duty free will be available. 100-ton travel-lift. Chandlery. Repair facilities.

Limassol Marina
✆ +357 25 020 020
Email info@limassolmarina.com
www.limassolmarina.com
www.cnmarinas.com

LIMASSOL – ST RAPHAEL MARINA

34°42'·8N 33°11'·0E

☆ Entrance Fl(2)10s9m10M/Fl.G.2s3M

VHF Ch 09, 16 (callsign *St-Raphael Marina*).

Berths Where directed. Laid moorings.

Shelter Good shelter.

Data 237 berths. Limited visitors' berths. Max LOA 30m. Depths 3–5m. Charge band 3.

Facilities Water. 220V. Telephone. Showers and toilets. Fuel quay. 60-ton travel-hoist. Some yacht repairs. Limited provisions. Restaurant.

Remarks Entry/exit procedures may be completed in the marina.

St Raphael Marina
✆ 25 636 100
Email marina@raphael.com.cy
www.raphael.com.cy

VASSILIKOS

34°42'·7N 33°18'·7E (F.R.6M)
TR 343

☆ F.R.110m1M. S breakwater head Fl.R.5s. N breakwater head Oc.G.

VHF Ch 12, 16.

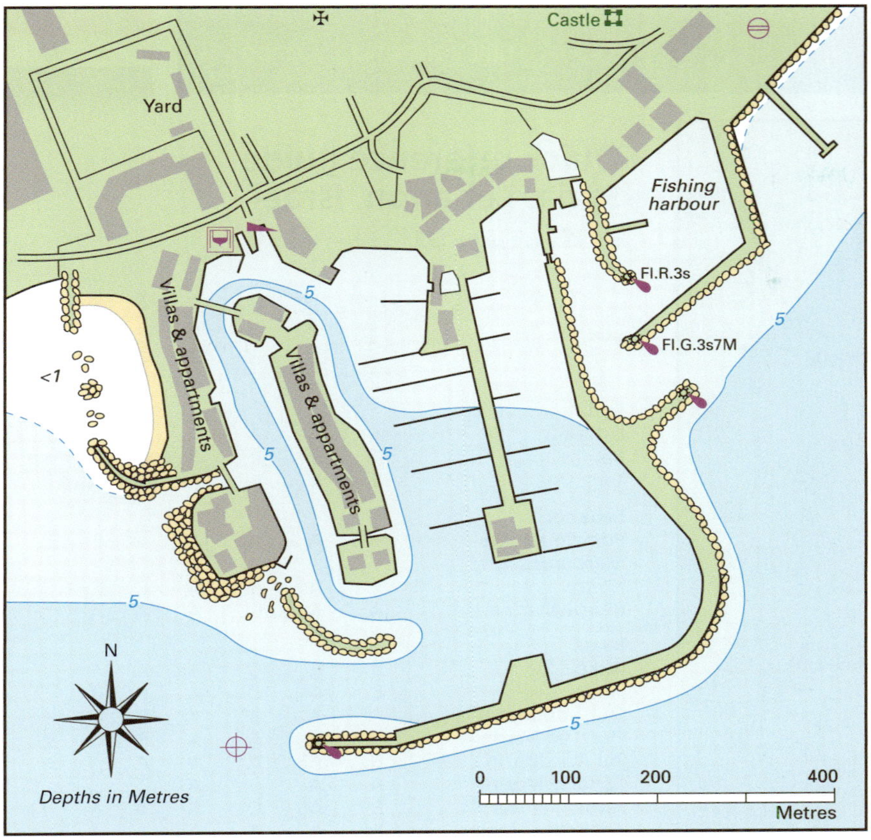

LIMASSOL MARINA

LARNACA

34°55'·1N 33°38'·6E
BA 848 TR 343
34M Limassol ←→ Jounié 111M

☆ Ak Kiti Fl(3)15s20m13M. Fishing harbour entrance Fl(2)R.10s4M/ Fl(2)G.10s4M. Marina entrance F.R.1M. Commercial port entrance Fl.WR.5s8m10/5M / F.G.5m3M

VHF Ch 14, 16 for port authorities (0800–1400).

Note Work on the new marina and cruise ship terminal have been put on hold due to funding issues following the financial crisis. It is unlikely that any work will start before 2016.

Navigation Care needed of the reef and shoal water off Ak Kiti.

Berths Where directed.

Shelter Good shelter.

Data c.200 berths. Max LOA 35m. Depths 1·5–5m.

Facilities Water and electricity. Showers and WC. Laundry. Provisions and restaurants nearby.

Remarks A port of entry.

Larnaca Marina ✆ +357 24 65 31 10 / 13
Email larnaca.marina@cytanet.com.cy

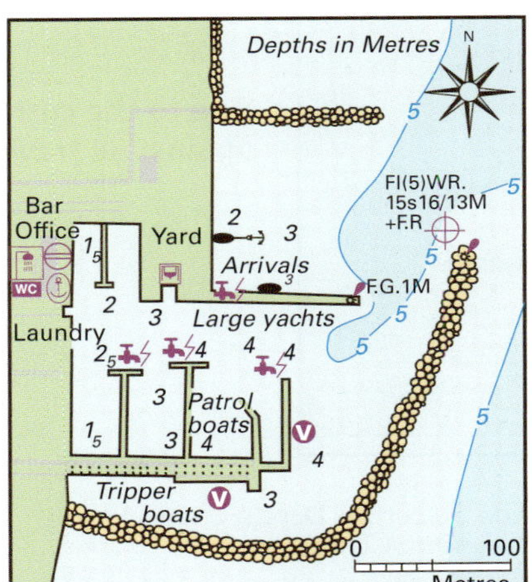

LARNACA

MAKRONISOS MARINA (Ayia Thekla)

The go-ahead has recently been given for a 600-berth marina and residential project in the Ayia Thekla area, 2·5M W of Ayia Napa. At the time of writing construction had not started, and no completion date is available.

10.14 Syria

TIME ZONE UT+2 ✆ IDD +963

Quick reference guide Syria, Lebanon, Israel

For Key see page 139

	Shelter	Mooring	Fuel	Water	Provisions	Eating out	Charge band
Syria							
Lattakia	A	A	A	A	A	A	3
Banias	A	B	B	A	B	O	
Tartoûs	B	B	B	A	A	A	
Lebanon							
Port de Jounié	A	A	A	A	A	B	2
Marina Joseph Koury	A	A	B	A	C	C	
Beirut Marina	A	A	B	A	A	A	
Israel							
Akko	B	A	O	A	A	A	
Haifa	B	A	O	A	B	B	
Quishon Marina	A	A	B	A	B	B	
Herzliya Marina	A	B	A	A	B	O	3
Tel Aviv Marina	B	AB	A	A	A	A	3
Ashdod Marina	A	A		A			
Jaffa	B	AB	O	A	A	A	2/3
Ashkelon Marina	A	A	A	A	A	A	2
Eilat Marina	A	A	B	A	B	A	

Due to the current instability the FCO advises against all travel to Syria

LATTAKIA (AL'LADHIQIYAH, PORT DE LATTAQUIE)

35°31'·9N 35°45'·3E (Fl.G.5M)
BA 1579 SHOM 7513

☆ Al Burj Fl(2)9s22m10M.
Leading lights 115·5° Front Fl(2)R.5s6M Rear F(2)R.5s6M.
Breakwater LFl.G.4s4m5M.
Marina N breakwater Fl.R.3s.
S breakwater Fl.G.5s

VHF Ch 12, 14, 16 for authorities. Ch 11, 16 for pilots. Pilot compulsory. Ch 16, 73 for Syrian Yacht Club.

Navigation Arrival by day preferred. Call up pilots when 2–5 M off with ETA.

Berths Yachts are required to berth in the fishing harbour to the N of the commercial port. The Syrian Yacht Club maintains the quay immediately to port on entering the harbour. Go alongside or stern or bows-to the quay. The dredged harbour has 2–6m depths.

Data 50 berths. Depths 2–6m. Max LOA 40m. Charge band 3.

Shelter Good all-round shelter.

Facilities Water. 220V. WC and showers. Laundry. Fuel station. 30-ton crane. chandlers. Some repairs through Khalife Agency. Good provisions and market. Restaurants.

Remarks A port of entry. Suggested as the best first port to arrive at in Syria. Officials helpful although it may take some time to get a visa.

Syrian Yacht Club
✆ 041 311 110 / 988 901 010
Email syrianyachtclub@yahoo.com or syrychtclb@mail.sy
www.syrianyachtclub.com
Khalife Forwarding and Transport Co
✆ 041 234 641

JABLAH (PORT DE JEBLA)

35°21'·6N 35°55'·6E (Q.R.4M)

☆ Entrance Q.G.7m4M/Q.R.6m5M

Remarks Not a port of entry.

NAHR HURAYSUN

BA 1579
35°13'·4N 35°56'·7E (Fl.R.10s3M)

☆ Entrance Fl.5s6m4M/Fl.R.10s6m3M

Remarks Not a port of entry. Oil-loading terminal.

BANIAS

35°11'·4N 35°56'·5E
BA 1579 SHOM 7513

Navigation Yachts should head for the fishing harbour. Silting around entrance to the harbour. Approach the channel parallel to the beach in 2·5–3m and keep close off the breakwater. Pilotage into the port by the harbourmaster. Not recommended for yachts drawing over 1·8m.

Berths Where directed by the harbourmaster.

Shelter Good.

Facilities Water. Fuel by taxi from town. Provisions.

Remarks The oil terminal port is the official port of entry but is unsuitable for yachts which use the fishing harbour. Banias should not therefore be the first port of call in Syria (go to Lattakia).

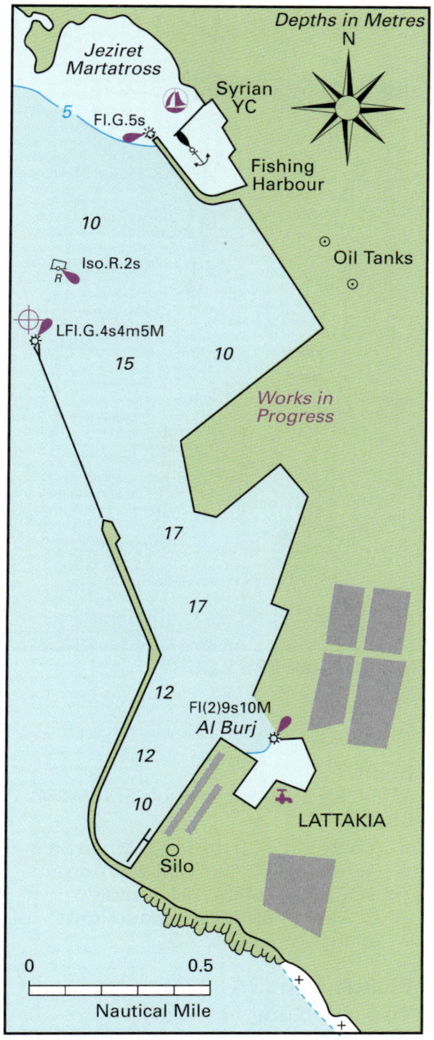

LATTAKIA

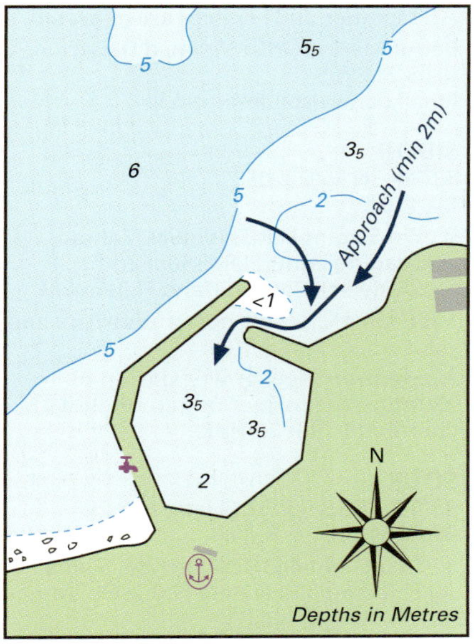

BANIAS FISHING HARBOUR

TARTUS (PORT DE TARTOUS)

34°54′·6N 35°51′·2E
BA 1579

☆ E breakwater head Fl.R.4s7m5M

VHF Ch 08, 10, 16 for port authorities. Pilot compulsory.

Navigation Normally a number of ships anchored in the roadstead. Call up pilots with an ETA.

Berths Alongside at the head of basin 1 or 2.

Shelter Good shelter but uncomfortable from the wash of tugs, pilot boats and bum boats coming and going.

Facilities Water. Fuel by taxi from town. Provisions and restaurants.

Remarks A port of entry. Not recommended compared to Lattakia because of the difficulties with berthing.

JAZIRAT ARWAD (ILE DE ROUAD)

34°51′·4N 35°51′·6E (Q.G.1M)
BA 2633

☆ Main lights Fl.5s20m12M. Entrance Q.G.3m1M/Q.R.3m1M

Anchorage possible behind the island with permission from the authorities. Permission is obtained by taking a ferry from Tartus to Arwad Island and requesting permission from the harbourmaster there. A yacht must return to Tartus to clear out of Syria.

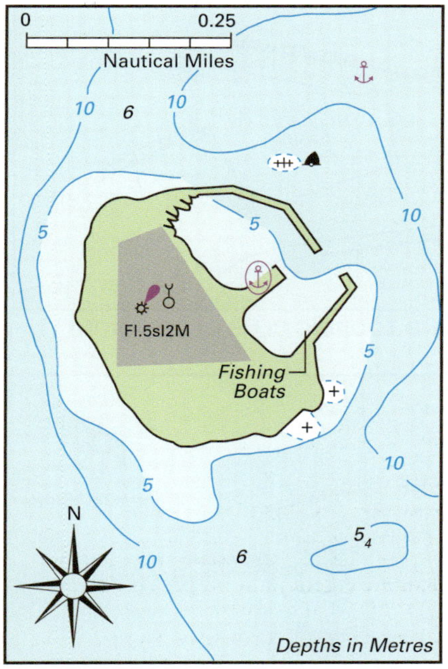

ILE DE ROUAD

10.15 Lebanon

TIME ZONE UT+2 ◑ IDD +961

Yachts are not permitted to proceed from Israel to Lebanon.

TRIPOLI

34°27′·9N 35°49′·5E (Jetée du Large Head Fl.G.4·5s5M)
BA 1561

☆ Ramkin Islet Fl.3·3s22m18M. Entrance Fl.G.4·5s10m5M/ Fl.R.3s9m5M. Tower of Lions F.R.3M. Kalmoun Fl.3s5m3M. Enfe Fl.G.3s5m3M. Chekka Fl.R.3s3m3M. Batrun Fl.G.2s5m3M. Fad'ous Fl.R.2s7m3M. R¸s Aamchîte. Terouel Fl.2s6m3M

VHF Ch 16, 11 for port authorities and pilot. Call *Oscar November* on Ch 16 while still in international waters (12M+ offshore) to request entry.

Navigation New power station with conspic chimney reported 2km N of Tripoli.

Remarks Not really suitable for yachts. Minimum payment for one month.

JEBAIL

34°07′·5N 35°38′·5E (Fl.R.3s5M)

☆ Entrance Fl.R.3s15m5M/Fl.G.3s7m5M. Tabarja Fl.3s10m5M. Aquamarina Fl.3s

PORT DE JOUNIÉ

33°59′·2N 35°37′·4E
BA 1563

☆ Yacht basin entrance Fl.R.3s8m5M/Fl(2)G.3s8M. Naval basin entrance Fl.G.3s10m8M. S entrance Fl.R. Adonis fishing harbour Fl.2s

VHF Ch 11, 16. Call *Oscar Charlie* on Ch 11, 16 while still in international waters (12M+) to request entry. Only after receiving a clearance number should you proceed.

Navigation Entry should be made in daylight hours only. Pilotage is not compulsory for vessels of less than 50 NRT. Two red-and-white striped chimneys at the power station S of Jounié are conspicuous. Closer in, the marina breakwater is obvious.

Berths Go on the fuel jetty to be cleared in. You will then be directed to a berth. Go stern or bows-to and in most cases you will have to use your own anchor although some berths have laid moorings.

Shelter Good.

Data Visitors' berths available. First three days mooring free. After that, charge band 2.

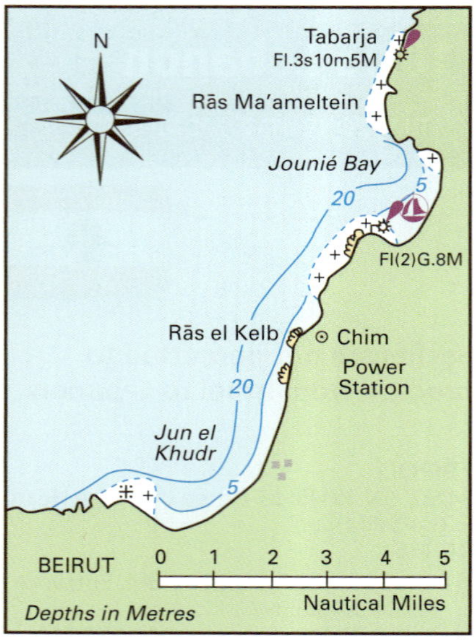

APPROACHES TO BEIRUT AND JOUNIÉ

Remarks To clear in and out there is a flat fee of US$80. Any skipper who is not the owner of the vessel should have a letter of authority from the owner.

Facilities Diesel and petrol at fuel jetty. Chandlery near marina gate. Several good supermarkets in the town. Weather forecasts from marina office.

Jounie Yacht Club ☏ 9932 020 / 640 220
Email atcl@inco.com.lb

MARINA JOSEPH KOURY

33°56'·09N 35°35'·0E

VHF Ch 16.

Navigation Marina JK is located at the N end of Beirut.

Data 600 berths. Visitors' berths. Max LOA 85m. Depths 6–9m.

Facilities Water. 220V. Showers and WC. Fuel quay. 500-ton hydraulic lift. Restaurant.

Marina Joseph Khoury
☏ 04 418 826 / 03 744 676 / 03 713 230
Email info@lamarinajk.com
www.lamarinajk.com

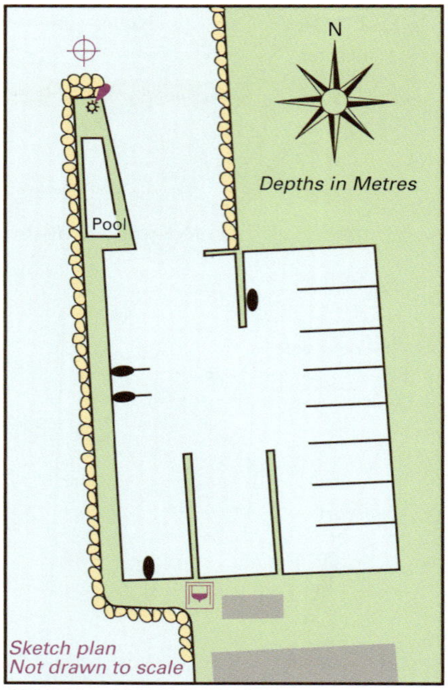

MARINA JOSEPH KOURY

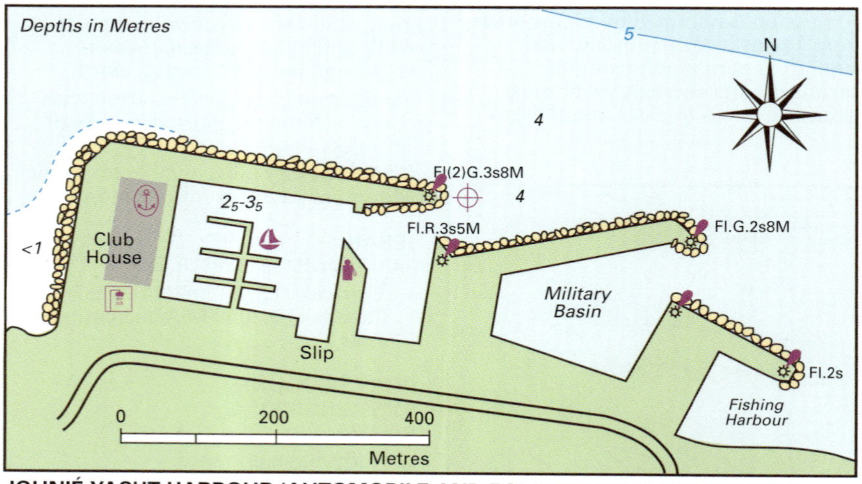

JOUNIÉ YACHT HARBOUR (AUTOMOBILE AND TOURING CLUB OF LEBANON)

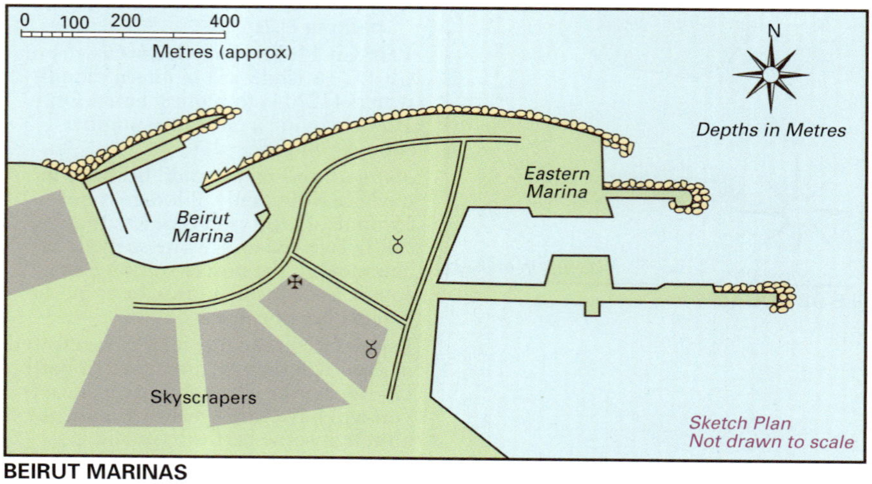

BEIRUT MARINAS

BEIRUT

33°54'·6N 35°31'·4E (N mole Fl.G.5s8M)
BA 1563

☆ Rās Beirut Fl(2)10s52m22M. Airfield Aero Fl.WG.4s42m17M and Aero Mo(BL)G.12s43m17M. N mole Fl.G.5s14m8M. All harbour lights extinguished (T) 2000.

BEIRUT MARINA

Two new basins in a marina development close to the city centre.

Projected data 300 berths. Max LOA 50m.

All facilities and services are expected.

Beirut Marina (Attn Mr Imad Dana)
☏ 03 211 705
Email danai@solidere.com.lb

SIDON

33°34'·3N 35°22'·0E
BA 1561

☆ Ziri S point Fl.R.3s10m6M. Zahrani Leading lights Fl.R.2s56m and 2F.R(vert)42m. Sarafand Fl.3s5m3M

VHF Ch 14, 16 for port authorities and pilot.

Navigation New power station in Zahrani, the former oil terminal, with chimney 150m conspic.

SOUR

33°16'·5N 33°11'·5E (S jetty Fl.R.2s)
BA 1561

☆ Main light Fl(3)12s15m12M. S jetty Fl.R.2s6m3M. N jetty Fl.G.2s6m3M.

10.16 Israel

TIME ZONE UT+2 ☽ IDD +972

Note At the present time anyone travelling to Israel should seek advice from the Foreign Office. For further information see www.fco.gov.uk/travel

AKKO (ACRE)

32°55′·1N 35°04′·1E
BA 1585

☆ Main light Fl(2)7s16m10M. Breakwater head Q(3)R.5s1M / Q(3)G.5s3M

VHF Ch 11, 16. 24/24 (callsign *Marina Acre*).

Navigation Care needed of the reef around the rock (Tower of the Flies) in the approaches. The approach should be made leaving Tower of the Flies to starboard.

Berths Stern or bows-to where directed. Crowded so check if a berth is available.

Shelter Adequate shelter. Uncomfortable in SW winter gales.

Data 80 berths. Five visitors' berths. Max LOA 12m. Depths 1–3m.

Facilities Water. 220V. Showers and toilets. Provisions and restaurants.

Remarks There are plans to expand the number of berths to 300 in the future.

Marina manager Gideon Shmueli, Akko Marina ☽ 04 991 9287

HAIFA

32°49′·6N 35°00′·9E (Breakwater head Fl(2)G.4s2M)
BA 1585

☆ Har Karmel Fl.5s179m30M. Commercial Port entrance Fl(2)G.4s15m2M/Fl.R.3s14m5M. Haifa Bay 2Fl. Qishon Harbour entrance Q(2)R.5s10m6M/Q(2)G.5s6m4M. Jast E Zarka Fl(4)G.11s3M/Fl(2)R.7s3M

A night entry is difficult as ships anchored in the roadstead and the loom of the town lights tend to obscure the harbour lights.

VHF Ch 12, 14, 16 for port authorities and pilot. Contact *Israeli Navy* on Ch 16. Ch 16, 12, 14 for Quishon Marina (callsign *Haifa Port*).

Navigation Four chimneys at the power station are conspicuous. Yachts should head for Quishon Marina.

QUISHON MARINA

(Kishon Marina and Fishing Port)
32°49′N 35°00′E

Navigation Yachts should make for Quishon and not the Carmel YC.

VHF Ch 16, 12, 14 (callsign *Haifa Port*)

Data 200 berths. Depths 3m.

Remarks A port of entry in conjunction with Haifa.

☽ 04 842 2106

HADERA (POWER STATION)

32°28′·2N 34°51′·8E (Jetty head F.R)
BA 2634, 1591

☆ Jetty head F.R.19m2M. Boat harbour entrance Fl.G.2s9m3M / Fl.R.5s9m2M

VHF Ch 10, 16.

Remarks Only use in an emergency.

HERZLIYA MARINA (HERZLIA)

32°09′·94N 34°47′·56E

☆ Main Breakwater Fl.G.5s12M. Lee breakwater Fl.R.5s12M

VHF Ch 11, 16. 24/24.

Navigation Difficult to identify from seaward. Buoyed channel.

Berths Where directed. Finger pontoons.

Shelter Good shelter.

Data 800 berths. Max LOA 60m. Depths 2–5m. Charge band 3.

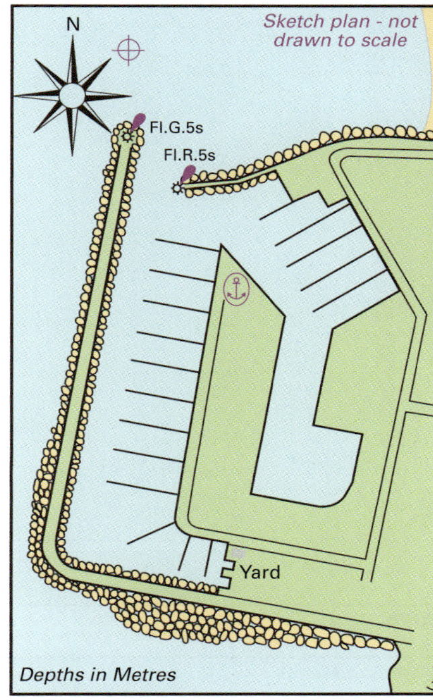

HERZLIYA MARINA

Facilities Water. 220V. Showers and toilets. Waste pump-out. Fuel quay. 50-ton travel-lift. Yacht repairs. Provisions can be found.

Remarks Port of entry. Herzlia is a chic upmarket suburb 15M N of Tel Aviv.

Herzlia Marina ☽ 09 956 5591 / 5 / 6
Email mail@herzliya-marina.co.il
www.herzliya-marina.co.il

SEANERGY

Yacht management and maintenance services.

Seanergy Ltd. Itay Singer (CEO), Haogen, Marina ☽ 99 548 548
www.seanergyachts.com

TEL AVIV POWER STATION

☆ Breakwater Fl(2)R.5s2M. Basin F.R/F.G

TEL AVIV MARINA

32°05′·3N 34°46′·0E
BA 2634, 1591

☆Breakwater head Fl(5)G.20s

VHF Ch 10, 16 (office hours, callsign *Tel Aviv Marina*).

Navigation Foreign yachts are not permitted to enter at night. In daylight hours contact the marina for a pilot to guide you in. Buoyed channel.

Berths Berth alongside the fuel quay just inside the entrance and await clearance. Afterwards berth where directed. The marina is very crowded and you should enquire in advance for a berth.

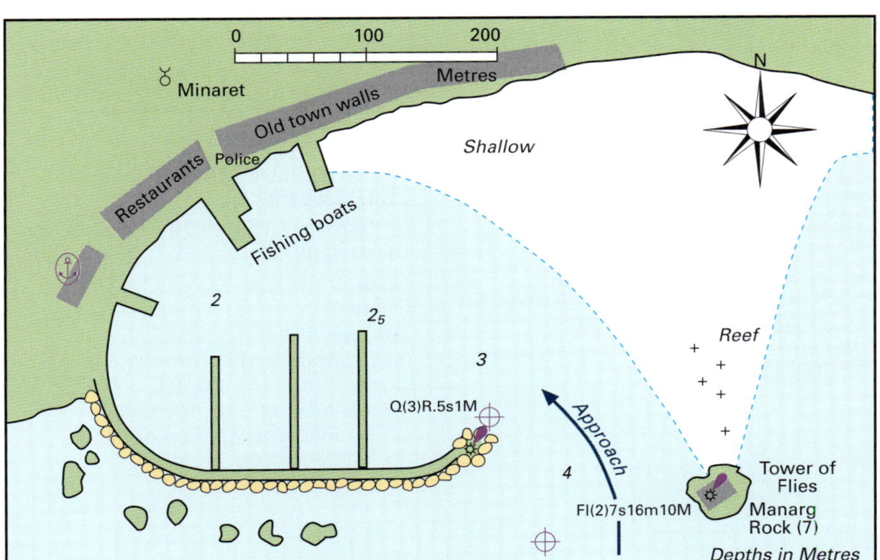

AKKO MARINA

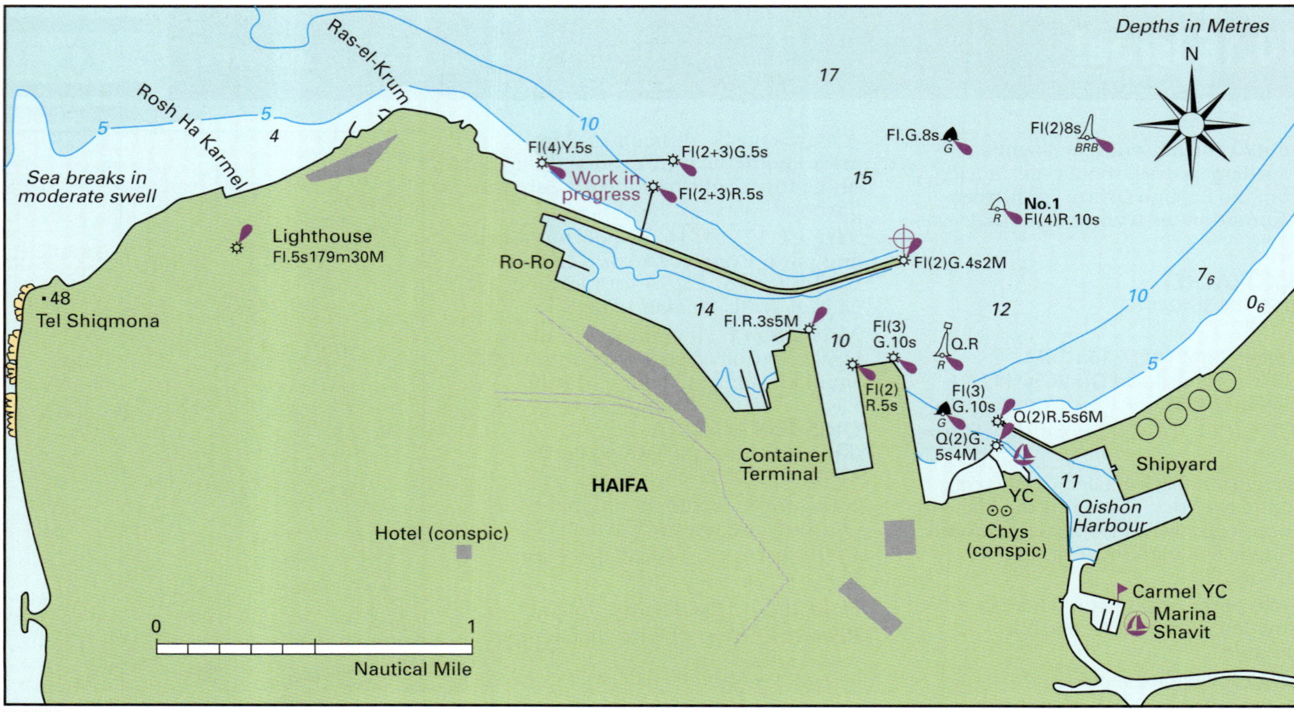

HAIFA

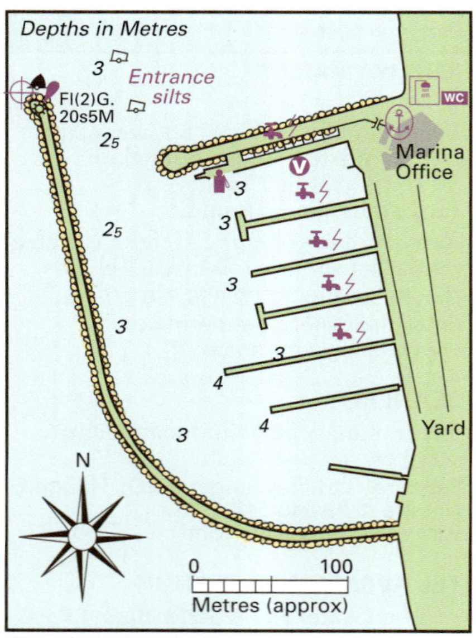

TEL AVIV MARINA

Shelter Uncomfortable with strong SW gales.

Data 320 berths. Max LOA 20m. Depths 1·5–2·5m. Charge band 3.

Facilities Water. 220V. Showers and toilets. Washing machines. Fuel quay. 20-ton crane. Chandlers. Yacht repairs. Provisions and restaurants.

Remarks Port of entry where immigration and customs can be carried out in the marina.

Note Refurbishment of berths and facilities has been completed.

Marina Tel Aviv ✆ 03 527 2596
Email marinata@zahav.net.il
www.telaviv-marina.co.il

JAFFA

32°03'·3N 34°45'·1E (Front leading light F.R)
BA 1591

☆ Leading lights 129° (occas) Front F.R Rear F.R. Breakwater head Fl.G.4s7M

VHF Ch 11, 16 (callsign *Jaffa Marina*).

Navigation Care needed of Andromeda Rocks at the entrance. They can be left to port on 123° on St Peters Church belfry. If in difficulty call up the marina who will send a boat out to guide you in.

Berths The marina is usually fully booked so enquire in advance for a berth.

Shelter Normally good in the summer. Uncomfortable with strong SW winds.

Data 100 berths. Max LOA 16m. Depths 1·5m. Charge band 2/3.

Facilities Water. 220V. 35-ton travel-hoist. Provisions and restaurants.

Remarks Port of entry.

Jaffa Marina ✆ 03 683 2255

ASHDOD

31°50'N 34°38'·2E (Main breakwater Fl.G.2s7M)
BA 1585

☆ Main light Fl(3)20s76m22M. Breakwater head Fl.G.2s7M. N breakwater Fl.R.2s7M / Fl(2)R5s7M / Fl.5s3m2M. Lee breakwater

Remarks A commercial port with no facilities for yachts.

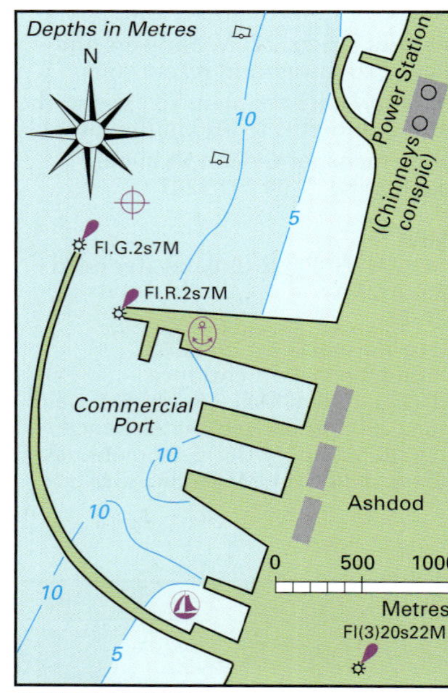

ASHDOD PORT

ASHDOD BLUE MARINA

31°47'·5N 34°37'·3E

☆ Entrance Oc(2)G.8s7m/Oc(2)R.8s7m

VHF Ch 09, 16, 11, 10 (24/24)

Data 574 berths. Max LOA 30m. Depths 4m.

Remarks Port of entry where immigration and customs can be carried out in the marina.

Marina Ashdod ✆ 08 855 7246
Email bmarina@netvision.net.il

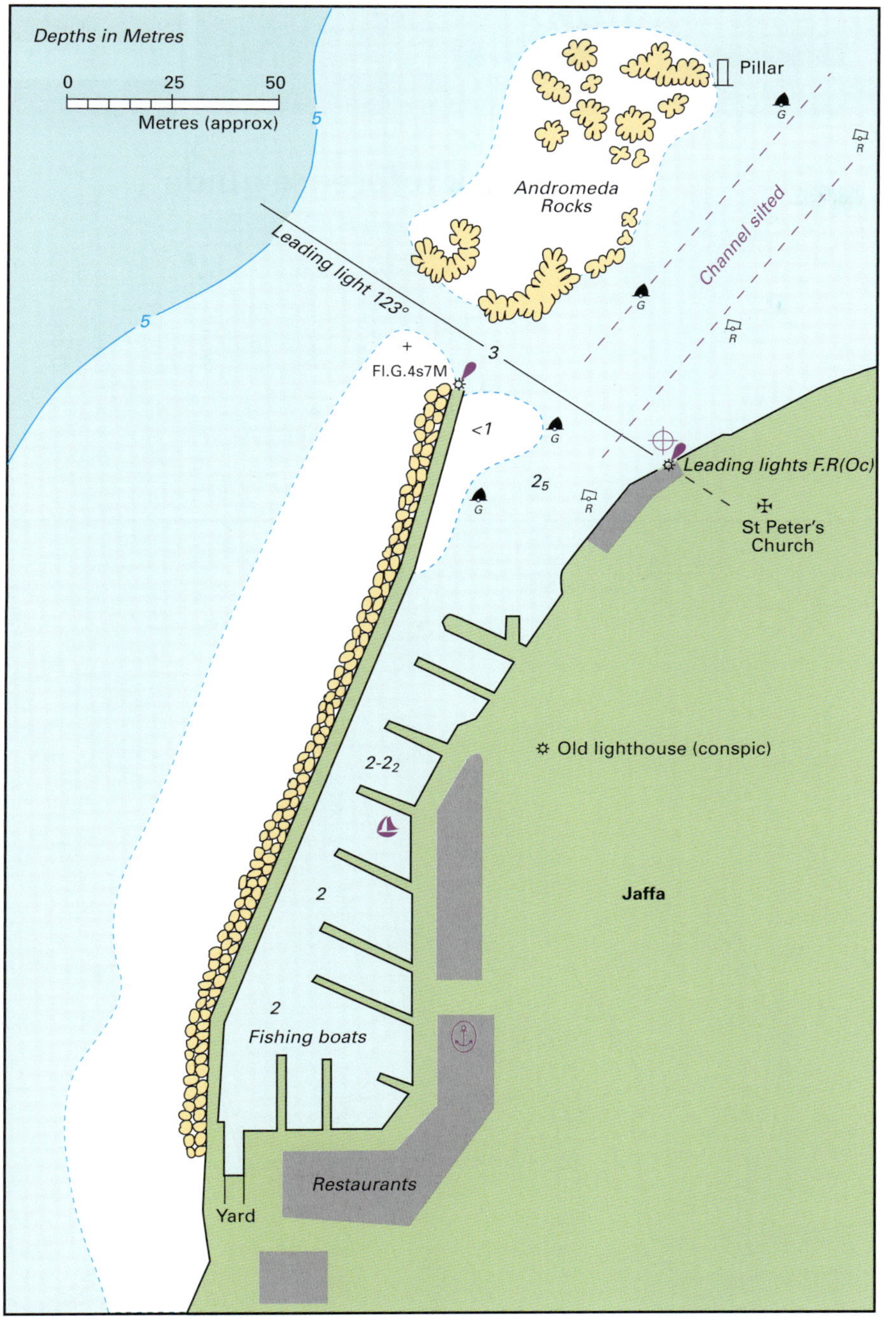

JAFFA MARINA

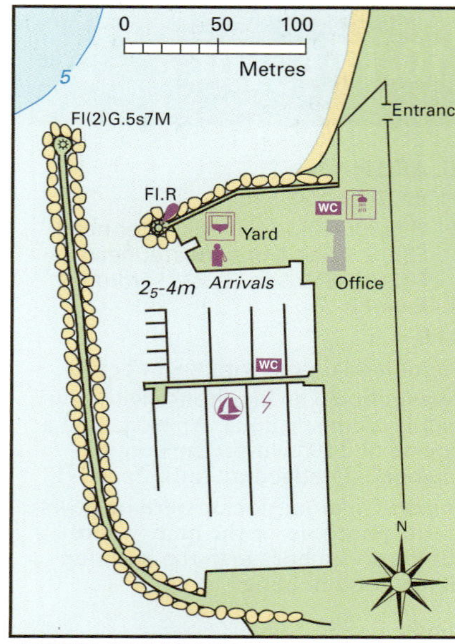

ASHKELON MARINA

ASHKELON MARINA

31°41′·2N 34°33′·4E

☆ Main light Fl(2)10s15M. Marina Fl(2)G.5s7M/Fl.R. Harbour outer breakwater Fl(2)G.6s4M. Inner breakwater Fl(2)R.10s. S end Fl.R.4s. S breakwater Fl.G.4s

VHF Ch 11, 16 (24/24).

Navigation A tall chimney 1M S of the marina is conspicuous (lit at night with four white lights vert). The marina is difficult to make out from the distance but, closer in, the breakwater will be seen.

Berths Stern or bows-to with a line to a pile where directed.

Shelter Good.

Data 600 berths. Visitors' berths. Max LOA 54m. Depths 1·5–3m. Charge band 2.

Facilities Water, 220V. Showers and toilets. Fuel. 100-ton lift. Yacht repairs. Provisions and restaurants.

Remarks Port of entry. Immigration and customs can be carried out in the marina. A useful first port of call for boats that have come through the Suez Canal.

Ashkelon Marina ☏ 08673 3780
Email marin_nm@netvision.net.il
www.ashkelon-marina.co.il

EILAT MARINA (Red Sea)

29°33′N 34°58′E

☆ Eilat main light Fl.10s21M. Marina Fl(1+3+6)R.2M

VHF Ch 16, 11 (0830–1700).

Navigation Lift bridge must be opened to enter marina.

Data 300 berths. Depths 2·5–3m.

☏ 08 637 6761

10.17 Egypt

TIME ZONE UT+2 IDD +20

Quick reference guide

For Key see page 139

	Shelter	Mooring	Fuel	Water	Provisions	Eating out	Charge band
Egypt							
Port Said	A	A	B	A	A	A	5
Alexandria	B	ABC	A	A	A	A	
Porto Marina	A	A		A	B	B	

EL ARISH

31°09'·7N 33°50'·15E

☆ Fl.5s39m18M. W breakwater head Fl(3)G.5s8M. E breakwater head Fl(3)R.5s8M. Ldg Lts 213° *Front* F.R. *Rear* F.R

VHF Ch 16

Commercial port with yacht berths.

Navigation The lighthouse with b/w bands is conspicuous. Approach on a course of 210° within the buoyed channel. (Dredged to 7m.) Open NE.

Berths Go alongside or stern or bows-to the pontoons or the quay where directed. Anchorage in the harbour. Sand, good holding.

PORT SAID

31°18'·1N 32°21'·5E (El Bahar light)
BA 240

☆ E Main light Fl.10s47m20M. Aero Oc.R.2·5s100m. El Bahar Tower Iso.2s42m15M. E breakwater head Oc.R.6s. Leading lights (217°40') Front F.R.36m6M. Rear Oc(2)R.10s46m7M. E Port E breakwater head F.R

The lights of ships at anchor in the roadstead obscure the lights in the approach.

VHF Ch 13, 16 for port authorities. Pilot Ch 12. Port Fouad Yacht Centre Ch 12, 16. Call *Port Said One* on Ch 16, 12 when 10M off. You will be directed to call again when 2M off and transferred to a pilot boat, usually on Ch 12. The pilot may ask for *backsheesh*.

Navigation There may be an early morning fog in the winter exacerbated by air pollution around Port Said. There are numerous ships either under way or at anchor in the approaches. Follow the buoyed channel into the harbour as the W breakwater is just under the water for a considerable length. Care needed of oil rigs off the coast.

Berths Stern or bows-to at Port Fouad Yacht Centre. Charge band 5.

Shelter Good shelter although there is wash from passing ships.

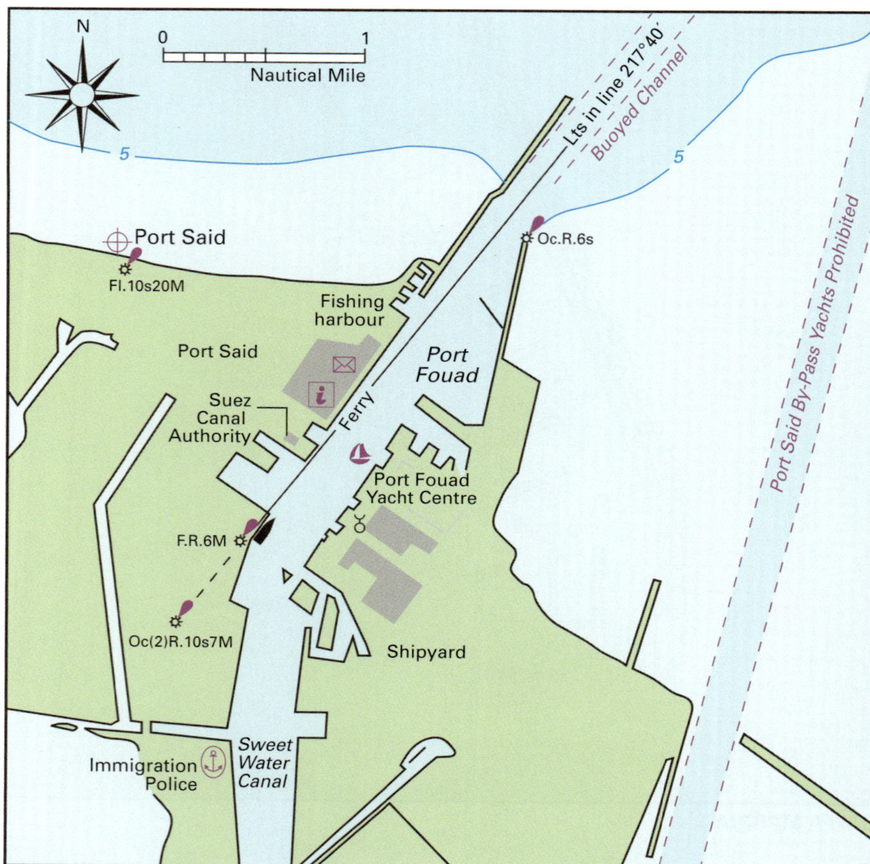

PORT SAID

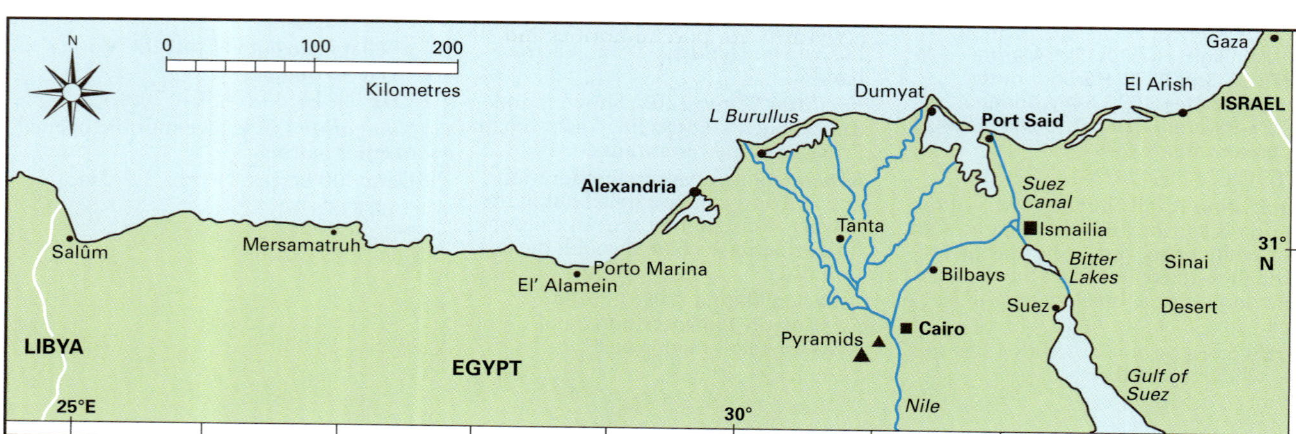

Facilities Water. 220V. Showers and toilets. Fuel by arrangement. Limited yacht repairs. Provisions and restaurants.

Remarks Agents will approach you at Port Fouad. Most yachts now use an agent.

SUEZ CANAL
31°15'·1N 32°21'·6E (E breakwater FW)
BA 233, 240

☆ Breakwater E side F. Breakwater W side F. New channel km 2·378 E side Fl(2)R.10s25m W side Fl(2)G.10s25m. Ismailia quay F.R.11m8M

VHF Port Said 1 Ch 16. Port Said 2 Ch 12. Port Said 3 Ch 09, 13, 73. Port authorities Ch 16. Pilot Ch 12. Measurement office Ch 73.
Port Suez. Port Tewfik 1 Ch 16.
Port Tewfik 2 Ch 11.
Port Tewfik 3 Ch 09, 14, 74.
Port authorities Ch 16. Pilot Ch 11. Inside harbour Ch 14. Measurement office Ch 74.

Navigation Pilotage is compulsory for the canal. Enquire at Port Fouad Yacht Centre for advice or consult other yachtsmen regarding the fees and reliability of agents. Recently fees for yachts using the canal have been standardised.

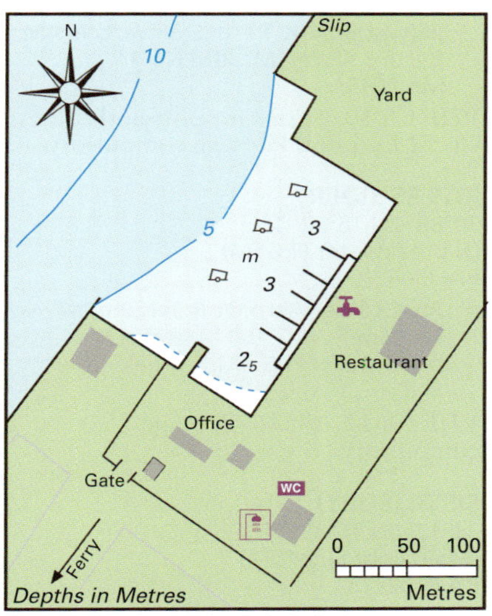

PORT FOUAD YACHT CENTRE

PORT TEWFIK-SUEZ
29°56'·5N 32°34'·3E

Port at the S end of the Suez Canal.

SUEZ CANAL AGENTS
Felix Agency, (Nagib Latif) ✆ 66 33 33 132
Email felix@felix-eg.com
VHF Ch 12.

The Prince of the Red Sea (Mohammed F Soukar or his son Heebi) ✆ 62 222 126
Email princeoftheredsea@gega.net
VHF Ch 16.

Fees
Fees for 12m yacht:
Southbound approx US$350.
Northbound approx US$250.

DAMIETTA MOUTH
31°31'·4N 31°50'·9E
(Entrance E side light Fl(2)30s20M)
BA 2578

☆ Entrance Fl(2)30s47m20M/Fl.G.10s14m8M. El Girbi Fl.G.3s4m5M

DAMIETTA PORT
31°29'·3N 31°45'·6E
(E breakwater Fl(2)R.10s6M)
BA 2578

☆ DirLt 191·5° Front F.R.33m10M. Rear F.R.4m10M
Entrance Fl.G.5s6M/Fl(2)R.10s6M. No.37 Fl.Bu.2·5s7M. Barge canal E end N side No.35 Fl.G.5s6M. S side No.36 Fl(2)R.10s8M. W end S side No.33 Fl.G.5s7M. N side No.34 Fl(2)R.10s7M

VHF Ch 16 for port authorities and pilot.

Navigation Pilotage compulsory.

EL MA'DÎYA
31°16'·4N 30°09'·2E
(W breakwater head Fl.G.5s2M)

☆ Entrance Fl.G.5s / Fl(2)Y.5s4m2M / Fl.R.5s. Leading lights (177·5°) Front F.WR(vert)4M. Rear F.WR(vert)4M

VHF Ch 69.

Navigation Pilotage compulsory.

ALEXANDRIA (EL ISKANDARIYA)
31°12'·9N 29°53'·7E
(Eastern Harbour)
BA 302

☆ Eastern harbour entrance Fl.R.5s14m5M/Fl.G.5s21m8M/F.Y. Rās el-Tîn Fl(2+1)30s52m21M. Agamy Fl(2)15s17m15M. Great Pass entrance S side (Bn) Fl.4s21m16M. Leading lights 113°
Front 2F.R(vert)18m5M+F.13m5M.
Rear 2F(vert)38m10M.
North Shoal Fl.R.5s5M.
El Dikheila Airport Aero Al.Fl.WG.9m.
Outer breakwater Fl.R.3s20m8M.
Quarantine breakwater Fl.G.3s20m8M. Petroleum harbour entrance Fl.G.5s5m2M/Fl.R.5s2M.
Inner harbour coal quay Fl(2)R.10s7m.
Arsenal basin W mole Fl.R.3s18m.
Arsenal quay Fl.G.
El Dikheila leading lights 173°
Front Fl.3s14m14M.
Rear Iso.2s31m17M.
Breakwater head Fl.9m5M
Fl.R.6m(×2) / Fl.G.6m(×2)
Jetty Fl.R.4s2M. Platform 3Mo(U)15s10M+Horn Mo(U)30s

VHF Ch 16 for port authorities and pilot. Pilot compulsory for sailing yachts over 100 tons and motor yachts over 150 tons.

Navigation Yachts normally make for the Eastern Harbour where the Yacht Club of Egypt arranges berthing.

Berths Anchorage on the W side.

Shelter Uncomfortable with strong N winds.

Facilities Water at YC. Fuel. Slipway and limited yacht repairs. Provisions and restaurants.

SIDIR KERIR
31°03'·4N 29°40'·2E (2F.R.9m5M)
BA 3325

☆ Leading lights 142° Front 2F.R.9m5M. Rear 2F.R.13m5M.
N breakwater Fl.G.2s5M. E breakwater Fl.R.4s5M

VHF Ch 16, 78, 79.

PORTO MARINA
30°50'·4N 29°01'·7E

A new marina project near Alamein on the Mediterranean coast of Egypt.

Navigation Entrance channel into marina on 210°M. Depths 5–7m. Care needed of shoals on either side of the channel.

Data 500 berths. Max LOA 100m. Depths 2·5–7m. Charge band 2.

Facilities Water. 220V. Fuel. Waste pump-out. Hauling and repair facilities.
✆ 046 445 2711
Email cap.tawfikonsi@yahoo.com

EL'ALAMEIN (MERSA EL HAMRA)
30°58'N 28°51'E
BA 3326

VHF Ch 10, 12, 14, 16.

MERSA EL FALLAH
31°21'·0N 27°20'·8E (Jetty N end F.G)
BA 2574

☆ Jetty N end F.G(occas). S end F.G(occas). Reef N end F.R(occas)

MERSA MATRUH
31°22'·2N 27°13'·7E
BA 3400

☆ No. 1 Q.G.6m5M. No. 2 Q.R.6m5M

SALÛM HARBOUR
31°33'·7N 25°09'·9E

☆ Pier head Fl(3)20s14m12M

10.18 Libya

TIME ZONE UT+1 ✆ IDD +218

Due to the current instability the FCO advises against all travel to Libya.

Prior to the overthrow of Gaddafi, Libya was developing its tourism infrastructure, and this included plans for several new marinas, free-trade zones and associated development. Places earmarked for such development include Benghazi (Al Madinah al Hurra), Tripoli (Hay-al Andalus), the Green river, and Farwa Island.

Following the overthrow of the Gaddafi regime it is not known whether these projects will continue.

PORT BARDIA
31°45'·6N 25°06'·5E
(Mingar Raai Ruhah light Fl.5s12M)
BA 3401

☆ Mingar Raai Ruhah Fl.5s98m12M. Raz Azzaz Fl.3s16m10M

MERSA TOBRUCH (TOBRUK)
32°05'·3N 23°59'·4E
(Main light Fl(3)15s15M)
BA 3657

☆ Main light Fl(3)15s53m15M. Punta Tòbruch Fl.G.5s6m6M. Marsa Umm Esc-sciausc Leading lights 224°48' Front Q.21m7M. Rear Iso.2s26m7M. Marsa El Hariga Oil Terminal E end F.R.9m2M. Berth No. 2 E end 2F.G(vert)10m2M. W end 2F.G(vert)10m2M. T-jetty 2F.G.2M. Commercial Pier head Q.R. No. 1 Quay W end Oc.RG.15s

VHF Ch 09, 12, 16, 19 for port authorities and pilot. Pilotage compulsory.

DERNA (DARNAH)
32°45'·9N 22°39'·8E
(N mole light Fl(2)G.6s7M)
BA 3401

☆ Main light Fl(4)20s60m20M. Entrance Q.G.8M/Q.R.8M

VHF Ch 16 for port authorities and pilot. Pilotage compulsory.

BHENGHAZI (BANGHAZI)
32°06'·9N 20°01'·6E
(N breakwater light Fl.R.3s6M)
BA 3352

☆ Main light (Musselman Cemetery) Fl.3s41m17M. Main harbour entrance Fl.R.3s13m6M/Fl.G.3s13m6M. Dir Lt 066° DirF.WRG.13m14-9M. No.4 berth Q.R.5m1M. No.3 berth Q.5m3M. Central mole head Q.G.5m1M. Inner basin mole head Fl.R.3s5m2M. No.1/18 berth Fl.3s5m4M. No.19/M8 berth Q.5m3M. MB berth Fl(3)10s5m3M. No.22A berth Q.R.5m1M. No.22 berth Fl(3)R.10s5m2M. Outer harbour W breakwater S head Q.R.13m4M. Head Iso.5s10m6M. Head Fl(3)G.10s13m4M/Q.5m3M

VHF Ch 12, 16 for port authorities and pilot. (Callsign *Bhenghazi Port Control*).

EZ ZUEITINA (AZ ZUWAYTINAH)
30°56'N 20°00'E
(Terminal light float Mo(Z)10s10M)
BA 3346

☆ Radio Mast Q.R.137m15M/F.R.97m/F.R.56m. Leading lights 135° Front Fl.Y.1·5s7m10M. Rear Oc.Y.10s13m10M. Waffeya Fl(6)10s5M/Fl(2)13s31m16M. LPG berth Q.R

VHF Ch 13, 16 (callsign *Zueitina Marina*).

MARSA EL BREGA (AL BURAYQAH)
30°25'·1N 19°35'·4E
(W breakwater head Fl.G.3s15M)
BA 3350

☆ W breakwater head Fl.G.3s12m15M. E breakwater head Q.R.12m15M. Leading lights (143°41') Front Q.R Rear Fl.R. Approach lights (in line on 235°05') Rear F.R. Common Front Oc.R. Approach lights (in line on 239·1°) Rear F.R. Leading lights (167°38') Front IQ.8s Rear IQ.15s. No. 2 berths (lights in line 145°48') Oc.R Common rear Q.R. Lights in line 147°33' Front Oc.R. Mooring island No. 3 berth F.R.28m. Inner harbour leading lights (223°58') Front F.Y Rear F.Y. Gas jetty SE end F.G, NE end F.R. Intake Fl.G

VHF Ch 09, 12, 13, 16 for port authorities and pilot. Pilotage compulsory. (Callsign *Brega Port Control*).

Data 10 moorings.

RĀS LANUF
30°30'·4N 18°35'·7E
(Main breakwater head Oc(2)G.10s5M)
BA 3343

☆ Water Tower Q(2)5s50m15M/F.R.52m. Entrance Fl(2)G.10s18m5M/Fl(2)R.10s18m5M. Leading lights (287·5°) Front F.12m9M. Rear F.17m4M. Jetty Berth 1 2F(vert)9m4M. Berth 2 3F(vert)9m4M. Berth 3 4F.9m4M. SBM No.4 Mo(U)15s.

VHF Ch 10, 16, 22 for port authorities. Ch 12 for pilot. Pilotage compulsory.

RĀS ES SIDER
30°38'·2N 18°22'·1E
(N breakwater Fl.G5M)
BA 3344

☆ Rās Es Sider Aero.Oc.R.3s120m8M/F.R.94m/F.WRG. Rijl Matratin N breakwater Fl.G.5M. S breakwater Fl.R

VHF Ch 12, 14, 16. Pilotage compulsory.

SIRTE (SURT)
31°12'·5N 16°35'·6E
(Main light Fl.5s15M)
BA 3402

☆ Main light Fl.5s35m15M

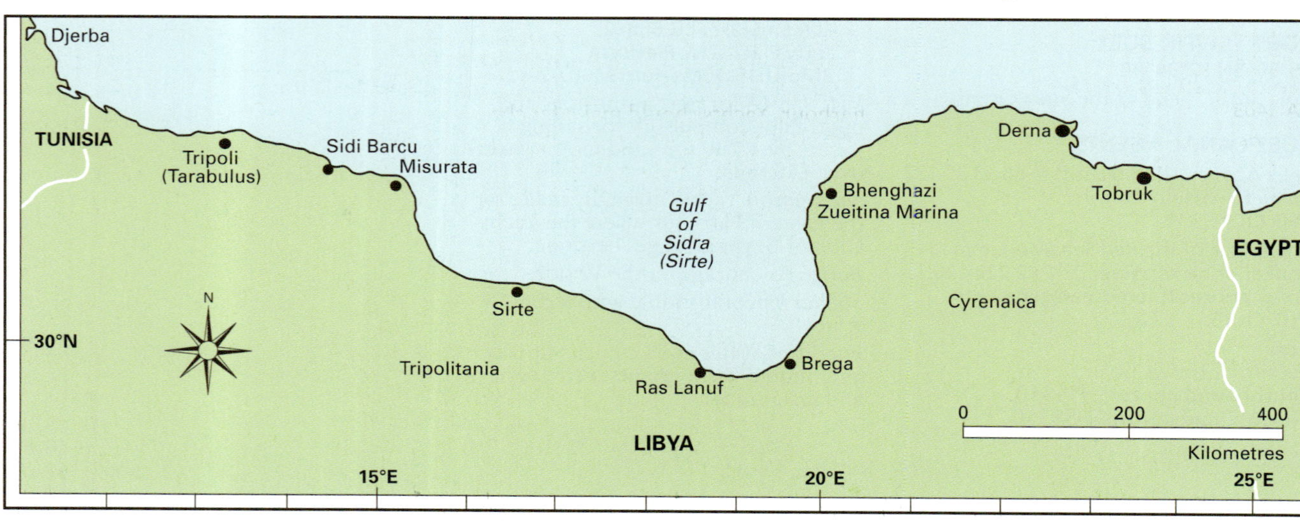

QASR AHMED (MISURATA)
32°22'·4N 15°13'·7E
(N breakwater light Fl.G.10s)
BA 3402

☆ Rãs Zarrùgh Fl.5s24m8M. Entrance Fl.G.10s/Fl.R.5s. Leading lights (270°) Front Fl.G.5s Rear Fl.G.12s

VHF Ch 12, 16 for port authorities and pilot (0800–2000). Pilotage compulsory.

Free trade port.

SIDI BARCU
32°38'·4N 14°20'·0E (Jetty F.R)

☆ Jetty F.R

AL KHUMS
37°40'·9N 14°16'·1E

Commercial cargo and fishing harbour.

TRIPOLI (TARABULUS)
32°54'·3N 13°10'·7E
(Spanish mole main light Fl(2)10s12M)
BA 248

☆ Spanish mole main light Fl(2)10s60m12M. No. II Leading lights (175°) Front F.R.17m Rear F.R.25m. No. 1 Fl.G.3s13m10M. No. 2 Fl.R.3s13m10M. No. 4Fl(2)R.6s13m 10M. NE breakwater head LFl.G.8s10m. NW breakwater head LFl.R.8s10m. Spanish mole pier head Iso.G.4s10m 4M. Karamanli mole head Fl(2)R.6s10m4M. Marsa Dila Fl.4s24m

VHF Ch 08, 12, 14, 16 for port authorities and pilot (0600–1800). Pilotage compulsory.

MARINA ANDALUS
32°53'·1N 13°09'·0E

New marina under development as part of the Hi Elandalous Village in western Tripoli. Hotel, golf course, spa and shopping centre all planned. Basic construction complete but continued fighting in the area means it is unlikely to open in the near future.

ZAWIA
32°47'·5N 12°40'·9E (Jetty Fl.RG.7s)
BA 3403

☆ Jetty head Fl.RG.7s

VHF Ch 12, 16, 22, 27. Pilotage compulsory.

ZUARA (ZUWARAH)
32°55'·4N 12°07'·2E
(N mole head Fl.G.3s3M)
BA 3403

☆ Fl.5s15m12M. Entrance VQ.G.8M/VQ.R.8M

VHF Ch 16 for port authorities.

Fishing harbour.

ABBU KAMMASH
33°05'·7N 11°50'E (Jetty E head light VQ.R)

☆ Industrial complex Jetty E head VQ.R. W head VQ.G

VHF Ch 10, 11, 16.

10.19 Tunisia

TIME ZONE UT+1 ✆ IDD +216

Quick reference guide

For Key see page 139

Tunisia	*Shelter*	*Mooring*	*Fuel*	*Water*	*Provisions*	*Eating out*	*Charge band*
Zarzis	A	BC	A	A	A	A	
Ajim	B	AB	A	A	O	O	
Djerba Marina	B	A	A	A	A	A	
Gabes	A	B	A	A	A	A	
Maharés	O	B	A	A	A	A	
Sidi Youssef	A	C	O	A	O	C	
Port de Najet	B	B	A	A	O	C	
El Ataya	A	A	A	A	C	O	
Sfax	C	AB	A	A	A	A	
La Chebba	O	AB	A	A	C	B	
Mahdia	A	AB	A	A	A	A	
Teboulba	B	B	A	A	B	B	
Monastir Harbour	A	AB	A	A	C	C	
Monastir Marina	A	A	A	A	A	A	2
El Kantaoui	A	A	A	A	A	A	2/3
Yasmine Hammamet	A	A	A	A	C	C	2/3
Ben Khiar	C	AB	A	A	O	O	
Kelibia	O	B	A	A	A	A	2
La Goulette	A	A	A	A	A	A	
Sidi Bou Said	B	A	A	A	C	C	2/3
Bizerte	B	A	A	A	A	A	2
Bizerte Marina	A	A	A	A	A	A	
Tabarka	A	AB	A	A	A	A	2

East coast

EL KETEF
33°11'·1N 11°29'·3E
BA 3403

☆ Entrance Iso.G.6s5M/Q(3)R.10s5M

ZARZIS
33°30'·0N 11°08'·5E
BA 3403 SHOM 4245, 7524

☆ Main light Oc(2+1)12s15m15M (180°-vis-090°) (270°). Emergency light F.R.10M. Fishing harbour Fl.G.4s7M / Fl.R.5s6m8M. Breakwater head Fl(2+1)15s11m12M

VHF Ch 10 (24/24) for port control. Ch 16 (0600–2000) for harbourmaster.

Navigation Buoyed channel into harbour. Yachts should make for the inner harbour in the NW corner.

Berths Alongside in inner basin or anchorage in the middle of the inner harbour clear of E side.

Shelter Good shelter.

Facilities Water. WC and showers. Fuel. 50-ton slipway. Mechanical and engineering repairs. Provisions and restaurants. PO. Bank.

Remarks A 3km walk to the town centre.

Note Port of entry.

Harbourmaster ✆ 568 0304
Port Control ✆ 568 0850

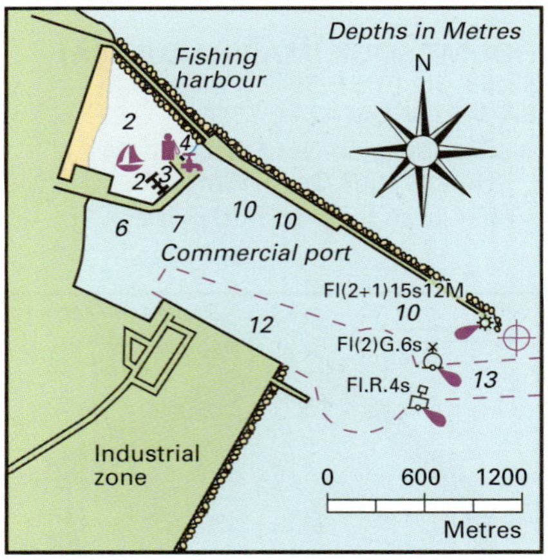

ZARZIS

AJIM (DJERBA)
33°42'·75N 10°44'·5E
BA 3403 SHOM 4242, 7524

☆ Passe Ouest Fl(2)9s5m7M. No. 1 Buoy in port channel Fl(3)G.15s5m5M. Jetty head Fl(5)R.20s5M

Navigation Ferry and fishing port reached by an awkward buoyed channel.

Berths Stern or bows-to or alongside outermost pier or anchorage to SW.

Data Five berths. Max LOA 12m.

Facilities Water. Fuel. Café.

APIP Port Authority ✆ 75 655 002

HOUMT SOUK (MARINA DJERBA)

33°53′·3N 10°51′·5E
BA 3403 SHOM 4244, 7524

☆ Rās Tourg-en-Nes Fl.5s64m24M.
Houmt Souk Oc(2)7s9m14M

VHF Ch 16 for port authorities.

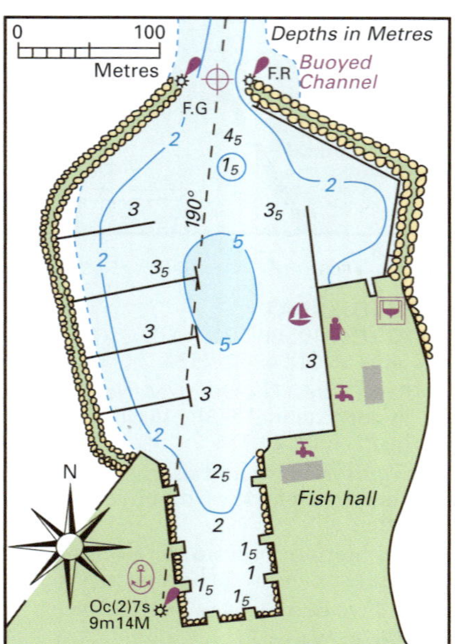

HOUMT SOUK (MARINA DJERBA)

Navigation Entrance is via a buoyed channel 4M long on 190°. Flood stream sets W and ebb E.

Data 200 yacht berths. Max LOA 20m. Depths 1·5–4m.

Berths Where directed on pontoons. Laid moorings. Anchorage on W side.

Shelter Adequate in the summer.

Facilities Water. 220V. Fuel. 40-ton travel-lift. Provisions and restaurants.

Remarks Village 2km away.

Note Port of entry.

Marina Djerba
✆ 71 806 392 / 75 652 211
Email marina.djerba@marinadjerba.com

ZARAT

33°42′·0N 10°21′·8E
BA 3403 SHOM 4242, 7524

☆ Entrance Fl(3)G.10s6m5M/
LFl.R.10s6m5M

Small fishing port. 0·5–1·5m depths.

GABES

33°53′·7N 10°07′·3E
BA 9 SHOM 4241, 7524

☆ Main light Fl(2)6s13m20M. Entrance Fl(2)G.9s10m6M/Fl.R.6·5s10m6M

VHF Ch 16 for port authorities (24/24).

Navigation Care needed as the entrance silts around the ends of the breakwaters.

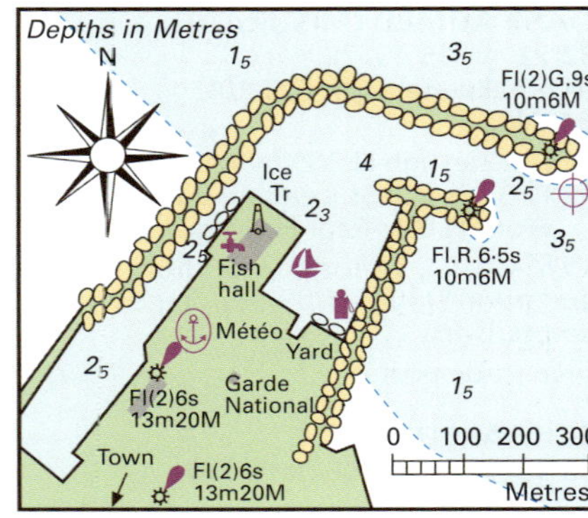

GABES

Berths On SE side of central pier (fish hall).

Shelter Good shelter.

Data 10 visitors' berths. Max LOA 19m. Depths 2–4·5m.

Facilities Water. Laundry Fuel quay. 200-ton travel-hoist. Some mechanical repairs. Provisions and restaurants. PO. Banks.

Harbourmaster ✆ 527 0367

PORT DE GHANNOUCHE

33°55′·5N 10°06′·7E
(Jetée Nord Fl.G.3s15M)
BA 9 SHOM 4240, 7524

☆ Entrance Fl.G.4s12m8·3M/
Fl.R.5s12m10M

VHF Ch 12, 15, 16, 17 for port authorities and pilot. Pilotage compulsory.

Phosphate port 2M N of Gabes. Commercial vessels only.

LA SKHIRA

34°17′·0N 10°06′·0E
BA 9 SHOM 4239, 7524

☆ Baie des Sur-Kenis Fl.G.3s32m20M. Oil jetty head F.R.32m5M.

Note a number of beacons Nos 1–3, 6–11, Fl.R and Fl.G plus Fl.G.4s and Fl.R.4s have been established to mark the channel to the oil terminal which has been expanded.

VHF Ch 16 for port authorities and pilot.

Data Depths 1–2m.

Facilities Water. Fuel. Some provisions.

Remarks Tidal range 1·8m.

The fishing harbour 3M SW from the port is full of fishing boats and is also unsuitable for yachts.

MAHARÈS

34°30′·5N 10°29′·9E
BA 3403 SHOM 4315, 4239

☆ DirF.WRG.8m3M. Bn No. 1 Q.G.8m3M

VHF Ch 16 for port authorities.

Navigation Harbour built at the end of a causeway. Access via a dredged channel 356° on new minaret.

Berths Alongside outer pontoons.

Shelter Adequate in the summer.

Data 124 berths. Seven visitors' berths. Max LOA 12m. Depths 1·8m in channel and 1–2m in basin.

Facilities Water. Fuel quay. Provisions and restaurants. PO. Bank.
APIP Port office ☏ 74 290 543 (0830–1330).

Iles Kerkennah

SIDI YOUSSEF (ILE GHARBI)
34°39′·3N 10°57′·5E

☆ Mole Sud head Fl(2)G.6s8m5M. Mole Nord head Fl(3)R.12s8m5M. Dir light DirOc(2)WRG.9·6s9-7M. Entrance F.R.2M/F.G.2M

VHF Ch 16 (24/24).

Navigation Entrance is via a buoyed channel on 112°. Care needed of tidal stream.

Berths Anchor with a long line ashore in N corner. Keep well clear of ferry turning area.

Shelter Good shelter.

Data 10 visitors' berths. Max LOA 20m. Basin dredged to 3·5m.

Facilities Water. Café.

Remarks Village of Melita is 5km away. Ferry to Sfax.

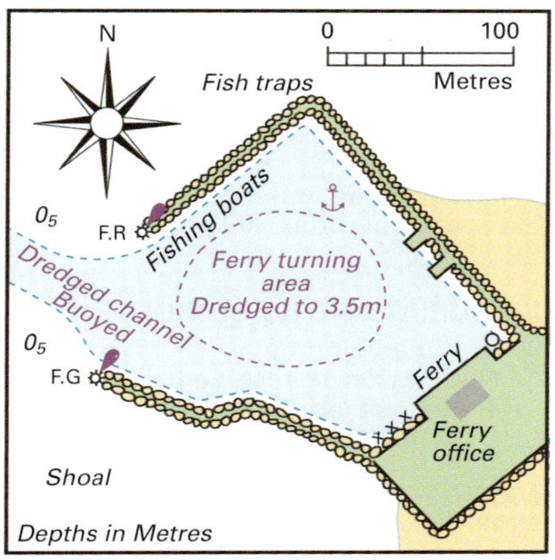

SIDI YOUSSEF

PORT DE NAJET (ILE CHERGUI)
34°49′·7N 11°15′·4E

☆ Rās Djila Fl(2)10s10m6M. Ennajet E jetty head Fl(2)R.10s5M/Fl.G on west jetty. El Awabed No.2 Fl.R.3s3M / Fl.G.3s nearby. Mole head Fl.3s5M

Navigation Care needed of sand banks in the approaches.

Berths Alongside.

Data 10 visitors' berths. Max LOA 12m. Depths 1–2m.

Facilities Water. Fuel. Café.
APIP Port Authority ☏ 74 487 450

EL ATAYA (ILE CHERGUI)
34°43′·7N 11°17′·7E

Navigation Access via Oued Mimoun channel marked by two buoys and palm fronds. Minimum depth 3·5m.

Berths Stern or bows-to N or E quay.

Shelter Good shelter.

Data 30 berths. Max LOA 12m. Depths 2–3·5m in basin.

Facilities Water. Fuel. 100-ton travel-hoist. Limited provisions.

SFAX
34°43′·0N 10°47′·0E
BA 1162 SHOM 4238, 4228

☆ Rās Tina Fl(2)10s55m24M. Quai du Commerce DirOc(2)8s18m13M. Fishing harbour S breakwater N head Fl.R.5s10M. N jetty SW end Fl.G.4s10M. Breakwater N head Iso.R.6s10M/Fl.Y.10s/Fl.Y.20s4M. Six pairs of lightbuoys mark the approach channel Fl.G/Fl.R

VHF Ch 14, 16 for port authorities.

Navigation Access via buoyed channel. Branch channel to fishing port at buoy Sfax 7 and 8.

Berths Clear in at commercial port under Dir light. Yacht berths at inner basin of commercial port. The fishing harbour is usually full.

Shelter Good shelter.

Data 10 visitors' berths. Depths minimum 3m.

Facilities Water. 220V at some berths. Fuel. 150-ton travel-hoist. 250-ton travel-hoist and slipway. Provisions and restaurants.

Remarks Fishing port oily and smelly.

Note Port of entry. Tidal range 1·5m.
Harbour captain ☏ 74 225 040 / 644
Fishing port harbourmaster ☏ 74 296 888

LA LOUZA (PORT DE LA LOUATA)
35°02′·5N 11°02′·1E
BA 3403 SHOM 4236

☆ Entrance Fl.R.5s7m6M / Fl.G.4s7m6M Bn No.2 Fl.R.4s3M. Bn No.1 Fl.G.4s. NR1 Fl.3s. NR6 Fl.4s. NR4 Fl.4s. NR5 Fl.3s.

VHF Ch 16.

Data Five visitors' berths. Max LOA 12m. Depths 1–2m.

Facilities Water. Fuel. Limited provisions.

Remarks Small fishing port.
APIP Port Authority ☏ 74 896 091
Harbourmaster ☏ 223 717

LA CHEBBA (SHEBBA)
35°13′·5N 11°10′·0E (Fl(2)G.9s6M)
BA 3403 SHOM 4227

☆ Tour Khadidja Fl(2)WR.9s27m19/14M (325°-R-135°). Lightbuoys Fl.G/Fl.R. Entrance Fl(2)G.9s8m6M/ Fl.R.6·5s8m6M

VHF Ch 16, 10 (0830–1800)

Navigation Access via dredged buoyed channel.

Berths Stern or bows-to or alongside outer pier.

Shelter Adequate in the summer.

Data 10 visitors' berths. Max LOA 25m. Depths 1·5–4m.

Facilities Water. Fuel quay. 50-ton slipway. Limited yacht repairs. Limited provisions. Restaurant.

Remarks Town 4km away.
Harbourmaster ☏ 73 643 044

SALAKTA
35°23′·8N 11°03′·0E

☆ Iso.R.4s

VHF Ch 16, 24.

Data 10 visitors' berths. Max LOA 12m. Depths 2-4m. Liable to silting.

Facilities Water. Fuel. Repairs.

Remarks Busy fishing harbour.
APIP Port Authority ☏ 73 666 415

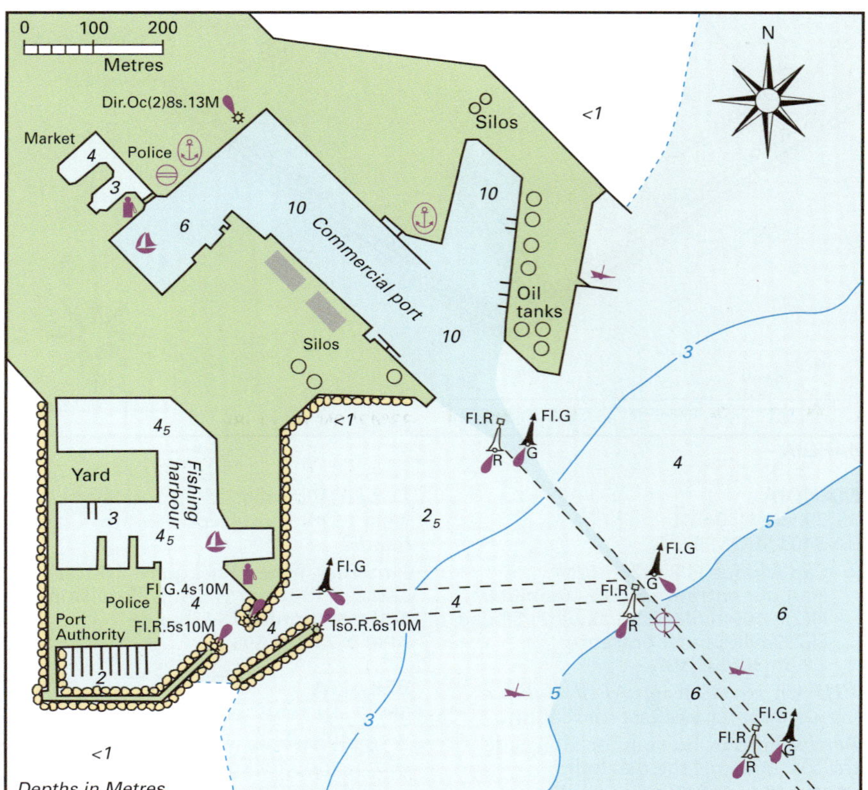

SFAX

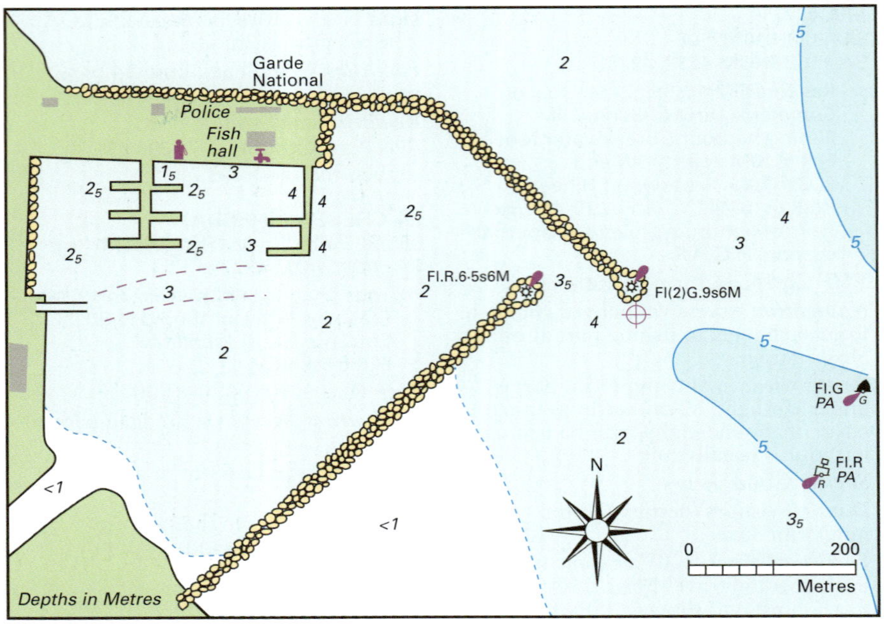

LA CHEBBA

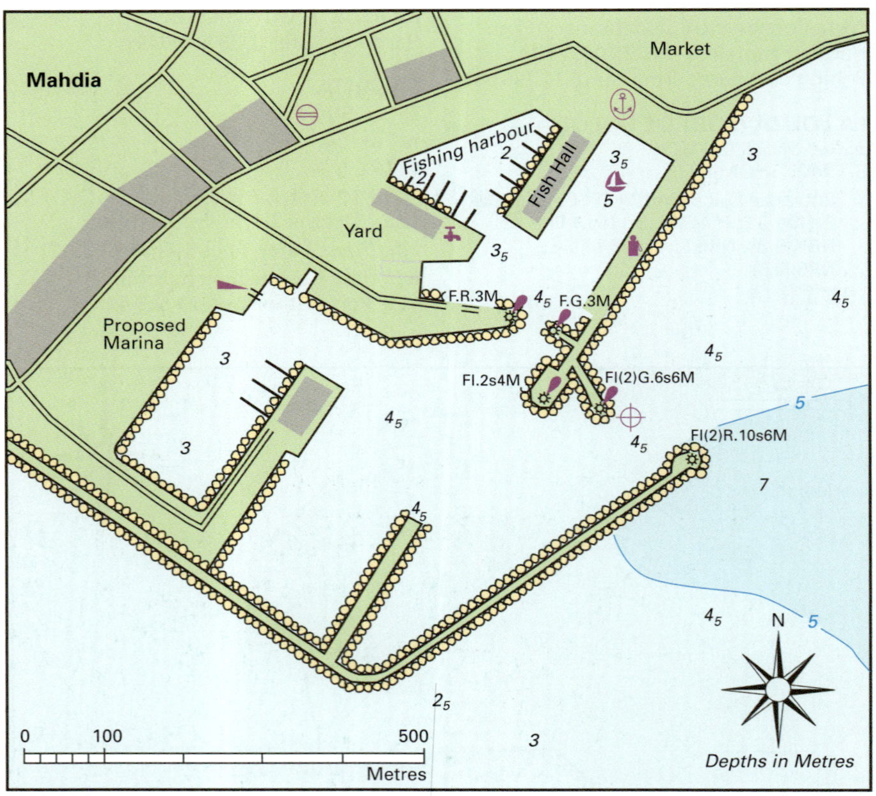

MAHDIA

MAHDIA

35°29′·8N 11°04′·1E
BA 3403 SHOM 4227

☆ Cap Afrique Fl.R.5s26m17M. Harbour entrance Fl(2)G.10s6m6M/ Fl(2)R.10s4m6M. E breakwater S head Fl.2s9m4M. Inner entrance F.R.5m3M/F.G.3M

VHF Ch 16. (Callsign *APIP Mahdia*). Ch 10 weather forecast on request.

Berths Stern or bows-to or alongside the SW quay off the fish hall.

Shelter Good shelter.

Data 610 berths. 15 visitors' berths. Max LOA 30m. Depths 2–5m. Charge band 2.

Facilities Water. Fuel quay. 10-ton crane. 250-ton travel-lift. Provisions and restaurants. PO. Banks

APIP ✆ 73 281 695

BEKALTA

35°37′·4N 11°03′·0E

A small harbour which is liable to silting and blocking with seaweed.

TEBOULBA

35°39′·5N 10°57′·4E
BA 1162 SHOM 4226

☆ Entrance LFl.G.10s7m5M/LFl.R.10s7m5M. Secondary Ch No.1 Fl.G.6s2M. No.2 Fl.R.6s2M. The channel to Teboula is marked by light bns.

VHF Ch 16.

Navigation Access via a dredged channel marked by a pair of buoys. Depths in the entrance channel are around 3–3·5m. Depths in the outer harbour are variable though mostly 3m but with some 1·5m patches. Care needed.

Berths Alongside.

Data Max LOA 20m. Depths 1–2m.

Facilities Water. Fuel quay. 130-ton hoist. Mechanical and engineering repairs. Other repairs possible although the yard is mostly used to fishing boats. Chandlery. Restaurant.

Remarks Village 3km away.

SAYADA

35°40′·4N 10°53′·6E

☆ NW jetty head Fl.G.4s7m5M. NE jetty head Fl(3)R.12s7m6M

A small fishing harbour reached via a dredged buoyed channel. Depths around 2m. Yachts berth on the SE quay.

Facilities Water and fuel in the harbour. Provisions, PO and bank in the village.

ILE KURIAT AND ILE CONIGLIERA

☆ Ile Kuriat lighthouse Fl.WR.5s30m18/14M. Centrale Thermique jetty Oc.G.5s8m5M/ Oc(2)10s8m5M

MONASTIR FISHING PORT

35°45′·28N 10°50′·41E WGS84

☆ Bordj el Kelb Fl(2)R.6s26m10M. Old fishing harbour shelter mole head Fl.R.5s12m5M. Entrance Fl.G.4s12m5M / Fl.R.5s12m5M

VHF Ch 16.

Navigation The fortress near Monastir marina entrance is conspicuous. Continue S past the old fishing harbour and the entrance to this new fishing harbour will be seen. The light Bordj el Kelb near the entrance is conspicuous.

Berths Limited yacht berths in this large new fishing harbour.

Shelter Good shelter.

Facilities Water. 220V. Toilets and showers. 300-ton travel-hoist. Large area hard standing. Limited security. Engineering work. Basic provisions and restaurant in the harbour. Town 3km.

Chantier Naval and Elite Services ✆ 73 449 037

Engineer Gamel Kouraichi ✆ 73 425 368

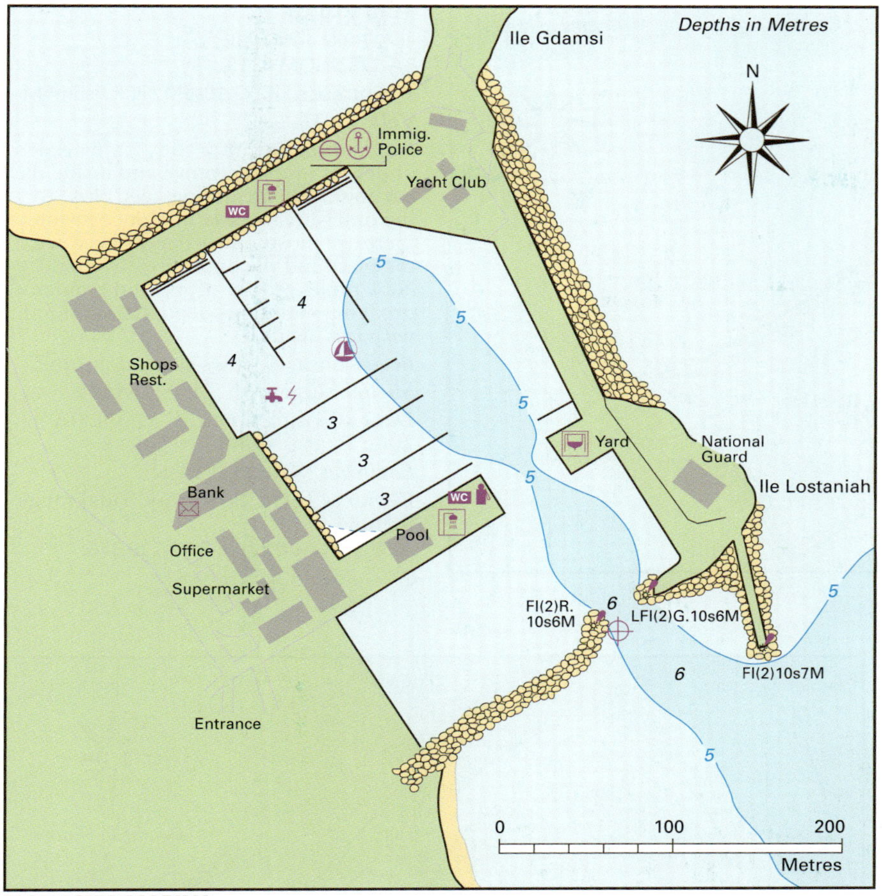

MONASTIR MARINA

EL KANTAOUI MARINA

35°53'·45N 10°36'·36E WGS84
BA 1162 SHOM 4315

☆ Entrance Fl.G.6s6M / Fl.R.6s9m6M. Channel buoys sometimes lit Fl.G/Fl.R

VHF Ch 06, 16.

Navigation Access via buoyed channel on 305°. Channel silts and is periodically dredged.

Berths Where directed. Laid moorings tailed to buoys.

Shelter Good shelter.

Data 340 berths. Visitors' berths. Max LOA 40m. Depths 2–4m. Charge band 2/3.

Facilities Water. 220V/380V. Showers and toilets. Laundry. Telephone. TV. Fuel quay. 40-ton travel-hoist. 5-ton crane. Limited yacht repairs. Provisions and restaurants. PO. Bank.

Remarks Also a swimming pool, tennis courts and a golf course.

Port El Kantaoui ✆ 73 348 600 / 799
Email capitainerie@portelkantaoui.com.tn

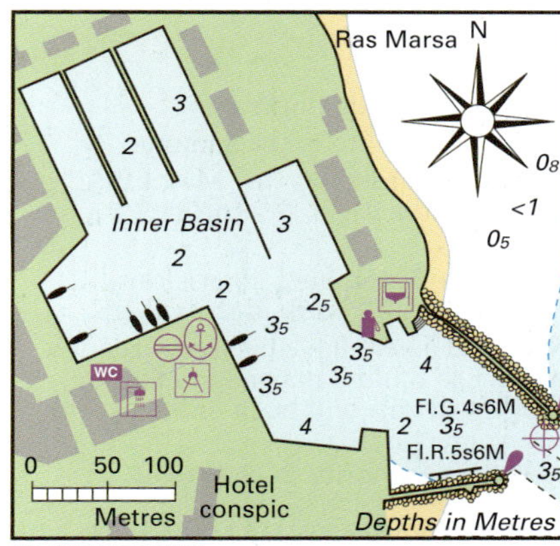

EL KANTAOUI

MONASTIR MARINA

35°46'·61N 10°50'·30E WGS84
BA 1162 SHOM 4226

☆ Ile Kuriat Fl.WR.5s30m14/18M. Entrance Fl(2)10s11m7M / Fl.G.4s8m6M / Fl.R.5s8m6M

VHF Ch 16 (0800–1800).

Berths Stern or bows-to where directed. Finger pontoons or laid moorings tailed to buoys.

Shelter Good shelter and security.

Data 400 berths. 200 visitors' berths. Max LOA 45m. Depths 3–5·5m. Approach channel 6m min. Charge band 2.

Facilities Water. 220V/380V. Toilets and showers. Laundry. Telephone and television connections for berths 12m+. Fuel quay. 35-ton travel-hoist. Yacht repairs. Camping Gaz. Provisions and restaurants. Telephone and fax service.

Remarks Also other facilities including tennis courts, swimming pool and YC. Close to town centre. Very popular with yachts over-wintering.

Jalel Ben Salem, Responsable du Port, Marina Cap Monastir ✆ 73 462 305
Email capitaineriemonastir@topnet.tn

SOUSSE

35°49'·40N 10°39'·53E WGS84
BA 1162 SHOM 4102

☆ Kasbah Fl.4s70m22M. Jetée Abri Oc.WR.4s12m10/6M. Entrance Fl.G.4s10m8M / Fl.R.5s10m8M. Lightbuoy LFl.G.6s5M

VHF Ch 16 for port authorities.

Large commercial harbour. Yachts are directed to the marina, except in emergencies.

Harbourmaster ✆ 73 255 755

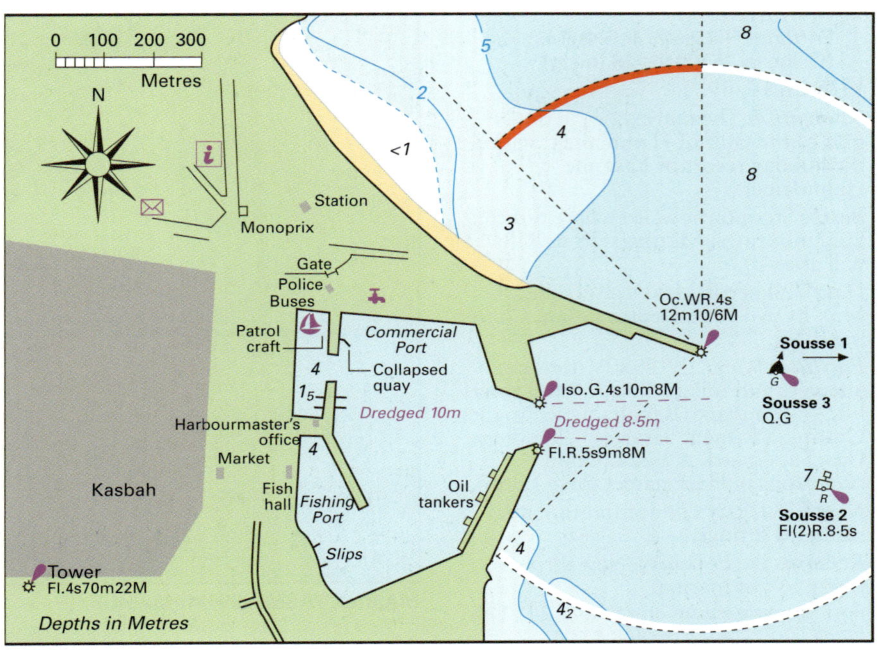

SOUSSE

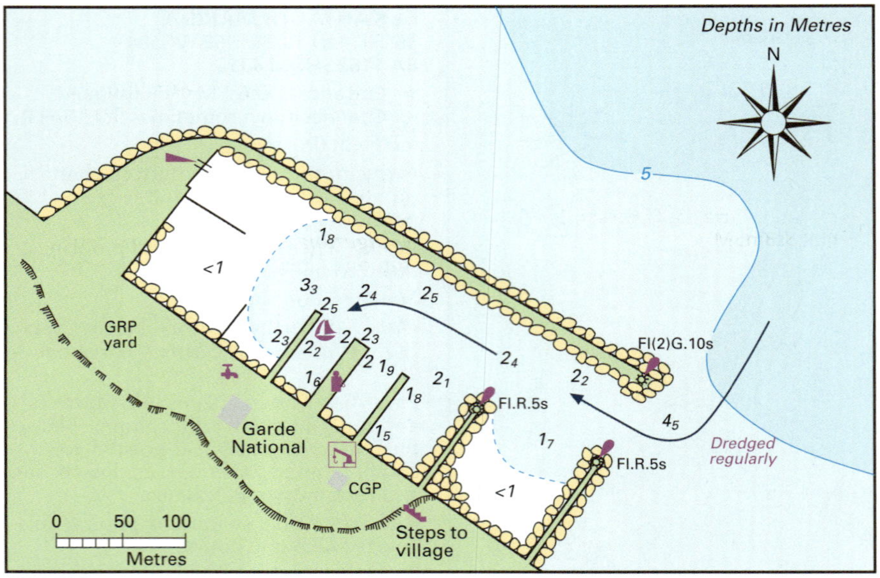

HERGLA

BENI KHIAR

36°27'·0N 10°47'·8E
BA 176 SHOM 4315

☆ Entrance Fl(2)G.10s6M / Fl.R.5s5m6M

VHF Ch 16.

Navigation Entrance silts. Care needed of depths in the entrance and inside the harbour. When entering keep close to the outer breakwater and once inside there are mostly 2m+ depths between the piers and the outer breakwater. New moles reduce silting and regular dredging maintains depths around 3m, with less inside.

Berths Stern or bows-to or alongside.

Shelter Surge with SW–SE winds.

Data 20 visitors' berths. Max LOA 20m. Depths 1–3m (irregular).

Facilities Water. WC. Fuel.

Remarks Town 2km away. Tidal range 0·5m.

APIP Port Authority ☏ 72 229 376

HERGLA

36°01'·9N 10°30'·7E
BA 176 SHOM 4315

☆ Entrance Fl(2)G.10s5m6M/ Fl.R.5s9m6M. Nouvelle jetée sud head Fl.R.5s9m6M

VHF Ch 16.

Berths Alongside finger pier.

Shelter Adequate in the summer.

Data 10 visitors' berths. Max LOA 12m. Depths 0·1–2·5m (prone to silting).

Facilities Water. Fuel. Provisions, market PO and bank in the village.

Remarks There have been reports of a project to build a marina in Hergla. Further details will be in online supplements.

APIP Port Authority ☏ 73 251 464

MARINA YASMINE HAMMAMET

36°22'·01N 10°32'·70E WGS84

☆ Fl(2)15s12M.
Entrance Fl.R5s6M/ Fl.G.4s6M.
NE corner VQ(3)10s4M (buoy)

VHF Ch 16, 09.

Navigation The marina lies in the N part of the Gulf of Hammamet, within the holiday resort of Yasmine Hammamet.

Berths Stern or bows-to where directed. Laid moorings. Marina staff in RIBs will assist.

Data 720 berths. 100 visitors' berths. Max LOA 110m. Depths 2–6m. Charge band 2/3.

Facilities Water. 220/380V. Internet. Showers and toilets. Fuel. 80-ton travel-lift. 40-ton crane. Repairs by Rodrigues Group SNP Yacht Services. Chandlery. Gas. Supermarket. Bank. Good provisions in Hammamet town (5km).

Note Electricity connections are not standard fittings.

Remarks Port of entry. New airport 20km SW of marina.

Port Yasmine Hammamet ☏ 72 241 111
Email contact@portyasmine.com.tn
www.portyasmine.com.tn

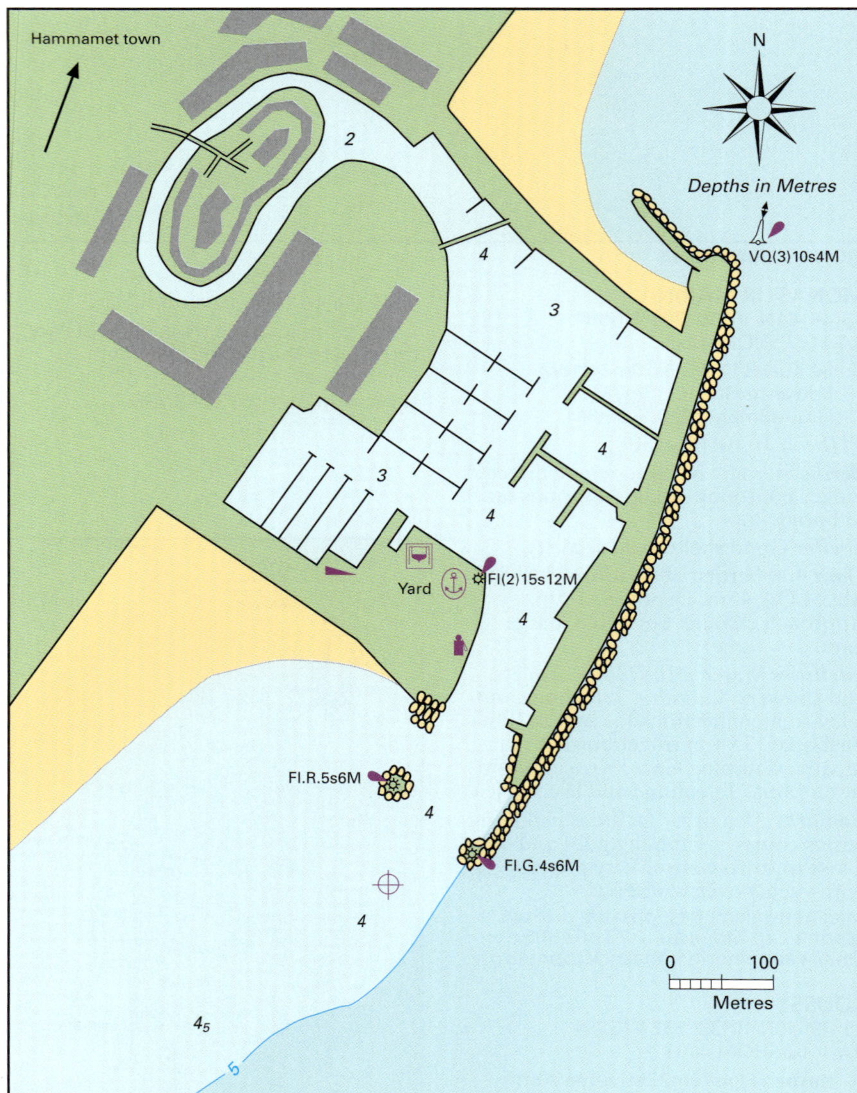

MARINA YASMINE HAMMAMET

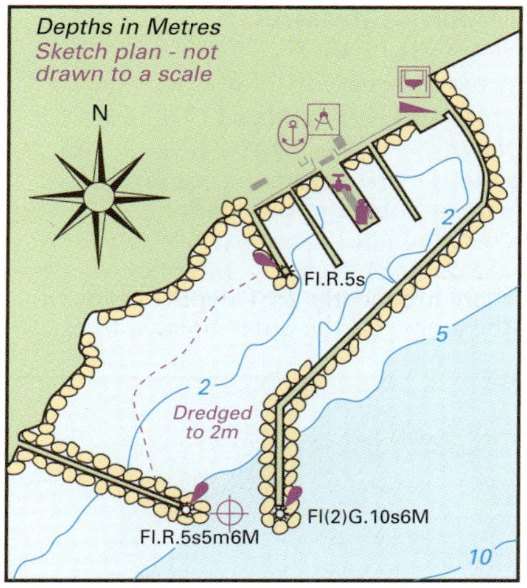

BENI KHIAR

KELIBIA
36°50′·1N 11°06′·6E
BA 2122 SHOM 4183

☆ Fortress Fl(4)20s82m23M. S Jetée head Fl(2)8s.5m5M. Entrance Fl.G.4s5m2M/Fl.R.2s5m2M

VHF Ch 16 for port authorities (24/24).

Berths Rafted out alongside either side of Navy pier. Charge band 2.

Shelter Adequate in the summer. Frequent squalls from the NW.

Facilities Water. 220V. Fuel quay. 250-ton travel-hoist. Limited yacht repairs. Provisions and restaurants.

Remarks Useful port of entry from Malta or Sicily. Town 2km away.

Note Radio Keliba transmits weather reports on VHF Ch 16/72 at 0600 and 1000.

APIP Port Authority ✆ 72 273 639 / 074

North coast

Ilot Zembra

ZEMBRA
37°07′·0N 10°48′·4E

☆ Djamour es Srir Fl.4s59m6M. Djamour el Kebir entrance Fl.G.4s5m5M / Fl.R.5s3m5M

EL HAOUARIA
37°04′·5N 10°58′·6E

A new port. Only suitable for shoal draught craft.

SIDI DAOUD
37°01′·3N 10°54′·3E
BA 2122 SHOM 4191

☆ Entrance Fl(2)R.10s3m6M/ Fl(2)G.10s3m6M

VHF Ch 16 (0730–1330).

Fishing port. Wind generators are conspicuous behind the harbour. Entrance via winding channel. The entrance to the harbour has two set nets outside it marked by cardinal buoys. However to get into the harbour you need to go between the N buoy of the S net and the W buoy of the N net. The channel has been reported dredged but is shallow outside of the channel. Inside the harbour there is a rocky area with 1m over and depths are irregular 0·5–2m. Care needed.

Berths Go stern or bows-to or alongside the S pier where there are depths around 2m. A dangerous wreck lies in the centre of the port, between the end of the S breakwater and the entrance to the S part of the harbour.

Facilities Water. Fuel. 30-ton slipway.

LA GOULETTE (TUNIS)
36°48′·3N 10°18′·9E
BA 1184 SHOM 6062

☆ Main light Jetée Nord S corner Fl(3)12s13m11M. Chimney 1M SW of entrance Fl.R.1·5s102m8M. Digue Nord Fl(2)G.10s5M. Port side F.R.5M. Digue Sud Fl.R.5s6M/Fl(2)Y.9s6M.

VHF Ch 10, 16 for YC.

Navigation A new 800m long cruise ship quay lies inside the commercial harbour.

Berths Stern or bows-to at YC in the N corner. Laid moorings on the pontoons.

Shelter Good shelter.

Data 150 berths. 30 visitors' berths. Max LOA 12m. Depths 2–5m.

Facilities Water. 220V. Showers and toilets. Fuel. 3-ton crane. Larger mobile crane can be arranged. Limited yacht repairs. Provisions and restaurants. Laundry.

Note The channel through the port leads up into Tunis city centre. Larger vessels may be permitted to navigate up here. There have been plans to develop a marina in this central location, but no details are available.

Remarks No longer a port of entry. Naval base. At times yachts have been turned away from here.

Commercial Harbourmaster ✆ 71 730 141
Port Authority ✆ 71 736 430
YC ✆ 71 736 284

SIDI BOU SAID
36°51′·8N 10°21′·0E
BA 1184 SHOM 6062

☆ Cap Carthage Fl.5s146m22M. Lightbuoy Fl(3)G.5s1M. Entrance Fl.G.5·5s6m4M/Fl.R.3s6m4M

VHF Ch 16, 09 (0730–1830).

Navigation Entrance liable to silt. Approach on a N course towards the conspicuous hotel, before turning parallel to the beach and heading towards the port side of the entrance. Entry is dangerous in strong winds NE–S.

Berths Stern or bows-to where directed. Laid moorings. Two underwater obstructions are reported close off the central pier. Max depth over 1·5m.

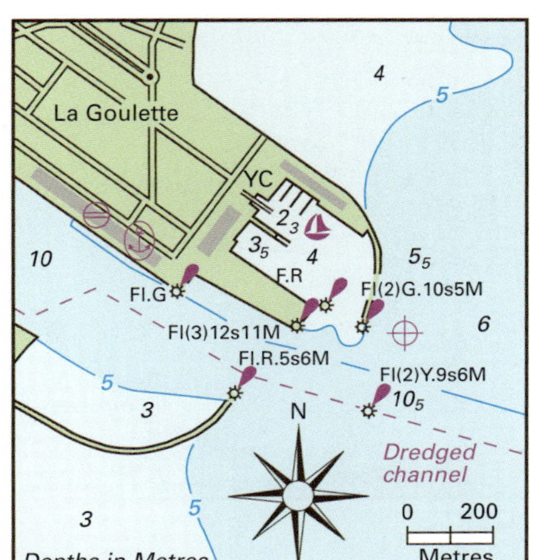

LA GOULETTE

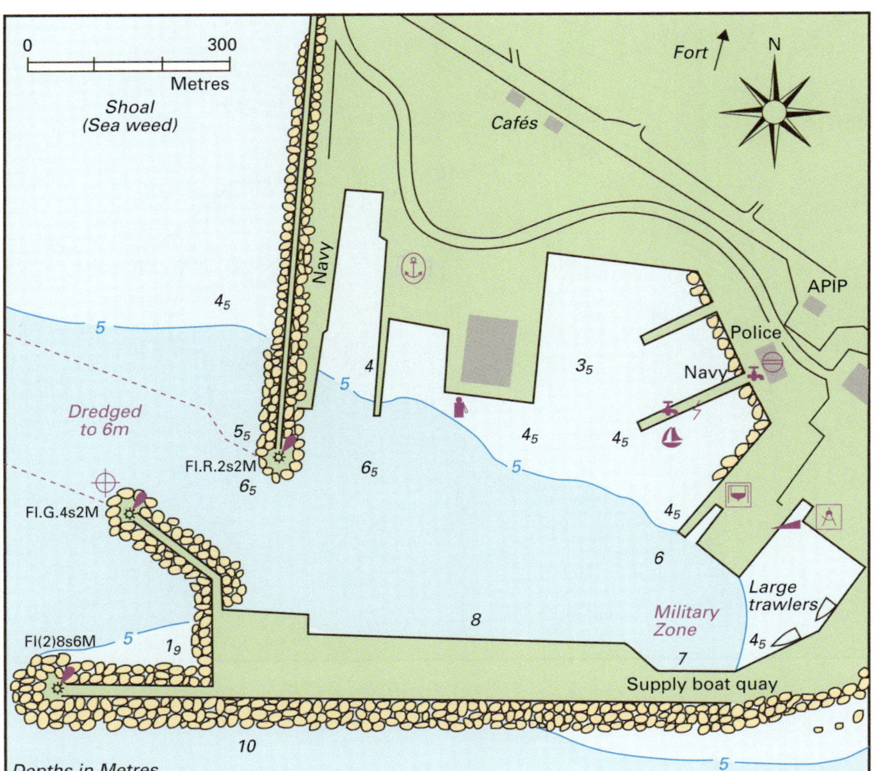

KELIBIA

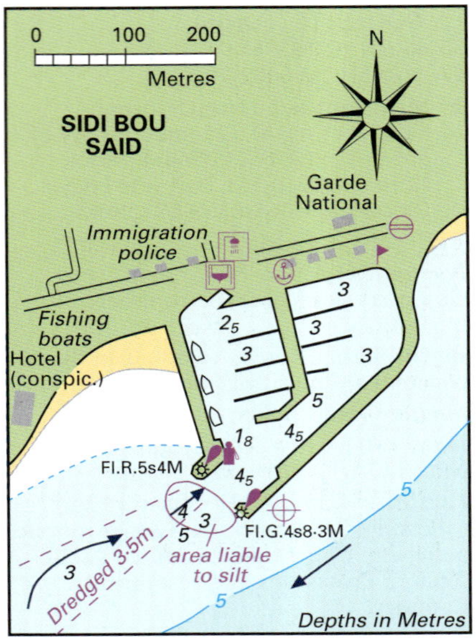

SIDI BOU SAID

Shelter Uncomfortable with SE–W winds.

Data 380 berths. 30 visitors' berths. Max LOA 30m. Depths 2–4·5m. Charge band 2/3.

Facilities Water. 220V/380V. Showers and toilets. Laundry. Fuel quay. 15-ton travel-hoist. Limited yacht repairs. Chandlers. Some provisions and restaurant.

Remarks A 10-minute taxi ride to La Marsa. Port of entry.

Harbourmaster ☏ 71 741 645
Fax 71 744 217
Email port.sbs@gnet.tn
YC ☏ 71 951 466

MARINA GAMMARTH

36°55'·2N 10°18'·7E

A new marina 5M N of Carthage.

Data 400 berths. Max LOA 25m.

Facilities Water. 220V. Showers and toilets. Cafés, bars and restaurants as part of hotel and residential development.

☏ 7128 6431
Email info@labaiedegammarth.com

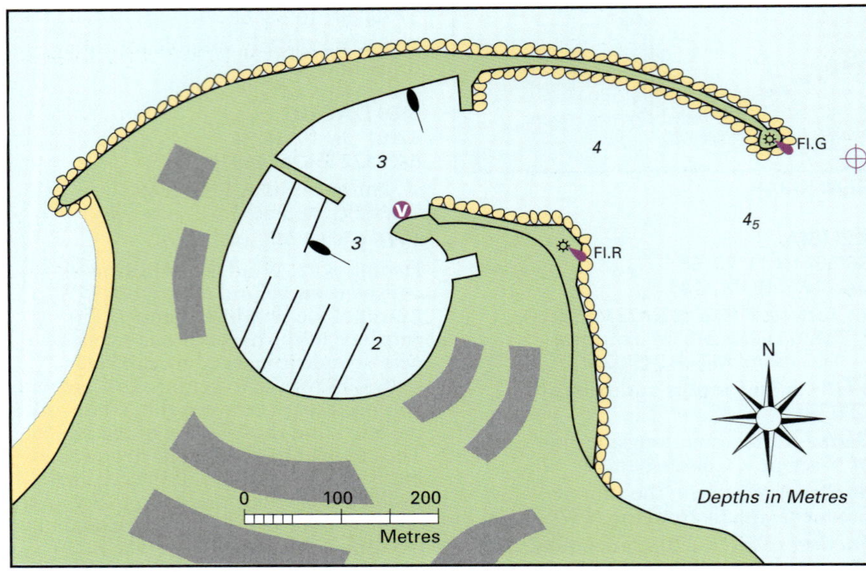

MARINA GAMMARTH

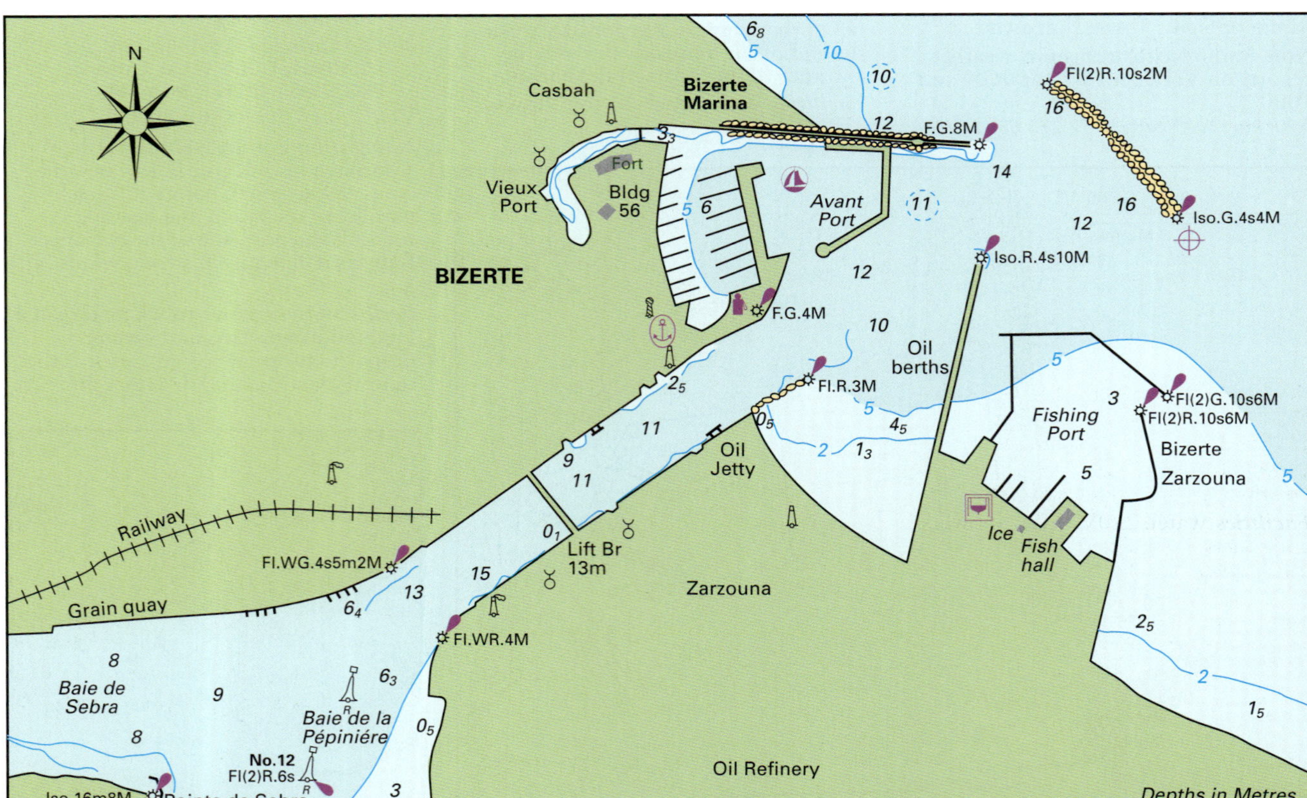

BIZERTE

TUNISBAY FINANCIAL HARBOUR

A new city project on the coast 15km N of Carthage airport. Centred around a marina basin, with apartments, hotels, university, shopping centre and golf course.

As yet there is no timescale for the project.

GHAR EL MELH (PORTO FARINA)

37°08′·6N 10°12′·4E
BA 2122 SHOM 4250

☆ Ile Plane Fl(2)WR.10s15/11M. Entrance Fl.G.4s5m6M / F.R.5s5m3·6M

VHF Ch 16.

Small fishing port. Entrance silts. Normally 2–4m in harbour. Yacht berth rafted up alongside.

Remarks The village is a long walk away.

CAP ZEBIB

37°16′·0N 10°04′·2E

☆ Fishing harbour jetty head Fl.G.4s6M/Fl.R.5s7M/Fl.R.5s3M

VHF Ch 16.

A remote harbour prone to silting. Depths inside 2–4m. Max LOA (after dredging) 15m.

BIZERTE ZARZOUNA

37°16′·5N 09°53′·8E

☆ Entrance Fl(2)G.10s6m6M/ Fl(2)R.10s6M

Fishing harbour. Depths 2–6m. 110/250-ton travel-hoist. Café and provisions.

BIZERTE MARINA

37°16′·9N 09°53′·5E (Fl(2)R.10s2M)
BA 1569 SHOM 5281

☆ Digue Exteriéure S head Iso.G.4s15m4M. N head Fl(2)R.10s10m2M. Avant Port entrance F.G.15m8M/ Iso.R.4s24m10M. Entrée du Goulet F.G.5m4M/Fl.R.5m3M. Goulet du Lac Quai Nord No. 9 Fl.G.4s2M. Quai sud No. 10 Fl.R.4s2M.

VHF Ch 11, 16, 04, 72.

Navigation Yachts should head for the new marina.

Berths Strong currents can make mooring difficult.

Shelter Adequate in the summer.

Data 800 berths. Max LOA 110m. Depths 1–6m. Charge band 3/4.

Facilities Water. 220V. WiFi. Showers and toilets. Fuel. Gas. 300-ton travel-lift. Limited yacht repairs (SEMB boatyard). Provisions and restaurants.

Bizerte Marina ☎ 98 708 819
Email info@marinabizerte.com
www.marinabizerte.com
Port de La Liberte ☎ 72 436 610
Tunisia Yacht Services (S&D Yachts, Malta) ☎ 72 431 480
Email siren@planet.tn
SEMB ☎ 72 592 677
Harbourmaster ☎ 72 431 688

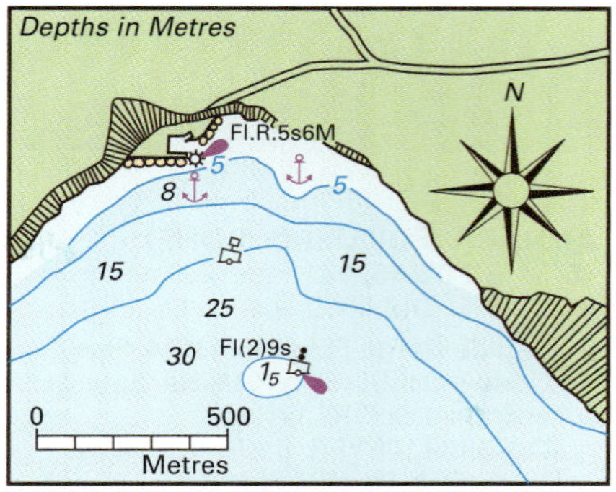

ILE DE GALITE. SOUTH ANCHORAGE

ILE DE GALITE

37°31′·5N 08°56′·5E
BA 1712 SHOM 5698

☆ Galiton de l'Ouest (37°29′·9N 08°52′·6E) Fl(4)20s168m24M/ F.R.160m22M

Anchorage and small port on S side of island. Anchor in 3–8m where convenient. Sheltered from the N but open S. Some shelter from SE winds in the cove on the N side opposite S anchorage.

TABARKA

36°57′·5N 08°45′·9E
BA 1712 SHOM 4087

☆ Ile de Tabarka Fl.5s72m17M. Fish harbour. Digue nord head Fl.G.4s10m6M. Digue est elbow Fl.R.5s10m6M. Digue interior Fl.R.5s8m5M

VHF Ch 16, 08, 10, 14.

Berths Where directed alongside or stern-to near the harbourmasters office on the breakwater. Laid moorings.

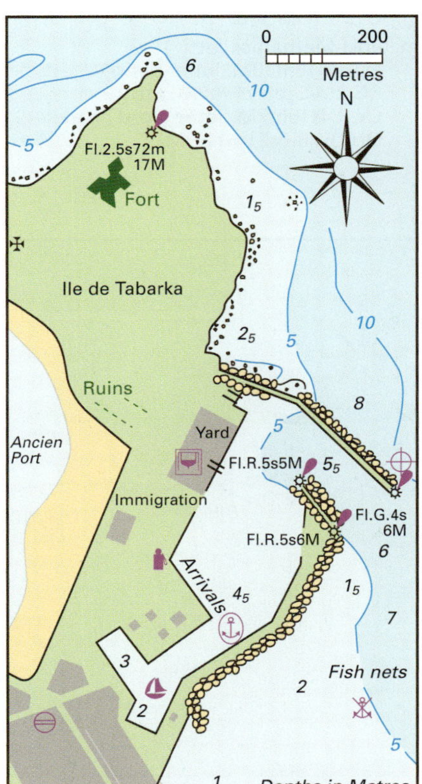

TABARKA

Shelter Good shelter.

Data 100 berths. 70 visitors' berths. Max LOA 40m. Depths 2–4·5m. Charge band 2.

Facilities Water. 220/380V. Shower and WC. Fuel quay. 250-ton travel-hoist. Limited yacht repairs. Provisions and restaurants. PO. Bank.

Remarks Seiche up to 2m reported. Port of entry.

Port de Plaisance ☎ 78 670 599
APIP Port Authority ☎ 78 643 112

SEAMTECH

A sails and canvas agent for all of Tunisia run under French management. Also agents for Profurl, International paints and Plastimo. Liferaft servicing.
☎ 984 56549
Email manu@seamtech.com
www.seamtech.com

10.20 Algeria

TIME ZONE UT+1 IDD +213

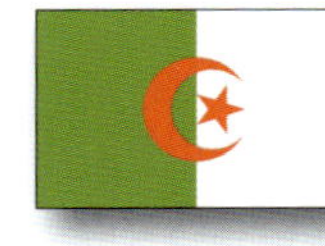

Note The current situation in Algeria appears calmer than in previous years, but you should contact the Foreign Office for up-to-date advice on travel. It is important if you do visit that you apply for a visa in advance, otherwise you will not be permitted to leave the port, or in some cases, to leave your vessel. Coastguard services can offer assistance without charge.

www.fco.gov.uk/travel

Quick reference guide

For Key see page 139

	Shelter	*Mooring*	*Fuel*	*Water*	*Provisions*	*Eating out*
Algeria						
Annaba	B	B	A	O	O	O
Stora	O	B	A	O	C	C
Bejaia	B	B	A	A	B	C
Sidi Ferruch	A	A	O	A	C	B
Cherchell	O	B	A	A	B	B
Mostaganem	B	B	B	A	B	C
Arzew	A	B	A	A	B	B
Oran	A	A	A	A	C	B

EL KALA
36°54′N 08°26′·6E

☆ Entrance Iso.R.4s17m9M

Small fishing port. Entry dangerous with strong NW winds. Liable to silting.

POINTE DU CIMETIÈRE
36°54′·1N 08°27′·5E (Fl.G.4s2M)

☆ Jetty Fl.G.4s10m2M. N quay F.R

ANNABA (FORMERLY BÔNE)
36°54′·3N 07°46′·9E
BA 1567 SHOM 5669

☆ Cap de Garde Fl.5s143m30M. Fort Génois Oc(2)6s61m10M. Harbour entrance Oc(3)G.12s9M/ Oc(2)R.6s10M/F.R. Basin F.G.3m2M/ F.R.3m2M. Pier F.G.2M/F.G.

VHF Ch 14.

Large commercial harbour. YC in N basin.

Berths Yachts are usually directed to the SW quay.

Facilities Fuel on the quay in the fishing harbour.

Note This harbour was closed to yachts in 2004. Port of entry.

CHETAIBI (MERSA TAKOUCH, FORMERLY HERBILLON)
37°04′·0N 07°23′·2E
BA 1712 SHOM 3024

☆ Cap Takouch Oc.WR.4s128m8/5M. Harbour Jetée Est F.G.9m2M. Jetée Ouest F.R.8m

Harbour open NE–E.

PORT METHANIER
36°53′·8N 06°57′·0E

A new oil terminal. Entry easy in most conditions. Open E.

Note Port of entry.

SKIKDA (FORMERLY PHILIPPEVILLE)
36°53′·6N 06°56′·9E
BA 855 SHOM 5787

☆ Port Methanier Jetty 1 Fl.G.4s16m10M. Inner basin W jetty F.G.2M/E jetty F.R.2M. Jetty 2 Oc.R.4s10m7M. Jetée Nord head Oc(2)WR.6s21m12/9M.

VHF Ch 12, 14, 16 for port authorities.

Large commercial harbour. Heavy surge makes entry difficult in strong N winds. The old yacht basin is no longer in use.

STORA
36°54′·1N 06°52′·9E
BA 855 SHOM 3061

☆ Ile Srigina Fl.R.5s54m20M. Ilôt des Singes Iso.WG.17m10/6M (216°-W-023°). Entrance.F.G/F.R

Small fishing harbour.

Berths Finger piers for pleasure boats.

Shelter Uncomfortable with N winds.

Facilities Fuel quay. Limited provisions and restaurants.

Note Prohibited entry to yachts 2004.

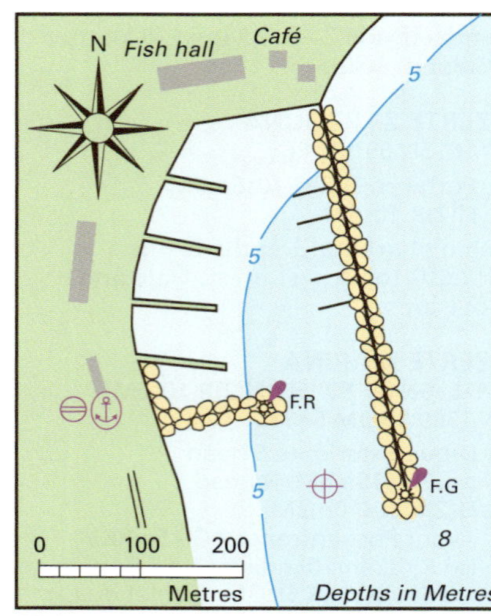

STORA

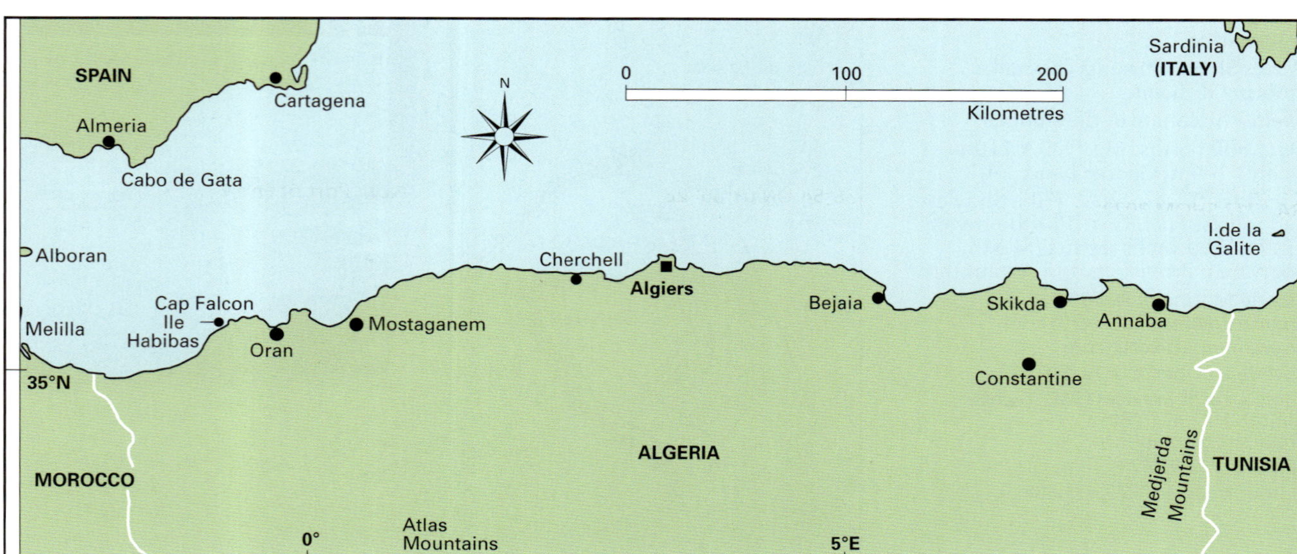

ALGERIA

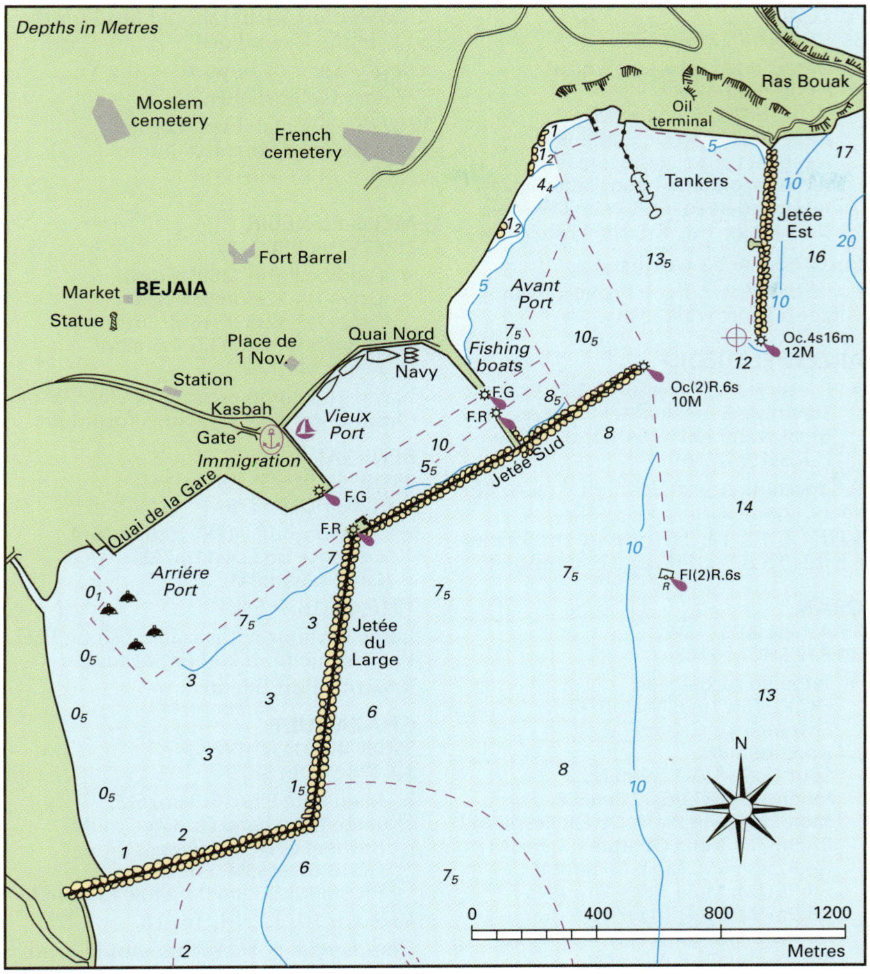

BEJAIA

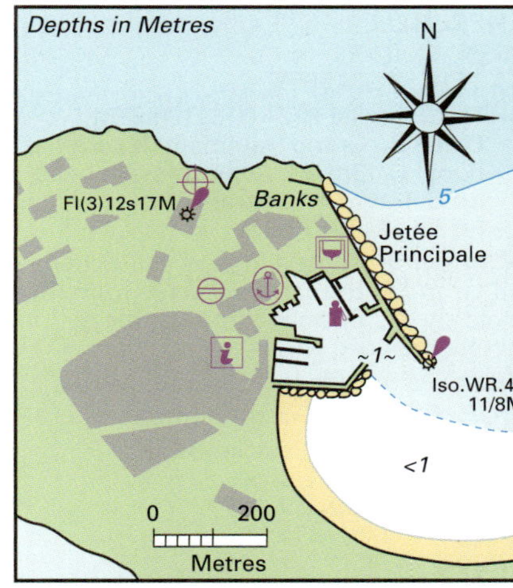

SIDI FERRUCH MARINA (SIDI FREDJ)

COLLO
37°00'·3N 06°34'·5E
BA 1712 SHOM 3023

☆ Cap Collo Fl.G.5s26m12M. Jetty F.G

Anchorage.

Note Port of entry.

DJEN DJEN
36°50'·3N 05°53'·8E

☆ Entrance Oc.G.4s8M / Iso.R.4s8M

Large new commercial harbour. No facilities for yachts.

Note Port of entry.

JIJEL
36°49'·6N 05°47'E
BA 1712 SHOM 3023

☆ Rās el Afia Fl.R.5s43m24M. Aux. light Fl.R.4s28m10M. Jetée Nord main light Fl(2+1)WR.12s19m12/9M (096°-R-101°). Entrance Iso.G.4s9m/Fl.R.4s7m3M/Fl.R.4s. Inner harbour N side F.R/F.G

Naval Base. Yachts prohibited from entering.

BEJAÏA (formerly BOUGIE)
36°45'·2N 05°06'·2E
BA 1710 SHOM 5641

☆ Rās Carbon Fl(3)20s220m28M. Aux. light Fl.WR.1·5s32m10/7M. Entrance Oc.4s16m12M/Oc(2)R.6s11m10M. Passe Abdelkader S side spur Fl(2)R.6s8m8M. Passe de la Kasbah Fl(2)R.7s8m8M

VHF Ch 10, 12, 14, 16 for port authorities and pilot (0800–1200/1400–1800).

Large commercial port. Yachts use the Vieux Port.

Facilities Water. Fuel. Ferry to Marseille and Algerian ports.

AZZEFOUN
36°54'·2N 04°25'·3E

☆ Entrance Fl.R.2s/Fl.G.2s

DELLYS
36°54'·9N 03°55'·2E
BA 1710 SHOM 3036, 3043

☆ Cap Bengut Fl(4)15s63m30M. Pointe de Dellys F.R.41m15M. Entrance Oc.4s12m9M / Oc(2)R.8s12m5M

VHF Ch 10, 11, 12, 13, 14, 16.

Commercial and fishing port.

Note Port of entry

ZEMMOURI BAHAR (formerly COURBET MARINE)
36°48'·4N 03°33'·8E

☆ NE pier head Q.16m10M. NW pier Fl.G.5s17m7M. Hbr entrance F.G.5m6M/F.R.5m6M

Shallow harbour. Depths <1–4m.

LA PÉROUSE
36°48'·3N 03°13'·9E
BA 855

☆ Pier head Iso.R.2s7M

ALGIERS
36°45'·8N 03°04'·7E
BA 855 SHOM 5638

☆ Roche M' Tahen Q(3)10s12m8M. Memorial du Martyr Fl.R (by day F.R). Port d'Alger, Jetée Kheir Fl(2)3s23m20M. Harbour Jetée de Mustapha head Iso.G.4s12m12M. Passe Sud Oc.R.4s12m13M. Jetée du Vieux Port Fl.R.4s10m12M. Bassin de L'Agha F.R/F.G/F.R/F.G

VHF Ch 10, 12, 16 for port authorities and pilot. Military commercial and fishing port.

May only be used by yachts in an emergency, and with authorisation obtained on VHF in advance.

SIDI FERRUCH (SIDI FREDJ MARINA)
36°46'·0N 02°50'·9E
BA 1910 SHOM 3030

☆ Rās Caxine Fl.5s64m30M. Sidi Fredj Marina Fl(3)12s42m17M. Jetée Principale Iso.WG.4s14m11/8M. Marina entrance F.G./F.R.

Navigation Entrance has silted to 1m and less.

Berths Stern or bows-to outer mole.

Shelter Good shelter.

Facilities Water. Showers. 16-ton travel-hoist. Meagre provisions. Restaurants.

Note Port of entry.

BOU HAROUN
36°37'·7N 02°39'·3E
SHOM 3030

☆ Jetée Est F.R.8m5M

PORT DE KHEMISTI
36°37'·8N 02°39'·6E

☆ W jetty F.G.7m6M

TIPASA
36°35'·7N 02°27'·1E

☆ Rās El Kalia Oc.4s32m12M. Entrance F.G.8m6M/F.R.11m. Port de Plaisance F.G.6m

Anchorage.

CHERCHELL
36°36'·8N 02°11'·5E
BA 1710 SHOM 5699

☆ Fort Joinville Fl(2+1)15s37m21M. Ecueil du Grand Hammam (N cardinal buoy) Q.13m7M. Jetée Joinville head Iso.G.4s10m7M. Entrance F.G.7m5M/F.R.7m6M

Navigation Approach between Ecueil du Grand Hammam and Jetée Joinville from the N. Entrance impassable in strong onshore winds.
Berths Alongside local fishing boats.
Shelter Adequate in the summer.
Facilities Water. Provisions and restaurants.
Note Port of entry.

TÉNÈS
36°31'·6N 01°19'·1E
BA 178 SHOM 5708

☆ Cap Ténès Fl(2)10s89m31M. Detached breakwater W head Q.10m10M. E Head Iso.G.4s10m5M. Entrance Oc(2)G.6s10m7M / Oc(2)R.6s10m9M. Dir light DirF.WG.8M

VHF Ch 10, 11, 13, 14, 16 for port authorities. Commercial port.
Note Port of entry.

MOSTAGANEM
35°56'·1N 00°04'·2E
BA 1909 SHOM 5696, 5951

☆ Harbour entrance Fl(4)WR.12s17m13/10M 197°-R-234°. Spur head Oc(2)R.6s7M. Mole de Independance head Fl.G.4s6M. Inner basin Oc(2)G.6s13m5M

VHF Ch 11, 12, 14, 16.
Commercial port.
Berths Go alongside the customs quay in the SE corner to complete formalities. Yachts are then directed, usually, to the NE quay.
Facilities Water. Provisions in town.

ARZEW
35°51'·6N 00°17'·4W

☆ Detached breakwater E head Fl(3)G.5s11m7M / W head Fl(3)R.5s11m7M. Jetée Abri head Oc.G.4s9m9M. Jetée du Large Q(4)6s15m12M. Jetée Secondaire head Fl.R.4s6m2M. Jetée Sud head Iso.R.2s4m2M. Mole No.3 F.R.2m1M / F.G. No.4 F.G.2m1M

Entry easy in all weathers.
Facilities Water. Fuel. Provisions in village a short walk away.

ARZEW EL DJEDID

☆ E jetty Fl.R.2s. W jetty Fl.G.2s. Port de Servitude E breakwater Fl(2)R.6s. W breakwater Fl(2)G.6s. Ilot d'Arzew Fl.R.5s19m16M

A supertanker port 2M S of Arzew. No yacht facilities.
VHF Ch 12, 14, 16 for port authorities. Ch 12, 16 pilot. Pilotage compulsory.

ORAN
35°43'·2N 00°37'·5W
BA 812 SHOM 5763

☆ Jetée du Large head Fl(2+1)15s21m22M Horn 60s. Entrance Iso.G.4s8m7M / Iso.R.4s9m8M. Spur Oc(2+1)G.12s9m6M. Inner spur Oc(3)G.12s9m6M. Mole du Ravin Blanc Oc(2)R.6s9m7M / F.R.9m7M. Mole Oblique F.R.9m3M / Iso.R.2s8m6M. Mole Millerand F.R.9m7M. Mole Jules-Giraud F.R.9m7M/Oc(4)R.12s7M. Ibn Tofail NE corner Oc.4s3m10M. NW corner Oc.R.4s9m7M. Mole du Centre NE corner F.R.9m7M. Vieux Port entrance Iso.G.4s9m6M/F.R.6m7M

VHF Ch 12, 14, 16 for port authorities and pilot.
Navigation Yachts should head for the YC in the Vieux Port.
Berths Stern or bows-to at the YC.
Shelter Good shelter.
Facilities Water. Fuel. Limited provisions at Port. Restaurants.
Note Port of entry.

MERS-EL-KÉBIR
35°43'·3N 00°42'·2W

☆ Leading lights (259°) Front Oc(2+1)R.12s53m9M. Rear Oc(2+1)R.12s67m16M. Entrance VQ(4)2s13m9M/Fl.G.4s5m3M/ Fl.R.4s14m12M

Naval and commercial port close W of Oran. Entrance by yacht is forbidden.

BENI-SAF
35°18'·6N 01°23'·2W
BA 178 SHOM 5876

☆ Ile Rachgoun Fl(2)R.10s81m16M. Entrance Iso.G.4s11m7M/ Oc(2)R.6s9m8M

VHF Ch 16.
Large harbour with sizable fishing fleet. Entry difficult in N–NW winds.
Remarks Port of entry.

GHAZAOUET
35°06'·4N 01°52'·1W
BA 178 SHOM 5873

☆ Main light Fl(3)15s92m26M. Jetée Nord head Oc.R.4s17m8M. Rocher Les Deux Frères Fl(2)G.6s26m5M. Entrance F.R.8m6M/F.G.8m5M. Mole F.G.8m5M

VHF Ch 10, 12, 14, 16, 18.
Commercial port. Yachts should head for inner fishing port.
Note Port of entry.

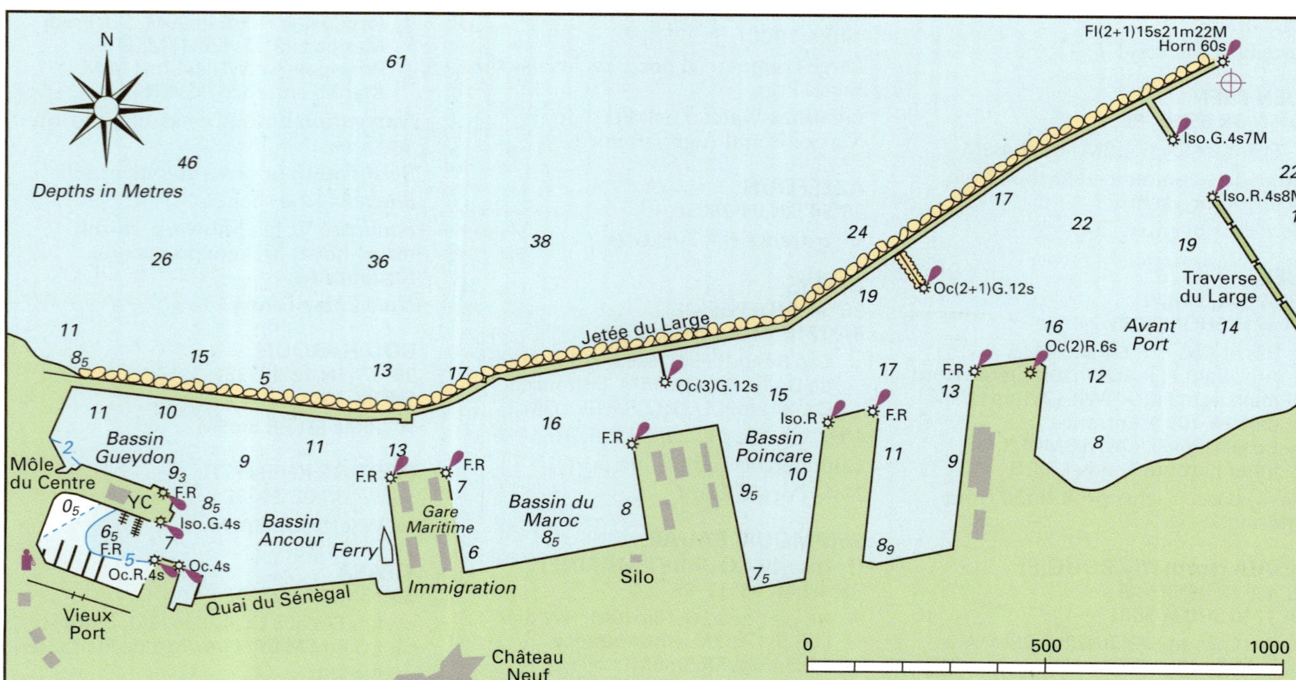

ORAN

10.21 Morocco

TIME ZONE UT+1 ☏ IDD +212

Note Yachts should clear in at one of the main tourist ports, preferably Marina Smir, before proceeding to ports towards the Algerian border. There is some smuggling activity along the eastern coast and there may be difficulties if you arrive unannounced in smaller harbours or anchorages. *Kif* (marijuana) is grown around the area close to the Algerian border and most of it is smuggled into Spain. The Spanish coastguard keep a close watch on traffic between Morocco and Spain and you can expect to be watched on your return from Morocco to Spain or Gibraltar.

Quick reference guide

For Key see page 139

	Shelter	*Mooring*	*Fuel*	*Water*	*Provisions*	*Eating out*	*Charge band*
Morocco							
Marina Saida	B	A	A	A	C	C	2
Ras El Ma	A	B	O	A	C	C	
Melilla	A	A	A	A	A	A	2
Al Hoceïma	A	AB	O	O	C	C	
Torres de Al Cala	B	B	B	B	C	C	
El Jebha	B	B	B	B	C	B	
M'diq	B	A	A	A	A	A	
Kabila Marina	A	B	O	A	C	B	
Marina Smir	A	AB	A	A	C	B	3
Puerto Deportivo de Ceuta	A	B	A	A	A	A	3
Tanger	A	AB	A	A	B	B	2
Rabat Marina	A	A	A	A	A	B	
Mohammedia	A	AB	A	A	B	C	
Casablanca	A	AB	A	A	C	C	
Jorf Lasfar	A	B	B	A	C	B	
Agadir Marina	A	A	A	A	B	B	3

Mediterranean coast

SAIDIA MARINA

35°06'.0N 02°17'·0W

Berths Where directed. Laid moorings tailed to pontoons.

Data 800 berths. Max LOA 50m. Depths 3–6m. Charge band 2.

Facilities Water. 220/380V. WC and showers. Fuel quay. Waste pump-out.100-ton travel-lift. 8-ton crane. Chandler. Repairs.

Remarks Extension works in progress.

☏ 36 62 4793 or 0801 009 009
Email medsaidia1@gmail.com
www.medsaidia.com

RĀS EL MA (RĀS KEBDANA)

35°08'·9N 02°25'·2W
BA 2437 SHOM 6570

☆ Rās Kebdana Fl(2)6s42m8M. Port de Rās Kebdana Dir Lt 294° DirF.WRG.9m10-7M. Entrance Iso.G.6s12m10M/ Iso.R.6s13m10M

Navigation Keep close to outer N breakwater in entrance.

Berths Alongside N or W quay.

Shelter Good shelter.

Facilities Water. Some provisions. Restaurants.

NADOR

35°17'·1N 02°55'·2W (Fl(2)R.6s)

☆ Muelle de Beni Enzar head Fl(2)R.6s5M. Wharf No.1 NE Q.R. Wharf No.2 NE VQ(4)R.

Commercial port close S of Melilla.

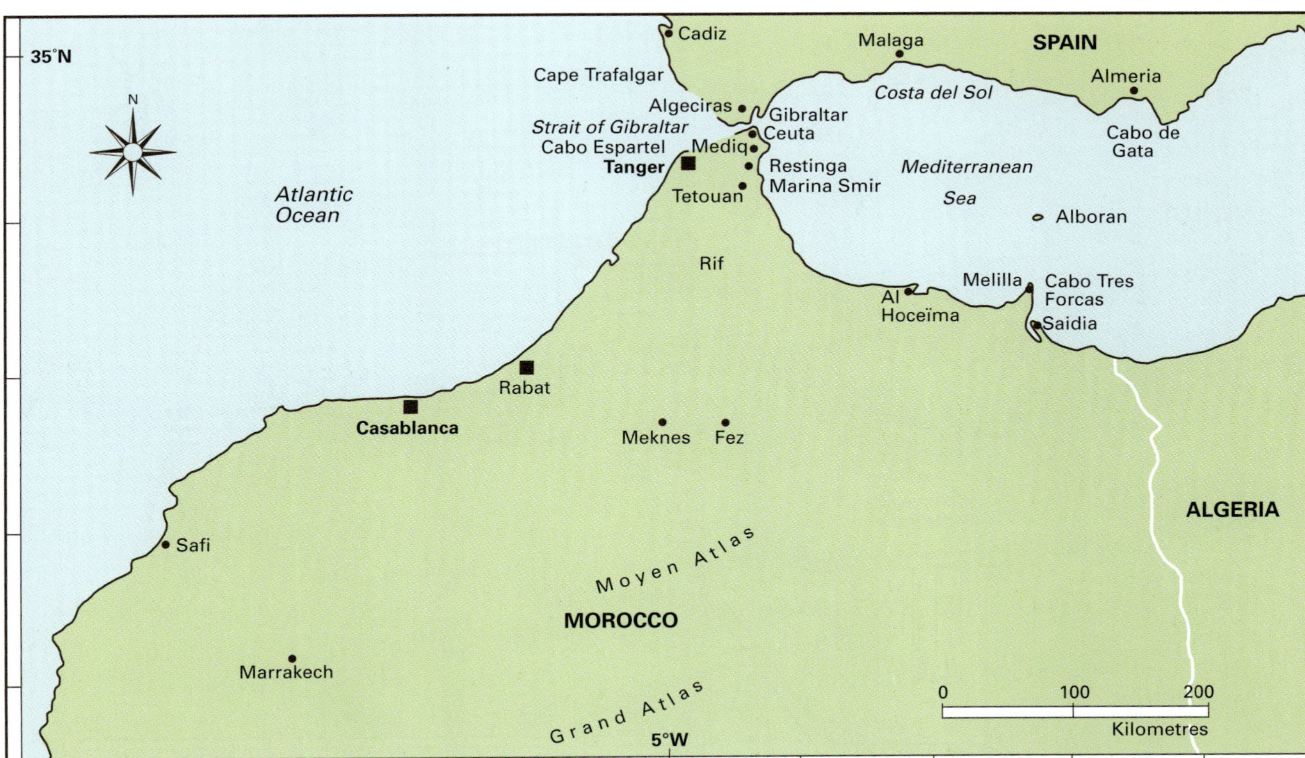

MOROCCO

MELILLA (SPANISH)

35°17′·4N 02°55′·6W
BA 580 SHOM 5864 Sp 4331

☆ Los Farallones Iso.Y.2s21m6M. Melilla main light Oc(2)6s40m14M. NE breakwater Fl.G.4s32m7M / Fl.G.4s5M. Dique Nordeste Espigón 1 head Fl(2)G.7s3M. Dique outer Fl.R.5s5M / Q(3)10s3M / Fl.G.4s1M. Muelle de Ribera Fl(2+1)G.12s1M. Ore loading pier Fl(2+1)R.12s3M. Basin entrance Fl(4)G.11s1M / Fl(4)R.11s1M

VHF Ch 11, 12, 14, 16.

Navigation Yachts should head for the marina on the W side of the harbour.

Berths Stern or bows-to. In the marina there are depths of 3m in the entrance, and 2m at the end of the pontoons, shallowing toward the quay. Visiting yachts often berth along the outer breakwater. Berth where directed. Alternatively you may get a berth at the yacht club in the old fishing basin. Charge band 2.

Shelter Good shelter in the marina and the fishing basin.

Facilities Water. 220V (in the marina). WC and showers. Fuel quay on the S mole. 65-ton travel-hoist. Chandleries.

Remarks Theft is a problem in parts of the port, but the marina has good security.

Club Maritimo ✆ 052 683 559 / 683 559

CALA TRAMONTANA

35°24′·1N 03°00′·6W

☆ Rās Baraket Oc(2+1)12s49m9M

Anchorage protected from the NE–S.

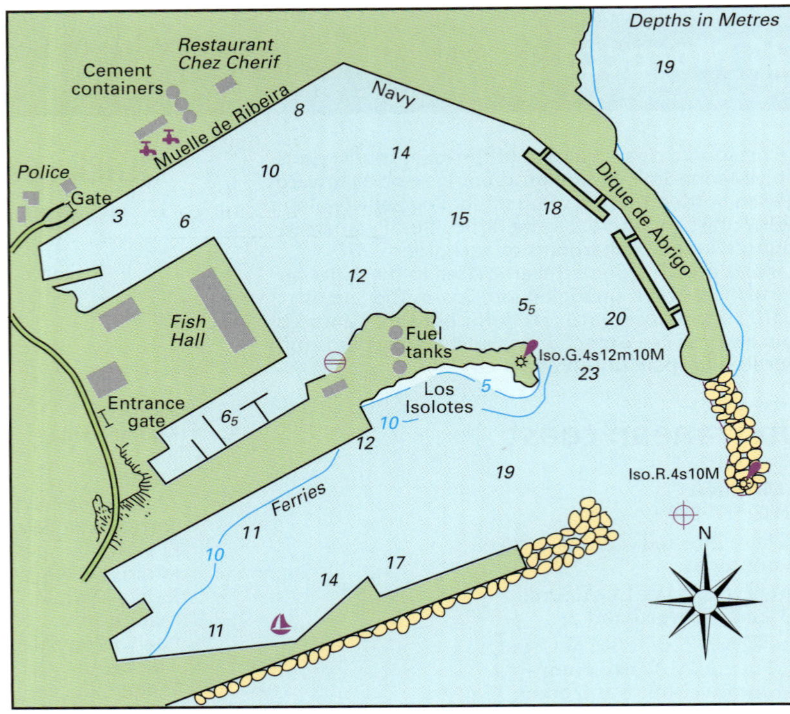

AL HOCEIMA

AL HOCEÏMA

35°14′·9N 03°55′·1W
BA 580 SHOM 5864

☆ Leading lights (274°) Front F.R.25m3M. Rear F.R.47m3M. Leading lights (330°) Front Oc.G.27m10M. Rear Oc.G.46m10M. Entrance Iso.G.4s12m10M / Iso.R.4s12m10M

VHF Ch 16.

Berths Harbour works have been completed. Berths outside customs building for impounded vessels only. The N side of the new harbour is for ferries only. Yachts may use the S quay, but mooring bollards are few and far between.

Shelter Good shelter.

Data 20 berths.

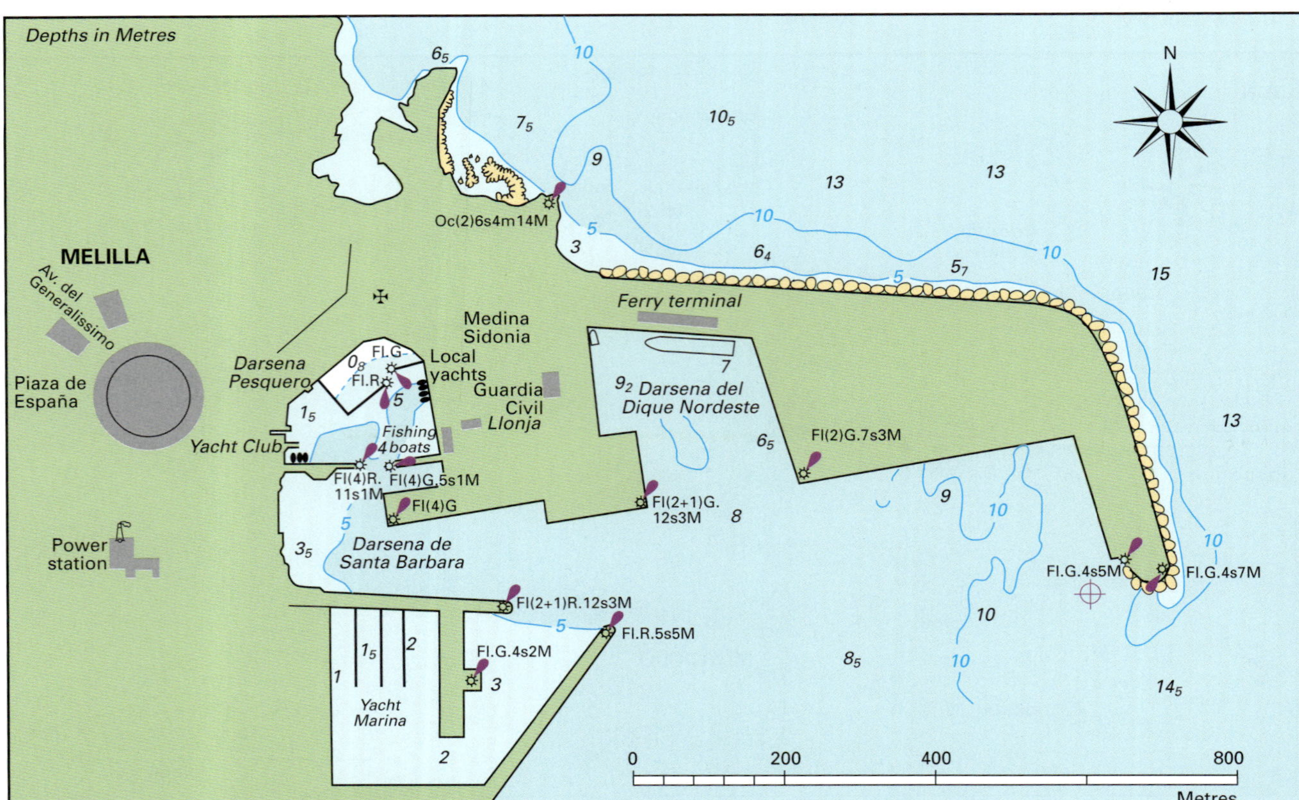

MELILLA

Facilities Fuel can be delivered. Some provisions. Restaurants.
Note Port of entry.

CALA IRIS
35°09'·0N 04°22'·2W

New fishing harbour. Yachts can berth alongside on the S quay. Simple restaurant ashore.

EL JEBHA
35°13'·0N 04°40'·8W
BA 773 SHOM 1711

☆ Punta de Pescatores Fl(2)10s38m18M. Port de Peche S jetty Iso.G.4s8M.

Fishing harbour. Good shelter. Harbour is full of fishing boats. Yachts go alongside fisheries protection vessel. Limited provisions.

PORTO AL MARTIL
35°37'·1N 05°16'·6W
(Puerto de Rio Martin lights Fl.4s10M)

☆ Puerto de Rio Martin. Leading lights Front F.WRG.11m Rear F.WRG.15m. Port has silted

M'DIQ
35°41'·0N 05°18'·5W
BA 142 SHOM 1711, 7042

☆ Ras El Aswad Fl(2+1)135m20M. E pier head Q.12m13M. Entrance F.G/F.R

Home of Royal Yachting Club of M'Diq.
✆ 039 975 659
www.rycmdiq.com

KABILA MARINA
35°43'·3N 05°20'1W

☆ E pier head Fl.10s. Entrance Fl.R.5s/Fl.G.5s

VHF Ch 09, 16.
Dangers The entrance of the marina has not been dredged for several years and has now silted to less than 1m. It is not suitable except for small shallow draught motor boats. The facilities are dilapidated and the marina has little to offer.
Navigation 2M S of Marina Smir. Entrance difficult and possibly dangerous with strong onshore winds.
Berths Where directed. Finger pontoons.
Shelter Good shelter.
Data 250 berths. 80 visitors' berths. Max LOA 16m. Depths 1·5–2·5m.
Facilities Water. Showers and toilets. Fuel. 15-ton crane. Some provisions.
Kabila Marina ✆ 039 666 264

MARINA SMIR (RESTINGA SMIR)
35°45'·2N 05°20'·2W
BA 142 SHOM 7042

☆ Iso.G.4s11m4M/Iso.R.4s7m4M

VHF 09, 16.
Navigation Do not stray too close to the coast in the approach.
Berths Yachts should go alongside the customs and fuel quay before being directed to a berth.
Shelter Good shelter.
Data 450 berths. 100 visitors' berths. Max LOA 60m. Charge band 3.
Facilities Water. 220/380V. Telephone. TV. Showers and toilets. Fuel. 150-ton travel-hoist. 10-ton crane. Large hardstanding area. Yacht repairs. Some provisions. Restaurants.
Remarks Duty free port.
Port Marina Smir ✆ 039 977 251
Email portmarinasmir@menara.ma
www.portmarinasmir.com

CEUTA (SPANISH)
35°53'·8N 05°18'·6W
BA 2742 SHOM 7503 Sp 4511

☆ Punta Almina Fl(2)10s148m22M. Entrance Fl.G.5s13m5M / Fl.R.5s13m5M. Spur E corner Fl(2)G.8s1M. Muelle de España head W corner Fl(2+1)R.12s3M. Muelle del

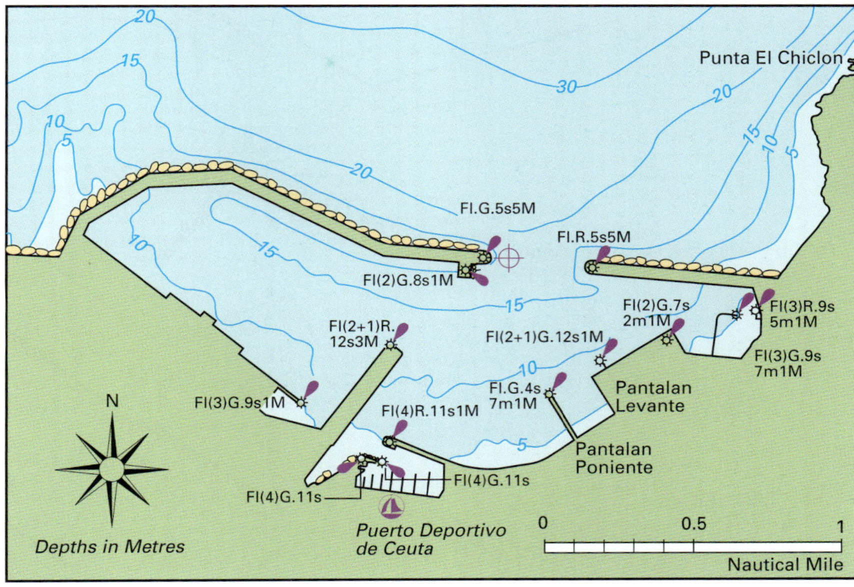

CEUTA

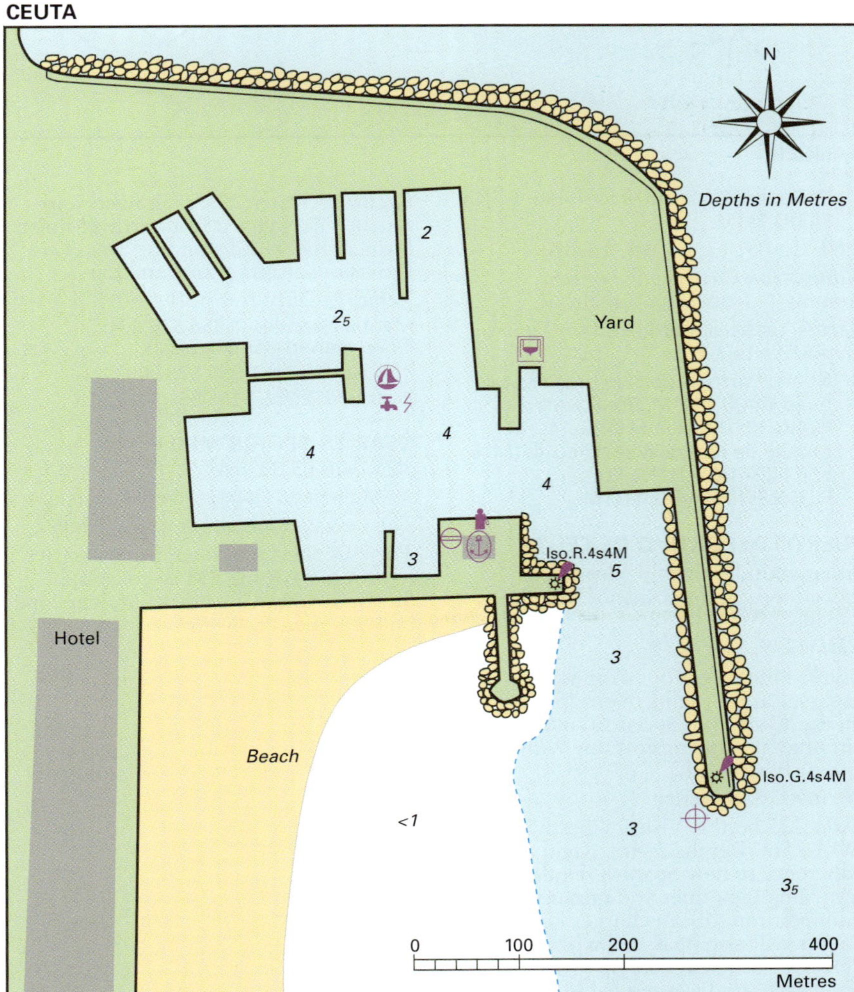

MARINA SMIR

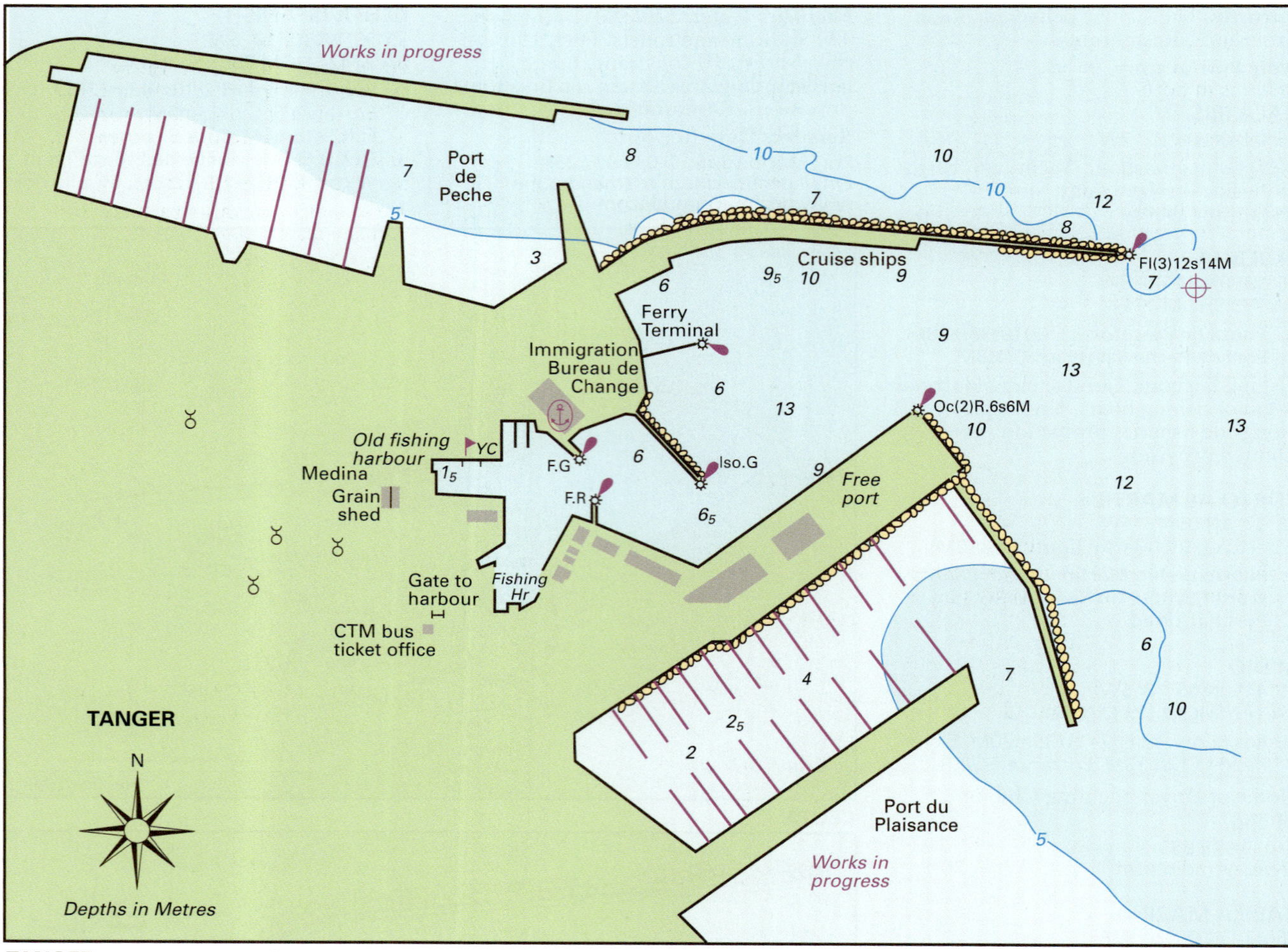

TANGER

Canonero Dato entrance head Fl(3)G.9s1M.

VHF Ch 09, 12, 13, 14, 15, 16.

Navigation Care needed of reef running N from Baja Isabel.

Berths Yachts should head for Puerto Deportivo de Ceuta.

☆ Nuevo Porto Deportivo breakwater head Fl(4)R.11s1M. Breakwater Fl(4)G.11s1M. Head Fl(4)G.11s1M. Muelle de Ribera W end Fl.G.4s1M. E end Fl(2+1)G.21s1M. Corner Fl(3)G.9s1M/Fl(4)G.11s1M

PUERTO DEPORTIVO DE CEUTA

Situated under the old Muelle de Pescadores on the E side of Muelle Espana.

VHF Ch 9.

Berths Finger pontoons for most yachts. Larger yachts might find a berth on the W side of the central mole, although it is uncomfortable with wash and dirty with oil.

Shelter Good shelter.

Data 325 berths. Visitors' berths. Max LOA 25m. Depths 2–4m. Rigid adherence to new Spanish regulations regarding light dues and midnight–midnight rates mean charges have risen. Yachts will also be issued with a *Permisso* which allows up to six visits in one year and is intended to reduce congestion here. Charge band 3.

Facilities Water. 220V. Showers and toilets. Fuel quay. 250-ton travel-hoist. 8-ton crane. Hard standing area. Gas. Provisions. Restaurants and bars.

Remarks Duty-free port.

Marina Hercules ✆ 956 525 001
Email mahersa@mahersa.es
Port Authority ✆ 956 528 000
Boatyard ✆ 956 511 985

KSÁR-ES-SEGHIR MED PORT

35°51'·0N 05°33'·6W

☆ Mole head Fl(4)12s16m8M

The new commercial port for Tanger.

The complex consists of three massive harbours covering 5M of coastline SE from Punta Cires for containers and bulk cargoes.

Atlantic coast

Note Care is needed along the Moroccan Atlantic coast where strong onshore winds can make the entrance to some harbours danagerous.

TANGER

35°47'·6N 05°47'·5W
BA 1912 SHOM 1701 Sp 4461

☆ Cabo Espartel Fl(4)20s95m30M. Punta Malabata Fl.5s76m22M. Monte Dirección Oc(3)WRG.12s88m16-11M (140°-G-174·5°-W-200°-R-225°). Entrance Fl(3)12s14M/ Oc(2)R.6s7m6M. NW inner jetée Iso.G.4s6m6M. Basin F.G.4m6M/F.R.4m6M

VHF Ch 06, 14 for port authorities. Pilot Ch 12, 16. Ch 11 for RYCT.

Berths The harbour has been reopened to yachts, with a new pontoon and dredged basin, at Royal YC Tanger. Charge band 2.

Go stern or bows-to where directed on the pontoon on the N side of the old fishing harbour.

Shelter Good shelter although there can be a surge which makes things uncomfortable.

Facilities Water. Showers. 220V (YC). Fuel by drums. Provisions and restaurants.

Note Port of entry.

As a free port, passports are retained in exchange for shore passes while the vessel is in port.

Remarks The whole structure of Tangers harbour is being reorganised. All commercial shipping has been relocated to the new ports to the E of Tangiers. The old commercial basin is being redesigned as a cruise ship and ferry terminal. Work is in progress developing a port de plaisance in a new basin to the S of the main harbour. A new fishing harbour has been built to the N of the main harbour. At present yachts still berth in the inner harbour.

RYCT ✆ 039 938 909

ASILAH

35°47'·6N 05°55'·3W (Cabo Espartel)

☆ Cap Spartel Fl(4)20s30M.
Entrance Leading Lights 140°
Front F.R.6m. Rear F.R.9m

A shallow harbour, and entry should only be attempted in calm weather. Care needed of sandbanks in the approaches. Depths change after Atlantic storms. New marina plans for Asilah and another between Tanger and Asilah have been shelved.

LARACHE

35°12'·3N 06°09'·3W

☆ Oc(4)15s15m17M

A harbour on the river Oued Loukkas. Entry is difficult, with sand bars and strong currents.

MEHDIA & KENITRA

34°16'·0N 06°41'·4W

☆ Oc.R.6s5M/Iso.G.4s6M

Two harbours on the river Oued Sebon.

RABAT

34°02'·1N 06°50'·8W (Rabat Lt Ho)

☆ Oc(2)6s16M

The city and harbour on the river Oued Regreg.

BOUREGREG MARINA (RABAT)

VHF Ch 10.

Navigation A pilot will come out to guide you up the river. Depths reported sufficient for 2·35m draught.

Entry is dangerous with any onshore swell.

Data 240 berths. Max LOA 30m. Charge band 2.

Facilities Water. 220V. WiFi. Fuel. Chandlers. Restaurants. Ferry to Medina.

Bouregreg Marina ✆ 05 37 849 900
Email marinabouregreg@gmail.com
www.bouregregmarina.com

MARINA SABLE D'OR

A prestigious marina whose development was halted by the building of a palace close by for the King.

The breakwaters are complete but yachts are not permitted to use the harbour.

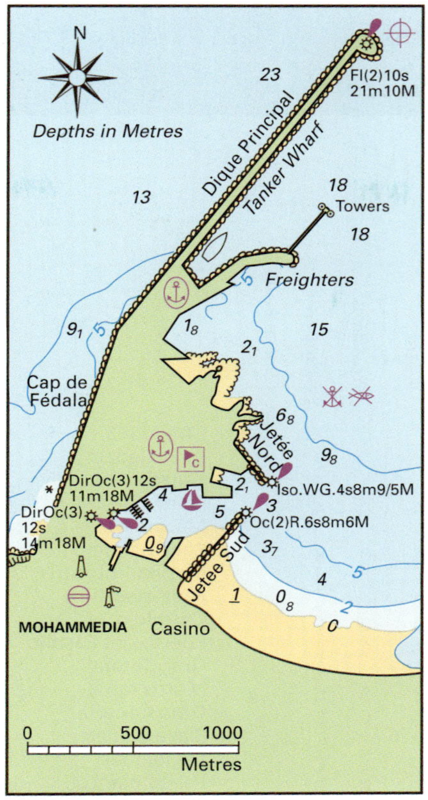

MOHAMMEDIA

MOHAMMEDIA

33°44'·0N 07°23'·2W

☆ Outer breakwater head Fl(2)10s21m10M. Ldg Lts 130° front Oc(2)WG.6s14/11M, rear Oc(2)6s18M. Harbour entrance Ldg Lts 265° (front and rear) DirOc(3)12s18M. N and S breakwater head Iso.WG.4s9/5M/Oc(2)R.6s6M

VHF Ch 16, 11, 13, 10.

Navigation Club Nautique in SW corner of the large harbour. Entry possible in onshore winds.

Berths Stern or bows-to on the yacht pontoons. The YC welcomes visiting yachts. Otherwise anchor off outside of the YC.

Remarks Port of entry.

YC Maroc Marina ✆ 023 134 747
Email marina.ycm@menara.ma
www.yachtclubdumaroc.com

CASABLANCA

33°37'·2N 07°35'·1W

☆ Oc(2)G.6s5m5M

VHF Ch 16, 12, 14.

A major redevelopment project of central Casablanca to include business and residential buildings, an aquarium and a marina. Work is ongoing.

Remarks Port of entry and naval base.

Data (when completed) 135 berths. Max LOA 25m. Depths 2-5m.

Berths Until completion yacht berths in the basin in the SW corner are restricted.

Casablanca Marina
✆ 05 22 45 36 36
www.casablancamarina.ma

JORF LASFAR

33°10'N 08°37'W

Phosphate export port. Entry straightforward in all weather, with S-facing entrance. Useful port of refuge, with yachts welcome in *Capitainerie* basin (4th on starboard hand before the large commercial dock).

Tie alongside or raft to a tug with agreement. 18km to town.

Remarks Port of entry.

SAFI

32°19'·0N 09°15'·4W

☆ Iso.G.4s11M / Oc.R.4s6M.
Ldg lights Q.12M on 150°

Commercial port. Yachts welcome.

Remarks Port of entry.

VHF Ch 16.

AGADIR

30°25'·2N 09°37'·0W

New marina outside the main port on the SE side. Only 220M from the Canaries.

Data 300 berths. Max LOA 30m. Depths 4m.

Facilities Water. 220V. Toilets and showers. 60-ton travel-lift. Fuel. Charge band 3.

Remarks Port of entry.

Marina Agadir ✆ 0528 828 686
Email info@portmarinaagadir.com

MOROCCO RIVIERA

28°41'7N 11°07'9W

Another vast project for hotels, apartments, golf courses and a 700-berth marina. Further details will follow in the supplement.

TAN TAN

28°29'N 11°20'W

☆ Cap Nachtigal Fl.5s15M. Main SW jetty Fl.10m / F.R / F.G

A new commercial harbour close to Cap Nachtigal.

CHBIKA MARINA

28°18'·1N 11°31'·7W

A new residential and leisure development around Chbika lagoon. The marina entrance will lie close N of the lagoon. Completion date is given as 2015. Further details will follow in the supplement.

www.chbika.ma

10.22 Atlantic Islands

Quick reference guide *For Key see page 139*

	Shelter	Mooring	Fuel	Water	Provisions	Eating out	Charge band
Atlantic Islands							
AZORES							
Faial							
Horta	A	AB	A	A	A	A	2
Flores							
Porto das Lajes	C	AC	C	B	B	B	
Pico							
Madalena	B	C	C	B	C	C	
Cais do Pico	B	BC	C	B	B	C	
Sta Cruz das Ribeiras	B	C	C	A	C	C	
São Jorge							
Vila das Velas	C	C	C	B	B	C	
Calheta	B	C	C	A	C	C	
Graciosa							
Vila da Praia	B	BC	B	O	C	C	
Santa Cruz	C	C	C	B	B	B	
Terceira							
Angra do Heroismo Marina	A	A	A	A	A	A	2
Praia da Vitoria Marina	A	A	B	A	B	B	2
São Miguel							
Ponta Delgada	A	B	A	A	A	A	2
Vila Franca do Campo	C	B	A	A	C	C	
Santa Maria							
Vila do Porto	B	AC	C	B	B	C	2
MADEIRA							
Baia de Porto Santo	B	A	A	A	A	A	
Funchal	A	B	A	A	A	A	2/3
Quinta do Lorde Marina	B	B	A	A	C	C	3
Marina do Lugar de Baixo	A	A	A*	A*	C	C	
Porto de Recreio da Calheta	A	A	A*	A*	C	C	

	Shelter	Mooring	Fuel	Water	Provisions	Eating out	Charge band
CANARIES							
La Sociedad	B	A	C	B	C	C	2
Lanzarote							
Puerto de Los Mármoles	A	C	C	B	B	B	
Puerto Calero	A	B	A	A	B	B	2/3
Marina Rubicon	A	B	A	A	B	B	2/3
Fuerteventura							
Corralejo	C	A	C	A	B	B	
Puerto del Castillo	B	B	A	A	B	C	3
Gran Tarajal	B	C	C	B	C	C	2
Morro Jable	B	AC	C	C	C	C	2
Gran Canaria							
Playa Blanca	O	B	O	B	B	B	
Las Palmas	A	A	A	A	A	A	2
Pasito Blanco	C	B	A	A	C	C	2
Puerto Rico	A	A	A	A	A	A	2
Puerto de Mogan	A	A	A	A	A	A	
Tenerife							
Marina de Tenerife	B	A	O	A	C	C	2
Puerto Chico	B	A	A	A	C	C	2
Marina del Atlantico	A	A	O	A	A	A	2
Puerto Radazul	B	AB	O	A	C	C	
Puerto Deportivo de Colon	A	A	A	A	C	C	
Puerto Deportivo de Los Gigantes	C	B	A	A	B	B	
Gomera							
Marina La Gomera	B	AB	A	A	B	B	2
La Palma							
Santa Cruz	B	B	BC	B	B	B	
Hierro							
La Estaca	B	C	C	B	C	C	

Azores

TIME ZONE UT–1 ☽ IDD +351

Tides
Max mean range at springs 1·4m

AZORES MARINAS
www.marinasazores.com

Ilha do Flores

PORTO DAS LAJES

39°22'·8N 31°09'·7W B/w head

☆ Ponta des Lajes Fl(3)28s87m26M. Breakwater head Fl(2)R.12s14m9M

VHF Ch 16, 14.

Main ferry and ship port for Flores. A small marina is planned. Yachts berth bows-to on the quay or anchor off. Often rolly at anchor. Water near the quay.

Note Marina plans deferred. Yacht pontoons planned.

Remarks Entry formalities may be completed here.

Clube Naval das Lajes das Flores
☽ 292 592 542
HM ☽ 292 593 437
Email lajes.flores@aptosa.com

Ilha do Faial

HORTA

38°32'·10N 28°37'·14W WGS84
BA 1957 Portuguese 46403
Imray-Iolaire E1

☆ Breakwater end Fl.R.3s20m11M. Boa Viagem Dir.Iso.WRG.6s12m9/6M. Ldg Lts (196°) Front Iso.G.2s13m2M. Rear Iso.G.2s15m2M

VHF Ch 16, 11 for port authority. Ch 16, 10 for Horta Marina (0800–1200, 1400–2000).

Navigation Yachts should make for the marina on the W side.

Berths Report to the reception quay for a berth. You may be rafted four or five boats out here. Friendly and efficient check-in procedure. Yachts up to 12m are directed to the N basin, on finger pontoons; yachts of about 10–19m more usually raft alongside the wall. Larger yachts tend to be directed to the S basin, stern-to with laid moorings or alongside. Very large yachts go alongside or stern-to the outer breakwater. Yachts waiting for a berth anchor off the S basin. Most yachts will be offered a berth within 36hrs of arrival.

Shelter Good shelter inside the N harbour. At times there can be a surge on the arrivals quay which can cause damage. There is also some surge in the

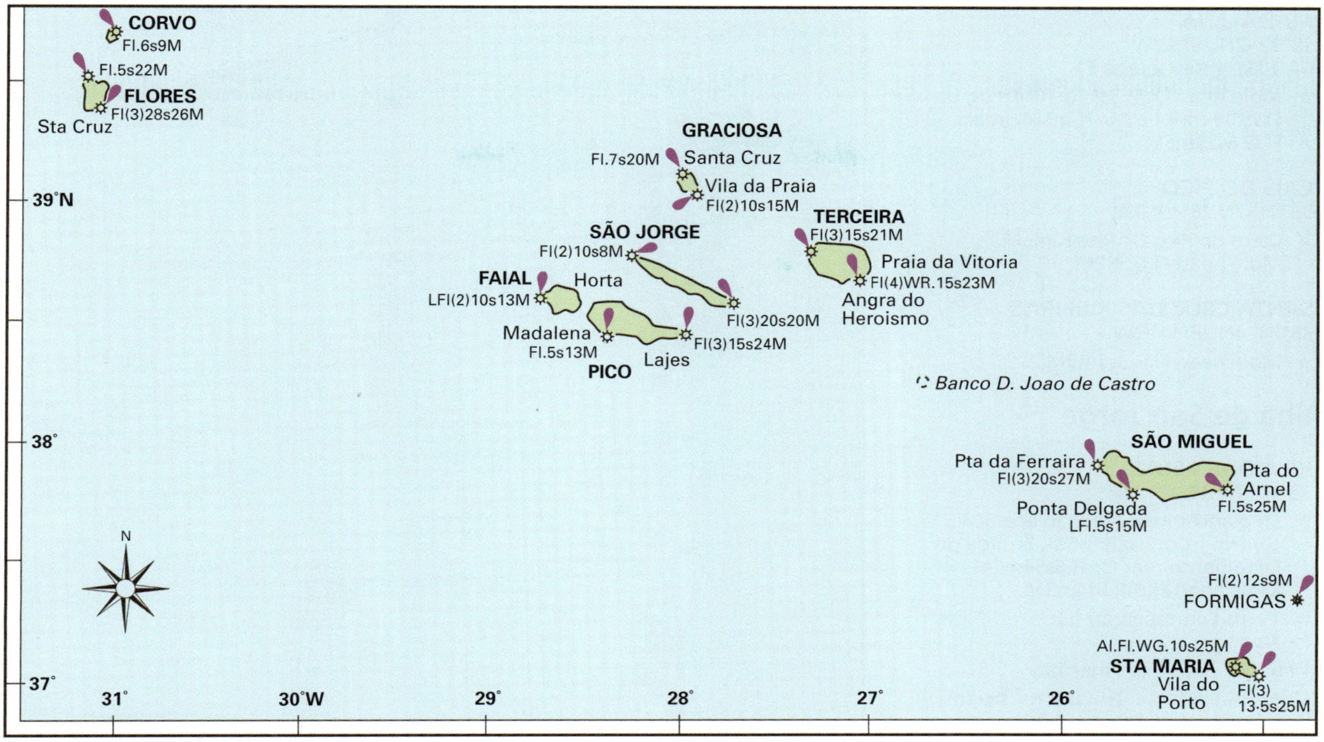

THE AZORES

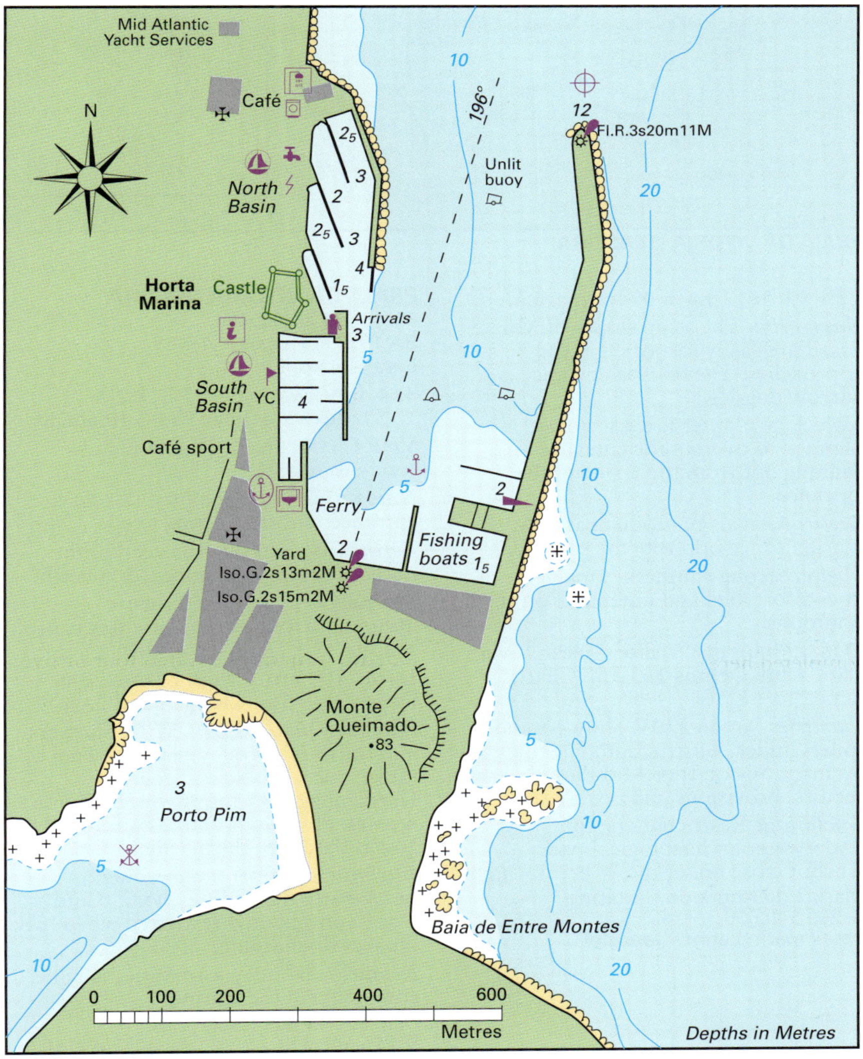

HORTA (FAIAL)

S harbour. In May, June and July Horta is full to overflowing and yachts are often four to five deep on the wall.

Data 300 berths. Visitors' berths. Max LOA around 40m. Depths 1–6m. Charge band 2.

Facilities Water. 220V. Showers and toilets. Self-service laundry in the marina as well as full collection/ delivery services. Fuel quay. 22-ton travel-hoist. 25-ton crane. Yacht repairs. Sailmaker. Chandlers. Provisions and restaurants nearby.

Horta Port Authority ✆ 292 293 453
Email portohorta@mail.telepac.pt
www.portohorta.com

Horta Marina ✆ 292 391 693 / 292 208 300
Email hortamarina@aptosa.pt

Clube Naval (fuel station) ✆ 292 200 680
Email secretariado@cnhorta.pt
www.cnhorta.org

Mid Atlantic Yacht Services
✆ 292 391 616
Email mays@mail.telepac.pt
VHF Ch 77.

Ilha do Pico

LAJES DO PICO MARINA

38°23'·7N 28°15'·1W

VHF Ch 16.

Navigation Follow the buoyed channel into the harbour.

Data 48 berths. Max LOA c.18m

Berths Where directed on pontoons with finger pontoons.

Marina ✆ 292 672 121
Email recreio.lajes@sapo.pt

MADALENA
38°32′·2N 28°32′W
BA 1957 Imray-Iolaire E1

☆ Mole head Oc.R.3s11m10M. Ldg Lts (139°) Front Fl.G.6s15m5M. Rear Fl.G.6s20m5M

CAIS DO PICO
38°31′·7N 28°19′·3W

☆ Caios do Pico Oc.R.6s10m6M. Mole head Fl.G.3s2M

SANTA CRUZ DAS RIBEIRAS
38°24′·4N 28°11′·2W

☆ Mole head Fl.R.3s7m3M

Ilha de São Jorge

VILA DAS VELAS
38°40′·7N 28°12′·3W

☆ Ship anchorage lights in line 304·3° central front Iso.R.5s6M. Ermida do Livramento rear Oc.R.6s54m7M. Mole head Fl(3)R.9s4m3M

Ferry and commercial harbour. New marina.

VHF Ch 16, 10 for marina.

Data 76 berths. c.10 visitors' berths. Depths 3m. Charge band 2.

Facilities Water. 220V. Showers and toilets. Laundry. Fuel. Travel-hoist.

Velas Marina ✆ 295 412 047 / 963 698 900
Email saojorge@aptosa.com

CALHETA
38°35′·95N 28°00′·5W

☆ Calheta Fl.R.3s12m10M. New b/w head is lit, char unknown.

Yachts berth alongside new quayed breakwater (depths 4m), or the old quay (1·7–3m). May be asked to move when ferry is due.

Ilha Graciosa

VILA DA PRAIA
39°03′·1N 27°58′·0W
BA 1957 Imray-Iolaire E1

☆ Breakwater Fl.G.3s13m9M

New fishing harbour/marina complete.

Data c.40 berths (when pontoon in place). Otherwise go alongside quay on breakwater head.

SANTA CRUZ
39°05′·4N 28°00′·5W
BA 1957 Imray-Iolaire E1

☆ Santa Cruz Fl.R.4s6m6M

Ilha Terceira

ANGRA DO HEROISMO MARINA
38°38′·5N 27°12′·8W
BA 1957 Imray-Iolaire E1

☆ Pta do Farol Monte Brasil Oc.WR.10s27m12M (191°-R-295°). Mole head Fl.G.3s11m6M. Ldg Lts (341°) Front Fl.R.4s20m7M. Rear Oc.R.6s54m7M

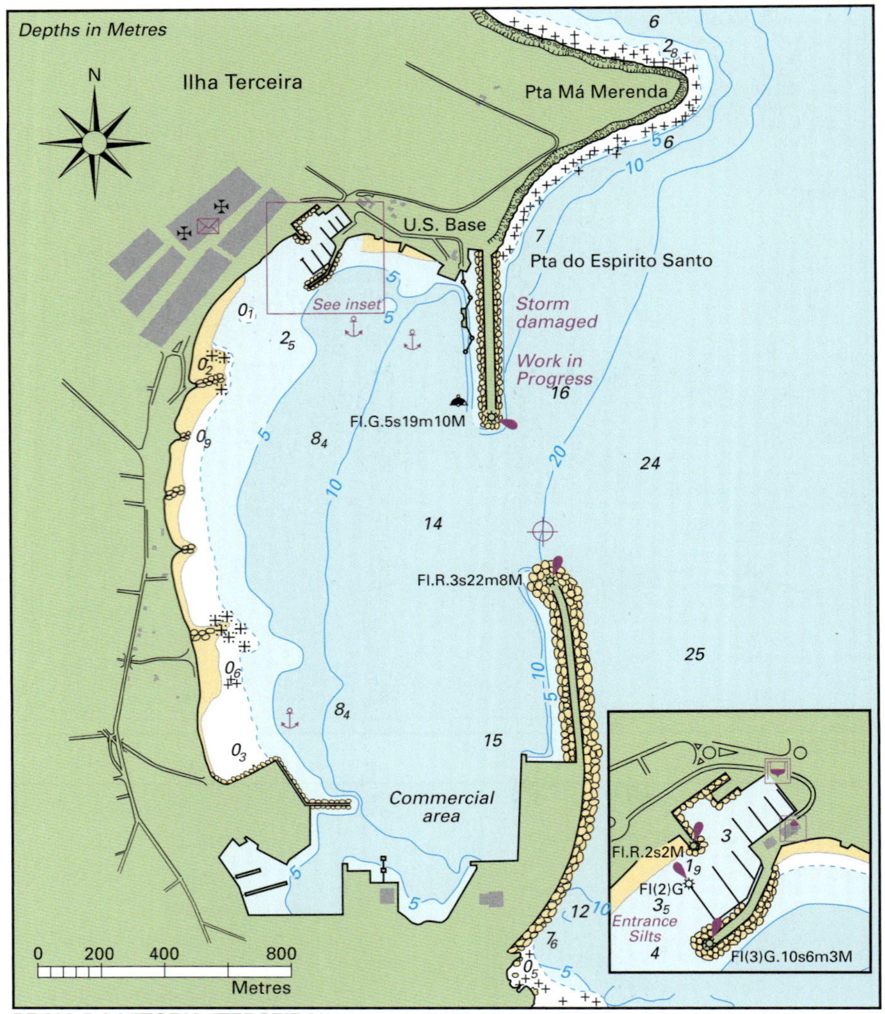

PRAIA DA VITORIA (TERCEIRA)

VHF Ch 16, 10. Ch 09 for marina.

Navigation The steep slopes of Monte Brasil are easily identified in the approaches. The marina entrance is a narrow dog-leg.

Note A new outer breakwater is planned to overlap the entrance running out from the E side of the entrance.

Berths Arrivals pontoon near new marina office opposite the entrance.

Shelter Strong southerlies make it uncomfortable, and untenable on the E pontoons.

Data 260 berths. Visitors' berths. Max LOA 18m. Depths 1–3·5m. Charge band 2.

Facilities Water. 220V. Showers and toilets under construction. Fuel quay. Security. 50-ton travel-lift. Some repairs. Provisions and restaurants.

Anchorage Restricted due to underwater archaeological park. Anchor close under the W breakwater.

Marina de Angra do Heroismo
✆ 295 540 000
Email marina.angra@aptg.pt

PRAIA DA VITÓRIA MARINA
38°43′·6N 27°03′·1W
BA 1957 Portuguese 46405
Imray-Iolaire E1

☆ N breakwater head Fl.R.2s2M. S breakwater head Fl(3)G.10s6m3M

VHF Ch 09, 16 (0830–2000 daily June–August)

Navigation Entrance silts. Depths in entrance reported 1·9m.

Berths Go alongside the head of the outer pontoon and report for a berth.

Shelter Good all-round shelter although strong southerlies may cause a surge.

Data 210 berths. Max LOA c.20m. Depths 2–3·5m. Charge band 2.

Facilities Water. 220V. WiFi. Showers and toilets. Fuel quay planned. Fuel by tanker for >200 litres. Security. Gardiennage. 35-ton travel-lift. Some repairs. Provisions and restaurants. US Naval Base E of the marina.

Anchorage Shelter under either breakwater depending on wind and sea. Reported only restricted when fuel tankers discharging.

Remarks All entry formalities may be completed in the marina.

Marina da Praia da Vitoria
✆ 295 540 219
Email marina@cmpv.pt www.cmpv.pt

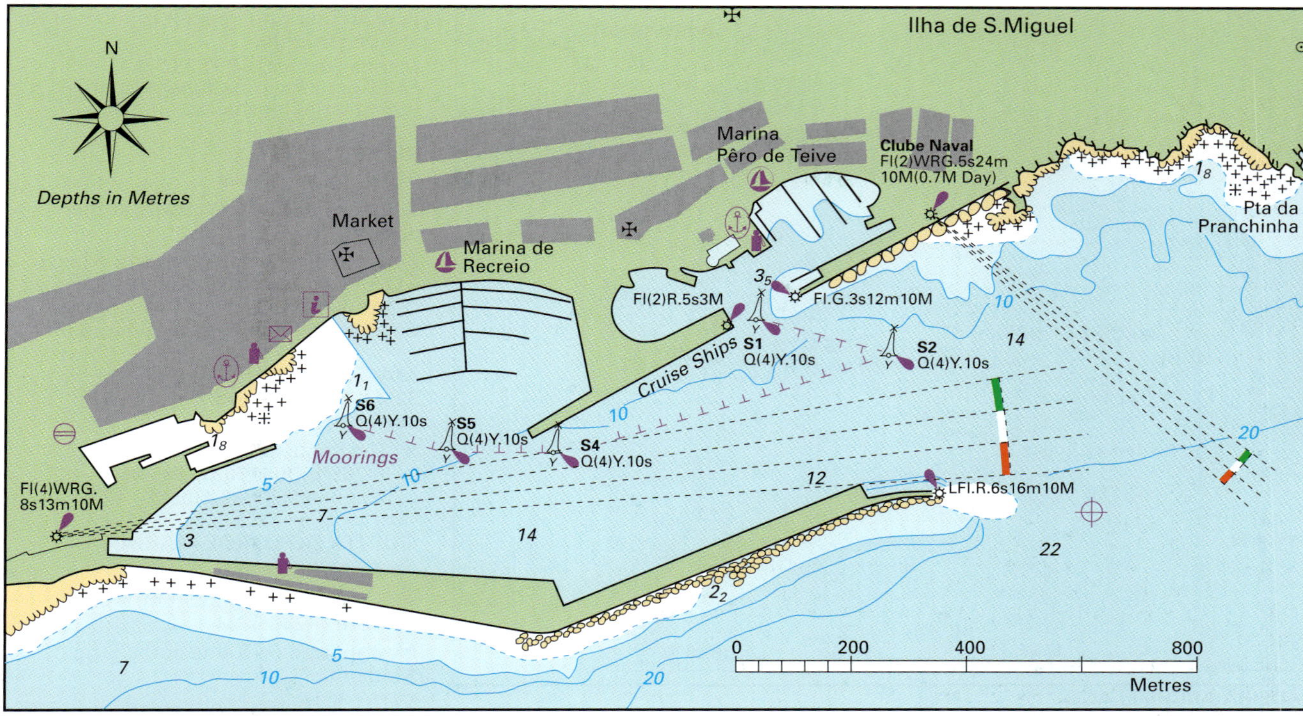

PONTA DELGADA (S.MIGUEL)

Ilha de São Miguel

PONTA DELGADA

37°44'·20N 25°39'·09W WGS84
BA 1895 Portuguese 46406 Imray-Iolaire E1

☆ Ponta Delgada mole head LFl.R.6s16m10M. Marina mole Fl.G.3s12m10M. Naval Club Fl(2)WRG.5s24m10M. S Brás Fort SE corner Fl(4)WRG.8s13m10M, by day Fl(4)WRG.8s13m1M. Santa Clara LFl.W.5s26m15M

VHF Ch 16, 09 for the marina (May–September, Monday–Friday 0900–1800; weekends 0900–1730).

Navigation Care needed of underwater extension to breakwater for 50m approximately. Yachts should head for the marina.

Note New marina berths and cruise ship berths to the W of the marina are now complete.

MARINA PÊRO DE TEIVE

Berths Go on the fuel quay on the N side of the entrance to complete formalities and to be allocated a berth. Finger pontoons for smaller yachts. Otherwise go stern or bows-to on pontoons, some laid moorings.

Shelter There is some surge on the arrivals quay. Good shelter at most berths.

Data 640 berths. Visitors' berths. Max LOA 18m/60m. Depths 3–8m. 3m depths in entrance at MLWS. Charge band 2.

Facilities Water. 220V. WC and showers. Laundry. Fuel quay. 25-ton travel-hoist. Some mechanical repairs. Limited yacht repairs. Provisions and restaurants.

Remarks Up to 4-day forecast available in the marina office.

Marina Pêro de Teive
✆ 296 281 510 / 511 / 512
Email marinapdl@apsm.pt
www.marinasazores.com

VILA FRANCA DO CAMPO MARINA

37°42·7N 25°25'·6W

Small marina 11M E of Ponta Delgada. Care needed of off-lying rocks. Approach on a course of 317° using leading lights close W of the harbour.

New breakwater improves shelter and increases number of berths.

Data 125 berths. Max LOA 14m. Depths 2·5-3·5m. Charge band 2.

Facilities Water. 220V. ATM. Provisions and restaurants ashore.

Marina da Vila ✆ 296 581 222 / 488
Email marinaem@sapo.pt
www.marinadavila.com

Ilha de Santa Maria

VILA DO PORTO MARINA

36°56'·4N 25°09'·0W
BA 1959 Portuguese 46407 Imray-Iolaire E1

☆ Pta Malmerendo Fl(2)10s49m12M. Breakwater head LFl.R.5s14m5M. Ldg lights 173·4° Front Fl.3s12m10M. Rear LFl.6s20m10M

VHF Ch 16, 10 for marina.

Data 120 berths. Water. 220V. Showers and toilets. Laundry. Travel-hoist. Charge band 2.

Berths On the yacht pontoon with finger pontoons in the SW corner of the harbour.

Vila do Porto Marina ✆ 296 882 282
Email marinavdp@marinasazores.com
Clube Naval de Santa Maria
✆ 296 883 230

Madeira

TIME ZONE UT ✆ IDD +351

Tides
Max mean range at springs 2·2m

Ilha de Porto Santo

BAIA DE PORTO SANTO

33°03'·3N 16°18'·6W
BA 1689 Portuguese 36401
Imray-Iolaire E3

☆ Ilhéu de Cima Fl(3)15s123m21M. Baia de Porto Santo breakwater head Fl.G.4s6M. N breakwater head Fl.R.4s7M

Two pontoons accommodate visiting yachts.

VHF Ch 09 for Marina Porto Santo.

Data 135 berths. Depths 2–6m. Larger yachts berth alongside concrete pier. Charge band 2/3.

Note Charges to anchor inside the harbour approx €14 (12m). Higher charges to anchor outside.

Facilities Water. 220V. Toilets and showers. Fuel on the ferry (jetfoil) quay. 35-ton travel-hoist. Provisions and restaurants.

Marina Porto Santo ✆ 291 980 080
Email geral@marinadoportosanto.com
marinaportosanto@quintadolorde.pt

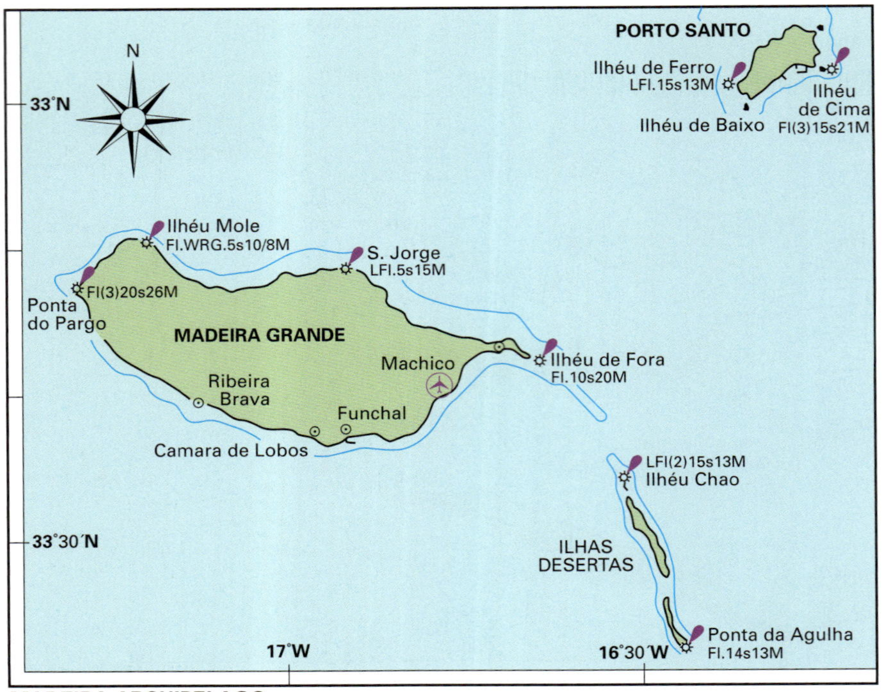

MADEIRA ARCHIPELAGO

Ilha da Madeira

FUNCHAL

32°38'·3N 16°54'·2W
BA 1689 Portuguese 36402 Imray-Iolaire E3

☆ Breakwater head Fl.R.5s14m8M. Marina entrance F.G/F.R

VHF Ch 16, 09.

Berths Yachts should head for the marina on the N side of the entrance. Berth where directed or where possible. Visitors usually have to find a place rafted onto the inside of the outer marina mole.

Shelter Reasonable shelter, although SW winds make it very uncomfortable and warps will chafe through quickly with the surge.

Data Nominally 240 berths. 12 visitors' berths. Max LOA 20m. Charge band 2/3.

Facilities Water on the quay in the marina. 220V. WiFi. Showers and toilets. Fuel quay. 25-ton travel-lift. Slipway. Some yacht repairs. Modest chandlers. Provisions and restaurants.

Remarks The marina is often full in the season. Yachts can anchor off E of the marina but this anchorage is exposed to onshore winds. There are reports that a new marina is to be built to the E of the existing marina.

Marina Funchal ✆ 291 232 717
Email geral@marina-funchal.com
www.marinafunchal.pt

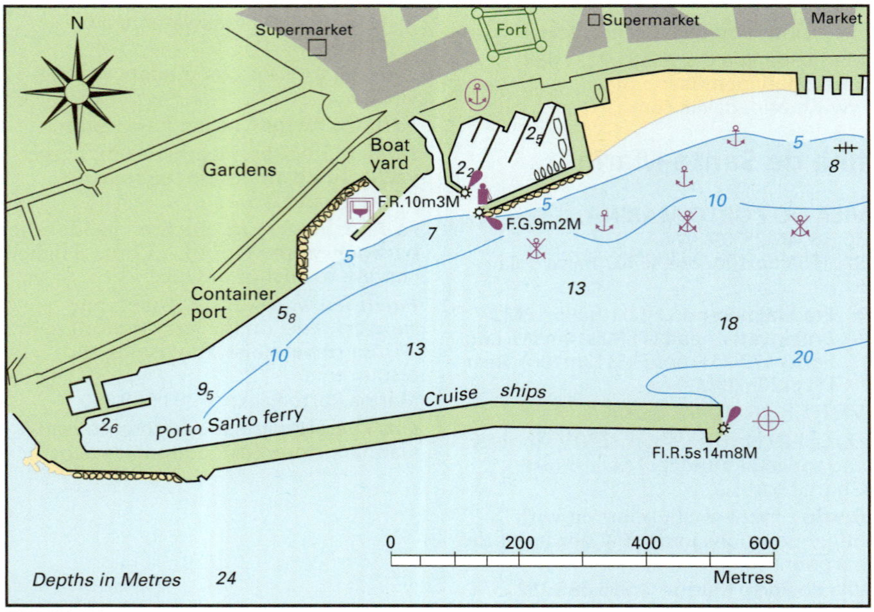

FUNCHAL

REP MARITIMA

32°42'·0N 16°46'·0W

Boatyard under the runway at the airport.

Data 85 places. Max 35-tons. Max LOA 16m. Max beam 5·2m.

✆ 291 969 800
Email estaleiroap@repmaritima.com

MACHICO

32°42'·6N 16°45'·6W
Portuguese 154

☆ São Roque LFl.WR.5s11m9/7M (230°-R-265°). Quay Fl(3)G.8s6m6M Pier head Fl(3)R8s6m5M

QUINTA DO LORDE MARINA

32°44'·0N 16°44'·0W

☆ S mole head Fl(2)G.5s6M. N mole head Fl(2)R.5s3M

New marina on S side of the E tip of Madeira.

VHF Ch 16, 09.

Navigation No dangers in the approaches, but the W-facing entrance lies close-in to the cliffs and requires a sharp 090° turn. Entry could be dangerous in even moderate onshore winds.

Berths Go alongside the reception berth along the W mole, or where directed. Finger pontoons. Larger yachts go alongside the W pontoon.

Data Visitors' berths. Max LOA 50m. Depths 2–5m. Charge band 3.

Facilities Water. 220V. Showers and toilets. Fuel quay. Café in the marina. Shops and restaurants are planned. Provisions and restaurants in Canical.

Remarks Port of entry.

Quinta do Lorde Marina ✆ 291 969 607
Email marina@quintadolorde.pt
www.quintadolorde.com

CANICAL

32°44'·0N 16°44'·0W

Commercial and fishing port.

Few yacht berths.

Facilities Fishing Co-op 300-ton travel-hoist. Madeira Engineering Syncro-lift up to 100m LOA.

APRAM (Co-op contact) ✆ 291 208 600
Madeira Eng ✆ 291 220 191

MARINA DO LUGAR DE BAIXO

32°40'·5N 17°05'·3W

Marina 11M W of Funchal.

Remarks Problems with shelter. Breakwaters damaged (again). Marina unlikely to open in near future.

PORTO DE RECREIO DA CALHETA
32°43′·0N 17°10′·3W
New marina 16M W of Funchal. Main construction is complete, and shore-side development continues.
VHF Ch 16, 10.
Data c.320 berths. Max LOA 20m. Depths 1–5m. Charge band 3.
Facilities Water. 220V. WiFi. Showers and toilets. Laundry. Fuel.
Remarks Port of entry.
✆ 291 824 003
Email portoderecreiodacalheta@netmadeira.com

The Canary Islands

TIME ZONE UT ✆ **IDD +34**

Note The prevailing winds are the NE trades which tend to get channelled between the high islands to produce strong gusty conditions in places. While the wind over the open sea may be Force 3–4, where it is channelled it can get up to Force 5–6. Areas known for increased wind strength and gusts are the NE side of Palma, E side of Gomera, E side of Hierro, all around Tenerife, W and E sides of Gran Canaria, SE side of Lanzarote, and the S tip of Fuerteventura.

Tides

Max mean range at springs 2·2m

Canaries Traffic Separation Schemes
New TSS between Fuerteventura and Gran Canaria, and Gran Canaria and Tenerife.

Areas to be avoided

Zones of particularly sensitive areas have been established as Marine Reserves are developed:

Lanzarote N coast, Gran Canaria SW coast, Tenerife SW coast – Gomera, La Palma and Hierro coasts.

Restrictions to yachts may apply in the future.

Fish farms

Many new fish farms have been established around the coasts of the Canaries. Care needed as they can be close in on the approaches to harbours and marinas. Most are lit, but caution is advised when making a night approach.

Light dues

Yachts staying in municipal ports are obliged to pay light dues in addition to port dues. On a daily basis they can double the cost of a berth. Paid on a monthy or annual basis the charges are far less and cover all public harbours.

Isla Graciosa

LA SOCIEDAD
29°13′·60N 13°30′·12W WGS84
☆ Entrance Fl.G.5s3M/Fl.R.5s3M
Small fishing harbour with two yacht pontoons with fingers in the S of the harbour. Max LOA 15m. Depths 2–5m. More berths on pontoons along N breakwater. Go alongside or raft up to another yacht. Charge band 2.
Shelter Good shelter although there may be some surge with strong SW winds.
Facilities Water on fuel quay. Provisions and restaurants.
Data c.40 visitors' berths.
Remarks Anchorage to the S of the harbour.

Isla de Lanzarote

PUERTO DE LOS MÁRMOLES/ PUERTO DE NAOS
28°57′·8N 13°31′·6W (Fl.G.5s11M)
BA 1863, 1862 Sp 502, 504
Imray-Iolaire E2

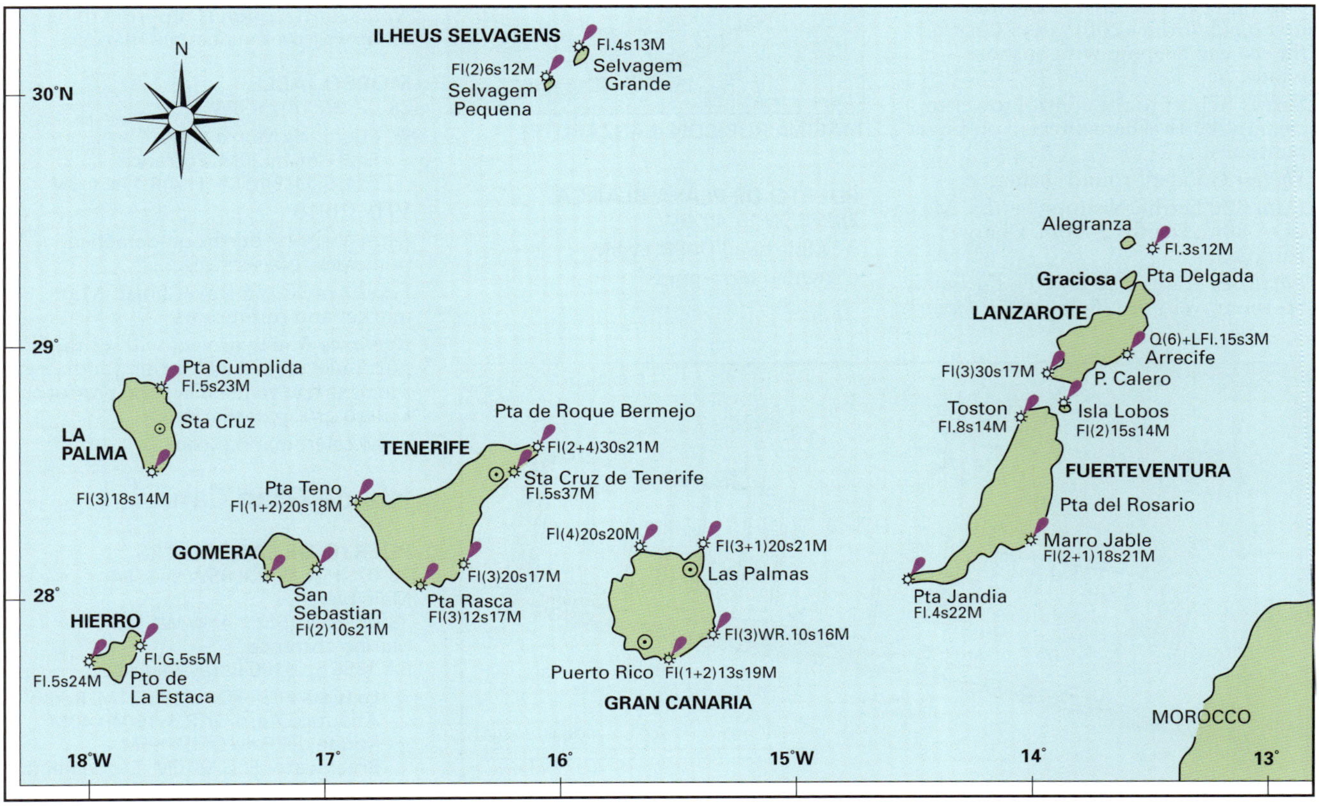

THE CANARY ISLANDS

☆ Puerto de Arrecife mole head Q(6)+LFl.15s10m3M. Marmoles pier head Fl.G.5s5M. Muelle de Contenedores E head Fl(2+1)R.10s3M. W head Fl(3)G.9s5m3M. Puerto de Naos mole head Fl(2)R.7s5m3M. No.1 buoy Fl(4).G.11s. No.2 buoy Fl(3)R.9s. No.3 mark Fl.G.5s. No.4 buoy. Fl(4).R.11s.

VHF Ch 16 for port authorities and pilots.

MARINA LANZAROTE

VHF Ch 09 for marina.

Navigation Care needed following channel to S end of Puerto de Naos.

The buoyed channel is dredged to 5m.

Berths Stern or bows-to on pontoons in the S of the harbour. Laid moorings tailed to the pontoons.

Shelter Good shelter.

Data 430 berths. Max LOA 80m. Charge band 2/3.

Facilities Water. 220/380V. WiFi. Showers and toilets. Laundry. Fuel quay. 100-ton travel-lift. Provisions and restaurants nearby.

Remarks Part of the Calero Marinas group.

Marina Lanzarote ☎ 648 524649
Email marina@marinalanzarote.com

PUERTO CALERO MARINA

28°54'·88N 13°42'·43W WGS84

☆ S mole head Fl(3)G.14s9m6M and buoys.

VHF Ch 09,16.

Navigation The marina lies in the NW side of the bay. At night it should not be confused with the smaller fishing harbour 2M to the SE which has the same light characteristic. Depths come up quickly from >200m to <20m, and the sea can heap up with onshore winds.

Berths Report to the control tower to clear in. Berth where directed on finger pontoons.

Shelter Good all-round shelter.

Data 420 berths. Visitors' berths. Max LOA 80m. Depths 2–10m. Charge band 2/3.

Facilities Water. 220V. WiFi. Fuel quay. 90-ton travel-hoist. Some yacht repairs. Provisions, bars and restaurants.

Remarks New superyacht berths completed on NW side of the marina.

Puerto Calero ☎ 928 510 850
Email reservas@puertocalero.com
www.puertocalero.com

MARINA RUBICON

28°51'·4N 13°49'·1W

☆ Marina entrance Fl(4)G.15s3m5M/Fl(4)R.15s1m5M. Spur Fl.G.5s. Inner N mole Fl.R.5s1M.

Marina and development on the S coast of Lanzarote, across the bay from Playa Blanca.

VHF Ch 09, 16.

Berths Report to the 'lighthouse' control tower. Berth where directed on long finger pontoons.

Shelter Good all-round shelter.

Data 500 berths. 200 visitors' berths. Max LOA 45m. Depths <1–5m. Charge band 2/3.

Facilities Water. 220/380V. WiFi. Showers and toilets. Fuel quay. 90-ton travel-hoist. Some repairs. Provisions and restaurants are increasing in number.

Marina Rubicon ☎ 928 519 012
Email info@marinarubicon.com
www.marinarubicon.com

Waterline Yacht Service ☎ 928 018 262
Email mail@waterlineyachtservice.com

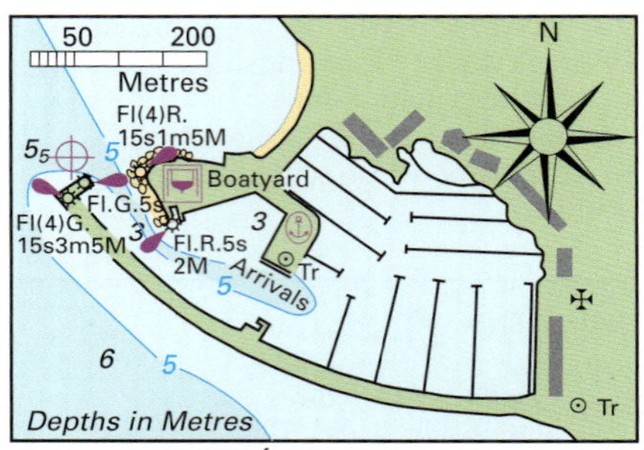

MARINA RUBICÓN (LANZAROTE)

PUERTO DE PLAYA BLANCA

28°51'·5N 13°49'·9W

☆ Mole head Fl(4)R.11s5M

Crowded ferry port.

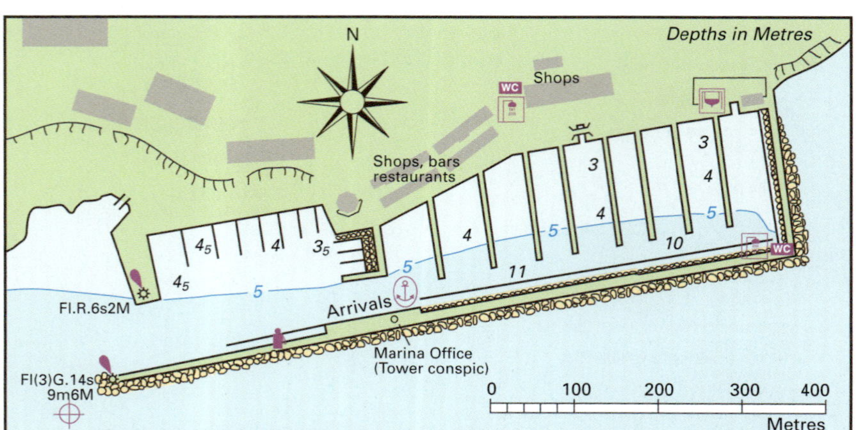

PUERTO CALERO (LANZAROTE)

Isla de Fuerteventura

CORRALEJO

28°44'·3N 13°51'·6W
BA 1862 Sp 503 Imray-Iolaire E2

☆ Cerro Martiño (Isla de Lobos) Fl(2)15s28m14M. Breakwater head Fl.G.3s8m4M

Small ferry and fishing port. Yacht berths usually full.

PUERTO DEL ROSARIO

28°29'·5N 13°51'·2W

☆ Entrance Fl.G.5s13m5M/Q(3)10s3M

Commercial port.

PUERTO DEL CASTILLO

28°23'·4N 13°51'·3W

☆ Mole head Fl(2)G.12s9m5M

VHF Ch 09, 16.

Navigation A dangerous reef extends 250m E and 500m S from the breakwater. It is now marked with S cardinal beacon. Keep well clear and approach on a course due N towards the breakwater head, through the buoyed channel.

Data 100 berths. 20 vistors berths. Max LOA 16m. Depths 1–4m. Charge band 3.

Facilities Water. 220V. Fuel. Some repairs. Provisions and restaurants in the holiday resort.

Marina ☎ 928 163 514

GRAN TARAJAL

28°12'·3N 14°01'·3W

☆ Pier head Fl(3)G.7s5M/Fl(3)R.7s5M

Berths Go alongside the breakwater and enquire about berths on the yacht pontoon.

Note Construction is reported to be underway on the planned marina.

MORRO JABLE

28°02'·8N 14°21'·8W

☆ Puerto de Morro Jable Fl(2)10s61m20M. Entrance Fl(4)G.11s9m5M / Fl(4)R.11s5m3M

VHF Ch 10

Data Visitors' berths on detached pontoons. No services.

Facilities 30-ton travel-hoist. Mini-market and restaurants.

Remarks A new project will see the port redeveloped as Marina Jandia over the next few years. It will be part of the Calero group of marinas.

www.caleromarinas.com

Isla de Gran Canaria

PUERTO DE LAS PALMAS

28°07'·15N 15°23'·85W WGS84
Main b/w
28°07'·68N 15°25'·41W WGS84
Marina entrance
BA 1856 Sp 6100 Imray-Iolaire E2

☆ La Isleta Fl(3+1)20s248m21M. Radio Atlantico Aero Oc.R.3s1604m40M. Roque del Palo Q(3)10s6M. Breakwater Fl.G.5s10M. Dique Reina Sofia elbow Q(2)G.6s7m4M/ Q(3)5s8M/Fl(3)G.8s3M/

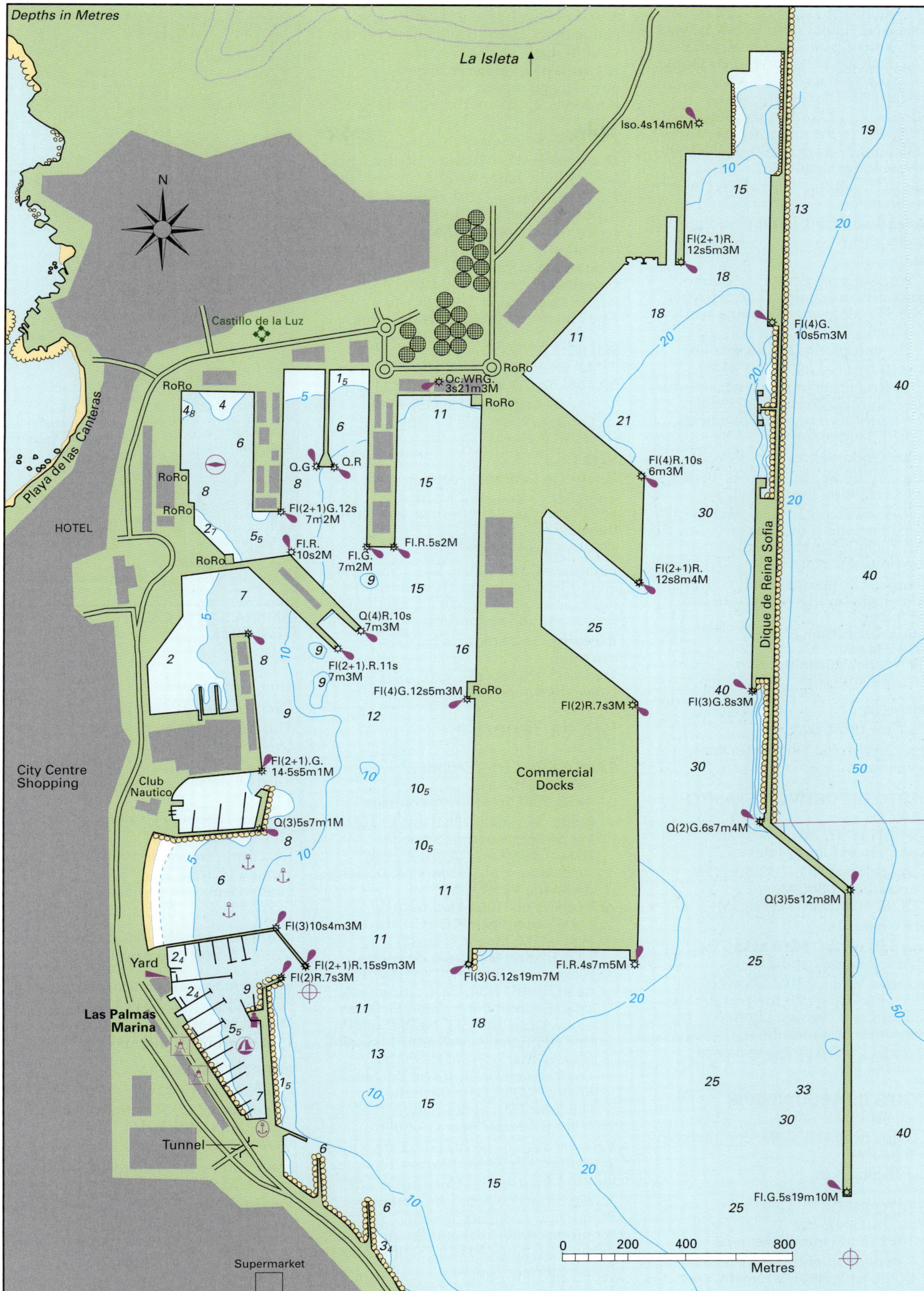

LAS PALMAS (GRAN CANARIA)

Fl(4)G.10s3M. Dique Leon y Castillo head NE Fl(2)R.7s3M / SE Fl.R.5s5M. W Fl(3)G.12s19m7M. S jetty, inner elbow (Ciudad Jardin) Fl(2)R.7s3M. N (outer) elbow Fl(3)10s3M. Head Fl(2+1)R.12s4M

VHF Ch 10, 12, 16 for port authorities. Ch 12, 14, 16 for pilots. Ch 11, 16 for Las Palmas Marina (0900–1400/1600–1900 Monday–Saturday).

Note VHF calls may not always be answered.

Navigation Yachts should head for the marina.

Note

1. Work in progress on the outer breakwater is ongoing. The extension to the S is complete. Widening work continues.

2. The entrance to the marina lies between two red lights (*see plan*).

Berths Reception pontoon near the fuel berth. Marina office is now close to here. Berth stern or bows-to where directed. Laid moorings.

Shelter Good shelter.

Data c.1,200 berths. Visitors' berths. Max LOA 45m. Depths 2–12m.

Facilities Water. 220V. Showers and toilets. Fuel quay. 60-ton travel-lift. Most yacht repairs. Chandlers. Provisions and restaurants.

Remarks The marina is full with ARC yachts from mid-October until late November.

Marina de Las Palmas
☎ 928 234 960
Email marina@palmasport.es
www.palmasport.es

ARINAGA

27°50'·6N 15°24'·0W

New commercial harbour under development.

PUERTO DEPORTIVO DE PASITO BLANCO

27°44'·7N 15°37'·2W
BA 1861 Sp 611 Imray-Iolaire E2

☆ Maspalomas Fl(1+2)13s59m19M. Entrance F.R.8m3M/ Q(2)R.4s3m3M/Fl.G.3s3m3M

VHF Ch 06, 16.

Data 350 berths. Max LOA 20m approx. Charge band 2.

Facilities Water. 220V. Showers and toilets. Fuel quay. 70-ton travel-hoist. Limited yacht repairs. Limited provisions. Restaurant/bar.

Puerto Deportivo de Pasito Blanco
☎ 928 142 194

PUERTO DE ARGUINEGUIN

27°45'·4N 15°41'·2W

☆ Dique head Fl.G.5s3M. Contradique Fl.R.5s3M

Busy fishing port.

PUERTO RICO

27°46'·7N 15°42'·6W
BA 1861 Sp 611 Imray-Iolaire E2

☆ East harbour entrance W breakwater Q(2)R.4s10m4M/F.G.10m4M. West harbour entrance Fl.G.3s5m4M/ F.R.10m5M

VHF Ch 08, 16 (1800–1600).

Navigation Yachts should head for the E harbour.

Berths Where directed. Visitors normally go on one of the outer pontoons. Laid moorings tailed to the quay.

Shelter Good shelter.

Data 400 berths. Visitors' berths. Max LOA 45m. Charge band 2.

Facilities Water. 220V. Showers and toilets. Fuel quay. 30-ton travel-hoist. Limited yacht repairs. Provisions and restaurants.

Remarks Apartment and hotel complexes cover the landscape.

Puerto Rico Marina ☎ 928 561 141
Email pricomarina@puertoricosa.com

PUERTO DE MOGAN

27°48'·9N 15°45'·7W
BA 1861 Sp 611 Imray-Iolaire E2

☆ Pta del Castillete Fl.5s113m17M. Entrance Fl(3)R.8·5s12m3M/ Fl(2)G.7s2m4M

VHF Ch 12, 16.

Berths Go onto the reception quay just inside the N entrance where a berth will be allocated. Laid moorings tailed to the quay.

Shelter Good shelter.

Facilities Water. 220V. WiFi. Showers and toilets. Fuel quay. 30-ton travel-hoist. Some yacht repairs. Chandlers. Provisions and restaurants.

Remarks Pre-booking a berth is essential.

Marina ☎ 928 565 151
Email info@puertomogan.es

Isla de Tenerife

SANTA CRUZ DE TENERIFE

28°29'·5N 16°12'·6W
BA 1858, 1847 Sp 6120 Imray-Iolaire E2

☆ Punta del Hidalgo Fl(3)16s51m16M. Pta de Roque Bermejo Anaga Fl(2+4)30s246m21M. Los Rodeos Airfield Aero Fl.5s650m37M. Dársena de Anaga S pier head Fl(2)R.7s18m10M. Club Náutico breakwater head Fl.G.5s5m1M. Elbow Fl.4s5m1M. Muelle N head Fl(2)G.7s5m1M. Muelle de Enlace ferry pier W head Fl(4)Y.11s1M. E head Fl(4)Y.11s8m1M. E entrance W side/SE corner E side Q.R/Q.G. Dique elbow Q(3)10s8m5M. Head E and W side Fl(3)G.9s12m9M/Fl(4)G.11s5m3M. Muelle interior head Fl.G.5s1M. Contradique Fl(3)R.10s7m9M. Muelle Ribera Fl(4)R.11s7m3M. RoRo Fl.R.5s5m1M. Leading Lights 354° Front Q.12m3M Rear Q.12m3M

VHF Ch 12, 14, 16 for port authorities and pilots. Ch 09 for Marina Tenerife, Puerto Chico and Marina Santa Cruz.

Navigation The N basin Darsena Pesquera for Marina Tenerife (pontoons on E side) and Puerto Chico, or the S basin for Marina Santa Cruz.

Berths Stern or bows-to.

Data Marina Tenerife 220 berths. Limited visitors' berths. Max LOA

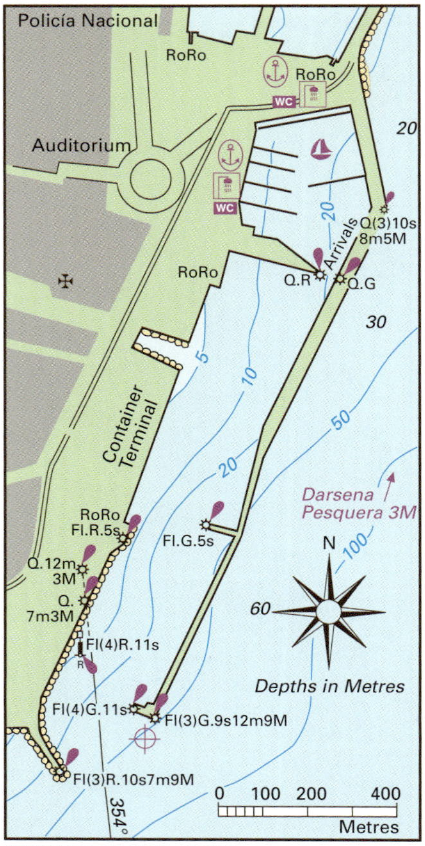

MARINA SANTA CRUZ (TENERIFE)

16m. Charge band 2.

Puerto Chico 40 berths. Fuel.

Marina Santa Cruz 300 berths. Max LOA 80m. Depths 4-10m.

Facilities Water. 220V. Showers and toilets. Fuel in Puerto Chico and Santa Cruz.

Marina Tenerife 70-ton travel-lift. Storage and repairs.

Excellent provisions and restaurants in Santa Cruz.

Puerto Deportivo Marina Tenerife
☎ 922 591 247
Email
marinatenerife@nauticaydeportes.com
Marina Tenerife Boatyard ☎ 922 591 313
Email
varaderosanaga@nauticaydeportes.com
Puerto Chico ☎ 922 549 818
Marina Santa Cruz ☎ 922 292 184
Email reservas@marinasantacruz.com

PUERTO RADAZUL

28°24'·0N 16°19'·5W

☆ Entrance Fl(2)G.10s9m5M/ Fl(2)R.7s3M/Q(6)+LFl.15s9m3M.

VHF Ch 16.

Data 200 berths. Limited visitors' berths. Max LOA 18m. Depths 3–4m.

Facilities Water. 220V. Showers and toilets. 30-ton travel-hoist. Yacht repairs. Limited provisions. Restaurant.

Remarks Some distance from Santa Cruz.

☎ 922 680 550
Email ptoradaz@vanaga.com

LA GALERA
28°21'·5N 16°21'·9W
Small craft harbour.
Data c.70 berths. Max LOA c.10m.

CANDELARIA
28°21'·3N 16°22'·1W
Small fishing harbour with craft kept on moorings behind the breakwater.

PUERTO DE GUIMAR
28°17'·1N 16°22'·7W
Small marina usually full of local craft.
Data Max LOA c.12m. Depths 1–2m.

MARINA SAN MIGUEL
28°01'·1N 16°37'·5W
VHF Ch 09, 16.
Navigation Care needed as depths are uneven. Dredged periodically.
Data 340 berths. Visitors' berths. Max LOA 20m. Charge band 2/3.
Shelter Reasonable shelter, but with S winds the entrance is difficult and berths uncomfortable.
Facilities Water. 220V. Showers and toilets. Fuel. Travel-hoist. Provisions and restaurants.
✆ 922 785 124
Email reservas@marinasanmiguel.com
www.marinasanmiguel.com

LAS GALLETAS
28°00'·3N 16°39'·6W
☆ Las Galletas breakwater head Fl(4)G.11s4m3M

LOS CRISTIANOS
28°02'·7N 16°42'·9W
BA 1861 Sp 5140 Imray-Iolaire E2
☆ Pta Răsca Fl(3)12s50m17M. Entrance Fl.R.5s12m5M/Fl(2+1)G.21s2M/Fl(2)R.7s3M
Busy ferry and tripper boat port. Boatyard hauls yachts.
Note Reports of theft in the harbour. Precautions advised.
Confradia de Pescadores (boatyard)
✆ 922 790 014

PUERTO DEPORTIVO DE COLON
28°04'·7N 16°44'·2W
BA 1861 Sp 514 Imray-Iolaire E2
☆ Entrance Fl(2)G.7s5M/Fl(2)R.7s3M. Elbow Q(9)15s6M
VHF Ch 16, 09.
Berths Go alongside the reception quay at the N entrance and report for a berth.
Shelter Good shelter.
Facilities Water. 220V. Showers and toilets. Fuel quay. 20-ton travel-hoist. Limited yacht repairs. Some provisions and restaurants.
Remarks Frequently full, so check ahead.
Puerto Deportivo de Colon
✆ 922 714 211
Email puertocolon@terra.es

SAN JUAN
28°10'·6N 16°48'·7W
☆ Mole head Fl(3)R.10s12m2M

PUERTO DEPORTIVO DE LOS GIGANTES
28°14'·9N 16°50'·5W
☆ Breakwater corner Q(9)15s10m4M. Head Fl.G.6s10m3M. Pier head Fl(2)G.7s5m1M. Elbow Fl(3)G.9s5m1M. Outer breakwater head Fl.G.5s3M
VHF Ch 16 (0900–1300/1500–1900).
Navigation Extreme caution advised in the approaches. The entrance is prone to silting and with any swell waves break before reaching the marina entrance.
Data 300 berths. Visitors' berths. Max LOA 20m.
Facilities Water. 220V. Showers and toilets. Fuel quay. 60-ton travel-hoist. Limited yacht repairs. Provisions and restaurants.
Remarks The harbour is prone to a surge with S winds.
Marina ✆ 922 868 002
Email lgmoffice@losgigantesmarina.com

Isla Gomera

SAN SEBASTIAN
28°05'·1N 17°06'·4W
BA 1861 Sp 517 Imray-Iolaire E2
☆ Pta de San Cristóbal Fl(2)10s83m21M. Marina basin Fl(2)G.7s6m3M / Fl(4)R.12s6m3M. Head E elbow Fl.G.5s15m6M. W corner Fl(2)G.7s6m3M
VHF Ch 09, 16 for Marina La Gomera.
Navigation The marina is in the NE corner of the harbour.
Berths Call ahead for a berth. The reception is on the E side of the entrance to the marina. Visitors' berths with finger pontoons. When full yachts raft up alongside the E quay.
Shelter Good shelter in the marina. Strong S winds make E side visitors' berths uncomfortable.
Data 300 berths. Visitors' berths. Max LOA 20m. Depths 2–6m. Charge band 2.
Facilities Water. 220V. WiFi. Showers and toilets. Fuel. Provisions and restaurants in the town.
Note Exit stamps are given to those leaving for the Caribbean.
Remarks Anchoring is forbidden inside the harbour.
Marina ✆ 922 141 769
Email info@marinalagomera.es
www.marinalagomera.es

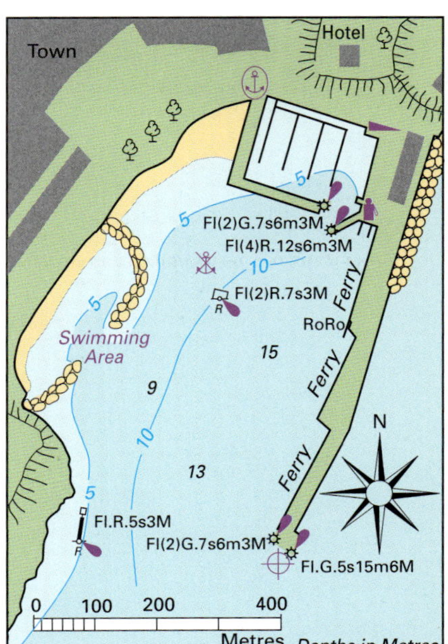

LA GOMERA MARINA

PUERTO DE SANTIAGO
28°01'·5N 17°11'·7W
☆ Entrance Fl(2)R.7s12m3M / Fl(2)G.7s5M

PUERTO DE VUELTAS (VALLE GRAN REY)
28°04'·7N 17°19'·8W
☆ Breakwater head Fl(3)R.9s1m5M
Port development underway to enlarge the harbour. New breakwater complete. No yacht berths available yet.

Isla de la Palma

SANTA CRUZ DE LA PALMA
28°40'·3N 17°45'·8W
☆ Breakwater Fl.G.5s5M. MarinaFl(2)G.7s3M / Fl(2)R.7s4m3M
VHF Ch 06, 16 for Port Authority. Ch 09 for Marina La Palma.
Berths Stern or bows-to. Finger pontoons.
Shelter Reasonable shelter in the marina but there can be some surge.
Data 180 berths. Max LOA 25m. Depths 6m. Charge band 2.

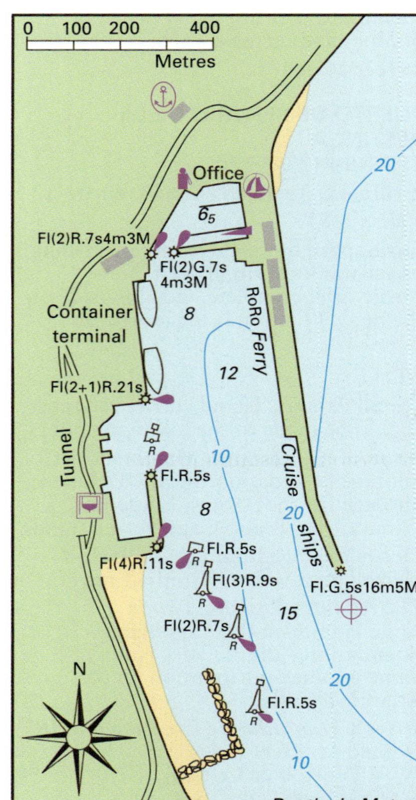

SANTA CRUZ MARINA (LA PALMA)

Facilities Water. 220/380V. Showers and toilets. Laundry. WiFi. Fuel. 70-ton travel-hoist. Chandlers. Provisions and restaurants.

Marina ✆ 922 410 289
Email info@marinalapalma.es
www.marinalapalma.es

Yacht Club ✆ 922 411 346
Email vela@rcnlapalma.com

Note The marina is part of the Calero group.

PUERTO REFUGIO DE TAZACORTE
28°38'·5N 17°56'·5W

☆ Mole head Fl(2)R.7s16m5M. Breakwater Q(9)15s9m3M. E head Fl(2)R.7s6m5M. Muelle de Combustible, S Corner Fl(3)R.9s6m1M

Marina under development. Marina pontoons (with finger pontoons) in place.

Data c.150 berths. Limited visitors' berths. Max LOA c.15m. Charge band 2.

Facilities Water. 220V. Travel-hoist.

Isla del Hierro

PUERTO DE LA ESTACA
27°46'·9N 17°53'·9W
BA 1861 Sp 6150 Imray-Iolaire E2

☆ Breakwater head Fl.G.5s13m5M. Inner breakwater head Fl(2)G.7s3M. Outer breakwater head Fl(2)R.7s3M

VHF Ch 16.

Breakwater extension and inner moles completed. High quay walls make mooring difficult. Limited services and facilities.

Remarks There are plans to install pontoons to increase yacht berths here.
✆ 922 550 160

PUERTO DE REFUGIO DE LA RESTINGA
27°38'·3N 17°58'·7W

☆ Breakwater head F(2)G.7s14m1M

VHF Ch 81.

Little space for yachts amongst fishing boats and local small craft. New breakwater complete. Go alongside on the quay. Pontoon is for local craft.

NOTE

For all Atlantic Island entries reference should be made to the following pilots.

Atlantic Islands Anne Hammick (RCC Pilotage Foundation/Imray). Detailed pilotage for the Azores, Madeira, Canary Islands and Cape Verde islands.

Ocean Passages and Landfalls Rod Heikell and Andy O'Grady (Imray)

The Atlantic Crossing Guide Anne Hammick (RCC Pilotage Foundation/Adlard Coles Nautical). Some pilotage information on the Atlantic Islands.

Street's Transatlantic Crossing Guide Donald M Street Jnr (W W Norton & Co Ltd).

Admiralty *West Coasts of Spain and Portugal Pilot NP67*. Covers the Atlantic Islands.

11. CALENDAR 2015

January						
Su	M	Tu	W	Th	F	Sa
				1	2	3
4	5	6	7	8	9	10
11	12	13	14	15	16	17
18	19	20	21	22	23	24
25	26	27	28	29	30	31

February						
Su	M	Tu	W	Th	F	Sa
1	2	3	4	5	6	7
8	9	10	11	12	13	14
15	16	17	18	19	20	21
22	23	24	25	26	27	28

March						
Su	M	Tu	W	Th	F	Sa
1	2	3	4	5	6	7
8	9	10	11	12	13	14
15	16	17	18	19	20	21
22	23	24	25	26	27	28
29	30	31				

April						
Su	M	Tu	W	Th	F	Sa
			1	2	3	4
5	6	7	8	9	10	11
12	13	14	15	16	17	18
19	20	21	22	23	24	25
26	27	28	29	30		

May						
Su	M	Tu	W	Th	F	Sa
					1	2
3	4	5	6	7	8	9
10	11	12	13	14	15	16
17	18	19	20	21	22	23
24	25	26	27	28	29	30
31						

June						
Su	M	Tu	W	Th	F	Sa
	1	2	3	4	5	6
7	8	9	10	11	12	13
14	15	16	17	18	19	20
21	22	23	24	25	26	27
28	29	30				

July						
Su	M	Tu	W	Th	F	Sa
			1	2	3	4
5	6	7	8	9	10	11
12	13	14	15	16	17	18
19	20	21	22	23	24	25
26	27	28	29	30	31	

August						
Su	M	Tu	W	Th	F	Sa
						1
2	3	4	5	6	7	8
9	10	11	12	13	14	15
16	17	18	19	20	21	22
23	24	25	26	27	28	29
30	31					

September						
Su	M	Tu	W	Th	F	Sa
		1	2	3	4	5
6	7	8	9	10	11	12
13	14	15	16	17	18	19
20	21	22	23	24	25	26
27	28	29	30			

October						
Su	M	Tu	W	Th	F	Sa
				1	2	3
4	5	6	7	8	9	10
11	12	13	14	15	16	17
18	19	20	21	22	23	24
25	26	27	28	29	30	31

November						
Su	M	Tu	W	Th	F	Sa
1	2	3	4	5	6	7
8	9	10	11	12	13	14
15	16	17	18	19	20	21
22	23	24	25	26	27	28
29	30					

December						
Su	M	Tu	W	Th	F	Sa
		1	2	3	4	5
6	7	8	9	10	11	12
13	14	15	16	17	18	19
20	21	22	23	24	25	26
27	28	29	30	31		

Full moon

New moon

11. CALENDAR 2016

January

Su	M	Tu	W	Th	F	Sa
					1	2
3	4	5	6	7	8	9
10	11	12	13	14	15	16
17	18	19	20	21	22	23
24	25	26	27	28	29	30
31						

February

Su	M	Tu	W	Th	F	Sa
	1	2	3	4	5	6
7	8	9	10	11	12	13
14	15	16	17	18	19	20
21	22	23	24	25	26	27
28	29					

March

Su	M	Tu	W	Th	F	Sa
		1	2	3	4	5
6	7	8	9	10	11	12
13	14	15	16	17	18	19
20	21	22	23	24	25	26
27	28	29	30	31		

April

Su	M	Tu	W	Th	F	Sa
					1	2
3	4	5	6	7	8	9
10	11	12	13	14	15	16
17	18	19	20	21	22	23
24	25	26	27	28	29	30

May

Su	M	Tu	W	Th	F	Sa
1	2	3	4	5	6	7
8	9	10	11	12	13	14
15	16	17	18	19	20	21
22	23	24	25	26	27	28
29	30	31				

June

Su	M	Tu	W	Th	F	Sa
			1	2	3	4
5	6	7	8	9	10	11
12	13	14	15	16	17	18
19	20	21	22	23	24	25
26	27	28	29	30		

July

Su	M	Tu	W	Th	F	Sa
					1	2
3	4	5	6	7	8	9
10	11	12	13	14	15	16
17	18	19	20	21	22	23
24	25	26	27	28	29	30
31						

August

Su	M	Tu	W	Th	F	Sa
	1	2	3	4	5	6
7	8	9	10	11	12	13
14	15	16	17	18	19	20
21	22	23	24	25	26	27
28	29	30	31			

September

Su	M	Tu	W	Th	F	Sa
				1	2	3
4	5	6	7	8	9	10
11	12	13	14	15	16	17
18	19	20	21	22	23	24
25	26	27	28	29	30	

October

Su	M	Tu	W	Th	F	Sa
						1
2	3	4	5	6	7	8
9	10	11	12	13	14	15
16	17	18	19	20	21	22
23	24	25	26	27	28	29
30	31					

November

Su	M	Tu	W	Th	F	Sa
		1	2	3	4	5
6	7	8	9	10	11	12
13	14	15	16	17	18	19
20	21	22	23	24	25	26
27	28	29	30			

December

Su	M	Tu	W	Th	F	Sa
				1	2	3
4	5	6	7	8	9	10
11	12	13	14	15	16	17
18	19	20	21	22	23	24
25	26	27	28	29	30	31

Full moon

New moon

INDEX OF LIGHTS

See 6.4 List of Major Lights

GENERAL INDEX